NINTH EDITION

American Constitutional Law

Introductory Essays and Selected Cases

ALPHEUS THOMAS MASON

Princeton University

DONALD GRIER STEPHENSON, JR.

Franklin and Marshall College

COMMEMORATING THE BICENTENNIAL
OF THE FIRST SESSION OF THE UNITED STATES
SUPREME COURT AND THE BICENTENNIAL
OF THE RATIFICATION OF THE BILL OF RIGHTS

Prentice Hall
Englewood Cliffs, New Jersey 07632

Library of Congress Cataloging-in-Publication Data

MASON, ALPHEUS THOMAS (date)
    American constitutional law : introductory essays and selected
cases / Alpheus Thomas Mason, Donald Grier Stephenson, Jr.—9th
ed.

    p.   cm.
    Includes bibliographies and indexes.
    ISBN 0-13-024803-7
    1. United States—Constitutional law—Cases.   I. Stephenson, D.
Grier.   II. Title.
KF4549.M3 1990
342.73′0264—dc19
[347.3020264]   88-35976
                                                   CIP

Editorial/production supervision and
    interior design: Mary Anne Shahidi
Cover design: Edsal Enterprises
Manufacturing buyer: Peter Havens

 © 1990, 1987, 1983, 1978, 1972, 1968, 1964, 1959, 1954 by Prentice-Hall, Inc.
A Division of Simon & Schuster
Englewood Cliffs, New Jersey 07632

Printed in the United States of America
10   9   8   7   6   5   4   3   2

ISBN 0-13-024803-7

Prentice-Hall International (UK) Limited, *London*
Prentice-Hall of Australia Pty. Limited, *Sydney*
Prentice-Hall Canada Inc., *Toronto*
Prentice-Hall Hispanoamericana, S.A., *Mexico*
Prentice-Hall of India Private Limited, *New Delhi*
Prentice-Hall of Japan, Inc., *Tokyo*
Simon & Schuster Asia Pte. Ltd., *Singapore*
Editora Prentice-Hall do Brasil, Ltda., *Rio de Janeiro*

For
George Thomas and *Mary Ellen Neal Walker*
and in Memory of
Herbert Adams and *Helen Davenport Gibbons*
and
Bradley Rau Dewey
with Loving Appreciation

Contents

4 Federalism   122

5 Commerce Power and State
Power   159

10   First Amendment Freedoms   371

12   Equal Protection of the Laws   478

Appendix   528

Noteworthy Decisions: 1988–89 Term   549

Index of Cases   563

Index of Names   571

Preface

Celebrations of the 200th anniversaries of the first session of the United States Supreme Court and the ratification of the Bill of Rights highlight the continuing vitality of the nation's fundamental charter.

This edition, following the pattern of earlier versions, is rooted in the conviction that constitutional law is an intricate blend of history and politics. Judicial decisions are but one of its dimensions. Others are the economic and political climate in which these are rendered and the theory that rationalizes both decision and social preference.

A distinctive feature is the introductory essay preceding each chapter, which supplies the historical and political context and traces the meandering thread of constitutional doctrine through major decisions. Additional material in both essays and cases reflects new judicial concerns: review in the Introduction of President Reagan's struggle to shape the Supreme Court, including the defeat of the Bork nomination; discussion in Chapter 1 of the 1988 overhaul of the Court's appellate jurisdiction, the first in over 60 years; an overview of approaches to constitutional interpretation in Chapter 2; heightened separation-of-powers concerns in Chapter 3; judicial federalism in Chapter 4; the Court's "takings" jurisprudence and the "new property" in Chapter 8; understanding when a search is a "search" in Chapter 9; private clubs and the First Amendment in Chapter 10; a new chapter (11) on the right to privacy; continued interest in affirmative action in Chapter 12. Some very recent decisions from the 1988–89 term, handed down while this book was in production, are included at the end of the book.

Sparingly selected cases are set in this variegated framework. Although relatively small in number, the cases feature generous excerpts, not snippets. To assist students in learning how to study cases, Chapter 1 includes suggestions on "Reading a Supreme Court Decision." Relevant to both essays and cases, and designed to aid discussion and further study, are queries and a list of key terms following the essay in each chapter. Each term is defined in the chapter essay and relates to the cases which follow. Acknowledging the outpouring of scholarship on the Constitution in recent years, the selected readings for each chapter have been reworked, as well as updated.

Throughout, names of cases discussed in the essays which are also reprinted in the book appear in boldface italics. Citations to cases discussed in the essays now appear in the index of cases. Tabular data in the appendix show Court appointments by president and party affiliation, as well as by court periods. The index of names indicates at a glance where opinions by individual justices are reprinted. Headnotes contain the voting alignments of each case.

The Supreme Court does not function in a vacuum. Besides briefs of counsel, it is influenced by the giants of American constitutional interpretation—Kent, Story, Cooley, Thayer. Perhaps more than any other commentator of his time, Edward S. Corwin illustrates his incisive observation: "If judges make law, so do commentators." This book owes a great debt to him.

To a greater extent than earlier editions, this one includes relevant extrajudicial material. The student is thus alerted to illuminating debates, sometimes unstaged, outside the Court: in Chapter 2, Alexander Hamilton and Robert Yates's sharply divergent prognoses concerning the possible consequences of judicial review; differences as to the judicial function echoed in the Marshall-Gibson encounter; poignant statements by presidents Jackson and Lincoln, laid alongside the Court's pronouncement in *Cooper* v. *Aaron,* highlighting the question of who has the last word in debate over what the Constitution means; and clashing approaches to constitutional interpretation in statements by Judge Bork and Professor Tribe. Chapter 8 includes Justice Brewer's fervent advocacy in 1893 of a "strengthened judiciary" and Professor Thayer's closely reasoned plea that the Court resist "stepping into the shoes of the lawmaker." Chapter 9, which now contains the materials relating to the origins of the Bill of Rights as well as the incorporation doctrine, recalls Jefferson's drive for a Bill of Rights in the face of Hamilton and James Wilson's vigorous refutation of its necessity. Justice Cardozo's unpublished concurring opinion in the Minnesota Moratorium case of 1934 and Justice Frankfurter's letter of 1940 to Justice Stone regarding the first Flag Salute case, reproduced in Chapters 8 and 10, respectively, portray an essential ingredient in the judicial decision-making process, bargaining.

The goal of this broad approach is better understanding of the present in light of the past, and of the past in light of the present. Revealed, among other things, is the Supreme Court as participant in the governing process. Under the impact of various pressures, judicial decisions reflect the sometimes capricious selection of hard alternatives rather than the easy dictate of a brooding omnipresence or soulless command of mechanics.

No casebook, however current, can ever stay completely abreast of Supreme Court action. This handicap is not insuperable. For very recent decisions, one can easily make available at the outset copies of major cases, say three or four, that have come down since publication. In this way, the student is introduced not only to current issues but also to the Court's present membership and its divergent approaches to constitutional interpretation.

Many persons cooperated in shaping the contents and organization of this book. Through the years since publication of the first edition in 1954, users, teachers and students alike, contributed to its betterment. Their suggestions, reflected in both omissions and additions, indicate the measure of our indebtedness. Thanks in particular go to Henry J. Abraham, Jeffrey S. Harwin, Joseph Rish, Harold J. Spaeth, H.L. Pohlman, and John H. Vanderzell. We are grateful to Paul R. Benson, Jr. of The Citadel, William Haltom of the University of Puget Sound, and Kristine L. Olsen of California State University, Los Angeles, who carefully reviewed the eighth edition and made suggestions for the ninth. Frank A. Mosier, Jr., assisted with the indexes.

Special gratitude, as always, is owed our families—Christine, Ellen, Louise, Todd, and Claire—whose love, encouragement, and understanding are necessary ingredients in a book of this magnitude.

Alpheus Thomas Mason
Donald Grier Stephenson, Jr.

Introduction
to the Ninth Edition:
The Supreme Court
in American Politics

Nothing tends more to render judges careful in their decisions and anxiously
solicitous to do exact justice than the consciousness that every act of theirs
is to be subject to the intelligent scrutiny of their fellow men, and to their candid
criticism. . . . In the case of judges having a life tenure, indeed, their very
independence makes the right freely to comment on their decisions of greater importance,
because it is the only practical and available instrument in the hands of a free
people to keep such judges alive to the reasonable demands of those they serve.

—WILLIAM HOWARD TAFT (1895)

It was one of George Washington's first concerns as president: Who would sit on the Supreme Court of the United States? "Impressed with a conviction that the true administration of justice is the firmest pillar of good government," he wrote his future Attorney General Edmund Randolph in 1789, "I have considered the first arrangement of the judicial department as essential to the happiness of our country and the stability of its political system." Under the Articles of Confederation, which the recently ratified Constitution replaced, there had been no national judiciary. The Court's precise role in the new political system was unclear, but Washington realized the impact the Court might have in the young Republic. This required, he told Randolph, "the selection of the fittest characters to expound the laws and dispense justice. . . ." As he selected the six justices Congress had authorized, Washington also made sure that each section of the nation was represented and that the six were strong supporters of the new Constitution.

The first session of the newly constituted Supreme Court was scheduled for February 1, 1790, in the Exchange Building at the foot of Broad Street in New York City. The occasion was inauspicious. Only three of the six justices were present, so the Court adjourned until February 2. By then a fourth justice had arrived. In contrast to the black robes worn today, the justices were dressed in black and red gowns. A newspaper account of the day reported, "As no business appeared to require immediate notice, the Court was adjourned."

Two centuries ago, the justices had not carved out their role in American government. Months would pass before the Supreme Court even decided its first cases. Yet the time was near when observers could say with near accuracy, "[E]very decision becomes a page of history."* The Court's place in the American constitutional system is the subject of this

---

* Attorney General George W. Wickersham, in a memorial address following Chief Justice Melville Fuller's death, 1910 (219 U.S. xv).

book. Though Alexander Hamilton labeled the Court "the least dangerous" branch, regarding it as the weakest of the three, the justices have had an impact on American life that can scarcely be exaggerated. This fact describes a reality made possible by, and bound up with, democratic politics and a written Constitution.

CONSTITUTIONAL INTERPRETATION AND POLITICAL CHOICE

". . . [W]e must never forget that it is a *constitution** we are expounding." With this commanding reminder, serviceable to Supreme Court justices and students of constitutional interpretation, Chief Justice John Marshall interrupted a closely reasoned argument in *McCulloch* v. *Maryland* (1819).** He did not pause to spell out what he had in mind. His meaning emerges from other passages in the opinion.

As Chapter Four will show, Chief Justice Marshall in *McCulloch* found in the Constitution a deep reservoir of congressional power and a subordinate place for the states in the federal system. Even without express authorization in the Constitution, Congress could charter a national bank. Furthermore, Maryland and other states could not tax it. The Supreme Court, as expounder of the Constitution, would correspondingly have a narrow but nonetheless important role, guarding national over state interests. The results of *McCulloch* have been far-reaching.

In *McCulloch* Marshall made *constitutional law*. Constitutional law or jurisprudence consists of the prevailing meaning of the Constitution as found in decisions by the United States Supreme Court. As law, these decisions are "legal," to be sure, but the law they announce is not ordinary law. Because it deals with fundamental matters such as the organization of government and the authority of officials over the lives of citizens, constitutional law is a very special kind of law, fusing politics, history, political thought, ethics, and economics. This art of interpreting the Constitution is a lawyer's art only in the narrow sense that justices of the Supreme Court have been lawyers. But they have had to be more than mere legal technicians. Successful constitutional interpretation has required that they rise to the demands of political theory and that they excel in statecraft.

Interpreting the Constitution has meant that the Court, almost from the beginning, has been an institution that has blended contradictions. From John Jay and John Marshall to Warren Burger and William Rehnquist, justices have been guardians of particular interests and promoters of preferred values. Nevertheless, the myth articulated by Chief Justice Marshall endures: "Courts are the mere instruments of the law, and can will nothing," he wrote in *Osborn* v. *Bank* (1824). The Supreme Court's version of the Constitution, unlike that of any other organ or agency of government, has the special virtue of never seeming to mangle or change the original instrument.

The theme of this book is *interpretation*. After 200 years, the Constitution is far more than a historic relic on display for tourists visiting the National Archives in Washington. The Constitution is the vital foundation of our political system. Broad or narrow, the prevailing interpretation of the Constitution at different times has been a major influence on the kind of nation and society Americans have enjoyed. Interpretation requires choice and is always the product of contending values. Some of these values have promoted centralized power; others, control by the states. Some have enlarged, whereas others have diminished, the influence of one branch of the national government. Some have expanded

---

* Emphasis within quotations, including judicial opinions, is in the original, unless otherwise indicated.
** Boldface italic type is used throughout to indicate those cases reprinted in the book.

individual liberties; others have expanded the powers of government, state and national, at the expense of the individual. Still others have allowed the powers of government to grow in order to protect minorities from majorities.

Constitutional interpretation occurs when the Supreme Court and other courts decide *cases* that require judges to give meaning to particular words and passages in the Constitution. Cases are disputes handled by a court. They may pit one individual against another, the government against an individual or corporation, and so forth. Cases are thus the raw material of the judicial process. Although many cases do not involve conflicting interpretations of the Constitution, those that do enable courts to apply the nation's fundamental law— largely crafted for an agrarian society near the end of the eighteenth century—to the needs of a technological nation on the brink of the twenty-first century.

The justices established the Supreme Court as the oracle of the Constitution through the power of *judicial review:* the authority to set aside laws passed by Congress and the state legislatures as being contrary to the Constitution. As discussed in Chapter Two, judicial review is, accordingly, law steeped in politics. The development of judicial review has meant that two branches of the national government—Congress and the presidency—are preoccupied with partisan pressures. The third branch—the judiciary—is preoccupied with constitutional principles packed with political significance. Constitutional interpretation is political in the broadest sense because it makes courts, especially the Supreme Court, participants in the process of government. American courts are therefore distinctive because they routinely speak the language of the fundamental values of the political system.

THE POLITICS OF SUPREME COURT APPOINTMENTS, 1968–1988

Attesting to the Supreme Court's place in the political system is the inordinate attention the justices and their decisions receive. The separated powers mandated by the Constitution make possible the Court's considerable independence from partisan politics, but the role of interpretation the Constitution allows and the significance of the decisions the justices render make impossible a complete isolation of the Court from the partisan life of the nation. "The great tides and currents which engulf the rest of men do not turn aside in their course and pass the judges by," acknowledged Judge (later Justice) Benjamin Cardozo. Little wonder the selection of justices is of paramount concern to presidents, senators, and citizens alike.

From Warren to Burger. On June 26, 1968, President Lyndon Johnson announced Chief Justice Earl Warren's intention to resign. Warren had been on the Court since President Dwight Eisenhower named him chief justice in 1953. His tenure had been one of the most active and remarkable in American history. Hardly an aspect of life had gone untouched by landmark decisions on race discrimination, legislative apportionment, and the Bill of Rights. His Court initiated a revolution during the quiescent Eisenhower years that is measured by Ike's latter-day lament over Warren's appointment: "The biggest damn fool mistake I ever made."

On June 27, President Johnson nominated a close friend, Associate Justice Abe Fortas, to succeed the controversial chief justice. Only two associate justices had been advanced to the center chair—Edward Douglass White in 1910 and Harlan Fiske Stone in 1941. Accusing President Johnson of "cronyism," opposition formed immediately.

Fortas was charged with various improprieties, including participation in White House strategy conferences on the Vietnam War and acceptance of high lecture fees raised by wealthy business executives who happened to be clients of Fortas's former law partner, Paul

Porter. After four days, the Senate voted 45 to 43 to cut off debate, 14 votes short of the two-thirds necessary to end the anti-Fortas filibuster. Two days later the ill-fated justice withdrew his name. For the first time, nomination of a Supreme Court justice had been blocked by a Senate filibuster.

It was a Pyrrhic victory. For the time being, critics of the Warren Court had to reconcile themselves to the continued presence of Chief Justice Warren. "If they don't confirm Abe," the chief justice commented cheerfully, while Fortas's fate hung in the balance, "they will have me." So they did for one more year.

When the Senate blocked Fortas's nomination, President Johnson refused to submit another name. L.B.J., a lame duck president, left this high-level appointment to President Richard M. Nixon, whose campaign for the White House had been in part a campaign against the Warren Court.

Finding himself in a similar situation in 1801, President John Adams, much to Thomas Jefferson's chagrin, followed an altogether different course. A few weeks before he left the White House, Adams named Secretary of State John Marshall Chief Justice of the United States. If Adams had taken President Johnson's route, Chief Justice Ellsworth's successor probably would have been the ardent defender of states' rights, Spencer Roane. In that event, history during the crucial formative years would have been drastically altered, perhaps for the worse.

Appointment of a chief justice is a rare occurrence. There have been 41 presidents, only 16 chief justices. John Marshall sat in the Court's center chair 34 years, from 1801 to 1835. During that time there were six presidents. The contrast is significant substantively as well as statistically, a fact that prompted John Quincy Adams to rate the office of chief justice as "more important than that of President."

President Nixon's first step toward fulfilling his 1968 campaign promise to strengthen the "peace forces as against the criminal forces of the country" was the selection of Warren Earl Burger, 61, chief judge, United States Court of Appeals for the District of Columbia Circuit. Judge Burger's confirmation, June 9, 1969, by a vote of 74 to 3, was hasty—almost pro forma. Earl Warren waited five months for the Senate vote, Burger only 18 days.

Fortas Resigns. In the spring of 1969, *Life* magazine revealed that Justice Fortas had received a yearly $20,000 fee from the Family Foundation of Louis Wolfson, then serving a prison term for selling unregistered stock. Once again judicial fat was in the political fire. Fortas's resignation, May 16, 1969, opened the way for President Nixon's nomination of Clement F. Haynsworth, Jr., chief judge, United States Court of Appeals for the Fourth Circuit. As a circuit court judge, Haynsworth had taken a restrictive view of school desegregation and had also been insensitive to proprieties in ways that involved finance and conflict of interest. After weeks of heated debate the Senate, in a surprise vote, rejected the president's nominee 55 to 45.

The Senate's rejection of Haynsworth strengthened President Nixon's determination to "pack" the Court with "strict constructionists." His next nominee, G. Harrold Carswell, had served seven years as a federal district judge in Tallahassee and six months on the United States Court of Appeals for the Fifth Circuit. In 1948, he had said, "I yield to no man as a fellow candidate [he was then running for political office] or as a fellow citizen in the firm, vigorous belief in the principles of White Supremacy, and I shall always be so governed."

Quite apart from Judge Carswell's avowed racism (which he now disavowed), critics charged that President Nixon's nominee was in fact mediocre. Accepting the criticism, Nebraska Senator Hruska tried to convert it into an asset: "Even if he is mediocre, there are a lot of mediocre judges and people and lawyers. They are entitled to a little representation, aren't they, and a little chance? We can't have all Brandeises, Cardozos and Frankfurters and stuff like that there."

Judge Carswell was rejected 51 to 45. Even prominent members of the president's own party voted against him. To fill the place vacated by Justice Fortas, President Nixon turned to Chief Justice Burger's longtime Minnesota friend, Judge Harry A. Blackmun of the Court of Appeals for the Eighth Circuit. A product of Harvard College and Harvard Law School and former counsel to the Mayo Clinic, Blackmun aroused little opposition and was promptly confirmed 94–0, and sworn in on June 9, 1970, too late to participate in any of the term's decisions.

Defenders of Judges Haynsworth and Carswell, piqued by defeat, launched a counteroffensive, calling for the impeachment of libertarian Justice William O. Douglas. When Michigan Congressman Gerald Ford, spearhead of the drive, was asked to define "impeachable offense," he replied, "The only honest answer is that an impeachable offense is whatever a majority of the House of Representatives considers it to be at a given moment in history; conviction results from whatever offense or offenses two-thirds of the other body considers to be sufficiently serious to require removal of the accused from office." Ford's definition was not unprecedented. When, with President Jefferson's support, impeachment proceedings were instigated against Justice Samuel Chase, Senator Giles explained,

> A trial and removal of a judge upon impeachment need not imply any criminality or corruption in him . . . [but] was nothing more than a declaration of Congress to this effect: You hold dangerous opinions, and if you are suffered to carry them into effect you will work the destruction of the nation. *We want your offices,* for the purpose of giving them to men who will fill them better.

Applied to Justice Douglas, this open-ended definition failed.

Powell and Rehnquist. In the fall of 1970, President Nixon was still determined to appoint a southerner to the Supreme Court. The most likely spot to be vacated was that occupied by 84-year-old Justice Hugo Black. Asked for his reaction, Black replied, "I think it would be nice to have *another* Southerner up here."

In June 1971, Justice Black selected his law clerks for the 1971–1972 term, a sure sign that he intended to carry on. The justice had moved into third place in length of service. The longevity goal was in sight; fate defeated its realization. In September 1971, Justices Black and John Harlan, both ailing, resigned within days of each other. Hugo Black died on September 25, Harlan on December 29, 1971. Had Black remained on the bench eight months longer, he would have exceeded Stephen J. Field's record, having served 34 years, 6 months, and 13 days.

In October 1971, Richard Nixon enjoyed an opportunity no president had experienced since 1940—that of simultaneously filling two Supreme Court vacancies. The president nominated Lewis F. Powell, Jr., 64, a distinguished Richmond lawyer, and William H. Rehnquist, 47, law clerk, 1952–1953, to the late Justice Robert H. Jackson, and the Nixon administration's assistant attorney general in charge of the Office of Legal Counsel.

Powell, arousing little or no objection, was confirmed 89 to 1 on December 6, emphatically disproving Nixon's widely publicized lament of 1969 that the Senate, as then constituted, would not confirm a southerner. Rehnquist ran into stormy waters. Among other things, critics charged that he had supported curtailment of defendants' rights in criminal cases, use of electronic surveillance, preventive detention, and "no knock" police entry. He had proclaimed virtually unlimited war power for the president and sanctioned mass arrest of demonstrators. Confronted with these barbed attacks, Rehnquist told the Judiciary Committee: "My fundamental commitment, if I am confirmed, will be to totally disregard my own personal belief." Rehnquist received Senate approval on December 10, 1971, 68 to 26.

Douglas Retires. The Court's personnel remained unchanged until November 1975, when President Ford nominated John Paul Stevens, a 55-year-old Appeals Court judge from the Seventh Circuit, to fill the vacancy created by the retirement of William O. Douglas. The previous New Year's Eve Douglas had suffered a stroke. He had served 36 years on the high bench, surpassing the record long held by Justice Field.

Justice Douglas's reluctance to retire raised again the thorny question of how to remove an incapacitated Supreme Court justice. The Constitution supplies no answer, but history does. On more than one occasion, the power of persuasion exerted on a faltering justice by the Court itself has proved effective.

In 1869, Associate Justice Field convinced Justice Grier that he was too ill to continue. Later, when Justice Field became incapacitated, the first Justice Harlan asked his colleague whether he remembered urging Grier to retire. "Yes," Field snapped, "and a dirtier day's work I never did in my life." After Justice McKenna's all too obvious demonstration of mental slowdown, Chief Justice Taft reluctantly persuaded him to retire. Justice Holmes, older than McKenna, then a bystander, was sure he would be "intellectually honest in judging my condition and my product." But the 91-year-old justice gave up only after Chief Justice Hughes requested him to do so. Ignoring or eluding pressure from whatever source, Douglas reached his own decision, on November 12, 1975, to leave the Court, almost a year after he was stricken. His death came in January 1980.

Douglas's successor, though relatively unknown, seemed eminently qualified. He had established a brilliant academic record. After graduating first in his class at Northwestern University Law School, he served two years as Supreme Court Justice Rutledge's law clerk. The Senate quickly confirmed 98–0; on December 19, 1975, Stevens was sworn in.

Ford's successor in the White House was Jimmy Carter, whose one-term administration had mixed impact on the federal judiciary. In one respect, Carter's influence survived his presidency. He was able to make more appointments to the district and appeals courts than any previous president, thanks in part to a Democratic Congress willing to enlarge both benches substantially. Moreover, although not overlooking the importance of merit, Carter also appointed more females and nonwhites to the federal courts than all of his predecessors combined. In another respect, however, Carter's influence was nil. He was the first president to serve *at least* a full four-year term who did not have the opportunity to fill a single vacancy on the Supreme Court. Even James Garfield, who served less than a year before he was assassinated, was able to appoint Justice Stanley Matthews.

The First Woman Justice. The judiciary figured in the national campaign of 1980 in a way it did not in 1976, when Jimmy Carter wrested the presidency from Gerald Ford. The Republicans had good reason to be wary of judicial appointments at all levels. Along with everyone else they noted that five years had passed without a Supreme Court vacancy on a bench where more than half the justices were above 70 years of age. Moreover, the Court only seven years before had injected itself into the most divisive of contemporary moral issues by declaring abortion to be a constitutional right. Three Nixon appointees had voted with the majority, and one of them—Justice Blackmun—had written the majority opinion. This case alone was reminder enough that recent Republican presidents had not been notably adept in picking nominees who accorded with their political views. Warren, Brennan, Blackmun, and Stevens had all proven to be "surprises" in various ways. This time, conservative Republicans wanted to be more careful.

The Republican platform therefore called for judges "who respect traditional family values and the sanctity of innocent human life." The second part was a code word for opposition to abortion. Denounced by the National Organization for Women for "medieval stances on women's issues," Reagan confounded the campaign by promising to name a woman to fill one of "the first Supreme Court vacancies in my administration."

As if to accommodate, the justices dropped the notation "Mr. Justice" in their orders on November 18, replacing it simply with "Justice." As the most junior member, Justice Stevens relayed the message to the Clerk's Office but declined to discuss with the press the reasons for the change. "You can probably guess," he acknowledged.

President Reagan soon had his chance. At age 66, Potter Stewart, appointed by President Eisenhower in 1958 and long regarded as a "swing vote" among the justices, announced his retirement on June 18, 1981. Reagan's choice for a successor was Judge Sandra Day O'Connor, age 51, of the Arizona Court of Appeals, who had been a law student with Justice Rehnquist at Stanford University (he finished first, she third, in the class of 1952). Not only was Judge O'Connor to be the first woman to sit on the High Court, she was the first since Brennan to have had experience as a state judge. More significantly perhaps, she was the first since Justice Harold Burton, Stewart's predecessor, to have served as a state legislator. Criticized by some for injecting gender into justice, Reagan's fulfillment of a campaign pledge placed him squarely in established tradition: Other presidents have considered region, religion, and race in making appointments to the Court.

Questions about Judge O'Connor shortly developed—from the right. The Moral Majority and "right-to-life" groups claimed that she was "unsound" on abortion. The debate temporarily split political conservatives. Possessing impeccable conservative credentials, Senator Barry Goldwater of Arizona called on "all good Christians" to kick the leader of the Moral Majority in his posterior. Opponents to the O'Connor nomination were clearly looking beyond her to other opportunities Reagan might have. "I'm not sure we'll defeat her," said Peter Gemma of the National Pro-Life Political Action Committee. "But we want to send the President a clear signal at how much of an insult this is, and how his next appointment had better be pro-life." Opposition remained more outside than inside the Senate, where she was confirmed 99–0 on September 21.

The Court in the 1984 Presidential Campaign. With the approach of the 1984 presidential race, the Court's future again became an issue. And with good reason. Some saw the coming election as a referendum on the Constitution. The High Bench was the second oldest in history, just behind the "Nine Old Men" of Franklin Roosevelt's first term in the 1930s. On election day, five of the justices were 75 years of age or older. Although justices sometimes defy the actuarial tables, of the 93 since 1789 who completed their service before 1984, only eight stayed on after their 80th birthdays. Reagan's opponents feared a Court that would not be merely conservative but potentially radical, discarding settled constitutional doctrine.

In headline-generating remarks, Justice Rehnquist tried to minimize the impact of any president on the Court. "Presidents who wish to pack the Supreme Court, like murder suspects in a detective novel, must have both motive and opportunity," Rehnquist declared at the University of Minnesota Law School. Even with both, "a number of factors militate against a president having anything more than partial success." Chief among them was that neither presidents nor nominees "are usually vouchsafed the foresight to see what the great issues of 10 or 15 years hence are to be."

There was another reason why the 1984 election was so important for the Constitution and the Court: nominations by the president to the district and appeals benches. During his first term, President Reagan appointed about one-quarter of all federal judges. By late 1988, he had appointed about one-half of the entire federal bench not counting the Supreme Court, surpassing the prior record holder, President Carter. Numbers are important in assessing any president's impact on the courts, but in Reagan's case he clearly wanted a change in the ideological balance of the federal courts. Assisting in this effort was the President's Committee on Judicial Selection. Court scholar Sheldon Goldman found "the formal mechanism of the committee [to be] the most consistent ideological or policy-orientation screening of judicial candidates since the first term of Franklin Roosevelt."

Whose Supreme Court Is It? On June 17, 1986, President Reagan announced the retirement of Chief Justice Warren Burger and his intention to nominate Justice William Rehnquist as chief justice and Judge Antonin Scalia, age 50, of the United States Court of Appeals for the District of Columbia Circuit as associate justice. Upon confirmation at age 61 by the Senate as the nation's sixteenth chief justice, Rehnquist, an associate justice since 1971, would become only the third to have been selected from the Court itself.

President Reagan had learned three weeks earlier of Burger's intention to step down. At age 78 and chief justice for 17 years, Burger served longer than any other chief justice nominated thus far in the twentieth century. Although President Richard Nixon named Burger to the Court in 1969 to fulfill a campaign pledge against judicial activism, the Court during Burger's time did not overturn outright a single major decision of the activist Warren Court (1953–1969). The persistence of the Warren Court's jurisprudence is all the more remarkable when it is remembered that by 1986, only three members of the Warren Court were still serving, and of the three only two (Justices Brennan and Marshall) had been closely identified with the Warren Court's major accomplishments. Although some of the Warren Court's landmark rulings on criminal procedure were restricted—most notably the exclusionary rule (see Chapter Nine)—the Burger Court practiced its own kind of judicial activism, especially with respect to racial and sexual equality, abortion, and other privacy issues (see Chapters Eleven and Twelve). With the possible exception of William Howard Taft, Warren Burger was the most active chief justice *outside* the Supreme Court. He treated his office like a pulpit from which to campaign energetically for changes in legal education, professional standards for bench and bar, criminal sanctions, prisons, and the administration of justice.

Judge Scalia would become the first Italian American to serve on the nation's highest court. He graduated *summa cum laude* from Georgetown University in 1957 and received his legal training at Harvard, where he was an editor of the *Law Review*. He was an assistant attorney general in the U.S. Department of Justice between 1974 and 1977 and had been a member of the law faculties at the University of Chicago, the University of Virginia, Georgetown University, and Stanford University before President Reagan appointed him to the Court of Appeals in 1982. Like Rehnquist, he was widely regarded as a politically conservative legal thinker.

From the outset the Rehnquist nomination encountered intense opposition. If the president took a nominee's views into account, should not the Senate do the same? Preferring to forget their party's opposition to Abe Fortas in 1965 and 1968, Republican leaders wanted to limit the Senate to a consideration of character and merit. Yet the Senate historically has been less deferential to nominations to the Supreme Court than to nominations to a president's cabinet. Since 1789 only nine cabinet nominees have met defeat. Of 141 nominations to the Supreme Court submitted to the Senate between 1789 and 1986, 26 were not approved (12 confirmed persons declined to serve), some clearly because the candidates' views were unacceptable to a majority of the Senate.

Now, some Democrats seemed intent on ensuring a coordinate role for the Senate. "The framers envisioned a major role for the Senate in the appointment of judges," argued Senator Kennedy. "It is historical nonsense to suggest that all the Senate has to do is to check the nominee's I.Q., be sure he has a law degree and no arrests, and rubber stamp the President's choice." If Rehnquist's vision of the Constitution was properly the Senate's concern, how much should it matter? Neither the Constitution nor Senate tradition offered a conclusive answer.

The Rehnquist nomination was unusual because it offered a rare second chance to vote on the *results* of a justice's career, not just on its prospects. Yet some senators instead directed questions to other, perhaps surrogate, issues that cast doubt on Rehnquist's fitness to serve. As a Republican activist in Phoenix, Arizona, in 1962 and 1964, Rehnquist was supposed to have intimidated voters. He denied the charges. In a deed for a house Rehnquist had purchased in Vermont in 1974, a 1933 covenant (now legally unenforceable) barred sale or lease to a person of "the Hebrew race." Rehnquist explained that he was unaware of the existence of the restriction and promised that he would have the offensive language removed.

A third charge turned on the propriety of Rehnquist's participation in a free speech case in 1972, *Laird* v. *Tatum,* which dismissed a suit challenging surveillance by the Army of domestic political groups. In October 1972, Rehnquist issued a 16-page opinion,* explaining that he had not taken part in the government's case and that he did not know much about the evidence.

In August 1986, opponents claimed that Rehnquist knew more than he admitted in 1972 and more than he acknowledged in late July when the matter arose during the confirmation hearings. On August 12, Rehnquist responded to questions from Senator Charles Mathias of Maryland, writing that he had "no recollection of any participation in the formulation of policy" on the surveillance.

Hearings by the Judiciary Committee on the Rehnquist nomination consumed four days, and Senate floor debate five. Confirmation, 65–33, came on September 17. Not since 1836, when the Senate confirmed Roger Taney, had a nominee for chief justice been approved by a ratio of less than two to one.

Perhaps because the Senate's scrutiny of Justice Rehnquist was so intense, Judge Scalia's nomination generated only mild turbulence. The Judiciary Committee's hearings on Judge Scalia lasted only two days. Floor debate did not exceed five minutes. Following the vote on Rehnquist, the Senate confirmed, 98–0.

From Powell to Kennedy. At the end of Rehnquist's first term as chief justice, Justice Lewis Powell announced his retirement on June 26, 1987. For several years Powell had been in a pivotal position on the Court, especially in abortion, privacy, church-state, and affirmative action cases. The president now had a chance to advance his social agenda judicially, parts of which had been rebuffed by Congress: prayer in the schools, restrictions on abortions, and limits on affirmative action.

Reagan's announcement on July 1 was not a surprise. At his side was Robert H. Bork, age 60, who had been passed over in favor of Scalia the year before. Since 1982 Bork had been a judge on the United States Court of Appeals for the District of Columbia Circuit. From 1962 to 1981 he had been a member of the faculty at Yale Law School, taking time out from 1973 to 1977 to serve as solicitor general. It was as the third-ranking official in the Department of Justice that Bork found himself caught up in the "Saturday Night Massacre" on October 20, 1973, in the Watergate affair. Refusing to obey President Nixon's order to fire special prosecutor Archibald Cox, Attorney General Elliot Richardson and Deputy Attorney General William Ruckelshaus resigned. As the ranking officer in the department, Bork carried out the president's command. Some senators still considered Bork's actions legally and ethically dubious.

He was also a prolific writer. Not since Felix Frankfurter's appointment in 1939 had the Senate considered a Supreme Court nominee with so many publications. Of particular

---

* Memorandum on Motion to Recuse, 409 U.S. 824 (1972).

interest was a 1971 article in the *Indiana Law Journal*. Among other things, it called into question the constitutional underpinnings of *Griswold* v. *Connecticut,* the landmark 1965 ruling on a right of privacy and birth control. If *Griswold* rested on dubious ground, so presumably did *Roe* v. *Wade,* the 1973 abortion decision (see Chapter Eleven). Bork had testified in the 1982 Senate hearings on his appointment to the Court of Appeals, "I do not know any way to apply the Constitution that I regard as legitimate other than in terms of the intent of the framers, as best as that can be determined."

Bork's nomination was guaranteed to be rancorous. The midterm elections in 1986 had converted a 53–47 Republican majority in the Senate into a 54–46 Democratic one. Moreover, some southern Democrats in the Senate could not have been elected without the black votes they received. Joseph Biden, not Strom Thurmond, chaired the Senate Judiciary Committee. Two of the Democrats on the committee (Biden and Paul Simon) were running for president. Moreover, Reagan himself was politically weaker in mid-1987 than in mid-1986. Intervening were revelations of the Iran-contra affair, which had shaken public confidence in the administration.

Before the Judiciary Committee began its record-setting 12 days of hearings on the nomination on September 15 (Bork would testify and be questioned on five of those days), the battle lines had already been drawn. Hesitation expressed in 1986 over close scrutiny of a nominee's judicial philosophy all but disappeared. Some Democrats, including Biden, let it be known well before the hearings started that they would vote against the nomination.

Cooperating with Democrats in the Senate was the Leadership Conference on Civil Rights, an umbrella organization of nearly 200 groups. It coordinated a massive public relations drive to galvanize public opposition. Nearly 2,000 law school professors (about 40 percent of all law faculty in the nation) signed a petition urging rejection. Old-timers recalled that only 300 law professors publicly opposed Carswell in 1970. The American Civil Liberties Union repealed a 50-year-old rule so that it could take a public stance against the nomination. Direct mail, television and newspaper advertisements, and other techniques of modern interest-group politics for the first time were aimed squarely against a Supreme Court nominee. The attempt was to make Bork appear not as a conservative but as a radical, as someone who would take away rights the people thought the Constitution protected. Not since Woodrow Wilson nominated Louis Brandeis in 1916 had a confirmation battle become so vitriolic.

On October 23, Judge Bork's Senate opponents prevailed, 58–42, a larger negative vote than either Haynsworth and Carswell had suffered in 1969 and 1970.

In place of Bork, President Reagan's advisers recommended a conservative without the years of scholarly writing that had made the Bork nomination a lightning rod. Senate Minority Leader Robert Dole advised anyone with ambitions to sit on the Supreme Court not to "write a word. I would hide in the closet until I was nominated."

On October 29, Reagan selected one of Bork's colleagues, Judge Douglas H. Ginsburg of the Court of Appeals for the District of Columbia Circuit. At age 41, Ginsburg had been an appeals judge for less than a year, was the first Jew chosen since Abe Fortas went on the bench in 1965, and was the youngest nominee to the Court since William O. Douglas in 1939. A clerk to Justice Thurgood Marshall in 1974–1975, Ginsburg taught law at Harvard until joining the Office of Management and Budget and then the Justice Department in the Antitrust Division in 1983.

Senators never got a chance to query Judge Ginsburg. Questions surfaced almost instantly. As an official in the Justice Department, he had handled a major case regarding the cable television industry while owning $140,000 worth of stock in a Canadian cable company. Then Ginsburg acknowledged disclosures that he had smoked marijuana as a student in the 1960s and more recently as a member of the Harvard law faculty in the 1970s. On November 7, he withdrew his name from consideration.

Not since 1970 had a president had to make a third nomination to fill a single vacancy. Time was critical. Reagan was nearing the start of his last year in office. "Lame duck" talk abounded. Like Johnson with Fortas in 1968, the vacancy might carry over to his successor in 1989.

On November 10 Reagan made his next move, nominating long-time acquaintance Anthony M. Kennedy, age 51, who had been a judge on the Ninth Circuit Court of Appeals since leaving private practice in 1975. With an undergraduate degree in political science from Stanford and a law degree from Harvard, Kennedy had been Chief of Staff Howard Baker's first choice after the Bork debacle, when Attorney General Edwin Meese convinced the president to pick Ginsburg. Democrats could find little wrong with Kennedy. His 500 opinions as an appeals judge suggested to them that his appointment would not dramatically change the direction of the Supreme Court.

An hour's debate in the Senate on February 3, 1988, preceded the vote to confirm, 97–0. Anthony Kennedy was sworn in on February 18 as the Court's 105th justice, ending a seven-month struggle over Justice Powell's successor.

The fight to replace Powell will have consequences apart from Kennedy's career on the Court. The tentative senatorial probing of ideology in the nominations of Rehnquist and Scalia in 1986 gave way to searching scrutiny in 1987. The Senate firmly reestablished the precedent that judicial philosophy is relevant and important. One of President Reagan's contributions to American government was no doubt unintended: he helped to make the Senate a more equal partner in shaping the Supreme Court.

Justice Kennedy had barely taken his seat on the Supreme Court when the presidential campaign of 1988 began. Although opposing political forces had waged a battle over the Court in 1987, the Court was not a prominent issue in the race between George Bush and Michael Dukakis. Strategists for both sides may have concluded that each candidate had more to lose than to gain by characterizing a vote for president as a vote for the future of the Supreme Court. Fundamentally, however, it was.

The Court and the rest of the federal judiciary will remain at the storm center of politics. Reagan's appointments at all levels will influence American life well into the twenty-first century, as will those of his successor, George Bush. Like Court-conscious Presidents Taft, Franklin Roosevelt, and Nixon before him, Reagan's aspirations to shape the Constitution through judicial nominations meant that presidential influence survives long after a presidential term expires. Even without deliberate efforts to mold the Court, a president's grasp may well exceed his reach.

KEY TERMS

constitutional law	cases	Warren Court
constitutional interpretation	judicial review	

QUERIES

1. What standards should the Senate apply during confirmation proceedings on a judicial nomination?

2. Can the Senate's rejection of Judge Bork in 1987 be explained mainly in terms of the fact that Democratic senators outnumbered Republican senators?

3. In November 1986, Senator Joseph Biden said he would have to vote for a qualified conservative like Judge Bork. He recanted in July after Bork's nomination, explaining that he had in mind a situation in which a conservative would be replacing another conservative. Is Biden's position supportable? Does the Senate have a constitutional or political obligation to ensure an ideologically balanced Supreme Court?

4. Why do some presidents make ideology or judicial philosophy a more obvious criterion in their selection of nominees to the bench?

SELECTED READINGS ON THE SUPREME COURT, THE JUDICIAL PROCESS, AND CONSTITUTIONAL INTERPRETATION*

ABRAHAM, HENRY J. *Freedom and the Court,* 5th ed. New York: Oxford University Press, 1988.

————. *The Judicial Process,* 5th ed. New York: Oxford University Press, 1986.

————. *The Judiciary,* 7th ed. Boston: Allyn & Bacon, 1987.

————. *Justices and Presidents: A Political History of Appointments to the Supreme Court,* 2d ed. New York: Oxford University Press, 1985.

BERGER, RAOUL. *Government by Judiciary: The Transformation of the Fourteenth Amendment.* Cambridge, Mass.: Harvard University Press, 1977.

BLASI, VINCENT, ed. *The Burger Court: The Counter-Revolution That Wasn't.* New Haven, Conn.: Yale University Press, 1983.

BORK, ROBERT H. "Neutral Principles and Some First Amendment Problems." 47 *Indiana Law Journal* 1 (1971).

CAPLAN, LINCOLN. *The Tenth Justice: The Solicitor General and the Rule of Law.* New York: Knopf, 1987.

CARDOZO, BENJAMIN. *The Nature of the Judicial Process.* New Haven, Conn.: Yale University Press, 1932.

CARTER, LEIF. *Reason in Law,* 3d ed. Boston: Little, Brown, 1988.

CUOMO, MARIO. "The Constitution, the Courts, and Judicial Competence." 116 *USA Today* 34 (July 1987).

CURRIE, DAVID P. *The Constitution in the Supreme Court: The First Hundred Years, 1789–1888.* Chicago: University of Chicago Press, 1985.

FUNSTON, RICHARD Y. *Constitutional Counter-Revolution? The Warren Court and the Burger Court.* Cambridge: Schenkman, 1977.

GABIN, SANFORD B. "Judicial Review, James Bradley Thayer and the 'Reasonable Doubt' Test." 3 *Hastings Constitutional Law Quarterly* 96 (1976).

GARRATY, JOHN, ed. *Quarrels That Have Shaped the Constitution,* rev. ed. New York: Harper & Row, 1987.

GOLDMAN, SHELDON. "Reaganizing the Judiciary: The First Term Appointments." 68 *Judicature* 313 (1985).

JACKSON, ROBERT H. *The Struggle for Judicial Supremacy.* New York: Knopf, 1941.

* Bibliographic entries for periodicals follow the legal form: volume number, name of periodical, and beginning page number, if any.

————. *The Supreme Court and the American System of Government.* Cambridge, Mass.: Harvard University Press, 1955.

KAMMEN, MICHAEL. *A Machine That Would Go of Itself: The Constitution in American Culture.* New York: Knopf, 1986.

KELLY, ALFRED H., WINFRED A. HARBISON, and HERMAN BELZ. *The American Constitution; Its Origins and Development,* 6th ed. New York: Norton, 1983.

LEVI, EDWARD H. *An Introduction to Legal Reasoning.* Chicago: University of Chicago Press, 1948.

MCCLOSKEY, ROBERT G. *The American Supreme Court.* Chicago: University of Chicago Press, 1960.

MCFEELEY, NEIL D. *Appointment of Judges, The Johnson Presidency.* Austin: University of Texas Press, 1987.

MARCUS, MAEVA, and JAMES E. PERRY, eds. *The Documentary History of the Supreme Court of the United States, 1789–1800: Vol. 1; Parts I and II, Appointments and Proceedings.* New York: Columbia University Press, 1985.

MASON, ALPHEUS T. "The Burger Court in Historical Perspective." 89 *Political Science Quarterly* 27 (1974).

————. "Eavesdropping on Justice: A Review Essay." 95 *Political Science Quarterly* 295 (1980).

————. *The Supreme Court from Taft to Burger.* Baton Rouge: Louisiana State University Press, 1979.

————, and GORDON E. BAKER. *Free Government in the Making,* 4th ed. New York: Oxford University Press, 1985.

MILLER, CHARLES A. *The Supreme Court and the Uses of History.* Cambridge, Mass.: Harvard University Press, 1969.

MORGAN, DONALD G. "The Origin of Supreme Court Dissent." 10 *William and Mary Quarterly* (3d series) 353 (1953).

MURPHY, WALTER F. *Elements of Judicial Strategy.* Chicago: University of Chicago Press, 1964.

————, and C. HERMAN PRITCHETT. *Courts, Judges, and Politics,* 4th ed. New York: Random House, 1986.

The Oliver Wendell Holmes Devise History of the Supreme Court of the United States. New York: Macmillan, 1971–. Volumes to date include: JULIUS GOEBEL, *Antecedents and Beginnings to 1801,* Vol. I (1971); GEORGE LEE HASKINS, and HERBERT A. JOHNSON, *Foundations of Power: John Marshall, 1801–15,* Vol. II (1981); G. EDWARD WHITE, *The Marshall Court and Cultural Change, 1815–35,* Vols. III and IV (1988); CARL B. SWISHER, *The Taney Period, 1836–64,* Vol. V (1974); CHARLES FAIRMAN, *Reconstruction and Reunion 1864–88,* Vols. VI and VII (1971, 1987); CHARLES FAIRMAN, *Five Justices and the Electoral Commission of 1877,* supplement to Vol. VII (1988); ALEXANDER M. BICKEL and BENNO C. SCHMIDT, JR., *The Judiciary and Responsible Government, 1910–21,* Vol. IX (1984).

REHNQUIST, WILLIAM H. *The Supreme Court: How It Was, How It Is.* New York: William Morrow, 1987.

SCHMIDHAUSER, JOHN R. *Judges and Justices: The Federal Appellate Judiciary.* Boston: Little, Brown, 1979.

SHOGAN, ROBERT A. *A Question of Judgment: The Fortas Case and the Struggle for the Supreme Court.* Indianapolis: Bobbs-Merrill, 1972.

SIMON, JAMES F. *In His Own Image: The Supreme Court in Richard Nixon's America.* New York: David McKay, 1973.

SPAETH, HAROLD J. *Supreme Court Policy Making.* San Francisco: W. H. Freeman, 1979.

STEAMER, ROBERT J. *Chief Justice: Leadership and the Supreme Court.* Columbia: University of South Carolina Press, 1986.

TRIBE, LAURENCE H. *American Constitutional Law,* 2d ed. Mineola, N.Y.: Foundation Press, 1988.

WARREN, CHARLES. *The Supreme Court in United States History,* 2 vols. Boston: Little, Brown, 1926.

SELECTED BIOGRAPHIES

BEVERIDGE, ALBERT J. *The Life of John Marshall,* 4 vols. Boston: Houghton Mifflin, 1916.

BOLES, DONALD E. *Mr. Justice Rehnquist, Judicial Activist: The Early Years.* Ames: Iowa State University Press, 1987.

CORWIN, EDWARD S. *John Marshall and the Constitution.* New Haven, Conn.: Yale University Press, 1919.

DANELSKI, DAVID J., and JOSEPH F. TULCHIN, eds. *The Autobiographical Notes of Charles Evans Hughes.* Cambridge, Mass.: Harvard University Press, 1973.

DUNNE, GERALD T. *Hugo Black and the Judicial Revolution.* New York: Simon & Schuster, 1977.

————. *Justice Joseph Story and the Rise of the Supreme Court.* New York: Simon & Schuster, 1970.

FAIRMAN, CHARLES. *Mr. Justice Miller and the Supreme Court, 1862–1890.* Cambridge, Mass.: Harvard University Press, 1939.

FINE, SIDNEY. *Frank Murphy,* 3 vols. Ann Arbor: University of Michigan Press, 1975–1984 (for Vols. 1 and 3); Chicago: University of Chicago Press, 1979 (for Vol. 2).

HENDEL, SAMUEL. *Charles Evans Hughes and the Supreme Court.* New York: Columbia University Press, 1951.

HIGHSAW, ROBERT B. *Edward Douglass White; Defender of the Conservative Faith.* Baton Rouge: Louisiana State University Press, 1981.

HIRSCH, H. N. *The Enigma of Felix Frankfurter.* New York: Basic Books, 1981.

HOWARD, J. WOODFORD. *Mr. Justice Murphy: A Political Biography.* Princeton, N.J.: Princeton University Press, 1968.

KING, WILLARD L. *Melville Weston Fuller.* New York: Macmillan, 1950.

LASH, JOSEPH P., ed. *Diaries of Felix Frankfurter* (1882–1965). New York: Norton, 1975.

LERNER, MAX. *The Mind and Faith of Mr. Justice Holmes.* Garden City, N.Y.: Halcyon House Reprint, 1948.

MAGRATH, C. PETER. *Morrison R. Waite.* New York: Macmillan, 1963.

MASON, ALPHEUS THOMAS. *Brandeis: A Free Man's Life.* New York: Viking, 1946.

————. *Harlan Fiske Stone: Pillar of the Law.* New York: Viking, 1956.

_____ . *William Howard Taft: Chief Justice.* New York: Simon & Schuster, 1964.

PASCHAL, J. FRANCIS. *Mr. Justice Sutherland.* Princeton, N.J.: Princeton University Press, 1951.

SCHWARTZ, BERNARD. *Super Chief: Earl Warren and His Supreme Court.* New York: New York University Press, 1983.

SIMON, JAMES F. *Independent Journey: The Life of William O. Douglas.* New York: Harper & Row, 1980.

STRUM, PHILIPPA. *Louis D. Brandeis: Justice for the People.* Cambridge, Mass.: Harvard University Press, 1984.

SWISHER, CARL B. *Roger B. Taney.* Washington, D.C.: Brookings, 1935.

_____ . *Stephen J. Field: Craftsman of the Law.* Washington, D.C.: Brookings, 1930.

WHITE, G. EDWARD. *Earl Warren: A Public Life.* New York: Oxford University Press, 1982.

ONE

Jurisdiction
and Organization
of the Federal Courts

Whoever attentively considers the different
departments of power must perceive that, in a
government in which they are separated from each
other, the judiciary, from the nature of its
functions, will always be the least dangerous
to the political rights of the Constitution. . . .

—ALEXANDER HAMILTON (1788)

American constitutional law represents a tiny fraction of the entire corpus of the law. Run-of-the-mill litigation between private parties seldom falls into the category of "cases" to which the judicial power of the Supreme Court extends. Even cases involving constitutional questions may be sidestepped. The Court decides, as we shall see, only those cases that meet certain prescribed standards. The Supreme Court of the United States is not "a super legal aid bureau."

This chapter presents certain rules and procedures guiding the justices in choosing the cases they will decide and sketches the major steps in the decision-making process. The rules and decisions governing jurisdiction and standing to sue vest in the justices considerable discretionary power. They control their workload by selecting the cases that require judicial remedy at the highest level. In the governing process, the Supreme Court has an important, though circumscribed, role to play.

THE JUDICIAL POWER

The Constitution in Article III makes possible the resolution of certain legal disputes in national, as opposed to state, courts. One significant difference between American government under the Articles of Confederation and the Constitution was the provision in the latter for a system of national courts. Under the Articles, there was not even a Supreme Court.

Federal and State Courts. Courts in the United States comprise 51 separate judicial systems: the court systems of the 50 states and the courts of the United States. The latter are commonly referred to, somewhat misleadingly, as federal courts.

The federal judicial power granted in Article III includes (1) cases arising under the Constitution, the laws of the United States, and treaties made under the authority of the United States; (2) admiralty and maritime cases; (3) controversies between two or more states; (4) controversies to which the United States is a party, even where the other party is a state; and (5) cases begun by a state against a citizen of another state or against another country.*

In contrast, the courts of the 50 states receive their authority from the constitutions and statutes of their respective states. This dual system of courts means that almost everyone in any of the 50 states is simultaneously within the *jurisdiction,* or reach, of two judicial systems, one state and the other federal. *Jurisdiction* refers to the authority a court has to decide a case. The term has two basic dimensions: who and what. The first identifies the parties who may take a case into a particular court. The second refers to the subject matter the parties may raise in their case.

Constitutional Courts and Legislative Courts. The Constitution vests judicial power of the United States in "one Supreme Court and in such inferior courts as the Congress may from time to time ordain and establish" (Art. III, Sec. 1). This provision is not self-executing, and Congress has established the following so-called constitutional courts: (1) courts of appeals for each of the 11 judicial circuits, plus one for the District of Columbia; (2) district courts, of which there are now 91 (89 in the 50 states, plus one in the District of Columbia and one in Puerto Rico); and (3) special courts, such as the Court of Appeals for the Federal Circuit. This thirteenth appeals court is the newest and, unlike the other 12, has both a different and a national jurisdiction. A merger of the old Court of Claims and the Court of Custom and Patent Appeals, this court accepts appeals in patent and trademark cases from any district court as well as all appeals from the Claims Court and the Court of International Trade.

Under power granted to it by other clauses in the Constitution, Congress has set up so-called legislative courts such as the United States Tax Court, which hears appeals from Treasury tax rulings; the Court of Military Appeals; and "local" courts for the District of Columbia (a trial court called the Superior Court and an appellate court known as the District of Columbia Court of Appeals). Since these courts are "legislative" as opposed to "constitutional," the tenure of the judges rests with statutes passed by Congress. Other legislative courts include the district courts established for the territories (one each in Guam, Northern Mariana Islands, and the Virgin Islands). Even though the judges on the United States District Court in Puerto Rico sit for terms of eight years, as opposed to life tenure, this court is considered "constitutional" rather than "legislative."

These distinctions are important in determining the power of Congress over the federal courts. Thus a constitutional court is governed by the doctrine of the separation of powers, and no legislative or administrative functions may be given it. In Hayburn's Case (1792), for example, the Court rejected an attempt by the legislature to impose on federal courts the duty of passing on pension claims. A legislative court, on the other hand, may be given nonjudicial functions, since the doctrine of separation of powers is inapplicable; and Congress has full power over the salary and tenure of its judges.

It does not follow, however, that because a court is a legislative body it may not exercise judicial power. The power exercised by such courts is not, however, that defined

* *Chisholm* v. *Georgia* (1793) (see Chapter Four) precipitated the Eleventh Amendment, which says that a state may not be a defendant in federal court in an action initiated by a citizen of another state or country. And the principle of sovereign immunity shields a state from a suit in federal courts initiated by its own citizens (*Hans* v. *Louisiana,* 1890). A suit may nonetheless be brought against state officers to bar them from executing an unconstitutional statute. Furthermore, the Eleventh Amendment is not a barrier to enforcement of a citizen's rights under the Fourteenth Amendment (*Fitzpatrick* v. *Bitzer,* 1976).

and granted by Article III but a power conferred by Congress in the execution of other provisions of the Constitution.

Jurisdiction of the Supreme Court. The Supreme Court's jurisdiction is in two parts: original and appellate. A court has *original jurisdiction* when a case begins or originates there, *appellate* when a case involves review of the decision of a lower court.

The Supreme Court's original jurisdiction is specified in Article III and can be neither diminished nor enlarged by Congress. It includes four kinds of disputes: (1) cases between one of the states and the national government; (2) cases between two or more states; (3) cases involving foreign ambassadors, ministers, or consuls; and (4) cases begun by a state against a citizen of another state or against another country. Only controversies between states qualify today exclusively as original cases in the Supreme Court. For the others, Congress has given concurrent jurisdiction to the lower federal courts. As a result, almost all of the Court's cases come from its appellate jurisdiction.

According to Article III, the Supreme Court has appellate jurisdiction "in all other cases . . . both as to law and fact, with such exceptions, and under such regulations as the Congress shall make." Congress, in other words, decides which categories of cases in the lower courts qualify for review by the Court. Not until 1889, for example, was there a right of appeal to the High Court in most federal criminal cases. Perhaps Congress could even deprive the Court of all appellate review and make final the decisions of lower courts. An extreme example occurred in 1869 when Congress, fearing that the Court would invalidate the Reconstruction Acts, hastily withdrew the Court's jurisdiction under the Habeas Corpus Act of 1867. The Court thus became powerless to pass on a case in which argument had been heard (***Ex parte McCardle***, in Chapter Two).

The major change in the appellate jurisdiction of the Supreme Court since 1789 has been in the proportion of cases qualifying for obligatory, as opposed to discretionary, review. Although the Judiciary Act of 1789 allowed Supreme Court review of certain cases from the state and lower federal courts by way of a writ of error, it was not until 1891, with passage of the Circuit Courts of Appeals Act, that the justices had some discretion over the cases they would decide.

The Judges Act of 1925 further reduced the mandatory jurisdiction. As a result, most cases raising a *federal question*—that is, involving the Constitution, statutes, or treaties of the United States—reached the Court on *certiorari*. Review in this category was plainly discretionary. The justices could select for decision those cases it considered of greatest national importance. A much smaller number of cases (about 5 percent of the total filings in the mid-1980s) came to the Court on *appeal*. These cases qualified by statute for obligatory review, without regard to the importance of the issue raised or its impact on the government or the general public. By the mid-1980s, the appeals category accounted for one-third of all cases the Court decided on the merits each term. Because the justices disposed of some appeals summarily without the usual briefing and oral argument (see the section on Supreme Court Decision Making), decisions were of murky precedential value and sometimes resulted in confusion for lower courts.

In 1988 Congress enacted a major overhaul of the Supreme Court's jurisdiction, a move supported by all sitting justices. With the start of the October 1988 term, the Court's appellate jurisdiction became almost entirely discretionary. Access to the Court is now mainly by certiorari. The mandatory "appeals" category has been nearly abolished, except for decisions by three-judge district courts (required by Congress in a few instances), which go to the Supreme Court on *direct appeal,* bypassing the courts of appeals.

Jurisdiction of the Courts of Appeals. Congress has given the courts of appeals jurisdiction in appeals taken from the federal district courts sitting in their respective circuits, from judgments of the Tax Court, and from the rulings of particular administrative and regulatory agencies such as the National Labor Relations Board and the Securities and Exchange Commission. The heaviest responsibility for reviewing decisions of administrative tribunals falls on the Court of Appeals for the District of Columbia Circuit. In addition, courts of appeals may review cases from the district courts in the territories. (For example, Guam and the Northern Mariana Islands are considered part of the Ninth Circuit.)

Jurisdiction of the District Courts. The district courts have appellate jurisdiction only with respect to a few classes of cases tried before U.S. magistrates (formerly U.S. commissioners). Their original jurisdiction includes cases involving more than $50,000, where the parties are citizens of different states, and cases that raise a federal question. Two wholly independent bases of jurisdiction are thus provided. The United States District Court for the District of Columbia has a special responsibility in reviewing changes in local electoral practices in certain states by virtue of the Voting Rights Act.

Self-Imposed Limitations on Judicial Power. In many cases where the federal courts, including the Supreme Court, would appear to have jurisdiction, one or more other requirements may prevent a court from accepting and deciding the case. Some of these self-denying ordinances were set forth by Justice Brandeis, concurring, in *Ashwander* v. *TVA* (1936). Summarized briefly, these rules are

1. The Court will not pass upon the constitutionality in a friendly, nonadversary, proceeding.
2. The Court will not anticipate a question of constitutional law in advance of the necessity for deciding it.
3. The Court will not formulate a rule of law broader than the facts of the case require.
4. If possible, the Court will dispose of a case on nonconstitutional grounds.
5. The Court will not pass upon the validity of a statute on complaint of one who fails to show injury to person or property.
6. The Court will not pass upon the constitutionality of a statute at the instance of one who has accepted its benefits.
7. Whenever possible, statutes will be construed so as to avoid a constitutional issue.

A commonly invoked rule is that requiring *standing to sue,* that is, a direct personal interest on the part of the litigant allegedly infringed by the law or government action. Hayburn's Case, for example, has long been understood to bar federal courts from issing *advisory opinions,* or extrajudicial advice. Instead, in terms of Article III, a real "case" or "controversy" must be present.

Standing is a threshold question. Without standing, litigants do not get to press the merits or substance of their dispute. In *Massachusetts* v. *Mellon* (1923) a state was not allowed to challenge the validity of the Federal Maternity Act on behalf of its citizens. And although state taxpayers are allowed to bring suit in state courts based on the unconstitutionality of state laws and official acts, *Frothingham* v. *Mellon* (1923) denied standing to a federal taxpayer who sought to challenge the Federal Maternity Act. The Court distinguished the status of federal and state taxpayers by concluding that the interest of the former was minute and indeterminable. In spite of this decision, the Court in 1968 conceded standing to a federal taxpayer who sought to challenge an alleged breach of the First Amendment's establishment-of-religion clause through federal expenditures under a 1965 act for textbooks and instructional costs in sectarian schools (*Flast* v. *Cohen*). The Court distinguished this situation from the typical taxpayer suit by viewing the establishment clause itself as a limitation on the taxing and spending power of Congress; hence taxpayers can urge more than their general interest in the expenditure of federal funds. But *Flast* has limits. In 1982, the Court denied standing in a case where surplus government property had been transferred to a sectarian school (*Valley Forge Christian College* v. *Americans United for Separation of Church and State*). The majority regarded the transfer as an executive action under the Property Clause (Article IV), not congressional action under the Taxing and Spending Clause, as had been the case in *Flast*. So *Flast's* easier standing rules did not apply.

Another requirement is that the case must present a *live dispute*. In *De Funis* v. *Odegaard* (1974) the Court held, 5–4, that a case brought by a white law student, challenging a University of Washington preferential admissions program for minorities, was *moot*. *De Funis* aroused national interest, with 26 amicus curiae briefs, yet the majority concluded that since the student had been admitted to law school by court order and was about to graduate, he suffered no injury.

A case must also be "ripe for review." It must have reached a certain stage of *ripeness* or maturity before the Court will hear and decide it on the merits. A 1972 decision, *Laird* v. *Tatum*, held 5–4 that the petitioners' attack on the Army's civilian surveillance system was not ripe. For the majority allegations of a "subjective chill [of First Amendment rights] are not an adequate substitute for a claim of objective harm or a threat of specific future harm."

Absence of an actual controversy, ripeness, standing, or jurisdiction makes a case *nonjusticiable,* or inappropriate for settlement by a court. Justiciability merges into the *political question doctrine*. Discussed more fully in **Baker** v. **Carr** (1962) in Chapter Two, a political question is one that the Court believes should be decided by the "political branches" of the government—Congress or the presidency. Today, political questions include certain foreign-policy matters, the Constitution's stipulation of a "republican form of government" for every state, and the ratification of constitutional amendments. At one time apportionment of legislative districts was deemed "political" and hence out of judicial bounds.

Modesty pervades these self-denials, but the justices differ markedly in applying them. *Judicial activists* (those more eager to intervene and to substitute their views for those of other policymakers) tend to gloss over such matters as "technical." *Judicial restraintists* (those inclined to defer to decisions made elsewhere in the political system) can frequently avoid a decision on the merits by insisting that a litigant has run afoul of one or more limiting rules.

SUPREME COURT DECISION MAKING

Article III of the Constitution establishes "the judicial power of the United States" in "one Supreme Court." Initially staffed by six justices, since 1869 the Supreme Court has had nine justices.

Access to the Supreme Court. Having a case decided by a state or lower federal court by no means assures the losing litigant of review, ultimately, by the United States Supreme Court. In fact, the justices reject many more cases than they decide. In recent terms, the justices have annually denied review in about 4,000 cases and have decided only about 160 cases with full opinion. Some 750 cases are usually carried over for action the following term.

Mystery surrounds selection of cases, but experience suggests that the presence of one or more of the following factors increases the likelihood that the justices will accept a case for decision: (1) The United States is a party to the case and requests Supreme Court review, (2) courts of appeals have issued conflicting decisions on the question, (3) the issue is one some justices are eager to engage, (4) the court below has made a decision clearly at odds with established Supreme Court interpretation of a law or constitutional provision, (5) the Court's workload seems to permit accepting another case for decision, and (6) the case raises an issue of overriding importance to the nation.

A minimum of four justices must vote to accept the case. This is the so-called *rule of four*. Deciding what to decide is therefore an important stage in the judicial process. Statements by losing counsel that they will take their case "all the way to the Supreme Court" should, therefore, be regarded as threats, not promises.

The Justices at Work. The actual work of the Supreme Court falls under four headings: reading various papers, oral argument, conference, opinions and decisions.

(1) *The reading stage.* Each petition for review generates extensive reading material for the justices and their law clerks. In documents called briefs, counsel submit lengthy statements and cite substantial portions of the lower court record to demonstrate why the Court should (or should not) accept the case for decision. (A denial of review leaves in force the decision of the most immediate court below.) When the justices accept a case, opposing counsel submit yet another round of briefs. Persons and organizations interested in, but not parties to, a case may add to the justices' reading assignments still further by filing their own briefs as *amici curiae,* or "friends of the Court."

(2) *Oral argument.* In addition to reading the printed briefs submitted by counsel, the Court listens to oral argument. During the chief justiceship of John Marshall (1801–1835) arguments were well-nigh interminable. Daniel Webster, a leading attorney of that day, used to run on for days. In 1849, the Court reduced the time for oral argument to two hours: one for appellant or petitioner (the party seeking the review) and one for appellee or respondent (the defendant on review). More recently, opposing counsel must be content with dividing an hour between themselves. The Court allots additional time only in exceptional circumstances. The Court sits from the first Monday in October through June and sometimes into early July, with arguments being heard from October until the end of April. Monday, Tuesday, and Wednesday of two consecutive weeks are set aside for oral argument, with at least two weeks following being reserved for the preparation of opinions. The justices hear arguments on those days from 10:00 A.M. until 3:00 P.M., with an hour recess at noon for lunch.

(3) *Conference.* Wednesday and Friday are conference days—the time set apart primarily for discussion and decision of cases argued during the week. According to Chief Justice Rehnquist,

As soon as we come off the bench Wednesday afternoon around three o'clock, we go into private "conference" in a room adjoining the chambers of the Chief Justice. At our Wednesday afternoon meeting we deliberate and vote on the four cases which we heard argued the preceding Monday. The Chief Justice begins the discussion of each case with a summary of the facts, his analysis of the law, and an announcement of his proposed vote (that is, whether to affirm, reverse, modify, etc.). The discussion then passes to the senior Associate Justice, presently Mr. Justice Brennan, who does likewise. It then goes on down the line to the junior Associate Justice. When the discussion of one case is concluded, the discussion of the next one is immediately taken up, until all the argued cases on the agenda for that particular Conference have been disposed of.*

* "Sunshine in the Third Branch," 16 *Washburn Law Journal* 559, 559–660, n. 1:1977.

In cases of great importance, discussion may take place at more than one conference before the justices are prepared to reach a decision. All cases are decided by majority vote. For conference action on petitions for review, the chief justice uses a "Discuss List." This is a timesaving device. Any justice may add a case to the "Discuss List," but unless a case makes the list—and about 70 percent do not—review is automatically denied, without discussion.

(4) *Opinions and decisions.* On Monday after a two-week argument session the chief justice circulates an assignment list to the justices. If the chief justice is of the majority, he assigns the task of writing the opinion for the Court; if not, the senior justice of the majority makes the assignment. Preparation of the majority opinion requires much "give and take," with an opinion going through as many as a dozen drafts. The goal is an *opinion of the Court,* representing the consensus of the majority, not merely the views of the writer. A decision for which no majority opinion can be agreed on is referred to as "the judgment of the Court." The justices' positions are fluid. Up to the moment—weeks or months after the opinion writing began—the writer announces the decision in open Court, the justices are free to change their votes.

In only about a quarter of the decisions each term is the Court unanimous. In the rest dissenters file one or more opinions explaining their differences with the majority. According to Chief Justice Hughes, *dissents* are "an appeal to the brooding spirit of the law, to the intelligence of a future day, when a later decision may possibly correct the error into which the dissenting judge believes the court to have been betrayed." *Concurring opinions,* increasingly prevalent in recent years, indicate a justice's acceptance of the majority decision but unwillingness to adopt all the reasoning contained in the opinion of the Court or a desire to say something additionally.

An Overworked Bench? Although the number of cases the Court decides with formal written opinion has not changed significantly during the past two or three decades, the number of cases from which the justices choose this number has grown drastically. In 1930, the justices found 1,039 cases on their docket. In 1951, about 1,200 cases were filed. By 1970 the number had tripled to 3,600. The 1979–1980 docket contained 3,985 new filings, with 796 additional cases carried over from prior terms. This trend has led some to worry about the Court's workload and its ability to do its work competently. Chief Justice Burger warned that it may become "impossible" for a chief justice "to perform his duties well and survive very long." Justice Blackmun has worried "about the cases that we 'barely' do not take, namely, those that almost assuredly would have been taken twenty years ago."

To deal with the caseload, a study group headed by Professor Paul A. Freund and selected by Chief Justice Burger recommended in 1972 the establishment of a National Court of Appeals to share the task of screening requests for High Court action each year. The new court would review the Supreme Court docket, referring only the most important cases to the justices and disposing of the rest itself.

The proposal stirred controversy within the Court and among lawyers and lower-court judges. Without formal endorsement, Chief Justice Burger pressed for action to relieve the Court's burden, citing the Freund Commission's recommendations as worthy of consideration. The chief justice also encouraged the establishment of a federal commission, headed by Nebraska Senator Roman L. Hruska, which recommended an intermediate court to decide about 150 cases a year referred to it either by the Supreme Court or existing courts of appeals. However, all its rulings would be subject to Supreme Court review.

Congressional elimination in 1988 of almost all the Court's mandatory appellate jurisdiction, discussed earlier in this chapter, may marginally affect the number of annual filings. It will surely affect the way the justices allocate their time. Other proposed changes call for eliminating categories of cases that currently qualify for Supreme Court review and establishing an intercircuit panel to deal with conflicting rulings among the courts of appeals. It seems certain that debate on the Court's workload and various remedies will continue. Proposals to change the jurisdiction of the Supreme Court and the organization of the federal court system have been controversial throughout American history because such changes involve considerations of access and power, as well as efficiency.

SOURCE MATERIALS

Supreme Court Decisions. The reported opinions of the Supreme Court form the basic material for the study of constitutional law. There are three editions of these reports.

(1) *United States Reports* (the official edition, now published by the Government Printing Office, Washington, D.C.). Until 1875, the reports were cited according to the name of the reporter, with the reporter's name usually abbreviated. Beginning with Volume 91 in 1875, the reports have been cited only by volume number and the designation "U.S." (For example, a case cited as 444 U.S. 130 is located in volume 444 of the *U.S. Reports,* beginning on page 130.)

1789–1800 Dallas	(1–4 Dall., 1–4 U.S.)
1801–1815 Cranch	(1–9 Cr., 5–13 U.S.)
1816–1827 Wheaton	(1–12 Wheat., 14–25 U.S.)
1828–1842 Peters	(1–16 Pet., 26–41 U.S.)
1843–1860 Howard	(1–24 How., 42–65 U.S.)
1861–1862 Black	(1–2 Bl., 66–67 U.S.)
1863–1874 Wallace	(1–23 Wall., 68–90 U.S.)
1875–	(91– U.S.)

The number of volumes of the *United States Reports* has now passed the 500 mark.

(2) *United States Supreme Court Reports, Lawyers' Edition* (published by the Lawyers' Cooperative Publishing Company, Rochester, New York, a commercial publisher). The advantage of this complete edition lies in the inclusion of material from the briefs of opposing counsel and a substantial number of notes and annotations on various topics of constitutional law. *Lawyers' Edition* is cited as L.Ed. (e.g., 96 L.Ed. 954).

(3) *Supreme Court Reporter* (published by West Publishing Company, St. Paul, Minnesota). This is similar in concept to *Lawyers' Edition* but is not a complete edition of all cases since 1789. It is cited as S.Ct. (e.g., 58 S.Ct. 166).

The foregoing publishers issue preliminary or advance sheets of the reports, those of the commercial publishers appearing much earlier than the government's. The earliest publication of the full opinions appears in the *United States Law Week,* published by the Bureau of National Affairs. Some very recent cases cited in this volume carry the *Law Week* citation (e.g., 56 U.S.L.W. 4818). In addition, the Clerk's Office at the Supreme Court has a very limited number of "slip opinions" available when decisions are handed down.

The "record" of each decided case contains valuable material in the form of briefs of counsel, proceedings in lower courts, and exhibits. Unfortunately, these are not nearly so widely available as the Supreme Court decisions themselves. Some 25 law libraries across the nation are designated depositories and routinely receive copies of such documents from the clerk of the Supreme Court. Other libraries may subscribe to microfiche editions. University Publications of America in Washington, D.C., publishes *Landmark Briefs and Arguments of the Supreme Court of the United States: Constitutional Law*. With new volumes added annually, this set contains the complete extant record, plus transcripts of oral arguments where available, of major constitutional decisions of the Supreme Court, beginning in 1793, including many of the cases selected for this book. Information about pending cases appears in *Preview*, published from September through May by the Public Education Division of the American Bar Association.

Lower Federal Court Decisions. Lower federal court opinions are published by West: The decisions of the courts of appeals appear in *Federal Reporter* in 300 numbered volumes, subsequently numbered in a second series; they are cited as F. or F.2d. Selected decisions of the district courts appear in *Federal Supplement,* cited as F. Supp.

For current developments in judicial organization, jurisdictional changes, and appointments, consult *The Third Branch,* a monthly bulletin of the federal courts published by the Federal Judicial Center in Washington, D.C.

Legislative and Administrative Records. The statutes may be found chronologically in *United States Statutes at Large,* of which a new volume appears annually, and are available in an analytical form in the *United States Code* (U.S. Government Printing Office), *United States Code Annotated* (West Publishing Co.), and in *United States Code Service* (Lawyers' Cooperative Publishing Co.).

Debates in Congress are available under the following titles and have been officially published since 1873:

Annals of Congress, 1789–1824

Register of Debates in Congress, 1824–1837

Congressional Globe, 1833–1873

Congressional Record, 1873–

Administrative rules and orders are published chronologically in the *Federal Register* and are presented analytically in the *Code of Federal Regulations.* Administrative and congressional activity is followed by *Congressional Quarterly Weekly Report* (published by Congressional Quarterly, Inc., of Washington, D.C.) and by *National Journal* (published by Government Research Corp., of Washington, D.C.).

State Court Decisions. The decisions of the highest state courts are published separately by either the state or a commercial publisher. A sectional reporter system, which combines selected decisions of the courts of several states in one publication, is also available in most law libraries.

Law Review Material. In addition to a substantial body of books and monographs, many of which are cited at the ends of essays throughout this book, there is a vast output of articles in legal periodicals on all phases of constitutional law. Consult the *Index to Legal Periodicals* (published by H. W. Wilson Co. of New York City), which is organized on a subject-matter and author basis.

Other Research Aids. Bibliographic sources include the massive set compiled by Kermit L. Hall, *A Comprehensive Bibliography of American Constitutional and Legal History, 1896–1979,* 5 vols. (Millwood, N.Y.: Kraus International Publications, 1984). More concise are Alpheus Thomas Mason and D. Grier Stephenson, Jr., *American Constitutional Development* (Arlington Heights, Ill.: AHM Publishing Co., 1977), and D. Grier Stephenson, Jr., *The Supreme Court and the American Republic: An Annotated Bibliography* (New York: Garland Publishing, 1981). The latter volume includes a guide to the location of the papers of Supreme Court Justices.

Study of individual Justices is now considerably aided by Linda A. Blandford and Patricia Russell Evans, eds., *Supreme Court of the United States 1789–1980: An Index to Opinions Arranged by Justice*, 2 vols. (Millwood, N.Y.: Kraus International Publications, 1983). Biographical essays are contained in Leon Friedman and Fred L. Israel, *The Justices of the United States Supreme Court 1789–1969: Their Lives and Major Opinions*, 4 vols. (New York: Chelsea House, 1969). A fifth volume, edited by Friedman, covers the years 1969–1978 and supplements the first four. General information on almost all aspects of the work of the Supreme Court is contained in Congressional Quarterly's *Guide to the U.S. Supreme Court* (1979). Constitutional analysis, to supplement this text, appears in *The Constitution of the United States: Analysis and Interpretation* (Washington, D.C.: Government Printing Office, 1973, with later supplements), and in J. W. Peltason's *Corwin and Peltason's Understanding the Constitution*, 11th ed. (New York: Holt, Rinehart & Winston, 1988). An invaluable resource is Kermit L. Hall, ed., *United States Constitutional and Legal History*, 20 vols. (New York: Garland Publishing, 1987), which reprints more than 450 articles. Also helpful are Leonard W. Levy, Kenneth L. Karst, and Dennis J. Mahoney, eds., *Encyclopedia of the American Constitution*, 4 vols. (New York: Macmillan, 1986), and Robert J. Janosik, ed., *Encyclopedia of the American Judicial System*, 3 vols. (New York: Scribner's, 1987). Other sources to consult on the Court, past and present, include the *Yearbook* of the Supreme Court Historical Society; the *ABA Journal*, published by the American Bar Association; and *Judicature*, published by the American Judicature Society.

READING A SUPREME COURT DECISION

Every discipline has its own literature, and the literature of the study of the Constitution includes judicial opinions. It is essential, therefore, to acquire a talent for reading cases because they represent the medium through which a court speaks. Students will find it helpful to take careful notes in the form of an outline on the cases they read. Making the outline is called *briefing a case*. Thorough case briefing consists of a summary of at least seven elements.

Name of the Case. Always located at the beginning, the name or title identifies the parties to the case. The name of the person or entity bringing the case to the Supreme Court appears first; the party being brought to the Court is listed second. The *v.* stands for "versus" or "against." So in ***Davis*** v. ***Bandemer*** (1986) (see Chapter Two), Davis was one of several Indiana officials. Bandemer was one of several Indiana Democrats who had convinced a district court that Davis and the others were maintaining a constitutionally invalid legislative apportionment plan. Having lost in the court below, Davis wanted the Supreme Court to overturn the district court. In cases on certiorari the *petitioner* brings the case against the *respondent*. In cases on appeal, the *appellant* brings the case against the *appellee*. At times the terminology becomes confusing in a criminal case, in which the person charged with the crime in the trial court is often called "the defendant." In the Supreme Court the defendant may now be the petitioner, respondent, appellant, or appellee, but the justices in their opinions may refer to "the defendant" in one paragraph and "the respondent" in another and still be referring to the same individual.

Facts. Cases are real, not hypothetical, controversies between parties. The issues of a case arise from circumstances or events that have prompted one or both parties to seek redress or resolution in court. The facts of a case may or may not be in dispute, but they are always a factor in how cases are decided.

Question(s). The facts of a case present one or more issues or questions for decision. Most of a judicial opinion is an effort to answer those questions. Although even a relatively simple case may generate many questions, counsel in the Supreme Court seek review only of those of the gravest importance—to the parties involved and to the nation. Ordinarily, the Supreme Court decides questions of law, not fact. In reviewing a criminal conviction, for instance, the Court is rarely concerned with a defendant's actual guilt or innocence. Rather, the justices focus on procedural issues, such as the admissibility of evidence or the lawfulness of an arrest.

Decision. A decision is the result or outcome of a case. The Court's opinion provides answers to the question(s) the case raises. For example, a government agency has, or has not, exceeded its authority under the law or the Constitution. Typically in the Supreme Court, decisions take the form of *affirming* (accepting) or *reversing* (rejecting and setting aside) the judgment of the court below. When reversing, the justices will often *remand* (send back) a case to the lower court for action "not inconsistent" with the Court's decision.

Reasoning of the Majority Opinion. As explained in the previous section, the goal of the Court's decision-making process is a statement reflecting the consensus of a majority of the justices. It explains why a certain question requires a certain answer. An exercise in persuasion, the majority opinion attempts to justify the decision the Court has reached.

Reasoning of Separate Opinions. Concurring and dissenting opinions should be examined closely because they may shed light on what has been decided. Dissenting opinions highlight weaknesses in the majority's reasoning. Concurring opinions may indicate the limits to a line of reasoning beyond which certain members of the majority are not willing to go. Both may highlight legal trends—where a decision has come from and where it might be going.

Votes. The Supreme Court sits as a collegial body. That is, all justices normally take part in each decision. The Court's quorum now stands at six. Awareness of the votes of individual justices can alert the reader to shifts in a justice's position. Throughout this book, the headnote for each excerpted case contains the voting alignment.

KEY TERMS

federal courts	mootness	concurring opinion
state courts	ripeness	briefing a case
jurisdication	nonjusticiable	petitioner
constitutional courts	political question	respondent
legislative courts	judicial activist	appellant
original jurisdiction	judicial restraintist	appellee
appellate jurisdiction	rule of four	affirm
federal question	amicus curiae	reverse
certiorari	oral argument	remand

appeal   conference   majority opinion

direct appeal   opinion of the court   separate opinions

Ashwander rules   dissent   advisory opinion

standing to sue

QUERIES

1. Why are the decisions of state and lower federal courts important in helping to shape American constitutional law?

2. How can "threshold questions" such as standing be crucial in the outcome of a constitutional case?

3. Attempts to alter the jurisdiction of the Supreme Court usually arouse controversy. Why?

4. Explain recent proposals to ease the workload of the Supreme Court. Can you suggest others? From what sources are support and opposition for these proposals most likely to come?

SELECTED READINGS

BURGER, WARREN E. "The Time Is Now for an Intercircuit Panel." 71 *ABA Journal* 86 (April 1985).

CASPER, GERHARD, and RICHARD A. POSNER. *The Workload of the Supreme Court.* Chicago: American Bar Foundation, 1976.

ESTREICHER, SAMUEL, and JOHN SEXTON. *Redefining the Supreme Court's Role: A Theory of Managing the Federal Justice Process.* New Haven, Conn.: Yale University Press, 1986.

FISH, PETER G. *The Politics of Federal Judicial Administration.* Princeton, N.J.: Princeton University Press, 1973.

FRANKFURTER, FELIX, and J. M. LANDIS. *The Business of the Supreme Court.* New York: Macmillan, 1928.

HOWARD, J. WOODFORD, JR. *Courts of Appeals in the Federal Judicial System.* Princeton, N.J.: Princeton University Press, 1981.

MARCUS, MAEVA, and ROBERT TEIR. "*Hayburn's Case:* A Misinterpretation of Precedent." 1988 *Wisconsin Law Review* 527 (1988).

NEUBORNE, BURT. "Justiciability, Remedies, and the Burger Court." In Herman Schwartz, ed., *The Burger Years.* New York: Penguin, 1988.

PROVINE, DORIS MARIE. *Case Selection in the United States Supreme Court.* Chicago: University of Chicago Press, 1980.

SPAETH, HAROLD J. "Jurisdiction," in 2 *Encyclopedia of the American Judicial System* 825 (New York: Scribner's, 1987).

STERN, ROBERT L., EUGENE GRESSMAN, and STEPHEN M. SHAPIRO. *Supreme Court Practice,* 6th ed. Washington, D.C.: Bureau of National Affairs, 1986.

WASBY, STEPHEN L. *The Supreme Court in the Federal Judicial System,* 3d ed. Chicago: Nelson-Hall, 1988.

TWO

The Constitution, the Supreme Court, and Judicial Review

*How easily men satisfy themselves that the Constitution
is exactly what they wish it to be.*

—JUSTICE JOSEPH STORY (1845)

The Constitution of 1787 and its 26 amendments can be read in about half an hour. One could memorize the written document word for word, as many schoolchildren once did, and still know little or nothing of its meaning. The reason is that the body of rules known as constitutional law consists primarily of decisions and opinions of the United States Supreme Court—the gloss that the justices have spread on the formal document. Charles Warren asked us not to forget that "however the Court may interpret the provisions of the Constitution, it is still the Constitution which is law and not decisions of the Court." But Charles Evans Hughes bluntly asserted that "The Constitution is what the Judges say it is." Furthermore, recurrent declarations of reverence for "our Ark of Covenant," as Chief Justice Taft called the Constitution, stand in sharp contrast to the reality that most Americans do not adequately understand the Constitution. Popular perceptions about the Constitution are frequently at odds with the document itself, making the American Constitution in its broadest sense greater than the sum of its parts. Myth wars with fact both within and without the Court.

GRANTING AND LIMITING POWER

In the United States the Constitution alone is supreme. All agencies of government stand in the relationship of creator to creatures. There is, Woodrow Wilson observed, "no sovereign government in America." But Wilson was not blind to the fact that government means action. "Power belongs to government, is lodged in organs of initiative; control belongs to the community, is lodged with the voters"—and the courts.

American *constitutionalism*—the belief in limiting government power by a written charter—deals with the problem James Madison posed in *The Federalist,* No. 51: "In framing a government which is to be administered by men over men, the great difficulty lies in this: you must first enable the government to control the governed; and in the next place oblige it to control itself." The Constitution both grants and limits power. Article I lists the powers of Congress; Article II invests executive power in the president; Article III confers judicial power on one Supreme Court and on such other courts as Congress may establish. Article I, Section 9, sets limits on national power; Article I, Section 10, restricts the states. Chief Justice Marshall called this section, the only one in the original Constitution limiting state power, "a bill of rights for the people of the states." The Constitution provides no definition of either powers or limitations, nor does the Constitution state how its words are to be interpreted.

In ways both obvious and subtle, the Constitution appears to be an instrument of rights, of limitations, rather than of powers. Certain things Congress is expressly forbidden to do. It may not pass an ex post facto law or a bill of attainder; it may not tax exports from any state; and it may not—except in great emergencies—suspend the writ of habeas corpus. The Bill of Rights (Amendments I through VIII) contains a longer list of things the national government is powerless to do. The state governments are likewise forbidden to do specific things. Article I, Section 10, declares that a state may not enact ex post facto laws, impair the obligation of contracts, coin money, emit bills of credit, or enter into any treaty or alliance with a foreign state. Certain restrictions imposed by the Bill of Rights on the national government have now been largely "incorporated" in the Fourteenth Amendment as limits on the states, as Chapter Nine explains.

Government is also circumscribed in less specific ways. The Constitution separates and limits power, even as it confers it. Congress is endowed with "legislative" power; it may not, therefore (except as a result of a specific grant or by implication), exercise executive or judicial power. The same restrictions apply to the other branches of the national government: The terms *judicial power* and *executive power,* like *legislative power,* have a technical meaning. In the exercise of their respective functions, neither Congress, president, nor judiciary may, under the principle of separation of powers, encroach on fields allocated to the other branches of government. Instead of requiring that the departments be kept absolutely separate and distinct, however, the Constitution mingles their functions. Congress is granted legislative power, but the grant is not exclusive. Lawmaking is shared by the president in his exercise of the veto. The appointing authority is vested in the president; but on certain appointments the Senate must give its advice and consent.

The second power-limiting principle, federalism, means a constitutional system in which two authorities, each having a complete government system, exist in the same territory and act on the same people. In its American manifestation, federalism is a complicated arrangement whereby the national government exercises enumerated, implied, and inherent powers, all others being "reserved to the States respectively, or to the people." Each government is supreme within its own sphere; neither is supreme within the sphere of the other. Federalism, like separation of powers and checks and balances, is a means of obliging government to control itself. None of these limiting principles is spelled out; they are either implicit in the organization and structure of the Constitution, or as with judicial review, deducible from "the theory of our government."

Madison and the Founding Fathers generally called this intricate system "free government." The power surrendered by the people is first divided between two distinct governments (the national government and the states) and then the portion allotted to each subdivided among distinct and separate departments. Hence a double security is provided for the rights of the people. Distinct governments will exercise control over each other and at the same time each will be checked by itself. "Vibrations of power" (the "genius" of free government, Hamilton called it) are inherent in this complexus of restraints. Just how such controls were to be enforced the Constitution does not specify.

THE DOCTRINE OF JUDICIAL REVIEW

For correctives against abuse of power, Americans have not been content to rely on *political checks*. Public opinion and the ballot box, the essential safeguards in most free societies, are not enough. In America, government is kept within bounds, not only by the electoral process, but also through separation of powers, federalism, and (as an adjunct to all these) *judicial review*.

Views of the Framers. The framers made the Constitution "the supreme law of the land," but they left unanswered the question of who was to sustain this supremacy. In the Philadelphia Convention debates of 1787, it was suggested that each house of Congress might, when in doubt, call on the judges for an opinion concerning the validity of national legislation. Madison declared that a "law violating a constitution established by the people themselves would be considered by the judges as null and void." It was repeatedly urged that Supreme Court justices be joined with the executive in a council of revision and be empowered to veto congressional legislation. Certain delegates objected to this proposal, contending that the justices would have this power anyway in cases properly before them. Any such provision would give the Court a double check. It would compromise "the impartiality of the Court by making them go on record before they were called in due course, to give . . . their exposition of the laws, which involved a power of deciding on their constitutionality." Other members of the Convention, though not denying that the Court could exercise such power, asserted that it would violate the principle of separation of powers and have the effect, as Elbridge Gerry remarked, of "making statesmen of judges." In the end the power of judicial review was not expressly authorized.

Professor Corwin suggested that for the Constitution's framers, judicial review rested "upon certain general principles [government under law, separation of powers, federalism, Bill of Rights] which, in their estimation, made specific provision for it unnecessary." Accordingly, James Wilson, Oliver Ellsworth, and John Marshall, all destined for appointment to the Supreme Court, subscribed to the doctrine of judicial review in their respective ratifying conventions. On January 17, 1788, Ellsworth of Connecticut declared,

> If the United States go beyond their powers, if they make a law which the constitution does not authorize, it is void; and the judicial power, the national judges, who, to secure their impartiality, are to be made independent, will declare it to be void. On the other hand, if the States go beyond their limits, if they make a law which is an usurpation upon the general government, the law is void; and upright independent judges will declare it so.

Robert Yates, Philadelphia Convention delegate from New York, and a nonsigner of the Constitution, probed these realities and predicted that judicial review, which he took for granted, would enable the justices "to mould the government into almost any shape they please. . . . Men placed in this situation will generally soon feel themselves independent of Heaven itself."

Yates raised a hard question and made a serious charge. To answer it, Hamilton fused faith and reason. Judicial review, he argued in *The Federalist,* No. 78, does not suppose "a superiority of the judicial to the legislative power. It only supposes that the power of the people (whose will the Constitution embodies) is superior to both." Thanks to judicial review, the "intentions of the people" would prevail over "the intentions of their agents." Hamilton, apparently realizing that such reasoning bordered on deception, went the whole way toward legerdemain: "It may be truly said that the judiciary has neither force nor will, but merely judgment." For Hamilton, in exercising this high authority the judges claim no supremacy: They claim only to administer the public will. If an act of the legislature is held void, it is not because judges have any control over legislative power but because the act is forbidden by the Constitution and because the will of the people, which is declared supreme, is paramount to that of their representatives. Hence the ideal government of laws and not of men. Hence also the intriguing paradox of judicial review: While wearing the magical habiliments of the law, Supreme Court justices take sides on vital social and political issues. This unstaged debate between Yates and Hamilton is excerpted in this chapter.

The Written and Unwritten Constitution. The American Constitution, unlike the British, cannot be changed by an ordinary act of legislation; this is its distinctive feature, not that it is written. No constitution, including our own, is either altogether written or altogether unwritten. The British constitution, though supposedly made up of custom and tradition, is partly written. Magna Charta, Petition of Right, Bill of Rights, Act of Settlement, and Parliament Act of 1911 are written. In the Constitution, there is no mention of the president's cabinet and no reference to senatorial courtesy, to political parties, or to the national nominating conventions for choosing candidates for election. The electoral college is expressly provided for in the written Constitution; usage has, for all practical purposes, discarded it. Thus the Constitution is only the original trunk. Important new branches have been added, through formal amendment; custom and usage; and above all, judicial inter-pretation. The American Constitution "in operation," Woodrow Wilson wrote, "is manifestly a very different thing from the Constitution of the books."

Marbury v. *Madison.* Several weeks before Thomas Jefferson's inauguration as president in 1801, Congress, lame duck and Federalist-dominated, passed the District of Columbia Act, which authorized the appointment of 42 new justices of the peace. President Adams made the appointments, but in the waning hours of his administration, Chief Justice John Marshall, also serving as secretary of state, failed to deliver all of the commissions of office to the would-be justices of the peace. Upon assuming office on March 4, Jefferson held back delivery to some of Adams's appointees. Later that year, William Marbury and three others whom Adams had named filed suit in the Supreme Court against Secretary of State James Madison. They wanted the Court to issue a *writ of mandamus,* directing Madison to hand over the undelivered commissions. (A writ of mandamus is an order to a public official directing performance of a ministerial, or nondiscretionary, act.)

When the Court heard argument in February 1803, it was apparent that the justices were in a predicament. Because of tense partisan differences between the Federalists and the Democratic-Republicans, Jefferson and Madison would probably disregard the writ. There would then be no one to enforce the order. Yet for the Court to rule that Marbury was not entitled to the judgeship would be an open and painful acknowledgement of weakness.

Marshall's opinion in *Marbury* v. *Madison* avoided both dangers and claimed power for the Court. He announced that, although Marbury and the others were entitled to their jobs, the Court was powerless to help because the Court had no authority to issue the writ. Whereas Section 13 of the Judiciary Act of 1789 gave the Court authority to issue the writ as part of the Court's *original,* as opposed to *appellate,* jurisdiction, Marshall noted that the Court's original jurisdiction is spelled out in Article III. Article III includes no reference to writs of mandamus. By enlarging the Court's original jurisdiction, Section 13 conflicted with the Constitution. Was the Court to apply an unconstitutional statute? To do so would make the statute (and Congress) superior to the Constitution. Section 13 was, therefore, void.

According to Marshall, the most distinctive feature of our Constitution is that it is *law,* paramount, supreme law, and subject to interpretation by the Supreme Court in cases properly before it. Judicial review is an implied, not a substantive power; it is implied from, and is incidental to, the Court's judicial power—the power to interpret law and decide cases. Chief Justice Marshall portrayed judicial review as a necessary adjunct to both a written Constitution and a government deriving its power from the people. Nor does judicial power, he maintained, give the Supreme Court any practical or real omnipotence. The Court is simply exercising judicial power conferred by the Constitution and sustained by the principle of separation of powers. "It is, emphatically, the province and duty of the Judicial department to say what the law is." The effect, in theory, is not to elevate Court over legislature, but rather to make "the power of the people superior to both."

Marshall's argument was not unanswerable, as Justice Gibson's trenchant criticism in *Eakin* v. *Raub* makes clear. In 1803, and for quite some time thereafter, *Marbury* v. *Madison* aroused comment and criticism, not because the "great Chief Justice" asserted the power of judicial review, but because he went out of his way to read a lecture to President Jefferson and Secretary of State Madison concerning their official duties under the Constitution. Earlier, Democratic-Republicans had severely criticized the Alien-Sedition Law and incorporation of the national bank as unconstitutional. The effects of judicial review are both negative and positive; it can veto as well as authenticate.

Finality of Supreme Court Decisions. Jefferson himself never denied the power of the Supreme Court to pass on the validity of acts of Congress in the course of deciding cases. But he did deny that such a decision was binding on the president in the performance of his purely executive function. Jefferson stated his position in 1804: "The judges, believing the [Alien-Sedition] law constitutional, had a right to pass a sentence of fine and imprisonment, because that power was placed in their hands by the Constitution. But the Executive, believing the law to be unconstitutional, was bound to remit the execution of it, because that power has been confided to him by the Constitution. That instrument meant that its coordinate branches should be checks on each other. But the opinion which gives to the judges the right to decide what laws are constitutional, and what not, not only for themselves in their own sphere of action, but for the legislative and Executive also in their spheres, would make the Judiciary a despotic branch." Jefferson accepted the finality of judicial *decisions* in cases where their effects were primarily on the judiciary, as in *Marbury;* he rejected their binding effect on coordinate branches of the government.

Other presidents, notably Jackson, Lincoln, Franklin Roosevelt, Nixon, and Reagan, have also on occasion refused to accept Supreme Court decisions as foreclosing further debate on the meaning of the Constitution. Their view is that all constitutional officers, not the justices alone, play a part in constitutional interpretation. An "unstaged debate" on the finality of Supreme Court decisions appears in this chapter.

Dred Scott. The "despotic" potential of the judicial veto, at least in Marshall's time, was less onerous than is sometimes imagined. It was not until 1857 and the ill-fated Dred Scott decision that the second act of Congress ran afoul of the Constitution. Rejecting Marshall's view of a constitution intended to endure, Chief Justice Taney affirmed that the Constitution "speaks not only with the same words, but with the same meaning and intent" as when it came from the hands of the framers. Taney did not confine his opinion to the question of black citizenship but proceeded to discuss the extent of congressional power over the territories. Congress had no power to prohibit slavery in the territories, and therefore the Missouri Compromise of 1820 violated the constitution.

Dred Scott marked a major expansion in the scope of judicial review. Unlike the statute in *Marbury,* the invalidated act did not pertain to the Judicial Department nor contravene a precise, unambiguous provision of the Constitution. The Court vetoed a major legislative policy, forestalling future congressional efforts to deal with the foremost political issue of the day. *Dred Scott,* not *Marbury,* foreshadowed future controversies concerning the scope of judicial review. For Marshall's doctrine of *national* supremacy, Taney substituted *judicial* supremacy.

Supreme Court Review of State Court Decisions. More important than judicial review of acts of Congress is the control federal courts exercise over state acts and state court decisions. The first Congress, apparently believing that the purpose of the supremacy clause (Art. VI, Para. 2) was to make the judiciary the final resort for all cases arising in the states, enacted Section 25 of the Judiciary Act of 1789, authorizing the Supreme Court to pass on the validity of state legislation and to review decisions of state tribunals wherein constitutional questions had been answered in favor of the state, or adversely to national power. Though Section 25 recognized the important role that state courts might play in interpreting and applying the Constitution, federal law, and treaties, it had the effect of strengthening national power by making explicit a function of the Supreme Court left to inference in the Constitution itself.

The number of congressional acts invalidated has been comparatively small (see Table 2.1), just over a hundred to date, not counting the potentially broad swath cut by *I.N.S. v. Chadha* (see Chapter three) on legislative vetoes found in several hundred congressional statutes. Quite otherwise has been the effect of judicial review of state action. Since 1810, when the Court overturned the first state act in *Fletcher* v. *Peck,* about 900 state laws and perhaps 100 local ordinances have been struck down. The seeming inconsistency between the doctrine of judicial review of congressional legislation and the need for effective government did not become a serious public issue until the last quarter of the nineteenth century. Prior to 1900 the Court had invoked its authority against Congress so sparingly that Justice Holmes could predict that "the United States would not come to an end if we lost our power to declare an Act of Congress void." "I do think," Holmes added, "the Union would be imperilled if we could not make that declaration as to the laws of the several states." One in his position could observe, "how often a local policy prevails with those who are not trained to national views."

During the formative period of our history, it was of first importance to establish an effective barrier against state action hostile to the Constitution and the Union it created. Thomas Jefferson voiced the hope "that some peaceable means should be contrived for the federal head to enforce compliance on the part of the States." The Philadelphia Convention delegates, keenly aware of the necessity of establishing external control over state action, suggested various limitations. One proposal gave Congress a negative on state laws; another provided for federal appointment of state governors and gave the general government a negative on state acts. All these were rejected. In its final form "this Constitution," and the laws "made in pursuance thereof, and all treaties made, or which shall be made, under the authority of the United States," are declared to be "the supreme law of the land; and the judges in every state are bound thereby, anything in the Constitution or laws of any State to the contrary notwithstanding."

In the Virginia Ratifying Convention, John Marshall envisioned judicial review as an alternative to revolution. "What is the service or purpose of a judiciary but to execute the laws in a peaceful, orderly manner, without shedding blood, or creating a contest, or availing yourselves of force?" Madison reinforced Marshall: "A political system that does not provide for a peaceable and effectual decision of all controversies arising among the parties is not a Government, but a mere Treaty between independent nations, without any resort for

Table 2.1: Congressional Acts Invalidated by the Supreme Court

Period	Chief Justice	U.S. Statutes Declared Unconstitutional
1789–1800	Jay, Rutledge, Ellsworth	0
1801–1835	Marshall	1
1836–1864	Taney	1
1865–1873	Chase	9
1874–1888	Waite	8
1888–1910	Fuller	14
1910–1921	White	11
1921–1930	Taft	15
1930–1941	Hughes	13
1941–1946	Stone	2
1946–1953	Vinson	1
1953–1969	Warren	19
1969–1986	Burger	25
1986–	Rehnquist	1

terminating disputes but negotiations, and that failing, the sword." Failure to lodge this power in the federal judiciary, he added in 1832, "would be as much a mockery as a scabbard put into the hands of a soldier without a sword in it."

APPROACHES TO CONSTITUTIONAL INTERPRETATION

A long-standing consensus that the Supreme Court is the chief expositor of the Constitution dissolves, however, over the question *how* judges are supposed to interpret the Constitution. The answer to this question partly determines the values the Constitution protects. Four of the most common approaches to constitutional interpretation are discussed below.

Literalism and "Clear Meaning." For some, constitutional interpretation is a mechanical process, much like the dry-goods clerk measuring fabric or the grocer weighing coffee. "When an act of Congress is appropriately challenged in the courts as not conforming to constitutional mandate," explained Justice Owen J. Roberts in *United States* v. *Butler* (1936), "the judicial branch of the Government has only one duty—to lay the article of the Constitution which is invoked beside the statute which is challenged and to decide whether the latter squares with the former" (see Chapter Seven). Seen this way, the Constitution's meaning is clear. The judge's task is to point out what is plainly there. Of course, some parts of the Constitution do have a clear meaning. The president's term is four years, a senator's six. Yet these are rarely, if ever, involved in litigation. More common and more troublesome are the "commerce" Article I empowers Congress to regulate (see Chapters Five and Six) or the "speech" the First Amendment protects (see Chapter Ten).

Adaptation. Even judges who sometimes rest on the Constitution's clear meaning will also employ adaptation. Here, the judge reasons from the Constitution by first identifying principles or values the Constitution contains, and then applying them to contemporary circumstances. As much as any other method, deductive reasoning enables the Court to accommodate the Constitution to situations and problems the framers did not confront.

Original Intent. Clear meaning and adaptation may be involved in a third approach, *original intent*. Originalists look for what the framers of a constitutional provision meant. The question combines historicity with contemporary application: identifying how those who wrote (and perhaps those who ratified) the Constitution would resolve a question facing judges today. As illustrated by Justice George Sutherland's dissenting opinion in *West Coast Hotel* v. *Parrish* (1937).

> [T]o say . . . that the words of the Constitution mean today what they did not mean when written—that is, that they do not apply to a situation now to which they would have applied then—is to rob that instrument of the essential element that continues it in force as the people have made it until they, and not their official agents, have made it otherwise. . . . The judicial function is that of interpretation; it does not include the power of amendment under the guise of interpretation. To miss the point of difference between the two is to miss all that the phrase "supreme law of the land" stands for and to convert what was intended as inescapable and enduring mandates into mere moral reflections.

Original intent is not without its difficulties. These are explored in the "unstaged debate" between Judge Robert Bork and Professor Laurence Tribe later in this chapter.

Structuralism. Some cases are decided by *structuralism,* which draws principles not so much from the words of single passages but from the structure or framework the Constitution establishes or from the relation of one clause to another. Chief Justice Marshall's opinion in *Marbury* v. *Madison* is a good example of structuralism at work. Examining the system of limited government created by the Constitution, Marshall found the basis of judicial review. Structuralism lies at the heart of recent separation-of-powers decisions like *Morrison* v. *Olson* (1988), in Chapter Three.

With any interpretative approach, judges have considerable leeway. Agreement on the method to be used by no means guarantees agreement on the outcome in individual cases.

JUDGING SELF-JUDGED

Justice Brewer maintained in the late 1800s that judges "make no laws, establish no policy, never enter into the domain of popular action. They do not govern." "All the court does, or can do," Justice Roberts declared in 1936, "is to announce its considered judgment. . . . The only power it has, if such it may be called, is the power of judgment. This court neither approves nor condemns any legislative policy." Through the years, Supreme Court justices have continued to profess judicial impotence, but hardly ever without rousing incredulity. In its dual role of symbol and instrument of authority, the Supreme Court has always been confronted with the difficult task of reconciling the profession of judicial aloofness with the reality of personal discretion and political power. With refreshing candor, Justice Jackson observed, "We are not final because we are infallible, but we are infallible only because we are final" (*Brown* v. *Allen,* 1953).

Supreme Court justices are appointed for life—or during "good behavior." They may be impeached, but impeachment proved in practice to be not even a "scarecrow," as Jefferson said. Nevertheless, the Court is subject to various direct and indirect controls. The dramatic repudiation of its own decisions in 1937, on the heels of President Roosevelt's Court-packing threat, contradicted Justice Stone's self-effacing dictum that "the only check upon our own exercise of power is our own sense of self-restraint." Decisions on constitutional issues may be changed, by constitutional amendment, as in the Income Tax Case of 1895. Decisions involving statutory interpretation can be altered by an act of Congress, as was done by the Civil Rights Restoration Act of 1988, which overturned *Grove City College* v. *Bell* (1984). In *Grove City,* the Court had interpreted the Education Amendments of 1972 to require a cutoff of federal funds to a discriminatory program, but not to the whole institution. Clarifying the law in 1988, Congress left no doubt that it intended the cutoff of aid to be institution-wide, even if only a part of an institution was found not to be in compliance with the law.

The Constitution expressly gives Congress control over the Court's appellate jurisdiction. To prevent the Court from passing on the constitutionality of the Reconstruction Acts, Congress denied the Court's jurisdiction in a case then pending. "What, then, is the effect of the Repealing Act?" Chief Justice Chase asked deferentially. "We cannot doubt as to this. Without jurisdiction the Court cannot proceed at all in any cause. Jurisdiction is power to declare the law; when it ceases to exist, the only function remaining to the Court is that of announcing the fact and dismissing the cause" (**Ex parte McCardle,** 1869).

Moreover, a president may, by discriminating appointments, if the opportunity presents itself, change the voting balance within the Court. This occurred in the Legal Tender Cases (1871) and after John F. Kennedy's replacement of Felix Frankfurter with Arthur Goldberg. President Roosevelt's Court-packing proposal failed of enactment, but it was not without effect. Justice Roberts told a congressional committee in 1954 that he had been "fully conscious of the tremendous strain and threat to the existing court," stemming from F.D.R.'s audacious assault, discussed in Chapter Six. Presidents Nixon and Reagan were able to alter the tone of constitutional jurisprudence as it had prevailed in Chief Justice Warren's day. Ours is "a government of laws and not of men" only in a qualified sense.

ENTERING THE "POLITICAL THICKET"

If "judges can open it [the Constitution] at all," Chief Justice Marshall commented in *Marbury* v. *Madison,* "what part of it are they forbidden to read or obey?" A self-disabling answer, at odds with the Chief Justice's inference, was given in *Luther* v. *Borden* (1849). The justices, speaking through Chief Justice Taney, decided that the question whether the government of Rhode Island or any other state is "republican" (as guaranteed by Art. IV, Sec. 4) was "political" in nature, and must be determined either by Congress through its acceptance or rejection of stae representatives or by presidential acts in response to requests for assistance in putting down domestic violence. Decisions of the political departments concerning the international relations of the United States are likewise considered binding on the Court. Another question termed "political," and therefore requiring solution, if at all, through political agencies, is determination of whether a state has ratified a proposed constitutional amendment (*Coleman* v. *Miller,* 1939). The Court has also refused to decide whether use by a state of the initiative and referendum is a denial of "a republican form of government" (*Pacific States Tel. & Tel. Co.* v. *Oregon,* 1912).

One of the most important fields in which the Court once invoked this self-imposed limitation on judicial power is legislative apportionment. In *Colegrove* v. *Green* (1946), Justice Frankfurter termed this issue one "of a peculiarly political nature and therefore not meet for judicial determination." Voters seeking relief from Illinois's malapportioned congressional districts were told to turn to the state legislature or Congress, not to the Court. "Courts ought not to enter this 'political thicket,' " Frankfurter warned. "It is hostile to a democratic system to involve the judiciary in the politics of the people. . . . The remedy for unfairness in districting is to secure state legislatures that will apportion properly, or to invoke the ample powers of Congress."

A contrary view prevailed in *Gomillion* v. *Lightfoot* (1960). Involved was an act of the Alabama legislature changing the boundaries in the city of Tuskegee from a simple square into a 28-sided monster. The result was to remove from the city all but a handful of black voters, while leaving white voters unaffected. Justice Frankfurter, in spite of a contention made in his *Colegrove* opinion, that this was a "political question," ruled that the Fifteenth Amendment guarantee against racial discrimination justified judicial action. Left unanswered was the question of whether the Fourteenth Amendment's equal protection clause might provide a basis for judicial remedy of nonracial discrimination, specifically that based on urban versus rural residence.

An affirmative answer was given in **Baker** v. **Carr** (1962). Finding no obstacle in the "political question" doctrine, Justice Brennan ruled that malapportionment of state legislatures may constitute a violation of the equal protection clause and that federal courts are empowered to provide a remedy.

One Person, One Vote. In making belated entrance into this "political thicket," the justices neglected (or refused) to lay down guidelines along which reapportionment might proceed. That came the next year, in *Gray* v. *Sanders* (1963), in which the Court, applying the one person-one vote principle, invalidated the Georgia county unit system of primary election in statewide offices. Said Justice Douglas, "Once the geographical unit for which a representative is to be chosen is designated, all who participate in the election are to have an equal vote—whatever their race, whatever their sex, whatever their occupation, whatever their income, and wherever their home may be in that geographical unit. This is required by the equal protection clause of the Fourteenth Amendment."

In 1964, the Court (*Wesberry* v. *Sanders*, 1964) extended the same principle to congressional districts, holding that the Constitution had the "plain objective of making equal representation for equal numbers of people the fundamental goal for the House of Representatives." "As nearly as practicable," the Court declared, "one man's vote in a congressional election is to be worth as much as another's." The conclusion of the three-round battle, set in motion by *Baker* v. *Carr*, came in **Reynolds** v. **Sims**. By applying the now familiar principle of one person, one vote, the justices challenged the constitutionality of at least 40 state legislatures.

Since 1964, the justices have applied the one person-one vote principle in a variety of apportionment cases. Only in the most unusual situations, and then only if congressional districts are not at issue, will the Court make an exception. For instance, in *Brown* v. *Thompson* (1983), five justices approved an apportionment plan for the Wyoming House of Representatives with an average deviation of 16 percent from population equality and a maximum deviation of 89 percent. Crucial in the majority's view were the isolation and vast distances separating some sparsely settled areas of the state.

Yet on the same day in *Karcher* v. *Daggett* (1983), a somewhat different combination of five justices disallowed a New Jersey apportionment plan for the state's 14 congressional districts, with a maximum deviation of less than 1 percent. The seemingly contradictory decision in *Karcher* was the closest the Supreme Court had come to entering the thicket of partisan *gerrymandering*. In *Baker*, Frankfurter had warned against the justices' becoming entangled in the brambles of such party-related matters. Justice Stewart's opinion in the 1964 reapportionment cases decided with *Reynolds* revealed how complex the subject of representation could be. Now Republicans claimed that Democrats had unfairly advantaged themselves at the former's expense in drawing district lines. The *Karcher* majority concluded that the population deviations, though small, were not the result of a "good faith effort to achieve population equality." Silently persuasive perhaps were the unusually strange shapes of some of the districts. One resembled a swan and took in parts of seven counties. Another looked like a fishhook. Justice Stevens made it clear in a concurring opinion that the "judiciary is not powerless to provide a constitutional remedy in egregious cases" of gerrymandering.

Gerrymandering. A majority accepted Stevens's assessment in 1986. In a challenge to the apportionment plan for the Indiana legislature, the Court concluded in *Davis* v. *Bandemer* that partisan gerrymandering presented a justiciable issue under the equal protection clause. Yet only two justices found a constitutional defect in the Indiana plan. For future cases, the Court announced a standard much less precise than one person, one vote: "Unconstitutional discrimination occurs only when the electoral system is arranged in a manner that will consistently degrade a voter's or a group of voters' influence on the political process as a whole." Left in doubt is the kind of evidence and the period of time required to prove an unconstitutional gerrymander. Complicating any such litigation is the requirement that legislatures be reapportioned after each decennial census.

When Chief Justice Warren left the Court in 1969, he was asked to identify his major contribution. The somewhat surprising answer was categorical: reapportionment, especially *Reynolds* v. *Sims*. Why? The right to vote freely and equitably for the candidates of one's choice is the essence of a democratic society. Untrammeled exercise of this right is essential to the preservation of all others—"the bedrock of our political system," he called it. To hold that a vote in one county or electoral district is worth ten times as much as the vote in another runs counter to "our fundamental ideas of democratic representation."

JUDICIAL REVIEW—A DISTINCTIVELY AMERICAN CONTRIBUTION

The pervasiveness of judicial power is now one of the most conspicuous aspects of the American political system. It is hard to think of a feature of life left untouched by the Court's decrees. Its docket reads like a policy agenda for the nation. "The restraining power of the judiciary does not manifest its chief worth," Judge Cardozo observed, "in the few cases in which the legislature has gone beyond the lines that mark the limits of discretion." Its primary value has been in "making vocal and audible the ideals that might otherwise be silenced. . . ." Had this not been so, a document framed in the context of agrarianism, and largely unamended except by constitutional interpretation, could not serve the expanding needs of government in a complex technological society.

Within consensus, however, lies conflict. To believe that the Court *can* exercise judicial review is not necessarily to acknowledge that the Court always *should*. To recognize the Court's place in principle is not to approve its intervention in particular cases or in particular arenas of public policy. "What is unique about the Supreme Court," John Vanderzell has written, "is its constant responsibility to justify itself and public policy in terms of enduring but adaptable fundamental principles as they appear and are made to appear in the Constitution through time."

What was true in the time of Yates, Hamilton, and Marshall remains true today. Constitutional law in the American context is concerned with the nature and scope of judicial power. That concern finds its way explicitly or implicitly into every case reprinted in this book. The concern is no idle, useless relic from eighteenth-century minds and jurisprudence. It remains indisputably alive in the last decade of the twentieth century.

Applying standards drawn from the Constitution, the Supreme Court is the ultimate guardian of individual privilege and governmental prerogative alike. It is, Woodrow Wilson observed, "the balance-wheel of our entire system." "The greatest statesmen," he added, "are always those who attempt their task with imagination, with a large vision of things to come. . . . And so, whether by force of circumstance or by deliberate design, we have married legislation with adjudication and look for statesmanship in our courts." Thanks largely to statesmanship within the Supreme Court, the Constitution has been more than "a mere lawyer's document." It has been "a vehicle of the nation's life."

KEY TERMS

constitutionalism	original jurisdiction	structuralism
free government	appellate jurisdiction	political question
political checks	judicial supremacy	political thicket
judicial review	literalism	one person, one vote
unwritten constitution	adaptation	gerrymandering
writ of mandamus	original intent	

QUERIES

1. Did Judge Gibson in *Eakin* v. *Raub* provide an effective rebuttal to Chief Justice Marshall's opinion in *Marbury* v. *Madison?*

2. Several theories have dominated judicial discourse on constitutional interpretation. One holds that the "intention of the framers" is the sole guide. Another favors an adaptive approach. Which judicial opinions in this chapter support these views? What problems will a judge probably encounter with each approach?

3. Consider what Justice Frankfurter called one's "rooted notions regarding the scope and limits of a judge's authority." What references to judicial role can you find in the opinions in this chapter?

4. What are the bones of contention between Robert Yates ("Letters of Brutus") and Alexander Hamilton (*Federalist,* No. 78)? Explore the safeguards against abuse of judicial power.

SELECTED READINGS

AGRESTO, JOHN. *The Supreme Court and Constitutional Democracy.* Ithaca, N.Y.: Cornell University Press, 1984.

BLOCH, SUSAN LOW, and MAEVA MARCUS. "John Marshall's Selective Use of History in *Marbury* v. *Madison.*" 1987 *Wisconsin Law Review* 301 (1987).

BURTON, HAROLD H. "The Cornerstone of Constitutional Law: The Extraordinary Case of Marbury v. Madison." 36 *American Bar Association Journal* 805 (1950).

CHOPER, JESSE H. *Judicial Review and the National Political Process: A Functional Reconsideration.* Chicago: University of Chicago Press, 1980.

ELLIOTT, WARD E. Y. *The Rise of Guardian Democracy: The Supreme Court's Role in Voting Rights Disputes.* Cambridge, Mass.: Harvard University Press, 1974.

ELY, JOHN HART. *Democracy and Distrust: A Theory of Judicial Review.* Cambridge, Mass.: Harvard University Press, 1980.

FEHRENBACHER, DON E. *The Dred Scott Case.* New York: Oxford University Press, 1978.

GUNTHER, GERALD. "Congressional Power to Curtail Federal Court Jurisdiction: An Opinionated Guide to the Ongoing Debate." 36 *Stanford Law Review* 895 (1984).

HALPERN, STEPHEN C., and CHARLES M. LAMB, eds. *Supreme Court Activism and Restraint.* Lexington, Mass.: D. C. Heath, 1982.

HENKIN, LOUIS. "Is There a 'Political Question' Doctrine?" 85 *Yale Law Journal* 597 (1971).

HOBSON, CHARLES F. "The Negative on State Laws: James Madison, the Constitution, and the Crisis of Republican Government." 36 *William and Mary Quarterly* (3d series) 215 (1979).

LOSS, RICHARD, ed. *Corwin on the Constitution: Volume One, The Foundations of American Constitutional and Political Thought, the Powers of Congress, and the President's Power of Removal.* Ithaca, N.Y.: Cornell University Press, 1981.

LUSKY, LOUIS. *By What Right? A Commentary on the Supreme Court's Power to Revise the Constitution.* Charlottesville, Va.: Michie, 1976.

MCCLOSKEY, ROBERT G. "Foreword: The Reapportionment Case." 75 *Harvard Law Review* 54 (1962).

MASON, ALPHEUS T. *The Supreme Court: Palladium of Freedom.* Ann Arbor: University of Michigan Press, 1962.

O'CONNOR, SANDRA DAY. "Reflections on Preclusion of Judicial Review in England and the United States." 27 *William and Mary Law Review* 643 (1986).

SEDDIG, ROBERT G. "John Marshall and the Origins of Supreme Court Leadership." 36 *University of Pittsburgh Law Review* 785 (1975).

VISHNESKI, JOHN S., III. "What the Court Decided in *Dred Scott* v. *Sandford.*" 32 *American Journal of Legal History* 373 (1988).

WOLFE, CHRISTOPHER. *The Rise of Modern Judicial Review.* New York: Basic Books, 1986.

Unstaged Debate of 1788:
Robert Yates v. Alexander Hamilton

*This power in the judicial will enable them [judges] to mould the
Government into almost any shape they please*

—ROBERT YATES, *Letters of Brutus,* 1788*

BRUTUS, NO. XI 31 January 1788

. . . Much has been said and written upon the subject of this new system on both sides, but I have not met with any writer, who has discussed the judicial powers with any degree of accuracy. . . . The real effect of this system of government will therefore be brought home to the feelings of the people through the medium of the judicial power. It is, moreover, of great importance, to examine with care the nature and extent of the judicial power, because those who are to be vested with it, are to be placed in a situation altogether unprecedented in a free country. They are to be rendered totally independent, both of the people and the legislature, both with respect to their offices and salaries. No errors they may commit can be corrected by any power above them, if any such power there be, nor can they be removed from office for making ever so many erroneous adjudications.

The only causes for which they can be displaced, is, conviction of treason, bribery, and high crimes and misdemeanors.

This part of the plan is so modelled, as to authorize the courts, not only to carry into execution the powers expressly given, but where these are wanting or ambiguously expressed, to supply what is wanting by their own decisions. . . .

They [the courts] will give the sense of every article of the constitution, that may from time to time come before them. And in their decisions they will not confine themselves to any fixed or established rules, but will determine, according to what appears to them, the reason and spirit of the

constitution. The opinions of the supreme court, whatever they may be, will have the force of law, because there is no power provided in the constitution, that can correct their errors, or controul their adjudications. From this court there is no appeal. And I conceive the legislature themselves, cannot set aside a judgment of this court, because they are authorized by the constitution to decide in the last resort. The legislature must be controuled by the constitution, and not the constitution by them. They have therefore no more right to set aside any judgment pronounced upon the construction of the constitution, than they have to take from the president, the chief command of the army and navy, and commit it to some other person. The reason is plain; the judicial and executive derive their authority from the same source, that the legislature do theirs; and therefore in all cases, where the constitution does not make the one responsible to, or controulable by the other, they are altogether independent of each other.

The judicial power will operate to effect, in the most certain, but yet silent and imperceptible manner, what is evidently the tendency of the constitution:—I mean, an entire subversion of the legislative, executive and judicial powers of the individual states. Every adjudication of the supreme court, on any question that may arise upon the nature and extent of the general government, will affect the limits of the state jurisdiction. In proportion as the former enlarge the exercise of their powers, will that of the latter be restricted.

That the judicial power of the United States, will lean strongly in favour of the general government, it will give such an explanation to the constitution, as will favour an extension of its jurisdiction, is very evident from a variety of considerations.

1st. The constitution itself strongly countenances such a mode of construction. Most of the articles

* Published in the *New York Journal and Weekly Register,* Numbers 11, 12, and 15. Reprinted in E. S. Corwin, *Court over Constitution* (Princeton, N.J.: Princeton University Press, 1938), Appendix, pp. 231–62.

in this system, which convey powers of any considerable importance, are conceived in general and indefinite terms, which are either equivocal, ambiguous, or which require long definitions to unfold the extent of their meaning. . . . The clause which vests the power to pass all laws which are proper and necessary, to carry the powers given into execution . . . leaves the legislature at liberty, to do every thing, which in their judgment is best. . . .

2d. Not only will the constitution justify the courts in inclining to this mode of explaining it, but they will be interested in using this latitude of interpretation. Every body of men invested with office are tenacious of power; they feel interested, and hence it has become a kind of maxim, to hand down their offices, with all its rights and privileges, unimpaired to their successors; the same principle will influence them to extend their power, and increase their rights; this of itself will operate strongly upon the courts to give such a meaning to the constitution in all cases where it can possibly be done, as will enlarge the sphere of their own authority. . . .

3d. Because they will have precedent to plead, to justify them in it. It is well known, that the courts in England, have by their own authority, extended their jurisdiction far beyond the limits set them in their original institution, and by the laws of the land. . . .

This power in the judicial, will enable them to mould the government, into almost any shape they please. . . .

BRUTUS, NO. XV   20 March 1788

I do not object to the judges holding their commissions during good behaviour. I suppose it a proper provision provided they were made properly responsible. But I say, this system has followed the English government in this, while it has departed from almost every other principle of their jurisprudence, under the idea, of rendering the judges independent; which, in the British constitution, means no more than that they hold their places

during good behaviour, and have fixed salaries, they have made the judges *independent,* in the fullest sense of the word. There is no power above them, to controul any of their decisions. There is no authority that can remove them, and they cannot be controuled by the laws of the legislature. In short, they are independent of the people, of the legislature, and of every power under heaven. Men placed in this situation will generally soon feel themselves independent of heaven itself. . . .

The supreme court then have a right, independent of the legislature, to give a construction of the constitution and every part of it, and there is no power provided in this system to correct their construction or do it away. If, therefore, the legislature pass any laws, inconsistent with the sense the judges put upon the constitution, they will declare it void; and therefore in this respect their power is superior to that of the legislature. . . .

Had the construction of the constitution been left with the legislature, they would have explained it at their peril; if they exceeded their powers, or sought to find, in the spirit of the constitution, more than was expressed in the letter, the people from whom they derived their power could remove them, and do themselves right; and indeed I can see no other remedy that the people can have against their rulers for encroachments of this nature. A constitution is a compact of a people with their rulers; if the rulers break the compact, the people have a right and ought to remove them and do themselves justice; but in order to enable them to do this with the greater facility, those whom the people chuse at stated periods, should have the power in the last resort to determine the sense of the compact; if they determine contrary to the understanding of the people, an appeal will lie to the people at the period when the rulers are to be elected, and they will have it in their power to remedy the evil; but when this power is lodged in the hands of men independent of the people, and of their representatives, and who are not, constitutionally, accountable for their opinions, no way is left to controul them but *with a high hand and an outstretched arm.*

*The Judiciary is beyond comparison the weakest of the three
departments of power*

—ALEXANDER HAMILTON, *The Federalist*, No. 78*

HAMILTON'S REPLY TO "BRUTUS"

We proceed now to an examination of the judiciary department of the proposed government. . . .

Whoever attentively considers the different departments of power must perceive, that, in a government in which they are separated from each other, the judiciary, from the nature of its functions, will always be the least dangerous to the political rights of the Constitution; because it will be least in a capacity to annoy or injure them. . . . The judiciary . . . has no influence over either the sword or the purse; no direction either of the strength or of the wealth of the society; and can take no active resolution whatever. It may truly be said to have neither FORCE nor WILL, but merely judgment; and must ultimately depend upon the aid of the executive arm even for the efficacy of its judgments.

This simple view of the matter suggests several important consequences. It proves incontestably, that the judiciary is beyond comparison the weakest of the three departments of power; that it can never attack with success either of the other two; and that all possible care is requisite to enable it to defend itself against their attacks. It equally proves, that though individual oppression may now and then proceed from the courts of justice, the general liberty of the people can never be endangered from that quarter; I mean so long as the judiciary remains truly distinct from both the legislature and the Executive. . . .

Some perplexity respecting the right of courts to pronounce legislative acts void, because contrary to the Constitution, has arisen from an imagination that the doctrine would imply a superiority of the judiciary to the legislative power. It is urged that the authority which can declare the acts of another void, must necessarily be superior to the one whose acts may be declared void. As this doctrine is of great importance in all the American constitutions,

a brief discussion of the ground on which it rests cannot be unacceptable.

There is no position which depends on clearer principles, than that every act of a delegated authority, contrary to the tenor of the commission under which it is exercised, is void. No legislative act, therefore, contrary to the Constitution, can be valid. To deny this, would be to affirm, that the deputy is greater than his principal; that the servant is above his master; that the representatives of the people are superior to the people themselves; that men acting by virtue of powers, may do not only what their powers do not authorize, but what they forbid.

If it be said that the legislative body are themselves the constitutional judges of their own powers, and that the construction they put upon them is conclusive upon the other departments, it may be answered, that this cannot be the natural presumption, where it is not to be collected from any particular provisions in the Constitution. It is not otherwise to be supposed, that the Constitution could intend to enable the representatives of the people to substitute their *will* to that of their constituents. It is far more rational to suppose, that the courts were designed to be an intermediate body between the people and the legislature, in order, among other things, to keep the latter within the limits assigned to their authority. The interpretation of the laws is the proper and peculiar province of the courts. A constitution is, in fact, and must be regarded by the judges, as a fundamental law. It therefore belongs to them to ascertain its meaning, as well as the meaning of any particular act proceeding from the legislative body. If there should happen to be an irreconcilable variance between the two, that which has the superior obligation and validity ought, of course, to be preferred; or, in other words, the Constitution ought to be preferred to the statute, the intention of the people to the intention of their agents.

Nor does this conclusion by any means suppose a superiority of the judicial to the legislative power. It only supposes that the power of the people is

* Henry Cabot Lodge, ed., *The Federalist* (New York: G. P. Putnam's Sons, 1904).

superior to both; and that where the will of the legislature, declared in its statutes, stands in opposition to that of the people, declared in the Constitution, the judges ought to be governed by the latter rather than the former. They ought to regulate their decisions by the fundamental laws, rather than by those which are not fundamental. . . .

If, then, the courts of justice are to be considered as the bulwarks of a limited Constitution against legislative encroachments, this consideration will afford a strong argument for the permanent tenure of judicial offices, since nothing will contribute so much as this to that independent spirit in the judges which must be essential to the faithful performance of so arduous a duty.

This independence of the judges is equally requisite to guard the Constitution and the rights of individuals from the effects of those ill humors, which the arts of designing men, or the influence of particular conjectures, sometimes disseminate among the people themselves, and which, though they speedily give place to better information, and more deliberate reflection, have a tendency, in the meantime, to occasion dangerous innovations in the government, and serious oppressions of the minor party in the community. . . .

But it is not with a view to infractions of the Constitution only, that the independence of the judges may be an essential safeguard against the effects of occasional ill humors in the society. These sometimes extend no farther than to the injury of the private rights of particular classes of citizens, by unjust and partial laws. Here also the firmness of the judicial magistracy is of vast importance in mitigating the severity and confining the operation of such laws. . . .

There is yet a further and a weightier reason for the permanency of the judicial offices, which is deducible from the nature of the qualifications they require. It has been frequently remarked, with great propriety, that a voluminous code of laws is one of the inconveniences necessarily connected with the advantages of a free government. To avoid an arbitrary discretion in the courts, it is indispensable that they should be bound down by strict rules and precedents, which serve to define and point out their duty in every particular case that comes before them; and it will readily be conceived from the variety of controversies which grow out of the folly and wickedness of mankind, that the records of those precedents must unavoidably swell to a very considerable bulk, and must demand long and laborious study to acquire a competent knowledge of them. Hence it is, that there can be but few men in the society who will have sufficient skill in the laws to qualify them for the stations of judges. And making the proper deductions for the ordinary depravity of human nature, the number must be still smaller of those who unite the requisite integrity with the requisite knowledge. These considerations apprise us, that the government can have no great option between fit character; and that a temporary duration in office, which would naturally discourage such characters from quitting a lucrative line of practice to accept a seat on the bench, would have a tendency to throw the administration of justice into hands less able, and less well qualified, to conduct it with utility and dignity. . . .

Marbury v. Madison
5 U.S. (1 Cranch) 137, 2 L.Ed. 60 (1803)

Shortly before the end of President Adams's term, he nominated Marbury and three others to be justices of the peace in the District of Columbia. Their nominations were confirmed and commissions signed by the president, but the secretary of state, John Marshall, had not delivered them. Jefferson's new secretary of state, James Madison, refused to deliver the commissions, claiming that delivery was necessary to complete the appointments. The four men asked the Supreme Court to issue a writ of mandamus ordering delivery in the exercise of its original jurisdiction. Mandamus was not sought from lower federal courts. Majority: Marshall, Chase, Paterson, Washington. Not participating: Cushing, Moore.

The opinion of the court was delivered by the CHIEF JUSTICE [MARSHALL]. . . .

The first object of inquiry is—Has the applicant a right to the commission he demands? . . . [The court finds that as Marbury's appointment was complete he has a right to the commission.]

2. This brings us to the second inquiry; which is: If he has a right, and that right has been violated, do the laws of this country afford him a remedy? . . . [The court finds that they do.]

3. It remains to be inquired whether he is entitled to the remedy for which he applies? This depends on 1st. The nature of the writ applied for; and 2d. The power of this court.

1st. . . . This, then, is a plain case for a *mandamus,* either to deliver the commission, or a copy of it from the record; and it only remains to be inquired, whether it can issue from this court.

The act to establish the judicial courts of the United States authorizes the supreme court "to issue writs of *mandamus,* in cases warranted by the principles and usages of law, to any courts appointed, or persons holding office, under the authority of the United States." . . . The constitution vests the whole judicial power of the United States in one supreme court, and such inferior courts as congress shall, from time to time, ordain and establish. This power is expressly extended to all cases arising under the laws of the United States; and consequently, in some form, may be exercised over the present case; because the right claimed is given by a law of the United States.

In the distribution of this power, it is declared, that "the supreme court shall have original jurisdiction, in all cases affecting ambassadors, other public ministers and consuls, and those in which a state shall be a party. In all other cases, the supreme court shall have appellate jurisdiction." . . . If it had been intended to leave it in the discretion of the legislature, to apportion the judicial power between the supreme and inferior courts, according to the will of that body, it would certainly have been useless to have proceeded further than

to have defined the judicial power, and the tribunals in which it should be vested. The subsequent part of the section is mere surplusage—is entirely without meaning, if such is to be the construction. If congress remains at liberty to give this court appellate jurisdiction, where the constitution has declared their jurisdiction shall be original; and original jurisdiction where the constitution has declared it shall be appellate; the distribution of jurisdiction, made in the constitution, is form without substance. . . . To enable this court, then, to issue a *mandamus,* it must be shown to be an exercise of appellate jurisdiction, or to be necessary to enable them to exercise appellate jurisdiction. . . . It is the essential criterion of appellate jurisdiction, that it revises and corrects the proceedings in a cause already instituted, and does not create that cause. Although therefore, a *mandamus* may be directed to courts, yet to issue such a writ to an officer, for the delivery of a paper, is, in effect, the same as to sustain an original action for that paper, and therefore, seems not to belong to appellate, but to original jurisdiction. Neither is it necessary in such a case as this to enable the court to exercise its appellate jurisdiction. The authority, therefore, given to the supreme court, by the act establishing the judicial courts of the United States, to issue writs of *mandamus* to public officers, appears not to be warranted by the constitution; and it becomes necessary to inquire whether a jurisdiction so conferred can be exercised.

The question, whether an act, repugnant to the constitution, can become the law of the land, is a question deeply interesting to the United States: but, happily, not of an intricacy proportioned to its interest. It seems only necessary to recognize certain principles, supposed to have been long and well established, to decide it. That the people have an original right to establish, for their future government, such principles as, in their opinion, shall most conduce to their own happiness, is the basis on which the whole American fabric has been erected. The exercise of this original right is a very great exertion; nor can it, nor ought it, to be frequently repeated. The principles, therefore, so established, are deemed fundamental: and as the authority from which they proceed is supreme, and can seldom act, they are designed to be permanent.

This original and supreme will organizes the government, and assigns to different departments their respective powers. It may either stop here, or establish certain limits not to be transcended by those departments. The government of the United States is of the latter description. The powers of the legislature are defined and limited; and that those limits may not be mistaken, or forgotten, the constitution is written. To what purpose are powers limited, and to what purpose is that limitation committed to writing, if these limits may, at any time, be passed by those intended to be restrained? The distinction between a government with limited and unlimited powers is abolished, if those limits do not confine the persons on whom they are imposed, and if acts prohibited and acts allowed, are of equal obligation. It is a proposition too plain to be contested, that the constitution controls any legislative act repugnant to it; or, that the legislature may alter the constitution by an ordinary act.

Between these alternatives, there is no middle ground. The constitution is either a superior paramount law, unchangeable by ordinary means, or it is on a level with ordinary legislative acts, and, like other acts, is alterable when the legislature shall please to alter it. If the former part of the alternative be true, then a legislative act, contrary to the constitution, is not law; if the latter part be true, then written constitutions are absurd attempts, on the part of the people, to limit a power, in its own nature, illimitable.

Certainly, all those who have framed written constitutions contemplate them as forming the fundamental and paramount law of the nation, and consequently, the theory of every such government must be, that an act of the legislature, repugnant to the constitution, is void. This theory is essentially attached to a written constitution, and is, consequently, to be considered, by this court, as one of the fundamental principles of our society. It is not, therefore, to be lost sight of, in the further consideration of this subject.

If an act of the legislature, repugnant to the constitution, is void, does it, notwithstanding its invalidity, bind the courts, and oblige them to give it effect? Or, in other words, though it be not law, does it constitute a rule as operative as if it was a law? This would be to overthrow, in fact, what was established in theory; and would seem, at first view, an absurdity too gross to be insisted on. It shall, however, receive a more attentive consideration.

It is, emphatically, the province and duty of the judicial department, to say what the law is. Those who apply the rule to particular cases, must of necessity expound and interpret that rule. If two laws conflict with each other, the courts must decide on the operation of each. So, if a law be in opposition to the constitution; if both the law and the constitution apply to a particular case, so that the court must either decide that case, conformably to the law, disregarding the constitution; or conformably to the constitution, disregarding the law; the court must determine which of these conflicting rules governs the case: this is of the very essence of judicial duty. If then, the courts are to regard the constitution, and the constitution is superior to any ordinary act of the legislature, the constitution, and not such ordinary act, must govern the case to which they both apply.

Those, then, who controvert the principle, that the constitution is to be considered, in court, as a paramount law, are reduced to the necessity of maintaining that courts must close their eyes on the constitution, and see only the law. This doctrine would subvert the very foundation of all written constitutions. It would declare that an act which, according to the principles and theory of our government, is entirely void, is yet, in practice, completely obligatory. It would declare, that if the legislature shall do what is expressly forbidden, such act, notwithstanding the express prohibition, is in reality effectual. It would be giving to the legislature a practical and real omnipotence, with the same breath which professes to restrict their powers within narrow limits. It is prescribing limits, and declaring that those limits may be passed at pleasure. That it thus reduces to nothing, what we have deemed the greatest improvement on political institutions, a written constitution, would, of itself, be sufficient, in America, where written constitutions have been viewed with so much reverence, for rejecting the construction. But the peculiar expressions of the constitution of the United States furnish additional arguments in favor of its rejection. The judicial power of the United States is extended to all cases arising under the constitution. Could it be the intention of those who gave this power, to say, that in using it, the constitution should not be looked into? That a case arising under the constitution should be decided, without examining the instrument under which it arises? This is too extravagant to be maintained. In some cases, then, the constitution must be looked into by the judges. And if they can open it at all, what part of it are they forbidden to read or to obey?

There are many other parts of the constitution which serve to illustrate this subject. It is declared, that "no tax or duty shall be laid on articles exported from any state." Suppose, a duty on the export of cotton, of tobacco, or of flour; and a suit instituted to recover it. Ought judgment to be rendered in such a case? Ought the judges to close their eyes on the constitution, and only see the law?

The constitution declares "that no bill of attainder or *ex post facto* law shall be passed." If, however, such a bill should be passed, and a person should be prosecuted under it, must the court condemn to death those victims whom the constitution endeavors to preserve?

"No person," says the constitution, "shall be convicted of treason, unless on the testimony of two witnesses to the same overt act, or on confession in open court." Here, the language of the constitution is addressed especially to the courts. It prescribes, directly for them, a rule of evidence not to be departed from. If the legislature should change that rule, and declare one witness, or a confession out of court, sufficient for conviction, must the constitutional principle yield to the legislative act?

From these, and many other selections which might be made, it is apparent, that the framers of the constitution contemplated that instrument as a rule for the government of courts, as well as of the legislature. Why otherwise does it direct the judges to take an oath to support it? This oath certainly applies, in an especial manner, to their conduct in their official character. How immoral to impose it on them, if they were to be used as the instruments, and the knowing instruments, for violating what they swear to support!

The oath of office, too, imposed by the legislature, is completely demonstrative of the legislative opinion on this subject. It is in these words: "I do solemnly swear, that I will administer justice, without respect to persons, and do equal right to the poor and to the rich; and that I will faithfully and impartially discharge all the duties incumbent on me as———, according to the best of my abilities and understanding, agreeable to the constitution and laws of the United States." Why does a judge swear to discharge his duties agreeably to the constitution of the United States, if that constitution forms no rule for his government? If it is closed upon him, and cannot be inspected by him? If such be the real state of things, this is worse than solemn mockery. To prescribe, or to take this oath, becomes equally a crime.

It is also not entirely unworthy of observation, that in declaring what shall be the supreme law of the land, the constitution itself is first mentioned; and not the laws of the United States, generally, but those only which shall be made in pursuance of the constitution, have that rank.

Thus, the particular phraseology of the constitution of the United States confirms and strengthens the principle, supposed to be essential to all written constitutions, that a law repugnant to the constitution is void; and that courts, as well as other departments, are bound by that instrument.

The rule must be discharged.

Eakin v. Raub
12 Sergeant and Rawle (Pennsylvania Supreme Court) 330 (1825)

The dissenting opinion by Justice Gibson of the Pennsylvania Supreme Court in this unimportant 1825 case is generally recognized as the most effective answer to Marshall's famous argument supporting judicial review. Justice Gibson's opinion, Professor J. B. Thayer observed, "has fallen strangely out of sight. It is much the ablest discussion of the question [of the power of the judiciary to declare legislative acts unconstitutional] which I have ever seen, not excepting the judgment of Marshall in *Marbury* v. *Madison*, which as I venture to think has been overpraised." Justice Gibson's bold and impressive argument was a substantial factor in preventing his own appointment to the Supreme Court on the death of Justice Washington in 1830. In 1845 Gibson himself recanted, because the legislature of Pennsylvania had "sanctioned the pretensions of the courts to deal freely with the acts of the legislature, and from experience of the necessity of the case" (see *Norris* v. *Clymer*, 2 Pa. 281).

GIBSON, J. . . .

I am aware, that a right [in the judiciary] to declare all unconstitutional acts void . . . is generally held as a professional dogma, but, I apprehend, rather as a matter of faith than of reason. I admit that I once embraced the same doctrine, but without examination, and I shall therefore state the arguments that impelled me to abandon it, with great respect for those by whom it is still maintained. But I may premise, that it is not a little remarkable, that although the right in question has all along been claimed by the judiciary, no judge has ventured to discuss it, except Chief Justice Marshall, and if the argument of a jurist so distinguished for the strength of his ratiocinative powers be found inconclusive, it may fairly be set down to the weakness of the position which he attempts to defend. . . .

I begin, then, by observing that in this country, the powers of the judiciary are divisible into those that are POLITICAL and those that are purely civil. Every power by which one organ of the government is enabled to control another, or to exert an influence over its acts, is a political power. . . .

The constitution and the right of the legislature to pass the act, may be in collision. But is that a legitimate subject for judicial determination? If it be, the judiciary must be a peculiar organ, to revise the proceedings of the legislature, and to correct its mistakes; and in what part of the constitution are we to look for this proud pre-eminence? Viewing the matter in the opposite direction, what would be thought of an act of assembly in which it should be declared that the supreme court had, in a particular case, put a wrong construction on the constitution of the United States, and that the

judgment should therefore be reversed? It would doubtless be thought a usurpation of judicial power. But it is by no means clear, that to declare a law void which has been enacted according to the forms prescribed in the constitution, is not a usurpation of legislative power. . . .

But it has been said to be emphatically the business of the judiciary, to ascertain and pronounce what the law is; and that this necessarily involves a consideration of the constitution. It does so: but how far? If the judiciary will inquire into anything besides the form of enactment, where shall it stop? . . .

. . . In theory, all the organs of the government are of equal capacity; or, if not equal, each must be supposed to have superior capacity only for those things which peculiarly belong to it; and as legislation peculiarly involves the consideration of those limitations which are put on the law-making power, and the interpretation of the laws when made, involves only the construction of the laws themselves, it follows that the construction of the constitution in this particular belongs to the legislature, which ought therefore to be taken to have superior capacity to judge of the constitutionality of its own acts. . . .

When the entire sovereignty was separated into its elementary parts, and distributed to the appropriate branches, all things incident to the exercise of its powers were committed to each branch exclusively. The negative which each part of the legislature may exercise, in regard to the acts of the other, was thought sufficient to prevent material infractions of the restraints which were put on the power of the whole; for, had it been intended to interpose the judiciary as an additional barrier, the matter would surely not have been left in doubt. The judges would not have been left to stand on the insecure and ever shifting ground of public opinion as to constructive powers; they would have been placed on the impregnable ground of an express grant. They would not have been compelled to resort to debates in the convention, or the opinion that was generally entertained at the time. . . .

The power is said to be restricted to cases that are free from doubt or difficulty. But the abstract existence of a power cannot depend on the clearness or obscurity of the case in which it is to be exercised; for that is a consideration that cannot present itself, before the question of the existence of the power shall have been determined; and, if its existence be conceded, no considerations of policy arising from the obscurity of the particular case, ought to influence the exercise of it. . . .

To say, therefore, that the power is to be exercised but in perfectly clear cases, is to betray a doubt of the propriety of exercising it at all. Were the same caution used in judging of the existence of the power that is inculcated as to the exercise of it, the profession would perhaps arrive at a different conclusion. The grant of a power so extraordinary ought to appear so plain, that he who should run might read. . . .

What I have in view in this inquiry, is the supposed right of the judiciary to interfere, in cases where the constitution is to be carried into effect through the instrumentality of the legislature, and where that organ must necessarily first decide on the constitutionality of its own act. The oath to support the constitution is not peculiar to the judges, but is taken indiscriminately by every officer of the government, and is designed rather as a test of the political principles of the man, than to bind the officer in the discharge of his duty: otherwise it is difficult to determine what operation it is to have in the case of a recorder of deeds, for instance, who, in the execution of his office, has nothing to do with the constitution. But granting it to relate to the official conduct of the judge, as well as every other officer, and not to his political principles, still it must be understood in reference to supporting the constitution, *only as far as that may be involved in his official duty;* and, consequently, if his official duty does not comprehend an inquiry into the authority of the legislature, neither does his oath. . . .

But do not the judges do a positive act in violation of the constitution, when they give effect to an unconstitutional law? Not if the law has been passed according to the forms established in the constitution. The fallacy of the question is, in supposing that the judiciary adopts the acts of the legislature as its own. . . . The fault is imputable to the legislature, and on it the responsibility exclusively rests. . . .

But it has been said, that this construction would deprive the citizen of the advantages which are peculiar to a written constitution, by at once declaring the power of the legislature in practice to be illimitable. . . . But there is no magic or inherent power in parchment and ink, to command respect and protect principles from violation. In the business of government a recurrence to first principles answers the end of an observation at sea with a view to correct the dead reckoning; and for this purpose, a written constitution is an instrument of inestimable value. It is of inestimable value, also, in rendering its first principles familiar to the mass of people; for, after all, there is no effectual guard against legislative usurpation but public opinion, the force of which, in this country is inconceivably great. . . . Once let public opinion be so corrupt as to sanction every misconstruction of the constitution and abuse of power which the temptation of the moment may dictate, and the party which may happen to be predominant, will laugh at the puny efforts of a dependent power to arrest it in its course.

For these reasons, I am of [the] opinion that it rests with the people, in whom full and absolute sovereign power resides, to correct abuses in legislation, by instructing their representatives to repeal the obnoxious act. . . . It might, perhaps, have been better to vest the power in the judiciary; as it might be expected that its habits of deliberation, and the aid derived from the arguments of counsel, would more frequently lead to accurate conclusions. On the other hand, the judiciary is not infallible; and an error by it would admit of no remedy but a more distinct expression of the public will, through the extraordinary medium of a convention; whereas, an error by the legislature admits of a remedy by an exertion of the same will, in the ordinary exercise of the right of suffrage,—a mode better calculated to attain the end, without popular excitement. . . .

But in regard to an act of [a state] assembly,

which is found to be in collision with the constitution, laws, or treaties of the *United States,* I take the duty of the judiciary to be exactly the reverse. By becoming parties to the federal constitution, the states have agreed to several limitations of their individual sovereignty, to enforce which, it was thought to be absolutely necessary to prevent them from giving effect to laws in violation of those limitations, through the instrumentality of their own judges. Accordingly, it is declared in the sixth article and second section of the federal constitution, that "This constitution, and the laws of the *United States* which shall be made in pursuance thereof, and all treaties made, or which shall be made under the authority of the *United States,* shall be the *supreme* law of the land; and the *judges* in every *state* shall be BOUND thereby: anything in the *laws* or *constitution* of any *state* to the contrary notwithstanding." . . .

Scott v. *Sandford**
60 U.S. (19 Howard) 393, 15 L.Ed. 691 (1857)

In 1834, Dr. John Emerson, an Army surgeon, took his slave Dred Scott from Missouri to Illinois, where slavery was forbidden. In 1836 Emerson took Scott to Fort Snelling, north of 36° 30' in the Louisiana territory, where slavery had been banned by the Missouri Compromise. In 1838 Emerson returned to Missouri with Scott. After Emerson died, a suit was brought in the Missouri courts against his widow, claiming that Scott's residence in free territory had made him a free man. The lower court held for Scott, but the state Supreme Court reversed in 1852. Whatever Scott's legal status outside Missouri, it concluded, he remained a slave under Missouri law. By this time Mrs. Emerson had married Dr. C. C. Chaffee, an abolitionist from Massachusetts. To reopen the case, and to shield both his reputation and the friendly nature of the litigation, he transferred ownership of Scott to Mrs. Chaffee's brother, John Sanford, of New York. In 1853 Chaffee arranged for Roswell Field, an abolitionist attorney in St. Louis, to file suit on Scott's behalf against Sanford in the United States Circuit Court in Missouri. On a writ of error from an adverse judgment, Scott appealed to the Supreme Court. The justices twice heard arguments in the case, in February and December of 1856. Majority: Taney, Campbell, Catron, Daniel, Grier, Nelson, Wayne. Dissenting: Curtis, Nelson. (Not all members of the majority agreed with Taney's disposition of all points in the case.)

MR. CHIEF JUSTICE TANEY delivered the opinion of the Court.

. . . The question is simply this: Can a negro, whose ancestors were imported into this country, and sold as slaves, become a member of the political community formed and brought into existence by

* In Howard's *Reports,* Sanford's name is incorrectly spelled "Sandford."

the Constitution of the United States, and as such become entitled to all the rights, and privileges, and immunities guarantied by that instrument to the citizen? One of which rights is the privilege of suing in a court of the United States in the cases specified in the Constitution.

We think . . . [the people of the Negro race] . . . are not included, and were not intended to be included, under the words "citizens" in the

Constitution, and can therefore claim none of the rights and privileges which that instrument provides for and secures to citizens of the United States. On the contrary, they were at that time considered as a subordinate and inferior class of beings, who had been subjugated by the dominant race, and, whether emancipated or not, yet remained subject to their authority, and had no rights or privileges but such as those who held the power and the Government might choose to grant them. . . .

The question then arises, whether the provisions of the Constitution, in relation to the personal rights and privileges to which the citizen of the State should be entitled, embraced the negro African race, at that time in this country, or who might afterwards be imported, who had then or should afterwards be made free in any State; and to put it in the power of a single State to make him a citizen of the United States, and endue him with the full rights of citizenship in every other State without their consent? Does the Constitution of the United States act upon him whenever he shall be made free under the laws of a State, and raised there to the rank of a citizen, and immediately clothe him with all the privileges of a citizen in every other State, and in its own courts?

The court thinks the affirmative of these propositions cannot be maintained. And if it cannot, the plaintiff in error could not be a citizen of the State of Missouri, within the meaning of the Constitution of the United States, and, consequently, was not entitled to sue in its courts. . . .

No one, we presume, supposes that any change in public opinion or feeling, in relation to this unfortunate race, in the civilized nations of Europe or in this country, should induce the court to give to the words of the Constitution a more liberal construction in their favor than they were intended to bear when the instrument was framed and adopted. Such an argument would be altogether inadmissible in any tribunal called on to interpret it. If any of its provisions are deemed unjust, there is a mode prescribed in the instrument itself by which it may be amended; but while it remains unaltered, it must be construed now as it was understood at the time of its adoption. It is not only the same in words, but the same in meaning, and delegates the same powers to the Government, and reserves and secures the same rights and privileges to the citizen; and as long as it continues to exist in its present form, it speaks not only in the same words, but with the same meaning and intent with which it spoke when it came from the hands of its framers, and was voted on and adopted by the people of the United States. Any other rule of construction would abrogate the judicial character of this court, and make it the mere reflex of the popular opinion of the day. . . .

What the construction was at that time, we think can hardly admit of doubt. We have the language of the Declaration of Independence and of the Articles of Confederation, in addition to the plain words of the Constitution itself; we have the legislation of the different States, before, about the time, and since, the Constitution was adopted; we have the legislation of Congress, from the time of its adoption to a recent period; and we have the constant and uniform action of the Executive Department, all concurring together, and leading to the same result. And if anything in relation to the construction of the Constitution can be regarded as settled, it is that which we now give to the word "citizen" and the word "people." . . .

The act of Congress, upon which the plaintiff relies, declares that slavery and involuntary servitude, except as a punishment for crime, shall be forever prohibited in all that part of the territory ceded by France, under the name of Louisiana, which lies north of thirty-six degrees thirty minutes north latitude, and not included within the limits of Missouri. And the . . . inquiry is whether Congress was authorized to pass this law under any of the powers granted to it by the Constitution; for if the authority is not given by that instrument, it is the duty of this court to declare it void and inoperative, and incapable of conferring freedom upon any one who is held as a slave under the laws of any one of the States. . . .

. . . The powers of the Government and the rights and privileges of the citizen are regulated and plainly defined by the Constitution itself. And when the Territory becomes a part of the United States, the Federal Government enters into possession in the character impressed upon it by those who created it. It enters upon it with its powers over the citizen strictly defined, and limited by the Constitution, from which it derives its own existence, and by virtue of which alone it continues to exist and act as a Government and sovereignty. It has not power of any kind beyond it; and it cannot, when it enters a Territory of the United States, put off its character and assume discretionary or despotic powers which the Constitution has denied to it. It cannot create for itself a new character separated from the citizens of the United States, and the duties it owes them under the provisions of the Constitution. The Territory being a part of the United States, the Government and the citizen both enter it under the authority of the Constitution, with their respective rights defined and marked out; and the Federal Government can exercise no power over his person or property, beyond what that instrument confers, nor lawfully deny any right which it has reserved. . . .

. . . An Act of Congress which deprives a citizen of the United States of his liberty or property, merely because he came himself or brought his property into a particular Territory of the United States, and who had committed no offense against the laws, could hardly be dignified with the name of due process of law. . . .

Upon these considerations, it is the opinion of the court that the act of Congress which prohibited a citizen from holding and owning property of this kind in the territory of the United States north of the line therein mentioned, is not warranted by the Constitution, and is therefore void; and that neither Dred Scott himself, nor any of his family, were made free by being carried into this territory; even if they had been carried there by the owner, with the intention of becoming a permanent resident. . . .

MR. JUSTICE CURTIS, joined by MR. JUSTICE McLEAN, dissenting:

. . . To determine whether any free persons, descended from Africans held in slavery, were citizens of the United States under the Confederation, and consequently at the time of the adoption of the Constitution of the United States, it is only necessary to know whether any such persons were citizens of either of the States under the Confederation, at the time of the adoption of the Constitution.

Of this there can be no doubt. At the time of the ratification of the Articles of Confederation, all free native-born inhabitants of the States of New Hampshire, Massachusetts, New York, New Jersey, and North Carolina, though descended from African slaves, were not only citizens of those States, but such of them as had the other necessary qualifications possessed the franchise of electors, on equal terms with other citizens. . . .

Having first decided that they were bound to consider the sufficiency of the plea to the jurisdiction of the Circuit Court, and having decided that this plea showed that the Circuit Court had no jurisdiction, and consequently that this is a case to which the judicial power of the United States does not extend, they have gone on to examine the merits of the case as they appeared on the trial before the court and jury, on the issues joined on the pleas in bar, and so have reached the question of the power of Congress to pass the act of 1820. On so grave a subject as this, I feel obliged to say that, in my opinion, such an exertion of judicial power transcends the limits of the authority of the court, as described by its repeated decisions and, as I understand, acknowledged in this opinion of the majority of the court. . . .

Nor, in my judgment, will the position, that a prohibition to bring slaves into a Territory deprives any one of his property without due process of law, bear examination. . . .

Ex Parte McCardle
74 U.S. (7 Wall.), 19 L.Ed. 264 (1869)

During Reconstruction after the Civil War, a newspaper editor in Mississippi named William McCardle was jailed by a military commander for trial before a military commission for publishing "incendiary and libelous" articles. McCardle was a civilian and sought release on habeas corpus in the Circuit Court for the Southern District of Mississippi. After hearing his case the judge remanded McCardle to the custody of the military authorities. McCardle then took an appeal to the Supreme Court authorized by a statute passed by Congress in 1867. Following argument of his case in the Supreme Court and while the justices had it under advisement, Congress overrode President Johnson's veto and repealed the statute in 1868. The majority in Congress apparently feared that the constitutionality of much of its Reconstruction program was at stake in the litigation. Chief Justice Chase noted in his opinion that decision in the case had been delayed by his participation in the president's impeachment trial in the Senate. The *McCardle* case should be read in the light of *Ex parte Yerger* (1869) and *United States* v. *Klein* (1872). Majority: Chase, Clifford, Davis, Field, Grier, Miller, Nelson, Swayne.

MR. CHIEF JUSTICE CHASE delivered the opinion of the Court. . . .

The first question necessarily is that of jurisdiction; for, if the act of March, 1868, takes away the jurisdiction defined by the act of February, 1867, it is useless, if not improper, to enter into any discussion of other questions.

It is quite true, as was argued by the counsel for the petitioner, that the appellate jurisdiction of this court is not derived from acts of Congress. It is, strictly speaking, conferred by the Constitution. But it is conferred "with such exceptions and under such regulations as Congress shall make."

It is unnecessary to consider whether, if Congress had made no exceptions and no regulations, this court might not have exercised general appellate jurisdiction under rules prescribed by itself. For among the earliest acts of the first Congress, at its first session, was the act of September 24th, 1789, to establish the judicial courts of the United States. That act provided for the organization of this court, and prescribed regulations for the exercise of its jurisdiction.

The source of that jurisdiction, and the limitations of it by the Constitution, and by statute, have been on several occasions subjects of consideration here. . . .

The principle that the affirmation of appellate jurisdiction implies the negation of all such jurisdiction not affirmed having been thus established, it was an almost necessary consequence that acts of Congress, providing for the exercise of jurisdiction, should come to be spoken of as acts granting jurisdiction, and not as acts making exceptions to the constitutional grant of it.

The exception to appellate jurisdiction in the case before us, however, is not an inference from the affirmation of other appellate jurisdiction. It is made in terms. The provision of the act of 1867, affirming the appellate jurisdiction of this court in cases of *habeas corpus* is expressly repealed. It is hardly possible to imagine a plainer instance of positive exception.

We are not at liberty to inquire into the motives of the legislature. We can only examine into its power under the Constitution; and the power to make exceptions to the appellate jurisdiction of this court is given by express words.

What, then, is the effect of the repealing act upon the case before us? We cannot doubt as to this. Without jurisdiction the court cannot proceed at all in any cause. Jurisdiction is power to declare the law, and when it ceases to exist, the only function remaining to the court is that of announcing the fact and dismissing the cause. And this is not less clear upon authority than upon principle. . . .

It is quite clear, therefore, that this court cannot proceed to pronounce judgment in this case, for it has no longer jurisdiction of the appeal; and judicial duty is not less fitly performed by declining ungranted jurisdiction than in exercising firmly that which the Constitution and the laws confer.

Counsel seem to have supposed, if effect be given to the repealing act in question, that the whole appellate power of the court, in cases of *habeas corpus,* is denied. But this is an error. The act of 1868 does not except from that jurisdiction any cases but appeals from Circuit Courts under the act of 1867. It does not affect the jurisdiction which was previously exercised.

The appeal of the petitioner in this case must be dismissed for want of jurisdiction.

Baker v. *Carr*
369 U.S. 186, 82 S.Ct. 691, 7 L.Ed. 2d 663 (1962)

Appellants brought suit in United States District Court in Tennessee, under the Civil Rights Acts of 1875, to redress alleged violations of constitutional rights. They charged that a 1901 Tennessee statute arbitrarily and capriciously apportioned the seats in the General Assembly among the state's 95 counties. Failure subsequently to reapportion the seats, notwithstanding substantial growth and redistribution of the state's population, debased their votes and thus denied them equal protection of the laws guaranteed by the Fourteenth Amendment. The district court dismissed the complaint, ruling that it lacked jurisdiction of the subject matter and that no claim was stated upon which relief could be granted. Majority: Brennan, Black, Clark, Douglas, Stewart, Warren. Dissenting: Frankfurter, Harlan. Not participating: Whittaker.

JUSTICE BRENNAN delivered the opinion of the Court. . . .

The complaint alleges that the 1901 statute effects an apportionment that deprives the appellants of the equal protection of the laws in violation of the Fourteenth Amendment. . . .

We hold that the appellants do have standing to maintain this suit. Our decisions plainly support this conclusion. Many of the cases have assumed rather than articulated the premise in deciding the merits of similar claims. And *Colegrove* v. *Green* . . . squarely held that voters who allege facts showing disadvantage to themselves as individuals have standing to sue. [A footnote points out that the concurring opinion of Justice Rutledge and Justice Black's dissenting opinion held there was standing, and expressed doubt whether Justice Frankfurter's opinion intimated lack of it.] . . .

We hold that the claim pleaded here neither rests upon nor implicates the Guaranty Clause and that its justiciability is therefore not foreclosed by our decisions of cases involving that clause. The District Court misinterpreted *Colegrove* v. *Green* and other decisions of this Court on which it relied. Appellants' claim that they are being denied equal protection is justiciable, and if "discrimination is sufficiently shown, the right to relief under the equal protection clause is not diminished by the fact that the discrimination relates to political rights." . . . To show why we reject the argument based on the Guaranty Clause, we must examine the

authorities under it. But because there appears to be some uncertainty as to why those cases did present political questions, and specifically as to whether this apportionment case is like those cases, we deem it necessary first to consider the contours of the "political question" doctrine. . . . [The opinion proceeds to a consideration of foreign relations, "durations of hostilities," validity of enactments of constitutional amendments, and the status of Indian tribes.]

Prominent on the surface of any case held to involve a political question is found a textually demonstrable constitutional commitment of the issue to a coordinate political department; or a lack of judicially discoverable and manageable standards for resolving it; or the impossibility of deciding without an initial policy determination of a kind clearly for nonjudicial discretion; or the impossibility of a court's undertaking independent resolution without expressing lack of the respect due coordinate branches of government; or an unusual need for unquestioning adherence to a political decision already made; or the potentiality of embarrassment from multifarious pronouncements by various departments on one question.

Unless one of these formulations is inextricable from the case at bar, there should be no dismissal for nonjusticiability on the ground of a political question's presence. The doctrine of which we treat is one of "political questions," not one of "political cases." The courts cannot reject as "no lawsuit" a bona fide controversy as to whether some action denominated "political" exceeds constitutional authority. . . .

Several factors were thought by the Court in Luther [*Luther* v. *Borden*] to make the question there "political": the commitment to the other branches of the decision as to which is the lawful state government; the unambiguous action by the President, in recognizing the charter government as the lawful authority; the need for finality in the executive's decision; and the lack of criteria by which a court could determine which form of government was republican.

But the only significance that Luther could have for our immediate purposes is in its holding that the Guaranty Clause is not a repository of judicially manageable standards which a court could utilize independently in order to identify a State's lawful government. The Court has since refused to resort to the Guaranty Clause—which alone had been invoked for the purpose—as the source of a constitutional standard for invalidating state action. . . .

We come, finally to the ultimate inquiry whether our precedents as to what constitutes a nonjusticiable "political question" bring the case before us under the umbrella of that doctrine. A natural beginning is to note whether any of the common characteristics which we have been able to identify and label descriptively are present. We find none: The question here is the consistency of state action with the Federal Constitution. We have no question decided, or to be decided, by a political branch of government coequal with this Court. Nor do we risk embarrassment of our government abroad, or grave disturbance at home if we take issue with Tennessee as to the constitutionality of her action here challenged. Nor need the appellants, in order to succeed in this action, ask the Court to enter upon policy determinations for which judicially manageable standards are lacking. Judicial standards under the Equal Protection Clause are well developed and familiar, and it has been open to courts since the enactment of the Fourteenth Amendment to determine, if on the particular facts they review, that a discrimination reflects no policy, but simply arbitrary and capricious action. . . .

We conclude then that the nonjusticiability of claims resting on the Guaranty Clause which arises from their embodiment of questions that were thought "political," can have no bearing upon the justiciability of the equal protection claim presented in this case. Finally, we emphasize that it is the involvement in Guaranty Clause claims of the elements thought to define "political questions," and no other feature, which could render them nonjusticiable. Specifically, we have said that such claims are not held nonjusticiable because they touch matters of state governmental organization. . . .

Article 1, Sections 2, 4, and 5 and Amendment 14, Section 2 relate only to congressional elections and obviously do not govern apportionment of state legislatures. However, our decisions in favor of justiciability even in light of those provisions plainly afford no support for the District Court's conclusion that the subject matter of this controversy presents a political question. Indeed, the refusal to award relief in Colegrove resulted only from the controlling view of a want of equity. . . .

We conclude that the complaint's allegations of a denial of equal protection present a justiciable constitutional cause of action upon which appellants are entitled to a trial and a decision. The right asserted is within the reach of judicial protection under the Fourteenth Amendment. . . .

MR. JUSTICE FRANKFURTER dissenting, joined by MR. JUSTICE HARLAN.

The Court today reverses a uniform course of decision established by a dozen cases, including one by which the very claim now sustained was unanimously rejected only five years ago. . . . Such a massive repudiation of the experience of our whole past in asserting destructively novel judicial power demands a detailed analysis of the role of this Court in our constitutional scheme. Disregard of inherent limits in the effective exercise of the Court's "judicial Power" not only presages the futility of judicial intervention in the essentially political conflict of forces by which the relation between population and representation has time out of mind been and now is determined. It may well impair the Court's position as the ultimate organ of "the supreme Law of the Land" in that vast range of legal problems, often strongly entangled in popular feeling, on which this Court must pronounce. The Court's authority—possessed neither of the purse nor the sword—ultimately rests on sustained public confidence in its moral sanction. Such feeling must be nourished by the Court's complete detachment, in fact and in appearance, from political entanglements and by abstention from injecting itself into the clash of political forces in political settlements. . . .

For this Court to direct the District Court to enforce a claim to which the Court has over the years consistently found itself required to deny legal enforcement and at the same time to find it necessary to withhold any guidance to the lower court how to enforce this turnabout, new legal claim, manifests an odd—indeed an esoteric—conception of judicial propriety. . . .

Even assuming the indispensable intellectual disinterestedness on the part of judges in such matters, they do not have accepted legal standards or criteria or even reliable analogies to draw upon for making judicial judgments. To charge courts with the task of accommodating the incommensurable factors of policy that underlie these mathematical puzzles is to attribute, however flatteringly, omnicompetence to judges. . . .

We are soothingly told at the bar of this Court that we need not worry about the kind of remedy a court could effectively fashion once the abstract constitutional right to have courts pass on a statewide system of electoral districting is recognized as a matter of judicial rhetoric, because legislatures would heed the Court's admonition. This is not only an euphoric hope. It implies a sorry confession of judicial impotence in place of a frank acknowledgment that there is not under our Constitution a judicial remedy for every political mischief, for every undesirable exercise of legislative power. The Framers carefully and with deliberate forethought refused so to enthrone the judiciary. In this situation, as in others of like nature, appeal for relief does not belong here. Appeal must be to an informed, civically militant electorate. In a democratic society like ours, relief must come through an aroused popular conscience that sears the conscience of the people's representatives. In any event there is nothing judicially more unseemly nor more self-defeating than for this Court to make interrorem

pronouncements, to indulge in merely empty rhetoric, sounding a word of promise to the ear, sure to be disappointing to the hope. . . .

What, then, is this question of legislative apportionment? Appellants invoke the right to vote and to have their votes counted. But they are permitted to vote and their votes are counted. They go to the polls, they case their ballots, they send their representatives to the state councils. Their complaint is simply that the representatives are not sufficiently numerous or powerful—in short, that Tennessee has adopted a basis of representation with which they are dissatisfied. Talk of "debasement" or "dilution" is circular talk. One cannot speak of "debasement" or "dilution" of the value of a vote until there is first defined a standard of reference as to what a vote should be worth. What is actually asked of the Court in this case is to choose among competing bases of representation—ultimately, really, among competing theories of political philosophy—in order to establish an appropriate frame of government for the State of Tennessee and thereby for all the States of the Union. . . .

. . . What Tennessee illustrates is an old and still widespread method of representation—representation by local geographical division, only in part respective of population—in preference to others, others, forsooth, more appealing. Appellants contest this choice and seek to make this Court the arbiter of the disagreement. They would make the Equal Protection Clause the charter of adjudication, asserting that the equality which it guarantees comports, if not the assurance of equal weight to every voter's vote, at least the basic conception that representation ought to be proportionate to population, a standard by reference to which the reasonableness of apportionment plans may be judged.

To find such a political conception legally enforceable in the broad and unspecific guarantee of equal protection is to rewrite the Constitution. . . .

Reynolds v. Sims
377 U.S. 533, 84 S.Ct. 1362, 12 L.Ed. 2d 506 (1964)

The climax of a series of cases involving challenges to state apportionment arrangements came in 1964, when the Court invalidated the legislative apportionments of Alabama, Colorado, Delaware, Maryland, New York, and Virginia. The majority opinion in *Reynolds v. Sims* (the Alabama case) sets forth the basic principles applied in each of the six cases. Majority: Warren, Black, Brennan, Clark, Douglas, Goldberg, Stewart, White. Dissenting: Harlan. Justice Stewart, joined by Justice Clark, dissented in the New York and Colorado cases. His opinion is reprinted here following Justice Harlan's dissent.

MR. CHIEF JUSTICE WARREN delivered the opinion of the Court. . . .

Plaintiffs below alleged that the last apportionment of the Alabama Legislature was based on the 1900 federal census, despite the requirement of the State Constitution that the legislature be reapportioned decennially. They asserted that, since the population growth in the State from 1900 to 1960 had been uneven, Jefferson and other counties were now victims of serious discrimination with respect to the allocation of legislative representation. As a result of the failure of the legislature to reapportion itself, plaintiffs asserted, they were denied "equal suffrage in free and equal elections . . . and the equal protection of the laws" in violation of the Alabama Constitution and the Fourteenth Amendment to the Federal Constitution. The complaint asserted that plaintiffs had no other adequate remedy, and that they had exhausted all forms of relief other than that available through the federal courts. . . .

Undeniably the Constitution of the United States protects the right of all qualified citizens to vote, in state as well as in federal elections. A consistent line of decisions by this Court in cases involving attempts to deny or restrict the right of suffrage has made this indelibly clear. . . .

Legislators represent people, not trees or acres. Legislators are elected by voters, not farms or cities or economic interests. As long as ours is a representative form of government, and our legislatures are those instruments of government elected directly by and directly representative of the people, the right to elect legislators in a free and unimpaired fashion is a bedrock of our political system. It could hardly be gainsaid that a constitutional claim

had been asserted by an allegation that certain otherwise qualified voters had been entirely prohibited from voting for members of their state legislature. And, if a State should provide that the votes of citizens in one part of the State should be given two times, or five times, or 10 times the weight of votes of citizens in another part of the State, it could hardly be contended that the right to vote of those residing in the disfavored areas had not been effectively diluted. It would appear extraordinary to suggest that a state could be constitutionally permitted to enact a law providing that certain of the state's voters could vote two, five, or 10 times for their legislative representatives, while voters living elsewhere could vote only once. And it is inconceivable that a state law to the effect that, in counting votes for legislators, the votes of citizens in one part of the State would be multiplied by two, five or 10, while the votes of persons in another area would be counted only at face value, could be constitutionally sustainable. Of course, the effect of state legislative districting schemes which give the same number of representatives to unequal numbers of constituents is identical. . . .

State legislatures are, historically, the fountainhead of representative government in this country. . . .

Logically, in a society that is ostensibly grounded on representative government, it would seem reasonable that a majority of the people of the State could elect a majority of that State's legislators. To conclude differently, and to sanction minority control of state legislative bodies, would appear to deny majority rights in a way that far surpasses any possible denial of minority rights that might otherwise be thought to result. Since legislatures are responsible for enacting laws by which all citizens are to be governed, they should be bodies which are collectively responsive to the popular will. And the concept of equal protection has been traditionally viewed as requiring the uniform treatment of persons standing in the same relation to the governmental action questioned or challenged. With respect to the allocation of legislative representation, all voters, as citizens of a State, stand in the same relation regardless of where they live. Any suggested criteria for the differentiation of citizens are insufficient to justify any discrimination, as to the weight of their votes, unless relevant to the permissible purposes of legislative apportionment. Since the achieving of fair and effective representation for all citizens is concededly the basic aim of legislative apportionment, we conclude that the Equal Protection Clause guarantees the opportunity for equal participation by all voters in the election of state legislators. . . .

We are told that the matter of apportioning representation in a state legislature is a complex and many-faceted one. We are advised that States can rationally consider factors other than population in apportioning legislative representation. We are admonished not to restrict the power of the States to impose differing views as to political philosophy on their citizens. We are cautioned about the dangers of entering into political thickets and mathematical quagmires. Our answer is this: a denial of constitutionally protected rights demands judicial protection: our oath and our office require no less of us. . . .

To the extent that a citizen's right to vote is debased, he is that much less a citizen. The fact that an individual lives here or there is not a legitimate reason for overweighting or diluting the efficacy of his vote. The complexions of societies and civilizations change, often with amazing rapidity. A nation once primarily rural in character becomes predominantly urban. Representation schemes once fair and equitable become archaic and outdated. But the basic principle of representative government remains, and must remain, unchanged—the weight of a citizen's vote cannot be made to depend on where he lives. Population is, of necessity, the starting point for consideration and the controlling criterion for judgment in legislative apportionment controversies. A citizen, a qualified voter, is no more nor no less so because he lives in the city or on the farm. This is the clear and strong command of our Constitution's Equal Protection Clause. This is an essential part of the concept of a government of laws and not men. This is at the heart of Lincoln's vision of "government of the people, by the people, [and] for the people." The Equal Protection Clause demands no less than substantially equal state legislative representation for all citizens, of all places as well as of all races.

We hold that, as a basic constitutional standard, the Equal Protection Clause requires that the seats in both houses of a bicameral state legislature must be apportioned on a population basis. Simply stated, an individual's right to vote for state legislators is unconstitutionally impaired when its weight is in a substantial fashion diluted when compared with votes of citizens living in other parts of the State. Since, under neither the existing apportionment provisions nor under either of the proposed plans was either of the houses of the Alabama Legislature apportioned on a population basis, the District Court correctly held that all three of these schemes were constitutionally invalid. . . .

Much has been written since our decision in *Baker* v. *Carr* about the applicability of the so-called federal analogy to state legislative apportionment arrangements. After considering the matter, the court below concluded that no conceivable analogy could be drawn between the federal scheme and the apportionment of seats in the Alabama Legislature under the proposed constitutional amendment. We agree with the District Court and find the federal analogy inapposite and irrelevant to state legislative districting schemes. Attempted reliance on the federal analogy often appears to be little more than an after-the-fact rationalization offered in defense of maladjusted state apportionment arrangements. The original constitutions of 36 of our States provided that representation in both houses of the state legislatures would be based completely, or predominantly, on population. And the Founding Fathers clearly had no intention of establishing a pattern or model for the apportionment of seats in state legislatures when the system of representation in the Federal Congress was adopted. Demonstrative of this is the fact that the Northwest Ordinance, adopted in the same year, 1787, as the Federal Constitution, provided for the apportionment of seats in territorial legislatures solely on the basis of population.

The system of representation in the two Houses

of the Federal Congress is one ingrained in our Constitution, as part of the law of the land. It is one conceived out of compromise and concession indispensable to the establishment of our federal republic. Arising from unique historical circumstances, it is based on the consideration that in establishing our type of federalism a group of formerly independent States bound themselves together under one national government. . . .

Political subdivisions of States—counties, cities, or whatever—never were and never have been considered as sovereign entities. Rather, they have been traditionally regarded as subordinate governmental instrumentalities created by the State to assist in the carrying out of state governmental functions. . . .

We do not believe that the concept of bicameralism is rendered anachronistic and meaningless when the predominant basis of representation in the two state legislative bodies is required to be the same—population. A prime reason for bicameralism, modernly considered, is to insure mature and deliberate consideration of, and to prevent precipitate action on, proposed legislative measures. Simply because the controlling criterion for apportioning representation is required to be the same in both houses does not mean that there will be no differences in the composition and complexion of the two bodies. Different constituencies can be represented in the two houses. One body could be composed of single-member districts while the other could have at least some multimember districts. The length of terms of the legislators in the separate bodies could differ. The numerical size of the two bodies could be made to differ, even significantly, and the geographical size of districts from which legislators are elected could also be made to differ. And apportionment in one house could be arranged so as to balance off minor inequities in the representation of certain areas in the other house. In summary, these and other factors could be, and are presently in many States, utilized to engender differing complexions and collective attitudes in the two bodies of a state legislature, although both are apportioned substantially on a population basis. . . .

MR. JUSTICE HARLAN, dissenting.

. . . With these cases the Court approaches the end of the third round set in motion by the complaint filed in *Baker* v. *Carr.* What is done

today deepens my conviction that judicial entry into this realm is profoundly ill-advised and constitutionally impermissible. . . .

These decisions also cut deeply into the fabric of our federalism. What must follow from them may eventually appear to be the product of State Legislatures. Nevertheless, no thinking person can fail to recognize that the aftermath of these cases, however desirable it may be thought in itself, will have been achieved at the cost of a radical alteration in the relationship between the States and the Federal Government, more particularly the Federal Judiciary. Only one who has an overbearing impatience with the federal system and its political processes will believe that that cost was not too high or was inevitable.

Finally, these decisions give support to a current mistaken view of the Constitution and the constitutional function of this Court. This view, in a nutshell, is that every major social ill in this country can find its cure in some constitutional "principle," and that this Court should "take the lead" in promoting reform when other branches of government fail to act. The Constitution is not a panacea for every blot upon the public welfare, nor should this Court, ordained as a judicial body, be thought of as a general haven for reform movements. The Constitution is an instrument of government, fundamental to which is the premise that in a diffusion of governmental authority lies the greatest promise that this Nation will realize liberty for all its citizens. This Court, limited in function in accordance with that premise, does not serve its high purpose when it exceeds its authority, even to satisfy justified impatience with the slow workings of the political process. For when, in the name of constitutional interpretation, the Court *adds* something to the Constitution that was deliberately excluded from it, the Court in reality substitutes its view of what should be so for the amending process. . . .

MR. JUSTICE STEWART, whom MR. JUSTICE CLARK joins, dissenting [in the New York and Colorado cases].

. . . Simply stated, the question [in these cases] is to what degree, if at all, the Equal Protection Clause of the Fourteenth Amendment limits each sovereign State's freedom to establish appropriate electoral constituencies from which representatives to the State's bicameral legislative assembly are to be chosen. The Court's answer is a blunt one, and,

I think, woefully wrong. The Equal Protection Clause, said the Court, "requires that the seats in both houses of a bicameral state legislature must be apportioned on a population basis." . . .

With all respect, I think that this is not correct, simply as a matter of fact. It has been unanswerably demonstrated before now that this "was not the colonial system, it was not the system chosen for the national government by the Constitution, it was not the system exclusively or even predominantly practiced by the States at the time of adoption of the Fourteenth Amendment, it is not predominantly practiced by the States today." . . .

The Court's draconian pronouncement, which makes unconstitutional the legislatures of most of the 50 States, finds no support in the words of the Constitution, in any prior decision of this Court, or in the 175-year political history of our Federal Union. With all respect, I am convinced these decisions mark a long step backward into that unhappy era when a majority of the members of this Court were thought by many to have convinced themselves and each other that the demands of the Constitution were to be measured not by what it says, but by their own notions of wise political theory. . . .

What the Court has done is to convert a particular political philosophy into a constitutional rule, binding upon each of the 50 States, from Maine to Hawaii, from Alaska to Texas, without regard and without respect for the many individualized and differentiated characteristics stemming from each State's distinct history, distinct geography, distinct distribution of population, and distinct political heritage. My own understanding of the various theories of representative government is that no one theory has ever commanded unanimous assent among political scientists, historians, or others who have considered the problem. But even if it were thought that the rule announced today by the Court is, as a matter of political theory, the most desirable general rule which can be devised as a basis for the make-up of the representative assembly of a typical State, I could not join in the fabrication of a constitutional mandate which imports and forever freezes one theory of political thought into our Constitution, and forever denies to every State any opportunity for enlightened and progressive innovation in the design of its democratic institutions, so as to accommodate within a system of

representative government the interests and aspirations of diverse groups of people, without subjecting any group or class to absolute domination by a geographically concentrated or highly organized majority.

Representative government is a process of accommodating group interests through democratic institutional arrangements. Its function is to channel the numerous opinions, interests, and abilities of the people of a State into the making of the State's public policy. Appropriate legislative apportionment, therefore, should ideally be designed to insure effective representation in the State's legislature, in cooperation with other organs of political power, of the various groups and interests making up the electorate. In practice, of course, this ideal is approximated in the particular apportionment system of any State by a realistic accommodation of the diverse and often conflicting political forces operating within the State. . . .

The Court today declines to give any recognition to these considerations and countless others, tangible and intangible, in holding unconstitutional the particular systems of legislative apportionment which these States have chosen. Instead, the Court says that the requirements of the Equal Protection Clause can be met in any State only by the uncritical, simplistic, and heavy-handed application of sixth-grade arithmetic.

But legislators do not represent faceless numbers. They represent people, or, more accurately, a majority of the voters in their districts—people with identifiable needs and interests which require legislative representation, and which can often be related to the geographical areas in which these people live. The very fact of geographic districting, the constitutional validity of which the Court does not question, carries with it an acceptance of the idea of legislative representation of regional needs and interests. Yet if geographical residence is irrelevant, as the Court suggests, and the goal is solely that of equally "weighted" votes, I do not understand why the Court's constitutional rule does not require the abolition of districts and the holding of all elections at large. . . .

I think that the Equal Protection Clause demands but two basic attributes of any plan of state legislative apportionment. First, it demands that, in the light of the State's own characteristics and needs, the plan must be a rational one. Secondly, it demands that the plan must be such as not to permit the systematic frustration of the will of a majority of the electorate of the State. I think it is apparent that any plan of legislative apportionment which could be shown to reflect no policy, but simply arbitrary and capricious action or inaction, and that any plan which could be shown systematically to prevent ultimate effective majority rule, would be invalid under accepted Equal Protection Clause standards. But, beyond this, I think there is nothing in the Federal Constitution to prevent a State from choosing any electoral legislative structure it thinks best suited to the interests, temper, and customs of its people. . . .

Davis v. Bandemer
478 U.S. 109, 106 S.Ct. 2797, 92 L.Ed. 2d 85 (1986)

The Indiana legislature comprises a 100-member House and a 50-member Senate. House members serve two-year terms, with elections for all seats every two years. Senators serve four-year terms, with half of the seats up for election every two years. Senators are elected from single-member districts; representatives are elected from a mixture of single-member and multimember districts. Following the 1981 reapportionment based on 1980 census figures, Bandemer and others filed suit in United States District Court for the Southern District of Indiana, claiming that the 1981 reapportionment plan was a political gerrymander intended to disadvantage Democrats and so was a violation of the equal protection clause. Before the case went to trial, elections under the new plan were held in November 1982. Democratic candidates for the House received 51.9 percent of the votes cast statewide but only 43 out of the 100 seats to be filled. Democratic candidates for the Senate received 53.1 percent of the votes cast statewide, and 13 out of the 25 Democratic candidates were elected. In Marion and Allen Counties, both divided into multimember House districts, Democratic candidates received 46.6 percent of the vote but won only 3 of the 21 seats at stake. Relying primarily on these data, the district court invalidated the 1981 reapportionment plan and ordered the legislature to prepare a new plan. In the opinions that follow, note that six of the nine justices concluded that political gerrymanders presented a justiciable question, even though there was no "opinion of the Court." Majority: White, Blackmun, Brennan, Burger, Marshall, O'Connor, Rehnquist. Dissenting: Powell, Stevens.

JUSTICE WHITE announced the judgment of the Court and delivered an opinion in which JUSTICES BRENNAN, MARSHALL, and BLACKMUN joined. . . .

We address first the question whether this case presents a justiciable controversy or a nonjusticiable political question. . . .

The outlines of the political question doctrine were described and to a large extent defined in *Baker* v. *Carr*. . . .

This analysis applies equally to the question now before us. Disposition of this question does not involve us in a matter more properly decided by a coequal branch of our Government. There is no risk of foreign or domestic disturbance, and in light of our cases since *Baker* we are not persuaded that there are no judicially discernible and manageable standards by which political gerrymander cases are to be decided. . . .

Having determined that the political gerrymandering claim in this case is justiciable, we turn to the question whether the District Court erred in holding that appellees had alleged and proved a violation of the Equal Protection Clause. . . .

We also agree with the District Court that in order to succeed the Bandemer plaintiffs were required to prove both intentional discrimination against an identifiable political group and an actual discriminatory effect on that group. . . . Further, we are confident that if the law challenged here had discriminatory effects on Democrats, this record would support a finding that the discrimination was intentional. Thus, we decline to overturn the District Court's finding of discriminatory intent as clearly erroneous. . . .

We do not accept, however, the District Court's legal and factual bases for concluding that the 1981 Act visited a sufficiently adverse effect on the appellees' constitutionally protected rights to make out a violation of the Equal Protection Clause. The District Court held that because any apportionment scheme that purposely prevents proportional representation is unconstitutional, Democratic voters need only show that their proportionate voting influence has been adversely affected. . . . Our cases, however, clearly foreclose any claim that the Constitution requires proportional representation or that legislatures in reapportioning must draw district lines to come as near as possible to allocating seats to the contending parties in proportion to what their anticipated statewide vote will be. . . .

[T]he mere fact that a particular apportionment scheme makes it more difficult for a particular group in a particular district to elect the representatives of its choice does not render that scheme constitutionally infirm. This conviction, in turn, stems from a perception that the power to influence the political process is not limited to winning elections. An individual or a group of individuals who votes for a losing candidate is usually deemed to be adequately represented by the winning candidate and to have as much opportunity to influence that candidate as other voters in the district. We cannot presume in such a situation, without actual proof to the contrary, that the candidate elected

will entirely ignore the interests of those voters. This is true even in a safe district where the losing group loses election after election. Thus, a group's electoral power is not unconstitutionally diminished by the simple fact of an apportionment scheme that makes winning elections more difficult, and a failure of proportional representation alone does not constitute impermissible discrimination under the Equal Protection Clause. . . .

Rather, unconstitutional discrimination occurs only when the electoral system is arranged in a manner that will consistently degrade a voter's or a group of voters' influence on the political process as a whole. . . .

Based on these views, we would reject the District Court's apparent holding that *any* interference with an opportunity to elect a representative of one's choice would be sufficient to allege or make out an equal protection violation, unless justified by some acceptable state interest that the State would be required to demonstrate. In addition to being contrary to the above-described conception of an unconstitutional political gerrymander, such a low threshold for legal action would invite attack on all or almost all reapportionment statutes. District-based elections hardly ever produce a perfect fit between votes and representation. The one-person, one-vote imperative often mandates departure from this result as does the no-retrogression rule required by § 5 of the Voting Rights Act. Inviting attack on minor departures from some supposed norm would too much embroil the judiciary in second-guessing what has consistently been referred to as a political task for the legislature, a task that should not be monitored too closely unless the express or tacit goal is to effect its removal from legislative halls. We decline to take a major step toward that end, which would be so much at odds with our history and experience. . . .

The District Court's findings do not satisfy this threshold condition to stating and proving a cause of action. In reaching its conclusion, the District Court relied primarily on the results of the 1982 elections. . . .

Relying on a single election to prove unconstitutional discrimination is unsatisfactory. . . . Rather, we have required that there be proof that the complaining minority "had less opportunity . . . to participate in the political processes and to elect legislators of their choice." . . .

We recognize that our own view may be difficult

of application. Determining when an electoral system has been "arranged in a manner that will consistently degrade a voter's or a group of voters' influence on the political process as a whole" . . . is of necessity a difficult inquiry. Nevertheless, we believe that it recognizes the delicacy of intruding on this most political of legislative functions and is at the same time consistent with our prior cases regarding individual multi-member districts, which have formulated a parallel standard.

In sum, we hold that political gerrymandering cases are properly justiciable under the Equal Protection Clause. We also conclude, however, that a threshold showing of discriminatory vote dilution is required for a prima facie case of an equal protection violation. In this case, the findings made by the District Court of an adverse effect on the appellees do not surmount the threshold requirement. Consequently, the judgment of the District Court is

Reversed.

JUSTICE O'CONNOR, with whom THE CHIEF JUSTICE and JUSTICE REHNQUIST join, concurring in the judgment.

Today the Court holds that claims of political gerrymandering lodged by members of one of the political parties that make up our two-party system are justiciable under the Equal Protection Clause of the Fourteenth Amendment. Nothing in our precedents compels us to take this step, and there is every reason not to do so. I would hold that the partisan gerrymandering claims of major political parties raise a nonjusticiable political question that the judiciary should leave to the legislative branch as the Framers of the Constitution unquestionably intended. Accordingly, I would reverse the District Court's judgment on the grounds that appellees' claim is nonjusticiable.

There can be little doubt that the emergence of a strong and stable two-party system in this country has contributed enormously to sound and effective government. The preservation and health of our political institutions, state and federal, depends to no small extent on the continued vitality of our two-party system, which permits both stability and measured change. The opportunity to control the drawing of electoral boundaries through the legislative process of apportionment is a critical and traditional part of politics in the United States, and one that plays no small role in fostering active

participation in the political parties at every level. Thus, the legislative business of apportionment is fundamentally a political affair, and challenges to the manner in which an apportionment has been carried out—by the very parties that are responsible for this process—present a political question in the truest sense of the term.

To turn these matters over to the federal judiciary is to inject the courts into the most heated partisan issues. It is predictable that the courts will respond by moving away from the nebulous standard a plurality of the Court fashions today and toward some form of rough proportional representation for all political groups. The consequences of this shift will be as immense as they are unfortunate. I do not believe, and the Court offers not a shred of evidence to suggest, that the Framers of the Constitution intended the judicial power to encompass the making of such fundamental choices about how this Nation is to be governed. Nor do I believe that the proportional representation towards which the Court's expansion of equal protection doctrine will lead is consistent with our history, our traditions, or our political institutions. . . .

The standard the plurality proposes exemplifies the intractable difficulties in deriving a judicially manageable standard from the Equal Protection Clause for adjudicating political gerrymandering claims. The plurality rejects any standard that would require drawing "district lines to come as near as possible to allocating seats to the contending parties in proportion to what their anticipated statewide vote will be," . . . and states that "unconstitutional discrimination occurs only when the electoral system is arranged in a manner that will consistently degrade a voter's or a group of voters' influence on the political process as a whole." . . . In my view, this standard will over time either prove unmanageable and arbitrary or else evolve towards some loose form of proportionality. . . . Either outcome would be calamitous for the federal courts, for the States, and for our two-party system.

Vote dilution analysis is far less manageable when extended to major political parties than if confined to racial minority groups. First, an increase in the number of competing claims to equal group representation will make judicial review of apportionment vastly more complex. Designing an apportionment plan that does not impair or degrade the voting strength of several groups is more difficult than designing a plan that does not have such an effect on one group for the simple reason that, as the number of criteria the plan must meet increases, the number of solutions that will satisfy those criteria will decrease. Even where it is not impossible to reconcile the competing claims of political, racial, and other groups, the predictable result will be greater judicial intrusion into the apportionment process.

Second, while membership in a racial group is an immutable characteristic, voters can—and often do—move from one party to the other or support candidates from both parties. Consequently, the difficulty of measuring voting strength is heightened in the case of a major political party. It is difficult enough to measure "a voter's or a group of voters' influence on the political process as a whole" . . . when the group is a racial minority in a particular district or community. When the group is a major political party the difficulty is greater, and the constitutional basis for intervening far more tenuous.

Moreover, any such intervention is likely to move in the direction of proportional representation for political parties. This is clear by analogy to the problem that arises in racial gerrymandering cases: "in order to decide whether an electoral system has made it harder for minority voters to elect the candidates they prefer, a court must have an idea in mind of how hard it 'should' be for minority voters to elect their preferred candidates under an acceptable system." . . .

I would avoid the difficulties generated by the plurality's efforts to confine the effects of a generalized group right to equal representation by not recognizing such a right in the first instance. To allow district courts to strike down apportionment plans on the basis of their prognostications as to the outcome of future elections or future apportionments invites "findings" on matters as to which neither judges nor anyone else can have any confidence. Once it is conceded that "a group's electoral power is not unconstitutionally diminished by the simple fact of an apportionment scheme that makes winning elections more difficult" . . . the virtual impossibility of reliably predicting how difficult it will be to win an election in 2, or 4, or 10 years should, in my view, weigh in favor of holding such challenges nonjusticiable. Racial gerrymandering should remain justiciable, for the harms it engenders run counter to the central thrust of the Fourteenth

Amendment. But no such justification can be given for judicial intervention on behalf of mainstream political parties, and the risks such intervention poses to our political institutions are unacceptable. "Political affiliation is the keystone of the political trade. Race, ideally, is not." . . .

JUSTICE POWELL, with whom JUSTICE STEVENS joins, concurring in part and dissenting in part. . . .

The Equal Protection Clause guarantees citizens that their state will govern them impartially. . . . In the context of redistricting, that guarantee is of critical importance because the franchise provides most citizens their only voice in the legislative process. . . . Since the contours of a voting district powerfully may affect citizens' ability to exercise influence through their vote, district lines should be determined in accordance with neutral and legitimate criteria. When deciding where those lines will fall, the state should treat its voters as standing in the same position, regardless of their political beliefs or party affiliation. . . .

In light of the foregoing principles, I believe that the plurality's opinion is seriously flawed in several respects. First, apparently to avoid the forceful evidence that some district lines indisputably were designed to and did discriminate against Democrats, the plurality describes appellees' claim as alleging that "Democratic voters over the State as a whole, not Democratic voters in particular districts, have been subjected to unconstitutional discrimination." . . . This characterization is not inconsistent with appellees' proof, and the District Court's finding, of statewide discriminatory effect resulting from "individual districting" that "exemplif[ies] this discrimination." . . . If Democratic voters in a number of critical districts are the focus of unconstitutional discrimination, as the District Court found, the *effect* of that discrimination will be felt over the State as a whole.

The plurality also erroneously characterizes the harm members of the losing party suffer as a group when they are deprived, through deliberate and arbitrary distortion of district boundaries, of the opportunity to elect representatives of their choosing. It may be, as the plurality suggests, that representatives will not "entirely ignore the interests" of opposition voters. . . . But it defies political reality to suppose that members of a losing party have as much political influence over state government as do members of the victorious party. Even the most conscientious state legislators do not disregard opportunities to reward persons or groups who were active supporters in their election campaigns. Similarly, no one doubts that partisan considerations play a major role in the passage of legislation and the appointment of state officers. Not surprisingly, therefore, the District Court expressly found that "[c]ontrol of the General Assembly is crucial" to members of the major political parties in Indiana. . . . In light of those findings, I cannot accept the plurality's apparent conclusion that loss of this "crucial" position is constitutionally insignificant as long as the losers are not "entirely ignored" by the winners. . . .

The final and most basic flaw in the plurality's opinion is its failure to enunciate any standard that affords guidance to legislatures and courts. Legislators and judges are left to wonder whether compliance with "one person, one vote" completely insulates a partisan gerrymander from constitutional scrutiny, or whether a fairer but as yet undefined standard applies. The failure to articulate clear doctrine in this area places the plurality in the curious position of inviting further litigation even as it appears to signal the "constitutional green light" to would-be gerrymanderers. . . .

Unstaged Debate on the Finality of Supreme Court Decisions: Andrew Jackson and Abraham Lincoln v. the Supreme Court*

PRESIDENT JACKSON VETOES
THE BANK ACT

When Congress voted to continue the Bank of the United States in 1832, President Andrew Jackson vetoed the bill in part because he thought it unconstitutional. The Supreme Court in *McCulloch v. Maryland* (1819), a case reprinted in Chapter Four, had alread upheld the constitutionality of the bank. Jackson's words were drafted mainly by Roger Brooke Taney, whom Jackson soon appointed to succeed John Marshall as chief justice of the United States.

It is maintained by the advocates of the bank that its constitutionality in all its features ought to be considered as settled by precedent and by the decision of the Supreme Court. To this conclusion I can not assent.

If the opinion of the Supreme Court covered the whole ground of this act, it ought not to control the coordinate authorities of this Government. The Congress, the Executive, and the Court must each for itself be guided by its own opinion of the

Constitution. Each public officer who takes an oath to support the Constitution swears that he will support it as he understands it, and not as it is understood by others. It is as much the duty of the House of Representatives, of the Senate, and of the President to decide upon the constitutionality of any bill or resolution which may be presented to them for passage or approval as it is of the supreme judges when it may be brought before them for judicial decision. The opinion of the judges has no more authority over Congress than the opinion of Congress has over the judges, and on that point the President is independent of both. The authority of the Supreme Court must not, therefore, be permitted to control the Congress or the Executive when acting in their legislative ca-

* The Jackson and Lincoln messages appear in James D. Richardson, ed., *A Compilation of the Messages and Papers of the Presidents* (Washington, D.C.: Bureau of National Literature and Art, 1908) at Vol. 2, pp. 581–82, and at Vol. 6, p. 9, respectively.

pacities, but to have only such influence as the force of their reasoning may deserve.

PRESIDENT LINCOLN DELIVERS HIS FIRST INAUGURAL ADDRESS (1861)

I do not forget the position assumed by some, that constitutional questions are to be decided by the Supreme Court; nor do I deny that such decisions must be binding in any case, upon the parties to a suit, as to the object of that suit, while they are also entitled to a very high respect and consideration, in all parallel cases, by all other departments of government. And while it is obviously possible that such decision may be erroneous in any given case, still the evil effect following it, being limited to that particular case, with the chance that it may be over-ruled, and never become a precedent for other cases, can better be borne than could the evils of a different practice. At the same time the candid citizen must confess that if the policy of the government, upon vital questions, affecting the whole people, is to be irrevocably fixed by decisions of the Supreme Court, the instant they are made, in ordinary litigation between parties, in personal actions, the people will have ceased, to be their own rulers, having to that extent, practically resigned their government, into the hands of that eminent tribunal. Nor is there, in this view, any assault upon the court, or the judges. It is a duty, from which they may not shrink, to decide cases properly brought before them; and it is no fault of theirs, if others seek to turn their decisions to political purposes.

THE SUPREME COURT DECIDES
COOPER v. *AARON* (1958)

This case grew out of resistance in Little Rock, Arkansas, to the Supreme Court's 1954 school desegregation decision (**Brown v. Board of Education,** in Chapter Twelve). The opinion is unusual in that all nine justices signed it.

Opinion of the Court by THE CHIEF JUSTICE, MR. JUSTICE BLACK, MR. JUSTICE FRANKFURTER, MR. JUSTICE DOUGLAS, MR. JUSTICE BURTON, MR. JUSTICE CLARK, MR. JUSTICE HARLAN, MR. JUSTICE BRENNAN, and MR. JUSTICE WHITTAKER.

As this case reaches us it raises questions of the highest importance to the maintenance of our federal system of government. It necessarily involves a claim by the Governor and Legislature of a State that there is no duty on state officials to obey federal court orders resting on this Court's considered interpretation of the United States Constitution. Specifically it involves actions by the Governor and Legislature of Arkansas upon the premise that they are not bound by our holding in *Brown* v. *Board of Education*. . . .

What has been said, in the light of the facts developed, is enough to dispose of the case. However, we should answer the premise of the actions of the Governor and Legislature that they are not bound by our holding in the *Brown* case. It is necessary only to recall some basic constitutional propositions which are settled doctrine.

Article 6 of the Constitution makes the Constitution the "supreme Law of the Land." In 1803, Chief Justice Marshall, speaking for a unanimous Court, referring to the Constitution as "the fundamental and paramount law of the nation," declared in the notable case of *Marbury* v. *Madison* . . . that "It is emphatically the province and duty of the judicial department to say what the law is." This decision declared the basic principle that the federal judiciary is supreme in the exposition of the law of the Constitution, and that principle has ever since been respected by this Court and the Country as a permanent and indispensable feature of our constitutional system. It follows that the interpretation of the Fourteenth Amendment enunciated by this Court in the *Brown* Case is the supreme law of the land, and Art. 6 of the Constitution makes it of binding effect on the States "any Thing in the Constitution or Laws of any

State to the Contrary notwithstanding." Every state legislator and executive and judicial officer is solemnly committed by oath taken pursuant to Art. 6, ¶3 "to support this Constitution." Chief Justice Taney, speaking for a unanimous Court in 1859, said that this requirement reflected the framers' "anxiety to preserve it [the Constitution] in full force, in all its powers, and to guard against resistance to or evasion of its authority, on the part of a State. . . ."

No state legislator or executive or judicial officer can war against the Constitution without violating his undertaking to support it. Chief Justice Marshall spoke for a unanimous Court in saying that: "If the legislatures of the several states may, at will, annul the judgments of the courts of the United States, and destroy the rights acquired under those judgments, the constitution itself becomes a solemn mockery. . . ." A Governor who asserts a power to nullify a federal court order is similarly restrained. If he had such power, said Chief Justice Hughes, in 1932, also for a unanimous Court, "it is manifest that the fiat of a state Governor, and not the Constitution of the United States, would be the supreme law of the land; that the restrictions of the Federal Constitution upon the exercise of state power would be but impotent phrases. . . ."

Unstaged Debate of 1986:
Judge Bork v. Professor Tribe

ROBERT H. BORK,* *Original Intent and the Constitution,* 7 Humanities 22, 26–27 (Feb. 1986)

The phrase "original intent" has suddenly become the focus of national controversy, and none too soon. The controversy swirls around the question whether judges, who undertake to strike down laws and executive actions in the name of the Constitution, must do so only in accordance with the intentions of those who wrote, proposed, and ratified the Constitution's various provisions. This philosophy of originalism comports with what most people assume judges are, and should be, doing. But it is not what most academic constitutional specialists want of judges and it is apparently not what some judges conceive their function to be. They have evolved a philosophy of non-originalism according to which judges should create individual rights that supersede democratic decisions. . . .

It is argued by some legal theorists that the Constitution's meaning should evolve and that the

course of evolution should be determined by moral and political philosophy. It is not entirely clear why this method of changing the document's meaning, if it is legitimate, should be confined to individual freedoms, found primarily in the Bill of Rights and the Civil War amendments. It could as well be applied to the interpretation of the powers and structures of government laid out in the first three articles of the Constitution. That is rarely, if ever, proposed, probably because it would make embarrassingly clear that the professors are asking judges to remake our form of government. Yet one form of judicial creativity is no more illegitimate than the other. But the problem with the argument goes deeper. There is no single philosophy or method of philosophic reasoning upon which all Americans agree. . . .

Perhaps recognizing these difficulties, other constitutional theorists would have judges apply not philosophical analysis but something more akin to a sense, almost intuitive, of what "our evolving morality" demands at the moment. This idea rests upon the correct observation that a society's morality does evolve and that the American morality of today differs in a number of respects from the American morality of the late eighteenth century.

* Judge, United States Court of Appeals, District of Columbia Circuit, 1982–1988. Judge Bork's nomination to the Supreme Court was rejected by the Senate in 1987.

All quite true, but inadequate to support the conclusion. The Constitution's guarantees—freedom of speech, press, and religion; freedom from unreasonable searches and seizures; freedom from required self-incrimination; and much more—remain highly relevant today. Any free society must respect them. No theorist, to my knowledge, suggests that, if American morality evolves so that these freedoms are disliked, judges should abandon them—yet that is what would seem to be required by this approach. Again, however, the trouble goes deeper. To the degree that the morality that is evolving deserves the name of "our morality," it will be embodied in legislation and executive action. There will be no need for judges to tell the society what the society's morality is. Judges who undertake to apply "our evolving morality" to invalidate democratically enacted law will, in truth, be enforcing their own morality upon the rest of us and calling it the Constitution.

These considerations seem to me to leave only the method of original intent as a legitimate means of applying the Constitution. Only that can give us law that is something other than, and superior to, the judge's will. It is objected that the process of discerning the Framers' intentions can be manipulated and that, in any event, it is impossible to know what the Framers would have done in specific cases. Those things are true and, if they are insuperable objections, the only conclusion left is that the Constitution can never be law and judicial review should be abandoned. The objections are by no means fatal, however.

Any system of argument which is complex and involves questions of degree and of judgment is manipulable. Certainly, it will be easier to detect manipulation of historical materials than of philosophic concepts or subjective estimates of contemporary morality. The only ultimate solution is the selection of intellectually honest judges.

The objection that we can never know what the Framers would have done about specific modern situations is entirely beside the point. The originalist attempts to discern the principles the Framers enacted, the values they sought to protect. All that the philosophy of original intention requires is that the text, structure, and history of the Constitution provide the judge not with a conclusion about a specific case but with a premise from which to begin reasoning about that case. For instance, while

the Fourth Amendment, when framed, envisioned protection only against unwarranted searches and seizures by physical invasion, its intended prohibition of unreasonable intrusions by the state against the individual can certainly be applied in the context of electronic surveillance. . . .

Adherence to a philosophy of searching for original intent does not mean that judges will invariably decide cases the way the Framers would have, though many cases will be decided that way. At the very least, the originalist philosophy confines judges to areas the Framers assigned to them and reserves to democratic processes those areas of life the Framers placed there. That much is indispensable if judges are not to usurp the legitimate freedom of the people to govern themselves, and no philosophy other than that of original intent can provide that safeguard.

LAURENCE H. TRIBE,* *The Holy Grail of Original Intent,* 7 Humanities 23–25 (Feb. 1986)

. . . In today's highly visible and notably politicized constitutional discourse, a particular version of "history"—what some confidently claim to know our country's Founders and our Constitution's Framers "originally intended"—is offered as the only relevant, and indeed the definitive, source of the true meaning of each provision in the constitutional text. But, by standing on its head Santayana's injunction that those who forget the past are condemned to repeat it, these new "originalists" are busily *inventing* a particular past that might *dictate* our constitutional future. In doing so, they are claiming for history a decisive authority that is incompatible with the limits of what we can know and false to the nature of the Constitution itself. . . .

Those disputants who, like Judge Bork, define the values they deem themselves bound to protect in such a way as to reflect narrowly the specific practices and concrete concerns that moved the founding generation have made a choice to reject a higher level of abstraction and generality. For them, "liberty" is more likely to represent a *catalogue* of freedoms from particular abuses feared by the Framers than a general *concept* of personal

* Tyler Professor of Constitutional Law at Harvard Law School. Professor Tribe testified against Judge Bork's nomination to the Supreme Court in 1987.

autonomy. That is a choice that may be either attacked or defended, but it is by no means a choice mandated by what the Constitution expressly says, by what its authors and ratifiers demonstrably meant, or even by the virtue of confining the discretion of unelected judges.

To begin with, the very generality of many of the terms the Framers used—such as "liberty," "due process," and "equal protection"—strongly suggests an intent not to confine their meaning to the specific outcomes and contexts that occurred to those who first used them, but to invite the development of meanings in light of the needs and insights of succeeding generations. . . .

The originalists must accordingly persuade us that their own departure from that overarching original intent is justified—and that it may be coherently pursued despite the often conflicting things that the many who wrote, or voted to ratify, the Constitution's provisions had in mind. And they must, in addition, convince us that their program will succeed in its proclaimed objective of placing the interpretive enterprise beyond the reach of personal predilection and subjective judgment.

For my part, I gravely doubt that the program can come even close to succeeding. Consider the justices who wrote in *Dred Scott* that slaves are mere property, the justices who wrote in *Plessy* that racial separation by law need not deny equality, and the justices who wrote in *Lochner* that laws regulating hours and wages invade "freedom of contract." All of them invoked "original intent" with considerable conviction and plausibility. . . . If one wants to say—as I do, and as . . . Judge Bork seem[s] to—that those cases were wrongly decided, one must do much better than the originalists have yet done to explain away the awkward facts of history that weighed in on the wrong side of those disputes. Nor can the program of the originalists avoid the charge of subjective and even politically motivated selectivity and manipulation when those who advocate it so readily support the constitutionality of eminently sensible and currently indispensable policies that would certainly have

shocked those who framed the Constitution and the Bill of Rights—such as "stop and frisk" practices by police in urban areas, the extraction of coerced testimony in response to promises of immunity, and the authorization of police searches for mere evidence of crime as opposed to contraband. Finally, the originalist project can hardly succeed when even its most ardent proponents counsel that some constitutional decisions, even if originally wrong by their own test of the Framers' intent, have become so deeply rooted that it would be neither prudent nor necessary to roll back the clock. . . .

The major difference between those who insist that they are passively discerning and enforcing the specific intentions of the Framers, and those who concede that they are of necessity doing something more, is likely to come down to this: The originalists seek to deny their own responsibility for the choices they are making—and imposing upon the rest of us—whereas their opponents, for better or worse, accept such responsibility as inescapably theirs. . . .

To insist, as I would, that all judicial choices ought to be seriously constrained by constitutional text, structure, and tradition indeed requires one to confess that such choices are never merely the passive products of a single "original intent" existing in history and waiting to be discovered. The danger that judges might wield power in the name of the Constitution but in the service of nothing beyond their personal moral predilections is heightened, not reduced, by the habit of couching judicial determinations in the form of ineluctable readings of a purely external reality. However adorned by scholarly references to history, such claims are far less subject to meaningful dispute, and hence far less constrained by the requirements of persuasion, than are the more modest claims of those who admittedly base their constitutional arguments on a more eclectic, less determinate mix of appeals to language, precedent, and legal philosophy. . . . A candid avowal of the limits of originalism can open the process of constitutional interpretation to the full public debate without which it partakes only of miracle, mystery, and unquestioned authority.

THREE

Congress, the Court, and the President

[A] mere demarcation on parchment of the constitutional limits of the several departments is not a sufficient guard against those encroachments which lead to a tyrannical concentration of all the powers of government in the same hands.

—JAMES MADISON (1788)

The principle of separation of powers, propounded by seventeenth- and eighteenth-century political philosophers Harrington, Locke, and Montesquieu, was a device for limiting government power by taking from the monarch his ancient lawmaking power and vesting it in a legislature. The American development of this doctrine went much further. In place of the traditional division into legislative and executive, the American colonies adopted a threefold division, elevating the judiciary to coequal position and putting all three under the rule of law established by a written constitution.

SEPARATION OF POWERS

The federal Constitution contains no specific declaration concerning separation of powers. The principle is implicit in the organization of the first three articles: (1) "All legislative powers herein granted shall be vested in a Congress of the United States"; (2) "The executive power shall be vested in a President of the United States"; (3) "The judicial power shall be vested in one Supreme Court and in such inferior courts as the congress shall . . . ordain and establish." From this separation is derived the doctrine that certain functions, because of their essential nature, may properly be exercised by only a particular branch of the government; that such functions cannot be delegated to any other branch; and that one department may not interfere with another by usurping its powers or by supervising their exercise.

At the Convention of 1787, separation of powers was endorsed with virtual unanimity. "No political truth," Madison said, "is of greater intrinsic value." In *The Federalist, Nos.*

47, 48, and 51 (excerpted in this chapter), Madison explored the principle. Inherited from Montesquieu, it is inspired by the conviction that "every man vested with power is apt to abuse it; and carry his authority as far as it will go." "Is it not strange," Montesquieu asked, "that virtue itself has need of limits?"

Separation of powers is a misnomer. No precise line is or could be drawn between the three branches of the national government. The Constitution separates organs of government; it fuses functions and powers. Because of frequently voiced criticism of the blending of executive, legislature, and judiciary in the proposed Constitution, Madison felt compelled to restate the traditional theory. The sharing of powers through the scheme of checks and balances was, Madison explained, a valuable additional restraint on government that complemented the principle of separation of powers. Not only did the blending of powers limit government itself; it also provided weapons by which each department could defend its position in the constitutional system. The president's veto, it was urged, protected him against legislative encroachments, and his power of appointment gave him influence against judicial assault. The Court had the power to pass on legislation and was protected by life tenure. The Congress could impeach a president and members of the Court. The national lawmakers controlled the purse on which both the other departments depended, the Senate passed on presidential appointments, and the Congress controlled the appellate jurisdiction of the Supreme Court.

The legislature may exercise the executive power of pardon in the form of a grant of amnesty or immunity from prosecution. It may punish contempts and may provide in minute detail the rules of procedure to be followed by the courts. The power of Congress to control the issuance of injunctions by federal courts and to restrict their power to punish disobedience has also been sustained. Although the courts do not legislate in the strict sense of the word, their decisions may be regarded from a realistic point of view as a form of lawmaking. As upheld in **Morrison v. Olson** (1988) the courts, within limits, may exercise the executive power of appointment; and Congress may confer on them the power to suspend sentence, even though such power is legislative in nature. The president's power over foreign relations is such that the functions of advising and consenting to treaties and of "declaring" war, apparently entrusted by the Constitution to the legislature, have come largely under his control. Executive officers and administrative bodies also exercise functions that belong to other departments. Thus the commissioner of patents exercises judicial power in determining whether a patent shall be issued or renewed, and the independent regulatory commissions and the cabinet departments themselves exercise legislative and judicial powers. Moreover, under *Katzenbach* v. *Morgan* (1966), which found constitutional the ban on literacy tests for voting in the Voting Rights Act of 1965, the justices effectively shared the power of constitutional interpretation with Congress. The inference was that Congress is as entitled to determine legislatively what the Fourteenth Amendment means as the court is entitled to do so judicially.

THE CONGRESS

Delegation of Authority. Statutes cannot be so detailed as to contain every regulation and form of procedure by which the legislative policies set forth in them are to be carried out. The courts have consequently recognized that administrative officers must be permitted some discretion in the enforcement of laws, and that the effective operation of government often requires the exercise of legislative authority by the executive. Hence Congress may permit executive officers to determine when a given statute shall become operative and fill in the details of legislative enactments by appropriate regulations. An early case, *The Aurora* v. *United States* (1813), sustained the grant of power to the president to revive the Non-Intercourse Act when he shall have ascertained that certain conditions exist. *Hampton & Co.* v. *United States* (1928) sustained a flexible tariff act authorizing the president to raise or lower tariff rates by 50 percent to equalize the costs of production in the United States and competing foreign countries. For a unanimous court, Chief Justice Taft wrote,

> The field of Congress involves all and many varieties of legislative action and Congress has found it frequently necessary to use officers of the executive branch within defined limits, to secure the exact effect intended by acts of legislation, by vesting discretion in such officers to make public regulations interpreting a statute and directing the details of its execution, even to the extent of providing for penalizing a breach of such regulations. . . .
>
> Congress may feel itself unable conveniently to determine exactly when its exercise of the legislative power should become effective, because dependent on future conditions, and it may leave the determination of such time to the decision of an executive. . . .

Before 1935 no statute had ever been held invalid because of unconstitutional delegation of power to the executive. In each instance the standard set up by the legislature was held to be sufficiently definite, although some rather vague criteria were thus sustained. In *Panama Refining Co.* v. *Ryan* (Hot Oil Case) (1935), however, the Supreme Court held unconstitutional a provision of the National Industrial Recovery Act authorizing the president to prohibit the interstate shipment of oil produced or withdrawn in violation of state regulations. The Court declared that an absolute and uncontrolled discretion had been vested in the executive since the statute stated no policy and provided no standard by which the validity of the president's action could be judged.

Schechter Poultry Corporation v. *United States* (1935), decided shortly after the Hot Oil decision, condemned the attempted delegation to the president of code-approving authority. The discretion of the president under the National Industrial Recovery Act was, the Court said, "virtually unfettered," and Cardozo, in a concurring opinion, termed it "delegation run riot." The infirmities of these laws with respect to the attempted delegations were for the most part the result of hasty and inefficient legislative draftsmanship. By 1938 both Congress and the Court had learned a lesson. In the Fair Labor Standards Act, Congress, by adding a rather detailed, though uninstructive, list of factors to guide the administrators' judgment, provided satisfactory limits within which administrative discretion was to be exercised. In *Opp Cotton Mills* v. *Administrator* (1941), the Court unanimously upheld regulations against the charge, among other things, that the administrator was authorized to fix wages without adequate congressional guides or control.

Whether in war or in peace, delegations of rule-making authority became even more necessary in later years. Indeed, most "legislation" today is not enacted by Congress but is promulgated by dozens of administrative agencies. "The rise of administrative bodies probably has been the most significant legal trend of the last century," said Justice Jackson four decades ago. "They have become a veritable fourth branch of the Government, which has deranged our three-branch legal theories . . ." (*Federal Trade Commission* v. *Ruberoid Co.*, 1952). To control these agencies, Congress a half-century ago began writing a "veto" provision into various statutes. This "legislative veto" enabled Congress to have its cake and eat it too. Agencies could continue making rules, but Congress could "veto" or set aside such regulations by a one-house, two-house, or even a committee resolution. Of course, such "vetoes" were not subject to presidential vetoes, and here lay the rub. Congress seemed to be making law other than in the constitutionally prescribed fashion. This is the significance of *I.N.S.* v. *Chadha.* The justices have been willing to approve *delegation* of authority but unwilling to permit this form of tight legislative *control*. In the face of the Court's declaring the legislative veto unconstitutional, it remains to be seen what devices Congress will choose to keep control of the many agencies to which it has delegated rule-making authority.

A potentially broad-based challenge to delegation of legislative authority—and hence to the modern regulatory state—took the form of litigation over the Balanced Budget and Emergency Deficit Control Act of 1985 (commonly called the Gramm-Rudman-Hollings Act). The statute attempted to cope with massive budget deficits by requiring cuts in spending by the federal government. If Congress would not or could not make the cuts by the prescribed time, the comptroller general was to prepare a report detailing program-by-program budget reductions. The president would then issue a "sequestration" order for the cuts. As soon as the bill was signed into law, Congressman Mike Synar of Oklahoma brought suit, claiming, among other things, that Congress had unconstitutionally delegated budgetary decision making (a key legislative function) to bureaucrats.

In *Bowsher* v. *Synar* (1986), seven justices struck down the automatic reduction feature of the 1985 law. Significantly, however, the Court rejected Synar's principal objection. According to Warren Burger in his last opinion as chief justice, the defect in the statute was not delegation of Congress's spending power to bureaucrats but delegation of the president's power to execute the laws to an agent of Congress. The act violated the principle of separation of powers. Otherwise Congress would be executing the law itself. It made no difference that Congress had not once removed a comptroller since creation of the office in 1921. "[I]t is clear that Congress has consistently viewed the Comptroller General as an officer of the Legislative Branch," declared Burger. "Over the years, the Comptrollers General have also viewed themselves as part of the Legislative Branch. . . . [W]e see no escape from the conclusion that, because Congress has retained removal authority over the Comptroller General, he may not be entrusted with executive powers."

Legislative Investigations. A function of Congress, vying in importance with law-making itself, is investigation. Woodrow Wilson rated the "informing function" higher than that of legislation. In 1936 Senator Hugo L. Black, who the next year became a Supreme Court justice, referred to congressional investigations as "among the most useful and fruitful functions of the national legislature." Though derived immediately from the "necessary and proper" clause, the investigatory power is also grounded in the fact that Congress, like Parliament and the early state legislatures, is a deliberative body. Each house, separately or concurrently, may pass resolutions expressing its views on any subject it sees fit. To inform itself on matters likely to become subjects of legislation, Congress may establish committees. Such committees may *subpoena* witnesses (that is, compel their attendance) and take testimony. If witnesses refuse to cooperate, they may be punished for contempt. But legislative imprisonment may not extend beyond the session of Congress in which the offense was committed. Congress's investigatory power falls short of authority to make inquiry into the purely personal affairs of private individuals. Investigation must be related to some legislative purpose (*Kilbourn* v. *Thompson,* 1881).

Without basing its decision on the First Amendment, the Court in **Watkins** v. **United States** (1957) questioned the authority of either house to delve into the private lives of individuals—to "expose for the sake of exposure" or to deny freedom of speech or right of association. The 6-to-1 majority agreed that the power to conduct investigations "is inherent in the legislative process" but insisted that as a matter of due process of law all witnesses must be informed of the pertinency of the questions put to them. Reaction to the decision was hotly critical. Two years later, by construing the Watkins precedent narrowly, a divided court in **Barenblatt** v. **United States** (1959) reached a different result.

Membership and Privilege. On March 1, 1967, the House of Representatives voted to exclude Harlem Congressman Adam Clayton Powell on the ground that he had misused public funds and was contemptuous of the New York courts and committees of Congress. By a vote of 7 to 1 *(Powell v. McCormack),* the Supreme Court held that the House of Representatives lacked power to *exclude* from its membership a person duly elected who meets the age, citizenship, and residence requirements specified in Article I, Section 2, of the Constitution. (However, a restriction on the power of the House to *exclude* must not be equated with its power to *expel.*) Holding that "it is the responsibility of this Court to act as ultimate interpreter of the Constitution," Chief Justice Warren in his last major opinion, reversed the opinion of Appeals Judge Warren E. Burger, the man nominated to succeed him. Invoking separation of powers, Burger had dismissed Representative Powell's suit for reinstatement, contending that courts should not rule on a political issue fraught with possible conflict between Congress and courts. Chief Justice Warren disagreed: "A fundamental principle of our representative democracy is, in Hamilton's words, 'that the people should choose whom they please to govern them. . . .' As Madison pointed out in the Convention, this principle is undermined as much by limiting whom the people can elect as by limiting the franchise itself." As in so many of the Warren Court's rulings, judicial review, apparently at odds with popular government, was invoked to sustain government by the people.

The Court has also declined to allow Congress to be the sole judge of the scope of the privilege enshrined in the Speech or Debate Clause (Art. I, Sec. 6) of the Constitution. The protection against being "questioned in any other Place" is a major resource of legislative power and independence. The privilege extends "not only to a member but also to his aides insofar as the conduct of the latter would be a protected legislative act if performed by the member himself" *(Gravel v. United States,* 1972). Critical to the scope of the privilege is the definition of a "protected legislative act," by no means an all-inclusive term. Such protection extends to voting and preparing committee reports but not to newsletters and press releases, declared the Court in *Hutchinson v. Proxmire* (1979). Senator William Proxmire's "Golden Fleece of the Month Award" had ridiculed a researcher for studies done on animals. In a newsletter Proxmire had charged that the research had "made a monkey out of the American taxpayer." Without the protection of the Speech or Debate Clause, the Court ruled that the senator could be sued for damages.

THE PRESIDENT

Addressing himself to the executive in *The Federalist,* No. 70, Hamilton wrote,

> There is an idea, which is not without its advocates, that a vigorous executive is inconsistent with the genius of republican government. The enlightened well-wishers to this species of government must at least hope that the supposition is destitute of foundation. Energy in the Executive is a leading character in the definition of good government. It is essential to the protection of the community against foreign attacks; it is not less essential to the steady administration of the laws; to the protection of property against those irregular and high-handed combinations which sometimes interrupt the ordinary course of justice; to the security of liberty against the enterprises and assaults of ambition, of faction, and of anarchy.
>
> A feeble executive implies a feeble execution of the government. A feeble execution is but another phrase for a bad execution; and a government ill executed, whatever it may be in theory, must be, in practice, a bad government.
>
> The ingredients which constitute energy in the Executive are, first, unity: secondly, duration; thirdly, an adequate provision for its support; fourthly, competent powers.

Like most modern governments, the United States has manifested a tendency toward concentration of power in the hands of the executive. The president is the political head of the country in extraconstitutional affairs; he exercises the power to pardon, the veto power, and extensive war powers, and has an almost absolute control over foreign relations. Moreover, under certain limitations, Congress may give the executive its own power for use when swift and coordinated action is required. Finally, the conduct of government is increasingly in the multiple hands of administrative agencies.

The members of the Convention of 1787 who feared that the president inevitably would succumb to an all-powerful legislature have proved to be poor prophets. Although the Supreme Court has from the time of Marshall asserted and maintained a role of great significance, it is the presidential office that has expanded most in power and shown the greatest increase in both the number and variety of its activities. This swelling of executive power is not unique to America. The grand age of the legislature, when the dominance of the concept of limited government both required and permitted long debate preceding any change in government policy, and the paucity of government programs facilitated legislative surveillance of administration, is past. War, economic crises, and the complexity of problems confronting industrialized societies have thrust on the executive power and responsibility not contemplated in an earlier age. "Taken, by and large," Professor Corwin wrote in 1941, "the history of the presidency has been a history of aggrandizement." Only since 1970 has Congress attempted to regain influence and to reverse the trend toward presidential dominance.

Theories of Presidential Power. Three strikingly divergent theories purport to describe the nature and scope of presidential power: the *constitutional theory,* the *stewardship theory,* and the *prerogative theory.* The constitutional theory holds that Article II contains an enumeration of executive powers, and that the president must be prepared to justify all his actions on the basis of either enumerated or implied power. The best statement of the constitutional theory appears in W. H. Taft's book, *Our Chief Magistrate and His Powers* (1916). In opposition to Taft, Theodore Roosevelt contended that the president is a "steward of the people," and is therefore under the duty to do "anything that the needs of the nation demanded unless such action was forbidden by the Constitution and the laws." Taft denounced Roosevelt's theory as calculated to make the president a "universal Providence." As chief justice, however, he indicated greater sympathy for it. Going beyond the first Roosevelt's "stewardship" theory, Franklin D. Roosevelt's concept of his duties conforms essentially to John Locke's description of "prerogative"—"the power to act according to discretion for the public good, without the prescription of the law and sometimes even against it." During his long incumbency, President Roosevelt often sacrificed constitutional and legal restrictions on the altar of "emergency" and a commanding public interest.

Many dicta in *United States* v. *Curtiss Wright* (1936) seem to justify "inherent" power, at least in foreign affairs, where the president speaks and acts for the nation. In the domestic sphere, however, this is, as the Steel Seizure Case suggests, a highly dubious rationale for presidential action (*Youngstown* v. *Sawyer).* When this case was before the District Court, counsel for the United States, asked by the bench to specify the source of the president's power to seize the steel mills in peacetime, declared, ". . . We base the President's power on Sections 1, 2, and 3 of Article II of the Constitution, and whatever inherent, implied or residual powers may flow therefrom." "So you contend the Executive has unlimited power in time of an emergency?" the judge inquired. Government counsel replied that the president "has the power to take such action as is necessary to meet the emergency" and indicated that the only limitations on executive power in an emergency are the ballot box and impeachment. In argument before the Supreme Court, however, government counsel stressed the president's specific powers derived from the duty to execute the laws and as commander-in-chief. The Steel Seizure Case demonstrates that although the president may not be the subject of judicial orders limiting his actions in executing laws or implementing policy (*Mississippi* v. *Johnson*, 1867), his subordinate officers may be the objects of injunctive and other forms of relief when they act, or threaten to act, illegally.

In its unanimous decision in **United States v. Nixon** (1974), the Court held that the president himself must respond to a subpoena issued in connection with a pending trial of former government officials. Although sanctioning "executive privilege,"—the right of officials in the executive branch to refuse to appear before Congress and the courts and to provide requested documents—the justices ruled that neither the doctrine of separation of powers nor the alleged confidentiality of executive communications barred the federal courts from access to presidential tapes needed as evidence in a criminal case. Participating in the case were justices appointed by five presidents, three by President Nixon. In constitutional theory and political consequences, the decision is among the most remarkable in the Court's history. Vindicated was the ideal "government of laws and not of men." The Court has also upheld the Presidential Recordings and Materials Preservation Act, specifying control over, and access to, the White House papers and tape recordings from President Nixon's five and a half years in office (*Nixon* v. *Administrator of General Services,* 1977). The majority reached this conclusion in the face of Justice Rehnquist's charge that the statute, even though limited only to the Nixon materials, "poses a real threat to the ability of future Presidents to receive candid advice and to give candid instructions. This result . . . will daily stand as a veritable sword of Damocles over every succeeding President and his advisors."

Appointment and Removal of Officers. The Constitution provides that the president "shall nominate and, by and with the advice and consent of the Senate, shall appoint ambassadors . . . judges of the Supreme Court, and all other officers of the United States, whose appointments are not herein otherwise provided for and which shall be established by law; but the Congress may by law vest the appointment of such inferior officers, as they think proper, in the President alone, in the courts of law, or in the heads of departments" (Art. II, Sec. 2, Cl. 2). Persons appointed in a manner not specified by the Constitution are not "officers of the United States"; and although no precise definition of the term *inferior officers* has ever been made by the courts, it would seem to include all except those in whom the power of appointment might be vested.

The Constitution makes no provision for the removal of officers appointed under the preceding clause, but the power of removal is generally regarded as a power derived from the power to appoint. Following the decision of *Myers* v. *United States,* (1926), it was generally thought that the power of the president to remove officials appointed by him was plenary, free from any limitations by Congress. Nine years later, however, the Court whittled down the broad rule, holding that the removal of officials from certain independent agencies, such as the Federal Trade Commission, could be limited to causes defined by Congress (*Humphrey's Executor* v. *United States,* 1934). The Court distinguished positions in the traditional executive departments, for whose administration the president assumed primary responsibility, from those in agencies established by Congress to carry out legislative policy essentially free from any executive influence other than that resulting from appointment.

The definition of *inferior officer,* questions of appointment and removal, and separation of powers combined in **Morrison v. Olson** (1988), which Geoffrey Miller characterized as "one of those great cases that organize and define the national political life for many years to come." The case challenged the provision in the Ethics in Government Act of 1978 for an independent counsel to investigate criminal wrongdoing by high officials in the executive branch.

Under the terms of the statute, upon receiving information suggesting criminal conduct, the attorney general conducts a preliminary inquiry and then may refer the matter to a division of the Court of Appeals for the District of Columbia Circuit. This division appoints the independent counsel. Once named, the independent counsel can be removed only for cause, and the removal is subject to judicial review. The independent counsel may use the full investigative and prosecutorial functions of the Department of Justice with respect to the matters within the scope of the referral. In essence Congress decreed that criminal investigation at the highest levels be done by an attorney not subject to routine control by the president.

Olson's attack on the independent counsel provision grew out of an interbranch and largely partisan conflict stemming from a congressional investigation of the Environmental Protection Agency and the cleanup of toxic wastes. Opponents of the 1978 law claimed it was more likely to open wide the door to political retribution than to deter and punish crime in the executive branch. Supporters claimed the law was especially needed when Justice Department officials were not inclined toward vigorous enforcement.

Looking back to *Myers* (which recognized broad removal powers) and to *Humphrey's Executor* (which narrowed the reach of the removal power), eight justices agreed that Congress could place the independent counsel under the terms of the latter. Counsel's independence, Chief Justice Rehnquist explained, did not impermissibly interfere "with the President's exercise of his constitutionally appointed functions." The Court faced two conflicting views of separation of powers. One allowed some blurring of distinctions among the branches in order to retain an additional check in the scheme of checks and balances. The other maintained the hierarchical integrity of a branch limited ultimately only by the people through the ballot box and Congress through impeachment. Choosing the first, the majority effected "a revolution in our constitutional jurisprudence," Justice Scalia charged in his lone dissent. To take away prosecutorial discretion from the president is "to remove the core of the prosecutorial function"—"a quintessentially executive function."

Immunity. If presidents may have the constitutionality of their policies challenged in court, to what degree may a president be subjected to personal lawsuits because of a disregard of legal and constitutional limits? As in other areas, the Nixon administration (1969–1974) generated controversies that had to be settled by the judiciary. According to the Supreme Court, one's avenues of redress do not include a personal suit against the president. In *Nixon* v. *Fitzgerald* (1982), five justices bestowed on the president an absolute immunity (shared also by federal judges and prosecutors) from private lawsuit. The immunity was a "functionally mandated incident of his unique office," declared Justice Powell, "rooted in the constitutional tradition of the separation of powers and supported by the Nation's history." This immunity extends to all acts within what the Court called "the outer perimeter" of his official duties. Probably important in this decision was the presence of the impeachment remedy, the availability of Congressional and public oversight, and concern for one's "place in history." Presidential aides, however, do not enjoy the same unqualified protection. Instead, theirs is a "good faith" immunity, shielding them from damage suits as long as their conduct does not violate "clearly established" statutory or constitutional rights of which a reasonable person would have known (*Harlow* v. *Fitzgerald*, 1982).

Pardoning Power. The president is empowered to grant "reprieves" (a temporary suspension of legally imposed penalties) and "pardons" (a remission of sentence before or after conviction) except in cases of impeachment. Under Article II, Section 4, a president allegedly guilty of treason, bribery, or other high crimes and misdemeanors is subject to impeachment. The penalty is removal from office and disqualification for future office holding. An impeached president may be prosecuted, and if found guilty, the usual penalties are applicable. Without confessing criminal wrongdoing, President Nixon escaped impeachment by resignation in 1974. President Ford's "full, free and absolute" pardon saved his predecessor from prosecution for criminal conduct and also removed any political disqualification.

Protection against Domestic Violence. The president has the duty under Article IV, Section 4, to furnish military assistance to repress domestic violence upon call of a state legislature or governor. From the Whiskey Rebellion to the present, presidents have been called on for aid, either because of insurrection against the lawful state government or because of disorders arising from economic or social disputes. The action of the president in sending, or even agreeing to commit, troops to the aid of one of the contending factions in a state dispute is a recognition that there is a lawful government in that state (*Luther* v. *Borden*, 1849). If the disorder results in the violation of federal laws, the president may then act in accordance with his duty to "take care that the laws be faithfully executed. . . ." In either case, in the actual direction of troops he acts in his capacity of commander-in-chief.

Execution of the Laws. With or without approval of a state governor, the president may use military force or any other means deemed necessary to fulfill his obligation faithfully to execute the laws of the United States (*In re Debs*, 1895). Earlier the Court exempted from state prosecution a special officer appointed by direction of the president to guard Justice Field when the officer shot and killed a man who had threatened and accosted the Supreme Court justice (*In re Neagle*, 1890). The justification given in the Neagle Case was the president's duty to execute the laws, which the Court interpreted broadly to include the protection of officials carrying out their lawful duties. In other words, the president was not required to cite a specific statute authorizing each of his actions.

Impoundment. Particularly in recent years the president, at odds with Congress, has refused to spend appropriated funds. In 1972, President Nixon directed the administrator of the Environmental Protection Agency to allot to the states several billion dollars less than authorized by the Federal Water Pollution Control Act. In *Train* v. *New York City* (1975), the Court avoided the constitutional issue of impoundment but concluded as a matter of statutory interpretation that Congress had not intended to allow the president such discretion. In 1974, the Congressional Budget and Impoundment Control Act became law, as the senators and representatives attempted to strengthen their influence over the "purse." Title X of the statute creates a procedure for legislative review of impoundments. Involved is a complex political struggle that does not lend itself to easy judicial resolution.

Foreign Affairs. In foreign affairs, presidential power is limited by Congress only with great difficulty. Congressional control of the purse provides a check of growing importance at a time when foreign aid is a serious consideration in diplomatic relations. Of great importance to presidential power, however, is the theory of sovereignty set forth in Justice Sutherland's *Curtiss-Wright* opinion and the great reservoir of inherent power possessed by the president as representative of the United States in dealing with other nations. Treaties, it is true, must receive the consent of two-thirds of the Senate. Once it is passed, a treaty may then be the basis of implementing legislation that otherwise would not be within the power of Congress (*Missouri v. Holland*). On the other hand, Congress may by statute alter or negate the effect of a treaty on domestic law. The tendency of modern presidents to use *executive agreements* in place of the treaty has freed them from dependency on the Senate. Such agreements have the same legal effect as treaties (*United States* v. *Belmont*, 1937; *United States* v. *Pink*, 1942).

With the increasing importance and complexity of foreign policy, therefore, the president has found it necessary to play a role unhindered by the ability of one-third-plus-one of the Senate to frustrate his actions. A case in point was President Carter's notification in December 1978 to terminate this country's Mutual Defense Treaty with Taiwan on January 1, 1980, without congressional approval. Opponents of his efforts couched their objections in constitutional terms. The Senate had ratified the treaty, and even though its terms provided for termination on a year's notice by either signatory, they claimed the president could not do it alone. So they filed suit. After a defeat in the district court, the court of appeals upheld Carter's unilateral authority. The Senate's authority to ratify does not imply a role in termination, the judges held. The Senate had approved a treaty that provided for terms of a year's notice. It was up to the president to give that notice, as the nation's representative in foreign affairs. In *Goldwater* v. *Carter* (1979), the Supreme Court refused to address the merits of the suit. Six justices directed the lower court to dismiss the complaint. Two would have assigned the case for full review and decision. Only Justice Brennan reached the merits, siding with the president.

In this situation as in many others in American constitutional interpretation, the past informs the present and the present sheds light on the past. Bearing on the Taiwan treaty termination is *Myers* v. *United States,* reviewed earlier. President Wilson had fired Myers, an executive officer, without approval of Congress. Voting 6 to 3, the Supreme Court found the president's power of removal to be incident to his power of appointment, not to the Senate's power of advising and consenting to the appointment. If the removal power is incident to appointment, may not the termination of a treaty be considered incident to negotiation? The fact that the *Myers* case involved internal rather than external affairs strengthened the constitutional case for President Carter. The president, declared Justice Sutherland in *Curtiss-Wright,* "makes treaties with the advice and consent of the Senate; but he alone negotiates. Into the field of negotiation the Senate cannot intrude; the Congress itself is powerless to invade it."

Military Powers. The power of the federal government over the armed forces of the nation is divided between the president and Congress. The legislature has been given the important powers of raising armies and providing a navy (Art. I, Sec. 8, Cl. 14); the president, as commander-in-chief of the armed forces (Art. II, Sec. 2, Cl. 1), may issue regulations of his own and may take charge of all military operations in time of peace as well as in war.

Two different approaches to the problem of waging war successfully can be found in American history. Under Lincoln, Congress was ignored or asked to ratify executive actions already accomplished or under way. In World Wars I and II, on the other hand, Congress passed a vast number of general statutes of wide scope delegating to the president, or to persons designated by him, vast discretionary powers. The widest of these delegations was upheld (e.g., *Bowles* v. *Willingham,* 1944). When statutory authority is thus added to the president's already expansive powers as commander-in-chief, all constitutional limitations virtually disappear, as seen in the Japanese relocation cases (***Korematsu* v. *United States,*** 1944). Even without the support of statute, presidential power in wartime is subject to few limitations. The president can control the movement of the armed forces and prescribe rules, including judicial procedures, for the government of captured territory. He may direct the seizure of former enemy officers and officials after the conclusion of hostilities and set up military commissions to try them in proceedings that are not limited by the Constitution (*In re Yamashita,* 1946).

Does war suspend the guarantees of the Constitution? Justice Holmes remarked in 1919 (*Frohwerk* v. *U.S.*), "We do not lose our right to condemn either measures or men because the country is at war." Yet under the "inherent" powers doctrine, Attorney General John Mitchell argued in 1971 that "the President, acting through the Attorney General, may constitutionally authorize the use of electronic surveillance in cases where he had determined that, in order to preserve national security the use of such surveillance is reasonable." Countervailing values were asserted in the Court's far-reaching decision in **United States v. United States District Court** (1972).

Article I, Section 9, of the Constitution seemingly limits Congress's power of suspending the writ of habeas corpus (a protection against unlawful confinement) to "cases of rebellion or invasion." Yet President Lincoln during the Civil War suspended the writ without congressional authorization and ordered his officers to refuse service of a writ of habeas corpus issued by Chief Justice Taney. Subsequently, Congress authorized the president to suspend the writ in certain cases; the Supreme Court, however, refused to pass on the validity of the president's action (*Ex parte Vallandigham*, 1864). Lincoln provided another extreme example of executive power when he imposed martial law on portions of the northern states and substituted trial by military commission for the regular processes of law in dealing with traitors and others charged with violations of wartime statutes.

In *Ex parte Milligan* (1866) the Court held that Lincoln had exceeded his authority, the regular courts of Indiana, where the military commission had convicted Milligan, being open and prepared to handle the charges against him. Five members of the Court went further and stated that martial rule could never exist where the courts were open. Four members thought that Congress could have sanctioned what the executive could not. In World War II a similar result followed when the governor-general of Hawaii, pursuant to presidential authorization, invoked martial rule and gave to military commissions jurisdiction over all criminal offenses. In a 6-to-2 decision, the Court held such action invalid on the basis of the Milligan decision (*Duncan* v. *Kahamanmoku*, 1946). In both cases, final judicial decisions followed the end of hostilities. In time of war officials do what seems to be necessary to ensure survival.

The framers made war making a joint enterprise. Congress is authorized to "declare war"; the president is designated "commander in chief." Technology has expanded the president's role and correspondingly curtailed the power of Congress. In recognition of vastly changed conditions after World War II, Congress itself endorsed executive aggrandizement. Only recently have the legislators attempted to regain their constitutional share of war making, or war avoiding.

In the face of rising public protest against the undeclared Vietnam War in the 1970s, Congress enacted (over President Nixon's veto) the widely debated War Powers Resolution of 1973, designed to curb presidential discretion in committing the armed forces of the nation to combat. The 1973 resolution was a far cry from the Gulf of Tonkin Resolution of 1964, which declared "that Congress approves and supports the determination of the President as commander-in-chief, to take all necessary measures to repel any armed attack against the forces of the United States and to prevent further aggression." President Lyndon Johnson viewed the Tonkin Resolution as the functional equivalent of a declaration of war.

In contrast, under the **War Powers Resolution**, the president can commit troops only (1) if Congress has declared war, (2) if Congress authorizes military action by statute, or (3) if a national emergency arises following an attack on the nation or its armed forces. The third condition is the most controversial. Under it, the president is supposed to consult with Congress whenever possible *prior* to committing troops, and in any event he is supposed to inform Congress of what he has done within 48 hours. Unless Congress authorizes continued action, use of troops must cease after 60 days. Furthermore, Congress by concurrent resolution (not subject to presidential veto) may order the president to withdraw the troops from combat. *Chadha* has cast doubt on the constitutionality of this use of the legislative veto.

Experience since 1973 casts doubt on whether the War Powers Act amounts to a significant restraint on presidential power. Most presidents have considered the act unconstitutional and have generally failed to "invoke" the act by claiming the law does not apply to military operations they have initiated. Moreover, Congress has yet to display sufficient political will to ensure compliance. If the Court's reluctance to consider the unconstitutionality of Vietnam-type "undeclared wars" is any guide, the justices will probably not intervene in War Powers Resolution disputes. (See the opinions by Justices Marshall and Douglas in *Holtzman* v. *Schlesinger*, 1973.)

The president is under a positive obligation "to take care that the laws be faithfully executed." His power must be adapted to changed and changing conditions. But, in fulfilling this responsibility, he must also take into account those principles and provisions of the Constitution that restrict as well as enlarge his powers. As commander-in-chief, he cannot pick and choose the provisions of the Constitution he executes. Congress's share in war making must be adapted to unforeseen developments. Otherwise, technological evolution will vastly alter the constitutional balance.

The power of Congress in this sensitive area was not meant to cripple and impede; it was designed to produce a wiser course of action. Sound in 1787, it is no less so today.

KEY TERMS

separation of powers

delegation

legislative veto

checks and balances

subpoena

exclusion

expulsion

Speech or Debate
  Clause

constitutional theory

stewardship theory

prerogative theory

executive privilege

inferior officer

good-faith immunity

reprieve

pardon

impoundment

executive agreement

martial law

War Powers
  Resolution

QUERIES

1. Some have argued that the judicial function, as originally conceived, was narrow and relatively simple, amounting to little more than "policing" the frontiers separating the spheres of government. What insight can be gleaned from Chief Justice Burger's opinion in *United States* v. *Nixon?*

2. How was statutory interpretation significant in *United States* v. *United States District Court?* What are the sources of Justice Powell's comments on the nature of political power?

3. According to Justice Sutherland in *United States* v. *Curtiss-Wright,* what is the source of the president's powers in foreign relations? Is the majority's position in the Steel Seizure Case a rejection of Sutherland's view?

4. If the executive branch was on the losing side in *Morrison* v. *Olson,* does this mean that Congress was on the winning side?

SELECTED READINGS

BARBER, S. A. *The Constitution and the Delegation of Congressional Power.* Chicago: University of Chicago Press, 1975.

BERGER, RAOUL, *Congress and the Supreme Court.* Cambridge, Mass. Harvard University Press, 1969.

_____. *Executive Privilege*. Cambridge, Mass: Harvard University Press, 1974.

_____. *Impeachment*. Cambridge, Mass.: Harvard University Press, 1973.

CORWIN, EDWARD S. *The President, Office and Powers*, 4th ed. New York: New York University Press, 1957.

_____. "The Steel Seizure Case," 53 *Columbia Law Review* 53 (1953).

CRAIG, BARBARA HINKSON. *Chadha*. New York: Oxford University Press, 1988.

FELLMAN, DAVID. "The Separation of Powers and the Judiciary," 37 *Review of Politics* 357 (1975).

FISHER, LOUIS. *Constitutional Conflicts Between Congress and the President*. Princeton, N.J.: Princeton University Press, 1985.

GOLDWIN, ROBERT A., and ART KAUFMAN, eds. *Separation of Powers—Does It Still Work?* (Washington, D.C.: American Enterprise Institute, 1986).

HENKIN, LOUIS. *Foreign Affairs and the Constitution*. Mineola, N.Y.: Foundation Press, 1972.

LOFGREN, CHARLES A. *Government from Reflection and Choice: Constitutional Essays on War, Foreign Relations, and Federalism*. New York: Oxford University Press, 1988.

MARCUS, MAEVA. *Truman and the Steel Seizure Case: The Limits of Presidential Power*. New York: Columbia University Press, 1977.

MOYNIHAN, DANIEL P. "The Modern Role of Congress in Foreign Affairs." 9 *Cardozo Law Review* 1489 (1988).

RANDALL, J. G. *Constitutional Problems under Lincoln*, rev. ed. Urbana: University of Illinois Press, 1951.

ROSSITER, CLINTON. *The Supreme Court and the Commander-in-Chief*. Ithaca, N.Y.: Cornell University Press, 1951.

STEPHENSON, D. GRIER, JR., " 'The Mild Magistracy of the Law': *U.S. v. Richard Nixon*." 103 *Intellect* 288 (1975).

Symposium: "Congress' Role and Responsibility in the Federal Balance of Power." 21 *Georgia Law Review* 1 (1986).

TAYLOR, TELFORD. *The Grand Inquest: The Story of Congressional Investigations*. New York: Simon & Schuster, 1955.

WORMUTH, FRANCIS DUNHAM. *To Chain the Dog of War: The War Power of Congress in History and Law*. Dallas: Southern Methodist University Press, 1986.

The Federalist, No. 47 (Madison)

One of the principal objections inculcated by the more respectable adversaries to the Constitution, is its supposed violation of the political maxim, that the legislative, executive, and judiciary departments ought to be separate and distinct. In the structure of the federal government, no regard, it is said, seems to have been paid to this essential precaution in favor of liberty. The several departments of power are distributed and blended in such a manner as at once to destroy all symmetry and beauty of form, and to expose some of the essential parts of the edifice to the danger of being crushed by the disproportionate weight of other parts.

No political truth is certainly of greater intrinsic value, or is stamped with the authority of more enlightened patrons of liberty, than that on which the objection is founded. The accumulation of all powers, legislative, executive, and judiciary, in the same hands, whether of one, a few, or many, and whether hereditary, self-appointed, or elective may justly be pronounced the very definition of tyranny. . . .

The oracle who is always consulted and cited on this subject is the celebrated Montesquieu. If he be not the author of this invaluable precept in the science of politics, he has the merit at least of displaying and recommending it most effectually to the attention of mankind. . . . In saying "There can be no liberty where the legislative and executive powers are united in the same person, or body of magistrates," or, "if the power of judging be not separated from the legislative and executive powers," he did not mean that these departments ought to have no PARTIAL AGENCY in, or no CONTROL over, the acts of each other. His meaning, as his own words import, and still more conclusively as illustrated by the example in his eye, can amount to no more than this, that where the WHOLE power of one department is exercised by the same hands which possess the WHOLE power of another department, the fundamental principles of a free constitution are subverted. . . .

The reasons on which Montesquieu grounds his maxim are a further demonstration of his meaning. "When the legislative and executive powers are united in the same person or body," says he, "there can be no liberty, because apprehensions may arise lest THE SAME monarch or senate should ENACT tyrannical laws to EXECUTE them in a tyrannical manner," Again: "Were the power of judging joined with the legislative, the life and liberty of the subject would be exposed to arbitrary control, for THE JUDGE would then be THE LEGISLATOR. Were it joined to the executive power, THE JUDGE might behave with all the violence of AN OPPRESSOR." Some of these reasons are more fully explained in other passages; but briefly stated as they are here, they sufficiently establish the meaning which we have put on this celebrated maxim of the celebrated author.

The Federalist, No. 48 (Madison)

It is agreed on all sides, that the powers properly belonging to one of the departments ought not to be directly and completely administered by either of the other departments. It is equally evident, that none of them ought to possess, directly or indirectly, an overruling influence over the others, in the administration of their respective powers. It will not be denied, that power is of an encroaching nature, and that it ought to be effectually restrained from passing the limits assigned to it. After discriminating, therefore, in theory, the several classes of power, as they may in their nature be legislative, executive, or judiciary, the next and most difficult task is to provide some practical security for each, against the invasion of the others. What this security ought to be, is the great problem to be solved.

Will it be sufficient to mark, with precision, the boundaries of these departments, in the constitution of the government, and to trust to these parchment barriers against the encroaching spirit of power? This is the security which appears to have been principally relied on by the compilers of most of the American constitutions. But experience assures us, that the efficacy of the provision has been greatly overrated; and that some more adequate defense is indispensably necessary for the more feeble, against the more powerful, members of the government. The legislative department is everywhere extending the sphere of its activity, and drawing all power into its impetuous vortex.

The legislative department derives a superiority in our governments from other circumstances. Its constitutional powers being at once more extensive, and less susceptible of precise limits, it can, with the greater facility, mask, under complicated and indirect measures, the encroachments which it makes on the coordinate departments. . . . On the other side, the executive power being restrained within a narrower compass, and being more simple in its nature, and the judiciary being described by landmarks still less uncertain, projects of usurpation by either of these departments would immediately betray and defeat themselves. Nor is this all: as the legislative department alone has access to the pockets of the people, and has in some constitutions full discretion, and in all a prevailing influence, over the pecuniary rewards of those who fill the other departments, a dependence is thus created in the latter, which gives still greater facility to encroachments of the former. . . .

The conclusion which I am warranted in drawing from these observations is, that a mere demarcation on parchment of the constitutional limits of the several departments, is not a sufficient guard against those encroachments which lead to a tyrannical concentration of all the powers of government in the same hands.

The Federalist, No. 51 (Madison)

To what expedient, then, shall we finally resort, for maintaining in practice the necessary participation of power among the several departments, as laid down in the Constitution? The only answer that can be given is, that as all these exterior provisions are found to be inadequate, the defect must be supplied, by so contriving the interior structure of the government as that its several constituent parts may, by their mutual relations, be the means of keeping each other in their proper places. . . .

In order to lay a due foundation for that separate and distinct exercise of the different powers of government, which to a certain extent is admitted on all hands to be essential to the preservation of liberty, it is evident that each department should have a will of its own; and consequently should be so constituted that the members of each should have as little agency as possible in the appointment of the members of the others. . . .

But the great security against a gradual concentration of the several powers in the same department, consists in giving to those who administer each department the necessary constitutional means and personal motives to resist encroachments of the others. The provision for defence must in this, as in all other cases, be made commensurate to the danger of attack. Ambition must be made to counteract ambition. The interest of the man must be connected with the constitutional rights of the place. It may be a reflection on human nature, that such devices should be necessary to control the abuses of government. But what is government itself, but the greatest of all reflections on human nature? If men were angels, no government would be necessary. If angels were to govern men, neither external nor internal controls on government would be necessary. In framing a government which is to be administered by men over men, the great difficulty lies in this: you must first enable the government to control the governed; and in the next place oblige it to control itself. A dependence on the people is, no doubt, the primary control on the government; but experience has taught mankind the necessity of auxiliary precautions.

This policy of supplying, by opposite and rival interests, the defect of better motives, might be traced through the whole system of human affairs, private as well as public. We see it particularly displayed in all the subordinate distributions of power, where the constant aim is to divide and arrange the several offices in such a manner as that each may be a check on the other—that the private interest of every individual may be a sentinel over the public rights. These inventions of prudence cannot be less requisite in the distribution of the supreme powers of the State. . . .

Watkins v. United States*
354 U.S. 178, 77 S.Ct. 1173, 1 L.Ed. 2d 1273 (1957)

The broad investigating power of Congress was upheld in *McGrain v. Daugherty* (1927), where the purpose was to obtain information about alleged wrongdoing by the attorney general and the Department of Justice. Increasingly in the period after World War II, Congress turned its attention to the activities within the United States of alleged members and officers of the Communist Party. Frequently, witnesses invoked the Fifth Amendment in refusing to answer committee questions. In *Watkins,* the witness based this refusal to answer on different grounds. The facts are given in the following opinion. Majority: Warren, Black, Brennan, Douglas, Frankfurter, Harlan. Dissenting: Clark. Not participating: Burton, Whittaker.

MR. CHIEF JUSTICE WARREN delivered the opinion of the Court. . . .

On April 29, 1954, petitioner appeared as a witness in compliance with a subpoena issued by a Subcommittee of the Committee on Un-American Activities of the House of Representatives. . . .

We start with several basic premises on which there is general agreement. The power of the Congress to conduct investigations is inherent in the legislative process. That power is broad. It encompasses inquiries concerning the administration of existing laws as well as proposed or possibly needed statutes. It includes surveys of defects in our social, economic or political system for the purpose of enabling the Congress to remedy them. It comprehends probes into departments of the Federal

Government to expose corruption, inefficiency or waste. But broad as is this power of inquiry, it is not unlimited. There is no general authority to expose the private affairs of individuals without justification in terms of the functions of the Congress. This was freely conceded by the Solicitor General in his argument of this case. . . .

It is unquestionably the duty of all citizens to cooperate with the Congress in its efforts to obtain the facts needed for intelligent legislative action. It is their unremitting obligation to respond to subpoenas, to respect the dignity of the Congress and its committees and to testify fully with respect to matters within the province of proper investigation. This, of course, assumes that the constitutional rights of witnesses will be respected by the Congress as they are in a court of justice.

In the decade following World War II, there appeared a new kind of congressional inquiry un-

*This case should also be read in connection with Chapter Ten.

known in prior periods of American history. Principally this was the result of the various investigations into the threat of subversion of the United States Government, but other subjects of congressional interest also contributed to the changed scene. This new phase of legislative inquiry involved a broad-scale intrusion into the lives and affairs of private citizens. It brought before the courts novel questions of the appropriate limits of congressional inquiry. Prior cases . . . had defined the scope of investigative power in terms of the inherent limitations of the sources of that power. In the more recent cases, the emphasis shifted to problems of accommodating the interest of the Government with the rights and privileges of individuals. The central theme was the application of the Bill of Rights as a restraint upon the assertion of governmental power in this form.

It was during this period that the Fifth Amendment privilege against self-incrimination was frequently invoked and recognized as a legal limit upon the authority of a committee to require that a witness answer its questions. Some early doubts as to the applicability of the privilege before a legislative committee never matured. When the matter reached this Court, the Government did not challenge in any way that the Fifth Amendment protection was available to the witness, and such a challenge could not have prevailed. It confined its argument to the character of the answers sought and to the adequacy of the claim of privilege. . . .

A far more difficult task evolved from the claim by witnesses that the committees' interrogations were infringements upon the freedoms of the First Amendment. Clearly, an investigation is subject to the command that the Congress shall make no law abridging freedom of speech or press or assembly. While it is true that there is no statute to be reviewed, and that an investigation is not a law, nevertheless an investigation is part of lawmaking. It is justified solely as an adjunct to the legislative process. The First Amendment may be invoked against infringement of the protected freedoms by law or by lawmaking.

Abuses of the investigative process may imperceptibly lead to abridgement of protected freedoms. The mere summoning of a witness and compelling him to testify, against his will, about his beliefs, expressions or associations is a measure of governmental interference. And when those forced reve-

lations concern matters that are unorthodox, unpopular, or even hateful to the general public, the reaction in the life of the witness may be disastrous. . . .

. . . It is the responsibility of the Congress, in the first instance, to insure that compulsory process is used only in furtherance of a legislative purpose. That requires that the instructions to an investigating committee spell out that group's jurisdiction and purpose with sufficient particularity. Those instructions are embodied in the authorizing resolution. That document is the committee's charter. Broadly drafted and loosely worded, however, such resolutions can leave tremendous latitude to the discretion of investigators. The more vague the committee's charter is, the greater becomes the possibility that the committee's specific actions are not in conformity with the will of the parent House of Congress.

The authorizing resolution of the Un-American Activities Committee was adopted in 1938 when a select committee, under the chairmanship of Representative Dies, was created. Several years later, the Committee was made a standing organ of the House with the same mandate. It defines the Committee's authority as follows:

[Rule XI]

The Committee on Un-American Activities, as a whole or by subcommittee, is authorized to make from time to time investigations of (i) the extent, character, and objects of un-American propaganda activities in the United States, (ii) the diffusion within the United States of subversive and un-American propaganda that is instigated from foreign countries or of a domestic origin and attacks the principle of the form of government as guaranteed by our Constitution, and (iii) all other questions in relation thereto that would aid Congress in any necessary remedial legislation.

It would be difficult to imagine a less explicit authorizing resolution. Who can define the meaning of "un-American"? . . .

. . . Plainly these committees are restricted to the missions delegated to them, i.e., to acquire certain data to be used by the House or the Senate in coping with a problem that falls within its legislative sphere. No witness can be compelled to make disclosures on matters outside that area. . . .

When the definition of jurisdictional pertinency is as uncertain and wavering as in the case of the Un-American Activities Committee, it becomes extremely difficult for the Committee to limit its inquiries to statutory pertinency.

In fulfillment of their obligation under this statute, the courts must accord to the defendants every right which is guaranteed to defendants in all other criminal cases. Among these is the right to have available, through a sufficiently precise statute, information revealing the standard of criminality before the commission of the alleged offense. Applied to persons prosecuted under § 192, this raises a special problem in that the statute defines the crime as refusal to answer "any question pertinent to the question under inquiry." Part of the standard of criminality, therefore, is the pertinency of the questions propounded to the witness.

The problem attains proportion when viewed from the standpoint of the witness who appears before a congressional committee. He must decide at the time the questions are propounded whether or not to answer. . . .

It is obvious that a person compelled to make this choice is entitled to have knowledge of the subject to which the interrogation is deemed pertinent. That knowledge must be available with the same degree of explicitness and clarity that the Due Process Clause requires in the expression of any element of a criminal offense. The "vice of vagueness" must be avoided here as in all other crimes. There are several sources that can outline the "question under inquiry" in such a way that the rules against vagueness are satisfied. The authorizing resolution, the remarks of the chairman or members of the committee, or even the nature of the proceedings themselves might sometimes make the topic clear. This case demonstrates, however, that these sources often leave the matter in grave doubt. . . .

. . . The conclusions which we have reached in this case will not prevent the Congress, through its committees, from obtaining any information it needs for the proper fulfillment of its role in our scheme of government. The legislature is free to determine the kinds of data that should be collected. It is only those investigations that are conducted by use of compulsory process that give rise to a need to protect the rights of individuals against illegal encroachment. That protection can be readily achieved through procedures which prevent the separation of power from responsibility and which provide the constitutional requisites of fairness for witnesses. A measure of added care on the part of the House and the Senate in authorizing the use of compulsory process and by their committees in exercising that power would suffice. That is a small price to pay if it serves to uphold the principles of limited, constitutional government without constricting the power of the Congress to inform itself.

The judgment of the Court of Appeals is reversed, and the case is remanded to the District Court with instructions to dismiss the indictment.

It is so ordered.

MR. JUSTICE CLARK, dissenting.

As I see it the chief fault in the majority opinion is its mischievous curbing of the informing function of the Congress. While I am not versed in its procedures, my experience in the executive branch of the Government leads me to believe that the requirements laid down in the opinion for the operation of the committee system of inquiry are both unnecessary and unworkable. . . .

It may be that at times the House Committee on Un-American Activities has, as the Court says, "conceived of its task in the grand view of its name." And, perhaps, as the Court indicates, the rules of conduct placed upon the Committee by the House admit of individual abuse and unfairness. But that is none of our affair. So long as the object of a legislative inquiry is legitimate and the questions propounded are pertinent thereto, it is not for the courts to interfere with the committee system of inquiry. To hold otherwise would be an infringement on the power given the Congress to inform itself, and thus a trespass upon the fundamental American principle of separation of powers. The majority has substituted the judiciary as the grand inquisitor and supervisor of congressional investigations. It has never been so. . . .

Barenblatt v. United States*
360 U.S. 109, 79 S.Ct. 1081, 3 L.Ed. 2d 1115 (1959)

Lloyd Barenblatt, a former college teacher, was called as a witness before a subcommittee of the House Un-American Activities Committee investigating Communist infiltration in education. Disclaiming any reliance on the Fifth Amendment, he refused to answer questions regarding past affiliation with the Communist Party, contending that the subcommittee has no power to inquire into political beliefs and associations. The Supreme Court vacated his conviction for contempt of Congress, remanding the case for further consideration in light of the *Watkins* decision. His conviction was again upheld by the court of appeals. Majority: Harlan, Clark, Frankfurter, Stewart, Whittaker. Dissenting: Black, Brennan, Douglas, Warren.

MR. JUSTICE HARLAN delivered the opinion of the Court.

Once more the Court is required to resolve the conflicting constitutional claims of congressional power and of an individual's right to resist its exercise. The congressional power in question concerns the internal process of Congress in moving within its legislative domain; it involves the utilization of its committees to secure "testimony needed to enable it efficiently to exercise a legislative function belonging to it under the Constitution."
. . .

Broad as it is, the power is not, however, without limitations. Since Congress may only investigate into those areas in which it may potentially legislate or appropriate, it cannot inquire into matters which are within the exclusive province of one of the other branches of the Government. . . . And the Congress, in common with all branches of the Government, must exercise its powers subject to the limitations placed by the Constitution on governmental action, more particularly in the context of this case the relevant limitations of the Bill of Rights. . . .

In the present case congressional efforts to learn the extent of a nationwide, indeed worldwide, problem have brought one of its investigating committees into the field of education. Of course, broadly viewed, inquiries cannot be made into the teaching that is pursued in any of our educational institutions. When academic teaching-freedom and

its corollary learning-freedom, so essential to the well-being of the Nation, are claimed, this Court will always be on the alert against intrusion by Congress into this constitutionally protected domain. But this does not mean that the Congress is precluded from interrogating a witness merely because he is a teacher. An educational institution is not a constitutional sanctuary from inquiry into matters that may otherwise be within the constitutional legislative domain merely for the reason that inquiry is made of someone within its walls. . . .

At the outset it should be noted that Rule XI authorized this Subcommittee to compel testimony within the framework of the investigative authority conferred on the Un-American Activities Committee. Petitioner contends that *Watkins* v. *United States* . . . nevertheless held the grant of this power in all circumstances ineffective because of the vagueness of Rule XI in delineating the Committee jurisdiction to which its exercise was to be appurtenant. . . .

The Watkins case cannot properly be read as standing for such a proposition. A principal contention in *Watkins* was that the refusals to answer were justified because the requirement . . . that the questions asked be "pertinent to the question under inquiry" had not been satisfied. . . . This Court reversed the conviction solely on that ground, holding that Watkins had not been adequately apprised of the subject matter of the Subcommittee's investigation or the pertinency thereto of the questions he refused to answer. . . . In so deciding the Court drew upon Rule XI only as one of the facets in the total *mise en scène* in its search for

* This case should also be read in connection with Chapter Ten.

the "question under inquiry" in that particular investigation. . . . In short, while *Watkins* was critical of Rule XI, it did not involve the broad and inflexible holding petitioner now attributes to it. . . .

. . . What we deal with here is whether petitioner was sufficiently apprised of "the topic under inquiry" thus authorized "and the connective reasoning whereby the precise questions asked related to it." . . . In light of this prepared memorandum of constitutional objectives there can be no doubt that this petitioner was well aware of the Subcommittee's authority and purpose to question him as it did. . . . In addition the other sources of this information which we recognized in *Watkins* . . . leave no room for a "pertinency" objection on this record. The subject matter of the inquiry had been identified at the commencement of the investigation as Communist infiltration into the field of education. . . .

The protections of the First Amendment, unlike a proper claim of the privilege against self-incrimination under the Fifth Amendment, do not afford a witness the right to resist inquiry in all circumstances. Where First Amendment rights are asserted to bar governmental interrogation, resolution of the issue always involves a balancing by the courts of the competing private and public interests at stake in the particular circumstances shown. These principles were recognized in the Watkins case. . . .

. . . An investigation of advocacy or of preparation for overthrow certainly embraces the right to identify a witness as a member of the Communist Party . . . and to inquire into various manifestations of the Party's tenets. The strict requirements of a prosecution under the Smith Act . . . are not the measure of the permissible scope of a congressional investigation into "overthrow," for of necessity the investigatory process must proceed step by step. Nor can it fairly be concluded that this investigation was directed at controlling what is being taught at our universities rather than at overthrow. . . .

Nor can we accept the further contention that this investigation should not be deemed to have been in futherance of a legislative purpose because the true objective of the Committee and of the Congress was purely "exposure." So long as Congress acts in pursuance of its constitutional power, the Judiciary lacks authority to intervene on the basis of the motives which spurred the exercise of that power. . . .

We conclude that the balance between the individual and the governmental interests here at stake must be struck in favor of the latter, and that therefore the provisions of the First Amendment have not been offended. . . .

MR. JUSTICE BLACK, with whom the CHIEF JUSTICE and MR. JUSTICE DOUGLAS concur, dissenting. . . .

I do not agree that laws directly abridging First Amendment freedoms can be justified by a congressional or judicial balancing process. . . .

To apply the Court's balancing test under such circumstances is to read the First Amendment to say "Congress shall pass no law abridging freedom of speech, press, assembly and petition, unless Congress and the Supreme Court reach the joint conclusion that on balance the interest of the Government in stifling these freedoms is greater than the interest of the people in having them exercised." This is closely akin to the notion that neither the First Amendment nor any other provision of the Bill of Rights should be enforced unless the Court believes it is reasonable to do so. . . .

But even assuming what I cannot assume, that some balancing is proper in this case, I feel that the Court after stating the test ignores it completely. At most it balances the right of the Government to preserve itself, against Barenblatt's right to refrain from revealing Communist affiliations. Such a balance, however, mistakes the factors to be weighed. In the first place, it completely leaves out the real interest in Barenblatt's silence, the interest of the people as a whole in being able to join organizations, advocate causes and make political "mistakes" without later being subjected to governmental penalties for having dared to think for themselves. It is this right, the right to err politically, which keeps us strong as a Nation. For no number of laws against communism can have as much effect as the personal conviction which comes from having heard its arguments and rejected them, or from having once accepted its tenets and later recognized their worthlessness. Instead, the obloquy which results from investigations such as this not only stifles "mistakes" but prevents all but the most courageous from hazarding any views which might at some later time become disfavored. This result, whose importance cannot be overestimated, is doubly crucial when it affects the universities, on which we must largely rely for the experimentation and development of new ideas essential to our country's welfare. It is these interests of society, rather than Barenblatt's own right to silence, which I think the Court should put on the balance against the demands of the Government, if any balancing process is to be tolerated. . . .

Immigration and Naturalization Service v. Chadha
462 U.S. 919, 103 S.Ct. 2764, 77 L.Ed. 2d 317 (1983)

Section 244(a)(1) of the Immigration and Nationality Act authorized the attorney general, in his discretion, to suspend the deportation of a deportable alien. Under Section 244(c)(1), the attorney general was required to report such suspension to Congress. Section 244(c)(2) of the act authorized *either* house of Congress by resolution to invalidate the suspension before the end of the session following the one during which the suspension occurred. The attorney general discharged his responsibilities through the Immigration and Naturalization Service (INS), a division of the Department of Justice.

Jagdish Rai Chadha is an East Indian who was born in Kenya and who was lawfully admitted to the United States in 1966 on a non-immigrant student visa. He remained in the United States after his visa had expired in 1972 and was soon ordered by the INS to show cause why he should not be deported. Chadha then applied for suspension of the deportation order, and in 1974 an immigration judge, acting for the attorney general, ordered the suspension. On December 16, 1975, the House of Representatives exercised the veto authority reserved to it under Section 244(c)(2). Without action by either house of Congress, Chadha's deportation proceedings would have been cancelled after Congress adjourned on December 19, 1975, and his status would have become that of permanent resident alien. Since the House acted under Section 244(c)(2), the resolution was not like an ordinary law. That is, it was not submitted to the Senate and was not presented to the president for his signature.

The immigration judge then reopened the deportation proceedings, but Chadha moved to block further action, arguing that Section 244(c)(2) violated the Constitution. The immigration judge ruled that he had no authority to question the constitutionality of the law and directed that Chadha be deported as the House had directed. Chadha appealed that order to the Board of Immigration Appeals, which upheld the immigration judge. Chadha next asked the Court of Appeals for the Ninth Circuit to review the deportation order. The INS joined Chadha in arguing that Section 244 (c)(2) was unconstitutional. At this point, the court of appeals invited both the Senate and the House of Representatives to file briefs amici curiae. This invitation was important since the principal arguments in support of the validity of the legislative veto came from counsel representing the House and Senate. The court of appeals ruled in 1981 that the House of Representatives lacked constitutional authority to order Chadha's deportation. Majority: Burger, Blackmun, Brennan, Marshall, O'Connor, Powell, Stevens. Dissenting: White, Rehnquist.

CHIEF JUSTICE BURGER delivered the opinion of the Court.

We granted certiorari . . . [to consider] a challenge to the constitutionality of the provision in § 244(c)(2) of the Immigration and Nationality Act, 8 U.S.C. § 1254(c)(2), authorizing one House of Congress, by resolution, to invalidate the decision of the Executive Branch, pursuant to authority delegated by Congress to the Attorney General of the United States, to allow a particular deportable alien to remain in the United States. . . .

[The chief justice first rejects arguments that the case is a "friendly, non-adversary proceeding" and that it presents "a non-justiciable political question."]

We turn now to the question whether action of one House of Congress under §244(c)(2) violates strictures of the Constitution. We begin, of course, with the presumption that the challenged statute is valid. Its wisdom is not the concern of the courts; if a challenged action does not violate the Constitution, it must be sustained. . . .

Explicit and unambiguous provisions of the Constitution prescribe and define the respective functions of the Congress and of the Executive in the legislative process. Since the precise terms of those familiar provisions are critical to the resolution of this case, we set them out verbatim. Art. I provides:

"All legislative Powers herein granted shall be vested in a Congress of the United States, which shall consist of a Senate *and* a House of Representatives." Art. I, § 1. (Emphasis added.)

"Every Bill which shall have passed the House of Representatives *and* the Senate, *shall,* before it become a Law, be presented to the President of the United States; . . ." Art. I, § 7, cl. 2. (Emphasis added.)

"*Every* Order, Resolution, or Vote to which the Concurrence of the Senate and House of Representatives may be necessary (except on a question of Adjournment) *shall be* presented to the President of the United States; and before the Same shall take Effect, *shall be* approved by him, or being disapproved by him, *shall be* repassed by two thirds of the Senate

and House of Representatives, according to the Rules and Limitations prescribed in the Case of a Bill." Art. I, § 7, cl. 3. (Emphasis added.)

The records of the Constitutional Convention reveal that the requirement that all legislation be presented to the President before becoming law was uniformly accepted by the Framers. Presentment to the President and the Presidential veto were considered so imperative that the draftsmen took special pains to assure that these requirements could not be circumvented. . . .

The bicameral requirement of Art. I, §§ 1, 7 was of scarcely less concern to the Framers than was the Presidential veto and indeed the two concepts are interdependent. By providing that no law could take effect without the concurrence of the prescribed majority of the Members of both Houses, the Framers reemphasized their belief, already remarked upon in connection with the Presentment Clauses, that legislation should not be enacted unless it has been carefully and fully considered by the Nation's elected officials. . . .

The Constitution sought to divide the delegated powers of the new federal government into three defined categories, legislative, executive and judicial, to assure, as nearly as possible, that each Branch of government would confine itself to its assigned responsibility. The hydraulic pressure inherent within each of the separate Branches to exceed the outer limits of its power, even to accomplish desirable objectives, must be resisted.

Although not "hermetically" sealed from one another, . . . the powers delegated to the three Branches are functionally identifiable. When any Branch acts, it is presumptively exercising the power the Constitution has delegated to it. . . .

Beginning with this presumption, we must nevertheless establish that the challenged action under § 244(c)(2) is of the kind to which the procedural requirements of Art. I, § 7 apply. Not every action taken by either House is subject to the bicameralism and presentment requirements of Art. I. . . . Whether actions taken by either House are, in law and fact, an exercise of legislative power depends not on their form but upon "whether they contain matter which is properly to be regarded as legislative in its character and effect." . . .

Examination of the action taken here by one House pursuant to § 244(c)(2) reveals that it was essentially legislative in purpose and effect. In purporting to exercise power defined in Art. I, § 8, cl. 4 to "establish an uniform Rule of Naturalization," the House took action that had the purpose and effect of altering the legal rights, duties and relations of persons, including the Attorney General, Executive Branch officials and Chadha, all outside the legislative branch. . . .

The choices we discern as having been made in the Constitutional Convention impose burdens on governmental processes that often seem clumsy, inefficient, even unworkable, but those hard choices were consciously made by men who had lived under a form of government that permitted arbitrary governmental acts to go unchecked. There is no support in the Constitution or decisions of this Court for the proposition that the cumbersomeness and delays often encountered in complying with explicit Constitutional standards may be avoided, either by the Congress or by the President. . . . With all the obvious flaws of delay, untidiness, and potential for abuse, we have not yet found a better way to preserve freedom than by making the exercise of power subject to the carefully crafted restraints spelled out in the Constitution.

We hold that the Congressional veto provision in § 244(c)(2) is . . . unconstitutional. Accordingly, the judgment of the Court of Appeals is

Affirmed.

JUSTICE WHITE, dissenting.

Today the Court not only invalidates § 244(c)(2) of the Immigration and Nationality Act, but also sounds the death knell for nearly 200 other statutory provisions in which Congress has reserved a "legislative veto." For this reason, the Court's decision is of surpassing importance. . . .

The prominence of the legislative veto mechanism in our contemporary political system and its importance to Congress can hardly be overstated. It has become a central means by which Congress secures the accountability of executive and independent agencies. Without the legislative veto, Congress is faced with a Hobson's choice: either to refrain from delegating the necessary authority, leaving itself with a hopeless task of writing laws with the requisite specificity to cover endless special circumstances across the entire policy landscape, or in the alternative, to abdicate its lawmaking function to the executive branch and independent agencies. To choose the former leaves major national problems unresolved; to opt for the latter risks unaccountable policymaking by those not elected to fill that role. Accordingly, over the past five decades, the legislative veto has been placed in nearly 200 statutes. The device is known in every field of governmental concern: reorganization, budgets, foreign affairs, war powers, and regulation of trade, safety, energy, the environment and the economy. . . .

. . . The Court's holding today that all legislative-type action must be enacted through the lawmaking process ignores that legislative authority is routinely delegated to the Executive branch, to the independent regulatory agencies, and to private individuals and groups. . . .

This Court's decisions sanctioning such delegations make clear that Article I does not require all action with the effect of legislation to be passed as a law. . . .

The wisdom and the constitutionality of these broad delegations are matters that still have not been put to rest. But for present purposes, these cases establish that by virtue of congressional delegation, legislative power can be exercised by independent agencies and Executive departments without the passage of new legislation. For some time, the sheer amount of law—the substantive rules that regulate private conduct and direct the operation of government—made by the agencies has far outnumbered the lawmaking engaged in by Congress through the traditional process. There is no question but that agency rulemaking is lawmaking in any functional or realistic sense of the term. . . .

If Congress may delegate lawmaking power to independent and executive agencies, it is most difficult to understand Article I as forbidding Congress from also reserving a check on legislative power for itself. Absent the veto, the agencies receiving delegations of legislative or quasi-legislative power may issue regulations having the force of law without bicameral approval and without the President's signature. It is thus not apparent why the reservation of a veto over the exercise of that legislative power must be subject to a more exacting test. In both cases, it is enough that the initial statutory authorizations comply with the Article I requirements. . . .

The Court also takes no account of perhaps the most relevant consideration: However resolutions of disapproval under § 244(c)(2) are formally characterized, in reality, a departure from the status quo occurs only upon the concurrence of opinion among the House, Senate, and President. Reservations of legislative authority to be exercised by Congress should be upheld if the exercise of such reserved authority is consistent with the distribution of and limits upon legislative power that Article I provides. . . .

Section 244(a)(1) authorizes the Attorney General, in his discretion, to suspend the deportation of certain aliens who are otherwise deportable and, upon Congress' approval, to adjust their status to that of aliens lawfully admitted for permanent residence. In order to be eligible for this relief, an alien must have been physically present in the United States for a continuous period of not less than seven years, must prove he is of good moral character, and must prove that he or his immediate family would suffer "extreme hardship" if he is deported. Judicial review of a denial of relief may

be sought. Thus, the suspension proceeding "has two phases: a determination whether the statutory conditions have been met, which generally involves a question of law, and a determination whether relief shall be granted, which [ultimately] . . . is confided to the sound discretion of the Attorney General [and his delegates]." . . .

There is also a third phase to the process. Under § 244(c)(1) the Attorney General must report all such suspensions, with a detailed statement of facts and reasons, to the Congress. Either House may then act, in that session or the next, to block the suspension of deportation by passing a resolution of disapproval. § 244(c)(2). Upon Congressional approval of the suspension—by its silence—the alien's permanent status is adjusted to that of a lawful resident alien.

The history of the Immigration Act makes clear that § 244(c)(2) did not alter the division of actual authority between Congress and the Executive. At all times, whether through private bills, or through affirmative concurrent resolutions, or through the present one-House veto, a permanent change in a deportable alien's status could be accomplished only with the agreement of the Attorney General, the House, and the Senate. . . .

Ex Parte Milligan
71 U.S. (4 Wall.) 2, 18 L.Ed. 281 (1866)

In 1864, Lambdin P. Milligan, self-educated teacher and lawyer, a southern sympathizer living in Indiana, was seized and tried on charges of disloyalty by a military commission in the military district of Indiana. Not in the military forces and a citizen of Indiana, in which neither war nor insurrection existed and in which the civil courts were functioning, Milligan objected to the jurisdiction of the military commission and sought a writ of habeas corpus in the circuit court. An Act of 1863 had authorized suspension of the writ, but Milligan still insisted that the commission had no jurisdiction of his case. Sharply divided, the circuit court judges decided that this important case should be heard by the highest court in the land. The following questions were therefore certified by the Supreme Court: (1) Ought a writ of habeas corpus be issued? (2) Should the petitioner be discharged from custody? (3) Had the military commission jurisdiction to try and sentence Milligan? Majority: Davis, Chase, Clifford, Field, Grier, Miller, Nelson, Swayne, Wayne. Note that concurring justices Chase, Swayne, Miller, and Wayne did not accept Davis's sweeping restriction on Congress.

MR. JUSTICE DAVIS delivered the opinion of the Court. . . .

During the late wicked Rebellion, the temper of the times did not allow that calmness and deliberation in discussion so necessary to a correct conclusion of a purely judicial question. *Then,* considerations of safety were mingled with the exercise of power, and feelings and interests prevailed which are happily terminated. *Now* that the public safety is assured, this question, as well as all others, can be discussed and decided without passion or the admixture of any element not required to form the legal judgment. We approach the investigation of this case, fully sensible of the magnitude of the inquiry and of the necessity of full and cautious deliberation.

The controlling question in the case is this: Upon the facts stated in Milligan's petition, and the exhibits filed, had the military commission mentioned in it jurisdiction, legally, to try and sentence him? Milligan, not a resident of one of the rebellious States, or a prisoner of war, but a citizen of Indiana for twenty years past, and never in the military or naval service, is while at his home, arrested by the military power of the United States, imprisoned, and, on certain criminal charges preferred against him, tried, convicted, and sentenced to be hanged by a military commission, organized under the direction of the military commander of the military district of Indiana. Had this tribunal the legal power and authority to try and punish this man? . . .

The Constitution of the United States is a law for rulers and people, equally in war and in peace, and covers with the shield of its protection all classes of men, at all times, and under all circumstances. No doctrine involving more pernicious consequences was ever invented by the wit of man than that any of its provisions can be suspended during any of the great exigencies of government. Such a doctrine leads directly to anarchy or despotism, but the theory of necessity on which it is based is false; for the government, within the Constitution, has all the powers granted to it which are necessary to preserve its existence; as has been happily proved by the result of the great effort to throw off its just authority.

Have any of the rights guaranteed by the Constitution been violated in the case of Milligan? and if so, what are they?

Every trial involves the exercise of judicial power; and from what source did the military commission that tried him derive their authority? Certainly no part of the judicial power of the country was conferred on them; because the Constitution expressly vests it "in one supreme court and such inferior courts as the Congress may from time to time ordain and establish," and it is not pretended that the commission was a court ordained and established by Congress. They cannot justify on the mandate of the President, because he is controlled by law, and has his appropriate sphere of duty, which is to execute, not to make, the laws; and there is "no unwritten criminal code to which resort can be had as a source of jurisdiction." . . .

Why was he not delivered to the Circuit Court of Indiana to be proceeded against according to law? No reason of necessity could be urged against it; because Congress had declared penalties against the offenses charged, provided for their punishment, and directed that court to hear and determine them. And soon after this military tribunal was ended, the Circuit Court met, peacefully transacted its business, and adjourned. It needed no bayonets to protect it, and required no military aid to execute its judgments. It was held in a State, eminently distinguished for patriotism, by judges commissioned during the Rebellion, who were provided with juries, upright, intelligent, and selected by a marshal appointed by the President. The government had no right to conclude that Milligan, if guilty, would not receive in that court merited punishment. . . .

Another guarantee of freedom was broken when Milligan was denied a trial by jury. . . .

The discipline necessary to the efficiency of the army and navy required other and swifter modes of trial than are furnished by the common-law courts; and, in pursuance of the power conferred by the Constitution, Congress has declared the kinds of trial, and the manner in which they shall be conducted, for offenses committed while the party is in the military or naval service. Every one connected with these branches of the public service is amenable to the jurisdiction which Congress has created for their government, and, while thus serving, surrenders his right to be tried by the civil courts. All other persons, citizens of States where the courts are open, if charged with crime, are guaranteed the inestimable privilege of trial by jury. . . .

It is claimed that martial law covers with its broad mantle the proceedings of this military commission. The proposition is this: that in a time of war the commander of an armed force (if, in his opinion, the exigencies of the country demand it, and of which he is the judge) has the power, within the lines of his military district, to suspend all civil rights and their remedies, and subject citizens as well as soldiers to the rule of his will; and in the exercise of this lawful authority cannot be restrained, except by his superior officer or the President of the United States.

If this position is sound to the extent claimed, then when war exists, foreign or domestic, and the country is subdivided into military departments for mere convenience, the commander of one of them can, if he chooses, within his limits, on the plea of necessity, with the approval of the Executive, substitute military force for, and to the exclusion of, the laws, and punish all persons, as he thinks right and proper, without fixed or certain rules.

The statement of this proposition shows its importance; for, if true, republican government is a failure, and there is an end of liberty regulated by law. . . .

This nation, as experience has proved, cannot always remain at peace, and has no right to expect that it will always have wise and humane rulers, sincerely attached to the principles of the Constitution. Wicked men, ambitious of power, with hatred of liberty and contempt of law, may fill the place once occupied by Washington and Lincoln; and if this right is conceded, and the calamities of war again befall us, the dangers to human liberty are frightful to contemplate. . . .

The two remaining questions in this case must be answered in the affirmative. The suspension of the privilege of the writ of *habeas corpus* does not suspend the writ itself. The writ issues as a matter of course; and on the return made to it the court decides whether the party applying is denied the right of proceeding any further with it.

If the military trial of Milligan was contrary to law, then he was entitled, on the facts stated in his petition, to be discharged from custody by the terms of the act of Congress of March 3, 1868. . . . THE CHIEF JUSTICE [CHASE] delivered the following opinion. . . .

We agree in the proposition that no department of the government of the United States—neither President, nor Congress, nor the Courts—possesses any power not given by the Constitution. . . .

We think . . . that the power of Congress, in the government of the land and naval forces and of the militia, is not at all affected by the fifth or any other amendment. It is not necessary to attempt any precise definition of the boundaries of this power. But may it not be said that government includes protection and defence as well as the regulation of the internal administration? And is it impossible to imagine cases in which citizens conspiring or attempting the destruction or great injury of the national forces may be subjected by Congress to military trial and punishment in the just exercise of this undoubted constitutional power? Congress is but the agent of the nation, and does not the security of individuals against the abuse of this, as of every other power, depend on the intelligence and virtue of the people, on their zeal for public and private liberty, upon official responsibility secured by law, and upon the frequency of elections, rather than upon doubtful constructions of legislative powers? . . .

In Indiana, for example, at the time of the arrest of Milligan and his co-conspirators, it is established by the papers in the record, that the state was a military district, was the theatre of military operations, had been actually invaded, and was constantly threatened with invasion. It appears, also, that a powerful secret association, composed of citizens and others, existed within the state, under military organization, conspiring against the draft, and plotting insurrection, the liberation of the prisoners of war at various depots, the seizure of the state and national arsenals, armed cooperation with the enemy, and war against the national government.

We cannot doubt that, in such a time of public danger, Congress had power, under the Constitution, to provide for the organization of a military commission, and for trial by that commission of persons engaged in this conspiracy. The fact that the Federal courts were open was regarded by Congress as a sufficient reason for not exercising the power; but that fact could not deprive Congress of the right to exercise it. Those courts might be open and undisturbed in the execution of their functions, and yet wholly incompetent to avert threatened danger, or to punish, with adequate promptitude and certainty, the guilty conspirators. . . .

MR. JUSTICE WAYNE, MR. JUSTICE SWAYNE, and MR. JUSTICE MILLER concur with me in these views.

Missouri v. Holland
252 U.S. 416, 40 S.Ct. 382, 64 L.Ed. 641 (1920)

By a treaty of 1916 the United States and Great Britain undertook the regulation and protection of birds migrating between Canada and various parts of the United States. An act of 1918 gave effect to the treaty by establishing closed seasons and other rules. The state of Missouri brought a bill in equity to prevent a game warden of the United States from enforcing the act, and appealed from the district court's dismissal of the bill. Majority: Holmes, Brandeis, Clarke, Day, McKenna, McReynolds, White. Dissenting: Pitney, Van Devanter.

MR. JUSTICE HOLMES delivered the opinion of the Court. . . .

. . . The question raised is the general one whether the treaty and statute are void as an interference with the rights reserved to the States.

To answer this question it is not enough to refer to the Tenth Amendment, reserving the powers not delegated to the United States, because by Article II, § 2, the power to make treaties is delegated expressly, and by Article VI treaties made under the authority of the United States, along with the Constitution and laws of the United States made in pursuance thereof, are declared the supreme law of the land. If the treaty is valid there can be no dispute about the validity of the statute under Article I, §8, as a necessary and proper means to execute the powers of the Government. The language of the Constitution as to the supremacy of treaties being general, the question before us is narrowed to an inquiry into the ground upon which the present supposed exception is placed.

It is said that a treaty cannot be valid if it infringes the Constitution, that there are limits, therefore, to the treaty-making power, and that one such limit is that what an act of Congress could not do unaided, in derogation of the powers reserved to the States a treaty cannot do. An earlier act of Congress that attempted by itself and not in pursuance of a treaty to regulate the killing of migratory birds within the States had been held bad in the District Court. Those decisions were supported by arguments that migratory birds were owned by the States in their sovereign capacity for the benefit of their people and that . . . this control was one that Congress had no power to displace. The same argument is supposed to apply now with equal force.

. . . Acts of Congress are the supreme law of the land only when made in pursuance of the Constitution, while treaties are declared to be so when made under the authority of the United States. It is open to question whether the authority of the United States means more than the formal acts prescribed to make the convention. We do not mean to imply that there are no qualifications to the treaty-making power; but they must be ascertained in a different way. It is obvious that there may be matters of the sharpest exigency for the national well-being that an act of Congress could not deal with but that a treaty followed by such an act could, and it is not lightly to be assumed that, in matters requiring national action, "a power which must belong to and somewhere reside in every civilized government" is not to be found. . . . [W]hen we are dealing with words that also are a constituent act, like the Constitution of the United States, we must realize that they have called into life a being the development of which could not have been foreseen completely by the most gifted of its begetters. It was not enough for them to realize or to hope that they had created an organism; it has taken a century and has cost their successors much sweat and blood to prove that they created a nation. The case before us must be considered in the light of our whole experience and not merely in that of what was said a hundred years ago. The treaty in question does not contravene any prohibitory words to be found in the Constitution. The only question is whether it is forbidden by some invisible radiation from the general terms of the Tenth Amendment. We must consider what this country has become in deciding what that Amendment has reserved.

The State as we have intimated founds its claim of exclusive authority upon an assertion of title to migratory birds, an assertion that is embodied in statute. No doubt it is true that as between a State and its inhabitants the State may regulate the killing and sale of such birds, but it does not follow that its authority is exclusive of paramount powers. To put the claim of the State upon title is to lean upon a slender reed. Wild birds are not in the possession of anyone; and possession is the beginning of ownership. The whole foundation of the State's rights is the presence within their jurisdiction of birds that yesterday had not arrived, tomorrow may be in another State and in a week a thousand miles away. If we are to be accurate we cannot put the case of the State upon higher ground than that the treaty deals with creatures that for the moment are within the State borders, that it must be carried out by officers of the United States within the same territory, and that but for the treaty the State would be free to regulate this subject itself. . . .

Here a national interest of very nearly the first magnitude is involved. It can be protected only by national action in concert with that of another power. The subject matter is only transitorily within the State and has no permanent habitat therein. But for the treaty and the statute there soon might be no birds for any powers to deal with. We see nothing in the constitution that compels the Government to sit by while a food supply is cut off and the protectors of our forests and our crops are destroyed. It is not sufficient to rely upon the States. The reliance is vain, and were it otherwise, the question is whether the United States is forbidden to act. We are of opinion that the treaty and statute must be upheld.

Decree affirmed.

United States v. Curtiss-Wright
299 U.S. 304, 57 S.Ct. 216, 81 L.Ed. 255 (1936)

This landmark case involving the powers of the president in foreign affairs grew out of the efforts of Congress to limit a war between Bolivia and Paraguay by granting to the president the power to prohibit the sale of arms and munitions to the warring nations. The defendant corporation, charged with conspiring to sell 15 machine guns to Bolivia, demurred to the indictment on the ground that the delegation of power to the president was invalid. The district court sustained the demurrer. Majority: Sutherland, Brandeis, Butler, Car-

dozo, Hughes, Roberts, Van Devanter. Dissenting: McReynolds. Not participating: Stone.

MR. JUSTICE SUTHERLAND delivered the opinion of the Court. . . .

Whether, if the Joint Resolution had related solely to internal affairs, it would be open to the challenge that it constituted an unlawful delegation of legislative power to the Executive, we find it unnecessary to determine. The whole aim of the resolution is to affect a situation entirely external to the United States, and falling within the category of foreign affairs. The determination which we are called to make, therefore, is whether the Joint Resolution, as applied to that situation, is vulnerable to attack under the rule that forbids a delegation of the lawmaking power. In other words, assuming (but not deciding) that the challenged delegation, if it were confined to internal affairs, would be invalid, may it nevertheless be sustained on the ground that its exclusive aim is to afford a remedy for a hurtful condition within foreign territory?

It will contribute to the elucidation of the question if we first consider the differences between the powers of the federal government in respect of foreign or external affairs and those in respect of domestic or internal affairs. That there are differences between them, and that these differences are fundamental, may not be doubted.

The two classes of powers are different, both in respect of their origin and their nature. The broad statement that the federal government can exercise no powers except those specifically enumerated in the Constitution, and such implied powers as are necessary and proper to carry into effect the enumerated powers, is categorically true only in respect of our internal affairs. In that field, the primary purpose of the Constitution was to carve from the general mass of legislative powers *then possessed by the states* such portions as it was thought desirable to vest in the federal government leaving those not included in the enumeration still in the states. . . . That this doctrine applies only to powers which the states had is self-evident. And since the states severally never possessed international powers, such powers could not have been carved from the mass of state powers but obviously were transmitted to the United States from some other source. During the Colonial period, those powers were possessed exclusively by and were entirely under the control of the Crown. By the Declaration of Independence, "the Representatives of the United States of America" declared the United (not the several) Colonies to be free and independent states, and as such to have "full Power to levy War, conclude Peace, contract Alliances, establish Commerce and to do all other Acts and Things which Independent States may of right do."

As a result of the separation from Great Britain by the colonies, acting as a unit, the powers of external sovereignty passed from the Crown not to the colonies severally, but to the colonies in their collective and corporate capacity as the United States of America. . . . When, therefore, the external sovereignty of Great Britain in respect of the colonies ceased, it immediately passed to the Union. . . . That fact was given practical application almost at once. The treaty of peace, made on September 3, 1783, was concluded between his Britannic Majesty and the "United States of America." . . .

The Union existed before the Constitution, which was ordained and established among other things to form "a more perfect Union." Prior to that event, it is clear that the Union declared by the Articles of Confederation to be "perpetual," was the sole possessor of external sovereignty, and in the Union it remained without change save in so far as the Constitution in express terms qualified its exercise. The Framers' Convention was called and exerted its powers upon the irrefutable postulate that though the states were several their people in respect of foreign affairs were one. . . .

It results that the investment of the federal government with the powers of external sovereignty did not depend upon the affirmative grants of the Constitution. The powers to declare and wage war, to conclude peace, to make treaties, to maintain diplomatic relations with other sovereignties, if they had never been mentioned in the Constitution, would have vested in the federal government as necessary concomitants of nationality. . . . As a member of the family of nations, the right and power of the United States in that field are equal to the right and power of the other members of the international family. Otherwise, the United States is not completely sovereign. . . .

Not only, as we have shown, is the federal

power over external affairs in origin and essential character different from that over internal affairs, but participation in the exercise of the power is significantly limited. In this vast external realm, with its important, complicated, delicate and manifold problems, the President alone has the power to speak or listen as a representative of the nation. He *makes* treaties with the advice and consent of the Senate; but he alone negotiates. Into the field of negotiation the Senate cannot intrude; and Congress itself is powerless to invade it. . . .

It is important to bear in mind that we are here dealing not alone with an authority vested in the President by an exertion of legislative power, but with such an authority plus the very delicate, plenary and exclusive power of the President as the sole organ of the federal government in the field of international relations—a power which does not require as a basis for its exercise an act of Congress, but which, of course, like every other governmental power, must be exercised in subordination to the applicable provisions of the Constitution. It is quite apparent that if, in the maintenance of our international relations, embarrassment—perhaps serious embarrassment—is to be avoided and success for our aims achieved, congressional legislation which

is to be made effective through negotiation and inquiry within the international field must often accord to the President a degree of discretion and freedom from statutory restriction which would not be admissible were domestic affairs alone involved. . . . Indeed, so clearly is this true that the first President refused to accede to a request to lay before the House of Representatives the instructions, correspondence and documents relating to the negotiation of the Jay Treaty—a refusal the wisdom of which was recognized by the House itself and has never been doubted. . . .

Both upon principle and in accordance with precedent, we conclude there is sufficient warrant for the broad discretion vested in the President to determine whether the enforcement of the statute will have a beneficial effect upon the reestablishment of peace in the affected countries; whether he shall make proclamation to bring the resolution into operation; whether and when the resolution shall cease to operate and to make proclamation accordingly; and to prescribe limitations and exceptions to which the enforcement of the resolution shall be subject. . . .

Reversed

Korematsu v. United States*
323 U.S. 214, 65 S.Ct. 193, 89 L.Ed. 194 (1944)

Shortly after America entered World War II, President Roosevelt issued an executive order authorizing creation of military areas from which persons suspected of sabotage and espionage might be excluded. In pursuance of this order, military commanders were authorized to prescribe regulations controlling the right of persons to enter, leave, or remain in the areas. For violation of these regulations, Congress provided penalties.

Acting under these executive and congressional authorizations, the Western Defense Command divided the Pacific Coast into two military areas, imposing restrictions on persons living in them, including a curfew that applied only to aliens and persons of Japanese ancestry.

* This case should also be read in connection with Chapter Twelve.

The curfew was upheld (*Hirabayashi* v. *United States,* 1943) as a legitimate wartime measure.

Later, the commanding general removed all Japanese, including many American citizens, to War Relocation Centers. Korematsu, an American citizen who refused to leave his home, was convicted in a federal district court for violation of the restriction order. The circuit court of appeals affirmed his conviction. Majority: Black, Douglas, Frankfurter, Reed, Rutledge, Stone. Dissenting: Jackson, Murphy, Roberts.

MR. JUSTICE BLACK delivered the opinion of the Court.

. . . In the light of the principles we announced in the Hirabayashi Case, we are unable to conclude that it was beyond the war power of Congress and the Executive to exclude those of Japanese ancestry from the West Coast war area at the time they did. True, exclusion from the area in which one's home is located is a far greater deprivation than constant confinement to the home from 8 p.m. to 6 a.m. Nothing short of apprehension by the proper military authorities of the gravest imminent danger to the public safety can constitutionally justify either. But exclusion from a threatened area, no less than curfew, has a definite and close relationship to the prevention of espionage and sabotage. The military authorities, charged with the primary responsibility of defending our shores, concluded that curfew provided inadequate protection and ordered exclusion. They did so, as pointed out in our Hirabayashi opinion, in accordance with congressional authority to the military to say who should, and who should not, remain in the threatened areas.

In this case the petitioner challenges the assumptions upon which we rested our conclusions in the Hirabayashi Case. He also urges that by May 1942, when Order No. 34 was promulgated, all danger of Japanese invasion of the West Coast had disappeared. After careful consideration of these contentions we are compelled to reject them. . . .

Like curfew, exclusion of those of Japanese origin was deemed necessary because of the presence of an unascertained number of disloyal members of the group, most of whom we have no doubt were loyal to this country. It was because we could not reject the finding of the military authorities that it was impossible to bring about an immediate segregation of the disloyal from the loyal that we sustained the validity of the curfew order as applying to the whole group. In the instant case, temporary exclusion of the entire group was rested by the military on the same ground. The judgment that exclusion of the whole group was for the same reason a military imperative answers the contention that the exclusion was in the nature of group punishment based on antagonism to those of Japanese origin. That there were members of the group who retained loyalties to Japan has been confirmed by investigations made subsequent to the exclusion. Approximately five thousand American citizens of Japanese ancestry refused to swear unqualified allegiance to the United States and to renounce allegiance to the Japanese Emperor, and several thousand evacuees requested repatriation to Japan.

We uphold the exclusion order as of the time it was made and when the petitioner violated it. . . . In doing so, we are not unmindful of the hardships imposed by it upon a large group of American citizens. . . . But hardships are part of war, and war is an aggregation of hardships. All citizens alike, both in and out of uniform, feel the impact of war in greater or lesser measure. Citizenship has its responsibilities as well as its privileges, and in time of war the burden is always heavier. Compulsory exclusion of large groups of citizens from their homes, except under circumstances of direst emergency and peril, is inconsistent with our basic governmental institutions. But when under conditions of modern warfare our shores are threatened by hostile forces, the power to protect must be commensurate with the threatened danger. . . .

It is said that we are dealing here with the case of imprisonment of a citizen in a concentration camp solely because of his ancestry, without evidence or inquiry concerning his loyalty and good disposition towards the United States. Our task would be simple, our duty clear, were this a case involving the imprisonment of a loyal citizen in a concentration camp because of racial prejudice. Regardless of the true nature of the assembly and relocation centers—and we deem it unjustifiable to call them concentration camps with all the ugly connotations that term implies—we are dealing specifically with nothing but an exclusion order. To cast this case into outlines of racial prejudice, without reference to the real military dangers which were presented, merely confuses the issue. Korematsu was not excluded from the Military Area because of hostility to him or his race. He *was* excluded because we are at war with the Japanese Empire, because the properly constituted military authorities feared an invasion of our West Coast and felt constrained to take proper security measures, because they decided that the military urgency of the situation demanded that all citizens of Japanese ancestry be segregated from the West Coast temporarily, and finally, because Congress, reposing its confidence in this time of war in our military leaders—as inevitably it must—determined that they should have the power to do just this. . . . We cannot—by availing ourselves of the calm perspective of hindsight—now say that at the time these actions were unjustified.

Affirmed.

MR. JUSTICE JACKSON, dissenting:

The limitation under which courts always will labor in examining the necessity for a military order are illustrated by this case. How does the Court know that these orders have a reasonable basis in necessity? No evidence whatever on that subject has been taken by this or any other court. There is sharp controversy as to the credibility of the DeWitt report. So the Court, having no real evidence before it, has no choice but to accept General DeWitt's own unsworn, self-serving statement, untested by any cross-examination, that what he did was reasonable. And thus it will always be when courts try to look into the reasonableness of a military order.

In the very nature of things military decisions are not susceptible of intelligent judicial appraisal. They do not pretend to rest on evidence, but are made on information that often would not be admissible and on assumptions that could not be proved. Information in support of an order could not be disclosed to courts without danger that it would reach the enemy. Neither can courts act on communications made in confidence. Hence courts can never have any real alternative to accepting the mere declaration of the authority that issued the order that it was reasonably necessary from a military viewpoint.

Much is said of the danger to liberty from the Army program for deporting and detaining these citizens of Japanese extraction. But a judicial construction of the due process clause that will sustain this order is a far more subtle blow to liberty than the promulgation of the order itself. A military order, however unconstitutional, is not apt to last longer than the military emergency. Even during that period a succeeding commander may revoke it all. But once a judicial opinion rationalizes such an order to show that it conforms to the Constitution, or rather rationalizes the Constitution to show that the Constitution sanctions such an order, the Court for all time has validated the principle of racial discrimination in criminal procedure and of transplanting American citizens. The principle then lies about like a loaded weapon ready for the hand of any authority that can bring forward a plausible claim of an urgent need. Every repetition imbeds that principle more deeply in our law and thinking and expands it to new purposes. All who observe the work of the courts are familiar with what Judge Cardozo described as "the tendency of a principle to expand itself to the limit of its logic." A military commander may overstep the bounds of constitutionality, and it is an incident. But if we review and approve, that passing incident becomes the doctrine of the Constitution. There it has a generative power of its own, and all that it creates will be in its own image. Nothing better illustrates this danger than does the Court's opinion in this case.

It argues that we are bound to uphold the conviction of Korematsu because we upheld one in *Hirabayashi* v. *United States* . . . when we sustained these orders in so far as they applied a curfew requirement to a citizen of Japanese ancestry. I think we would learn something from that experience.

In that case we were urged to consider only the curfew feature, that being all that technically was involved, because it was the only count necessary to sustain Hirabayashi's conviction and sentence. We yielded, and the Chief Justice guarded the opinion as carefully as language will do. He said:

"Our investigation here does not go beyond the inquiry whether, in the light of all the relevant circumstances preceding and attending their promulgation, the challenged orders and statute *afforded a reasonable basis for the action taken in imposing the curfew.*". . . "We decide only the issue as we have defined it—we decide only that the *curfew order* as applied, and at the time it was applied, was within the boundaries of the war power." . . . And again: "It is unnecessary to consider whether or to what extent *such findings would support orders differing from the curfew order.*" . . . [Italics supplied.] However, in spite of our limiting words we did validate a discrimination on the basis of ancestry for mild and temporary deprivation of liberty. Now the principle of racial discrimination is pushed from support of mild measures to very harsh ones, and from temporary deprivations to indeterminate ones. And the precedent which it is said requires us to do so is *Hirabayashi.* The Court is now saying that in *Hirabayashi* we did decide the very things we there said we were not deciding. Because we said that these citizens could be made to stay in their homes during the hours of dark, it is said we must require them to leave home entirely; and if that, we are told they may also be taken into custody for deportation; and if that, it is argued they may also be held for some undetermined time in detention camps. How far the principle of this case would be extended before plausible reasons would play out, I do not know. . . .

Of course the existence of a military power resting on force, so vagrant, so centralized, so necessarily heedless of the individual, is an inherent threat to liberty. But I would not lead people to rely on this Court for a review that seems to me wholly delusive. The military reasonableness of these orders can only be determined by military superiors. If the people ever let command of the war power fall into irresponsible and unscrupulous hands, the courts wield no power equal to its restraint. The chief restraint upon those who command the physical forces of the country, in the future as in the past, must be their responsibility to the political judgments of their contemporaries and to the moral judgments of history.

My duties as a justice as I see them do not require me to make a military judgment as to whether General DeWitt's evacuation and detention program was a reasonable military necessity. I do not suggest that the courts should have attempted to interfere with the Army in carrying out its task. But I do not think they may be asked to execute a military expedient that has no place in law under the Constitution. I would reverse the judgment and discharge the prisoner.*

---

* Calling the internment "part of an unfortunate episode in our nation's history," the Justice Department in 1983 successfully petitioned the United States District Court in San Francisco to set aside Fred Korematsu's conviction. Claiming the government exaggerated the wartime security risks on the West Coast, Korematsu and other Japanese-Americans then filed a suit for damages against the government. In 1984, the District Court for the District of Columbia ruled that the Korematsu litigation was barred by a six-year rule of the statute of limitations, for suits against the government. Reversing the district court, the court of appeals held 2-1 in 1986 that previously uncompensated internees could press their suit for damages. Important in the ruling was evidence that the government had concealed information that those interned did not pose a danger to national security during World War II. In *United States* v. *Hohri* (1987), the Supreme Court vacated the appeals court decision because the appeal should have been heard by the Court of Appeals for the Federal Circuit. During oral argument in *Hohri,* Solicitor General Charles Fried described the 1944 *Korematsu* ruling as the "greatest departure from the values for which we were fighting" during World War II. He accepted Justice Murphy's contention that the decision was based on "amateur socioanthropology" with a "racist cast." In 1988 the Supreme Court denied certiorari in *Hohri* v. *United States,* in which the Court of Appeals for the Federal Circuit had held that the statute of limitations barred the claims under the Takings Clause of the Fifth Amendment pressed by the interned citizens and their descendants.—Ed.

Youngstown Co. v. Sawyer
343 U.S. 579, 72 S.Ct. 863, 96 L.Ed. 1153 (1952)

A labor dispute in the steel industry began in 1951 and resulted in a 1952 presidential order authorizing the secretary of commerce to seize and operate steel mills. The presidential order was not based on any statute, but rather was premised on the national emergency created by the threatened strike in an industry vital to defense production. Additional details are contained in the opinion. The steel companies then obtained an injunction from a federal district court restraining Secretary of Commerce Sawyer, and a court of appeals decision stayed the injunction. Majority: Black, Burton, Clark, Douglas, Frankfurter, Jackson. Dissenting: Vinson, Minton, Reed.

MR. JUSTICE BLACK delivered the opinion of the Court.

We are asked to decide whether the President was acting within his constitutional power when he issued an order directing the Secretary of Commerce to take possession of and operate most of the Nation's steel mills. The mill owners argue that the President's order amounts to law making, a legislative function which the Constitution has expressly confided to the Congress and not to the President. The Government's position is that the order was made on findings of the President that his action was necessary to avert a national catastrophe which would inevitably result from a stoppage of steel production, and that in meeting this grave emergency the President was acting within the aggregate of his constitutional powers as the Nation's Chief Executive and the Commander in Chief of the Armed Forces of the United States. . . .

The President's power, if any, to issue the order must stem either from an act of Congress or from the Constitution itself. There is no statute that expressly authorizes the President to take possession of property as he did here. Nor is there any act of Congress to which such a power can fairly be implied. Indeed, we do not understand the Government to rely on statutory authorization for this seizure. . . .

Moreover, the use of the seizure technique to solve labor disputes in order to prevent work stoppages was not only unauthorized by any congressional enactment; prior to this controversy, Congress had refused to adopt that method of settling labor disputes. When the Taft-Hartley Act was under consideration in 1947, Congress rejected an amendment which would have authorized such governmental seizures in case of emergency. . . .

It is clear that if the President had authority to issue the order he did, it must be found in some provision of the Constitution. And it is not claimed that express constitutional language grants this power to the President. The contention is that presidential power should be implied from the aggregate of his powers under the Constitution. Particular reliance is placed on provisions in Article II which say that "the executive Power shall be vested in a President. . . ."; that "he shall take Care that the Laws be faithfully executed"; and that he "shall be Commander in Chief of the Army and Navy of the United States."

The order cannot properly be sustained as an exercise of the President's military power as Commander in Chief of the Armed Forces. The Government attempts to do so by citing a number of cases upholding broad powers in military commanders engaged in day-to-day fighting in a theater of war. Such cases need not concern us here. Even though "theater of war" be an expanding concept, we cannot with faithfulness to our constitutional system hold that the Commander in Chief of the Armed Forces has the ultimate power as such to take possession of private property in order to keep labor disputes from stopping production. This is a job for the Nation's lawmakers, not for its military authorities.

Nor can the seizure order be sustained because of the several constitutional provisions that grant executive power to the President. In the framework of our Constitution, the President's power to see that the laws are faithfully executed refutes the idea that he is to be a lawmaker. The Constitution limits his functions in the lawmaking process to the recommending of laws he thinks wise and the vetoing of laws he thinks bad. And the Constitution is neither silent nor equivocal about who shall make laws which the President is to execute. . . .

The Founders of this Nation entrusted the lawmaking power to the Congress alone in both good and bad times. It would do no good to recall the historical events, the fears of power and the hopes for freedom that lay behind their choice. Such a review would but confirm our holding that this seizure order cannot stand.

The judgment of the District Court is

Affirmed.

MR. JUSTICE JACKSON, concurring in the judgment and opinion of the Court. . . .

A judge, like an executive adviser, may be surprised at the poverty of really useful and unambiguous authority applicable to concrete problems of executive power as they actually present themselves. Just what our forefathers did envision, or would have envisioned had they foreseen modern conditions, must be divined from materials almost as enigmatic as the dreams Joseph was called upon to interpret for Pharaoh. A century and a half of partisan debate and scholarly speculation yields no net result but only supplies more or less apt quotations from respected sources on each side of any question. They largely cancel each other. And court decisions are indecisive because of the judicial practice of dealing with the largest questions in the most narrow way.

The actual art of governing under our Constitution does not and cannot conform to judicial definitions of the power of any of its branches based on isolated clauses or even single Articles torn from context. While the Constitution diffuses power the better to secure liberty, it also contemplates that practice will integrate the dispersed powers into a workable government. It enjoins upon its branches separateness but interdependence, autonomy but reciprocity. Presidential powers are not fixed but fluctuate, depending upon their disjunction or conjunction with those of Congress. We may well begin by a somewhat oversimplified grouping of practical situations in which a President may doubt, or others may challenge, his powers. . . .

1. When the President acts pursuant to an express or implied authorization of Congress his authority is at its maximum, for it includes all that he possesses in his own right plus all that Congress can delegate. In these circumstances, and in these only, may he be said (for what it may be worth) to personify the federal sovereignty. If his act is held unconstitutional under these circumstances, it usually means that the Federal Government as an undivided whole lacks power. A seizure executed by the President pursuant to an Act of Congress would be supported by the strongest of presumptions and the widest latitude of judicial interpretation, and the burden of persuasion would rest heavily upon any who might attack it.

2. When the President acts in absence of either a congressional grant or denial of authority, he can only rely upon his own independent powers, but there is a zone of twilight in which he and Congress may have concurrent authority, or in which its distribution is uncertain. Therefore, congressional inertia, indifference or quiescence may sometimes, at least as a practical matter, enable, if not invite, measures on independent presidential responsibility. In this area, any actual test of power is likely to depend on the imperatives of events and contemporary imponderables rather than on abstract theories of law.

3. When the President takes measures incompatible with the expressed or implied will of Congress, his power is at its lowest ebb, for then he can rely only upon his own constitutional powers minus any constitutional powers of Congress over the matter. Courts can sustain exclusive presidential control in such a case only by disabling the Congress from acting upon the subject. Presidential claim to a power at once so conclusive and preclusive must be scrutinized with caution, for what is at stake is the equilibrium established by our constitutional system.

Into which of these classifications does this executive seizure of the steel industry fit? It is eliminated from the first by admission, for it is conceded that no congressional authorization exists for this seizure. That takes away also the support of the many precedents and declarations which were made in relation, and must be confined, to this category.

Can it then be defended under flexible tests available to the second category? It seems clearly eliminated from that class because Congress has not left seizure of private property an open field but has covered it by three statutory policies inconsistent with this seizure. In cases where the purpose is to supply needs of the Government itself, two courses are provided: one, seizure of a plant which fails to comply with obligatory orders placed by the Government, another, condemnation of facilities, including temporary use under the power of eminent domain. The third is applicable where it is the general economy of the country that is to be protected rather than exclusive governmental interests. None of these were invoked. In choosing a different and inconsistent way of his own, the President cannot claim that it is necessitated or invited by failure of Congress to legislate upon the occasions, grounds and methods for seizure of industrial properties. . . .

The Solicitor General seeks the power of seizure in three clauses of the Executive Article, the first reading, "The executive Power shall be vested in a President of the United States of America." Lest I be thought to exaggerate, I quote the interpretation which his brief puts upon it: "In our view, this clause constitutes a grant of all the executive powers of which the Government is capable." If that be true, it is difficult to see why the forefathers bothered to add several specific items, including some trifling ones.

The example of such unlimited executive power that must have most impressed the forefathers was the prerogative exercised by George III, and the description of its evils in the Declaration of Independence leads me to doubt that they were creating their new Executive in his image. Continental European examples were no more appealing. And if we seek instruction from our own times, we can match it only from the executive powers in those governments we disparagingly describe as totalitarian. I cannot accept the view that this clause is a grant in bulk of all conceivable executive power but regard it as an allocation to the presidential office of the generic powers thereafter stated.

The clause on which the Government next relies is that "The President shall be Commander in Chief of the Army and Navy of the United States. . . ." These cryptic words have given rise to some of the most persistent controversies in our constitutional history. Of course, they imply something more than an empty title. But just what authority goes with the name has plagued presidential advisers who would not waive or narrow it

by nonassertion yet cannot say where it begins or ends. It undoubtedly puts the Nation's armed forces under presidential command. Hence, this loose appellation is sometimes advanced as support for any presidential action, internal or external, involving use of force, the idea being that it vests power to do anything, anywhere, that can be done with an army or navy.

That seems to be the logic of an argument tendered at our bar—that the President having, on his own responsibility, sent American troops abroad derives from that act "affirmative power" to seize the means of producing a supply of steel for them. To quote, "Perhaps the most forceful illustration of the scope of presidential power in this connection is the fact that American troops in Korea, whose safety and effectiveness are so directly involved here, were sent to the field by an exercise of the President's constitutional powers." Thus, it is said he has invested himself with "war powers."

I cannot foresee all that it might entail if the Court should endorse this argument. Nothing in our Constitution is plainer than that declaration of a war is entrusted only to Congress. Of course, a state of war may in fact exist without a formal declaration. But no doctrine that the Court could promulgate would seem to me more sinister and alarming than that a President whose conduct of foreign affairs is so largely uncontrolled, and often even is unknown, can vastly enlarge his mastery over the internal affairs of the country by his own commitment of the Nation's armed forces to some foreign venture. I do not, however, find it necessary or appropriate to consider the legal status of the Korean enterprise to discountenance argument based on it. . . .

We should not use this occasion to circumscribe, much less to contract, the lawful role of the President as Commander-in-Chief. I should indulge the widest latitude of interpretation to sustain his exclusive function to command the instruments of national force, at least when turned against the outside world for the security of our society. But, when it is turned inward, not because of rebellion but because of a lawful economic struggle between industry and labor, it should have no such indulgence. . . .

The third clause in which the Solicitor General finds seizure powers is that "he shall take Care that the Laws be faithfully executed. . . ." That authority must be matched against words of the Fifth Amendment that "No person shall be . . .

deprived of life, liberty or property, without due process of law. . . ."

One gives a governmental authority that reaches so far as there is law, the other gives a private right that shall go no farther. These signify about all there is of the principle that ours is a government of laws, not of men, and that we submit ourselves to rulers only if under rules.

The Solicitor General lastly grounds support of the seizure upon nebulous, inherent powers never expressly granted but said to have accrued to the office from the customs and claims of preceding administrations. The plea is for a resulting power to deal with a crisis or an emergency according to the necessities of the case, the unarticulated assumption being that necessity knows no law. . . .

Contemporary foreign experience may be inconclusive as to the wisdom of lodging emergency powers somewhere in a modern government. But it suggests that emergency powers are consistent with free government only when their control is lodged elsewhere than in the Executive who exercises them. That is the safeguard that would be nullified by our adoption of the "inherent powers" formula. . . .

In the practical working of our Government we already have evolved a technique within the framework of the Constitution by which normal executive powers may be considerably expanded to meet an emergency. Congress may and has granted extraordinary authorities which lie dormant in normal times but may be called into play by the Executive in war or upon proclamation of a national emergency. . . .

In view of the ease, expedition and safety with which Congress can grant and has granted large emergency powers, certainly ample to embrace this crisis, I am quite unimpressed with the argument that we should affirm possession of them without statute. Such power either has no beginning or it has no end. If it exists, it need submit to no legal restraint. I am not alarmed that it would plunge us straightaway into dictatorship, but it is at least a step in that wrong direction. . . .

The essence of our free Government is "leave to live by no man's leave, underneath the law"— to be governed by those impersonal forces which we call law. Our Government is fashioned to fulfill this concept so far as humanly possible. The Executive, except for recommendation and veto, has no legislative power. The executive action we have

here originates in the individual will of the President and represents an exercise of authority without law. No one, perhaps not even the President, knows the limits of the power he may seek to exert in this instance and the parties affected cannot learn the limit of their rights. We do not know today what powers over labor or property would be claimed to flow from Government possession if we should legalize it, what rights to compensation would be claimed or recognized, or on what contingency it would end. With all its defects, delays and inconveniences, men have discovered no technique for long preserving free government except that the Executive be under the law, and that the law be made by parliamentary deliberations.

Such institutions may be destined to pass away. But it is the duty of the Court to be last, not first, to give them up.

MR. CHIEF JUSTICE VINSON, with whom MR. JUSTICE REED and MR. JUSTICE MINTON join, dissenting. . . .

Those who suggest that this is a case involving extraordinary powers should be mindful that these are extraordinary times. A world not yet recovered from the devastation of World War II has been forced to face the threat of another and more terrifying global conflict. . . .

The steel mills were seized for a public use. The power of eminent domain, invoked in this case, is an essential attribute of sovereignty and has long been recognized as a power of the Federal Government. . . .

Admitting that the Government could seize the mills, plaintiffs claim that the implied power of eminent domain can be exercised only under an Act of Congress; under no circumstances, they say, can that power be exercised by the President unless he can point to an express provision in enabling legislation. This was the view adopted by the District Judge when he granted the preliminary injunction. Without an answer, without hearing evidence, he determined the issue on the basis of his "fixed conclusion . . . that defendant's acts are illegal" because the President's only course in the face of an emergency is to present the matter to Congress and await the final passage of legislation which will enable the Government to cope with threatened disaster.

Under this view, the President is left powerless at the very moment when the need for action may be most pressing and when no one, other than he, is immediately capable of action. Under this view, he is left powerless because a power not expressly given to Congress is nevertheless found to rest exclusively with Congress. . . .

In passing upon the grave constitutional question presented in this case, we must never forget, as Chief Justice Marshall admonished, that the Constitution is "intended to endure for ages to come, and, consequently, to be adapted to the various *crises* of human affairs," and that "[i]ts means are adequate to its ends. . . ."

A review of executive action demonstrates that our Presidents have on many occasions exhibited the leadership contemplated by the Framers when they made the President Commander in Chief, and

imposed upon him the trust to "take care that the Laws be faithfully executed." With or without explicit statutory authorization, Presidents have at such times dealt with national emergencies by acting promptly and resolutely to enforce legislative programs, at least to save those programs until Congress could act. Congress and the courts have responded to such executive initiative with consistent approval. . . .

The absence of a specific statute authorizing seizure of the steel mills as a mode of executing the laws—both the military procurement program and the anti-inflation program—has not until today been thought to prevent the president from executing the laws.

New York Times Company v. *United States*
403 U.S. 713, 91 S.Ct. 2140, 29 L.Ed. 2d 822 (1971)

(This case is reprinted in Chapter Ten beginning on page 416.)

United States v. *United States District Court**
407 U.S. 297, 92 S.Ct. 2125, 32 L.Ed. 2d 752 (1972)

During pretrial proceedings in a prosecution in the United States District Court for the Eastern District of Michigan for conspiracy to destroy government property, the court ordered the government to make full disclosure to one of the defendants of his conversations overheard by electronic surveillance instituted without a search warrant. The United States Court of Appeals for the Sixth Circuit denied the government's petition for a writ of mandamus to compel the district judge to vacate the disclosure order. Majority: Powell, Blackmun, Brennan, Burger, Douglas, Marshall, Stewart, White. Not participating: Rehnquist.

MR. JUSTICE POWELL delivered the opinion of the Court.

The issue before us is an important one for the people of our country and their Government. It

involves the delicate question of the President's power, acting through the Attorney General, to authorize electronic surveillance in internal security matters without prior judicial approval. Successive Presidents for more than one quarter of a century have authorized such surveillance in varying degrees, without guidance from the Congress or a definitive

---

* This case should also be read in connection with Chapter Nine.

decision of this Court. This case brings the issue here for the first time. Its resolution is a matter of national concern, requiring sensitivity both to the Government's right to protect itself from unlawful subversion and attack and to the citizen's right to be secure in his privacy against unreasonable Government intrusion. . . .

Title III of the Omnibus Crime Control and Safe Streets Act . . . authorizes the use of electronic surveillance for classes of crimes carefully specified. . . . The Act represents a comprehensive attempt by Congress to promote more effective control of crime while protecting the privacy of individual thought and expression. . . .

Together with the elaborate surveillance requirements in Title III, there is the following proviso, 18 USC § 2511 (3):

> Nothing contained in this chapter or in section 605 of the Communications Act of 1934 shall limit the constitutional power of the President to take such measures as he deems necessary to protect the Nation against actual or potential attack or other hostile acts of a foreign power, to obtain foreign intelligence information deemed essential to the security of the United States, or to protect national security information against foreign intelligence activities. *Nor shall anything contained in this chapter be deemed to limit the constitutional power of the President to take such measures as he deems necessary to protect the United States against the overthrow of the Government by force or other unlawful means, or against any other clear and present danger to the structure or existence of the Government.* The contents of any wire or oral communication intercepted by authority of the President in the exercise of the foregoing powers may be received in evidence in any trial hearing or other proceeding only where such interception was reasonable, and shall not be otherwise used or disclosed except as is necessary to implement that power. (Emphasis supplied.)

The Government relies on § 2511 (3). It argues that "in excepting national security surveillances from the Act's warrant requirement Congress recognized the President's authority to conduct such surveillances without prior judicial approval." . . . The section thus is viewed as a recognition or affirmance of a constitutional authority in the President to conduct warrantless domestic security surveillance such as that involved in this case.

We think the language of § 2511 (3), as well as the legislative history of the statute, refutes this interpretation. The relevant language is that:

> Nothing contained in this chapter . . . shall limit the constitutional power of the President to take such measures as he deems necessary to protect . . .

against the dangers specified. At most, this is an implicit recognition that the President does have certain powers in the specified areas. Few would doubt this, as the section refers—among other things—to protection "against actual or potential attack or other hostile acts of a foreign power." But so far as the use of the President's electronic surveillance power is concerned, the language is essentially neutral.

Section 2511 (3) certainly confers no power, as the language is wholly inappropriate for such a purpose. It merely provides that the Act shall not be interpreted to limit or disturb such power as the President may have under the Constitution. In short, Congress simply left presidential powers where it found them. . . .

. . . [N]othing in § 2511 (3) was intended to *expand* or to *contract* or to *define* whatever presidential surveillance powers existed in matters affecting the national security. If we could accept the Government's characterization of § 2511 (3) as a congressionally prescribed exception to the general requirement of a warrant, it would be necessary to consider the question of whether the surveillance in this case came within the exception and, if so, whether the statutory exception was itself constitutionally valid. But viewing § 2511 (3) as a congressional disclaimer and expression of neutrality, we hold that the statute is not the measure of the executive authority asserted in this case. Rather, we must look to the constitutional powers of the President.

It is important at the outset to emphasize the limited nature of the question before the Court. This case . . . requires no judgment on the scope of the President's surveillance power with respect to the activities of foreign powers, within or without this country. The Attorney General's affidavit in this case states that the surveillances were "deemed necessary to protect the nation from attempts of *domestic organizations* to attack and subvert the existing structure of Government" (emphasis supplied). There is no evidence of any involvement, directly or indirectly, of a foreign power.

Our present inquiry, though important, is therefore a narrow one. . . .

Though the Government and respondents debate their seriousness and magnitude, threats and acts of sabotage against the Government exist in sufficient number to justify investigative powers with respect to them. The covertness and complexity of potential unlawful conduct against the Government and the necessary dependency of many conspirators upon the telephone make electronic surveillance an effective investigatory instrument in certain circumstances. The marked acceleration in technological developments and sophistication in their use have resulted in new techniques for the planning, commission and concealment of criminal activites. It would be contrary to the public interest for Government to deny to itself the prudent and lawful employment of those very techniques which are employed against the Government and its law-abiding citizens. . . .

But a recognition of these elementary truths does not make the employment by Government of electronic surveillance a welcome development—even when employed with restraint and under judicial supervision. There is, understandably, a deep-seated uneasiness and apprehension that this capability will be used to intrude upon cherished privacy of law-abiding citizens.

We look to the Bill of Rights to safeguard this privacy. Though physical entry of the home is the chief evil against which the wording of the Fourth Amendment is directed, its broader spirit now shields private speech from unreasonable surveillance. . . .

History abundantly documents the tendency of Government—however benevolent and benign its motives—to view with suspicion those who most fervently dispute its policies. Fourth Amendment protections become the more necessary when the targets of official surveillance may be those suspected of unorthodoxy in their political beliefs. The danger to political dissent is acute where the Government attempts to act under so vague a concept as the power to protect "domestic security." Given the difficulty of defining the domestic security interest, the danger of abuse in acting to protect that interest becomes apparent. . . . The price of lawful public dissent must not be a dread of subjection to an unchecked surveillance power. Nor must the fear of unauthorized official eavesdropping deter vigorous citizen dissent and discussion of Government action in private conversation. For private dissent, no less than open public discourse, is essential to our free society.

As the Fourth Amendment is not absolute in its terms, our task is to examine and balance the basic values at stake in this case: the duty of Government to protect the domestic security, and the potential danger posed by unreasonable surveillance to individual privacy and free expression. If the legitimate need of Government to safeguard domestic security requires the use of electronic surveillance, the question is whether the needs of citizens for privacy and free expression may not be better protected by requiring a warrant before such surveillance is undertaken. We must also ask whether a warrant requirement would unduly frustrate the efforts of Government to protect itself from acts of subversion and overthrow directed against it. . . .

. . . Fourth Amendment freedoms cannot properly be guaranteed if domestic security surveillances may be conducted solely within the discretion of the executive branch. The Fourth Amendment does not contemplate the executive officers of Government as neutral and disinterested magistrates. Their duty and responsibility is to enforce the laws, to investigate and to prosecute. . . .

The Fourth Amendment contemplates a prior judicial judgment, not the risk that executive discretion may be reasonably exercised. This judicial role accords with our basic constitutional doctrine that individual freedoms will best be preserved through a separation of powers and division of functions among the different branches and levels of Government. . . . The independent check upon executive discretion is not satisfied, as the Government argues, by "extremely limited" post-surveillance judicial review. Indeed, post-surveillance review would never reach the surveillances which failed to result in prosecutions. Prior review by a neutral and detached magistrate is the time-tested means of effectuating Fourth Amendment rights. . . .

The Government argues that the special circumstances applicable to domestic security surveillances necessitate a further exception to the warrant requirement. It is urged that the requirement of prior judicial review would obstruct the President in the discharge of his constitutional duty to protect domestic security. We are told further that these surveillances are directed primarily to the collecting and maintaining of intelligence with respect to subversive forces and are not an attempt to gather evidence for specific criminal prosecutions. It is said that this type of surveillance should not be subject to traditional warrant requirements which were established to govern investigation of criminal activity, not on-going intelligence gathering. . . .

The Government further insists that courts "as a practical matter would have neither the knowledge nor the techniques necessary to determine whether there was probable cause to believe that surveillance was necessary to protect national security." These security problems, the Government contends, involve "a large number of complex and subtle factors" beyond the competence of courts to evaluate. . . .

As a final reason for exemption from a warrant requirement, the Government believes that disclosure to a magistrate of all or even a significant portion of the information involved in domestic security surveillances "would create serious potential dangers to the national security and to the lives of informants and agents. . . . Secrecy is the essential ingredient in intelligence gathering; requiring prior judicial authorization would create a greater 'danger of leaks . . . because in addition to the judge, you have the clerk, the stenographer and some other official like a law assistant or bailiff who may be apprised of the nature' of the surveillance." . . .

. . . There is, no doubt, pragmatic force to the Government's position.

But we do not think a case has been made for the requested departure from Fourth Amendment standards. The circumstances described do not justify complete exemption of domestic security surveillance from prior judicial scrutiny. . . .

We cannot accept the Government's argument that internal security matters are too subtle and complex for judicial evaluation. Courts regularly deal with the most difficult issues of our society. There is no reason to believe that federal judges will be insensitive to or uncomprehending of the issues involved in domestic security cases. Certainly courts can recognize that domestic security surveillance involves different considerations from the surveillance of ordinary crime. If the threat is too subtle or complex for our senior law enforcement officers to convey its significance to a court, one may question whether there is probable cause for surveillance.

Nor do we believe prior judicial approval will fracture the secrecy essential to official intelligence gathering. The investigation of criminal activity has long involved imparting sensitive information to judicial officers who have respected the confidentialities involved. Judges may be counted upon to be especially conscious of security requirements in national security cases. . . .

Thus, we conclude that the Government's concerns do not justify departure in this case from the customary Fourth Amendment requirement of judicial approval prior to initiation of a search or surveillance. Although some added burden will be imposed upon the Attorney General, this inconvenience is justified in a free society to protect constitutional values. Nor do we think the Government's domestic surveillance powers will be impaired to any significant degree. A prior warrant establishes presumptive validity of the surveillance and will minimize the burden of justification in post-surveillance judicial review. By no means of least importance, will be the reassurance of the public generally that indiscriminate wiretapping and bugging of law-abiding citizens cannot occur. . . .

The judgment of the Court of Appeals is hereby *Affirmed.*

United States v. *Nixon*
418 U.S. 683, 94 S.Ct. 3090, 41 L.Ed. 2d 1039 (1974)

Following the indictment of seven high-ranking White House officials—including former presidential assistants H.R. Haldeman and
John Ehrlichman and former Attorney General John Mitchell—for
conspiracy to defraud the U.S. government and obstruction of justice,
the special prosecutor obtained a subpoena *duces tecum* directing
President Richard M. Nixon to deliver to the trial judge certain tape
recordings and memoranda of conversations held in the White House.
Nixon produced some of the subpoenaed material but withheld other
portions, invoking executive privilege, which placed confidential presidential documents beyond judicial reach. The trial judge denied the
president's claim, and he appealed to the court of appeals. The
special prosecutor asked the Supreme Court to review the case before
the court of appeals had passed judgment. Majority: Burger, Blackmun, Brennan, Douglas, Marshall, Powell, Stewart, White. Not participating: Rehnquist.

MR. CHIEF JUSTICE BURGER delivered the opinion
of the Court. . . .

We turn to the claim that the subpoena should
be quashed because it demands "confidential conversations between a President and his close advisors
that it would be inconsistent with the public interest
to produce." . . . The first contention is a broad
claim that the separation of powers doctrine precludes judicial review of a President's claim of
privilege. The second contention is that if he does
not prevail on the claim of absolute privilege, the
court should hold as a matter of constitutional law
that the privilege prevails over the subpoena duces
tecum.

In the performance of assigned constitutional
duties each branch of the Government must initially
interpret the Constitution, and the interpretation
of its powers by any branch is due great respect
from the others. The President's counsel . . . reads
the Constitution as providing an absolute privilege
of confidentiality for all presidential communications. Many decisions of this Court, however, have
unequivocally reaffirmed the holding of *Marbury v.
Madison* that "it is emphatically the province and
duty of the judicial department to say what the
law is.". . .

No holding of the Court has defined the scope
of judicial power specifically relating to the enforcement of a subpoena for confidential presidential
communications for use in a criminal prosecution,
but other exercises of powers by the Executive
Branch and the Legislative Branch have been found
invalid as in conflict with the Constitution. . . .
Since this Court has consistently exercised the power
to construe and delineate claims arising under express powers, it must follow that the Court has
authority to interpret claims with respect to powers
alleged to derive from enumerated powers.

In support of his claim of absolute privilege,
the President's counsel urges two grounds, one of
which is common to all governments and one of
which is peculiar to our system of separation of
powers. The first ground is the valid need for
protection of communications between high government officials and those who advise and assist
them in the performance of their manifold duties;
the importance of this confidentiality is too plain
to require further discussion. . . . Whatever the
nature of the privilege of confidentiality of presidential communications in the exercise of Art. II
powers, the privilege can be said to derive from
the supremacy of each branch within its own assigned area of constitutional duties. Certain powers
and privileges flow from the nature of enumerated
powers; the protection of the confidentiality of presidential communications has similar constitutional
underpinnings.

The second ground asserted by the President's
counsel in support of the claim of absolute privilege
rests on the doctrine of separation of powers. Here

it is argued that the independence of the Executive Branch within its own sphere . . . insulates a president from a judicial subpoena in an ongoing criminal prosecution, and thereby protects confidential presidential communications.

However, neither the doctrine of separation of powers, nor the need for confidentiality of high level communications, without more, can sustain an absolute, unqualified presidential privilege of immunity from judicial process under all circumstances. The President's need for complete candor and objectivity from advisers calls for great deference from the courts. However, when the privilege depends solely on the broad, undifferentiated claim of public interest in the confidentiality of such conversations, a confrontation with other values arises. Absent a claim of need to protect military, diplomatic or sensitive national security secrets, we find it difficult to accept the argument that even the very important interest in confidentiality of presidential communications is significantly diminished by production of such material for *in camera* inspection with all the protection that a district court will be obliged to provide.

The impediment that an absolute, unqualified privilege would place in the way of the primary constitutional duty of the Judicial Branch to do justice in criminal prosecutions would plainly conflict with the function of the courts under Art. III. In designing the structure of our Government and dividing and allocating the sovereign power among three coequal branches, the Framers of the Constitution sought to provide a comprehensive system, but the separate powers were not intended to operate with absolute independence. . . .

Since we conclude that the legitimate needs of the judicial process may outweigh presidential privilege, it is necessary to resolve those competing interests in a manner that preserves the essential functions of each branch. The right and indeed the duty to resolve that question does not free the judiciary from according high respect to the representations made on behalf of the President.

The expectation of a President to the confidentiality of his conversations and correspondence, like the claim of confidentiality of judicial deliberations, for example, has all the values to which we accord deference for the privacy of all citizens and added to those values the necessity for protection of the public interest in candid, objective, and even blunt

or harsh opinions in presidential decision making. . . . These are the considerations justifying a presumptive privilege for presidential communications. The privilege is fundamental to the operation of government and inextricably rooted in the separation of powers under the Constitution. In *Nixon v. Sirica* . . . (1973), the Court of Appeals held that such presidential communications are "presumptively privileged" . . . and this position is accepted by both parties in the present litigation. We agree with Mr. Chief Justice Marshall's observation, therefore, that "in no case of this kind would a court be required to proceed against the President as against an ordinary individual."

But this presumptive privilege must be considered in light of our historic commitment to the rule of law. This is nowhere more profoundly manifest than in our view that "the twofold aim of criminal justice is that guilt shall not escape or innocence suffer." We have elected to employ an adversary system of criminal justice in which the parties contest issues before a court of law. The need to develop all relevant facts in the adversary system is both fundamental and comprehensive. The ends of criminal justice would be defeated if judgments were to be founded on a partial or speculative presentation of the facts. The very integrity of the judicial system and public confidence in the system depend on full disclosure of all the facts, within the framework of the rules of evidence. To ensure that justice is done, it is imperative to the function of courts that compulsory process be available for the production of evidence needed either by the prosecution or by the defense.

In this case the President challenges a subpoena served on him as a third party requiring the production of materials for use in a criminal prosecution on the claim that he has a privilege against disclosure of confidential communications. He does not place his claim of privilege on the ground they are military or diplomatic secrets. As to these areas of Art. II duties, the courts have traditionally shown the utmost deference to presidential responsibilities. . . . No case of the Court . . . has extended this high degree of deference to a President's generalized interest in confidentiality. Nowhere in the Constitution . . . is there any explicit reference to a privilege of confidentiality, yet to the extent this interest relates to the effective discharge of a President's powers, it is constitutionally based.

The right to the production of all evidence at a criminal trial similarly has constitutional dimensions. The Sixth Amendment explicitly confers upon every defendant in a criminal trial the right "to be confronted with the witnesses against him" and "to have compulsory process for obtaining witnesses in his favor." Moreover, the Fifth Amendment also guarantees that no person shall be deprived of liberty without due process of law. It is the manifest duty of the courts to vindicate those guarantees and to accomplish that it is essential that all relevant and admissible evidence be produced. . . .

. . . A President's acknowledged need for confidentiality in the communications of his office is general in nature, whereas the constitutional need for production of relevant evidence in a criminal proceeding is specific and central to the fair adjudication of a particular criminal case in the administration of justice. Without access to specific facts a criminal prosecution may be totally frustrated. . . .

We conclude that when the ground for asserting privilege as to subpoenaed materials sought for use in a criminal trial is based only on the generalized interest in confidentiality, it cannot prevail over the fundamental demands of due process of law in the fair administration of criminal justice. The generalized assertion of privilege must yield to the demonstrated, specific need for evidence in a pending criminal trial. . . .

Affirmed

Rostker v. Goldberg
453 U.S. 57, 101 S.Ct. 2646, 69 L.Ed. 2d 478 (1981)

(This case is reprinted in Chapter Twelve, beginning on page 517.)

Morrison v. Olson
56 U.S.L.W. 4835 (1988)

In 1982 two subcommittees of the House of Representatives directed the Environmental Protection Agency (EPA) to produce certain documents relating to the Superfund Law and the cleanup of toxic wastes. Theodore Olson at that time was assistant attorney general for the Office of Legal Counsel in the Department of Justice, Edward Schmults was deputy attorney general, and Carol Dinkins was the assistant attorney general for the Land and Resources Division. Acting on the advice of the Justice Department, President Reagan ordered Anne Burford, administrator of the EPA, to invoke executive privilege and to withhold particular documents. The House then held the administrator in contempt. In 1983 the Reagan administration granted the House limited access to the documents.

In 1984 the House Judiciary Committee investigated the Justice Department's role in the controversy over the documents. Olson was called to testify. In 1985 the Judiciary Committee issued a report suggesting that Olson had given false and misleading testimony to the committee and that Schmults and Dinkins had wrongfully withheld documents from the committee. The chair of the committee requested Attorney General Edwin Meese to appoint an independent counsel to investigate the allegations.

The Ethics in Government Act of 1978 provides for the appointment of an independent counsel to investigate and, if appropriate, to prosecute high-ranking officials of the executive branch for violation of federal criminal laws. Once appointed, an independent counsel is removable only for cause. Under the terms of the act, Meese conducted a preliminary investigation and applied to the Special Division of the Court of Appeals for the District of Columbia Circuit for an independent counsel to investigate Olson alone. The Special Division designated Alexia Morrison as independent counsel. When Morrison caused a grand jury to issue subpoenas to Olson, Schmults, and Dinkins, they moved to quash the subpoenas because the provision in the 1978 act authorizing an independent counsel was unconstitutional.

In 1987 the district court upheld the act. In 1988, a divided court of appeals reversed, concluding (1) that the independent counsel is not an "inferior officer" in terms of the appointments clause, (2) that the delegation of powers to the Special Division violated the limitations of Article III, (3) that the act's restrictions on the attorney general's power to remove an independent counsel infringed the separation of powers, and (4) that the act violated the executive's duty to "take care that the Laws be faithfully executed." Majority: Rehnquist, Blackmun, Brennan, Marshall, O'Connor, Stevens, White. Dissenting: Scalia. Not participating: Kennedy.

CHIEF JUSTICE REHNQUIST delivered the opinion of the Court.

This case presents us with a challenge to the independent counsel provisions of the Ethics in Government Act of 1978. . . . We hold today that these provisions of the Act do not violate the Appointments Clause of the Constitution, Art. II, §2, cl. 2, or the limitations of Article III, nor do they impermissibly interfere with the President's authority under Article II in violation of the constitutional principle of separation of powers. . . .

The Appointments Clause of Article II reads as follows:

"[The President] shall nominate, and by and with the Advice and Consent of the Senate, shall appoint Ambassadors, other public Ministers and Consuls, Judges of the supreme Court, and all other Officers of the United States, whose Appointments are not herein otherwise provided for, and which shall be established by Law: but the Congress may by Law vest the Appointment of such inferior Officers, as they think proper, in the President alone, in the Courts of Law, or in the Heads of Departments.". . .

First, appellant is subject to removal by a higher Executive Branch official. Although appellant may not be "subordinate" to the Attorney General (and the President) insofar as she possesses a degree of independent discretion to exercise the powers delegated to her under the Act, the fact that she can be removed by the Attorney General indicates that she is to some degree "inferior" in rank and authority. Second, appellant is empowered by the Act to perform only certain, limited duties. . . .

Third, appellant's office is limited in jurisdiction. Not only is the Act itself restricted in applicability to certain federal officials suspected of certain serious federal crimes, but an independent counsel can only act within the scope of the jurisdiction that has been granted by the Special Division pursuant to a request by the Attorney General. Finally, appellant's office is limited in tenure. There is concededly no time limit on the appointment of a particular counsel. Nonetheless, the office of independent counsel is "temporary" in the sense that an independent counsel is appointed essentially to accomplish a single task, and when that task is over the office is terminated, either by the counsel herself or by action of the Special Division. . . .

This does not, however, end our inquiry under the Appointments Clause. Appellees argue that even if appellant is an "inferior" officer, the Clause does not empower Congress to place the power to appoint such an officer outside the Executive Branch. They contend that the Clause does not contemplate congressional authorization of "interbranch appointments," in which an officer of one branch is appointed by officers of another branch. The relevant language of the Appointments Clause is worth repeating. It reads: " . . . but the Congress may by Law vest the Appointment of such inferior Officers, as they think proper, in the President alone, in the courts of Law, or in the Heads of Departments." On its face, the language of this "excepting clause" admits of no limitation on interbranch appointments. . . .

We do not mean to say that Congress' power to provide for interbranch appointments of "inferior officers" is unlimited. In addition to separation of powers concerns, which would arise if such provisions for appointment had the potential to impair the constitutional functions assigned to one of the branches . . . Congress' decision to vest the appointment power in the courts would be improper if there was some "incongruity" between the functions normally performed by the courts and the performance of their duty to appoint. . . .

Congress of course was concerned when it created the office of independent counsel with the conflicts of interest that could arise in situations when the Executive Branch is called upon to investigate its own high-ranking officers. If it were to remove the appointing authority from the Executive Branch, the most logical place to put it was in the Judicial Branch. In the light of the Act's provision making the judges of the Special Division ineligible to participate in any matters relating to an independent counsel they have appointed, we do not think that appointment of the independent counsels by the court runs afoul of the constitutional limitation on "incongruous" interbranch appointments.

Appellees next contend that the powers vested in the Special Division by the Act conflict with Article III of the Constitution. We have long recognized that by the express provision of Article III, the judicial power of the United States is limited to "Cases" and "Controversies." As a general rule, we have broadly stated that "executive or administrative duties of a nonjudicial nature may not be imposed on judges holding office under Art. III of the Constitution.". . .

Most importantly, the Act vests in the Special Division the power to choose who will serve as independent counsel and the power to define his or her jurisdiction. Clearly, once it is accepted that the Appointments Clause gives Congress the power to vest the appointment of officials such as the independent counsel in the "courts of Law," there can be no Article III objection to the Special Division's exercise of that power, as the power itself derives from the Appointments Clause, a source of authority for judicial action that is independent of Article III. . . .

This said, we do not think that Congress may give the Division *unlimited* discretion to determine the independent counsel's jurisdiction. In order for the Division's definition of the counsel's jurisdiction to be truly "incidental" to its power to appoint, the jurisdiction that the court decides upon must be demonstrably related to the factual circumstances that gave rise to the Attorney General's investigation and request for the appointment of the independent counsel in the particular case. . . .

We now turn to consider whether the Act is invalid under the constitutional principle of separation of powers. Two related issues must be addressed: The first is whether the provision of the Act restricting the Attorney General's power to remove the independent counsel to only those instances in which he can show "good cause," taken by itself, impermissibly interferes with the President's exercise of his constitutionally appointed functions. The second is whether, taken as a whole, the Act violates the separation of powers by reducing the President's ability to control the prosecutorial powers wielded by the independent counsel.

Two Terms ago we had occasion to consider whether it was consistent with the separation of powers for Congress to pass a statute that authorized a government official who is removable only by Congress to participate in what we found to be "executive powers." We held in *Bowsher* [v. *Synar*] that "Congress cannot reserve for itself the power of removal of an officer charged with the execution of the laws except by impeachment." A primary antecedent for this ruling was our 1925 decision in *Myers v. United States*. . . .

Unlike both *Bowsher* and *Myers,* this case does not involve an attempt by Congress itself to gain a role in the removal of executive officials other than its established powers of impeachment and conviction. The Act instead puts the removal power squarely in the hands of the Executive Branch; an independent counsel may be removed from office, "only by the personal action of the Attorney General, and only for good cause." There is no requirement of congressional approval of the Attorney General's removal decision, though the decision is subject to judicial review. In our view, the removal provisions of the Act make this case more analogous to *Humphrey's Executor v. United States*. . . .

At the other end of the spectrum from *Myers,* the characterization of the agencies in *Humphrey's Executor* . . . as "quasi-legislative" or "quasi-judicial" in large part reflected our judgment that it was not essential to the President's proper execution of his Article II powers that these agencies be headed up by individuals who were removable at will. We do not mean to suggest that an analysis of the functions served by the officials at issue is irrelevant. But the real question is whether the removal restrictions are of such a nature that they impede the President's ability to perform his constitutional duty, and the functions of the officials in question must be analyzed in that light. . . .

The final question to be addressed is whether the Act taken as a whole, violates the principle of separation of powers by unduly interfering with the role of the Executive Branch. . . .

We observe first that this case does not involve an attempt by Congress to increase its own powers at the expense of the Executive Branch. . . .

Similarly, we do not think that the Act works any *judicial* usurpation of properly executive functions. . . .

Finally, we do not think that the Act "impermissibly undermine[s]" the powers of the Executive Branch, or "disrupts the proper balance between the coordinate branches [by] prevent[ing] the Executive Branch from accomplishing its constitutionally assigned functions." It is undeniable that the Act reduces the amount of control or supervision that the Attorney General and, through him, the President exercises over the investigation and prosecution of a certain class of alleged criminal activity. The Attorney General is not allowed to appoint the individual of his choice; he does not determine the counsel's jurisdiction; and his power to remove a counsel is limited. Nonetheless, the Act does give the Attorney General several means of supervising or controlling the prosecutorial powers that may be wielded by an independent counsel. Most importantly, the Attorney General retains the power to remove the counsel for "good cause," a power that we have already concluded provides the Executive with substantial ability to ensure that the laws are "faithfully executed" by an independent counsel. No independent counsel may be appointed without a specific request by the Attorney General, and the Attorney General's decision not to request appointment if he finds "no reasonable grounds to believe that further investigation is warranted" is committed to his unreviewable discretion. . . .

In sum, we conclude today that it does not violate the Appointments Clause for Congress to vest the appointment of independent counsels in the Special Division; that the powers exercised by the Special Division under the Act do not violate Article III; and that the Act does not violate the separation of powers principle by impermissibly interfering with the functions of the Executive Branch. The decision of the Court of Appeals is therefore

Reversed.

JUSTICE SCALIA, dissenting. . . .

The framers of the Federal Constitution . . . viewed the principle of separation of powers as the absolutely central guarantee of a just government. . . .

That is what this suit is about. Power. The allocation of power among Congress, the President and the courts in such fashion as to preserve the equilibrium the Constitution sought to establish— so that "a gradual concentration of the several powers in the same department" can effectively be resisted. Frequently an issue of this sort will come before the Court clad, so to speak, in sheep's clothing: the potential of the asserted principle to effect important change in the equilibrium of power is not immediately evident and must be discerned by a careful and perceptive analysis. But this wolf comes as a wolf. . . .

If to describe this case is not to decide it, the concept of a government of separate and coordinate powers no longer has meaning. The Court devotes most of its attention to such relatively technical details as the Appointments Clause and the removal power, addressing briefly and only at the end of its opinion the separation of powers. . . . I think that has it backwards. . . .

The Court concedes that "[t]here is no real dispute that the functions performed by the independent counsel are 'executive,' " though it qualifies that concession by adding "in the sense that they are 'law enforcement' functions that typically have been undertaken by officials within the Executive Branch." The qualifier adds nothing but atmosphere. In what *other* sense can one identify "the executive Power" that is supposed to be vested in the President (unless it includes everything the Executive Branch is given to do) *except* by reference to what has always and everywhere—if conducted by Government at all—been conducted never by the legislature, never by the courts, and always by the executive. There is no possible doubt that the independent counsel's functions fit this description. She is vested with the "full power and independent authority to exercise all *investigative and prosecutorial* functions and powers of the Department of Justice [and] the Attorney General." Governmental investigation and prosecution of crimes is a quintessentially executive function.

As for the . . . question, whether the statute before us deprives the President of exclusive control over that quintessentially executive activity: The Court does not, and could not possibly, assert that it does not. That is indeed the whole object of the statute. Instead, the Court points out that the President, through his Attorney General, has at least *some* control. That concession is alone enough to invalidate the statute, but I cannot refrain from pointing out that the Court greatly exaggerates the extent of that "some" presidential control. "Most importan[t]" among these controls, the Court asserts, is the Attorney General's "power to remove the counsel for 'good cause.' " This is somewhat like referring to shackles as an effective means of locomotion. As we recognized in *Humphrey's Executor v. United States*—indeed, what *Humphrey's Executor* was all about—limiting removal power to

"good cause" is an impediment to, not an effective grant of, presidential control. We said that limitation was necessary with respect to members of the Federal Trade Commission, which we found to be "an agency of the legislative and judicial departments," and "wholly disconnected from the executive department," because "it is quite evident that one who holds his office only during the pleasure of another, cannot be depended upon to maintain an attitude of independence against the latter's will." What we in *Humphrey's Executor* found to be a means of eliminating presidential control, the Court today considers the "most importan[t]" means of assuring presidential control. Congress, of course, operated under no such illusion when it enacted this statute, describing the "good cause" limitation as "protecting the independent counsel's ability to act independently of the President's direct control" since it permits removal only for "misconduct." . . .

Finally, the Court points out that the Act directs the independent counsel to abide by general Justice Department policy, except when not "possible." The exception alone shows this to be an empty promise. Even without that, however, one would be hard put to come up with many investigative or prosecutorial "policies" (other than those imposed by the Constitution or by Congress through law) that are absolute. Almost all investigative and prosecutorial decisions—including the ultimate decision whether, after a technical violation of the law has been found, prosecution is warranted—involve the balancing of innumerable legal and practical considerations. . . .

[This] is the very essence of prosecutorial discretion. To take this away is to remove the core of the prosecutorial function, and not merely "some" presidential control. . . .

It is not for us to determine, and we have never presumed to determine, how much of the purely executive powers of government must be within the full control of the President. The Constitution prescribes that they *all* are. . . .

While the separation of powers may prevent us from righting every wrong, it does so in order to ensure that we do not lose liberty. The checks against any Branch's abuse of its exclusive powers are twofold: First, retaliation by one of the other Branch's use of *its* exclusive powers: Congress, for example, can impeach the Executive who willfully fails to enforce the laws; the Executive can decline to prosecute under unconstitutional statutes; and the courts can dismiss malicious prosecutions. Second, and ultimately, there is the political check that the people will replace those in the political branches . . . who are guilty of abuse. Political pressures produced special prosecutors—for Teapot Dome and for Watergate, for example—long before this statute created the independent counsel. . . .

. . . [T]he basic separation-of-powers principles I have discussed are what give life and content to our jurisprudence concerning the President's power to appoint and remove officers. . . .

. . . I think it preferable to look to the text of the Constitution and the division of power that it establishes. These demonstrate, I think, that the independent counsel is not an inferior officer because she is not *subordinate* to any officer in the Executive Branch (indeed, not even to the President). . . .

To be sure, it is not a *sufficient* condition for "inferior" officer status that one be subordinate to a principal officer. . . . But it is surely a *necessary* condition for inferior officer status that the officer be subordinate to another officer. . . .

Since our 1935 decision in *Humphrey's Executor v. United States* which was considered by many at the time the product of an activist, anti-New Deal court bent on reducing the power of President Franklin Roosevelt—it has been established that the line of permissible restriction upon removal of principal officers lies at the point at which the powers exercised by those officers are no longer purely executive. . . . By its short-sighted action today, I fear the Court has permanently encumbered the Republic with an institution that will do it great harm.

Worse than what it has done, however, is the manner in which it has done it. A government of laws means a government of rules. Today's decision on the basic issue of fragmentation of executive power is ungoverned by rule, and hence ungoverned by law. It extends into the very heart of our most significant constitutional function the "totality of the circumstances" mode of analysis that this Court has in recent years become fond of. Taking all things into account, we conclude that the power taken away from the President here is not really *too* much. . . .

The ad hoc approach to constitutional adjudication has real attraction, even apart from its work-saving potential. It is guaranteed to produce a result, in every case, that will make a majority of the Court happy with the law. The law is, by definition, precisely what the majority thinks, taking all things into account, it *ought* to be. I prefer to rely upon the judgment of the wise men who constructed our system, and of the people who approved it, and of two centuries of history that have shown it to be sound. Like it or not, that judgment says, quite plainly, that "[t]he executive Power shall be vested in a President of the United States."

War Powers Resolution
87 Stat. 555 (1973)

A peace accord to end American military involvement in Vietnam was signed in January 1973 following several years of domestic discontent over the nation's Indochina policy. After U.S. bombing of Cambodia later in the year, Congress passed the War Powers Resolution in the fall of 1973 in an attempt to provide a legal check on the president's authority to commit American forces abroad without congressional approval. President Richard Nixon vetoed the resolution on October 24, calling it both "dangerous" and "unconstitutional." By a vote of 284 to 135 (four more than the required two-thirds margin) in the House and 75 to 18 in the Senate, Congress overrode

Nixon's veto on November 7, 1973. Eighty-six of the 189 Republican representatives and 25 of the 40 Republican senators sided against the president. Nixon's political troubles over Watergate probably contributed to the successful congressional effort to thwart his veto.

Resolved by the Senate and House of Representatives of the United States of America in Congress assembled, That: . . .

Sec. 2. (a) It is the purpose of this joint resolution to fulfill the intent of the framers of the Constitution of the United States and insure that the collective judgment of both the Congress and the President will apply to the introduction of United States Armed Forces into hostilities, or into situations where imminent involvement in hostilities is clearly indicated by the circumstances, and to the continued use of such forces in hostilities or in such situations.

(b) Under article I, section 8, of the Constitution, it is specifically provided that the Congress shall have the power to make all laws necessary and proper for carrying into execution, not only its own powers but also all other powers vested by the Constitution in the Government of the United States, or in any department or officer thereof.

(c) The constitutional powers of the President as Commander-in-Chief to introduce United States Armed Forces into hostilities, or into situations where imminent involvement in hostilities is clearly indicated by the circumstances, are exercised only pursuant to (1) a declaration of war, (2) specific statutory authorization, or (3) a national emergency created by attack upon the United States, its territories or possessions, or its armed forces.

Sec. 3. The President in every possible instance shall consult with Congress before introducing United States Armed Forces into hostilities or into situations where imminent involvement in hostilities is clearly indicated by the circumstances, and after every such introduction shall consult regularly with the Congress until United States Armed Forces are no longer engaged in hostilities or have been removed from such situations.

Sec. 4. (a) In the absence of a declaration of war, in any case in which United States Armed Forces are introduced—

(1) into hostilities or into situations where imminent involvement in hostilities is clearly indicated by the circumstances;

(2) into the territory, airspace or waters of a foreign nation, while equipped for combat, except for deployments which relate solely to supply, replacement, repair, or training of such forces; or

(3) in numbers which substantially enlarge United States Armed Forces equipped for combat already located in a foreign nation;

The President shall submit within 48 hours to the Speaker of the House of Representatives and to the President pro tempore of the Senate a report, in writing, setting forth—

(A) the circumstances necessitating the introduction of United States Armed Forces;

(B) the constitutional and legislative authority under which such introduction took place; and

(C) the estimated scope and duration of the hostilities or involvement.

(b) The President shall provide such other information as the Congress may request in the fulfillment of its constitutional responsibilities with respect to committing the Nation to war and to the use of United States Armed Forces abroad.

(c) Whenever United States Armed Forces are introduced into hostilities or into any situation described in subsection (a) of this section, the President shall, so long as such armed forces continue to be engaged in such hostilities or situation, report to the Congress periodically on the status of such hostilities or situation as well as on the scope and duration of such hostilities or situation, but in no event shall he report to the Congress less often than once every six months.

Sec. 5. (a) Each report submitted pursuant to section 4(a)(1) shall be transmitted to the Speaker of the House of Representatives and to the President pro tempore of the Senate on the same calendar day. Each report so transmitted shall be referred to the Committee on Foreign Affairs of the House of Representatives and to the Committee on Foreign Relations of the Senate for appropriate action. If, when the report is transmitted, the Congress has adjourned sine die or has adjourned for any period in excess of three calendar days, the Speaker of the House of Representatives and the President pro tempore of the Senate, if they deem it advisable (or if petitioned by at least 30 percent of the membership of their respective Houses) shall jointly request the President to convene Congress in order that it may consider the report and take appropriate action pursuant to this section.

(b) Within sixty calendar days after a report is submitted or is required to be submitted pursuant to section 4(a)(1), whichever is earlier, the President shall terminate any use of United States Armed Forces with respect to which such report was submitted (or required to be submitted), unless the Congress (1) has declared war or has enacted a specific authorization for such use of United States Armed Forces, (2) has extended by law such sixty-day period, or (3) is physically unable to meet as a result of an armed attack upon the United States. Such sixty-day period shall be extended for not more than an additional thirty days if the President determines and certifies to the Congress in writing that unavoidable military necessity respecting the safety of United States Armed Forces requires the continued use of such armed forces in the course of bringing about a prompt removal of such forces.

(c) Notwithstanding subsection (b), at any time that United States Armed Forces are engaged in hostilities outside the territory of the United States, its possessions and territories without a declaration of war or specific statutory authorization, such forces shall be removed by the President if the Congress so directs by concurrent resolution.

[Sections 6 and 7, dealing with congressional consideration of resolutions introduced pursuant to sections 5(b) and 5(c), are omitted.]

Sec. 8. (a) Authority to introduce United States Armed Forces into hostilities or into situations wherein involvement in hostilities is clearly indicated by the circumstances shall not be inferred—

(1) from any provision of law (whether or not in effect before the date of the enactment of this joint resolution), including any provision contained in any appropriation Act, unless such provision specifically authorizes the introduction of United States Armed Forces into hostilities or into such situations and states that it is intended to constitute specific statutory authorization within the meaning of this joint resolution; or

(2) from any treaty heretofore or hereafter ratified unless such treaty is implemented by legislation specifically authorizing the introduction of United States Armed Forces into hostilities or into such situations and stating that it is intended to constitute specific statutory authorization within the meaning of this joint resolution.

(b) Nothing in this joint resolution shall be construed to require any further specific statutory authorization to permit members of United States Armed Forces to participate jointly with members of the armed forces of one or more foreign countries in the headquarters operations of high-level military commands which were established prior to the date of enactment of this joint resolution and pursuant to the United Nations Charter or any treaty ratified by the United States prior to such date.

(c) For purposes of this joint resolution, the term "introduction of United States Armed Forces" includes the assignment of members of such armed forces to command, coordinate, participate in the movement of, or accompany the regular or irregular military forces of any foreign country or government when such military forces are engaged, or there exists an imminent threat that such forces will become engaged, in hostilities.

(d) Nothing in this joint resolution—

(1) is intended to alter the constitutional authority of the Congress or of the President, or the provisions of existing treaties; or

(2) shall be construed as granting any authority to the President with respect to the introduction of United States Armed Forces into hostilities or into situations wherein involvement in hostilities is clearly indicated by the circumstances which authority he would not have had in the absence of this joint resolution.

Sec. 9. If any provision of this joint resolution or the application thereof to any person or circumstance is held invalid, the remainder of the joint resolution and the application of such provision to any other person or circumstance shall not be affected thereby.

Sec. 10. This joint resolution shall take effect on the date of its enactment.

FOUR

Federalism

The Constitution, in all its provisions, looks to an indestructible Union, composed of indestructible States.

—CHIEF JUSTICE SALMON P. CHASE (1869)

Although judicial review has been considered America's unique contribution to political science, it may be that federalism will continue to be of greater influence on other nations and of unending concern at home. Unfortunately for those who look upon federalism as the key to world order under law, our history—unless one takes the long view—is not reassuring.

The United States is governed by *federalism*—that is, a dual system in which government powers are distributed between central (national) and local (state) authorities. The reasons for the adoption of such a government are both historical and rational. During the revolutionary period the states regarded themselves as independent sovereignties. Under the Articles of Confederation, little of their power over internal affairs was surrendered to the Continental Congress. In the face of proved inability of the Confederation to cope with the problems confronting it, local patriotism had to yield.

When the Constitutional Convention met, compromise between the advocates of a strong central government and supporters of states' rights was necessary. Federalism fitted into Madison's basic requirement, reflecting his purpose, as stated in *The Federalist*, No. 51, to so contrive "the interior structure of the government as that its several constituent parts may, by their mutual relations, be the means of keeping each other in their proper places." Hamilton, in *The Federalist*, No. 23, listed four chief purposes to be served by union: common defense, public peace, regulation of commerce, and foreign relations. General agreement that these objectives required unified government drew together representatives of small and large states alike.

SOURCES OF CONTENTION

One point on which the nationalists at the Philadelphia Convention remained firm was their determination that no precise line should be drawn dividing national power from state power. The powers of the national government were enumerated but not defined. Alert to possible inroads on the states, Hugh Williamson of North Carolina objected that the effect might be to "restrain the States from regulating their internal affairs." Elbridge Gerry objected that indefinite power in the central authority might "enslave the States." Hamilton, Madison, and James Wilson would not budge, contending that a line dividing state and national power would unduly weaken national authority. "When we come near the line," Wilson explained, "it cannot be found. . . . A discretion must be left on one side or the other. . . . Will it not be most safely lodged on the side of the National Government? . . . What danger is there that the whole will unnecessarily sacrifice a part? But reverse the case, and leave the whole at the mercy of each part, and will not the general interest be continually sacrificed to local interests?"

Mincing no words, Wilson declared flatly that national power could not truly be limited if it were to reach national objects. "We find on an examination of all its parts," he said, "that the objects of this government are such as extend beyond the bounds of the particular States. This is the line of distinction between this government and the particular State governments." This unequivocal avowal of *national supremacy* from one whom President Washington would shortly appoint to the Supreme Court evoked from opponents of the Constitution an expected query: "[W]here is the bill of rights which shall check the power of this congress, which shall say, *thus far shall ye come and no farther?* The safety of the people depends on a bill of rights."

In the First Congress, Madison and others made good on their promise to make the addition of a bill of rights one of the first orders of business for the new government. (Documents relating to the development of a bill of rights are reprinted in Chapter Nine.) The *Antifederalists,* those who had opposed ratification in 1787–1788, had conjured up the image of the central government as a colossus, determined to swallow defenseless states. To quiet their fears, Madison included among the amendments submitted on June 8, 1789, the one that became the Tenth: "The powers not delegated by this constitution, nor prohibited by it to the States, are reserved to the States respectively, or to the people."

Madison was on record shortly before the Convention as having said that the states should be retained insofar as they could be "subordinately useful." Equally well known was Madison's early aversion to including a bill of rights. "It was obviously and self-evidently the case," Madison had insisted, "that every thing not granted is reserved." Now with an amendment on the floor he resisted efforts to convert it into a substantive check on national power. "It was impossible," Madison told Congress, "to confine a government to the exercise of express powers; there must necessarily be admitted powers by implication, unless the Constitution descended to recount every minutia."

What Madison said on the floor of Congress about the Tenth Amendment bears out Chief Justice Marshall's observation in *McCulloch* v. *Maryland.* It was designed, Marshall said, "for the purpose of quieting excessive jealousy which had been excited." In the House of Representatives debates, Madison stated his position tersely on August 15, 1789: "While I approve of these amendments [the Ninth and Tenth] I should oppose the consideration at this time of such as are likely to change the principles of the government." And when, three days later, Thomas Tucker proposed to add the word *expressly* to the proposed Tenth Amendment, making it read, "the powers not *expressly* delegated by this Constitution,"

Madison objected. "It was impossible," he explained, "to confine a Government to the exercise of express powers; there must necessarily be admitted powers by implication." Tucker's motion was defeated. Gerry's effort of August 21, to get the word *expressly* inserted, suffered the same fate, the vote being 32 to 17.

The unavailing struggle to give meaning to the Tenth Amendment underscores the conclusion that for many Antifederalists, *states'* rights weighed more heavily than their concern for *personal* rights. This would explain why so many Antifederalists were disappointed with the amendments as they emerged from Congress. To William Grayson, for one, the amendments were "so mutilated and gutted that in fact they are good for nothing. . . ." Richard Henry Lee still saw "the most essential danger" arising from the Constitution's "tendency to a consolidated government, instead of a union of Confederated States. . . ." Instead of "substantial amendments," complained South Carolina's Pierce Butler, here were a "few milk-and-water amendments . . . such as liberty of conscience, a free press, and one or two general things already well secured." Georgia's Congressman Jackson agreed: the amendments were not worth "a pinch of salt." Antifederalists had failed to make the Tenth Amendment a limit on national power.

The distribution of powers agreed on in the Convention, and the reassurance given the states by the Ninth and Tenth Amendments, did not preclude conflict. The struggle continued in politics and in the courts, and when prolonged debate and bitter controversy failed to yield a conclusive verdict, the contestants carried this baffling issue of political and constitutional theory to the battlefield in 1861 for settlement by the arbitrament of the sword. Even this holocaust was not conclusive.

The problem of determining the extent of national and state power and of resolving the conflicts between the two centers of authority was ultimately left to the Supreme Court. One of the ironies of American constitutional history is that the Supreme Court achieved, on occasion, through interpretation what the First Congress did not—insertion of the word *expressly* in the Tenth Amendment.

NATURE OF NATIONAL AUTHORITY

Delegated and Reserved Powers. Theoretically, the powers of the national government are limited to those delegated to it by the Constitution, expressly or by implication; the powers "not delegated . . . nor prohibited by it to the states" are "reserved to the states respectively or to the people" (Tenth Amendment).

Express and Implied Powers. As a second dimension, the national government may use any and all means to give effect to any power specifically granted. This doctrine of implied powers finds its verbal basis in the power granted to Congress to make all laws necessary and proper for carrying into execution those powers expressly delegated to it (Art. I, Sec. 8, Cl. 18). No new or additional powers are granted by the "necessary and proper" clause; it merely enables the federal government to maintain its supremacy in the limited sphere of its activity. The supremacy clause in Article VI, Paragraph 2, the keystone of the federal system, supplies a third dimension of national power. It indicates that if the legitimate powers of state and nation conflict, that of the national government shall prevail.

Thus national power is of three dimensions: (1) the enumeration in which the grant of power is couched, (2) the discretionary choice of means that Congress has for carrying its enumerated powers into execution, (3) the fact of supremacy. Under this three-dimensional theory of national authority, no subject matter whatever is withdrawn from control or regulation by the United States simply because it also lies within the usual domain of state power. Since the Tenth Amendment merely asserts a truism—powers not delegated are reserved—the coexistence of state governments does not limit national power.

Resulting Powers. Resulting powers are derived by implication from the mass of delegated powers or from a group of them. Such powers include the taking of property by eminent domain for a purpose not specified in the Constitution, the power to carry into effect treaties entered into by the United States, the power to maintain the supremacy of the national government within its sphere of authority, and the power to control relations with the Indians.

Exclusive and Concurrent Powers. The powers of the national government may also be classified as exclusive or concurrent. Powers delegated to Congress by the Constitution are exclusive under the following conditions:

1. Where the right to exercise the power is made exclusive by express provision of the Constitution. Article I, Section 8, Clause 17, for example, gives Congress exclusive power over the District of Columbia and over property purchased from a state with the consent of the legislature.

2. Where one section of the Constitution grants an express power to Congress and another section prohibits the states from exercising a similar power. For example, Congress is given the power to coin money (Art. I, Sec. 8. Cl. 5), and the states are expressly prohibited from exercising such power (Art. I, Sec. 10, Cl. 1).

3. Where the power granted to Congress, though not in terms exclusive, is such that the exercise of a similar power by the states would be utterly incompatible with national power. In *Cooley* v. *Board of Wardens* (1851) (see Chapter Five), the Court admitted the existence of a concurrent power to control interstate commerce but limited state power to matters of local concern. Where the subject matter is national in scope and requires uniform legislative treatment, such as the federal government alone can provide, the power of Congress is exclusive. "Exclusive" is here used in a special sense, since the disability of the states arises not from the Constitution but from the nature of the subject matter to which the power is applied. Such power has been termed "latent concurrent power" since Congress may consent to its exercise by the state.

Exclusive and concurrent powers relate to preemption, discussed later in this chapter.

CONCEPTS OF FEDERALISM

As was inevitable, the formal distribution of powers between the national government and the states proved to be a subject of diverse interpretations. Those who strove to safeguard state sovereignty feared broad construction of national powers; many who viewed the continuance of state power as the enemy of national strength tended for tactical reasons to conceal their satisfaction with the increased scope of national authority.

The Federalism of John Marshall. As John Adams left the presidency, he installed John Marshall, a strong party man and an ardent nationalist, as chief justice. Marshall read into our constitutional law a concept of federalism that magnified national at the expense of state power. Important precedents existed to aid his pronationalist labors. Besides the House of Representatives debates out of which the Tenth Amendment emerged, there was the 1793 case of *Chisholm* v. *Georgia* in which state sovereignty pretensions were denied by a vote of 4 to 1.

The Court's decision holding the state of Georgia amenable to the jurisdiction of the national judiciary and suable by a citizen of another state in the federal courts provoked prompt and largely unfavorable reaction and prompted immediate steps toward constitutional amendment. On January 8, 1798, three years before Marshall was appointed chief justice, the Eleventh Amendment became a part of the Constitution, overturning *Chisholm*. Nearly a decade before Chief Justice Marshall's assertion of judicial review in *Marbury* v. *Madison* (see Chapter Two) the Court's version of the Constitution was equated with the document itself.

Marshall's tenure (1801–1835), covering a period in which his political enemies dominated the political branches of the government, made his fervent nationalism stand out even more dramatically than if he had represented merely the judicial element in a broad nationalist movement. It was not until 1819, however, that the chief justice found himself face to face with the dreaded issue of "clashing sovereignties" *(McCulloch* v. *Maryland)*. The state of Maryland had levied a tax on the Second Bank of the United States, raising questions not only about the powers of Congress to charter a bank but also about the place of the states in the federal system. The Constitution, Marshall argued, was "ordained and established in the name of the people"; it was not a compact among states, as counsel for Maryland contended. Nor did it result from the action of the people of the states or of their governments. The Constitution, he declared, altered the former position of the states as sovereign entities. Unlike the Congress under the Articles of Confederation, the national government operated directly on individuals. Within the sphere of its enumerated powers Congress was supreme.

Furthermore, the *necessary and proper clause* gave Congress a discretionary choice of means for implementing the granted powers, and the Tenth Amendment served in no way to limit this freedom of selection. In reply to the argument that the taxing power was reserved to the states by the Tenth Amendment, and hence could operate even against a legitimate national instrumentality, Marshall went out of his way to deny state power to tax national instrumentalities. Thus, Marshall established not only the proposition that national powers must be liberally construed but also the equally decisive principle that the Tenth Amendment does not create in the states an independent limitation on such authority.

Two years later, in *Cohens* v. *Virginia* (1821), the chief justice refuted the argument that the highest state court had a power coequal with that of the Supreme Court in interpreting and applying the Constitution. "The American States," he said, "as well as the American People, have believed a close and firm Union to be essential to their liberty, and to their happiness." As a consequence the people had surrendered portions of state sovereignty to the national government. Finally, the supremacy clause and the principle of judicial review required that final decisions on constitutional issues "arising" in the state courts be made only by the Supreme Court.

Albert J. Beveridge described Marshall's opinion as "one of the strongest and most enduring strands of that mighty cable woven to hold the American people together as a united and imperishable nation." Jefferson condemned it as indicating judicial determination "to undermine the foundations of our confederated fabric." Denouncing the justices as a "subtle corps of sappers and miners constantly working underground," Jefferson charged that they had transformed the federal system into "a general and supreme one alone."

Marshall's doctrine of national supremacy built on the proposition that the central government and states confront each other in the relationship of superior and subordinate— if the exercise of Congress's enumerated powers be legitimate, the fact that their exercise encroaches on the states' traditional authority is of no significance. Finally, the Court's duty as arbiter of the federal system is not to preserve state sovereignty but to protect national power against state encroachments. As to federalism, the Court functions not as an umpire but as an agency of national authority. For Marshall, as for Madison in 1788, the principal danger of the federal system lay in erosive state action. Effective political limitations existed against national efforts to impinge on state power, but only the Supreme Court could peacefully restrain state action from infringing on the authority of the national government.

Marshall's doctrine of federalism did not go unchallenged. In a review of Kent's

Commentaries in 1828, Hugh Swinton Legaré, later attorney general and secretary of state under President Tyler, commented, "The government has been fundamentally altered by the progress of opinion—that instead of being any longer one of enumerated powers and a circumscribed sphere, as it was beyond all doubt intended to be, it knows absolutely no bounds but the will of a majority of Congress . . . and threatens in the course of a few years, to control in the most offensive and despotic manner, all the pursuits, the interests, the opinions and the conduct of men." "That argument," Legaré concluded, "cannot be sound which necessarily converts a government of enumerated into one of indefinite powers, and a confederacy of republics into a gigantic and consolidated empire." As if to answer these fears, Marshall's successor, Roger Brooke Taney of Maryland, strove valiantly during his long tenure (1836–1864) to redefine federalism in terms more favorable to state power.

Taney and Dual Federalism. The concept of federalism common to Marshall's critics insisted that the Constitution was a compact of sovereign states, not an ordinance of the people. It was the view that the national government and the states face each other as equals across a precise constitutional line defining their respective jurisdictions. This concept of national-state equality had been the basis of Virginia's anarchical arguments in *Cohens* v. *Virginia*. It was argued that state courts had a power equal with that of the United States Supreme Court to interpret and apply the Constitution; and that in all cases "arising" in their courts, state judges had authority to interpret, with finality, the Constitution and the United States laws and treaties made under its authority.

Accepting the basic creed of nation-state equality, the Taney Court stripped it of its anarchic implications. Within the powers reserved by the Tenth Amendment the states were sovereign, but final authority to determine the scope of state powers rested with the national judiciary, an arbitrator standing aloof from the sovereign pretensions of both nation and states. "This judicial power [Taney wrote in *Ableman* v. *Booth*, 1859] was justly regarded as indispensable, not merely to maintain the supremacy of the laws of the United States, but also to guard the states from any encroachment upon their reserved rights by the general government. . . . So long . . . as this Constitution shall endure, this tribunal must exist with it, deciding in the peaceful forum of judicial proceeding the angry and irritating controversies between sovereignties, which in other countries have been determined by the arbitrament of force." Marshall and Taney were agreed on one essential point: The Supreme Court provided a forum for keeping "revolution" within peaceful bounds. For John Marshall's concept of national supremacy, the Taney Court substituted a theory of federal equilibrium, later called "dual sovereignty."

Taney's passionate concern for states' rights should not, however, obscure the fact that in the context of his times the state *police power* (see Chapter Eight) was the only available weapon with which government could face the pressing problems of the day. Taney called it "the power to *govern men and things.* . . ." In a period in which the national government was not yet prepared to deal realistically with economic and social problems, the theory of national supremacy had the effect of posing the unexercised commerce power of Congress or the contract clause as barriers to any government action. Taney's dual federalism in the period 1837–1855 enabled the states to deal experimentally with problems that the national government would not face until another half-century had elapsed.

Marshall headed the Court for 34 years, Taney for 28, leaving two official conceptions of federalism succeeding justices were free to apply as their inclinations or needs of the time dictated.

National Supremacy and Dual Federalism, 1864–1937. Chief Justice Chase's observation (*Texas* v. *White*, 1869) that the Constitution "in all its provisions, looks to an indestructible Union, composed of indestructible states" was not mere rhetoric. In a series of cases arising under the Civil War amendments and various laws designed to fasten national standards on state political and social systems, the Supreme Court displayed stubborn resistance to extreme theories of national supremacy (e.g. **Slaughterhouse Cases,** 1873; **Civil Rights Cases,** 1883.) As a corollary, the Court tended to regard state police power legislation with a generous eye *(Munn* v. *Illinois,* 1877). When state power ran into preferred judicial values, however, the Court did not hesitate to impose a constitutional check, especially after 1890 *(Lochner* v. *New York,* 1905). With national legislation, the Marshall and Taney theories of federalism were called into service alternately, depending on judicial agreement with the policy objectives Congress sought. Cases such as *Swift* v. *United States* (1905) and *Hoke* v. *United States* (1913), which dealt with meat packing and prostitution respectively, looked to Marshall. In contrast, decisions such as *Hammer* v. *Dagenhart* (1918) (involving child labor) looked to Taney.

Initially, it was said that the powers of the national government were "enumerated," those of the states "reserved." Beginning with Taney, this order of things began to change; the Tenth Amendment was turned upside down. Thanks to judicial review, Congress no longer enjoyed a discretionary choice of means for carrying its enumerated powers into execution. The justices ruled, for example, that there were certain subject matters "expressly" reserved to the states, and, therefore, beyond national control. These included manufacturing *(United States* v. *E. C. Knight,* 1895), employer-employee relations *(Hammer* v. *Dagenhart),* and agriculture *(United States* v. *Butler,* 1936). In these areas, the states enjoyed enumerated powers, not by the Constitution but by judicial mandate. The effect was to eliminate the second dimension of national power in these areas.*

This wavering fealty to national supremacy lay bare a truth in debates on constitutional theory: One concept of federalism or another was chosen because of the policies it would in turn encourage or discourage. Flirtation with Taney's "dual federalism" reached a peak during the 1930s, resulting in the Court-packing fight discussed in Chapter Six. As a consequence, the Court embraced Marshall's doctrine of national supremacy after 1937.

Independence of State and National Governments. In addition to the express limitations and prohibitions on national and state power contained in the Constitution, the justices have developed a considerable number of limitations stemming from federalism itself. Practical considerations involved in the maintenance of a federal form of government in which two sovereignties must operate side by side led to the adoption of the doctrine that neither government may interfere with the government functions of the other, nor with the agencies and officials through which those functions are executed.

The doctrine of *governmental immunity* had its inception in *McCulloch* v. *Maryland.* On the premise that "the power to tax involves the power to destroy," Chief Justice Marshall declared, "The states have no power, by taxation or otherwise, to retard, impede, burden, or in any manner control the operations of the constitutional laws enacted by Congress to carry into execution the powers vested in the general government."

Marshall's immunity doctrine was based on the theory of the supremacy of the national government in its sphere of activity. Regarded in this light, it is quite consistent with his attitude toward the role of the central government in a federal system. Accordingly, he denied emphatically the proposition that "every argument which would sustain the right of the general government to tax banks chartered by the states will equally sustain the right of the state to tax banks chartered by the general government." "The difference," he explained, "is that which always exists, and always must exist, between the action of the whole on the part, and the part on the whole—between the laws of a government declared

---

* Slaughterhouse Cases, *Munn* v. *Illinois,* and *Lochner* v. *New York* appear in Chapter Eight, Civil Rights Cases in Chapter Twelve, *United States* v. *Butler* in Chapter Seven, and *United States* v. *E. C. Knight* and *Hammer* v. *Dagenhart* in Chapter Six.

to be supreme, and those of a government, which, when in opposition to those laws, is not supreme."

In *Collector* v. *Day* (1871), ruling that the salaries of state court judges were immune from a national income tax, the justices established the doctrine of reciprocal immunity, based on the theory of the equality of national and state authority under the federal system. In time, the doctrine of reciprocal immunity was carried to such lengths as to deny both governments fruitful sources of taxation. *Graves* v. *New York* (1939) overruled *Day* so far as it recognized "an implied constitutional immunity from income taxation of salaries of officers or employees of the national or state government or their instrumentalities." The immunity doctrine as to the states had been qualified even earlier in *South Carolina* v. *United States* (1905), which upheld a federal tax on South Carolina's liquor-dispensing business. In **New York v. United States** (1946) the Court refused to distinguish South Carolina's traffic in liquor from New York's traffic in mineral water. As explained further in Chapter Seven, the Court has continued to make inroads on the reciprocal immunity doctrine. *South Carolina* v. *Baker* (1988) explicitly held that interest derived from municipal bonds is not immune from federal tax.

CONTEMPORARY FEDERALISM

With the exception of one decision discussed in the next section, the Supreme Court since 1937 has invalidated no act of Congress because of conflicting state prerogatives. This fact hardly means that federalism has ceased to be an important element in the constitutional system. For one thing, federalism shapes American politics and dictates the way many national policies are both developed and implemented. For another, the Court has continued to be wary of state laws that intrude on protected national interests.

Cooperative Federalism. Although conflicts between the two governments are sometimes avoided by maintaining the independence of each, there are times when cooperation is both desirable and necessary. The Constitution does not prevent such comity. The interaction of the two governments is most apparent where concurrent legislative power is exercised. Congress may choose to leave the states free to act, either by failing to legislate itself or by specifically consenting to state legislation in the field. On the other hand, state laws may be adopted outright, or Congress may provide that the operation of its law shall depend on or be qualified by existing state laws.

In the zeal to examine the niceties of legal conflict, the constructive purposes federalism may serve have sometimes been overlooked. Of greatest significance is the use of grants-in-aid by the national government to the states in initiating and administering welfare programs. The national government may appropriate funds in aid of such state activities as education, road building, and unemployment relief. It may grant such funds to the respective states on condition that a like amount or a specified proportion thereof be raised by them for similar purposes, or on condition that the funds be spent in ways specified by federal law. Changing views on the "proper" roles of nation and states amply demonstrate that federalism is now, as always, in flux. Moreover, what presidents, governors, and members of Congress and state legislatures have to say about their respective responsibilities is today as important as are judicial decisions in deciding what federalism, American style, means.

Preemption. The *supremacy clause* means that state statutes and constitutional provisions must give way when they conflict with the Constitution, treaties, and valid laws of the United States. The latter *preempt* or supersede the former. What is the outcome when state and national governments choose to legislate on the same topic without enacting conflicting laws? Sometimes Congress explicitly recognizes a concurrent state interest and so approves complementary state statutes. At other times, Congress explicitly rules out a role for the states. A more difficult issue arises when state policies do not conflict and there is no expressed congressional intent to welcome or to displace action by the states.

In *Pennsylvania* v. *Nelson* (1956), for example, the Court was confronted with a state statute criminalizing sedition against the United States. In the Smith Act of 1940 (see Chapter Ten) Congress had prohibited the same thing. In holding that the Smith Act preempted the Pennsylvania law, Chief Justice Warren noted three conditions that suggest supersession: First, the scheme of federal regulation is "so pervasive as to make reasonable the inference that Congress left no room for the states to supplement it. . . ." Second, the national interest is so dominant on a subject that the federal system must "be assumed to preclude enforcement of state laws on the same subject." Third, there is a danger of conflict between state and federal enforcement efforts. The presence of the three conditions in *Nelson* meant that Congress had presumably chosen to "occupy the field."

Regulation of nuclear power generation raises a preemption question too. For instance, California has imposed a moratorium on the certification of new nuclear power plants until a state commission finds that technology has been developed and approved for the permanent disposal of high-level nuclear waste. Electric utilities in the state argued that the Atomic Energy Act of 1954 and later federal legislation preempted the state's role in the nuclear field. In *Pacific Gas & Electric Co.* v. *Energy Resources Conservation & Development Commission* (1983), the Court found that Congress intended both state and national agencies to have a nuclear role. The latter possess complete control over safety and operation; the former may establish the need for additional generating capacity, decide the type of facility to be licensed, and exercise control over land use and rate setting. Viewing the state's interest as "economic" and not safety-related, the Court found no preemption, and the moratorium remained in force.

Judicial Federalism. Because a large part of the Supreme Court's docket each term consists of cases from state courts, the justices are active players in the game of federalism, not simply referees between state policies and the dictates of the Constitution and congressional acts. Interaction between state and federal courts is called *judicial federalism*. One dimension of judicial federalism involves Supreme Court review of state court decisions, which arguably rest on the state, not the national, constitution.

As explained in Chapter One, the Court may sit in judgment on the decisions of the highest court of each state when *federal questions* are involved. A case raises a federal question when the correct interpretation of a provision of the United States Constitution, a treaty, or a national statute is at issue, or when a state court decision resting on the state constitution or law results in a restriction of a federally protected right. A provision in the Constitution may not mean "less" in a state court than it does in a federal court. Once a federal question is present, the Court becomes the ultimate arbiter of its resolution. This rule encourages uniformity among the states. In contrast, the absence of a federal question encourages diversity because the final resolution of an issue rests with the individual states.

What happens when a state court gives greater protection to a right found in both state and federal constitutions and rests its decision on the former? Noninterference by the Supreme Court in such situations allows states to expand liberties that have parallel protections in both constitutions. The Supreme Court, however, will not accept a state court's interpretation of the federal Constitution at variance with its own, even if the state's decision is more protective of individual liberty. Nor will the Court accept as dispositive merely an assertion that the state ruling rests on an "adequate and independent state ground."

In *Michigan* v. *Long* (1983), the Supreme Court of Michigan decided that the police had infringed Long's rights when making a search of his car. But which rights? Those protected by the Fourth Amendment in the United States Constitution or those in parallel provisions in the Michigan constitution? Long argued that the Michigan court had relied mainly on the state constitution. The United States Supreme Court thought otherwise and concluded that the police had acted correctly under the Fourth Amendment. Justice O'Connor's opinion for the majority asserted a strong presumption of federal jurisdiction when a state court decision (1) "fairly appears to rest primarily on federal law," or to be "interwoven with federal law," and (2) when "the adequacy and independence of any possible state-law ground is not clear from the face of the opinion."

To be served, O'Connor said, were the twin goals of allowing states to develop their own jurisprudence "unimpeded by federal interference" and preserving "the integrity of federal law." Still, *Long* demonstrates that state judges must be wary in developing state jurisprudence in a federal system, lest they find themselves reversed on appeal because they cited federal court decisions and constitutional provisions.

THE TENTH AMENDMENT RESUSCITATED?

From nearly the beginning, the Tenth Amendment has had a prominent role in the story of American federalism, more prominent indeed than its authors imagined. For those who proposed it to the First Congress and for Chief Justice Marshall, it seemed little more than a device to soothe the concerns of those who feared unchecked national powers: All that is not given is retained. Its detractors in that First Congress agreed; for them the Tenth Amendment did too little. But it was not long before the Tenth Amendment became a rallying point for opposition to congressional action. Failing to defeat a measure on the merits, one attacked the policy by arguing that Congress had invaded the reserved powers of the states. As noted, this was the heart of "dual federalism," a doctrine the Supreme Court favored with varying enthusiasm from Chief Justice Taney's day until 1937.

In 1941, the Court made a complete about-face, with Justice Stone labeling the Tenth Amendment a "truism" in **United States** v. **Darby** (see Chapter Six). The unanimous position in *Darby* that the Tenth Amendment did not serve as an independent limit on national power seemed to mark both the end of an era and the demise of "dual federalism."

Indeed, it was not until 1976 that the Court once again used the Tenth Amendment as an effective check on national power. Five justices, led by William Rehnquist, declared in *National League of Cities* v. *Usery* that Congress could not extend the minimum wage and maximum hours provisions of the Fair Labor Standards Act to almost all employees of states and their political subdivisions. The majority noted the

> limits upon the power of Congress to override state sovereignty, even when exercising its otherwise plenary powers to tax or to regulate commerce. . . . [T]here are attributes of sovereignty attaching to every state government which may not be impaired by Congress, not because Congress may lack an affirmative grant of legislative authority to reach the matter, but because the Constitution prohibits it from exercising the authority in that manner.

In 1981, holding that the Surface Mining and Reclamation Act of 1977 did not violate the Tenth Amendment by usurping state authority over land use regulations, the Court laid out a three-prong test for applying *National League of Cities.*

> First, there must be a showing that the challenged statute regulates the "States as States." . . . Second, the federal regulation must address matters that are indisputably "attribute[s] of state

sovereignty." . . . And third, it must be apparent that the States' compliance with the federal law would directly impair their ability "to structure integral operations in areas of traditional governmental functions." *(Hodel* v. *Virginia Surface Mining and Reclamation Association,* 1981)

United Transportation Union v. *Long Island Rail Road Company* (1982) found all nine justices in rare agreement that application of the Railway Labor Act to a state-owned railroad was not prohibited by the Tenth Amendment. Under *Usery,* operating a railroad was not viewed as an integral part of traditional state activities, nor was there any significant undermining of "the role of states in our federal system." Even so, *National League of Cities* meant that virtually every congressional statute when applied to states was a candidate for constitutional attack before the Supreme Court. *National League of Cities* had placed the justices once more at the center of the lawmaking process, deciding what kinds of regulations were permissible and what kinds were not.

By 1985, the division on the Court seemed sharp between those whose fealty lay with Marshall's national supremacy and those who would breathe new life into the Tenth Amendment as a substantive check on congressional power. If *National League of Cities* prevailed, the Tenth Amendment would be anything but Stone's "truism" or Marshall's balm to quiet "the excessive state jealousies which had been excited." *National League of Cities* had restored the discretion the Court once enjoyed over the substance of a broad range of national policy.

In *Garcia* v. *San Antonio Metropolitan Transit Authority* (1985), the *National League of Cities* dissenters seemed to carry the day. At issue was the extent to which SAMTA could be subjected to the minimum-wage and overtime requirements of the Fair Labor Standards Act. Justice Blackmun, himself a reluctant member of the *National League of Cities* majority, announced for a bare majority of five that "the attempt to draw the boundaries of state regulatory immunity in terms of 'traditional governmental function' is not only unworkable but is inconsistent with established principles of federalism. . . . That case, accordingly, is overruled." Reaffirmed was a view of the Constitution in which "special restraints on federal power over the States inhered principally in the workings of the National Government itself, rather than in discrete limitations on the objects of federal authority." The "basic limit on the federal commerce power" would come "through state participation in federal governmental action" and the "internal safeguards of the political process."

If *National League of Cities* is overruled, does the Tenth Amendment nonetheless retain vitality? Without mentioning the Tenth directly, the *Garcia* majority, significantly perhaps, recognized explicitly the "special and specific position in our constitutional system" that the states occupy and that "the scope of Congress' authority under the Commerce Clause must reflect that position." The dissenters—Chief Justice Burger and Justices Powell, Rehnquist, and O'Connor—took that assumption as a starting point. "[J]udicial enforcement of the Tenth Amendment is essential to maintaining the federal system," declared Powell. Rehnquist was even more forthcoming. "I do not think it incumbent . . . to spell out further the fine points of a principle that will, I am confident, in time again command the support of a majority of this Court." That principle, added O'Connor, "requires the Court to enforce affirmative limits on federal regulation of the States to complement the judicially crafted expansion of the interstate commerce power."

Although the Tenth Amendment may be a "truism," it nonetheless remains a compelling reminder of America's search for *union without unity.* Whether in terms of the differing visions of Chief Justices John Marshall and Roger Taney or of Presidents Franklin Roosevelt and Ronald Reagan, federalism is a prominent feature of American politics and government. Its prominence springs from the fact that federalism concerns the allocation of power. This allocation is important because it helps to determine which of the many contending political groups will have the dominant voice and, therefore, which of many possible policy objectives government will pursue. Deciding *who* will act often decides *what* will be done.

KEY TERMS

federalism	resulting powers	preemption
national supremacy	exclusive powers	cooperative
Antifederalists	concurrent powers	federalism
Tenth Amendment	necessary and proper	supremacy clause
delegated powers	clause	federal question
reserved powers	dual federalism	judicial federalism
express powers	police power	reciprocal immunity
implied powers	governmental	
	immunity	

QUERIES

1. In *McCulloch* v. *Maryland,* on what checks did Marshall rely to guard against abuse of power? Was his view in *McCulloch* consistent with his view in *Marbury* v. *Madison?*

2. What is "the integral role of the Tenth Amendment in our constitutional theory" to which Justice Powell referred in *Garcia* v. *San Antonio Metropolitan Transit Authority?*

3. What significance does *Chisholm* v. *Georgia* have in the development of the Court's role in American government?

4. What is Chief Justice Chase's understanding of the nature of the union in *Texas* v. *White?*

SELECTED READINGS

BERGER, RAOUL. *Federalism: The Founders' Design.* Norman: University of Oklahoma Press, 1987.

CORWIN, EDWARD S. "The Passing of Dual Federalism," 36 *Virginia Law Review* 1 (1950).

ELAZAR, DANIEL J. *Exploring Federalism.* Tuscaloosa: University of Alabama Press, 1986.

FINO, SUSAN P. *The Role of State Supreme Courts in the New Judicial Federalism.* Westport, Conn.: Greenwood, 1987.

GOLDWIN, ROBERT, ed. *A Nation of States: Essays on the American Federal System.* Chicago: Rand McNally, 1974. See especially Martin Diamond, "What the Framers Meant by Federalism," and Walter Berns, "The Meaning of the 10th Amendment."

"Judge Spencer Roane of Virginia: Champion of States' Rights—Foe of John Marshall." 66 *Harvard Law Review* 1242 (1953).

KINCAID, JOHN. "The New Judicial Federalism." 61 *Journal of State Government* 163 (1988).

LOFGREN, CHARLES A., "The Origins of the Tenth Amendment; History, Sovereignty and the Problem of Constitutional Intention." In Ronald K. L. Collins, ed. *Constitutional Government in America*. Durham, N.C.: Carolina Academic Press, 1980.

MASON, ALPHEUS T. *The States Rights Debate: Antifederalism and the Constitution*. New York: Oxford University Press, 1972.

MATHIS, DOYLE. "*Chisholm* v. *Georgia:* Background and Settlement." 54 *Journal of American History* 19 (1967).

POWELL, JEFF. "The Compleat Jeffersonian: Justice Rehnquist and Federalism." 91 *Yale Law Journal* 1317 (1982).

RANNEY, JOHN C. "The Basis of American Federalism." 3 *William and Mary Quarterly* (3d series) 1 (1982).

SCHMIDHAUSER, JOHN R. *The Supreme Court as Final Arbiter in Federal-State Relations, 1789–1957*. Chapel Hill: University of North Carolina Press, 1958.

SPAETH, HAROLD J. "Burger Court Review of State Court Civil Liberties Decisions." 68 *Judicature* 285 (1985).

STEPHENSON, D. GRIER, JR., and BARRY MICHAEL LEVINE. "Vicarious Federalism: The Modern Supreme Court and the Tenth Amendment." 19 *The Urban Lawyer* 683 (1987).

STORING, HERBERT J., ed. *The Complete Anti-Federalist,* 7 vols. Chicago: University of Chicago Press, 1981.

ZUCKERT, MICHAEL P. "Federalism and the Founding: Toward a Reinterpretation of the Constitutional Convention." 48 *Review of Politics* 166 (1986).

Chisholm v. Georgia
2 U.S. (2 Dall.) 419, 1 L.Ed. 440 (1793)

On October 31, 1777, the Executive Council of Georgia authorized State Commissioners Thomas Stone and Edward Davies to purchase much-needed supplies from Robert Farquhar, a Charleston, South Carolina, merchant. For his merchandise, Stone and Davies agreed to pay Farquhar $169,613.33 in Continental Currency or in indigo at Carolina prices, if currency was not available. Farquhar never received payment. His claims were still unsatisfied when he was hit by the boom of a pilot boat headed for Savannah. A short time after his death Alexander Chisholm, a Charleston merchant, was qualified as Farquhar's executor and began to press for payment of Farquhar's claim. When Georgia refused to pay, the executor brought suit against the state in the United States Circuit Court for the District of Georgia. Alleging its sovereign and independent status under the federal Constitution, Georgia answered that it could not be made a party to any suit by a South Carolina citizen. Judges James Iredell and Nathaniel Pendleton upheld, for different reasons, Georgia's objections.

In 1792, Chisholm filed suit in the Supreme Court. When Georgia failed to appear, the Court pointedly asked, "Any person having authority to speak for the State of Georgia is required to come forth and appear accordingly." When Georgia persisted in its refusal, the case again was postponed until February 4, 1793. No one appeared, and again the justices issued another invitation. Still nothing happened, and the decision came down February 19, 1793. All five justices delivered opinions; only Justice Iredell, holding to the view he announced in the circuit court, dissented. In the face of assurances made by Hamilton, Madison, and Marshall during the ratification debates that a state could not, without its consent, be made party defendant in the federal courts by a citizen of another state, the Court took jurisdiction and decided against the state.

The negative reaction was strong and prompt. A House resolution calling for amendment to the Constitution was filed the day of the decision, followed the next day by a supportive Senate resolution. The Eleventh Amendment was proposed by Congress on March 4, 1794, and ratification was completed in 11 months. Official announcement of ratification was not made until January 8, 1798, when President John Adams in a message to Congress declared that it "may now be deemed to be a part of the Constitution." Congress's prompt resort to the formal amending process as a corrective for a decision that flew in the face of reassurances made while ratification of the Constitution was pending is a testimonial to the stature of the judiciary. Congress, in proposing the Eleventh Amendment, and the states, in ratifying it, had within a markedly short time equated the Court's interpretation of the Constitution with the document itself. Majority: Wilson, Blair, Cushing, Jay. Dissenting: Iredell.

WILSON, JUSTICE:—This is a case of uncommon magnitude. One of the parties to it is a state; certainly respectable, claiming to be sovereign. The question to be determined is whether this state, so respectable, and whose claim soars so high, is amenable to the jurisdiction of the supreme court of the United States? This question, important in itself, will depend on others, more important still; and, may, perhaps, be ultimately resolved into one, no less radical than this—"do the people of the United States form a nation?" . . .

To the Constitution of the United States the term sovereign is totally unknown. There is but one place where it could have been used with propriety. But, even in that place it would not, perhaps, have comported with the delicacy of those who ordained and established that constitution. They might have announced themselves "sovereign" people of the United States: But serenely conscious of the fact, they avoided the ostentatious declaration.
. . .

With the strictest propriety, therefore, classical and political, our national scene opens with the most magnificent object which the nation could present. "The people of the United States" are the first personages introduced. Who were those people? They were the citizens of thirteen states, each of which had a separate constitution and government, and all of which were connected together by articles of confederation. . . .

The question now opens fairly to our view, could the people of those states, among whom were those of Georgia, bind those states, and Georgia, among the others, by the legislative, executive, and judicial power so vested? If the principles on which I have founded myself are just and true, this question must, unavoidably, receive an affirmative answer.
. . .

The next question under this head is—Has the constitution done so? Did those people mean to exercise this, their undoubted power? These questions may be resolved, either by fair and conclusive deductions, or by direct and explicit declarations. In order, ultimately, to discover, whether the people of the United States intended to bind those states by the judicial power vested by the national constitution, a previous inquiry will naturally be: Did those people intend to bind those states by the legislative power vested by that constitution? The articles of confederation, it is well known, did not

operate upon individual citizens, but operated only upon states. This defect was remedied by the national constitution, which, as all allow, has an operation on individual citizens. But if an opinion, which some seem to entertain, be just; the defect remedied, on one side, was balanced by a defect introduced on the other: for they seem to think, that the present constitution operates only on individual citizens, and not on states. This opinion, however, appears to be altogether unfounded. When certain laws of the states are declared to be "subject to the revision and control of the congress"; it cannot, surely be contended, that the legislative power of the national government was meant to have no operation on the several states. The fact, uncontrovertibly established in one instance, proves the principle in all other instances, to which the facts will be found to apply. We may then infer, that the people of the United States intended to bind the several states, by the legislative power of the national government. . . .

But, in my opinion, this doctrine rests not upon the legitimate result of fair and conclusive deduction from the constitution; it is confirmed, beyond all doubt, by the direct and explicit declaration of the constitution itself. "The judicial power of the United States shall extend to controversies between two States." Two States are supposed to have a controversy between them; this controversy is supposed to be brought before those vested with the judicial power of the United States; can the most consummate degree of professional ingenuity devise a mode by which this "controversy between two States" can be brought before a court of law, and yet neither of those States be a defendant? "The judicial power of the United States shall extend to controversies between a State and citizens of another State." Could the strictest legal language; could even that language which is peculiarly appropriated to an art, deemed by a great master to be one of the most honorable, laudable, and profitable things in our law; could this strict and appropriate language describe with more precise accuracy the cause now pending before the tribunal? Causes, and not parties to causes, are weighed by justice in her equal scales; on the former, solely, her attention is fixed; to the latter she is, as she is painted, blind. . . .

JAY, CHIEF JUSTICE:—The question we are now to decide has been accurately stated, viz.: Is a state suable by individual citizens of another state? . . .

The revolution, or rather the Declaration of Independence, found the people already united for general purposes, and at the same time, providing for their more domestic concerns, by state conventions, and other temporary arrangements. . . . [T]hey made a confederation of the States, the basis of a general Government. Experience disappointed the expectations they had formed from it; and then the people, in their collective and national capacity, established the present Constitution. It is remarkable that in establishing it, the people exercised their own rights, and their own proper sovereignty, and conscious of the plentitude of it, they declared with becoming dignity, "We the people of the United States," "do ordain and establish this Constitution." Here we see the people acting as sovereigns of the whole country; and in the language of sovereignty, establishing a Constitution by which it was their will, that the State Governments should be bound, and to which the State Constitutions should be made to conform. Every State Constitution is a compact made by and between the citizens of a state to govern themselves in a certain manner; and the Constitution of the United States is likewise a compact made by the people of the United States to govern themselves as to general objects, in a certain manner. By this great compact however, many prerogatives were transferred to the national Government, such as those of making war and peace, contracting alliances, coining money, &c. . . .

It is politic, wise and good, that not only the controversies in which a state is plaintiff, but also those in which a state is defendant, should be settled; both cases, therefore, are within the reason of the remedy; and ought to be so adjudged, unless the obvious, plain and literal sense of the words forbid it. If we attend to the words, we find them to be express, positive, free from ambiguity, and without room for such implied expressions: "The judicial power of the United States shall extend to controversies between a state and citizens of another state." If the constitution really meant to extend these powers only to those controversies in which a state might be plaintiff, to the exclusion of those in which citizens had demands against a state, it is inconceivable, that it should have attempted to convey that meaning in words, not only so incompetent, but also repugnant to it; if it meant to exclude a certain class of these controversies, why were they not expressly excepted; on the contrary, not even an intimation of such intention appears in any part of the Constitution. . . . When power is thus extended to a controversy, it necessarily, as to all judicial purposes, is also extended to those between whom it subsists. . . .

IREDELL, JUSTICE:—[Dissenting]

A general question of great importance here occurs. What controversy of a civil nature can be maintained against a state by an individual? The framers of the constitution, I presume, must have meant one of two things—Either, 1. In the conveyance of that part of the judicial power which did not relate to the execution of the other authorities of the general government . . . to refer to antecedent laws for the construction of the general words they use: or, 2. To enable congress in all such cases to pass all such laws as they might deem necessary and proper to carry the purposes of this constitution into full effect, either absolutely at their discretion, or, at least, in cases where prior laws were deficient for such purposes, if any such deficiency existed.

The attorney-general has indeed suggested another construction, a construction, I confess, that I never heard of before, nor can I now consider it grounded on any solid foundation, though it appeared to me to be the basis of the attorney-general's argument. His construction I take to be this: "That the moment a supreme court is formed, it is to exercise all the judicial power vested in it by the constitution, by its own authority, whether the legislature has prescribed methods of doing so, or not." My conception of the constitution is entirely different. I conceive, that all the courts of the United States must receive, not merely their *organization* as to the number of judges of which they are to consist; but all their authority, as to the manner of their proceeding, from the legislature only. . . .

McCulloch v. Maryland
17 U.S. (4 Wheat.) 316, 4 L.Ed. 579 (1819)

This famous case resulted from the attempt of the Maryland legislature in 1818 to tax banks and bank branches not chartered by the state legislature. James McCulloch, cashier of the Baltimore branch of the Second Bank of the United States, against which the law was directed, failed to pay the $15,000 annual fee or comply with the alternative requirement by affixing tax stamps to the bank notes issued. Mc-Culloch brought a writ of error against the Court of Appeals of the State of Maryland, which had upheld a lower court judgment against him. Majority: Marshall, Duvall, Johnson, Livingston, Story, Todd, Washington.

MARSHALL, CHIEF JUSTICE, delivered the opinion of the Court.

In the case now to be determined, the defendant, a sovereign state, denies the obligation of a law enacted by the legislature of the Union; and the plaintiff, on his part, contests the validity of an act which has been passed by the legislature of that state. . . . No tribunal can approach such a question without a deep sense of its importance, and of the awful responsibility involved in its decision. But it must be decided peacefully, or remain a source of hostile legislation, perhaps of hostility of a still more serious nature; and if it is to be so decided, by this tribunal alone can the decision be made. On the supreme court of the United States has the constitution of our country devolved this important duty.

The first question made in the case is, has congress power to incorporate a bank? . . .

In discussing this question, the counsel for the state of Maryland have deemed it of some importance, in the construction of the constitution, to consider that instrument not as emanating from the people, but as the act of sovereign and independent states. The powers of the general government, it has been said, are delegated by the states, who alone are truly sovereign; and must be exercised in subordination to the states, who alone possess supreme dominion. It would be difficult to sustain this proposition. The convention which framed the constitution was, indeed, elected by the state legislatures. But the instrument, when it came from their hands, was a mere proposal, without obligation, or pretensions to it. It was reported to the

then existing congress of the United States, with a request that it might "be submitted to a convention of delegates, chosen in each state by the people thereof, under the recommendation of its legislature, for their assent and ratification." This mode of proceeding was adopted; and by the convention, by congress, and by the state legislatures, the instrument was submitted to the *people*. They acted upon it, in the only manner in which they can act safely, effectively, and wisely, on such a subject by assembling in convention. It is true, they assembled in their several states; and where else should they have assembled? No political dreamer was ever wild enough to think of breaking down the lines which separate the states, and of compounding the American people into one common mass. Of consequence, when they act, they act in their states. But the measures they adopt do not, on that account, cease to be the measures of the people themselves, or become the measures of the state governments.

From these conventions the constitution derives its whole authority. The government proceeds directly from the people; is "ordained and established" in the name of the people; and is declared to be ordained, "in order to form a more perfect union, establish justice, insure domestic tranquillity, and secure the blessings of liberty, to themselves and to their posterity." The assent of the States, in their sovereign capacity, is implied in calling a convention, and thus submitting that instrument to the people. . . .

This government is acknowledged by all to be one of enumerated powers. . . . [T]hat principle is now universally admitted. But the question respecting the extent of the powers actually granted, is perpetually arising, and will probably continue to arise, as long as our system shall exist. In discussing these questions, the conflicting powers of the general and state governments must be brought into view, and the supremacy of their respective laws, when they are in opposition, must be settled.

If any one proposition could command the universal assent of mankind, we might expect that it would be this—that the government of the Union, though limited in its powers, is supreme within its sphere of action. This would seem to result, necessarily, from its nature. It is the government of all; its powers are delegated by all; it represents all, and acts for all. Though any one state may be willing to control its operations, no state is willing to allow others to control them. The nation, on those subjects on which it can act, must necessarily bind its component parts. But this question is not left to mere reason: the people have, in express terms, decided it, by saying, "this constitution, and the laws of the United States, which shall be made in pursuance thereof," "shall be the supreme law of the land," and by requiring that the members of the state legislatures, and the officers of the executive and judicial departments of the states, shall take the oath of fidelity to it. The government of the United States, then, though limited in its powers, is supreme; and its laws, when made in pursuance of the constitution, form the supreme law of the land, "anything in the constitution or laws of any state, to the contrary notwithstanding."

Among the enumerated powers, we do not find that of establishing a bank or creating a corporation. But there is no phrase in the instrument which, like the articles of confederation, excludes incidental or implied powers; and which requires that everything granted shall be expressly and minutely described. Even the 10th amendment, which was framed for the purpose of quieting the excessive jealousies which had been excited, omits the word "expressly," and declares only that the powers "not delegated to the United States, nor prohibited to the states, are reserved to the states or to the people;" thus leaving the question, whether the particular power which may become the subject of contest, has been delegated to the one government, or prohibited to the other, to depend on a fair construction of the whole instrument. The men who drew and adopted this amendment had experienced the embarrassments resulting from the insertion of this word in the articles of confederation, and probably omitted it, to avoid those embarrassments. A constitution, to contain an accurate detail of all the subdivisions of which its great powers will admit, and of all the means by which they may be carried into execution, would partake of the prolixity of a legal code, and could scarcely be embraced by the human mind. It would, probably, never be understood by the public. Its nature, therefore, requires, that only its great outlines should be marked, its important objects designated, and the minor ingredients which compose those objects, be deduced from the nature of the objects themselves. That this idea was entertained by the framers of the American constitution, is not only to be inferred from the nature of the instrument, but from the language. Why else were some of the limitations, found in the 9th section of the 1st article, introduced? It is also, in some degree, warranted, by their having omitted to use any restrictive term which might prevent its receiving a fair and just interpretation. In considering this question, then, we must never forget, that it is *a constitution* we are expounding.

Although, among the enumerated powers of government, we do not find the word "bank," or "incorporation," we find the great powers, to lay and collect taxes; to borrow money; to regulate commerce; to declare and conduct war; and to raise and support armies and navies. The sword and the purse, all the external relations, and no inconsiderable portion of the industry of the nation, are intrusted to its government. It can never be pretended, that these vast powers draw after them others of inferior importance, merely because they are inferior. Such an idea can never be advanced. But it may with great reason be contended, that a government, intrusted with such ample powers, on the due execution of which the happiness and prosperity of the nation so vitally depends, must also be intrusted with ample means for their execution. The power being given, it is the interest of the nation to facilitate its execution. It can never be their interest, and cannot be presumed to have been their intention, to clog and embarrass its execution, by withholding the most appropriate means. Throughout this vast republic, from the St.

Croix to the Gulf of Mexico, from the Atlantic to the Pacific, revenue is to be collected and expended, armies are to be marched and supported. The exigencies of the nation may require, that the treasure raised in the north should be transported to the south, that raised in the east, conveyed to the west, or that this order should be reversed. Is that construction of the constitution to be preferred, which would render these operations difficult, hazardous, and expensive? Can we adopt that construction (unless the words imperiously require it), which would impute to the framers of that instrument, when granting these powers for the public good, the intention of impeding their exercise by withholding a choice of means? . . .

But the constitution of the United States has not left the right of congress to employ the necessary means, for the execution of the powers conferred on the government, to general reasoning. To its enumeration of powers is added, that of making "all laws which shall be necessary and proper, for carrying into execution the foregoing powers, and all other powers vested by this constitution, in the government of the United States, or in any department thereof." . . .

But the argument on which most reliance is placed, is drawn from the peculiar language of this clause. Congress is not empowered by it to make all laws, which may have relation to the powers conferred on the government, but only such as may be "necessary and proper" for carrying them into execution. The word "necessary" is considered as controlling the whole sentence, and as limiting the right to pass laws for the execution of the granted powers, to such as are indispensable, and without which the power would be nugatory. That it excludes the choice of means, and leaves to Congress, in each case, that only which is most direct and simple.

Is it true, that this is the sense in which the word "necessary" is always used? Does it always import an absolute physical necessity, so strong, that one thing, to which another may be termed necessary, cannot exist without that other? We think it does not. If reference be had to its use, in the common affairs of the world, or in approved authors, we find that it frequently imports to more than that one thing is convenient, or useful, or essential to another. To employ the means necessary to an end, is generally understood as employing any means

calculated to produce the end, and not as being confined to those single means, without which the end would be entirely unattainable. . . .

. . . This provision is made in a constitution, intended to endure for ages to come, and consequently to be adapted to the various *crises* of human affairs. To have prescribed the means by which government should, in all future times, execute its powers, would have been to change, entirely, the character of the instrument, and give it the properties of a legal code. It would have been an unwise attempt to provide, by immutable rules, for exigencies which, if foreseen at all, must have been seen dimly, and which can be best provided for as they occur. To have declared, that the best means shall not be used, but those alone, without which the power given would be nugatory, would have been to deprive the legislature of the capacity to avail itself of experience, to exercise its reason, and to accommodate its legislation to circumstances. If we apply this principle of construction to any of the powers of the government, we shall find it so pernicious in its operation that we shall be compelled to discard it. . . .

But the argument which most conclusively demonstrates the error of the construction contended for by the counsel for the state of Maryland, is founded on the intention of the convention, as manifested in the whole clause. . . . This clause, as construed by the state of Maryland, would abridge, and almost annihilate, this useful and necessary right of the legislature to select its means. That this could not be intended is, we should think, had it not been already controverted, too apparent for controversy.

We think so for the following reasons: 1st. The clause is placed among the powers of congress, not among the limitations on those powers. 2d. Its terms purport to enlarge, not to diminish the powers vested in the government. It purports to be an additional power, not a restriction on those already granted. No reason has been, or can be assigned, for thus concealing an intention to narrow the discretion of the national legislature, under words which purport to enlarge it. The framers of the constitution wished its adoption, and well knew that it would be endangered by its strength, not by its weakness. Had they been capable of using language which would convey to the eye one idea, and, after deep reflection, impress on the mind, another, they would rather have disguised the grant of power, than its limitation. If then, their intention had been, by this clause, to restrain the free use of means which might otherwise have been implied, that intention would have been inserted in another place, and would have been expressed in terms resembling these. "In carrying into execution the foregoing powers and all others," &c., "no laws shall be passed but such as are necessary and proper." Had the intention been to make this clause restrictive, it would unquestionably have been so in form as well as in effect. . . .

We admit, as all must admit, that the powers of the government are limited, and that its limits are not to be transcended. But we think the sound construction of the constitution must allow to the national legislature that discretion, with respect to the means by which the powers it confers are to be carried into execution, which will enable that body to perform the high duties assigned to it, in the manner most beneficial to the people. Let the end be legitimate, let it be within the scope of the constitution, and all means which are appropriate, which are plainly adapted to that end, which are not prohibited, but consistent with the letter and spirit of the constitution, are constitutional. . . .

It being the opinion of the court, that the act incorporating the bank is constitutional; and that the power of establishing a branch in the state of Maryland might be properly exercised by the bank itself, we proceed to inquire—

Whether the state of Maryland may, without violating the constitution, tax that branch? . . . But such is the paramount character of the constitution, that its capacity to withdraw any subject from the action of even this power, is admitted. . . .

On this ground, the counsel for the bank place its claim to be exempted from the power of a state to tax its operations. There is no express provision for the case, but the claim has been sustained on a principle which so entirely pervades the constitution, is so intermixed with the materials which compose it, so interwoven with its web, so blended with its texture, as to be incapable of being separated from it, without rending it into shreds. This great principle is, that the constitution and the laws made in pursuance thereof are supreme; that they control the constitution and laws of the respective states, and cannot be controlled by them. From this, which may be almost termed an axiom, other propositions are deduced as corollaries, on the truth or error of which, and on their application to this case, the cause has been supposed to depend. These are, 1st: That a power to create implies a power to preserve: 2d. That a power to destroy, if wielded by a different hand, is hostile to, and incompatible with, these powers to create and preserve: 3d. That where this repugnancy exists, that authority which is supreme must control, not yield to that over which it is supreme. . . .

The sovereignty of a state extends to everything which exists by its own authority, or is introduced by its permission; but does it extend to those means which are employed by Congress to carry into execution—powers conferred on that body by the people of the United States? We think it demonstrable that it does not. Those powers are not given by the people of a single state. They are given by the people of the United States, to a government whose laws, made in pursuance of the constitution, are declared to be supreme. Consequently, the people of a single state cannot confer a sovereignty which will extend over them.

If we measure the power of taxation residing in a state, by the extent of sovereignty which the people of a single state possess, and can confer on its government, we have an intelligible standard, applicable to every case to which the power may be applied. We have a principle which leaves the power of taxing the people and property of a state unimpaired; which leaves to a state the command of all its resources, and which places beyond its reach, all those powers which are conferred by the people of the United States on the government of the Union, and all those means which are given for the purpose of carrying those powers into execution. We have a principle which is safe for the states, and safe for the Union. We are relieved, as we ought to be, from clashing sovereignty; from interfering powers; from a repugnancy between a right in one government to pull down, what there is an acknowledged right in another to build up; from the incompatibility of a right in one government to destroy, what there is an acknowledged right in another to build up; from the incompatibility of a right in one government to destroy, what there is a right in another to preserve. We are not driven to the perplexing inquiry, so unfit for the judicial department, what degree of taxation is a legitimate use, and what degree may amount to the abuse of the power. The attempt to use it on the means employed by the government of the Union, in pursuance of the constitution, is itself an abuse, because it is the usurpation of a power, which the people of a single state cannot give. We find, then, on just theory, a total failure of this original right to tax the means employed by the government of the Union, for the execution of its powers. The right never existed, and the question whether it has been surrendered, cannot arise.

But, waiving this theory for the present, let us resume the inquiry, whether this power can be exercised by the respective states, consistently with a fair construction of the constitution? That the power to tax involves the power to destroy; that the power to destroy may defeat and render useless the power to create; that there is a plain repugnancy in conferring on one government a power to control the constitutional measures of another, which other, with respect to those very measures, is declared to be supreme over that which exerts the control, are propositions not to be denied. But all inconsistencies are to be reconciled by the magic of the word *confidence*. Taxation, it is said, does not necessarily and unavoidably destroy. To carry it to the excess of destruction, would be an abuse, to presume which, would banish that confidence which is essential to all government. But is this a case of confidence? Would the people of any one state trust those of another with a power to control the most significant operations of their state government? We know they would not. Why, then, should we suppose, that the people of any one state should be willing to trust those of another with a power to control the operations of a government to which they have confided their most important and most valuable interests? In the legislature of the Union alone, all are represented. The legislature of the Union alone, therefore, can be trusted by the people with the power of controlling measures which concern all, in the confidence that it will not be abused. This, then is not a case of confidence, and we must consider it as it really is.

If we apply the principle for which the state of Maryland contends, to the constitution generally, we shall find it capable of changing totally the character of that instrument. We shall find it capable of arresting all the measures of the government, and of prostrating it at the foot of the states. The American people have declared their constitution and the laws made in pursuance thereof, to be supreme; but this principle would transfer the supremacy, in fact, to the states. If the states may tax one instrument, employed by the government in the execution of its powers, they may tax any and every other instrument. They may tax the mail; they may tax the mint; they may tax patent rights; they may tax the papers of the custom-house; they may tax judicial process; they may tax all the means employed by the government, to an excess which would defeat all the ends of government. This was not intended by the American people. They did not design to make their government dependent on the states. . . .

. . . If the controlling power of the states be established; if their supremacy as to taxation be acknowledged; what is to restrain their exercising this control in any shape they may please to give it? Their sovereignty is not confined to taxation; that is not the only mode in which it might be displayed. The question is, in truth, a question of supremacy, and if the right of the states to tax the means employed by the general government be conceded, the declaration that the constitution, and the laws made in pursuance thereof, shall be the supreme law of the land, is empty and unmeaning declamation. . . .

It has also been insisted, that, as the power of taxation in the general and state governments is acknowledged to be concurrent, every argument which would sustain the right of the general government to tax banks chartered by the states, will equally sustain the rights of the states to tax banks chartered by the general government. But the two cases are not the same reason. The people of all the states have created the general government, and have conferred upon it the general power of taxation. The people of all the states, and the states themselves, are represented in congress, and, by their representatives, exercise this power. When they tax the chartered institutions of the states, they tax their constituents; and these taxes must be uniform. But when a state taxes the operations of the government of the United States, it acts upon institutions created, not by their own constituents, but by people over whom they claim no control. It acts upon the measures of a government created by others as well as themselves, for the benefit of others in common with themselves. The difference is that which always exists, and always must exist, between the action of the whole on a part, and the action of a part on the whole—between the laws of a government declared to be supreme, and those of a government which, when in opposition to those laws, is not supreme. . . .

The court has bestowed on this subject its most deliberate consideration. The result is a conviction that the states have no power, by taxation or otherwise, to retard, impede, burden, or in any manner control, the operations of the constitutional laws enacted by congress to carry into execution the powers vested in the general government. This is, we think, the unavoidable consequence of that supremacy which the constitution has declared. We are unanimously of opinion, that the law passed by the legislature of Maryland, imposing a tax on the Bank of the United States, is unconstitutional and void. . . .

Cohens v. Virginia
19 U.S. (6 Wheat.) 264, 5 L.Ed. 257 (1821)

In 1802 Congress passed a law authorizing the District of Columbia to conduct a lottery. P.J. and M.J. Cohen were arrested in Norfolk Virginia, and convicted of selling lottery tickets in violation of a state statute. On the merits of the case, the Court upheld the Cohens' conviction, declaring that the federal law afforded no immunity to prosecution beyond the limits of the District of Columbia. The portion of the opinion that follows pertains solely to the question of jurisdiction. Majority: Marshall, Duvall, Johnson, Livingston, Story, Todd. Not participating: Washington.

MR. CHIEF JUSTICE MARSHALL delivered the opinion of the Court. . . .

Judgment was rendered against the defendants; and the court in which it was rendered being the highest court of the state in which the cause was cognizable, the record has been brought into this court by a writ of error.

The defendant in error moves to dismiss this writ, for want of jurisdiction.

In support of this motion, three points have been made, and argued with the ability which the importance of the question merits. These points are—

1st. That a state is a defendant.

2nd. That no writ of error lies from this court to a state court.

[Point 3 has been omitted.]

The questions presented to the court by the two first points made at the bar are of great magnitude, and may truly be said vitally to affect the Union. They exclude the inquiry whether the constitution and laws of the United States have been violated by the judgment which the plaintiffs in error seek to review; and maintain that, admitting such violation, it is not in the power of the government to apply a corrective. They maintain that the nation does not possess a department capable of restraining, peaceably, and by authority of law, any attempts which may be made, by a part, against the legitimate powers of the whole; and that the government is reduced to the alternative of submitting to such attempts, or of resisting them by force. They maintain that the constitution of the United States has provided no tribunal for the final construction of itself, or of the laws or treaties of the nation; but that this power may be exercised in the last resort by the courts of every state of the Union. That the constitution, laws and treaties may receive as many constructions as there are states; and that this is not a mischief, or, if a mischief is irremediable. . . .

1st. The first question to be considered is, whether

the jurisdiction of this court is excluded by the character of the parties, one of them being a state, and the other a citizen of that state? . . .

The American states, as well as the American people, have believed a close and firm Union to be essential to their liberty and to their happiness. They have been taught by experience, that this Union cannot exist without a government for the whole; and they have been taught by the same experience that this government would be a mere shadow, that must disappoint all their hopes, unless invested with large portions of that sovereignty which belongs to independent states. Under the influence of this opinion, and thus instructed by experience, the American people, in the conventions of their respective states, adopted the present constitution.

If it could be doubted whether, from its nature, it were not supreme in all cases where it is empowered to act, that doubt would be removed by the declaration that "this constitution, and the laws of the United States which shall be made in pursuance thereof and all treaties made, or which shall be made, under the authority of the United States, shall be the supreme law of the land; and the judges in every state shall be bound thereby, anything in the constitution or laws of any state to the contrary notwithstanding."

This is the authoritative language of the American people; and, if gentlemen please, of the American states. It marks with lines too strong to be mistaken, the characteristic distinction between the government of the Union and those of the states. The general government, though limited as to its objects, is supreme with respect to those objects. This principle is a part of the constitution; and if there be any who deny its necessity, none can deny its authority.

To this supreme government ample powers are confided; and if it were possible to doubt the great purposes for which they were so confided, the people of the United States have declared that they are given "in order to form a more perfect union, establish justice, insure domestic tranquillity, provide for the common defense, promote the general welfare, and secure the blessings of liberty to themselves and their posterity."

With the ample powers confided to this supreme government, for these interesting purposes, are connected many express and important limitations on the sovereignty of the states, which are made for the same purposes. The powers of the Union on the great subjects of war, peace, and commerce, and on many others, are in themselves limitations of the sovereignty of the states; but in addition to these, the sovereignty of the states is surrendered in many instances where the surrender can only operate to the benefit of the people, and where, perhaps, no other power is conferred on congress than a conservative power to maintain the principles established in the constitution. The maintenance of these principles in their purity is certainly among the great duties of the government. One of the instruments by which this duty may be peaceably performed is the judicial department. It is authorized to decide all cases, of every description, arising under the constitution or laws of the United States. From this general grant of jurisdiction, no exception is made of those cases in which a state may be a party. When we consider the situation of the government of the Union and of a state, in relation to each other; the nature of our constitution; the subordination of the state governments to that constitution; the great purpose for which jurisdiction over all cases arising under the constitution and laws of the United States, is confided to the judicial department; are we at liberty to insert in this general grant, an exception of those cases in which a state may be a party? Will the spirit of the constitution justify this attempt to control its words? We think it will not. We think a case arising under the constitution or laws of the United States, is cognizable in the courts of the Union, whoever may be the parties of that case. . . .

One of the express objects, then, for which the judicial department was established, is the decision of controversies between states, and between a state and individuals. The mere circumstance, that a state is a party, gives jurisdiction to the court. How, then, can it be contended, that the very same instrument, in the very same section, should be so construed, as that this same circumstance should withdraw a case from the jurisdiction of the court, where the constitution or laws of the United States are supposed to have been violated? . . .

The mischievous consequences of the construction contended for on the part of Virginia, are also entitled to great consideration. It would prostrate, it has been said, the government and its laws at the feet of every state in the Union. And would not this be its effect? What power of the government could be executed by its own means, in any state disposed to resist its execution by a course of legislation? The laws must be executed by individuals acting within the several states. If these individuals may be exposed to penalties, and if the courts of the Union cannot correct the judgments by which these penalties may be enforced, the course of the government may be, at any time, arrested by the will of one of its members. Each member will possess a *veto* on the will of the whole. . . .

These collisions may take place in times of no extraordinary commotion. But a constitution is framed for ages to come, and is designed to approach immortality as nearly as human institutions can approach it. Its course cannot always be tranquil. It is exposed to storms and tempests, and its framers must be unwise statesmen indeed, if they have not provided it, as far as its nature will permit, with the means of self-preservation from the perils it may be destined to encounter. No government ought to be so defective in its organization, as not to contain within itself the means of securing the execution of its own laws against other dangers than those which occur every day. Courts of justice are the means most usually employed; and it is reasonable to expect that a government should repose on its own courts, rather than on others. There is certainly nothing in the circumstances under which our constitution was formed; nothing in the history of the times, which would justify the opinion that the confidence reposed in the states was so implicit as to leave in them and their tribunals the power of resisting or defeating, in the form of law, the legitimate measures of the Union. . . .

. . . If jurisdiction depended entirely on the character of the parties, and was not given where the parties have not an original right to come into court, that part of the 2d section of the 3d article, which extends the judicial power to all cases arising under the constitution and laws of the United States, would be surplusage. It is to give jurisdiction where the character of the parties would not give it, that this very important part of the clause was inserted. . . .

It is most true, that this court will not take jurisdiction if it should not; but it is equally true, that it must take jurisdiction, if it should. The judiciary cannot, as the legislature may, avoid a measure, because it approaches the confines of the constitution. We cannot pass it by, because it is doubtful. With whatever doubts, with whatever difficulties, a case may be attended, we must decide it, if it be brought before us. We have no more right to decline the exercise of jurisdiction which is given, than to usurp that which is not given. The one or the other would be treason to the constitution. Questions may occur, which we would gladly avoid; but we cannot avoid them. All we can do is, to exercise our best judgment, and conscientiously to perform our duty. In doing this, on the present occasion, we find this tribunal invested with appellate jurisdiction in all cases arising under the constitution and laws of the United States. We find no exception to this grant, and we cannot insert one. . . .

This leads to a consideration of the 11th amendment. It is in these words: "The judicial power of the United States shall not be construed to extend to any suit in law or equity commenced or prosecuted against one of the United States, by citizens of another state, or by citizens or subjects of any foreign state." It is a part of our history, that, at the adoption of the constitution, all the states were greatly indebted; and the apprehension that these debts might be prosecuted in the federal courts, formed a very serious objection to that instrument. Suits were instituted; and the court maintained its jurisdiction. The alarm was general; and, to quiet the apprehensions that were so extensively entertained, this amendment was proposed in Congress, and adopted by the state legislatures.* That its motive was not to maintain the sovereignty of a state from the degradation supposed to attend a compulsory appearance before the tribunal of the nation, may be inferred from the terms of the amendment. It does not comprehend controversies between two or more states, or between a state and a foreign state. The jurisdiction of the court still extends to these cases; and in these a state may still be sued. We must ascribe the amendment, then, to some other cause than the dignity of a state. There is no difficulty in finding this cause. Those who were inhibited from commencing a suit against a state, or from prosecuting one which might be commenced before the adoption of the amendment, were persons who might probably be

---

* The Eleventh Amendment was proposed and ratified shortly after the Court's decision in *Chisholm* v. *Ga.* (1793).—ED.

its creditors. There was not much reason to fear that foreign or sister states would be creditors to any considerable amount, and there was reason to retain the jurisdiction of the court in those cases, because it might be essential to the preservation of peace. The amendment, therefore, extended to suits commenced or prosecuted by individuals, but not to those brought by states. . . .

Under the Judiciary Act, the effect of a writ of error is simply to bring the record into court, and submit the judgment of the inferior tribunal to reexamination. It does not in any manner act upon the parties; it acts only on the record. It removes the record into the supervising tribunal. Where, then, a state obtains a judgment against an individual, and the court rendering such judgment overrules a defense set up under the constitution or laws of the United States, the transfer of this record into the supreme court for the sole purpose of inquiring whether the judgment violates the constitution of the United States, can, with no propriety, we think, be denominated a suit commenced or prosecuted against the state whose judgment is so far reexamined. Nothing is demanded from the state. No claim against it of any description is asserted or prosecuted. The party is not to be restored to the possession of anything. Essentially, it is an appeal on a single point; and the defendant who appeals from a judgment rendered against him, is never said to commence or prosecute a suit against the plaintiff who has obtained the judgment. . . .

It is, then, the opinion of the court, that the defendant who removes a judgment rendered against him by a state court into this court, for the purpose of reexamining the question, whether that judgment be in violation of the constitution or laws of the United States, does not commence or prosecute a suit against the state. . . .

2d. The second objection to the jurisdiction of the court is, that its appellate power cannot be exercised, in any case, over the judgment of a state court. . . .

. . . America has chosen to be, in many respects, and to many purposes, a nation; and for all these purposes, her government is complete; to all these objects it is competent. The people have declared, that in the exercise of all powers given for these objects, it is supreme. It can, then, in effecting these objects, legitimately control all individuals or governments within the American territory. The constitution and laws of a state, so far as they are repugnant to the constitution and laws of the United States, are absolutely void. These states are constituent parts of the United States; they are members of one great empire—for some purposes sovereign, for some purposes subordinate.

In a government so constituted, is it unreasonable, that the judicial power should be competent to give efficacy to the constitutional laws of the legislature? That department can decide on the validity of the constitution or law of a state, if it be repugnant to the constitution or to a law of the United States. Is it unreasonable, that it should also be empowered to decide on the judgment of a state tribunal enforcing such unconstitutional law? . . .

The propriety of entrusting the construction of the constitution, and laws made in pursuance thereof, to the judiciary of the Union has not, we believe, as yet, been drawn into question. It seems to be a corollary from this political axiom, that the federal courts should either possess exclusive jurisdiction in such cases, or a power to revise the judgment rendered in them, by the state tribunals. If the federal and state courts have concurrent jurisdiction in all cases arising under the constitution, laws, and treaties of the United States; and if a case of this description brought in a state court cannot be removed before judgment, nor revised after judgment, then the construction of the constitution, laws, and treaties of the United States is not confided particularly to their judicial department, but is confided equally to that department and to the state courts, however they may be constituted. "Thirteen independent courts," says a very celebrated statesman (and we have now more than twenty such courts), "of final jurisdiction over the same causes, arising upon the same laws, is a hydra in government, from which nothing but contradiction and confusion can proceed."

Dismissing the unpleasant suggestion, that any motives which may not be fairly avowed, or which ought not to exist, can ever influence a state or its courts, the necessity of uniformity, as well as correctness in expounding the constitution and laws of the United States, would itself suggest the propriety of vesting in some single tribunal the power of deciding, in the last resort, all cases in which they are involved.

We are not restrained, then, by the political relations between the general and state governments, from construing the words of the constitution, defining the judicial power, in their true sense. We are not bound to construe them more restrictively than they naturally import.

They give to the supreme court appellate jurisdiction in all cases arising under the constitution, laws, and treaties of the United States. The words are broad enough to comprehend all cases of this description, in whatever court they may be decided. . . .

This opinion has been already drawn out to great length to admit of entering into a particular consideration of the various forms in which the counsel who made this point has, with much ingenuity, presented his argument to the court. The argument, in all its forms, is essentially the same. It is founded, not on the words of the constitution, but on its spirit—a spirit extracted, not from the words of the instrument, but from his view of the nature of our Union, and of the great fundamental principles on which the fabric stands. To this argument, in all its forms, the same answer must be given. Let the nature and objects of our Union be considered; let the great fundamental principles, on which the fabric stands, be examined; and we think, the result must be, that there is nothing so extravagantly absurd, in giving to the court of the nation the power of revising the decisions of local tribunals, on questions which affect the nation, as to require the words which import this power should be restricted by a forced construction. . . .

Judgment affirmed

[On the merits of the case, the Court held that the federal statute authorizing a lottery in the District of Columbia had no effect outside the limits of the district, and it therefore upheld the conviction under the Virginia statute.]

Texas v. White
74 U.S. (7 Wall.) 700, 19 L.Ed. 227 (1869)

In 1851 Congress provided that $10 million in U.S. bonds should be transferred to the state of Texas, payable to the state or bearer and redeemable in 1864. In receiving the bonds, the Texas legislature stipulated that endorsement by the governor of the state was necessary to make any of the bonds valid in the hands of individual holders. [This act was repealed in 1862 by the insurgent Texas legislature, which authorized use of the bonds to obtain war supplies. In 1866 the Reconstruction government sought to block payment of bonds to George White and others out of state who held them] The defense interposed was that the Supreme Court lacked jurisdiction to entertain this original action because the plaintiff was not a state of the Union. The Supreme Court heard the case on an original bill. In his opinion Chief Justice Chase simultaneously espoused the Lincoln theory of secession and, without passing on the validity of any particular Reconstruction statute, acknowledged Congress's authority to maintain provisional governments in the southern states. Majority: Chase, Clifford, Davis, Field, Nelson. Dissenting: Grier, Miller, Swayne.

THE CHIEF JUSTICE [CHASE] delivered the opinion of the Court. . . .

Texas took part, with the other Confederate States, in the war of the rebellion, which these events made inevitable. During the whole of that war there was no governor, or judge, or any other State official in Texas, who recognized the National authority. Nor was any officer of the United States permitted to exercise any authority whatever under the National government within the limits of the

State, except under the immediate protection of the National military forces.

Did Texas, in consequence of these acts, cease to be a State? Or, if not, did the State cease to be a member of the Union?

It is needless to discuss, at length, the question whether the right of a State to withdraw from the Union for any cause, regarded by herself as sufficient, is consistent with the Constitution of the United States.

The Union of the States never was a purely artificial and arbitrary relation. It began among the Colonies, and grew out of common origin, mutual sympathies, kindred principles, similar interests, and geographical relations. It was confirmed and strengthened by the necessities of war, and received definite form, and character, and sanction from the Articles of Confederation. By these the Union was solemnly declared to "be perpetual." And when these Articles were found to be inadequate to the exigencies of the country, the Constitution was ordained "to form a more perfect Union." It is difficult to convey the idea of indissoluble unity more clearly than by these words. What can be indissoluble if a perpetual Union, made more perfect, is not?

But the perpetuity and indissolubility of the Union, by no means implies the loss of distinct and individual existence, or of the right of self-government by the States. Under the Articles of Confederation, each State retained its sovereignty, freedom, and independence, and every power, jurisdiction, and right not expressly delegated to the United States. Under the Constitution, though the powers of the States were much restricted, still, all powers not delegated to the United States, nor prohibited to the States, are reserved to the States respectively, or to the people. . . . Not only therefore can there be no loss of separate and independent autonomy to the States, through their union under the Constitution, but it may be not unreasonably said the preservation of the States, and the maintenance of their governments, are as much within the design and care of the Constitution as the preservation of the Union and the maintenance of the National government. The Constitution, in all its provisions, looks to an indestructible Union, composed of indestructible States.

When, therefore, Texas became one of the United States, she entered into an indissoluble relation. All

the obligations of perpetual union and all the guarantees of republican government in the Union, attached at once to the State. The act which consummated her admission into the Union was something more than a compact; it was the incorporation of a new member into the political body. And it was final. The union between Texas and the other States was as complete, as perpetual, and as indissoluble as the union between the original States. There was no place for reconsideration, or revocation, except through revolution, or through consent of the States.

Considered therefore as transactions under the Constitution, the ordinance of secession, adopted by the convention and ratified by a majority of the citizens of Texas, and all the acts of her legislature intended to give effect to that ordinance, were absolutely null. They were utterly without operation in law. The obligations of the State, as a member of the Union, and of every citizen of the State, as a citizen of the United States, remained perfect and unimpaired. It certainly follows that the State did not cease to be a State, nor her citizens to be citizens of the Union. If this were otherwise, the State must have become foreign, and her citizens foreigners. The war must have ceased to be a war for the suppression of rebellion, and must have become a war of conquest and subjugation.

Our conclusion therefore is, that Texas continued to be a State, and a State of the Union, notwithstanding the transactions to which we have referred. And this conclusion, in our judgment, is not in conflict with any act or declaration of any department of the National government, but entirely in accordance with the whole series of such acts and declarations, since the first outbreak of rebellion.

But in order to the exercise, by a State, of the right to sue in this court, there needs to be a State government, competent to represent the State in its relations with the National government, so far at least as the institution and prosecution of a suit is concerned. . . .

All admit that, during this condition of civil war, the rights of the State as a member, and her people as citizens of the Union, were suspended. The government and the citizens of the State, refusing to recognize their constitutional obligations, assumed the character of enemies, and incurred the consequences of rebellion.

These new relations imposed new duties upon

the United States. The first was that of suppressing the rebellion. The next was that of re-establishing the broken relations of the State with the Union. The first of these duties having been performed, the next necessarily engaged the attention of the National government. . . .

There being then no government in Texas in constitutional relations with the Union, it became the duty of the United States to provide for the restoration of such a government. But the restoration of the government which existed before the rebellion, without a new election of officers, was obviously impossible; and before any such election could be properly held, it was necessary that the old constitution should receive such amendments as would conform its provisions to the new conditions created by emancipation, and afford adequate security to the people of the State.

In the exercise of the power conferred by the guaranty clause, as in the exercise of every other constitutional power, a discretion in the choice of means is necessarily allowed. It is essential only that the means must be necessary and proper for carrying into execution the power conferred, through the restoration of the State to its constitutional relations, under a republican form of government, and that no acts be done, and no authority exerted, which is either prohibited or unsanctioned by the Constitution. . . .

Nothing in the case before us requires the court to pronounce judgment upon the constitutionality of any particular provision of these acts.

But it is important to observe that these acts themselves show that the governments, which had been established and had been in actual operation under executive direction, were recognized by Congress as provisional, as existing, and as capable of continuance. . . .

[The right of Texas to bring suit was affirmed and a decree issued enjoining White and others from setting up any claim to the bonds.]

MR. JUSTICE GRIER, dissenting. . . .

The original jurisdiction of this court can be invoked only by one of the United States. The Territories have no such right conferred on them by the Constitution, nor have the Indian tribes who are under the protection of the military authorities of the government.

Is Texas one of these United States? Or was she such at the time the bill was filed, or since?

This is to be decided as *a political fact*, not as *a legal fiction*. This court is bound to know and notice the public history of the nation.

If I regard the truth of history for the last eight years, I cannot discover the State of Texas as one of these United States. . . .

New York v. United States*
326 U.S. 572, 66 S.Ct. 310, 90 L.Ed. 326 (1946)

In 1932, the United States imposed a tax on the sale of bottled mineral water. An attempt to collect this tax on mineral waters bottled and sold by a New York State public benefit corporation, the Saratoga Springs Authority, was resisted by New York, and from an adverse judgment the state sought review. Majority: Frankfurter, Burton, Murphy, Reed, Rutledge, Stone. Dissenting: Douglas, Black. Not participating: Jackson.

* This case should also be read in connection with Chapter Seven.

MR. JUSTICE FRANKFURTER announced the judgment of the Court and delivered an opinion in which MR. JUSTICE RUTLEDGE joined. . . .

Enactments levying taxes made in pursuance of the Constitution are, as other laws are, "the supreme Law of the Land." . . . The first of the powers conferred upon Congress is the power "To lay and collect Taxes, Duties, Imposts and Excises. . . ." By its terms the Constitution has placed only one limitation upon this power, other than limitations upon methods of laying taxes not here relevant: Congress can lay no tax "on Articles exported from any State." . . . Barring only exports, the power of Congress to tax "reaches every subject." But the fact that ours is a federal constitutional system, as expressly recognized in the Tenth Amendment, carries with it implications regarding the taxing power as in other aspects of government. . . . Thus, for Congress to tax State activities while leaving untaxed the same activities pursued by private persons would do violence to the presuppositions derived from the fact that we are a Nation composed of States. . . .

In the meantime, cases came here . . . in which States claimed immunity from a federal tax imposed generally on enterprises in which the State itself was also engaged. This problem did not arise before the present century, partly because State trading did not actively emerge until relatively recently, and partly because of the narrow scope of federal taxation. In *South Carolina* v. *United States,* immunity from a federal tax on a dispensary system, whereby South Carolina monopolized the sale of intoxicating liquors, was denied by drawing a line between taxation of the historically recognized governmental functions of a State, and business engaged in by a State of a kind which theretofore had been pursued by private enterprise. . . . It could hardly remain a satisfactory constitutional doctrine that only such State activities are immune from federal taxation as were engaged in by the States in 1787. Such a static concept of government denies its essential nature. . . .

When this Court came to sustain the federal taxing power upon a transportation system operated by a State, it did so in ways familiar in developing the law from precedent to precedent. It edged away from reliance on a sharp distinction between the "governmental" and the "trading" activities of a State, by denying immunity from federal taxation

to a State when it "is undertaking a business enterprise of a sort that is normally within the reach of the federal taxing power and is distinct from the usual governmental functions that are immune from federal taxation in order to safeguard the necessary independence of the State." But this likewise does not furnish a satisfactory guide for dealing with such a practical problem as the constitutional power of the United States over State activities. To rest the federal taxing power on what is "normally" conducted by private enterprise in contradiction to the "usual" governmental functions is too shifting a basis for determining constitutional power and too entangled in expediency to serve as a dependable legal criterion. The essential nature of the problem cannot be hidden by an attempt to separate manifestations of indivisible governmental powers. . . .

In the older cases, the emphasis was on immunity from taxation. The whole tendency of recent cases reveals a shift in emphasis to that of limitation upon immunity. They also indicate an awareness of the limited rôle of courts in assessing the relative weight of the factors upon which immunity is based. Any implied limitation upon the supremacy of the federal power to levy a tax like that now before us, in the absence of discrimination against State activities, brings fiscal and political factors into play. The problem cannot escape issues that do not lend themselves to judgment by criteria and methods of reasoning that are within the professional training and special competence of judges. Indeed the claim of implied immunity by States from federal taxation raises questions not wholly unlike provisions of the Constitution, such as that of Art. IV, § 4, guaranteeing States a republican form of government, which this Court has deemed not within its duty to adjudicate. . . .

There are, of course, State activities and State-owned property that partake of uniqueness from the point of view of intergovernmental relations. These inherently constitute a class by themselves. Only a State can own a Statehouse; only a State can get income by taxing. These could not be included for purposes of federal taxation in any abstract category of taxpayers without taxing the State as a State. But so long as Congress generally taps a source of revenue by whomsoever earned and not uniquely capable of being earned only by a State, the Constitution of the United States does not forbid it merely because its incidence falls also on a State. If Congress desires, it may of course leave untaxed enterprises pursued by States for the public good while it taxes like enterprises organized for private ends. . . .

The process of Constitutional adjudication does not thrive on conjuring up horrible possibilities that never happen in the real world and devising doctrines sufficiently comprehensive in detail to cover the remotest contingency. . . . So we . . . find no restriction upon Congress to include the States in levying a tax exacted equally from private persons upon the same subject matter.

Judgment affirmed.

MR. JUSTICE DOUGLAS, with whom MR. JUSTICE BLACK concurs, dissenting. . . .

I do not believe *South Carolina* v. *United States* states the correct rule. A State's project is as much a legitimate governmental activity whether it is traditional, or akin to private enterprise, or conducted for profit. . . . A State may deem it as essential to its economy that it own and operate a railroad, a mill, or an irrigation system as it does to own and operate bridges, street lights, or a sewage disposal plant. What might have been viewed in an earlier day as an improvident or even dangerous extension of state activities may today be deemed indispensable. But as MR. JUSTICE WHITE said in his dissent in *South Carolina* v. *United States,* any activity in which a State engages within the limits of its police power is a legitimate governmental activity. Here a State is disposing of some of its natural resources. Tomorrow it may issue securities, sell power from its public power project, or manufacture fertilizer. Each is an exercise

of its power of sovereignty. Must it pay the federal government for the privilege of exercising that inherent power? If the Constitution grants it immunity from a tax on the issuance of securities, on what grounds can it be forced to pay a tax when it sells power or disposes of other natural resources? . . .

The notion that the sovereign position of the States must find its protection in the will of a transient majority of Congress is foreign to and a negation of our constitutional system. There will often be vital regional interests represented by no majority in Congress. The constitution was designed to keep the balance between the States and the Nation outside the field of legislative controversy.

The immunity of the States from federal taxation is no less clear because it is implied. . . . The Constitution is a compact between sovereigns. The power of one sovereign to tax another is an innovation so startling as to require explicit authority if it is to be allowed. If the power of the federal government to tax the States is conceded, the reserved power of the States guaranteed by the Tenth Amendment does not give them the independence which they have always been assumed to have. They are relegated to a more servile status. They become subject to interference and control both in the functions which they exercise and the methods which they employ. They must pay the federal government for the privilege of exercising the powers of sovereignty guaranteed them by the Constitution, whether, as here, they are disposing of their natural resources, or tomorrow they issue securities or perform any other acts within the scope of their police power. . . .

Pacific Gas & Electric Co. v. *Energy Resources Conservation and Development Commission*
461 U.S. 190, 103 S. Ct. 1713, 75 L.Ed.2d 752 (1983)

The California Public Resources Code, as amended in 1976, provides in Section 25524.1(b) that, before a nuclear power plant may be built, the state's Energy Resources Conservation and Development Commission must determine on a case-by-case basis that there will be adequate capacity for interim storage of the plant's spent fuel at the time the plant requires such storage. Section 25524.2 imposes a moratorium on the certification of new nuclear plants until the commission finds that approved technology has been developed for the permanent disposal of high-level nuclear wastes. Electric utilities convinced the district court in 1980 that the provisions were invalid under the supremacy clause because they were preempted by the Atomic Energy Act of 1954 and other federal legislation. In 1981 the Ninth Circuit Court of Appeals held that the challenge to Section 25524.1(b) was not "ripe for review" (see Chapter One for a discussion of ripeness) and that Section 25524.2 was not preempted because Congress intended states to regulate nuclear power plants for reasons other than protection against radiation hazards. The Supreme Court agreed that the attack on Section 25524.1(b) lacked ripeness but that the challenge to the moratorium in Section 25524.2 was ripe for review. The following excerpts from Justice White's opinion focus on the question of preemption. Majority: White, Blackmun, Brennan, Burger, Marshall, O'Connor, Powell, Rehnquist, Stevens.

JUSTICE WHITE delivered the opinion of the Court.

The turning of swords into plowshares has symbolized the transformation of atomic power into a source of energy in American society. To facilitate this development the Federal Government relaxed its monopoly over fissionable materials and nuclear technology, and in its place, erected a complex scheme to promote the civilian development of nuclear energy, while seeking to safeguard the public and the environment from the unpredictable risks of a new technology. Early on, it was decided that the States would continue their traditional role in the regulation of electricity production. The interrelationship of federal and state authority in the nuclear energy field has not been simple; the federal regulatory structure has been frequently amended to optimize the partnership.

This case emerges from the intersection of the Federal Government's efforts to ensure that nuclear power is safe with the exercise of the historic state authority over the generation and sale of electricity. At issue is whether provisions in the 1976 amendments . . . which condition the construction of nuclear plants on findings by the State Energy Resources Conservation and Development Commission that adequate storage facilities and means of disposal are available for nuclear waste, are preempted by the Atomic Energy Act of 1954, so amended. . . .

It is well-established that within Constitutional limits Congress may preempt state authority by so

stating in express terms. Absent explicit preemptive language, Congress' intent to supercede state law altogether may be found from a "scheme of federal regulation so pervasive as to make reasonable the inference that Congress left no room to supplement it," "because the Act of Congress may touch a field in which the federal interest is so dominant that the federal system will be assumed to preclude enforcement of state laws on the same subject," or because "the object sought to be obtained by the federal law and the character of obligations imposed by it may reveal the same purpose." Even where Congress has not entirely displaced state regulation in a specific area, state law is preempted to the extent that it actually conflicts with federal law. Such a conflict arises when "compliance with both federal and state regulations is a physical impossibility," or where state law "stands as an obstacle to the accomplishment and execution of the full purposes and objectives of Congress."

Petitioners, the United States, and supporting amici, present three major lines of argument as to why § 25524.2 is preempted. First, they submit that the statute—because it regulates construction of nuclear plants and because it is allegedly predicated on safety concerns—ignores the division between federal and state authority created by the Atomic Energy Act, and falls within the field that the federal government has preserved for its own exclusive control. Second, the statute, and the judgments that underlie it, conflict with decisions concerning the nuclear waste disposal issue made by Congress and the Nuclear Regulatory Commission. Third, the California statute frustrates the federal goal of developing nuclear technology as a source of energy. We consider each of these contentions in turn.

. . . From the passage of the Atomic Energy Act in 1954, through several revisions, and to the present day, Congress has preserved the dual regulation of nuclear-powered electricity generation: the federal government maintains complete control of the safety and "nuclear" aspects of energy generation; the states exercise their traditional authority over the need for additional generating capacity, the type of generating facilities to be licensed, land use, ratemaking, and the like. . . .

At the outset, we emphasize that the statute does not seek to regulate the construction or operation of a nuclear power plant. It would clearly be impermissible for California to attempt to do so, for such regulation, even if enacted out of non-safety concerns, would nevertheless directly conflict with the NRC's exclusive authority over plant construction and operation. Respondents appear to concede as much. Respondents do broadly argue, however, that although safety regulation of nuclear plants by states is forbidden, a state may completely prohibit new construction until its safety concerns are satisfied by the federal government. We reject this line of reasoning. State safety regulation is not preempted only when it conflicts with federal law. Rather, the federal government has occupied the entire field of nuclear safety concerns, except the limited powers expressly ceded to the states. When the federal government completely occupies a given field or an identifiable portion of it, as it has done here, the test of preemption is whether "the matter on which the state asserts the right to act is in any way regulated by the federal government." A state moratorium on nuclear construction grounded in safety concerns falls squarely within the prohibited field. . . .

That being the case, it is necessary to determine whether there is a non-safety rationale for § 25524.2. . . .

Although [several] indicia of California's intent in enacting § 25524.2 are subject to varying interpretation, there are two reasons why we should not become embroiled in attempting to ascertain California's true motive. First, inquiry into legislative

motive is often an unsatisfactory venture. What motivates one legislator to vote for a statute is not necessarily what motivates scores of others to enact it. Second, it would be particularly pointless for us to engage in such inquiry here when it is clear that the states have been allowed to retain authority over the need for electrical generating facilities easily sufficient to permit a state so inclined to halt the construction of new nuclear plants by refusing on economic grounds to issue certificates of public convenience in individual proceedings. In these circumstances, it should be up to Congress to determine whether a state has misused the authority left in its hands.

Therefore, we accept California's avowed economic purpose as the rationale for enacting § 25524.2. Accordingly, the statute lies outside the occupied field of nuclear safety regulation.

Petitioners' second major argument concerns federal regulation aimed at the nuclear waste disposal problem itself. It is contended that § 25524.2 conflicts with federal regulation of nuclear waste disposal, with the NRC's decision that it is permissible to continue to license reactors, notwithstanding uncertainty surrounding the waste disposal problem, and with Congress' recent passage of legislation directed at that problem. . . .

The NRC's imprimatur, however, indicates only that it is safe to proceed with such plants, not that it is economically wise to do so. Because the NRC order does not and could not compel a utility to develop a nuclear plant, compliance with both it and § 25524.2 are possible. Moreover, because the NRC's regulations are aimed at insuring that plants are safe, not necessarily that they are economical, § 25524.2 does not interfere with the objective of the federal regulation.

Nor has California sought through § 25524.2 to impose its own standards on nuclear waste disposal. The statute accepts that it is the federal responsibility to develop and license such technology. As there is no attempt on California's part to enter this field, one which is occupied by the federal government, we do not find § 25524.2 preempted any more by the NRC's obligations in the waste disposal field than by its licensing power over the plants themselves. . . .

Finally, it is strongly contended that § 25524.2 frustrates the Atomic Energy Act's purpose to develop the commercial use of nuclear power. . . .

There is little doubt that a primary purpose of the Atomic Energy Act was, and continues to be, the promotion of nuclear power. The Act itself states that it is a program "to encourage widespread participation in the development and utilization of atomic energy for peaceful purposes to the maximum extent consistent with the common defense and security and with the health and safety of the public." The House and Senate Reports confirmed that it was "a major policy goal of the United States" that the involvement of private industry would "speed the further development of the peaceful uses of atomic energy." The same purpose is manifest in the passage of the Price-Anderson Act, which limits private liability from a nuclear accident. The Act was passed "in order to protect the public and to encourage the development of the atomic energy industry. . . ."

. . . The Court of Appeals is right . . . that the promotion of nuclear power is not to be accomplished "at all costs." The elaborate licensing and safety provisions and the continued preservation of state regulation in traditional areas belie that. Moreover, Congress has allowed the States to determine—as a matter of economics—whether a nuclear plant vis-a-vis a fossil fuel plant should be built. The decision of California to exercise that authority does not, in itself, constitute a basis for preemption. Therefore, while the argument of petitioners and the United States has considerable force, the legal reality remains that Congress has left sufficient authority in the states to allow the development of nuclear power to be slowed or even stopped for economic reasons. Given this statutory scheme, it is for Congress to rethink the division of regulatory authority in light of its possible exercise by the states to undercut a federal objective. The courts should not assume the role which our system assigns to Congress.

The judgment of the Court of Appeals is

Affirmed.

Garcia v. *San Antonio Metropolitan Transit Authority**
469 U.S. 528, 105 S.Ct. 1005, 83 L.Ed. 2d 1016 (1985)

San Antonio Metropolitan Transit Authority (SAMTA) operates a public mass-transit system in San Antonio, Texas, and the surrounding area. Following *National League of Cities* v. *Usery* in 1976, the transit authority (then known as the San Antonio Transit System) informed its employees that this decision relieved the transit system of its overtime pay obligations under the Fair Labor Standards Act (FLSA). (SAMTA did not attempt to avoid the minimum wage provisions of the FLSA.) In 1979, the Wage and Hour Administration of the Department of Labor informed SAMTA that its operations were covered by FLSA, in spite of *National League of Cities*. SAMTA then asked the United States District Court for the Western District of Texas for a declaratory judgment that the 1976 decision precluded application of the FLSA's overtime requirements to SAMTA's operations. At the same time, Joe Garcia and several other SAMTA employees filed suit against SAMTA in district court for overtime pay under the FLSA. In 1981, the district court ruled that, under *National League of Cities,*

---

* This case should also be read in connection with Chapter Six.

SAMTA was immune from the requirements of the FLSA. The Secretary of Labor and Garcia appealed directly to the Supreme Court.

While the San Antonio case was in progress, the Supreme Court ruled in *Transportation Union* v. *Long Island Railroad Co.* (1982) that commuter rail service provided by a state-owned railroad did not constitute a "traditional governmental function" and so did not qualify for immunity under *National League of Cities*. The Court vacated the district court's judgment in the SAMTA case, remanding for further consideration in light of *Long Island Railroad*. On remand, the district court maintained its original view and decided in favor of SAMTA. Majority: Blackmun, Brennan, Marshall, Stevens, White. Dissenting: Powell, Burger, O'Connor, Rehnquist.

JUSTICE BLACKMUN delivered the opinion of the Court.

We revisit in these cases an issue raised in *National League of Cities* v. *Usery*. . . . In that litigation, this Court, by a sharply divided vote, ruled that the Commerce Clause does not empower Congress to enforce the minimum-wage and overtime provisions of the Fair Labor Standards Act (FLSA) against the States "in areas of traditional governmental functions." . . . Although *National League of Cities* supplied some examples of "traditional governmental functions," it did not offer a general explanation of how a "traditional" function is to be distinguished from a "nontraditional" one. Since then, federal and state courts have struggled with the task, thus imposed, of identifying a traditional function for purposes of state immunity under the Commerce Clause. . . .

Our examination of this "function" standard applied in these and other cases over the last eight years now persuades us that the attempt to draw the boundaries of state regulatory immunity in terms of "traditional governmental function" is not only unworkable but is inconsistent with established principles of federalism and, indeed, with those very federalism principles on which *National League of Cities* purported to rest. That case, accordingly, is overruled. . . .

The present controversy concerns the extent to which SAMTA may be subjected to the minimum-wage and overtime requirements of the FLSA. . . .

We therefore now reject, as unsound in principle and unworkable in practice, a rule of state immunity from federal regulation that turns on a judicial appraisal of whether a particular governmental function is "integral" or "traditional." Any such rule

leads to inconsistent results at the same time that it disserves principles of democratic self-governance, and it breeds inconsistency precisely because it is divorced from those principles. If there are to be limits on the Federal Government's power to interfere with state functions—as undoubtedly there are—we must look elsewhere to find them. We accordingly return to the underlying issue that confronted this Court in *National League of Cities*—the manner in which the Constitution insulates States from the reach of Congress' power under the Commerce Clause.

The central theme of *National League of Cities* was that the States occupy a special position in our constitutional system and that the scope of Congress' authority under the Commerce Clause must reflect that position. . . .

What has proved problematic is not the perception that the Constitution's federal structure imposes limitations on the Commerce Clause, but rather the nature and content of those limitations. . . .

We doubt that courts ultimately can identify principled constitutional limitations on the scope of Congress' Commerce Clause powers over the States merely by relying on *a priori* definitions of state sovereignty. In part, this is because of the elusiveness of objective criteria for "fundamental" elements of state sovereignty, a problem we have witnessed in the search for "traditional governmental functions." There is, however, a more fundamental reason: the sovereignty of the States is limited by the Constitution itself. A variety of sovereign powers, for example, are withdrawn from the States by Article I, § 10. Section 8 of the same Article works an equally sharp contraction of state sovereignty by authorizing Congress to exercise a wide range of legislative powers and (in conjunction with the Supremacy Clause of Article VI) to displace contrary state legislation. . . . By providing for final review of questions of federal law in this Court, Article III curtails the sovereign power of the States' judiciaries to make authoritative determinations of law. . . . Finally, the developed application, through the Fourteenth Amendment, of the greater part of the Bill of Rights to the States limits the sovereign authority that States otherwise would possess to legislate with respect to their citizens and to conduct their own affairs. . . .

As a result, to say that the Constitution assumes the continued role of the States is to say little about the nature of that role. . . . With rare exceptions, like the guarantee, in Article IV, § 3, of state territorial integrity, the Constitution does not carve out express elements of state sovereignty that Congress may not employ its delegated powers to displace. James Wilson reminded the Pennsylvania ratifying convention in 1787: "It is true, indeed, sir, although it presupposes the existence of state governments, yet this Constitution does not suppose them to be the sole power to be respected." . . . The power of the Federal Government is a "power to be respected" as well, and the fact that the States remain sovereign as to all powers not vested in Congress or denied them by the Constitution offers no guidance about where the frontier between state and federal power lies. In short, we have no license to employ freestanding conceptions of state sovereignty when measuring congressional authority under the Commerce Clause. . . .

In short, the Framers chose to rely on a federal system in which special restraints on federal power over the States inhered principally in the workings of the National Government itself, rather than in discrete limitations on the objects of federal authority. State sovereign interests, then, are more properly protected by procedural safeguards inherent in the structure of the federal system than by judicially created limitations on federal power.

Insofar as the present cases are concerned, then, we need go no further than to state that we perceive nothing in the overtime and minimum-wage requirements of the FLSA, as applied to SAMTA, that is destructive of state sovereignty or violative of any constitutional provision. SAMTA faces nothing more than the same minimum-wage and over-time obligations that hundreds of thousands of other employers, public as well as private, have to meet. . . .

Of course, we continue to recognize that the States occupy a special and specific position in our constitutional system and that the scope of Congress' authority under the Commerce Clause must reflect that position. But the principal and basic limit on the federal commerce power is that inherent in all congressional action—the built-in restraints that our system provides through state participation in federal governmental action. The political process ensures that laws that unduly burden the States will not be promulgated. In the factual setting of these cases the internal safeguards of the political process have performed as intended. . . .

Though the separate concurrence* providing the fifth vote in *National League of Cities* was "not untroubled by certain possible implications" of the decision . . . the Court in that case attempted to articulate affirmative limits on the Commerce Clause power in terms of core governmental functions and fundamental attributes of state sovereignty. But the model of democratic decisionmaking the Court there identified underestimated, in our view, the solicitude of the national political process for the continued vitality of the States. Attempts by other courts since then to draw guidance from this model have proved it both impracticable and doctrinally barren. In sum, in *National League of Cities* the Court tried to repair what did not need repair.

We do not lightly overrule recent precedent. We have not hesitated, however, when it has become apparent that a prior decision has departed from a proper understanding of congressional power under the Commerce Clause. . . . Due respect for the reach of congressional power within the federal system mandates that we do so now.

National League of Cities v. *Usery* . . . is overruled. The judgment of the District Court is reversed, and these cases are remanded to that court for further proceedings consistent with this opinion.

It is so ordered.

JUSTICE POWELL, with whom THE CHIEF JUSTICE, JUSTICE REHNQUIST, and JUSTICE O'CONNOR join, dissenting. . . .

. . . A unique feature of the United States is the *federal* system of government guaranteed by

---

* Justice Blackmun refers to himself.—ED.

the Constitution and implicit in the very name of our country. Despite some genuflecting in the Court's opinion to the concept of federalism, today's decision effectively reduces the Tenth Amendment to meaningless rhetoric when Congress acts pursuant to the Commerce Clause.

To leave no doubt about its intention, the Court renounces its decision in *National League of Cities* because it "inevitably invites an unelected federal judiciary to make decisions about which state policies its favors and which ones it dislikes." . . . In other words, the extent to which the States may exercise their authority, when Congress purports to act under the Commerce Clause, henceforth is to be determined from time to time by political decisions made by members of the federal government, decisions the Court says will not be subject to judicial review. I note that it does not seem to have occurred to the Court that *it*—an unelected majority of five Justices—today rejects almost 200 years of the understanding of the constitutional status of federalism. In doing so, there is only a single passing reference to the Tenth Amendment. Nor is so much as a dictum of any court cited in support of the view that the role of the States in the federal system may depend upon the grace of elected federal officials, rather than on the Constitution as interpreted by this Court. . . .

Much of the initial opposition to the Constitution was rooted in the fear that the national government would be too powerful and eventually would eliminate the States as viable political entities. This concern was voiced repeatedly until proponents of the Constitution made assurances that a bill of rights, including a provision explicitly reserving powers in the States, would be among the first business of the New Congress. Samuel Adams argued, for example, that if the several States were to be joined in "one entire Nation, under one Legislature, the Powers of which shall extend to every Subject of Legislation, and its Laws be supreme & controul the whole, the Idea of Sovereignty in these States must be lost." . . .

This history, which the Court simply ignores, documents the integral role of the Tenth Amendment in our constitutional theory. It exposes as well, I believe, the fundamental character of the Court's error today. Far from being "unsound in principle" . . . judicial enforcement of the Tenth Amendment is essential to maintaining the federal

system so carefully designed by the Framers and adopted in the Constitution. . . .

Thus, the harm to the States that results from federal overreaching under the Commerce Clause is not simply a matter of dollars and cents. . . . Nor is it a matter of the wisdom or folly of certain policy choices. . . . Rather, by usurping functions traditionally performed by the States, federal overreaching under the Commerce Clause undermines the constitutionally mandated balance of power between the States and the federal government, a balance designed to protect our fundamental liberties. . . .

JUSTICE O'CONNOR, with whom JUSTICE POWELL and JUSTICE REHNQUIST join, dissenting. . . .

Due to the emergence of an integrated and industrialized national economy, this Court has been required to examine and review a breath-taking expansion of the powers of Congress. In doing so the Court correctly perceived that the Framers of our Constitution intended Congress to have sufficient power to address national problems. But the Framers were not single-minded. The Constitution is animated by an array of intentions. . . . Just as surely as the Framers envisioned a National Government capable of solving national problems, they also envisioned a republic whose vitality was assured by the diffusion of power not only among the branches of the Federal Government, but also between the Federal Government and the States. . . . In the 18th century these intentions did not conflict because technology had not yet converted every local problem into a national one. A conflict has now emerged, and the Court today retreats rather than reconciles the Constitution's dual concerns for federalism and an effective commerce power. . . .

Incidental to this expansion of the commerce power, Congress has been given an ability it lacked prior to the emergence of an integrated national economy. Because virtually every *state* activity, like virtually every activity of a private individual, arguably "affects" interstate commerce, Congress can now supplant the States from the significant sphere of activities envisioned for them by the Framers. It is in this context that recent changes in the workings of Congress, such as the direct election of Senators and the expanded influence of national interest groups . . . become relevant. These changes may well have lessened the weight Congress gives to the legitimate interests of States as States. As a result, there is now a real risk that Congress will gradually erase the diffusion of power between state and nation on which the Framers based their faith in the efficiency and vitality of our Republic. . . .

It is worth recalling the cited passage in *McCulloch* v. *Maryland* . . . that lies at the source of the recent expansion of the commerce power. "Let the end be legitimate, let it be within the scope of the constitution," Chief Justice Marshall said, "and all means which are appropriate, which are plainly adapted to that end, which are not prohibited, but consist with the letter *and spirit* of the constitution, are constitutional" (emphasis added). The *spirit* of the Tenth Amendment, of course, is that the States will retain their integrity in a system in which the laws of the United States are nevertheless supreme. . . .

This . . . requires the Court to enforce affirmative limits on federal regulation of the States to complement the judicially crafted expansion of the interstate commerce power. . . .

FIVE

Commerce Power
and State Power

*The desire of the Forefathers to federalize regulation of foreign
and interstate commerce stands in sharp contrast to their jealous
preservation of the State's power over its internal affairs. No
other federal power was so universally assumed to be necessary.
No other state power was so readily relinquished.*

—JUSTICE ROBERT H. JACKSON (1949)

No one familiar with state and local government today can fail to notice the wide variety
of regulations enacted by legislatures and city councils across the land on virtually every
aspect of commercial life. These laws are examples of the "police power," that general,
residual, and regulatory power retained by the states under the Constitution. Yet Section 8
of Article I of the Constitution declares, "The Congress shall have Power . . . To regulate
Commerce with foreign Nations, and among the several States, and with the Indian
Tribes. . . ." What is this power over commerce? To what degree does the national
commerce power limit or even prohibit state laws that affect commerce?

VIEWS OF THE FRAMERS

Removal of the obstructions on commercial relations imposed by the "sovereign" states was
a moving cause of the Philadelphia Convention of 1787. For protection against these burdens
and restrictions, James Madison, as a member of the Continental Congress, had advocated
general authority over commerce. Later on he was conspicuous among those who set in
motion the sequence of events leading to the successful meeting at Philadelphia. There
seems to be no doubt that the commerce clause was inserted in the Constitution primarily
to prevent the states from interfering with the freedom of commercial intercourse. Yet all
the plans offered by the Convention apparently envisioned a positive power in the national
government to regulate commerce, and subsequent developments converted this clause into
a most important source of national authority. Was this the intention of the men who
framed the Constitution? The record of the Convention of 1787 affords no conclusive answer.

On September 15, 1787, Madison, commenting on the question whether, under Article I, Section 10, a tonnage tax could be levied by the states for purposes of clearing and dredging harbors, said, "It depends on the extent of the commerce power. These terms—to regulate commerce—are vague but seem to exclude this power of the states. He [Madison] was more and more convinced that the regulation of commerce was in its nature indivisible and ought to be wholly under one authority." Immediately following this statement, Roger Sherman of Connecticut observed, "The Power of the United States to regulate trade, being Supreme, can control interferences of the State regulations where such interferences happen; so that there is no danger to be apprehended from a concurrent jurisdiction."

"Had the issue been clearly posed and unequivocally settled," Albert S. Abel commented, "it must perhaps have eliminated decades of judicial groping and guessing; on the other hand it might have broken up the convention."

Certain inferences about the nature and scope of the commerce power may be drawn from changes the Convention made in the wording of the commerce clause itself. In the Pinckney Plan the word *exclusive* was used before *power*. Draft VII of the Committee of Detail used *exclusive,* but in Draft IX it was deleted and reported out in its present form. No evidence has been presented concerning the significance of this deletion. *Exclusive* is used as a description of congressional power only in Clause 17 (laws for the District of Columbia). Even the power of Congress to declare war is not stated to be "exclusive," but Article I, Section 10, explicitly limits state action.

One becomes aware of a noticeable lack of specific restraints, such as those spelled out in Article I, Section 10. The only restriction of a commercial nature forbids duty on imports (or exports), except for the amount necessary to meet inspection cost. This seems to suggest freedom of the states to pass other laws regulating commerce.

Because of the partisan motives of the speakers, contemporary opinion on the meaning of the clause is no sure guide. Those opposed to the new Constitution stressed its centralizing tendencies in lurid colors; supporters, on the other hand, minimized the significance of the commerce power. James McHenry of the Maryland delegation said, "We almost shuddered at the fate of commerce of Maryland should we be unable to make any change in this extraordinary power." In the Virginia ratifying convention, Edmund Randolph agreed that the broad power over commerce was a sine qua non of the Union, and yet he favored a two-thirds vote by Congress for national commerce acts. Richard Henry Lee, also of Virginia, reported a widespread fear that the clause would be used to discriminate against southern states by the establishment of northern monopolies.

The writers of that skillful campaign document *The Federalist* employed their usual tactics. They made clear the dangers of not giving a broad power over commerce to the general government but blurred the precise limits of national power. In No. 7 Hamilton stated, "The competitions of commerce would be another fruitful source of contention. . . . Each state or separate confederacy would pursue a system of commercial policy peculiar to itself. . . .The infraction of these [state] regulations on one side, the efforts to prevent and repel them on the other, would naturally lead to outrages, and these to reprisals and war." In No. 42 Madison glossed over the nature of the commerce power by discussing it chiefly as a supplement to the power over foreign commerce and by stressing the unfairness of permitting coastal states to levy a toll on states in the interior. In No. 45 Madison again hinted that the commerce power would be exercised chiefly on foreign commerce.

Many years later, in 1829, after the "Father of the Constitution" had become a proponent of states' rights, Madison wrote to J. C. Cabell that the power to regulate commerce was designed to prevent abuses by the states rather than for positive purposes of the national government: ". . . .[I]t is very certain that it . . . was intended as a negative and preventive provision against injustice among the States themselves, rather than as a power to be used for the positive purposes of the General Government, in which alone, however, the remedial power could be lodged."

THE MARSHALL DOCTRINE

The intriguing question, What does the commerce clause mean? was first presented to the Court in 1824. *Gibbons* **v.** *Ogden* involved the unpopular New York "steamboat monopoly." Chancellor Kent of the New York court upheld the monopoly and maintained that Congress did not have any direct jurisdiction over internal commerce or waters. Daniel Webster, arguing for Gibbons on appeal to the Supreme Court, asserted that Congress alone could regulate "high branches" of commerce. Counsel for the monopoly claimed that a concurrent power existed whenever such a power was not clearly denied by the Constitution. Webster's prophetic construction of commerce as comprehending "almost all the business and intercourse of life" was countered by the definition of commerce as "the transportation and sale of commodities." Both sides agreed that if an actual collision of state and national power occurred the latter must prevail, but counsel for the monopoly held that state power gave way only to the extent needed to give effect to the federal law. Accordingly navigation on state waters remained under state control.

In a separate opinion, Marshall could have solved the case simply by finding that both state and nation had acted within their powers, but since the state law conflicted with the federal licensing act it must give way. He chose instead to examine the nature of the commerce power before finding the existence of a conflict. Commerce was more than traffic; "it is intercourse," and comprehended navigation. He reiterated the point that commerce "among" the states cannot stop at state lines but "may be introduced into the interior." The power to regulate was "complete in itself, may be exercised to its utmost extent, and acknowledges *no limitations,* other than are prescribed in the Constitution." Though the states retained authority to enact inspection, pilotage, and health laws, even here Congress could enter the field if it chose.

In a separate opinion, Justice William Johnson went beyond Marshall. Even in the absence of the licensing act, the state monopoly must give way. Johnson's forthright remarks on the effect of the coasting license stand in bold contrast to those of Marshall. The national commerce power, Johnson contended, embraces all the power enjoyed by the states before the Constitution. It is a grant of the whole power carrying the whole subject exclusively into the hands of the national government.

With the exception of monopolists and southern slave-owners who feared the consequence of a broad definition of national power over commerce, public opinion welcomed the rebuke given holders of special privilege. Following the decision, the number of steamboats plying in and out of New York harbor increased in one year from six to 43.

Three years later, in *Brown* v. *Maryland* (1827) the Court held that national power over foreign commerce excluded state regulation in the form of licensing and taxing importers. Marshall pointed out that state actions of this nature violated both the prohibition of state taxes on imports (Art. I, Sec. 10) and the limitations on state power implicit in the commerce clause. In his effort to draw a line between commerce that could be regulated by the states and commerce that could not, he formulated the *original package doctrine,* adding the dictum "we suppose the principles laid down in this case to apply equally to importations from a sister state."

By barring state taxation of goods before they had mixed with the commerce of a state, Marshall moved to protect the shipment of commercial products across the land from crippling restraints that might be imposed by a state through which the merchandise entered.

In *Leisy* v. *Hardin* (1890), the Court accepted Marshall's dictum (statements by a judge not necessary to the decision of a case) and applied the doctrine to commodities produced inside the United States and transported to another state. In both the objective was a nondiscriminatory state policy that did not depend on the foreign origin of the goods.

Though Marshall described the subject matter of commerce and national power to regulate it in the most sweeping terms, he did not overlook the tremendous power reserved to the states. But on what authority would state policy rest?

Marshall's view on this question comes out most clearly in *Willson* v. *Black Bird Creek Marsh Co.* (1829). The Delaware legislature had authorized the Black Bird Creek Marsh Company to build a dam across the creek for the purpose of reclaiming marshland. Willson, who owned a sloop licensed under national authority, broke through the dam and continued to navigate the creek. The company sued for trespass. Upholding the Delaware Act, Marshall ruled,

> The act of assembly by which the plaintiffs were authorized to construct their dam, shows plainly that this is *one of those many creeks,* passing through a deep, level marsh, adjoining the Delaware, up which the tide flows for some distance. The value of the property on its banks must be enhanced by excluding the water from the marsh, and the *health of the inhabitants probably improved.* Measures calculated to produce these objects, provided they do not come into collision with the powers of the general government, are undoubtedly within those which are reserved to the states. . . .
>
> The counsel for the plaintiffs in error insist that it comes in conflict with the power of the United States "to regulate commerce . . . among the several states." If Congress had passed any act which bore upon the case; any act in execution of the power to regulate commerce, the object of which was to control state legislation over *those small navigable creeks* into which the tide flows, and *which abound throughout the lower country of the middle and southern states,* we should feel not much difficulty in saying that a state law coming in conflict with such act would be void. But Congress has passed no such act. . . .
>
> We do not think, that the act empowering the Black Bird Creek Marsh company to place a dam across the creek, can, *under all the circumstances of the case,* be considered as repugnant to the power to regulate commerce in its dormant state, or as being in conflict with any law passed on the subject. [Italics are the authors'.]

Marshall was at pains to show the bearing of the dam on land values and the health of the community. As a health measure, enacted under police power, the act was valid until it collided with national authority. One notes also that he passed over the fact that the sloop in question was licensed under an act of Congress—the vital consideration in the Gibbons case. Moreover, for the first time Marshall applied the word *dormant* to the commerce power. It refers to the restraint the commerce clause imposes on the states even in the absence of national legislation. The clause thus has two dimensions: a grant of authority to Congress and a limit on state policies. Only the first requires positive action by Congress to be operative.

THE DOCTRINE OF THE TANEY COURT

During Taney's tenure as chief justice (1836–1864) the Court squarely faced the question Marshall had pointedly sidestepped in *Gibbons* v. *Ogden:* May the states regulate commerce in the absence of federal regulation? The importance of the answer cannot be overstressed.

Congress was not likely to react positively during this period. Thus the invalidation of state laws regulating commerce meant that commerce was likely to be free from all regulation.

In *New York* v. *Miln* (1837), the Taney Court, in a confused set of opinions, upheld as a police-power regulation a state act requiring the ship's master on incoming vessels to furnish information concerning his passengers. Justice Thompson, originally assigned the task of writing the opinion, treated the state act as a police measure and permissible—in the absence of national action. Because four members of the Court balked at Thompson's analysis, Justice Barbour wrote an opinion holding the state law valid purely as a police measure. In his opinion, however, Barbour added some expressions about the commerce power with which other members did not agree, but since it was delivered on the last day of the term, they could do nothing to show their displeasure. Barbour's gratuitous remarks on commerce, with which Taney later indicated agreement, stated in effect that persons were not "subjects of commerce," a pronouncement highly pleasing to the slave states.

In 1847, the even more confused opinions in the License Cases revealed how difficult it was for the Court to settle on any one view of commerce power. Taney favored state regulation of the liquor trade. In one case, upholding a state act, he adopted the "original package" doctrine. In another he said that a state could regulate articles in original packages in the absence of national regulation, thus countering Marshall's dictum in *Brown* v. *Maryland,* a case in which Taney had been counsel for the state. Some members of the Court reasoned in terms of "police power"; others argued that only intrastate commerce was involved.

In the Passenger Cases (1849), taxes on passengers on incoming vessels were challenged. These cases were argued on three different occasions over a four-year period. Daniel Webster, who as counsel opposed the state acts, was convinced of the accuracy of his position but feared the absence of a "strong and leading mind" on the Court. Martin Van Buren, for the states, stressed the popular support for the state acts and state sovereignty. Webster won a 5-to-4 decision. Each of the five justices stated his views in such a way, however, that the reporter could enter as a headnote only that the act was invalid. Three of the four dissenters wrote separate opinions. Taney held that since states could expel undesirable immigrants, they could reject them in the first place, and he cited *New York* v. *Miln* to the effect that persons were not "subjects of commerce." The majority split—two justices ruling congressional power over foreign commerce to be exclusive, three holding that this was unnecessary for the decision since the state act conflicted with existing national legislation. The one happy note in this confusion was that the judges did not follow sectional or party lines. Nevertheless, disappointment and frustration greeted the decision.

The law was in this muddle when President Fillmore, in 1851, appointed Benjamin R. Curtis to the Court. Curtis, a brilliant Massachusetts lawyer, was destined to be the mediator between the two tenuous coalitions and the effective medium through whom a compromise was reached. In the famous case of **Cooley** v. **Board of Port Wardens** (1851), a state pilotage fee was declared valid against the charge that it conflicted with the national commerce power. Complicating the situation was a congressional act of 1789 stating that pilots should be regulated in conformity "with such laws as the states may hereafter enact . . . until further legislative provision shall be made by Congress." Curtis, combining elements of the "exclusive" and "concurrent" doctrines, fashioned a new formula. His middle ground was this: Subjects national in scope admit only of uniform regulation; these require congressional legislation, and in the absence of such legislation the states cannot act. As to subjects of a local character, not requiring uniform legislation, the states may legislate (according to Curtis) until Congress, by acting on the same subject, displaces the state law. Where national and state laws are in conflict, the federal rule prevails. Though Taney did not agree with Curtis's analysis, he silently joined in the opinion.

The opinions delivered under the leadership of Marshall and Taney contained ammunition for those advocating or opposing commercial regulation by either state or nation. For future courts, however, substantial difficulties existed, despite the "balanced" formula fashioned in *Cooley*. What was a subject matter requiring a national (or uniform) regulation? When was a state law affecting commerce in conflict with national legislation? The awkward question of the extent of state power to tax one or more aspects of interstate commerce was left to the future. The answers the Court might give had more than logical or semantic importance because, with the national government incapable or unwilling to regulate, a theory of broad national power, combined with a narrow definition of what required local regulation, meant that commerce would be free of all regulation.

COMMERCE POWER AND STATE ACTION: 1865–1890

Under the Cooley doctrine, in the absence of congressional legislation, the Court's first duty was to determine the nature of the subject matter regulated. If it required national regulation, state action was foreclosed. If the subject matter permitted state or local regulation, two questions remained: Did the state law discriminate against interstate commerce and in favor of local commerce? Did the state act, although nondiscriminatory, place an unreasonable burden on interstate commerce? Socioeconomic fact and theory, flavored by judicial bias, entered inevitably into the attempt to answer these questions.

Remember that in the post-Civil War period especially, state legislatures were under pressure to solve the problems arising from a burgeoning industrialism. At least before 1890, regulation—if it was to come at all—would be state regulation. Conflicts over the desirability of regulation continued to be translated into debates over the meaning of the commerce clause.

[margin note: flourishing]

State legislation regulating the railroads focused judicial attention on the limits of state power in the absence of congressional action. In *Munn v. Illinois* (see Chapter Eight) and the other "Granger" Cases (1877) the Court upheld an Illinois regulation of elevator and railroad rates. Although "instruments" of interstate commerce were the subject of the legislation and "may become connected with interstate commerce," they were not necessarily so; until Congress acted, the states could control the rates, even though this regulation had an indirect effect on interstate commerce.

By 1886, however, the Court was prepared to shift from the position apparently taken in the Granger Cases of 1877. It is noteworthy that between 1877 and 1886 the Court set aside 14 state commercial regulations; in only two instances was national legislation involved. The facts in the historic Wabash case (*Wabash, St. Louis & Pacific Ry. Co.* v. *Illinois*, 1886) showed that the railroad charged 15 cents per pound from Peoria, Illinois, and 25 cents per pound from Gilman, Illinois, on shipments of similar chattels to New York City. Since Gilman was 86 miles closer to New York, the two rates ran afoul of an Illinois statute banning long-short haul rate discrimination. With most of the distance for each shipment lying outside Illinois, the state was in effect regulating interstate commerce.

The majority in *Wabash* found the state law an invalid intrusion on the national commerce power. "This is commerce of national character," Justice Miller said, "and national regulation is required." As to *Munn*, Justice Miller insisted that it had never been "the deliberate opinion of a majority of this court that a statute of a State which attempts to regulate the fares and charges of a railroad company within its limits, for a transportation which constitutes a part of commerce among the States, is a valid law."

Wabash was significant in helping to bring about a climate of opinion favorable to national regulation of interstate railroad rates through passage of the Interstate Commerce

Act of 1887. This law established the Interstate Commerce Commission, the first permanent federal regulatory agency created by Congress with broad quasi-legislative, executive, and judicial powers. Although state railroad rate regulation, therefore, became virtually meaningless after 1887, state police-power legislation affecting transportation continued unabated.

STATE LEGISLATION AND THE COMMERCE POWER: 1890–1989

After 1890 two dominant themes pervade the application of the commerce clause: (1) use of the commerce power by Congress to accomplish broad social and economic purposes (a subject covered in the following chapter), and (2) further development of the commerce clause as a restriction on state action affecting commerce.

At the outset cases on the latter subject revealed no clear pattern. In **Leisy v. Hardin** (1890), the Fuller Court rejected the Taney Court's ruling in the License Cases on the ground that beer was a genuine article of commerce, the sale of which could be prohibited only by congressional action. Yet four years later in *Plumley* v. *Massachusetts,* the Court held that a state law prohibiting the sale of colored oleomargarine only "incidentally affected" trade between the states and was, therefore, a legitimate measure to prevent the defrauding of purchasers. Increasingly, the Court, after ascertaining that the subject matter was not one requiring national regulation, examined the state law to see whether it discriminated against or burdened interstate commerce.

By the 1940s, three basic positions emerged. All justices agreed that even in the absence of congressional action, no state could discriminate against interstate commerce in order to gain for itself a commercial advantage. One group of justices, led by Hugo Black, would have stopped there. A second group, led by Chief Justice Stone and later joined by Black, preferred a "balancing-of-interests" rule, as illustrated by **Southern Pacific v. Arizona** (1945). Here the Court had to decide whether the state's regulation limiting the size of interstate and intrastate trains could stand. Another group led by Justice Robert Jackson found the first two positions equally objectionable. Neither gave due weight to the danger the commerce clause was designed to avert "Balkanization," which would permit individual states to raise barriers to commerce. According to this view, even in the absence of congressional legislation, the commerce clause of its own force prohibited states from doing anything to burden, obstruct, hinder, or restrain interstate commerce. Furthermore, it was the duty of the Supreme Court to guard national commerce from such local encroachments. Jackson articulated his position in *Hood* v. *Dumond* (1949), which overturned an administrative ruling in New York that blocked a milk processor from establishing an additional milk-receiving station in the state.

Variations of these positions continue to be reflected in decisions reviewing the many ways state regulations arguably affect commerce.

Transportation. Initially, the court was rather generous in upholding state acts regulating motor transportation, such as the licensing of vehicles using state roads (*Buck* v. *Kuykendall,* 1925). In the important 1938 case of *South Carolina* v. *Barnwell,* a statute prohibiting trucks with loads over 20,000 pounds and widths exceeding 90 inches from using state roads was upheld. Justice Stone thought that in the absence of congressional legislation it was a reasonable measure to protect roads built and maintained by the state, especially since no discrimination or attempt to burden interstate commerce had been shown.

Most often today in such situations the justices are inclined toward the balancing-of-interests approach reflected in Stone's opinion in *Southern Pacific* v. *Arizona.* In recent truck-length cases, the Court has ruled that state bans on 65-foot double trailers, especially where neighboring states permit them on the highways, violate the commerce clause (*Raymond Motor Transportation, Inc.* v. *Rice,* 1978; *Kassel* v. *Consolidated Freightways Corp.,* 1981). As Justice Powell maintained in *Kassel,* "[T]he incantation of a purpose to promote the public health or safety does not insulate a state law from Commerce Clause attack. Regulations designed for that salutary purpose nevertheless may further the purpose so marginally, and interfere with commerce so substantially, as to be invalid. . . ." The judicial task in these cases is at heart both empirical and political—a weighing of one benefit against another.

Commercial Regulation. Articulation of worthy purposes alone will not necessarily be enough to save a statute under the commerce clause. Generally, burdens on commerce become "undue" (and therefore unconstitutional) when the laws in question discriminate against interstate commerce or, under *Cooley,* when they disrupt a desired uniformity. For example, states may not engage in protectionism (favoring local economic interests at the expense of those from out of state). Neither may a state, under the guise of guarding the public health, exclude, say, out-of-state foods that are pure. But a state may, under the commerce clause, prohibit the shipment outside the state of citrus fruits that are judged to be damaged or otherwise unfit for consumption (*Sligh* v. *Kirkwood,* 1915).

These concerns are reflected in the majority and dissenting opinions in **Reeves** v. **Stake** (1980). Here the justices examined the sales policies of a state-owned cement plant where the state chose to supply in-state customers first, after a cut in production. As a result, an out-of-state concrete business was unable to purchase any more cement and had to reduce its own production by 76 percent. For the majority, Justice Blackmun drew on a novel distinction the Court first employed in *Hughes* v. *Alexandria Scrap Corp.* (1976) between the state as market participant and the state as market regulator. Since the state was acting in the role of the former, there was no violation of the commerce clause even though the state's policy clearly placed out-of-state buyers at a disadvantage.

The participant/regulator distinction was important in *New England Power Co.* v. *New Hampshire* (1982). Here, the public utility commission in New Hampshire had ordered the privately owned power company to sell within the state the electricity it produced in the state. The Court reaffirmed the view that the commerce clause precludes a state's giving residents a preferred right of access to its natural resources or to products derived from those resources.

Taxation. State taxation of interstate business is another practice that presents difficult application of commerce clause principles. Justice Frankfurter confessed in 1946 that the "history of this problem is spread over hundreds of volumes of our Reports." By then there were already 300 full opinions on the question. "To attempt to harmonize all that has been said . . . ," he acknowledged, "would neither clarify what has gone before nor guide the future." More than any other area of constitutional law perhaps, "in this field opinions must be read in the setting of the particular cases and as the product of preoccupation with their special facts" (*Freeman* v. *Hewit*).

Complete Auto Transit v. *Brady* (1977) demonstrates the Court's recent approach to the limits the commerce clause places on a state's taxing power. In this case, Mississippi applied a tax for "the privilege of doing business" in the state to an interstate motor carrier that transported automobiles assembled out of state between points in the state. Holding that such taxes were not "per se unconstitutional," Justice Blackmun's majority opinion developed a four-prong test by which to evaluate this kind of taxation under the commerce clause. To pass, the Court would look to see whether the tax "is applied to an activity with a substantial nexus with the taxing state, is fairly apportioned, does not discriminate against interstate commerce, and is fairly related to the services provided by the state." Choosing between interstate trade that is free and that which is not, the Court opted for commerce that can be required to "pay its own way." "Substantial nexus" means that a state must have considerable authority over the goods or transactions before the tax is levied. Also, where several states have such a nexus, taxes must be fairly apportioned to prevent taxation that is entirely too burdensome.

In 1987, *American Trucking Associations, Inc*. v. *Scheiner* refined *Complete Auto Transit* by making explicit an "internal consistency test." Until 1982, Pennsylvania imposed a flat $25 annual marker fee on trucks using the state's roadways. That fee was replaced by a $36 per-axle tax. For vehicles registered in Pennsylvania the fee and tax were included in the state's registration fees and so amounted to no additional charge.

Especially because Pennsylvania-registered trucks used the state's roads more than trucks registered out of state, Justice Stevens declared for a majority of five that the fee and tax "penalize some travel within the free trade area . . . [and] threaten the free movement of commerce by placing a financial barrier around the State of Pennsylvania." To pass the internal consistency test, "a state tax must be of a kind that, if applied by every jurisdiction, there would be no impermissible interference with free trade." For Stevens, if every state imposed the same kind of flat tax, "there is no conceivable doubt that commerce among the States would be deterred." Required were "more finely calibrated user charges." The new rule would be waived only if administrative burdens made such calibrations impractical.

Presumably such calibrations are not needed for severance taxes, which the Court has accepted under the commerce clause. For example, because of the energy crisis in the 1970s, Montana sharply increased its severance tax on coal mined in the state. The significance of the tax was revealed by its role in funding state expenditures. In 1972, revenues generated by the tax amounted to 0.4 percent of total state revenues, but by 1976 that percentage had jumped 28 fold to 11.4. Although state residents using coal mined in Montana were treated the same as users outside the state, the effect of the tax was to draw an increased percentage of state revenues from non-Montanans since the great majority of coal users resided or were in business elsewhere. Justice Marshall concluded,

> [W]hen the measure of a tax is reasonably related to the taxpayer's activities or presence in the State—from which it derives some benefit such as the substantial privilege of mining coal— the taxpayer will realize, in proper proportion to the taxes it pays, "[t]he only benefit to which the taxpayer is constitutionally entitled . . .[:] that derived from his enjoyment of the privileges of living in an organized society, established and safeguarded by the devotion of taxes to public purposes" (*Commonwealth Edison Co*. v. *Montana,* 1981).

Quality of Life. State and local regulations to protect the environment or to improve the quality of life may meet similar challenges under the commerce clause. In *Burbank* v. *Lockheed Air Terminal* (1973), the Court struck down an ordinance banning takeoffs and landings by certain jet aircraft at an airport during late-night hours. Although finding no express preemption by national statutes, Justice Douglas for the Court found an implied one: "If we were to uphold the Burbank ordinance and a significant number of municipalities followed suit, it is obvious that fractionalized control of the timing of takeoffs and landings would severely limit the flexibility of the FAA in controlling air traffic flow. The difficulties of scheduling flights to avoid congestion and the concomitant decrease in safety would be compounded."

In 1978, Justice Stewart spoke for a seven-member majority in overturning a New Jersey statute that prohibited the importation of most "solid or liquid waste which originated or was collected outside the territorial limits of the State" (***Philadelphia*** v. ***New Jersey***). The obvious intent of the law was to prevent the state from becoming a dumping ground for its more populous neighbors of New York and Pennsylvania. "The New Jersey law blocks the importation of waste in an . . . effort to saddle those outside the State with the entire burden of slowing the flow of refuse into New Jersey's remaining landfill sites. That legislative effort is clearly impermissible under the Commerce Clause. . . ." Avoiding the accumulation of garbage in the first place appears to present fewer constitutional obstacles. In *Minnesota* v. *Clover Leaf Creamery Co.* (1981), the Court upheld a statute banning the sale of milk in plastic (but not paperboard), nonreturnable containers. According to Justice Brennan, the requirement was not unduly burdensome on interstate commerce and was not protectionist. The decision bears on the validity of similar laws in other states taxing or otherwise regulating containers in which soft drinks are bottled.

A CONTINUING JUDICIAL ROLE

"The material success that has come to inhabitants of the states which make up this federal free trade unit has been the most impressive in the history of commerce, but the established interdependence of the States only emphasizes the necessity of protecting interstate movement of goods against local burdens and repressions." Justice Jackson's observation points to the Court's important role in interpreting the commerce clause.

From this chapter certain conclusions can be drawn. First, the rule in *Cooley* has not been used to frustrate state legislation simply because one might argue that a national rule would be more efficient or desirable. Second, judicial generosity toward state action has in fact permitted the erection of modest trade barriers (motor carrier limitations, taxes, inspection laws, safety laws). Third, Congress for many reasons has not chosen to regulate all subjects that lie within the reach of its commerce power. Fourth, the permissible limits of the state taxing power are not clearly defined, although, in general, nondiscriminatory and apportioned taxes have a good chance of being upheld. Fifth, cases testing state power under the commerce clause unavoidably require the exercise of judicial discretion.

Throughout, the Supreme Court has undertaken the role of guardian of the national market against most obviously discriminatory and parochial efforts to reerect the type of trade barriers that marked the preconstitutional era. But the Court has increasingly recognized the danger of leaving large areas of commercial activity free from all regulation, which would be the inescapable result if Congress cannot or will not act and the states are forbidden to act. The commerce clause in its twin dimensions has been a "prolific source of conflict" between state interests and national prerogatives and, as Chapter Six will show, an equally "prolific source of national power."

KEY TERMS

police power

commerce

original package doctrine

dormant commerce power

Cooley doctrine

Balkanization

protectionist legislation

dictum

internal consistency test

QUERIES

1. According to Chief Justice Marshall in *Gibbons* v. *Ogden,* what authority do the states possess to regulate commerce?

2. What questions, left unanswered by *Gibbons* v. *Ogden,* did *Cooley* v. *Board of Wardens* resolve?

3. In cases such as *Southern Pacific* v. *Arizona, Reeves* v. *Stake,* and *Philadelphia* v. *New Jersey,* what role have federalism and the commerce clause bequeathed to the Supreme Court?

4. According to opinions reviewing state regulatory policies under the commerce clause, what values do the justices most often seem to be protecting? What dangers do they want to guard against?

SELECTED READINGS

BENSON, PAUL R., JR. *The Supreme Court and the Commerce Clause, 1937–1970.* Cambridge, Mass.: Dunellen, 1970.

COLLINS, RICHARD B. "Economic Union as a Constitutional Value." 63 *New York University Law Review* 43 (1988).

CORWIN, EDWARD S. *The Commerce Power Versus States Rights.* Princeton, N.J.: Princeton University Press, 1936.

CURRIE, DAVID P. "The Constitution in the Supreme Court: The Protection of Economic Interests, 1889–1910." 52 *University of Chicago Law Review* 324 (1985).

DOWLING, NOEL T. "Interstate Commerce and the State Power," 47 *Columbia Law Review* 547 (1947).

EULE, JULIAN N. "Laying the Dormant Commerce Clause to Rest." 91 *Yale Law Journal* 425 (1982).

FRANKFURTER, FELIX. *The Commerce Clause under Marshall, Taney and Waite.* Chapel Hill: University of North Carolina Press, 1937.

"*Hood* v. *Dumond:* A Study of the Supreme Court and the Ideology of Capitalism." 134 *University of Pennsylvania Law Review* 657 (1986).

Gibbons v. *Ogden*
22 U.S. (9 Wheat.) 1, 6 L.Ed. 23 (1824)

In 1811 the state of New York granted the fifth in a series of monopolies to jurist and diplomat Robert Livingston and steamboat pioneer Robert Fulton to operate steamboats on the waterways of New York. The monopoly required all persons navigating by steam in New York to obtain a license from Livingston and Fulton. Any unlicensed vessel, "together with the engine, tackle and apparel thereof," would be forfeited to them. Aaron Ogden operated a licensed steam-powered ferry between New York and New Jersey. In 1819 his former associate Thomas Gibbons, who held a "coasting license" under a 1793 act of Congress, began to run boats along the same route in competition with Ogden. Gibbons's boats were not licensed under the New York monopoly. Ogden brought action in the New York Court of Chancery to stop his rival. Chancellor James Kent ruled for Ogden, holding that the congressional statute was not in conflict with the New York monopoly and conferred no right on Gibbons to navigate on New York waters. The New York Court of Errors affirmed in 1820, and Gibbons appealed. This dispute gave rise to the first important case in the Supreme Court concerning the meaning of the commerce clause. Writing a century after the decision, Albert J. Beveridge found that Marshall's opinion "has done more to knit the American people into an indivisible Nation than any other one force in our history, excepting only war." Majority: Marshall, Duvall, Johnson, Story, Todd, Washington. Not participating: Thompson.

MARSHALL, CH. J., delivered the opinion of the Court. . . .

This instrument [the Constitution] contains an enumeration of powers expressly granted by the people to their government. It has been said, that these powers ought to be construed strictly. But why ought they to be so construed? Is there one sentence in the constitution which gives countenance to this rule? In the last of the enumerated powers, that which grants, expressly, the means for carrying all others into execution, congress is authorized "to make all laws which shall be necessary and proper" for the purpose. But this limitation on the means which may be used, is not extended to the powers which are conferred; nor is there one sentence in the constitution, which has been pointed out by the gentlemen of the bar, or which we have been able to discern, that prescribes this rule. We do not, therefore, think ourselves justified in adopting it. What do gentlemen mean, by a strict construc-

tion? If they contend only against that enlarged construction, which would extend words beyond their natural and obvious import, we might question the application of the term, but should not controvert the principle. If they contend for that narrow construction which, in support of some theory not to be found in the constitution, would deny to the government those powers which the words of the grant, as usually understood, import, and which are consistent with the general views and objects of the instrument—for that narrow construction, which would cripple the government, and render it unequal to the objects for which it is declared to be instituted, and to which the powers given, as fairly understood, render it competent—then we cannot perceive the propriety of this strict construction, nor adopt it as the rule by which the constitution is to be expounded. As men whose intentions require no concealment, generally employ the words which most directly and aptly express the ideas they intend to convey, the enlightened patriots who framed our constitution, and the people who adopted it, must be understood to have employed words in their natural sense, and to have intended what they have said. If, from the imperfection of human language, there should be serious doubts respecting the extent of any given power, it is a well settled rule, that the objects for which it was given, especially, when those objects are expressed in the instrument itself, should have great influence in the construction. . . . We know of no rule for construing the extent of such powers, other than is given by the language of the instrument which confers them, taken in connection with the purposes for which they were conferred.

The words are: "Congress shall have power to regulate commerce with foreign nations, and among the several states, and with the Indian tribes." The subject to be regulated is commerce; and our constitution being, as was aptly said at the bar, one of enumeration, and not of definition, to ascertain the extent of the power, it becomes necessary to settle the meaning of the word. The counsel for the appellee would limit it to traffic, to buying and selling, or the interchange of commodities, and do not admit that it comprehends navigation. This would restrict a general term, applicable to many objects, to one of its significations. Commerce, undoubtedly, is traffic, but it is something more—it is intercourse. It describes the commercial intercourse between nations, and parts of nations, in all its branches, and is regulated by prescribing rules for carrying on that intercourse. The mind can scarcely conceive a system for regulating commerce between nations which shall exclude all laws concerning navigation, which shall be silent on the admission of the vessels of the one nation into the ports of the other, and confined to prescribing rules for the conduct of individuals, in the actual employment of buying and selling or of barter. If commerce does not include navigation, the government of the Union has no direct power over that subject, and can make no law prescribing what shall constitute American vessels, or requiring that they shall be navigated by American seamen. Yet this power has been exercised from the commencement of the government, has been exercised with the consent of all, and has been understood by all to be a commercial regulation. All America understands, and has uniformly understood, the word

"commerce," to comprehend navigation. It was so understood, and must have been so understood, when the constitution was framed. The power over commerce, including navigation, was one of the primary objects for which the people of America adopted their government, and must have been contemplated in forming it. The convention must have used the word in that sense, because all have understood it in that sense; and the attempt to restrict it comes too late. If the opinion that "commerce," as the word is used in the constitution, comprehends navigation also, requires any additional confirmation, that additional confirmation is, we think, furnished by the words of the instrument itself. It is a rule of construction, acknowledged by all, that the exceptions from a power mark its extent: for it would be absurd, as well as useless, to except from a granted power, that which was not granted—that which the words of the grant could not comprehend. If, then, there are in the constitution plain exceptions from the power over navigation, plain inhibitions to the exercise of that power in a particular way, it is a proof that those who made these exceptions, and prescribed these inhibitions, understood the power to which they applied as being granted. The 9th section of the last article declares, that "no preference shall be given, by any regulation of commerce or revenue, to the ports of one state over those of another." This clause cannot be understood as applicable to those laws only which are passed for the purposes of revenue, because it is expressly applied to commercial regulations; and the most obvious preference which can be given to one port over another, in regulating commerce, relates to navigation. But the subsequent part of the sentence is still more explicit. It is, "nor shall vessels bound to or from one state, be obliged to enter, clear or pay duties in another." These words have a direct reference to navigation. . . .

The word used in the constitution, then, comprehends, and has been always understood to comprehend, navigation within its meaning; and a power to regulate navigation, is as expressly granted, as if that term had been added to the word "commerce." To what commerce does this power extend? The constitution informs us, to commerce "with foreign nations, and among the several states, and with the Indian tribes." It has, we believe, been universally admitted, that these words comprehend every species of commercial intercourse between the United States and foreign nations. No sort of trade can be carried on between this country and any other, to which this power does not extend. It has been truly said, that commerce, as the word is used in the constitution, is a unit, every part of which is indicated by the term. . . .

But, in regulating commerce with foreign nations, the power of congress does not stop at the jurisdictional lines of the several states. It would be a very useless power, if it could not pass those lines. The commerce of the United States with foreign nations is that of the whole United States; every district has a right to participate in it. The deep streams which penetrate our country in every direction pass through the interior of almost every state in the Union, and furnish the means of exercising this right. If congress has the power to regulate it, that power must be exercised whenever the subject exists. If it exists within the states, if a foreign voyage may commence or terminate at a port within a state, then the power of congress may be exercised within a state.

This principle is, if possible, still more clear, when applied to commerce "among the several states." They either join each other, in which case they are separated by a mathematical line, or they are remote from each other, in which case other states lie between them. What is commerce "among" them; and how is it to be conducted? Can a trading expedition between two adjoining states, commence and terminate outside of each? And if the trading intercourse be between two states remote from each other, must it not commence in one, terminate in the other, and probably pass through a third? Commerce among the states must of necessity, be commerce with the states. In the regulation of trade with the Indian tribes, the action of the law, especially, when the constitution was made, was chiefly within a state. The power of congress, then, whatever it may be, must be exercised within the territorial jurisdiction of the several states. The sense of the nation on this subject, is unequivocally manifested by the provisions made in the laws for transporting goods, by land, between Baltimore and Providence, between New York and Philadelphia, and between Philadelphia and Baltimore.

We are now arrived at the inquiry—what is this power? It is the power to regulate; that is, to prescribe the rule by which commerce is to be governed. This power, like all others vested in congress, is complete in itself, may be exercised to its utmost extent, and acknowledges no limitations, other than are prescribed in the constitution. These are expressed in plain terms, and do not affect the questions which arise in this case, or which have been discussed at the bar. If, as has always been understood, the sovereignty of congress, though limited to specified objects, is plenary as to those objects, the power over commerce with foreign nations, and among the several states, is vested in congress as absolutely as it would be in a single government, having in its constitution the same restrictions on the exercise of the power as are found in the constitution of the United States. The wisdom and the discretion of congress, their identity with the people, and the influence which their constituents possess at elections, are, in this, as in many other instances, as that, for example, of declaring war, the sole restraints on which they have relied, to secure them from its abuse. They are the restraints on which the people must often rely solely, in all representative governments. . . .

But it has been urged, with great earnestness, that although the power of congress to regulate commerce with foreign nations, and among the several states, be co-extensive with the subject itself, and have no other limits than are prescribed in the constitution, yet the states may severally exercise the same power within their respective jurisdictions. In support of this argument, it is said that they possessed it as an inseparable attribute of sovereignty before the formation of the constitution, and still retain it, except so far as they have surrendered it by that instrument; that this principle results from the nature of the government, and is secured by the tenth amendment; that an affirmative grant of power is not exclusive, unless in its own nature it be such that the continued exercise of it by the former possessor is inconsistent with the grant, and that this is not of that description. The appellant conceding these postulates, except the last, contends that full power to regulate a particular subject implies the whole power, and leaves no residuum; that a grant of the whole is incompatible with the existence of a right in another to any part of it. . . .

The grant of the power to lay and collect taxes is, like the power to regulate commerce, made in general terms, and has never been understood to interfere with the exercise of the same power by the states; and hence has been drawn an argument which has been applied to the question under consideration. But the two grants are not, it is conceived, similar in their terms or their nature. Although many of the powers formerly exercised by the states are transferred to the government of the Union, yet the state governments remain, and constitute a most important part of our system. The power of taxation is indispensable to their existence, and is a power which, in its own nature, is capable of residing in, and being exercised by, different authorities at the same time. We are accustomed to see it placed, for different purposes, in different hands. Taxation is the simple operation of taking small portions from a perpetually accumulating mass, susceptible of almost infinite division; and a power in one to take what is necessary for certain purposes, is not in its nature incompatible with a power in another to take what is necessary for other purposes. Congress is authorized to lay and collect taxes, etc., to pay the debts, and provide for the common defense and general welfare of the United States. This does not interfere with the power of the states to tax for the support of their own governments; nor is the exercise of that power by the states an exercise of any portion of the power that is granted to the United States. In imposing taxes for state purposes, they are not doing what congress is empowered to do. Congress is not empowered to tax for those purposes which are within the exclusive province of the States. When, then, each government exercises the power of taxation, neither is exercising the power of the other. But when a state proceeds to regulate commerce with foreign nations, or among the several states, it is exercising the very power that is granted to congress, and is doing the very thing which congress is authorized to do. There is no analogy then, between the power of taxation and the power of regulating commerce. . . .

But the inspection laws are said to be regulations of commerce, and are certainly recognized in the constitution as being passed in the exercise of a power remaining with the states.

That inspection laws may have a remote and considerable influence on commerce, will not be denied; but that a power to regulate commerce is the source from which the right to pass them is derived, cannot be admitted. The object of inspection laws, is to improve the quality of articles produced by the labor of a country; to fit them for exportation; or it may be, for domestic use. They act upon the subject, before it becomes an article of foreign commerce, or of commerce among the states, and prepare it for that purpose. They form a portion of that immense mass of legislation, which embraces everything within the territory of a state, not surrendered to a general government; all of which can be most advantageously exercised by the states themselves. Inspection laws, quarantine laws, health laws of every description, as well as laws for regulating the internal commerce of a state, and those which respect turnpike roads, ferries, etc., are component parts of this mass.

No direct general power over these objects is granted to congress, and, consequently, they remain subject to state legislation. If the legislative power of the Union can reach them, it must be, where the power is expressly given for a special purpose, or is clearly incidental to some power which is expressly given. It is obvious, that the government of the Union, in the exercise of its express powers, that, for example, of regulating commerce with foreign nations and among the states, may use means that may also be employed by a state, in the exercise of its acknowledged powers; that, for example, of regulating commerce within the state. If congress licenses vessels to sail from one port to another, in the same state, the act is supposed to be, necessarily, incidental to the power expressly granted to congress, and implies no claim of a direct power to regulate the purely internal commerce of a state, or to act directly on its system of police. So, if a state, in passing laws on subjects acknowledged to be within its control, and with a view to those subjects, shall adopt a measure of the same character with one which congress may adopt, it does not derive its authority from the particular power which has been granted, but from some other which remains with the state. . . .

Since, however, in exercising the power of regulating their own purely internal affairs, whether of trading or police, the states may sometimes enact laws, the validity of which depends on their [not] interfering with, and being contrary to, an act of congress passed in pursuance of the constitution, the court will enter upon the inquiry whether the laws of New York, as expounded by the highest tribunal of that state, have, in their application to this case, come into collision with an act of congress, and deprived a citizen of a right to which that act entitles him. Should this collision exist, it will be immaterial whether those laws were passed in virtue of a concurrent power "to regulate commerce with foreign nations and among the several States," or, in virtue of a power to regulate their domestic trade and police. In one case and the other, the acts of New York must yield to the law of congress, and the decision sustaining the privilege they confer, against a right given by a law of the Union, must be erroneous.

This opinion has been frequently expressed in this court, and is founded, as well on the nature of the government, as on the words of the constitution. In argument, however, it has been contended, that if a law passed by a state, in the exercise of its acknowledged sovereignty comes into conflict with a law passed by congress in pursuance of the constitution, they affect the subject, and each other, like equal opposing powers.

But the framers of our constitution foresaw this state of things, and provided for it, by declaring the supremacy not only of itself, but of the laws made in pursuance of it. The nullity of any act, inconsistent with the constitution, is produced by the declaration, that the constitution is the supreme law. . . . In every such case, the act of congress, or the treaty, is supreme; and the law of the state, though enacted in the exercise of powers not controverted, must yield to it. . . .

Powerful and ingenious minds, taking, as postulates, that the powers expressly granted to the government of the Union are to be contracted, by construction, into the narrowest possible compass, and that the original powers of the States are retained, if any possible construction will retain them, may, by a course of well digested, but refined and metaphysical reasoning, founded on these premises, explain away the constitution of our country, and leave it a magnificent structure indeed, to look at, but totally unfit for use. They may so entangle and perplex the understanding, as to obscure principles which were before thought quite plain, and induce doubts where, if the mind were to pursue its own course, none would be perceived. In such a case, it is peculiarly necessary to recur to safe and fundamental principles to sustain those principles, and, when sustained, to make them the tests of the arguments to be examined.

JOHNSON, JUSTICE. . . .

. . . Power to regulate foreign commerce, is given in the same words, and in the same breath, as it were, with that over the commerce of the states and with the Indian tribes. But the power to regulate foreign commerce is necessarily exclusive. The states are unknown to foreign nations; their sovereignty exists only with relation to each other and the general government. Whatever regulations foreign commerce should be subjected to in the ports of the Union, the general government would be held responsible for them; and all other regulations, but those which congress had imposed, would be regarded by foreign nations as trespasses and violations of national faith and comity.

But the language which grants the power as to one description of commerce, grants it as to all; and, in fact, if ever the exercise of a right, or acquiescence in a construction, could be inferred from contemporaneous and continued assent, it is that of the exclusive effect of this grant. . . .

It is impossible, with the views which I entertain of the principle on which the commercial privileges of the people of the United States among themselves, rests [sic], to concur in the view which this court takes of the effect of the coasting license in this cause. I do not regard it as the foundation of the right set up in behalf of the appellant. If there was any one object riding over every other in the adoption of the constitution, it was to keep the commercial intercourse among the states free from all invidious and partial restraints. And I cannot overcome the conviction, that if the licensing act was repealed tomorrow, the rights of the appellant to a reversal of the decision complained of, would be as strong as it is under this license. . . .

. . . This court doth further direct, order and decree, that the bill of the said Aaron Ogden be dismissed, and the same is hereby dismissed accordingly.

Cooley v. Board of Wardens
53 U.S. (12 How.) 299, 13 L.Ed. 996 (1851)

A state pilotage law of 1803 required that vessels leaving Philadelphia should pay a one-half fee for use of the Society for the Relief of Distressed and Decayed Pilots, their Widows and Children, if a pilot were not hired. An act of the United States of 1789 declared that state pilotage acts should continue in effect. Cooley, the consignee of two vessels outward bound from Philadelphia, refused to pay the state fee. From judgments against him in the state courts, he brought writs of error. Majority: Curtis, Catron, Daniel, Grier, McKinley, Nelson, Taney. Dissenting: McLean, Wayne.

MR. JUSTICE CURTIS delivered the opinion of the Court. . . .

It remains to consider the objection that it [the state act] is repugnant to the third clause of the eighth section of the first article. "The Congress shall have power to regulate commerce with foreign nations and among the several states, and with the Indian tribes."

That the power to regulate commerce includes the regulation of navigation, we consider settled. . . .

The act of 1789 . . . already referred to, contains a clear legislative exposition of the Constitution by the first Congress, to the effect that the power to regulate pilots was conferred on Congress by the Constitution. . . . And a majority of the court are of opinion that a regulation of pilots is a regulation of commerce, within the grant to Congress of the commercial power, contained in the third clause of the eighth section of the first article of the Constitution.

It becomes necessary, therefore, to consider whether this law of Pennsylvania, being a regulation of commerce, is valid.

The act of Congress of the 7th of August, 1789, sec. 4, is as follows:

That all pilots in the bays, inlets, rivers, harbors, and ports of the United States shall continue to be regulated in conformity with the existing laws of the states, respectively wherein such pilots may be, or with such laws as the states may respectively hereafter enact for the purpose, until further legislative provision shall be made by Congress.

If the law of Pennsylvania, now in question, had been in existence at the date of this act of Congress, we might hold it to have been adopted by Congress, and thus made a law of the United States, and so valid. Because this act does, in effect, give the force of an act of Congress, to the then existing state laws on this subject, so long as they should continue unrepealed by the state which enacted them.

But the law on which these actions are founded was not enacted till 1803. What effect then can be attributed to so much of the act of 1789, as declares, that pilots shall continue to be regulated in conformity "with such laws as the states may respectively hereafter enact for the purpose, until further legislative provision shall be made by Congress"?

If the states were divested of the power to legislate on this subject by the grant of the commercial power to Congress, it is plain this act could not confer upon them power thus to legislate. If the Constitution excluded the states from making any law regulating commerce, certainly Congress cannot regrant, or in any manner reconvey to the states that power. And yet this act of 1789 gives its sanction only to laws enacted by the States. This necessarily implies a constitutional power to legislate; for only a rule created by the sovereign power of a state acting in its legislative capacity, can be deemed a law enacted by a state; and if the state has so limited its sovereign power that it no longer extends to a particular subject, manifestly it cannot, in any proper sense, be said to enact law thereon. Entertaining these views, we are brought directly and unavoidably to the consideration of the question, whether the grant of the commercial power to congress, did per se deprive the states of all power to regulate pilots. This question has never been decided by this court, nor, in our judgment, has any case depending upon all the considerations which must govern this one, come before this court. The grant of commercial power to Congress does not contain any terms which expressly exclude the states from exercising an authority over its subject matter. If they are excluded, it must be because the nature of the power, thus granted to Congress, requires that a similar authority should not exist in the states. . . .

. . . Now the power to regulate commerce embraces a vast field, containing not only many, but exceedingly various subjects, quite unlike in their nature; some imperatively demanding a single uniform rule, operating equally on the commerce of the United States in every port; and some, like the subject now in question, as imperatively demanding that diversity which alone can meet the local necessities of navigation.

Either absolutely to affirm, or deny that the nature of this power requires exclusive legislation by Congress, is to lose sight of the nature of the subjects of this power, and to assert concerning all of them, what is really applicable but to a part. Whatever subjects of this power are in their nature national, or admit only of one uniform system, or plan of regulation, may justly be said to be of such a nature as to require exclusive legislation by Congress. That this cannot be affirmed of laws for the regulation of pilots and pilotage is plain. The act of 1789 contains a clear and authoritative declaration by the first Congress that the nature of this subject is such that until Congress should find it necessary to exert its power, it should be left to the legislation of the states; that it is local and not national; that it is likely to be the best provided for, not by one system, or plan or regulation but by as many as the legislative discretion of the several states should deem applicable to the local peculiarities of the ports within their limits.

Viewed in this light, so much of this act of 1789 as declares that pilots shall continue to be regulated "by such laws as the states may respectively hereafter enact for that purpose," instead of being held to be inoperative, as an attempt to confer on the states a power to legislate, of which the Constitution had deprived them, is allowed an appropriate and important signification. It manifests the understanding of Congress, at the outset of the government, that the nature of this subject is not such as to require its exclusive legislation. . . .

It is the opinion of a majority of the court that the mere grant to Congress of the power to regulate commerce did not deprive the states of power to regulate pilots, and that although Congress has legislated on this subject, its legislation manifests an intention, with a single exception not to regulate this subject, but to leave its regulation to the several states. To these precise questions, which are all we are called on to decide, this opinion must be understood to be confined. It does not extend to the question what other subjects, under the commercial power, are within the exclusive control of Congress, or may be regulated by the states in the absence of all congressional legislation; nor to the general question, how far any regulation of a subject by Congress, may be deemed to operate as an exclusion of all legislation by the states upon the same subject. We decide the precise questions before us, upon what we deem sound principles, applicable to this particular subject in the state in which the legislation of Congress has left it. We go no further. . . .

We are of opinion that this state law was enacted by virtue of a power, residing in the state to legislate; that it is not in conflict with any law of Congress; that it does not interfere with any system which Congress has established by making regulations, or by intentionally leaving individuals to their own unrestricted action: that this law is therefore valid, and the judgment of the Supreme Court of Pennsylvania in each case must be affirmed.

Leisy v. *Hardin*
135 U.S. 100, 10 S.Ct. 681, 34 L.Ed. 128 (1890)

A statute of Iowa prohibited the manufacture, sale, or dispensing of intoxicating liquors except for specified purposes, which required a permit. Leisy, an Illinois brewer, shipped beer in the original barrels and case to Iowa, where the property was seized by Hardin, a constable, while it was in the possession of Leisy's agent. The trial and Superior courts of Iowa held the state statute invalid, but the Supreme Court of Iowa held that the statute was constitutional. Majority: Fuller, Blatchford, Bradley, Field, Lamar, Miller. Dissenting: Gray, Brewer, Harlan.

MR. CHIEF JUSTICE FULLER . . . delivered the opinion of the Court. . . .

Whenever, however, a particular power of the general government is one which must necessarily be exercised by it, and Congress remains silent, this is not only not a concession that the powers reserved by the States may be exerted as if the specific power had not been elsewhere reposed, but, on the contrary, the only legitimate conclusion is that the general government intended that power should not be affirmatively exercised, and the action of the States cannot be permitted to effect that which would be incompatible with such intention. Hence, inasmuch as interstate commerce, consisting in the transportation, purchase, sale, and exchange of commodities, is national in its character, and must be governed by a uniform system, so long as Congress does not pass any law to regulate it, or allowing the States so to do, it thereby indicates its will that such commerce shall be free and untrammelled. . . .

That ardent spirits, distilled liquors, ale and beer, are subjects of exchange, barter and traffic, like any other commodity in which a right of traffic exists, and are so recognized by the usages of the commercial world, the laws of Congress and the decisions of courts, is not denied. Being thus articles of commerce, can a State, in the absence of legislation on the part of Congress prohibit their importation from abroad or from a sister State? or when imported prohibit their sale by the importer? If the importation cannot be prohibited without the consent of Congress, when does property imported from abroad, or from a sister State, so become part of the common mass of property within

a State as to be subject to its unimpeded control? . . .

The doctrine now firmly established is . . . [this]: "It is only after the importation is completed, and the property imported has mingled with and become a part of the general property of the State, that its regulations can act upon it, except so far as may be necessary to insure safety in the disposition of the import until thus mingled."

The conclusion follows that, as the grant of the power to regulate commerce among the States, so far as one system is required, is exclusive, the States cannot exercise that power without the assent of Congress, and, in the absence of legislation, it is left for the courts to determine when State action does or does not amount to such exercise, or, in other words, what is or is not a regulation of such commerce. When that is determined, controversy is at an end. . . .

The plaintiffs in error are citizens of Illinois, are not pharmacists, and have no permit, but import into Iowa beer, which they sell in original packages, as described. Under our decision in *Bowman* v. *Chicago, & c. Railway Co.*, they had the right to import this beer into that State, and in the view which we have expressed they had the right to sell it, by which act alone it would become mingled in the common mass of property within the State. Up to that point of time, we hold that in the absence of congressional permission to do so, the State had no power to interfere by seizure, or any other action, in prohibition of importation and sale of the foreign or non-resident importer. Whatever our individual views may be as to the deleterious or dangerous qualities of particular articles, we cannot hold that any articles which Congress recognizes as subjects of interstate commerce are not such, or that whatever are thus recognized can be controlled by state laws amounting to regulations, while they retain that character; although, at the same time, if directly dangerous in themselves, the State may take appropriate measures to guard against injury before it obtains complete jurisdiction over them. To concede to a State the power to exclude directly or indirectly, articles so situated, without congressional permission, is to concede to a majority of the people of a State, represented in the State legislature, the power to regulate commercial intercourse between the States, by determining what shall be its subjects, when that power was distinctly granted to be exercised by the people of the United States, represented by Congress, and its possession by the latter was considered essential to that more perfect Union which the Constitution was adopted to create. . . .

The legislation in question is to the extent indicated repugnant to the third clause of section 8 of Art. I of the Constitution of the United States, and therefore the judgment of the Supreme Court of Iowa is

Reversed.

MR. JUSTICE GRAY, with whom concurred MR. JUSTICE HARLAN and MR. JUSTICE BREWER, dissenting. . . .

The statutes in question were enacted by the State of Iowa in the exercise of its undoubted power to protect its inhabitants against the evils, physical, moral, and social, attending the free use of intoxicating liquors. They are not aimed at interstate commerce. They have no relation to the movement of goods from one State to another, but operate only on intoxicating liquors within the territorial limits of the State. They include all such liquors without discrimination, and do not even mention where they are made or whence they come. They affect commerce much more remotely and indirectly than laws of a State (the validity of which is unquestioned), authorizing the erection of bridges and dams across navigable waters within its limits, which wholly obstruct the course of commerce and navigation; or than quarantine laws, which operate directly upon all ships and merchandise coming into the ports of the State. . . .

The silence and inaction of Congress upon the subject, during the long period since the decision of the *License Cases*, appear to us to require the inference that Congress intended that the law should remain as thereby declared by this court; rather than to warrant the presumption that Congress intended that commerce among the States should be free from the indirect effect of such an exercise of the police power for the public safety, as had been adjudged by that decision to be within the constitutional authority of the States. . . .

Southern Pacific v. Arizona
325 U.S. 761, 65 S.Ct. 1515, 89 L.Ed. 1915 (1945)

The Arizona Train Limit Law of 1912 made it unlawful to operate within the state a railroad train of more than 14 passenger or 70 freight cars. In 1940, when the state sought to collect penalties for violations of the act, the appellant company objected, claiming that the act was unconstitutional. The Supreme Court of Arizona upheld the constitutionality of the law, and the company appealed. The portion of the opinion of Chief Justice Stone holding that there was no conflict between the state act and federal legislation has been omitted. Majority: Stone, Frankfurter, Jackson, Murphy, Reed, Roberts, Rutledge. Dissenting: Black, Douglas.

MR. CHIEF JUSTICE STONE delivered the opinion of the Court. . . .

. . . We are . . . brought to appellant's contention, that the state statute contravenes the commerce clause of the Federal Constitution.

Although the commerce clause conferred on the national government power to regulate commerce, its possession of the power does not exclude all state power of regulation. Ever since *Willson* v. *Black Bird Creek Marsh Co.* and *Cooley* v. *Board of Wardens* . . . it has been recognized that, in the absence of conflicting legislation by Congress, there is a residuum of power in the state to make laws governing matters of local concern which nevertheless in some measure affect interstate commerce or even, to some extent, regulate it. . . . Thus the states may regulate matters which, because of their number and diversity, may never be adequately dealt with by Congress. . . . When the regulation of matters of local concern is local in character and effect, and its impact on the national commerce does not seriously interfere with its operation, and the consequent incentive to deal with them nationally is slight, such regulation has been generally held to be within state authority. . . .

But ever since *Gibbons* v. *Ogden* . . . the states have not been deemed to have authority to impede substantially the free flow of commerce from state to state, or to regulate those phases of the national commerce which, because of the need of national uniformity, demand that their regulation, if any, be prescribed by a single authority. . . .

For a hundred years it has been accepted constitutional doctrine that the commerce clause, without the aid of Congressional legislation, thus affords some protection from state legislation inimical to the national commerce, and that in such cases, where Congress has not acted, this Court, and not the state legislature, is under the commerce clause the final arbiter of the competing demands of state and national interests. . . .

Congress has undoubted power to redefine the distribution of power over interstate commerce. It may either permit the states to regulate the commerce in a manner which would otherwise not be permissible . . . or exclude state regulation even of matters of peculiarly local concern which nevertheless affect interstate commerce. . . .

But in general Congress has left it to the courts to formulate the rules thus interpreting the commerce clause in its application, doubtless because it has appreciated the destructive consequences to the commerce of the nation if their protection were withdrawn and has been aware that in their application state laws will not be invalidated without the support of relevant factual material which will "afford a sure basis" for an informed judgment. . . .

Hence the matters for ultimate determination here are the nature and extent of the burden which the state regulation of interstate trains, adopted as a safety measure, imposes on interstate commerce, and whether the relative weights of the state and national interests involved are such as to make inapplicable the rule, generally observed, that the free flow of interstate commerce and its freedom from local restraints in matters requiring uniformity of regulation are interests safeguarded by the commerce clause from state interference. . . .

The findings show that the operation of long trains, that is trains of more than fourteen passenger and more than seventy freight cars, is standard practice over the main lines of the railroads of the United States, and that, if the length of trains is to be regulated at all, national uniformity in the regulation adopted, such as only Congress can prescribe, is practically indispensable to the operation of an efficient and economical national railway system. . . .

The unchallenged findings leave no doubt that the Arizona Train Limit Law imposes a serious burden on the interstate commerce conducted by appellant. It materially impedes the movement of appellant's interstate trains through that state and interposes a substantial obstruction to the national policy proclaimed by Congress, to promote adequate, economical and efficient railway transportation service. . . . Enforcement of the law in Arizona, while train lengths remain unregulated or are regulated by varying standards in other states, must inevitably result in an impairment of uniformity of efficient railroad operation because the railroads are subjected to regulation which is not uniform in its application. Compliance with a state statute limiting train lengths requires interstate trains of a length lawful in other states to be broken up and reconstituted as they enter each state according as it may impose varying limitations upon train lengths. The alternative is for the carrier to conform to the lowest train limit restriction of any of the states through which its trains pass, whose laws thus control the carriers' operations both within and without the regulating state. . . .

The trial court found that the Arizona law had no reasonable relation to safety, and made train operation more dangerous. Examination of the evidence and the detailed findings makes it clear that this conclusion was rested on facts found which indicate that such increased danger of accident and personal injury as may result from the greater length of trains is more than offset by the increase in the number of accidents resulting from the larger number of trains when train lengths are reduced. In considering the effect of the statute as a safety measure, therefore, the factor of controlling significance for present purposes is not whether there is basis for the conclusion of the Arizona Supreme Court that the increase in length of trains beyond the statutory maximum has an adverse effect upon safety of operation. The decisive question is whether in the circumstances the total effect of the law as a safety measure in reducing accidents and casualties is so slight or problematical as not to outweigh the national interest in keeping interstate commerce free from interferences which seriously impede it and subject it to local regulation which does not have a uniform effect on the interstate train journey which it interrupts. . . .

We think, as the trial court found, that the Arizona Train Limit Law, viewed as a safety measure, affords at most slight and dubious advantage, if any, over unregulated train lengths, because it results in an increase in the number of trains and train operations and the consequent increase in train accidents of a character generally more severe than those due to slack action. Its undoubted effect on the commerce is the regulation, without securing uniformity, of the length of trains operated in interstate commerce, which lack is itself a primary cause of preventing the free flow of commerce by delaying it and by substantially increasing its cost and impairing its efficiency. In these respects the case differs from those where a state, by regulatory measures affecting the commerce, has removed or reduced safety hazards without substantial interference with the interstate movement of trains. . . .

Appellees especially rely on the full train crew cases, . . . and also on *South Carolina State Highway Dept.* v. *Barnwell Bros.*, as supporting the state's authority to regulate the length of interstate

trains. While the full train crew laws undoubtedly placed an added financial burden on the railroads in order to serve a local interest, they did not obstruct interstate transportation or seriously impede it.

South Carolina State Highway Dept. v. *Barnwell Bros.*, was concerned with the power of the state to regulate the weight and width of motor cars passing interstate over its highways, a legislative field over which the state has a far more extensive control than over interstate railroads. In that case. . . we were at pains to point out that there are few subjects of state regulation affecting interstate commerce which are so peculiarly of local concern as is the use of the state's highways. Unlike the railroads local highways are built, owned and maintained by the state or its municipal subdivisions. The state is responsible for their safe and economical administration. Regulations affecting the safety of their use must be applied alike to intrastate and interstate traffic. The fact that they affect alike shippers in interstate and intrastate commerce in great numbers, within as well as without the state, is a safeguard against regulatory abuses. Their regulation is akin to quarantine measures, game laws, and like local regulations of rivers, harbors, piers, and docks, with respect to which the state has exceptional scope for the exercise of its regulatory power, and which, Congress not acting, have been sustained even though they materially interfere with interstate commerce.

The contrast between the present regulation and the full train crew laws in point of their effects on the commerce, and the like contrast with the highway safety regulations, in point of the nature of the subject of regulation and the state's interest in it, illustrate and emphasize the considerations which enter into a determination of the relative weights of state and national interests where state regulation affecting commerce is attempted. Here examination of all the relevant factors makes it plain that the state interest is outweighed by the interest of the Nation in an adequate, economical and efficient railway transportation service, which must prevail.

Reversed.

MR. JUSTICE BLACK, dissenting. . . .

I think that legislatures, to the exclusion of courts, have the constitutional power to enact laws limiting train lengths, for the purpose of reducing injuries brought about by "slack movements." Their power is not less because a requirement of short trains might increase grade crossing accidents. This latter fact raises an entirely different element of danger which is itself subject to legislative regulation. For legislatures may, if necessary, require railroads to take appropriate steps to reduce the likelihood of injuries at grade crossings. . . . And the fact that grade-crossing improvements may be expensive is no sufficient reason to say that an unconstitutional "burden" is put upon a railroad even though it be an interstate road. . . .

There have been many sharp divisions of this Court concerning its authority, in the absence of congressional enactment, to invalidate state laws as violating the Commerce Clause. . . . That discussion need not be renewed here, because even the broadest exponents of judicial power in this field have not heretofore expressed doubt as to a state's power, absent a paramount congressional declaration, to regulate interstate trains in the interest of safety. . . .

This record in its entirety leaves me with no doubt whatever that many employees have been seriously injured and killed in the past, and that many more are likely to be so in the future, because of "slack movement" in trains. Everyday knowledge as well as direct evidence presented at the various hearings, substantiates the report of the Senate Committee that danger from slack movement is greater in long trains than in short trains. It may be that offsetting dangers are possible in the operation of short trains. The balancing of these probabilities, however, is not in my judgment a matter for judicial determination, but one which calls for legislative consideration. Representatives elected by the people to make their laws, rather than judges appointed to interpret those laws, can best determine the policies which govern the people. That at least is the basic principle on which our democratic society rests. I would affirm the judgment of the Supreme Court of Arizona.

Philadelphia v. *New Jersey*
437 U.S. 617, 98 S.Ct. 2531, 57 L.Ed. 2d 475 (1978)

In 1974 a New Jersey law (referred to in the following opinions as Chapter 363) went into effect that provided, "No person shall bring into this State any solid or liquid waste which originated or was collected outside the territorial limits of the State, except garbage to be fed to swine in the State . . . until the commissioner [of the state Department of Environmental Protection] shall determine that such action can be permitted without endangering the public health, safety and welfare and has promulgated regulations permitting and regulating the treatment and disposal of such waste in this State." As authorized, the commissioner issued regulations permitting four categories of waste to enter the state, mainly for recycling and reprocessing. The city of Philadelphia, other out-of-state cities, and private landfills—all affected by the statute—challenged the law on various state and federal grounds. The trial court invalidated the law because it discriminated against interstate commerce, and the New Jersey Supreme Court affirmed. On appeal to the United States Supreme Court, the justices remanded the case to the state court in light of passage of the Resources Conservation and Recovery Act of 1976. The New Jersey Supreme Court found no federal preemption of the 1974 law. The United States Supreme Court later disposed of the preemption issue in a single sentence: "We agree with the New Jersey court that the state law has not been pre-empted by federal legislation." (See Chapter Four for a discussion of preemption.) Majority: Stewart, Blackmun, Brennan, Marshall, Powell, Stevens, White. Dissenting: Rehnquist, Burger.

MR. JUSTICE STEWART delivered the opinion of the Court.

A New Jersey law prohibits the importation of most "solid or liquid waste which originated or was collected outside the territorial limits of the State. . . ." In this case we are required to decide whether this statutory prohibition violates the Commerce Clause of the United States Constitution. . . .

The crucial inquiry, therefore, must be directed to determining whether ch. 363 is basically a protectionist measure, or whether it can fairly be viewed as a law directed to legitimate local concerns, with effects upon interstate commerce that are only incidental.

The purpose of ch. 363 is set out in the statute itself as follows:

"The Legislature finds and determines that . . . the volume of solid and liquid waste continues to rapidly increase, that the treatment and disposal of these wastes continues to pose an even greater threat to the quality of the environment of New Jersey, that the available and appropriate land fill sites within the State are being diminished, that the environment continues to be threatened by the treatment and disposal of waste which originated or was collected outside the State and that the public health, safety and welfare require that the treatment and disposal within this State of all wastes generated outside of the State be prohibited."

The New Jersey Supreme Court accepted this statement of the state legislature's purpose. The state court additionally found that New Jersey's existing landfill sites will be exhausted within a few years; that to go on using these sites or to develop new ones will take a heavy environmental toll, both from pollution and from loss of scarce open lands; that new techniques to divert waste from landfills to other methods of disposal and resource recovery processes are under development, but that these changes will require time; and finally, that "the extension of the lifespan of existing land-

fills, resulting from the exclusion of out-of-state waste, may be of crucial importance in preventing further virgin wetlands or other undeveloped lands from being devoted to landfill purposes." Based on these findings, the court concluded that ch. 363 was designed to protect not the State's economy, but its environment, and that its substantial benefits outweigh its "slight" burden on interstate commerce.

The appellants strenuously contend that ch. 363, "while outwardly cloaked 'in the currently fashionable garb of environmental protection'. . . is actually no more than a legislative effort to suppress competition and stabilize the cost of solid waste disposal for New Jersey residents. . . ."

This dispute about ultimate legislative purpose need not be resolved, because its resolution would not be relevant to the constitutional issue to be decided in this case. Contrary to the evident assumption of the state court and the parties, the evil of protectionism can reside in legislative means as well as legislative ends. Thus, it does not matter whether the ultimate aim of ch. 363 is to reduce the waste disposal costs of New Jersey residents or to save remaining open lands from pollution, for we assume New Jersey has every right to protect its residents' pocketbooks as well as their environment. And it may be assumed as well that New Jersey may pursue those ends by slowing the flow of *all* waste into the State's remaining landfills, even though interstate commerce may incidentally be affected. But whatever New Jersey's ultimate purpose, it may not be accomplished by discriminating against articles of commerce coming from outside the State unless there is some reason, apart from their origin, to treat them differently. Both on its face and in its plain effect, ch. 363 violates this principle of nondiscrimination.

The Court has consistently found parochial legislation of this kind to be constitutionally invalid. . . .

The New Jersey law at issue in this case falls squarely within the area that the Commerce Clause puts off-limits to state regulation. On its face, it imposes on out-of-state commercial interests the full burden of conserving the State's remaining landfill space. It is true that in our previous cases the scarce natural resource was itself the article of commerce, whereas here the scarce resource and the article of commerce are distinct. But that difference is without consequence. In both instances, the State has overtly moved to slow or freeze the flow of commerce for protectionist reasons. It does not matter that the State has shut the article of commerce inside the State in one case and outside the State in the other. What is crucial is the attempt by one State to isolate itself from a problem common to many by erecting a barrier against the movement of interstate trade. . . .

It is true that certain quarantine laws have not been considered forbidden protectionist measures, even though they were directed against out-of-state commerce. . . . But those quarantine laws banned the importation of articles such as diseased livestock that required destruction as soon as possible because their very movement risked contagion and other evils. Those laws thus did not discriminate against interstate commerce as such, but simply prevented traffic in noxious articles, whatever their origin.

The New Jersey statute is not such a quarantine law. There has been no claim here that the very movement of waste into or through New Jersey endangers health, or that waste must be disposed of as soon and as close to its point of generation as possible. The harms caused by waste are said to arise after its disposal in landfill sites, and at that point, as New Jersey concedes, there is no basis to distinguish out-of-state waste from domestic waste. If one is inherently harmful, so is the other. Yet New Jersey has banned the former while leaving its landfill sites open to the latter. The New Jersey law blocks the importation of waste in an obvious effort to saddle those outside the State with the entire burden of slowing the flow of refuse into New Jersey's remaining landfill sites. That legislative effort is clearly impermissible under the Commerce Clause of the Constitution.

Today, cities in Pennsylvania and New York find it expedient or necessary to send their waste into New Jersey for disposal, and New Jersey claims the right to close its borders to such traffic. Tomorrow, cities in New Jersey may find it expedient or necessary to send their waste into Pennsylvania or New York for disposal, and those States might then claim the right to close their borders. The Commerce Clause will protect New Jersey in the future, just as it protects her neighbors now, from efforts by one State to isolate itself in the stream of interstate commerce from a problem shared by all.

The judgment is reversed.

MR. JUSTICE REHNQUIST, with whom THE CHIEF JUSTICE joins, dissenting. . . .

The health and safety hazards associated with landfills presents appellees with a currently unsolvable dilemma. Other, hopefully safer, methods of disposing of solid wastes are still in the development stage and cannot presently be used. But appellees obviously cannot completely stop the tide of solid waste that its citizens will produce in the interim. For the moment, therefore, appellees must continue to use sanitary landfills to dispose of New Jersey's own solid waste despite the critical environmental problems thereby created. . . .

The Court recognizes that States can prohibit the importation of items "which, on account of their existing condition, would bring in and spread disease, pestilence, and death, such as rags or other substances infected with the germs of yellow fever or the virus or smallpox, or cattle or meat or other provisions that are diseased or decayed, or otherwise, from their condition and quality, unfit for human use or consumption."

In my opinion, these cases are dispositive of the present one. Under them, New Jersey may require germ-infected rags or diseased meat to be disposed of as best as possible within the State, but at the same time prohibit the *importation* of such items for disposal at the facilities that are set up within New Jersey for disposal of such material generated *within* the State. The physical fact of life that New Jersey must somehow dispose of its own noxious items does not mean that it must serve as a depository for those of every other State. Similarly, New Jersey should be free under our past precedents to prohibit the importation of solid waste because of the health and safety problems that such waste poses to its citizens. The fact that New Jersey continues to, and indeed must continue to, dispose of its own solid waste does not mean that New Jersey may not prohibit the importation of even more solid waste into the State. I simply see no way to distinguish solid waste, on the record of this case, from germ-infected rags, diseased meat, and other noxious items.

The Court's effort to distinguish these prior cases

is unconvincing. It first asserts that the quarantine laws which have previously been upheld "ban the importation of articles such as diseased livestock that required destruction as soon as possible because their very movement risked contagion and other evils." According to the Court, the New Jersey law is distinguishable from these other laws, and invalid, because the concern of New Jersey is not with the *movement* of solid waste but of the present inability to safely *dispose* of it once it reaches its destination. But I think it far from clear that the State's law has as limited a focus as the Court imputes to it: Solid waste which is a health hazard when it reaches its destination may in all likelihood be an equally great health hazard in transit. . . .

Second, the Court implies that the challenged laws must be invalidated because New Jersey has left its landfills open to domestic waste. But, as the Court notes, this Court has repeatedly upheld quarantine laws "even though they appear to single out interstate commerce for special treatment." The fact that New Jersey has left its landfill sites open for domestic waste does not, of course, mean that solid waste is not innately harmful. Nor does it mean that New Jersey prohibits importation of solid waste for reasons other than the health and safety of its population. New Jersey must out of sheer necessity treat and dispose of its solid waste in some fashion, just as it must treat New Jersey cattle suffering from hoof-and-mouth disease. It does not follow that New Jersey must, under the Commerce Clause, accept solid waste or diseased cattle from outside its borders and thereby exacerbate its problems. . . .

Reeves, Inc. v. *Stake*
447 U.S. 429, 100 S.Ct. 2271, 65 L.Ed. 2d 244 (1980)

For many years the state of South Dakota has operated a cement plant. Between 1970 and 1977, some 40 percent of the plant's production was shipped to buyers outside the state. Reeves, Inc., a ready-mix concrete distributor in Wyoming, from 1958 until 1978 obtained 95 percent of its cement from the state-owned plant. In 1978, various difficulties at the cement plant forced a cut in production. The State Cement Commission chose to supply all South Dakota customers first and to honor other contract commitments. Being out of state and lacking a long-term contract, Reeves was unable to purchase any more cement and was obliged to reduce its own concrete production by 76 percent when no other adequate suppliers could be found. Reeves then sued the commission in district court, which "reasoned that South Dakota's 'hoarding' was inimical to the national free market envisioned by the Commerce Clause." The Court of Appeals for the Eighth Circuit reversed. Justice Blackmun's majority opinion and Justice Powell's dissent, reprinted below, refer to *Hughes* v. *Alexandria Scrap Corp.* (1976). In that case Maryland offered a "bounty" for every Maryland-titled junk car converted into scrap. Documentation requirements were more exacting for out-of-state processors, making it less profitable for suppliers to transfer vehicles outside Maryland. Thus, in-state processors of junk cars were favored over those out of state. Upholding the policy, the Court declared, "Nothing in the purposes animating the Commerce Clause prohibits a State, in the absence of congressional action, from participating in the market and exercising the right to favor its own citizens over others." In *Alexandria Scrap,* Justice Powell wrote the opinion of the Court, and Justices Brennan, White, and Marshall dissented. Majority: Blackmun, Burger, Marshall, Rehnquist, Stewart. Dissenting: Powell, Brennan, Stevens, White.

Mr. Justice Blackmun delivered the opinion of the Court. . . .

The basic distinction drawn in *Alexandria Scrap* between States as market participants and States as market regulators makes good sense and sound law. As that case explains, the Commerce Clause responds principally to state taxes and regulatory measures impeding free private trade in the national marketplace. . . . There is no indication of a constitutional plan to limit the ability of the States themselves to operate freely in the free market. . . .

Restraint in this area is also counseled by considerations of state sovereignty, the role of each State " 'as guardian and trustee for its people' ". . . and "the long recognized right of trader or manufacturer, engaged in an entirely private business, freely to exercise his own independent discretion as to parties with whom he will deal." . . . Moreover, state proprietary activities may be, and often are, burdened with the same restrictions imposed on private market participants. Evenhandedness suggests that, when acting as proprietors, States should similarly share existing freedoms from federal constraints, including the inherent limits of the Commerce Clause. . . . Finally, as this case illustrates, the competing considerations in cases involving state proprietary action often will be subtle, complex, politically charged, and difficult to assess under traditional Commerce Clause analysis. Given these factors, *Alexandria Scrap* wisely recognizes that, as a rule, the adjustment of interests in this context is a task better suited for Congress than this Court.

South Dakota, as a seller of cement, unquestionably fits the "market participant" label more comfortably than a State acting to subsidize local scrap processors. Thus, the general rule of *Alexandria Scrap* plainly applies here. . . .

In finding a Commerce Clause violation, the District Court emphasized "that the Commission . . . made an election to become part of the interstate commerce system." . . . The gist of this reasoning, repeated by petitioner here, is that one good turn deserves another. Having long exploited the interstate market, South Dakota should not be permitted to withdraw from it when a shortage arises. This argument is not persuasive. It is somewhat self-serving to say that South Dakota has "exploited" the interstate market. An equally fair characterization is that neighboring States have long benefited from South Dakota's foresight and industry. . . .

Our rejection of petitioner's market-exploitation theory fundamentally refocuses analysis. It means that to reverse we would have to void a South Dakota "residents only" policy even if it had been enforced from the plant's very first days. Such a holding, however, would interfere significantly with a State's ability to structure relations exclusively with its own citizens. It would also threaten the future fashioning of effective and creative programs for solving local problems and distributing government largesse. . . . A healthy regard for federalism and good government renders us reluctant to risk these results. . . .

Undaunted by these considerations, petitioner advances four more arguments for reversal:

First, petitioner protests that South Dakota's preference for its residents responds solely to the "non-governmental objective" of protectionism. . . . Therefore, petitioner argues the policy is *per se* invalid. . . .

We find the label "protectionism" of little help in this context. The State's refusal to sell to buyers other than South Dakotans is "protectionist" only in the sense that it limits benefits generated by a state program to those who fund the state treasury and whom the State was created to serve. Petitioner's argument apparently also would characterize as "protectionist" rules restricting to state residents the enjoyment of state educational institutions, energy generated by a state-run plant, police and fire protection, and agricultural improvement and business development programs. Such policies, while perhaps "protectionist" in a loose sense, reflect the essential and patently unobjectionable purpose of state government—to serve the citizens of the State.

Second, petitioner echoes the District Court's warning.

If a state in this union, were allowed to hoard its commodities or resources for the use of their own residents only, a drastic situation might evolve. For example, Pennsylvania or Wyoming might keep their coal, the northwest its timber, and the mining states their minerals. The result being that embargo may be retaliated by embargo and commerce would be halted at state lines. . . .

This argument, although rooted in the core purpose of the Commerce Clause, does not fit the present facts. Cement is not a natural resource, like coal, timber, wild game, or minerals. . . . It is the end-product of a complex process whereby a costly physical plant and human labor act on raw materials. South Dakota has not sought to limit access to the State's limestone or other materials used to make cement. Nor has it restricted the ability of private firms or sister States to set up plants within its borders. . . .

Third, it is suggested that the South Dakota program is infirm because it places South Dakota suppliers of ready-mix concrete at a competitive advantage in the out-of-state market; Wyoming suppliers, such as petitioner, have little chance against South Dakota suppliers who can purchase cement from the State's plant and freely sell beyond South Dakota's borders.

The force of this argument is seriously diminished, if not eliminated, by several considerations. The argument necessarily implies that the South Dakota scheme would be unobjectionable if sales in other States were totally barred. It therefore proves too much, for it would tolerate even a greater measure of protectionism and stifling of interstate commerce than the challenged system allows. . . . Finally, the competitive plight of out-of-state ready-mix suppliers cannot be laid solely at the feet of South Dakota. It is attributable as well to their own States' not providing or attracting alternative sources of supply and to the suppliers' own failure to guard against shortages by executing long-term supply contracts with the South Dakota plant.

In its last argument, petitioner urges that, had South Dakota not acted, free market forces would have generated an appropriate level of supply at free market prices for all buyers in the region. Having replaced free market forces, South Dakota should be forced to replicate how the free market would have operated under prevailing conditions.

This argument appears to us to be simplistic and speculative. The very reason South Dakota built its plant was because the free market had failed adequately to supply the region with cement. . . .

We conclude, then, that the arguments for invalidating South Dakota's resident-preference program are weak at best. Whatever residual force inheres in them is more than offset by countervailing considerations of policy and fairness. Reversal would discourage similar state projects, even though this project demonstrably has served the needs of state residents and has helped the entire region for more than a half century. Reversal also would rob South Dakota of the intended benefit of its foresight, risk, and industry. Under these circumstances, there is no reason to depart from the general rule of *Alexandria Scrap*.

The judgment of the United States Court of Appeals is affirmed.

It is so ordered.

Mr. Justice Powell, with whom Mr. Justice Brennan, Mr. Justice White and Mr. Justice Stevens join, dissenting. . .

The need to ensure unrestricted trade among the States created a major impetus for the drafting of the Constitution. . . .

The Commerce Clause has proved an effective weapon against protectionism. The Court has used it to strike down limitations on access to local goods, be they animal. . . vegetable . . . or mineral. . . .

This case presents a novel constitutional question. The Commerce Clause would bar legislation imposing on private parties the type of restraint on commerce adopted by South Dakota. . . . Conversely, a private business constitutionally could adopt a marketing policy that excluded customers who come from another State. This case falls between those polar situations. The State, through its Commission, engages in a commercial enterprise and restricts its own interstate distribution. The question is whether the Commission's policy should be treated like state regulation of private parties or like the marketing policy of a private business.

The application of the Commerce Clause to this case should turn on the nature of the governmental activity involved. If a public enterprise undertakes an "integral operatio[n] in areas of traditional governmental functions" . . . the Commerce Clause is not directly relevant. If, however, the State enters the private market and operates a commercial enterprise for the advantage of its private citizens, it may not evade the constitutional policy against economic balkanization.

This distinction derives from the power of governments to supply their own needs. . . and from the purpose of the Commerce Clause itself, which is designed to protect "the natural functioning of the interstate market," *Hughes* v. *Alexandria Scrap.* . . . In procuring goods and services for the operation of government, a State may act without regard to the private marketplace and remove itself from the reach of the Commerce Clause. . . . But when a State itself becomes a participant in the private market for other purposes, the Constitution forbids actions that would impede the flow of interstate commerce. These categories recognize no more than the "constitutional line between the State as Government and the State as trader."

The threshold issue is whether South Dakota has undertaken integral government operations in an area of traditional governmental functions, or whether it has participated in the marketplace as a private firm. If the latter characterization applies, we also must determine whether the State Commission's marketing policy burdens the flow of interstate trade. This analysis highlights the differences between the state action here and that before the Court in *Hughes* v. *Alexandria Scrap Corp.* . . .

. . . *Alexandria Scrap* determined that Maryland's bounty program constituted direct state participation in the market for automobile hulks. . . But the critical question—the second step in the opinion's analysis—was whether the bounty program constituted an impermissible burden on interstate commerce. Recognizing that the case did not fit neatly into conventional Commerce Clause theory . . . we found no burden on commerce. . . .

Unlike the market subsidies at issue in *Alexandria Scrap,* the marketing policy of the South Dakota Cement Commission has cut off interstate trade. . . . The effect on interstate trade is the same as if the state legislature had imposed the policy on private cement producers. The Commerce Clause prohibits this severe restraint on commerce.

I share the Court's desire to preserve state sovereignty. But the Commerce Clause long has been recognized as a limitation on that sovereignty, consciously designed to maintain a national market and defeat economic provincialism. The Court today approves protectionist state policies. In the absence of contrary congressional action, those policies now can be implemented as long as the State itself directly participates in the market.

By enforcing the Commerce Clause in this case, the Court would work no unfairness on the people of South Dakota. They still could reserve cement for public projects and share in whatever return the plant generated. They could not, however, use the power of the State to furnish themselves with cement forbidden to the people of neighboring States.

The creation of a free national economy was a major goal of the States when they resolved to unite under the Federal Constitution. The decision today cannot be reconciled with that purpose.

SIX

Congressional Power under the Commerce Clause

Powerful and ingenious minds . . . may so entangle and perplex the understanding, as to obscure principles which were before thought quite plain, and induce doubts where, if the mind were to pursue its own course, none would be perceived. In such a case, it is peculiarly necessary to recur to safe and fundamental principles. . . .

—CHIEF JUSTICE JOHN MARSHALL (1824)

The commerce clause as a reservoir of congressional power did not become a constitutional issue until after the Civil War, when a truly national economy, tied together by the railroads, developed. Then, two major questions arose. First, what was the "commerce" that Congress was empowered to regulate? Did it, for instance, extend to manufacturing? Second, what was the reach of the *commerce power?* Could the commerce power touch matters and relationships traditionally regarded as local in nature? Answers to these questions have greatly affected national policy for over a century. The course the Supreme Court has generally followed since 1937 undergirds the modern regulatory state.

THE NEED FOR NATIONAL ACTION

Initially, as seen in Chapter Five, the Court was generally concerned with the commerce clause as it limited state action affecting interstate commerce. In 1877, for example, the Justices in **Munn** v. **Illinois** (see Chapter Eight) and other Granger Cases held that state legislatures—in the absence of legislation by Congress—could regulate railroad and other rates for interstate as well as for intrastate shipments. This led to such great confusion that nearly a decade later the Court, in the history-making *Wabash Railway Co.* v. *Illinois* (1886), was obligated to repudiate its former view. As explained in Chapter Five, the Court suggested that since interstate rates were of "national character," any regulation "should be done by the Congress . . . under the commerce clause of the Constitution." Enacted the next year was the Interstate Commerce Act, which represented Congress's first major regulatory effort using the commerce power and which established the Interstate Commerce Commission, the nation's first independent regulatory commission.

Three years later, in 1890, the Sherman Anti-Trust Act showed that Congress was determined to use its commerce power to accomplish purposes far beyond anything hitherto attempted. The business community strenuously resisted this bold national effort to control American industrial and commercial life, finding useful constitutional weapons in both the due process and commerce clauses.

Difficult questions arose at the very outset concerning the applicability of the Sherman Act to industrial and commercial enterprise. The rationale of the act was that certain combinations and conspiracies that had the effect of restraining or monopolizing interstate commerce should be prohibited. In **United States v. E. C. Knight** (the Sugar Trust Case, 1895) a monopoly in the production of refined sugar was held exempt from the Sherman Act. To Chief Justice Fuller, commerce meant primarily transportation—the physical movement of goods following manufacture. The effect of contracts and combinations to control manufacture, "however inevitable and whatever its extent," would be "indirect," the chief justice held, and therefore beyond congressional reach. Yet he recognized that goods are manufactured *only* because they can be sold, that manufacture and commerce are part of a seamless web. Much disturbed by the implications of an integrated national economy for federal power, the chief justice said, "Slight reflection will show that if the national power extends to all contracts and combinations in manufacture, agriculture, mining, and other productive industries, whose ultimate result may affect external commerce, comparatively little of business operations and affairs would be left for state control."

In 1904, however (*Northern Securities Co.* v. *United States*), a scheme by which a holding company had been established to hold the stock of competing railroads was held contrary to the Sherman Act. In another broad interpretation of the commerce power (*Swift* v. *United States,* 1905), a combination of meat packers was held unlawful under the act, on the ground that their activities, though geographically "local," were important incidents in a current of interstate commerce. The Sugar Trust Case was seriously undermined.

JUDICIAL CHOICES IN CONSTITUTIONAL INTERPRETATION

A series of cases between 1903 and World War I clearly established the principle that the commerce power could be used as a device for accomplishing purely social goals. These decisions meant that Congress in effect possessed a *national police power,* alongside the police power ("the power to govern men and things," Chief Justice Taney called it) the states had always enjoyed. (See Chapter Eight for a discussion of the development of state police power.)

In the first case (*Champion* v. *Ames,* 1903) a federal act prohibiting the interstate shipment of lottery tickets was upheld. Whereas the opinion contained frequent references to the evil quality of these tickets, the dissent pointed out that the evil began only with their illegal use at the point of destination. On similar grounds, the Pure Food and Drug Act withstood attack in 1911 (*Hipolite Egg Co.* v. *United States*). In *Hoke* v. *United States* (1913), the Court approved the Mann Act, making it a felony to transport a woman from one state to another for immoral purposes. In *Houston, E. & W. Texas Ry. Co.* v. *United States* (the Shreveport Case), the Court upheld in 1914 an Interstate Commerce Commission order fixing intrastate railroad rates because of their effect on interstate commerce, suggesting Marshall's view that national commerce power extends to all commerce that "affects more than one state."

The pattern then became confused. In ***Hammer*** v. ***Dagenhart*** the Court in 1918 followed the Sugar Trust Case and drew a distinction between commerce and manufacturing. Congress had prohibited the transportation in interstate commerce of products produced by child labor (age 16 in mines, age 14 in factories, or more than 48 hours a week for the age group 14–16 years). Justice Day, for the Court, characterized the precedents involving lotteries, food, and white slavery as attempts to regulate where transportation was used to accomplish harmful results; production and its incidents, on the other hand, were (in Day's opinion) local matters.

Two subsequent cases seemed to indicate once again that the Court might be prepared to accept a broad construction of the commerce power. In ***Stafford*** v. ***Wallace*** (1922), Chief Justice Taft delivered an opinion upholding the Packers and Stockyards Act of 1921, an attempt to regulate trade practices in the Chicago meat-packing industry. Taft stated that although in a geographic sense the packers were conducting a local business, in an economic sense their activities were only an incident in a continuing interstate market. Following the same line of reasoning, the Court in 1925 upheld the National Motor Theft Act, making it a crime to transport or conceal a stolen automobile (*Brooks* v. *United States*). These cases cast doubt on the value of *Hammer* v. *Dagenhart* as a precedent and seemed to portend a return to the broad doctrines of Chief Justice Marshall.

In 1935, when the Court was faced with the necessity of passing on the New Deal legislation enacted under the commerce clause, it had before it two viable lines of precedents: (1) The doctrines established by John Marshall, which had inspired the Court's decisions in *Swift* v. *United States* and *Stafford* v. *Wallace;* and (2) the restrictive interpretations of the Sugar Trust Case and *Hammer* v. *Dagenhart.*

THE NEW DEAL IN COURT

Franklin D. Roosevelt was inaugurated president in 1933 in the depths of the Great Depression. His administration achieved rapid passage in Congress of a series of measures designed to aid economic recovery. The first phase of F.D.R.'s domestic reform program (called the New Deal) involved agricultural and business regulation, price stabilization, public works, and banking and finance regulation. Prominent legislation included the National Industrial Recovery Act (NIRA) and the Agricultural Adjustment Act (AAA), both enacted in 1933. The second phase began in 1935 and emphasized social and economic legislation— such as the Social Security Act and the Fair Labor Standards Act—to benefit working people directly.

The first New Deal reform measure reached the Supreme Bench for argument in December 1934 under circumstances that did not augur well for the validity of executive orders issued under NIRA. The Panama Refining Company had challenged the act's prohibition against shipment of "hot oil" (that exceeding state allowances) across state lines. Early in the argument government counsel disclosed that criminal penalties attaching to the violation of the relevant code provisions had been inadvertently omitted from the executive order. Judicial curiosity was immediately aroused, and concern deepened when opposing counsel bitterly complained that his client had been arrested, indicted, and held several days in jail for violating this nonexistent "law." With these points against it the government was at a disadvantage in pressing its argument that Congress could constitutionally empower the president in his discretion to ban hot oil from interstate commerce. Eight justices held Section 9(c) of the NIRA invalid as an unconstitutional delegation of legislative power to the chief executive (*Panama Refining Co.* v. *Ryan, 1935*). Congress, they said, established no "primary standard," thus leaving "the matter to the President without standard or rule, to be dealt with as he pleased." For the first time the maxim *delegata potestas non potest delegari* (a delegated power cannot be delegated), a principle not found in the Constitution, formed the basis of a judicial decision overturning an act of Congress.

Before the dust thrown up by the hot oil decision had fairly settled, the Court made headlines again in its 5-to-4 decision scuttling the recently enacted railroad retirement scheme, which required the carriers to subscribe to a pension plan for old employees (*Railroad Retirement Board* v. *Alton R. R. Co., 1935*). For the majority, Mr. Justice Roberts ridiculed the statute. Brushing the legislation aside as based on "the contentment and satisfaction theory" of social progress, he inquired, "Is it not apparent that they [pensions] are really and essentially related solely to the social welfare of the worker, and therefore remote from any regulation of commerce as such?" Congress might, he agreed, require outright dismissal of all aged workers, but it could not give them pensions. If superannuation is a danger, Roberts argued in effect, the commerce clause authorizes compulsory retirement—without a pension! Congressional effort to compel railroads to pension off older workers failed for want of any relation between the pensioning system and the efficiency or safety of the national rail network.

Taken together, the Panama Refining and the Railroad Retirement cases forecast the New Deal's doom. The blow fell on May 27, 1935, "Black Monday," when NIRA (symbolized by the Blue Eagle) was guillotined out of the recovery program (*Schechter Poultry Co.* v. *United States*).

The Schechter brothers, wholesale poultry dealers in Brooklyn, were charged with violating NIRA's Live Poultry Code by ignoring minimum wage and maximum hour requirements and by giving special treatment to preferred customers. The Court, speaking through Chief Justice Hughes, found the act wanting as an unconstitutional delegation of legislative power. Government counsel conceded that congressional authority to regulate the Schechter business had to be based on the commerce clause, but the Court held the defendants' business was neither interstate commerce in itself nor closely enough connected with it to "affect" such commerce.

Stone and Cardozo, in a separate opinion written by the latter, agreed with the Court's disposition of the case. "This," they said, "is delegation running riot." Nor could they find support in the commerce clause "for the regulation of wages and hours of labor in the intrastate transactions that make up the defendants' business." Without characterizing all production as "local," Stone and Cardozo rejected "a view of causation that would obliterate the distinction between what is national and what is local in the activities of commerce." Somewhat more cautious than their brethren, however, they subtly indicated a desire to treat such problems as they arose without anticipating and deciding in sweeping language all the constitutional issues of the decade.

On May 18, 1936, the justices ruled 6 to 3 that Congress had exceeded its authority in enacting the Guffey-Snyder Bituminous Coal Conservation Act of 1935 (**Carter** v. **Carter Coal Co.**). Through a complex system of wage and price controls administered by a commission, the statute attempted to provide remedies for the notoriously distressed bituminous coal industry. The situation was so urgent and the benefits of the legislation so evident that President Roosevelt had taken the unusual step of asking the congressional subcommittee, while the coal act was pending, not to "permit doubts as to constitutionality, however reasonable," to block the suggested legislation. Five justices, apparently undisturbed by the consequences of inaction, were moved by considerations (to them) of even greater concern: ". . . it is of vital moment," Justice Sutherland said for the majority, "that, in order to preserve the fixed balance intended by the Constitution, the powers of the general government be not so extended as to embrace any not within the express terms of the several grants or the implications necessary to be drawn therefrom."

Sutherland's opinion was clear-cut and unequivocal on the nature of the distinction between direct and indirect effects. "The local character of mining, of manufacturing, and of crop growing is a fact, and remains a fact, whatever may be done with the products," Sutherland said. Going back to Chief Justice Fuller's opinion in the Sugar Trust Case and paraphrasing his words, Sutherland declared, "Such effect as they [working conditions] may have upon commerce, however extensive it may be, is secondary and indirect. An increase in the greatness of the effect adds to its importance. It does not alter its character." In the teeth of the congressional declaration that the act's price-fixing and labor provisions were separable, Sutherland held that they were united inextricably, and therefore must stand or fall together. They must fall, he ruled, because the labor provisions here, like those involved in the Schechter Case, bore no "direct" relation to interstate commerce. Thus, *dual federalism* (see Chapter Four) remained an independent check on the extent of Congress's power under the commerce clause.

As far as the commerce power was concerned, the Court by 1936 seemed to have adopted the view that certain subjects were local in nature and beyond the power of Congress even though they required national or uniform regulations if they were to be regulated at all. On the other hand, effective state-by-state regulation was clearly impossible; even if it were attempted it might, if any state regulation were found to have any substantial effect on interstate commerce, run afoul of the *dormant commerce power*. The Court thus had narrowed the commerce doctrines of Marshall by withdrawing from congressional power certain subject matters, such as production, agriculture, and the employer-employee relationship. In effect, the Court had created a category other than those enumerated in the Cooley Case, viz., those objects that could not in practice be regulated by either government— a "twilight zone," a "no man's land." As Justice Stone wrote to his sister at the end of the Court's term in June 1936, "we seem to have tied Uncle Sam up in a hard knot." Indeed, in the years 1934–1936 the Supreme Court in 12 decisions had declared unconstitutional all or part of 11 New Deal measures.*

THE COURT-PACKING THREAT

By the spring of 1936 it looked as if the Court had put the New Deal firmly on the rack of unconstitutionality. Loud acclaim resounded in the ranks of the Old Guard. Addressing the 1936 Republican National Convention, former President Herbert Hoover expressed heartfelt thanks "to Almighty God for the Constitution and the Supreme Court." Chief Justice Hughes joined in this triumphant chorus. "I am happy to report," he remarked in his American Law Institute address, "that the Supreme Court is still functioning." Members

---

* Economy Act of 1933 in *Lynch* v. *United States* (1934); Agricultural Adjustment Act of 1933 in *United States* v. *Butler* (1936); Joint Resolution of June 5, 1933, in *Perry* v. *United States* (1935) (but plaintiff was held not entitled to recover); National Industrial Recovery Act of 1933 in *Schechter Poultry Corp.* v. *United States* (1935) and *Panama Refining Co.* v. *Ryan* (1935); Independent Offices Appropriation Act of 1933 in *Booth* v. *United States* (1934); 1933 Amendments to Home Owners' Loan Act in *Hopkins Savings Assn.* v. *Cleary* (1935); 1934 Amendments to Bankruptcy Act of 1898 in *Ashton* v. *Cameron County Dist.* (1936); Railroad Retirement Act of 1934 in *Railroad Retirement Board* v. *Alton R. Co.* (1935); Frazier-Lemke Act of 1934 in *Louisville Bank* v. *Radford* (1935); AAA Amendments of 1935 in *Rickert Rice Mills* v. *Fontenot* (1936); Bituminous Coal Conservation Act of 1935 in *Carter* v. *Carter Coal Co.* (1936).

and guests of the institute vigorously applauded the announcement, obliging the speaker "to pause for more than two minutes."

All this rejoicing was in response to the stark fact that nine Supreme Court justices, sometimes only five, had rendered government impotent. The entire legislative program overwhelmingly approved by the American people in 1932, 1934, and 1936 was, as Assistant Attorney General Robert Jackson said, in danger of being lost in "a maze of constitutional metaphors."

Various correctives were open. The president and Congress might limit the jurisdiction of the Supreme Court, increase the number of judges to override the present arrogant majority, or sponsor constitutional amendments limiting the Court's power. Though many members of Congress urged that something be done, they were uncertain what to do, not quite sure whether the trouble was the fault of the Constitution or of judges. The president and his party were uncertain, too, at least on the most feasible remedy politically. The Democratic Party platform in 1936 said, "If these problems [social and economic] cannot be effectively solved by legislation within the Constitution, we shall seek such clarifying amendments as [we] . . . shall find necessary, in order adequately to regulate commerce, protect public health and safety and safeguard economic liberty. Thus we propose to maintain the letter and spirit of the Constitution." Throughout the campaign Democratic orators muted the discord, giving no hint that President Roosevelt would, if reelected, wage all-out war on the judiciary.

Even in the face of his overwhelming electoral triumph, the president could not be sure that the Court would give ground. Did not the traditional theory insist that the justices are, and must be, immune to election returns? In no mood to take chances, the president, on February 5, 1937, sent to Congress his message proposing a drastic shake-up in the judiciary. In a word, the president's solution was to give a Supreme Court justice past 70 six months in which to retire. A justice who failed to retire within the appointed time could continue in office, but the chief executive would appoint an additional justice, up to a maximum bench of 15 justices—presumably younger and better able to carry the heavy load. Since there were six justices in this category, Roosevelt would have been able to make six appointments at once.

In presenting his proposal the president gave no hint of wishing to stem the tide of anti-New Deal decisions. He tendered the hemlock cup to the elderly jurists on the elevated ground that they slowed the efficient dispatch of judicial business. "Can it be said," the president observed, "that full justice is achieved when a court is forced by the sheer necessity of keeping up with its business to decline, without even an explanation, to hear 87 percent of the cases presented to it by private litigants?"

Roosevelt had awaited the propitious moment. Early February 1937 seemed well-nigh perfect. With Roosevelt's carrying 46 of the 48 states, the election had, as one newspaper said, yielded "a roar in which cheers for the Supreme Court were drowned out." Congressional opinion appeared overtly hostile.

Yet from the very start "Court packing" ran into terrific public opposition. Overnight, Supreme Court justices were again pictured as demigods, weighing public policy in the delicate scales of the law. "Constitutionality" was talked about as if it were a tangible fact, undeviating and precise, not merely the current judicial theory of what ought and what ought not to be done. The same members of Congress who, before the president's message, had demanded the scalps of reactionary justices, were "shocked beyond measure" and turned on Roosevelt in an attitude of anguished surprise. Closing ranks with bar associations, the newspapers lined up almost solidly against Court packing. The idea implicit in Roosevelt's scheme, that the Court may change its interpretation in such a way as to sustain legislative power to meet national needs, was called as "false in theory, as it would be ruinous in practice." The press and the bar had hit a responsive chord. Said Walter Lippmann, "No issue so great or so deep has been raised in America since secession." Throughout the ensuing months debate waxed furiously. Clergy, educators, business leaders, and lawyers trekked to Washington and testified for or against the plan.

Everyone who could read knew that the justices were not the vestal virgins of the Constitution. Yet through the years, and despite increasing evidence that judicial interpretation and not fundamental law shackled the power to govern, the American people had come to regard the Court as the symbol of their freedom. Tarnished though the symbol was, it made, like the English monarchy, for national stability and poise in crisis; moreover, like its English counterpart, the Supreme Court commanded the loyalty of the citizenry, providing perhaps an impregnable barrier against dictatorship and personal government. "The President wants to control the Supreme Court" was hammered home incessantly. If the plan were accepted, the anti-New Deal press averred, nothing would stand between Roosevelt and the absolute dictatorship of the United States.

Roosevelt, quick to sense that his initial approach had been a major blunder, moved closer to the real issue on March 4, when he likened the judiciary to an unruly horse on the government gang plough, unwilling to pull with its teammates, the executive and Congress. As he saw it now, the crucial question was not whether the Court had kept up with its calendar but whether it had kept up with the country. The president's false assertion that the judges lagged in their work blurred the issue, diverting public attention so completely that his later effort to face the difficulty squarely never quite succeeded.

In a nationwide Fireside Chat on March 9, the president threw off the cloak of sophistry and frankly explained: "The Court has been acting not as a judicial body, but as a policy-making body. . . . That is not only my accusation, it is the accusation of most distinguished Justices of the present Supreme Court. . . . In holding the AAA unconstitutional, Justice Stone said of the majority opinion that it was 'a tortured construction of the Constitution' and two other Justices agreed with him. In the case holding the New York Minimum Wage Law unconstitutional [*Morehead* v. *New York ex rel. Tipaldo*, 1936], Justice Stone said that the majority were actually reading into the Constitution their own 'personal economic predilections' . . . and two other justices agreed with him."

A vigorous campaign against the president's bill was being waged in the Senate under the leadership of Senator Burton K. Wheeler. Tom Corcoran, then a White House adviser, tried vainly to dissuade the Montana senator from making a fight; the president himself told Wheeler of the futility of opposing a measure certain to pass in any event. "A liberal cause," Wheeler explained bluntly, "was never won by stacking a deck of cards, by stuffing a ballot box or packing a Court."

Meanwhile, those able to make the most realistic estimate of the condition of the Court's docket—the justices themselves—maintained a discreet silence. Finally, Senator Wheeler nervously sought an interview with Justice Brandeis.

Much to his surprise he found Brandeis most cooperative. "Why don't you call on the Chief Justice?" Brandeis suggested. "But I don't know the Chief Justice," the Montana senator demurred. "Well," said Brandeis, somewhat impatiently, "the Chief Justice knows you and knows what you are doing."

This was late Friday afternoon. The next day Senator Wheeler went to see Chief Justice Hughes. The senator wanted to know from the justices themselves whether the president's oft-repeated allegations about the swollen Court docket, lack of efficiency, and so on had any basis in fact. As Brandeis had indicated, the chief justice was not only enlisted but enthusiastic. Though Wheeler had not reached him until Saturday, March 20, he was able somehow to prepare a long and closely reasoned document for the senator's use the following Monday, March 22. "The baby is born," he said with a broad smile, as he put the letter into Wheeler's hand late Sunday afternoon.

Hughes's letter not only scotched the president's charge that the "old men" were not abreast of their docket but also revealed its composer as a canny dialectician. Though carefully refraining from open opposition to the plan, the letter suggests that the president's idea of an enlarged Court and the hearing of cases in divisions might run counter to the constitutional provision for "one Supreme Court." It was extraordinary enough, some of his colleagues thought, for a justice to go out of his way to meet constitutional issues unnecessary for deciding a case; Hughes went further and handed down advisory opinion on a burning political issue, and did so, moreover, in flat opposition to the stand he had taken in his book of 1928, *The Supreme Court of the United States.*

Hughes also managed to convey the erroneous impression that the entire Court endorsed his statement. Ignoring the customary disavowal of authority to speak for members of a body not consulted, he was "confident that it [the statement] is in accord with the views of the justices," though he admitted "on account of the shortness of time, I have not been able to consult with members of the Court generally." Cardozo and Stone, at least, objected strongly to Hughes's "extra-official-expression on a constitutional question." "I did not see the Chief Justice's letter, or know of it until I read it in the papers," Stone exploded; "I certainly would not have joined in that part of it which undertakes to suggest, what is and what is not constitutional."

The chief justice's letter, combined with the Court's forthcoming about-face, put a fatal crimp in the president's project. The Court's victory was not, however, unmixed. Roosevelt's plan was defeated, but without the appointment of a single new justice, he won from the embattled Court decisions favorable to the New Deal. As Robert Jackson put it, "In politics the black-robed reactionary Justices had won over the master liberal politician of our day. In law the President defeated the recalcitrant Justices in their own Court." As the fight raged about them, the justices began destruction of their most recent handiwork.

A SWITCH IN TIME

At the end of the 1935–1936 term, the really big issue facing Court and country was posed by the Wagner Labor Relations Act. Would the justices turn their backs on the Schechter and Guffey Coal rulings and permit the national government to substitute law for naked force in labor relations? Several cases were argued on February 10 and 11, 1937. In the heat of the court fight, industrial peace—or war—seemed to hang in the balance. Then, on April 12, 1937, Chief Justice Hughes put forward a broad and encompassing definition of interstate commerce and conceded to Congress the power to protect the lifelines of the national economy from private industrial warfare (**National Labor Relations Board v. Jones & Laughlin Steel Corp.**).

Arguments that had proved effective in the Schechter and Guffey Coal cases now availed nothing. "Those cases," the chief justice commented summarily, "are not controlling here." They were not controlling because he now chose to consider that "fundamental" distinction between "direct and indirect effects" as one of degree rather than kind. They were not binding now because he minimized the point much stressed in the Schechter case, namely, that the "fundamental" nature of the distinction between direct and indirect effects of intrastate transactions on interstate commerce arises from the fact that it is "essential" to the maintenance of "our constitutional system." Since interstate commerce was now seen as a "practical conception," interference with that commerce "must be appraised by a judgment that does not ignore actual experience."

Treating the earlier approach somewhat disdainfully, the chief justice declared that, in light of the industry's "farflung activities," it was "idle to say" that interference by strikes or other labor disturbances "would be indirect or remote. It is obvious that it would be immediate and might be catastrophic." "We are asked to shut our eyes to the plainest facts of our national life," the chief justice continued, "and to deal with the question of direct and indirect effects in an intellectual vacuum."

"When industries organize themselves on a national scale, making their relation to interstate commerce the dominant factor in their activities, how can it be maintained that their industrial labor relations constitute a forbidden field into which Congress may not enter when it is necessary to protect interstate commerce from the paralyzing consequences of industrial war?" The chief justice's sweeping doctrine did not apply solely to large-scale industries, such as steel. He proceeded immediately to apply the same doctrine to two small concerns, a trailer company and a men's clothing manufacturer. By a vote of 5 to 4 a major New Deal enactment was sustained.

Chief Justice Hughes's insistence that the new interpretation, while the Court was under fire, was unrelated to the president's bold determination to reorganize the judiciary provoked cynical reaction among both professional and lay commentators. "We are told," a skeptical paragrapher noted, "that the Supreme Court's about-face was not due to outside clamor. It seems that the new building has a sound-proof room, to which the Justices may retire to change their minds."

Two things should be noted: First, there is little in the majority opinion that does not find its counterpart in *Gibbons* v. *Ogden* (see Chapter Five). Second, this was not a "packed" Court. The same justices had defeated the NIRA and the Guffey Coal Act.

THE NATIONAL VIEW OF COMMERCE

In *United States* v. *Darby* (1941) the Court upheld the Fair Labor Standards Act, which fixed minimum wages and maximum hours for producers of goods shipped in interstate commerce and which banned the interstate shipment of goods manufactured under substandard conditions or by children. In his opinion, Justice Stone included this significant comment: "The motive and purpose of a regulation of interstate commerce are matters for the legislative judgment upon the exercise of which the Constitution places no restriction and over which the Courts are given no control." *Hammer* v. *Dagenhart,* he said, was overruled. Finally, in *Wickard* v. *Filburn* (1942), the Court went full circle by upholding the validity of the wheat-marketing provisions of the Agricultural Adjustment Act as applied to wheat grown for home consumption.

Decisions upholding the 1964 Civil Rights Act cast further light on the modern Court's conception of congressional power over commerce. In *Heart of Atlanta Motel* v. *United States* and in *Katzenback* v. *McClung* (1964), the justices upheld the application of provisions of the act barring racial discrimination not only to an establishment serving interstate travelers (*Atlanta Motel*), but also to a local restaurant using food that had "moved" in commerce between the states (*McClung*). It may be asked whether there is now any commercial activity beyond the reach of congressional power.

The extensive reach of the 1964 act is manifest in *Daniel* v. *Paul* (1969), where a recreational facility near Little Rock, Arkansas, was found to be a "public accommodation" affecting commerce. The entire 232-acre establishment with its golf, swimming, dancing, and other activities was held to be within the act's provisions because three of the four items sold at the snack bar had originated outside of the state, thus making it a public accommodation.

Various anticrime statutes provide other examples of how congressional control of the channels and instrumentalities of interstate commerce can be used to regulate or prohibit activities formerly considered essentially local. As the earlier lottery, oleomargarine, and Mann Act decisions indicate, congressional control based on the commerce clause seems virtually unlimited. In 1961 Congress passed antiracketeering acts, forbidding traveling in interstate commerce with intent to do a number of enumerated crime-related acts, such as sending or carrying bookmaking articles in interstate commerce or receiving a firearm shipped in interstate commerce if the recipient has been convicted of a crime. Two provisions of the 1968 Civil Rights Act adopt the same format. One prohibits traveling in interstate commerce, or using its instrumentalities, with intent to cause a riot. Another is directed against those who, by teaching or acts, contribute to a civil disorder that may "obstruct, delay, or adversely affect commerce." Clearly, there are almost endless opportunities to extend federal power against antisocial behavior, using the techniques of the 1961 and 1968 acts.

So far as the commerce power is concerned, the constitutional revolution of 1937 thus appears not so much a revolution as a counterrevolution. In the period from 1890 to 1936, when the Court began to develop a series of implied limitations on the exercise of the commerce power, it was not doing so in response to any rule of law announced by the Marshall or Taney Courts. Marshall, although not denying the power of the states to regulate certain local matters, defined the commerce power broadly. Taney's Court, although more generous to local regulation in the absence of federal legislation, made it clear that Congress's power was broad and to the extent exercised would be upheld, and that the Court would undertake to determine the validity of state acts by measuring the need for uniform regulation in each case. The Court, in other words, would play the difficult role of ascertaining the limits of state power over commerce until Congress should act.

In the period 1890–1936 the Court inverted the role of the Taney Court. At one time it would use the commerce power to frustrate state acts where they interfered with national commerce; but at other times it would imply limits on the national power to regulate certain aspects of commerce by evolving rules denying to mining, agriculture, and manufacturing any relationship with interstate commerce.

If one is inclined to protest that the Founders never dreamed of AAA, FLSA, and NLRA, the answer is that of course they did not. This argument, it might be pointed out, could be used to reject the great bulk of modern state and national regulatory acts. But as Marshall said in *McCulloch* v. *Maryland* (1819), "This provision [necessary and proper clause] is made in a constitution, intended to endure for ages to come, and consequently, to be adapted to the various crises of human affairs. To have prescribed the means by which government should, in all future time, execute its powers, would have been to change, entirely, the character of the instrument, and give it the properties of a legal code. It would have been an unwise attempt to provide, by immutable rules, for exigencies which, if foreseen at all, must have been seen dimly, and which can be best provided for as they occur." In the light of this philosophy the growth of national power through the commerce clause can be described as the necessary response by government to economic and social change. Those adversely affected by regulation clamored "back to the Constitution." Back to which constitution—that of 1787, as interpreted by John Marshall, or that of 1890–1936?

Until 1976, events dictated the answer. Then, in an extraordinary about-face, the justices voted, 5 to 4, in *National League of Cities* v. *Usery* that the 1974 amendments to the Fair Labor Standards Act extending the minimum wage and maximum hour provisions to employees of states and their subdivisions exceeded congressional power under the commerce clause. For the majority, the constitutional barrier was the Tenth Amendment. Revived was the Court-created doctrine of dual federalism.

Nearly a decade later in **Garcia v. San Antonio Metropolitan Transit Authority** (1985), five justices overruled *National League of Cities*. In place of the Tenth Amendment as a check on the commerce power would be "state participation in federal governmental action" and the "internal safeguards of the political process." (*Garcia*, turning as it does on the doctrine of dual federalism, is discussed and reprinted in Chapter Four.) It remains to be seen whether *Garcia*'s slim majority will hold, especially in view of Justice Rehnquist's assurance that the principle represented by *National League of Cities* "will . . . in time again command the support of . . . this Court."

KEY TERMS

direct and indirect effects

national police power

Tenth Amendment

New Deal

dual federalism

commerce

Court-packing plan

constitutional revolution

dormant commerce power

QUERIES

1. In cases testing congressional power under the commerce clause before 1937, evaluate the influence of the judicially created concepts "direct and indirect effects" and "dual federalism."

2. When President Franklin Roosevelt's New Deal was put on the anvil of constitutionality, two lines of precedents, moving in opposite directions, were available as a basis of decision by the Supreme Court. Explain.

3. In the Court-packing struggle of 1937, both sides won; both sides lost. Explain.

4. In light of *Wickard* v. *Filburn, Heart of Atlanta Motel* v. *United States,* and *Garcia* v. *San Antonio Metropolitan Transit Authority* (from Chapter Four), do any judicially enforceable constitutional checks remain on congressional power under the commerce clause?

SELECTED READINGS

CORWIN, EDWARD S. *The Commerce Power Versus States Rights*. Princeton, N.J.: Princeton University Press, 1936.

————. *Constitutional Revolution, Ltd*. Westport, Conn.: Greenwood, 1977 (reissue of the 1941 edition).

CURRIE, DAVID P. "The Constitution in the Supreme Court: The New Deal, 1931–1940." 54 *University of Chicago Law Review* 504 (1987).

CUSHMAN, ROBERT E. "National Police Power under the Commerce Clause." In *3 Selected Essays on Constitutional Law*. Chicago: Foundation Press, 1938.

EPSTEIN, RICHARD A. "The Proper Scope of the Commerce Power," 73 *Virginia Law Review* 1387 (1987).

GORDON, DAVID. "*Swift & Co.* v. *United States:* The Beef Trust and the Stream of Commerce Doctrine." 28 *American Journal of Legal History* 244 (1984).

MASON, ALPHEUS T. "Charles Evans Hughes: An Appeal to the Bar of History." 6 *Vanderbilt Law Review* 1 (1952).

————— "Harlan Fiske Stone and FDR's Court Plan." 61 *Yale Law Journal* 791 (1952).

————— *The Supreme Court: Instrument of Power or of Revealed Truth, 1930–1937.* Boston: Boston University Press, 1953.

STEAMER, ROBERT J. *Supreme Court in Crisis.* Amherst: University of Massachusetts Press, 1971.

United States v. E. C. Knight Co.
156 U.S. 1, 15 S.Ct. 249, 39 L.Ed. 325 (1895)

The American Sugar Refining Company, which controlled a majority of the sugar-refining companies of the United States, attempted to attain an almost complete monopoly by purchasing control of the E. C. Knight Company and three other companies, which together produced about one-third of the national output. Alleging that the defendant companies (American Sugar, E. C. Knight, and three others) had entered into contracts that constituted combinations in restraint of trade, and that these companies had conspired to restrain trade, both contrary to the Sherman Anti-Trust Act of 1890, the government sought to obtain a court order canceling the various agreements. The lower federal courts refused to grant this relief on the ground that the combination or conspiracy involved in this case pertained to manufacturing and not to interstate commerce. Majority: Fuller, Brewer, Brown, Field, Gray, Jackson, Shiras, White. Dissenting: Harlan.

MR. CHIEF JUSTICE FULLER . . . delivered the opinion of the Court. . . .

The fundamental question is, whether conceding that the existence of a monopoly in manufacture is established by the evidence, that monopoly can be directly suppressed under the act of Congress in the mode attempted by this bill.

It cannot be denied that the power of a state to protect the lives, health, and property of its citizens, and to preserve good order and the public morals, "the power to govern men and things within the limits of its dominion," is a power originally and always belonging to the States, not surrendered by them to the general government, nor directly restrained by the Constitution of the United States, and essentially exclusive. The relief of the citizens of each State from the burden of monopoly and the evils resulting from the restraint of trade among such citizens was left with the States to deal with, and this court has recognized their possession of that power even to the extent of holding that an employment or business carried on by private individuals, when it becomes a matter of such public interest and importance as to create a common charge or burden upon the citizen; in other words, when it becomes a practical monopoly, to which the citizen is compelled to resort and by means of which a tribute can be exacted from the community, is subject to regulation by state legislative power. On the other hand, the power of Congress to regulate commerce among the several States is also exclusive. The Constitution does not provide that interstate commerce shall be free, but, by the grant of this exclusive power to regulate it, it was left free except as Congress might impose restraints. . . . That which belongs to commerce is within the jurisdiction of the United States, but that which does not belong to commerce is within the jurisdiction of the police power of the State. . . .

The argument is that the power to control the manufacture of refined sugar is a monopoly over a necessary of life, to the enjoyment of which by a large part of the population of the United States interstate commerce is indispensable, and that, therefore, the general government in the exercise of the power to regulate commerce may repress such monopoly directly and set aside the instruments which have created it. But this argument cannot be confined to necessaries of life merely, and must include all articles of general consumption. Doubtless the power to control the manufacture of a given thing involves in a certain sense the control of its disposition, but this is a secondary and not the primary sense; and although the exercise of that power may result in bringing the operation of commerce into play, it does not control it, and affects it only incidentally and indirectly. Commerce succeeds to manufacture, and is not a part of it. The power to regulate commerce is the power to prescribe the rule by which commerce shall be governed, and is a power independent of the power to suppress monopoly. But it may operate in repression of monopoly whenever that comes within the rules by which commerce is governed or whenever the transaction is itself a monopoly of commerce. . . .

It is vital that the independence of the commercial power and of the police power, and the delimitation between them, however sometimes perplexing, should always be recognized and observed, for while the one furnishes the strongest bond of union, the other is essential to the preservation of the autonomy of the States as required by our dual form of government; and acknowledged evils, however grave and urgent they may appear to be, had better be borne, than the risk be run, in the effort to suppress them, of more serious consequences by resort to expedients of even doubtful constitutionality. . . .

. . . Slight reflection will show that if the national power extends to all contracts and combinations in manufacture, agriculture, mining, and other productive industries, whose ultimate result may affect external commerce, comparatively little of business operations and affairs would be left for state control.

It was in the light of well-settled principles that the act of July 2, 1890, was framed. Congress did not attempt thereby to assert the power to deal with monopoly directly as such. . . . Aside from the provisions applicable where Congress might exercise municipal power, what the law struck at was combinations, contracts, and conspiracies to monopolize trade and commerce among the several States or with foreign nations; but the contracts and acts of the defendants related exclusively to the acquisition of the Philadelphia refineries and the business of sugar refining in Pennsylvania, and bore no direct relation to commerce between the States or with foreign nations. . . .

Decree affirmed.

Mr. Justice Harlan, dissenting. . . .

. . . If this combination, so far as its operations necessarily or directly affect interstate commerce, cannot be restrained or suppressed under some power granted to Congress, it will be cause for regret that the patriotic statesmen who framed the Constitution did not foresee the necessity of investing the national government with power to deal with gigantic monopolies holding in their grasp, and injuriously controlling in their own interest, the entire trade *among the States* in food products that are essential to the comfort of every household in the land. . . .

The power of Congress covers and protects the absolute freedom of such intercourse and trade among the States as may or must succeed manufacture and precede transportation from the place of purchase. This would seem to be conceded; for, the court in the present case expressly declares that "*contracts to buy,* sell, or exchange goods *to be transported among the several States,* the transportation and its instrumentalities, and articles bought, sold, or exchanged for the purpose of such transit among the States, or put in the way transit, *may be regulated,* but this is *because they form part of interstate trade or commerce.*" Here is a direct admission—one which the settled doctrines of this court justify—that contracts to buy and the purchasing of goods *to be transported from one State to another,* and transportation, with its instrumentalities, are all *parts* of interstate trade or commerce. Each part of such trade is then under the protection of Congress. And yet, by the opinion and judgment in this case, if I do not misapprehend them, Congress is without power to protect the commercial intercourse that such purchasing necessarily involves against the restraints and burdens arising from the existence of *combinations* that meet purchasers, from whatever State they come, with the threat—for it is nothing more or less than a threat—that they *shall not* purchase what they desire to purchase, *except at the prices fixed by such combinations.*

. . . The common government of all the people is the only one that can adequately deal with a matter which directly and injuriously affects the entire commerce of the country, which concerns equally all the people of the Union, and which, it must be confessed, cannot be adequately controlled by any one State. Its authority should not be so weakened by construction that it cannot reach and eradicate evils that, beyond all question, tend to defeat an object which that government is entitled, by the Constitution, to accomplish. . . .

Champion v. *Ames*
(The Lottery Case)
188 U.S. 321, 23 S.Ct. 321, 47 L.Ed. 492 (1903)

An Act of Congress of 1895 made it an offense to send or conspire to send lottery tickets in interstate commerce. The defendants, who were convicted under the statute, appealed from a circuit court order dismissing a writ of habeas corpus. Majority: Harlan, Brown, Holmes, McKenna, White. Dissenting: Fuller, Brewer, Peckham, Shiras.

MR. JUSTICE HARLAN . . . delivered the opinion of the Court.

The appellant insists that the carrying of lottery tickets from one State to another State by an express company engaged in carrying freight and packages, from State to State, although such tickets may be contained in a box or package, does not constitute, and cannot by any act of Congress be legally made to constitute, *commerce* among the states within the meaning of the clause of the Constitution of the United States providing that Congress shall have power "to regulate commerce with foreign nations, and among the several states, and with the Indian tribes"; consequently, that Congress cannot make it an offense to cause such tickets to be carried from one State to another. . . .

What is the import of the word "commerce" as used in the Constitution? It is not defined by that instrument. Undoubtedly, the carrying from one State to another by independent carriers of things or commodities that are ordinary subjects of traffic, and which have in themselves a recognized value in money, constitutes interstate commerce. But does not commerce among the several States include something more? Does not the carrying from one State to another, by independent carriers, of lottery tickets that entitle the holder to the payment of a certain amount of money therein specified, also constitute commerce among the States? . . .

The leading case under the commerce clause of the Constitution is *Gibbons* v. *Ogden*. . . .

. . . The cases cited . . . show that commerce among the States embraces navigation, intercourse, communication, traffic, the transit of persons, and the transmission of messages by telegraph. They also show that the power to regulate commerce among the several States is vested in Congress as absolutely as it would be in a single government, having in its constitution the same restrictions on the exercise of the power as are found in the Constitution of the United States; that such power is plenary, complete in itself, and may be exerted by Congress to its utmost extent, subject *only* to such limitations as the Constitution imposes upon the exercise of the powers granted by it; and that in determining the character of the regulations to be adopted Congress has a large discretion which is not to be controlled by the courts, simply because, in their opinion, such regulations may not be the best or most effective that could be employed.

We come then to inquire whether there is any solid foundation upon which to rest the contention that Congress may not regulate the carrying of lottery tickets from one State to another, at least by corporations or companies whose business it is, for hire, to carry tangible property from one State to another. . . .

We are of opinion that lottery tickets are subjects of traffic, and therefore are subjects of commerce, and the regulation of the carriage of such tickets from State to State, at least by independent carriers, is a regulation of commerce among the several States.

But it is said that the statute in question does not regulate the carrying of lottery tickets from State to State, but by punishing those who cause them to be so carried Congress in effect prohibits such carrying; that in respect of the carrying from one State to another of articles or things that are, in fact, or according to usage in business, the subjects of commerce, the authority given Congress was not to *prohibit*, but only to *regulate*. . . .

If a State, when considering legislation for the suppression of lotteries within its own limits, may properly take into view the evils that inhere in the raising of money, in that mode, why may not Congress, invested with the power to regulate commerce among the several States, provide that such commerce shall not be polluted by the carrying of lottery tickets from one State to another? In this connection it must not be forgotten that the power of Congress to regulate commerce among the States is plenary, is complete in itself, and is subject to no limitations except such as may be found in the Constitution. What provision in that instrument can be regarded as limiting the exercise of the power granted? . . .

If it be said that the act of 1895 is inconsistent with the Tenth Amendment, reserving to the States respectively, or to the people, the powers not delegated to the United States, the answer is that the power to regulate commerce among the States has been expressly delegated to Congress. . . .

. . .We should hesitate long before adjudging that an evil of such appalling character, carried on through interstate commerce, cannot be met and crushed by the only power competent to that end. . . .

It is said, however, that if, in order to suppress lotteries carried on through interstate commerce, Congress may exclude lottery tickets from such commerce, that principle leads necessarily to the conclusion that Congress may arbitrarily exclude from commerce among the States any article, commodity, or thing, of whatever kind or nature, or however useful or valuable, which it may choose, no matter with what motive, to declare shall not be carried from one State to another. It will be time enough to consider the constitutionality of such legislation when we must do so. The present case does not require the court to declare the full extent of the power that Congress may exercise in the regulation of commerce among the States. We may, however, repeat, in this connection, what the court has heretofore said, that the power of Congress to regulate commerce among the States, although plenary, cannot be deemed arbitrary, since it is subject to such limitations or restrictions as are prescribed by the Constitution. . . .

Affirmed.

Mr. Chief Justice Fuller . . . dissenting: . . .

The power of the State to impose restraints and burdens on persons and property in conservation and promotion of the public health, good order, and prosperity is a power originally and always belonging to the States, not surrendered by them to the general government, nor directly restrained by the Constitution of the United States, and essentially exclusive, and the suppression of lotteries as a harmful business falls within this power, commonly called, of police. . . .

It is urged, however, that because Congress is empowered to regulate commerce between the several States, it, therefore, may suppress lotteries by prohibiting the carriage of lottery matter. Congress may, indeed, make all laws necessary and proper for carrying the powers granted to it into execution, and doubtless an act prohibiting the carriage of lottery matter would be necessary and proper to the execution of a power to suppress lotteries; but that power belongs to the States and not to Congress. To hold that Congress has general police power would be to hold that it may accomplish objects not intrusted to the General Government, and to defeat the operation of the Tenth Amendment. . . .

. . . To say that the mere carrying of an article which is not an article of commerce in and of itself nevertheless becomes such the moment it is to be transported from one State to another, is to transform a non-commercial article into one simply because it is transported. I cannot conceive that any such result can properly follow. . . .

This in effect breaks down all the differences between that which is, and that which is not, an article of commerce, and the necessary consequence is to take from the States all jurisdiction over the subject so far as interstate communication is concerned. It is a long step in the direction of wiping out all traces of state lines, and the creation of a centralized Government.

Does the grant to Congress of the power to regulate interstate commerce impart the absolute power to prohibit it? . . .

The power to prohibit the transportation of diseased animals and infected goods over railroads or on steamboats is an entirely different thing, for they would be in themselves injurious to the transaction of interstate commerce, and, moreover, are essentially commercial in their nature. And the exclusion of diseased persons rests on different ground, for nobody would pretend that persons could be kept off the trains because they were going from one state to another to engage in the lottery business. However enticing that business may be, we do not understand how these pieces of paper themselves can communicate bad principles by contact. . . .

I regard this decision as inconsistent with the views of the framers of the Constitution, and of Marshall, its great expounder. Our form of government may remain notwithstanding legislation or decision, but, as long ago observed, it is with governments, as with religions, the form may survive the substance of the faith.

In my opinion the act in question in the particular under consideration is invalid, and the judgments below ought to be reversed, and my brothers Brewer, Shiras and Peckham concur in this dissent.

Hammer v. Dagenhart
247 U.S. 251, 38 S.Ct. 529, 62 L.Ed. 1101 (1918)

An Act of Congress of 1916 forbade the shipment in interstate commerce of products of child labor. A father of two children who worked in a North Carolina cotton mill sought and obtained an injunction against enforcement of the act, on the ground that it was unconstitutional. Majority: Day, McReynolds, Pitney, Van Devanter, White. Dissenting: Holmes, Brandeis, Clarke, McKenna.

MR. JUSTICE DAY delivered the opinion of the Court. . . .

The controlling question for decision is: Is it within the authority of Congress in regulating commerce among the States to prohibit the transportation in interstate commerce of manufactured goods, the product of a factory in which, within thirty days prior to their removal therefrom, children under the age of fourteen have been employed or permitted to work, or children between the ages of fourteen and sixteen years have been employed or permitted to work more than eight hours in any day, or more than six days in any week, or after the hour of 7 o'clock P.M. or before the hour of 6 o'clock A.M.?

The power essential to the passage of this act, the Government contends, is found in the commerce clause of the Constitution which authorizes Congress to regulate commerce with foreign nations and among the States. . . .

. . . [I]t is insisted that adjudged cases in this court establish the doctrine that the power to regulate given to Congress incidentally includes the authority to prohibit the movement of ordinary commodities and therefore that the subject is not open for discussion. The cases demonstrate the contrary. They rest upon the character of the particular subjects dealt with and the fact that the scope of governmental authority, state or national, possessed over them is such that the authority to prohibit is as to them but the exertion of the power to regulate. . . .

In each of these instances the use of interstate transportation was necessary to the accomplishment of harmful results. In other words, although the power over interstate transportation was to regulate, that could only be accomplished by prohibiting the use of the facilities of interstate commerce to effect the evil intended.

This element is wanting in the present case. The thing intended to be accomplished by this statute is the denial of the facilities of interstate commerce to those manufacturers in the States who employ children within the prohibited ages. The act in its effect does not regulate transportation among the States, but aims to standardize the ages at which children may be employed in mining and manufacturing within the States. The goods shipped are of themselves harmless. The act permits them to be freely shipped after thirty days from the time of their removal from the factory. When offered for shipment, and before transportation begins, the labor of their production is over, and the mere fact that they were intended for interstate commerce transportation does not make their production subject to federal control under the commerce power. . . .

That there should be limitations upon the right to employ children in mines and factories in the interest of their own and the public welfare, all will admit. That such employment is generally deemed to require regulation is shown by the fact that the brief of counsel states that every State in the Union has a law upon the subject, limiting the right to thus employ children. In North Carolina, the State wherein is located the factory in which the employment was had in the present case, no child under twelve years of age is permitted to work.

It may be desirable that such laws be uniform, but our Federal Government is one of enumerated powers; "this principle," declared Chief Justice Marshall in *McCulloch* v. *Maryland* . . . "is universally admitted." . . .

In interpreting the Constitution it must never be forgotten that the nation is made up of States to which are entrusted the powers of local government. And to them and to the people the powers not expressly [*sic*] delegated to the national government are reserved. . . . Thus the act in a twofold sense is repugnant to the Constitution. It not only transcends the authority delegated to Congress over commerce but also exerts a power as to a purely local matter to which the federal authority does not extend. The far-reaching result of upholding the act cannot be more plainly indicated than by pointing out that if Congress can thus regulate matters entrusted to local authority by prohibition of the movement of commodities in interstate commerce, all freedom of commerce will be at an end, and the power of the states over local matters may be eliminated, and thus our system of government be practically destroyed.

For these reasons we hold that this law exceeds the constitutional authority of Congress. It follows that the decree of the District Court must be

Affirmed.

MR. JUSTICE HOLMES, dissenting. . . .

The first step in my argument is to make plain what no one is likely to dispute—that the statute in question is within the power expressly given to Congress if considered only as to its immediate effects and that if invalid it is so only upon some collateral ground. The statute confines itself to prohibiting the carriage of certain goods in interstate or foreign commerce. Congress is given power to regulate such commerce in unqualified terms. It would not be argued today that the power to regulate does not include the power to prohibit. Regulation means the prohibition of something, and when interstate commerce is the matter to be regulated I cannot doubt that the regulation may prohibit any part of such commerce that Congress sees fit to forbid. At all events it is established by the Lottery Case and others that have followed it that a law is not beyond the regulative power of Congress merely because it prohibits certain transportation out and out. . . . So I repeat that this statute in its immediate operation is clearly within the Congress's constitutional power.

The question then is narrowed to whether the exercise of its otherwise constitutional power by Congress can be pronounced unconstitutional because of its possible reaction upon the conduct of the States in a matter upon which I have admitted that they are free from direct control. I should have thought that that matter had been disposed of so fully as to leave no room for doubt. I should have thought that the most conspicuous decisions of this Court had made it clear that the power to regulate commerce and other constitutional powers could not be cut down or qualified by the fact that it might interfere with the carrying out of the domestic policy of any State. . . .

The notion that prohibition is any less prohibition when applied to things now thought evil I do not understand. But if there is any matter upon which civilized countries have agreed—far more unanimously than they have with regard to intoxicants and some other matters over which this country is now emotionally aroused—it is the evil of premature and excessive child labor. I should have thought that if we were to introduce our own moral conceptions where in my opinion they do not belong, this was preeminently a case for upholding the exercise of all its powers by the United States.

But I had thought that the propriety of the exercise of a power admitted to exist in some cases was for the consideration of Congress alone and that this Court always had disavowed the right to intrude its judgment upon questions of policy or morals. It is not for this Court to pronounce when prohibition is necessary to regulation if it ever may be necessary—to say that it is permissible as against strong drink but not as against the product of ruined lives.

The act does not meddle with anything belonging to the States. They may regulate their internal affairs and their domestic commerce as they like. But when they seek to send their products across the state line they are no longer within their rights. If there were no Constitution and no Congress their power to cross the line would depend upon their neighbors. Under the Constitution such commerce belongs not to the States but to Congress to regulate. . . .

MR. JUSTICE MCKENNA, MR. JUSTICE BRANDEIS and MR. JUSTICE CLARKE concur in this opinion.

Stafford v. *Wallace*
258 U.S. 495, 42 S.Ct. 397, 66 L.Ed. 735 (1922)

The Packers and Stockyards Act of 1921 attempted to regulate certain practices of meat packers that allegedly restricted and burdened interstate commerce in meat products. Stafford unsuccessfully sought an injunction against the enforcement of the act. Majority: Taft, Brandeis, Clarke, Holmes, McKenna, Pitney, Van Devanter. Dissenting: McReynolds. Not participating: Day.

MR. CHIEF JUSTICE TAFT . . . delivered the opinion of the Court. . . .

The Packers and Stockyards Act of 1921 seeks to regulate the business of the packers done in interstate commerce and forbids them to engage in unfair, discriminatory or deceptive practices in such commerce, or to subject any person to unreasonable prejudice therein, or to do any of a number of acts to control prices or establish a monopoly in the business. . . .

The object to be secured by the act is the free and unburdened flow of live stock from the ranges and farms of the West and the Southwest through the great stockyards and slaughtering centers on the borders of that region, and thence in the form of meat products to the consuming cities of the country in the Middle West and East, or, still as live stock, to the feeding places and fattening farms in the Middle West or East for further preparation for the market.

The chief evil feared is the monopoly of the packers, enabling them unduly and arbitrarily to lower prices to the shipper who sells, and unduly and arbitrarily to increase the price to the consumer who buys. Congress thought that the power to maintain this monopoly was aided by control of the stockyards. Another evil which it sought to provide against by the act, was exorbitant charges, duplication of commissions, deceptive practices in respect of prices, in the passage of the live stock through the stockyards, all made possible by collusion between the stockyards management and the commission men, on the one hand, and the packers and dealers on the other.

The stockyards are not a place of rest or final destination. Thousands of head of live stock arrive daily by carload and trainload lots, and must be promptly sold and disposed of and moved out to give place to the constantly flowing traffic that presses behind. The stockyards are but a throat through which the current flows, and the transactions which occur therein are only incident to this current from the West to the East, and from one State to another. Such transactions cannot be separated from the movement to which they contribute and necessarily take on its character. . . . The stockyards and the sales are necessary factors in the middle of this current of commerce.

The act, therefore, treats the various stockyards of the country as great national public utilities to promote the flow of commerce from the ranges and farms of the West to the consumers in the East. It assumes that they conduct a business affected by a public use of a national character and subject to national regulation. That it is a business within the power of regulation by legislative action needs no discussion. That has been settled since the case of *Munn* v. *Illinois.* . . . Nor is there any doubt that in the receipt of live stock by rail and in their delivery by rail the stockyards are an interstate commerce agency. . . . The only question here is whether the business done in the stockyards between the receipt of the live stock in the yards and the shipment of them therefrom is a part of interstate commerce, or is so associated with it as to bring it within the power of national regulation. A similar question has been before this court and had great consideration in *Swift & Co.* v. *United States.* The judgment in that case gives a clear and comprehensive exposition which leaves to us in this case little but the obvious application of the principles there declared. . . .

The application of the commerce clause of the Constitution in the Swift Case was the result of the natural development of interstate commerce under modern conditions. It was the inevitable recognition of the great central fact that such streams of commerce from one part of the country to another which are ever flowing are in their very essence the commerce among the States and with foreign nations which historically it was one of the chief purposes of the Constitution to bring under national protection and control. This court declined to defeat this purpose in respect of such a stream and take it out of complete national regulation by a nice and technical inquiry into the non-interstate character of some of its necessary incidents and facilities

when considered alone and without reference to their association with the movement of which they were an essential but subordinate part. . . .

Of course, what we are considering here is not a bill in equity or an indictment charging conspiracy to obstruct interstate commerce, but a law. The language of the law shows that what Congress had in mind primarily was to prevent such conspiracies by supervision of the agencies which would be likely to be employed in it. If Congress could provide for punishment or restraint of such conspiracies after their formation through the Anti-Trust Law as in the Swift Case, certainly it may provide regulation to prevent their formation. The reasonable fear by Congress that such acts, usually lawful and affecting only intrastate commerce when considered alone, will probably and more or less constantly be used in conspiracies against interstate commerce or constitute a direct and undue burden on it, expressed in this remedial legislation, serves the same purpose as the intent charged in the Swift indictment to bring acts of a similar character into the current of interstate commerce for federal restraint. Whatever amounts to more or less constant practice, and threatens to obstruct or unduly to burden the freedom of interstate commerce is within the regulatory power of Congress under the commerce clause, and it is primarily for Congress to consider and decide the fact of danger and meet it. This court will certainly not substitute its judgment for that of Congress in such a matter unless the relation of the subject to interstate commerce and its effect upon it are clearly nonexistent. . . .

The orders of the District Court refusing the interlocutory injunctions are

Affirmed.

MR. JUSTICE MCREYNOLDS dissents.

Carter v. Carter Coal Co.
298 U.S. 238, 56 S.Ct. 855, 80 L.Ed. 1160 (1936)

In the Bituminous Coal Conservation Act of 1935 Congress attempted to stabilize the production and marketing of coal. The act provided for a National Bituminous Coal Commission with general supervisory powers over the industry through a Bituminous Coal Code. In each of 23 districts, boards were to be given the power to fix minimum coal prices. National hours of labor and district minimum wage agreements were to be effective when the producers of two-thirds of the annual tonnage and representatives of more than one-half of the employed workers agreed to terms. A labor board in the Department of Labor was given the duty of protecting the collective bargaining process and adjudicating labor disputes.

Producers were to be induced to accept these codes by a tax provision that allowed 90 percent of a tax of 15 percent on sales at the mines to be refunded to those producers who accepted the code provisions. In the act, Congress also stated that the provisions of the act were separable, and the possible invalidity of one should not affect the constitutionality of other sections. A number of cases involving suits to bar payment of the tax and acceptance of the code were consolidated on certiorari from circuit courts of appeals and from district courts. The majority of the Supreme Court held the delegation of code-drafting power to a part of the producers and workers to be invalid. The following excerpts from the opinion deal principally with the issue of whether federal regulation of mining activities was permissible under the commerce clause. Majority: Sutherland, Butler, Hughes, McReynolds, Roberts, Van Devanter. Dissenting: Cardozo, Brandeis, Stone.

MR. JUSTICE SUTHERLAND delivered the opinion of the Court. . . .

The general rule with regard to the respective powers of the national and the state governments under the Constitution is not in doubt. The States were before the Constitution; and, consequently, their legislative powers antedated the Constitution. Those who framed and those who adopted that instrument meant to carve from the general mass of legislative powers, then possessed by the States, only such portions as it was thought wise to confer upon the federal government; and in order that there should be no uncertainty in respect of what was taken and what was left, the national powers of legislation were not aggregated but enumerated— with the result that what was not embraced by the enumeration remained vested in the States without change or impairment. . . . While the States are not sovereign in the true sense of that term, but only *quasi*-sovereign, yet in respect of all powers reserved to them they are supreme— "as independent of the general government as that government within its sphere is independent of the States." And since every addition to the national legislative power to some extent detracts from or invades the power of the States, it is of vital moment that, in order to preserve the fixed balance intended by the Constitution, the powers of the general government be not so extended as to embrace any not within the express terms of the several grants or implications necessarily to be drawn therefrom. It is no longer open to question that the general government, unlike the States . . . possesses no *inherent* power in respect of the internal affairs of the States; and emphatically not with regard to legislation. The question in respect of the inherent power of that government as to the external affairs of the nation and in the field of international law is a wholly different matter which it is not necessary now to consider. . . .

. . . Every journey to a forbidden end begins with the first step; and the danger of such a step by the federal government in the direction of taking over the powers of the states is that the end of the journey may find the states so despoiled of their powers, or—what may amount to the same thing—so relieved of the responsibilities which possession of the powers necessarily enjoins, as to reduce them to little more than geographical subdivisions of the national domain. It is safe to say that if, when the Constitution was under consideration, it had been thought that any such danger lurked behind its plain words, it would never have been ratified. . . .

. . . Since the validity of the act depends upon whether it is a regulation of interstate commerce, the nature and extent of the power conferred upon Congress by the commerce clause becomes the determinative question in this branch of the case. . . . We first inquire, then—What is commerce? The term, as this court many times has said, is one of extensive import. No all-embracing definition has ever been formulated. The question is to be approached both affirmatively and negatively—that is to say, from the points of view as to what it includes and what it excludes. . . .

That commodities produced or manufactured within a State are intended to be sold or transported outside the State does not render their production or manufacture subject to federal regulation under the commerce clause. . . .

We have seen that the word "commerce" is the equivalent of the phrase "intercourse for the purposes of trade." Plainly, the incidents leading up to and culminating in the mining of coal do not constitute such intercourse. The employment of men, the fixing of their wages, hours of labor, and working conditions, the bargaining in respect of these things—whether carried on separately or collectively—each and all constitute intercourse for the purposes of production, not of trade. The latter is a thing apart from the relation of employer and employee, which in all producing occupations is purely local in character. Extraction of coal from the mine is the aim and the completed result of local activities. Commerce in the coal mined is not brought into being by force of these activities, but by negotiations, agreements and circumstances entirely apart from production. Mining brings the subject matter of commerce into existence. Commerce disposes of it.

A consideration of the foregoing . . . renders inescapable the conclusion that the effect of the labor provisions of the act, including those in respect of minimum wages, wage agreements, collective bargaining, and the Labor Board and its powers, primarily falls upon production and not upon commerce; and confirms the further resulting conclusion that production is a purely local activity. It follows that none of these essential antecedents of production constitutes a transaction in or forms any part of interstate commerce. . . .

But § 1 (the preamble) of the act now under review declares that all production and distribution of bituminous coal "bear upon and directly affect its interstate commerce"; and that regulation thereof is imperative for the protection of such commerce. The contention of the government is that the labor provisions of the act may be sustained in that way.

That the production of every commodity intended for interstate sale and transportation has some effect upon interstate commerce may be, if it has not already been, freely granted: and we are brought to the final and decisive inquiry, whether here that effect is direct, as the "preamble" recites, or indirect. The distinction is not formal, but substantial in the highest degree as we pointed out in the Schechter case. . . . "If the commerce clause were construed," we there said, "to reach all enterprises and transactions which could be said to have an indirect effect upon interstate commerce, the federal authority would embrace practically all the activities of the people and the authority of the State over its domestic concerns would exist only by sufferance of the federal government. Indeed, on such a theory, even the development of the State's commercial facilities would be subject to federal control." It was also pointed out . . . "that the distinction between direct and indirect effects of intrastate transactions upon interstate commerce must be recognized as a fundamental one, essential to the maintenance of our constitutional system."

Whether the effect of a given activity or condition is direct or indirect is not always easy to determine. The word "direct" implies that the activity or condition invoked or blamed shall operate proximately—not mediately, remotely, or collaterally—to produce the effect. It connotes the absence of an efficient intervening agency or condition. And the extent of the effect bears no logical relation to its character. The distinction between a direct and an indirect effect turns, not upon the magnitude of either the cause or the effect, but entirely upon the manner in which the effect has been brought about. If the production by one man of a single ton of coal intended for interstate sale and shipment, and actually so sold and shipped, affects interstate commerce indirectly, the effect does not become direct by multiplying the tonnage, or increasing the number of men employed, or adding to the expense or complexities of the business, or by all combined.

It is quite true that rules of law are sometimes qualified by considerations of degree, as the government argues. But the matter of degree has no bearing upon the question here, since that question is not—What is the *extent* of the local activity or condition, or the *extent* of the effect produced upon interstate commerce? but—What is the *relation* between the activity or condition and the effect?

Much stress is put upon the evils which come from the struggle between employers and employees over the matter of wages, working conditions, the right of collective bargaining, etc., and the resulting strikes, curtailment, and irregularity of production and effect on prices; and it is insisted that interstate commerce is greatly affected thereby. But, in addition to what has just been said, the conclusive answer is that the evils are all local evils over which the federal government has no legislative control. The relation of employer and employee is a local relation. . . . Such effect as they may have upon commerce, however extensive it may be, is secondary and indirect. An increase in the greatness of the effect adds to its importance. It does not alter its character. . . .

. . . Finally, we are brought to the price-fixing provisions of the code. The necessity of considering the question of their constitutionality will depend upon whether they are separable from the labor provisions so that they can stand independently. . . .

Since both were adopted, we must conclude that both were thought essential. The regulations of labor on the one hand and prices on the other furnish mutual aid and support; and their associated force—not one or the other but both combined—was deemed by Congress to be necessary to achieve the end sought. The statutory mandate for a code upheld by two legs at once suggests the improbability that Congress would have assented to a code supported by only one. . . .

. . . The conclusion is unavoidable that the price-fixing provisions of the code are so related to and dependent upon the labor provisions as considerations or compensations, as to make it clearly probable that the latter being held bad, the former would not have been passed. The fall of the latter, therefore, carries down with it the former. . . .

The price-fixing provisions of the code are thus disposed of without coming to the question of their constitutionality; but neither this disposition of the matter, nor anything we have said, is to be taken as indicating that the court is of opinion that these provisions, if separately enacted, could be sustained. . . .

It is so ordered.

MR. JUSTICE CARDOZO, dissenting. . . .

. . . I am satisfied that the Act is within the power of the central government in so far as it provides for minimum and maximum prices upon sales of bituminous coal in the transactions of interstate commerce and in those of intrastate commerce where interstate commerce is directly or intimately affected. Whether it is valid also in other provisions that have been considered and condemned in the opinion of the court, I do not find it necessary to determine at this time. Silence must not be taken as importing acquiescence. . . . As a system of price fixing the Act is challenged upon three grounds: (1) because the governance of prices is not within the commerce clause; [(2) and (3) omitted].

(1) With reference to the first objection, the obvious and sufficient answer is, so far as the Act is directed to interstate transactions, that sales made in such conditions constitute interstate commerce, and do not merely "affect" it. . . . To regulate the price for such transactions is to regulate commerce itself, and not alone its antecedent conditions or its ultimate consequences. The very act of sale is limited and governed. Prices in interstate transactions may not be regulated by the States. They must therefore be subject to the power of the nation unless they are to be withdrawn altogether from governmental supervision. . . . If such a vacuum were permitted, many a public evil incidental to interstate transactions would be left without a remedy. . . .

Regulation of prices being an exercise of the commerce power in respect of interstate transactions, the question remains whether it comes within that power as applied to intrastate sales where interstate prices are directly or intimately affected. Mining and agriculture and manufacture are not interstate commerce considered by themselves, yet their relation to that commerce may be such that for the protection of the one there is need to regulate the other. . . . Sometimes it is said that the relation must be "direct" to bring that power into play. In many circumstances such a description will be sufficiently precise to meet the needs of the occasion.

But a great principle of constitutional law is not susceptible of comprehensive statement in an adjective. The underlying thought is merely this, that "the law is not indifferent to considerations of degree." . . . It cannot be indifferent to them without an expansion of the commerce clause that would absorb or imperil the reserved powers of the States. At times, as in the case cited, the waves of causation will have radiated so far that their undulatory motion, if discernible at all, will be too faint or obscure, too broken by crosscurrents, to be heeded by the law. In such circumstances the holding is not directed at prices or wages considered in the abstract, but at prices or wages in particular conditions. The relation may be tenuous or the opposite according to the facts. Always the setting of the facts is to be viewed if one would know the closeness of the tie. Perhaps, if one group of adjectives is to be chosen in preference to another, "intimate" and "remote" will be found to be as good as any. At all events, "direct" and "indirect," even if accepted as sufficient, must not be read too narrowly. . . . A survey of the cases shows that the words have been interpreted with suppleness of adaptation and flexibility of meaning. The power is as broad as the need that evokes it. . . .

I am authorized to state that MR. JUSTICE BRANDEIS and MR. JUSTICE STONE join in this opinion.

National Labor Relations Board
v. *Jones & Laughlin Steel Corporation*
301 U.S. 1, 57 S.Ct. 615, 81 L.Ed. 893 (1937)

The National Labor Relations Act of 1935 was designed to protect the right of workers to organize and to encourage collective bargaining procedures. In this case the National Labor Relations Board ordered the defendant corporation to cease and desist from certain "unfair labor practices," and when the corporation failed to comply, unsuccessfully petitioned the circuit court of appeals (as provided in the act) to enforce the board's order. Majority: Hughes, Brandeis, Cardozo, Roberts, Stone. Dissenting: McReynolds, Butler, Sutherland, Van Devanter.

MR. CHIEF JUSTICE HUGHES delivered the opinion of the Court. . . .

The Act is challenged in its entirety as an attempt to regulate all industry, thus invading the reserved powers of the States over their local concerns. . . .

If this conception of terms, intent and consequent inseparability were sound, the Act would necessarily fall by reason of the limitation upon the federal power which inheres in the constitutional grant, as well as because of the explicit reservation of the Tenth Amendment. . . . The authority of the federal government may not be pushed to such an extreme as to destroy the distinction, which the commerce clause itself establishes, between commerce "among the several States" and the internal concerns of a State. That distinction between what is national and what is local in the activities of commerce is vital to the maintenance of our federal system. . . .

We think it clear that the National Labor Relations Act may be construed so as to operate within the sphere of constitutional authority. The jurisdiction conferred upon the Board, and invoked in this instance, is found in § 10 (a), which provides:

"Sec. 10(a). The Board is empowered, as hereinafter provided, to prevent any person from engaging in any unfair labor practice (listed in § 8) affecting commerce."

The critical words of this provision, prescribing the limits of the Board's authority in dealing with the labor practices, are "affecting commerce." . . .

There can be no question that the commerce thus contemplated by the Act (aside from that within a Territory or the District of Columbia) is interstate and foreign commerce in the constitutional sense. The Act also defines the term "affecting commerce" (§ 2(6)):

"The term 'affecting commerce' means in commerce, or burdening or obstructing commerce or the free flow of commerce, or having led or tending to lead to a labor dispute burdening or obstructing commerce or the free flow of commerce."

This definition is one of exclusion as well as inclusion. The grant of authority to the Board does not purport to extend to the relationship between all industrial employees and employers. Its terms do not impose collective bargaining upon all industry regardless of effects upon interstate or foreign commerce. It purports to reach only what may be deemed to burden or obstruct that commerce and, thus qualified, it must be construed as contemplating the exercise of control within constitutional bounds. . . .

Respondent says that whatever may be said of employees engaged in interstate commerce, the industrial relations and activities in the manufacturing department of respondent's enterprise are not subject to federal regulation. The argument rests upon the proposition that manufacturing in itself is not commerce. . . .

. . . Reference is made to our decision sustaining the Packers and Stockyards Act. . . . The Court found that the stockyards were but a "throat" through which the current of commerce flowed and the transactions which there occurred could not be separated from that movement. . . .

Respondent contends that the instant case presents material distinction. Respondent says that the Aliquippa plant is extensive in size and represents a large investment in buildings, machinery and equipment. The raw materials which are brought to the plant are delayed for long periods and, after being subjected to manufacturing processes "are changed substantially as to character, utility and value." . . .

We do not find it necessary to determine whether these features of defendant's business dispose of the asserted analogy to the "stream of commerce" cases. The instances in which that metaphor has been used are but particular, and not exclusive, illustrations of the protective power which the Government invokes in support of the present Act. The congressional authority to protect interstate commerce from burdens and obstructions is not limited to transactions which can be deemed to be an essential part of a "flow" of interstate or foreign commerce. Burdens and obstructions may be due to injurious action springing from other sources. The fundamental principle is that the power to regulate commerce is the power to enact "all appropriate legislation" for "its protection and advancement." . . . That power is plenary and may be exerted to protect interstate commerce "no matter what the source of the dangers which threaten it." . . . Although activities may be intrastate in character when separately considered, if they have such a close and substantial relation to interstate commerce that their control is essential or appropriate to protect that commerce from burdens and obstructions, Congress cannot be denied the power to exercise that control. . . . Undoubtedly the scope of this power must be considered in the light of our dual system of government and may not be extended so as to embrace effects upon interstate commerce so indirect and remote that to embrace them, in view of our complex society, would effectually obliterate the distinction between what is national and what is local and create a completely centralized government. . . . The question is necessarily one of degree. . . .

It is thus apparent that the fact that the employees here concerned were engaged in production is not determinative. The question remains as to the effect upon interstate commerce of the labor practice involved. In the Schechter case, we found that the effect there was so remote as to be beyond the federal power. To find "immediacy or directness" there was to find it "almost everywhere," a result inconsistent with the maintenance of our federal system. In the Carter case, the Court was of the opinion that the provisions of the statute relating to production were invalid upon several grounds—that there was improper delegation of legislative power, and that the requirements not only went beyond any sustainable measure of protection of interstate commerce but were also inconsistent with due process. These cases are not controlling here.

Giving full weight to respondent's contention with respect to a break in the complete continuity of the "stream of commerce" by reason of respondent's manufacturing operations, the fact remains that the stoppage of those operations by industrial strife would have a most serious effect upon interstate commerce. In view of respondent's farflung activities, it is idle to say that the effect would be indirect or remote. It is obvious that it would be immediate and might be catastrophic. We are asked to shut our eyes to the plainest facts of our national life and to deal with the question of direct and indirect effects in an intellectual vacuum. Because there may be but indirect and remote effects upon interstate commerce in connection with a host of local enterprises throughout the country, it does not follow that other industrial activities do not have such a close and intimate relation to interstate commerce as to make the presence of industrial strife a matter of the most urgent national concern. When industries organize themselves on a national scale, making their relation to interstate commerce the dominant factor in their activities, how can it be maintained that their industrial labor relations constitute a forbidden field into which Congress may not enter when it is necessary to protect interstate commerce from the paralyzing consequences of industrial war? We have often said that interstate commerce itself is a practical conception. It is equally true that interferences with that commerce must be appraised by a judgment that does not ignore actual experience. . . .

Our conclusion is that the order of the Board was within its competency and that the Act is valid as here applied. The judgment of the Circuit Court of Appeals is reversed and the case is remanded for further proceedings in conformity with this opinion.

Reversed.

MR. JUSTICE MCREYNOLDS, dissenting.

MR. JUSTICE VAN DEVANTER, MR. JUSTICE SUTHERLAND, MR. JUSTICE BUTLER and I are unable to agree with the decisions just announced. . . .

The Court as we think departs from well-established principles followed in *Schechter Poultry Corp.* v. *United States* . . . and *Carter* v. *Carter Coal Co.* . . . Every consideration brought forward to uphold the Act before us was applicable to support the Acts held unconstitutional in cases decided within two years. And the lower courts rightly deemed them controlling. . . .

Any effect on interstate commerce by the discharge of employees shown here, would be indirect and remote in the highest degree, as consideration of the facts will show. In No. 419 (*National Labor Relations Board* v. *Jones & Laughlin Steel Corp.*) ten men out of ten thousand were discharged; in the other cases only a few. The immediate effect in the factory may be to create discontent among all those employed and a strike may follow, which, in turn, may result in reducing production, which ultimately may reduce the volume of goods moving in interstate commerce. By this chain of indirect and progressively remote events we finally reach the evil with which it is said the legislation under consideration undertakes to deal. A more remote and indirect interference with interstate commerce or a more definite invasion of the powers reserved to the States is difficult, if not impossible, to imagine. The constitution still recognizes the existence of States with indestructible powers; the Tenth Amendment was supposed to put them beyond controversy.

United States v. *Darby*
312 U.S. 100, 61 S.Ct. 451, 85 L.Ed. 609 (1941)

The Fair Labor Standards Act of 1938 provided for the fixing of minimum wages and maximum hours for employees in industries whose products were shipped in interstate commerce. The act declared that the production of goods for commerce under substandard conditions and by children causes the channels of commerce to be used to "spread and perpetuate such labor conditions among the workers of the several States; burdens commerce and the free flow of goods in commerce; constitutes an unfair method of competition in commerce; leads to labor disputes burdening and obstructing commerce; and interferes with the orderly and fair marketing of goods in commerce." A district court judgment quashed an indictment against an alleged violator of the act. Majority: Stone, Black, Douglas, Frankfurter, Hughes, Murphy, Reed, Roberts.

MR. JUSTICE STONE delivered the opinion of the Court.

The two principal questions raised by the record in this case are, *first,* whether Congress has constitutional power to prohibit the shipment in interstate commerce of lumber manufactured by employees whose wages are less than a prescribed minimum or whose weekly hours of labor at that wage are greater than a prescribed maximum, and, *second,* whether it has power to prohibit the employment of workmen in the production of goods "for interstate commerce" at other than prescribed wages and hours.

The demurrer, so far as now relevant to the appeal, challenged the validity of the Fair Labor Standards Act under the Commerce Clause and the Fifth and Tenth Amendments. The district court quashed the indictment in its entirety upon the broad grounds that the Act, which it interpreted as a regulation of manufacture within the states, is unconstitutional. It declared that manufacture is not interstate commerce and that the regulation by the Fair Labor Standards Act of wages and hours of employment of those engaged in the manufacture of goods which it is intended at the time of production "may or will be" after production "sold in interstate commerce in part or in whole" is not within the congressional power to regulate interstate commerce.

The effect of the court's decision and judgment are thus to deny the power of Congress to prohibit shipment in interstate commerce of lumber produced for interstate commerce under the proscribed substandard labor conditions of wages and hours, its power to penalize the employer for his failure to conform to the wage and hour provisions in the case of employees engaged in the production of lumber which he intends thereafter to ship in interstate commerce in part or in whole according to the normal course of his business and its power to compel him to keep records of hours of employment as required by the statute and the regulations of the administrator. . . .

. . . It is conceded that the power of Congress to prohibit transportation in interstate commerce includes noxious articles . . . stolen articles . . . kidnapped persons . . . and articles such as intoxicating liquor or convict made goods, traffic in which is forbidden or restricted by the laws of the state of destination. . . .

But it is said that the present prohibition falls within the scope of none of these categories; that while the prohibition is nominally a regulation of the commerce its motive or purpose is regulation of wages and hours of persons engaged in manufacture, the control of which has been reserved to the states and upon which Georgia and some of the states of destination have placed no restriction; that the effect of the present statute is not to exclude the prescribed articles from interstate commerce in aid of state regulation . . . but instead, under the guise of a regulation of interstate commerce, it undertakes to regulate wages and hours within the state contrary to the policy of the state which has elected to leave them unregulated. . . .

The motive and purpose of the present regulation is plainly to make effective the Congressional conception of public policy that interstate commerce should not be made the instrument of competition in the distribution of goods produced under substandard labor conditions, which competition is injurious to the commerce and to the states from and to which the commerce flows. The motive and purpose of a regulation of interstate commerce are matters for the legislative judgment upon the exercise of which the Constitution places no restriction and over which the courts are given no control. . . . Whatever their motive and purpose, regulations of commerce which do not infringe some constitutional prohibition are within the plenary power conferred on Congress by the Commerce Clause. Subject only to that limitation . . . we conclude that the prohibition of the shipment interstate of goods produced under the forbidden substandard labor conditions is within the constitutional authority of Congress.

In the more than a century which has elapsed since the decision of *Gibbons* v. *Ogden,* these principles of constitutional interpretation have been so long and repeatedly recognized by this Court as applicable to the Commerce Clause, that there would be little occasion for repeating them now were it not for the decision of this Court twenty-two years ago in *Hammer* v. *Dagenhart.* . . .

Hammer v. *Dagenhart* has not been followed. The distinction on which the decision was rested that Congressional power to prohibit interstate commerce is limited to articles which in themselves have some harmful or deleterious property—a distinction which was novel when made and unsupported by any provision of the Constitution—has long since been abandoned. . . .

The conclusion is inescapable that *Hammer* v. *Dagenhart* was a departure from the principles which have prevailed in the interpretation of the commerce clause both before and since the decision and that such vitality, as a precedent, as it then had has long since been exhausted. It should be and now is overruled. . . .

Section 15(a) (2) and §§ 6 and 7 require employers to conform to the wage and hour provisions with respect to all employees engaged in the production of goods for interstate commerce. As appellees' employees are not alleged to be "engaged in interstate commerce" the validity of the prohibition turns on the question whether the employment, under other than the prescribed labor standards, of employees engaged in the production of goods for interstate commerce is so related to the commerce and so affects it as to be within the reach of the power of Congress to regulate it. . . .

Congress, having by the present Act adopted the policy of excluding from interstate commerce all goods produced for the commerce which do not conform to the specified labor standards, it may choose the means reasonably adapted to the attainment of the permitted end, even though they involve control of interstate activities. Such legislation has often been sustained with respect to powers, other than the commerce power granted to the national government, when the means chosen, although not themselves within the granted power, were nevertheless deemed appropriate aids to the accomplishment of some purpose within an admitted power of the national government. . . .

Our conclusion is unaffected by the Tenth Amendment which provides: "The powers not delegated to the United States by the Constitution nor prohibited by it to the states are reserved to the states respectively or to the people." The amendment states but a truism that all is retained which has not been surrendered. There is nothing in the history of its adoption to suggest that it was more than declaratory of the relationship between the national and state governments as it had been established by the Constitution before the amendment or that its purpose was other than to allay fears that the new national government might seek to exercise powers not granted, and that the states might not be able to exercise fully their reserved powers. . . .

Reversed.

Wickard v. *Filburn*
317 U.S. 111, 63 S.Ct. 82, 87 L.Ed. 122 (1942)

The Agricultural Adjustment Act of 1938 was passed by Congress in an effort to stabilize agricultural production. The basic scheme as applied to wheat involved an annual proclamation by the secretary of agriculture of a national acreage allotment, which was then apportioned to states and eventually passed on in the form of quotas to the individual farmer. If more than one-third of the farmers subject to the act disapproved by referendum the proposed national quota, the effect of the act was to be suspended. Penalties were imposed for production in excess of an agreed-upon quota. Roscoe Filburn raised chickens in Ohio. Each year he planted wheat to feed his livestock and poultry on his own farm. He accepted an Agricultural Marketing Agreement allotment of 11.1 acres, but actually planted 23 acres and grew 239 bushels in excess of his assigned quota. Filburn resisted payment of the penalty by seeking an injunction against Secretary of Agriculture Claude R. Wickard and other officials. The excerpt that follows deals with the main constitutional issue of whether the regulation was within the commerce power. Majority: Jackson, Black, Douglas, Frankfurter, Murphy, Reed, Roberts, Stone.

MR. JUSTICE JACKSON delivered the opinion of the Court. . . .

It is urged that under the Commerce Clause of the Constitution, Art. I, § 8, Cl. 3, Congress does not possess the power it has in this instance sought to exercise. The question would merit little consideration since our decision in *United States* v. *Darby* . . . sustaining the federal power to regulate production of goods for commerce except for the fact that this Act extends federal regulation to production not intended in any part for commerce but wholly for consumption on the farm. . . . [T]he Federal Government fixes a quota including all that the farmer may harvest for sale or for his own farm needs, and declares that wheat produced on excess acreage may neither be disposed of nor used except upon payment of the penalty or except it is stored as required by the Act or delivered to the Secretary of Agriculture.

Appellee says that this is a regulation of production and consumption of wheat. Such activities are, he urges, beyond the reach of Congressional power under the Commerce Clause, since they are local in character, and their effects upon interstate commerce are at most "indirect." In answer the Government argues that the statute regulates neither production nor consumption, but only marketing; and, in the alternative, that if the Act does go beyond the regulation of marketing it is sustainable as a "necessary and proper" implementation of the power of Congress over interstate commerce. . . .

We believe that a review of the course of decision under the Commerce Clause will make plain . . . that questions of the power of Congress are not to be decided by reference to any formula which would give controlling force to nomenclature such as "production" and "indirect" and foreclose consideration of the actual effects of the activity in question upon interstate commerce. . . .

The Court's recognition of the relevance of the economic effects in the application of the Commerce Clause . . . has made the mechanical application of legal formulas no longer feasible. Once an economic measure of the reach of the power granted to Congress in the Commerce Clause is accepted, questions of federal power cannot be decided simply be finding the activity in question to be "production" nor can consideration of its economic effects be foreclosed by calling them "indirect." . . .

Whether the subject of the regulation in question was "production," "consumption," or "marketing" is, therefore, not material for purposes of deciding the question of federal power before us. That an activity is of local character may help in a doubtful case to determine whether Congress intended to reach it. The same consideration might help in determining whether in the absence of Congressional action it would be permissible for the state to exert its power on the subject matter, even though in so doing it to some degree affected interstate commerce. But even if appellant's activity be local and though it may not be regarded as commerce, it may still, whatever its nature, be reached by Congress if it exerts a substantial economic effect on interstate commerce and this irrespective of whether such effect is what might at some earlier time have been defined as "direct" or "indirect." . . .

The effect of consumption of home-grown wheat

on interstate commerce is due to the fact that it constitutes the most variable factor in the disappearance of the wheat crop. Consumption on the farm where grown appears to vary in an amount greater than 10 per cent of average production. The total amount of wheat consumed as food varies but relatively little, and use as seed is relatively constant. . . .

It is well established by decisions of this Court that the power to regulate commerce includes the power to regulate the prices at which commodities in that commerce are dealt in and practices affecting such prices. One of the primary purposes of the Act in question was to increase the market price of wheat and to that end to limit the volume thereof that could affect the market. It can hardly be denied that a factor of such volume and variability as home-consumed wheat would have a substantial influence on price and market conditions. This may arise because being in marketable condition such home-grown wheat overhangs the market and if induced by rising prices tends to flow into the market and check price increases. But if we assume that it is never marketed, it supplies a need of the man who grew it which would otherwise be reflected by purchases in the open market.

Home-grown wheat in this sense competes with wheat in commerce. The stimulation of commerce is a use of a regulatory function quite as definitely as prohibitions or restrictions thereon. This record leaves us in no doubt that Congress may properly have considered that wheat consumed on the farm where grown if wholly outside the scheme of regulation would have a substantial effect in defeating and obstructing its purpose to stimulate trade therein at increased prices.

It is said, however, that this Act, forcing some farmers into the market to buy what they could provide for themselves, is an unfair promotion of the markets and prices of specializing wheat growers. It is of the essence of regulation that it lays a restraining hand on the self-interest of the regulated and that advantages from the regulation commonly fall to others. The conflicts of economic interest between the regulated and those who advantage by it are wisely left under our system to resolution by the Congress under its more flexible and responsible legislative process. Such conflicts rarely lend themselves to judicial determination. And with the wisdom, workability, or fairness, of the plan of regulation we have nothing to do. . . .

Reversed.

Heart of Atlanta Motel v. United States
379 U.S. 241, 85 S.Ct. 348, 13 L.Ed. 2d 258 (1964)
Katzenbach v. McClung
379 U.S. 294, 85 S.Ct. 377, 13 L.Ed. 2d 290 (1964)

In the Civil Rights Act of 1964 Congress sought, among other purposes, to eliminate racial discrimination in hotels, motels, restaurants, and similar places, basing its action on both the equal protection of the laws clause and Section 5 of the Fourteenth Amendment and the commerce clause. In the Atlanta Motel case, the act was applied to an establishment where 75 percent of the guests were from out of state. McClung's Barbecue, in Birmingham, Alabama, was a local restaurant to which the act was applied under a provision covering any restaurant that "serves or offers to serve interstate travelers or a substantial portion of the food which it serves . . . has moved in commerce." Approximately half the food served at McClung's, though purchased within Alabama, had "moved" in commerce. Although two justices, Douglas and Goldberg, would have upheld the act under the Fourteenth Amendment provisions as well as the commerce clause, the commerce clause was chosen by the majority as justifying the act, and the portions of the opinions that follow deal principally with the commerce power. The motel appealed from a three-judge district court injunction against its refusal to accept black lodgers, and the attorney general appealed in *McClung* from a three-judge district court holding that the act could not be applied to the restaurant. A brief excerpt from Justice Clark's opinion for the Court in *Atlanta Motel* is followed by a somewhat longer extract from his opinion in *McClung*. Majority: Clark, Black, Brennan, Douglas, Goldberg, Harlan, Stewart, Warren, White.

MR. JUSTICE CLARK delivered the opinion of the Court. . . . (*Heart of Atlanta*)

It is admitted that the operation of the motel brings it within the provisions of § 201(a) of the Act and that appellant refused to provide lodging for transient Negroes because of their race or color and that it intends to continue that policy unless restrained. . . .

. . . The determinative test of the exercise of power by the Congress under the Commerce Clause is simply whether the activity sought to be regulated is "commerce which concerns more than one state" and has a real and substantial relation to the national interest. . . .

It is said that the operation of the motel here is of a purely local character. But, assuming this to be true, "if it is interstate commerce that feels the pinch, it does not matter how local the operation that applies the squeeze." . . .

. . . The power of Congress to promote interstate commerce also includes the power to regulate the local incidents thereof, including local activities in both the States of origin and destination, which might have a substantial and harmful effect upon that commerce. One need only examine the evidence which we have discussed above to see that Congress may—as it has—prohibit racial discrimination by motels serving travelers, however "local" their operations may appear. . . .

Affirmed.

MR. JUSTICE CLARK delivered the opinion of the Court. . . . (*Katzenbach* v. *McClung*)

. . . The activities that are beyond the reach of Congress are "those which are completely within a particular State, which do not affect other States, and with which it is not necessary to interfere, for the purpose of executing some of the general powers

of the government." . . . *Gibbons* v. *Ogden*. This rule is as good today as it was when Chief Justice Marshall laid it down almost a century and a half ago.

This Court has held time and again that this power extends to activities of retail establishments, including restaurants, which directly or indirectly burden or obstruct interstate commerce. We have detailed the cases in *Heart of Atlanta Motel* . . . and will not repeat them here. . . .

Here, as there, Congress has determined for itself that refusals of service to Negroes have imposed burdens both upon the interstate flow of food and upon the movement of products generally. Of course, the mere fact that Congress has said when particular activity shall be deemed to affect commerce does not preclude further examination by this Court. But where we find that the legislators, in light of the facts and testimony before them, have a rational basis for finding a chosen regulatory scheme necessary to the protection of commerce, our investigation is at an end. . . .

Confronted as we are with the facts laid before Congress, we must conclude that it had a rational basis for finding that racial discrimination in restaurants had a direct and adverse effect on the free flow of interstate commerce. . . .

The absence of direct evidence connecting discriminatory restaurant service with the flow of interstate food, a factor on which the appellees place much reliance, is not, given the evidence as to the effect of such practices on other aspects of commerce, a crucial matter.

The power of Congress in this field is broad and sweeping; where it keeps within its sphere and violates no express constitutional limitation it has been the rule of this Court, going back almost to the founding days of the Republic, not to interfere. The Civil Rights Act of 1964, as here applied, we find to be plainly appropriate in the resolution of what the Congress found to be a national commercial problem of the first magnitude. We find it in no violation of any express limitations of the Constitution and we therefore declare it valid.

MR. JUSTICE BLACK, concurring. . . .

. . . I recognize that every remote possible, speculative effect on commerce should not be accepted as an adequate constitutional ground to uproot and throw into the discard all our traditional distinctions between what is purely local, and therefore controlled by state laws, and what affects the national interest and is therefore subject to control by federal laws. I recognize too that some isolated and remote lunch room which sells only to local people and buys almost all its supplies in the locality may possibly be beyond the reach of the power of Congress to regulate commerce, just as such an establishment is not covered by the present Act. But in deciding the constitutional power of Congress in cases like the two before us we do not consider the effect on interstate commerce of only one isolated, individual, local event, without regard to the fact that this single local event when added to many others of a similar nature may impose a burden on interstate commerce by reducing its volume or distorting its flow. . . .

MR. JUSTICE DOUGLAS, concurring.

Though I join the Court's opinion, I am somewhat reluctant here . . . to rest solely on the Commerce Clause. My reluctance is not due to any conviction that Congress lacks power to regulate commerce in the interests of human rights. It is rather my belief that the right of people to be free of state action that discriminates against them because of race, like the "right to persons to move freely from State to State" . . . "occupies a more protected position in our constitutional system than does the movement of cattle, fruit, steel and coal across state lines." . . .

Hence I would prefer to rest on the assertion of legislative power contained in § 5 of the Fourteenth Amendment which states: "The Congress shall have power to enforce, by appropriate legislation, the provisions of this article"—a power which the Court concedes was exercised at least in part in this Act.

A decision based on the Fourteenth Amendment* would have a more settling effect, making unnecessary litigation over whether a particular restaurant or inn is within the commerce definitions of the Act or whether a particular customer is an interstate traveler. Under my construction, the Act would apply to all customers in all the enumerated places of public accommodation. And that construction would put an end to all obstructionist strategies and finally close one door on a bitter chapter in American history.

---

* The Supreme Court rejected the Fourteenth Amendment as a basis for a public accommodations statute in 1883. See the Civil Rights Cases, in Chapter Twelve—ED.

Garcia v. San Antonio Metropolitan Transit Authority
469 U.S. 528, 105 S.Ct. 1005, 83 L.Ed. 2d 1016 (1985)

(This case is reprinted in Chapter Four, beginning on page 154.)

SEVEN

National Taxing and Spending Power

It is . . . particularly true of constitutional government that its atmosphere is opinion. . . . It does not remain fixed in any unchanging form, but grows with the growth and is altered with the change of the nation's needs and purposes.

—WOODROW WILSON (1908)

Government, like individual citizens, must have regular income to pay bills and maintain credit. In addition, government must have coercive power to collect taxes. No government can carry on if it has to depend, as did the Congress under the Articles of Confederation, on requisitions and voluntary contributions. Indeed, the principal weakness of the central government under the Articles was want of power to levy taxes. National expenditures were defrayed out of a common treasury, supplied by the states in proportion to the occupied land in each state, and upon requisition of Congress. The states reserved the right to levy taxes for this purpose and were, in fact, delinquent in making payments.

Therefore, it is not surprising that, although members of the federal Convention were sharply divided on many issues, they were almost unanimous in their insistence that Congress should have broad power to tax and spend. Heading the list of enumerated powers in Article I, Section 8, stands the provision that Congress shall have power "to lay and collect taxes, duties, imposts and excises, to pay the debts and provide for the common defense and general welfare of the United States."

It would be difficult to fashion more sweeping language. In the exercise of its taxing and spending power, the national government acts directly on individual citizens and their property, acts as directly as though there were no states. Nor are there any limits (apart from those imposed on Congress at the ballot box) on the amount Congress may attempt to collect through taxation. The only limitations on taxing power are those that the Constitution specifically provides in Article I, Section 9, and those that the Supreme Court has established through its various decisions. Article I, Section 9, specifically prohibits the national government from granting a preference to one state's ports over another's and forbids a tax on exports (a concession made in 1787 to southern exporters). These provisions have occasioned no difficulties.

LIMITATIONS THROUGH INTERPRETATION

In addition to express limitations, the Supreme Court has developed two others through interpretation. The first is the doctrine of *reciprocal immunity* of the state and national governments and their instrumentalities from taxation by the other. The second is the *independent constitutional bar*. As a check on the national taxing and spending powers, both today are mere shadows of their former selves.

Reciprocal Immunity. Originally Chief Justice Marshall argued that this immunity was enjoyed only by the national government (*McCulloch* v. *Maryland,* in Chapter Four), but with the ascendancy of the concept of dual federalism, the Court extended the immunity to state governments and their instrumentalities. *Collector* v. *Day* (1871), in which the Court recognized an implied immunity of state and municipal officers from income taxation, was finally overruled in *Graves* v. *New York* (1938). The immunity of the states, however, was qualified in 1905. In *South Carolina* v. *United States,* involving a federal tax on the state of South Carolina's liquor-dispensing business, the state claimed immunity under the doctrine of *Collector* v. *Day,* but without success. In denying immunity, the Court made this distinction: Whenever the state embarks on a business enterprise, in contrast to what the Court called the exercise of government functions, the state loses its Court-created immunity. This is still good law, though what is and what is not a government function is not easily decided today, with state governments entering more and more fields previously under private management (e.g., water and power utilities and transit systems). In the New York Mineral Waters Case, as seen in Chapter Four, the Court split three ways.

With respect to a federal tax on the income derived from municipal bonds, *South Carolina* v. *Baker* (1988) explicitly overruled *Pollock* v. *Farmers' Loan & Trust Co.* (1895, first hearing), which held that municipal bond interest was immune from federal tax. In upholding the Tax Equity and Fiscal Responsibility Act of 1982, which removed the federal income tax exemption from interest earned on bearer (as opposed to registered) municipal bonds, Justice Brennan, for a seven-justice majority, explained that the sources of state and federal immunity were different: "the state immunity arises from the constitutional structure and a concern for protecting state sovereignty whereas the federal immunity arises from the Supremacy Clause." Under current intergovernmental tax immunity doctrine, therefore,

> the States can never tax the United States directly, but can tax any private parties with whom it does business, even though the financial burden falls on the United States, as long as the tax does not discriminate against the United States or those with whom it deals. . . . The rule with respect to state tax immunity is essentially the same . . . except that at least some nondiscriminatory federal taxes can be collected directly from the States even though a parallel state tax could not be collected directly from the Federal Government.

Independent Constitutional Bar. This second judge-made limitation was first considered in the Child Labor Tax Case of 1922 (*Bailey* v. *Drexel Furniture Co.*) but was not fully developed until 1936 in the case challenging the Agricultural Adjustment Act (*United States* v. *Butler*). Justice Roberts, speaking for the Court, declared that the reserved powers of the states (Tenth Amendment) prevented Congress from using the taxing and spending power as an indirect method of regulating certain activities that traditionally belonged to the states, of which agricultural production was one example. This view was hardly announced, however, before it was retracted one year later in *Steward Machine Company* v. *Davis.*

DIRECT AND INDIRECT TAXES

The constitution declares that taxes are of two kinds, and sets forth briefly the rules by which Congress may use each. Article I, Section 9, declares that direct taxes shall be levied according to the rule of apportionment among the several states on the basis of census enumeration or population. Indirect taxes shall be levied according to the rule of uniformity, which means geographical uniformity, as *Knowlton* v. *Moore* (1900) made clear. That is to say, a tax must be laid at the same rate and on the same basis in all parts of the United States. The meaning of indirect taxes, which include all excises and duties, has rarely troubled the Court, but the definition of direct taxes has provided substantial difficulties.

Views of the Framers. Madison's notes throw no light on the mystery of what is a direct tax. The single entry on this question runs, "Mr. Davie of North Carolina rose to ask the meaning of the direct taxes. Mr. King said he did not know." Like so many other terms in the Constitution, the meaning of *direct taxes* had to be spelled out by judicial construction. The Court first spoke on the subject in 1796 in **Hylton** v. **United States,** where a federal tax on carriages was held to be an indirect tax and therefore not subject to apportionment. The Court's holding was based first on the nature of the carriage tax, which it considered a levy on the privilege of using carriages, and second, on the impossibility of fairly apportioning a tax of this kind since the ratio of carriages to population was obviously not the same in each state. The justices agreed that the only direct taxes were capitation and land taxes, and these categories remained frozen for a century.

The Income Tax Case. In accordance with its belief that the Court would adhere to this definition, Congress levied an income tax during the Civil War. It was challenged unsuccessfully in *Springer* v. *United States* (1881) and stood until the 1890s, when Congress enacted another income tax law, levied, as the Civil War tax had been, as if it were indirect. This time, in **Pollock** v. **Farmers' Loan & Trust Co.,** the Court changed its mind, boldly correcting the definition of direct taxes given in *Hylton*, thus righting, by a margin of one vote, "a century of error." In his brief attacking the validity of the income tax (on the theory that it was direct and had to be apportioned), Joseph H. Choate, one of the leaders of the American bar, referred to the tax in violent terms—he called it "communism," "socialism," and "populism." Adopting Choate's sulphurous language, Justice Field in a concurring opinion warned, "The present assault upon capital is but the beginning . . . the stepping stone to others . . . till our political contests will become a war of the poor against the rich." He insisted that this kind of class struggle had to be stopped. The dissenting judges decried in equally fervent language what they deemed a disastrous blow at congressional power and an unwarranted expansion of judicial review.

The immediate effect of this decision was to add income taxes to the category of direct taxes, and since it was not feasible to apportion income taxes, Congress was deprived of this fruitful source of revenue for nearly 20 years. To correct this judge-made amendment of the Constitution, Congress and the states resorted finally to the cumbersome formal amending process, which in 1913 resulted in the Sixteenth Amendment: "The Congress shall have power to lay and collect taxes on incomes, from whatever source derived, without apportionment among the several states, and without regard to any census or enumeration."

This seemingly comprehensive language, however, was not allowed to mean all that it seemed to say. By judicial construction, the amendment was held to mean only that income taxes need not be apportioned and was not interpreted as authorizing taxes on all incomes. The salaries of federal judges, the Court ruled in 1920 in *Evans* v. *Gore,* were still exempt from the income tax—the justices thus preferred their own judge-made exemption to the clear language of a constitutional amendment. However, without any revision of the

Sixteenth Amendment, *Evans* v. *Gore* was overruled in 1939. In *O'Malley* v. *Woodrough* Justice Frankfurter observed, "To suggest that it [a nondiscriminatory income tax] makes inroads upon the independence of judges . . . by making them bear their aliquot share of the cost of maintaining the government is to trivialize the great historic experience on which the framers based the safeguards of Article 3, Section 1."

REGULATION THROUGH TAXATION

The most obvious and normal purpose of taxation is the raising of revenue, but this is not taxation's only legitimate purpose. Whether a tax is primarily for revenue or regulation is frequently a difficult question, a matter of degree, for strictly speaking, no tax is or can be solely a revenue measure.

Taxation and Enumerated Powers. One aspect of this question has been definitely settled: Congress may use its taxing power primarily for purposes of regulation, or even destruction, when the tax serves to aid Congress in exercising one of its other delegated powers, such as regulating interstate commerce, controlling the currency, or maintaining a postal service. An illustrative case is *Veazie Bank* v. *Fenno* (1869), involving an act of Congress in placing a 10 percent tax on state bank note issues to protect the notes of the new national banks from the state banks' competition. The tax was of course destructive, as it was intended to be; yet the Court upheld it on the ground that Congress could have achieved the same end by absolute prohibition of state bank notes under the currency power.

Taxation and Unenumerated Powers. A more controversial question remains. May Congress use a tax primarily as a regulatory device, that is, to enforce some social or economic policy, when no enumerated power of Congress can be invoked in justification? For a long period the Court's answers to this question wavered between a clear yes and an equally clear no.

The leading affirmative case is **McCray v. United States** (1904), which concerned the validity of a destructive tax on oleomargarine colored to resemble butter. That the primary purpose of the tax was regulation and not revenue was clear from the much higher tax on colored oleomargarine (ten cents per pound) as compared with uncolored oleomargarine (one-quarter cent per pound). Yet the Court held that since Congress had virtually unlimited discretion in the selection of the objects of taxation, it was no part of the judicial function to explore congressional motives. Under this judicial hands-off policy, Congress proceeded to regulate by taxation the manufacture of phosphorus matches and narcotics and the retail sale of certain firearms. It should be observed that the doctrine of *McCray* came close to making the question of the validity of destructive and regulatory taxation a political question.

In due course, the Court evolved a more effective technique for imposing limitations on the destructive use of the federal taxing power for purposes of social control and regulation. The change came in 1922 in *Bailey* v. *Drexel Furniture Co.*, which involved the constitutionality of a 10 percent federal tax on the net income of any employer of child labor, regardless of the number of children employed. In addition the act set up an elaborate code for regulating each employer's conduct, a matter over which Congress admittedly had no direct control. Speaking through Chief Justice Taft, an all but unanimous Court condemned the act primarily because it was a "penalty" and not a tax, and secondarily because by regulating production the act invaded the reserved powers of the states.

United States v. Butler. In 1935–1936, when taxation provisions of New Deal programs were tested, two lines of precedents were available. If the Court chose to sustain a measure under the taxing power, it could employ the generous principle of *McCray*. If, on the other hand, the Court chose to set aside the legislation, it could look on the tax—as Chief Justice Taft did in *Bailey*—as a "penalty," a form of "regulation," an invasion of domain reserved to the states.

One of the planks in the platform on which F.D.R. was elected—a commitment equal in emphasis to the Democratic candidate's campaign promise to balance the budget—was his solemn vow to restore agricultural prosperity. Under the Agricultural Adjustment Act (AAA), a processing tax was levied on basic commodities such as wheat, corn, and cotton. From the funds thus accumulated, money was paid out to farmers as "inducement" to reduce their acreage. Here, at long last, was a self-financing scheme to subsidize farmers as the protective tariff had long subsidized industry.

High expectations arose from the first years of its administration, until one December day in 1935 the entire scheme became shrouded in constitutional doubt. Attacking the act's constitutionality was Philadelphia's most eminent lawyer, George Wharton Pepper. Perfectly cast for the role, Pepper observed, "I have tried very hard to argue this case calmly and dispassionately, because it seems to me that this is the best way in which an advocate can discharge his duty to this Court. But I do not want Your Honors to think my feelings are not involved and that my emotions are not deeply stirred. Indeed, may it please Your Honors, I believe I am standing here today to plead the cause of the America I have loved; and I pray Almighty God that not in my time may 'the land of the regimented' be accepted as a worthy substitute for 'the land of the free.' " For Pepper, economic dogma, no less than congressional taxing power, was at stake.

The former senator's prayer was soon answered. Within a month the Court announced its decision. According to Justice Roberts, Pepper's former student at the University of Pennsylvania Law School, the processing tax could not be upheld as a tax. "The word has never been thought to connote the expropriation of money from one group for the benefit of another." If valid, the exaction could be supported only as an exercise of the disputed power to tax and spend for the general welfare. The Court was thus face to face with an unresolved issue dating from Washington's first administration.

Was the power to tax and spend for the general welfare a substantive, independent power, as Hamilton maintained? Or was it no power at all, but rather an appendage of Congress's other enumerated powers, as Madison contended? Through many administrations, regardless of party, appropriations of money had been made to accomplish purposes not identified with those that Congress is authorized to promote under its other powers. Hamilton had upheld this view in his famous *Report on Manufactures,* and Justice Roberts emphatically embraced it. No sooner had he adopted the Hamiltonian theory, however, than the justice proceeded to enforce, for all practical purposes, the narrow Madisonian theory he had just repudiated. Congress, the justice agreed, might appropriate money for an objective designated as the general welfare, but it could attach no terms or conditions to the use of funds so appropriated unless such terms or conditions were themselves authorized by another specific congressional grant. Federal money might be spent for the broad purposes outlined by Hamilton, but Congress could control the expenditure only if the objectives were within the narrow scope Madison gave the general welfare clause.

Probing deeply into congressional motives, Justice Roberts discovered that this was not a tax at all but payment of benefits to farmers to induce (or coerce) them into curtailing production. Congress, he said, has no power to regulate production. The tax was thus in effect an ingenious disguise of such regulation, an invalid invasion of the reserved domain of the states.

Justice Roberts thus placed the taxing and spending provisions in a special category, doing for Congress's power to tax and spend what Justice Day had done in 1918 (*Hammer v. Dagenhart*) for Congress's power to regulate interstate commerce. In both instances the judiciary wrote *expressly* into the Tenth Amendment. "It is an established principle," Justice

Roberts concluded, "that the attainment of a prohibited end may not be accomplished under the pretext of the exertion of powers which are granted."

Justice Stone in his dissent did more than attack the majority's view of the taxing and spending power. He blasted judicial usurpation as such. Justice Roberts had raised the specter of "legislative power, without restriction or limitation," "vested in a parliament . . . subject to no restrictions except the discretion of its members." But Stone countered, consider the status of our own power. Whereas the executive and Congress are restrained by "the ballot box and the processes of democratic government [and] subject to judicial restraint, the only check upon our own exercise of power is our own sense of self-restraint." Precisely because it is unfettered, Stone argued, judicial responsibility should be discharged with finer conscience and humility than that of any other agency of government.

Stone's words, frequently quoted, rarely if ever queried, were too sweeping. They overlooked the control Congress and the president may exert. In less than a year after Stone uttered those words, President Roosevelt demonstrated how a president may influence judicial decisions merely by threatening to "pack" the Court with justices of his own political persuasion (see Chapter Six).

Thus in *United States* v. *Butler* the Court chose to follow a narrow construction of the taxing power, only to revert back, in upholding the Social Security Act in *Steward Machine*, to the more generous rule of *McCray*. Justice Cardozo set forth a strongly nationalistic theory of the taxing power which, in effect, held that Congress has full power to tax and spend for the general welfare. His opinion represented a significant shift in political theory as well as constitutional interpretation.

Taxing, Spending, and the Bill of Rights. What happens when exercise of the taxing or spending power collides with a protection in the Bill of Rights? The Federal Wagering Tax statutes, for example, required gamblers to procure a license and to pay a substantial tax. Many forms of gambling, however, were illegal under federal as well as state law. Information gathered through the licensing and taxing provisions of the statutes was readily available to state, local, and federal law-enforcement authorities. Gamblers violated the law if they did not comply and furnished evidence of a crime if they did. The Supreme Court in *United States* v. *Kahriger* (1953) upheld the policy but changed its mind in *Marchetti* v. *United States* (1968). Seven justices considered that the Fifth Amendment's privilege against self-incrimination was a complete defense against prosecution under the wagering tax laws.

Chief Justice Warren, the sole dissenter, would have affirmed Marchetti's conviction on the basis of *Kahriger.* Warren was concerned lest the Court open to attack other federal registration statutes touching allegedly illegal activities. Among the legislation in jeopardy was the Federal Marijuana Tax Act, prohibiting sale of the drug without an official order form, which six justices upheld the following year in *Minor* v. *United States* (1969). Distinguishing marijuana dealers from gamblers, Justice White reasoned that there was no real possibility that the order form the law required would incriminate sellers since a buyer would probably not be willing to comply with the law's demand that the order form state the buyer's name and address.

In another example of the use of the taxing and spending power to enforce public policy, Congress enacted the *Solomon Amendment,* tying federal aid for college students to draft registration. Males not registering are ineligible for federal aid, and late registration to obtain financial aid amounts to a declaration that one has been in violation of the draft law. In *Selective Service System* v. *Minnesota Public Interest Research Group* (1984), six justices rejected a *Marchetti*-styled attack on Fifth Amendment grounds.

A Uniform Drinking Age? The 1980s witnessed an attempt by Congress to cope with alcohol-related traffic accidents by imposing indirectly a national drinking age. The National Minimum Drinking Age Amendment of 1982 directed the secretary of transportation to withhold 5 percent of allotted federal highway funds from states with a legal drinking age under 21. Justice Roberts in *Butler* had relied on the Tenth Amendment to block indirect federal regulation of agriculture. Now South Dakota contended that the Twenty-first Amendment limited this new use of the spending power. **South Dakota v. Dole** (1987) rejected the state's claim. Although eight justices left open the question whether Congress could legislate a national drinking age directly, they had little doubt about doing so by way of disbursement of funds. Only Justice O'Connor dissented, paying special attention to Roberts's reasoning in *Butler*. "The immense size and power of the Government of the United States ought not obscure its fundamental character. It remains a Government of enumerated powers."

Clearly, Congress's broad powers to spend—and tax—continue to raise questions under the Constitution.

KEY TERMS

Articles of	direct taxes	Hamiltonian theory
Confederation	indirect taxes	
reciprocal immunity	enumerated powers	
independent	unenumerated powers	
constitutional bar	Madisonian theory	

QUERIES

1. How does *Hylton* v. *United States* anticipate *Marbury* v. *Madison?*

2. According to Justice O'Connor in *South Dakota* v. *Dole,* what is the source of limitations on Congress's spending power?

3. Appraise Justice Roberts's opinion in *United States* v. *Butler.*

4. What does *Marchetti* v. *United States* say about Congress's powers of taxation?

SELECTED READINGS

"Validity of Federal Tax as Affected by Restrictive, Suppressive, or Other Ulterior Purpose." 99 *U.S. Supreme Court Reports, Lawyers' Edition* 481.

CORWIN, EDWARD S. *Court Over Constitution.* Princeton, N.J.: Princeton University Press, 1938.

———. "The Spending Power of Congress." 36 *Harvard Law Review* 548 (1923).

CUSHMAN, ROBERT E. "Social and Economic Control Through Federal Taxation," 18 *Minnesota Law Review* 757 (1934).

LAWSON, J. F. *The General Welfare Clause.* Washington D.C.: J. F. Lawson, 1926.

LUND, NELSON. "Congressional Power over Taxation and Commerce: The Supreme Court's Lost Chance to Devise a Consistent Doctrine." 18 *Texas Tech Law Review* 729 (1987).

MASON, ALPHEUS T. "Owen Josephus Roberts." *Dictionary of American Biography, Supplement Five.* New York: Scribner's, 1977.

Hylton v. United States
3 U.S. (3 Dall.) 171, 1 L.Ed 556 (1796)

Hylton claimed that a congressional act of 1794 levying a tax of $16 on each carriage was a direct tax and must be laid in proportion to the census. With an ownership of 125 carriages, Hylton obtained review of an adverse judgment in the circuit court. Majority: Chase, Iredell, Paterson, Wilson. Not participating: Ellsworth, Cushing.

CHASE, JUSTICE.—By the case stated, only one question is submitted to the opinion of this court—whether the law of Congress of the 5th of June 1794, entitled, "An act to lay duties upon carriages for the conveyance of persons," is unconstitutional and void?

The principles laid down, to prove the above law void, are these: that a tax on carriages is a direct tax, and, therefore, by the constitution, must be laid according to the census, directed by the constitution to be taken, to ascertain the number of representatives from each state. And that the tax in question on carriages is not laid by that rule of apportionment, but by the rule of uniformity, prescribed by the constitution in the case of duties, imposts and excises; and a tax on carriages is not within either of those descriptions. . . .

I think, an annual tax on carriages, for the conveyance of persons, may be considered as within the power granted to congress to lay duties. . . .

I am inclined to think but of this I do not give a judicial opinion, that the direct taxes contemplated by the constitution, are only two, to wit, a capitation or poll tax, simply, without regard to property, profession or any other circumstance; and a tax on land. I doubt, whether a tax, by a general assessment of personal property, within the United States, is included within the term direct tax. . . .

PATERSON, JUSTICE.—. . .

. . . Whether direct taxes, in the sense of the constitution, comprehend any other tax than a capitation tax, and tax on land, is a questionable point. If congress, for instance, should tax, in the aggregate, or mass, things that generally pervade all the states in the Union, then, perhaps, the rule of apportionment would be the most proper, especially, if an assessment was to intervene. This appears by the practice of some of the states, to have been considered as a direct tax. Whether it be so, under the constitution of the United States, is a matter of some difficulty; but as it is not before the court, it would be improper to give any decisive opinion upon it. I never entertained a doubt that the principal, I will not say, the only, objects, that the framers of the constitution contemplated, as falling within the rule of apportionment, were a capitation tax and a tax on land. Local considerations, and the particular circumstances, and relative situation of the states, naturally lead to this view of the subject. The provision was made in favor of the southern states; they possessed a large number of slaves; they had extensive tracts of territory, thinly settled, and not very productive. A majority of the states had but few slaves, and several of them a limited territory, well settled, and in a high state of cultivation. The southern states, if no provision had been introduced in the constitution, would have been wholly at the mercy of the other states. Congress in such case, might tax slaves, at discretion or arbitrarily, and land in every part of the Union, after the same rate or measure: so much a head in the first instance, and so much an acre, in the second. To guard them against imposition, in these particulars, was the reason of introducing the clause in the constitution, which directs that representatives and direct taxes shall be apportioned among the states, according to their respective numbers. . . .

IREDELL, JUSTICE.—. . .

As all direct taxes must be apportioned, it is evident, that the constitution contemplated none as direct, but such as could be apportioned. If this cannot be apportioned, it is, therefore, not a direct tax in the sense of the constitution.

That this tax cannot be apportioned, is evident. Suppose, ten dollars contemplated as a tax on each chariot, or post chaise, in the United States, and the number of both in all the United States be computed at 105, the number of representatives in congress.

This would produce in the whole $1,050.00
The share of Virginia being 19/105 parts, would be $190.00
The share of Connecticut being 7/105 parts, would be 70.00
Then suppose Virginia had 50 carriages, Connecticut 2,
The share of Virginia being $190, this must, of

course, be collected from the owners of carriages, and there would, therefore, be collected from each carriage 3.80
The share of Connecticut being $70, each carriage would pay 35.00

If any state had no carriages, there could be no apportionment at all. This mode is too manifestly absurd to be supported, and has not even been attempted in debate. . . .

BY THE COURT.—Let the judgment of the circuit court be affirmed.

Pollock v. Farmers' Loan & Trust Company
158 U.S. 601, 15 S.Ct. 673, 39 L.Ed. 1108 (1895) (Rehearing)

An Act of Congress of 1894 imposed a tax on income derived from various classes of property as well as that resulting from personal services. In the first decision (April 8, 1895) involving the act, the Court, with one justice absent, declared the act invalid insofar as it was applied to the income from real estate or the interest on municipal bonds. The Court split on other questions presented. In May 1895, the Court granted a rehearing so that these questions might receive authoritative answers. Majority: Fuller, Brewer, Field, Gray, Shiras. Dissenting: Harlan, Brown, Jackson, White.

MR. CHIEF JUSTICE FULLER delivered the opinion of the Court. . . .

. . . The Constitution divided Federal taxation into two great classes, the class of direct taxes and the class of duties, imposts, and excises, and prescribed two rules which qualified the grant of power as to each class.

The power to lay direct taxes, apportioned among the several States in proportion to their representation in the popular branch of Congress, a representation based on population as ascertained by the census, was plenary and absolute, but to lay direct taxes without apportionment was forbidden. The power to lay duties, imposts, and excises was subject to the qualification that the imposition must be .uniform throughout the United States.

Our previous decision was confined to the consideration of the validity of the tax on the income

from real estate, and on the income from municipal bonds. . . .

We are now permitted to broaden the field of inquiry, and determine to which of the two great classes a tax upon a person's entire income, whether derived from rents, or products, or otherwise, of real estate, or from bonds, stocks or other forms of personal property, belongs; and we are unable to conclude that the enforced subtraction from the yield of all the owner's real or personal property, in the manner prescribed, is so different from a tax upon the property itself, that it is not a direct, but an indirect tax, in the meaning of the Constitution. . . .

We know of no reason for holding otherwise than that the words "direct taxes" on the one hand, and "duties, imposts, and excises" on the other, were used in the Constitution in their natural and obvious sense, nor, in arriving at what those terms embrace, do we perceive any ground for enlarging them beyond, or narrowing them within, their natural and obvious import at the time the Constitution was framed and ratified. . . .

The reasons for the clauses of the Constitution in respect of direct taxation are not far to seek. The States, respectively, possessed plenary powers of taxation. . . . They retained the power of direct taxation, and to that they looked as their chief resource; but even in respect of that, they granted the concurrent power, and if the tax were placed by both governments on the same subject, the claim of the United States had preference. Therefore, they did not grant the power of direct taxation without regard to their own condition and resources as States; but they granted the power of apportioned direct taxation, a power just as efficacious to serve the needs of the general government, but securing to the States the opportunity to pay the amount apportioned, and to recoup from their own citizens in the most feasible way, and in harmony with their systems of local self-government. . . .

It is said that a tax on the whole income of property is not a direct tax in the meaning of the Constitution, but a duty, and, as a duty, leviable without apportionment, whether direct or indirect. We do not think so. Direct taxation was not restricted in one breath, and the restriction blown to the winds in another. . . .

. . . Thus we find Mr. Hamilton, while writing to induce the adoption of the Constitution, *first,* dividing the power of taxation into *external* and *internal,* putting into the former the power of imposing duties on imported articles and into the latter all remaining powers; and, *second,* dividing the latter into *direct* and *indirect,* putting into the latter, duties and excises on articles of consumption.

It seems to us to inevitably follow that in Mr. Hamilton's judgment at that time all internal taxes, except duties and excises on articles of consumption, fell into the category of direct taxes. . . .

. . . He gives, however, it appears to us, a definition which covers the question before us. A tax upon one's whole income is a tax upon the annual receipts from his whole property, and as such falls within the same class as a tax upon that property, and is a direct tax, in the meaning of the Constitution. And Mr. Hamilton in his report on the public credit, in referring to contracts with citizens of a foreign country, said: "This principle,

which seems critically correct, would exempt as well the income as the capital of the property. It protects the use, as effectually as the thing. What, in fact, is property, but a fiction, without the beneficial use of it? In many cases, indeed, the *income* or *annuity* is the property itself." . . .

Whatever the speculative views of political economists or revenue reformers may be, can it be properly held that the Constitution, taken in its plain and obvious sense, and with due regard to the circumstances attending the formation of the government, authorizes a general unapportioned tax on the products of the farm and the rents of real estate, although imposed merely because of ownership and with no possible means of escape from payment, as belonging to a totally different class from that which includes the property from which the income proceeds?

There can be only one answer, unless the constitutional restriction is to be treated as utterly illusory and futile, and the object of its framers defeated. We find it impossible to hold that a fundamental requisition, deemed so important as to be enforced by two provisions, one affirmative and one negative, can be refined away by forced distinctions between that which gives value to property and the property itself.

Nor can we perceive any ground why the same reasoning does not apply to capital in personalty held for the purpose of income or ordinarily yielding income, and to the income therefrom. All the real estate of the country, and all its invested personal property, are open to the direct operation of the taxing power if an apportionment be made according to the Constitution. The Constitution does not say that no direct tax shall be laid by apportionment on any other property than land; on the contrary, it forbids all unapportioned direct taxes; and we know of no warrant for excepting personal property from the exercise of the power, or any reason why an apportioned direct tax cannot be laid and assessed. . . .

We have considered the act only in respect of the tax on income derived from real estate, and from invested personal property, and have not commented on so much of it as bears on gains or profits from business, privileges, or employments, in view of the instances in which taxation on business, privileges, or employments has assumed the guise of an excise tax and been sustained as such.

Being of opinion that so much of the sections of this law as lays a tax on income from real and personal property is invalid, we are brought to the question of the effect of that conclusion upon these sections as a whole.

It is elementary that the same statute may be in part constitutional and in part unconstitutional, and if the parts are wholly independent of each other, that which is constitutional may stand while that which is unconstitutional will be rejected. And in the case before us there is no question as to validity of this act, except sections twenty-seven to thirty-seven inclusive, which relate to the subject which has been under discussion; and as to them we think that the rule laid down by Chief Justice Shaw [of the Massachusetts Supreme Court] in *Warren* v. *Charlestown,* 2 Gray, 84, is applicable, that if the different parts "are so mutually connected with and dependent on each other, as conditions, considerations or compensations for each other, as to warrant the belief that the legislature intended them as a whole, and that, if all could not be carried into effect, the legislature would not pass the residue independently, and some parts are unconstitutional, all the provisions which are thus dependent, conditional or connected, must fall with them.". . .

Our conclusions may, therefore, be summed up as follows:

First. We adhere to the opinion already announced, that, taxes on real estate being indisputably direct taxes, taxes on the rents or incomes of real estate are equally direct taxes.

Second. We are of opinion that taxes on personal property, or on the income of personal property, are likewise direct taxes.

Third. The tax imposed by sections twenty-seven to thirty-seven, inclusive, of the act of 1894, so far as it falls on the income of real estate and of personal property, being a direct tax within the meaning of the Constitution, and, therefore, unconstitutional and void because not apportioned according to representation, all those sections, constituting one entire scheme of taxation, are necessarily invalid.

The decrees hereinbefore entered in this court will be vacated; the decrees below will be reversed, and the case remanded, with instructions to grant the relief prayed.

MR. JUSTICE HARLAN dissenting. . . .

In my judgment a tax on *income* derived from real property ought not to be, and until now has never been, regarded by any court as a direct tax on such property within the meaning of the Constitution. As the great mass of lands in most of the States do not bring any rents, and as incomes from rents vary in different States, such a tax cannot possibly be apportioned among the States on the basis merely of numbers with any approach to equality of right among taxpayers, any more than a tax on carriages or other personal property could be so apportioned. And, in view of former adjudications, beginning with the Hylton case and ending with the Springer case, a decision now that a tax on income from real property can be laid and collected only by apportioning the same among the States, on the basis of numbers, may, not improperly, be regarded as a judicial revolution, that may sow the seeds of hate and distrust among the people of different sections of our common country. . . .

In my judgment—to say nothing of the disregard of the former adjudications of this court, and of the settled practice of the government—this decision may well excite the gravest apprehensions. It strikes at the very foundations of national authority, in that it denies to the general government a power which is, or may become, vital to the very existence and preservation of the Union in a national emergency, such as that of war with a great commercial nation, during which the collection of all duties upon imports will cease or be materially diminished. It tends to reestablish that condition of helplessness in which Congress found itself during the period of the Articles of Confederation, when it was without authority by laws operating directly upon individuals, to lay and collect, through its own agents, taxes sufficient to pay the debts and defray the expenses of government, but was dependent, in all such matters, upon the good will of the States, and their promptness in meeting requisitions made upon them by Congress.

Why do I say that the decision just rendered impairs or menaces the national authority? The reason is so apparent that it need only be stated. In its practical operation this decision withdraws from national taxation not only all incomes derived from real estate, but tangible personal property, *invested* personal property, bonds, stocks, investments of all kinds, and the income that may be derived from such property. This results from the fact that by the decision of the court, all such personal property and all incomes from real estate and personal property are placed beyond national taxation otherwise than by *apportionment* among the States *on the basis* simply *of population*. No such apportionment can possibly be made without doing gross injustice to the many for the benefit of the favored few in particular States. Any attempt upon the part of Congress to apportion among the States, upon the basis simply of their population, taxation of personal property or of incomes, would tend to arouse such indignation among the freemen of America that it would never be repeated. When therefore, this court adjudges, as it does now adjudge, that Congress cannot impose a duty or tax upon personal property, or upon income arising either from rents of real estate or from personal property, including invested personal property, bonds, stocks, and investments of all kinds, except by apportioning the sum to be so raised among the States according to population, it *practically* decides that, *without an amendment of the Constitution*—two-thirds of both Houses of Congress and three-fourths of the States concurring—such property and incomes can never be made to contribute to the support of the national government. . . .

I dissent from the opinion and judgment of the court.

McCray v. United States
195 U.S. 27, 24 S.Ct. 769, 49 L.Ed. 78 (1904)

The Oleomargarine Act, passed by Congress in 1886 and amended in 1902, levied a tax of one-quarter cent per pound on uncolored oleomargarine and ten cents per pound on oleomargarine colored yellow. McCray, a licensed dealer, failed to pay the higher tax in making sales of the colored product and was fined. Majority: White, Brewer, Day, Harlan, Holmes, McKenna. Dissenting: Fuller, Brown, Peckham.

MR. JUSTICE WHITE . . . delivered the opinion of the court. . . .

That the acts in question on their face impose excise taxes which Congress had the power to levy is so completely established as to require only statement. . . .

It is, however, argued if a lawful power may be exerted for an unlawful purpose, and thus by abusing the power it may be made to accomplish a result not intended by the Constitution, all limitations of power must disappear, and the grave function lodged in the judiciary, to confine all the departments within the authority conferred by the Constitution, will be of no avail. This, when reduced to its last analysis, comes to this, that, because a particular department of the government may exert its lawful powers with the object or motive of reaching an end not justified, therefore it becomes the duty of the judiciary to restrain the exercise of a lawful power wherever it seems to the judicial mind that such lawful power has been abused. But this reduces itself to the contention that, under our constitutional system, the abuse by one department of the government of its lawful powers is to be corrected by the abuse of its powers by another department. . . .

It is, of course, true, as suggested, that if there be no authority in the judiciary to restrain a lawful exercise of power by another department of the government, where a wrong motive or purpose has impelled to the exertion of the power, that abuses of a power conferred may be temporarily effectual. The remedy for this, however, lies, not in the abuse by the judicial authority of its functions, but in the people, upon whom, after all, under our institutions, reliance must be placed for the correction of abuses committed in the exercise of a lawful power. . . .

It being thus demonstrated that the motive or purpose of Congress in adopting the acts in question may not be inquired into, we are brought to consider the contentions relied upon to show that the acts assailed were beyond the power of Congress, putting entirely out of view all considerations based upon purpose or motive. . . .

Since . . . the taxing power conferred by the Constitution knows no limits except those expressly stated in that instrument, it must follow, if a tax be within the lawful power, the exertion of that power may not be judicially restrained because of the results to arise from its exercise. . . .

Whilst undoubtedly both the Fifth and Tenth Amendments qualify, in so far as they are applicable, all the provisions of the Constitution, nothing in those amendments operates to take away the grant of power to tax conferred by the Constitution upon Congress. The contention on this subject rests upon the theory that the purpose and motive of Congress in exercising its undoubted powers may be inquired into by the courts, and the proposition is therefore disposed of by what has been said on that subject.

The right of Congress to tax within its delegated powers being unrestrained, except as limited by the Constitution, it was within the authority conferred on Congress to select the objects upon which an excise should be laid. It therefore follows that, in exerting its power, no want of due process of law could possibly result, because that body chose to impose an excise on artificially colored oleomargarine and not upon natural butter artificially colored. The judicial power may not usurp the functions of the legislative in order to control that branch of the government in the performance of its lawful duties. . . .

Let us concede that if a case was presented where the abuse of the taxing power was so extreme as to be beyond the principles which we have previously stated, and where it was plain to the judicial mind that the power had been called into play not for revenue but solely for the purpose of destroying rights which could not be rightfully destroyed consistently with the principles of freedom and justice upon which the Constitution rests, that it would be the duty of the courts to say that such an arbitrary act was not merely an abuse of a delegated power, but was the exercise of an authority not conferred. This concession, however, like the one previously made, must be without influence upon the decision of this case for the reasons previously stated; that is, that the manufacture of artificially colored oleomargarine may be prohibited by a free government without a violation of fundamental rights.

Affirmed.

United States v. Butler
297 U.S. 1, 56 S.Ct. 312, 80 L.Ed. 477 (1936)

In 1933 Congress attempted to benefit farm producers through the Agricultural Adjustment Act. The basic scheme adopted was the payment of various amounts to farmers in return for the farmers' promise to reduce crop acreage. A processing tax designed to finance the program of benefit payments was levied on the first processor of the commodity involved and was to be measured by the difference between current average farm prices and the price prevailing in an earlier period (1909–1914). Butler, the receiver for a processor, refused to pay the tax. The district court ordered it paid, but the court of appeals reversed the order. Majority: Roberts, Butler, Hughes, McReynolds, Sutherland, Van Devanter. Dissenting: Stone, Brandeis, Cardozo.

MR. JUSTICE ROBERTS delivered the opinion of the Court. . . .

There should be no misunderstanding as to the function of this court in such a case. It is sometimes said that the court assumes a power to overrule or control the action of the people's representatives. This is a misconception. The Constitution is the supreme law of the land ordained and established by the people. All legislation must conform to the principles it lays down. When an act of Congress is appropriately challenged in the courts as not conforming to the constitutional mandate, the judicial branch of the Government has only one duty—to lay the article of the Constitution which is invoked beside the statute which is challenged and to decide whether the latter squares with the former. All the court does, or can do, is to announce its considered judgment upon the question. The only power it has, if such it may be called, is the power of judgment. This court neither approves nor condemns any legislative policy. Its delicate and difficult office is to ascertain and declare whether the legislation is in accordance with, or in contravention of, the provisions of the Constitution; and having done that, its duty ends. . . .

The clause thought to authorize the legislation . . . confers upon the Congress power "to lay and collect Taxes, Duties, Imposts and Excises, to pay the Debts and provide for the common Defense and general Welfare of the United States. . . ." It is not contended that this provision grants power to regulate agricultural production upon the theory that such legislation would promote the general welfare. The government concedes that the phrase "to provide for the general welfare" qualifies the power "to lay and collect taxes." The view that the clause grants power to provide for the general welfare, independently of the taxing power, has never been authoritatively accepted. Mr. Justice Story points out that, if it were adopted, "it is obvious that under color of the generality of the words, to 'provide for the common defence and general welfare,' the government of the United States is, in reality, a government of general and unlimited powers, notwithstanding the subsequent enumeration of specific powers." The true construction undoubtedly is that the only thing granted is the power to tax for the purpose of providing funds for payment for the nation's debts and making provision for the general welfare.

Nevertheless, the Government asserts that warrant is found in this clause for the adoption of the Agricultural Adjustment Act. The argument is that Congress may appropriate and authorize the spending of moneys for the "general welfare"; that the phrase should be liberally construed to cover anything conducive to national welfare; that decision as to what will promote such welfare rests with Congress alone, and the courts may not review its determination; and, finally, that the appropriation under attack was in fact for the general welfare of the United States.

The Congress is expressly empowered to lay taxes to provide for the general welfare. . . .

Since the foundation of the nation, sharp differences of opinion have persisted as to the true interpretation of the phrase. Madison asserted it amounted to no more than a reference to the other powers enumerated in the subsequent clauses of the same section; that, as the United States is a government of limited and enumerated powers, the grant of power to tax and spend for the general national welfare must be confined to the enumerated legislative fields committed to the Congress. In this view the phrase is mere tautology, for taxation and appropriation are or may be necessary incidents of the exercise of any of the enumerated legislative powers. Hamilton, on the other hand, maintained the clause confers a power separate and distinct from those later enumerated, is not restricted in meaning by the grant of them, and Congress consequently has a substantive power to tax and to appropriate, limited only by the requirement that it shall be exercised to provide for the general welfare of the United States. Each contention has had the support of those whose views are entitled to weight. This court has noticed the question, but has never found it necessary to decide which is the true construction. Mr. Justice Story, in his Commentaries, espouses the Hamiltonian position. We shall not review the writings of public men and commentators or discuss the legislative practice. Study of all these leads us to conclude that the reading advocated by Mr. Justice Story is the correct one. While, therefore, the power to tax is not unlimited, its confines are set in the clause which confers it and not in those of Section 8 which bestow and define the legislative powers of the Congress. It results that the power of Congress to authorize expenditure of public moneys for public purposes is not limited by the direct grants of legislative power found in the Constitution.

But the adoption of the broader construction leaves the power to spend subject to limitations. . . .

Story says that if the tax be not proposed for the common defence or general welfare, but for other objects wholly extraneous, it would be wholly indefensible upon constitutional principles. And he makes it clear that the powers of taxation and appropriation extend only to matters of national, as distinguished from local welfare. . . .

We are not now required to ascertain the scope of the phrase "general welfare of the United States" or to determine whether an appropriation in aid of agriculture falls within it. Wholly apart from that question, another principle embedded in our Constitution prohibits the enforcement of the Agricultural Adjustment Act. The act invades the reserved rights of the states. It is a statutory plan to regulate and control agricultural production, a matter beyond the powers delegated to the federal government. The tax, the appropriation of the funds raised, and the direction for their disbursement, are but parts of the plan. They are but means to an unconstitutional end.

From the accepted doctrine that the United States is a government of delegated powers, it follows that those not expressly granted, or reasonably to be implied from such as are conferred, are reserved to the states or to the people. To forestall any suggestion to the contrary, the Tenth Amendment was adopted. The same proposition, otherwise stated, is that powers not granted are prohibited. None to regulate agricultural production is given, and therefore legislation by Congress for that purpose is forbidden. . . .

If the act before us is a proper exercise of the federal taxing power, evidently the regulation of all industry throughout the United States may be accomplished by similar exercises of the same power. . . .

Until recently no suggestion of the existence of any such power in the federal government has been advanced. The expressions of the framers of the Constitution, the decisions of this court interpreting that instrument and the writings of great commentators will be searched in vain for any suggestion that there exists in the clause under discussion or elsewhere in the Constitution, the authority whereby every provision and every fair implication from that instrument may be subverted, the independence of the individual states obliterated, and the United States converted into a central government exercising uncontrolled police power in every state of the Union, superseding all local control or regulation of the affairs or concerns of the states. . . .

Affirmed.

MR. JUSTICE STONE, dissenting. . . .

The power of courts to declare a statute unconstitutional is subject to two guiding principles of decision which ought never to be absent from judicial consciousness. One is that courts are concerned only with the power to enact statutes, not with their wisdom. The other is that while unconstitutional exercise of power by the executive and legislative branches of the government is subject to judicial restraint, the only check upon our own exercise of power is our own sense of self-restraint. For the removal of unwise laws from the statute books appeal lies not to the courts but to the ballot and to the processes of democratic government. . . .

It is upon the contention that state power is infringed by purchased regulation of agricultural production that chief reliance is placed. It is insisted that, while the Constitution gives to Congress, in specific and unambiguous terms, the power to tax and spend, the power is subject to limitations which do not find their origin in any express provision of the Constitution and to which other expressly delegated powers are not subject. . . .

The spending power of Congress is in addition to the legislative power and not subordinate to it. This independent grant of the power of the purse, and its very nature, involving in its exercise the duty to insure expenditure within the granted power presuppose freedom of selection among diverse ends and aims, and the capacity to impose such conditions as will render the choice effective. It is a contradiction in terms to say that there is power to spend for the national welfare, while rejecting any power to impose conditions reasonably adapted to the attainment of the end which alone would justify the expenditure.

The limitation now sanctioned must lead to absurd consequences. The government may give seeds to farmers, but may not condition the gift upon their being planted in places where they are most needed or even planted at all. The government may give money to the unemployed, but may not ask that those who get it shall give labor in return, or even use it to support their families. It may give money to sufferers from earthquake, fire, tornado, pestilence or flood, but may not impose conditions—health precautions designed to prevent the spread of disease, or induce the movement of population to safer or more sanitary areas. All that, because it is purchased regulation infringing state powers, must be left for the states, who are unable or unwilling to supply the necessary relief. . . .

That the governmental power of the purse is a great one is not now for the first time announced. . . .

The suggestion that it must now be curtailed by judicial fiat because it may be abused by unwise use hardly rises to the dignity of the arguments. So may judicial power be abused. "The power to tax is the power to destroy," but we do not, for that reason, doubt its existence, or hold that its efficacy is to be restricted by its incidental or collateral effects upon the states. . . .

A tortured construction of the Constitution is not to be justified by recourse to extreme examples of reckless congressional spending which might occur if courts could not prevent expenditures which, even if they could be thought to effect any national purpose, would be possible only by action of a legislature lost to all sense of public responsibility. Such suppositions are addressed to the mind accustomed to believe that it is the business of courts to sit in judgment on the wisdom of legislative action. Courts are not the only agency of government that must be assumed to have capacity to govern. Congress and the courts both unhappily may falter or be mistaken in the performance of their constitutional duty. But interpretation of our great charter of government which proceeds on any assumption that the responsibility for the preservation of our institutions is the exclusive concern of any one of the three branches of government, or that it alone can save them from destruction is far more likely, in the long run, "to obliterate the constituent members" of "an indestructible union of indestructible states" than the frank recognition that language, even of a constitution, may mean what it says: that the power to tax and spend includes the power to relieve a nationwide economic maladjustment by conditional gifts of money.

MR. JUSTICE BRANDEIS and MR. JUSTICE CARDOZO joined in this opinion.

Steward Machine Co. v. Davis
301 U.S. 548, 57 S.Ct. 883, 81 L.Ed. 1279 (1937)

The Social Security Act of 1935 required that employers of eight or more workers pay a federal excise tax based on their annual payroll. The taxpayer was allowed to credit against the federal tax (up to 90 percent thereof) amounts contributed to a state unemployment fund, provided the state fund met federal standards. The Steward Company, after paying the tax, filed a claim for refund and sued unsuccessfully in district court, claiming that the statute's primary aim was to force the states to enact unemployment laws at the behest of the federal government. Majority: Cardozo, Brandeis, Hughes, Roberts, Stone. Dissenting: Butler, McReynolds, Sutherland, Van Devanter.

MR. JUSTICE CARDOZO delivered the opinion of the Court. . . .

The assault on the statute proceeds on an extended front. Its assailants take the ground that the tax is not an excise; that it is not uniform throughout the United States as excises are required to be; that its exceptions are so many and arbitrary as to violate the Fifth Amendment; that its purpose was not revenue, but an unlawful invasion of the reserved powers of the states; and that the states in submitting to it have yielded to coercion and have abandoned governmental functions which they are not permitted to surrender. . . .

. . . The case for the petitioner is built on the contention that here an ulterior aim is wrought into the very structure of the act, and what is even more important that the aim is not only ulterior, but essentially unlawful. In particular, the 90 percent credit is relied upon as supporting that conclusion. But before the statute succumbs to an assault upon these lines, two propositions must be made out by the assailant. . . . There must be a showing in the first place that separated from the credit the revenue provisions are incapable of standing by themselves. There must be a showing in the second place that the tax and the credit in combination are weapons of coercion, destroying or impairing the autonomy of the states. The truth of each proposition being essential to the success of the assault, we pass for convenience to a consideration of the second, without pausing to inquire whether there has been a demonstration of the first.

To draw the line intelligently between duress and inducement there is need to remind ourselves of facts as to the problem of unemployment that are now matters of common knowledge. . . .

In the presence of this urgent need for some remedial expedient, the question is to be answered whether the expedient adopted has overleapt the bounds of power. The assailants of the statute say that its dominant end and aim is to drive the state legislatures under the whip of economic pressure into the enactment of unemployment compensation laws at the bidding of the central government. Supporters of the statute say that its operation is not constraint, but the creation of a larger freedom, the states and the nation joining in coöperative endeavor to avert a common evil. . . .

The Social Security Act is an attempt to find a method by which all these public agencies may work together to a common end. Every dollar of the new taxes will continue in all likelihood to be used and needed by the nation as long as states are unwilling, whether through timidity or for other motives, to do what can be done at home. At least the inference is permissible that Congress so believed, though retaining undiminished freedom to spend the money as it pleased. On the other hand

fulfilment of the home duty will be lightened and encouraged by crediting the taxpayer upon his account with the Treasury of the nation to the extent that his contributions under the laws of the locality have simplified or diminished the problem of relief and the probable demand upon the resources of the fisc. Duplicated taxes, or burdens that approach them, are recognized hardships that government, state or national, may properly avoid. . . . If Congress believed that the general welfare would better be promoted by relief through local units than by the system then in vogue, the coöperating localities ought not in all fairness to pay a second time.

Who then is coerced through the operation of this statute? Not the taxpayer. He pays in fulfillment of the mandate of the local legislature. Not the state. Even now she does not offer a suggestion that in passing the unemployment law she was affected by duress. . . . For all that appears she is satisfied with her choice, and would be sorely disappointed if it were now to be annulled. The difficulty with the petitioner's contention is that it confuses motive with coercion. "Every tax is in some measure regulatory. To some extent it interposes an economic impediment to the activity taxed as compared with others not taxed." . . . In like manner every rebate from a tax when conditioned upon conduct is in some measure a temptation. But to hold that motive or temptation is equivalent to coercion is to plunge the law in endless difficulties. The outcome of such a doctrine is the acceptance of a philosophical determinism by which choice becomes impossible. Till now the law has been guided by a robust common sense which assumes the freedom of the will as a working hypothesis in the solution of its problems. The wisdom of the hypothesis has illustration in this case. Nothing in the case suggests the exertion of a power akin to undue influence, if we assume that such a concept can ever be applied with fitness to the relations between the state and nation. Even on that assumption the location of the point at which pressure turns into compulsion, and ceases to be inducement, would be a question of degree,—at times, perhaps, of fact. . . .

The judgment is

Affirmed.

MR. JUSTICE BUTLER, dissenting. . . .

I am also of the opinion that, in principle and

as applied to bring about and to gain control over state unemployment compensation, the statutory scheme is repugnant to the Tenth Amendment: "The powers not delegated to the United States by the Constitution, nor prohibited by it to the States, are reserved to the States respectively, or to the people." The Constitution grants to the United States no power to pay unemployed persons or to require the states to enact laws or to raise or disburse money for that purpose. The provisions in question, if not amounting to coercion in a legal sense, are manifestly designed and intended directly to affect state action in the respects specified. And, if valid as so employed, this "tax and credit" device may be made effective to enable federal authorities to induce, if not indeed to compel, state enactments for any purpose within the realm of state power,

and generally to control state administration of state laws. . . .

Federal agencies prepared and took draft bills to state legislatures to enable and induce them to pass laws providing for unemployment compensation in accordance with federal requirements, and thus to obtain relief for the employers from the impending federal exaction. Obviously the Act creates the peril of federal tax not to raise revenue but to persuade. . . .

The terms of the measure make it clear that the tax and credit device was intended to enable federal officers virtually to control the exertion of powers of the states in a field in which they alone have jurisdiction and from which the United States is by the Constitution excluded.

Marchetti v. *United States**
390 U.S. 39, 88 S.Ct. 697, 19 L.Ed. 2d 889 (1968)

James Marchetti was convicted in United States District Court in Connecticut for violating the federal wagering tax statutes (26 U.S.C. 4411 and 4412). He argued unsuccessfully in the Second Circuit Court of Appeals that the registration requirement and occupation tax imposed on gamblers by the wagering laws infringed the Fifth Amendment privilege against self-incrimination. In *United States* v. *Kahriger* (1953) and *Lewis* v. *United States* (1955), the Supreme Court had rejected this constitutional attack. Justice Harlan's majority opinion, which follows, contains a detailed account of the operation of the tax laws. Majority: Harlan, Black, Brennan, Douglas, Fortas, Stewart, White. Dissenting: Warren. Not participating: Marshall.

MR. JUSTICE HARLAN delivered the opinion of the Court.

The provisions in issue here are part of an interrelated statutory system for taxing wagers. The system is broadly as follows. Section 4401 of Title 26 imposes upon those engaged in the business of accepting wagers an excise tax of 10% on the gross amount of all wagers they accept, including the value of chances purchased in lotteries conducted

for profit. Parimutuel wagering enterprises, coin-operated devices, and state-conducted sweepstakes are expressly excluded from taxation. . . . Section 4411 imposes in addition an occupational tax of $50 annually, both upon those subject to taxation under §4401 and upon those who receive wagers on their behalf.

The taxes are supplemented by ancillary provisions calculated to assure their collection. In particular, §4412 requires those liable for the occupational tax to register each year with the director of their internal revenue district. The registrants

* This case should also be read in connection with Chapter Nine.

must submit Internal Revenue Service Form 11-C, and upon it must provide their residence and business addresses, must indicate whether they are in the business of accepting wagers, and must list the names and addresses of their agents and employees. The statutory obligations to register and to pay the occupational tax are essentially inseparable elements of a single registration procedure; Form 11-C thus constitutes both the application for registration and the return for the occupational tax.

In addition, registrants are obliged to post the revenue stamps which denote payment of the occupational tax "conspicuously" in their principal places of business, or, if they lack such places, to keep the stamps on their persons, and to exhibit them upon demand to any Treasury officer. They are required to preserve daily records indicating the gross amount of the wagers as to which they are liable for taxation, and to permit inspection of their books of account. Moreover, each principal internal revenue office is instructed to maintain for public inspection a listing of all who have paid the occupational tax, and to provide certified copies of the listing upon request to any state or local prosecuting officer. Finally, payment of the wagering taxes is declared not to "exempt any person from any penalty provided by a law of the United States or of any State for engaging" in any taxable activity.

The issue before us is *not* whether the United States may tax activities which a State or Congress has declared unlawful. The Court has repeatedly indicated that the unlawfulness of an activity does not prevent its taxation, and nothing that follows is intended to limit or diminish the vitality of those cases. . . . The issue is instead whether the methods employed by Congress in the federal wagering tax statutes are, in this situation, consistent with the limitations created by the privilege against self-incrimination guaranteed by the Fifth Amendment. We must for this purpose first examine the implications of these statutory provisions.

Wagering and its ancillary activities are very widely prohibited under both federal and state law. Federal statutes impose criminal penalties upon the interstate transmission of wagering information; upon interstate and foreign travel or transportation in aid of racketeering enterprises, defined to include gambling; upon lotteries conducted through use of the mails or broadcasting; and upon the interstate transportation of wagering paraphernalia.

State and local enactments are more comprehensive. The laws of every State, except Nevada, include broad prohibitions against gambling, wagering, and associated activities. Every State forbids, with essentially minor and carefully circumscribed exceptions, lotteries. Even Nevada, which permits many forms of gambling, retains criminal penalties upon lotteries and certain other wagering activities taxable under these statutes. . . .

Information obtained as a consequence of the federal wagering tax laws is readily available to assist the efforts of state and federal authorities to enforce these penalties. Section 6107 of Title 26 requires the principal internal revenue offices to provide to prosecuting officers a listing of those who have paid the occupational tax. Section 6806(c) obliges taxpayers either to post the revenue stamp "conspicuously" in their principal places of business, or to keep it on their persons, and to produce it on the demand of Treasury officers. Evidence of the possession of a federal wagering tax stamp, or of payment of the wagering taxes, has often been admitted at trial in state and federal prosecutions for gambling offenses; such evidence has doubtless proved useful even more frequently to lead prosecuting authorities to other evidence upon which convictions have subsequently been obtained. Finally, we are obliged to notice that a former Commissioner of Internal Revenue has acknowledged that the Service "makes available" to law enforcement agencies the names and addresses of those who have paid the wagering taxes, and that it is in "full cooperation" with the efforts of the Attorney General of the United States to suppress organized gambling.

In these circumstances, it can scarcely be denied that the obligations to register and to pay the occupational tax created for petitioner "real and appreciable," and not merely "imaginary and unsubstantial," hazards of self-incrimination. . . .

. . . We emphasize that we do not hold that these wagering tax provisions are as such constitutionally impermissible; we hold only that those who properly assert the constitutional privilege as to these provisions may not be criminally punished for failure to comply with their requirements. If, in different circumstances, a taxpayer is not confronted by substantial hazards of self-incrimination, or if he is otherwise outside the privilege's protection, nothing we decide today would shield him from the various penalties prescribed by the wagering tax statutes.

The judgment of the Court of Appeals is

Reversed.

MR. CHIEF JUSTICE WARREN, dissenting. . . .

[The chief justice's dissent was appended to the companion case of *Grosso* v. *United States* (1968), decided on the same day as *Marchetti*.]

In addition to being in disagreement with the Court on the result it reaches in these cases, I am puzzled by the reasoning process which leads it to that result. The Court professes to recognize and accept the power of Congress legitimately to impose taxes on activities which have been declared unlawful by federal or state statutes. Yet, by its sweeping declaration that the congressional scheme for enforcing and collecting the taxes imposed on wagers and gamblers is unconstitutional, the Court has stripped from Congress the power to make its taxing scheme effective. A reading of the registration requirement of 26 USC §4412, as implemented by Internal Revenue Service Form 11-C, reveals that the information demanded of gamblers is no more than is necessary to assure that the tax collection process will be effective. Registration of those liable for special taxes is a common and integral feature of the tax laws. . . . So also is the requirement of public disclosure. And the reach of the registration and disclosure requirements extends to both lawful and unlawful activities. Because registration and disclosure are so pervasive in the Internal Revenue Code, it is clear that such requirements have been imposed by Congress to aid in the collection of taxes legitimately levied. Because most forms of gambling have been declared illegal in this country, gamblers necessarily operate furtively in the dark shadows of the underworld. Only by requiring that such individuals come forward under pain of criminal sanctions and reveal the nature and scope of their activities can Congress confidently expect that revenue derived from that outlawed occupation will be subject to the legitimate reach of the tax laws. Indeed, it seems to me that the very secrecy which surrounds the business of gambling demands disclosure. Those legislative committees and executive commissions which have studied the problems of illicit gambling activities have found it impossible to determine with any precision the gross revenues derived from that business. . . .

South Dakota v. *Dole*
483 U.S. 203, 107 S.Ct. 2793, 97 L.Ed. 2d 171 (1987)

In 1984 Congress enacted the National Minimum Drinking Age Amendment, referred to in the following opinions as §158. It directed the secretary of transportation to withhold 5 percent of federal highway funds from states "in which the purchase or public possession of any alcoholic beverage by a person who is less than twenty-one years of age is lawful." At the time South Dakota permitted persons 19 years of age or older to purchase beer containing 3.2 percent alcohol. The state sued in district court, asserting that the law exceeded Congress's spending power and that it violated the Twenty-first Amendment. The district court rejected South Dakota's claims, and the Court of Appeals for the Eighth Circuit affirmed. Majority: Rehnquist, Blackmun, Marshall, Powell, Scalia, Stevens, White. Dissenting: Brennan, O'Connor.

CHIEF JUSTICE REHNQUIST delivered the opinion of the Court. . . .

Despite the extended treatment of the question by the parties . . . we need not decide in this case whether that Amendment would prohibit an attempt by Congress to legislate directly a national minimum drinking age. Here, Congress has acted indirectly under its spending power to encourage uniformity in the States' drinking ages. As we explain below, we find this legislative effort within constitutional bounds even if Congress may not regulate drinking ages directly. . . .

The spending power is of course not unlimited, but is instead subject to several general restrictions articulated in our cases. The first of these limitations is derived from the language of the Constitution itself: the exercise of the spending power must be in pursuit of "the general welfare." In considering whether a particular expenditure is intended to serve general public purposes, courts should defer substantially to the judgment of Congress. Second, we have required that if Congress desires to condition the States' receipt of federal funds, it "must do so unambiguously . . . enabl[ing] the States to exercise their choice knowingly, cognizant of the consequences of their participation." Third, our cases have suggested (without significant elaboration) that conditions on federal grants might be illegitimate if they are unrelated "to the federal interest in particular national projects or programs." . . . Finally, we have noted that other constitutional provisions may provide an independent bar to the conditional grant of federal funds. . . .

South Dakota does not seriously claim that §158 is inconsistent with any of the first three restrictions mentioned above.

[T]he basic point of disagreement between the parties—is whether the Twenty-first Amendment constitutes an "independent constitutional bar" to the conditional grant of federal funds. Petitioner, relying on its view that the Twenty-first Amendment prohibits *direct* regulation of drinking ages by Congress, asserts that "Congress may not use the spending power to regulate that which it is prohibited from regulating directly under the Twenty-first Amendment." But our cases show that this "independent constitutional bar" limitation on the spending power is not of the kind petitioner suggests. *United States* v. *Butler,* for example, established that the constitutional limitations on Congress when exercising its spending power are less exacting than those on its authority to regulate directly.

We have also held that a perceived Tenth Amendment limitation on congressional regulation of state affairs did not concomitantly limit the range of conditions legitimately placed on federal grants. . . .

These cases establish that the "independent constitutional bar" limitation on the spending power is not, as petitioner suggests, a prohibition on the indirect achievement of objectives which Congress is not empowered to achieve directly. Instead, we think that the language in our earlier opinions stands for the unexceptionable proposition that the power may not be used to induce the States to engage in activities that would themselves be unconstitutional. Thus, for example, a grant of federal funds conditioned on invidiously discriminatory state action or the infliction of cruel and unusual punishment would be an illegitimate exercise of the Congress' broad spending power. But no such claim can be or is made here. Were South Dakota to succumb to the blandishments offered by Congress and raise its drinking age to 21, the State's action in so doing would not violate the constitutional rights of anyone.

Our decisions have recognized that in some circumstances the financial inducement offered by Congress might be so coercive as to pass the point at which "pressure turns into compulsion." Here, however, Congress has directed only that a State desiring to establish a minimum drinking age lower than 21 lose a relatively small percentage of certain federal highway funds. Petitioner contends that the coercive nature of this program is evident from the degree of success it has achieved. We cannot conclude, however, that a conditional grant of federal money of this sort is unconstitutional simply by reason of its success in achieving the congressional objective.

When we consider, for a moment, that all South Dakota would lose if she adheres to her chosen course as to a suitable minimum drinking age is 5% of the funds otherwise obtainable under specified highway grant programs, the argument as to coercion is shown be more rhetoric than fact. . . .

Accordingly, the judgment of the Court of Appeals is

Affirmed.

JUSTICE O'CONNOR, dissenting. . . .

[T]he Court's application of the requirement that the condition imposed be reasonably related to the purpose for which the funds are expended, is cursory and unconvincing. We have repeatedly said that Congress may condition grants under the Spending Power only in ways reasonably related to the purpose of the federal program. . . .

Aside from these "concessions" by counsel, the Court asserts the reasonableness of the relationship between the supposed purpose of the expenditure—"safe interstate travel"—and the drinking age condition. The Court reasons that Congress wishes that the roads it builds may be used safely, that drunk drivers threaten highway safety, and that young people are more likely to drive while under the influence of alcohol under existing law than would be the case if there were a uniform national drinking age of 21. It hardly needs saying, however, that if the purpose of §158 is to deter drunken driving, it is far too over- and under-inclusive. It is over-inclusive because it stops teenagers from drinking even when they are not about to drive on interstate highways. It is under-inclusive because teenagers pose only a small part of the drunken driving problem in this Nation. . . .

There is a clear place at which the Court can draw the line between permissible and impermissible conditions on federal grants. It is the line identified in the Brief for the National Conference of State Legislatures as *Amici Curiae:*

"Congress has the power to *spend* for the general welfare, it has the power to *legislate* only for delegated purposes. . . .

"The appropriate inquiry, then, is whether the spending requirement or prohibition is a condition on a grant or whether it is regulation. The difference turns on whether the requirement specifies in some way how the money should be spent, so that Congress' intent in making the grant will be effectuated. Congress has no power under the Spending Clause to impose requirements on a grant that go beyond specifying how the money should be spent. A requirement that is not such a specification is not a condition, but a regulation, which is valid only if it falls within one of Congress' delegated regulatory powers."

This approach harks back to *United States* v. *Butler,* the last case in which this Court struck down an Act of Congress as beyond the authority granted by the Spending Clause. There the Court wrote that "[t]here is an obvious difference between a statute stating the conditions upon which moneys shall be expended and one effective only upon assumption of a contractual obligation to submit to a regulation which otherwise could not be enforced." The *Butler* Court saw the Agricultural Adjustment Act for what it was—an exercise of regulatory, not spending, power. The error in *Butler* was not the Court's conclusion that the Act was essentially regulatory, but rather its crabbed view of the extent of Congress' regulatory power under the Commerce Clause. . . .

While *Butler*'s authority is questionable insofar as it assumes that Congress has no regulatory power over farm production, its discussion of the Spending Power and its description of both the power's breadth and its limitations remains sound. The Court's decision in *Butler* also properly recognizes the gravity of the task of appropriately limiting the Spending Power. If the Spending Power is to be limited only by Congress' notion of the general welfare, the reality, given the vast financial resources of the Federal Government, is that the Spending Clause gives "power to the Congress to tear down the barriers, to invade the states' jurisdiction, and to become a parliament of the whole people, subject to no restrictions save such as are self-imposed." This, of course, as *Butler* held, was not the Framers' plan and it is not the meaning of the Spending Clause.

Of the other possible sources of congressional authority for regulating the sale of liquor only the Commerce Power comes to mind. But in my view, the regulation of the age of the purchasers of liquor, just as the regulation of the price at which liquor may be sold, falls squarely within the scope of those powers reserved to the States by the Twenty-first Amendment. . . . Accordingly, Congress simply lacks power under the Commerce Clause to displace state regulation of this kind.

The immense size and power of the Government of the United States ought not obscure its fundamental character. It remains a Government of enumerated powers. . . .

EIGHT

The Contract Clause, Property Rights, and the Development of Due Process

Great constitutional provisions must be administered with caution. Some play must be allowed for the joints of the machine, and it must be remembered that legislatures are the ultimate guardians of the liberties and welfare of the people in quite as great a degree as the court.

—JUSTICE OLIVER WENDELL HOLMES, JR. (1904)

Heretofore we have been concerned with national power—the power of Congress to regulate commerce and to tax and spend, and the relation of congressional authority to state power in the same areas. Out of the Court's interpretation of national power emerged one of the first great antinomies of constitutional law—national supremacy versus dual federalism. By 1937 the Court had largely resolved that conflict in favor of national power.

This chapter features another major antinomy—the doctrines of vested rights versus state police power. Throughout much of our history, the state *police power* (the power to promote the health, safety, morals, and general welfare) has been limited by the commerce clause.* We are now to explore the limitations of state power that flow from the doctrine of vested rights. The chapter concludes with a review of Fifth Amendment "takings" and constitutional issues generated by the "new property."

The struggle between vested rights and police power is a variant of the earlier conflict between theories of natural rights, on the one hand, and the principle of legislative supremacy, on the other. On this side of the Atlantic, these two doctrines represent the reaction on each other of the prerevolutionary contest between the natural rights of the colonists and parliamentary supremacy. The same phenomenon was manifest after 1776 in the efforts of state legislative majorities to regulate the property and contract rights of individual citizens.

---

* The term *police power* itself appears in *Brown* v. *Maryland* (1827). Marshall speaks of the police power as residual, comprising what is left over of the state's power beyond those other great prerogatives, eminent domain and taxation.

THE DOCTRINE OF VESTED RIGHTS

Of the two doctrines, that of *vested rights* is of earlier origin, being rooted in the notion that property is the basic social institution. Antedating civil society itself, property fixes the limits within which even supreme legislative authority may properly operate. Indeed, the main function of government, its *raison d'être,* is to protect property. "The right of acquiring and possessing property and having it protected," Justice Paterson wrote in an early circuit court opinion, "is one of the natural inherent and unalienable rights of man. Men have a sense of property: property is necessary to their subsistence, and correspondent to their natural wants and desires; its security was one of the objects that induced them to unite in society. No man would become a member of a community in which he could not enjoy the fruits of his honest labor and industry. The preservation of property, then, is a primary object of the social compact" (*Van Horne's Lessee* v. *Dorrance,* 1795).

Among the major causes of the federal Convention of 1787 was the "injustice" of state laws concerning property, bringing into question "the fundamental principle of republican government, that the majority who rule in such governments are the safest guardians both of public good and private rights." The point is illustrated in the colloquy that occurred in the early days of the Philadelphia Convention between Roger Sherman and James Madison. Sherman had enumerated the objects of the Convention as defense against foreign danger and internal disputes and the need for a central authority to make treaties with foreign nations and to regulate foreign commerce. Madison agreed that these objects were important but insisted on combining with them "the necessity of providing more effectually for *the security of private rights* and the steady dispensation of justice within the states." "Interferences with these," Madison added, "were evils which had, more perhaps than anything else, produced this convention." What Madison had in mind was state legislation on behalf of the financially embarrassed but politically dominant small-farmer class, led by such rabble-rousers as Daniel Shays in Massachusetts—men seeking special legislation to alter under the standing law the rights of designated parties; intervention by state legislatures in private controversies pending in, or already decided by, the ordinary courts; and legislation setting aside judgments, granting new hearings, voiding valid wills, or validating void wills. Those who wished to see the menace of special legislation and state legislative supremacy abated, those who felt the need for outside protection of the rights of property and of contract, naturally supported the movement afoot for a Constitutional Convention.

But how were the framers to secure such protection? Various measures were proposed, but every motion looking to the imposition of property qualification for suffrage or office holding failed. The suggestion that the Senate be organized as a barrier for property was also defeated. The difficult and delicate matter of suffrage was ultimately left to the states. As the Constitution came from the hands of the framers, it contained only one brief clause that might afford vested rights protection against state legislative majorities—Article 1, Section 10: "No State shall . . . pass any . . . ex post facto law or laws impairing the obligation of contracts. . . ." When it came up for interpretation in *Calder* v. *Bull,* even this clause was given a very narrow interpretation. Confining the application of ex post facto to retroactive penal legislation, the Court held that it was not "inserted to secure the citizen in his private rights of either property or contracts." This decision, creating a wide breach in the constitutional protection afforded civil rights, aroused widespread criticism. Even Justice Chase, who delivered the opinion, seemed apologetic, suggesting that legislation adversely affecting vested rights might be set aside as violation of natural law. "There are certain vital principles," Chase observed, "in our free republican governments which will determine and overrule an apparent and flagrant abuse of legislative power. An act of the legislature (for I cannot call it a law) contrary to the great principles of the social compact cannot be considered a rightful exercise of the legislative authority."

But Chase's associate Justice Iredell questioned the validity of natural law limitations on legislative power. He characterized such talk as the plaything of "some speculative jurists" and said that if the Constitution itself imposed no checks on legislative power, "whatever the legislature chose to enact would be lawfully enacted, and the judicial power could never interpose to pronounce it void." "The ideas of natural justice are regulated by no fixed standard," Iredell commented. "The ablest and purest of men have differed upon the subject, and all that the Court could properly say in such an event would be that the legislature . . . had passed an act which, in the opinion of the judges, was inconsistent with abstract principles of justice."

Which of these views on the scope of judicial power has prevailed? In appearance Iredell's, but (as we shall see) at the end of the nineteenth century Chase's views were for all practical purposes triumphant. By 1890 the Court achieved, under the due process clause of the Fourteenth Amendment, the very power to supervise and control legislative action in relation to abstract principles of justice against which Iredell had so strongly protested.

THE EXPANSION OF THE CONTRACT CLAUSE

Calder v. *Bull* was a binding precedent in 1810, when *Fletcher* v. *Peck* came before Chief Justice Marshall. "Marshall," Professor Corwin observed, found in *Fletcher* v. *Peck* "a task of restoration awaiting him in that great field of Constitutional Law which defines state power in relation to private rights." Hamilton had laid solid foundations for an effective national government; no such preliminary work had been done in the task now confronting the chief justice. Indeed, *Calder* v. *Bull* presented a well-nigh insuperable barrier.

Fletcher v. *Peck* illustrates the speculative spirit rife in America at the close of the 1700s. Land companies found Georgia an especially inviting field. Between 1789 and 1795 speculators badgered the Georgia legislators without success. Finally, however, on January 7, 1795, the governor of Georgia signed a bill granting the greater part of what is now Alabama and Mississippi to four groups of purchasers, known as the Yazoo Land Companies, at 1½ cents per acre. The "purchasers" included men of national reputation and local politicians (all but one member of the Georgia legislature who voted for the act held shares in one or more of the companies). Indignation ran high and in 1796 a new legislature repealed the land-grab act. By the time of repeal some of the lands had passed into the hands of purchasers, mostly Boston capitalists, who in turn sold extensively to investors in New England and the Middle Atlantic states.

Contending that the repeal act of 1796 could not constitutionally divest them of their titles, these innocent purchasers decided to test their rights in the federal courts. The case, an "arranged" suit, first came before the Supreme Court in the 1809 term; it was reargued the next year, and a decision was rendered on March 16, 1810. Sustaining the contention of the Yazoo claimants, Chief Justice Marshall held that the 1796 repeal act was an unconstitutional impairment of the obligation of a contract. At the outset Marshall suggested that the rescinding act of the Georgia legislature was void as a violation of vested rights, and hence contrary to the underlying principles of society and government. But apparently realizing that a decision based on such flimsy ground would be less secure than one grounded in the Constitution, he turned to the contract clause. In doing this, he was confronted with two difficulties: First, the sort of contract the framers had in mind must have been executory— a contract in which the obligation of performance is still to be discharged. Marshall got around this by saying that every grant is attended by an implied contract on the part of the grantor not to reassert his or her right to the thing granted. Therefore, the clause covered executed contracts in which performance has been fulfilled as well as executory contracts.

The greater difficulty was that the contract before the Court was *public,* not private. In private contracts it is easy enough to distinguish the contract as an agreement between the parties from the obligation that comes from the law and holds the parties to their agreement. Who, in this case, was to hold Georgia to its engagement? Certainly not Georgia, which had passed the rescinding act, nor the Georgia state court. Marshall escaped the dilemma by ruling that Georgia's obligation was moral and that this moral injunction had been elevated to legal status by Article 1, Section 10—"a Bill of Rights for the people of each State," Marshall called it.

But the chief justice was uncertain at the very end. The last paragraph of his opinion states that Georgia was restrained from passing the rescinding act "either by general principles that are common to our free institutions, or by particular provisions of the Constitution."

Fletcher v. *Peck* went a long way toward bridging the gap opened by *Calder* v. *Bull* in the constitutional protection of private rights. But since Marshall's ruling was somewhat ambiguous, there remained the question of whether the obligation-of-contract clause safeguarded corporate charters as well as public grants against legislative interference. In 1819, by his opinion in the **Dartmouth College Case,** Marshall filled in the breach Justice Chase had created in the constitutional protection of vested rights.

The college's original charter was granted by the King of England. Parliament could have destroyed it at any time before 1776, and before 1788 the state of New Hampshire could have wiped it out. After that year, Marshall held that it must continue in perpetuity. His opinion adds up to these propositions: The college was not public, but a "private eleemosynary institution"; its charter was the outgrowth of a contract between the original donors and the Crown; the trustees represented the interest of the donors; the Constitution protects this representative interest.

Marshall agonized at only one point. The requirement of the obligation-of-contract clause was admittedly designed to protect those having a vested beneficial interest. No one then living, not even the trustees, had any such interest in Dartmouth College. But Marshall held that the case came within the spirit, if not the words, of the Constitution.

The nub of Marshall's decision is the proposition that any ambiguity in a charter must be construed in favor of the adventurers and against the state. With perpetuity thus implied, the college charter was placed beyond the reach of the legislature. By that same token, the charters of profit-seeking corporations were likewise beyond the control of legislative majorities. In short, the doctrine of vested rights, heretofore having no safeguard except the principles of natural law, now enjoyed the solid protection of a specific provision of the Constitution—the impairment-of-contract clause.

In a separate opinion in the Dartmouth College Case, Marshall's scholarly colleague Joseph Story suggested the means by which states might in the future avoid the restrictive effect of Marshall's holding. Speaking of the state's power over corporations, Story observed that there was "no other control, than what is expressly or implicitly reserved by the charter itself."

As early as 1805 Virginia had used a *reservation clause* (reserving to the state the power to alter, amend, or repeal a charter) in special incorporation acts. In 1827, following the Dartmouth decision, New York enacted a general law making all charters "hereafter granted . . . subject to alteration, suspension and repeal, in the discretion of the legislature." All states now have such a provision in their constitutions, in general acts, or in both.

By 1830, the doctrine of vested rights, as limiting legislative power, was nevertheless accepted in a majority of the states and by leading lawyers and judges. This meant that property rights fixed the contours within which the legislature exercised its powers. The Court felt obliged to enforce these limitations even in the absence of specific provisions of the Constitution. In Justice Story's words, "That government can scarcely be deemed to be free where the rights of property are left solely dependent upon the will of a legislative body without any restraint. The fundamental maxims of a free government seem to require that the rights of personal liberty and private property should be sacred." These were America's "preferred freedoms"—values so generally recognized and accepted that no such phrase was needed to describe them.

THE DEVELOPMENT OF THE POLICE POWER

Meanwhile political forces of great significance for the development of constitutional law were taking shape. The year 1828 saw the election as president of the democratically inclined Andrew Jackson; in the same decade Massachusetts, New York, and Virginia called conventions to remove certain constitutional safeguards for economic privilege and to liberalize the suffrage. Out of all this emerged the doctrine of *popular sovereignty,* the notion that the will of the people is to be discovered at the ballot box, not merely in a document framed in 1787. The juristic expression of popular sovereignty is the doctrine of the police power, which was given classic expression and interpretation in 1837 by Jackson's appointee and Marshall's successor, Roger Brooke Taney.

The two cases of Dartmouth College and **Charles River Bridge** illustrate two alternate approaches to progress. Chief Justice Marshall's thoughts turned toward security of property and contract rights against government encroachment. Without losing sight of these values, Chief Justice Taney argued that the community also has rights and it is the object and end of government to promote the prosperity and happiness of all.

In the License Cases of 1847, Taney gave the state police power succinct definition: "The power to *govern men and things* within the limits of its own dominion." A concept of incalculable potential, "police power" came to mean not only legislative authority to remove government-created privilege, as in the Charles River Bridge Case, but also sanction for state legislation having broad social purpose. Coming in 1837 at the peak of Jackson's power and prestige, Taney's doctrine of the police power did in fact stimulate considerable legislative activity.

After the Charles River Bridge decision, rejecting *implied contracts,* the contract clause never regained its earlier stature as a barrier against legislative encroachment on property rights. Indeed, in 1934, in one of the first cases foreshadowing the ultimately favorable constitutional fate of the New Deal (*Home Building and Loan Association* v. *Blaisdell*), the justices, voting 5 to 4, refused to hold that the contract clause had been breached by a state statute changing the terms of mortgage contracts. The legislation seemed to fly in the face of Article 1, Section 10. Distinguishing between the *obligation* of the contract and the *remedy,* Chief Justice Hughes tried to demonstrate that the moratorium placed on mortgage foreclosures did not impair the obligation; the statute merely modified the remedy, explaining that "while emergency does not create power, emergency may furnish the occasion for the exercise of power." Justices Cardozo and Stone read the chief justice's first draft with misgivings so serious that each considered writing a concurring opinion. The former actually prepared a draft (reprinted in this chapter), and Stone submitted a long memorandum.

The chief justice's opinion, as finally announced, included long passages from Cardozo's unpublished concurring opinion and from Stone's memorandum. But he kept intact the legalistic logomachy about "emergency," thus exposing himself to dissenting Justice Sutherland's broadside.

In *El Paso* v. *Simmons* (1965), the Court's flexible interpretation of the obligation-of-contract clause won well-nigh unanimous support. Eight justices, only Black dissenting, held that not every modification of a contractual promise, even one embodied in a state statute, impairs the obligation of contract. Denying that the Minnesota Moratorium decision furnished foundations for the majority's decision, Justice Black accused his colleagues of "balancing away the plain guarantee of Article 1, Section 10 . . . ," of justifying a state in taking "a man's private property for public use without compensation in violation of the plain guarantee of the Fifth Amendment, made applicable to the States by the Fourteenth. . . ." That some life remains in the contract clause is evident from Justice Blackmun's opinion in *United States Trust Co.* v. *New Jersey,* decided in 1977.

THE ORIGINS OF DUE PROCESS

Meanwhile a new judicial formula had been found for defeating government action under the police power. The 1830s had seen the establishment of the public school system; the 1840s witnessed the first steps toward regulation of the liquor traffic and primitive factory legislation. The character and volume of social legislation created the need for a new constitutional weapon. Special credit for the invention of that weapon must go to the New York Court of Appeals—and to the leading case of *Wynehamer* v. *New York* (1856).

The defendant, Wynehamer, was indicted and convicted by a jury in the Court of Sessions of Erie County for selling liquor in small quantities contrary to the act, passed April 9, 1855, "for the prevention of intemperance, pauperism and crime." It was admitted that the defendant owned the liquors in question before and at the time the law took effect. But on appeal Wynehamer's counsel insisted that he was entitled to an acquittal on the ground, among others, that the statute was unconstitutional and void. The Court agreed.

Judge Comstock, who spoke for the New York court, noted that, although "the legislative power" is vested in the legislature, it is subject to special constitutional limitations, "which are of very great interest and importance" in that they prohibit the deprivation of life, liberty, and property without due process of law.

He thus introduced a constitutional injunction of tremendous possibilities—"due process." What does it mean? To the lay mind this phrase suggests procedural limitations— that is, if it limits legislative power at all, it does so in terms not of what can be done but of *how* something must be done. Comstock and the concurring justices made clear that they had something more sweeping in mind. Since the legislature has only limited powers, it cannot encroach, Comstock contended, on the rights of any species of property, even where the action would be of "absolute benefit" to the people of the state. To allow the legislature such a power, even in the public interest, would "subvert the fundamental idea of property." "In a government like ours," Comstock observed, "theories of public good or public necessity may be so plausible, or even so truthful, as to command popular majorities. But whether truthful or plausible merely, and by whatever numbers they are assented to, there are some absolute private rights beyond their reach, and among these the constitution places the right of property." According to Comstock, due process placed *substantive* as well as procedural restraints on legislative power.

Thus, by mid-nineteenth century two great forces were meeting head on: the doctrine of vested rights and the doctrine of the police power. Professor Edward Corwin suggested that on the eve of the Civil War, courts and country were faced with a reincarnation of the old conundrum: What happens when an irresistible force—the doctrine of the police power—meets an immovable object—the doctrine of vested rights? What, moreover, was to be the role of the courts in this situation?

Confronted with cases such as that of Charles River Bridge, Edward Corwin suggested that the courts might have done one of two things: surrender the view that rights of property and of contract set absolute barriers against the exercise of public power, or cast about for a new constitutional formula to protect vested rights against regulatory legislative power. Would the phrase *due process* serve this purpose? Could a term suggesting procedural limitations only be fashioned into a limitation on substantive lawmaking? The great significance of *Wynehamer* is that it evoked in 1856 due process of law as a constitutional measure not only of *how* but also of *what* legislative power should be exercised.

JUDICIAL RESTRAINT AND THE FOURTEENTH AMENDMENT

Two major events made 1868 a landmark in the development of "due process": the publication of Thomas M. Cooley's classic work *Constitutional Limitations* and the adoption of the Fourteenth Amendment. Cooley's treatise contains chapters of special interest: Chapter 11, "Protection of Property by the Law of the Land," and Chapter 16, "The Police Power and the States." "Thus was the national Supreme Court," Corwin observed, ". . . supplied with a double set of answers, each duly authenticated by supporting precedents . . . touching the vital problem of the relation of legislative power to the property right." The Fourteenth Amendment added a weapon of untold potentialities to the judicial arsenal; henceforth the battles to protect property rights against state regulation were destined to revolve around "due process." Accordionlike in its contour, it was broad enough to embrace the concept of natural law.

Despite the unlimited potential latent in the Fourteenth Amendment for the enhancement of the Court's supervisory power, the justices were at first reluctant to exploit this new source of authority. In the **Slaughterhouse Cases** of 1873, Justice Miller and four colleagues refused to construe the privileges and immunities clause as breaking down the distinction between state and national citizenship. The purpose of the framers of the Fourteenth Amendment was not to confer on the national government the duty of protecting both kinds of citizenship. National citizenship included the right of coming to the seat of the government, the right to enjoy government offices, and the right to government protection on the high seas, whereas state citizenship included, among other rights, the fundamental right to acquire and possess property. Since the rights allegedly infringed in the Slaughterhouse Cases were derived from state citizenship, the butchers of New Orleans could not, in Miller's opinion, look beyond the state for protection.

Justice Miller was equally cool to the application of the equal protection and due process clauses. As for equal protection, he doubted its relevance except in cases involving the rights of blacks. Due process had not yet been the subject of much construction, but under no interpretation he had yet seen could the challenged statute be held lacking in due process. Why did Miller take such a narrow view of judicial power? Essentially it grew out of his conception of the Union—"the structure and spirit of our institutions." The Fourteenth Amendment did not change "the whole theory of the relations of the State and Federal governments to each other and of both these governments to the people." "Such a ruling," Miller said, "would constitute this Court a perpetual censor upon all legislation of the states on the civil rights of their own citizens, with authority to nullify such as it did not approve."

Involved was a theory of federalism. Justice Miller noted that the framers had "divided on the line which should separate the powers of the national government from those of the state governments." The prevailing sense of danger from federal power had motivated the drive for adoption of the first 11 amendments. The Civil War alerted the nation to the fact that "the true danger to the perpetuity of the Union" was "the capacity of the state organizations . . . for determined resistance to the General Government." The Civil War amendments, especially the Fourteenth, reflect this fear. Now, the Court felt duty-bound to curb any effort to change the federal balance, even by the amending process.

Judicial hands-off was maintained four years later in *Munn* v. *Illinois* in which a statute fixing rates for grain elevators was challenged. Harking back to principles of common law, Chief Justice Waite reasoned that when a man devotes his property to a use in which the public has an interest, the property ceases to be private; it becomes "affected with a public interest," and hence subject to a greater degree of regulation. The legislature, not the Court, was to determine how much regulation was permissible, whether it was arbitrary, and whether the business was so affected.

For almost a century the existence of the due process clause in the Fifth Amendment had not created any serious limitation on the substance of national legislation. But the clause was no sooner inserted in the Fourteenth Amendment than it became a rallying point for those who resisted the effort of government to regulate and control the expanding industrial economy. The next decade was to see the latter view prevail. Thus the breach left by *Munn* in the wall of protection around vested rights was destined to be closed, just as the same breach had been bridged by Chief Justice Marshall when he expanded the scope of the contract clause to overcome the decision in *Calder* v. *Bull*. Various forces and factors were joined in this movement.

THE FOURTEENTH AMENDMENT JUDICIALLY AMENDED

In 1878, one year after *Munn*, the American Bar Association was organized. By 1881 it was embarked on a deliberate and persistent campaign of education designed to reverse the Court's broad conception of legislative power. The chief burden of the association's campaign was to convince the nation that judges "discover" law rather than "make" it. In the annual addresses of the president and the titles of various papers, it is evident that the association stood with John Stuart Mill for individualism, agreed with Charles Darwin's view of the inevitability of the human struggle, and accepted Herbert Spencer's evolutionary theories of politics. Extracts from addresses reveal such thoughts as "The great curse of the world is too much government"; "Forces which make for growth should be left absolutely free to all"; "Ownership and responsibility are now individual"; "If trusts are a defensive weapon of property interests against the communistic trend, they are desirable"; "Monopoly is often a necessity and an advantage."

A shift in the Court's view, embodied in *Munn* v. *Illinois,* came swiftly. In 1882, Roscoe Conkling made his famous argument in *San Mateo Co.* v. *Southern Pacific R.R.* (1883). Conkling, who had been a member of the Joint Congressional Committee that drafted the Fourteenth Amendment in 1866, revealed for the first time a manuscript Journal of the Joint Committee. From this authoritative source he selected extensive quotations to show that he and his colleagues in drafting the equal protection and the due process clauses purposefully used the word *person* as including corporations. Within a few years after Conkling's revelations, the Court began veering away from the narrow black-race protection theory expounded by Miller in the Slaughterhouse Cases, away from the narrow conception of judicial review under due process propounded by Waite in *Munn* v. *Illinois,* and accepted Conkling's theory that corporations were persons under the due process clause (*Santa Clara Co.* v. *Southern Pacific R.R.,* 1886). Yet scholarly research has revealed that Conkling sold the Court a constitutional bill of goods. In 1938, Howard Jay Graham showed that Conkling's "conspiracy" theory of the Fourteenth Amendment was a fraud, or at least a trick unworthy of a great lawyer. Graham's conclusion was that Conkling "suppressed" pertinent facts and misrepresented others; he "deliberately misquoted the Journal [of the Joint Committee] and even arranged his excerpts so as to give his listeners a false impression of the record and his own relation thereto."

Nevertheless, Conkling's argument received strong support. The impending shift for which the dissenters in the Munn and Slaughterhouse cases had argued was evidenced in majority opinions. Justice Harlan, speaking for the Court in *Mugler* v. *Kansas* (1887), commented, "It does not at all follow that every statute enacted ostensibly for the promotion of these ends [morals and welfare] is to be accepted as a legitimate exertion of the police powers of the state." Legitimacy was to be determined by the Court. "The courts are not bound by mere forms, nor are they to be misled by mere pretenses. They are at liberty—indeed, are under a solemn duty—to look at the substance of things."

Three factors had been at work to effect this judicial revolution—the bar association's propaganda campaign, Conkling's so-called conspiracy theory of the Fourteenth Amendment, and powerful dissenting opinions. In 1887 and 1890 a fourth element was added—change in judicial personnel. Between 1877 and 1890 seven justices who had participated in the Slaughterhouse and Munn cases resigned or died. Field lived on, and in 1888 he was joined by his nephew David J. Brewer and Chief Justice Melville W. Fuller.

With new Justices came a repudiation of the hands-off approach of *Munn*. In *Chicago, Milwaukee & St. Paul R.R. Co.* v. *Minnesota* (1890) six justices decided that the question of the reasonableness of rates could not be left by the legislature to a state commission but must be subject to judicial review. This decision completed a judicial revolution. The Court had now become what Justice Miller had feared—a "perpetual censor" of state legislation under the due process clause of the Fourteenth Amendment. "From that decision," Judge Charles M. Hough wrote, "I date the flood."

The new view was reflected in remarks Justice David J. Brewer made to the New York Bar Association in 1893. Linking Herbert Spencer, the British sociologist, with Plato, taking account of the state of affairs and of popular and professional protest against the expansion of judicial power, Brewer advocated judicial activism—"Strengthening the judiciary." Brewer believed with Judge John F. Dillon that the Supreme Court was "the only breakwater against the haste and the passions of the people—against the tumultuous ocean of democracy."

The most reasoned response to Justice Brewer's advocacy of judicial activism came from Harvard law professor James Bradley Thayer, who proclaimed the standard for judicial self-restraint. Justice Frankfurter later rated Thayer's article of 1893 "the most important single essay in constitutional law . . . , the great guide for judges, and the great guide for understanding by nonjudges." Excerpts from both Thayer and Brewer appear as an "unstaged debate" in this chapter.

MEASURING THE IMMEASURABLE

Until the Court's about-face in 1937 (see Chapter Six), Thayer's sober counsel was to no avail. Armed with the power to decide matters of "right" and "wrong," the Court played a role it had earlier spurned. Virtually a superlegislature, the Court proceeded to discharge the delicate responsibility of mediating between public power and private rights. Due process was a poor measuring instrument because it varied according to the user. But its very uncertainty as a test of what the legislatures might do was useful for judges who wanted to be able to say no, and yet plead inability to say what might be done in the future or precisely what was wrong with that which had been done in the past. It would seem, then, that Justice Iredell's scorn of natural law as a limitation on state legislative power in *Calder* v. *Bull* might be applied equally well to due process. Since this concept provided no "fixed standard," all the Court could properly say in raising it as a constitutional bar was that the legislature had passed an act that, in the opinion of the judges, was inconsistent with abstract principles of justice.

Once the Court abandoned its previous attitude of judicial self-restraint, how could the justices avoid reading their own predilections into the Constitution? The problem was squarely presented in 1905 in the famous Bake Shop Case (***Lochner* v. *New York***). Justice Peckham's measure of "due process" in delivering the Court's opinion contrasts sharply with that of Holmes in dissent. Peckham invoked that most unscientific test, "common understanding"; "to common understanding," said Peckham in striking down New York's maximum hours law for bakers, "the trade of a baker has never been regarded as an unhealthy one."

Holmes denounced any such use of due process: The Constitution had not enacted Herbert Spencer's social statics or any other social or economic theory. Against Peckham's test of "common understanding," Holmes argued for the "natural outcome of a dominant opinion." Although the legislature was limited by prohibitory words in the Constitution, and by whether "a rational and fair man necessarily would admit that the statute proposed would infringe fundamental principles as they have been understood by the traditions of our people and our law," the presumed reasonableness of legislative majorities should be the rule, unreasonableness the exception. But was it not somewhat presumptuous for Holmes to suggest that the five justices in the majority were less "rational and fair" than himself and the three who agreed with him?

Justice Harlan, also dissenting, came to grips more effectively than Holmes with the central issue in the case: What is the proper scope of judicial power in this area, and how should this power be exercised? "If," Harlan answered, "the end the legislature seeks to accomplish be one to which its power extends, and if the means employed to that end, although not the wisest or best, are yet not plainly and palpably unauthorized by law, then the Court cannot interfere."

The dissenter was not content to let the matter rest there. Peckham indicated that if a real and substantial relation between the health of bakers and the hours they worked could be shown, the New York act might be sustained. Acting on this suggestion, meeting the majority on its own grounds, Justice Harlan proceeded to demonstrate by recourse to nonlegal sources (ignored by both Peckham and Holmes) that " 'the labor of the bakers is among the hardest and most laborious imaginable.' " Not only had hours of labor long been "a subject of consideration among civilized people," but "we also judicially know that the number of hours that should constitute a day's labor in particular occupations . . . has been the subject of enactments by Congress and by nearly all the states." Therefore, the New York statute could "not be held to be in conflict with the Fourteenth Amendment, without enlarging the scope of the amendment far beyond its original purpose, and without bringing under the supervision of this court matters which have been supposed to belong exclusively to the legislative departments of the several states when exerting their conceded power to guard the health and safety of their citizens by such regulations as they in their wisdom deem best."

THE BRANDEIS BRIEF

From the Lochner decision Justice Harlan anticipated "consequences of a far-reaching and mischievous character." Reformers shared these forebodings; they realized that if social legislation were to be saved from judicial obscurantism, a different approach would have to be made. In 1907 the National Consumers League, learning that the Oregon ten-hour law for women was soon to be contested in the Supreme Court, began a search for outstanding counsel to present the case in support of the Oregon law. Joseph H. Choate, one of the most distinguished and successful lawyers of his time, the man who had blocked the "march of Communism" in the Income Tax Case of 1895 (see Chapter Seven), refused a retainer, saying that he saw no reason why "a big husky Irish woman should not work more than ten hours in a laundry if she and her employers so desired." The day after Choate's refusal, Louis D. Brandeis of Boston accepted the retainer and began work on his now famous factual brief in *Muller* v. *Oregon* (1908).

At the turn of the century judges generally disliked hours-of-labor regulation. "In our judgment," Peckham had said in *Lochner,* "it is not possible *in fact* to discover the connection between the number of hours a baker must work in a bakery and the healthful quality of the bread made by the workman" (emphasis added). Brandeis, accepting this challenge, took a bold and unprecedented step: He furnished the Court with the requisite social and economic statistics to *demonstrate* this factual relationship between working hours and public health and safety. Heretofore no lawyer had had confidence in his ability to make the judges see a "reasonable" relation grounded in facts whether they wanted to see it or not. Brandeis had confidence in both himself and the judges.

Instead of the usual array of legal precedents, Brandeis produced facts and statistics on women's health needs in order to show that the legislation was within the legal principles already enumerated by the Court. He brought to a court disposed to make economic and social judgments—a power, one may well argue, never intended—a method for performing its task more intelligently and more fairly. His brief contained two pages of conventional legal arguments and over 100 pages of factual data drawn from the reports and studies of government bureaus, legislative committees, commissions on hygiene, and factory inspections— all proving that long hours are, *as a matter of fact,* dangerous to women's health, safety, and morals, and that short hours result in general social and economic benefits.

The ten-hour law was upheld and a more tolerant judicial attitude soon became apparent. In 1917 the Court upheld (*Bunting* v. *Oregon*) a ten-hour-day law with an overtime provision for men. "There is a contention made," the Court observed, "that the law, even regarded as regulating hours of service, is not either necessary or useful for the preservation of the health of employees in mills, factories and manufacturing establishments. The record contains no facts to support the contention and against it is the judgment of the legislature and the Supreme Court [of Oregon]." The burden of proof had been shifted from the state to those contesting the legislation.

Such "liberalism" was short-lived. Brandeis himself was appointed to the bench in 1916, but his appointment did little more than balance President Woodrow Wilson's earlier elevation of his attorney general, James C. McReynolds, to associate justice. Within a few years Warren G. Harding succeeded Wilson and named William Howard Taft chief justice and George Sutherland associate justice. So skepticism continued to mark the conservative justices' attitudes toward facts. For example, Justice Sutherland, confronted in 1923 with a mass of sociological data in support of the validity of a District of Columbia act regulating women's wages, brushed all such extralegal matter aside as "interesting, but only mildly persuasive" (*Adkins* v. *Children's Hospital*). "Freedom of contract is the general rule," Sutherland commented in setting aside the wage law, "restraint the exception."

In contrast, Justice Brandeis considered the Court's function circumscribed whether he approved or disapproved of a particular economic policy. In 1925 the Oklahoma legislature provided that no one could engage in the manufacture of ice for sale without obtaining a license. If on investigation the state commission found that the community was adequately served, it might turn down the bid of a would-be competitor, and in this way, perhaps, advance monopoly. On its face, this legislation encouraged precisely the trend Brandeis had tried to prevent. "The control here asserted," the Court ruled in a 6-to-2 opinion setting aside the act, "does not protect against monopoly, but tends to foster it." Yet Brandeis, in dissent, voted to uphold the regulation. "Our function," he wrote, "is only to determine the reasonableness of the legislature's belief in the existence of evils and in the effectiveness of the remedy provided." Amid economic emergency "more serious than war," Brandeis observed,

> There must be power in the States and the Nation to remould, through experimentation, our economic practices and institutions to meet changing social and economic needs. . . . This Court has the power to prevent an experiment. We may strike down the statute which embodies it on the ground that, in our opinion, the measure is arbitrary, capricious, or unreasonable. . . . But in the exercise of this high power, we must be ever on guard, lest we erect our prejudices into legal principles. If we would guide by the light of reason, we must let our minds be bold. (*New State Ice Co.* v. *Liebmann*, 1932)

THE DECLINE OF SUBSTANTIVE DUE PROCESS

Two cases decided in 1934 indicated a return to judicial restraint. In **Home Building and Loan Assn. v. Blaisdell,** a Minnesota emergency statute postponing the foreclosure of farm loans was upheld. In **Nebbia v. New York** the Court sustained a New York statute fixing minimum and maximum milk prices. Justice Roberts, rejecting the old "business affected with a public interest" concept as a limitation on state action, observed, "There is no closed class or category of business affected with a public interest." Concerning the high barrier earlier decisions had erected about wages and prices, Roberts observed, "The due process clause makes no mention of sales or of prices any more than it speaks of business or contract. . . . The thought seems nevertheless to have persisted that there is something peculiarly sacrosanct about the price one may charge for what he makes or sells."

"With the wisdom of the policy adopted," Justice Roberts added, "the Courts are both incompetent and unauthorized to deal." "But plainly," Justice McReynolds retorted in dissent, "I think this Court must have regard to the wisdom of the enactment."

Both *Blaisdell* and *Nebbia* were decided by votes of 5 to 4, but in 1936 (*Morehead* v. *New York ex rel. Tipaldo*) the justices virtually returned, in the face of these more recent rulings, to the discredited *Adkins* precedent of 1923. Nevertheless, it was soon evident that *Nebbia* had marked the beginning of the end of due process as a substantive limitation on legislation affecting economic rights. The death blow came in 1937 in *West Coast Hotel Co.* v. *Parrish,* where *Adkins* was expressly overruled. Upholding the minimum wage for women, Chief Justice Hughes asked, "What is freedom? The Constitution does not speak of liberty of contract. It speaks of liberty and prohibits the deprivation of liberty without due process of law. In prohibiting that deprivation, the Constitution does not recognize an absolute and uncontrollable liberty. Liberty in each of its phases has its history and connotation. But the liberty safeguarded is liberty in a social organization which requires the protection of law against the evils which menace the health, safety, morals and welfare of the people." Liberty could be infringed by forces other than government, and infringement by those forces may require the affirmative action of government for its protection.

The Court relinquished a self-acquired guardianship. Due process would no longer serve as a shield against the substance of commercial regulations. Within a year, without a single change in judicial personnel, "self-restraint" became the order of the day. Only President Roosevelt's Court-packing threat, reviewed in Chapter Six, had intervened.

If it would be extreme to say that the Court has completely abandoned its supervisory role in such matters, decisions since 1937 point strongly toward the position advocated by Holmes, Brandeis, and Stone. As Justice Black emphasized in 1963 (**Ferguson v. Skrupa**), "The doctrine that prevailed in Lochner . . . and like cases—that due process authorizes courts to hold laws unconstitutional when they believe the legislature has acted unwisely—has long since been discarded. We have returned to the original constitutional proposition that courts do not substitute their social and economic beliefs for the judgment of legislative bodies, who are elected to pass laws."

THE SEARCH FOR A ROLE: THE CAROLENE PRODUCTS FOOTNOTE

At the very moment the Court relaxed its supervisory control over social and economic policy, Justice Stone outlined "an affirmative thrust" for due process. In contrast with his expression of judicial tolerance of economic regulation, he suggested that political freedoms enjoy a special status in the Bill of Rights. In reviewing state or national action affecting speech, press, or religion, for instance, should the Court employ assumptions and presumptions that differ from those relied on in other cases where the question of constitutionality was raised? In other words, should the Court envision a hierarchy of Constitution-protected values, with the First Amendment freedoms at the apex and property rights placed further down?

In the otherwise obscure case of *United States* v. *Carolene Products Co.* (1938), Stone tentatively explored the subject. In the body of his opinion upholding a congressional ban on the shipment of "filled milk" against a challenge on due process grounds, he wrote, "Regulatory legislation affecting ordinary commercial transactions is not to be pronounced unconstitutional unless in the light of the facts made known or generally assumed it is of such a character as to preclude the assumption that it rests upon some rational basis within the knowledge and experience of the legislators." He would not go so far as to say that no economic legislation would ever violate constitutional restraints, but he did suggest strictly confining the Court's role. Attached to this proposition was footnote four:

> There may be narrower scope for operation of the presumption of constitutionality when legislation appears on its face to be within a specific prohibition of the Constitution, such as those of the first ten amendments, which are deemed equally specific when held to be embraced within the Fourteenth. . . .
>
> It is unnecessary to consider now whether legislation which restricts those political processes which can ordinarily be expected to bring about repeal of undesirable legislation, is to be subjected to more exacting judicial scrutiny under the general prohibitions of the Fourteenth Amendment than are most other types of legislation. . . .
>
> Nor need we enquire whether similar considerations enter into the review of statutes

directed at particular religious . . . or national . . . or racial minorities . . . whether prejudice against discrete and insular minorities may be a special condition, which tends seriously to curtail the operation of those political processes ordinarily to be relied upon to protect minorities, and which may call for a correspondingly more searching judicial inquiry. . . .

This footnote of three paragraphs contains a corresponding number of ideas. The first suggests that when legislation, on its face, contravenes the specific constitutional negatives set out in the Bill of Rights, the usual presumption of constitutionality may be curtailed or even waived. The second paragraph indicates that the judiciary has a special responsibility as defender of those liberties prerequisite to the effective functioning of political processes. The Court thus becomes the ultimate guardian against abuses that would poison the primary check on government—the ballot box. It must protect those liberties on which the effectiveness of political action depends. The third paragraph suggests a special role for the Court as protector of minorities and of unpopular groups peculiarly helpless at the polls in the face of discriminatory or repressive assault.

Under the self-restraint banner, the justices would leave protection of property to what Madison called the "primary control," "dependence on the people"—the ballot box. Judicial activism old-style was dead; judicial activism new-style was just around the corner. Judicial supervision would continue to be an important part of the political system, but new concerns would replace the old. These concerns are largely the topics covered in Chapters Nine through Twelve.

TAKINGS, LAND USE, AND THE FIFTH AMENDMENT

With the decline of the due process clause as a defense against commercial regulation, the takings clause of the Fifth Amendment has become a battleground for those who oppose public restrictions on property—especially with laws governing land use. The clause states; "nor shall property be taken for public use, without just compensation." As explained in Chapter Nine, the takings clause was the first provision of the Bill of Rights to be applied to the states through the due process clause of the Fourteenth Amendment (*Chicago, B. & Q. R. Co.* v. *Chicago,* 1897).

In its plainest sense the takings clause restricts the power of *eminent domain,* government's authority to acquire control of property. When that is done, "just compensation" must be paid. The takings clause thus disperses the costs of public policy. A taking without compensation places the burden squarely on the property owner. A taking with compensation distributes the burden or costs among the public.

The clause gives rise to at least three questions: First, what constitutes a "taking"? Second, what is "public use"? And finally, what compensation is "just"?

Takings. "[Q]uite simply," confessed Justice Brennan in 1978, the Supreme Court "has been unable to develop any 'set formula' for determining when justice and fairness require that economic injuries caused by public action be compensated by the government. . . ." Whether a Fifth Amendment "taking" has occurred depends instead on the circumstances of individual cases. Several factors seem significant: the economic impact of the regulation, the extent to which the regulation adversely affects "investment-backed" expectations, and the public interest the regulation serves. In the Court's eyes, most zoning laws and other regulations of property are not takings. Neither are taxes, even though they can negatively affect economic values.

Generally, land use regulations today do not effect a taking if they promote a legitimate state interest without denying all economically viable use of the land. Moreover, government's power to ban certain uses of land to advance a legitimate interest includes the power to condition such use on some concession by the owner. This relationship between the interest and the concession was apparently crucial to the outcome of *Nollan* v. *California Coastal Commission* (1987). Five justices invalidated a state regulation that beachfront property owners had to allow public access across their beach as a condition for obtaining a permit to replace a house with a larger one. Absent in this case, according to Justice Scalia's opinion for the majority, was a close nexus between the restriction and the public interest it was supposed to serve.

Public Use. A taking must be for public, not private, use. Although this stipulation has not been nearly so troublesome as the definition of a taking, it has become clear that the Court does not confine "public use" to property maintained by a government agency and accessible to the general public.

Hawaii Housing Authority v. *Midkiff* (1984) presented a situation in which the state required large landowners to sell their property to others. Against the charge that the law took private property for private use, all eight participating justices decided that Hawaii's plan served a public purpose. "Where the legislature's purpose is legitimate and its means are not irrational," declared Justice O'Connor, "our cases make clear that empirical debates over the wisdom of takings—no less than debates over the wisdom of other kinds of socioeconomic legislation—are not to be carried out in the federal courts."

Just Compensation. If a property owner is not satisfied with the price a government agency is willing to pay, courts ultimately settle the dispute. Owners are "entitled to receive what a willing buyer would pay in cash to a willing seller at the time of the taking," the Court announced in *United States* v. *564.54 Acres of Land* (1979). Just compensation is the fair market value of the property taken, not apparently the cost of replacement facilities. Exceptions include situations "where market value has been too difficult to find, or when . . . injustice to owner or public [would result]."

THE "NEW PROPERTY" AND DUE PROCESS OF LAW

Expanded economic and social roles for government at all levels are a hallmark of America today. In the 1960s, government increasingly became a *provider*, not merely the *regulator*. As a result, substantial numbers of people now depend on the government for income support, employment, or services essential to economic well-being. These interests have been labeled "the new property." To what degree are government benefits or *entitlements* constitutionally protected? Put another way, although government may not be constitutionally required to license drivers or to hire college teachers, for example, what constitutional standards, if any, apply when a state suspends a license or fires an instructor? Constitutional protection means that the entitlement, once extended, may not be withdrawn without due process of law.

New property questions differ, therefore, from other issues in this chapter. With *Lochner* v. *New York* or *Ferguson* v. *Skrupa*, the *substance* of the regulation was at stake. Could a state constitutionally limit the hours of work in a bakery or restrict debt adjustment to lawyers? Raising procedural concerns, new property cases assume the legitimacy of the entitlement or regulatory policy. At issue is *procedure*—the manner in which entitlements are curtailed.

A Protected Interest. Having a constitutionally protected entitlement depends on whether the benefit involves a "liberty" or "property" interest within the meaning given the due process clauses of the Fifth and Fourteenth Amendments. In *Goldberg* v. *Kelly* (1970), for example, the Supreme Court concluded that welfare benefits are more "like property than a 'gratuity.' Much of the existing wealth in this country," wrote Justice Brennan, "takes the form of rights that do not fall within traditional common law concepts of property." Thus a state could not stop public assistance payments without affording the recipient "the opportunity for an evidentiary hearing prior to termination."

Public employment may also be "property" if government specifies that a person can be discharged only "for cause" or if an understanding to that effect exists. In *Perry* v. *Sindermann* (1972), the Court held that a fourth-year instructor may have been entitled to a hearing before a junior college decided not to renew his contract. Even without explicit tenure rules, "there may be an unwritten 'common law' . . . that certain employees shall have the equivalent of tenure." But the majority found no such property interest in *Board of Regents* v. *Roth* (1972), where an instructor was let go after a single year of teaching. According to state law, the "decision whether to rehire a nontenured teacher for another year" was left "to the unfettered discretion of university officials." Unlike *Perry*, there was no other basis such as past practice on which to base the property interest.

Government action implicates a "liberty" interest when a person's good name, reputation, honor, or integrity is at stake. *Goss* v. *Lopez* (1975), for instance, held that the due process clause protected students from suspension from a public school in Columbus, Ohio. A state statute permitting up to a ten-day suspension with neither notice nor a hearing was found constitutionally defective because it infringed on both liberty and property interests. Dissenting, Justice Powell argued that the *Roth* Court had said that an interest is defined by statute or an understanding. "Thus the very legislation which 'defines' the 'dimension' of the student's entitlement, while providing a right to education generally, does not establish this right free of discipline imposed in accord with . . . the entire package of statutory provisions governing education in Ohio—of which the power to suspend is one."

A closely divided Court in *Bishop* v. *Wood* (1976) appeared to retreat from the positions taken in *Perry* and *Goss,* demonstrating that it is not always clear when constitutional protection adheres. Carl Bishop had worked for three and a half years as a police officer in Marion, North Carolina, when he was fired without a hearing. He maintained that he had "either an express or an implied right to continued employment." According to an ordinance, the city could discharge a permanent employer for failure "to perform work up to the standard of his classification, or if he is negligent, inefficient, or unfit to perform his duties." Did Bishop have a property interest in continued employment? On its face, explained Justice Stevens for the majority, "the ordinance . . . may fairly be read as conferring such a guarantee. However . . . [this] is not the only possible interpretation. . . ." In the eyes of the court below—a view accepted by the Supreme Court—Bishop "held his position at the will and pleasure of the city." Loss of his job was not therefore deprivation of a property interest within the scope of the due process clause.

What Process Is Due? If a court decides that the due process clause applies, it must then determine the process that is due. At one extreme, criminal trials (discussed in the next chapter) demand formal proceedings guided by a host of rules designed to ensure fairness. At the other extreme are brief, informal exchanges, which usually occur before a decision is made. In *Goss,* just discussed, although the majority concluded that the due process clause applied to school suspensions, only the barest process was due: (1) oral or written notice of the charge against a student and (2) an opportunity for a student to present his or her side of the story. There need be no delay between the moment of "notice" and the "hearing." The latter amounted to little more than "an informal give-and-take between student and disciplinarian, preferably prior to the suspension. . . ."

Mathews v. *Elridge* (1976) attempted to establish guidelines for the process various situations require. At issue was termination of disability insurance payments under the Social Security program. Existing procedures allowed the recipient to submit additional information by mail prior to termination and, within six months of the cutoff, to seek reconsideration in a hearing. Elridge demanded an evidentiary hearing prior to termination. Speaking for six of the eight participating justices, Justice Powell explained that a decision rested on several factors:

> First, the private interest that will be affected by the official action; second, the risk of an erroneous deprivation of such interest through the procedures used, and the probable value, if any, of additional or substitute procedural safeguards; and finally, the Government's interest, including the function involved and the fiscal and administrative burdens that the additional or substitute procedural requirement would entail.

Measured by this formulation, existing procedure satisfied the Constitution. "[T]he prescribed procedures not only provide the claimant with an effective process for asserting his claim prior to any administrative action, but also assure a right to an evidentiary hearing, as well as to subsequent judicial review, before the denial of his claim becomes final."

Elridge is significant because it makes explicit the balancing of interests involved, not in deciding whether a constitutionally protected interest is threatened, but in deciding the process by which it may be withdrawn. The thinking in *Elridge* is economic—the weighing of benefits of added procedure (which would minimize the risks of error) against its costs (which might come out of the resources available for social welfare programs). *Elridge* also leans in favor of a presumption of the adequacy of existing procedure and away from a heightened judicial scrutiny of what the state has offered.

Like any balancing test, justices disagree over its application. Consider **Mackey** v. **Montrym** (1979). Massachusetts law mandated suspension of a driver's license because of a refusal to take a breath analysis test upon arrest for driving while under the influence of alcohol. Only after surrender of the license could the registrar of motor vehicles conduct a hearing. Downplaying the risk of error or deliberate misrepresentation by the arresting officer, five justices found the statute constitutional. Four believed the law violated "the most elemental principles of due process. . . ."

The procedural standards accorded liberty and property interests make this subset one of the most encompassing in all constitutional law. Few if any constitutional safeguards touch more citizens directly and on a day-to-day basis. Perhaps in no other subset are more Americans likely at some time in their lives to experience infringement of what may be their constitutionally protected liberty or property.

KEY TERMS

police power	implied contract	takings
vested rights	due process	eminent domain
contract clause	Fourteenth	public use
ex post facto law	Amendment	just compensation
reservation clause	Brandeis brief	new property
popular sovereignty	footnote four	entitlements

QUERIES

1. How did Chief Justice Marshall resolve the conflict between the police power and property and contract rights in *Dartmouth College* v. *Woodward?* How did Chief Justice Taney resolve it in *Charles River Bridge* v. *Warren Bridge?*

2. It has been suggested that use of the contract and due process clauses to protect property represented an effort to amend the Constitution judicially, to add to the document what the framers failed to include. Discuss this statement in the light of the Slaughterhouse Cases and *Munn* v. *Illinois*.

3. In 1893, Justice David J. Brewer and Professor James Bradley Thayer spoke out on the issue of judicial activism versus judicial restraint. What did they recommend concerning the Court's role?

4. In the realm of "new property" does *Mackey* v. *Montrym* represent a departure from the standards the Court established in *Mathews* v. *Elridge?*

SELECTED READINGS

ACKERMAN, BRUCE. *Private Property and the Constitution*. New Haven, Conn.: Yale University Press, 1977.

BAKER, C. EDWIN. "Property and Its Relation to Constitutionally Protected Liberty." 134 *University of Pennsylvania Law Review* 741 (1986).

CORWIN, EDWARD S. "The Basic Doctrine of American Constitutional Law." 12 *Michigan Law Review* 247 (1914). Reprinted in Alpheus T. Mason and Gerald Garvey, eds. *American Constitutional History: Essays by Edward S. Corwin*. Gloucester, Mass.: Peter Smith, 1970.

————. "The Doctrine of Due Process of Law before the Civil War." 24 *Harvard Law Review* 366 (1911).

EPSTEIN, RICHARD A. "Toward a Revitalization of the Contract Clause." 51 *University of Chicago Law Review* 703 (1984).

HAMILTON, WALTON. "The Path of Due Process of Law." In Conyers Read, ed. *The Constitution Reconsidered*. New York: Columbia University Press, 1938.

HUMBACH, JOHN A. "Constitutional Limits on the Power to Take Private Property." 66 *Oregon Law Review* 547 (1987).

MCCLOSKEY, ROBERT G. "Economic Due Process and the Supreme Court: An Exhumation and Reburial." 1962 *Supreme Court Review* 34.

MCLAUGHLIN, ANDREW C. "The Courts, the Corporation, and Conkling." 46 *American Historical Review* 45 (1940).

MAGRATH, C. PETER. *Yazoo—Law and Politics in the New Republic*. Providence, R.I.: Brown University Press, 1966.

MALTZ, EARL M. "Fourteenth Amendment Concepts in the Antebellum Era." 32 *American Journal of Legal History* 305 (1988).

MASON, ALPHEUS T., *Brandeis, Lawyer and Judge in the Modern State*. Princeton, N.J.: Princeton University Press, 1933. See chapter VI: "The Brandeis Brief."

————. "The Conservative World of Mr. Justice Sutherland." 32 *American Political Science Review* 443 (1938).

PAUL, ARNOLD M. *Conservative Crisis and Rule of Law: Attitudes of Bar and Bench, 1887–1895*. Ithaca, N.Y.: Cornell University Press, 1960.

PHILLIPS, MICHAEL J. "Another Look at Economic Substantive Due Process," 1987 *Wisconsin Law Review* 265 (1987).

SIEGAN, BERNARD H. *Economic Liberties and the Constitution*. Chicago: University of Chicago Press, 1981.

STEPHENSON, D. GRIER, JR. "The Supreme Court and Constitutional Change: *Lochner* v. *New York* Revisited." 21 *Villanova Law Review* 217 (1976).

STRONG, FRANK R. *Substantive Due Process of Law: A Dichotomy of Sense and Nonsense*. Durham, N.C.: Carolina Academic Press, 1986.

TWISS, BENJAMIN R. *Lawyers and the Constitution*. Princeton, N.J.: Princeton University Press, 1942.

WRIGHT, BENJAMIN F. *The Contract Clause of the Constitution*. Cambridge, Mass.: Harvard University Press, 1938.

Calder v. Bull
3 U.S. (3 Dall.) 386, 1 L.Ed. 648 (1798)

The legislature of Connecticut passed a law granting a new hearing to Bull and his wife, after their right to appeal a probate court decree had expired. At the second hearing, Bull was successful, and Calder, the other claimant, after appealing unsuccessfully to the highest Connecticut court, brought his case to the Supreme Court on a writ of error. The opinions of Justices Chase and Iredell are important, not only for their definition of ex post facto laws, but also for the views expressed about natural law and judicial review. Majority: Chase, Cushing, Iredell, Paterson. Not participating: Ellsworth.

CHASE, JUSTICE.— . . .

The counsel for the plaintiffs in error contend, that the . . . law of the legislature of Connecticut, granting a new hearing, in the above case, is an *ex post facto* law, prohibited by the constitution of the United States; that any law of the federal government, or of any of the state governments, contrary to the constitution of the United States, is void; and that this court possess the power to declare such law void. . . .

Whether the legislature of any of the states can revise and correct by law, a decision of any of its courts of justice, although not prohibited by the constitution of the state, is a question of very great importance, and not necessary now to be determined; because the resolution or law in question does not go so far. I cannot subscribe to the omnipotence of a state legislature, or that it is absolute and without control; although its authority should not be expressly restrained by the constitution, or fundamental law of the state. The people of the United States erected their constitution or forms of government, to establish justice, to promote the general welfare, to secure the blessings of liberty, and to protect their persons and property from violence. The purposes for which men enter into society will determine the nature and terms of the social compact; and as they are the foundation of the legislative power, they will decide what are the proper objects of it. The nature and ends of legislative power will limit the exercise of it. This fundamental principle flows from the very nature of our free republican governments, that no man should be compelled to do what the laws do not require, nor to refrain from acts which the laws

permit. There are acts which the federal or state legislature cannot do, without exceeding their authority. There are certain vital principles in our free republican governments which will determine and overrule an apparent and flagrant abuse of legislative power; as to authorize manifest injustice by positive law; or to take away that security for personal liberty, or private property, for the protection whereof the government was established. An act of the legislature (for I cannot call it a law), contrary to the great first principles of the social compact, cannot be considered a rightful exercise of legislative authority. The obligation of a law in governments established on express compact, and on republican principles, must be determined by the nature of the power on which it is founded.

A few instances will suffice to explain what I mean. A law that punished a citizen for an innocent action, or, in other words, for an act which, when done, was in violation of no existing law; a law that destroys, or impairs, the lawful private contracts of citizens; a law that makes a man a judge in his own cause; or a law that takes property from A, and gives it to B. It is against all reason and justice for a people to intrust a legislature with such powers; and, therefore, it cannot be presumed that they have done it. The genius, the nature, and the spirit of our state governments amount to a prohibition of such acts of legislation; and the general principles of law and reason forbid them. The legislature may enjoin, permit, forbid and punish; they may declare new crimes, and establish rules of conduct for all its citizens in future cases; they may command what is right, and prohibit what is wrong; but they cannot change innocence into guilt, or punish innocence as a crime; or violate the right of an antecedent lawful private contract; or the right of private property. To maintain that our federal or state legislature possesses such powers, if they had not been expressly restrained, would, in my opinion, be a political heresy altogether inadmissible in our free republican governments. . . .

The Constitution of the United States, Art. 1, § 9, prohibits the legislature of the United States from passing an *ex post facto* law; and in section 10 lays several restrictions on the authority of the legislatures of the several states; and among them, "that no state shall pass any *ex post facto* law." . . .

I will state what laws I consider *ex post facto* laws, within the words and the intent of the prohibition. 1st. Every law that makes an action done before the passing of the law, and which was innocent when done, criminal; and punishes such action. 2d. Every law that aggravates a crime, or makes it greater than it was, when committed. 3d. Every law that changes the punishment, and inflicts a greater punishment, than the law annexed to the crime, when committed. 4th. Every law that alters the legal rules of evidence, and receives less, or different testimony, than the law required at the time of the commission of the offense, in order to convict the offender. All these, and similar laws, are manifestly unjust and oppressive. In my opinion, the true distinction is between *ex post facto* laws, and retrospective laws. Every *ex post facto* law must necessarily be retrospective; but every retrospective law is not an *ex post facto* law; the former only are prohibited. Every law that takes away or impairs rights vested, agreeably to existing laws, is retrospective, and is generally unjust, and may be oppressive; and it is a good general rule, that a law should have no retrospect; but there are cases in which laws may justly, and for the benefit of the community, and also of individuals, relate to a time antecedent to their commencement; as statutes of oblivion or of pardon. They are certainly retrospective, and literally both concerning and after the facts committed. But I do not consider any law *ex post facto,* within the prohibition, that mollifies the rigor of the criminal law; but only those that create or aggravate the crime; or increase the punishment, or change the rules of evidence, for the purpose of conviction. Every law that is to have an operation before the making thereof, as to commence at an antecedent time; or to save time from the statute of limitations; or to excuse acts which were unlawful, and before committed, and the like, is retrospective. But such laws may be proper or necessary, as the case may be. There is a great and apparent difference between making an unlawful act lawful; and the making an innocent action criminal, and punishing it as a crime. . . .

It is not to be presumed that the federal or state legislatures will pass laws to deprive citizens of rights vested in them by existing laws; unless for the benefit of the whole community; and on making full satisfaction. The restraint against making any *ex post facto* laws was not considered, by the framers of the constitution, as extending to prohibit the depriving a citizen even of a vested right to property; or the provision, "that private property should not be taken for public use, without just compensation," was unnecessary.

It seems to me that the right of property, in its origin, could only arise from compact express or implied, and I think it the better opinion, that the right, as well as the mode or manner of acquiring property, and of alienating or transferring, inheriting or transmitting it, is conferred by society, is regulated by civil institution, and is always subject to the rules prescribed by positive law. When I say that a right is vested in a citizen, I mean, that he has the power to do certain actions, or to possess certain things, according to the law of the land. . . .

I am of opinion that the decree of the supreme court of errors of Connecticut be affirmed, with costs.

IREDELL, JUSTICE.— . . .

If . . . a government, composed of legislative, executive and judicial departments, were established, by a constitution which imposed no limits on the legislative power, the consequence would inevitably be, that whatever the legislative power chose to enact, would be lawfully enacted, and the judicial power could never interpose to pronounce it void. It is true, that some speculative jurists have held, that a legislative act against natural justice must, in itself, be void; but I cannot think that, under such a government any court of justice would possess a power to declare it so. . . . [I]t has been the policy of all the American states, which have, individually, framed their state constitutions, since the revolution, and of the people of the United States, when they framed the federal constitution, to define with precision the objects of legislative power, and to restrain its exercise within marked and settled boundaries. If any act of congress, or of the legislature of the state, violates those constitutional provisions, it is unquestionably void; though, I admit, that as the authority to declare it void is of a delicate and awful nature, the court will never resort to that authority, but in a clear and urgent case. If, on the other hand, the legislature of the Union, or the legislature of any member of the Union, shall pass a law, within the general scope of their constitutional power, the court cannot pronounce it to be void, merely because it is, in their judgment, contrary to the principles of natural justice. The ideas of natural justice are regulated by no fixed standards: the ablest and the purest men have differed upon the subject; and all that the court could properly say, in such an event, would be, that the legislature (possessed of an equal right of opinion) had passed an act which, in the opinion of the judges, was inconsistent with the abstract principles of natural justice. . . .

Still, however, in the present instance, the act or resolution of the legislature of Connecticut, cannot be regarded as an *ex post facto* law; for the true construction of the prohibition extends to criminal, not to civil issues. . . .

The policy, the reason and humanity of the prohibition, do not . . . extend to civil cases, to cases that merely affect the private property of citizens. Some of the most necessary and important acts of legislation are, on the contrary, founded upon the principle, that private rights must yield to public exigencies. Highways are run through private grounds; fortifications, lighthouses, and other public edifices, are necessarily sometimes built upon the soil owned by individuals. In such, and similar cases, if the owners should refuse voluntarily to accommodate the public, they must be constrained, so far as the public necessities require; and justice is done, by allowing them a reasonable equivalent. Without the possession of this power, the operations of government would often be obstructed, and society itself would be endangered. It is not sufficient to urge, that the power may be abused, for such is the nature of all power—such is the tendency of every human institution. . . . We must be content to limit power, where we can, and where we cannot, consistently with its use, we must be content to repose a salutary confidence. It is our consolation, that there never existed a government, in ancient or modern times, more free from danger in this respect, than the governments of America. . . .

Judgment affirmed.

Dartmouth College v. Woodward
17 U.S. (4 Wheat.) 518, 4 L.Ed. 629 (1819)

The Dartmouth College Case involved rival claimants to the records, the seal, and other objects signifying control of the college. The trustees of the college, basing their claim on a charter granted in 1769 by King George III, sought to regain control from a group whose authority had been created by three legislative acts of 1816 that amended the original charter by increasing the number of trustees and vesting the future power of appointment of trustees in the governor and his council. The New Hampshire Superior Court of Judicature upheld Woodward and the new control group. Majority: Marshall, Johnson, Livingston, Story, Washington. Dissenting: Duvall. Not participating: Todd.

The opinion of the Court was delivered by MAR-SHALL, CH. J.— . . .

It can require no argument to prove, that the circumstances of this case constitute a contract. An application is made to the crown for a charter to incorporate a religious and literary institution. In the application, it is stated, that large contributions have been made for the object, which will be conferred on the corporation, as soon as it shall be created. The charter is granted, and on its faith the property is conveyed. Surely, in this transaction every ingredient of a complete and legitimate contract is to be found. The points for consideration are, 1. Is this contract protected by the constitution of the United States? 2. Is it impaired by the acts under which the defendant holds? . . .

If the act of incorporation be a grant of political power, if it creates a civil institution, to be employed in the administration of the government, or if the funds of the college be public property, or if the state of New Hampshire, as a government, be alone interested in its transactions, the subject is one in which the legislature of the state may act according to its judgment, unrestrained by any limitation of its power imposed by the constitution of the United States.

But if this be a private eleemosynary institution, endowed with a capacity to take property, for objects unconnected with government, whose funds are bestowed by individuals, on the faith of the charter; if the donors have stipulated for the future disposition and management of those funds, in the manner prescribed by themselves; there may be more difficulty in the case, although neither the persons who have made these stipulations, nor those for whose benefit they were made, should be parties to the cause. . . .

A corporation is an artificial being, invisible, intangible, and existing only in contemplation of law. Being the mere creature of law, it possesses only those properties which the charter of its creation confers upon it, either expressly or as incidental to its very existence. These are such as are supposed best calculated to effect the object for which it was created. Among the most important are immortality, and, if the expression may be allowed, individuality; properties by which a perpetual succession of many persons are considered as the same, and may act as a single individual. . . . It is no more a state instrument than a natural person

exercising the same powers would be. If, then, a natural person, employed by individuals in the education of youth, or for the government of a seminary in which youth is educated, would not become a public officer, or be considered as a member of the civil government, how is it that this artificial being, created by law for the purpose of being employed by the same individuals for the same purposes, should become a part of the civil government of the country? . . .

From the fact, then, that a charter of incorporation has been granted, nothing can be inferred which changes the character of the institution, or transfers to the government any new power over it. . . .

From this review of the charter, it appears that Dartmouth College is an eleemosynary institution, incorporated for the purpose of perpetuating the application of the bounty of the donors to the specified objects of the bounty; that its trustees or governors were originally named by the founder, and invested with the power of perpetuating themselves; that they are not public officers, nor is it a civil institution, participating in the administration of government; but a charity school, or a seminary of education, incorporated for the preservation of its property, and the perpetual application of that property to the objects of its creation.

Yet a question remains to be considered of more real difficulty, on which more doubt has been entertained than on all that have been discussed. The founders of the college, at least those whose contributions were in money, have parted with the property bestowed upon it, and their representatives have no interest in that property. The donors of land are equally without interest so long as the corporation shall exist. Could they be found, they are unaffected by any alteration in its constitution, and probably regardless of its form or even of its existence. The students are fluctuating, and no individual among our youth has a vested interest in the institution which can be asserted in a court of justice. Neither the founders of the college, nor the youth for whose benefit it was founded, complain of the alteration made in its charter, or think themselves injured by it. The trustees alone complain, and the trustees have no beneficial interest to be protected. Can this be such a contract as the constitution intended to withdraw from the power of state legislation? Contracts, the parties to which have a vested beneficial interest, and those only, it has been said, are the objects about which the constitution is solicitous, and to which its protection is extended.

The court has bestowed on this argument the most deliberate consideration, and the result will be stated. Dr. Wheelock, acting for himself and for those who, at his solicitation, had made contributions to his school, applied for this charter, as the instrument which should enable him and them to perpetuate their beneficent intention. It was granted. An artificial, immortal being was created by the crown, capable of receiving and distributing forever, according to the will of the donors, the donations which should be made to it. On this being, the contributions which had been collected were immediately bestowed. These gifts were made, not indeed to make a profit for the donors or their posterity, but for something, in their opinion, of inestimable value; for something which they deemed a full equivalent for the money with which it was purchased. The consideration for which they stipulated, is the perpetual application of the fund to its objects, in the mode prescribed by themselves. Their descendants may take no interest in the preservation of this consideration. But in this respect their descendants are not their representatives. They are represented by the corporation. The corporation is the assignee of their rights, stands in their place, and distributes their bounty, as they would themselves have distributed it had they been immortal. So with respect to the students who are to derive learning from this source. The corporation is a trustee for them also. Their potential rights, which, taken distributively, are imperceptible, amount collectively to a most important interest. These are, in the aggregate, to be exercised, asserted, and protected by the corporation. They were as completely out of the donors, at the instant of their being vested in the corporation, and as incapable of being asserted by the students, as at present. . . .

This is plainly a contract to which the donors, the trustees, and the crown (to whose rights and obligations New Hampshire succeeds) were the original parties. It is a contract made on a valuable consideration. It is a contract for the security and disposition of property. It is a contract on the faith of which real and personal estate has been conveyed to the corporation. It is then a contract within the letter of the constitution, and within its spirit also,

unless the fact that the property is invested by the donors in trustees, for the promotion of religion and education, for the benefit of persons who are perpetually changing, though the objects remain the same, shall create a particular exception, taking this case out of the prohibition contained in the constitution. . . .

On what safe and intelligible ground can this exception stand? There is no expression in the constitution, no sentiment delivered by its contemporaneous expounders, which would justify us in making it. . . .

If the insignificance of the object does not require that we should exclude contracts respecting it from the protection of the constitution, neither, as we conceive, is the policy of leaving them subject to legislative alteration so apparent, as to require a forced construction of that instrument, in order to effect it. These eleemosynary institutions do not fill the place, which would otherwise be occupied by government, but that which would otherwise remain vacant. They are complete acquisitions to literature. They are donations to education; donations, which any government must be disposed rather to encourage than to discountenance. It requires no very critical examination of the human mind, to enable us to determine, that one great inducement to these gifts is the conviction felt by the giver, that the disposition he makes of them is immutable. . . . All such gifts are made in the pleasing, perhaps delusive hope, that the charity will flow forever in the channel which the givers have marked out for it. If every man finds in his own bosom strong evidence of the universality of this sentiment, there can be but little reason to imagine, that the framers of our constitution were strangers to it, and that, feeling the necessity and policy of giving permanence and security to contracts, of withdrawing them from the influence of legislative bodies, whose fluctuating policy, and repeated interferences, produced the most perplexing and injurious embarrassments, they still deemed it necessary to leave these contracts subject to those interferences. The motives for such an exception must be very powerful, to justify the construction which makes it. . . .

2. We next proceed to the inquiry, whether its obligation has been impaired by those acts of the legislature of New Hampshire, to which the special verdict refers? . . .

It has been already stated, that the act "to

amend the charter, and enlarge and improve the corporation of Dartmouth College," increases the number of trustees of twenty-one, gives the appointment of the additional members to the executive of the state, and creates a board of overseers, to consist of twenty-five persons, of whom twenty-one are also appointed by the executive of New Hampshire, who have power to inspect and control the most important acts of the trustees.

On the effect of this law [of 1816], two opinions cannot be entertained. Between acting directly, and acting through the agency of trustees and overseers, no essential difference is perceived. The whole power of governing the college is transferred from trustees appointed according to the will of the founder, expressed in the charter, to the executive of New

Hampshire. The management and application of the funds of this eleemosynary institution, which are placed by the donors in the hands of trustees named in the charter, and empowered to perpetuate themselves, are placed by this act under the control of the government of the state. The will of the state is substituted for the will of the donors, in every essential operation of the college. This is not an immaterial change. . . .

It results from this opinion, that the acts of the legislature of New Hampshire, which are stated in the special verdict found in this cause, are repugnant to the constitution of the United States; and that the judgment on this special verdict ought to have been for the plaintiffs. The judgment of the State Court must, therefore, be reversed.

Charles River Bridge v. *Warren Bridge*
36 U.S. (11 Pet.) 420, 9 L.Ed. 773 (1837)

In 1785 the Massachusetts legislature granted to the Charles River Bridge Company the right to construct a bridge between Charlestown and Boston, with the power to collect tolls for 40 years (later extended to 70 years). This franchise replaced an exclusive ferry right formerly possessed by Harvard College, but which the college yielded in return for annual payments during the life of the bridge charter. In 1828, the legislature chartered the Warren Bridge Company, with the power to collect tolls on a bridge that it constructed sufficiently close to the Charles River Bridge to deprive its owners of their anticipated tolls. When a state court rejected the plaintiff company's bill for an injunction and other relief, review was sought on a writ of error. A very short excerpt from the 65-page dissenting opinion of Justice Story follows Taney's opinion for the Court. Majority: Taney, Baldwin, Barbour, Catron, McKinley, Wayne. Dissenting: McLean, Story, Thompson.

MR. CHIEF JUSTICE TANEY delivered the opinion of the Court. . . .

This brings us to the act of the legislature of Massachusetts, of 1785, by which the plaintiffs were incorporated by the name of "The Proprietors of the Charles River Bridge"; and it is here, and in the law of 1792, prolonging their charter, that we must look for the extent and nature of the franchise conferred upon the plaintiffs.

Much has been said in the argument of the principles of construction by which this law is to be expounded, and what undertakings, on the part of the state, may be implied. The court thinks there can be no serious difficulty on that head. It is the grant of certain franchises by the public to a private corporation, and in a matter where the public interest is concerned. The rule of construction in such cases is well settled, both in England and by the decisions of our own tribunals. . . . "This, like many other cases, is a bargain between a company of adventurers and the public, the terms of which are expressed in the statute; and the rule of construction, in all such cases, is now fully established to be this; that any ambiguity in the terms of the contract must operate against the adventurers, and in favor of the public, and the plaintiffs can claim nothing that is not clearly given them by the act." And the doctrine thus laid down is abundantly sustained by the authorities referred to in this decision.

. . . The argument in favour of the proprietors of the Charles River bridge, is . . . . that the power claimed by the state, if it exists, may be so used as to destroy the value of the franchise they have granted to the corporation. . . . The existence of the power does not, and cannot depend upon the circumstance of its having been exercised or not. . . .

. . . The object and end of all government is to promote the happiness and prosperity of the community by which it is established, and it can never be assumed, that the government intended to diminish its powers of accomplishing the end for which it was created. And in a country like ours, free, active, and enterprising, continually advancing in numbers and wealth, new channels of communication are daily found necessary, both for travel and trade; and are essential to the comfort, convenience, and prosperity of the people. A state ought never to be presumed to surrender this power, because, like the taxing power, the whole community has an interest in preserving it undiminished. And when a corporation alleges, that a state has surrendered, for seventy years, its power of improvement and public accommodation, in a great and important line of travel, along which a vast number of its citizens must daily pass, the community has a right to insist, in the language of this court above quoted, "that its abandonment ought not to be presumed in a case in which the deliberate purpose of the state to abandon it does not appear." The continued existence of a government would be of no great value, if by implications and presumptions it was disarmed by the powers necessary to accomplish the ends of its creation; and the functions it was designed to perform, transferred to the hands of privileged corporations. . . . While the rights of private property

are sacredly guarded, we must not forget that the community also has rights, and that the happiness and well-being of every citizen depends on their faithful preservation.

Adopting the rule of construction above stated as the settled one, we proceed to apply it to the charter of 1785, to the proprietors of the Charles River bridge. This act of incorporation is in the usual form, and the privileges such as are commonly given to corporations of that kind. It confers on them the ordinary faculties of a corporation, for the purpose of building the bridge; and establishes certain rates of toll, which the company is authorized to take: this is the whole grant. There is no exclusive privilege given to them over the water of Charles River, above or below their bridge; no right to erect another bridge themselves, nor to prevent other persons from erecting one, no engagement from the state, that another shall not be erected; and no undertaking not to sanction competition, not to make improvements that may diminish the amount of its income. Upon all these subjects, the charter is silent; and nothing is said in it about a line of travel, so much insisted on in the argument, in which they are to have exclusive privileges. . . .

. . . In short, all the franchises and rights of property, enumerated in the charter, and there mentioned to have been granted to it, remain unimpaired. But its income is destroyed by the Warren bridge; which, being free, draws off the passengers and property which would have gone over it, and renders their franchise of no value. This is the gist of the complaint. For it is not pretended, that the erection of the Warren bridge would have done them any injury, or in any degree affected their right of property, if it had not diminished the amount of their tolls. In order, then, to entitle themselves to relief, it is necessary to show, that the legislature contracted not to do the act of which they complain; and that they impaired, or in other words, violated, that contract by the erection of the Warren bridge.

The inquiry, then, is, does the charter contain such a contract on the part of the state? Is there any such stipulation to be found in that instrument? It must be admitted on all hands, that there is none; no words that even relate to another bridge, or to the diminution of their tolls, or to the line of travel. If a contract on that subject can be gathered from the charter, it must be by implication; and cannot be found in the words used. Can such an agreement be implied? The rule of construction before stated is an answer to the question; in charters of this description, no rights are taken from the public, or given to the corporation, beyond those which the words of the charter, by their natural and proper construction, purport to convey. There are no words which import such a contract as the plaintiffs in error contend for, and none can be implied. . . .

Indeed, the practice and usage of almost every state in the Union, old enough to have commenced the work of internal improvement, is opposed to the doctrine contended for on the part of the plaintiffs in error. Turnpike roads have been made in succession, on the same line of travel; the later ones interfering materially with the profits of the first. These corporations have, in some instances, been utterly ruined by the introduction of newer and better modes of transportation and traveling. In some cases, railroads have rendered the turnpike roads on the same line of travel so entirely useless, that the franchise of the turnpike corporation is not worth preserving. Yet in none of these cases have the corporations supposed that their privileges were invaded, or any contract violated on the part of the state. . . .

And what would be the fruits of this doctrine of implied contracts, on the part of the states, and of property in a line of travel by a corporation, if it should now be sanctioned by this court? To what results would it lead us? . . . Let it once be understood, that such charters carry with them these implied contracts, and give this unknown and undefined property in a line of travelling; and you will soon find the old turnpike corporations awakening from their sleep and calling upon this court to put down the improvements which have taken their place. The millions of property which have been invested in railroads and canals, upon lines of travel which had been before occupied by turnpike corporations, will be put in jeopardy. We shall be thrown back to the improvements of the last century, and obliged to stand still, until the claims of the old turnpike corporations shall be satisfied; and they shall consent to permit these states to avail themselves of the lights of modern science, and to partake of the benefit of those improvements

which are now adding to the wealth and prosperity, and the convenience and comfort, of every other part of the civilized world. . . . This court is not prepared to sanction principles which must lead to such results. . . .

The judgment of the supreme judicial court of the commonwealth of Massachusetts, dismissing the plaintiff's bill, must therefore, be affirmed with costs.

MR. JUSTICE STORY, dissenting. . . .

. . . We are to give this act of incorporation a rational and fair construction, according to the general rules which govern in all cases of the exposition of public statutes. We are to ascertain the legislative intent; and that once ascertained, it is our duty to give it a full and liberal operation. . . .

I admit, that where the terms of a grant are to impose burdens upon the public, or to create a restraint injurious to the public interests, there is sound reason for interpreting the terms, if ambiguous, in favor of the public. But at the same time, I insist, that there is not the slightest reason for saying, even in such a case, that the grant is not to be construed favourably to the grantee, so as to secure him in the enjoyment of what is actually granted. . . .

For my own part, I can conceive of no surer plan to arrest all public improvements, founded on private capital and enterprise, than to make the outlay of that capital uncertain, and questionable both as to security, and as to productiveness. No man will hazard his capital in any enterprise, in which, if there be a loss, it must be borne exclusively by himself; and if there be success, he has not the slightest security of enjoying the rewards of that success for a single moment. . . .

Upon the whole, my judgment is that the act of the legislature of Massachusetts granting the charter of Warren Bridge, is an act impairing the obligation of the prior contract and grant to the proprietors of Charles River bridge; and, by the Constitution of the United States, it is, therefore, utterly void. I am for reversing the decree of the state court (dismissing the bill), and for remanding the cause to the state court for further proceedings. . . .

Home Building & Loan Association v. Blaisdell
290 U.S 398, 54 S.Ct. 231, 78 L.Ed. 413 (1934)

The Minnesota Mortgage Moratorium Law, passed in 1933, was designed to prevent the foreclosure of mortgages during the emergency produced by economic depression. The act authorized judicial action by which the redemption period of mortgages could be extended under conditions set by the court. The act was to remain in effect "only during the continuance of the emergency and in no event beyond May 1, 1935." Blaisdell had mortgaged a house and lot to the appellant company; when the company foreclosed, Blaisdell sought an extension of the period of redemption on the ground that he would not be able to redeem by the date fixed by the law in effect when the mortgage had been foreclosed. The court extended the redemption period on condition that certain monthly payments be made. The Supreme Court of Minnesota affirmed the judgment. Majority: Hughes, Brandeis, Cardozo, Roberts, Stone. Dissenting: Sutherland, Butler, McReynolds, Van Devanter.

MR. CHIEF JUSTICE HUGHES delivered the opinion of the Court. . . .

The state court upheld the statute as an emergency measure. Although conceding that the obligations of the mortgage contract were impaired, the court decided that what it thus described as an impairment was, notwithstanding the contract clause of the Federal Constitution, within the police power of the state as that power was called into exercise by the public economic emergency which the legislature had found to exist. . . .

The statute does not impair the integrity of the mortgage indebtedness. The obligation for interest remains. The statute does not affect the validity of the sale or the right of a mortgagee-purchaser to title in fee, or his right to obtain a deficiency judgment, if the mortgagor fails to redeem within the prescribed period. Aside from the extension of time, the other conditions of redemption are unaltered. While the mortgagor remains in possession, he must pay the rental value as that value has been determined, upon notice and hearing, by the court. The rental value so paid is devoted to the carrying of the property by the application of the required payments to taxes, insurance, and interest on the mortgage indebtedness. While the mortgagee-purchaser is debarred from actual possession, he has, so far as rental value is concerned, the equivalent of possession during the extended period.

In determining whether the provision for this temporary and conditional relief exceeds the power of the state by reason of the clause in the Federal Constitution prohibiting impairment of the obligations of contracts, we must consider the relation of emergency to constitutional power, the historical setting of the contract clause, the development of the jurisprudence of this Court in the construction of that clause, and the principles of construction which we may consider to be established.

Emergency does not create power. Emergency does not increase granted power or remove or diminish the restrictions imposed upon power granted or reserved. . . .

While emergency does not create power, emergency may furnish the occasion for the exercise of power. . . . The constitutional question presented in the light of an emergency is whether the power possessed embraces the particular exercise of it in response to particular conditions. Thus, the war power of the federal government is not created by the emergency of war, but it is a power given to meet that emergency. It is a power to wage war successfully, and thus it permits the harnessing of the entire energies of the people in a supreme cooperative effort to preserve the nation. But even the war power does not remove constitutional limitations safeguarding essential liberties. When the provisions of the Constitution, in grant or restriction, are specific, so particularized as not to admit of construction, no question is presented. . . . But, where constitutional grants and limitations of power are set forth in general clauses, which afford a broad outline, the process of construction is essential to fill in the details. That is true of the contract clause. . . .

In the construction of the contract clause, the debates in the Constitutional Convention are of little aid. But the reasons which led to the adoption of that clause, and of the other prohibitions of Section 10 of Article I, are not left in doubt, and have frequently been described with eloquent emphasis. The widespread distress following the revolutionary period, and the plight of debtors had called forth in the state an ignoble array of legislative schemes for the defeat of creditors and the invasion of contractual obligations. Legislative interferences had been so numerous and extreme that the confidence essential to propserous trade had been undermined and the utter destruction of credit was threatened. . . .

It is manifest . . . that there has been a growing appreciation of public needs and of the necessity of finding ground for a rational compromise between individual rights and public welfare. . . .

It is no answer to say that this public need was not apprehended a century ago, or to insist that what the provision of the Constitution meant to the vision of that day it must mean to the vision of our time. If by the statement that what the Constitution meant at the time of its adoption it means today, it is intended to say that the great clauses of the Constitution must be confined to the interpretation which the framers, with the conditions and outlook of their time, would have placed upon them, the statement carries its own refutation. It was to guard against such a narrow conception that Chief Justice Marshall uttered the memorable warning: "We must never forget, that it is *a constitution* we are expounding"; "a constitution intended to endure for ages to come, and consequently, to be adapted to the various *crises* of human affairs." . . .

. . . The vast body of law which has been developed was unknown to the fathers, but it is believed to have preserved the essential content and the spirit of the Constitution. With a growing recognition of public needs and the relation of individual right to public security, the Court has

sought to prevent the perversion of the clause through its use as an instrument to throttle the capacity of the states to protect their fundamental interests. . . .

We are of the opinion that the Minnesota statute as here applied does not violate the contract clause of the Federal Constitution. Whether the legislation is wise or unwise as a matter of policy is a question with which we are not concerned. . . .

The judgment of the Supreme Court of Minnesota is affirmed.

Judgment affirmed.

MR. JUSTICE SUTHERLAND, dissenting. . . .

A provision of the Constitution, it is hardly necessary to say, does not admit of two distinctly opposite interpretations. It does not mean one thing at one time and an entirely different thing at another time. If the contract impairment clause, when framed and adopted, meant that the terms of a contract for the payment of money could not be altered *in invitum* by a state statute enacted for the relief of hardly pressed debtors to the end and with the effect of postponing payment or enforcement during and because of an economic or financial emergency, it is but to state the obvious to say that it means the same now. . . .

The provisions of the Federal Constitution, undoubtedly, are pliable in the sense that in appropriate cases they have the capacity of bringing within their grasp every new condition which falls within their meaning. But, their *meaning* is changeless; it is only their *application* which is extensible. . . . Constitutional grants of power and restrictions upon the exercise of power are not flexible as the doctrines of the common law are flexible. These doctrines, upon the principles of the common law itself, modify or abrogate themselves whenever they are or whenever they become plainly unsuited to different or changed conditions. . . .

The whole aim of construction, as applied to a provision of the Constitution, is to discover the meaning, to ascertain and give effect to the intent, of its framers and the people who adopted it. . . . And if the meaning be at all doubtful, the doubt should be resolved, wherever reasonably possible to do so, in a way to forward the evident purpose with which the provision was adopted. . . .

A candid consideration of the history and circumstances which led up to and accompanied the framing and adoption of this clause will demonstrate conclusively that it was framed and adopted with the specific and studied purpose of preventing legislation designed to relieve debtors *especially* in time of financial distress. Indeed, it is not probable that any other purpose was definitely in the minds of those who composed the framers' convention or the ratifying state conventions which followed, although the restriction has been given a wider application upon principles clearly stated by Chief Justice Marshall in the Dartmouth College Case. . . .

The present exigency is nothing new. From the beginning of our existence as a nation, periods of depression, of industrial failure, of financial distress, of unpaid and unpayable indebtedness, have alternated with years of plenty. The vital lesson that expenditure beyond income begets poverty, that public or private extravagance, financed by promises to pay, either must end in complete or partial repudiation or the promises be fulfilled by self-denial and painful effort, though constantly taught by bitter experience, seems never to be learned; and the attempt by legislative devices to shift the misfortune of the debtor to the shoulders of the creditor without coming into conflict with the contract impairment clause has been persistent and oft-repeated.

The defense of the Minnesota law is made upon grounds which were discountenanced by the makers of the Constitution and have many times been rejected by this court. That defense should not now succeed, because it constitutes an effort to overthrow the constitutional provision by an appeal to facts and circumstances identical with those which brought it into existence. With due regard for the process of logical thinking, it legitimately cannot be urged that conditions which produced the rule may now be invoked to destroy it.

. . . The opinion concedes that emergency does not create power, or increase granted power, or remove or diminish restrictions upon power granted or reserved. It then proceeds to say, however, that while emergency does not create power, it may furnish the occasion for the exercise of power. I can only interpret what is said on that subject as meaning that while an emergency does not diminish a restriction upon power it furnishes an occasion for diminishing it; and this, as it seems to me, is merely to say the same thing by the use of another set of words, with the effect of affirming that which has just been denied. . . .

The Minnesota statute either impairs the obligation of contracts or it does not. If it does not, the occasion to which it relates becomes immaterial, since then the passage of the statute is the exercise of a normal, unrestricted, state power and requires no special occasion to render it effective. If it does, the emergency no more furnishes a proper occasion for its exercise than if the emergency were non-existent. And so, while, in form, the suggested distinction seems to put us forward in a straight line, in reality it simply carries us back in a circle, like bewildered travelers lost in a wood, to the point where we parted company with the view of the state court. . . .

I am authorized to say that MR. JUSTICE VAN DEVANTER, MR. JUSTICE MCREYNOLDS and MR. JUSTICE BUTLER concur in this opinion.

MR. JUSTICE CARDOZO concurring in an *unpublished* opinion.* . . .

. . . The economic and social changes wrought by the industrial revolution and by the growth of population have made it necessary for government at this day to [do] a thousand things that were beyond the experience or the thought of a century ago. With the growing recognition of this need, courts have awakened to the truth that the contract clause is perverted from its proper meaning when it throttles the capacity of the states to exert their governmental power in response to crying needs. . . . The early cases dealt with the problem as one affecting the conflicting rights and interests of individuals and classes. This was the attitude of the courts up to the Fourteenth Amendment; and the tendency to some extent persisted even later. . . . The rights and interests of the state itself were involved, as it seemed, only indirectly and remotely, if they were thought to be involved at all. We know better in these days, with the passing of the frontier and of the unpeopled spaces of the west. With these and other changes, the welfare of the social organism in any of its parts is bound up more inseparably than ever with the welfare of the whole. A gospel of *laissez-faire*—of individual initiative—of thrift and industry and sacrifice—may be adequate in that great society we live in to

---

* This is part of a draft of an unpublished concurring opinion Justice Cardozo wrote and sent to Chief Justice Hughes. Hughes incorporated some of Cardozo's ideas into his own majority opinion. Harlan Fiske Stone Papers, Library of Congress.—ED.

point the way to salvation, at least for economic life. The state when it acts today by statutes like the one before us is not furthering the selfish good of individuals or classes as ends of ultimate validity. It is furthering its own good by maintaining the economic structure on which the good of all depends. Such at least is its endeavor, however much it miss the mark. The attainment of that end, so august and impersonal, will not be barred and thwarted by the obstruction of a contract set up along the way.

Looking back over the century, one perceives a process of evolution too strong to be set back. . . . [T]he court in its interpretation of the contract clause has been feeling its way toward a rational compromise between private rights and public welfare. From the beginning it was seen that something must be subtracted from the words of the Constitution in all their literal and stark significance. . . . Contracts were still to be preserved. There was to be no arbitrary destruction of their

binding force, nor any arbitrary impairment. There was to be no impairment, even though not arbitrary, except with the limits of fairness, of moderation, and of pressing and emergent need. But a promise exchanged between individuals was not to paralyze the state in its endeavor in times of direful crisis to keep its life-blood flowing.

To hold this may be inconsistent with things that men said in 1787 when expounding to compatriots the newly written constitution. They did not see the changes in the relation between states and nation or in the play of social forces that lay hidden in the womb of time. It may be inconsistent with things that they believed or took for granted. Their beliefs to be significant must be adjusted to the world they knew. It is not in my judgment inconsistent with what they would say today, nor with what today they would believe, if they were called upon to interpret "in the light of our whole experience" the constitution that they framed for the needs of an expanding future.

United States Trust Co. of New York v. New Jersey
431 U.S. 1, 97 S.Ct. 1505, 52 L.Ed. 2d 92 (1977)

The Port Authority of New York and New Jersey was established by the two states to coordinate and improve commerce in the port of New York. In 1962 an agreement between the two states, growing out of a construction project and the acquisition of a railroad, limited the ability of the Port Authority to subsidize rail passenger transportation from revenues and reserves pledged as security for bonds floated by the authority. In 1974, in the wake of a national energy crisis, the states repealed the 1962 Covenant. The bank brought suit in the New Jersey Superior Court, alleging an unconstitutional impairment of the states' contract with the bondholders. The state court dismissed the complaint after trial, and the New Jersey Supreme Court affirmed. Majority: Blackmun, Burger, Rehnquist, Stevens. Dissenting: Brennan, Marshall, White. Not participating: Powell, Stewart.

MR. JUSTICE BLACKMUN delivered the opinion of the Court. . . . [The first part of Justice Blackmun's opinion contains a lengthy statement of the facts and background of the case.]

Home Building & Loan Assn. v. *Blaidell* . . . is regarded as the leading case in the modern era

of Contract Clause interpretation. At issue was the Minnesota Mortgage Moratorium Law, enacted in 1933, during the depth of the Depression and when that State was under severe economic stress, and appeared to have no effective alternative. . . .

This Court's most recent Contract Clause decision

is *El Paso* v. *Simmons*. . . . That case concerned a 1941 Texas statute that limited to a 5-year period the reinstatement rights of an interest-defaulting purchaser of land from the State. . . . The Court recognized that "the power of a State to modify or affect the obligation of contract is not without limit," but held that "the objects of the Texas statute make abundantly clear that it impairs no protected right under the Contract Clause." . . .

Both of these cases eschewed a rigid application of the Contract Clause to invalidate state legislation. Yet neither indicated that the Contract Clause was without meaning in modern constitutional jurisprudence, or that its limitation on state power was illusory. Whether or not the protection of contract rights comports with current views of wise public policy, the Contract Clause remains a part of our written Constitution. . . .

Although the Contract Clause appears literally to proscribe "any" impairment, this Court observed in *Blaisdell* that "the prohibition is not an absolute one and is not to be read with literal exactness like a mathematical formula." . . . Thus, a finding that there has been a technical impairment is merely a preliminary step in resolving the more difficult question whether that impairment is permitted under the Constitution. . . .

We can only sustain the repeal of the 1962 covenant if that impairment was both reasonable and necessary to serve the admittedly important purposes claimed by the State.*

The more specific justification offered for the repeal of the 1962 covenant was the States' plan for encouraging users of private automobiles to shift to public transportation. The States intended to discourage private automobile use by raising bridge and tunnel tolls and to use the extra revenue from those tolls to subsidize improved commuter railroad service. Appellees contend that repeal of the 1962 covenant was necessary to implement this plan because the new mass transit facilities could not possibly be self-supporting and the covenant's "permitted deficits" level had already been exceeded.

We reject this justification because the repeal was neither necessary to achievement of the plan nor reasonable in light of the circumstances.

The determination of necessity can be considered on two levels. First, it cannot be said that total repeal of the covenant was essential; a less drastic modification would have permitted the contemplated plan without entirely removing the covenant's limitations on the use of Port Authority revenues and reserves to subsidize commuter railroads. Second, without modifying the covenant at all, the States could have adopted alternative means of achieving their twin goals of discouraging automobile use and improving mass transit. Appellees contend, however, that choosing among these alternatives is a matter for legislative discretion. But a State is not completely free to consider impairing obligations of its own contracts on a par with other policy alternatives. Similarly, a State is not free to impose a drastic impairment when an evident and more moderate course would serve its purposes equally well. In *El Paso* v. *Simmons* . . . the imposition of a five-year statute of limitations on what was previously a perpetual right of redemption was regarded by this Court as "quite clearly necessary" to achieve the State's vital interest in the orderly administration of its school lands program. . . . In the instant case the State has failed to demonstrate that repeal of the 1962 covenant was similarly necessary.

We also cannot conclude that repeal of the covenant was reasonable in light of the surrounding circumstances. In this regard a comparison with *El Paso* v. *Simmons* . . . again is instructive. There a 19th century statute had effects that were unforeseen and unintended by the legislature when originally adopted. As a result speculators were placed in a position to obtain windfall benefits. The Court held that adoption of a statute of limitation was a reasonable means to "restrict a party to those gains reasonably to be expected from the contract" when it was adopted. . . .

By contrast, in the instant case the need for mass transportation in the New York metropolitan area was not a new development, and the likelihood that publicly owned commuter railroads would produce substantial deficits was well known. As early as 1922, over a half century ago, there were pressures to involve the Port Authority in mass transit. It was with full knowledge of these concerns that

---

* The dissent suggests.. . . . that such careful scrutiny is unwarranted in this case because the harm to bondholders is relatively small. For the same reason, however, contractual obligations of this magnitude need not impose barriers to changes in public policy. The States remain free to exercise their powers of eminent domain to abrogate such contractual rights, upon payment of just compensation. . . .

the 1962 covenant was adopted. Indeed, the covenant was specifically intended to protect the pledged revenues and reserves against the possibility that such concerns would lead the Port Authority into greater involvement in deficit mass transit.

During the 12-year period between adoption of the covenant and its repeal, public perception of the importance of mass transit undoubtedly grew because of increased general concern with environmental protection and energy conservation. But these concerns were not unknown in 1962, and the subsequent changes were of degree and not of kind. We cannot say that these changes caused the covenant to have a substantially different impact in 1974 than when it was adopted in 1962. And we cannot conclude that the repeal was reasonable in the light of changed circumstances.

We therefore hold that the Contract Clause of the United States Constitution prohibits the retroactive repeal of the 1962 covenant. The judgment of the Supreme Court of New Jersey is reversed.

It is so ordered.

MR. JUSTICE BRENNAN, with whom MR. JUSTICE WHITE and MR. JUSTICE MARSHALL join, dissenting.

Decisions of this Court for at least a century have construed the Contract Clause largely to be powerless in binding a State to contracts limiting the authority of successor legislatures to enact laws in furtherance of the health, safety, and similar collective interests of the polity. In short, those decisions established the principle that lawful exercises of a State's police powers stand paramount to private rights held under contract. Today's decision, in invalidating the New Jersey Legislature's 1974 repeal of its predecessor's 1962 covenant, rejects this previous understanding and remolds the Contract Clause into a potent instrument for overseeing important policy determinations of the state legislature. At the same time, by creating a constitutional safe haven for property rights embodied in a contract, the decision substantially distorts modern constitutional jurisprudence governing regulation of private economic interests. . . .

Nowhere are we told why a state policy, no matter how responsive to the general welfare of its citizens, can be reasonable only if it confronts issues that previously were absolutely unforeseen. Indeed, this arbitrary perspective seems peculiarly inappropriate in a case like this where at least three new

and independent congressional enactments between the years 1962 and 1974 summoned major urban centers like New York and New Jersey to action in the environmental, energy, and transportation fields. In short, on this record, I can neither understand nor accept the Court's characterization of New Jersey's action as unreasonable.

If the Court's treatment of New Jersey's legitimate policy interests is inadequate, its consideration of the countervailing injury ostensibly suffered by the appellant is barely discernible at all. For the Court apparently holds that a mere "technical impairment" of contract suffices to subject New Jersey's repealer to serious judicial scrutiny and invalidation under the Contract Clause. . . . The Court's modest statement of the economic injury that today attracts its judicial intervention is, however, understandable. For fairly read, the record before us makes plain that the repeal of the 1962 covenant has occasioned only the most minimal damage on the part of the Authority's bondholders.

Obviously, the heart of the obligation to the bondholders—and the interests ostensibly safeguarded by the 1962 covenant—is the periodic payment of interest and the repayment of principal when due. The Court does not, and indeed cannot, contend that either New Jersey or the Authority has called into question the validity of these underlying obligations. No creditor complains that public authorities have defaulted on a coupon payment or failed to redeem a bond that has matured. In fact, the Court does not even offer any reason whatever for fearing that, as a result of the covenant's repeal, the securities in appellant's portfolio are jeopardized. . . .

One of the fundamental premises of our popular democracy is that each generation of representatives can and will remain responsive to the needs and desires of those whom they represent. Crucial to this end is the assurance that new legislators will not automatically be bound by the policies and undertakings of earlier days. In accordance with this philosophy, the Framers of our Constitution conceived of the Contract Clause primarily as protection for economic transactions entered into by purely private parties, rather than obligations involving the State itself. . . . The Framers fully recognized that nothing would so jeopardize the legitimacy of a system of government that relies upon the ebbs and flows of politics to "clean out the rascals" than the possibility that those same rascals might perpetuate their policies simply by locking them into binding contracts.

Following an early opinion of the Court, however, that took the first step of applying the Contract Clause to public undertakings . . . later decisions attempted to define the reach of the Clause consistently with the demands of our governing processes. The central principle developed by these decisions, beginning at least a century ago, has been that Contract Clause challenges such as that raised by appellant are to be resolved by according unusual deference to the lawmaking authority of state and local governments. Especially when the State acts in furtherance of the variety of broad social interests that came clustered together under the rubric of "police powers" . . . in particular, matters of health, safety, and the preservation of natural resources—the decisions of this Court pursued a course of

steady return to the intention of the Constitution's Framers by closely circumscribing the scope of the Contract Clause. . . .

I would not want to be read as suggesting that the States should blithely proceed down the path of repudiating their obligations, financial or otherwise. Their credibility in the credit market obviously is highly dependent on exercising their vast lawmaking powers with self restraint and discipline, and I, for one, have little doubt that few, if any, jurisdictions would choose to use their authority "so foolish[ly] as to kill a goose that lays golden eggs for them." . . . But in the final analysis, there is no reason to doubt that appellant's financial welfare is being adequately policed by the political processes and the bond marketplace itself. The role to be played by the Constitution is at most a limited one. . . .

Slaughterhouse Cases
83 U.S. (16 Wall.) 36, 21 L.Ed. 394 (1873)

In 1869 the Louisiana legislature granted a monopoly to a slaughterhouse company with a schedule of fees for the sheltering and slaughtering of animals within the city limits of New Orleans. Various butchers then unsuccessfully sought an injunction against the monopoly in the state courts. Majority: Miller, Clifford, Davis, Hunt, Strong. Dissenting: Field, Bradley, Chase, Swayne.

MR. JUSTICE MILLER . . . delivered the opinion of the Court. . . .

The statute is denounced not only as creating a monopoly and conferring odious and exclusive privileges upon a small number of persons at the expense of the great body of the community of New Orleans, but it is asserted that it deprives a large and meritorious class of citizens—the whole of the butchers of the city—of the right to exercise their trade, the business to which they have been trained and on which they depend for the support of themselves and their families; and that the unrestricted exercise of the business of butchering is necessary to the daily subsistence of the population of the city. . . .

The statute . . . does not, as has been asserted, prevent the butcher from doing his own slaughtering. On the contrary, the Slaughter House Company is required, under a heavy penalty, to permit any person who wishes to do so, to slaughter in their houses; and they are bound to make ample provision for the convenience of all slaughtering for the entire city. The butcher then is still permitted to slaughter, to prepare, and to sell his own meats; but he is required to slaughter at a specified place and to pay reasonable compensation for the use of the accommodations furnished him at that place.

The wisdom of the monopoly granted by the legislature may be open to question, but it is difficult to see a justification for the assertion that the butchers are deprived of the right to labor in their occupation, or the people of their daily service in preparing food, or how this statute, with the duties and guards imposed upon the company, can be said to destroy the business of the butcher, or seriously interfere with its pursuit.

The power here exercised by the legislature of Louisiana is, in its essential nature, one which has been, up to the present period in the constitutional history of this country, always conceded to belong to the States, however it may *now* be questioned in some of its details. . . .

The plaintiffs in error . . . allege that the statute is a violation of the Constitution of the United States in these several particulars:

That it creates an involuntary servitude forbidden by the thirteenth article of amendment;

That it abridges the privileges and immunities of citizens of the United States;

That it denies to the plaintiffs the equal protection of the laws; and,

That it deprives them of their property without due process of law; contrary to the provisions of the first section of the fourteenth article of amendment.

This court is thus called upon for the first time to give construction to these articles.

. . . On the most casual examination of the language of these amendments [the Thirteenth, Fourteenth, and Fifteenth], no one can fail to be impressed with the one pervading purpose found in them all, lying at the foundation of each, and without which none of them would have even been suggested; we mean the freedom of the slave race, the security and firm establishment of that freedom, and the protection of the newly-made freeman and citizen from the oppressions of those who had formerly exercised unlimited dominion over him. It is true that only the fifteenth amendment, in terms, mentions the negro by speaking of his color and his slavery. But it is just as true that each of the other articles was addressed to the grievances of that race, and designed to remedy them as the fifteenth.

We do not say that no one else but the negro can share in this protection. . . . But what we do say, and what we wish to be understood is, that in any fair and just construction of any section or phrase of these amendments, it is necessary to look to the purpose which we have said was the pervading spirit of them all, the evil which they were designed to remedy, and the process of continued addition to the Constitution, until that purpose was supposed to be accomplished, as far as constitutional law can accomplish it. . . .

The next observation is more important in view of the arguments of counsel in the present case. It is, that the distinction between citizenship of the United States and citizenship of a State is clearly recognized and established. Not only may a man be a citizen of the United States without being a citizen of a State, but an important element is necessary to convert the former into the latter. He must reside within the State to make him a citizen of it, but it is only necessary that he should be born or naturalized in the United States to be a citizen of the Union.

It is quite clear, then, that there is a citizenship of the United States, and a citizenship of a State, which are distinct from each other, and which depend upon different characteristics or circumstances in the individual.

We think this distinction and its explicit recognition in this amendment of great weight in this argument, because the next paragraph of this same section, which is the one mainly relied on by the plaintiffs in error, speaks only of privileges and immunities of citizens of the United States, and does not speak of those of citizens of the several States. The argument, however, in favor of the plaintiffs rests wholly on the assumption that the citizenship is the same, and the privileges and immunities guaranteed by the clause are the same.

The language is, "No State shall make or enforce any law which shall abridge the privileges or immunities of citizens of *the United States*." It is a little remarkable, if this clause was intended as a protection to the citizen of a State against the legislative power of his own State, that the word citizen of the State should be left out when it is so carefully used, and used in contradistinction to citizens of the United States, in the very sentence which precedes it. It is too clear for argument that the change in phraseology was adopted understandingly and with a purpose.

Of the privileges and immunities of the citizen of the United States, and of the privileges and immunities of the citizen of the State, and what they respectively are, we will presently consider; but we wish to state here that it is only the former which are placed by this clause under the protection of the Federal Constitution, and that the latter, whatever they may be, are not intended to have any additional protection by this paragraph of the amendment.

If, then, there is a difference between the privileges and immunities belonging to a citizen of the United States as such, and those belonging to the citizen of the State as such the latter must rest for their security and protection where they have heretofore rested; for they are not embraced by this paragraph of the amendment. . . .

Fortunately we are not without judicial construction of this clause of the Constitution. The first and the leading case on the subject is that of *Corfield* v. *Coryell* decided by Mr. Justice Washington in the Circuit Court for the District of Pennsylvania in 1823.

"The inquiry," he says, "is, what are the privileges and immunities of citizens of the several States? We feel no hesitation in confining these expressions to those privileges and immunities which are fundamental; which belong of right to the citizens of all free governments, and which have at all times been enjoyed by citizens of the several States which compose this Union, from the time of their becoming free, independent, and sovereign. What these fundamental principles are, it would be more tedious than difficult to enumerate. They may all, however, be comprehended under the following general heads: protection by the government, with the right to acquire and possess property of every kind, and to pursue and obtain happiness and safety, nevertheless, to such restraints as the government may prescribe for the general good of the whole.". . . .

It would be the vainest show of learning to attempt to prove by citations of authority, that up to the adoption of the recent amendments, no claim or pretense was set up that those rights depended on the Federal government for their existence or protection, beyond the very few express limitations which the Federal Constitution imposed upon the States—such, for instance, as the prohibition against ex post facto laws, bills of attainder, and laws impairing the obligation of contracts. But with the

exception of these and a few other restrictions, the entire domain of the privileges and immunities of the citizens of the States, as above defined, lay within the constitutional and legislative power of the States, and without that of the Federal government. Was it the purpose of the Fourteenth Amendment, by the simple declaration that no State should make or enforce any law which shall abridge the privileges and immunities of *citizens of the United States,* to transfer the security and protection of all the civil rights which we have mentioned, from the States to the Federal government? And where it is declared that Congress shall have the power to enforce that article, was it intended to bring within the power of Congress the entire domain of civil rights heretofore belonging exclusively to the States?

All this and more must follow, if the proposition of the plaintiffs in error be sound. For not only are these rights subject to the control of Congress whenever in its discretion any of them are supposed to be abridged by State legislation, but that body may also pass laws in advance, limiting and restricting the exercise of legislative power by the States, in their most ordinary and usual functions, as in its judgment it may think proper on all such subjects. And still further, such a construction followed by the reversal of the judgments of the Supreme Court of Louisiana in these cases, would constitute this court a perpetual censor upon all legislation of the States, on the civil rights of their own citizens, with authority to nullify such as it did not approve as consistent with those rights, as they existed at the time of the adoption of this amendment. The argument we admit is not always the most conclusive which is drawn from the consequences urged against the adoption of a particular construction of an instrument. But when, as in the case before us, these consequences are so serious, so far-reaching and pervading, so great a departure from the structure and spirit of our institutions; when the effect is to fetter and degrade the State governments by subjecting them to the control of Congress, in the exercise of powers heretofore universally conceded to them of the most ordinary and fundamental character; when in fact it radically changes the whole theory of the relations of the State and Federal governments to each other and of both these governments to the people; the argument has a force that is irresistible, in the absence of language which expresses such a purpose too clearly to admit of doubt.

We are convinced that no such results were intended by the Congress which proposed these amendments, nor by the legislatures of the States which ratified them. . . .

The argument has not been much pressed in these cases that the defendant's charter deprives the plaintiffs of their property without due process of law, or that it denies to them the equal protection of the law. The first of these paragraphs has been in the Constitution since the adoption of the fifth amendment, as a restraint upon the Federal power. It is also to be found in some form of expression in the constitutions of nearly all the states, as a restraint upon the power of the States. This law, then, has practically been the same as it now is during the existence of the government except so far as the present amendment may place the restraining power over the States in this matter in the hands of the Federal government.

We are not without judicial interpretation, therefore, both State and National, of the meaning of this clause. And it is sufficient to say that under no construction of that provision that we have ever seen, or any that we deem admissible, can the restraint imposed by the State of Louisiana upon the exercise of their trade by the butchers of New Orleans be held to be a deprivation of property within the meaning of that provision.

"Nor shall any State deny to any person within its jurisdiction the equal protection of the laws."

In the light of the history of these amendments, and the pervading purpose of them, which we have already discussed, it is not difficult to give a meaning to this clause. The existence of laws in the States where the newly emancipated negroes resided, which discriminated with gross injustice and hardship against them as a class, was the evil to be remedied by this clause, and by it such laws are forbidden.

If, however, the States did not conform their laws to its requirements, then by the fifth section of the article of amendment Congress was authorized to enforce it by suitable legislation. We doubt very much whether any action of a State not directed by way of discrimination against the negroes as a class, or on account of their race, will ever be held to come within the purview of this provision. It is so clearly a provision for that race and that

emergency, that a strong case would be necessary for its application to any other. . . .

The judgments of the Supreme Court of Louisiana in these cases are

Affirmed.

MR. JUSTICE FIELD, dissenting. . . .

The question presented is . . . one of the gravest importance, not merely to the parties here, but to the whole country. It is nothing less than the question whether the recent amendments to the Federal Constitution protect the citizens of the United States against the deprivation of their common rights by legislation. In my judgment the fourteenth amendment does afford such protection, and was so intended by the Congress which framed and the States which adopted it.

The amendment does not attempt to confer any new privileges or immunities upon citizens, or to enumerate or define those already existing. It assumes that there are such privileges and immunities which belong of right to citizens as such, and ordains that they shall not be abridged by State legislation. If this inhibition has no reference to privileges and immunities of this character, but only refers, as held by the majority of the court in their opinion, to such privileges and immunities as were before its adoption specially designated in the Constitution or necessarily implied as belonging to citizens of the United States, it was a vain and idle enactment, which accomplished nothing, and most unnecessarily excited Congress and the people on its passage. With privileges and immunities thus designated or implied no State could ever have interfered by its laws and no new constitutional provision was required to inhibit such interference. The supremacy of the Constitution and the laws of the United States always controlled any State legislation of that character. But if the amendment refers to the natural and inalienable rights which belong to all citizens, the inhibition has a profound significance and consequence.

What, then, are the privileges and immunities which are secured against abridgment by State legislation? . . .

The terms, "privileges and immunities" are not new in the Amendment; they were in the Constitution before the Amendment was adopted. They are found in the 2d section of the 4th article, which declares that "the citizens of each State shall be entitled to all privileges and immunities of citizens in the several States," and they have been the subject of frequent consideration in judicial decisions. In *Corfield* v. *Coryell* . . . Mr. Justice Washington said he had "no hesitation in confining these expressions to those privileges and immunities which were, in their nature, fundamental; which belong of right to citizens of all free governments, and which have at all times been enjoyed by the citizens of the several States which compose the Union, from the time of their becoming free, independent, and sovereign"; and in considering what those fundamental privileges were, he said that perhaps it would be more tedious than difficult to enumerate them, but that they might be "all comprehended under the following general heads: protection by the government; the enjoyment of life and liberty, with the right to acquire and possess property of every kind, and to pursue and obtain happiness and safety, subject, nevertheless to such restraints as the government may justly prescribe for the general good of the whole." This appears to me to be a sound construction of the clause in question. The privileges and immunities designated are those *which of right belong to the citizens of all free governments*. Clearly among these must be placed the right to pursue a lawful employment in a lawful manner, without other restraint than such as equally affects all persons. . . .

This equality of right, with exemption from all disparaging and partial enactments, in the lawful pursuits of life, throughout the whole country, is the distinguishing privilege of citizens of the United States. To them, everywhere, all pursuits, all professions, all avocations are open without other restrictions than such as are imposed equally upon all others of the same age, sex, and condition. The State may prescribe such regulations for every pursuit and calling of life as will promote the public health, secure the good order and advance the general prosperity of society, but when once prescribed the pursuit or calling must be free to be followed by every citizen who is within the conditions designated, and will conform to the regulations. This is the fundamental idea upon which our institutions rest, and unless adhered to in the legislation of the country our government will be a republic only in name. . . .

I am authorized by the CHIEF JUSTICE [CHASE], MR. JUSTICE SWAYNE, and MR. JUSTICE BRADLEY, to state that they concur with me in this dissenting opinion.

Munn v. Illinois
94 U.S. 113, 24 L.Ed. 77 (1877)

Article XIII of the Constitution of Illinois, adopted in 1870, declared grain elevators to be "public warehouses" and gave to the general assembly the power of passing laws relating to the storage of grain. An act of 1871 fixed the rates warehouse owners might charge, required licenses, and made other regulations governing the conduct of warehousemen. Munn was convicted of operating a warehouse without a license and other unlawful practices and he sought review from an adverse judgment in the Illinois Supreme Court. That part of the chief justice's opinion dealing with the commerce clause is omitted. Majority: Waite, Bradley, Clifford, Davis, Hunt, Miller, Swayne. Dissenting: Field, Strong.

MR. CHIEF JUSTICE WAITE delivered the opinion of the Court.

The question to be determined in this case is whether the general assembly of Illinois can, under the limitations upon the legislative powers of the States imposed by the Constitution of the United States, fix by law the maximum of charges for the storage of grain in warehouses at Chicago and other places in the State having not less than one hundred thousand inhabitants, "in which grain is stored in bulk, and in which the grain of different owners is mixed together, or in which grain is stored in such a manner that the identity of different lots or parcels cannot be accurately preserved." . . .

When one becomes a member of society, he necessarily parts with some rights or privileges which, as an individual not affected by his relations to others, he might retain. "A body politic," as aptly defined in the preamble of the Constitution of Massachusetts, "is a social compact by which the whole people covenants with each citizen, and each citizen with the whole people, that all shall be governed by certain laws for the common good." This does not confer power upon the whole people to control rights which are purely and exclusively private . . . but it does authorize the establishment of laws requiring each citizen to so conduct himself, and so use his own property, as not unnecessarily to injure another. This is the very essence of government, and has found expression in the maxim, *sic utere tuo ut alienum non laedas.* [So use your own as not to injure others.] From this source come the police powers, which, as was said by Mr. Chief Justice Taney in the License Cases, "are nothing more or less than the powers of government inherent in every sovereignty . . . that is to say . . . the power to govern men and things." Under these powers the government regulates the conduct of its citizens one towards another, and the manner in which each shall use his own property, when such regulation becomes necessary for the public good. In their exercise it has been customary in England from time immemorial, and in this country from its first colonization, to regulate ferries, common carriers, hackmen, bakers, millers, wharfingers, inn-keepers, &c., and in so doing to fix a maximum of charge to be made for services rendered, accommodations furnished, and articles sold. To this day, statutes are to be found in many of the States upon some or all these subjects; and we think it has never yet been successfully contended that such legislation came within any of the constitutional prohibitions against interference with private property. With the Fifth Amendment in force, Congress in 1820 conferred power upon the city of Washington "to regulate . . . the rates of wharfage at private wharves . . . the sweeping of chimneys, and to fix the rates of fees therefor . . . and the weight and quality of bread" . . . and, in 1848, "to make all necessary regulations respecting hackney carriages and the rates of fare of the same,

and the rates of hauling by cartmen, wagoners, carmen, and draymen, and the rates of commission of auctioneers." . . .

From this it is apparent that, down to the time of the adoption of the Fourteenth Amendment, it was not supposed that statutes regulating the use, or even the price of the use, of private property necessarily deprived an owner of his property without due process of law. Under some circumstances they may, but not under all. The amendment does not change the law in this particular: it simply prevents the States from doing that which will operate as such a deprivation.

This brings us to inquire as to the principles upon which this power of regulation rests, in order that we may determine what is within and what is without its operative effect. Looking, then, to the common law, from whence came the right which the Constitution protects, we find that when private property is "affected with a public interest, it ceases to be *juris privati* only." This was said by Lord Chief Justice Hale more than two hundred years ago, in his treatise *De Portibus Maris* . . . and has been accepted without objection as an essential element in the law of property ever since. Property does become clothed with a public interest, when used in a manner to make it of public consequence, and affect the community at large. When, therefore, one devotes his property to a use in which the public has an interest, he, in effect, grants to the public an interest in that use, and must submit to be controlled by the public for the common good, to the extent of the interest he has thus created. He may withdraw his grant by discontinuing the use; but, so long as he maintains the use, he must submit to the control. . . .

. . . It is difficult to see why, if the common carrier, or the miller, or the ferryman, or the innkeeper, or the wharfinger, or the baker, or the cartman, or the hackney-coachman, pursues a public employment and exercises "a sort of public office," these plaintiffs in error do not. They stand, to use again the language of their counsel, in the very "gateway of commerce," and take toll from all who pass. Their business most certainly "tends to a common charge, and has become a thing of public interest and use." Every bushel of grain for its passage "pays a toll, which is a common charge," and, therefore, according to Lord Hale, every such warehouseman "ought to be under public regulation, viz., that he . . . take but reasonable toll."

Certainly, if any business can be clothed "with a public interest and cease to be *juris privati* only," this has been. It may not be made so by the operation of the Constitution of Illinois or this statute, but it is by the facts.

. . . For our purposes we must assume that, if a state of facts could exist that would justify such legislation, it actually did exist when the statute now under consideration was passed. For us the question is one of power, not of expediency. If no state of circumstances could exist to justify such a statute, then we may declare this one void, because in excess of the legislative power of the State. But if it could, we must presume it did. Of the propriety of legislative interference within the scope of legislative power, the legislature is the exclusive judge. . . .

It is insisted, however, that the owner of property is entitled to a reasonable compensation for its use, even though it be clothed with a public interest, and that what is reasonable is a judicial and not a legislative question.

As has already been shown, the practice had been otherwise. In countries where the common law prevails, it has been customary from time immemorial for the legislature to declare what shall be a reasonable compensation under such circumstances, or, perhaps more properly speaking, to fix a maximum beyond which any charge made would be unreasonable. Undoubtedly, in mere private contracts, relating to matters in which the public has no interest, what is reasonable must be ascertained judicially. But this is because the legislature has no control over such a contract. So, too, in matters which do affect the public interest, and as to which legislative control may be exercised, if there are no statutory regulations upon the subject, the courts must determine what is reasonable. The controlling fact is the power to regulate at all. If that exists, the right to establish the maximum of charge, as one of the means of regulation, is implied. . . .

We know that this is a power which may be abused; but that is no argument against its existence. For protection against abuses by legislatures the people must resort to the polls, not to the courts. . . .

Judgment affirmed.

MR. JUSTICE FIELD, dissenting. . . .

The declaration of the Constitution of 1870, that private buildings used for private purposes shall be deemed public institutions, does not make them so. The receipt and storage of grain in a building erected by private means for that purpose does not constitute the building a public warehouse. There is no magic in the language, though used by a constitutional convention, which can change a private business into a public one, or alter the character of the building in which the business is transacted. A tailor's or a shoemaker's shop would still retain its private character, even though the assembled wisdom of the State should declare, by organic act or legislative ordinance, that such a place was a public workshop, and that the workmen were public tailors or public shoemakers. One might as well attempt to change the nature of colors, by giving them a new designation. The defendants were no more public warehousemen, as justly observed by counsel, than the merchant who sells his merchandise to the public is a public merchant, or blacksmith who shoes horses for the public is a public blacksmith and it was a strange notion that by calling them so they would be brought under legislative control. . . .

. . . The doctrine declared is that property "becomes clothed with a public interest when used in a manner to make it of public consequence, and affect the community at large"; and from such clothing the right of the legislature is deduced to control the use of the property, and to determine the compensation which the owner may receive for it. When Sir Matthew Hale, and the sages of the law in his day, spoke of property as affected by a public interest, and ceasing from that cause to be *juris privati* solely, that is ceasing to be held merely in private right, they referred to property dedicated by the owner to public uses, or to property the use of which was granted by the government, or in connection with which special privileges were conferred. Unless the property was thus dedicated or some right bestowed by the government was held with the property, either by specific grant or by prescription of so long a time as to imply a grant originally, the property was not affected by any public interest so as to be taken out of the category of property held in private right. But it is not in any such sense that the terms "clothing property with a public interest" are used in this case. From the nature of the business under consideration—the storage of grain—which, in any sense in which the words can be used, is a private business, in which the public are interested only as they are interested in the storage of other products of the soil, or in articles of manufacture, it is clear that the court intended to declare that, whenever one devotes his property to a business which is useful to the public—"affects the community at large,"—the legislature can regulate the compensation which the owner may receive for its use, and for his own services in connection with it. . . .

If this be sound law, if there be no protection, either in the principles upon which our republican government is founded, or in the prohibitions of the Constitution against such invasion of private rights, all property and all business in the State are held at the mercy of a majority of its legislature. The public has no greater interest in the use of buildings for the storage of grain than it has in the use of buildings for the residences of families, nor, indeed, any thing like so great an interest; and, according to the doctrine announced, the legislature may fix the rent of all tenements used for residences, without reference to the cost of their erection. If the owner does not like the rates prescribed, he may cease renting his houses. He has granted to the public, says the court, an interest in the use of the buildings, and "he may withdraw his grant by discontinuing the use; but, so long as he maintains the use, he must submit to the control." . . .

The same liberal construction which is required for the protection of life and liberty, in all particulars in which life and liberty are of any value, should be applied to the protection of private property. If the legislature of a State, under pretense of providing for the public good, or for any other reason, can determine, against the consent of the owner, the uses to which private property shall be devoted, or the prices which the owner shall receive for its uses,

it can deprive him of the property as completely as by a special act for its confiscation or destruction. If, for instance, the owner is prohibited from using his building for the purposes for which it was designed, it is of little consequence that he is permitted to retain the title and possession; or, if he is compelled to take as compensation for its use less than the expenses to which he is subjected by its ownership, he is, for all practical purposes, deprived of the property, as effectually as if the legislature had ordered his forcible dispossession. If it be admitted that the legislature has any control over the compensation, the extent of that compensation becomes a mere matter of legislative discretion. . . .

There is nothing in the character of the business of the defendants as warehousemen which called for the interference complained of in this case. Their buildings are not nuisances; their occupation of receiving and storing grain infringes upon no rights of others, disturbs no neighborhood, infects not the air, and in no respect prevents others from using and enjoying their property as to them may seem best. The legislation in question is nothing less than a bold assertion of absolute power by the state to control at its discretion the property and business of the citizen, and fix the compensation he shall receive. . . .

I deny the power of any legislature under our government to fix the price which one shall receive for his property of any kind. If the power can be exercised as to one article, it may as to all articles, and the prices of every thing, from a calico gown to a city mansion, may be the subject of legislative direction. . . .

I am of opinion that the judgment of the Supreme Court of Illinois should be reversed.

Unstaged Debate of 1893:
Justice Brewer v. Professor Thayer

JUSTICE DAVID J. BREWER, *THE MOVEMENT OF COERCION,* AN ADDRESS BEFORE THE NEW YORK STATE BAR ASSOCIATION, JANUARY 17, 1893

Three things differentiate the civilized man from the savage—that which he knows, that which he is, and that which he has. That which he knows: The Knowledge of the savage is limited to the day, and bounded by the visible horizon. The civilized man looks backward through all history, and beholds the present limits of the universe. The accumulations of the centuries are his. The logic of Aristotle and Bacon determines the processes of his mind. The philosophy of Plato and Herbert Spencer is his wisdom. . . .

It is the unvarying law, that the wealth of a community will be in the hands of a few; and the greater the general wealth, the greater the individual accumulations. The large majority of men are unwilling to endure that long self-denial and saving which makes accumulation possible; they have not the business tact and sagacity which bring about large combinations and great financial results; and hence it always has been, and until human nature is remodeled always will be true, that the wealth of a nation is in the hands of a few, while the many subsist upon the proceeds of their daily toil. But security is the chief end of government; and other things being equal, that government is best which protects to the fullest extent each individual, rich or poor, high or low, in the possession of his property and the pursuit of his business. It was the boast of our ancestors in the old country, that they were able to wrest from the power of the king so much security for life, liberty and property. . . .

Here there is no monarch threatening trespass upon the individual. The danger is from the multitudes—the majority, with whom is the power. . . .

This movement expresses itself in two ways: First, in the improper use of labor organizations to destroy the freedom of the laborer, and control the uses of capital. . . .

The other form of this movement assumes the guise of a regulation of the charges for the use of property subjected, or supposed to be, to a public use. This acts in two directions: One by extending the list of those things, charges for whose use the government may prescribe; until now we hear it affirmed that whenever property is devoted to a use in which the public has an interest, charges for that use may be fixed by law. And if there be any property in the use of which the public or some portion of it has no interest, I hardly know what it is or where to find it. And second, in so reducing charges for the use of property, which in fact is subjected to a public use, that no compensation or income is received by those who have so invested their property. By the one it subjects all

property and its uses to the will of the majority; by the other it robs property of its value. Statutes and decisions both disclose that this movement, with just these results, has a present and alarming existence. . . .

. . . It may be said that that majority will not be so foolish, selfish and cruel as to strip that property of its earning capacity. I say that so long as constitutional guaranties lift on American soil their buttresses and bulwarks against wrong, and so long as the American judiciary breathes the free air of courage, it cannot. . . .

As might be expected, they who wish to push this movement to the extreme, who would brook no restraint on aught that seems to make for their gain, are unanimous in crying out against judicial interference, and are constantly seeking to minimize the power of the courts. . . . The argument is that judges are not adapted by their education and training to settle such matters as these; that they lack acquaintance with affairs and are tied to precedents; that the procedure in the courts is too slow and that no action could be had therein until long after the need of action has passed. It would be folly to assert that this argument is barren of force. . . . But the great body of judges are as well versed in the affairs of life as any, and they who unravel all the mysteries of accounting between partners, settle the business of the largest corporations and extract all the truth from the mass of scholastic verbiage that falls from the lips of expert witnesses in patent cases, will have no difficulty in determining what is right and wrong between employer and employees, and whether proposed rates of freight and fare are reasonable as between the public and the owners; while as for speed, is there anything quicker than a writ of injunction? . . .

The mischief-makers in this movement ever strive to get away from courts and judges, and to place the power of decision in the hands of those who will the more readily and freely yield to the pressure of numbers, that so-called demand of the majority. . . .

And so it is, that because of the growth of this movement, of its development in many directions, and the activity of those who are in it, and especially because of the further fact that, carrying votes in its hand, it ever appeals to the trimming politician and time-serving demagogue, and thus enters into so much of legislation, arises the urgent need of giving to the judiciary the utmost vigor and efficiency. Now, if ever in the history of this country, must there be somewhere and somehow a controlling force which speaks for justice, and for justice only. . . .

What, then, ought to be done? My reply is, strengthen the judiciary. . . .

It may be said that this is practically substituting government by the judges for government by the people, and thus turning back the currents of history. The world has seen government by chiefs, by kings and emperors, by priests and by nobles. All have failed, and now government by the people is on trial. Shall we abandon that and try government by judges? But this involves a total misunderstanding of the relations of judges to government. There is nothing in this power of the judiciary detracting in the least from the idea of government of and by the people. The courts hold neither purse nor sword; they cannot corrupt nor arbitrarily control. They make no laws, they establish no policy, they never enter into the domain of popular action. They do not govern. Their functions in relation to the State are limited to seeing that popular action does not trespass upon right and justice as it exists in written constitutions and natural law. So it is that the utmost power of the courts and judges works no interference with true liberty, no trespass on the fullest and highest development of government of and by the people; it only means security to personal rights—the inalienable rights, life, liberty and the pursuit of happiness. . . .

I am firmly persuaded that the salvation of the Nation, the permanence of government of and by the people, rests upon the independence and vigor of the judiciary. To stay the waves of popular feeling, to restrain the greedy hand of the many from filching from the few that which they have honestly acquired, and to protect in every man's possession and enjoyment, be he rich or poor, that which he hath, demands a tribunal as strong as is consistent with the freedom of human action, and as free from all influences and suggestions other than is compassed in the thought of justice, as can be created out of the infirmities of human nature. To that end the courts exist. . . .

JAMES BRADLEY THAYER, *THE ORIGIN AND SCOPE OF THE AMERICAN DOCTRINE OF CONSTITUTIONAL LAW,* AN ADDRESS BEFORE

THE CONGRESS ON JURISPRUDENCE AND LAW REFORM, AUGUST 9, 1893. 7 *HARVARD LAW REVIEW, 129–156 (1893)*

How did our American doctrine, which allows to the judiciary the power to declare legislative Acts unconstitutional, and to treat them as null, come about, and what is the true scope of it? . . .

. . . The court's duty, we are told, is the mere and simple office of construing two writings and comparing one with another, as two contracts or two statutes are construed and compared when they are said to conflict; of declaring the true meaning of each, and, if they are opposed to each other, of carrying into effect the constitution as being of superior obligation—an ordinary and humble judicial duty, as the courts sometimes describe it. This way of putting it easily results in the wrong kind of disregard of legislative considerations; not merely in refusing to let them directly operate as grounds of judgment, but in refusing to consider them at all. Instead of taking them into account and allowing for them as furnishing possible grounds of legislative action, there takes place a pedantic and academic treatment of the texts of the constitution and the laws. And so we miss that combination of a lawyer's rigor with a statesman's breadth of view which should be found in dealing with this class of questions in constitutional law. . . .

The courts have perceived with more or less distinctness that this exercise of the judicial function does in truth go far beyond the simple business which judges sometimes describe. If their duty were in truth merely and nakedly to ascertain the meaning of the text of the constitution and of the impeached Act of the legislature, and to determine, as an academic question, whether in the court's judgment the two were in conflict, it would, to be sure, be an elevated and important office, one dealing with great matters, involving large public considerations, but yet a function far simpler than it really is. Having ascertained all this, yet there remains a question—the really momentous question—whether, after all, the court can disregard the Act. It cannot do this as a mere matter of course—merely because it is concluded that upon a just and true construction the law is unconstitutional. That is precisely the significance of the rule of administration that the courts lay down. It can only disregard the Act when those who have the right to make laws have not merely made a mistake, but have made a very clear one—so clear that it is not open to rational question. That is the standard of duty to which the courts bring legislative Acts; that is the test which they apply—not merely their own judgment as to constitutionality, but their conclusion as to what judgment is permissible to another department which the constitution has charged with the duty of making it. This rule recognizes that, having regard to the great, complex, ever-unfolding exigencies of government, much which will seem unconstitutional to one man, or body of men, may reasonably not seem so to another; that the constitution often admits of different interpretations; that there is often a range of choice and judgment; that in such cases the constitution does not impose upon the legislature any one specific opinion, but leaves open this range of choice; and that whatever choice is rational is constitutional. . . . [A legislator] may vote against a measure as being, in his judgment, unconstitutional; and, being subsequently placed on the bench, when this measure, having been passed by the legislature in spite of his opposition, comes before him judicially, may there find it his duty, although he has in no degree changed his opinion, to declare it constitutional. . . .

The legislature in determining what shall be done, what it is reasonable to do, does not divide its duty with the judges, nor must it conform to their conception of what is prudent or reasonable legislation. The judicial function is merely that of fixing the outside border of reasonable legislative action, the boundary beyond which the taxing power, the power of eminent domain, police power, and legislative power in general, cannot go without violating the prohibitions of the constitution or crossing the line of its grants. . . .

. . . *[T]he ultimate question is not what is the true meaning of the constitution, but whether legislation is sustainable or not.* . . .

. . . What really took place in adopting our theory of constitutional law was this: we introduced for the first time into the conduct of government through its great departments a judicial sanction, as among these departments, not full and complete, but partial. The judges were allowed, indirectly and in a degree, the power to revise the action of other departments and to pronounce it null. In simple truth, while this is a mere judicial function, it involves, owing to the subject matter with which it deals, taking a part, a secondary part, in the political conduct of government. If that be so, then the judges must apply methods and principles that befit their task. In such a work there can be no permanent or fitting *modus vivendi* between the different departments unless each is sure of the full cooperation of the others, as long as its own action conforms to any reasonable and fairly permissible view of its constitutional power. The ultimate arbiter of what is rational and permissible is indeed always the courts, so far as litigated cases bring the question before them. This leaves to our courts a great and stately jurisdiction. It will only imperil the whole of it if it is sought to give them more. They must not step into the shoes of the lawmaker. . . .

I am not stating a new doctrine, but attempting to restate more exactly and truly an admitted one. If what I have said be sound, it is greatly to be desired that it should be more emphasized by our courts, in its full significance. It has been often remarked that private rights are more respected by the legislatures of some countries which have no written constitution, than by ours. No doubt our doctrine of constitutional law had had a tendency to drive out questions of justice and right, and to fill the mind of legislators with thoughts of mere legality, of what the constitution allows. And, moreover, even in the matter of legality, they have felt little responsibility; if we are wrong, they say, the courts will correct it. If what I have been saying is true, the safe and permanent road towards reform is that of impressing upon our people a far stronger sense than they have of the great range of possible harm and evil that our system leaves open, and must leave open, to the legislatures, and of the clear limits of judicial power; so that responsibility may be brought sharply home where it belongs. . . . Under no system can the power of courts go far to save a people from ruin; our chief protection lies elsewhere. . . .

Lochner v. *New York*
198 U.S. 45, 25 S.Ct. 539, 49 L.Ed 937 (1905)

Joseph Lochner, a bakery owner in Utica, was convicted of violating a New York law that limited the hours of employment in bakeries and confectionery establishments to ten hours a day and sixty hours a week. The New York appellate courts sustained the conviction. Majority: Peckham, Brewer, Brown, Fuller, McKenna. Dissenting: Harlan, Day, Holmes, White.

MR. JUSTICE PECKHAM . . . delivered the opinion of the Court. . . .

The statute necessarily interferes with the right of contract between the employer and employés, concerning the number of hours in which the latter may labor in the bakery of the employer. The general right to make a contract in relation to his business is part of the liberty of the individual protected by the Fourteenth Amendment of the federal constitution. Under that provision no state can deprive any person of life, liberty, or property without due process of law. The right to purchase or to sell labor is part of the liberty protected by this amendment, unless there are circumstances which exclude the right. There are, however, certain powers, existing in the sovereignty of each state in the Union, somewhat vaguely termed police powers, the exact description and limitation of which have not been attempted by the courts. Those powers, broadly stated, and without, at present, any attempt at a more specific limitation, relate to the safety, health, morals and general welfare of the public. Both property and liberty are held on such reasonable conditions as may be imposed by the governing power of the state in the exercise of those powers, and with such conditions the Fourteenth Amendment was not designed to interfere.

It must, of course, be conceded that there is a limit to the valid exercise of the police power by the state. There is no dispute concerning this general proposition. Otherwise the Fourteenth Amendment would have no efficacy and the legislatures of the states would have unbounded power, and it would be enough to say that any piece of legislation was enacted to conserve the morals, the health, or the safety of the people; such legislation would be valid, no matter how absolutely without foundation the claim might be. The claim of the police power

would be a mere pretext—become another and delusive name for the supreme sovereignty of the state to be exercised free from constitutional restraint. This is not contended for. In every case that comes before this court, therefore, where legislation of this character is concerned, and where the protection of the federal Constitution is sought, the question necessarily arises: Is this a fair, reasonable, and appropriate exercise of the police power of the state, or is it an unreasonable, unnecessary, and arbitrary interference with the right of the individual to his personal liberty, or to enter into those contracts in relation to labor which may seem to him appropriate or necessary for the support of himself and his family? Of course the liberty of contract relating to labor includes both parties to it. The one has as much right to purchase as the other to sell labor.

This is not a question of substituting the judgment of the court for that of the legislature. If the act be within the power of the state it is valid, although the judgment of the court might be totally opposed to the enactment of such a law. But the question would still remain: Is it within the police power of the state? and that question must be answered by the court.

The question whether this act is valid as a labor law, pure and simple, may be dismissed in a few words. There is no reasonable ground for interfering with the liberty of person or the right of free contract, by determining the hours of labor, in the occupation of a baker. There is no contention that bakers as a class are not equal in intelligence and capacity to men in other trades or manual occupations, or that they are not able to assert their rights and care for themselves without the protecting arm of the state, interfering with their independence of judgment and of action. They are in no sense wards of the state. Viewed in the light of a purely labor law, with no reference whatever to the question of health, we think that a law like the one before us involves neither the safety, the morals, nor the welfare, of the public, and that the interest of the public is not in the slightest degree affected by such an act. The law must be upheld, if at all, as a law pertaining to the health of the individual engaged in the occupation of a baker. It does not affect any other portion of the public than those who are engaged in that occupation. Clean and wholesome bread does not depend upon whether the baker works but ten hours per day or only sixty hours a week. The limitation of the hours of labor does not come within the police power on that ground. . . .

We think that there can be no fair doubt that the trade of a baker, in and of itself, is not an unhealthy one to that degree which would authorize the legislature to interfere with the right to labor, and with the right of free contract on the part of the individual, either as employer or employé. In looking through statistics regarding all trades and occupations, it may be true that the trade of a baker does not appear to be as healthy as some other trades, and is also vastly more healthy than still others. To the common understanding the trade of a baker has never been regarded as an unhealthy one. Very likely physicians would not recommend the exercise of that or of any other trade as a remedy for ill health. Some occupations are more healthy than others, but we think there are none which might not come under the power of the legislature to supervise and control the hours of working therein, if the mere fact that the occupation is not absolutely and perfectly healthy is to confer that right upon the legislative department of the government. It might be safely affirmed that almost all occupations more or less affect the health. . . . But are we all, on that account, at the mercy of legislative majorities? . . .

We do not believe in the soundness of the views which uphold this law. On the contrary we think that such a law as this, although passed in the assumed exercise of the police power, and as relating to the public health, or the health of the employés named, is not within that power, and is invalid. The act is not, within any fair meaning of the term, a health law, but is an illegal interference with the rights of individuals, both employers and

employes, to make contracts regarding labor upon such terms as they may think best, or which they may agree upon with the other parties to such contracts. . . .

Reversed.

MR. JUSTICE HARLAN, with whom MR. JUSTICE WHITE and MR. JUSTICE DAY concurred, dissenting. . . .

There are many reasons of a weighty, substantial character, based upon the experience of mankind, in support of the theory that, all things considered, more than ten hours' steady work each day, from week to week, in a bakery or confectionery establishment, may endanger the health and shorten the lives of the workmen, thereby diminishing their physical and mental capacity to serve the state and to provide for those dependent upon them.

If such reasons exist that ought to be the end of this case, for the state is not amenable to the judiciary, in respect of its legislative enactments, unless such enactments are plainly, palpably, beyond all question, inconsistent with the Constitution. . . .

MR. JUSTICE HOLMES, dissenting. . . .

This case is decided upon an economic theory which a large part of the country does not entertain. If it were a question whether I agree with that theory, I should desire to study if further and long before making up my mind. But I do not conceive that to be my duty, because I strongly believe that my agreement or disagreement has nothing to do with the right of a majority to embody their opinions in law. It is settled by various decisions of this court that state Constitutions and state laws may regulate life in many ways which we as legislators might think as injudicious, or if you like as tyrannical as this, and which, equally with this, interfere with the liberty to contract. Sunday laws and usury laws are ancient examples. A more modern one is the prohibition of lotteries. The liberty of the citizen to do as he likes so long as he does not interfere with the liberty of others to do the same, which has been a shibboleth for some well-known writers, is interfered with by school laws, by the post office, by every state or municipal institution which takes his money for purposes thought desirable, whether he likes it or not. The Fourteenth Amendment does not enact Mr. Herbert Spencer's Social Statics. . . . [A] constitution is not intended to embody a particular economic theory, whether of paternalism and the organic relation of the citizen to the state or of *laissez faire*. It is made for people of fundamentally differing views, and the accident of our finding certain opinions natural and familiar, or novel, and even shocking, ought not to conclude our judgment upon the question whether statutes embodying them conflict with the Constitution of the United States.

General propositions do not decide concrete cases. The decisions will depend on a judgment or intuition more subtle than any articulate major premise. But I think that the proposition just stated, if it is accepted, will carry us far toward the end. Every opinion tends to become a law. I think that the word "liberty," in the Fourteenth Amendment, is perverted when it is held to prevent the natural outcome of a dominant opinion, unless it can be said that a rational and fair man necessarily would admit that the statute proposed would infringe fundamental principles as they have been understood by the traditions of our people and our law. It does not need research to show that no such sweeping condemnation can be passed upon the statute before us. . . .

Nebbia v. *New York*
291 U.S. 502, 54 S.Ct. 505, 78 L.Ed. 940 (1934)

To combat some of the effects of economic depression on the milk industry, the legislature of New York in 1933 adopted a Milk Control Law under which minimum prices could be set. The board constituted by the law set a minimum price for the retail sale of milk, which Leo Nebbia, a grocery store proprietor in Rochester, violated. The New York Court of Appeals affirmed his conviction. Many commentators saw the Court's decision in this case, especially the proposition that "the power to promote the general welfare is inherent in government," as indicating judicial approval of the New Deal. Majority: Roberts, Brandeis, Cardozo, Hughes, Stone. Dissenting: McReynolds, Butler, Sutherland, Van Devanter.

Mr. Justice Roberts delivered the opinion of the Court. . . .

Under our form of government the use of property and the making of contracts are normally matters of private and not of public concern. The general rule is that both shall be free of governmental interference. But neither property rights nor contract rights are absolute; for government cannot exist if the citizen may at will use his property to the detriment of his fellows, or exercise his freedom of contract to work them harm. Equally fundamental with the private right is that of the public to regulate it in the common interest. . . .

These correlative rights, that of the citizen to exercise exclusive dominion over property and freely to contract about his affairs, and that of the state to regulate the use of property and the conduct of business, are always in collision. No exercise of the private right can be imagined which will not in some respect, however slight, affect the public; no exercise of the legislative prerogative to regulate the conduct of the citizen which will not to some extent abridge his liberty or affect his property. But subject only to constitutional restraint the private right must yield to the public need.

The Fifth Amendment, in the field of federal activity, and the Fourteenth, as respects state action, do not prohibit governmental regulation for the public welfare. They merely condition the exertion of the admitted power, by securing that the end shall be accomplished by methods consistent with due process. And the guaranty of due process, as has often been held, demands only that the law shall not be unreasonable, arbitrary, or capricious, and that the means selected shall have a real and substantial relation to the object sought to be attained. It results that a regulation valid for one sort of business, or in given circumstances, may be invalid for another sort, or for the same business under other circumstances, because the reasonableness of each regulation depends upon the relevant facts. . . .

But we are told that because the law essays to control prices it denies due process. . . . The argument runs that the public control of rates or prices is per se unreasonable and unconstitutional, save as applied to businesses affected with a public interest; that a business so affected is one in which property is devoted to an enterprise of a sort which the public itself might appropriately undertake, or one whose owner relies on a public grant or franchise for the right to conduct the business, or in which he is bound to serve all who apply; in short, such as is commonly called a public utility; or a business in its nature a monopoly. The milk industry, it is said, possesses none of these characteristics, and, therefore, not being affected with a public interest, its charges may not be controlled by the state. Upon the soundness of this contention the appellant's case against the statute depends.

We may as well say at once that the dairy industry is not, in the accepted sense of the phrase, a public utility. We think the appellant is also right in asserting that there is in this case no suggestion of any monopoly or monopolistic practice. It goes without saying that those engaged in the business are in no way dependent upon public grants or franchises for the privilege of conducting their activities. But if, as must be conceded, the industry is subject to regulation in the public interest, what constitutional principle bars the state from correcting existing maladjustments by legislation touching prices? We think there is no such principle. The due process clause makes no mention of sales or prices any more than it speaks of business or contracts or buildings or other incidents of property. The thought seems nevertheless to have persisted that there is something peculiarly sacrosanct about the price one may charge for what he makes or sells, and that, however able to regulate other elements of manufacture or trade, with incidental

effect upon price, the state is incapable of directly controlling the price itself. This view was negatived many years ago. . . .

The phrase "affected with a public interest" can, in the nature of things, mean no more than that an industry, for adequate reason, is subject to control for the public good. . . .

So far as the requirement of due process is concerned, and in the absence of other constitutional restriction, a state is free to adopt whatever economic policy may reasonably be deemed to promote public welfare, and to enforce that policy by legislation adapted to its purpose. The courts are without authority either to declare such policy, or, when it is declared by the legislative arm, to override it. If the laws passed are seen to have a reasonable relation to a proper legislative purpose and are neither arbitrary nor discriminatory, the requirements of due process are satisfied. . . . With the wisdom of the policy adopted, with the adequacy or practicability of the law enacted to forward it, the courts are both incompetent and unauthorized to deal. . . .

Price control, like any other form of regulation, is unconstitutional only if arbitrary, discriminatory, or demonstrably irrelevant to the policy the legislature is free to adopt, and hence an unnecessary and unwarranted interference with individual liberty.

Tested by these considerations we find no basis in the due process clause of the Fourteenth Amendment for condemning the provision of the Agriculture and Markets Law here drawn into question.

The judgment is

Affirmed.

Separate opinion of MR. JUSTICE McREYNOLDS. . . .

If . . . liberty or property may be struck down because of difficult circumstances, we must expect that hereafter every right must yield to the voice of an impatient majority when stirred by distressful exigency. . . . Certain fundamentals have been set beyond experimentation; the Constitution has released them from control by the state. . . .

The exigency is of a kind which inevitably arises when one set of men continue to produce more than all others can buy. The distressing result of the producer followed his ill-advised but voluntary effort. . . .

Of the assailed statute the Court of Appeals says . . . "With the wisdom of the legislation we have naught to do. . . ."

But plainly, I think, this Court must have regard to the wisdom of the enactment.

The Legislature cannot lawfully destroy guaranteed rights of one man with the prime purpose of enriching another, even if for the moment, this may seem advantageous to the public. And the adoption of any "concept of jurisprudence" which permits facile disregard of the Constitution as long interpreted and respected will inevitably lead to its destruction. Then, all rights will be subject to the caprice of the hour; government by stable laws will pass. . . .

. . . Grave concern for embarrassed farmers is everywhere; but this should neither obscure the rights of others nor obstruct judicial appraisement of measures proposed for relief. The ultimate welfare of the producer, like that of every other class, requires dominance of the Constitution. And zealously to uphold this in all its parts is the highest duty intrusted to the courts.

The judgment of the court below should be reversed.

MR. JUSTICE VAN DEVANTER, MR. JUSTICE SUTHERLAND, and MR. JUSTICE BUTLER authorize me to say that they concur in this opinion.

Ferguson v. Skrupa
372 U.S. 726, 83 S.Ct. 1028, 10 L.Ed. 2d 93 (1963)

The relevant facts are included in the opinion. Majority: Black, Brennan, Clark, Douglas, Goldberg, Harlan, Stewart, Warren, White.

MR. JUSTICE BLACK delivered the opinion of the Court.

In this case, properly here on appeal . . . we are asked to review the judgment of a three-judge District Court enjoining, as being in violation of the Due Process Clause of the Fourteenth Amendment, a Kansas statute making it a misdemeanor for any person to engage "in the business of debt adjusting" except as an incident to "the lawful practice of law in this state." The statute defines "debt adjusting" as "the making of a contract, express, or implied with a particular debtor whereby the debtor agrees to pay a certain amount of money periodically to the person engaged in the debt adjusting business who shall for a consideration distribute the same among certain specified creditors in accordance with a plan agreed upon." . . .

. . . The three-judge court heard evidence by Skrupa tending to show the usefulness and desirability of his business and evidence by the state officials tending to show that "debt adjusting" lends itself to grave abuses against distressed debtors, particularly in the lower income brackets, and that these abuses are of such gravity that a number of

States have strictly regulated "debt adjusting" or prohibited it altogether. The court found that Skrupa's business did fall within the Act's proscription and concluded, one judge dissenting, that the Act was prohibitory, not regulatory, but that even if construed in part as regulatory it was an unreasonable regulation of a "lawful business," which the court held amounted to a violation of the Due Process Clause of the Fourteenth Amendment. The court accordingly enjoined enforcement of the statute. . . .

Under the system of government created by our Constitution, it is up to legislatures, not courts, to decide on the wisdom and utility of legislation. There was a time when the Due Process Clause was used by this Court to strike down laws which were thought unreasonable, that is, unwise or incompatible with some particular economic or social philosophy. . . .

We have returned to the original constitutional proposition that courts do not substitute their social and economic beliefs for the judgment of legislative bodies, who are elected to pass laws. . . .

We conclude that the Kansas Legislature was

free to decide for itself that legislation was needed to deal with the business of debt adjusting. Unquestionably, there are arguments showing that the business of debt adjusting has social utility, but such arguments are properly addressed to the legislature, not to us. We refuse to sit as a "superlegislature to weigh the wisdom of legislation," and we emphatically refuse to go back to the time when courts used the Due Process Clause "to strike down state laws, regulatory of business and industrial conditions, because they may be unwise,

improvident, or out of harmony with a particular school of thought." Nor are we able or willing to draw lines by calling a law "prohibitory" or "regulatory." Whether the legislature takes for its textbook Adam Smith, Herbert Spencer, Lord Keynes, or some other is no concern of ours. The Kansas debt adjusting statute may be wise or unwise. But relief, if any be needed, lies not with us but with the body constituted to pass laws for the State of Kansas. . . .

Reversed.

Hawaii Housing Authority v. Midkiff
467 U.S. 229, 104 S.Ct. 2321, 81 L.Ed. 2d 186 (1984)

This case involved the constitutionality of the Hawaiian Land Reform Act of 1967 as measured by the public use standard of the Fifth Amendment. The facts of the case appear in Justice O'Connor's opinion of the Court. Majority: O'Connor, Blackmun, Brennan, Burger, Powell, Rehnquist, Stevens, White. Not participating: Marshall.

JUSTICE O'CONNOR delivered the opinion of the Court.

The Hawaiian Islands were originally settled by Polynesian immigrants from the eastern Pacific. These settlers developed an economy around a feudal land tenure system in which one island high chief, the ali'i nui, controlled the land and assigned it for development to certain subchiefs. The subchiefs would then reassign the land to other lower ranking chiefs, who would administer the land and govern the farmers and other tenants working it. All land was held at the will of the ali'i nui and eventually had to be returned to his trust. There was no private ownership of land. . . .

Beginning in the early 1800's, Hawaiian leaders and American settlers repeatedly attempted to divide the lands of the kingdom among the crown, the chiefs, and the common people. The efforts proved largely unsuccessful, however, and the land remained in the hands of a few. In the mid-1960's, after extensive hearings, the Hawaii Legislature discovered that, while the State and Federal Governments owned almost 49% of the State's land, another 47% was in the hands of only 72 private

landowners. . . . The legislature further found that 18 landholders, with tracts of 21,000 acres or more, owned more than 40% of this land and that, on Oahu, the most urbanized of the islands, 22 landowners owned 72.5% of the fee simple titles. . . . The legislature concluded that concentrated land ownership was responsible for skewing the State's residential fee simple market, inflating land prices, and injuring the public tranquility and welfare.

To redress these problems, the legislature decided to compel the large landowners to break up their estates. . . .

Under the Act's condemnation scheme, tenants living on single-family residential lots within development tracts at least five acres in size are entitled to ask the Hawaii Housing Authority (HHA) to condemn the property on which they live. . . . When 25 eligible tenants, or tenants on half the lots in the tract, whichever is less, file appropriate applications, the Act authorizes HHA to hold a public hearing to determine whether acquisition by the State of all or part of the tract will "effectuate the public purposes" of the Act. . . . If HHA finds that these public purposes will be served, it is authorized to designate some or all of the lots in the tract for acquisition. It then acquires, at prices set either by condemnation trial or by negotiation between lessors and lessees, the former fee owners' full "right, title, and interest" in the land. . . .

After compensation has been set, HHA may sell the land titles to tenants who have applied for fee simple ownership. . . .

In April 1977, HHA held a public hearing concerning the proposed acquisition of some of appellees' lands. HHA made the statutorily required finding that acquisition of appellees' lands would effectuate the public purposes of the Act. Then, in October 1978, it directed appellees to negotiate with certain lessees concerning the sale of the designated properties. Those negotiations failed, and HHA subsequently ordered appellees to submit to compulsory arbitration.

Rather than comply with the compulsory arbitration order, appellees filed suit, in February 1979, in United States District Court, asking that the Act be declared unconstitutional and that its enforcement be enjoined. . . . The District Court found that the Act's goals were within the bounds of the State's police powers and that the means the legislature had chosen to serve those goals were not arbitrary, capricious, or selected in bad faith.

The Court of Appeals for the Ninth Circuit reversed. . . . [T]he Court of Appeals determined that the Hawaii Land Reform Act could not pass the requisite judicial scrutiny of the Public Use Clause. It found that the transfers contemplated by the Act were unlike those of takings previously held to constitute "public uses" by this Court. The court further determined that the public purposes offered by the Hawaii Legislature were not deserving of judicial deference. The court concluded that the Act was simply "a naked attempt on the part of the state of Hawaii to take the private property of A and transfer it to B solely for B's private use and benefit." . . .

The starting point for our analysis of the Act's constitutionality is the Court's decision in *Berman* v. *Parker* (1954). In *Berman,* the Court held constitutional the District of Columbia Redevelopment Act of 1945. That Act provided both for the comprehensive use of the eminent domain power to redevelop slum areas and for the possible sale or lease of the condemned lands to private interests.

In discussing whether the takings authorized by that Act were for a "public use" . . . the Court stated

> We deal . . . with what traditionally has been known as the police power. . . . Subject to specific constitutional limitations, when the legislature has spoken, the public interest has been declared in terms well-nigh conclusive. In such cases the legislature, not the judiciary, is the main guardian of the public needs to be served by social legislation. . . .

The Court explicitly recognized the breadth of the principle it was announcing, noting:

> . . . Once the object is within the authority of Congress, the means by which it will be attained is also for Congress to determine. Here one of the means chosen is the use of private enterprise for redevelopment of the area. Appellants argue that this makes the project a taking from one businessman for the benefit of another businessman. But the means of executing the project are for Congress and Congress alone to determine, once the public purpose has been established. . . .

The "public use" requirement is thus coterminous with the scope of a sovereign's police powers. . . .

On this basis, we have no trouble concluding that the Hawaii Act is constitutional. The people of Hawaii have attempted, much as the settlers of the original 13 Colonies did, to reduce the perceived social and economic evils of a land oligopoly traceable to their monarchs. The land oligopoly has, according to the Hawaii Legislature, created artificial deterrents to the normal functioning of the State's residential land market and forced thousands of individual homeowners to lease, rather than buy, the land underneath their homes. Regulating oligopoly and the evils associated with it is a classic exercise of State's police powers. . . .

Nor can we condemn as irrational the Act's approach to correcting the land oligopoly problem. The Act presumes that when a sufficiently large number of persons declare that they are willing but unable to buy lots at fair prices the land market is malfunctioning. . . . This is a comprehensive and rational approach to identifying and correcting market failure.

Of course, this Act, like any other, may not be successful in achieving its intended goals. But "whether *in fact* the provision will accomplish its objectives is not the question: the [constitutional requirement] is satisfied if . . . the . . . [state] Legislature *rationally could have believed* that the [act] would promote its objective." . . . When the legislature's purpose is legitimate and its means are not irrational, our cases make clear that empirical debates over the wisdom of takings—no less than debates over the wisdom of other kinds of socio-economic legislation—are not to be carried out in the federal courts. Redistribution of fees simple to correct deficiencies in the market determined by the state legislature to be attributable to land oli-gopoly is a rational exercise of the eminent domain

power. Therefore, the Hawaii statute must pass the scrutiny of the Public Use Clause. . . .

The Hawaii Legislature enacted its Land Reform Act not to benefit a particular class of identifiable individuals but to attack certain perceived evils of concentrated property ownership in Hawaii—a le-gitimate public purpose. Use of the condemnation power to achieve this purpose is not irrational. Since we assume for purposes of this appeal that the weighty demand of just compensation has been met, the requirements of the Fifth and Fourteenth Amendments have been satisfied. Accordingly, we reverse the judgment of the Court of Appeals, and remand these cases for further proceedings in con-formity with this opinion.

It is so ordered.

Nollan v. California Coastal Commission
483 U.S. 825, 107 S.Ct. 3141, 97 L.Ed. 2d 677 (1987)

In 1982 the California Coastal Commission granted a permit to James and Marilyn Nollan to replace a small bungalow on their beachfront lot in Ventura County with a larger house. With the permit came the condition that the Nollans allow the public an easement to pass *across* their beach, which was located between two public beaches. The Nollans' property affected by the easement was bounded by the mean high-tide line on one side and their seawall on the other side. The county Superior Court granted the Nollans a writ of administrative mandamus and directed that the permit condition be removed. In 1986 the state Court of Appeals reversed the Superior Court, ruling that imposition of the condition did not violate the takings clause of the Fifth Amendment. Majority: Scalia, O'Connor, Powell, Rehn-quist, White. Dissenting: Brennan, Blackmun, Marshall, Stevens.

JUSTICE SCALIA delivered the opinion of the Court. . . .

Had California simply required the Nollans to make an easement across their beachfront available to the public on a permanent basis in order to increase public access to the beach, rather than conditioning their permit to rebuild their house on their agreeing to do so, we have no doubt there would have been a taking. To say that the appro-priation of a public easement across a landowner's premises does not constitute the taking of a property

interest but rather "a mere restriction on its use," is to use words in a manner that deprives them of all their ordinary meaning. Indeed, one of the principal uses of the eminent domain power is to assure that the government be able to require conveyance of just such interests, so long as it pays for them. Perhaps because the point is so obvious, we have never been confronted with a controversy that required us to rule upon it, but our cases' analysis of the effect of other governmental action leads to the same conclusion. We have repeatedly held that, as to property reserved by its owner for private use, "the right to exclude [others is] 'one of the most essential sticks in the bundle of rights that are commonly characterized as property.' " [W]here governmental action results in "[a] permanent physical occupation" of the property, by the government itself or by others, "our cases uniformly have found a taking to the extent of the occupation, without regard to whether the action achieves an important public benefit or has only minimal economic impact on the owner." We think a "permanent physical occupation" has occurred, for purposes of that rule, where individuals are given a permanent and continuous right to pass to and fro, so that the real property may continuously be traversed, even though no particular individual is permitted to station himself permanently upon the premises. . . .

Given, then, that requiring uncompensated conveyance of the easement outright would violate the Fourteenth Amendment, the question becomes whether requiring it to be conveyed as a condition for issuing a land use permit alters the outcome. We have long recognized that land use regulation does not effect a taking if it "substantially advance[s] legitimate state interests" and does not "den[y] an owner economically viable use of his land." . . . Our cases have not elaborated on the standards for determining what constitutes a "legitimate state interest" or what type of connection between the regulation and the state interest satisfies the requirement that the former "substantially advance" the latter. They have made clear, however, that a broad range of governmental purposes and regulations satisfies these requirements. . . . The Commission argues that among these permissible purposes are protecting the public's ability to see the beach, assisting the public in overcoming the "psychological barrier" to using the beach created by a developed shorefront, and preventing congestion on the public beaches. We assume, without deciding, that this is so—in which case the Commission unquestionably would be able to deny the Nollans their permit outright if their new house (alone, or by reason of the cumulative impact produced in conjunction with other construction) would substantially impede these purposes, unless the denial would interfere so drastically with the Nollans' use of their property as to constitute a taking.

The Commission argues that a permit condition that serves the same legitimate police-power purpose as a refusal to issue the permit should not be found to be a taking if the refusal to issue the permit would not constitute a taking. We agree. Thus, if the Commission attached to the permit some condition that would have protected the public's ability to see the beach notwithstanding construction of the new house—for example, a height limitation, a width restriction, or a ban on fences—so long as the Commission could have exercised its police power (as we have assumed it could) to forbid construction of the house altogether, imposition of the condition would also be constitutional. Moreover (and here we come closer to the facts of the present case), the condition would be constitutional even if it consisted of the requirement that the Nollans provide a viewing spot on their property for passersby with whose sighting of the ocean their new house would interfere. Although such a requirement, constituting a permanent grant of continuous access to the property, would have to be considered a taking if it were not attached to a development permit, the Commission's assumed power to forbid construction of the house in order to protect the public's view of the beach must surely include the power to condition construction upon some concession by the owner, even a concession of property rights, that serves the same end. . . .

The evident constitutional propriety disappears, however, if the condition substituted for the prohibition utterly fails to further the end advanced as the justification for the prohibition. When that essential nexus is eliminated, the situation becomes the same as if California law forbade shouting fire in a crowded theater, but granted dispensations to those willing to contribute $100 to the state treasury. While a ban on shouting fire can be a core exercise of the State's police power to protect the public safety, and can thus meet even our stringent standards for regulation of speech, adding the unrelated condition alters the purpose to one which, while it may be legitimate, is inadequate to sustain the ban. Therefore, even though, in a sense, requiring a $100 tax contribution in order to shout fire is a lesser restriction on speech than an outright ban, it would not pass constitutional muster. Similarly here, the lack of nexus between the condition and the original purpose of the building restriction converts that purpose to something other than what it was. The purpose then becomes, quite simply, the obtaining of an easement to serve some valid governmental purpose, but without payment of compensation. Whatever may be the outer limits of "legitimate state interests" in the takings and land use context, this is not one of them. In short, unless the permit condition serves the same governmental purpose as the development ban, the building restriction is not a valid regulation of land use but "an out-and-out plan of extortion." . . .

. . . It is quite impossible to understand how a requirement that people already on the public beaches be able to walk across the Nollans' property reduces any obstacles to viewing the beach created by the new house. It is also impossible to understand how it lowers any "psychological barrier" to using the public beaches, or how it helps to remedy any additional congestion on them caused by construction of the Nollans' new house. . . .

We are left, then, with the Commission's justification for the access requirement unrelated to land use regulation:

Finally, the Commission notes that there are several existing provisions of pass and repass lateral access benefits already given by past Faria Beach Tract applicants as a result of prior coastal permit decisions. The access required as a condition of this permit is part of a comprehensive program to provide continuous public access along Faria Beach as the lots undergo development or redevelopment.

That is simply an expression of the Commission's belief that the public interest will be served by a continuous strip of publicly accessible beach along the coast. The Commission may well be right that it is a good idea, but that does not establish that the Nollans (and other coastal residents) alone can be compelled to contribute to its realization. Rather, California is free to advance its "comprehensive program," if it wishes, by using its power of eminent domain for this "public purpose;" but if it wants an easement across the Nollans' property, it must pay for it.

Reversed.

JUSTICE BRENNAN, with whom JUSTICE MARSHALL joins, dissenting. . . .

Even if we accept the Court's unusual demand for a precise match between the condition imposed and the specific type of burden on access created by the appellants, the State's action easily satisfies this requirement. First, the lateral access condition serves to dissipate the impression that the beach that lies behind the wall of homes along the shore is for private use only. It requires no exceptional imaginative powers to find plausible the Commission's point that the average person passing along the road in front of a phalanx of imposing permanent residences, including the appellants' new home, is likely to conclude that this particular portion of the shore is not open to the public. If, however, that person can see that numerous people are passing and repassing along the dry sand, this conveys the message that the beach is in fact open for use by the public. Furthermore, those persons who go down to the public beach a quarter-mile away will be able to look down the coastline and see that persons have continuous access to the tidelands, and will observe signs that proclaim the public's right of access over the dry sand. The burden produced by the diminution in visual access—the impression that the beach is not open to the public—is thus directly alleviated by the provision for public access over the dry sand. The Court therefore has an unrealistically limited conception of what measures could reasonably be chosen to mitigate the burden produced by a diminution of visual access.

The second flaw in the Court's analysis of the fit between burden and exaction is more fundamental. The Court assumes that the only burden with which the Coastal Commission was concerned was blockage of visual access to the beach. This is incorrect. The Commission specifically stated in its report in support of the permit condition that "[t]he Commission finds that the applicants' proposed development would present an increase in view blockage, *an increase in private use of the shorefront,* and that this impact would burden the public's ability to traverse to and along the shorefront." . . .

. . . As the Commission observed in its report, "The Faria Beach shoreline fluctuates during the year depending on the seasons and accompanying storms, and the public is not always able to traverse the shoreline below the mean high tide line." As a result, the boundary between publicly owned tidelands and privately owned beach is not a stable one, and "[t]he existing seawall is located very near to the mean high water line." When the beach is at its largest, the seawall is about 10 feet from the mean high tide mark; "[d]uring the period of the year when the beach suffers erosion, the mean high water line appears to be located either on or beyond the existing seawall." Expansion of private development on appellants' lot toward the seawall would thus "increase private use immediately adjacent to public tidelands, which has the potential of causing adverse impacts on the public's ability to traverse the shoreline." . . .

The deed restriction on which permit approval was conditioned would directly address this threat to the public's access to the tidelands. It would provide a formal declaration of the public's right of access, thereby ensuring that the shifting character of the tidelands, and the presence of private development immediately adjacent to it, would not jeopardize enjoyment of that right. . . .

The fact that the Commission's action is a legitimate exercise of the police power does not, of course, insulate it from a takings challenge, for when "regulation goes too far it will be recognized as a taking." Conventional takings analysis underscores the implausibility of the Court's holding, for it demonstrates that this exercise of California's police power implicates none of the concerns that underlie our takings jurisprudence.

In reviewing a Takings Clause claim, we have regarded as particularly significant the nature of the governmental action and the economic impact of regulation, especially the extent to which regulation interferes with investment-backed expectations. The character of the government action in this case is the imposition of a condition on permit approval, which allows the public to continue to have access to the coast. The physical intrusion permitted by the deed restriction is minimal. The public is permitted the right to pass and re-pass along the coast in an area from the seawall to the mean high tide mark. This area is at its *widest* 10 feet, which means that *even without the permit condition,* the public's right of access permits it to pass on average within a few feet of the seawall. Passage closer to the 8-foot high rocky seawall will make the appellants even less visible to the public than passage along the high tide area farther out on the beach. The intrusiveness of such passage is even less than the intrusion resulting from the required dedication of a sidewalk in front of private residences, exactions which are commonplace conditions on approval of development. Furthermore, the high tide line shifts throughout the year, moving up to and beyond the seawall, so that public passage for a portion of the year would either be impossible or would not occur on appellant's property. Finally, although the Commission had the authority to provide for either passive or active recreational use of the property, it chose the least intrusive alternative: a mere right to pass and repass. . . . State agencies . . . require considerable flexibility in responding to private desires for development in a way that guarantees the preservation of public access to the coast. They should be encouraged to regulate development in the context of the overall balance of competing uses of the shoreline. The Court today does precisely the opposite, overruling an eminently reasonable exercise of an expert state agency's judgment, substituting its own narrow view of how this balance should be struck. Its reasoning is hardly suited to the complex reality of natural resource protection in the twentieth century. I can only hope that today's decision is an aberration, and that a broader vision ultimately prevails.

Mackey v. Montrym
443 U.S. 1, 99 S.Ct. 2612, 61 L.Ed. 2d 321 (1979)

On May 15, 1976, Donald Montrym was involved in an automobile accident in Acton, Massachusetts, and was charged with several offenses, including that of operating a vehicle while intoxicated. At the police station, Montrym refused a request by police to take a breathalyzer examination. Twenty minutes later, Montrym tried to retract his refusal, but the police, believing the law gave them no discretion, declined to administer the test. On June 2, 1976, a state court dismissed the charge of drunken driving, apparently because the police had not administered the test after Montrym changed his mind.

Massachusetts law mandates automatic suspension of a driver's license when a driver refuses to take a breathalyzer test upon arrest for driving while intoxicated. Accordingly, the registrar of motor vehicles formally suspended Montrym's license for 90 days on June 7. Montrym took an appeal to the Board of Appeals, but before the board acted, he filed suit in district court, claiming that the statute was unconstitutional on its face. A three-judge panel agreed, holding that due process requires a presuspension hearing.

The following opinions refer to *Dixon* v. *Love* (1977), in which the Supreme Court (1) recognized a constitutionally protected property interest in a driver's license and (2) upheld the constitutionality of an Illinois statute authorizing summary suspension of a driver's license prior to an evidentiary hearing, where there was a record of repeated traffic offenses. Majority: Burger, Blackmun, Powell, Rehnquist, White. Dissenting: Stewart, Brennan, Marshall, Stevens.

MR. CHIEF JUSTICE BURGER delivered the opinion of the Court. . . .

The Registrar concedes here that suspension of a driver's license for statutorily defined cause implicates a protectible property interest; accordingly, the only question presented by this appeal is what process is due to protect against an erroneous deprivation of that interest. Resolution of this inquiry requires consideration of a number of factors. . . .

The first step in the balancing process mandated by *Eldridge* is identification of the nature and weight of the private interest affected by the official action challenged. Here, as in *Love*, the private interest affected is the granted license to operate a motor vehicle. More particularly, the driver's interest is in continued possession and use of his license pending the outcome of the hearing due him. As we recognized in *Love*, that interest is a substantial one, for the Commonwealth will not be able to make a driver whole for any personal inconvenience and economic hardship suffered by reason of any delay in readdressing and erroneous suspension through post-suspension review procedures.

But, however substantial Montrym's property interest may be, it is surely no more substantial than the interest involved in *Love*. The private interest involved here actually is *less* substantial, for the Massachusetts statute authorizes suspension for

a maximum of only 90 days, while the Illinois scheme permitted suspension for as long as a year and even allowed for the possibility of indefinite revocation of a license. . . .

Because a primary function of legal process is to minimize the risk of erroneous decisions, the second stage of the *Eldridge* inquiry requires consideration of the likelihood of an erroneous deprivation of the private interest involved as a consequence of the procedures used. And, although this aspect of the *Eldridge* test further requires an assessment of the relative reliability of the procedures used and the substitute procedures sought, the Due Process Clause has never been construed to require that the procedures used to guard against an erroneous deprivation of a protectible "property" or "liberty" interest be so comprehensive as to preclude any possibility of error. The Due Process Clause simply does not mandate that all governmental decisionmaking comply with standards that assure perfect, error-free determinations.

As was the case in *Love*, the predicates for a driver's suspension under the Massachusetts scheme are objective facts either within the personal knowledge of an impartial government official or readily ascertainable by him. Cause arises for license suspension if the driver has been arrested for driving while under the influence of an intoxicant, probable cause exists for arrest, and the driver refuses to take a breathalyzer test. The facts of the arrest and the driver's refusal will inevitably be within the personal knowledge of the reporting officer; indeed, Massachusetts requires that the driver's refusal be witnessed by two officers. At the very least, the arresting officer ordinarily will have provided the driver with an informal opportunity to tell his side of the story and, as here, will have had the opportunity to observe the driver's condition and behavior before effecting any arrest.

The District Court, in holding that the Due Process Clause mandates that an opportunity for a further hearing before the Registrar *precede* a driver's suspension, overstated the risk of error inherent in the statute's initial reliance on the corroborated affidavit of a law-enforcement officer. The officer whose report of refusal triggers a driver's suspension is a trained observer and investigator. He is, by reason of his training and experience, well-suited for the role the statute accords him in the pre-suspension process. . . .

Moreover, as this case illustrates, there will rarely be any genuine dispute as to the historical facts providing cause for a suspension. It is significant that Montrym does *not* dispute that he was arrested, or that probable cause existed for his arrest, or that he initially refused to take the breathalyzer test at the arresting officer's request. The allegedly "factual" dispute that he claims a constitutional right to raise and have determined by the Registrar prior to his suspension really presents questions of law; namely, whether the state court's subsequent finding that the police *later* refused to administer a breathalyzer test at Montrym's request is binding on the Registrar as a matter of collateral estoppel; and, if so, whether that finding undermines the validity of Montrym's suspension, which may well be justified under the statute solely on the basis of Montrym's initial refusal to take the breathalyzer test and notwithstanding the officer's subsequent refusal to honor Montrym's belated request for the test.* The Commonwealth must have the authority, if it is

to protect people from drunk drivers, to require that the breathalyzer test record the alcoholic content of the bloodstream at the earliest possible moment. . . .

The third leg of the *Eldridge* balancing test requires us to identify the governmental function involved; also, to weigh in the balance the state interests served by the summary procedures used, as well as the administrative and fiscal burdens, if any, that would result from the substitute procedures sought.

Here, as in *Love,* the statute involved was enacted in aid of the Commonwealth's police function for the purpose of protecting the safety of its people. . . .

The Commonwealth's interest in public safety is substantially served by the summary suspension of those who refuse to take a breathalyzer test upon arrest in several ways. First, the very existence of the summary sanction of the statute serves as a deterrent to drunk driving. Second, it provides strong inducement to take the breathalyzer test and thus effectuates the Commonwealth's interest in obtaining reliable and relevant evidence for use in subsequent criminal proceedings. Third, in promptly removing such drivers from the road, the summary sanction of the statute contributes to the safety of public highways. . . .

We conclude, as we did in *Love,* that the compelling interest in highway safety justifies the Commonwealth in making a summary suspension effective pending the outcome of the prompt post-suspension hearing available.

Accordingly, the judgment of the District Court is reversed and the case is remanded for further proceedings consistent with this opinion.

Reversed and remanded.

MR. JUSTICE STEWART, with whom MR. JUSTICE BRENNAN, MR. JUSTICE MARSHALL and MR. JUSTICE STEVENS, join, dissenting

The question in this case, simply put, is whether a person who is subject to losing his driver's license for three months as a penalty for allegedly refusing a demand to take a breathalyzer test is constitutionally entitled to some sort of hearing before his license is taken away. In Massachusetts, such suspensions are effected by the Registrar of Motor Vehicles solely upon the strength of a policeman's affidavit recounting *his* version of an encounter between the police and the motorist. The driver is

* An evidentiary hearing into the historical facts would be ill-suited for resolution of such questions of law. Indeed, it is not clear whether the Registrar even has the plenary authority to resolve such questions. Ultimately, any legal questions must be resolved finally by the Massachusetts courts on judicial review of the decision of the Board of Appeal after any appeal taken from the ruling of the Registrar.

afforded no opportunity, before this deprivation occurs, to present his side of the story in a forum other than a police station. He is given no notice of any entitlement he might have to a "same day" hearing before the Registrar. The suspension penalty itself is concededly imposed not as an emergency measure to remove unsafe drivers from the roads, but as a sanction to induce drivers to submit to breathalyzer tests. In short, the critical fact that triggers the suspension is noncooperation with the police, not drunken driving. In my view, the most elemental principles of due process forbid a State from extracting this penalty without first affording the driver an opportunity to be heard. . . .

When a deprivation is irreversible—as is the case with a license suspension that can at best be shortened but cannot be undone—the requirement of some kind of hearing before a final deprivation takes effect is all the more important. . . .

The case of *Dixon* v. *Love* is not, as the Court seems to suggest, to the contrary. At issue in *Love* was a statute permitting the summary revocation of the license of a repeat traffic offender on the strength of a cumulative record of traffic convictions and suspensions. The Court in *Love* stressed that the appellee had not contested the factual basis for his license revocation and had not contested the procedures followed in securing his previous convictions. Instead, the *Dixon* appellee had merely asserted a right to appear in person in advance to ask for leniency. . . .

A breathalyzer suspension is premised upon three factors: reasonable grounds for an arrest for driving while intoxicated; a proper request by the officer that the driver submit to a breathalyzer test; and a refusal to do so by the driver. The petitioner in this case was indeed arrested, after a collision in which his car was struck in the rear by a motorcycle, for driving while intoxicated. Moreover, he admitted that he initially refused to take a breathalyzer test. But he consistently contended that he was not informed of the sanction, as is required [by the statute] . . . and he vigorously disputed the accuracy of the police affidavit that said he was so informed. His further claim—that he requested a test as soon as he learned by inadvertence of the sanction, and that the police then refused to administer the test—was apparently accepted by the Massachusetts judge who subsequently dismissed the criminal charges against him. Thus, there was clearly a significant factual dispute in this case.

That dispute . . . concerned a critical element of the statutory basis for a suspension—in this instance whether there was indeed a refusal to take a breathalyzer test after a proper demand. The Court suggests nonetheless that the "fact" of an informed refusal, as well as the other statutory factual bases for a suspension, are somehow so routine, objective, and reliable as to be equivalent to routinely maintained official records of criminal convictions. I find this equation highly dubious. . . .

I am not persuaded that the relative infrequency with which a driver may be able successfully to show that he did not refuse to take a breathalyzer test should excuse the State from the constitutional need to afford a prior hearing to any person who wishes to make such a challenge. The question whether or not there was such a refusal is one classically subject to adjudicative factfinding, and one that plainly involves issues of credibility and veracity. . . .

The State has urged, and the Court seems to agree, that summary procedures are nevertheless required to further the State's interest in protecting the public from unsafe drivers. It cannot be doubted that the interest in "removing drunken drivers from the road" is significant. But the precedents supporting *ex parte* action have not turned simply on the significance of the governmental interest asserted. To the contrary, they have relied upon the extent to which that interest will be frustrated by the delay necessitated by a prior hearing. . . .

The State's basic justification for its summary suspension scheme, as the Court recognizes, lies in the unremarkable idea that a prior hearing might give drivers a significant incentive to refuse to take the test. Related to this argument is the suggestion that the availability of a prior hearing might encourage a driver to demand such a hearing as a "dilatory" tactic, and thus might increase administrative costs by generating a "sharp increase in the number of hearings." In sum, the State defends the *ex parte* suspension as essential to enlist the cooperation of drivers and also as a cost-saving device. I cannot accept either argument.

The three-month driver's license suspension alone is obviously sufficient to promote the widespread use of the breathalyzer test, if drivers are informed not only of this sanction for a refusal but also realize that cooperation may conclude the entire case in their favor. Moreover, as is generally the case when a person's ability to protect his interests will ultimately depend upon a swearing contest with a law-enforcement officer, the deck is already stacked heavily against the motorist under this statute. . . . The argument that a prior hearing might encourage "dilatory" tactics on the part of the motorist, true as it might be to human nature, is likewise wholly inconsistent with the simple Fourteenth Amendment guarantee that every "person" is entitled to be heard, before he may be deprived of his property by the State. Finally, the all-too-familiar cost-saving arguments raised by the State have regularly been made here and have as regularly been rejected as a justification for dispensing with the guarantees of the Fourteenth Amendment. For if costs were the criterion, the basic procedural protections of the Fourteenth Amendment could be read out of the Constitution. Happily, the Constitution recognizes higher values than "speed and efficiency." . . .

Finally, the Registrar—according to the Court's own description of the Massachusetts scheme—quite possibly does not have authority to resolve even the most basic questions that might be raised about the validity of a breathalyzer suspension. And, if the Registrar has no final authority to resolve the "legal" question the Court perceives in this case, it can hardly be concluded that there exists the prompt postsuspension relief that is said to excuse the State from any need to provide a prior hearing. For, if a prompt postsuspension hearing is even to be eligible for consideration as minimally adequate to satisfy the demands of procedural due process, it must provide for an impartial decisionmaker with authority to resolve the basic dispute and to provide prompt relief. . . .

NINE

Criminal Justice
and the Nationalization
of the Bill of Rights

The history of American freedom is in no small measure the history of procedure.

—JUSTICE FELIX FRANKFURTER (1945)

Preceding chapters have shown that the Supreme Court's regard for certain strictures in the Constitution dates from the earliest years of the Republic. Aside from property interests, however, judicial attention to the Bill of Rights, though part of the Constitution since 1791, is largely of recent origin. Most cases that have shaped the meaning of constitutionally protected expression (the First Amendment) and that have defined personal liberty and the rights of persons accused of crimes (the Fourth, Fifth, Sixth, and Eighth Amendments) have been decided in the twentieth century. As late as the 1935–1936 term, only two of the Court's 160 decisions concerned nonproperty issues in civil liberties and civil rights.* In 1960–1961 the number increased to 54 of the 120 cases decided by full opinion. Disproportionate judicial concern for these matters continues. In 1987–1988, cases involving the Bill of Rights and related provisions accounted for 64 of the term's 148 decisions. These statistics reflect not only an enhanced interest in the Bill of Rights but also the result of a process by which the Court applied the Bill of Rights to the states.

THE BILL OF RIGHTS

State constitutions adopted in 1776 and in subsequent years usually contained a separate bill of rights or other provisions that achieved the same purpose. As the national Constitution came from the hands of the framers in 1787, the powers of the national government were

---

* There is no precise distinction in usage between civil liberties and civil rights. Some Americans use the terms interchangeably, referring to any constitutionally or legally protected right. *Civil liberties* usually include the freedoms to act or not to act and to be free from unwarranted government intrusion in one's life. *Civil rights*

enumerated but not defined. Without specification or definition, other powers were reserved to the states or to the people. The Constitution was drafted, submitted to state conventions, and ratified without a bill of rights. While the states pondered ratification, Jefferson urged specific restraints on national authority. Arguing that "a bill of rights is what the people are entitled to against every government on earth," he insisted that natural rights "should not be refused or rest on inference."

Alexander Hamilton and James Wilson demurred. Both contended that a bill of rights was unnecessary. Why make exceptions to power not granted? "In a government of enumerated powers," Wilson declared, "such a measure would not only be unnecessary, but preposterous and dangerous." For Hamilton, bills of rights "would sound much better in a treatise on ethics than in a constitution of government."

Thanks to Jefferson, these arguments did not prevail. Insisting on curbs over and beyond structural checks, he advocated "binding up the several branches of the government by certain laws, which when they transgress their acts become nullities." This would "render unnecessary an appeal to the people, or in other words a rebellion on every infraction of their rights." When a reluctant James Madison yielded to Jefferson's plea for a bill of rights and deduced supporting reasons, Jefferson singled out the argument of "great weight" for him—the legal check it puts in the hands of the judiciary. In presenting bill of rights amendments to the first Congress, Madison made Jefferson's argument his own. Thanks to the Bill of Rights, "independent tribunals of justice" would be "an impenetrable bulwark against every assumption of power in the legislative or executive." The Jefferson-Madison correspondence (1787–1789) is excerpted before the cases in this chapter.

As a member of the First Congress elected under the new Constitution, Madison had drawn up 17 amendments. After a two-year delay, ten were ratified. The first eight constitute the Bill of Rights. Urged but not ratified on Madison's list was number 14: "No state shall infringe the right of trial by jury in criminal cases, nor the right of conscience, nor the freedom of speech or press." Believing that there was more danger of abuse of power by state governments than by the government of the United States, Madison conceived number 14 to be "the most valuable amendment in the whole list. If there were any reason to restrain the Government of the United States from infringing these essential rights, it was equally necessary that they should be secured against the State governments."

Madison's concern was prophetic. It anticipated the adoption of the Fourteenth Amendment 79 years later. It foreshadowed the drive to apply the specific provisions of the Bill of Rights to state action under the Fourteenth Amendment's due process clause. Incorporation was significant. Without application of the Bill of Rights to the states, the full impact of Justice Stone's *Carolene Products* footnote, discussed in the previous chapter, could not be felt.

Fundamental rights gain no greater moral sanctity by being written into the Constitution, but individuals could thereafter look to courts for their protection. In Jefferson's words, "tho' written constitutions may be violated in moments of passion or delusion, yet they furnish a text to which those who are watchful may again rally and recall the people; they fix too for the people principles for their political creed." Rights formerly natural became civil.

---

usually encompass participatory rights—a citizen's right under the law to participate in society and in the political system on an equal footing with others. Civil liberties are the subject of Chapters Nine through Eleven. Some important civil rights are discussed in Chapter Twelve.

THE ARGUMENT FOR INCORPORATION

It was not until 1833 that the Supreme Court answered the question of whether the first eight amendments limited state as well as national action. To Marshall this was a question "of great importance, but not of much difficulty" (*Barron* v. *Baltimore*). The City of Baltimore, under acts of the Maryland legislature, had diverted the flow of several streams. As a result of the changes, silt was deposited around Barron's wharf, making it unfit for shipping and, in Barron's opinion, depriving him of property without just compensation. Denying the Supreme Court's jurisdiction to declare the state acts repugnant to the Constitution, Marshall observed, "We are of the opinion, that the provision in the Fifth Amendment to the Constitution, declaring that private property shall not be taken for public use without just compensation is intended solely as a limitation of the power of the United States, and is not applicable to the legislation of the states." In support of this conclusion, the chief justice pointed out that the limitations set forth in the Constitution in general terms, as well as the powers conferred, applied to the "government created by the instrument." In addition, he cited proceedings in the state ratifying conventions culminating in the demand for a bill of rights to furnish "security against the apprehended encroachments of the general government."

A contrary ruling would have had immense consequences for the jurisdiction of the Court. As it was, most legal disputes between a state government and one of its citizens remained outside the federal judicial system, unless the commerce or contract clause was at issue. This is important to remember, because until recent decades government action and government policy largely meant the action and policy of state and local governments.

Shortly after the end of the Civil War, the question of the applicability of the Bill of Rights to the states reappeared. This time there was a difference. The Fourteenth Amendment had become part of the Constitution in 1868. Did it have the effect of incorporating the Bill of Rights, either through the privileges and immunities clause or by virtue of the due process clause?

In the 1884 case of *Hurtado* v. *California,* the Court had to decide whether the due process clause of the Fourteenth Amendment prevented a state from substituting a prosecutor's affidavit (information) for grand jury indictment in criminal cases. The Fifth Amendment required a grand jury indictment in federal criminal cases, as did most state constitutions for state criminal trials. Did the Fourteenth mandate grand jury indictments for the states? For the majority, Justice Matthews said no. He rejected the view that "any proceeding . . . not . . . sanctioned by usage, or which supersedes and displaces one that is, cannot be regarded as due process of law. . . . [T]o hold that such a characteristic is essential to due process of law, would be to deny every quality of the law but its age, and to render it incapable of progress or improvement. It would be to stamp upon our jurisprudence the unchangeableness attributed to the laws of the Medes and Persians."

Besides, the fact that the Fifth Amendment already contained a due process clause meant that "due process" was not intended to include the particular safeguards of the Bill of Rights. If the Fourteenth Amendment required use of grand jury indictments, "it would have embodied, as did the Fifth Amendment, express declarations to that effect." What, therefore, did "due process" allow? "[A]ny legal proceeding . . . whether sanctioned by age and custom, or newly devised . . . in furtherance of the general public good, which regards and preserves these principles of liberty and justice, must be held to be due process of law. . . ." For Justice Harlan in dissent, the majority's argument proved too much by *excluding* from the due process clause the most fundamental protections.

Thirteen years later in *Chicago, Burlington & Q. R. Co.* v. *Chicago* (1897), the Court cast doubt on the *Hurtado* doctrine by ruling that the Fourteenth Amendment's due process clause limited the taking of property for public use without just compensation. The Fifth

Amendment contained the same safeguard. Then *Twining* v. *New Jersey* (1908) took another step beyond *Hurtado.* Laid to rest was the view that the inclusion of a right in the Bill of Rights necessarily excluded that right from the protection offered by the due process clause of the Fourteenth Amendment. "[I]t is possible," acknowledged Moody, "that some of the personal rights safeguarded by the first eight Amendments against national action may also be safeguarded against state action. . . . If this is so, it is not because those rights are enumerated in the first eight Amendments, but because they are of such a nature that they are included in the conception of due process of law."

By 1937, the Supreme Court had agreed that the "liberty" protected by the Fourteenth Amendment included some First Amendment freedoms (for example, see *Gitlow* v. *New York,* in Chapter Ten). *Palko* v. *Connecticut* (1937) presented the Court with yet another procedural claim—double jeopardy. Here the justices reaffirmed their long-held view that the *entire* Bill of Rights was not incorporated in the Fourteenth Amendment. Building on *Twining,* Justice Cardozo attempted to justify the selective process.

> There emerges the perception of a rationalizing principle which gives to discrete instances a proper order and coherence. The right to trial by jury and the immunity from prosecution except as a result of an indictment may have value and importance. Even so, they are not of the very essence of a scheme of ordered liberty. To abolish them is not to violate a "principle of justice so rooted in the traditions and conscience of our people as to be ranked as fundamental. . . ."
>
> We reach a different plane of social and moral values when we pass to the privileges and immunities that have been taken over from the earlier articles of the Federal Bill of Rights and brought within the Fourteenth Amendment by a process of absorption. These in their origin were effective against the federal government. If the Fourteenth Amendment has absorbed them, the process of absorption has had its source in the belief that neither liberty nor justice would exist if they were sacrificed.

This "ordered liberty" method of selecting and discarding rights did not go unchallenged. Consider Justice Black's dissenting opinion in *Adamson* v. *California* (1947).

> My study of the historical events that culminated in the Fourteenth Amendment, and the expressions of those who sponsored and favored, as well as those who opposed its submission and passage, persuades me that one of the chief objects that the provisions of the Amendment's first section, separately, and as a whole were intended to accomplish, was to make the Bill of Rights applicable to the states. . . .The "natural law" formula should be abandoned as an incongruous excrescence on our Constitution. I believe that formula to be itself a violation of our Constitution, in that it subtly conveys to courts, at the expense of legislatures, ultimate power over public policies in fields where no specific provision of the Constitution limits legislative power. . . . I fear to see the consequences of the Court's practice of substituting its own concept of decency and fundamental justice for the language of the Bill of Rights as its point of departure in interpreting and enforcing that Bill of Rights.

Today, almost all of the provisions of the Bill of Rights that have contemporary significance have been brought to bear selectively against the states. The consequences for federalism and judicial power have been enormous, especially when coupled with an increased sensitivity to police and courtroom procedure during the second half of the Warren Court (1961–1969). Incorporation was so nearly complete that Justice Black observed with some relish in *Duncan* v. *Louisiana* that the process of selectivity had finally accomplished piecemeal what he would have done at once in *Adamson.* Also of significance today are the protections enshrined in due process beyond those strictly enumerated in the Bill of Rights.

It is here that Justice Black's *total incorporation* approach (this much, and no more) stops, and a variation on Justice Cardozo's ordered liberty doctrine begins. If the Fourteenth Amendment's due process clause is not bound to the meaning of the Bill of Rights, it remains a source of inspiration for those who wish to enlarge the list of constitutionally protected liberties.

Today, no one would accept Sir Henry Maine's nineteenth-century characterization of the Bill of Rights as a "certain number of amendments on comparatively unimportant points."

THE DOUBLE STANDARD—STATE AND FEDERAL CRIMINAL JUSTICE

For a long time, not only did the Court refuse to incorporate the entire Bill of Rights, or even its more important procedural guarantees, but also it refrained for several decades from any realistic review of state convictions to determine whether "due" or "fair" process had been followed.

The Fair Trial Rule. At least until the 1920s, the Supreme Court reviewed state criminal trials only to the extent necessary to determine that the state court had exercised jurisdiction properly and provided a corrective process for possible trial errors (*Frank* v. *Mangum*, 1915). In other words, a state trial that seemingly complied with the state's formal rules as interpreted by the state's highest court satisfied the Supreme Court's Fourteenth Amendment standard of due process of law. This superficial and essentially meaningless federal review began to change with *Moore* v. *Dempsey* (1923). In this case, the Court held that the federal district court was duty-bound to conduct a hearing on the facts when state prisoners alleged that their trial and conviction lacked due process as the result of mob pressure and inflammatory newspaper accounts. Still, citizens were subject to a double standard of justice under the Constitution, as *Palko* v. *Connecticut* demonstrates. At most, construing due process as requiring basically a "fair trial" meant that the states in the 1920s and 1930s were subject to only minimal procedural demands under the Fourteenth Amendment.

The Constitution and Federal Criminal Justice. For a defendant standing trial, the federal constitutional rights one enjoyed depended therefore on whether the trial was in state or federal court. Supreme Court review was far more demanding of the latter than the former. Moreover, the Supreme Court tended to impose on federal officials and federal trial courts rules that on the whole were more protective of individual rights than those applied by state courts under their own legal systems. The Supreme Court even went beyond the Bill of Rights and federal statutes by invoking its supervisory powers as the highest court in the federal judicial system to justify prescribing rules of procedure and penalties for improper conduct that were not required by any constitutional provision.

For example, one of the thorniest problems in criminal procedure has resulted from the Supreme Court's decision in 1914 to impose an *exclusionary rule* as a means of enforcing the Fourth Amendment's protection against unreasonable searches and seizures. In English common law, material and relevant evidence has always been held admissible at a trial even though officials may have obtained it through an improper search and seizure. In an early case, *Boyd* v. *United States* (1886), the Court refused to allow the government to compel an individual to produce papers that might help convict him of a violation of customs law, combining the protections against self-incrimination and unreasonable seizures. Then *Weeks* v. *United States* (1914) laid down the broad rule that evidence produced by illegal searches was inadmissible at federal trials. But *Weeks* applied only to trials in federal courts. Moreover, as late as 1961, nearly half the states still admitted unlawfully seized evidence in state trials.

Another difficult question involved the right to assistance of counsel in the Sixth Amendment. Historically, the Sixth Amendment had meant that the government could not deny a person the opportunity to retain counsel. A decision by the Supreme Court in 1938 (*Johnson* v. *Zerbst*) construed that provision so that every defendant in federal criminal trials was to be offered counsel, at the government's expense if necessary. Twenty-five years later, some states had still not adopted the *Zerbst* rule on their own.

For the pretrial stage, *McNabb* v. *United States* (1943) and *Mallory* v. *United States* (1957) read as mandatory the federal rule requiring prompt arraignment of a defendant after arrest. (At an *arraignment,* the court informs the defendant of the charges brought against him or her, and the defendant pleads guilty or not guilty.) These decisions meant that even a voluntary confession made to police between arrest and a delayed arraignment before a United States commissioner was inadmissible at trial. Again, as late as 1961, courts of 34 states had expressly rejected the *McNabb* rule for their own legal systems.

The Constitution and State Criminal Justice. Once the Supreme Court and lower federal courts abandoned their hands-off policy and began a more realistic, if restrained, examination of state criminal proceedings in the 1930s, they found many discrepancies between state practice and due process standards. The 1931 Report of the Wickersham Commission, *Lawlessness in Law Enforcement,* documented the use by the police of physical and psychological coercion in inducing confessions, detention incommunicado of suspects, unfairness in prosecutor bargaining, and other departures from fair procedures in the period before trial. In the following year, **Powell** v. **Alabama** revealed how the widely assumed right of indigent defendants to have the assistance of counsel could be frustrated even in the most serious cases. In *Powell,* the justices held that in capital cases, indigent, young, inexperienced, and illiterate defendants had to receive the assistance of counsel appointed by the state, and the appointment had to be one that made possible a reasonably efficient defense. Four years later, in *Brown* v. *Mississippi* (1936), a unanimous bench reversed three murder convictions marked by what Chief Justice Hughes called "compulsion by torture to extort a confession. . . . It would be difficult to conceive of methods more revolting to the sense of justice than those taken to procure the confessions of these petitioners, and the use of the confessions thus obtained as the basis for conviction and sentence was a clear denial of due process." In the course of reaching its decisions in *Powell* and *Brown,* the Supreme Court revealed again some of the realities of pretrial procedure in the states, especially in those cases in which authorities were under pressure to obtain convictions.

THE MERGING OF STATE AND FEDERAL CRIMINAL JUSTICE

As the crime rate rose dramatically in the 1960s, the Supreme Court devoted more and more time to criminal cases, both state and national. The result was what some have termed the "due process revolution." Never before had an American court brought such rapid and extensive change to virtually all stages of criminal justice.

A Clash of Rights. The conflict of interests presented in the cases in this chapter is frequently stated in misleading terms. It is a struggle between two cherished and not necessarily antithetical values, a clash of rights, not of wrongs. The conflict is between the public's interest in safety and the public's interest in the protection of individual liberty. It is inaccurate simply to view the struggle as a contest between the safety of good people and the protection of criminals. Constitutional protections belong to all people, innocent and guilty alike. The judicial task is one of determining how much protection can be accorded each individual without unduly hampering the effort of government to maintain order and peace, without which there can be no freedom. Small wonder the framers of our national and state constitutions gave special attention to procedural rights. Far from demonstrating fondness for technicalities, this emphasis highlights the conviction that without limits to authority, America would be a far different place in which to live.

The Due Process Revolution. Once the Supreme Court decided that the Constitution actively protected the rights of state defendants too, and that federal courts were available forums to those seeking vindication of their rights, the pattern was set for a continuing feud between state and federal judges and other officials. If some state officials were upset by the application of the fair trial rule, allowing federal judges to examine the totality of the facts and circumstances of each case, they were greatly disturbed by the bombshells in the 1960s by which virtually all of the procedural guarantees of the Bill of Rights were incorporated into the Fourteenth Amendment. By 1969, there had ceased to be any significant difference under the U.S. Constitution between individual rights applicable in federal courts and individual rights applicable in state courts. The venerable double standard had vanished. In what became one of the hallmarks of the Warren Court, the justices nationalized the Bill of Rights.

A DEFENDANT'S RIGHTS TODAY

What follows is a brief survey of some of the topics in criminal procedure, with a review of the major cases. The field is too vast to include them all. Cases on criminal justice are as myriad as the variety of citizen-police-courtroom encounters themselves.

The Exclusionary Rule. After *Weeks* v. *United States* in 1914, as noted, federal courts excluded from trial evidence obtained illegally. In 1949 *Wolf* v. *Colorado* held the Fourth Amendment guaranty against unreasonable search and seizure applicable to the states but refrained from imposing the federal exclusionary rule, asserting with more confidence than accuracy that other remedies were available to state victims of illegal searches and seizures. By 1961 the Supreme Court had learned what others had long known—civil tort remedies against offending police officers or criminal prosecution failed to provide redress. *Mapp* v. *Ohio* did what *Wolf* had failed to do and applied the exclusionary rule to the states. In his opinion, Justice Clark emphasized the twin pillars for suppressing illegally seized evidence: deterrence of unlawful police conduct and the maintenance of judicial integrity. *Mapp* marked the beginning of heightened concern with the realities of criminal justice at the state level and signaled the abandonment of the fair trial approach. Indeed, *Mapp required* that the justices pay close attention to the day-to-day business of state and local police departments.

Mapp has remained the linchpin for much of the due process revolution set loose by the Warren Court. Most citizen encounters with law-enforcement authorities are with state and local police. Court decisions specifying proper police procedure for stops, searches, and arrests thus have real impact on the criminal justice system when coupled with the exclusionary rule. No wonder Supreme Court decisions interpreting the Fourth Amendment attract such widespread attention, for they define constitutionally correct conduct for all law-enforcement officers in the land. *Mapp* gave those rules teeth because a violation of the Fourth Amendment meant a loss of otherwise useful, reliable, and probative evidence.

Yet because of the social costs of the rule—a defendant does not benefit directly from its operation *unless* incriminating evidence is found—it has been a center of controversy. Two years after becoming chief justice, Warren Burger used a dissenting opinion to advocate a change. "Suppressing unchallenged truth has set guilty criminals free but demonstrably has neither deterred deliberate violations of the Fourth Amendment nor decreased those errors in judgment that will inevitably occur given the pressures inherent in police work having to do with serious crimes" (*Bivens* v. *Six Unknown Federal Narcotics Agents*, 1971). Burger, however, was unwilling to leave the Fourth Amendment unprotected. "I do not question the need for some remedy to give meaning and teeth to the constitutional guarantees against unlawful conduct by government officials. Without some effective sanction, these protections would constitute little more than rhetoric." The Court, therefore, should not abandon the exclusionary rule "until meaningful alternatives can be developed." That task lay with Congress.

Chief Justice Burger's patience was exhausted by 1976. In *Stone* v. *Powell* Burger advised those who favored "the continued existence of this judge-made rule" to demonstrate that "it serves its declared deterrent purpose and to show that the results outweigh the rule's heavy costs to rational enforcement of the criminal law. . . ." The alternative remedies he had called for in *Bivens* had not come forth.

Justice White, whom President Kennedy had named to the Court the year after *Mapp,* was equally prepared to act.

> I . . . would join four or more other Justices in substantially limiting the reach of the exclusionary rule as presently administered under the Fourth Amendment in federal and state criminal trials. . . . [T]he rule should be substantially modified so as to prevent its application in those many circumstances where the evidence at issue was seized by an officer acting in the good-faith belief that his conduct comported with existing law and having reasonable grounds for this belief.

Even though the preferences of Burger and White did not prevail in *Stone,* the majority was still willing to cut back on a defendant's chances to raise Fourth Amendment questions that involved the exclusionary rule. Under existing federal habeas corpus practice, persons convicted of state crimes could challenge their convictions collaterally by claiming one or more violations of constitutional rights.

Stone held that where prisoners had already had a "full and fair" hearing in state court on the Fourth Amendment issues, they could not bring habeas corpus actions to test once more the constitutionality of searches or arrests. In such situations, the majority was not persuaded that the deterrent value of the exclusionary rule outweighed the "rule's heavy cost to a rational enforcement of criminal law." *Stone* was important in the Court's evolving attitude toward the exclusionary rule for at least two reasons. First, *Mapp* to the contrary, the rule was viewed as a "judge-made" device to enforce a constitutional right, not a part of the Constitution itself. Second, the decision revealed that most justices thought of Fourth Amendment violations as being very different from Fifth and Sixth Amendment violations. That is, an unconstitutional seizure of evidence, for example, would not normally affect the integrity or reliability of that evidence. In contrast, a coerced confession (in violation of the Fifth Amendment) is inherently an untrustworthy confession, and a trial without counsel (in violation of the Sixth Amendment) would place in doubt the integrity of a courtroom's entire fact-finding process.

Eight years later, justices antagonistic to the exclusionary rule got results. In ***United States* v. *Leon,*** the Court modified the exclusionary rule to permit a limited "good-faith" or "reasonable mistake" exception. On the facts of the case, Justice White's majority opinion applied only to searches with warrants, not warrantless searches, so *Leon* does not affect *all* Fourth Amendment cases. However, in *Illinois* v. *Krull* (1987) a 6–3 Court extended *Leon* to situations in which police place objectively reasonable reliance on a statute that authorizes warrantless administrative searches but which is later declared unconstitutional.*

---

* A different problem arises when police fail to preserve lawfully obtained evidence potentially useful to the defense. In *Arizona* v. *Youngbood* (1988), a case challenging the conviction of a 47-year-old man for sexually assaulting a 10-year-old boy, the Court held that, unless the defendant could show "bad faith" on the part of the police, even their negligent failure to preserve evidence that might have exonerated the accused is not a denial of due process of law.

Arrests, Searches, and Seizures. Few areas of the law are as confusing and uncertain as the interpretation of the Fourth Amendment: "The right of the people to be secure in their persons, houses, papers, and effects, against unreasonable searches and seizures, shall not be violated, and no Warrants shall issue, but upon probable cause, supported by Oath or affirmation, and particularly describing the place to be searched, and the persons or things to be seized." The language of the Constitution raises questions immediately. What makes a search "unreasonable"? Do all searches and arrests require warrants (that is, prior judicial authorization, issued by a "neutral" magistrate or justice of the peace)? What is "probable cause"? Answers evolve from judicial decisions, and these decisions clarifying the Fourth Amendment have immense significance whenever the exclusionary rule is applicable.

(1) *Probable cause.* Probable cause is more than a "hunch" that someone is engaged in illegal activity, but it is less than the degree of certainty a prosecutor needs at trial to establish guilt beyond a reasonable doubt. Justice Rutledge once characterized the standard in this manner:

> In dealing with probable cause . . . we deal with probabilities. These are not technical; they are the factual and practical considerations of everyday life on which reasonable and prudent men, not legal technicians, act. . . . Probable cause exists where the facts and circumstances within [the officers'] knowledge, and of which they had reasonably trustworthy information, [are] sufficient in themselves to warrant a man of reasonable caution in the belief that an offense has been or is being committed.

Probable cause, Rutledge said, seeks "to safeguard citizens from rash and unreasonable interferences with privacy and from unfounded charges of crime. [It also seeks] to give fair leeway for enforcing the law in the community's protection." For the Court to require "more would unduly hamper law enforcement. To allow less would be to leave law-abiding citizens at the mercy of the officers' whim or caprice" (*Brinegar* v. *United States*, 1949). More recently, the justices have emphasized that the standard "is to be applied, not according to a fixed and rigid formula, but rather in the light of the 'totality of the circumstances' made known to the magistrate" who issues the warrant. "[T]he task of a reviewing court," in overseeing the Fourth Amendment, "is not to conduct a de novo determination of probable cause, but only to determine whether there is substantial evidence in the record supporting the magistrate's decision to issue the warrant." (*Massachusetts* v. *Upton*, 1984.)

It is easy to see how probable cause can take on accordionlike qualities. Whatever its definition, it must be present for arrests and searches, although as noted below, the justices have approved limited detentions and searches on the basis of something less than probable cause. Moreover, the justices do not always require warrants.

(2) *Search incident to an otherwise lawful arrest.* The Court has almost always shown a preference in this century for searches and seizures authorized by warrants, as opposed to warrantless intrusions. Situations can be anticipated, however, in which the requirement for a warrant would be so impractical as seriously to hamper law enforcement. So over the years the justices have created exceptions to the warrant requirement, and as one might suppose, the scope and application of the various exceptions have been the source of much litigation.

An important exception to the provision for a search warrant was the curiously evolved doctrine that those places under the control of the arrestee could be searched to avoid the danger of concealed weapons or to prevent destruction of crime-related items. In *United States* v. *Rabinowitz* (1950) an entire office was thoroughly searched incident to a lawful arrest, and the admission at trial of forged stamps discovered during the search was approved. The 1969 decision in *Chimel* v. *California* represents the Court's effort to narrow the area subject to a warrantless search incident to an arrest and to induce greater use of search warrants.

(3) *The automobile exception.* The automobile itself has long been an exception to the general rule that warrants are needed in advance of searches. *Carroll* v. *United States* (1925) allowed the warrantless search of a car when there was probable cause to believe it was carrying contraband or was being used to violate the law. Not only are motor vehicles mobile, and so might quickly depart the jurisdiction while an officer attempted to obtain a warrant, but most justices also see them as involving lesser "expectations of privacy" than, say, someone's house or apartment.

If the automobile itself may be searched without a warrant, what about containers police find in the automobile that may contain contraband? Should it make any difference whether such containers are located in the passenger compartment or in the trunk? Such matters occupied the justices in *United States* v. *Ross* (1982). Justice Stevens's majority opinion provides a tour through the Court's decisions in this complex area of Fourth Amendment law.

(4) *Informers.* A factor complicating judicial oversight of police practices and behavior is the use of anonymous informers in establishing probable cause. Many of the affidavits signed by police officers recite certain details they learned secondhand from such people, anonymous even to the magistrate issuing the warrant. The constitutional objection to the use of informers on the ground that one cannot confront one's accusers was overcome by the Court in *McCray* v. *Illinois* (1967). So when *Chimel* called for a greater use of search warrants, *McCray* made it easier to get them.

Key to preventing anonymity from becoming a shield for fictitiousness is the requirement that the officer demonstrate the informant's reliability to the magistrate. The justices have differed over the degree to which the government must demonstrate such reliability when obtaining a warrant. Until 1983, the Court required police to demonstrate an informer's "reliability" and "basis of knowledge" before a magistrate could issue a warrant based on information provided by anonymous informers (*Spinelli* v. *United States*, 1969). But in *Illinois* v. *Gates*, a majority abandoned this "two-pronged test," substituting in its place a "totality of circumstances" approach. According to *Gates*, the magistrate must make a practical, "commonsense" decision whether, given all the information the officer provides, there is a fair probability that evidence of a crime will be found in a particular place. To uphold the drug-related convictions in *Gates*, the Court had to abandon the old test since the informer was anonymous even to the police. There was no way, therefore, that an officer could establish the informer's "reliability" and "basis of knowledge."

(5) *Stop and frisk.* For many years police had engaged in the practice of stopping persons behaving suspiciously and, to protect themselves, patting down or searching those who might be armed. Most civil libertarians criticized this process since the police normally lacked probable cause for an arrest and the law simply had no provision for a detention process less restrictive than arrest. The critics also claimed that stopping, questioning, and frisking for weapons was a police tactic too often directed toward racial and other minority groups. In *Terry* v. *Ohio* (1968), this practice was upheld by the Warren Court against the charge that it violated the Fourth Amendment. In so doing, the justices authenticated an important police tactic in the prevention and solution of crimes. Building on *Terry*, *Adams* v. *Williams* (1972) allowed the presence of an informer's tip, admittedly insufficiently reliable to constitute probable cause, to help establish the "reasonable suspicion"—a standard less demanding on police than probable cause—which *Terry* approved.

Terry remains an important law-enforcement weapon in the war against narcotics trafficking. *United States* v. *Place* (1983) extended *Terry* to a person's *effects*, in this case personal luggage. The government contended that when authorities have knowledge supporting a reasonable belief or suspicion—but a belief still short of probable cause—that a traveler's bags contain narcotics, police may briefly seize the luggage to pursue further investigation, including "sniffs" by trained narcotics-sensitive dogs. A majority agreed but reversed the conviction because detention of Place's bags for 90 minutes was too long to be considered "reasonable."

(6) *Arrests and other detentions.* Police may make felony arrests in public places without warrants where probable cause exists (*United States* v. *Watson*, 1976), but arrest warrants are required when police make routine felony arrests in a private residence (*Payton* v. *New York,* 1980) in the absence of exigent circumstances. What is a "reasonable" length of time for a detention on less than probable cause? The time involved in *Place* was seen as unreasonable, but two years later in *United States* v. *Sharpe* (1985), the Court approved a 20-minute roadside investigative stop, without probable cause, before officers were able to make a formal arrest based on probable cause. The variety of possible situations has made it difficult for the justices to write precise guidelines.

(7) *Administrative searches.* For searches by public officials other than law-enforcement agents, the Court employs a relaxed standard. Health and safety inspections of homes and most businesses, for example, require an administrative warrant if the occupant refuses entry, not a criminal warrant. The former does not have to have the particularity of the latter, nor does there need to be evidence of a violation. Rather, a reasonable plan of enforcement authorized by statute suffices. The Court has approved warrantless administrative searches for some "closely regulated" businesses such as automobile junkyards (*New York* v. *Burger,* 1987).

In a different context, the Court has ruled that public school officials and teachers are governed by the Fourth Amendment but that the amendment means less in school than it does on the street. In *New Jersey* v. *T.L.O.* (1985) a high school teacher found a 14-year-old freshman and her companion smoking cigarettes in the school lavatory, in violation of a school rule. During questioning by the assistant principal, one of the girls denied that she smoked at all. The assistant principal demanded to see the contents of her purse. Opening it, he found cigarettes but also noticed cigarette rolling papers commonly used with marijuana. A more thorough search turned up marijuana and drug-related items. The state then brought delinquency charges against her in juvenile court, against her claim that the search of her purse had violated the Fourth Amendment. Upholding the state, the Court struck a balance between a pupil's expectations of privacy and a school's need to preserve a sound learning environment, and eased the usual restrictions on searches. So not only are warrants unnecessary for such in-school searches, but also school officials may search on less than probable cause as long as the search seems "reasonable" under the circumstances. This means that the Fourth Amendment sets one standard for police officers conducting searches on school premises but a decidedly less demanding standard for school officials doing the same thing.

Similarly, five justices upheld a supervisor's warrantless search without probable cause of a public employee's office, desk, and file cabinets. Acknowledging the employee's expectation of privacy in his private office, Justice O'Connor explained that the employer's intrusion is nonetheless valid when it is reasonable in scope and justified by a work-related need or reasonable suspicion (*O'Connor* v. *Ortega,* 1987).

Electronic Surveillance. With the development of electronic means of surveillance in the twentieth century, the Court was faced with difficult questions concerning what kind of official invasions violate the Fourth Amendment. In **Olmstead** v. **United States** (1928), a sharply divided Court held that wiretapping did not violate the Fourth Amendment guaranty against unreasonable searches and seizures because there was no seizure of papers, tangible material effects, or actual physical invasion of the house.

Justice Brandeis's spirited dissenting opinion in *Olmstead* gave Chief Justice Marshall's famous dictum—"We must never forget it is *a constitution* we are expounding"—a new twist. Just as grants of power, as Marshall had reasoned, must be adapted to changed conditions, so Brandeis insisted that the Court take into account altered conditions in interpreting limitations on power. Here, too, Brandeis argued, "Time works changes. . . . Discovery and invention have made it possible for the government by means far more effective than stretching upon the rack to obtain disclosures in court of what is whispered in the closet."

Electronic surveillance by police at all levels continued for nearly 40 years without close federal judicial supervision. Only when there was an official physical trespass to the property subject to the wiretap or bugging was the Court prepared to find a Fourth Amendment violation (*Silverman* v. *United States,* 1961).

For different reasons both civil libertarians and law-enforcement agents welcomed **Katz** v. **United States** (1968), which expressly overruled *Olmstead. Olmstead* fell because of the Court's emphasis in *Katz* on one's "expectation of privacy." The "Fourth Amendment protects people, not places," declared Justice Stewart. But the individual's expectation must also be one society is prepared to acknowledge as a reasonable expectation. Moreover, while overturning a conviction based on evidence acquired by a listening device planted without a warrant on the outside of a telephone booth, the majority made it plain that Congress could establish constitutionally correct standards governing electronic surveillance with a warrant. The Court was willing to exchange legitimacy for controls.

Following *Katz,* the 1968 Omnibus Crime Control and Safe Streets Act authorized state and federal electronic surveillance in a wide variety of cases, but the statute by no means answered all the constitutional questions. In a highly significant interpretation of the act in 1972, all eight participating justices rejected the federal government's claim that electronic surveillance, endorsed by the attorney general but without judicial approval, was lawful under the president's power to protect national security at home (**United States** v. **U.S. District Court**). Congressional action to legitimize electronic surveillance in national security matters came in the Foreign Intelligence Surveillance Act of 1978. Special courts created by the act hear requests by the government for warrants to conduct electronic surveillance of "U.S. persons" believed to be working on behalf of a foreign power. More relaxed controls are allowed when the target of the surveillance is a "foreign power" or "agent of a foreign power."

The 1968 act continues to play an important role in crime fighting. As of 1987, 31 states, the District of Columbia, and the federal government had statutes authorizing electronic surveillance. According to the Administrative Office of the United States Courts, judges issued 237 federal and 437 state orders in 1987 (down from a high of 289 and 512 in 1984), which led to a total of 823,566 intercepted conversations (of which 18 percent were incriminating) by 65,939 persons. The average length of each original period of interception was 25 days; the average length of 402 extensions was 26 days.

Informers and electronic surveillance combine when an agent or informer is "wired for sound" while talking to a suspect. These situations are not counted in the preceding data. Even after *Katz,* with its emphasis on "expectation of privacy," the practice survived a constitutional challenge in *United States* v. *White* (1971). The Court has concluded that one takes one's chances when talking with anyone. Similarly, the warrantless use of a "beeper" to monitor the movement of an automobile on public roadways does not violate the Fourth Amendment (*United States* v. *Knotts,* 1983). Once the beeper inside a container transmits from inside a house and later from other locations, however, a warrant is necessary (*United States* v. *Karo,* 1984) because the beeper provides agents with information they could not have acquired by visual surveillance.

Defining a Search. In a Fourth Amendment case, an important threshold determination is whether a "search" or "seizure" has in fact occurred. If it has not, the constraints of the amendment do not apply. For example, searches of "open fields" in contrast to "curtilage" (the area immediately surrounding the home) do not implicate the Fourth Amendment because they are not searches of "persons, houses, papers or effects."

The Court attempted to mark the extent of the curtilage in *United States* v. *Dunn* (1987). At night and without a warrant, drug agents crossed a fence surrounding a 198-acre ranch to reach a barn that was surrounded by a wooden fence and was about 60 yards from the residence, itself also surrounded by a fence. Smelling a drug-related odor coming from the barn, agents peered inside with a flashlight to obtain the information needed for a search warrant for the rest of their investigation. Upholding the validity of the intrusion because the barn was outside the curtilage, Justice White explained that the extent of the curtilage depends on four factors: (1) "the proximity of the area claimed to be curtilage to the home"; (2) "whether the area is included within an enclosure surrounding the home"; (3) "the nature of the uses to which the area is put"; and (4) "the steps taken by the resident to protect the area from observation by people passing by." Justice Brennan, joined by Justice Marshall, thought the critical issue was Dunn's expectation of privacy in the barnyard itself: "When, as here, the public is excluded from an area immediately surrounding or adjacent to a business structure, that area is not . . . part of the open fields."

Being within the curtilage does not bar all police observation, however. In *California* v. *Ciraolo* (1986), aerial photographic surveillance by police of marijuana plants in the backyard of a house, even though surrounded by two fences, was not deemed a search. Although the fences certainly indicated the occupant's expectation of privacy, five justices concluded that *Katz's* second prong (that the expectation be reasonable) was not met. Observation occurred "from a public vantage point [above 1,000 feet] where [the officer] has a right to be and which renders the activities clearly visible," according to Chief Justice Rehnquist.

Outside the curtilage, expectation of privacy is central in deciding when a Fourth Amendment search has occurred. Consider *California* v. *Greenwood* (1988), in which police conducted warrantless searches of sacks of garbage left at curbside. Against the objection that "a single bag of trash testifies eloquently to the eating, reading, and recreational habits of the person who produced it," six justices upheld the search because the occupants of the house had "exposed their garbage to the public sufficiently to defeat their claim to Fourth Amendment protection."

The Right to Counsel. The fair trial rule with respect to counsel in state noncapital cases was overturned in *Gideon* v. *Wainwright* (1963), which imposed the federal rule on state procedures. Justice Black sought to give the impression that *Betts* v. *Brady* (1942), requiring appointment of counsel only where the totality of circumstances made it necessary for a fair trial, was a prior break with the precedents. To one who reexamines *Powell* v. *Alabama* and subsequent decisions, Black's reasoning was contrived. Yet Black was correct in stating, ". . . The right of one charged with crime to counsel may not be deemed fundamental and essential to fair trials in some countries, but it is in ours." For counsel at trial, the Burger Court broadened the *Gideon* rule to include petty offenses, when confinement for any period is part of the sentence. The trial judge's decision to appoint counsel thus affects the sentence imposed later if the defendant is found guilty (*Scott* v. *Illinois,* 1979, clarifying *Argersinger* v. *Hamlin,* 1972). Nevertheless, a defendant has a constitutional right to refuse counsel if the choice is made voluntarily and intelligently (*Faretta* v. *California,* 1975).

Right to counsel under the Sixth Amendment is now pervasive throughout the criminal justice process during and following the stage at which formal charges are brought against the accused. For instance, the Court has held that counsel must be available:

1. For the arraignment (*Hamilton* v. *Alabama,* 1961) [Assertion of right to counsel at the arraignment creates an absolute bar to further police-initiated questioning without counsel (*Michigan* v. *Jackson,* 1986).]

2. On an appeal by right, not where the appeal is discretionary (*Douglas* v. *California,* 1962; *Ross* v. *Moffitt,* 1974).

3. While in custody [A defendant's damaging statements overheard by a paid informer are inadmissible at trial (*Massiah* v. *United States,* 1964), as are statements coached by police (*Brewer* v. *Williams,* 1977).]

4. At police lineups, to avoid faulty identification (*United States* v. *Wade,* 1967) [but not including informal identification that occurs prior to initiation of criminal prosecution (*Kirby* v. *Illinois,* 1972)]

5. At some probation revocation proceedings (*Gagnon* v. *Scarpelli,* 1973)

The Fifth Amendment, discussed later, grants a right to counsel to those not formally charged who are in custodial interrogation.

Both at trial and on direct appeal the Court has clarified the Sixth Amendment to require *effective* assistance of counsel (*Strickland* v. *Washington,* 1984). The justices have concluded that a right to assistance of counsel means little if that right does not include effective assistance. But showing ineffective assistance is not easy. What is mandated is not an error-free defense. Rather, one must demonstrate that, but for counsel's mistakes, the result of the proceeding would have been different.

Closely akin to assistance of counsel, the Constitution now requires that an indigent defendant have access to "one competent psychiatrist" for the "assistance necessary to prepare an effective defense based on his mental condition, when his sanity at the time of the offense is seriously in question" (*Ake* v. *Oklahoma,* 1985). The broad contours of the due process clause recognize, declared Justice Marshall in a potentially far-reaching opinion, that "the assistance of a psychiatrist may well be crucial" because psychiatrists "ideally assist lay jurors to make a sensible and educated determination about the mental condition of the defendant. . . ." Not clear from *Ake* is whether the Constitution requires a state to permit a defense based on insanity.

Self-Incrimination and Identification of the Accused. The Fifth Amendment's assurance that "no person . . . shall be compelled in any criminal case to be a witness against himself" is a right "hard-earned by our fore-fathers," said Chief Justice Warren. The reasons "for its inclusion in the Constitution—and the necessities for its preservation—are to be found in the lessons of history." The right is a central feature of a system of criminal justice that presumes innocence—that is, which places the burden of proof on the prosecution to establish guilt. No one accused of a crime should have to assist the state in proving its case. The framers of the Bill of Rights, Leonard Levy explains, were "deeply committed to perpetuating a system that minimized the possibilities of convicting the innocent" but "were not less concerned about the humanity that the fundamental law should show even to the offender." The Fifth Amendment stands for the proposition that determining guilt and innocence by fair procedures is more important than punishing the guilty.

The extent of the guard against self-incrimination has nonetheless presented the Court with hard questions. How far should the needs of law enforcement be accommodated and how much freedom should be accorded the individual?

(1) *Immunity.* One may claim Fifth Amendment protection in refusing to testify before a grand jury, jury, or legislative committee or in being compelled to produce papers or other evidence (*Counselman* v. *Hitchcock,* 1892; *Quinn* v. *United States,* 1955). Yet the Court has allowed Congress to grant immunity from prosecution to extract testimony from reluctant witnesses, an especially useful technique in investigations of subversive activities and organized crime. "Immunity displaces the danger. Once the reason for the privilege ceases, the privilege ceases," reasoned Justice Frankfurter in *Ullman* v. *United States* (1956). The Immunity Act of 1954 challenged in *Ullman* provided for complete (or "transactional") immunity from both state and federal prosecution in exchange for testimony about various criminal activities. But the Organized Crime Control Act of 1970 permits a federal court, agency, or congressional committee to offer "use and derivative use" as opposed to "transactional" immunity in exchange for compelled testimony. The former is less generous to the witness than the latter because under "use immunity" the witness can still be prosecuted for crimes about which the witness has testified. The limitation on the government is that the prosecutor simply may not later *use* this testimony against the witness. Five justices found even this arrangement harmonious with the Fifth Amendment in *Kastigar* v. *United States* (1972).

(2) *Nontestimonial evidence.* Other examples demonstrate that constitutional rights are not self-defining. The Court has generally interpreted the protection against self-incrimination to include testimonial, but not nontestimonial, evidence. So in *Schmerber* v. *California* (1966), a narrow majority upheld a conviction for drunken driving based on a blood sample taken without the defendant's permission. In a case with strong overtones of the testimonial, a badly divided Court refused to void a California statute that required the driver of an automobile involved in an accident to stop and leave his name and address with the owner of the property he had damaged (*California* v. *Byers,* 1971).

(3) *Interrogations.* Police interrogation of suspects raises obvious Fifth Amendment questions. At least since *Brown* v. *Mississippi,* discussed earlier, the justices have overturned state convictions based on "coerced confessions." Some justices began to wonder whether interrogations could be anything but threatening and intimidating if the accused was denied the right to have a lawyer present. Thus, in *Escobedo* v. *Illinois* (1964), the Court condemned the police practice of preventing a suspect from consulting with a lawyer until the interrogation had ended. This and numerous other cases over the previous three decades had made the Court aware of a variety of law-enforcement practices that seemed unfair to accused persons, many of whom were young, ignorant, and members of minority groups. The Court inched toward what Herbert Packer termed the "due process model" of criminal justice (which stressed fairness and the rights of the accused), in contrast to the older "crime control model" (which stressed the powers of the prosecution). In **Miranda v. Arizona** (1966), the Court required federal and state officials to give suspects specified warnings or equivalent advice before beginning to interrogate them about alleged crimes. The Warren Court held that the privilege against self-incrimination can be secured in no other way. The justices were joining the Sixth Amendment's provisions for right to counsel with the Fifth Amendment's guard against self-incrimination. The belief was that events occurring in the station house greatly influence the outcome of events in the courthouse.

From a law-enforcement viewpoint, *Miranda* at first seemed a disaster. But statements made by a suspect after requesting a lawyer may still be used under certain circumstances. In cases today, the debate turns on whether the suspect has in fact waived the *Miranda* rights, whether a *Miranda*-type "interrogation" has in fact occurred, or whether incriminating but unwarned statements later taint incriminating and warned statements. Consider **Oregon v. Elstad** (1985), in which six justices upheld the validity of a confession following the suspect's voluntary, but unwarned, admission of guilt.

Miranda has spawned dozens of decisions. Generally the Burger and Rehnquist Courts have been hesitant to extend the ruling. Several cases have restricted its scope. For instance,

a. Statements, inadmissible as direct testimony because of a *Miranda* violation, may be used to attack credibility of statements the accused makes on the witness stand (*Harris* v. *New York,* 1971).

b. No Fifth Amendment interrogation occurred when a suspect asserted the right to silence and then, in a police car, responded with incriminating statements to comments made by officers (*Rhode Island* v. *Innis,* 1980).

c. Assertion of right to counsel in the interrogation is an absolute bar to subsequent uncounseled, police-initiated questioning (*Edwards* v. *Arizona,* 1981).

d. Questioning that occurs before arrest for a traffic offense does not amount to "custodial interrogation" within *Miranda's* reach (*Berkemer* v. *McCarty,* 1984).

e. Public safety allows police to ask a suspect the whereabouts of a gun before administering a *Miranda* warning (*New York* v. *Quarles,* 1984).

f. Police are under no constitutional obligation to tell a suspect whom they are questioning without a lawyer that a lawyer retained by a third party is attempting to get in touch with that suspect (*Moran* v. *Burbine,* 1985).

g. Waiver of *Miranda* rights is not considered involuntary because the defendant's "perception of coercion flowing from the 'voice of God,' however important or significant such a perception may be in other disciplines, is a matter to which the United States Constitution does not speak" (*Colorado* v. *Connelly,* 1986).

h. No interrogation occurred when police allowed a suspect's wife to talk to him in the officer's presence (*Arizona* v. *Mauro,* 1987).

The Court is rarely unanimous on *Miranda* issues. In cases decided against the defendant, dissenters claim that the holdings reward police misconduct, remove incentives to abide by *Miranda,* and generally undercut the spirit of the 1966 decision. Justices in the majority reply that the decisions strike the proper balance between society's legitimate law-enforcement interests and the protection of the defendant's Fifth Amendment rights.

(4) *Taxes, draft registration, and self-incrimination.* Often, public policies entail conflicts between different provisions of the Constitution. Even with Congress's broad power to tax, the justices have said that the Fifth Amendment provides a complete defense against violation of the Federal Wagering Tax statutes. **Marchetti v. United States** (1968) held that the federal government could not require wagerers to register and pay a tax where that information was readily available to local authorities for prosecution under state antigambling laws. Is there also a Fifth Amendment violation in the congressional inducement to young males to register for the draft? The Military Selective Service Act denies financial aid to male students between the ages of 18 and 26 who fail to register. The act also makes late registration a crime. A student who registers late to keep his financial aid is thus furnishing the government with information that would be necessary to prosecute him criminally. In *Selective Service System* v. *Minnesota Public Interest Research Group* (1984), six of the eight participating justices said that *Marchetti* did not apply because the young men in question had not registered and so could not yet assert their constitutional privilege.

Capital and Other Punishment. In *Furman* v. *Georgia* (1972) the Supreme Court ruled 5 to 4 that the death penalty, as then administered, was cruel and unusual punishment in violation of the Eighth and Fourteenth Amendments. Too much discretion in the hands of trial judges and juries made application of the death sentence capricious. Thirty-five states and Congress (for aircraft hijacking) then reinstated capital punishment with more carefully drawn statutes to meet the Court's objections in *Furman.* In **Gregg v. Georgia** (1976) a majority of the justices concluded that the death penalty was not inherently cruel and unusual and upheld a two-step sentencing scheme designed to set strict standards for trial courts. A jury would first decide the question of guilt and then in a separate proceeding impose punishment.

Following *Gregg*, nearly 2,000 convicted felons had been placed on "death row" by mid-1988, but only 100 were executed. One reason for this discrepancy is that the Court, although approving capital punishment in principle, has raised substantial obstacles to carrying it out. Some of the conditions that have led to an invalidation of a death sentence include

1. Complete removal of trial court discretion by making capital punishment mandatory (*Woodson v. North Carolina,* 1976)
2. Failure to allow the introduction of any mitigating circumstances (*Roberts v. Louisiana,* 1977)
3. Death penalty imposed for rape (*Coker v. Georgia,* 1977)
4. Death penalty for those who commit felonies in which murders occur but who themselves do not kill or attempt to kill, unless the felon's participation is "major" and his or her mental state one of "reckless indifference" to the value of human life (*Enmund v. Florida,* 1982, and *Tison v. Arizona,* 1987)
5. Onset of insanity while condemned prisoner is awaiting execution (*Ford v. Wainwright,* 1986)
6. Mandatory execution for prison inmate who commits murder while serving life sentence (*Sumner v. Shuman,* 1987)
7. Consideration by jury of "victim impact statements" (*Booth v. Maryland,* 1987)
8. Death sentence for person younger than 16 where there is no statute explicitly providing for execution of juveniles (*Thompson v. Oklahoma,* 1988)

In contrast to procedural attacks on the death penalty, **McCleskey v. Kemp** (1987) was the first frontal assault on capital punishment since *Gregg*. A complex statistical study showed that in Georgia in the 1970s killers of whites were 4.3 times as likely to receive the death penalty than killers of blacks. Although statistics have been sufficient to establish discrimination in jury selection and employment, five justices were unpersuaded by the numbers in this context. The study did not prove that race had been a factor in McCleskey's case. Because each capital jury is unique, explained Justice Powell, and because "discretion is essential to the criminal justice process, we would demand exceptionally clear proof before we would infer that the discretion has been abused."

Justices have only recently appeared willing to scrutinize noncapital sentences that might violate the Eighth Amendment because they are excessive. True, the Court in 1910 (*Weems v. United States*) struck down as excessive a sentence of a Philippine court which entailed, among other penalties, 12 years' imprisonment at hard labor, while chained day and night at the wrists and ankles. And in 1962 (*Robinson v. California*) the Court found "excessive" a 90-day jail term for the crime of being "addicted to the use of narcotics." As recently as 1980 in *Rummel v. Estelle,* however, a bare majority led by Justice Rehnquist refused to become involved in proportionality review of various lengths of prison terms. At issue was application of the Texas recidivist statute under which Rummel was sentenced to life imprisonment after conviction for his third felony for defrauding others. The total amount in question from Rummel's three run-ins with the law was about $230.

In 1983 an equally bare majority in *Solem v. Helm* "distinguished" *Rummel*. Stressing that *successful* challenges to the proportionality of particular sentences will be rare, Justice Powell declared,

[W]e hold as a matter of principle that a criminal sentence must be proportionate to the crime for which the defendant has been convicted. Reviewing courts, of course, should grant substantial deference to the broad authority that legislatures necessarily possess in determining the types and limits of punishments for crimes, as well as to the discretion that trial courts possess in sentencing convicted criminals. But no penalty is *per se* constitutional. . . .

In sum, a court's proportionality analysis under the Eighth Amendment should be guided by objective criteria, including (i) the gravity of the offense and the harshness of the penalty; (ii) the sentences imposed on other criminals in the same jurisdiction; and (iii) the sentences imposed for commission of the same crime in other jurisdictions.

Preventive detention—imprisonment before trial because of the danger the arrestee poses to the community—raises questions under both the Eighth Amendment and the due process clauses. The Bail Reform Act of 1984 for the first time permitted federal judges, following a hearing, to deny bail to an individual arrested for certain very serious offenses on the ground of dangerousness. Heretofore, bail was solely a device to ensure a person's presence for trial. Now bail could be denied because of the prediction of future criminal conduct. Opponents charged that the statute authorized punishment without trial and that denial of bail should not be used to protect the community. In *United States* v. *Salerno* (1987) six justices held that the act was punitive in neither purpose nor effect because of the procedural safeguards it contained. The government's interest in guarding the community from danger outweighed the individual's interest in liberty. *Salerno* had been anticipated by *Schall* v. *Martin* (1984), in which the Court upheld an elaborate New York system allowing detention of an accused juvenile after a finding of "serious risk" that the juvenile would commit a criminal act during the pretrial period.

A NEW DOUBLE STANDARD?

During the Warren Court (1953–1969), a majority often found itself pushing state criminal justice systems to provide a longer list of rights for the accused. A pro-prosecution ruling by a state supreme court stood a good chance of being reversed on appeal. With less enthusiasm among a majority of the Burger and Rehnquist Courts for the rights of criminal defendants, many state courts have maintained or enlarged these rights as a matter of *state* constitutional law.

"I [was] sworn in to uphold the state Constitution [and] I am going to uphold [it]," Vermont's Chief Justice Allen has asserted. The opportunity for expanded state protection is present because virtually all the states have bills of rights similar to, or even more lengthy, than the federal Bill of Rights. Protection of individual liberties by state courts interpreting state constitutions raises no federal constitutional questions, provided the minimum standards of the latter are met. Federalism means that a state may grant more freedom under its own constitution. In fact, Professor Ronald Collins has counted more than 450 instances— most of them since 1980—in which the highest courts of the states have set standards exceeding federal guarantees.

"Incorporation" (originally the vehicle for bringing the Bill of Rights to the states) is partly responsible for more than the continuing controversy surrounding many Warren Court decisions expanding liberties and Burger and Rehnquist Court decisions contracting them. Ironically, incorporation may have indirectly stimulated the growth of *state* constitutional rights. (See the section on judicial federalism in Chapter Four.)

Incorporating the Bill of Rights into the Fourteenth Amendment multiplied by thousands the occasions when the Constitution could command that the guilty go free. Without incorporation, a decision expanding, say, the protections afforded by the Fourth

Amendment would have only limited effects. With incorporation, such a ruling would affect every police department, district attorney's office, and courtroom in the land. Before incorporation, a decision contracting Fourth Amendment protection would directly affect only federal prosecutions. Now, a similar decision directly affects all components of the national system of criminal justice, unless state judges, using state constitutions, resist.

KEY TERMS

civil liberties	due process	open fields
civil rights	revolution	transactional
Bill of Rights	exclusionary rule	immunity
incorporation	habeas corpus	use immunity
due process of law	search warrant	*Miranda* warning
ordered liberty	probable cause	due process model
total incorporation	reasonable suspicion	crime-control model
fair trial rule	administrative	preventive detention
double standard	searches	
arraignment	curtilage	

QUERIES

1. Assess the arguments for a bill of rights in the exchange between Thomas Jefferson and James Madison.

2. What was the place of *Mapp* v. *Ohio* in the Warren Court's due process revolution?

3. Respond to the following question: "Why should the police have to abide by Marquis of Queensberry rules all the while criminals are acting like thugs?"

4. What questions regarding the right to counsel did *Gideon* v. *Wainwright* and *Miranda* v. *Arizona* leave unanswered? To what extent have these questions been answered by later cases?

SELECTED READINGS

BAKER, LIVA. *Miranda: Crime, Law and Politics*. New York: Atheneum, 1983.

BEANEY, WILLIAM M. *The Right to Counsel in American Courts*. Ann Arbor: University of Michigan Press, 1955.

BRANT, IRVING. *The Bill of Rights*. Indianapolis: Bobbs-Merrill, 1965.

BRENNAN, WILLIAM J., JR. "The Bill of Rights and the States: The Revival of State Constitutions as Guardians of Individual Rights." 61 *New York University Law Review* 535 (1986).

CHOPER, JESSE H. "Consequences of Supreme Court Decisions Upholding Individual Constitutional Rights." 83 *Michigan Law Review* 4 (1984).

CORTNER, RICHARD C. *A "Scottsboro" Case in Mississippi.* Jackson: University Press of Mississippi, 1986.

————. *The Supreme Court and the Second Bill of Rights: The Fourteenth Amendment and the Nationalization of Civil Liberties.* Madison: University of Wisconsin Press, 1981.

CURTIS, MICHAEL KENT. *No State Shall Abridge: The Fourteenth Amendment and the Bill of Rights.* Durham, N.C.: Duke University Press, 1986.

FAIRMAN, CHARLES. "Does the Fourteenth Amendment Incorporate the Bill of Rights: The Original Understanding." 2 *Stanford Law Review* 5 (1949).

GRAHAM, FRED P. *The Self-Inflicted Wound.* New York: Macmillan, 1970.

KAPLAN, JOHN. "The Limits of the Exclusionary Rule." 26 *Stanford Law Review* 1027 (1974).

KAMISAR, YALE. " 'Comparative Reprehensibility' and the Fourth Amendment Exclusionary Rule." 86 *Michigan Law Review* 1 (1987).

————. "The 'Police Practice' Phases of the Criminal Process and the Three Phases of the Burger Court." In Herman Schwartz, ed. *The Burger Years.* New York: Penguin, 1988.

LaFAVE, WAYNE R. *A Treatise on the Fourth Amendment,* 4 vols., 2d ed. St. Paul, Minn.: West, 1986.

LEVY, LEONARD. *Origins of the Fifth Amendment.* New York: Oxford University Press, 1968.

MASON, ALPHEUS T. "The Bill of Rights: An Almost Forgotten Appendage." In Stephen C. Halpern, ed. *The Future of Our Liberties.* Westport, Conn.: Greenwood, 1982.

RUTLAND, ROBERT A. *The Birth of the Bill of Rights, 1776–1791.* Chapel Hill: University of North Carolina Press, 1955.

WHITE, WELSH S. *The Death Penalty in the Eighties.* Ann Arbor: University of Michigan Press, 1987.

I. DRIVE FOR A BILL OF RIGHTS

Jefferson-Madison Correspondence, 1787–1789

THOMAS JEFFERSON to James Madison, 20 December 1787

. . . I like much the general idea of framing a government which should go on of itself peaceably, without needing continual recurrence to the state legislatures. I like the organization of the government into Legislative, Judiciary and Executive.

. . . There are other good things of less moment. I will now add what I do not like. First the omission of a bill of rights providing clearly and without the aid of sophisms for freedom of religion, freedom of the press, protection against standing armies, restriction against monopolies, the eternal and unremitting force of the habeas corpus laws, and trials by jury in all matters of fact triable by the laws of the land and not by the law of Nations. To say, as Mr. Wilson does, that a bill of rights was not necessary because all is reserved in the case of the general government which is not given, while in the particular ones all is given which is not reserved might do for the Audience to whom it was addressed, but is surely gratis dictum, opposed by strong inferences from the body of the instrument, as well as from the omission of the clause of our present confederation which had declared that in express terms. It was a hard conclusion to say because there has been no uniformity among the states as to the cases triable by jury, because some have been so incautious as to abandon this mode of trial, therefore the more prudent states shall be reduced to the same level of calamity. It would have been much more just and wise to have concluded the other way that as most of the states had judiciously preserved this palladium, those who had wandered should be brought back to it, and to have established general right instead of general wrong. Let me add that a bill of rights is what the people are entitled to against every government on earth, general or particular, and what no just government should refuse, or rest on inference. . . .

JAMES MADISON to Thomas Jefferson, 17 October 1788

. . . My own opinion has always been in favor of a bill of rights, provided it be so framed as not to imply powers not meant to be included in the enumeration. At the same time I have never thought the omission a material defect, nor been anxious to supply it even by *subsequent* amendment, for any other reason than that it is anxiously desired by others. I have favored it because I supposed it might be of use, and if properly executed could not be of disservice. I have not viewed it in an important light. . . .

. . . Experience proves the inefficacy of a bill of rights on those occasions when its control is most needed. Repeated violations of these parchment barriers have been committed by overbearing majorities in every State. In Virginia I have seen the bill of rights violated in every instance where it has been opposed to a popular current. Notwithstanding the explicit provision contained in that instrument for the rights of Conscience, it is well known that a religious establishment would have taken place in that State, if the Legislative majority had found as they expected, a majority of the people in favor of the measure; and I am persuaded that if a majority of the people were not of one sect, the measure would still take place and on narrower ground than was then proposed, notwithstanding the additional obstacle which the law has since created. Wherever the real power in a Government lies, there is the danger of oppression. In our Government, the real power lies in the majority of the Community, and the invasion of private rights is *chiefly* to be apprehended, not from acts of government contrary to the sense of its constituents, but from acts in which the Government is the mere instrument of the major number of the Constituents. This is a truth of great importance, but not yet sufficiently attended to; and is probably more strongly impressed on my mind by facts, and reflections suggested by them, than on yours which has contemplated abuses of power issuing from a very different quarter. Wherever there is an interest and power to do wrong, wrong will generally be done, and not less readily by a powerful & interested party than by a powerful and interested prince. . . .

. . . What use then it may be asked can a bill of rights serve in popular Governments? I answer the two following which, though less essential than in other Governments, sufficiently recommend the precaution: 1. The political truths declared in that solemn manner acquire by degrees the character of fundamental maxims of free Governments, and as they become incorporated with the national senti-

ment, counteract the impulses of interest and passion. 2. Altho, it be generally true as above stated that the danger of oppression lies in the interested majorities of the people rather than in usurped acts of the Government, yet there may be occasions on which the evil may spring from the latter source; and on such, a bill of rights will be a good ground for an appeal to the sense of the community. Perhaps too there may be a certain degree of danger, that a succession of artful and ambitious rulers may be gradual & well timed advances, finally erect an independent Government on the subversion of liberty. Should this danger exist at all, it is prudent to guard against it, especially when the precaution can do no injury. . . . It is a melancholy reflection that liberty should be equally exposed to danger whether the Government have too much or too little power, and that the line which divides these extremes should be so inaccurately defined by experience. . . .

THOMAS JEFFERSON to James Madison, 15 March 1789

. . . In the arguments in favor of a declaration of rights, you omit one which has great weight with me, the legal check which it puts into the hands of the judiciary. This is a body, which if rendered independent, and kept strictly to their own department merits great confidence for their learning and integrity. . . .

. . . Experience proves the inefficacy of a bill of rights. True. But tho it is not absolutely efficacious under all circumstances, it is of great potency always, and rarely inefficacious. A brace the more will often keep up the building which would have fallen with that brace the less. There is a remarkable difference between the characters of the inconven-

iences which attend a Declaration of rights, and those which attend the want of it. The inconveniences of the Declaration are that it may cramp government in its useful exertions. But the evil of this is short-lived, moderate and reparable. The inconveniences of the want of a Declaration are permanent, afflicting and irreparable: they are in constant progression from bad to worse. The executive in our government is not the sole, it is scarcely the principal object of my jealousy. The tyranny of the legislatures is the most formidable dread at present, and will be for long years. That of the executive will come in its turn, but it will be at a remote period. . . .

JAMES MADISON, Speech Placing the Proposed Bill of Rights Amendments before the House of Representatives, 8 June 1789

Mr. Madison rose, and reminded the House that this was the day that he had heretofore named for bringing forward amendments to the constitution, as contemplated in the fifth article of the constitution. . . .

The first of these amendments relates to what may be called a bill of rights. . . .

It has been said, that it is unnecessary to load the constitution with this provision, because it was not found effectual in the constitution of the particular States. It is true, there are a few particular States in which some of the most valuable articles have not, at one time or other, been violated; but it does not follow but they may have, to a certain degree, a salutary effect against the abuse of power. If they are incorporated into the constitution, independent tribunals of justice will consider themselves in a peculiar manner the guardians of those rights; they will be an impenetrable bulwark against every assumption of power in the legislative or executive; they will be naturally led to resist every encroachment upon rights expressly stipulated for in the constitution by the declaration of rights. Besides this security, there is a great probability that such a declaration in the federal system would be enforced; because the State Legislatures will jealously and closely watch the operations of this Government, and be able to resist with more effect every assumption of power, than any other power on earth can do; and the greatest opponents to a Federal Government admit the State Legislatures to be sure guardians of the people's liberty. I conclude, from this view of the subject, that it will be proper in itself, and highly politic, for the tranquility of the public mind, and the stability of the Government, that we should offer something, in the form I have proposed, to be incorporated in the system of Government, as a declaration of the rights of the people.

I wish also, in revising the constitution, we may throw into that section, which interdicts the abuse of certain powers in the State Legislatures, some other provisions of equal, if not greater importance than those already made. The words, "No State shall pass any bill of attainder, *ex post facto* law," &c. were wise and proper restrictions in the constitution. I think there is more danger of those powers being abused by the State Governments than by the Government of the United States. The same may be said of other powers which they possess, if not controlled by the general principle, that laws are unconstitutional which infringe the rights of the community. I should therefore wish to extend this interdiction, and add that no State shall violate the equal right of conscience, freedom of the press, or trial by jury in criminal cases; because it is proper that every Government should be disarmed of powers which trench upon those particular rights. I know, in some of the State constitutions, the power of the Government is controlled by such a declaration; but others are not. I cannot see any reason against obtaining even a double security on those points; and nothing can give a more sincere proof of the attachment of those who opposed this constitution to these great and important rights, than to see them join in obtaining the security I have now proposed: because it must be admitted, on all hands, that the State Governments are as liable to attack these invaluable privileges as the General Government is, and therefore ought to be as cautiously guarded against. . . . [An amendment providing for safeguards against the states was proposed, but it failed of adoption.]

II. NATIONALIZATION OF THE BILL OF RIGHTS

Palko v. *Connecticut*
302 U.S. 319, 58 S.Ct. 149, 82 L.Ed. 288 (1937)

By statute Connecticut permitted the state to appeal from rulings and decisions in its criminal courts on points of law. Palko, convicted of murder in the second degree and given a life sentence, was retried after a successful state appeal. His second trial, held in spite of his objection that he was being placed in jeopardy twice, resulted in a conviction for first-degree murder and a death sentence. Majority: Cardozo, Black, Brandeis, Hughes, Roberts, Sutherland, Stone, Van Devanter. Dissenting: Butler.

MR. JUSTICE CARDOZO delivered the opinion of the Court. . . .

The argument for appellant is that whatever is forbidden by the Fifth Amendment is forbidden by the Fourteenth Amendment also. . . .

[The] thesis is even broader. Whatever would be a violation of the original bill of rights (Amendments I to VIII) if done by the federal government is now equally unlawful by force of the Fourteenth Amendment if done by a state. There is no such general rule.

The Fifth Amendment provides, among other things, that no person shall be held to answer for a capital or otherwise infamous crime unless on presentment or indictment of a grand jury. This court has held that, in prosecutions by a state, presentment or indictment by a grand jury may give way to informations at the instance of a public officer. . . . The Fifth Amendment provides also that no person shall be compelled in any criminal case to be a witness against himself. This court has said that, in prosecutions by a state, the exemption will fail if the state elects to end it. . . . The Sixth Amendment calls for a jury trial in criminal cases and the Seventh for a jury trial in civil cases of common law where the value in controversy shall exceed twenty dollars. This court has ruled that consistently with those amendments trial by jury may be modified by a state or abolished altogether. . . .

On the other hand, the due process clause of the Fourteenth Amendment may make it unlawful for a state to abridge by its statutes the freedom of speech which the First Amendment safeguards against encroachment by the Congress . . . or the like freedom of the press . . . or the right of peaceable assembly, without which speech would be unduly trammeled. . . .

The line of division may seem to be wavering and broken if there is a hasty catalogue of the cases on the one side and the other. Reflection and analysis will induce a different view. There emerges the perception of a rationalizing principle which gives to discrete instances a proper order and coherence. The right to trial by jury and the immunity

from prosecution except as the result of an indictment may have value and importance. Even so, they are not of the very essence of a scheme of ordered liberty. To abolish them is not to violate a "principle of justice so rooted in the traditions and conscience of our people as to be ranked as fundamental." . . . Few would be so narrow or provincial as to maintain that a fair and enlightened system of justice would be impossible without them. What is true of jury trials and indictments is true also, as the cases show, of the immunity from compulsory self-incrimination. . . . This too might be lost, and justice still be done. Indeed, today as in the past there are students of our penal system who look upon the immunity as a mischief rather than a benefit, and who would limit its scope, or destroy it altogether. No doubt there would remain the need to give protection against torture, physical or mental. . . . Justice, however, would not perish if the accused were subject to a duty to respond to orderly inquiry. The exclusion of these immunities and privileges from the privileges and immunities protected against the action of the states has not been arbitrary or casual. It has been dictated by a study and appreciation of the meaning, the essential implications, of liberty itself.

We reach a different plane of social and moral values when we pass to the privileges and immunities that have been taken over from the earlier articles of the Federal Bill of Rights and brought within the Fourteenth Amendment by a process of absorption. These in their origin were effective against the federal government alone. If the Fourteenth Amendment has absorbed them, the process of absorption has had its source in the belief that neither liberty nor justice would exist if they were sacrificed. . . . This is true, for illustration, of freedom of thought and speech. Of that freedom one may say that it is the matrix, the indispensable condition, of nearly every other form of freedom. . . .

Our survey of the cases serves, we think, to justify the statement that the dividing line between them, if not unfaltering throughout its course, has been true for the most part to a unifying principle.

On which side of the line the case made out by the appellant has appropriate location must be the next inquiry and the final one. Is that kind of double jeopardy to which the statute has subjected him a hardship so acute and shocking that our policy will not endure it? Does it violate those "fundamental principles of liberty and justice which lie at the base of all our civil and political institutions?" . . . The answer surely must be "no." What the answer would have to be if the state were permitted after a trial free from error to try the accused over again or to bring another case against him, we have no occasion to consider. We deal with the statute before us and no other. The state is not attempting to wear the accused out by a multitude of cases with accumulated trials. It asks no more than this, that the case against him shall go on until there shall be a trial free from the corrosion of substantial legal error. . . .

The judgment is

Affirmed.

Adamson v. *California*
332 U.S. 46, 67 S.Ct. 1672, 91 L.Ed. 1903 (1947)

Adamson appealed from a judgment of the Supreme Court of California affirming his conviction of murder. The basis of his appeal was the alleged invalidity of a California code provision that permitted the prosecution and the court to comment on the failure of a defendant to take the witness stand to explain or deny evidence against him. In his trial Adamson, who had a record of three previous felony convictions, chose not to take the stand, thus causing adverse comments by the district attorney and court. However, if he had chosen to testify the district attorney could then have revealed his record of previous convictions in order to impeach his testimony. It should be noted that the majority of state jurisdictions and the federal courts did not permit comment on a defendant's failure to testify. Majority: Reed, Burton, Frankfurter, Jackson, Vinson. Dissenting: Black, Douglas, Murphy, Rutledge.

MR. JUSTICE REED delivered the opinion of the Court. . . .

. . . A right to a fair trial is a right admittedly protected by the due process clause of the Fourteenth Amendment. Therefore, appellant argues, the due process clause of the Fourteenth Amendment protects his privilege against self-incrimination. The due process clause of the Fourteenth Amendment, however, does not draw all the rights of the federal Bill of Rights under its protection. That contention was made and rejected in *Palko* v. *Connecticut*. . . .

Specifically, the due process clause does not protect, by virtue of its mere existence, the accused's freedom from giving testimony by compulsion in state trials that is secured to him against federal interference by the Fifth Amendment. . . . For a state to require testimony from an accused is not necessarily a breach of a state's obligation to give a fair trial. . . .

California, however, is one of a few states that permit limited comment upon a defendant's failure to testify. That permission is narrow. The California law . . . authorizes comment by court and counsel upon the "failure of the defendant to explain or so deny by his testimony any evidence or facts in the case against him." This does not involve any presumption, rebuttable or irrebuttable, either of guilt or of the truth of any fact, that is offered in evidence. It allows inferences to be drawn from proven facts. Because of this clause, the court can direct the jury's attention to whatever evidence there may be that a defendant could deny and the prosecution can argue as to inferences that may be drawn from the accused's failure to testify. . . . It seems quite natural that when a defendant has opportunity to deny or explain facts and determines not to do so, the prosecution should bring out the strength of the evidence by commenting upon defendant's failure to explain or deny it. The prosecution evidence may be of facts that may be beyond the knowledge of the accused. If so, his failure to testify would have little if any weight. But the facts may be such as are necessarily in the knowledge of the accused. In that case a failure to explain would point to an inability to explain. . . .

It is true that if comment were forbidden, an accused in this situation could remain silent and avoid evidence of former crimes and comment upon his failure to testify. We are of the view, however, that a state may control such a situation in accordance with its own ideas of the most efficient administration of criminal justice. The purpose of due process is not to protect an accused against a proper conviction but against an unfair conviction. When evidence is before a jury that threatens conviction, it does not seem unfair to require him to choose between leaving the adverse evidence unexplained and subjecting himself to impeachment through disclosure of former crimes. Indeed, this is a dilemma with which any defendant may be faced. If facts, adverse to the defendant, are proven by the prosecution, there may be no way to explain them favorably to the accused except by a witness who may be vulnerable to impeachment on cross-examination. The defendant must then decide whether or not to use such a witness. The fact that the witness may also be the defendant makes the choice more difficult but a denial of due process does not emerge from the circumstances. . . .

We find no other error that gives ground for our intervention in California's administration of criminal justice.

Affirmed.

MR. JUSTICE BLACK, dissenting. . . .

This decision reasserts a constitutional theory spelled out in *Twining* v. *New Jersey* . . . that this Court is endowed by the Constitution with boundless power under "natural law" periodically to ex-

pand and contract constitutional standards to conform to the Court's conception of what at a particular time constitutes "civilized decency" and "fundamental liberty and justice." Invoking this *Twining* rule, the Court concludes that although comment upon testimony in a federal court would violate the Fifth Amendment, identical comment in a state court does not violate today's fashion in civilized decency and fundamentals and is therefore not prohibited by the Federal Constitution as amended.

The *Twining* case was the first, as it is the only decision of this Court which has squarely held that states were free, notwithstanding the Fifth and Fourteenth Amendments, to extort evidence from one accused of crime. I agree that if *Twining* be reaffirmed, the result reached might appropriately follow. But I would not reaffirm the *Twining* decision. I think that decision and the "natural law" theory of the Constitution upon which it relies degrade the constitutional safeguards of the Bill of Rights and simultaneously appropriate for this Court a broad power which we are not authorized by the Constitution to exercise. . . .

My study of the historical events that culminated in the Fourteenth Amendment, and the expressions of those who sponsored and favored, as well as those who opposed its submission and passage, persuades me that one of the chief objects that the provisions of the Amendment's first section, separately, and as a whole, were intended to accomplish was to make the Bill of Rights applicable to the states. With full knowledge of the import of the *Barron* decision, the framers and backers of the Fourteenth Amendment proclaimed its purpose to be to overturn the constitutional rule that case had announced. This historical purpose has never received full consideration or exposition in any opinion of this Court interpreting the Amendment. . . .

For this reason I am attaching to this dissent an appendix which contains a resumé, by no means complete, of the Amendment's history. In my judgment that history conclusively demonstrates that the language of the first section of the Fourteenth Amendment taken as a whole, was thought by those responsible for its submission to the people, and by those who opposed its submission, sufficiently explicit to guarantee that thereafter no state could deprive its citizens of the privileges and protections of the Bill of Rights. . . .

I cannot consider the Bill of Rights to be an

outworn 18th-century "straight jacket" as the Twining opinion did. Its provisions may be thought outdated abstractions by some. And it is true that they were designed to meet ancient evils. But they are the same kind of human evils that have emerged from century to century wherever excessive power is sought by the few at the expense of the many. In my judgment the people of no nation can lose their liberty so long as a Bill of Rights like ours survives and its basic purposes are conscientiously interpreted, enforced and respected so as to afford continuous protection against old, as well as new, devices and practices which might thwart those purposes. I fear to see the consequences of the Court's practice of substituting its own concepts of decency and fundamental justice for the language of the Bill of Rights as its point of departure in interpreting and enforcing that Bill of Rights. If the choice must be between the selective process of the Palko decision applying some of the Bill of Rights to the States, or the Twining rule applying none of them, I would choose the Palko selective process. But rather than accept either of these choices, I would follow what I believe was the original purpose of the Fourteenth Amendment—to extend to all the people of the nation the complete protection of the Bill of Rights. To hold that this Court can determine what, if any, provisions of the Bill of Rights will be enforced, and if so to what degree, is to frustrate the great design of a written Constitution. . . .

MR. JUSTICE MURPHY, with whom MR. JUSTICE RUTLEDGE concurs, dissenting.

While in substantial agreement with the views of MR. JUSTICE BLACK, I have one reservation and one addition.

I agree that the specific guarantees of the Bill of Rights should be carried over intact into the first section of the Fourteenth Amendment. But I am not prepared to say that the latter is entirely and necessarily limited by the Bill of Rights. Occasions may arise where a proceeding falls so far short of conforming to fundamental standards of procedure as to warrant constitutional condemnation in terms of a lack of due process despite the absence of a specific provision in the Bill of Rights. . . .

Duncan v. Louisiana
391 U.S. 145, 88 S.Ct. 1444, 20 L.Ed. 2d 491 (1968)

Duncan was convicted of simple battery, a misdemeanor punishable under Louisiana law by two years' imprisonment and a $300 fine. His request for trial by jury was denied because the state constitution restricted trial by jury to capital offenses and those punishable by hard labor. The Louisiana Supreme Court denied his claim that his right to jury trial under the Sixth and Fourteenth Amendments had been violated. Majority: White, Black, Brennan, Douglas, Fortas, Marshall, Warren. Dissenting: Harlan, Stewart.

MR. JUSTICE WHITE delivered the opinion of the Court. . . .

The Fourteenth Amendment denies the States the power to "deprive any person of life, liberty, or property, without due process of law." In resolving conflicting claims concerning the meaning of this spacious language, the Court has looked increasingly to the Bill of Rights for guidance; many of the rights guaranteed by the first eight Amendments to the Constitution have been held to be protected against state action by the Due Process Clause of the Fourteenth Amendment. That clause now protects the right to compensation for property taken by the State;[1] the rights of speech, press, and religion covered by the First Amendment;[2] the Fourth Amendment rights to be free from unreasonable searches and seizures and to have

[1] *Chicago, B. & Q. R. Co.* v. *Chicago* (1897).
[2] See, e.g., *Fiske* v. *Kansas* (1927).

excluded from criminal trials any evidence illegally seized;[3] the right guaranteed by the Fifth Amendment to be free of compelled self-incrimination;[4] and the Sixth Amendment rights to counsel,[5] to a speedy[6] and public[7] trial, to confrontation of opposing witnesses,[8] and a compulsory process for obtaining witnesses.[9]

The test for determining whether a right extended by the Fifth and Sixth Amendments with respect to federal criminal proceedings is also protected against state action by the Fourteenth Amendment has been phrased in a variety of ways in the opinions of this Court. The question has been asked whether a right is among those " 'fundamental principles of liberty and justice which lie at the base of all our civil and political institutions,' " whether it is "basic in our system of jurisprudence," and whether it is "a fundamental right, essential to a fair trial." The claim before us is that the right to trial by jury guaranteed by the Sixth Amendment meets these tests. The position of Louisiana, on the other hand, is that the Constitution imposes upon the States no duty to give a jury trial in any criminal case, regardless of the seriousness of the crime or the size of the punishment which may be imposed. Because we believe that trial by jury in criminal cases is fundamental to the American scheme of justice, we hold that the Fourteenth Amendment guarantees a right of jury trial in all criminal cases which— were they to be tried in a federal court—would come within the Sixth Amendment's guarantee.[10]

[3] See *Mapp* v. *Ohio* (1961).

[4] *Malloy* v. *Hogan* (1964).

[5] *Gideon* v. *Wainwright* (1963).

[6] *Klopfer* v. *North Carolina* (1967).

[7] *In re Oliver* (1948).

[8] *Pointer* v. *Texas* (1965).

[9] *Washington* v. *Texas* (1967).

[10] In one sense recent cases applying provisions of the first eight Amendments to the States represent a new approach to the "incorporation" debate. Earlier the Court can be seen as having asked, when inquiring into whether some particular procedural safeguard was required of a state, if a civilized system could be imagined that would not accord the particular protection. . . . The recent cases, on the other hand, have proceeded upon the valid assumption that state criminal processes are not imaginary and theoretical schemes but actual systems bearing virtually every characteristic of the common-law system that has been developing contemporaneously in England and in this country. The question thus is whether given this kind of system a particular procedure is fundamental—whether, that is, a pro-

Since we consider the appeal before us to be such a case, we hold that the Constitution was violated when appellant's demand for jury trial was refused. MR. JUSTICE BLACK, with whom MR. JUSTICE DOUGLAS joins, concurring.

The Court today holds that the right to trial by jury guaranteed defendants in criminal cases in federal courts by Art. III of the United States Constitution and by the Sixth Amendment is also guaranteed by the Fourteenth Amendment to defendants tried in state courts. With this holding I agree for reasons given by the Court. I also agree because of reasons given in my dissent in *Adamson* v. *California*. . . . And I am very happy to support this selective process through which our Court has since the Adamson case held most of the specific Bill of Rights' protections applicable to the States to the same extent they are applicable to the Federal Government. . . .

---

cedure is necessary to an Anglo-American regime of ordered liberty. It is this sort of inquiry that can justify the conclusions that state courts must exclude evidence seized in violation of the Fourth Amendment; that state prosecutors may not comment on a defendant's failure to testify; and that criminal punishment may not be imposed for the status of narcotics addiction. Of immediate relevance for this case are the Court's holdings that the States must comply with certain provisions of the Sixth Amendment, specifically that the States may not refuse a speedy trial, confrontation of witnesses, and the assistance, at state expense if necessary, of counsel. . . . Of each of these determinations that a constitutional provision originally written to bind the Federal Government should bind the States as well it might be said that the limitation in question is not necessarily fundamental to fairness in every criminal system that might be imagined but is fundamental in the context of the criminal processes maintained by the American States.

When the inquiry is approached in this way the question whether the States can impose criminal punishment without granting a jury trial appears quite different from the way it appeared in the older cases opining that States might abolish jury trial. A criminal process which was fair and equitable but used no juries is easy to imagine. It would make use of alternative guarantees and protections which would serve the purposes that the jury serves in the English and American systems. Yet no American State has undertaken to construct such a system. Instead, every American State, including Louisiana, uses the jury extensively, and imposes very serious punishments only after a trial at which the defendant has a right to a jury's verdict. In every state, including Louisiana, the structure and style of the criminal process—the supporting framework and the subsidiary procedures—are of the sort that naturally complement jury trial, and have developed in connection with and in reliance upon jury trial.

What I wrote there in 1947 was the product of years of study and research. My appraisal of the legislative history followed 10 years of legislative experience as a Senator of the United States, not a bad way, I suspect, to learn the value of what is said in legislative debates, committee discussions, committee reports, and various other steps taken in the course of passage of bills, resolutions, and proposed constitutional amendments. My Brother Harlan's objections to my Adamson dissent history, like that of most of the objectors, relies most heavily on a criticism written by Professor Charles Fairman. . . . I have read and studied this article extensively, including the historical references, but am compelled to add that in my view it has completely failed to refute the inferences and arguments that I suggested in my Adamson dissent. Professor Fairman's "history" relied very heavily on what was *not* said in the state legislatures that passed on the Fourteenth Amendment. Instead of relying on this kind of negative pregnant, my legislative experience has convinced me that it is far wiser to rely on what *was* said, and most importantly, said by the men who actually sponsored the Amendment in the Congress. . . .

While I do not wish at this time to discuss at length my disagreement with Brother Harlan's forthright and frank restatement of the now discredited Twining doctrine, I do want to point out what appears to me to be the basic difference between us. His view, as was indeed the view of Twining, is that "due process is an evolving concept" and therefore that it entails a "gradual process of judicial inclusion and exclusion" to ascertain those "immutable principles of free government which no member of the Union may disregard." Thus the Due Process Clause is treated as prescribing no specific and clearly ascertainable constitutional command that judges must obey in interpreting the Constitution, but rather as leaving judges free to decide at any particular time whether a particular rule or judicial formulation embodies an "immutable principle of free government" or "is implicit in the concept of ordered liberty," or whether certain conduct "shocks the judge's conscience" or runs counter to some other similar, undefined and undefinable standard. Thus due process, according to my Brother Harlan, is to be a word with no permanent meaning, but one which is found to shift from time to time in accordance with judges'

predilections and understandings of what is best for the country. If due process means this, the Fourteenth Amendment, in my opinion, might as well have been written that "no person shall be deprived of life, liberty or property except by laws that the judges of the United States Supreme Court shall find to be consistent with the immutable principles of free government." It is impossible for me to believe that such unconfined power is given to judges in our Constitution that is a written one in order to limit governmental power. . . .

MR. JUSTICE HARLAN, whom MR. JUSTICE STEWART joins, dissenting. . . .

The Court's approach to this case is an uneasy and illogical compromise among the views of various Justices on how the Due Process Clause should be interpreted. The Court does not say that those who framed the Fourteenth Amendment intended to make the Sixth Amendment applicable to the States. And the Court concedes that it finds nothing unfair about the procedure by which the present appellant was tried. Nevertheless, the Court reverses his conviction: it holds, for some reason not apparent to me, that the Due Process Clause incorporates the particular clause of the Sixth Amendment that requires trial by jury in federal criminal cases—including, as I read its opinion, the sometimes trivial accompanying baggage of judicial interpretation in federal contexts. I have raised my voice many times before against the Court's continuing undiscriminating insistence upon fastening on the States federal notions of criminal justice, and I must do so again in this instance. With all respect, the Court's approach and its reading of history are altogether topsy-turvy. . . .

A few members of the Court have taken the position that the intention of those who drafted the first section of the Fourteenth Amendment was simply, and exclusively, to make the provisions of the first eight amendments applicable to state action. This view has never been accepted by this Court. In my view . . . the first section of the Fourteenth Amendment was meant neither to incorporate, nor to be limited to, the specific guarantees of the first eight amendments. The overwhelming historical evidence marshalled by Professor Fairman demonstrates, to me conclusively, that the Congressmen and state legislators who wrote, debated, and ratified the Fourteenth Amendment did not think they were "incorporating" the Bill of Rights and the very breadth and generality of the Amendment's provisions suggest that its authors did not suppose that the Nation would always be limited to mid-19th century conceptions of "liberty" and "due process of law" but that the increasing experience and evolving conscience of the American people would add new "intermediate premises." In short, neither history, nor sense, supports using the Fourteenth Amendment to put the States in a constitutional strait-jacket with respect to their own development in the administration of criminal or civil law. . . .

Apart from the approach taken by the absolute incorporationists, I can see only one method of analysis that has any internal logic. That is to start with the words "liberty" and "due process of law" and attempt to define them in a way that accords with American traditions and our system of government. This approach, involving a much more discriminating process of adjudication than does "incorporation," is, albeit difficult, the one that was followed throughout the nineteenth and most of the present century. It entails a "gradual process of judicial inclusion and exclusion," seeking, with due recognition of constitutional tolerance for state experimentation and disparity, to ascertain those "immutable principles of free government which no member of the Union may disregard." . . .

Through this gradual process, this Court sought to define "liberty" by isolating freedoms that Americans of the past and of the present considered more important than any suggested countervailing public objective. The Court also, by interpretation of the phrase "due process of law," enforced the Constitution's guarantee that no State may imprison an individual except by fair and impartial procedures.

The relationship of the Bill of Rights to this "gradual process" seems to me to be twofold. In the first place it has long been clear that the Due Process Clause imposes some restrictions on state action that parallel Bill of Rights restrictions on federal action. Second, and more important than this accidental overlap, is the fact that the Bill of Rights is evidence, at various points, of the content Americans find in the term "liberty" and of American standards of fundamental fairness. . . .

The argument that jury trial is not a requisite of due process is quite simple. The central proposition of *Palko* . . . a proposition to which I would adhere, is that "due process of law" requires only that criminal trials be fundamentally fair. As stated above, apart from the theory that it was historically intended as a mere shorthand for the Bill of Rights, I do not see what else "due process of law" can intelligibly be thought to mean. If due process of law requires only fundamental fairness, then the inquiry in each case must be whether a state trial process was a fair one. The Court has held, properly I think, that in an adversary process it is a requisite of fairness, for which there is no adequate substitute, that a criminal defendant be afforded a right to counsel and to cross-examine opposing witnesses. But it simply has not been demonstrated, nor, I think, can it be demonstrated, that trial by jury is the only fair means of resolving issues of fact. . . .

III. THE EXCLUSIONARY RULE

Mapp v. *Ohio*
367 U.S. 643, 81 S.Ct. 1684, 6 L.Ed. 2d 1081 (1961)

Cleveland police officers, acting on information that a bombing-case suspect and betting equipment might be found in Mrs. Mapp's house, forced their way in after being refused admission and, without a search warrant, subjected the house and its contents to thorough search. In a basement trunk materials were found that provided the basis for her conviction of possessing obscene materials. The Ohio Supreme Court upheld the conviction on the grounds that state law did not require the exclusion of illegally obtained evidence and that *Wolf* v. *Colorado* (1949) did not prevent Ohio from adopting such a rule. Majority: Clark, Black, Brennan, Douglas, Stewart, Warren. Dissenting: Harlan, Frankfurter, Whittaker.

MR. JUSTICE CLARK delivered the opinion of the Court. . . .

Today we once again examine *Wolf's* constitutional documentation of the right to privacy free from unreasonable state intrusion, and, after its dozen years on our books, are led by it to close the only courtroom door remaining open to evidence secured by official lawlessness in flagrant abuse of that basic right, reserved to all persons as a specific guarantee against that very same unlawful conduct. We hold that all evidence obtained by searches and seizures in violation of the Constitution is, by that same authority, inadmissible in a state court.

Since the Fourth Amendment's right of privacy has been declared enforceable against the States through the Due Process Clause of the Fourteenth, it is enforceable against them by the same sanction of exclusion as is used against the Federal Government. . . . [T]he admission of the new constitutional right by *Wolf* could not consistently tolerate denial of its most important constitutional privilege, namely, the exclusion of the evidence which an accused had been forced to give by reason of the unlawful seizure. To hold otherwise is to grant the right but in reality to withhold its privilege and enjoyment. . . .

Indeed, we are aware of no restraint, similar to that rejected today, conditioning the enforcement of any other basic constitutional right. The right to privacy, no less important than any other right carefully and particularly reserved to the people, would stand in marked contrast to all other rights declared as "basic to a free society." This Court has not hesitated to enforce as strictly against the State as it does against the Federal Government the rights of free speech and of a free press, the rights to notice and to a fair, public trial, including, as it does, the right not to be convicted by use of a coerced confession, however logically relevant it be, and without regard to its reliability. . . . And nothing could be more certain than that when a coerced confession is involved, "the relevant rules

of evidence" are overridden without regard to "the incidence of such conduct by the police," slight or frequent. Why should not the same rule apply to what is tantamount to coerced testimony by way of unconstitutional seizure of goods, papers, effects, documents, etc.? . . .

The ignoble shortcut to conviction left open to the State tends to destroy the entire system of constitutional restraints on which the liberties of the people rest. Having once recognized that the right to privacy embodied in the Fourth Amendment is enforceable against the States and that the right to be secure against rude invasions of privacy by state officers is, therefore, constitutional in origin, we can no longer permit that right to remain an empty promise. Because it is enforceable in the same manner and to like effect as other basic rights secured by the Due Process Clause, we can no longer permit it to be revocable at the whim of any police officer who, in the name of law enforcement itself, chooses to suspend its enjoyment. Our decision, founded on reason and truth, gives to the individual no more than that which the Constitution guarantees him, to the police officer no less than that to which honest law enforcement is entitled, and, to the courts, that judicial integrity so necessary in the true administration of justice. . . .

Reversed and remanded.

MR. JUSTICE BLACK, concurring. . . .

I am still not persuaded that the Fourth Amendment, standing alone, would be enough to bar the introduction into evidence against an accused of papers and effects seized from him in violation of its commands. For the Fourth Amendment does not itself contain any provisions expressly precluding the use of such evidence, and I am extremely doubtful that such a provision could properly be inferred from nothing more than the basic command against unreasonable searches and seizures. Reflection on the problem, however, in the light of cases coming before the Court since *Wolf*, has led me to conclude that when the Fourth Amendment's ban against unreasonable searches and seizures is considered together with the Fifth Amendment's ban against compelled self-incrimination, a constitutional basis emerges which not only justifies but actually requires the exclusionary rule. . . .

MR. JUSTICE HARLAN, whom MR. JUSTICE FRANKFURTER and MR. JUSTICE WHITTAKER join, dissenting. . . .

At the heart of the majority's opinion in this case is the following syllogism: (1) the rule excluding in federal criminal trials evidence which is the product of an illegal search and seizure is a "part and parcel" of the Fourth Amendment; (2) *Wolf* held that the "privacy" assured against federal action by the Fourth Amendment is also protected against state action by the Fourteenth Amendment; and (3) it is therefore "logically and constitutionally necessary" that the Weeks exclusionary rule should also be enforced against the States.

This reasoning ultimately rests on the unsound premise that because *Wolf* carried into the States, as part of "the concept of ordered liberty" embodied in the Fourteenth Amendment . . . it must follow that whatever configurations of the Fourth Amendment have been developed in the particularizing federal precedents are likewise to be deemed a part of "ordered liberty," and as such are enforceable against the States. For me, this does not follow at all.

It cannot be too much emphasized that what was recognized in *Wolf* was not that the Fourth Amendment *as such* is enforceable against the States as a facet of due process, a view of the Fourteenth Amendment which, as *Wolf* itself pointed out . . . has long since been discredited, but the principle of privacy "which is at the core of the Fourth Amendment." . . .

United States v. Leon
468 U.S. 897, 104 S.Ct. 3405, 82 L.Ed. 2d 677 (1984)

With information from a confidential informant, police officers in Burbank, California, undertook surveillance of Alberto Leon and others for suspected drug-trafficking activities. Based on an affidavit summarizing police observations, Officer Rombach prepared a warrant application to search three residences and the automobiles of the individuals who lived there. Several deputy district attorneys reviewed Rombach's application, and a state judge issued the warrant. The searches that followed turned up large quantities of illegal drugs and other evidence. Leon and his cohorts were indicted for violating federal drug laws, but the district court suppressed some of the evidence seized in the searches because the affidavit contained insufficient information to establish probable cause to search all of the residences. The Court of Appeals for the Ninth Circuit affirmed. The government's petition for certiorari did not claim that probable cause was present but raised only the question of whether a good-faith exception to the exclusionary rule should be recognized under the Fourth Amendment. Majority: White, Blackmun, Burger, O'Connor, Powell, Rehnquist. Dissenting: Brennan, Marshall, Stevens.

JUSTICE WHITE delivered the opinion of the Court.

This case presents the question whether the Fourth Amendment exclusionary rule should be modified so as not to bar the use in the prosecution's case-in-chief of evidence obtained by officers acting in reasonable reliance on a search warrant issued by a detached and neutral magistrate but ultimately found to be unsupported by probable cause. To resolve this question, we must consider once again the tension between the sometimes competing goals of, on the one hand, deterring official misconduct and removing inducements to unreasonable invasions of privacy and, on the other, establishing procedures under which criminal defendants are "acquitted or convicted on the basis of all the evidence which exposes the truth." . . .

The Fourth Amendment contains no provision expressly precluding the use of evidence obtained in violation of its commands, and an examination of its origin and purposes makes clear that the use of fruits of a past unlawful search or seizure "work[s] no new Fourth Amendment wrong." . . . The wrong condemned by the Amendment is "fully accomplished" by the unlawful search or seizure itself . . . and the exclusionary rule is neither intended nor able to "cure the invasion of the defendant's rights which he has already suffered." . . . The rule thus operates as "a judicially created remedy designed to safeguard Fourth Amendment rights generally through its deterrent effect, rather than a personal constitutional right of the person aggrieved." . . .

Whether the exclusionary sanction is appropriately imposed in a particular case, our decisions make clear, is "an issue separate from the question whether the Fourth Amendment rights of the party seeking to invoke the rule were violated by police conduct." . . . Only the former question is currently before us, and it must be resolved by weighing the costs and benefits of preventing the use in the prosecution's case-in-chief of inherently trustworthy tangible evidence obtained in reliance on a search warrant issued by a detached and neutral magistrate that ultimately is found to be defective.

The substantial social costs exacted by the exclusionary rule for the vindication of Fourth Amendment rights have long been a source of concern. . . .*

Particularly when law enforcement officers have acted in objective good faith or their transgressions have been minor, the magnitude of the benefit conferred on such guilty defendants offends basic concepts of the criminal justice system. . . .

To the extent that proponents of exclusion rely on its behavioral effects on judges and magistrates in these areas, their reliance is misplaced. First, the exclusionary rule is designed to deter police misconduct rather than to punish the errors of judges and magistrates. Second, there exists no evidence suggesting that judges and magistrates are inclined to ignore or subvert the Fourth Amendment or that lawlessness among these actors requires application of the extreme sanction of exclusion.

Third, and most important, we discern no basis, and are offered none, for believing that exclusion of evidence seized pursuant to a warrant will have a significant deterrent effect on the issuing judge or magistrate. Many of the factors that indicate that the exclusionary rule cannot provide an effective "special" or "general" deterrent for individual offending law enforcement officers apply as well to judges or magistrates. And, to the extent that the rule is thought to operate as a "systemic" deterrent on a wider audience, it clearly can have no such effect on individuals empowered to issue search warrants. Judges and magistrates are not adjuncts to the law enforcement team. . . . The threat of

---

* Researchers have only recently begun to study extensively the effects of the exclusionary rule on the disposition of felony arrests. One study suggests that the rule results in the nonprosecution or nonconviction of between 0.6% and 2.35% of individuals arrested for felonies. Davies, A Hard Look at What We Know (and Still Need to Learn) About the "Costs" of the Exclusionary Rule: The NIJ Study and Other Studies of "Lost" Arrests, 1983 A. B. F. Res. J. 611, 621. The estimates are

higher for particular crimes the prosecution of which depends heavily on physical evidence. Thus, the cumulative loss due to nonprosecution or nonconviction of individuals arrested on felony drug charges is probably in the range of 2.8% to 7.1%. Id., at 680. Davies' analysis of California data suggests that screening by police and prosecutors results in the release because of illegal searches or seizures of as many as 1.4% of all felony arrestees, id., at 650, that 0.9% of felony arrestees are released because of illegal searches or seizures at the preliminary hearing or after trial, id., at 653, and that roughly 0.5% of all felony arrestees benefit from reversals on appeal because of illegal searches. Id., at 654. Many of these researchers have concluded that the impact of the exclusionary rule is insubstantial, but the small percentages with which they deal mask a large absolute number of felons who are released because the cases against them were based in part on illegal searches or seizures. "[A]ny rule of evidence that denies the jury access to clearly probative and reliable evidence must bear a heavy burden of justification, and must be carefully limited to the circumstances in which it will pay its way by deterring official lawlessness." . . . Because we find that the rule can have no substantial deterrent effect in the sorts of situations under consideration in this case . . . we conclude that it cannot pay its way in those situations.

exclusion thus cannot be expected significantly to deter them. Imposition of the exclusionary sanction is not necessary meaningfully to inform judicial officers of their errors, and we cannot conclude that admitting evidence obtained pursuant to a warrant while at the same time declaring that the warrant was somehow defective will in any way reduce judicial officers' professional incentives to comply with the Fourth Amendment, encourage them to repeat their mistakes, or lead to the granting of all colorable warrant requests.

If exclusion of evidence obtained pursuant to a subsequently invalidated warrant is to have any deterrent effect, therefore, it must alter the behavior of individual law enforcement officers or the policies of their departments. . . .

. . . [E]ven assuming that the rule effectively deters some police misconduct and provides incentives for the law enforcement profession as a whole to conduct itself in accordance with the Fourth Amendment, it cannot be expected, and should not be applied, to deter objectively reasonable law enforcement activity. . . .

This is particularly true, we believe, when an officer acting with objective good faith has obtained a search warrant from a judge or magistrate and acted within its scope. In most such cases, there is no police illegality and thus nothing to deter. It is the magistrate's responsibility to determine whether the officer's allegations establish probable cause and, if so, to issue a warrant comporting in form with the requirements of the Fourth Amendment. In the ordinary case, an officer cannot be expected to question the magistrate's probable-cause determination or his judgment that the form of the warrant is technically sufficient. . . . Penalizing the officer for the magistrate's error, rather than his own, cannot logically contribute to the deterrence of Fourth Amendment violations.

We conclude that the marginal or nonexistent benefits produced by suppressing evidence obtained in objectively reasonable reliance on a subsequently invalidated search warrant cannot justify the substantial costs of exclusion. We do not suggest, however, that exclusion is always inappropriate in cases where an officer has obtained a warrant and abided by its terms. . . .

Suppression therefore remains an appropriate remedy if the magistrate or judge in issuing a warrant was misled by information in an affidavit that the affiant knew was false or would have known was false except for his reckless disregard of the truth. . . .

When the principles we have enunciated today are applied to the facts of this case, it is apparent that the judgment of the Court of Appeals cannot stand. . . .

Accordingly, the judgment of the Court of Appeals is

Reversed.

JUSTICE BRENNAN, with whom JUSTICE MARSHALL joins, dissenting. . . .

The majority ignores the fundamental constitutional importance of what is at stake here. While the machinery of law enforcement and indeed the nature of crime itself have changed dramatically since the Fourth Amendment became part of the Nation's fundamental law in 1791, what the Framers understood then remains true today—that the task of combatting crime and convicting the guilty will in every era seem of such critical and pressing concern that we may be lured by the temptations of expediency into forsaking our commitment to protecting individual liberty and privacy. It was for that very reason that the Framers of the Bill of Rights insisted that law enforcement efforts be permanently and unambiguously restricted in order to preserve personal freedoms. In the constitutional scheme they ordained, the sometimes unpopular task of ensuring that the government's enforcement efforts remain within the strict boundaries fixed by the Fourth Amendment was entrusted to the courts. . . .

At the outset, the Court suggests that society has been asked to pay a high price—in terms either of setting guilty persons free or of impeding the proper functioning of trials—as a result of excluding relevant physical evidence in cases where the police, in conducting searches and seizing evidence, have made only an "objectively reasonable" mistake concerning the constitutionality of their actions. . . . But what evidence is there to support such a claim?

Significantly, the Court points to none, and, indeed, as the Court acknowledges, . . . recent studies have demonstrated that the "costs" of the exclusionary rule—calculated in terms of dropped prosecutions and lost convictions—are quite low. Contrary to the claims of the rule's critics that exclusion leads to "the release of countless guilty criminals" . . . these studies have demonstrated that federal and state prosecutors very rarely drop cases because of potential search and seizure problems. For example, a 1979 study prepared at the request of Congress by the General Accounting Office reported that only 0.4% of all cases actually declined for prosecution by federal prosecutors were declined primarily because of illegal search problems. . . . If the GAO data are restated as a percentage of *all* arrests, the study shows that only 0.2% of all felony arrests are declined for prosecution because of potential exclusionary rule problems. . . .* Of course, these data describe only the costs attributable to the exclusion of evidence in all cases; the costs due to the exclusion of evidence in the narrower category of cases where police have made objectively reasonable mistakes must necessarily be even smaller. The Court, however, ignores this distinction and mistakenly weighs the aggregated costs of exclusion in *all* cases, irrespective of the circumstances that led to exclusion . . . against the

* In a series of recent studies, researchers have attempted to quantify the actual costs of the rule. A recent National Institute of Justice study based on data for the four year period 1976–1979 gathered by the California Bureau of Criminal Statistics showed that 4.8% of all cases that were declined for prosecution by California prosecutors were rejected because of illegally seized evidence. National Institute of Justice, Criminal Justice Research Report—The Effects of the Exclusionary Rule: A Study in California 1 (1982). However, if these data are calculated as a percentage of all arrests that were declined for prosecution, they show that only 0.8% of all arrests were rejected for prosecution because of illegally seized evidence. . . .

In another measure of the rule's impact—the number of prosecutions that are dismissed or result in acquittals in cases where evidence has been excluded—the available data again show that the Court's past assessment of the rule's costs has generally been exaggerated. For example, a study based on data from 9 mid-sized counties in Illinois, Michigan and Pennsylvania reveals that motions to suppress physical evidence were filed in approximately 5% of the 7,500 cases studied, but that such motions were successful in only 0.7% of all these cases. Nardulli, The Societal Cost of the Exclusionary Rule: An Empirical Assessment, 1983 Am. Bar Found. Res. J. 585, 596. The study also shows that only 0.6% of all cases resulted in acquittals because evidence had been excluded. . . . In the GAO study, suppression motions were filed in 10.5% of all federal criminal cases surveyed, but of the motions filed, approximately 80–90% were denied. . . . Evidence was actually excluded in only 1.3% of the cases studied, and only 0.7% of all cases resulted in acquittals or dismissals after evidence was excluded. . . . And in another study based on data from cases during 1978 and 1979 in San Diego and Jacksonville, it was shown that only 1% of all cases resulting in nonconviction were caused by illegal searches. Feeney, Dill & Weir, *Arrests Without Conviction: How Often They Occur and Why* (1983). . . .

potential benefits associated with only those cases in which evidence is excluded because police reasonably but mistakenly believe that their conduct does not violate the Fourth Amendment. . . .

When such faulty scales are used, it is little wonder that the balance tips in favor of restricting the application of the rule.

What then supports the Court's insistence that this evidence be admitted? Apparently, the Court's only answer is that even though the costs of exclusion are not very substantial, the potential deterrent effect in these circumstances is so marginal that exclusion cannot be justified. The key to the Court's conclusion in this respect is its belief that the prospective deterrent effect of the exclusionary rule operates only in those situations in which police officers, when deciding whether to go forward with some particular search, have reason to know that their planned conduct will violate the requirements of the Fourth Amendment. . . .

The flaw in the Court's argument, however, is that its logic captures only one comparatively minor element of the generally acknowledged deterrent purposes of the exclusionary rule. To be sure, the rule operates to some extent to deter future misconduct by individual officers who have had evidence suppressed in their own cases. But what the Court overlooks is that the deterrence rationale for the rule is not designed to be, nor should it be thought of as, a form of "punishment" of individual police officers for their failures to obey the restraints imposed by the Fourth Amendment. . . . Instead, the chief deterrent function of the rule is its tendency to promote institutional compliance with Fourth Amendment requirements on the part of law enforcement agencies generally. . . .

After today's decision, however, that institutional incentive will be lost. Indeed, the Court's "reasonable mistake" exception to the exclusionary rule will tend to put a premium on police ignorance of the law. Armed with the assurance provided by today's decision that evidence will always be admissible whenever an officer has "reasonably" relied upon a warrant, police departments will be encouraged to train officers that if a warrant has simply been signed, it is reasonable, without more, to rely on it. Since in close cases there will no longer be any incentive to err on the side of constitutional behavior, police would have every reason to adopt a "let's-wait-until-its-decided" approach in situations in which there is a question about a warrant's validity or the basis for its issuance. . . .

Although the Court brushes these concerns aside, a host of grave consequences can be expected to result from its decision to carve this new exception out of the exclusionary rule. A chief consequence of today's decision will be to convey a clear and unambiguous message to magistrates that their decisions to issue warrants are now insulated from subsequent judicial review. Creation of this new exception for good faith reliance upon a warrant implicitly tells magistrates that they need not take much care in reviewing warrant applications, since their mistakes will from now on have virtually no consequence: If their decision to issue a warrant was correct, the evidence will be admitted; if their decision was incorrect but the police relied in good faith on the warrant, the evidence will also be admitted. Inevitably, the care and attention devoted to such an inconsequential chore will dwindle. . . .

Moreover, the good faith exception will encourage police to provide only the bare minimum of information in future warrant applications. The police will now know that if they can secure a warrant, so long as the circumstances of its issuance are not "entirely unreasonable" . . . all police conduct pursuant to that warrant will be protected from further judicial review. . . .

JUSTICE STEVENS dissenting. . . .

. . . [U]nder our cases it has never been "reasonable" for the police to rely on the mere fact that a warrant has issued; the police have always known that if they fail to supply the magistrate with sufficient information, the warrant will be held invalid and its fruits excluded.*

The notion that a police officer's reliance on a magistrate's warrant is automatically appropriate is one the Framers of the Fourth Amendment would have vehemently rejected. The precise problem that the Amendment was intended to address was *the unreasonable issuance of warrants.* . . .

* The majority seems to be captivated by a vision of courts invalidating perfectly reasonable police conduct because of "technical" violations of the Fourth Amendment. In my view there is no such thing as a "technical" violation of the Fourth Amendment. No search or seizure can be unconstitutional unless it is "unreasonable." By definition a Fourth Amendment violation cannot be reasonable. . . .

IV. ELECTRONIC SURVEILLANCE AND UNREASONABLE SEARCHES AND SEIZURES

Olmstead v. *United States*
277 U.S. 438, 48 S.Ct. 564, 72 L.Ed. 944 (1928)

Olmstead and others were charged and convicted of conspiring to violate the national Prohibition Act. Evidence proving the conspiracy had been obtained by four federal agents who tapped the telephone lines of several of the defendants, without, however, committing any trespass on their property. A statute of the state of Washington made it a misdemeanor to "intercept, read or in any way interrupt or delay the sending of a message over any telegraph or telephone line. . . ." Majority: Taft, McReynolds, Sanford, Sutherland, Van Devanter. Dissenting: Brandeis, Butler, Holmes, Stone.

MR. CHIEF JUSTICE TAFT delivered the opinion of the court. . . .

The well-known historical importance of the Fourth Amendment, directed against general warrants and writs of assistance, was to prevent the use of governmental force to search a man's house, his person, his papers and his effects, and to prevent their seizure against his will. . . .

The amendment itself shows that the search is to be of material things—the person, the house, his papers, or his effects. The description of the warrant necessary to make the proceeding lawful is that it must specify the place to be searched and the person or *things* to be seized. . . . The language of the amendment cannot be extended and expanded to include telephone wires, reaching to the whole world from the defendant's house or office. The intervening wires are not part of his house or office, any more than are the highways along which they are stretched. . . .

Congress may, of course, protect the secrecy of telephone messages by making them, when intercepted, inadmissible in evidence in federal criminal trials, by direct legislation, and thus depart from the common law of evidence. But the courts may not adopt such a policy by attributing an enlarged and unusual meaning to the Fourth Amendment. The reasonable view is that one who installs in his house a telephone instrument with connecting wires intends to project his voice to those quite outside, and that the wires beyond his house, and messages while passing over them, are not within the protection of the Fourth Amendment. Here those who intercepted the projected voices were not in the house of either party to the conversation.

Neither the cases we have cited nor any of the many federal decisions brought to our attention hold the Fourth Amendment to have been violated as against a defendant, unless there has been an official search and seizure of his person or such a seizure of his papers or his tangible material effects or an actual physical invasion of his house "or curtilage" for the purpose of making a seizure.

We think, therefore, that the wire tapping here disclosed did not amount to a search or seizure within the meaning of the Fourth Amendment. . . .

. . . Our general experience shows that much evidence has always been receivable, although not obtained by conformity to the highest ethics. The history of criminal trials shows numerous cases of prosecutions of oathbound conspiracies for murder, robbery, and other crimes, where officers of the law have disguised themselves and joined the organizations, taken the oaths, and given themselves every appearance of active members engaged in the promotion of crime for the purpose of securing evidence. Evidence secured by such means has always been received.

A standard which would forbid the reception of evidence, if obtained by other than nice ethical conduct by government officials, would make society suffer and give criminals greater immunity than has been known heretofore. In the absence of controlling legislation by Congress, those who realize the difficulties in bringing offenders to justice may well deem it wise that the exclusion of evidence should be confined to cases where rights under the Constitution would be violated by admitting it. . . .

Affirmed.

MR. JUSTICE HOLMES: [dissenting]

My Brother Brandeis has given this case so exhaustive an examination that I desire to add but a few words. . . . It is desirable that criminals should be detected, and to that end that all available evidence should be used. It also is desirable that the Government should not itself foster and pay for other crimes, when they are the means by which the evidence is to be obtained. . . . We have to choose, and for my part I think it a less evil that some criminals should escape than that the Government should play an ignoble part. . . .

MR. JUSTICE BRANDEIS, dissenting. . . .

"We must never forget," said Mr. Chief Justice Marshall in *McCulloch* v. *Maryland,* "that it is *a constitution* we are expounding." Since then, this Court has repeatedly sustained the exercise of power by Congress, under various clauses of that instrument, over objects of which the Fathers could not have dreamed. . . . We have likewise held that general limitations on the powers of Government, like those embodied in the due process clauses of the Fifth and Fourteenth Amendments, do not forbid the United States or the States from meeting modern conditions by regulations which "a century ago, or even half a century ago, probably would have been rejected as arbitrary and oppressive." . . . Clauses guaranteeing to the individual protection against specific abuses of power, must have a similar capacity of adaptation to a changing world. . . .

When the Fourth and Fifth Amendments were adopted, "the form that evil had theretofore taken," had been necessarily simple. Force and violence were then the only means known to man by which a Government could directly effect self-incrimination. It could compel the individual to testify—a compulsion effected, if need be, by torture. It could secure possession of his papers and other articles incident to his private life—a seizure effected, if need be, by breaking and entry. Protection against such invasion of "the sanctities of a man's home and the privacies of life" was provided in the Fourth and Fifth Amendments, by specific language. But "time works changes, brings into existence new conditions and purposes." Subtler and more far-reaching means of invading privacy have become available to the government. Discovery and invention have made it possible for the government, by means far more effective than stretching upon the rack, to obtain disclosure in court of what is whispered in the closet.

Moreover, "in the application of a constitution, our contemplation cannot be only of what has been, but of what may be." The progress of science in furnishing the government with means of espionage is not likely to stop with wire-tapping. Ways may some day be developed by which the government, without removing papers from secret drawers, can reproduce them in court, and by which it will be enabled to expose to a jury the most intimate occurrences of the home. Advances in the psychic and related sciences may bring means of exploring unexpressed beliefs, thoughts and emotions.

. . . Can it be that the Constitution affords no protection against such invasions of individual security?

A sufficient answer is found in *Boyd* v. *United States* . . . a case that will be remembered as long as civil liberty lives in the United States. This court there reviewed the history that lay behind the Fourth and Fifth Amendments. We said with reference to Lord Camden's judgment in *Entick* v. *Carrington:* "The principles laid down in this opinion affect the very essence of constitutional liberty and security. They reach farther than the concrete form of the case there before the court, with its adventitious circumstances; they apply to all invasions on the part of the Government and its employés of the sanctities of a man's home and the privacies of life. It is not the breaking of his doors, and the rummaging of his drawers, that constitutes the essence of the offence: but it is the invasion of his indefeasible right of personal security,

personal liberty and private property, where that right has never been forfeited by his conviction of some public offence—it is the invasion of this sacred right which underlies and constitutes the essence of Lord Camden's judgment. Breaking into a house and opening boxes and drawers are circumstances of aggravation; but any forcible and compulsory extortion of a man's own testimony or of his private papers to be used as evidence of a crime or to forfeit his goods, is within the condemnation of that judgment. In this regard the Fourth and Fifth Amendments run almost into each other." . . .

Decisions of this Court applying the principle of the Boyd case have settled these things. Unjustified search and seizure violates the Fourth Amendment, whatever the character of the paper; whether the paper when taken by the federal officers was in the home, in an office or elsewhere; whether the taking was effected by force, by fraud, or in the orderly process of a court's procedure. From these decisions, it follows necessarily that the Amendment was violated by the officer's reading the paper without a physical seizure, without his even touching it; and that use, in any criminal proceeding, of the contents of the paper so examined—as where they are testified to by a federal officer who thus saw the document or where, through knowledge so obtained, a copy has been procured elsewhere—any such use constitutes a violation of the Fifth Amendment.

The protection guaranteed by the Amendments is much broader in scope. The makers of our Constitution undertook to secure conditions favorable to the pursuit of happiness. They recognized the significance of man's spiritual nature, of his feelings and of his intellect. They knew that only a part of the pain, pleasure and satisfactions of life are to be found in material things. They sought to protect Americans in their beliefs, their thoughts, their emotions and their sensations. They conferred, as against the Government, the right to be let alone—the most comprehensive of rights and the right most valued by civilized men. To protect that right, every unjustifiable intrusion by the Government upon the privacy of the individual, whatever the means employed, must be deemed a violation of the Fourth Amendment. And the use, as evidence in a criminal proceeding, of facts ascertained by such intrusion must be deemed a violation of the Fifth.

Applying to the Fourth and Fifth Amendments the established rule of construction, the defendant's objections to the evidence obtained by a wire-tapping must, in my opinion, be sustained. It is, of course, immaterial where the physical connection with the telephone wires leading into the defendants' premises was made. And it is also immaterial that the intrusion was in aid of law enforcement. Experience should teach us to be most on our guard to protect liberty when the government's purposes are beneficent. Men born to freedom are naturally alert to repel invasion of their liberty by evilminded rulers. The greatest dangers to liberty lurk in insidious encroachment by men of zeal, well-meaning, but without understanding. . . .

[JUSTICE BRANDEIS, in the remainder of his opinion, declared that the violation of the state statute by federal officers was an additional ground for holding the evidence to be inadmissible.]

Katz v. *United States*
389 U.S. 347, 88 S.Ct. 507, 19 L.Ed. 2d 576 (1967)

The petitioner, Katz, was convicted of transmitting wagering information by telephone from Los Angeles to Miami and Boston in violation of a federal statute. At the trial, the government was permitted to introduce evidence gathered from attaching an electronic listening device to the outside of a public telephone booth from which he placed his calls. The Supreme Court granted certiorari to determine if the recordings had been obtained in violation of the Fourth Amendment. Majority: Stewart, Brennan, Douglas, Fortas, Harlan, Warren, White. Dissenting: Black. Not participating: Marshall.

MR. JUSTICE STEWART delivered the opinion of the Court. . . .

The petitioner has strenuously argued that the booth was a "constitutionally protected area." The Government has maintained with equal vigor that it was not. But this effort to decide whether or not a given "area," viewed in the abstract, is "constitutionally protected" deflects attention from the problem presented by this case. For the Fourth Amendment protects people, not places. What a person knowingly exposes to the public, even in his own home or office, is not a subject of Fourth Amendment protection. . . . But what he seeks to preserve as private, even in an area accessible to the public, may be constitutionally protected. . . .

The Government stresses the fact that the telephone booth from which the petitioner made his calls was constructed partly of glass, so that he was as visible after he entered it as he would have been if he had remained outside. But what he sought to exclude when he entered the booth was not the intruding eye—it was the uninvited ear. He did not shed his right to do so simply because he made his calls from a place where he might be seen. No less than an individual in a business office, in a friend's apartment, or in a taxicab, a person in a telephone booth may rely upon the protection of the Fourth Amendment. One who occupies it, shuts the door behind him, and pays the toll that permits him to place a call, is surely entitled to assume that the words he utters into the mouthpiece will not be broadcast to the world. To read the Constitution more narrowly is to ignore the vital role that the public telephone has come to play in private communication.

The Government contends, however, that the activities of its agents in this case should not be tested by Fourth Amendment requirements, for the surveillance technique they employed involved no physical penetration of the telephone booth from which the petitioner placed his calls. It is true that the absence of such penetration was at one time thought to foreclose further Fourth Amendment inquiry. . . . That Amendment was thought to limit only searches and seizures of tangible property. But "[t]he premise that property interests control the right of the Government to search and seize has been discredited." Thus, although a closely divided Court supposed in *Olmstead* that surveillance without any trespass and without the seizure of any material object fell outside the ambit of the Constitution, we have since departed from the narrow view on which that decision rested. . . . Once this much is acknowledged, and once it is recognized that the Fourth Amendment protects people—and not simply "areas"—against unreasonable searches and seizures, it becomes clear that the reach of that Amendment cannot turn upon the presence or absence of a physical intrusion into any given enclosure.

. . . We conclude that the underpinnings of *Olmstead* . . . have been so eroded by our subsequent decisions that the "trespass" doctrine there enunciated can no longer be regarded as controlling. The Government's activities in electronically listening to and recording the petitioner's words violated the privacy upon which he justifiably relied while using the telephone booth and thus constituted a "search and seizure" within the meaning of the Fourth Amendment. The fact that the electronic device employed to achieve that end did not happen to penetrate the wall of the booth can have no constitutional significance.

The question remaining for decision, then, is whether the search and seizure conducted in this case complied with constitutional standards. In that regard, the Government's position is that its agents acted in an entirely defensible manner: They did not begin their electronic surveillance until investigation of the petitioner's activities had established a strong probability that he was using the telephone in question to transmit gambling information to persons in other States, in violation of federal law. Moreover, the surveillance was limited, both in scope and in duration, to the specific purpose of establishing the contents of the petitioner's unlawful telephonic communications. The agents confined their surveillance to the brief periods during which he used the telephone booth, and they took great care to overhear only the conversations of the petitioner himself.

Accepting this account of the Government's actions as accurate, it is clear that this surveillance was so narrowly circumscribed that a duly authorized magistrate, properly notified of the need for such investigation, specifically informed of the basis on which it was to proceed, and clearly apprised of the precise intrusion it would entail, could constitutionally have authorized, with appropriate safeguards, the very limited search and seizure that the Government asserts in fact took place. . . .

The Government . . . argues that surveillance of a telephone booth should be exempted from the usual requirement of advance authorization by a magistrate upon a showing of probable cause. We cannot agree. Omission of such authorization "bypasses the safeguards provided by an objective predetermination of probable cause, and substitutes instead the far less reliable procedure of an after-the-event justification for the . . . search, too likely to be subtly influenced by the familiar shortcomings of hindsight judgment." . . .

And bypassing a neutral predetermination of the *scope* of a search leaves individuals secure from Fourth Amendment violations "only in the discretion of the police." . . .

. . . The government agents here ignored "the procedure of antecedent justification . . . that is central to the Fourth Amendment," a procedure that we hold to be a constitutional precondition of the kind of electronic surveillance involved in this case. Because the surveillance here failed to meet that condition, and because it led to the petitioner's conviction, the judgment must be reversed.

It is so ordered.

MR. JUSTICE DOUGLAS, with whom MR. JUSTICE BRENNAN joins, concurring.

While I join the opinion of the Court, I feel compelled to reply to the separate concurring opinion of my Brother White, which I view as a wholly unwarranted green light for the Executive Branch to resort to electronic eavesdropping without a warrant in cases which the Executive Branch itself labels "national security" matters.

Neither the President nor the Attorney General is a magistrate. In matters where they believe national security may be involved they are not detached, disinterested, and neutral as a court or magistrate must be. Under the separation of powers created by the Constitution, the Executive Branch is not supposed to be neutral and disinterested. Rather it should vigorously investigate and prevent breaches of national security and prosecute those who violate the pertinent federal laws. The President and Attorney General are properly interested parties, cast in the role of adversary, in national security cases. They may even be the intended victims of subversive action. Since spies and saboteurs are as entitled to the protection of the Fourth Amendment as suspected gamblers like petitioner, I cannot agree that where spies and saboteurs are involved adequate protection of Fourth Amendment rights is assured when the President and Attorney General assume both the position of adversary-and-prosecutor and disinterested, neutral magistrate. . . .

MR. JUSTICE HARLAN, concurring. . . .

As the Court's opinion states, "the Fourth Amendment protects people, not places." The question, however, is what protection it affords to those people. Generally, as here, the answer to that question requires reference to a "place." My understanding of the rule that has emerged from prior decisions is that there is a twofold requirement, first that a person have exhibited an actual (subjective) expectation of privacy and second, that the expectation be one that society is prepared to recognize as "reasonable."

MR. JUSTICE WHITE, concurring.

In joining the Court's opinion, I note the Court's acknowledgment that there are circumstances in which it is reasonable to search without a warrant. In this connection . . . the Court points out that today's decision does not reach national security cases. Wiretapping to protect the security of the Nation has been authorized by successive Presidents. The present Administration would apparently save national security cases from restrictions against wiretapping. . . . We should not require the warrant procedure and the magistrate's judgment if the President of the United States or his chief legal officer, the Attorney General, had considered the requirements of national security and authorized electronic surveillance as reasonable.

MR. JUSTICE BLACK, dissenting. . . .

My basic objection is twofold: (1) I do not believe that the words of the Amendment will bear the meaning given them by today's decision, and (2) I do not believe that it is the proper role of this Court to rewrite the Amendment in order "to bring it into harmony with the times" and thus reach a result that many people believe to be desirable. . . .

The first clause protects "persons, houses, papers, and effects, against unreasonable searches and seizures. . . ." These words connote the idea of tangible things with size, form, and weight, things capable of being searched, seized, or both. The second clause of the Amendment still further establishes its Framers' purpose to limit its protection to tangible things by providing that no warrants shall issue but those "particularly describing the place to be searched and the person or things to be seized." A conversation overheard by eavesdropping whether by plain snooping or wiretapping, is not tangible and, under the normally accepted meanings of the words, can neither be searched nor seized. In addition the language of the second clause indicates that the Amendment refers to something not only tangible so it can be seized but to something already in existence so it can be described. Yet the Court's interpretation would have the Amendment apply to overhearing future conversations which by their very nature are nonexistent until they take place. How can one "describe" a future conversation, and if not, how can a magistrate issue a warrant to eavesdrop one in the future? It is argued that information showing what is expected to be said is sufficient to limit the boundaries of what later can be admitted into evidence; but does such general information really meet the specific language of the Amendment which says "particularly describing"? Rather than using language in a completely artificial way, I must conclude that the Fourth Amendment simply does not apply to eavesdropping.

Tapping telephone wires, of course, was an unknown possibility at the time the Fourth Amendment was adopted. . . . "In those days the eavesdropper listened by naked ear under the eaves of houses or their windows, or beyond their walls seeking out private discourse." . . . There can be no doubt that the Framers were aware of this practice, and if they had desired to outlaw or restrict the use of evidence obtained by eavesdropping, I believe that they would have used the appropriate language to do so in the Fourth Amendment. They certainly would not have left such a task to the ingenuity of language-stretching judges. . . .

In interpreting the Bill of Rights, I willingly go

as far as a liberal construction of the language takes me, but I simply cannot in good conscience give a meaning to words which they have never before been thought to have and which they certainly do not have in common ordinary usage. I will not distort the words of the Amendment in order to "keep the Constitution up to date" or "to bring it into harmony with the times." It was never meant for this Court to have such power, which in effect would make us a continuously functioning constitutional convention.

With this decision the Court has completed, I hope, its rewriting of the Fourth Amendment, which started only recently when the Court began referring incessantly to the Fourth Amendment not so much as a law against *unreasonable* searches and seizures as one to protect an individual's privacy. By clever word juggling the Court finds it plausible to argue that language aimed specifically at searches and seizures of things that can be searched and seized may, to protect privacy, be applied to eavesdropped evidence of conversations that can neither be searched nor seized. Few things happen to an individual that do not affect his privacy in one way or another. Thus, by arbitrarily substituting the Court's language, designed to protect privacy, for the Constitution's language, designed to protect against unreasonable searches and seizures, the Court has made the Fourth Amendment its vehicle for holding all laws violative of the Constitution which offend the Court's broadest concept of privacy. . . . .

United States v. United States District Court
407 U.S. 297, 92 S.Ct. 2125, 32 L.Ed. 2d 752 (1972)

(This case is reprinted in Chapter Three, beginning on page 108.)

Terry v. Ohio
392 U.S. 1, 88 S.Ct. 1868, 20 L.Ed. 2d 889 (1968)

This case examined the constitutionality of the "stop and frisk" by police and presented the Warren Court with a Fourth Amendment dilemma. Was the situation Officer McFadden observed sufficient to establish probable cause for arrest? If so, what would such a ruling do to the limits imposed on police behavior by the Constitution? If the Court found McFadden's actions constitutionally unacceptable, could the justices reasonably expect police officers in the future not to do precisely what McFadden had done? The reader should pay particular attention to Chief Justice Warren's recitation of, and emphasis on, the facts. Remember that the decision came down after several years of increasingly violent street crime. In the courts below, the convictions of Terry and his sidekick Chilton for carrying concealed weapons had been upheld. Majority: Warren, Black, Brennan, Fortas, Harlan, Marshall, Stewart, White. Dissenting: Douglas.

MR. CHIEF JUSTICE WARREN delivered the opinion of the Court. . . .

Petitioner Terry was convicted of carrying a concealed weapon and sentenced to the statutorily prescribed term of one to three years in the penitentiary. Following the denial of a pretrial motion to suppress, the prosecution introduced in evidence two revolvers and a number of bullets seized from Terry and a codefendant, Richard Chilton, by Cleveland Police Detective Martin McFadden. At the hearing on the motion to suppress this evidence, Officer McFadden testified that while he was patrolling in plain clothes in downtown Cleveland at approximately 2:30 in the afternoon of October 31, 1963, his attention was attracted by two men, Chilton and Terry, standing on the corner of Huron Road and Euclid Avenue. He had never seen the two men before, and he was unable to say precisely what first drew his eye to them. However, he testified that he had been a policeman for 39 years and a detective for 35 and that he had been assigned to patrol this vicinity of downtown Cleveland for shoplifters and pickpockets for 30 years. . . .

His interest aroused, Officer McFadden took up a post of observation in the entrance to a store 300 to 400 feet away from the two men. . . . He saw one of the men leave the other one and walk southwest on Huron Road, past some stores. The man paused for a moment and looked in a store window, then walked on a short distance, turned around and walked back toward the corner, pausing once again to look in the same store window. He rejoined his companion at the corner, and the two conferred briefly. Then the second man went through the same series of motions, strolling down Huron Road, looking in the same window, walking on a short distance, turning back, peering in the store window again, and returning to confer with the first man at the corner. The two men repeated this ritual alternately between five and six times apiece—in all, roughly a dozen trips. At one point, while the two were standing together on the corner, a third man approached them and engaged them briefly in conversation. This man then left the two others and walked west on Euclid Avenue. Chilton and Terry resumed their measured pacing, peering, and conferring. After this had gone on for 10 to 12 minutes, the two men walked off together, heading west on Euclid Avenue, following the path taken earlier by the third man.

By this time Officer McFadden had become thoroughly suspicious. He testified that after observing their elaborately casual and oft-repeated reconnaissance of the store window on Huron Road, he suspected the two men of "casing a job, a stick-up," and that he considered it his duty as a police officer to investigate further. He added that he feared "they may have a gun." Thus, Officer McFadden followed Chilton and Terry and saw them stop in front of Zucker's store to talk to the same man who had conferred with them earlier on the street corner. Deciding that the situation was ripe for direct action, Officer McFadden approached the three men, identified himself as a police officer and asked for their names. At this point his knowledge was confined to what he had observed. He was not acquainted with any of the three men by name or by sight, and he had received no information concerning them from any other source. When the men "mumbled something" in response to his inquiries, Officer McFadden grabbed petitioner Terry, spun him around so that they were facing the other two, with Terry between McFadden and the others, and patted down the outside of his clothing. In the left breast pocket of Terry's overcoat Officer McFadden felt a pistol. He reached inside the overcoat pocket, but was unable to remove the gun. At this point, keeping Terry between himself and the others, the officer ordered all three men to enter Zucker's store. As they went in, he removed Terry's overcoat completely, removed a .38-caliber revolver from the pocket and ordered all three men to face the wall with their hands raised. Officer McFadden proceeded to pat down the outer clothing of Chilton and the third man, Katz. He discovered another revolver in the outer pocket of Chilton's overcoat, but no weapons were found on Katz. . . .

Our first task is to establish at what point in this encounter the Fourth Amendment becomes relevant. That is, we must decide whether and when Officer McFadden "seized" Terry and whether and when he conducted a "search." . . . It is quite plain that the Fourth Amendment governs "seizures" of the person which do not eventuate in a trip to the station house and prosecution for a crime—"arrests" in traditional terminology. It must be recognized that whenever a police officer accosts an individual and restrains his freedom to walk away, he has "seized" that person. And it is nothing less than sheer torture of the English language to suggest that a careful exploration of the outer surfaces of a person's clothing all over his or her body in an attempt to find weapons is not a "search." . . .

The danger in the logic which proceeds upon distinctions between a "stop" and an "arrest," or "seizure" of the person, and between a "frisk" and a "search" is twofold. It seeks to isolate from constitutional scrutiny the initial stages of the contact between the policeman and the citizen. And by suggesting a rigid all-or-nothing model of justification and regulation under the Amendment, it obscures the utility of limitations upon the scope, as well as the initiation, of police action as a means of constitutional regulation. . . .

. . . We therefore reject the notions that the Fourth Amendment does not come into play at all as a limitation upon police conduct if the officers stop short of something called a "technical arrest" or a "full-blown search." . . .

[W]e cannot blind ourselves to the need for law enforcement officers to protect themselves and other prospective victims of violence in situations where they may lack probable cause for an arrest. When an officer is justified in believing that the individual whose suspicious behavior he is investigating at close range is armed and presently dangerous to the officer or to others, it would appear to be clearly unreasonable to deny the officer the power to take necessary measures to determine whether the person is in fact carrying a weapon and to neutralize the threat of physical harm.

We must still consider, however, the nature and quality of the intrusion on individual rights which must be accepted if police officers are to be conceded the right to search for weapons in situations where probable cause to arrest for crime is lacking. Even a limited search of the outer clothing for weapons constitutes a severe, though brief, intrusion upon cherished personal security, and it must surely be an annoying, frightening, and perhaps humiliating experience. . . .

We conclude that the revolver seized from Terry was properly admitted in evidence against him.

. . . Each case of this sort will, of course, have to be decided on its own facts. We merely hold today that where a police officer observes unusual conduct which leads him reasonably to conclude in light of his experience that criminal activity may be afoot and that the persons with whom he is dealing may be armed and presently dangerous, where in the course of investigating this behavior he identifies himself as a policeman and makes reasonable inquiries, and where nothing in the initial stages of the encounter serves to dispel his reasonable fear for his own or others' safety, he is entitled for the protection of himself and others in the area to conduct a carefully limited search of the outer clothing of such persons in an attempt to discover weapons which might be used to assault him.

Such a search is a reasonable search under the Fourth Amendment, and any weapons seized may properly be introduced in evidence against the person from whom they were taken.

Affirmed.

MR. JUSTICE DOUGLAS, dissenting.

I agree that petitioner was "seized" within the meaning of the Fourth Amendment. I also agree that frisking petitioner and his companions for guns was a "search." But it is a mystery how that "search" and that "seizure" can be constitutional by Fourth Amendment standards, unless there was "probable cause" to believe that (1) a crime had been committed or (2) a crime was in the process of being committed or (3) a crime was about to be committed. . . .

There have been powerful hydraulic pressures throughout our history that bear heavily on the Court to water down constitutional guarantees and give the police the upper hand. That hydraulic pressure has probably never been greater than it is today.

Yet if the individual is no longer to be sovereign, if the police can pick him up whenever they do not like the cut of his jib, if they can "seize" and "search" him in their discretion, we enter a new regime. The decision to enter it should be made only after a full debate by the people of this country.

Chimel v. California
395 U.S. 752, 89 S.Ct. 2034, 23 L.Ed. 2d 685 (1969)

After arresting the defendant in his home for burglary of a coin shop, police officers conducted a search of his entire three-bedroom house, including the attic, the garage, a small workshop, and various drawers. Certain items found through the search were admitted into evidence against him and he was convicted. Both the California Court of Appeal and the California Supreme Court affirmed the conviction, holding that although the officers had no search warrant, the search of the defendant's house had been justified on the ground that it had been incident to a valid arrest. Majority: Stewart, Brennan, Douglas, Fortas, Harlan, Marshall, Warren. Dissenting: White, Black.

MR. JUSTICE STEWART delivered the opinion of the Court.

This case raises basic questions concerning the permissible scope under the Fourth Amendment of a search incident to a lawful arrest. . . .

When an arrest is made, it is reasonable for the arresting officer to search the person arrested in order to remove any weapons that the latter might seek to use in order to resist or effect his escape. Otherwise, the officer's safety might well be endangered, and the arrest itself frustrated. In addition, it is entirely reasonable for the arresting officer to search for and seize any evidence on the arrestee's person in order to prevent its concealment or destruction. And the area into which an arrestee might reach in order to grab a weapon or evidentiary items must, of course, be governed by a like rule. A gun on a table or in a drawer in front of one who is arrested can be as dangerous to the arresting officer as one concealed in the clothing of the person arrested. There is ample justification, therefore, for a search of the arrestee's person and the area "within his immediate control"—construing that phrase to mean the area from within which he might gain possession of a weapon or destructible evidence.

There is no comparable justification, however, for routinely searching through all the desk drawers or other closed or concealed areas in that room itself. Such searches, in the absence of well recognized exceptions, may be made only under the authority of a search warrant. The "adherence to judicial processes" mandated by the Fourth Amendment requires no less. . . .

It is argued in the present case that it is "rea-

sonable" to search a man's house when he is arrested in it. But that argument is founded on little more than a subjective view regarding the acceptability of certain sorts of police conduct, and not on considerations relevant to Fourth Amendment interests. Under such an unconfined analysis, Fourth Amendment protection in this area would approach the evaporation point. It is not easy to explain why, for instance, it is less subjectively "reasonable" to search a man's house when he is arrested on his front lawn—or just down the street—than it is when he happens to be in the house at the time of arrest. . . .

Application of sound Fourth Amendment principles to the facts of this case produces a clear result. The search here went far beyond the petitioner's person and the area from within which he might have obtained either a weapon or something that could have been used as evidence against him. There was no constitutional justification, in the absence of a search warrant, for extending the search beyond that area. The scope of the search was, therefore, "unreasonable" under the Fourth and Fourteenth Amendments, and the petitioner's conviction cannot stand.

Reversed.

MR. JUSTICE WHITE, with whom JUSTICE BLACK joins, dissenting. . . .

The case provides a good illustration of my point that it is unreasonable to require police to leave the scene of an arrest in order to obtain a search warrant when they already have probable cause to search and there is a clear danger that the items for which they may reasonably search will be removed before they return with a warrant. Petitioner was arrested in his home after an arrest whose validity will be explored below, but which I will now assume was valid. There was doubtless probable cause not only to arrest petitioner, but also to search his house. He had obliquely admitted, both to a neighbor and to the owner of the burglarized store, that he had committed the burglary. In light of this, and the fact that the neighbor had seen other admittedly stolen property in petitioner's house, there was surely probable cause on which a warrant could have [been] issued to search the house for the stolen coins. Moreover, had the police simply arrested petitioner, taken him off to the station house, and later returned with a warrant, it seems very likely that petitioner's wife, who in view of petitioner's generally garrulous nature must have known of the robbery, would have removed the coins. For the police to search the house while the evidence they had probable cause to search out and seize was still there cannot be considered unreasonable. . . .

If circumstances so often require the warrantless arrest that the law generally permits it, the typical situation will find the arresting officers lawfully on the premises without arrest or search warrant. Like the majority, I would permit the police to search the person of a suspect and the area under his immediate control either to assure the safety of the officers or to prevent the destruction of evidence. And like the majority, I see nothing in the arrest alone furnishing probable cause for a search of any broader scope. However, where as here the existence of probable cause is independently established and would justify a warrant for a broader search for evidence, I would follow past cases and permit such a search to be carried out without a warrant, since the fact of arrest supplies an exigent circumstance justifying police action before the evidence can be removed, and also alerts the suspect to the fact of the search so that he can immediately seek judicial determination of probable cause in an adversary proceeding, and appropriate redress.

This view, consistent with past cases, would not authorize the general search against which the Fourth Amendment was meant to guard, nor would it broaden or render uncertain in any way whatsoever the scope of searches permitted under the Fourth Amendment. The issue in this case is not the breadth of the search since there was clearly probable cause for the search which was carried out. No broader search than if the officers had a warrant would be permitted. The only issue is whether a search warrant was required as a precondition to that search. It is agreed that such a warrant would be required absent exigent circumstances. I would hold that the fact of arrest supplies such an exigent circumstance, since the police had lawfully gained entry to the premises to effect the arrest and since delaying the search to secure a warrant would have involved the risk of not recovering the fruits of the crime. . . .

United States v. Ross
456 U.S. 798, 102 S.Ct. 2157, 72 L.Ed. 2d 572 (1982)

Warrantless searches of automobiles have long been a troubled area for Fourth Amendment jurisprudence and the Supreme Court. This decision from 1982 marks a major step toward drawing a "bright line" for police, clarifying the limits of a search without warrant once police have lawfully stopped a car.

Based on information from an informant, police in Washington, D.C., believed that a certain individual known as "Bandit" was selling narcotics, which he kept in the trunk of his maroon Chevrolet Malibu. Detectives Marcum and Cassidy and Sergeant Gonzales spotted the car as it turned a corner in front of them. Both car and driver matched the informant's description. After the officers stopped the car, Marcum and Cassidy told the driver (later identified as Albert Ross) to get out of the car. While they searched him, Gonzales discovered a bullet on the front seat of the car and then located a pistol in the glove compartment. Ross was then arrested and handcuffed. Cassidy took Ross's keys and opened the trunk, where he found a closed brown paper bag. Opening the bag, Cassidy saw a number of glassine bags containing a white powder, which later proved to be heroin. At the police station, Cassidy thoroughly searched the car. In addition to the paper bag, which had been opened at curbside, he found in the trunk a zippered red leather pouch. Inside the pouch was $3,200 in cash. At no point did police obtain a warrant.

At trial the heroin and currency were introduced in evidence and Ross was convicted for possession of heroin with intent to distribute. On appeal, a three-judge panel of the court of appeals reversed the conviction, holding that although police had probable cause to stop and search the car, including the trunk and the brown paper bag found inside, the warrantless search of the leather pouch was not valid. The entire court of appeals then voted to rehear the case *en banc* and rejected the distinction the three-judge panel had drawn between the bag and the pouch, concluding that the police should not have opened *either* container without first obtaining a warrant. Majority: Stevens, Blackmun, Burger, Powell, O'Connor, Rehnquist. Dissenting: Marshall, Brennan, White.

JUSTICE STEVENS delivered the opinion of the Court.

In *Carroll* v. *United States* . . . the Court held that a warrantless search of an automobile stopped by police officers who had probable cause to believe the vehicle contained contraband was not unreasonable within the meaning of the Fourth Amendment. The Court in *Carroll* did not explicitly address the scope of the search that is permissible. In this case, we consider the extent to which police officers—who have legitimately stopped an automobile and who have probable cause to believe that contraband is concealed somewhere within it—may conduct a probing search of compartments and containers within the vehicle whose contents are not in plain view. We hold that they may conduct a search of the vehicle that is as thorough as a magistrate could authorize in a warrant "particularly describing the place to be searched." . . .

The rationale justifying a warrantless search of an automobile that is believed to be transporting contraband arguably applies with equal force to any movable container that is believed to be carrying an illicit substance. That argument, however, was squarely rejected in . . . *Arkansas* v. *Sanders*. . . . In *Sanders*, a Little Rock police officer received information from a reliable informant that Sanders would arrive at the local airport on a specified flight that afternoon carrying a green suitcase containing marijuana. The officer went to the airport. Sanders arrived on schedule and retrieved a green suitcase from the airline baggage service. Sanders gave the suitcase to a waiting companion who placed it in the trunk of a taxi. Sanders and his companion drove off in the cab; police officers followed and stopped the taxi several blocks from the airport. The officers opened the trunk, seized the suitcase, and searched it on the scene without a warrant. As predicted, the suitcase contained marijuana.

The Arkansas Supreme Court ruled that the warrantless search of the suitcase was impermissible under the Fourth Amendment, and this Court affirmed. . . .

. . . In rejecting the State's argument that the warrantless search of the suitcase was justified on the ground that it had been taken from an automobile lawfully stopped on the street, the Court broadly suggested that a warrantless search of a container found in an automobile could never be sustained as part of a warrantless search of the automobile itself. . . .

Robbins v. *California* . . . however, was a case in which suspicion was not directed at a specific container. In that case the Court for the first time was forced to consider whether police officers who are entitled to conduct a warrantless search of an automobile stopped on a public roadway may open a container found within the vehicle. In the early morning of January 5, 1975, police officers stopped Robbins' station wagon because he was driving erratically. Robbins got out of the car, but later returned to obtain the vehicle's registration papers. When he opened the car door, the officers smelled marijuana smoke. One of the officers searched Robbins and discovered a vial of liquid; in a search of the interior of the car the officer found marijuana. The police officers then opened the tailgate of the station wagon and raised the cover of a recessed luggage compartment. In the compartment they found two packages wrapped in green opaque plastic. The police unwrapped the packages and discovered a large amount of marijuana in each.

Robbins was charged with various drug offenses and moved to suppress the contents of the plastic packages. The California Court of Appeal held that "[s]earch of the automobile was proper when the officers learned that appellant was smoking marijuana when they stopped him" and that the warrantless search of the packages was justified because "the contents of the packages could have been inferred from their outward appearance, so that appellant could not have held a reasonable expectation of privacy with respect to the contents." . . .

This Court reversed. Writing for a plurality, Justice Stewart rejected the argument that the outward appearance of the packages precluded Robbins from having a reasonable expectation of privacy in their contents. He also squarely rejected the argument that there is a constitutional distinction between searches of luggage and searches of "less worthy" containers. Justice Stewart reasoned that all containers are equally protected by the Fourth Amendment unless their contents are in plain view. . . .

In *Carroll* itself, the whiskey that the prohibition agents seized was not in plain view. It was dis-

covered only after an officer opened the rumble seat and tore open the upholstery of the lazyback. The Court did not find the scope of the search unreasonable. . .

[T]he decision in *Carroll* was based on the Court's appraisal of practical considerations viewed in the perspective of history. It is therefore significant that the practical consequences of the *Carroll* decision would be largely nullified if the permissible scope of a warrantless search of an automobile did not include containers and packages found inside the vehicle. Contraband goods rarely are strewn across the trunk or floor of a car; since by their very nature such goods must be withheld from public view, they rarely can be placed in an automobile unless they are enclosed within some form of container. . . .

A lawful search of fixed premises generally extends to the entire area in which the object of the search may be found and is not limited by the possibility that separate acts of entry or opening may be required to complete the search. Thus, a warrant that authorizes an officer to search a home for illegal weapons also provides authority to open closets, chests, drawers, and containers in which the weapon might be found. A warrant to open a footlocker to search for marijuana would also authorize the opening of packages found inside. A warrant to search a vehicle would support a search of every part of the vehicle that might contain the object of the search. When a legitimate search is under way, and when its purpose and its limits have been precisely defined, nice distinctions between closets, drawers, and containers, in the case of a home, or between glove compartments, upholstered seats, trunks, and wrapped packages, in the case of a vehicle, must give way to the interest in the prompt and efficient completion of the task at hand. . . .

The scope of a warrantless search based on probable cause is no narrower—and no broader— than the scope of a search authorized by a warrant supported by probable cause. Only the prior approval of the magistrate is waived; the search otherwise is as the magistrate could authorize.

The scope of a warrantless search of an automobile thus is not defined by the nature of the container in which the contraband is secreted. Rather, it is defined by the object of the search and the places in which there is probable cause to believe that it may be found. Just as probable cause to believe that a stolen lawnmower may be found in a garage will not support a warrant to search an upstairs bedroom, probable cause to believe that undocumented aliens are being transported in a van will not justify a warrantless search of a suitcase. Probable cause to believe that a container placed in the trunk of a taxi contains contraband or evidence does not justify a search of the entire cab.

Our decision today is inconsistent with the disposition in *Robbins* v. *California* and with the portion of the opinion in *Arkansas* v. *Sanders* on which the plurality in *Robbins* relied. Nevertheless, the doctrine of *stare decisis* does not preclude this action. Although we have rejected some of the reasoning in *Sanders,* we adhere to our holding in that case. . . .

We hold that the scope of the warrantless search authorized by that exception is no broader and no narrower than a magistrate could legitimately authorize by warrant. If probable cause justifies the search of a lawfully stopped vehicle, it justifies the search of every part of the vehicle and its contents that may conceal the object of the search.

The judgment of the Court of Appeals is reversed. The case is remanded for further proceedings consistent with this opinion.

It is so ordered.

JUSTICE MARSHALL, with whom JUSTICE BRENNAN joins, dissenting.

The majority today not only repeals all realistic limits on warrantless automobile searches, it repeals the Fourth Amendment warrant requirement itself. By equating a police officer's estimation of probable cause with a magistrate's, the Court utterly disregards the value of a neutral and detached magistrate. . . .

Our cases do recognize a narrow exception to the warrant requirement for certain automobile searches. Throughout our decisions, two major considerations have been advanced to justify the automobile exception to the warrant requirement. We have upheld only those searches that are actually justified by those considerations.

First, these searches have been justified on the basis of the exigency of the mobility of the automobile. . . .

In many cases, however, the police will, prior to searching the car, have cause to arrest the occupants and bring them to the station for booking. In this situation, the police can ordinarily seize the automobile and bring it to the station. Because the vehicle is now in the exclusive control of the authorities, any subsequent search cannot be justified by the mobility of the car. Rather, an immediate warrantless search of the vehicle is permitted because of the second major justification for the automobile exception: the diminished expectation of privacy in an automobile.

Because an automobile presents much of its contents in open view to police officers who legitimately stop it on a public way, is used for travel, and is subject to significant government regulation, this Court has determined that the intrusion of a warrantless search of an automobile is constitutionally less significant than a warrantless search of more private areas. . . .

The majority's rule is flatly inconsistent with these established Fourth Amendment principles concerning the scope of the automobile exception and the importance of the warrant requirement. . . .

The practical mobility problem—deciding what to do with both the car and the occupants if an immediate search is not conducted—is simply not present in the case of movable containers, which can easily be seized and brought to the magistrate. . . .

The majority's sleight-of-hand ignores the obvious differences between the function served by a magistrate in making a determination of probable cause and the function of the automobile exception. It is irrelevant to a magistrate's function whether the items subject to search are mobile, may be in danger of destruction, or are impractical to store, or whether an immediate search would be less intrusive than a seizure without a warrant. A magistrate's only concern is whether there is probable cause to search them. Where suspicion has focused not on a particular item but only on a vehicle, home, or office, the magistrate might reasonably authorize a search of closed containers at the location as well. But an officer on the beat who searches an automobile without a warrant is not entitled to conduct a broader search than the exigency obviating the warrant justifies. After all, what justifies the warrantless search is not probable cause alone, but *probable cause coupled with the mobility of the automobile.* Because the scope of a *warrantless* search should depend on the scope of the justification for dispensing with a warrant, the entire premise of the majority's opinion fails to support its conclusion.

The majority's rule masks the startling assumption that a policeman's determination of probable cause is the functional equivalent of the determination of a neutral and detached magistrate. This assumption ignores a major premise of the warrant requirement—the importance of having a neutral and detached magistrate determine whether probable cause exists. . . .

Finally, the majority's new rule is theoretically unsound and will create anomalous and unwarranted results. . . . The Court suggests that probable cause to search only a container does not justify a warrantless search of an automobile in which it is placed, absent reason to believe that the contents could be secreted elsewhere in the vehicle. . . . But why is such a container more private, less difficult for police to seize and store, or in any other relevant respect more properly subject to the warrant requirement, than a container that police discover in a probable cause search of an entire automobile? This rule plainly has peculiar and unworkable consequences: the Government "must show that the investigating officer knew enough but not too much, that he had sufficient knowledge to establish probable cause but insufficient knowledge to know exactly where the contraband was located." . . .

California v. Greenwood
56 U.S.L.W. 4409 (1988)

Investigator Jenny Stracner of the Laguna Beach, California, Police Department received information that Billy Greenwood might be engaged in narcotics trafficking. On April 6, 1984, she asked the regular trash collector to turn over to her the plastic garbage bags Greenwood had left on the curb in front of his house without mixing their contents with the garbage from other houses. Search of the rubbish revealed items suggesting narcotics use. She used them to obtain a warrant to search the Greenwood residence. Search of the house uncovered cocaine and hashish. Greenwood posted bail following his arrest. Later, with additional information indicating continued narcotics trafficking, Investigator Robert Rahaeuser obtained Greenwood's garbage on May 4 in the same manner. Another warrant search of the house led to a second arrest on narcotics charges. Concluding that warrantless trash searches violate the Fourth Amendment, the Superior Court dismissed the charges. The Court of Appeals affirmed, and the California Supreme Court denied review. Those parts of Justice White's majority opinion dealing with the impact of California law on the case are omitted. Majority: White, Blackmun, O'Connor, Rehnquist, Scalia, Stevens. Dissenting: Brennan, Marshall. Not participating: Kennedy.

JUSTICE WHITE delivered the opinion of the Court.

The issue here is whether the Fourth Amendment prohibits the warrantless search and seizure of garbage left for collection outside the curtilage of a home. We conclude, in accordance with the vast majority of lower courts that have addressed the issue, that it does not. . . .

The warrantless search and seizure of the garbage bags left at the curb outside the Greenwood house would violate the Fourth Amendment only if respondents manifested a subjective expectation of privacy in their garbage that society accepts as objectively reasonable. . . .

They assert, however, that they had, and exhibited, an expectation of privacy with respect to the trash that was searched by the police: The trash, which was placed on the street for collection at a fixed time, was contained in opaque plastic bags, which the garbage collector was expected to pick up, mingle with the trash of others, and deposit at the garbage dump. The trash was only temporarily on the street, and there was little likelihood that it would be inspected by anyone.

It may well be that respondents did not expect that the contents of their garbage bags would become known to the police or other members of the public. An expectation of privacy does not give rise to Fourth Amendment protection, however, unless society is prepared to accept that expectation as objectively reasonable.

Here, we conclude that respondents exposed their garbage to the public sufficiently to defeat their claim to Fourth Amendment protection. It is common knowledge that plastic garbage bags left on or at the side of a public street are readily accessible to animals, children, scavengers, snoops, and other members of the public. Moreover, respondents placed their refuse at the curb for the express purpose of conveying it to a third party, the trash collector, who might himself have sorted through respondents' trash or permitted others, such as the police, to do so. Accordingly . . . respondents could have had no reasonable expectation of privacy in the inculpatory items that they discarded.

Furthermore, as we have held, the police cannot reasonably be expected to avert their eyes from evidence of criminal activity that could have been observed by any member of the public. . . . We held in *Smith* v. *Maryland* (1979), for example, that the police did not violate the Fourth Amendment by causing a pen register to be installed at the telephone company's offices to record the telephone numbers dialed by a criminal suspect. An individual has no legitimate expectation of privacy in the numbers dialed on his telephone, we reasoned, because he voluntarily conveys those numbers to the telephone company when he uses the telephone. . . .

Similarly, we held in *California* v. *Ciraolo* (1986) that the police were not required by the Fourth Amendment to obtain a warrant before conducting surveillance of the respondent's fenced backyard from a private plane flying at an altitude of 1,000 feet. We concluded that the respondent's expectation that his yard was protected from such surveillance was unreasonable because "[a]ny member of the public flying in this airspace who glanced down could have seen everything that these officers observed." . . .

The judgment of the California Court of Appeal is therefore reversed, and this case is remanded for further proceedings not inconsistent with this opinion.

It is so ordered.

JUSTICE BRENNAN, with whom JUSTICE MARSHALL joins, dissenting. . . .

Scrutiny of another's trash is contrary to commonly accepted notions of civilized behavior. I suspect, therefore, that members of our society will be shocked to learn that the Court, the ultimate guarantor of liberty, deems unreasonable our expectation that the aspects of our private lives that are concealed safely in a trash bag will not become public. . . .

The Framers of the Fourth Amendment understood that "unreasonable searches" of "paper[s] and effects"—no less than "unreasonable searches" of "person[s] and houses"—infringe privacy. As early as 1878, this Court acknowledged that the contents of "[l]etters and sealed packages . . . in the mail are as fully guarded from examination and inspection . . . . as if they were retained by the parties forwarding them in their own domiciles." In short, so long as a package is "closed against inspection," the Fourth Amendment protects its contents, "wherever they may be," and the police must obtain a warrant to search it just "as is required when papers are subjected to search in one's own household." . . .

With the emergence of the reasonable-expectation-of-privacy analysis . . . we have reaffirmed this fundamental principle. . . .

Our precedent, therefore, leaves no room to doubt that had respondents been carrying their personal effects in opaque, sealed plastic bags—identical to the ones they placed on the curb—their privacy would have been protected from warrantless police intrusion. . . .

Respondents deserve no less protection just because Greenwood used the bags to discard rather than to transport his personal effects. Their contents are not inherently any less private, and Greenwood's decision to discard them, at least in the manner in which he did, does not diminish his expectation of privacy. . . .

. . . A single bag of trash testifies eloquently

to the eating, reading, and recreational habits of the person who produced it. A search of trash, like a search of the bedroom, can relate intimate details about sexual practices, health, and personal hygiene. Like rifling through desk drawers or intercepting phone calls, rummaging through trash can divulge the target's financial and professional status, political affiliations and inclinations, private thoughts, personal relationships, and romantic interests. It cannot be doubted that a sealed trash bag harbors telling evidence of the "intimate activity associated with the 'sanctity of a man's home and the privacies of life,' " which the Fourth Amendment is designed to protect. . . .

In evaluating the reasonableness of Greenwood's expectation that his sealed trash bags would not be invaded, the Court has held that we must look to "understandings that are recognized and permitted by society." Most of us, I believe, would be incensed to discover a meddler—whether a neighbor, a reporter, or a detective—scrutinizing our sealed trash containers to discover some detail of our personal lives. . . .

That is not to deny that isolated intrusions into opaque, sealed trash containers occur. . . .

Had Greenwood flaunted his intimate activity by strewing his trash all over the curb for all to see, or had some nongovernmental intruder invaded his privacy and done the same, I could accept the Court's conclusion that an expectation of privacy would have been unreasonable. Similarly, had police searching the city dump run across incriminating evidence that, despite commingling with the trash of others, still retained its identity as Greenwood's, we would have a different case. But all that Greenwood "exposed . . . to the public" were the exteriors of several opaque, sealed containers. Until the bags were opened by police, they hid their contents from the public's view every bit as much as did Chadwick's double-locked footlocker and

Robbins' green, plastic wrapping. Faithful application of the warrant requirement does not require police to "avert their eyes from evidence of criminal activity that could have been observed by any member of the public." Rather, it only requires them to adhere to norms of privacy that members of the public plainly acknowledge.

The mere *possibility* that unwelcome meddlers *might* open and rummage through the containers does not negate the expectation of privacy in its contents any more than the possibility of a burglary negates an expectation of privacy in the home; or the possibility of a private intrusion negates an expectation of privacy in an unopened package; or the possibility that an operator will listen in on a telephone conversation negates an expectation of privacy in the words spoken on the telephone. . . .

Nor is it dispositive that "respondents placed their refuse at the curb for the express purpose of conveying it to a third party . . . who might himself have sorted through respondents' trash or permitted others, such as police, to do so." In the first place, Greenwood can hardly be faulted for leaving trash on his curb when a county ordinance commanded him to do so. . . . More importantly, even the voluntary relinquishment of possession or control over an effect does not necessarily amount to a relinquishment of a privacy expectation in it. Were it otherwise, a letter or package would lose all Fourth Amendment protection when placed in a mail box or other depository. . . .

In holding that the warrantless search of Greenwood's trash was consistent with the Fourth Amendment, the Court paints a grim picture of our society. . . . The American society with which I am familiar "chooses to dwell in reasonable security and freedom from surveillance," and is more dedicated to individual liberty and more sensitive to intrusions on the sanctity of the home than the Court is willing to acknowledge.

V. RIGHT TO COUNSEL AND SELF-INCRIMINATION

Powell v. *Alabama*
287 U.S. 45, 53 S.Ct. 55, 77 L.Ed. 158 (1932)

The 1931 conviction in Scottsboro, Alabama, of seven black men charged with the rape of two white women resulted in a series of legal tests in the Supreme Court of the United States, of which this case was the first. The chief justice of the Alabama Supreme Court had dissented from that court's affirmance of the convictions, chiefly because of the hostile atmosphere that surrounded the trial and the speed and casualness with which the trial judge had dealt with the question of counsel for the defendants. Majority: Sutherland, Brandeis, Cardozo, Hughes, Roberts, Stone, Van Devanter. Dissenting: Butler, McReynolds.

MR. JUSTICE SUTHERLAND delivered the opinion of the court. . . .

The record shows that immediately upon the return of the indictment defendants were arraigned and pleaded not guilty. Apparently they were not asked whether they had, or were able to employ, counsel, or wished to have counsel appointed; or whether they had friends or relatives who might assist in that regard if communicated with. That it would not have been an idle ceremony to have given the defendants reasonable opportunity to communicate with their families and endeavor to obtain counsel is demonstrated by the fact that very soon after conviction, able counsel appeared in their behalf. . . .

It is hardly necessary to say that the right to counsel being conceded, a defendant should be afforded a fair opportunity to secure counsel of his own choice. Not only was that not done here, but such designation of counsel as was attempted was either so indefinite or so close upon the trial as to amount to a denial of effective and substantial aid in that regard. This will be amply demonstrated by a brief review of the record.

April 6, six days after indictment, the trials began. When the first case was called, the court inquired whether the parties were ready for trial. The state's attorney replied that he was ready to proceed. No one answered for the defendants or appeared to represent or defend them. Mr. Roddy,

a Tennessee lawyer not a member of the local bar, addressed the court, saying that he had not been employed, but that people who were interested had spoken to him about the case. He was asked by the court whether he intended to appear for the defendants, and answered that he would like to appear along with counsel that the court might appoint. . . .

And in this casual fashion the matter of counsel in a capital case was disposed of.

It thus will be seen that until the very morning of the trial no lawyer had been named or definitely designated to represent the defendants. . . .

. . . [D]uring perhaps the most critical period of the proceedings against these defendants, that is to say, from the time of their arraignment until the beginning of their trial, when consultation, thorough-going investigation and preparation were vitally important, the defendants did not have the aid of counsel in any real sense, although they were as much entitled to such aid during that period as at the trial itself.

The Constitution of Alabama provides that in all criminal prosecutions the accused shall enjoy the right to have the assistance of counsel; and a state statute requires the court in a capital case, where the defendant is unable to employ counsel, to appoint counsel for him. The state Supreme Court held that these provisions had not been infringed, and with that holding we are powerless to interfere.

The question, however, which it is our duty, and within our power, to decide, is whether the denial of the assistance of counsel contravenes the due process clause of the Fourteenth Amendment to the Federal Constitution. . . .

An affirmation of the right to the aid of counsel in petty offenses, and its denial in the case of crimes of the gravest character, where such aid is most needed, is so outrageous and so obviously a perversion of all sense of proportion that the rule was constantly, vigorously and sometimes passionately assailed by English statesmen and lawyers. . . .

The rule was rejected by the colonies. . .

The Sixth Amendment, in terms, provides that in all criminal prosecutions the accused shall enjoy the right "to have the Assistance of Counsel for his defence." In the face of the reasoning of the Hurtado case, if it stood alone, it would be difficult to justify the conclusion that the right to counsel, being thus specifically granted by the Sixth Amendment, was also within the intendment of the due process of law clause. But the Hurtado case does not stand alone. In the later case of *Chicago, Burlington & Q. R. Co.* v. *Chicago,* this court held that a judgment of a state court, even though authorized by statute, by which private property was taken for public use without just compensation, was in violation of the due process of law required by the Fourteenth Amendment, notwithstanding that the Fifth Amendment explicitly declares that private property shall not be taken for public use without just compensation. . . .

. . . The fact that the right involved is of such a character that it cannot be denied without violating those "fundamental principles of liberty and justice which lie at the base of all our civil and political institutions" is obviously one of those compelling considerations which must prevail in determining whether it is embraced within the due process clause of the Fourteenth Amendment, although it be specifically dealt with in another part of the Federal Constitution. . . . While the question has never been categorically determined by this court, a consideration of the nature of the right and a review of the expressions of this and other courts makes it clear that the right to the aid of counsel is of this fundamental character. . . .

What, then, does a hearing include? Historically and in practice, in our own country at least, it has always included the right to the aid of counsel when desired and provided by the party asserting the right. The right to be heard would be, in many cases, of little avail if it did not comprehend the right to be heard by counsel. Even the intelligent and educated layman has small and sometimes no skill in the science of law. If charged with crime, he is incapable, generally, of determining for himself whether the indictment is good or bad. He is unfamiliar with the rules of evidence. Left without the aid of counsel he may be put on trial without a proper charge, and convicted upon incompetent evidence, or evidence irrelevant to the issue or otherwise inadmissible. He lacks both the skill and knowledge adequately to prepare his defense, even though he have a perfect one. He requires the guiding hand of counsel at every step in the proceedings against him. Without it, though he be not guilty, he faces the danger of conviction because he does not know how to establish his innocence. If that be true of men of intelligence, how much more true is it of the ignorant and illiterate, or those of feeble intellect. If in any case, civil or criminal, a state or federal court were arbitrarily to refuse to hear a party by counsel, employed by and appearing for him, it reasonably may not be doubted that such a refusal would be a denial of a hearing, and, therefore, of due process in the constitutional sense. . . .

In the light of the facts outlined in the forepart of this opinion—the ignorance and illiteracy of the defendants, their youth, the circumstances of public hostility, the imprisonment and the close surveillance of the defendants by the military forces, the fact that their friends and families were all in other states and communication with them necessarily difficult, and above all that they stood in deadly peril of their lives—we think the failure of the trial court to give them reasonable time and opportunity to secure counsel was a clear denial of due process.

But passing that, and assuming their inability, even if opportunity had been given, to employ counsel, as the trial court evidently did assume, we are of opinion that, under the circumstances just stated, the necessity of counsel was so vital and imperative that the failure of the trial court to make an effective appointment of counsel was likewise a denial of due process within the meaning of the Fourteenth Amendment. Whether this would be so in other criminal prosecutions, or under other circumstances, we need not determine. All that it is necessary now to decide, as we do decide, is that in a capital case, where the defendant is unable to employ counsel, and is incapable adequately of making his own defense because of ignorance, feeblemindedness, illiteracy, or the like, it is the duty of the court, whether requested or not, to assign counsel for him as a necessary requisite of due process of law; and that duty is not discharged by an assignment at such a time or under such circumstances as to preclude the giving of effective aid in the preparation and trial of the case. . . .

The judgments must be reversed and the causes remanded for further proceedings not inconsistent with this opinion.

Judgments reversed.

Gideon v. *Wainwright*
372 U.S. 335, 83 S.Ct. 792, 9 L.Ed. 2d 799 (1963)

Clarence Gideon was charged in a Florida state court with breaking and entering a poolroom with the intent to commit a crime. This was a felony under Florida law. He appeared in court without a lawyer, and when he requested that the trial court appoint one for him because he could not afford retained counsel, the judge refused. Florida law at the time provided appointed counsel for indigents only in capital cases. Following conviction, Gideon filed a petition for habeas corpus in the Florida Supreme Court, which denied relief without opinion. Majority: Black, Brennan, Clark, Douglas, Goldberg, Harlan, Stewart, Warren, White.

MR. JUSTICE BLACK delivered the opinion of the Court. . . .

Since 1942, when *Betts* v. *Brady* . . . was decided by a divided Court, the problem of a defendant's federal constitutional right to counsel in a state court has been a continuing source of controversy and litigation in both state and federal courts. . . .

The facts upon which Betts claimed that he had been unconstitutionally denied the right to have counsel appointed to assist him are strikingly like the facts upon which Gideon here bases his federal constitutional claim. Betts was indicted for robbery in a Maryland state court. On arraignment, he told the trial judge of his lack of funds to hire a lawyer and asked the court to appoint one for him. Betts was advised that it was not the practice in that county to appoint counsel for indigent defendants except in murder and rape cases. He then pleaded not guilty, had witnesses summoned, crossexamined the State's witnesses, examined his own, and chose not to testify himself. He was found guilty by the judge, sitting without a jury, and sentenced to eight years in prison.

Like Gideon, Betts sought release by *habeas corpus,* alleging that he had been denied the right to assistance of counsel in violation of the Fourteenth Amendment. Betts was denied any relief, and on review this Court affirmed. It was held that a refusal to appoint counsel for an indigent defendant charged with a felony did not necessarily violate the Due Process Clause of the Fourteenth Amendment, which for reasons given the Court deemed to be the only applicable federal constitutional provision. The Court said,

> Asserted denial [of due process] is to be tested by an appraisal of the totality of facts in a given case. That which may, in one setting, constitute a denial of fundamental fairness, shocking to the universal sense of justice, may, in other circumstances, and in the light of other considerations, fall short of such denial. . . .

Treating due process as "a concept less rigid and more fluid than those envisaged in other specific and particular provisions of the Bill of Rights," the Court held that refusal to appoint counsel under the particular facts and circumstances in the Betts Case was not so "offensive to the common and fundamental ideas of fairness" as to amount to a denial of due process. . . .

We accept *Betts* v. *Brady's* assumption, based as it was on our prior cases, that a provision of the Bill of Rights which is "fundamental and essential to a fair trial" is made obligatory upon the States by the Fourteenth Amendment. We think the Court in *Betts* was wrong, however, in concluding that the Sixth Amendment's guarantee of counsel is not one of these fundamental rights. Ten years before *Betts* v. *Brady,* this Court, after full consideration of all the historical data examined in *Betts,* had unequivocally declared that "the right to the aid of counsel is of this fundamental character." While the Court at the close of its *Powell* opinion did by its language, as this Court frequently does, limit its holding to the particular facts and circumstances of that case, its conclusions about the fundamental nature of the right to counsel are unmistakable. . . .

The fact is that in deciding as it did—that "appointment of counsel is not a fundamental right, essential to a fair trial"—the Court in *Betts* v. *Brady* made an abrupt break with its own well-considered precedents. In returning to these old precedents, sounder we believe than the new, we but restore constitutional principles established to achieve a fair system of justice. Not only these precedents but also reason and reflection require us to recognize that in our adversary system of criminal justice, any person haled into court, who is too poor to hire a lawyer, cannot be assured a fair trial unless counsel is provided for him. This seems to us to be an obvious truth. Governments, both state and federal, quite properly spend vast sums of money to establish machinery to try defendants accused of crime. Lawyers to prosecute are everywhere deemed essential to protect the public's interest in an orderly society. Similarly, there are few defendants charged with crime, few indeed, who fail to hire the best lawyers they can get to prepare and present their defenses. That government hires lawyers to prosecute and defendants who have the money hire lawyers to defend are the strongest

indications of the widespread belief that lawyers in criminal courts are necessities, not luxuries. The right of one charged with crime to counsel may not be deemed fundamental and essential to fair trials in some countries, but it is in ours. From the very beginning, our state and national constitutions and laws have laid great emphasis on procedural and substantive safeguards designed to assure fair trials before impartial tribunals in which every defendant stands equal before the law. This noble ideal cannot be realized if the poor man charged with crime has to face his accusers without a lawyer to assist him.

The Court in *Betts* v. *Brady* departed from the sound wisdom upon which the Court's holding in *Powell* v. *Alabama* rested. Florida, supported by two other States, has asked that *Betts* v. *Brady* be left intact. Twenty-two States, as friends of the Court, argue that *Betts* was "an anachronism when handed down" and that it should now be overruled. We agree.

The judgment is reversed and the cause is remanded to the Supreme Court of Florida for further action not inconsistent with this opinion.

Reversed.

MR. JUSTICE HARLAN, concurring. . . .

I cannot subscribe to the view that *Betts* v. *Brady* represented "an abrupt break with its own well-considered precedents." . . . In 1932, in *Powell* v. *Alabama* . . . a capital case, this Court declared that under the particular facts there presented—"the ignorance and illiteracy of the defendants, their youth, the circumstances of public hostility . . . and above all that they stood in deadly peril of their lives" . . .—the state court had a duty to assign counsel for the trial as a necessary requisite of due process of law. It is evident that these limiting facts were not added to the opinion as an afterthought; they were repeatedly emphasized . . . and were clearly regarded as important to the result.

Thus when this Court, a decade later, decided *Betts* v. *Brady,* it did no more than to admit of the possible existence of special circumstances in noncapital as well as capital trials, while at the same time insisting that such circumstances be shown in order to establish a denial of due process. . . .

In noncapital cases, the "special circumstances" rule has continued to exist in form while its substance has been substantially and steadily eroded. In the first decade after *Betts,* there were cases in which the Court found special circumstances to be lacking, but usually by a sharply divided vote. However, no such decision has been cited to us, and I have found none, after *Quicksall* v. *Michigan* . . . decided in 1950. . . . The Court has come to recognize, in other words, that the mere existence of a serious criminal charge constituted in itself special circumstances requiring the services of coun-sel at trial. In truth the *Betts* v. *Brady* rule is no longer a reality.

This evolution, however, appears not to have been fully recognized by many state courts, in this instance charged with the front-line responsibility for the enforcement of constitutional rights. To continue a rule which is honored by this Court only with lip service is not a healthy thing and in the long run will do disservice to the federal system. . . .

Miranda v. Arizona
384 U.S. 436, 86 S.Ct. 1602, 16 L.Ed. 2d 694 (1966)

In reviewing four state criminal convictions in 1966 (in three the convictions had been upheld; in one, reversed) the Supreme Court, as on earlier occasions, was presented in each case with the question of whether a defendant's confession made in police custody was admissible under constitutional requirements. In each of these cases defendant had not been advised of his right to remain silent and to consult counsel. Although the interrogations took place for varying periods in the cases, in none was there an allegation of violence or threat of violence. In *Escobedo* v. *Illinois* (1964) the Court had reversed because the defendant was interrogated without being ad-vised of his right to remain silent and to consult with counsel and because his request to consult counsel was denied. Majority: Warren, Black, Brennan, Douglas, Fortas. Dissenting: Harlan, Clark, Stewart, White.

MR. CHIEF JUSTICE WARREN delivered the opinion of the Court. . . .

Our holding . . . briefly stated . . . is this: the prosecution may not use statements, whether exculpatory or inculpatory, stemming from custodial interrogation of the defendant unless it demonstrates the use of procedural safeguards effective to secure the privilege against self-incrimination. By custodial interrogation, we mean questioning initiated by law enforcement officers after a person has been taken into custody or otherwise deprived of his freedom of action in any significant way. As for the pro-cedural safeguards to be employed, unless other fully effective means are devised to inform accused persons of their right of silence and to assure a continuous opportunity to exercise it, the following measures are required. Prior to any questioning, the person must be warned that he has a right to remain silent, that any statement he does make may be used as evidence against him, and that he has a right to the presence of an attorney, either retained or appointed. The defendant may waive effectuation of these rights, provided the waiver is made voluntarily, knowingly and intelligently. If, however, he indicates in any manner and at any stage of the process that he wishes to consult with an attorney before speaking there can be no ques-tioning. Likewise, if the individual is alone and indicates in any manner that he does not wish to be interrogated, the police may not question him. The mere fact that he may have answered some questions or volunteered some statements on his own does not deprive him of the right to refrain from answering any further inquiries until he has consulted with an attorney and thereafter consents to be questioned.

The constitutional issue we decide in each of these cases is the admissibility of statements obtained from a defendant questioned while in custody and deprived of his freedom of action. In each, the defendant was questioned by police officers, detectives, or a prosecuting attorney in a room in which he was cut off from the outside world. In none of these cases was the defendant given a full and effective warning of his rights at the outset of the interrogation process. In all the cases, the questioning elicited oral admissions, and in three of them, signed statements as well which were admitted at their trials. They all thus share salient features—incommunicado interrogation of individuals in a police-dominated atmosphere, resulting in self-incriminating statements without full warnings of constitutional rights.

An understanding of the nature and setting of this in-custody interrogation is essential to our decisions today. . . .

. . . [T]he modern practice of in-custody interrogation is psychologically rather than physically oriented. . . . Interrogation still takes place in privacy. Privacy results in secrecy and this in turn results in a gap in our knowledge as to what in fact goes on in the interrogation rooms. A valuable source of information about present police practices, however, may be found in various police manuals and texts which document procedures employed with success in the past, and which recommend various other effective tactics. [The opinion here surveys manuals and texts.]

From these representative samples of interrogation techniques, the setting prescribed by the manuals and observed in practice becomes clear. In essence, it is this: To be alone with the subject is essential to prevent distraction and to deprive him of any outside support. The aura of confidence in his guilt undermines his will to resist. He merely confirms the preconceived story the police seek to have him describe. Patience and persistence, at times relentless questioning, are employed. To obtain a confession, the interrogator must "patiently maneuver himself or his quarry into a position from which the desired object may be obtained." When normal procedures fail to produce the needed result,

the police may resort to deceptive strategems such as giving false legal advice. It is important to keep the subject off balance, for example, by trading on his insecurity about himself or his surroundings. The police then persuade, trick, or cajole him out of exercising his constitutional rights.

Even without employing brutality, the "third degree" or the specific strategems described above, the very fact of custodial interrogation exacts a heavy toll on individual liberty and trades on the weakness of individuals.

In these cases, we might not find the defendants' statements to have been involuntary in traditional terms. Our concern for adequate safeguards to protect precious Fifth Amendment rights is, of course, not lessened in the slightest. To be sure, the records do not evince overt physical coercion or patented psychological ploys. The fact remains that in none of these cases did the officers undertake to afford appropriate safeguards at the outset of the interrogation to insure that the statements were truly the product of free choice. . . .

Today . . . there can be no doubt that the Fifth Amendment privilege is available outside of criminal court proceedings and serves to protect persons in all settings in which their freedom of action is curtailed from being compelled to incriminate themselves. . . .

The circumstances surrounding in-custody interrogation can operate very quickly to overbear the will of one merely made aware of his privilege by his interrogators. Therefore, the right to have counsel present at the interrogation is indispensable to the protection of the Fifth Amendment privilege under the system we delineate today. Our aim is to assure that the individual's right to choose between silence and speech remains unfettered throughout the interrogation process. . . .

Our decision is not intended to hamper the traditional function of police officers in investigating crime. . . . General on-the-scene questioning as to facts surrounding a crime or other general questioning of citizens in the fact-finding process is not affected by our holding. It is an act of responsible citizenship for individuals to give whatever information they may have to aid in law enforcement. In such situations the compelling atmosphere inherent in the process of in-custody interrogation is not necessarily present.

In dealing with statements obtained through

interrogation, we do not purport to find all confessions inadmissible. Confessions remain a proper element in law enforcement. Any statement given freely and voluntarily without any compelling influences is, of course, admissible in evidence. The fundamental import of the privilege while an individual is in custody is not whether he is allowed to talk to the police without the benefit of warnings and counsel, but whether he can be interrogated. There is no requirement that police stop a person who enters a police station and states that he wishes to confess to a crime, or a person who calls the police to offer a confession or any other statement he desires to make. Volunteered statements of any kind are not barred by the Fifth Amendment and their admissibility is not affected by our holding today. . . .

It is so ordered.

MR. JUSTICE HARLAN, whom MR. JUSTICE STEWART and MR. JUSTICE WHITE join, dissenting.

I believe the decision of the Court represents poor constitutional law and entails harmful consequences for the country at large. How serious these consequences may prove to be only time can tell. . . . The new rules are not designed to guard against police brutality or other unmistakably banned forms of coercion. Those who use third-degree tactics and deny them in court are equally able and destined to lie as skillfully about warnings and waivers. Rather, the thrust of the new rules is to negate all pressures, to reinforce the nervous or ignorant suspect, and ultimately to discourage any confession at all. The aim in short is toward "voluntariness" in a utopian sense, or to view it from a different angle, voluntariness with a vengeance.

To incorporate this notion into the Constitution requires a strained reading of history and precedent and a disregard of the very pragmatic concerns that alone may on occasion justify such strains. I believe that reasoned examination will show that the Due Process Clause provides an adequate tool for coping with confessions and that, even if the Fifth Amendment privilege against self-incrimination be invoked, its precedents taken as a whole do not sustain the present rules. Viewed as a choice based on pure policy, these new rules prove to be a highly debatable if not one-sided appraisal of the competing interests, imposed over widespread objection, at the very time when judicial restraint is most called for by the circumstances. . . .

The more important premise is that pressure on the suspect must be eliminated though it be only the subtle influence of the atmosphere and surroundings. The Fifth Amendment, however, has never been thought to forbid *all* pressure to incriminate oneself in the situations covered by it. . . . However, the Court's unspoken assumption that *any* pressure violates the privilege is not supported by the precedents and it has failed to show why the Fifth Amendment prohibits that relatively mild pressure the Due Process Clause permits. . . .

Examined as an expression of public policy, the Court's new regime proves so dubious that there can be no due compensation for its weakness in constitutional law. Foregoing discussion has shown, I think, how mistaken is the Court in implying that the Constitution has struck the balance in favor of the approach the Court takes. Rather, precedent reveals that the Fourteenth Amendment in practice has been construed to strike a different balance, that the Fifth Amendment gives the Court little solid support in this context, and that the Sixth Amendment should have no bearing at all. Legal history has been stretched before to satisfy deep needs of society. In this instance, however, the Court has not and cannot make the powerful showing that its new rules are plainly desirable in the context of our society, something which is surely demanded before those rules are engrafted onto the Constitution and imposed on every State and county in the land. . . .

. . . Until today, the role of the constitution has been only to sift out *undue* pressure, not to assure spontaneous confessions.

Marchetti v. *United States*
390 U.S. 39, 88 S.Ct. 697, 19 L.Ed. 2d 889 (1968)

(This case is reprinted in Chapter Seven, beginning on page 238.)

Oregon v. Elstad
470 U.S. 298, 105 S.Ct. 1285, 84 L.Ed. 2d 222 (1985)

The Court granted certiorari in this case to consider the question of whether the self-incrimination clause of the Fifth Amendment requires the suppression of a confession—made after proper *Miranda* warnings and a valid waiver of rights—solely because the arresting officers had obtained an earlier voluntary, but unwarned, admission from the defendant. The facts of the case are included in Justice O'Connor's opinion for the majority. Majority: O'Connor, Blackmun, Burger, Powell, Rehnquist, White. Dissenting: Brennan, Marshall, Stevens.

JUSTICE O'CONNOR delivered the opinion of the Court. . . .

In December, 1981, the home of Mr. and Mrs. Gilbert Gross, in the town of Salem, Polk County, Ore., was burglarized. Missing were art objects and furnishings valued at $150,000. A witness to the burglary contacted the Polk County Sheriff's Office, implicating respondent Michael Elstad, an 18-year-old neighbor and friend of the Grosses' teenage son. Thereupon, Officers Burke and McAllister went to the home of respondent Elstad, with a warrant for his arrest. Elstad's mother answered the door. She led the officers to her son's room where he lay on his bed, clad in shorts and listening to his stereo. The officers asked him to get dressed and to accompany them into the living room. Officer McAllister asked respondent's mother to step into the kitchen, where he explained that they had a warrant for her son's arrest for the burglary of a neighbor's residence. Officer Burke remained with Elstad in the living room. He later testified:

"I sat down with Mr. Elstad and I asked him if he was aware of why Detective McAllister and myself were there to talk to him. He stated no, he had no idea why we were there. I then asked him if he knew a person by the name of Gross, and he said yes, he did, and also added that he heard that there was a robbery at the Gross house. And at that point I told Mr. Elstad that I felt he was involved in that, and he looked at me and stated, 'Yes, I was there.' "

. . .

Elstad was transported to the Sheriff's headquarters and approximately one hour later, Officers Burke and McAllister joined him in McAllister's office. McAllister then advised respondent for the first time of his *Miranda* rights, reading from a standard card. Respondent indicated he understood his rights, and, having these rights in mind, wished to speak with the officers. Elstad gave a full statement, explaining that he had known that the Gross family was out of town and had been paid to lead several acquaintances to the Gross residence and show them how to gain entry through a defective sliding glass door. The statement was typed, reviewed by respondent, read back to him for correction, initialed and signed by Elstad and both officers. As an afterthought, Elstad added and initialed the sentence, "After leaving the house Robby & I went back to [the] van & Robby handed me a small bag of grass.". . . Respondent concedes that the officers made no threats or promises either at his residence or at the Sheriff's office.

Respondent was charged with first-degree burglary. He was represented at trial by retained counsel. Elstad waived his right to a jury and his case was tried by a Circuit Court Judge. Respondent moved at once to suppress his oral statement and signed confession. He contended that the statement he made in response to questioning at his house "let the cat out of the bag," citing *United States v. Bayer* (1947), and tainted the subsequent confession as "fruit of the poisonous tree," citing *Wong Sun v. United States* (1963). The judge ruled that the statement, "I was there," had to be excluded because the defendant had not been advised of his *Miranda* rights. The written confession taken after Elstad's arrival at the Sheriff's office, however, was admitted in evidence. . . . Elstad was found guilty of burglary in the first degree. He received a 5-year sentence and was ordered to pay $18,000 in restitution. . . .

. . . The Court of Appeals reversed respondent's conviction, identifying the crucial constitutional inquiry as "whether there was a sufficient break in the stream of events between [the] inadmissible statement and the written confession to insulate the latter statement from the effect of what went before." . . .

The Fifth Amendment prohibits use by the prosecution in its case in chief only of *compelled* testimony. Failure to administer *Miranda* warnings creates a presumption of compulsion. Consequently, unwarned statements that are otherwise voluntary within the meaning of the Fifth Amendment must nevertheless be excluded from evidence under *Miranda*. Thus, in the individual case, *Miranda's* preventive medicine provides a remedy even to the defendant who has suffered no identifiable constitutional harm. . . .

If errors are made by law enforcement officers in administering the prophylactic *Miranda* procedures, they should not breed the same irremediable consequences as police infringement of the Fifth Amendment itself. It is an unwarranted extension of *Miranda* to hold that a simple failure to administer the warnings, unaccompanied by any actual coercion or other circumstances calculated to undermine the suspect's ability to exercise his free will so taints the investigatory process that a subsequent voluntary and informed waiver is ineffective for some indeterminate period. . . .

. . . In these circumstances, a careful and thorough administration of *Miranda* warnings serves to cure the condition that rendered the unwarned statement inadmissible. The warning conveys the relevant information and thereafter the suspect's choice whether to exercise his privilege to remain silent should ordinarily be viewed as an "act of free will." . . .

The Oregon court nevertheless identified a subtle form of lingering compulsion, the psychological impact of the suspect's conviction that he has let the cat out of the bag and, in so doing, has sealed his own fate. . . .

This Court has never held that the psychological impact of voluntary disclosure of a guilty secret qualifies as state compulsion or compromises the voluntariness of a subsequent informed waiver. The Oregon court, by adopting this expansive view of Fifth Amendment compulsion, effectively immunizes a suspect who responds to pre-*Miranda* warning questions from the consequences of his subsequent informed waiver of the privilege of remaining silent. . . .

We must conclude that, absent deliberately coercive or improper tactics in obtaining the initial statement, the mere fact that a suspect has made an unwarned admission does not warrant a presumption of compulsion. A subsequent administration of *Miranda* warnings to a suspect who has given a voluntary but unwarned statement ordinarily should suffice to remove the conditions that precluded admission of the earlier statement. In such circumstances, the finder of fact may reasonably conclude that the suspect made a rational and intelligent choice whether to waive or invoke his rights.

Though belated, the reading of respondent's rights was undeniably complete. McAllister testified that he read the *Miranda* warnings aloud from a printed card and recorded Elstad's responses. There is no question that respondent knowingly and voluntarily waived his right to remain silent before he described his participation in the burglary. It is also beyond dispute that respondent's earlier remark was voluntary, within the meaning of the Fifth Amendment. Neither the environment nor the manner of either "interrogation" was coercive. The initial conversation took place at midday, in the living room area of respondent's own home, with his mother in the kitchen area, a few steps away. . . .

Respondent, however, has argued that he was unable to give a fully *informed* waiver of his rights because he was unaware that his prior statement could not be used against him. Respondent suggests that Deputy McAllister, to cure this deficiency, should have added an additional warning to those given him at the Sheriff's office. Such a requirement is neither practicable nor constitutionally necessary. In many cases, a breach of *Miranda* procedures may not be identified as such until long after full *Miranda* warnings are administered and a valid confession obtained. . . .

This Court has never embraced the theory that a defendant's ignorance of the full consequences of his decisions vitiates their voluntariness. . . . Thus we have not held that the *sine qua non* for a knowing and voluntary waiver of the right to remain silent is a full and complete appreciation of all of the consequences flowing from the nature and the quality of the evidence in the case. . . .

The Court today in no way retreats from the bright line rule of *Miranda*. We do not imply that good faith excuses a failure to administer *Miranda* warnings; nor do we condone inherently coercive police tactics or methods offensive to due process that render the initial admission involuntary and undermine the suspect's will to invoke his rights once they are read to him. A handful of courts has, however, applied our precedents relating to confessions obtained under coercive circumstances to situations involving wholly voluntary admissions, requiring a passage of time or break in events before a second, fully warned statement can be deemed voluntary. Far from establishing a rigid rule, we direct courts to avoid one; there is no warrant for presuming coercive effect where the suspect's initial inculpatory statement, though technically in violation of *Miranda,* was voluntary. The relevant inquiry is whether, in fact, the second statement was also voluntarily made. As in any such inquiry, the finder of fact must examine the surrounding circumstances and the entire course of police conduct with respect to the suspect in evaluating the voluntariness of his statements. The fact that a suspect chooses to speak after being informed of his rights is, of course, highly probative. . . .

The judgment of the Court of Appeals of Oregon is reversed, and the case is remanded for further proceedings not inconsistent with this opinion.

It is so ordered.

JUSTICE BRENNAN, with whom JUSTICE MARSHALL joins, dissenting. . . .

The threshold question is this: What effect should an admission or confession of guilt obtained in violation of an accused's *Miranda* rights be presumed to have upon the voluntariness of subsequent confessions that are preceded by *Miranda* warnings? Relying on the "cat out of the bag" analysis of *United States* v. *Bayer* . . . the Oregon Court of Appeals held that the first confession presumptively taints subsequent confessions in such circumstances. . . .

If this Court's reversal of the judgment below reflected mere disagreement with the Oregon court's

application of the "cat out of the bag" presumption to the particular facts of this case, the outcome, while clearly erroneous, would be of little lasting consequence. But the Court rejects the "cat out of the bag" presumption *entirely* and instead adopts a new rule presuming that "ordinarily" there is *no* causal connection between a confession extracted in violation of *Miranda* and a subsequent confession preceded by the usual *Miranda* warnings. . . .

The Court's marble-palace psychoanalysis is tidy, but it flies in the face of our own precedents, demonstrates a startling unawareness of the realities of police interrogation, and is completely out of tune with the experience of state and federal courts over the last 20 years. Perhaps the Court has grasped some psychological truth that has eluded persons far more experienced in these matters; if so, the Court owes an explanation of how so many could have been so wrong for so many years. . . .

The correct approach, administered for almost 20 years by most courts with no untoward results, is to presume that an admission or confession obtained in violation of *Miranda* taints a subsequent confession unless the prosecution can show that the taint is so attenuated as to justify admission of the subsequent confession. . . .

How can the Court possibly expect the authorities to obey *Miranda* when they have every incentive now to interrogate suspects without warnings or an effective waiver, knowing that the fruits of such interrogations "ordinarily" will be admitted, that an admissible subsequent confession "ordinarily" can be obtained simply by reciting the *Miranda* warnings shortly after the first has been procured and asking the accused to repeat himself, and that unless the accused can demonstrate otherwise his confession will be viewed as an "act of free will" in response to "legitimate law enforcement activity"? . . . By condoning such a result, the Court today encourages practices that threaten to reduce *Miranda* to a mere "form of words." . . .

VI. CAPITAL PUNISHMENT

Gregg v. Georgia
428 U.S. 153, 96 S.Ct. 2909, 49 L.Ed. 2d 859 (1976)

Furman v. *Georgia* (1972) held that, under Georgia's statutes, capital punishment constituted "cruel and unusual punishment" because juries had untrammeled discretion to impose or withhold the penalty. Georgia's amended statutory scheme, expressly drawn to meet the Court's objections, was sustained by the state supreme court. The United States Supreme Court affirmed. Although unable to join in an opinion, seven justices agreed that imposition of the death penalty for murder cases does not violate the Eighth and Fourteenth Amendments. Majority: Stewart, Blackmun, Burger, Powell, Rehnquist, Stevens, White. Dissenting: Brennan, Marshall.

Judgment of the Court, and opinion of MR. JUSTICE STEWART, MR. JUSTICE POWELL, and MR. JUSTICE STEVENS, announced by MR. JUSTICE STEWART.

. . .

We address initially the basic contention that the punishment of death for the crime of murder is, under all circumstances, "cruel and unusual" in violation of the Eighth and Fourteenth Amendments of the Constitution. . . .

Although this issue was presented and addressed in *Furman,* it was not resolved by the Court. Four Justices would have held that capital punishment is not unconstitutional per se; two Justices would have reached the opposite conclusion; and three Justices, while agreeing that the statutes then before the Court were invalid as applied, left open the question whether such punishment may ever be imposed. We now hold that the punishment of death does not invariably violate the Constitution. . . .

It is from the foregoing precedents that the Eighth Amendment has not been regarded as a static concept. As Chief Justice Warren said, in an oft-quoted phrase, "[the] amendment must draw its meaning from the evolving standards of decency that mark the progress of a maturing society." . . . Thus, an assessment of contemporary values concerning the infliction of a challenged sanction is relevant to the application of the Eighth Amendment. As we develop below more fully, this as-

sessment does not call for a subjective judgment. It requires, rather, that we look to objective indicia that reflect the public attitude toward a given sanction. . . .

But our cases also make clear that public perceptions of standards of decency with respect to criminal sanctions are not conclusive. A penalty also must accord with "the dignity of man," which is the "basic concept underlying the Eighth Amendment." . . . This means, at least, that the punishment not be "excessive." When a form of punishment in the abstract (in this case, whether capital punishment may ever be imposed as a sanction for murder) rather than in the particular (the propriety of death as a penalty to be applied to a specific defendant for a specific crime) is under consideration, the inquiry into "excessiveness" has two aspects. First, the punishment must not involve the unnecessary and wanton infliction of pain. Second, the punishment must not be grossly out of proportion to the severity of the crime. . . .

Of course, the requirements of the Eighth Amendment must be applied with an awareness of the limited role to be played by the courts. This does not mean that judges have no role to play, for the Eighth Amendment is a restraint upon the exercise of legislative power. . . .

The petitioners in the capital case before the Court today renew the "standards of decency" argument, but developments during the four years since *Furman* have undercut substantially the assumptions upon which their argument rested. Despite the continuing debate, dating back to the 19th century, over the morality and utility of capital punishment, it is now evident that a large proportion of American society continues to regard it as an appropriate and necessary sanction.

The most marked indication of society's endorsement of the death penalty for murder is the legislative response to *Furman*. The legislatures of at least 35 states have enacted new statutes that provide for the death penalty for at least some crimes that result in the death of another person. And the Congress of the United States, in 1974, enacted a statute providing the death penalty for aircraft piracy that results in death. . . .

. . . We now consider specifically whether the sentence of death for the crime of murder is a per se violation of the Eighth and Fourteenth Amendments to the Constitution. . . . We note first that history and precedent strongly support a negative answer to this question. . . .

It is apparent from the text of the Constitution itself that the existence of capital punishment was accepted by the framers. At the time the Eighth Amendment was ratified, capital punishment was a common sanction in every state. Indeed, the first Congress of the United States enacted legislation providing death as the penalty for specified crimes. . . .

For nearly two centuries, this Court, repeatedly and often expressly, has recognized that capital punishment is not invalid per se. . . .

Four years ago, the petitioners in *Furman* and its companion cases predicated their argument primarily upon the asserted proposition that standards of decency had evolved to the point where capital punishment no longer could be tolerated. The petitioners in those cases said, in effect, that the evolutionary process had come to an end, and that standards of decency required that the Eighth Amendment be construed finally as prohibiting capital punishment for any crime regardless of its depravity and impact on society. . . .

Although some of the studies suggest that the death penalty may not function as a significantly greater deterrent than lesser penalties, there is no convincing empirical evidence either supporting or refuting this view. We may nevertheless assume safely that there are murderers, such as those who act in passion, for whom the threat of death has little or no deterrent effect. But for many others, the death penalty undoubtedly is a significant deterrent. There are carefully contemplated murders, such as murder for hire, where the possible penalty of death may well enter into the cold calculus that precedes the decision to act. And there are some categories of murder, such as murder by a life prisoner, where other sanctions may not be adequate. . . .

In sum, we cannot say that the judgment of the Georgia Legislature that capital punishment may be necessary in some cases is clearly wrong. Considerations of federalism, as well as respect for the ability of a legislature to evaluate, in terms of its particular state the moral consensus concerning the death penalty and its social utility as a sanction, require us to conclude, in the absence of more convincing evidence, that the infliction of death as a punishment for murder is not without justification and thus is not unconstitutionally severe.

Finally, we must consider whether the punishment of death is disproportionate in relation to the crime for which it is imposed. There is no question that death as a punishment is unique in its severity and irrevocability. . . . When a defendant's life is at stake, the Court has been particularly sensitive to insure that every safeguard is observed. . . .

But we are concerned here only with the imposition of capital punishment for the crime of murder, and when a life has been taken deliberately by the offender, we cannot say that the punishment is invariably disproportionate to the crime. It is an extreme sanction, suitable to the most extreme of crimes.

We hold that the death penalty is not a form of punishment that may never be imposed, regardless of the circumstances of the offense, regardless of the character of the offender, and regardless of the procedure followed in reaching the decision to impose it.

We now consider whether Georgia may impose the death penalty on the petitioner in this case. . . .

The basic concern of *Furman* centered on those defendants who were being condemned to death capriciously and arbitrarily. Under the procedures before the Court in that case, sentencing authorities were not directed to give attention to the nature or circumstances of the crime committed or to the character or record of the defendant. Left unguided, juries imposed the death sentence in a way that could only be called freakish. The new Georgia sentencing procedures, by contrast, focus the jury's attention on the particularized nature of the crime and the particularized characteristics of the individual defendant. While the jury is permitted to consider any aggravating or mitigating circumstances, it must find and identify at least one statutory aggravating factor before it may impose a penalty of death. In this way the jury's discretion is channeled. No longer can a jury wantonly and freakishly impose the death sentence; it is always circumscribed by the legislative guidelines. In addition, the review function of the Supreme Court of Georgia affords additional assurance that the concerns that prompted our decision in *Furman* are not present to any significant degree in the Georgia procedure applied here.

For the reasons expressed in this opinion, we hold that the statutory system under which Gregg was sentenced to death does not violate the Constitution. Accordingly, the judgment of the Georgia Supreme Court is affirmed.

It is so ordered.

MR. JUSTICE BRENNAN, dissenting. . . .

This Court inescapably has the duty, as the ultimate arbiter of the meaning of our Constitution, to say whether, when individuals condemned to death stand before our bar, "moral concepts" require us to hold that the law has progressed to the point where we should declare that the punishment of death, like punishments on the rack, the screw and the wheel, is no longer morally tolerable in our civilized society. My opinion in *Furman* concluded that our civilization and the law had progressed to this point and therefore the punishment of death, for whatever crime and under all circumstances, is "cruel and unusual" in violation of the Eighth and Fourteenth Amendments of the Constitution. I shall not again canvass the reasons that led to that conclusion. I emphasize only that foremost among the "moral concepts" recognized in our cases and inherent in the clause is the primary moral principle that the state, even as it punishes, must treat its citizens in a manner consistent with their intrinsic worth as human beings—a punishment must not be so severe as to be degrading to human dignity. . . .

MR. JUSTICE MARSHALL, dissenting. . . .

Since the decision in *Furman*, the legislatures of 35 states have enacted new statutes authorizing the imposition of the death sentence for certain crimes, and Congress has enacted a law providing the death penalty for air piracy resulting in death. I would be less than candid if I did not acknowledge that these developments have a significant bearing on a realistic assessment of the moral acceptability of the death penalty to the American people. But if the constitutionality of the death penalty turns, as I have urged, on the opinion of an *informed* citizenry, then even the enactment of new death statutes cannot be viewed as conclusive. In *Furman*, I observed that the American people are largely unaware of the information critical to a judgment on the morality of the death penalty, and concluded that if they were better informed they would consider it shocking, unjust, and unacceptable. . . .

There remains for consideration, however, what might be termed the purely retributive justification for the death penalty—that the death penalty is appropriate, not because of its beneficial effect on society, but because the taking of the murderer's life is itself morally good. Some of the language of the plurality's opinion appears positively to embrace this notion of retribution for its own sake as a justification for capital punishment. . . .

. . . To be sustained under the Eighth Amendment, the death penalty must "[comport] with the basic concept of human dignity at the core of the amendment"; the objective in imposing it must be "[consistent] with our respect for the dignity of other men." Under these standards, the taking of life "because the wrongdoer deserves it" surely must fall, for such a punishment has as its very basis the total denial of the wrongdoer's dignity and worth.

The death penalty, unnecessary to promote the goal of deterrence or to further any legitimate notion of retribution, is an excessive penalty forbidden by the Eighth and Fourteenth Amendments. I respectfully dissent from the Court's judgment upholding the sentences of death imposed upon the petitioners in these cases.

McCleskey v. Kemp
481 U.S. 279, 107 S.Ct. 1756, 95 L.Ed. 2d 262 (1987)

In 1978 Warren McCleskey, a black man, was convicted of murder and sentenced to death in Superior Court of Fulton County, Georgia. He had been charged with the killing of a white police officer during the robbery of a furniture store. On appeal, the Georgia Supreme Court affirmed, and the United States Supreme Court denied certiorari. McCleskey then filed a petition for a writ of habeas corpus in state court. Relief was denied, the state supreme court affirmed, and again the United States Supreme Court denied certiorari. McCleskey next filed a petition for a writ of habeas corpus in United States district court. Among his claims was that the capital sentencing process in Georgia was administered in a racially discriminatory manner in violation of the Eighth and Fourteenth Amendments. In support, counsel put forth a statistical study by David C. Baldus, George Woodworth, and Charles Pulanski ["Comparative Review of Death Sentences: An Empirical Study of the Georgia Experience," 74 *Journal of Criminal Law and Criminology* 661 (1983)]. The study examined more than 2,000 murder cases in Georgia in the 1970s. Dividing the cases according to the combination of the race of the defendant and the race of the victim, the authors found that the death penalty was imposed in 22 percent of the cases involving a black defendant and a white victim, 8 percent of the cases with a white defendant and a white victim, 1 percent of the cases with a black defendant and a black victim, and 3 percent of the cases with a white defendant and a black victim. In further analysis, taking account of 39 nonracial variables, the authors showed that defendants charged with killing whites were 4.3 times as likely to receive the death sentence as those charged with killing blacks. McCleskey's counsel contended that black defendants who kill white victims have the greatest likelihood of receiving the death penalty.

In 1984 the district court questioned the study's methodology and concluded that the "statistics do not demonstrate a prima facie case in support of the contention that the death penalty was imposed upon him because of his race, because of the race of the victim, or because of any Eighth Amendment concern." In 1985 the Court of Appeals for the Eleventh Circuit, sitting *en banc*, assumed the validity of the study but found it "insufficient to demonstrate discriminatory intent or unconstitutional discrimination . . . [and] insufficient to show irrationality, arbitrariness and capriciousness under any kind of Eighth Amendment analysis." (Note: Racial discrimination is one of the topics covered in Chapter Twelve.) Majority: Powell, O'Connor, Rehnquist, Scalia, White. Dissenting: Brennan, Blackmun, Marshall, Stevens.

JUSTICE POWELL delivered the opinion of the Court.

This case presents the question whether a complex statistical study that indicates a risk that racial considerations enter into capital sentencing determinations proves that petitioner McCleskey's capital sentence is unconstitutional under the Eighth or Fourteenth Amendment. . . .

Our analysis begins with the basic principle that a defendant who alleges an equal protection violation has the burden of proving "the existence of purposeful discrimination." A corollary to this principle is that a criminal defendant must prove that the purposeful discrimination "had a discriminatory effect" on him. . . . Thus, to prevail under the Equal Protection Clause, McCleskey must prove that the decisionmakers in *his* case acted with discriminatory purpose. He offers no evidence specific to his own case that would support an inference that racial considerations played a part in his sentence. Instead, he relies solely on the Baldus study. McCleskey argues that the Baldus study compels an inference that his sentence rests on purposeful discrimination. McCleskey's claim that these statistics are sufficient proof of discrimination, without regard to the facts of a particular case, would extend to all capital cases in Georgia, at least where the victim was white and the defendant is black. . . .

Finally, McCleskey's statistical proffer must be viewed in the context of his challenge. McCleskey challenges decisions at the heart of the State's criminal justice system. "[O]ne of society's most basic tasks is that of protecting the lives of its citizens and one of the most basic ways in which it achieves the task is through criminal laws against murder." Implementation of these laws necessarily requires discretionary judgments. Because discretion is essential to the criminal justice process, we would demand exceptionally clear proof before we would infer that the discretion has been abused. The unique nature of the decisions at issue in this case also counsel against adopting such an inference from the disparities indicated by the Baldus study. Accordingly, we hold that the Baldus study is clearly insufficient to support an inference that any of the decisionmakers in McCleskey's case acted with discriminatory purpose. . . .

McCleskey also suggests that the Baldus study proves that the State as a whole has acted with a discriminatory purpose. He appears to argue that the State has violated the Equal Protection Clause by adopting the capital punishment statute and allowing it to remain in force despite its allegedly discriminatory application. . . .

As legislatures necessarily have wide discretion in the choice of criminal laws and penalties, and as there were legitimate reasons for the Georgia Legislature to adopt and maintain capital punishment . . . we will not infer a discriminatory purpose on the part of the State of Georgia. Accordingly, we reject McCleskey's equal protection claims.

McCleskey also argues that the Baldus study

demonstrates that the Georgia capital sentencing system violates the Eighth Amendment. We begin our analysis of this claim by reviewing the restrictions on death sentences established by our prior decisions under that Amendment. . . .

In sum, our decisions since *Furman* have identified a constitutionally permissible range of discretion in imposing the death penalty. First, there is a required threshold below which the death penalty cannot be imposed. In this context, the State must establish rational criteria that narrow the decisionmaker's judgment as to whether the circumstances of a particular defendant's case meet the threshold. Moreover, a societal consensus that the death penalty is disproportionate to a particular offense prevents a State from imposing the death penalty for that offense. Second, States cannot limit the sentencer's consideration of any relevant circumstance that could cause it to decline to impose the penalty. In this respect, the State cannot channel the sentencer's discretion, but must allow it to consider any relevant information offered by the defendant.

In light of our precedents under the Eighth Amendment, McCleskey cannot argue successfully that his sentence is "disproportionate to the crime in the traditional sense.". . .

On the other hand, he cannot base a constitutional claim on an argument that his case differs from other cases in which defendants *did* receive the death penalty. . . .

On the other hand, absent a showing that the Georgia capital punishment system operates in an arbitrary and capricious manner, McCleskey cannot prove a constitutional violation by demonstrating that other defendants who may be similarly situated did *not* receive the death penalty. In *Gregg*, the Court confronted the argument that "the opportunities for discretionary action that are inherent in the processing of any murder case under Georgia law," specifically the opportunities for discretionary leniency, rendered the capital sentences imposed arbitrary and capricious. We rejected this contention. . . .

Because McCleskey's sentence was imposed under Georgia sentencing procedures that focus discretion "on the particularized nature of the crime and the particularized characteristics of the individual defendant," we lawfully may presume that McCleskey's death sentence was not "wantonly and freakishly" imposed, and thus that the sentence is not disproportionate within any recognized meaning under the Eighth Amendment.

Although our decision in *Gregg* as to the facial validity of the Georgia capital punishment statute appears to foreclose McCleskey's disproportionality argument, he further contends that the Georgia capital punishment system is arbitrary and capricious in *application,* and therefore his sentence is excessive, because racial considerations may influence capital sentencing decisions in Georgia. We now address this claim.

To evaluate McCleskey's challenge, we must examine exactly what the Baldus study may show. Even Professor Baldus does not contend that his statistics *prove* that race enters into any capital sentencing decisions or that race was a factor in McCleskey's particular case. Statistics at most may show only a likelihood that a particular factor entered into some decisions. There is, of course, some risk of racial prejudice influencing a jury's decision in a criminal case. There are similar risks that other kinds of prejudice will influence other criminal trials. The question "is at what point that risk becomes constitutionally unacceptable." McCleskey asks us to accept the likelihood allegedly shown by the Baldus study as the constitutional measure of an unacceptable risk of racial prejudice influencing capital sentencing decisions. This we decline to do. . . .

At most, the Baldus study indicates a discrepancy that appears to correlate with race. Apparent disparities in sentencing are an inevitable part of our criminal justice system. . . .

Where the discretion that is fundamental to our criminal process is involved, we decline to assume that what is unexplained is invidious. In light of the safeguards designed to minimize racial bias in the process, the fundamental value of jury trial in our criminal justice system, and the benefits that discretion provides to criminal defendants, we hold that the Baldus study does not demonstrate a constitutionally significant risk of racial bias affecting the Georgia capital-sentencing process. . . .

Two additional concerns inform our decision in this case. First, McCleskey's claim, taken to its logical conclusion, throws into serious question the principles that underlie our entire criminal justice system. The Eighth Amendment is not limited in application to capital punishment, but applies to all penalties. Thus, if we accepted McCleskey's claim that racial bias has impermissibly tainted the capital

sentencing decision, we could soon be faced with similar claims as to other types of penalty. . . .

Second, McCleskey's arguments are best presented to the legislative bodies. It is not the responsibility—or indeed even the right—of this Court to determine the appropriate punishment for particular crimes. It is the legislatures, the elected representatives of the people, that are "constituted to respond to the will and consequently the moral values of the people." . . . Capital punishment is now the law in more than two thirds of our States. It is the ultimate duty of courts to determine on a case-by-case basis whether these laws are applied consistently with the Constitution. Despite McCleskey's wide ranging arguments that basically challenge the validity of capital punishment in our multi-racial society, the only question before us is whether in his case, the law of Georgia was properly applied. We agree with the District Court and the Court of Appeals for the Eleventh Circuit that this was carefully and correctly done in this case.

Accordingly, we affirm the judgment of the Court of Appeals for the Eleventh Circuit.

It is so ordered.

JUSTICE BRENNAN, with whom JUSTICE MARSHALL joins, and with whom JUSTICE BLACKMUN and JUSTICE STEVENS join in part, dissenting. . . .

It is important to emphasize at the outset that the Court's observation that McCleskey cannot prove the influence of race on any particular sentencing decision is irrelevant in evaluating his Eighth Amendment claim. Since *Furman* v. *Georgia,* the Court has been concerned with the risk of the imposition of an arbitrary sentence, rather than the proven fact of one. . . .

Defendants challenging their death sentences thus never have had to prove that impermissible considerations have actually infected sentencing decisions. We have required instead that they establish that the system under which they were sentenced posed a significant risk of such an occurrence. McCleskey's claim does differ, however, in one respect from these earlier cases: it is the first to base a challenge not on speculation about how a system *might* operate, but on empirical documentation of how it *does* operate. . . .

McCleskey's statistics have particular force because most of them are the product of sophisticated multiple-regression analysis. Such analysis is designed precisely to identify patterns in the aggregate, even though we may not be able to reconstitute with certainty any individual decision that goes to make up that pattern. Multiple-regression analysis is particularly well-suited to identify the influence of impermissible considerations in sentencing, since it is able to control for permissible factors that may explain an apparent arbitrary pattern. . . .

The Court cites four reasons for shrinking from the implications of McCleskey's evidence: the desirability of discretion for actors in the criminal-justice system, the existence of statutory safeguards against abuse of that discretion, the potential consequences for broader challenges to criminal sentencing, and an understanding of the contours of the judicial role. While these concerns underscore the need for sober deliberation, they do not justify rejecting evidence as convincing as McCleskey has presented.

The Court maintains that petitioner's claim "is antithetical to the fundamental role of discretion in our criminal justice system." It states that "[w]here the discretion that is fundamental to our criminal process is involved, we decline to assume that what is unexplained is invidious."

Reliance on race in imposing capital punishment, however, is antithetical to the very rationale for granting sentencing discretion. Discretion is a means, not an end. It is bestowed in order to permit the sentencer to "trea[t] each defendant in a capital case with that degree of respect due the uniqueness of the individual." . . .

The Court also declines to find McCleskey's evidence sufficient in view of "the safeguards designed to minimize racial bias in the [capital sentencing] process." . . .

It has now been over 13 years since Georgia adopted the provisions upheld in *Gregg*. Professor Baldus and his colleagues have compiled data on almost 2500 homicides committed during the period 1973–1979. They have taken into account the influence of 230 nonracial variables, using a multitude of data from the State itself, and have produced striking evidence that the odds of being sentenced to death are significantly greater than average if a defendant is black or his or her victim is white. The challenge to the Georgia system is not speculative or theoretical; it is empirical. . . .

The Court next states that its unwillingness to regard the petitioner's evidence as sufficient is based in part on the fear that recognition of McCleskey's

claim would open the door to widespread challenges to all aspects of criminal sentencing. Taken on its face, such a statement seems to suggest a fear of too much justice. . . .

In fairness, the Court's fear that McCleskey's claim is an invitation to descend a slippery slope also rests on the realization that any humanly imposed system of penalties will exhibit some imperfection. Yet to reject McCleskey's powerful evidence on this basis is to ignore both the qualitatively different character of the death penalty and the particular repugnance of racial discrimination, considerations which may properly be taken into account in determining whether various punishments are "cruel and unusual." Furthermore, it fails to take account of the unprecedented refinement and strength of the Baldus study. . . .

Certainly, a factor that we would regard as morally irrelevant, such as hair color, at least theoretically could be associated with sentencing results to such an extent that we would regard as arbitrary a system in which that factor played a significant role. The evaluation of evidence suggesting such a correlation must be informed not merely by statistics, but by history and experience. One could hardly contend that this nation has on the basis of hair color inflicted upon persons deprivation comparable to that imposed on the basis of race. Recognition of this fact would necessarily influence the evaluation of data suggesting the influence of hair color on sentencing, and would require evidence of statistical correlation even more powerful than that presented by the Baldus study. . . .

Finally, the Court justifies its rejection of McCleskey's claim by cautioning against usurpation of the legislatures' role in devising and monitoring criminal punishment. . . .

Those whom we would banish from society or from the human community itself often speak in too faint a voice to be heard above society's demand for punishment. It is the particular role of courts to hear these voices, for the Constitution declares that the majoritarian chorus may not alone dictate the conditions of social life. The Court thus fulfills, rather than disrupts, the scheme of separation of powers by closely scrutinizing the imposition of the death penalty, for no decision of a society is more deserving of the "sober second thought."

TEN

First Amendment Freedoms

*The Bill of Rights changed the original Constitution
into a new charter under which no branch of government
could abridge the people's freedoms of press, speech, religion, and assembly.*

—JUSTICE HUGO L. BLACK (1971)

The American political tradition has always been opposed to unlimited government power, and the Bill of Rights represents one of the "auxiliary precautions" against its emergence. In particular, the First Amendment is fundamental—free speech, free press, and the right of assembly make possible a continuing debate on issues large and small, without which the electoral process becomes an empty ritual. The free exercise of religion and the separation of church and state represent the American solution to one of the basic issues in the Western political tradition—the proper relation of state and church, of individuals to their God and their government. The religion clauses are central to the protection of religious beliefs and to the maintenance of civil peace in a religiously diverse culture.

THE NATIONALIZATION OF THE FIRST AMENDMENT

One of the most spectacular developments in American constitutional law has been the Supreme Court's expansion of the due process clause in the Fourteenth Amendment to include the Bill of Rights guarantees (see Chapter Nine). For the First Amendment, the change began when Justice McKenna (*Gilbert* v. *Minnesota,* 1920) assumed for the sake of argument that freedom of speech guaranteed in the First Amendment was applicable to state action. Justice Brandeis was more forthright: "I cannot believe," he declared, after citing a number of cases in which due process had been used to protect property rights, "that the liberty guaranteed by the Fourteenth Amendment includes only liberty to acquire and enjoy property."

371

This judicial about-face continued in *Gitlow* v. *New York* (1925). Gitlow had been convicted under the New York Criminal Anarchy Act of 1902 of circulating pamphlets urging workers to revolutionary mass action and "dictatorship of the proletariat." In Gitlow's defense his counsel argued that the New York statute deprived him of "liberty" without due process of law. Though the Court ruled that the 1902 act, as applied to Gitlow, did not unduly restrict freedom of speech or press, it accepted the view that the freedoms guaranteed in the First Amendment are safeguarded by the due process clause of the Fourteenth Amendment.

Incorporation of other First Amendment rights followed. In 1931 the Supreme Court voted 5 to 4 that freedom of the press is within the protection of the "liberty" guaranteed in the Fourteenth Amendment (*Near* v. *Minnesota*); in 1937 the right of peaceable assembly was included (*DeJonge* v. *Oregon*); and in 1940 the free exercise clause was used to invalidate a Connecticut statute requiring a permit of all solicitors for religious or charitable causes (*Cantwell* v. *Connecticut*). Then in 1947, the Court, while upholding 5 to 4 a New Jersey act providing bus service to all children attending public and parochial schools, served notice that the First Amendment provision denying to Congress the power to pass laws respecting establishment of religion was within the scope of the Fourteenth Amendment and was intended to create a "wall of separation" between church and state (*Everson* v. *Board of Education*). These rights in turn bred another in 1958: association. "It is beyond debate," declared the second Justice Harlan in *NAACP* v. *Alabama* (1958) "that freedom to engage in association for the advancement of beliefs and ideas is an inseparable aspect of the 'liberty' assured by the Due Process Clause of the Fourteenth Amendment, which embraces freedom of speech. . . ." As a result of these and other cases of similar import, all the rights of the First Amendment have been absorbed into the due process clause of the Fourteenth and now receive protection in federal courts against adverse action by the states or the national government. Expanded coverage of the First Amendment followed from the Court's recognition that free expression is vital to democratic politics.

THE TESTS OF FREEDOM

First Amendment freedoms confront the Court with a difficult task, one that is not present in all cases of judicial review. Where enumerated powers of Congress or the president are subject to interpretation, the Court's function is at an end when the action taken is found to be within the limits of constitutionally granted power. In reaching such a conclusion the Court is immeasurably aided by the well-established presumption of constitutionality that accompanies most legislative and executive actions.

In cases involving freedom of speech, of press, or of religion, the Court must interpret and apply a grant of power—frequently the "reserved" police power of the state—while at the same time it must interpret and apply a constitutional limitation on government power. Governments must have police power to maintain themselves against attacks from within, just as they must have military power to resist attacks from without. On the other hand, the Court is aware that unlimited government power negates the freedom the political system is designed to protect. Thus, the easy path to constitutional decision by way of presumption of constitutionality of legislative or administrative action is not readily available in this field.

When confronted with clashes between individual freedom and state power, the Court has formulated tests. Whatever measures are used, the Court's answers depend ultimately on the justices' view of correct social policy and their conception of the role of the judiciary in achieving balance between freedom and order. By 1925 the Court had two tests for First Amendment cases—"clear and present danger" (that seemed to express a preference for free speech) and "bad tendency" (a test more favorable to legislative action). Each emerged from post-World War I cases involving wartime national security legislation.

In later years, the Court developed the "overbreadth doctrine" for laws that not only address behavior that may constitutionally be regulated but include constitutionally protected activity as well. In free expression cases, such laws are sometimes also struck down because they have a "chilling effect"—that is, they may deter people from engaging in activity protected by the Constitution. In the First Amendment area, the Court for similar reasons may declare a law "void for vagueness." Due process requires that individuals have fair warning of prohibited conduct. A vague statute blurs the line between legal and illegal behavior and therefore may "chill" speech by causing people to censor themselves.

INTERNAL SECURITY

During the long period between 1787 and World War I, the First Amendment served as little more than a historical reminder of the lively concern for personal freedom expressed during the nation's formative years. Since the judicial revolution of 1937 (discussed in Chapters Six and Eight), however, the First Amendment has been one of the focal points of constitutional jurisprudence.

At the inception of the national government, the Federalists thought it necessary to curb the speech of their political opponents. Under the Alien and Sedition Acts of 1798 scandalous criticism of the president or Congress with intent to bring them into disrepute was proscribed in sweeping terms. These laws, generally judged unconstitutional, were never tested because Jefferson and the Republicans feared that the Federalist Supreme Court would declare the laws valid, thus establishing an unfortunate precedent. It is noteworthy that the Federalist proponents of these laws, many of whom had played leading roles in the dramatic formulation of the Constitution, used an argument that has become a familiar defense of speech limitations. Threats to national security, they argued, made restrictions inevitable; preservation of the Consituation is more important than protection of any one right it guarantees. Obviously, this logic may be used to justify destruction of all constitutional rights.

Barring Lincoln's unofficial suppression of northern critics of government policies during the Civil War, there was no national government action raising free speech issues until World War I. In 1917 and 1918 Congress passed two laws that resulted in extensive litigation, focusing public attention on basic issues of freedom of speech in wartime. The Espionage Act of 1917 prohibited and punished interferences with recruitment or acts adversely affecting military morale.

In *Schenck* v. *United States* (1919) Justice Holmes, in upholding the act as applied to antidraft leaflets, suggested the now famous "clear and present danger" test: "The question in every case is whether the words used are used in such circumstances and are of such a nature as to create a clear and present danger that they will bring about the substantive evils that Congress has a right to prevent." Holmes's test invited more questions than it answered. Enmeshed with highly complex issues of proximity, degree, and content, it nevertheless displayed a preference for a wide latitude of speech.

The Sedition Act of 1918 went far beyond the 1917 law, making punishable speech that in World War II or the Vietnam War would have been deemed mere political comment. It singled out for punishment any "disloyal, profane, scurrilous, or abusive language about the form of government, the Constitution, soldiers and sailors, flag or uniform of the armed forces," and in addition made unlawful any "word or act [favoring] the cause of the German Empire . . . or [opposing] the cause of the United States." This law was upheld, and its application sustained, in *Abrams* v. *United States* (1919), in which pamphlets opposing the Allied (and American) intervention in Russia after the revolution were held to be within its terms. When this flurry of litigation subsided, cases involving federal action vis-à-vis First Amendment rights virtually disappeared until World War II.

In the period between World Wars I and II, the states were more active in seeking curbs against radical action, principally through efforts to outlaw criminal syndicalism of the kind involved in *Gitlow* v. *New York.* In *Whitney* v. *California* (1927), for example the majority upheld a conviction under a state criminal syndicalism law, primarily because a criminal conspiracy was not within the bounds of free speech. Of particular interest in *Whitney* is Brandeis's concurring opinion, in which he reasserted and refashioned the merits and justification of the clear-and-present-danger test.

By World War II, "clear and present danger" was the accepted test of potential harm. Applied to both state and federal laws, it became the measure of the criminality of unpopular beliefs and potentially dangerous action.

It was not until the Court was confronted with a case testing the Smith Act of 1940, Section 1 of which made it a felony to advocate the violent overthrow of the government of the United States or to conspire to organize a group advocating such violence, that the clear-and-present-danger test "bowed out." In upholding the law as applied to 11 leaders of the American Communist Party (*Dennis* v. *United States,* 1951) the Supreme Court applied the test Judge Learned Hand suggested in his Second Circuit Court of Appeals opinion: "In each case Courts must ask whether the gravity of the 'evil,' discounted by its improbability, justifies such invasion of free speech as is necessary to avoid the danger." To Chief Justice Vinson, spokesperson for the Court, the clear-and-present-danger test, although applicable to the isolated speech of individuals or small groups, was inappropriate for testing words associated with a large-scale conspiratorial movement: "The situation with which Justices Holmes and Brandeis were concerned in *Gitlow* was a comparatively isolated event, bearing little relation in their minds to any substantial threat to the safety of the community." Vinson approved the trial judge's holding that as a matter of law, defendants' alleged activities presented "a sufficient danger of a substantive evil" to justify the application of the statute under the First Amendment. The chief justice's attempt to square Judge Hand's formula with the clear-and-present-danger test was highly reminiscent of the decisions obtained earlier by application of the "bad-tendency" test.

Dennis posed the dilemma every democracy faces sooner or later: what to do about antidemocratic forces, which were they to come to power, would surely destroy democratic politics as one of the first orders of business. Should the government wait until subversive elements have committed particular criminal *acts* (as Justices Black and Douglas advocated in their *Dennis* dissents), or should the government take steps to protect the nation and its constitutional processes only on the basis of the noxious *ideas* suspected subversives preach? If the latter option is chosen, how can the nation make the content of speech a crime, given the wording of the First Amendment? Moreover, if the government moves against those who wish the nation ill, how do law-enforcement agencies cast the net without placing dissent itself in danger?

In *Yates* v. *United States* (1957), the Court was again called on to examine the scope of the Smith Act. Its decision, taking a strict view of the proof necessary to convict, made it impossible for the government to retry the *Yates* defendants and others whose trials were pending. In the light of this decision, many thought that the membership provisions of the Smith Act would be held invalid once the Court was confronted with the issues. But in *Scales* v. *United States* (1961) the Court saved the constitutionality of the challenged clause by insisting that only active and knowledgeable membership was within the act's coverage. *Scales* and *Yates* thus had the effect of requiring the government to prove more to sustain a conviction under the Smith Act. In exchange for continuing the constitutionality of the Smith Act, the justices diminished the circle of people against whom the law could realistically be expected to apply.

Dennis turned out to be the high-water mark of judicial tolerance of various state and federal devices to uncover and punish those thought to be engaged in subversive activities. In a succession of cases lasting over a decade, the Court sometimes declared such policies unconstitutional or approved them in principle but required such exacting procedures that implementation of the various policies became more difficult. The justices seemed to be saying that the First Amendment does not prevent the nation from defending itself from internal threats but that, in defending itself, the nation must be careful not to tread too heavily on First Amendment guarantees.*

The prevailing view on the Court today is set firmly against almost all restrictions that are *content-based,* as **Brandenburg v. Ohio** (1969) illustrates. This case brought yet another state criminal syndicalism law before the justices, but the defendant this time was no leftist but a member of the Ku Klux Klan. Ohio banned "advocating . . . the duty, necessity, or propriety of crime, sabotage, violence or unlawful methods of terrorism as a means of accomplishing industrial or political reform." Brandenburg notified a Cincinnati reporter of a scheduled Klan rally, and later film clips of Brandenburg's remarks were telecast on a local station and on a national network. Recorded for posterity was his speech decrying government repression of the Caucasian race and references to the possibility of revenge. Some people in the crowd carried weapons. With this as evidence, the Ohio court fined him $1,000 and sentenced him to ten years in prison. The Supreme Court reversed, saying that a state cannot proscribe "advocacy of the use of force or of law violations except when it is directed to inciting or producing imminent lawless action and is likely to incite or produce such action." *Brandenburg* sets a tough standard for government restrictions aimed at dissident groups. It means that the First Amendment, with few exceptions, now bars virtually any conviction based on what someone *says.*

SPEECH AND ASSEMBLY: THE RIGHT TO PROTEST

When the Supreme Court was confronted by state and federal laws directed against Communist Party members, it dealt with a phenomenon of national and international significance. Viewed superficially, the Court should have an easier time in dealing with various municipal ordinances and administrative actions affecting freedom of speech and assembly. In practice the task has proved far from simple.

---

* For example, in reviewing actions directed against individuals and organizations accused of being subversive, the Supreme Court voided the automatic dismissal of a professor at the City College of New York who had invoked the Fifth Amendment at a congressional committee inquiry (*Slochower v. Board of Education*, 1956), but later upheld the dismissals of a public school teacher and a subway employee who had refused to answer questions from their supervisers about their loyalty (*Beilan v. Board of Education*, 1958; *Lerner v. Casey*, 1958). The justices' reactions were mixed in cases involving denials of admission to the bar when loyalty was in doubt (*Konigsberg v. State Bar*, 1957; *In re Anastaplo*, 1961). *Pennsylvania v. Nelson* (1956) struck down state versions of the Smith Act. *Albertson v. Subversive Activities Control Board* (1965) upheld the refusal of members of the Communist Party (USA) to register under the Subversive Activities Control Act of 1950. *Keyishian v. Board of Regents* (1967) threw out a New York loyalty oath requiring a denial of Communist affiliation as a prerequisite to teaching at a state university. Similarly, in *United States v. Robel* (1967) the Court invalidated a statute that made it a crime for any member of a Communist-action organization to hold a job in a defense facility.

Brandenburg v. *Ohio* instructs that violence must be exceedingly imminent before the state may intervene, yet police are charged with protection of life and property. A decision either way is bound to be viewed as wrong by those adversely affected. Moreover, unlike free speech cases that attacked laws banning particular messages, free speech claims today often arise from the application of laws that are not explicitly content-based, but can still be applied to restrict expression of particular points of view.

Demonstrations. The pre-*Brandenburg* decision of *Feiner* v. *New York* (1951) found the Court tolerant of police discretion. Feiner was a Syracuse University student whose sidewalk oratory featured derogatory language about various public officials (including President Harry Truman) and the American Legion. A small crowd clustered around him. Unrest and threatening movements prompted a police officer to order the speaker to stop and to arrest him when he refused. The Supreme Court, with three vehement dissenters, upheld the speaker's conviction. Citing with approval a statement in *Cantwell*, Chief Justice Vinson declared, "When clear and present danger of riot, disorder, interference with traffic upon the public streets, or other immediate threat to public safety, peace, or order, appears, the power of the state to prevent or punish is obvious." In this and similar cases, the confusion of facts that usually surrounds the allegedly illegal speech makes effective review by an appellate court extremely difficult. The trial court, by accepting the official version of the incidents involved, severely handicaps a speaker who wants to appeal his or her conviction.

Twelve years later in a setting more violence-prone than *Feiner*, the Court was less willing to accept the assessment of authorities on the scene if that meant a curtailing of First Amendment rights. *Edwards* v. *South Carolina* (1963) reversed breach-of-peace convictions of black students who had gathered near the South Carolina State House to protest racial discrimination. The arrests followed the gathering of a hostile crowd and the demonstrators' rejection of a police order to disperse. Distinguishing this case from *Feiner*, the majority relied heavily on the fact that petitioners had been convicted under a breach-of-peace statute rather than under a narrowly drawn ordinance designed to regulate traffic or establish reasonable hours of access to the State House. In this case the state had made criminal (through the use of a broad breach-of-peace statute) the expression of unpopular views. *Edwards* combined with *Brandenburg* thus make it very difficult to apply such laws to those who make their views known in dramatic fashion in public places.

Fighting Words. An exception may be "fighting words." In *Chaplinsky* v. *New Hampshire* (1942) the Court unanimously upheld the conviction of a Jehovah's Witness who in a dispute with a police officer used abusive language. The Court recognized Chaplinsky's words as "likely to provoke the average person to retaliation." In the opinion of Justice Murphy, certain utterances, of which fighting words are a part, "are no essential part of any exposition of ideas and are of such slight social value as a step to truth that any benefit that may be derived from them is clearly outweighed by the social interest in order and morality."

Even here, context is important. *Cohen* v. *California* (1971) found the Court reversing the conviction of a young man who, as a method of protest, emblazoned the words "F_ _ _ the draft" on his jacket. He was arrested in a courthouse corridor and charged with "disturbing the peace." "No individual actually or likely to be present could reasonably have regarded the words . . . as a direct personal insult," wrote patrician Justice Harlan. "Nor do we have here an instance of the exercise of the State's police power to prevent a speaker from intentionally provoking a given group to hostile reaction. . . . [W]hile the particular four-letter word being litigated here is perhaps more distasteful than most others of its genre, it is nevertheless often true that one man's vulgarity is another's lyric. Indeed . . . because government officials cannot make principled distinctions in this area . . . the Constitution leaves matters of taste and style so largely to the individual."

Symbolic Speech. Increasingly, those protesting government policy resort to "symbolic speech" to make clear their position, attract attention, and influence others. "Symbolic speech" refers to various kinds of actions designed to convey a message. A constitutional question arises when the actions, stripped of any message, are themselves illegal. Are otherwise illegal actions protected by the First Amendment when they have a speech content? The Supreme Court's reaction to such claims has understandably varied, but a standard approach seems to have emerged from several cases. First, to be considered "speech" at all, there must be an intent to convey a particular message and a reasonable likelihood that the message will be understood by an audience. Second, as with parades, the justices agree that speech symbolized by conduct is subject to reasonable time, place, and manner requirements. Third, symbolic speech may be prohibited or regulated if the conduct itself can constitutionally be regulated. Fourth, the regulation must be narrowly written and must further "a substantial governmental interest." Fifth, that interest must be unrelated to suppressing free speech.

In *United States* v. *O'Brien* (1968), the Court sustained a protestor's conviction for destroying his draft card in violation of federal law. But may a state protect the flag of the United States from defacement? In *Spence* v. *Washington* (1974), six justices were willing to regard as protected expression the display of an American flag to which had been affixed a peace symbol, even though a Washington State statute prohibited the exhibition of the flag of the United States with any attached figures or symbols. For most, said the Court, "the flag is a symbol of patriotism, of pride in the history of our country, and of the service, sacrifice, and valor of . . . millions of Americans. . . . " Even so, "we are confronted . . . with a case of prosecution for the expression of an idea through activity. . . . Given the protected character of his expression and in light of the fact that no interest the State may have in preserving the physical integrity of a privately owned flag was significantly impaired on these facts, the conviction must be invalidated."

Proper Forums. Closely related to conflicts over symbolic speech are efforts to draw the line between permissible and prohibited forums for the expression of ideas. The First Amendment protects "assembly" along with speech. So where may one constitutionally assemble?

A permissive answer came in *Brown* v. *Louisiana* (1966). Justice Fortas's plurality opinion made clear that the rights of free speech "are not confined to verbal expression," as the Court voted to overturn the convictions of five black males who protested the racial segregation of public library facilities in a Louisiana town by refusing to leave the library when asked. Their "speech" consisted of a "silent and reproachful presence."

Justice Black, normally a defender of First Amendment freedoms, had a different view. "Though the First Amendment guarantees the right of assembly . . . it does not guarantee to any person the right to use someone else's property, even that owned by government and dedicated to other purposes, as a stage to express dissident ideas."

Has Justice Black's position in *Brown* become the law of the land? ***Clark*** v. ***Community for Creative Non-Violence*** (1984) involved a different kind of silent protest—sleeping. The Park Service issued a permit to CCNV to stage a protest in Lafayette Park and the Mall in Washington, D.C., against Reagan administration policies regarding the homeless. But Park Service regulations banned camping and sleeping except in designated camping areas. CCNV maintained that sleeping was an integral part of the message it wanted to convey. Ruling against CCNV's position that sleeping across the street from the White House was symbolic expression protected by the First Amendment, the majority questioned whether the First Amendment even requires the Park Service to permit demonstrations of any kind in those park areas, which are "unique resources that the Federal Government holds in trust for the American people."

Picketing. Picketing is a special kind of symbolic expression that involves problems of the proper forum as well. To what extent does the Constitution protect one's right to advertise the facts of a labor dispute and to discourage public contact with the "struck" enterprise?

In 1940 peaceful picketing was brought under the protection of freedom of speech (*Thornhill* v. *Alabama*). In *Amalgamated Food Employees* v. *Logan Valley Plaza* (1968) the Court sustained the right of petitioners to picket at a privately owned shopping center. The majority reached back to *Marsh* v. *Alabama* (1946) for an analogy. In *Marsh,* the Court enforced the guaranties of the First Amendment on the streets of a "company town." "The similarities between the business block in Marsh and the shopping center in the present case are striking," Justice Marshall wrote. They were so striking that "the State may not delegate the power, through the use of its trespass laws, wholly to exclude those members of the public wishing to exercise their First Amendment rights on the premises in a manner and for a purpose generally consonant with the use to which the property is actually put."

In *Logan Valley,* the picketing was labor related, directed against a store in the shopping center. Would the Court extend *Logan Valley* to include other kinds of picketing or leafleting aimed not at a store but at a larger political or social issue not necessarily connected with any particular business at a shopping center? Four years later, a majority answered in the negative (*Lloyd Corp* v. *Tanner,* 1972), and *Logan Valley* was expressly overruled in *Hudgens* v. *NLRB* (1976).

It seems now, however, that free speech does not necessarily stop where the shopping mall begins. In *Prune Yard Shopping Center* v. *Robins* (1980) a unanimous bench allowed a state-created constitutional right of free speech at shopping centers to prevail against a challenge that it amounted to an unconstitutional state interference with the owner's property rights under the Fourteenth Amendment. What the Supreme Court is unwilling to read into the First Amendment is perfectly acceptable when read into state constitutions by state courts. *Logan Valley* has, practically speaking, been revived, if on a hobbled, state-option basis.

Residential picketing is another troublesome area of First Amendment policy, which provokes a clash not usually with property rights but with privacy. Even when such expression is confined to the public streets and sidewalks, "preserving the sanctity of the home, the one retreat to which men and women can repair to escape from the tribulations of their daily pursuits, is surely an important value," Justice Brennan acknowledged in 1980. Nonetheless, in *Frisby* v. *Schultz* (1988) the Court made it clear that an absolute ban on all residential picketing is constitutionally infirm. Accepted instead was a ban on the picketing of a single residence exclusively. Municipalities, however, have to allow picketing along the street or sidewalk of a targeted house, but may enforce regulations governing time, place, and manner, provided they are applied on a nondiscriminatory basis as to content. *Frisby* advises that picketers must patrol part of a neighborhood even if the target is a single home.

FREEDOM OF ASSOCIATION

At least since *NAACP* v. *Alabama* (1957), the Court has been sensitive to a First Amendment right of association. In that case a unanimous bench barred the state's order that a civil rights organization disclose its membership lists as a condition for continuing to do business in the state. Because of the hostile environment at that time, the justices believed that the directive would threaten the organization's existence and "chill" constitutionally protected liberties.

More recently state and local governments have restricted the right of association to eliminate racial and gender discrimination in certain private organizations and clubs. The view is that such discrimination denies women and racial minorities full participation in the business and professional life of a community. As explained in Chapter Twelve, discrimination by many clubs is forbidden by neither the Constitution nor, at present, federal law. Although continuing to recognize the importance of associational rights staked out in *NAACP* v. *Alabama,* the Court has nonetheless approved three antidiscrimination measures aimed at private organizations (*Roberts* v. *Jaycees,* 1984; *Rotary International* v. *Rotary Club of Duarte,* 1987; and **New York State Club Association v. New York City,** 1988).

In the New York City case, a 1984 ordinance banned discrimination in membership in clubs that have more than 400 members, that provide meal service, and in which some members' dues are paid by their employers or nonmembers routinely pay for use of the club. Clubs falling into this category were deemed "not distinctly private." Small clubs as well as benevolent and religious organizations were exempted as being legitimately private. Despite the clubs' insistence that the First Amendment right of association included the right to exclude women from membership, all justices concluded that government's "compelling interest" in combatting discrimination took priority. Moreover, the law did not affect "in any significant way" the ability of members to form associations that advocated various viewpoints. Further litigation, Justice White explained, could determine whether in particular instances certain clubs could not advocate their viewpoints while adhering to a nondiscrimination policy. The decision may encourage other locales and the federal government to adopt similar legislation.

THE ELECTORAL PROCESS

Cases like *NAACP* v. *Alabama,* defining a First Amendment right of association have not concerned traditional party politics. Still, they form an important backdrop as both Congress and state legislatures attempt to regulate various stages of political campaigns to prevent electoral abuses.

Restrictions on the source, amount, and use of funds in the political process impinge on the First Amendment. In *Buckley* v. *Valeo* (1976) the Court reviewed at length the constitutionality of the Federal Election Campaign Act, designed to reduce the influence of "big money" in national elections. In an extensive *per curiam* opinion and in a variety of concurring and dissenting opinions, which consumed almost 300 pages in the *United States Reports,* the Court disallowed the provisions of the statute that put a limit of $50,000 on the use by a presidential candidate of his own or his immediate family's money. This was seen as an unconstitutional infringement on the First Amendment. Endorsed, however, were ceilings on contributions of $1,000 and $5,000 from individuals and groups, respectively, to candidates seeking federal office. This restriction was regarded as a less "direct and substantial" restraint on expression. Combined, these holdings gave a distinct advantage to families with considerable wealth and to candidates with high name recognition. Because of limitations imposed on both gifts and spending, the news media now have a more prominent role in campaigns, as candidates in many instances are dependent on news coverage as a kind of "free advertising."

In recent presidential contests, independent "political action committees" (PAC) have played an important role. Federal law offers the presidential candidates of the major political parties the option (which each has accepted thus far) of receiving public financing, up to a specified maximum, for their general election campaigns. When a candidate accepted this option, the law made it a criminal offense for independent political committees to spend more than $1,000 on a candidate's behalf. ("Independent" of a candidate's campaign staff, these committees spend money on such things as radio, television, and newspaper advertising in support of the candidate the particular committee prefers. Such activities are in addition to the candidate's own campaign advertising, the funding for which comes from the federal treasury.) *Buckley* had held in 1976 that Congress could not constitutionally limit independent expenditures in presidential campaigns generally. Unclear was whether Congress could limit independent expenditures when the candidates had accepted federal funding. In ***Federal Election Commission* v. *National Conservative Political Action Committee*** (1985), the Court declared that independent expenditures "produce speech at the core of the First Amendment" and, finding no corruption or appearance of corruption in the practice, invalidated the spending limitation. For both NCPAC and the Fund for a Conservative Majority (another party to the case), "the First Amendment freedom of association is squarely implicated."

The Court has also expressed concern for the First Amendment interests of minor parties and their members and supporters. In 1982, the justices had occasion to examine an Ohio campaign disclosure law that required every political party to report names and addresses of campaign contributors and recipients of campaign disbursements. In *Brown v. Socialist Workers '74 Campaign Committee,* the Court invalidated application of the law to the Socialist Workers Party, which, with only 60 members, received less than 2 percent of the total vote cast in the state. What seemed important was "the threat to First Amendment rights that would result from requiring minor parties to disclose the recipients of campaign disbursements," declared Justice Marshall, echoing *NAACP* v. *Alabama.* This was especially so because of "evidence of private and Government hostility toward the SWP and its members" with "the reasonable probability of threats, harassment, or reprisals."

The First Amendment has brought the Court closer to the day-to-day world of American politics in other ways. *Cousins* v. *Wigoda* (1975) placed the justices in the midst of the credentials dispute from the 1972 Democratic National Convention. Wigoda was a member of the elected, but not seated, delegation from Cook County, Illinois. Cousins was a member of the defeated, but seated, delegation. Concluding that members of political parties enjoy a First Amendment right of association, the Court ruled for Cousins, according primacy to the national convention of a party in determining the qualifications and eligibility of its delegates. Similarly, the National Democratic Party's choice of closed presidential primaries prevailed when challenged by the open presidential primary preferred by Wisconsin (*Democratic Party v. LaFollette,* 1981). The question was not whether Wisconsin could have an open primary. "Rather, the question is whether, once Wisconsin has opened its presidential preference primary to voters who do not publicly declare their party affiliation, it may then bind the National Party to honor the binding results, even though those results were reached in a manner contrary to National Party rules." *Wigoda* provided the answer.

In *Tashjian* v. *Connecticut* (1986), however, state party preference prevailed, as five justices overturned a state law requiring that party primaries be "closed" rather than "open." Connecticut Republicans, knowing they were a minority, were convinced they could attract independent voters in the general election by allowing them to vote in its primary. Relying on associational rights, the Court concluded that parties, not state legislatures, should determine who participates in party affairs. Nonetheless, states still have an important role when it comes to the general election. For example, seven justices in 1986 rejected a constitutional challenge to a Washington State statute that required candidates of minor parties to receive at least 1 percent of the vote in the primary before the candidate's name would appear on the general election ballot. Outweighing the associational right was the state's interest in preserving the integrity of the electoral process by requiring evidence of prior support (*Munro v. Socialist Workers Party*).

COMMERCIAL SPEECH

First Amendment protections are by no means limited to political speech. Even though guarding the democratic process may have been uppermost in the minds of Madison and others who campaigned for the amendment, the Supreme Court has enlarged the shield to cover "commercial speech" as well. In *Virginia State Board of Pharmacy* v. *Virginia Consumer Council (1976)*, the justices set aside legislation barring price advertising of prescription drugs. From the drug store it was only a short distance to the law office the following year and a state bar's ban against advertising the fees lawyers charged clients for routine services (*Bates* v. *State Bar of Arizona*, 1977).

In 1980, Justice Powell offered an overview of the Court's position on commercial speech (*Central Hudson Gas & Electric Corp.* v. *Public Service Commission of New York*).

> In commercial speech cases . . . a four-part analysis has developed. At the outset, we must determine whether the expression is protected by the First Amendment. For commercial speech to come within that provision, it at least must concern lawful activity and not be misleading. Next, we ask whether the asserted governmental interest is substantial. If both inquiries yield positive answers, we must determine whether the regulation directly advances the governmental interest asserted, and whether it is not more extensive than is necessary to serve that interest.

The *Central Hudson* test, however, does not guarantee agreement among the justices. For example, the Court split 5 to 4 in *Posadas de Puerto Rico Associates* v. *Tourism Co.* (1986) in upholding Puerto Rico's ban on the advertising of casino gambling directed to its residents but not to tourists. Justice Rehnquist reasoned that "the greater power to completely ban casino gambling necessarily includes the lesser power to ban advertising of casino gambling." Rather than disallowing the conduct, Puerto Rico undertook to reduce the demand through restrictions on information. Countering, Justice Stevens asserted that Puerto Rico "discriminates in its punishment of speech depending on the publication, audience, and words employed."

FREEDOM OF THE PRESS

"A free press," declared Justice Frankfurter, "is indispensable to the workings of our democratic society." Whether through newspaper, magazine, radio, film, or television, journalism is an industry that "serves one of the most vital of all general interests," surmised Judge Learned Hand—"the dissemination of news from as many different sources, and with as many different facets and colors as is possible." Right conclusions "are more likely to be gathered out of a multitude of tongues, than through any kind of authoritative selection. To many this is, and always will be, folly; but we have staked upon it our all." The First Amendment lays down a claim for a free press, but the involvement of the press with "the workings of our democratic society" guarantees conflict between journalists and government.

Prior Restraints. At the very least, the First Amendment was designed to prevent "all such *previous restraints* upon publications as had been practised by other governments," noted Justice Holmes many years ago (*Patterson* v. *Colorado*, 1907). Prior censorship is still regarded as the most onerous kind of abridgement of press freedom and is a restriction the Court is most reluctant to approve.

In the landmark 1931 decision of *Near* v. *Minnesota,* the Court held unconstitutional a Minnesota statute that gave the state power to shut down any "malicious, scandalous and defamatory newspaper, magazine or periodical." Truth published with good motives was available as a defense. Near published *The Saturday Press,* which devoted several issues to violent attacks on various public officials. The attacks were anti-Semitic in tone and thoroughly tasteless, and the county attorney succeeded in having the law applied to Near. "This is . . . the essence of censorship," concluded Chief Justice Hughes, by a margin of one vote.

Near itself went on trial in June 1971, when the United States sought to enjoin first the *New York Times* and then the *Washington Post* from publishing the contents of a classified study the *Times* had obtained entitled "History of U.S. Decision-Making Process on Vietnam Policy" (***New York Times Co.* v. *United States***). Unlike the facts in *Near,* there was no express legislative authorization giving courts power to block continued publication of a newspaper, even to protect national security. With no time for anyone to write a majority opinion, the Court simply issued a brief *per curiam* order stating that the government had not met the necessary burden of "showing justification for the enforcement of such a restraint." The complexity of the issue was exemplified in the nine opinions filed in the case, six concurring and three dissenting. For Justices Black and Harlan, their opinions were the last they wrote.

Prior restraints on publication may be the hobgoblin of American constitutional interpretation, as some of the opinions in the Pentagon Papers Case suggest, but this presumption received its severest test when the federal government sought to prevent publication of an issue of *The Progressive* magazine. Officials were distressed by an article it was to contain: "The H-Bomb Secret; How We Got It, Why We're Telling It." The fear was not that the article would enable anyone to build a hydrogen bomb in the basement or garage, but that it contained information that would be a significant help to countries attempting to develop a nuclear capability. Unlike the government's position in the Pentagon Papers Case, there seemed this time to be statutory authority for a court to issue an injunction. In *United States* v. *Progressive, Inc.* (1979), Judge Warren of the United States District Court for the Western District of Wisconsin did just that. Before argument on appeal in the court of appeals, however, the *Madison* (Wisconsin) *Press Connection* published an 18-page letter recounting much of the same information that was to have appeared in *The Progressive.* The issue of prior restraint therefore became moot, and the Justice Department withdrew its suit. Although this case never received full judicial consideration higher than the district court level, it does illustrate the practical difficulties in trying to prevent publication of material people want to publish.

Direct restraints on publication are no more acceptable when the motive is protection of other constitutional rights. *Nebraska Press Association* v. *Stuart* (1976) involved a "gag order" applied to news media in a small Nebraska town to avoid adverse publicity in an effort to obtain a fair trial for the accused following a grisly murder. The Court unanimously concluded that the ban on publication of certain information before trial ran afoul of the First Amendment. "[T]he press may be arrogant, tyrannical, abusive, and sensationalist, just as it may be incisive, probing, and informative," wrote Justice Brennan in a concurring opinion. "But at least in the context of prior restraints on publication, the decision of what, when, and how to publish is for editors, not judges. . . ."

Libel. Although American judges historically have looked warily on prior restraints, the press has been on notice that it must take responsibility for what it publishes. The press may not be restrained in advance, but it may be punished for what it prints. Libel (written defamation of a person's reputation) is one of these subsequent punishments and has long been regarded as an exception to the press freedom protected by the First Amendment. In 1964, however, the justices virtually abolished the right of public officials to collect damages for libel (***New York Times* v. *Sullivan***). Under this decision, the press, and perhaps anyone else, has the right to publish libelous statements about public officials.

"Actual malice" must be shown by a plaintiff under the *Sullivan* rule. The Court's rationale has been summed up this way: "What is added to the field of libel is taken from the arena of debate, and democracy calls for robust, wide-open debate about public issues. Libel, then, that deals with public affairs is not evil; it serves a socially useful function."

In 1967 the Court extended the *Sullivan* rule to prominent people outside government (*Curtis Publishing Co.* v. *Butts*). For private individuals caught up in public events, the press enjoys less protection, but the plaintiff nonetheless bears the burden of proving falsity. The press does not have to prove the truthfulness of a story (*Philadelphia Newspapers* v. *Hepps,* 1986). Even parodies that are plainly false and intended to cause emotional distress are protected, the Court held in *Hustler Magazine* v. *Falwell* (1988). Here, a magazine had published a cartoon depicting a public figure in a drunken state and having an incestuous relationship with his mother in an outhouse.

Clearly, *Sullivan* has not ended libel suits by public officials and figures. Decisions have allowed more cases to go to trial by making the issue of malice one for the jury to decide. Furthermore, they have permitted plaintiffs to probe the minds of journalists in an effort to establish malice (*Herbert* v. *Lando,* 1979). By preserving the possibility of a successful libel action, libel law makes journalists understandably wary. Even if unsuccessful, a suit is costly because of the enormous amount of time a defense requires. A major television network may be able to absorb the costs, but a small newspaper would not and therefore might forgo the kind of controversial investigative reporting that might spark a libel suit.

Obscenity. State and national governments alike continue to be involved in the less dramatic function of protecting the morals and welfare of their citizens. Where these policies attempt to curtail sexually explicit materials (printed, filmed, or videotaped), First Amendment problems arise.

Roth v. *United States* (1957) was the Court's first formal acceptance under the First Amendment of state and federal action directed against pornography. In *Roth* Justice Brennan wrote for the majority that "obscenity is utterly without redeeming social importance." Therefore, it "is not within the area of constitutionally protected speech or press." The key of course was to define the obscene, and the constitutional standard became "whether to the average person, applying contemporary community standards, the dominant theme of the material taken as a whole appeals to prurient interest."

Roth raised perhaps as many questions as it answered and only began the Court's long struggle with what Harlan later called "the intractable obscenity problem." In effect, the justices became the censorship board for the nation. With unusual candor, Justice Stewart confessed in a 1964 case that the justices were trying "to define what may be indefinable."

> [U]nder the First and Fourteenth Amendments criminal laws in this area are constitutionally limited to hard-core pornography. I shall not today attempt further to define the kinds of material I understand to be embraced within that shorthand description; and perhaps I could never succeed in intelligibly doing so. But I know it when I see it. . . .

In 1966, in *Memoirs of a Woman of Pleasure* v. *Massachusetts* the justices tightened the *Roth* test and made it more difficult for government to maintain a successful obscenity prosecution. Although formally endorsed only by a plurality, the elements of proof now included a demonstration that the material in question be "patently offensive" and "utterly without redeeming social value." Definitional problems abounded, and as a result so did the number of obscenity cases on the Court's docket. Some of the justices found themselves with no choice but to look at the material in question. The Court staff obligingly set up a special viewing room, complete with projector.

In 1969, *Stanley* v. *Georgia* gave the strong hint that all obscenity laws were living on borrowed time. The Court held that mere private possession of obscene materials was protected by the First Amendment. Said Justice Marshall for the majority, "If the First Amendment means anything, it means that a State has no business telling a man, sitting alone in his own house, what books he may read or what films he may watch."

But the majority in 1973 pulled back from the logical implications of *Stanley* in *Miller* v. *California* and announced new definitional standards. Most significantly, the prosecution now had to show that the material in question lacked only "serious value," not that it was "utterly without" value. Today, no member of the Court is prepared to extend First Amendment protection to "child pornography." *Ferber* v. *New York* (1982) announced that a state may proscribe materials that photographically portray sexual acts or lewd exhibitions of genitalia by children even when the materials are not obscene under *Miller*.

Privilege and Access. A newer type of press litigation under the First Amendment involves privilege and access. Here the government actions in question are not aimed at preventing or punishing publication of certain information. Rather, a policy impedes or obstructs the press in carrying out tasks journalists assign to themselves. Does the First Amendment place journalists in an elite class, or are they citizens just like everyone else? For example, in **Branzburg v. Hayes** (1972) the issue was a constitutional privilege for newspersons refusing to reveal the identity of confidential sources before a grand jury. The slim majority of five relied on the maxim that the law is entitled to "every man's evidence," a point that became of greater interest two years later in the Nixon tapes case (see Chapter Three). In the wake of *Branzburg,* some states enacted "shield" laws to do statutorily what the Court had declined to do constitutionally. Such laws even predated *Branzburg* in other states. A state "shield" law is still subordinate to the Sixth Amendment's guaranty of a fair trial and so may not always grant as full a privilege as journalists desire.

Press interests won the approval of all eight participating justices in *Richmond Newspapers, Inc.* v. *Virginia* (1980). The Court set aside on First Amendment grounds a trial judge's order to close a trial for the purpose of limiting publicity, which might prove prejudicial to the rights of the accused. Said Justice Stevens, "This is a watershed case." It remains to be seen whether *Richmond Newspapers* will be applied only to trials or whether the Court will extend its application to other arenas as well. In most circumstances, the dominant view still seems to be, in Justice Stewart's words, that "the press is free to do battle against secrecy and deception in government. But the press cannot expect from the Constitution any guarantee that it will succeed."

Students and Free Expression. Young Americans relinquish some, but not all, constitutional rights when they walk through the schoolhouse door, according to the Supreme Court. A 1969 decision voided a school rule that barred students from wearing black armbands to protest the war in Vietnam. The First Amendment overrode the desire of administrators to avoid even the silent expression of a controversial point of view (*Tinker* v. *Des Moines Community School District*). Only if expression interfered with "appropriate discipline" could the rule be sustained. In 1986, in contrast, the Court with only two dissenters upheld the two-day suspension of a high school student in Washington State whose assembly speech contained sexual innuendo, although it was not legally obscene. Although no government agency could constitutionally punish the same speech off the school grounds, the Court denied that "the same latitude must be permitted to children in a public school." Rather, school personnel are empowered to say "what manner of speech in the classroom or in school asesembly is appropriate" (*Bethel School District* v. *Fraser*). In light of *Fraser,* what is left of *Tinker?* Consider **Hazelwood School District v. Kuhlmeier** (1988), where six justices upheld a principal's censorship of a high school newspaper. *Kuhlmeier* may prove to be more important for what it said than for what it did.

FREEDOM OF RELIGION

Working together, the establishment and free exercise clauses of the First Amendment are designed to safeguard individual conscience and to promote the civil peace in a religiously diverse land. Coupled with the ban on religious tests for public office in Article VI, the First Amendment achieves these ends by assuring the widest toleration for personal religious expression and by diminishing the possibility that any religious group can make itself the official church, thus potentially threatening other beliefs. The Constitution attempts to make sure that government remains off-limits as a prize in a nation of competing faiths.

The Establishment Clause. State laws first began receiving regular scrutiny under the establishment clause in *Everson* v. *Board of Education* (1947). Five justices, although allowing a state to pay the costs of bus transportation of children attending sectarian as well as public and nonsectarian private schools, set forth the principle that the religious clauses of the Constitution erected a "wall of separation" between church and state. Dissenting, Justice Rutledge issued a prophetic warning.

> Two great drives are constantly in motion to abridge, in the name of education, the complete division of religion and civil authority which our forefathers made. One is to introduce religious education and observances into the public schools. The other, to obtain public funds for the aid and support of various private religious schools. . . .
>
> In my opinion both avenues were closed by the Constitution. Neither should be opened by this Court. The matter is not one of quantity, to be measured by the amount of money expended. Now as in Madison's day it is one of principle, to keep separate the separate spheres as the First Amendment drew them; to prevent the first experiment upon our liberties; and to keep the question from becoming entangled in corrosive precedents. We should not be less strict to keep strong and untarnished the one side of the shield of religious freedom than we have been of the other.

The significance of the "wall" metaphor became more apparent in 1948, when the Court struck down a Champaign, Illinois, released-time program for religious instruction in *McCollum* v. *Board of Education*. But only four years later, in *Zorach* v. *Clauson* (1952) the Court upheld a New York released-time program, basing its different conclusion on factual distinctions between the two programs. Religion classes were held on school premises in the Illinois program but off school premises in New York. "We are a religious people whose institutions presuppose a Supreme Being," declared Justice Douglas in *Zorach*. "When the state encourages religious instruction or cooperates with religious authorities by adjusting the schedule of public events to sectarian needs, it follows the best of our traditions."

The first of Justice Rutledge's "great drives," however, continued to heat in the crucible of litigation. Any satisfaction to proponents of religion in public schools brought by *Zorach* was short-lived. Prayers and Bible reading in schools next came under fire. *Engel* v. *Vitale* (1962) invalidated the use in New York's public schools of a short prayer, approved by the Board of Regents, to be recited during opening exercises of each school day. In 1963, eight justices went further, declaring in *Abington Township* v. *Schempp* that Bible reading and recitation of the Lord's Prayer in class were also invalid. In deciding whether the "wall of separation" had been breached, Justice Clark explained, "[T]o withstand the strictures of the Establishment Clause, there must be a secular legislative purpose and a primary effect that neither advances nor inhibits religion."

Engel and *Schempp* did not end the school prayer controversy, however. Some school districts plainly ignored the decisions. In the early 1980s President Ronald Reagan campaigned for the restoration of prayer in the schools and advocated amending the Constitution to make that possible. "God never should have been expelled from America's classrooms," Reagan declared in his 1983 State of the Union address.

So it was not surprising that the justices faced the prayer issue yet again. This time the case involved a minute of silence "for meditation or voluntary prayer" in the public schools of Alabama. More than two dozen states had enacted laws similar to Alabama's. Even Justice Brennan's concurring opinion in *Schempp* had suggested that such moments of silence might not be unconstitutional. But in 1985, six justices thought the Alabama law was defective. "[T]he State intends to characterize prayer as a favored practice," announced Justice Stevens in *Wallace* v. *Jaffree.* "Such an end is not consistent with the established principle that the Government must pursue a course of complete neutrality toward religion." The Court's decision, with its flurry of separate opinions, seemed Solomonic. Strongly hinted was the constitutionality of a law setting aside a moment of silence "for meditation" where it was not obvious from the record that the state's purpose was one of making an "end run" around *Engel* and *Schempp.*

Louisiana's attempt to require the teaching of "creation science" alongside evolution therefore ran afoul of the establishment clause in *Edwards* v. *Aguillard* (1987). Looking at the legislative history of the act in question, Justice Brennan found that "[t]he pre-eminent purpose of the . . . legislature was clearly to advance the religious viewpoint that a supernatural being created humankind." Only Justice Scalia and Chief Justice Rehnquist accepted the state's reasoning that balanced treatment of both theories advanced the secular purpose of guarding academic freedom. For Scalia the majority's position was "Scopes-in-reverse," a reference to *Scopes* v. *State* (1927), in which the Tennessee courts upheld a conviction under a law banning the teaching of evolution.

Perhaps because of the impressionable nature of schoolchildren and the unique role public schools have long had in the life of the nation, the justices have been quicker to strike down religious influences in the classroom than in other official places. Outside the schoolroom, the justices appear more inclined to permit dominant religious groups greater leeway in expressing themselves in official settings. In *Marsh* v. *Chambers* (1983), for example, a majority of the Court found no constitutional objection to the Nebraska practice of having a chaplain for the state legislature paid out of public funds. Nor was a majority prepared to say that the First Amendment banned city officials in Pawtucket, Rhode Island, from annually erecting a municipally owned Christmas display, including a crèche, in a private park (*Lynch* v. *Donnelly,* 1984).

Litigation involving state aid to church-supported schools—the second of Justice Rutledge's "great drives"—has become a fixture on the Court's docket. Since *Everson* in 1947, the justices have allowed some forms of aid, but not most, to pass constitutional muster. Today, a three-prong test measures the constitutionality of such assistance: The state must demonstrate both "secular purpose" and "neutral effect" (from *Schempp*) and also convince the Court that the aid does not "excessively entangle" government and religion. (The "excessive entanglement" criterion first appeared in *Walz* v. *Tax Commission* (1970), when the justices upheld state tax exemptions for real property owned by religious institutions and used for religious purposes).

Applying the three-prong test in *Lemon* v. *Kurtzman* (1971), the justices found unconstitutional Pennsylvania and Rhode Island laws that, among other things, paid a 15 percent salary supplement to nonpublic schoolteachers of sectarian subjects. Although "excessive entanglement" had been used to *save* the tax exemption in *Walz,* that same standard proved the undoing of the parochial school aid policies challenged in *Lemon.* Efforts by the state to insure "neutral effect" were bound to create "excessive entanglement." Absent such "entanglement," the state could not be sure of a "neutral effect."

Application of the three-prong *Lemon* test has not produced predictable results.

Combining the holdings in *Meek* v. *Pittenger* (1975), *Wolman* v. *Walter* (1977), *Committee for Public Education* v. *Regan* (1980), and *Mueller* v. *Allen* (1983) with earlier decisions, the Court *will accept,* for example, on-premises diagnostic and off-premises therapeutic services for sectarian school pupils performed by state employees, supplemental grants to schools to pay for testing and scoring, textbook loans to pupils, bus transportation to and from school, tax deductions for public and private educational expenses, and construction funds for church-related colleges. Neither was the Court prepared to regard as facially invalid on establishment clause grounds the Adolescent Family Life Act (called by some the "chastity act"), which allows religious organizations to use federal funds to counsel adolescents on premartial sexual relations (*Bowen* v. *Kendrick,* 1988).

Not acceptable to a majority in establishment clause cases are state tuition tax credits to parents of parochial school pupils, state funds for school building maintenance, supplements for teachers' salaries, loans of instructional materials to sectarian schools, and bus transportation for field trips. Also unacceptable are "shared-time" programs in which supplemental classes in specialized subjects are taught by public school teachers to sectarian school pupils on sectarian school premises. Such a program funded by Congress to provide remedial instruction to educationally deprived children from low-income families was at issue in *Aguilar* v. *Felton* (1985).

The Free Exercise Clause. Cases under the establishment clause typically test public policies that arguably *aid* religion. Free exercise cases, in contrast, involve public policies that seem to *burden* religion. Religious persecution—that is, penalizing people *because* of their religious beliefs—was undoubtedly the most obvious evil the free exercise clause was intended to prevent. Litigation under this part of the First Amendment today, however, usually involves laws that were written with no particular religious group in mind but which happen to work a hardship when applied to members of one faith or another. Certainly, chaos would result if everyone received an exemption from a law just because it ran counter to the tenets of one's faith. Still, the free exercise clause suggests that the government should not always prevail when the commands of the state push in one direction and the dictates of conscience pull in another.

In one of the first applications of the free exercise clause to the states, the Court sustained a state act requiring all schoolchildren, including Jehovah's Witnesses to salute the flag (*Minersville School District* v. *Gobitis,* 1940).

Joined in Justice Frankfurter's seemingly reactionary decision were Justices Black, Douglas, and Murphy. Only Justice Stone dissented. In an effort to win Stone's support, Frankfurter wrote his colleague at length in a letter reprinted in this chapter, arguing that the case be decided "in the particular setting of our time and circumstances." "It is relevant," he pleaded, "to make the adjustment we have to make within the framework of present circumstances and those that are clearly ahead of us." The year was 1940, a few months after Hitler unleashed his diabolical blitzkrieg in Europe.

Two years later (*Jones* v. *Opelika,* 1942) Black, Douglas, and Murphy, in a remarkable about-face, recanted and explained:

> Since we joined in the opinion in the Gobitis case, we think this is an appropriate occasion to state that we now believe that it was also wrongly decided. Certainly our democratic form of government functioning under the historic Bill of Rights has a high responsibility to accommodate itself to the religious views of minorities however unpopular and unorthodox those views may be. The First Amendment does not put the right freely to exercise religion in a subordinate position. We fear, however, that the opinion in these and the Gobitis case do exactly that.

Encouraged by the *Opelika* dissent and the appointment of two new justices, Jackson and Rutledge, Walter Barnette and several other Jehovah's Witnesses brought suit to enjoin enforcement of the flag salute against their children. Voting 6 to 3 (**West Virginia Board of Ed. v. Barnett**), the Court reversed itself in 1943, holding that First Amendment freedoms may be restricted "only to prevent grave and immediate dangers." There are few instances in the Court's history in which the change of views and of judicial personnel were so quickly reflected in judicial decisions.

Sherbert v. *Verner* (1963) typifies present-day conflicts under this part of the First Amendment. At issue was application of South Carolina's law denying unemployment compensation to someone available for work who refused to accept a job. Adell Sherbert, a Seventh-day Adventist, refused to work on Saturday but was otherwise available for work. No one claimed that South Carolina passed this law to persecute members of this particular church, but as applied to her, the policy required her to choose between a job and religious disobedience, on the one hand, and no compensation and religious obedience, on the other. A majority of the justices found the law unconstitutional *as applied to Adell Sherbert,* because it unduly burdened her faith. For its part of the argument, the state had not convinced the justices that it had very good reasons for denying the unemployment benefits. Dissenters claimed the decision effectively made the Seventh-day Adventist Church an "established church" in South Carolina because it had now been singled out for preferential treatment.

Sherbert was authority for *Wisconsin* v. *Yoder* (1972) which exempted Old Order Amish from a state law requiring parents to send their children to school until the age of 16. An all but unanimous bench concluded that the rule compelled the Amish, whose church is a separatist sect and who do not provide formal education beyond the eighth grade, "to perform acts undeniably at odds with fundamental tenets of their religious beliefs. . . . [C]ompulsory school attendance . . . carries with it a very real threat of undermining the Amish community and religious practice as they exist today; they must either abandon belief and be assimilated into society at large, or be forced to migrate to some other and more tolerant region. . . ." Balanced was the threat to the faith posed by the law against the state's interest in uniform minimum school attendance for all.

Neither *Sherbert* nor *Yoder* should suggest that all free exercise claims prevail over government regulations. Especially when federal law is challenged, the Court appears reluctant to apply the free exercise clause with full force. So it would seem from *United States* v. *Lee* (1982), which denied an exemption for Amish from certain Social Security taxes. In 1986, a narrow majority upheld an Air Force ban on the wearing of headgear indoors even as applied to Simcha Goldman, an officer and an Orthodox Jew who regarded the wearing of the yarmulke as silent devotion akin to prayer (*Goldman* v. *Weinberger*). Then in 1988 the Court refused to block a road-building project by the U.S. Forest Service despite the Service's own finding that the road "would cause serious and irreparable damage to the sacred areas which are an integral and necessary part of the belief systems and lifeway of Northwest California Indian peoples" (**Lyng v. Northwest Indian Cemetery Protective Association**).

Free Exercise vs. Nonestablishment. Even though the religion clauses work to guard religious freedom, they focus on different threats and so at times may be in tension. Rigorous protection of nonestablishment values may infringe free exercise. Rigorous application of free exercise values may create an establishment of religion. In granting the exemption Adell Sherbert wanted, for example, the Court not only recognized the religious basis of her claim but aided religion as well. Justice O'Connor addressed this tension in *Wallace* v. *Jaffree:*

> It is disingenuous to look for a purely secular purpose when the manifest objective [of a policy] is to facilitate the free exercise of religion by lifting a government-imposed burden. Instead,

the Court should simply acknowledge that the religious purpose . . . is legitimated by the Free Exercise Clause . . . [I]ndividual perceptions . . . that a religious observer is exempted from a particular government requirement, would be entitled to little weight if the Free Exercise Clause strongly supported the exemption.

Crucial for O'Connor is that the burden on religion lifted by government be one that is imposed by government. This would explain *Thornton* v. *Caldor* (1985), which struck down as a religious establishment a requirement that an employer give employees the right not to work on their chosen Sabbath. *Sherbert* involved a burden imposed by the state; *Thornton* did not.

ARE THERE PREFERRED FREEDOMS?

During the past several decades the Court generally has maintained hostility to restrictions on First Amendment freedoms. Government policies or actions aimed at the content of speech, for example, enter the judicial process under heavy presumption of unconstitutionality. Only if the speech falls into one of several narrow exceptions is the Court inclined to be receptive to the government's position. Where a policy or action is not aimed at content of speech, but where the flow and distribution of speech are nonetheless inhibited, the Court weighs the effects of the former on the latter. Important in this calculus is the degree of construction on speech and the importance of the interest the state is pursuing. Interpretation of the First Amendment involves the balancing of recognized constitutional values.

If the balancing usually means that speech and other First Amendment rights prevail over competing interests, does this mean that the First Amendment is in a favored position? Are there preferred freedoms? Justice Stone's footnote four in *Carolene Products,* discussed in Chapter Eight, suggests precisely that. In response Justice Scalia contends that "the First Amendment is not everything." Regardless, constitutional rights are not rights against government so much as rights against the dominant majority represented by government. The Bill of Rights expresses the judgment of the founders that the majority is neither always right nor likely to be tolerant.*

First Amendment freedoms lie at the heart of democratic values and the democratic process. So much of the Constitution deals not with substance but with procedure. The Constitution speaks not nearly so often to *what* decisions are to be made as to *how* decisions are to be made. Freedom of expression and conscience are, therefore, integral components of democratic politics. Indeed, it is difficult to imagine politics being democratic when individuals with points of view in the minority cannot campaign to become the majority. Representative government and development of the human potential require a degree of tolerance for differing ideas, manners, and styles, and it is to forms of expression that the First Amendment largely addresses itself. This was the theme of Justice Jackson's opinion in the second flag-salute case when he argued, "The very purpose of a Bill of Rights was to withdraw certain subjects from the vicissitudes of political controversy, to place them beyond the reach of majorities."

---

* Stone himself later had second thoughts that the Court had carried the ideas in his *Carolene* footnote too far. "My more conservative brethren in the old days enacted their own economic prejudice into law. What they did placed in jeopardy a great and useful institution of government. The pendulum has now swung to the other extreme, and history is repeating itself. The Court is now in as much danger of becoming a legislative Constitution-making body, enacting into law its own predilections, as it was then." [To Irving Brant, Aug. 25, 1945. Quoted in Alpheus T. Mason, *The Supreme Court from Taft to Burger* (Baton Rouge: Louisiana State University Press, 1979), p. 168.]

KEY TERMS

First Amendment

Fourteenth
  Amendment

incorporation

clear-and-present-
  danger test

bad-tendency test

overbreadth doctrine

chilling effect

void for vagueness

prior restraint

libel

symbolic speech

commercial speech

obscenity

per curiam

Lemon test

establishment

free exercise

QUERIES

1. Review footnote four from *United States* v. *Carolene Products Co.*, reprinted in Chapter Eight. What are the footnote's implications in terms of judicial power and responsibility?

2. Trace the evolution of the protections afforded free speech as found in the cases in this chapter.

3. What accounts for the Court's approval of censorship in *Hazelwood School District* v. *Kuhlmeier,* in light of its resolute defense of press freedom in the Pentagon Papers Case?

4. In *Wallace* v. *Jaffree,* what is Justice Rehnquist's objection to the *Lemon* test? What alteration to the *Lemon* test does Justice O'Connor propose in her concurring opinion?

SELECTED READINGS

BARENDT, ERIC. *Freedom of Speech.* New York: Oxford University Press, 1986.

BERNS, WALTER. *The First Amendment and the Future of American Democracy.* New York: Basic Books, 1976.

BOLLINGER, LEE C. *The Tolerant Society.* New York: Oxford University Press, 1986.

CHAFEE, ZECHARIAH, JR. *Free Speech in the United States.* Cambridge, Mass.: Harvard University Press, 1942.

CORWIN, EDWARD S. "Bowing Out 'Clear and Present Danger' " 27 *Notre Dame Lawyer* 325 (1952).

CURRY, THOMAS J. *The First Freedoms: Church and State in America to the Passage of the First Amendment.* New York: Oxford University Press, 1986.

DANZIG, RICHARD J. "Justice Frankfurter's Opinions in the Flag Salute Cases." 36 *Stanford Law Review* 675 (1984).

EMERSON, THOMAS I. *The System of Freedom of Expression.* New York: Random House, 1970.

KALVEN, HARRY, JR. *A Worthy Tradition: Freedom of Speech in America.* New York: Harper & Row, 1988.

LEVY, LEONARD W. *Emergence of a Free Press.* New York: Oxford University Press, 1985 (a revision of Levy's 1960 work, *Legacy of Suppression*).

LIVELY, DONALD E. "The Supreme Court and Commercial Speech: New Words with an Old Message." 72 *Minnesota Law Review* 289 (1987).

MCCLOSKY, HERBERT, and ALIDA BRILL. *Dimensions of Tolerance: What Americans Believe about Civil Liberties.* New York: Russell Sage, 1983.

MEIKLEJOHN, ALEXANDER. "The First Amendment Is an Absolute." 1961 *Supreme Court Review* 245.

MENDELSON, WALLACE. "Clear and Present Danger—From Schenck to Dennis." 52 *Columbia Law Review* 313 (1952).

O'BRIEN, DAVID M. *The Public's Right to Know: The Supreme Court and the First Amendment.* New York: Praeger, 1981.

RABBAN, DAVID M. "The Emergence of Modern First Amendment Doctrine." 50 *University of Chicago Law Review* 1027 (1983).

REDLICH, NORMAN. "The Separation of Church and State: The Burger Court's Tortuous Journey." In Herman Schwartz, ed. *The Burger Years.* New York: Penguin, 1988.

SMOLLA, RODNEY A. *Suing the Press.* New York: Oxford University Press, 1986.

SORAUF, FRANK J. *The Wall of Separation: The Constitutional Politics of Church and State.* Princeton, N.J.: Princeton University Press, 1976.

STEPHENSON, D. GRIER, JR. "Religion and the Constitution: An Uncertain Consensus." 86 *South Atlantic Quarterly* 95 (1987).

SUNDERLAND, LANE V. *Obscenity.* Washington, D.C.: American Enterprise Institute, 1974.

I. INTERNAL SECURITY

Schenck v. United States
249 U.S. 47, 39 S.Ct. 247, 63 L.Ed. 470 (1919)

Schenck and others were convicted of conspiracy to obstruct the draft and other violations of the Espionage Act of 1917. Their specific offense was printing and distributing leaflets that opposed the war effort generally and conscription specifically. Majority: Holmes, Brandeis, Clarke, Day, McKenna, McReynolds, Pitney, Van Devanter, White.

MR. JUSTICE HOLMES delivered the opinion of the court. . . .

The document in question upon its first printed side recited the first section of the Thirteenth Amendment, said that the idea embodied in it was violated by the Conscription Act, and that a conscript is little better than a convict. In impassioned language it intimated that conscription was despotism in its worst form and a monstrous wrong against humanity in the interest of Wall Street's chosen few. It said "Do not submit to intimidation," but in form at least confined itself to peaceful measures such as a petition for the repeal of the act. The other and later printed side of the sheet was headed "Assert Your Rights." It stated reasons for alleging that any one violated the Constitution when he refused to recognize "your right to assert your opposition to the draft," and went on "If you do not assert and support your rights, you are helping to deny or disparage rights which it is the solemn duty of all citizens and residents of the United States to retain." It described the arguments on the other side as coming from cunning politicians and a mercenary capitalist press, and even silent consent to the conscription law as helping to support an infamous conspiracy. It denied the power to send our citizens away to foreign shores to shoot up the people of other lands, and added that words could not express the condemnation such cold-blooded ruthlessness deserves, &c., winding up "You must do your share to maintain, support and uphold the rights of the people of this country." Of course the document would not have been sent unless it had been intended to have some effect, and we do not see what effect it could be expected to have upon persons subject to the draft except to influence them to obstruct the carrying out of it. The defendants do not deny that the jury might find against them on this point.

But it is said, suppose that that was the tendency of this circular, it is protected by the First Amendment to the Constitution. Two of the strongest expressions are said to be quoted respectively from well-known public men. It well may be that the prohibition of laws abridging the freedom of speech is not confined to previous restraints, although to prevent them may have been the main purpose. . . . We admit that in many places and in ordinary times the defendants in saying all that was said in the circular would have been within their constitutional rights. But the character of every act depends upon the circumstances in which it is done. . . . The most stringent protection of free speech would not protect a man in falsely shouting fire in a theatre and causing a panic. It does not even protect a man from an injunction against uttering words that may have all the effect of force. . . . The question in every case is whether the words are used in such circumstances and are of such a nature as to create a clear and present danger that they will bring about the substantive evils that Congress has a right to prevent. It is a question of proximity and degree. When a nation is at war many things that might be said in time of peace are such a hindrance to its effort that their utterance will not be endured so long as men fight and that no Court could regard them as protected by any constitutional right. It seems to be admitted that if an actual obstruction of the recruiting service were proved, liability for words that produced that effect might be enforced. The statute of 1917 in § 4 punishes conspiracies to obstruct as well as actual obstruction. If the act (speaking, or circulating a paper), its tendency and the intent with which it is done are the same, we perceive no ground for saying that success alone warrants making the act a crime.

Judgments affirmed.

Gitlow v. New York
268 U.S. 652, 45 S.Ct. 625, 69 L.Ed. 1138 (1925)

Benjamin Gitlow, a member of the left-wing section of the Socialist Party, was convicted of the New York State statutory crime of criminal anarchy. Majority: Sanford, Butler, McReynolds, Sutherland, Taft, Van Devanter. Dissenting: Holmes, Brandeis. Not participating: Stone.

MR. JUSTICE SANFORD delivered the opinion of the Court. . . .

The contention here is that the statute, by its terms and as applied in this case, is repugnant to the due process clause of the Fourteenth Amendment. . . .

The indictment was in two counts. The first charged that the defendant had advocated, advised and taught the duty, necessity and propriety of overthrowing and overturning organized government by force, violence and unlawful means, by certain writings therein set forth entitled "The Left Wing Manifesto"; the second that he had printed, published and knowingly circulated and distributed a certain paper called "The Revolutionary Age," containing the writings set forth in the first count, advocating, advising and teaching the doctrine that organized government should be overthrown by force, violence and unlawful means. . . .

The precise question presented, and the only question which we can consider under this writ of error, then is, whether the statute, as construed and applied in this case by the state courts, deprived the defendant of his liberty of expression in violation of the due process clause of the Fourteenth Amendment.

The statute does not penalize the utterance or publication of abstract "doctrine" or academic discussion having no quality of incitement to any concrete action. It is not aimed against mere historical or philosophical essays. It does not restrain the advocacy of changes in the form of government by constitutional and lawful means. What it prohibits is language advocating, advising or teaching the overthrow of organized government by unlawful means. . . .

The Manifesto, plainly, is neither the statement of abstract doctrine nor, as suggested by counsel, mere prediction that industrial disturbances and revolutionary mass strikes will result spontaneously in an inevitable process of evolution in the economic system. It advocates and urges in fervent language mass action which shall progressively foment industrial disturbances and through political mass strikes and revolutionary mass action overthrow and destroy organized parliamentary government. It concludes with a call to action in these words: "The proletariat revolution and the Communist reconstruction of society—*the struggle for these*—is now indispensable. . . . The Communist International calls the proletariat of the world to the final struggle!" This is not the expression of philosophical abstractions, the mere prediction of future events; it is the language of direct incitement. . . .

For present purposes we may add and do assume that freedom of speech and of the press—which are protected by the First Amendment from abridgment by Congress—are among the fundamental personal rights and "liberties" protected by the due process clause of the Fourteenth Amendment from impairment by the states. . . .

. . . That utterances inciting to the overthrow of organized government by unlawful means, present a sufficient danger of substantive evil to bring their punishment within the range of legislative discretion, is clear. Such utterances, by their very nature, involve danger to the public peace and to the security of the State. They threaten breaches of the peace and ultimate revolution. And the immediate danger is none the less real and substantial, because the effect of a given utterance cannot be accurately foreseen. The State cannot reasonably be required to measure the danger from every such utterance in the nice balance of a jeweler's scale. A single revolutionary spark may kindle a fire that, smouldering for a time, may burst into a sweeping and destructive conflagration. It cannot be said that the State is acting arbitrarily or unreasonably when in the exercise of its judgment as to the measures necessary to protect the public peace and safety, it seeks to extinguish the spark without waiting until it has enkindled the flame or blazed into the conflagration. It cannot reasonably be required to defer the adoption of measures for its own peace and safety until the revolutionary utterances lead to actual disturbances of the public peace or imminent and immediate danger of its own destruction; but it may, in the exercise of its judgment, suppress the threatened danger in its incipiency. . . .

We cannot hold that the present statute is an arbitrary or unreasonable exercise of the police power of the State unwarrantably infringing the freedom of speech or press; and we must and do sustain its constitutionality. . . .

Affirmed.

MR. JUSTICE HOLMES, dissenting.

MR. JUSTICE BRANDEIS and I are of opinion that this judgment should be reversed. The general principle of free speech, it seems to me, must be taken to be included in the Fourteenth Amendment, in view of the scope that has been given to the word "liberty" as there used, although perhaps it may be accepted with a somewhat larger latitude of interpretation than is allowed to Congress by the sweeping language that governs or ought to govern the laws of the United States. If I am right, then I think that the criterion sanctioned by the full court in *Schenck* v. *United States* . . . applies. It is manifest that there was no present danger of an attempt to overthrow the government by force on the part of the admittedly small minority who shared the defendant's views. It is said that this manifesto was more than a theory, that it was an incitement. Every idea is an incitement. It offers itself for belief and if believed it is acted on unless some other belief outweighs it or some failure of energy stifles the movement at its birth. The only difference between the expression of an opinion and an incitement in the narrower sense is the speaker's enthusiasm for the result. Eloquence may set fire to reason. But whatever may be thought of the redundant discourse before us it had no chance of starting a present conflagration. If in the long run the beliefs expressed in proletarian dictatorship are destined to be accepted by the dominant forces of the community, the only meaning of free speech is that they should be given their chance and have their way.

If the publication of this document had been laid out as an attempt to induce an uprising against government at once and not at some indefinite time in the future it would have presented a different question. The object would have been one with which the law might deal, subject to the doubt whether there was any danger that the publication could produce any result, or in other words, whether it was not futile and too remote from possible consequences. But the indictment alleges the publication and nothing more.

Whitney v. *California*
274 U.S. 357, 47 S.Ct. 641, 71 L.Ed. 1095 (1927)

Anita Whitney was convicted of violating California's Criminal Syndicalism Act by organizing, assisting in organizing, and being a member of a group advocating unlawful force as a political weapon. Specifically, she was charged with participating in a convention of the Communist Labor Party of California, which was affiliated with the Communist International of Moscow. Evidence showed that she had personally proposed a resolution advocating a strictly political role for the party, which the convention had rejected in favor of a national program advocating various revolutionary measures including national strikes. She remained until the end of the convention and did not withdraw from the party. Majority: Sanford, Butler, Brandeis, Holmes, McReynolds, Stone, Sutherland, Taft, Van Devanter.

MR. JUSTICE SANFORD delivered the opinion of the Court. . . .

By enacting the provisions of the Syndicalism Act the State has declared, through its legislative body, that to knowingly be or become a member of or assist in organizing an association to advocate, teach or aid and abet the commission of crimes or unlawful acts of force, violence or terrorism as a means of accomplishing industrial or political changes, involves such danger to the public peace and the security of the State, that these acts should be penalized in the exercise of its police power. That determination must be given great weight. Every presumption is to be indulged in favor of the validity of the statute . . . and it may not be declared unconstitutional unless it is an arbitrary or unreasonable attempt to exercise the authority vested in the State in the public interest. . . .

Affirmed.

MR. JUSTICE BRANDEIS, concurring. . . .

Despite arguments to the contrary which had seemed to me persuasive, it is settled that the due process clause of the Fourteenth Amendment applies to matters of substantive law as well as to matters of procedure. Thus all fundamental rights comprised within the term liberty are protected by the Federal Constitution from invasion by the states. The right of free speech, the right to teach and the right of assembly are, of course, fundamental rights. . . . These may not be denied or abridged. But, although the rights of free speech and assembly are fundamental, they are not in their nature absolute. Their exercise is subject to restriction, if the particular restriction proposed is required in order to protect the state from destruction or from serious injury, political, economic or moral. That the necessity which is essential to a valid restriction does not exist unless speech would produce, or is intended to produce, a clear and imminent danger of some substantive evil which the state constitutionally may seek to prevent has been settled. . . .

This court has not yet fixed the standard by which to determine when a danger shall be deemed clear; how remote the danger may be and yet be deemed present; and what degree of evil shall be deemed sufficiently substantial to justify resort to abridgment of free speech and assembly as the means of protection. To reach sound conclusions on these matters, we must bear in mind why a state is, ordinarily, denied the power to prohibit dissemination of social, economic and political doctrine which a vast majority of its citizens believes to be false and fraught with evil consequence.

Those who won our independence believed that the final end of the state was to make men free to develop their faculties, and that in its government the deliberative forces should prevail over the arbitrary. They valued liberty both as an end and as a means. They believed liberty to be the secret of happiness and courage to be the secret of liberty. They believed that freedom to think as you will and to speak as you think are means indispensable to the discovery and spread of political truth; that without free speech and assembly discussion would be futile; that with them, discussion affords ordinarily adequate protection against the dissemination of noxious doctrine; that the greatest menace to freedom is an inert people; that public discussion is a political duty; and that this should be a fundamental principle of the American government. They recognized the risks to which all human institutions are subject. But they knew that order cannot be secured merely through fear of punishment for its infraction; that it is hazardous to discourage thought, hope and imagination; that fear breeds repression; that repression breeds hate; that hate menaces stable government; that the path of safety lies in the opportunity to discuss freely supposed grievances and proposed remedies; and that the fitting remedy for evil counsels is good ones. Believing in the power of reason as applied through public discussion, they eschewed silence coerced by law—the argument of force in its worst form. Recognizing the occasional tyrannies of governing majorities, they amended the Constitution so that free speech and assembly should be guaranteed.

Fear of serious injury cannot alone justify suppression of free speech and assembly. Men feared witches and burnt women. It is the function of speech to free men from the bondage of irrational fears. To justify suppression of free speech there must be reasonable ground to fear that serious evil will result if free speech is practiced. There must be reasonable ground to believe that the danger apprehended is imminent. There must be reasonable ground to believe that the evil to be prevented is a serious one. . . . The wide difference between advocacy and incitement, between preparation and attempt, between assembling and conspiracy, must be borne in mind. In order to support a finding of clear and present danger it must be shown either that immediate serious violence was to be expected or was advocated, or that the past conduct furnished reason to believe that such advocacy was then contemplated.

Those who won our independence by revolution were not cowards. They did not fear political change. They did not exalt order at the cost of liberty. To courageous, self-reliant men, with confidence in the power of free and fearless reasoning applied through the process of popular government, no danger flowing from speech can be deemed clear and present, unless the incidence of the evil apprehended is so imminent that it may befall before there is opportunity for full discussion. If there be time to expose through discussion the falsehood and fallacies, to avert the evil by the processes of education, the remedy to be applied is more speech, not enforced silence. Only an emergency can justify repression. Such must be the rule if authority is to be reconciled with freedom. Such, in my opinion, is the command of the Constitution. It is therefore always open to Americans to challenge a law abridg-

ing free speech and assembly by showing that there was no emergency justifying it.

Moreover, even imminent danger cannot justify resort to prohibition of these functions essential to effective democracy, unless the evil apprehended is relatively serious. Prohibition of free speech and assembly is a measure so stringent that it would be inappropriate as the means for averting a relatively trivial harm to society. A police measure may be unconstitutional merely because the remedy, although effective as means of protection, is unduly harsh or oppressive. . . . The fact that speech is likely to result in some violence or in destruction of property is not enough to justify its suppression. There must be the probability of serious injury to the State. Among free men, the deterrents ordinarily to be applied to prevent crime are education and punishment for violations of the law, not abridgment of the rights of free speech and assembly.

Whether in 1919, when Miss Whitney did the things complained of, there was in California such clear and present danger of serious evil, might have been made the important issue in this case. She might have required that the issue be determined either by the court or by the jury. She claimed below that the statute as applied to her violated the federal Constitution; but she did not claim that it was void because there was no clear and present danger of serious evil, nor did she request that the existence of these conditions of a valid measure thus restricting the rights of free speech and assembly be passed upon by the court or a jury. On the other hand, there was evidence on which the court or jury might have found that such danger existed. . . . [T]here was other testimony which tended to establish the existence of a conspiracy, on the part of members of the International Workers of the World, to commit present serious crimes, and likewise to show that such a conspiracy would be furthered by the activity of the society of which Miss Whitney was a member. Under these circumstances the judgment of the State court cannot be disturbed. . . .

MR. JUSTICE HOLMES joins in this opinion.

Dennis v. United States
341 U.S. 494, 71 S.Ct. 857, 95 L.Ed. 1137 (1951)

Dennis represents the last stage of the 1949 trial of the 11 leaders of the Communist Party of the United States for violations of the Smith Act of 1940. The Supreme Court granted certiorari, limited to a review of whether Sections 2 or 3 of the Smith Act, inherently or as construed and applied, violated the First or Fifth Amendments. Majority: Vinson, Burton, Frankfurter, Jackson, Minton, Reed. Dissenting: Black, Douglas. Not participating: Clark.

MR. CHIEF JUSTICE VINSON announced the judgment of the court and an opinion in which MR. JUSTICE REED, MR. JUSTICE BURTON, and MR. JUSTICE MINTON join. . . .

Sections 2 and 3 of the Smith Act, provide as follows:

Sec. 2

(a) It shall be unlawful for any person—

(1) to knowingly or willfully advocate, abet, advise, or teach the duty, necessity, desirability, or propriety of overthrowing or destroying any government in the United States by force or violence, or by the assassination of any officer of such government;

(2) with the intent to cause the overthrow or destruction of any government in the United States, to print, publish, edit, issue, circulate, sell, distribute, or publicly display any written or printed matter advocating, advising, or teaching the duty, necessity, desirability, or propriety of overthrowing or destroying any government in the United States by force or violence;

(3) to organize or help to organize any society, group, or assembly of persons who teach, advocate, or encourage the overthrow or destruction of any government in the United States by force or violence; or to be or become a member of, or affiliate with, any such society, group, or assembly of persons, knowing the purposes thereof. . . .

Sec. 3. It shall be unlawful for any person to attempt to commit, or to conspire to commit, any of the acts prohibited by the provisions of . . . this title. . . .

The obvious purpose of the statute is to protect existing Government, not from change by peaceable, lawful and constitutional means, but from change by violence, revolution and terrorism. . . . No one could conceive that it is not within the power of Congress to prohibit acts intended to overthrow the Government by force and violence. The question with which we are concerned here is not whether Congress has such *power*, but whether the *means* which it has employed conflict with the First and Fifth Amendments to the Constitution.

One of the bases for the contention that the means which Congress has employed are invalid takes the form of an attack on the face of the statute on the grounds that by its terms it prohibits academic discussion of the merits of Marxism-Leninism, that it stifles ideas and is contrary to all concepts of a free speech and a free press. . . .

The very language of the Smith Act negates the interpretation which petitioners would have us impose on that Act. It is directed at advocacy, not discussion. Thus, the trial judge properly charged the jury that they could not convict if they found that petitioners did "no more than pursue peaceful studies and discussions or teaching and advocacy in the realm of ideas." He further charged that it was not unlawful "to conduct in an American college or university a course explaining the philosophical theories set forth in the books which have been placed in evidence." Such a charge is in strict accord with the statutory language, and illustrates the meaning to be placed on those words. Congress did not intend to eradicate the free discussion of political theories, to destroy the traditional rights of Americans to discuss and evaluate ideas without fear of governmental sanction. Rather Congress was concerned with the very kind of activity in which the evidence showed these petitioners engaged. . . .

. . . The basis of the First Amendment is the hypothesis that speech can rebut speech, propaganda will answer propaganda, free debate of ideas will result in the wisest governmental policies. It is for this reason that this Court has recognized the inherent value of free discourse. An analysis of the leading cases in this Court which have involved direct limitations on speech, however, will demonstrate that both the majority of the Court and dissenters in particular cases have recognized that this is not an unlimited, unqualified right, but that the societal value of speech must, on occasion, be subordinated to other values and considerations. . . .

[The Court here discussed several post-World War I cases.]

The rule we deduce from these cases is that where an offense is specified by a statute in nonspeech or nonpress terms, a conviction relying upon speech or press as evidence of violation may be sustained only when the speech or publication created a "clear and present danger" of attempting or accomplishing the prohibited crime, e.g., interference with enlistment. The dissents, we repeat, in emphasizing the value of speech, were addressed to the argument of the sufficiency of the evidence. . . .

[The Court next discussed *Gitlow* and *Whitney*.]

Although no case subsequent to *Whitney* and *Gitlow* has expressly overruled the majority opinions in those cases, there is little doubt that subsequent opinions have inclined toward the Holmes-Brandeis rationale. . . . In this case we are squarely presented with the application of the "clear and present danger" test, and must decide what that phrase imports. . . .

Obviously, the words cannot mean that before the Government may act, it must wait until the putsch is about to be executed, the plans have been laid and the signal is awaited. If Government is aware that a group aiming at its overthrow is attempting to indoctrinate its members and to commit them to a course whereby they will strike when the leaders feel the circumstances permit, action by the Government is required. The argument that there is no need for Government to concern itself, for Government is strong, it possesses ample powers to put down a rebellion, it may defeat the revolution with ease needs no answer. For that is not the question. Certainly an attempt to overthrow the Government by force, even though doomed from the outset because of inadequate numbers or power of the revolutionists, is a sufficient

evil for Congress to prevent. The damage which such attempts create both physically and politically to a nation makes it impossible to measure the validity in terms of the probability of success, or the immediacy of a successful attempt. In the instant case the trial judge charged the jury that they could not convict unless they found that petitioners intended to overthrow the Government "as speedily as circumstances would permit." This does not mean, and could not properly mean, that they would not strike until there was certainty of success. What was meant was that the revolutionists would strike when they thought the time was ripe. We must therefore reject the contention that success or probability of success is the criterion.

The situation with which Justices Holmes and Brandeis were concerned in Gitlow was a comparatively isolated event, bearing little relation in their minds to any substantial threat to the safety of the community. . . . They were not confronted with any situation comparable to the instant one—the development of an apparatus designed and dedicated to the overthrow of the Government, in the context of world crisis after crisis.

Chief Judge Learned Hand, writing for the majority below, interpreted the phrase as follows: "In each case [courts] must ask whether the gravity of the 'evil,' discounted by its improbability, justifies such invasion of free speech as is necessary to avoid the danger." . . . We adopt this statement of the rule. As articulated by Chief Judge Hand, it is as succinct and inclusive as any other we might devise at this time. It takes into consideration those factors which we deem relevant, and relates their significances. More we cannot expect from words.

Likewise, we are in accord with the court below, which affirmed the trial court's finding that the requisite danger existed. The mere fact that from the period 1945 to 1948 petitioners' activities did not result in an attempt to overthrow the Government by force and violence is of course no answer to the fact that there was a group that was ready to make the attempt. The formation by petitioners of such a highly organized conspiracy, with rigidly disciplined members subject to call when the leaders, these petitioners, felt that the time had come for action, coupled with the inflammable nature of world conditions, similar uprisings in other countries, and the touch-and-go nature of our relations with countries with whom petitioners were in the very least ideologically attuned, convince us that their convictions were justified on this score. And this analysis disposes of the contention that a conspiracy to advocate, as distinguished from the advocacy itself, cannot be constitutionally restrained, because it comprises only the preparation. It is the existence of the conspiracy which creates the danger. . . . If the ingredients of the reaction are present, we cannot bind the government to wait until the catalyst is added. . . .

We agree that the standard as defined is not a neat, mathematical formulary. Like all verbalizations it is subject to criticism on the score of indefiniteness. But petitioners themselves contend that the verbalization, "clear and present danger" is the proper standard. We see no difference from the standpoint of vagueness, whether the standard of "clear and present danger" is one contained in haec verba within the statute, or whether it is the judicial measure of constitutional applicability. We have shown the indeterminate standard the phrase necessarily connotes. We do not think we have rendered that standard any more indefinite by our attempt to sum up the factors which are included within its scope. We think it well serves to indicate to those who would advocate constitutionally prohibited conduct that there is a line beyond which they may not go—a line, which they, in full knowledge of what they intend and the circumstances in which their activity takes place, will well appreciate and understand. . . .

Affirmed.

MR. JUSTICE FRANKFURTER, concurring in affirmance of the judgment. . . .

The language of the First Amendment is to be read not as barren words found in a dictionary but as symbols of historic experience illumined by the presuppositions of those who employed them. Not what words did Madison and Hamilton use, but what was it in their minds which they conveyed? Free speech is subject to prohibition of those abuses of expression which a civilized society may forbid. As in the case of every other provision of the Constitution that is not crystallized by the nature of its technical concepts, the fact that the First Amendment is not self-defining and self-enforcing neither impairs its usefulness nor compels its paralysis as a living instrument. . . .

. . . The demands of free speech in a democratic society as well as the interest in national security

are better served by candid and informed weighing of the competing interests, within the confines of the judicial process, than by announcing dogmas too inflexible for the non-Euclidian problems to be solved.

But how are competing interests to be assessed? Since they are not subject to quantitative ascertainment, the issue necessarily resolves itself into asking, who is to make the adjustment?—who is to balance the relevant factors and ascertain which interest is in the circumstances to prevail? Full responsibility for the choice cannot be given to the courts. Courts are not representative bodies. They are not designed to be a good reflex of a democratic society. Their judgment is best informed, and therefore most dependable, within narrow limits. Their essential quality is detachment, founded on independence. History teaches that the independence of the judiciary is jeopardized when courts become embroiled in the passions of the day and assume primary responsibility in choosing between competing political, economic and social pressures.

Primary responsibility for adjusting the interests which compete in the situation before us of necessity belongs to the Congress. The nature of the power to be exercised by this Court has been delineated in decisions not charged with the emotional appeal of situations such as that now before us. . . .

It is not for us to decide how we would adjust the clash of interests which this case presents were the primary responsibility for reconciling it ours. Congress has determined that the danger created by advocacy of overthrow justifies the ensuing restriction on freedom of speech. The determination was made after due deliberation, and the seriousness of the congressional purpose is attested by the volume of legislation passed to effectuate the same ends.

Can we then say that the judgment Congress exercised was denied it by the Constitution? Can we establish a constitutional doctrine which forbids the elected representatives of the people to make this choice? Can we hold that the First Amendment deprives Congress of what it deemed necessary for the Government's protection?

To make validity of legislation depend on judicial reading of events still in the womb of time—a forecast, that is, of the outcome of forces at best appreciated only with knowledge of the topmost secrets of nations—is to charge the judiciary with duties beyond its equipment. We do not expect courts to pronounce historic verdicts on bygone events. Even historians have conflicting views to this day on the origin and conduct of the French Revolution. It is as absurd to be confident that we can measure the present clash of forces and their outcome as to ask us to read history still enveloped in clouds of controversy. . . .

Civil liberties draw at best only limited strength from legal guaranties. Preoccupation by our people with the constitutionality, instead of with the wisdom of legislation or of executive action, is preoccupation with a false value. Even those who would most freely use the judicial brake on the democratic process by invalidating legislation that goes deeply against their grain, acknowledge, at least by paying lip service, that constitutionality does not exact a sense of proportion or the sanity of humor or an absence of fear. Focusing attention on constitutionality tends to make constitutionality synonymous with wisdom. When legislation touches freedom of thought and freedom of speech, such a tendency is a formidable enemy of the free spirit. Much that should be rejected as illiberal, because repressive and envenoming, may well be not unconstitutional. The ultimate reliance for the deepest needs of civilization must be found outside their vindication in courts of law; apart from all else, judges, howsoever they may conscientiously seek to discipline themselves against it, unconsciously are too apt to be moved by the deep undercurrents of public feeling. A persistent, positive translation of the liberating faith into the feelings and thoughts and actions of men and women is the real protection against attempts to strait-jacket the human mind. Such temptations will have their way, if fear and hatred are not exorcised. The mark of a truly civilized man is confidence in the strength and security derived from the inquiring mind. We may be grateful for such honest comforts as it supports, but we must be unafraid of its uncertitudes. Without open minds there can be no open society. And if society be not open the spirit of man is mutilated and becomes enslaved. . . .

Mr. Justice Black, dissenting. . . .

At the outset I want to emphasize what the crime involved in this case is, and what it is not. These petitioners were not charged with an attempt to overthrow the Government. They were not charged with overt acts of any kind designed to overthrow the Government. They were not even charged with saying anything or writing anything designed to overthrow the Government. The charge was that they agreed to assemble and to talk and publish certain ideas at a later date: The indictment is that they conspired to organize the Communist Party and to use speech or newspapers and other publications in the future to teach and advocate the forcible overthrow of the Government. No matter how it is worded, this is a virulent form of prior censorship of speech and press, which I believe the First Amendment forbids. I would hold § 3 of the Smith Act authorizing this prior restraint unconstitutional on its face and as applied. . . .

So long as this Court exercises the power of judicial review of legislation, I cannot agree that the First Amendment permits us to sustain laws suppressing freedom of speech and press on the basis of Congress's or our own notions of mere "reasonableness." Such a doctrine waters down the First Amendment so that it amounts to little more than an admonition to Congress. The Amendment as so construed is not likely to protect any but those "safe" or orthodox views which rarely need its protection. . . .

Mr. Justice Douglas, dissenting. . . .

If this were a case where those who claimed protection under the First Amendment were teaching the techniques of sabotage, the assassination of the President, the filching of documents from public files, the planting of bombs, the art of street warfare, and the like, I would have no doubts. The freedom to speak is not absolute; the teaching of methods of terror and other seditious conduct should be beyond the pale along with obscenity and immorality. This case was argued as if those were the facts. The argument imported much seditious conduct into the record. That is easy and it has popular appeal, for the activities of Communists in plotting and scheming against the free world are common knowledge. But the fact is that no such evidence was introduced at the trial. There is a statute which makes a seditious conspiracy unlawful. Petitioners, however, were not charged with a "conspiracy to overthrow" the Government. They were charged with a conspiracy to form a party and groups and assemblies of people who teach and advocate the overthrow of our Government by force or violence and with a conspiracy to advocate and teach its overthrow by force and violence. . . .

There comes a time when even speech loses its constitutional immunity. Speech innocuous one year may at another time fan such destructive flames that it must be halted in the interests of the safety of the Republic. That is the meaning of the clear and present danger test. When conditions are so critical that there will be no time to avoid the evil that the speech threatens, it is time to call a halt. Otherwise, free speech which is the strength of the Nation will be the cause of its destruction.

Yet free speech is the rule, not the exception. The restraint to be constitutional must be based on more than fear, on more than passionate opposition against the speech, on more than a revolted dislike for its contents. There must be some immediate injury to society that is likely if speech is allowed. . . .

How it can be said that there is a clear and present danger that this advocacy will succeed is, therefore, a mystery. Some nations less resilient than the United States, where illiteracy is high and where democratic traditions are only budding, might have to take drastic steps and jail these men for merely speaking their creed. But in America they are miserable merchants of unwanted ideas; their wares remain unsold. The fact that their ideas are abhorrent does not make them powerful. . . .

Vishinsky wrote in 1948 in *The Law of the Soviet State,* "In our state, naturally there can be no place for freedom of speech, press, and so on for the foes of socialism."

Our concern should be that we accept no such standard for the United States. Our faith should be that our people will never give support to these advocates of revolution, so long as we remain loyal to the purposes for which our Nation was founded.

Watkins v. *United States*
354 U.S. 178, 77 S.Ct. 1173, I L.Ed. 2d 1273 (1957)

(This case is reprinted in Chapter Three beginning on page 86.)

Barenblatt v. *United States*
360 U.S. 109, 79 S.Ct. 1081, 3 L.Ed. 2d 1115 (1959)

(This case is reprinted in Chapter Three beginning on page 89.)

II. PROTEST AND SYMBOLIC SPEECH

Brandenburg v. *Ohio*
395 U.S. 444, 89 S.Ct. 1827, 23 L.Ed. 2d 430 (1969)

This case tested the constitutionality of the Ohio criminal syndicalism statute. The facts are contained in the *per curiam* opinion that follows. (*Per curiam* means "by the Court" and is a designation the Supreme

Court uses for unsigned, and usually brief, opinions. A *per curiam* opinion sometimes indicates that the Court is only applying "settled law." At other times, a *per curiam* opinion is followed by a variety of separate opinions, as in *New York Times Co.* v. *United States,* when a signed majority opinion is not possible or desirable.) Majority: Warren, Black, Brennan, Douglas, Fortas, Harlan, Marshall, Stewart, White.

PER CURIAM.

The appellant, a leader of a Ku Klux Klan group, was convicted under the Ohio Criminal Syndicalism statute of "advocat[ing] . . . the duty, necessity, or propriety of crime, sabotage, violence, or unlawful methods of terrorism as a means of accomplishing industrial or political reform" and of "voluntarily assembl[ing] with any society, group or assemblage of persons formed to teach or advocate the doctrines of criminal syndicalism." . . . He was fined $1,000 and sentenced to one to 10 years' imprisonment. The appellant challenged the constitutionality of the criminal syndicalism statute under the First and Fourteenth Amendments to the United States Constitution, but the intermediate appellate court of Ohio affirmed his conviction without opinion. The Supreme Court of Ohio dismissed his appeal "for the reason that no substantial constitutional question exists herein." It did not file an opinion or explain its conclusions. Appeal was taken to this Court, and we noted probable jurisdiction. . . . We reverse.

The record shows that a man, identified at trial as the appellant, telephoned an announcer-reporter on the staff of a Cincinnati television station and invited him to come to a Ku Klux Klan "rally" to be held at a farm in Hamilton County. With the cooperation of the organizers, the reporter and a cameraman attended the meeting and filmed the events. Portions of the films were later broadcast on the local station and on a national network.

The prosecution's case rested on the films and on testimony identifying the appellant as the person who communicated with the reporter and who spoke at the rally. The State also introduced into evidence several articles appearing in the film, including a pistol, a rifle, a shotgun, ammunition, a Bible, and a red hood worn by the speaker in the films.

One film showed 12 hooded figures, some of whom carried firearms. They were gathered around a large wooden cross, which they burned. No one was present other than the participants and the newsmen who made the film. Most of the words uttered during the scene were incomprehensible when the film was projected, but scattered phrases could be understood that were derogatory of Negroes and, in one instance, of Jews*. Another scene on the same film showed the appellant, in Klan regalia, making a speech. The speech, in full, was as follows:

"This is an organizers' meeting. We have had quite a few members here today which are—we have hundreds, hundreds of members throughout the State of Ohio. I can quote from a newspaper clipping from the Columbus Ohio Dispatch, five weeks ago Sunday morning. The Klan has more members in the State of Ohio than does any other organization. We're not a revengent organization, but if our President, our Congress, our Supreme Court, continues to suppress the white, Caucasian race, it's possible that there might have to be some revengence taken.

"We are marching on Congress July the Fourth, four hundred thousand strong. From there we are dividing into two groups, one group to march on St. Augustine, Florida, the other group to march into Mississippi. Thank you."

The second film showed six hooded figures one of whom, later identified as the appellant, repeated

---

* The significant phrases that could be understood were:
"How far is the nigger going to—yeah"
"This is what we are going to do to the niggers"
"A dirty nigger"
"Send the Jews back to Israel"
"Let's give them back to the dark garden"
"Save America"
"Let's go back to constitutional betterment"
"Bury the niggers"
"We intend to do our part"
"Give us our state rights"
"Freedom for the whites"
"Nigger will have to fight for every inch he gets from now on."

a speech very similar to that recorded on the first film. The reference to the possibility of "revengence" was omitted, and one sentence was added: "Personally, I believe the nigger should be returned to Africa, the Jew returned to Israel." Though some of the figures in the films carried weapons, the speaker did not.

The Ohio Criminal Syndicalism Statute was enacted in 1919. From 1917 to 1920, identical or quite similar laws were adopted by 20 States and two territories. . . . In 1927, this Court sustained the constitutionality of California's Criminal Syndicalism Act . . . the text of which is quite similar to that of the laws of Ohio. *Whitney* v. *California.* . . . The Court upheld the statute on the ground that, without more, "advocating" violent means to effect political and economic change involves such danger to the security of the State that the State may outlaw it. . . . But *Whitney* has been thoroughly discredited by later decisions. See *Dennis* v. *United States.* . . . These later decisions have fashioned the principle that the constitutional guarantees of free speech and free press do not permit a State to forbid or proscribe advocacy of the use of force or of law violation except where such advocacy is directed to inciting or producing imminent lawless action and is likely to incite or produce such action. . . . "[T]he mere abstract teaching . . . of the moral propriety or even moral necessity for a resort to force and violence, is not the same as preparing a group for violent action and steeling it to such action." . . . A statute which fails to draw this distinction impermissibly intrudes upon the freedoms guaranteed by the First and Fourteenth Amendments. It sweeps within its condemnation speech which our Constitution has immunized from governmental control. . . .

Measured by this test, Ohio's Criminal Syndicalism Act cannot be sustained. The Act punishes persons who "advocate or teach the duty, necessity, or propriety" of violence "as a means of accomplishing industrial or political reform"; or who publish or circulate or display any book or paper containing such advocacy; or who "justify" the commission of violent acts "with intent to exemplify, spread or advocate the propriety of the doctrines of criminal syndicalism"; or who ". . . voluntarily assemble" with a group formed "to teach or advocate the doctrines of criminal syndicalism." Neither the indictment nor the trial judge's in-

structions to the jury in any way refined the statute's bald definition of the crime in terms of mere advocacy not distinguished from incitement to imminent lawless action.

Accordingly, we are here confronted with a statute which, by its own words and as applied, purports to punish mere advocacy and to forbid, on pain of criminal punishment, assembly with others merely to advocate the described type of action. Such a statute falls within the condemnation of the First and Fourteenth Amendments. The contrary teaching of *Whitney* v. *California* . . . cannot be supported, and that decision is therefore overruled.

Reversed.

MR. JUSTICE DOUGLAS, concurring.

While I join the opinion of the Court, I desire to enter a *caveat.* . . .

. . . I see no place in the regime of the First Amendment for any "clear and present danger" test whether strict and tight as some would make it or free-wheeling as the Court in *Dennis* rephrased it.

When one reads the opinions closely and sees when and how the "clear and present danger" test has been applied, great misgivings are aroused. First, the threats were often loud but always puny and made serious only by judges so wedded to the *status quo* that critical analysis made them nervous. Second the test was so twisted and perverted in *Dennis* as to make the trial of those teachers of Marxism an all-out political trial which was part and parcel of the Cold War that has eroded substantial parts of the First Amendment.

Action is often a method of expression and within the protection of the First Amendment.

Suppose one tears up his own copy of the Constitution in eloquent protest to a decision of this Court. May he be indicted?

Suppose one rips his own Bible to shreds to celebrate his departure from one "faith" and his embrace of atheism. May he be indicted? . . .

One's beliefs have long been thought to be sanctuaries which government could not invade. . . . I think that all matters of belief are beyond the reach of subpoenas or the probings of investigators. That is why the invasions of privacy made by investigating committees were notoriously unconstitutional. That is the deep-seated fault in the infamous loyalty-security hearings which, since 1947 when Truman launched them, have processed 20,000,000 men and women. Those hearings were primarily concerned with one's thoughts, ideas, beliefs, and convictions. They were the most blatant violations of the First Amendment we have ever known.

The line between what is permissible and not subject to control and what may be made impermissible and subject to regulation is the line between ideas and overt acts.

The example usually given by those who would punish speech is the case of one who falsely shouts fire in a crowded theatre.

This is, however, a classic case where speech is brigaded with action. . . . They are indeed inseparable and a prosecution can be launched for the overt acts actually caused. Apart from rare instances of that kind, speech is, I think, immune from prosecution.

Clark v. *Community for Creative Non-Violence*
468 U.S. 288, 104 S.Ct. 3065, 82 L.Ed. 2d 221 (1984)

In 1982, the National Park Service issued a permit to Community for Creative Non-Violence (CCNV) to conduct a demonstration in Lafayette Park and the Mall, which are national parks in Washington, D.C. CCNV wanted to protest the plight of the homeless, and the permit authorized erection of two symbolic tent cities. Relying on its regulations, however, the Park Service denied CCNV's request that demonstrators be allowed to sleep in the tents. CCNV then filed suit in United States District Court for the District of Columbia claiming that the Park Service regulations banning sleep violated the First Amendment. The district court granted summary judgment for the Park Service, but the Court of Appeals for the District of Columbia, sitting *en banc*, reversed 6 votes to 5. Majority: White, Blackmun, Burger, O'Connor, Powell, Rehnquist, Stevens. Dissenting: Marshall, Brennan.

JUSTICE WHITE delivered the opinion of the Court.

The issue in this case is whether a National Park Service regulation prohibiting camping in certain parks violates the First Amendment when applied to prohibit demonstrators from sleeping in Lafayette Park and the Mall in connection with a demonstration intended to call attention to the plight of the homeless. We hold that it does not and reverse the contrary judgment of the Court of Appeals.

The Interior Department, through the National Park Service, is charged with responsibility for the management and maintenance of the National Parks and is authorized to promulgate rules and regulations for the use of the parks in accordance with the purposes for which they were established. . . .

The network of National Parks includes the National Memorial-core parks, Lafayette Park and the Mall, which are set in the heart of Washington, D.C., and which are unique resources that the Federal Government holds in trust for the American people. Lafayette Park is a roughly seven-acre square located across Pennsylvania Avenue from the White House. . . .

We need not differ with the view of the Court of Appeals that overnight sleeping in connection with the demonstration is expressive conduct protected to some extent by the First Amendment. We assume for present purposes, but do not decide, that such is the case . . . but this assumption only begins the inquiry. Expression, whether oral or written or symbolized by conduct, is subject to reasonable time, place, and manner restrictions. We have often noted that restrictions of this kind are valid provided that they are justified without reference to the content of the regulated speech, that they are narrowly tailored to serve a significant governmental interest, and that they leave open ample alternative channels for communication of the information. . . .

It is also true that a message may be delivered by conduct that is intended to be communicative and that, in context, would reasonably be understood by the viewer to be communicative. . . . Symbolic expression of this kind may be forbidden or regulated if the conduct itself may constitutionally be regulated, if the regulation is narrowly drawn to further a substantial governmental interest, and if the interest is unrelated to the suppression of free speech.

The United States submits, as it did in the Court of Appeals, that the regulation forbidding sleeping is defensible either as a time, place, or manner restriction or as a regulation of symbolic conduct. We agree with that assessment. . . .

The requirement that the regulation be content neutral is clearly satisfied. The courts below accepted that view, and it is not disputed here that the prohibition on camping, and on sleeping specifically, is content neutral and is not being applied because of disagreement with the message presented. Neither was the regulation faulted, nor could it be, on the ground that without overnight sleeping the plight of the homeless could not be communicated in other ways. The regulation otherwise left the demonstration intact, with its symbolic city, signs, and the presence of those who were willing to take their turns in a day-and-night vigil. Respondents do not suggest that there was, or is, any barrier to delivering to the media, or to the public by other means, the intended message concerning the plight of the homeless.

It is also apparent to us that the regulation narrowly focuses on the Government's substantial interest in maintaining the parks in the heart of our capital in an attractive and intact condition, readily available to the millions of people who wish to see and enjoy them by their presence. To permit camping—using these areas as living accommodations—would be totally inimical to these purposes, as would be readily understood by those who have frequented the National Parks across the country and observed the unfortunate consequences of the activities of those who refuse to confine their camping to designated areas.

It is urged by respondents, and the Court of Appeals was of this view, that if the symbolic city of tents was to be permitted and if the demonstrators did not intend to cook, dig, or engage in aspects of camping other than sleeping, the incremental benefit to the parks could not justify the ban on sleeping, which was here an expressive activity said to enhance the message concerning the plight of the poor and homeless. We cannot agree. In the first place, we seriously doubt that the First Amendment requires the Park Service to permit a demonstration in Lafayette Park and the Mall involving a 24-hour vigil and the erection of tents to accommodate 150 people. Furthermore, although we have assumed for present purposes that the sleeping banned in this case would have an expressive element, it is evident that its major value to this demonstration would be facilitative. Without a permit to sleep, it would be difficult to get the poor and homeless to participate or to be present at all. . . .

Beyond this, however, it is evident from our cases that the validity of this regulation need not be judged solely by reference to the demonstration at hand. . . . Absent the prohibition on sleeping, there would be other groups who would demand permission to deliver an asserted message by camping in Lafayette Park. Some of them would surely have as credible a claim in this regard as does CCNV, and the denial of permits to still others would present difficult problems for the Park Service. With the prohibition, however, as is evident in the case before us, at least some around-the-clock demonstrations lasting for days on end will not materialize, others will be limited in size and duration, and the purposes of the regulation will thus be materially served. Perhaps these purposes would be more effectively and not so clumsily achieved by preventing tents and 24-hour vigils entirely in the core areas. But the Park Service's decision to permit non-sleeping demonstrations does not, in our view, impugn the camping prohibition as a valuable, but perhaps imperfect, protection to the parks. If the Government has a legitimate interest in ensuring that the National Parks are adequately protected, which we think it has, and if the parks would be more exposed to harm without the sleeping prohibition than with it, the ban is safe from invalidation under the First Amendment as a reasonable regulation on the manner in which a demonstration may be carried out. . . .

We have difficulty, therefore, in understanding why the prohibition against camping, with its ban on sleeping overnight, is not a reasonable time, place, and manner regulation that withstands constitutional scrutiny. Surely the regulation is not unconstitutional on its face. None of its provisions appears unrelated to the ends that it was designed to serve. Nor is it any less valid when applied to prevent camping in Memorial-core parks by those who wish to demonstrate and deliver a message to the public and the central government. Damage to the parks as well as their partial inaccessibility to other members of the public can as easily result from camping by demonstrators as by non-demonstrators. In neither case must the Government tolerate it. All those who would resort to the parks must abide by otherwise valid rules for their use, just as they must observe the traffic laws, sanitation regulations, and laws to preserve the public peace. This is no more than a reaffirmation that reasonable time, place, and manner restrictions on expression are constitutionally acceptable. . . .

Accordingly, the judgment of the Court of Appeals is

Reversed.

JUSTICE MARSHALL, with whom JUSTICE BRENNAN joins, dissenting.

The Court's disposition of this case is marked by two related failings. First, the majority is either unwilling or unable to take seriously the First Amendment claims advanced by respondents. Contrary to the impression given by the majority, respondents are not supplicants seeking to wheedle an undeserved favor from the Government. They are citizens raising issues of profound public importance who have properly turned to the courts for the vindication of their constitutional rights. Second, the majority misapplies the test for ascertaining whether a restraint on speech qualifies as a reasonable time, place, and manner regulation. In determining what constitutes a sustainable regulation, the majority fails to subject the alleged interests of the Government to the degree of scrutiny required to ensure that expressive activity protected by the First Amendment remains free of unnecessary limitations. . . .

The majority assumes, without deciding, that the respondents' conduct is entitled to constitutional protection. . . . The problem with this assumption is that the Court thereby avoids examining closely the reality of respondents' planned expression. The majority's approach denatures respondents' asserted right and thus makes all too easy identification of a government interest sufficient to warrant its abridgement. A realistic appraisal of the competing interests at stake in this case requires a closer look at the nature of the expressive conduct at issue and the context in which that conduct would be displayed. . . .

The Court has previously acknowledged the importance of context in determining whether an act can properly be denominated as "speech" for First Amendment purposes and has provided guidance concerning the way in which courts should "read" a context in making this determination. The leading case is *Spence* v. *Washington,* where this Court held that displaying a United States flag with a peace symbol attached to it was conduct protected by the First Amendment. The Court looked first to the intent of the speaker—whether there was an "intent to convey a particularized message"—and second to the perception of the audience—whether "the likelihood was great that the message would be understood by those who viewed it." . . . Here respondents clearly intended to protest the reality of homelessness by sleeping outdoors in the winter in the near vicinity of the magisterial residence of the President of the United States. In addition to accentuating the political character of their protest by their choice of location and mode of communication, respondents also intended to underline the meaning of their protest by giving their demonstration satirical names. Respondents planned to name the demonstration on the Mall "Congressional Village," and the demonstration in Lafayette Park, "Reaganville II."

Nor can there be any doubt that in the surrounding circumstances the likelihood was great that the political significance of sleeping in the parks would be understood by those who viewed it. Certainly the news media understood the significance of respondents' proposed activity; newspapers and magazines from around the Nation reported their previous sleep-in and their planned display. Ordinary citizens, too, would likely understand the political message intended by respondents. This likelihood stems from the remarkably apt fit between the activity in which respondents seek to engage and the social problem they seek to highlight. . . .

According to the majority, the significant government interest advanced by denying respondents' request to engage in sleep-speech is the interest in "maintaining the parks in the heart of our capital in an attractive and intact condition, readily available to the millions of people who wish to see and enjoy them by their presence." . . . That interest is indeed significant. However, neither the Government nor the majority adequately explains how prohibiting respondents' planned activity will substantially further that interest.

The majority's attempted explanation begins with the curious statement that it seriously doubts that the First Amendment requires the Park Service to permit a demonstration in Lafayette Park and the Mall involving a 24-hour vigil and the erection of tents to accommodate 150 people. . . . I cannot perceive why the Court should have "serious doubts" regarding this matter and it provides no explanation for its uncertainty. Furthermore, even if the majority's doubts were well-founded, I cannot see how such doubts relate to the problem at hand. The issue posed by this case is not whether the Government is constitutionally compelled to permit the erection of tents and the staging of a continuous 24-hour vigil; rather, the issue is whether any substantial government interest is served by banning sleep that is part of a political demonstration.

What the Court may be suggesting is that if the tents and the 24-hour vigil are permitted, but not constitutionally required to be permitted, then respondents have no constitutional right to engage in expressive conduct that supplements these activities. Put in arithmetical terms, the Court appears to contend that if X is permitted by grace rather than by constitutional compulsion, x + 1 can be denied without regard to the requirements the Government must normally satisfy in order to restrain protected activity. This notion, however, represents a misguided conception of the First Amendment. The First Amendment requires the Government to justify *every* instance of abridgement. . . .

The disposition of this case impels me to make two additional observations. First, in this case, as in some others involving time, place, and manner restrictions, the Court has dramatically lowered its scrutiny of governmental regulations once it has determined that such regulations are content neutral. The result has been the creation of a two-tiered approach to First Amendment cases: while regulations that turn on the content of the expression are subjected to a strict form of judicial review, regulations that are aimed at matters other than expression receive only a minimal level of scrutiny. The minimal scrutiny prong of this two-tiered approach has led to an unfortunate diminution of First Amendment protection. By narrowly limiting its concern to whether a given regulation creates a content-based distinction, the Court has seemingly overlooked the fact that content-neutral restrictions are also capable of unnecessarily restricting protected expressive activity. . . . The Court, however, has transformed the ban against content-distinctions from a floor that offers all persons at least equal liberty under the First Amendment into a ceiling that restricts persons to the protection of First Amendment equality—but nothing more. The consistent imposition of silence upon all may fulfill the dictates of an even-handed content-neutrality. But it offends our "profound national commitment to the principle that debate on public issues should be uninhibited, robust, and wide-open." . . .

Second, the disposition of this case reveals a mistaken assumption regarding the motives and behavior of government officials who create and administer content-neutral regulations. The Court's salutary skepticism of governmental decisionmaking in First Amendment matters suddenly dissipates once it determines that a restriction is not content-based. The Court evidently assumes that the balance struck by officials is deserving of deference so long as it does not appear to be tainted by content discrimination. What the Court fails to recognize is that public officials have strong incentives to overregulate even in the absence of an intent to censor particular views. This incentive stems from the fact that of the two groups whose interests officials must accommodate—on the one hand, the interests of the general public and on the other, the interests of those who seek to use a particular forum for First Amendment activity—the political power of the former is likely to be far greater than that of the latter. . . .

III. FREEDOM OF ASSOCIATION

New York State Club Association v. New York City*
56 U.S.L.W. 4653 (1988)

New York City's Human Rights Law forbids discrimination based on race, creed, sex, mental or physical handicap, and sexual orientation in places of "public accommodation, resort or amusement." A 1984 amendment (Local Law 63) extended the law to clubs other than benevolent orders (such as lodges and fraternal organizations) and religious groups if the clubs had more than 400 members, served meals, and received dues from the employers of members. An association of 125 clubs in New York State sued in state court that the law was unconstitutional on its face as a violation of the freedom of association protected by the First Amendment, as well as for other reasons. Some of the clubs had rules prohibiting female members. After defeats in the trial court, an intermediate appellate court, and the New York Court of Appeals, the Club Association appealed to the United States Supreme Court. Only months before this decision, Justice Blackmun resigned his membership in Washington's exclusive Cosmos Club, male-only at the time. Justice Kennedy resigned from San Francisco's male-only Olympic Club shortly before his nomination to the Court in 1987. The part of Justice White's opinion dealing with the validity of the law's exemption of benevolent and religious orders under the equal protection clause is omitted. Majority: White, Blackmun, Brennan, Kennedy, Marshall, O'Connor, Rehnquist, Scalia, Stevens.

JUSTICE WHITE delivered the opinion of the Court.

New York City has adopted a local law that forbids discrimination by certain private clubs. The New York Court of Appeals rejected a facial challenge to this law based on the First and Fourteenth Amendments. We sit in review of that judgment. . . .

. . . [A]ppellant brought this suit challenging the constitutionality of the statute on its face before any enforcement proceedings were initiated against any of its member associations. Although such facial challenges are sometimes permissible and often have been entertained, especially when speech protected by the First Amendment is at stake, to prevail on a facial attack the plaintiff must demonstrate that the challenged law either "could never be applied in a valid manner" or that even though it may

be validly applied to the plaintiff and others, it nevertheless is so broad that it "may inhibit the constitutionally protected speech of third parties." Properly understood, the latter kind of facial challenge is an exception to ordinary standing requirements, and is justified only by the recognition that free expression may be inhibited almost as easily by the potential or threatened use of power as by the actual exercise of that power. Both exceptions, however, are narrow ones: the first kind of facial challenge will not succeed unless the court finds that "every application of the statute created an impermissible risk of suppression of ideas," and the second kind of facial challenge will not succeed unless the statute is "substantially" overbroad, which requires the court to find "a realistic danger that the statute itself will significantly compromise recognized First Amendment protections of parties not before the Court."

We are unpersuaded that appellant is entitled

* This case should also be read in connection with Chapter Twelve.

to make either one of these two distinct facial challenges. Appellant conceded at oral argument, understandably we think, that the antidiscrimination provisions of the Law certainly could be constitutionally applied at least to some of the large clubs, under this Court's decisions in *Rotary* and *Roberts*. The clubs that are covered under the Law contain at least 400 members. They thus are comparable in size to the local chapters of the Jaycees that we found not to be protected private associations in *Roberts*, and they are considerably larger than many of the local clubs that were found to be unprotected in *Rotary*, some which included as few as 20 members. The clubs covered by Local Law 63 also provide "regular meal service" and receive regular payments "directly or indirectly from or on behalf of nonmembers for the furtherance of trade or business." The city found these two characteristics to be significant in pinpointing organizations which are "commercial" in nature, "where business deals are often made and personal contacts valuable for business purposes, employment and professional advancement are formed."

These characteristics are at least as significant in defining the nonprivate nature of these associations, because of the kind of role that strangers play in their ordinary existence, as is the regular participation of strangers at meetings, which we emphasized in *Roberts* and *Rotary*. It may well be that a considerable amount of private or intimate association occurs in such a setting, as is also true in many restaurants and other places of public accommodation, but that fact alone does not afford the entity as a whole any constitutional immunity to practice discrimination when the Government has barred it from doing so. Although there may be clubs that would be entitled to constitutional protection despite the presence of these characteristics, surely it cannot be said that Local Law 63 is invalid on its face because it infringes the private associational rights of each and every club covered by it.

The same may be said about the contention that the Law infringes upon every club member's right of expressive association. The ability and the opportunity to combine with others to advance one's views is a powerful practical means of ensuring the perpetuation of the freedoms the First Amendment has guaranteed to individuals as against the Government. "Effective advocacy of both public and private points of view, particularly controversial ones, is undeniably enhanced by group association, as this Court has more than once recognized by remarking upon the close nexus between the freedoms of speech and assembly." This is not to say, however, that in every setting in which individuals exercise some discrimination in choosing associates, their selective process of inclusion and exclusion is protected by the Constitution.

On its face, Local Law 63 does not affect "in any significant way" the ability of individuals to form associations that will advocate public or private viewpoints. It does not require the clubs "to abandon or alter" any activities that are protected by the First Amendment. If a club seeks to exclude individuals who do not share the views that the club's members wish to promote, the Law erects no obstacle to this end. Instead, the Law merely prevents an association from using race, sex, and the other specified characteristics as shorthand measures in place of what the city considers to be more legitimate criteria for determining membership. It is conceivable, of course, that an association might be able to show that it is organized for specific expressive purposes and that it will not be able to advocate its desired viewpoints nearly as effectively if it cannot confine its membership to those who share the same sex, for example, or the same religion. In the case before us, however, it seems sensible enough to believe that many of the large clubs covered by the Law are not of this kind. We could hardly hold otherwise on the record before us, which contains no specific evidence on the characteristics of *any* club covered by the Law.

The facial attack based on the claim that Local Law 63 is invalid in all of its applications must therefore fail. Appellant insists, however, that there are some clubs within the reach of the Law that are "distinctively private" and that the Law is therefore overbroad and invalid on its face. But as we have indicated, this kind of facial challenge also falls short.

The overbreadth doctrine is "strong medicine" that is used "sparingly and only as a last resort." A law is constitutional unless it is "substantially overbroad." To succeed in its challenge, appellant must demonstrate from the text of the Law and from actual fact that a substantial number of instances exist in which the Law cannot be applied constitutionally. Yet appellant has not identified those clubs for whom the antidiscrimination provisions will impair their ability to associate together or to advocate public or private viewpoints. No record was made in this respect, we are not informed of the characteristics of any particular clubs, and hence we cannot conclude that the Law threatens to undermine the associational or expressive purposes of any club, let alone a substantial number of them. We therefore cannot conclude that the Law is substantially overbroad and must assume that "whatever overbreadth may exist should be cured through case-by-case analysis of the fact sit-

uations to which its sanctions, assertedly, may not be applied." . . .

These opportunities for individual associations to contest the constitutionality of the Law as it may be applied against them are adequate to assure that any overbreadth under the Law will be curable through case-by-case analysis of specific facts. . . .

We therefore affirm the judgment below.

So ordered.

IV. THE ELECTORAL PROCESS

Federal Election Commission v. National Conservative Political Action Committee
470 U.S. 480, 105 S.Ct. 1459, 84 L.Ed. 2d 455 (1985)

This case involved the constitutionality of limits imposed by the Presidential Election Campaign Fund Act on money spent independently by political committees on behalf of a presidential candidate's campaign. The facts of the case are explained in the majority opinion. The first part of the majority opinion, not reprinted here, was concerned with whether the Democratic National Committee and the Democratic Party of the United States had standing, along with the Federal Election Commission, to file suit. On this question of standing, Justices Rehnquist, Blackmun, Powell, and O'Connor and Chief Justice Burger concluded that only the Federal Election Commission had standing. Justices Brennan, White, and Marshall dissented and would have granted standing to the Democratic National Committee. Justice Stevens did not think it necessary to decide standing. The second part of Justice Rehnquist's opinion for the majority, which follows, is concerned with the constitutionality of the spending limits. On this question, only Justices White and Marshall dissented from the majority position. Majority: Rehnquist, Blackmun, Burger, Brennan, O'Connor, Powell, Stevens. Dissenting: White, Marshall.

JUSTICE REHNQUIST delivered the opinion of the Court.

The Presidential Election Campaign Fund Act (Fund Act) offers the Presidential candidates of major political parties the option of receiving public financing for their general election campaigns. If a

Presidential candidate elects public financing, § 9012(f) makes it a criminal offense for independent "political committees," such as appellees National Conservative Political Action Committee (NCPAC) and Fund For A Conservative Majority (FCM), to expend more than $1,000 to further that candidate's election. A three-judge District Court for the Eastern District of Pennsylvania . . . held § 9012(f) unconstitutional on its face because it violated the First Amendment to the United States Constitution. . . . We . . . affirm its judgment as to the constitutional validity of § 9012(f). . . .

NCPAC is a nonprofit, nonmembership corporation formed under the District of Columbia Nonprofit Corporation Act in August 1975 and registered with the FEC as a political committee. Its primary purpose is to attempt to influence directly or indirectly the election or defeat of candidates for federal, state, and local offices by making contributions and by making its own expenditures. It is governed by a three-member board of directors which is elected annually by the existing board. The board's chairman and the other two members make all decisions concerning which candidates to support or oppose, the strategy and methods to employ, and the amounts of money to spend. Its contributors have no role in these decisions. It raises money by general and specific direct mail solicitations. . . .

FCM is incorporated under the laws of Virginia and is registered with the FEC as a multicandidate political committee. In all material respects it is identical to NCPAC.

Both NCPAC and FCM are self-described ideological organizations with a conservative political philosophy. They solicited funds in support of President Reagan's 1980 campaign, and they spent money on such means as radio and television advertisements to encourage voters to elect him President. On the record before us, these expenditures were "independent" in that they were not made at the request of or in coordination with the official Reagan election campaign committee or any of its agents. Indeed, there are indications that the efforts of these organizations were at times viewed with disfavor by the official campaign as counterproductive to its chosen strategy. NCPAC and FCM expressed their intention to conduct similar activities in support of President Reagan's reelection in 1984, and we may assume that they did so. . . .

The PACs in this case, of course, are not lone pamphleteers or street corner orators in the Tom Paine mold; they spend substantial amounts of money in order to communicate their political ideas through sophisticated media advertisements. And of course the criminal sanction in question is applied to the expenditure of money to propagate political views, rather than to the propagation of those views unaccompanied by the expenditure of money. But for purposes of presenting political views in connection with a nationwide Presidential election, allowing the presentation of views while forbidding the expenditure of more than $1,000 to present them is much like allowing a speaker in a public hall to express his views while denying him the use of an amplifying system. . . .

We also reject the notion that the PACs' form of organization or method of solicitation diminishes their entitlement to First Amendment protection. The First Amendment freedom of association is squarely implicated in this case. NCPAC and FCM are mechanisms by which large numbers of individuals of modest means can join together in organizations which serve to "amplif[y] the voice of their adherents." . . .

To say that their collective action in pooling their resources to amplify their voices is not entitled to full First Amendment protection would subordinate the voices of those of modest means as opposed to those sufficiently wealthy to be able to buy expensive media ads with their own resources.

Our decision in *FEC* v. *National Right to Work Committee* . . . is not to the contrary. That case turned on the special treatment historically accorded corporations. In return for the special advantages that the State confers on the corporate form, individuals acting jointly through corporations forgo some of the rights they have as individuals. . . . We held in *NRWC* that a rather intricate provision of the Federal Election Campaign Act dealing with the prohibition of corporate campaign contributions to political candidates did not violate the First Amendment. . . .

Like the National Right to Work Committee, NCPAC and FCM are also formally incorporated; however, this is not a "corporations" case because § 9012(f) applies not just to corporations but to any "committee, association, or organization (whether or not incorporated)" that accepts contributions or makes expenditures in connection with electoral campaigns. The terms of § 9012(f)'s prohibition apply equally to an informal neighborhood group that solicits contributions and spends money on a Presidential election as to the wealthy and professionally managed PACs involved in this case. . . .

Having concluded that the PAC's expenditures are entitled to full First Amendment protection, we now look to see if there is a sufficiently strong governmental interest served by § 9012(f)'s restriction on them and whether the section is narrowly tailored to the evil that may legitimately be regulated. . . .

We held in *Buckley* . . . that preventing corruption or the appearance of corruption are the only legitimate and compelling government interests thus far identified for restricting campaign finances. In *Buckley* we struck down the FECA's limitation on individuals' independent expenditures because we found no tendency in such expenditures, uncoordinated with the candidate or his campaign, to corrupt or to give the appearance of corruption. For similar reasons, we also find § 9012(f)'s limitation on independent expenditures by political committees to be constitutionally infirm.

Corruption is a subversion of the political process. Elected officials are influenced to act contrary to their obligations of office by the prospect of financial gain to themselves or infusions of money into their campaigns. The hallmark of corruption is the financial *quid pro quo:* dollars for political favors. But here the conduct proscribed is not contributions to the candidate, but independent expenditures in support of the candidate. The amounts given to the PACs are overwhelmingly small contributions, well under the $1,000 limit on contributions upheld in *Buckley;* and the contributions are by definition not coordinated with the campaign of the candidate. The Court concluded in *Buckley* that there was a fundamental constitutional difference between money spent to advertise one's views independently of the candidate's campaign and money contributed to the candidate to be spent on his campaign. . . .

We think that the same conclusion must follow here. It is contended that, because the PACs may by the breadth of their organizations spend larger amounts than the individuals in *Buckley,* the potential for corruption is greater. But precisely what the "corruption" may consist of we are never told with assurance. The fact that candidates and elected officials may alter or reaffirm their own positions on issues in response to political messages paid for by the PACs can hardly be called corruption, for one of the essential features of democracy is the presentation to the electorate of varying points of view. It is of course hypothetically possible here, as in the case of the independent expenditures forbidden in *Buckley,* that candidates may take notice of and reward those responsible for PAC expenditures by giving official favors to the latter in exchange for the supporting messages. But here, as in *Buckley,* the absence of prearrangement and coordination undermines the value of the expenditure to the candidate, and thereby alleviates the danger that expenditures will be given as a *quid pro quo* for improper commitments from the candidate. On this record, such an exchange of political favors for uncoordinated expenditures remains a hypothetical possibility and nothing more. . . .

The judgment of the District Court is affirmed as to the constitutionality of § 9012(f). . . .

It is so ordered.

JUSTICE WHITE, dissenting. . . .

Section 9012(f) . . . limits to $1000 the annual independent expenditures a PAC can make to further the election of a candidate receiving public funds. Because these expenditures "produce speech at the core of the First Amendment" . . . the majority concludes that they can only be regulated in order to avoid real or apparent corruption. Perceiving no such danger, since the money does not go directly to political candidates or their committees, it strikes down § 9012(f).

My disagreements with this analysis, which continues this Court's dismemberment of congressional efforts to regulate campaign financing, are many. First, I continue to believe that *Buckley* . . . was wrongly decided. . . .

In *Buckley,* I explained at some length why I am quite sure that regulations of campaign spending similar to that at issue here are constitutional. . . .

The burden on actual speech imposed by limitations on the spending of money is minimal and indirect. All rights of direct political expression and advocacy are retained. Even under the campaign laws as originally enacted, everyone was free to spend as much as they chose to amplify their views on general political issues, just not specific candidates. The restrictions, to the extent they do affect speech, are viewpoint-neutral and indicate no hostility to the speech itself or its effects. . . .

The credulous acceptance of the formal distinction between coordinated and independent expenditures blinks political reality. That the PACs' expenditures are not formally "coordinated" is too slender a reed on which to distinguish them from actual contributions to the campaign. The candidate cannot help but know of the extensive efforts "independently" undertaken on his behalf. In this realm of possible tacit understandings and implied agreements, I see no reason not to accept the congressional judgment that so-called independent expenditures must be closely regulated. . . .

Even if I accepted *Buckley* as binding precedent, I nonetheless would uphold § 9012(f). . . .

The majority never explicitly identifies whose First Amendment interests it believes it is protecting. However, its concern for rights of association and the effective political speech of those of modest means . . . indicates that it is concerned with the interests of the PACs' contributors. But the "contributors" are exactly that—contributors, rather than speakers. Every reason the majority gives for treating § 9012(f) as a restraint on speech relates to the effectiveness with which the donors can make their voices heard. In other words, what the majority purports to protect is the right of the contributors to make contributions.

But the contributors are not engaging in speech; at least, they are not engaging in speech to any greater extent than are those who contribute directly to political campaigns. *Buckley* explicitly distin-

guished between, on the one hand, using one's own money to express one's views, and, on the other, giving money to someone else in the expectation that that person will use the money to express views with which one is in agreement. This case falls within the latter category. As the *Buckley* Court stated with regard to contributions to campaigns, "the transformation of contributions into political debate involves speech by someone other than the contributor." . . . The majority does not explain the metamorphosis of donated dollars from money into speech by virtue of the identity of the donee. . . .

This case is in any event different enough from *Buckley* that that decision is not dispositive. . . .

Because it is an indispensable component of the public funding scheme, § 9012(f) is supported by governmental interests absent in *Buckley*. Rather than forcing Congress to abandon public financing because it is unworkable without constitutionally prohibited restrictions on independent spending, I would hold that § 9012(f) is permissible precisely because it is a necessary, narrowly-drawn means to a constitutional end. The need to make public financing, with its attendant benefits, workable is a constitutionally sufficient additional justification for the burden on First Amendment rights. . . .

V. FREEDOM OF THE PRESS

New York Times Company v. Sullivan
376 U.S. 254, 84 S.Ct. 710, 11 L.Ed. 2d 686 (1964)

Action for libel was brought in the Circuit Court of Montgomery County, Alabama, by a city commissioner of public affairs—whose duties included the supervision of the police department—against the *New York Times* for publication of a paid advertisement describing maltreatment in the city of black students protesting segregation and against four individuals whose names, among others, appeared in the advertisement. The jury awarded plaintiff damages of $500,000 against all defendants, and the judgment on the verdict was affirmed by the Supreme Court of Alabama on the grounds that the statements in the advertisement were libelous per se, false, and not privileged, and that the evidence showed malice on the part of the newspaper. The state court rejected the defendants' constitutional objections on the ground that the First Amendment does not protect libelous publications. Majority: Brennan, Black, Clark, Douglas, Goldberg, Harlan, Stewart, Warren, White.

MR. JUSTICE BRENNAN delivered the opinion of the Court.

We are required for the first time in this case to determine the extent to which the constitutional protections for speech and press limit a State's power to award damages in a libel action brought by a public official against critics of his official conduct. . . .

Respondent's complaint alleged that he had been libeled by statements in a full-page advertisement that was carried in the *New York Times* on March 29, 1960. Entitled "Heed Their Rising Voices," the advertisement began by stating that "As the whole world knows by now, thousands of Southern Negro students are engaged in widespread non-violent demonstrations in positive affirmation of the right to live in human dignity as guaranteed by the U.S. Constitution and the Bill of Rights." It went on to charge that "in their efforts to uphold these guarantees, they are being met by an unprecedented wave of terror by those who would deny and negate that document which the whole world looks upon as setting the pattern for modern freedom. . . ."

Of the 10 paragraphs of text in the advertisement, the third and a portion of the sixth were the basis of respondent's claim of libel. . . .

Although neither of these statements mentions respondent by name, he contended that the word "police" in the third paragraph referred to him as the Montgomery Commissioner who supervised the Police Department, so that he was being accused of "ringing" the campus with police. He further claimed that the paragraph would be read as imputing to the police, and hence to him, the padlocking of the dining hall in order to starve the students into submission. As to the sixth paragraph, he contended that since arrests are ordinarily made by the police, the statement "They have arrested [Dr. King] seven times" would be read as referring to him; he further contended that the "they" who did the arresting would be equated with the "they" who committed the other described acts and with the "Southern violators." . . .

We hold that the rule of law applied by the Alabama courts is constitutionally deficient for failure to provide the safeguards for freedom of speech and of the press that are required by the First and Fourteenth Amendments in a libel action brought by a public official against critics of his official conduct. We further hold that under the proper safeguards the evidence presented in this case is constitutionally insufficient to support the judgment for respondent. . . .

Respondent relies heavily, as did the Alabama courts, on statements of this Court to the effect that the Constitution does not protect libelous publications. Those statements do not foreclose our inquiry here. None of the cases sustained the use of libel laws to impose sanctions upon expression critical of the official conduct of public officials. . . . In the only previous case that did present the question of constitutional limitations upon the power to award damages for libel of a public official, the Court was equally divided and the question was not decided. . . .

The general proposition that freedom of expression upon public questions is secured by the First Amendment has long been settled by our decisions. . . .

Thus we consider this case against the background of a profound national commitment to the principle that debate on public issues should be uninhibited, robust, and wide-open, and that it may well include vehement, caustic, and sometimes unpleasantly sharp attacks on government and public officials. . . . The present advertisement, as an expression of grievance and protest on one of the major public issues of our time, would seem clearly to qualify for the constitutional protection. The question is whether it forfeits that protection by the falsity of some of its factual statements and by its alleged defamation of respondent. . . .

Authoritative interpretations of the First Amendment guarantees have consistently refused to recognize an exception for any test of truth, whether administered by judges, juries, or administrative officials—and especially not one that puts the burden of proving truth on the speaker. . . . The constitutional protection does not turn upon "the truth, popularity, or social utility of the ideas and beliefs which are offered." . . . As Madison said, "Some degree of abuse is inseparable from the proper use of every thing; and in no instance is this more true than in that of the press."

That erroneous statement is inevitable in free debate, and that it must be protected if the freedoms of expression are to have the "breathing space" that they "need . . . to survive" . . . [have been recognized].

Just as factual error affords no warrant for repressing speech that would otherwise be free, the same is true of injury to official reputation. . . .

If neither factual error nor defamatory content suffices to remove the constitutional shield from criticism of official conduct, the combination of the two elements is no less inadequate. . . .

A rule compelling the critic of official conduct to guarantee the truth of all his factual assertions—and to do so on pain of libel judgments virtually unlimited in amount—leads to a comparable "self-censorship." Allowance of the defense of truth, with the burden of proving it on the defendant, does not mean that only false speech will be deterred. Even courts accepting this defense as an adequate safeguard have recognized the difficulties of adducing legal proofs that the alleged libel was true in all its factual particulars. . . .

Under such a rule would-be critics of official conduct may be deterred from voicing their criticism, even though it is believed to be true and even though it is in fact true, because of doubt whether it can be proved in court or fear of the expense of having to do so. They tend to make only statements which "steer far wider of the unlawful zone." . . . The rule thus dampens the vigor and limits the variety of public debate. It is inconsistent with the First and Fourteenth Amendments.

The constitutional guarantees require, we think, a federal rule that prohibits a public official from recovering damages for a defamatory falsehood relating to his official conduct unless he proves that the statement was made with "actual malice"—that is, with knowledge that it was false or with reckless disregard of whether it was false or not. . . .

Applying these standards, we consider that the proof presented to show actual malice lacks the convincing clarity which the constitutional standard demands, and hence that it would not constitutionally sustain the judgment for respondent under the proper rule of law. The case of the individual petitioners requires little discussion. Even assuming that they could constitutionally be found to have authorized the use of their names on the advertisement, there was no evidence whatever that they were aware of any erroneous statements or were in any way reckless in that regard. The judgment against them is thus without constitutional support.

As to the *Times,* we similarly conclude that the facts do not support a finding of actual malice. . . . We think the evidence against the Times supports at most a finding of negligence in failing to discover the misstatements, and is constitutionally insufficient to show the recklessness that is required for a finding of actual malice. . . .

Reversed and remanded.

MR. JUSTICE BLACK, with whom MR. JUSTICE DOUGLAS joins, concurring.

I base my vote to reverse on the belief that the First and Fourteenth Amendments not merely "delimit" a State's power to award damages to "a public official against critics of his official conduct" but completely prohibit a State from exercising such a power. . . .

MR. JUSTICE GOLDBERG, with whom MR. JUSTICE DOUGLAS joins, concurring in the result.

. . . In my view, the First and Fourteenth Amendments to the Constitution afford to the citizen and to the press an absolute, unconditional privilege to criticize official conduct despite the harm which may flow from excesses and abuses. . . .

This is not to say that the Constitution protects defamatory statements directed against the private conduct of a public official or private citizen. Freedom of press and of speech insure that government will respond to the will of the people and that changes may be obtained by peaceful means. Purely private defamation has little to do with the political ends of a self-governing society. The imposition of liability for private defamation does not abridge the freedom of public speech.

New York Times Company v. United States*
403 U.S. 713, 91 S.Ct. 2140, 29 L.Ed. 2d 822 (1971)

The *New York Times* and the *Washington Post* acquired copies of a multivolume classified study of the evolution of the nation's Vietnam policy. Two federal district courts refused to enjoin publication. One decision was affirmed, one reversed by courts of appeals. The Supreme Court granted certiorari. The format of opinions was unusual— *per curiam,* with each justice delivering a separate opinion. Opinions by four justices are reprinted here. Majority: Black, Brennan, Douglas, Marshall, Stewart, White. Dissenting: Burger, Blackmun, Harlan.

PER CURIAM.

We granted certiorari in these cases in which the United States seeks to enjoin the *New York Times* and the *Washington Post* from publishing the contents of a classified study entitled "History of U.S. Decision-Making Process on Viet Nam Policy." . . .

"Any system of prior restraints of expression comes to this Court bearing a heavy presumption against its constitutional validity." . . . The Government "thus carries a heavy burden of showing justification for the enforcement of such a restraint." . . . The District Court for the Southern District of New York in the *New York Times* case and the District Court for the District of Columbia and the Court of Appeals for the District of Columbia Circuit in the *Washington Post* case held that the Government had not met that burden. We agree. . . .

MR. JUSTICE BLACK, with whom MR. JUSTICE DOUGLAS joins, concurring.

I adhere to the view that the Government's case against the *Washington Post* should have been dismissed and that the injunction against the *New York Times* should have been vacated without oral argument when the cases were first presented to this Court. I believe that every moment's continuance of the injunctions against these newspapers amounts to a flagrant, indefensible, and continuing violation of the First Amendment. . . . In my view it is unfortunate that some of my Brethren are apparently willing to hold that the publication

* This case should also be read in connection with Chapter Three.

of news may sometimes by enjoined. Such a holding would make a shambles of the First Amendment.

Our Government was launched in 1789 with the adoption of the Constitution. The Bill of Rights, including the First Amendment, followed in 1791. Now, for the first time in the 182 years since the founding of the Republic, the federal courts are asked to hold that the First Amendment does not mean what it says, but rather means that Government can halt the publication of current news of vital importance to the people of this country.

In seeking injunctions against these newspapers and in its presentation to the Court, the Executive Branch seems to have forgotten the essential purpose and history of the First Amendment. When the Constitution was adopted, many people strongly opposed it because the document contained no Bill of Rights to safeguard certain basic freedoms. They especially feared that the new powers granted to a central Government might be interpreted to permit the Government to curtail freedom of religion, press, assembly, and speech. In response to an overwhelming public clamor, James Madison offered a series of amendments to satisfy citizens that these great liberties would remain safe and beyond the power of government to abridge. . . . The amendments were offered to *curtail* and *restrict* the general powers granted to the Executive, Legislative, and Judicial Branches two years before in the original Constitution. The Bill of Rights changed the original Constitution into a new charter under which no branch of government could abridge the people's freedoms of press, speech, religion, and assembly. Yet the Solicitor General argues and some members of the Court appear to agree that the general powers of the Government adopted in the original Constitution should be interpreted to limit and restrict the specific and emphatic guarantees of the Bill of Rights adopted later. I can imagine no greater perversion of history. . . .

In the First Amendment the Founding Fathers gave the free press the protection it must have to fulfill its essential role in our democracy. The press was to serve the governed, not the governors. The Government's power to censor the press was abolished so that the press would remain forever free to censure the Government. The press was protected so that it could bare the secrets of government and inform the people. Only a free and unrestrained press can effectively expose deception in government. And paramount among the responsibilities of a free press is the duty to prevent any part of the government from deceiving the people and sending them off to distant lands to die of foreign fevers and foreign shot and shell. In my view, far from deserving condemnation for their courageous reporting, the *New York Times,* the *Washington Post,* and other newspapers should be commended for serving the purpose that the Founding Fathers saw so clearly. In revealing the workings of government that led to the Viet Nam war, the newspapers nobly did precisely that which the Founders hoped and trusted they would do. . . .

[W]e are asked to hold that despite the First Amendment's emphatic command, the Executive Branch, the Congress, and the Judiciary can make laws enjoining publication of current news and abridging freedom of the press in the name of "national security." The Government does not even attempt to rely on any act of Congress. Instead it makes the bold and dangerously far-reaching contention that the courts should take it upon themselves to "make" a law abridging freedom of the press in the name of equity, presidential power and national security, even when the representatives of the people in Congress have adhered to the command of the First Amendment and refused to make such a law. . . .

The word "security" is a broad, vague generality whose contours should not be invoked to abrogate the fundamental law embodied in the First Amendment. The guarding of military and diplomatic secrets at the expense of informed representative government provides no real security for our Republic. The Framers of the First Amendment, fully aware of both the need to defend a new nation and the abuses of the English and Colonial governments, sought to give this new society strength and security by providing that freedom of speech, press, religion, and assembly should not be abridged. This thought was eloquently expressed in 1937 by Mr. Chief Justice Hughes—great man and great Chief Justice that he was—when the Court held a man could not be punished for attending a meeting run by Communists.

> The greater the importance of safeguarding the community from incitements to the overthrow of our institutions by force and violence, the more imperative is the need to preserve inviolate the constitutional rights of free speech, free press and free assembly in order to maintain the opportunity for free political discussion, to the end that government may be responsive to the will of the people and that changes, if desired, may be obtained by peaceful means. Therein lies the security of the Republic, the very foundation of constitutional government.

MR. JUSTICE STEWART, with whom MR. JUSTICE WHITE joins, concurring.

In the governmental structure created by our Constitution, the Executive is endowed with enormous power in the two related areas of national defense and international relations. This power, largely unchecked by the Legislative and Judicial branches, has been pressed to the very hilt since the advent of the nuclear missile age. For better or for worse, the simple fact is that a President of the United States possesses vastly greater constitutional independence in these two vital areas of power than does, say, a prime minister of a country with a parliamentary form of government.

In the absence of the governmental checks and balances present in other areas of our national life, the only effective restraint upon executive policy and power in the areas of national defense and international affairs may lie in an enlightened citizenry—in an informed and critical public opinion which alone can here protect the values of democratic government. For this reason, it is perhaps here that a press that is alert, aware, and free most vitally serves the basic purpose of the First Amendment. For without an informed and free press there cannot be an enlightened people.

Yet it is elementary that the successful conduct

of international diplomacy and the maintenance of an effective national defense require both confidentiality and secrecy. Other nations can hardly deal with this Nation in an atmosphere of mutual trust unless they can be assured that their confidences will be kept. And within our own executive departments, the development of considered and intelligent international policies would be impossible if those charged with their formulation could not communicate with each other freely, frankly, and in confidence. In the area of basic national defense the frequent need for absolute secrecy is, of course, self-evident.

I think there can be but one answer to this dilemma, if dilemma it be. The responsibility must be where the power is. If the Constitution gives the Executive a large degree of unshared power in the conduct of foreign affairs and the maintenance of our national defense, then under the Constitution the Executive must have the largely unshared duty to determine and preserve the degree of internal security necessary to exercise that power successfully. It is an awesome responsibility, requiring judgment and wisdom of a high order. I should suppose that moral, political, and practical considerations would dictate that a very first principle of that wisdom would be an insistence upon avoiding secrecy for its own sake. For when everything is classified, then nothing is classified, and the system becomes one to be disregarded by the cynical or the careless, and to be manipulated by those intent on self-protection or self-promotion. . . . [I]t is clear to me that it is the constitutional duty of the Executive—as a matter of sovereign prerogative and not as a matter of law as the courts know law—through the promulgation and enforcement of executive regulations, to protect the confidentiality necessary to carry out its responsibilities in the fields of international relations and national defense.

This is not to say that Congress and the courts have no role to play. Undoubtedly Congress has the power to enact specific and appropriate criminal laws to protect government property and preserve government secrets. Congress has passed such laws, and several of them are of very colorable relevance to the apparent circumstances of these cases. And if a criminal prosecution is instituted, it will be the responsibility of the courts to decide the applicability of the criminal law under which the charge is brought. Moreover, if Congress should pass a specific law authorizing civil proceedings in this field, the courts would likewise have the duty to decide the constitutionality of such a law as well as its applicability to the facts proved.

But in the cases before us we are asked neither to construe specific regulations nor to apply specific laws. We are asked, instead, to perform a function that the Constitution gave to the Executive, not the Judiciary. We are asked, quite simply, to prevent the publication by two newspapers of material that the Executive Branch insists should not, in the national interest, be published. I am convinced that the Executive is correct with respect to some of the documents involved. But I cannot say that disclosure of any of them will surely result in direct, immediate, and irreparable damage to our Nation or its people. That being so, there can under the First Amendment be but one judicial resolution of the issues before us. I join the judgments of the Court.

MR. CHIEF JUSTICE BURGER, dissenting.

So clear are the constitutional limitations on prior restraint against expression, that from the time of *Near* v. *Minnesota* . . . until recently in *Organization for a Better Austin* v. *Keefe* (1971), we have had little occasion to be concerned with cases involving prior restraints against news reporting on matters of public interest. There is, therefore, little variation among the members of the Court in terms of resistance to prior restraints against publication. Adherence to this basic constitutional principle, however, does not make this case a simple one. In this case, the imperative of a free and unfettered press comes into collision with another imperative, the effective functioning of a complex modern government and specifically the effective exercise of certain constitutional powers of the Executive. Only those who view the First Amendment as an absolute in all circumstances—a view I respect, but reject—can find such a case as this to be simple or easy.

This case is not simple for another and more immediate reason. We do not know the facts of the case. No district Judge knew all the facts. No Court of Appeals judge knew all the facts. No member of this Court knows all the facts.

Why are we in this posture, in which only those judges to whom the First Amendment is absolute and permits of no restraint in any circumstances or for any reason, are really in a position to act?

I suggest we are in this posture because these cases have been conducted in unseemly haste. . . . [P]rompt judicial action does not mean unjudicial haste.

Here, moreover, the frenetic haste is due in large part to the manner in which the *Times* proceeded from the date it obtained the purloined documents. It seems reasonably clear now that the haste precluded reasonable and deliberate judicial treatment of these cases and was not warranted. The precipitous action of this Court aborting a trial not yet completed is not the kind of judicial conduct which ought to attend the disposition of a great issue.

The newspapers make a derivative claim under the First Amendment; they denominate this right as the public "right-to-know"; by implication, the *Times* asserts a sole trusteeship of that right by virtue of its journalistic "scoop." The right is asserted as an absolute. Of course, the First Amendment right itself is not an absolute, as Justice Holmes so long ago pointed out in his aphorism concerning the right to shout fire in a crowded theatre. There are other exceptions, some of which Chief Justice Hughes mentioned by way of example in *Near* v. *Minnesota*. There are no doubt other exceptions no one has had occasion to describe or discuss. Conceivably such exceptions may be lurking in these cases and would have been flushed had they been properly considered in the trial courts, free from unwarranted deadlines and frenetic pressures. A great issue of this kind should be tried in a judicial atmosphere conducive to thoughtful, reflective deliberation, especially when haste, in terms of hours, is unwarranted in light of the long period the *Times,* by its own choice, deferred publication.

It is not disputed that the *Times* has had unauthorized possession of the documents for three to four months, during which it has had its expert analysts studying them, presumably digesting them and preparing the material for publication. During all of this time, the *Times,* presumably in its capacity as trustee of the public's "right to know," has held up publication for purposes it considered proper and thus public knowledge was delayed. No doubt this was for a good reason; the analysis of 7,000 pages of complex material drawn from a vastly greater volume of material would inevitably take time and the writing of good news stories takes time. But why should the United States Government, from whom this information was illegally acquired by someone, along with all the counsel, trial judges, and appellate judges be placed under needless pressure? After these months of deferral, the alleged "right-to-know" has somehow and suddenly become a right that must be vindicated instanter. . . .

The consequence of all this melancholy series of events is that we literally do not know what we are acting on. . . .

We all crave speedier judicial processes but when judges are pressured as in these cases the result is a parody of the judicial process.

MR. JUSTICE HARLAN, with whom THE CHIEF JUSTICE and MR. JUSTICE BLACKMUN join, dissenting. . . .

With all respect, I consider that the Court has been almost irresponsibly feverish in dealing with these cases. . . .

This frenzied train of events took place in the name of the presumption against prior restraints created by the First Amendment. Due regard for the extraordinarily important and difficult questions involved in these litigations should have led the Court to shun such a precipitate timetable. . . .

Forced as I am to reach the merits of these cases, I dissent from the opinion and judgments of the Court. . . .

It is plain to me that the scope of the judicial function in passing upon the activities of the Executive Branch of the Government in the field of foreign affairs is very narrowly restricted. This view is, I think, dictated by the concept of separation of powers upon which our constitutional system rests. . . .

The power to evaluate the "pernicious influence" of premature disclosure is not, however, lodged in the Executive alone. I agree that, in performance of its duty to protect the values of the First Amendment against political pressures, the judiciary must review the initial Executive determination to the point of satisfying itself that the subject matter of the dispute does lie within the proper compass of the President's foreign relations power. Constitutional considerations forbid "a complete abandonment of judicial control." . . . Moreover, the judiciary may properly insist that the determination that disclosure of the subject matter would irreparably impair the national security be made by the head of the Executive Department concerned—here the Secretary of State or the Secretary of Defense—

after actual personal consideration by that officer. This safeguard is required in the analogous area of executive claims of privilege for secrets of state. . . .

Even if there is some room for the judiciary to override the executive determination, it is plain that the scope of review must be exceedingly narrow. I can see no indication in the opinions of either the District Court or the Court of Appeals, in the *Post* litigation that the conclusions of the Executive were given even the deference owing to an administrative agency, much less that owing to a co-equal branch of the Government operating within the field of its constitutional prerogative. . . .

Branzburg v. *Hayes*
408 U.S. 665, 92 S.Ct. 2646, 33 L.Ed. 2d 626 (1972)

Branzburg, Pappas, and Caldwell were reporters who were directed by grand juries conducting investigations to reveal the identity of news sources to whom each journalist had promised confidentiality. Branzburg had observed the processing of hashish from marijuana, and Pappas and Caldwell had observed activities of black militants. The Supreme Court combined the three cases for a ruling on a reporter's First Amendment privilege. Majority: White, Blackmun, Burger, Powell, Rehnquist. Dissenting: Stewart, Brennan, Douglas, Marshall.

Opinion of the Court by MR. JUSTICE WHITE, announced by THE CHIEF JUSTICE. . . .

Petitioners Branzburg and Pappas and respondent Caldwell press First Amendment claims that may be simply put: that to gather news it is often necessary to agree either not to identify the source of information published or to publish only part of the facts revealed, or both; that if the reporter is nevertheless forced to reveal these confidences to a grand jury, the source so identified and other confidential sources of other reporters will be measurably deterred from furnishing publishable information, all to the detriment of the free flow of information protected by the First Amendment. Although the newsmen in these cases do not claim an absolute privilege against official interrogation in all circumstances, they assert that the reporter should not be forced either to appear or to testify before a grand jury or at trial until and unless sufficient grounds are shown for believing that the reporter possesses information relevant to a crime the grand jury is investigating, that the information the reporter has is unavailable from other sources, and that the need for the information is sufficiently compelling to override the claimed invasion of First Amendment interests occasioned by the disclosure. Principally relied upon are prior cases emphasizing the importance of the First Amendment guarantees to individual development and to our system of representative government, decisions requiring that official action with adverse impact on First Amendment rights be justified by a public interest that is "compelling" or "paramount," and those precedents establishing the principle that justifiable governmental goals may not be achieved by unduly broad means having an unnecessary impact on protected rights of speech, press, or association. The heart of the claim is that the burden on news gathering resulting from compelling reporters to disclose confidential information outweighs any public interest in obtaining the information.

The sole issue before us is the obligation of reporters to respond to grand jury subpoenas as other citizens do and to answer questions relevant to an investigation into the commission of crime. Citizens generally are not constitutionally immune from grand jury subpoenas; and neither the First Amendment nor any other constitutional provision protects the average citizen from disclosing to a grand jury information that he has received in confidence. The claim is, however, that reporters are exempt from these obligations because if forced to respond to subpoenas and identify their sources or disclose other confidences, their informants will refuse or be reluctant to furnish newsworthy information in the future. . . .

The preference for anonymity of those confidential informants involved in actual criminal conduct is presumably a product of their desire to escape criminal prosecution, and this preference, while understandable, is hardly deserving of constitutional protection. It would be frivolous to assert—and no one does in these cases—that the First Amendment, in the interest of securing news or otherwise, confers a license on either the reporter or his news sources to violate valid criminal laws. Although stealing documents or private wiretapping could provide newsworthy information, neither reporter nor source is immune from conviction for such conduct, whatever the impact on the flow of news. Neither is immune, on First Amendment grounds, from testifying against the other, before the grand jury or at a criminal trial. . . .

Thus, we cannot seriously entertain the notion that the First Amendment protects a newsman's agreement to conceal the criminal conduct of his source, or evidence thereof, on the theory that it is better to write about crime than to do something about it. Insofar as any reporter in these cases undertook not to reveal or testify about the crime he witnessed, his claim of privilege under the First Amendment presents no substantial question. The crimes of news sources are no less reprehensible and threatening to the public interest when witnessed by a reporter than when they are not.

There remain those situations where a source is not engaged in criminal conduct but has information suggesting illegal conduct by others. Newsmen frequently receive information from such sources pursuant to a tacit or express agreement to withhold the source's name and suppress any information that the source wishes not published. Such informants presumably desire anonymity in order to avoid being entangled as a witness in a criminal trial or grand jury investigation. They may fear that disclosure will threaten their job security or personal

safety or that it will simply result in dishonor or embarrassment.

The argument that the flow of news will be diminished by compelling reporters to aid the grand jury in a criminal investigation is not irrational, nor are the records before us silent on the matter. But we remain unclear how often and to what extent informers are actually deterred from furnishing information when newsmen are forced to testify before a grand jury. . . .

The privilege claimed here is conditional, not absolute; given the suggested preliminary showings and compelling need, the reporter would be required to testify. Presumably, such a rule would reduce the instances in which reporters could be required to appear, but predicting in advance when and in what circumstances they could be compelled to do so would be difficult. Such a rule would also have implications for the issuance of compulsory process to reporters at civil and criminal trials and at legislative hearings. If newsmen's confidential sources are as sensitive as they are claimed to be, the prospect of being unmasked whenever a judge determines the situation justifies it is hardly a satisfactory solution to the problem. For them, it would appear that only an absolute privilege would suffice.

We are unwilling to embark the judiciary on a long and difficult journey to such an uncertain destination. The administration of a constitutional newsman's privilege would present practical and conceptual difficulties of a high order. Sooner or later, it would be necessary to define those categories of newsmen who qualified for the privilege, a questionable procedure in light of the traditional doctrine that liberty of the press is the right of the lonely pamphleteer who uses carbon paper or a mimeograph just as much as of the large metropolitan publisher who utilizes the latest photocomposition methods. . . .

In addition, there is much force in the pragmatic view that the press has at its disposal powerful mechanisms of communication and is far from helpless to protect itself from harassment or substantial harm. Furthermore, if what the newsmen urged in these cases is true—that law enforcement cannot hope to gain and may suffer from subpoenaing newsmen before grand juries—prosecutors will be loath to risk so much for so little. . . .

Finally, as we have earlier indicated, news gathering is not without its First Amendment protections, and grand jury investigations if instituted or conducted other than in good faith, would pose wholly different issues for resolution under the First Amendment. Official harassment of the press undertaken not for purposes of law enforcement but to disrupt a reporter's relationship with his news sources would have no justification. Grand juries are subject to judicial control and subpoenas to motions to quash. We do not expect courts will forget that grand juries must operate within the limits of the First Amendment as well as the Fifth. . . .

So ordered.

MR. JUSTICE STEWART, with whom MR. JUSTICE BRENNAN and MR. JUSTICE MARSHALL join, dissenting.

The Court's crabbed view of the First Amendment reflects a disturbing insensitivity to the critical role of an independent press in our society. The question whether a reporter has a constitutional right to a confidential relationship with his source is of first impression here, but the principles that should guide our decision are as basic as any to be found in the Constitution. . . . [T]he Court in these cases holds that a newsman has no First Amendment right to protect his sources when called before a grand jury. The Court thus invites state and federal authorities to undermine the historic independence of the press by attempting to annex the journalistic profession as an investigative arm of government. Not only will this decision impair performance of the press's constitutionally protected functions, but it will, I am convinced, in the long run harm rather than help the administration of justice.

I respectfully dissent.

The reporter's constitutional right to a confidential relationship with his source stems from the broad societal interest in a full and free flow of information to the public. It is this basic concern that underlies the Constitution's protection of a free press. . . .

Enlightened choice by an informed citizenry is the basic ideal upon which an open society is premised, and a free press is thus indispensable to a free society. Not only does the press enhance personal self-fulfillment by providing the people with the widest possible range of fact and opinion, but it also is an incontestable precondition of self-government. . . .

As private and public aggregations of power burgeon in size and the pressures for conformity necessarily mount, there is obviously a continuing need for an independent press to disseminate a robust variety of information and opinion through reportage, investigation, and criticism, if we are to preserve our constitutional tradition of maximizing freedom of choice by encouraging diversity of expression.

In keeping with this tradition, we have held that the right to publish is central to the First Amendment and basic to the existence of constitutional democracy. . . .

A corollary of the right to publish must be the right to gather news. The full flow of information to the public protected by the free-press guarantee would be severely curtailed if no protection whatever were afforded to the press by which news is assembled and disseminated. . . .

No less important to the news dissemination process is the gathering of information. News must not be unnecessarily cut off at its source, for without freedom to acquire information the right to publish would be impermissibly compromised. Accordingly, a right to gather news, of some dimensions, must exist. . . . As Madison wrote: "A popular Government, without popular information, or the means of acquiring it, is but a Prologue to a Farce or a Tragedy; or, perhaps both." . . .

The right to gather news implies, in turn, a right to a confidential relationship between a reporter and his source. This proposition follows as a matter of simple logic once three factual predicates are recognized: (1) newsmen require informants to gather news; (2) confidentiality—the promise or understanding that names or certain aspects of communications will be kept off the record—is essential to the creation and maintenance of a news-gathering relationship with informants; and (3) an unbridled subpoena power—the absence of a constitutional right protecting, in *any* way, a confidential relationship from compulsory process—will either deter sources from divulging information or deter reporters from gathering and publishing information. . . .

After today's decision, the potential informant can never be sure that his identity or off-the-record communications will not subsequently be revealed through the compelled testimony of a newsman. A public-spirited person inside government, who is not implicated in any crime, will now be fearful of revealing corruption or other governmental wrongdoing, because he will now know he can subsequently be identified by use of compulsory process. The potential source must, therefore, choose between risking exposure by giving information or avoiding the risk by remaining silent.

The reporter must speculate about whether contact with a controversial source or publication of controversial material will lead to a subpoena. In the event of a subpoena, under today's decision, the newsman will know that he must choose between being punished for contempt if he refuses to testify, or violating his profession's ethics and impairing his resourcefulness as a reporter if he discloses confidential information. . . .

Miller v. California
413 U.S. 5, 93 S.Ct. 2607, 37 L.Ed. 2d 419 (1973)

After a jury trial in the California state court, the defendant, who had mailed unsolicited advertising brochures containing pictures and drawings explicitly depicting sexual activities, was convicted of violating a California statute making it a misdemeanor knowingly to distribute obscene matter. On appeal, the Superior Court of California, County of Orange, affirmed. Majority: Burger, Blackmun, Powell, Rehnquist, White. Dissenting: Brennan, Douglas, Marshall, Stewart.

MR. CHIEF JUSTICE BURGER delivered the opinion of the Court.

This is one of a group of "obscenity-pornography" cases being reviewed by the Court in a reexamination of standards enunciated in earlier cases involving what Mr. Justice Harlan called "the intractable obscenity problem."

The brochures advertise four books entitled "Intercourse," "Man-Woman," "Sex Orgies Illustrated," and "An Illustrated History of Pornography," and a film entitled "Marital Intercourse." While the brochures contain some descriptive printed material, primarily they consist of pictures and drawings very explicitly depicting men and women in groups of two or more engaging in a variety of sexual activities, with genitals often prominently displayed. . . .

. . . [I]t is useful for us to focus on two of the landmark cases in the somewhat tortured history of the Court's obscenity decisions. In *Roth* v. *United States* (1957), the Court sustained a conviction under a federal statute punishing the mailing of "obscene, lewd, lascivious or filthy . . ." materials. The key to that holding was the Court's rejection of the claim that obscene materials were protected by the First Amendment. Five Justices joined in the opinion stating,

> All ideas having even the slightest redeeming social importance—unorthodox ideas, controversial ideas, even ideas hateful to the prevailing climate of opinion—have the full protection of the [First Amendment] guaranties, unless excludable because they encroach upon the limited area of more important interests. But implicit in the history of the First Amendment is the rejection of obscenity as utterly without redeeming social importance. . . .

Nine years later, in *Memoirs* v. *Massachusetts* (1966), the Court veered sharply away from the Roth concept and, with only three Justices in the plurality opinion, articulated a new test of obscenity. The plurality held that under the Roth definition

> . . . as elaborated in subsequent cases, three elements must coalesce: it must be established that (a) the dominant theme of the material taken as a whole appeals to a prurient interest in sex; (b) the material

is patently offensive because it affronts contemporary community standards relating to the description or representation of sexual matters; and (c) the material is utterly without redeeming social value. . . .

Apart from the initial formulation in the Roth case, no majority of the Court has at any given time been able to agree on a standard to determine what constitutes obscene, pornographic material subject to regulation under the States' police power. . . . We have seen a "variety of views among the members of the Court unmatched in any other course of constitutional adjudication." . . . This is not remarkable, for in the area of freedom of speech and press the courts must always remain sensitive to any infringement on genuinely serious literary, artistic, political, or scientific expression. This is an area in which there are few eternal verities. . . .

This much has been categorically settled by the Court, that obscene material is unprotected by the First Amendment. . . .

The basic guidelines for the trier of fact must be: (a) whether "the average person, applying contemporary community standards" would find that the work, taken as a whole appeals to the prurient interest, (b) whether the work depicts or describes, in a patently offensive way, sexual conduct specifically defined by the applicable state law, and (c) whether the work, taken as a whole, lacks serious literary, artistic, political, or scientific value. We do not adopt as a constitutional standard the "*utterly* without redeeming social value" test. . . . That concept has never commanded the adherence of more than three Justices at one time. . . . If a state law that regulates obscene material is thus limited, as written or construed, the First Amendment values applicable to the States through the Fourteenth Amendment are adequately protected by the ultimate power of appellate courts to conduct an independent review of constitutional claims when necessary. . . .

. . . We emphasize that it is not our function to propose regulatory schemes for the States. That must await their concrete legislative efforts. It is possible, however, to give a few plain examples of what a state statute could define for regulation:

(a) Patently offensive representations or descriptions of ultimate sexual acts, normal or perverted, actual or simulated.

(b) Patently offensive representations or descriptions of masturbation, excretory functions, and lewd exhibition of the genitals.

Sex and nudity may not be exploited without limit by films or pictures exhibited or sold in places of public accommodation any more than live sex and nudity can be exhibited or sold without limit in such public places. At a minimum, prurient, patently offensive depiction or description of sexual conduct must have serious literary, artistic, political, or scientific value to merit First Amendment protection. . . . For example, medical books for the education of physicians and related personnel necessarily use graphic illustrations and descriptions of human anatomy. In resolving the inevitably sensitive questions of fact and law, we must continue to rely on the jury system, accompanied by the safeguards that judges, rules of evidence, presumption of innocence and other protective features provide, as we do with rape, murder and a host of other offenses against society and its individual members. . . .

Under a national Constitution, fundamental First Amendment limitations on the powers of the States do not vary from community to community, but this does not mean that there are, or should or can be, fixed, uniform national standards of precisely what appeals to the "prurient interest" or is "patently offensive." These are essentially questions of fact, and our nation is simply too big and too diverse for this Court to reasonably expect that such standards could be articulated for all 50 States in a single formulation, even assuming the prerequisite consensus exists. When triers of fact are asked to decide whether "the average person, applying contemporary community standards" would consider certain materials "prurient," it would be unrealistic to require that the answer be based on some abstract formulation. The adversary system, with lay jurors as the usual ultimate fact-finders in criminal prosecutions, has historically permitted triers-of-fact to draw on the standards of their community, guided always by limiting instructions on the law. To require a State to structure obscenity proceedings around evidence of a *national* "community standard" would be an exercise in futility. . . .

It is neither realistic nor constitutionally sound to read the First Amendment as requiring that the people of Maine or Mississippi accept public depiction of conduct found tolerable in Las Vegas, or New York City. . . . People in different States vary in their tastes and attitudes, and this diversity is not to be strangled by the absolutism of imposed uniformity. . . .

The dissenting Justices sound the alarm of repression. But, in our view, to equate the free and robust exchange of ideas and political debate with commercial exploitation of obscene material demeans the grand conception of the First Amendment and its high purposes in the historic struggle for freedom. . . .

There is no evidence, empirical or historical, that the stern 19th century American censorship of public distribution and display of material relating to sex . . . anyway limited or affected expression of serious literary, artistic, political, or scientific ideas. On the contrary, it is beyond any question that the era following Thomas Jefferson to Theodore Roosevelt was an "extraordinarily vigorous period" not just in economics and politics, but in belles lettres and in "the outlying fields of social and political philosophies." . . .

In sum we (a) reaffirm the Roth holding that obscene material is not protected by the First Amendment, (b) hold that such material can be regulated by the States, subject to the specific safeguards enunciated above, without a showing that the material is "*utterly* without redeeming social value," and (c) hold that obscenity is to be determined by applying "contemporary community standards" . . . not "national standards." The judgment of the Appellate Department of the Superior Court, Orange County, California, is vacated and the case remanded to that court for further proceedings not inconsistent with the First Amendment standards established by this opinion.

MR. JUSTICE DOUGLAS, dissenting. . . .

Today the Court retreats from the earlier formulations of the constitutional test and undertakes to make new definitions. This effort, like the earlier ones, is earnest and well-intentioned. The difficulty is that we do not deal with constitutional terms, since "obscenity" is not mentioned in the Constitution or Bill of Rights. And the First Amendment makes no such exception from the "the press" which it undertakes to protect nor, as I have said on other occasions, is an exception necessarily implied, for there was no recognized exception to the free press at the time the Bill of Rights was adopted

which treated "obscene" publications differently from other types of papers, magazines, and books. So there are no constitutional guidelines for deciding what is and what is not "obscene." The Court is at large because we deal with tastes and standards of literature. What shocks me may be sustenance for my neighbor. What causes one person to boil up in rage over one pamphlet or movie may reflect only his neurosis, not shared by others. We deal here with problems of censorship which, if adopted, should be done by constitutional amendment after full debate by the people. . . .

MR. JUSTICE BRENNAN, with whom MR. JUSTICE STEWART and MR. JUSTICE MARSHALL join, dissenting. . . . [The following is taken from Brennan's dissent in the companion case to *Miller* v. *California, Paris Adult Theatre I* v. *Slaton,* 1973.]

Our experience with the Roth approach has certainly taught us that the outright suppression of obscenity cannot be reconciled with the fundamental principles of the First and Fourteenth Amendments. For we have failed to formulate a standard that sharply distinguishes protected from unprotected speech, and out of necessity, we have resorted to the Redrup approach, which resolves cases as between the parties, but offers only the most obscure guidance to legislation, adjudication by other courts, and primary conduct. By disposing of cases through summary reversal or denial of certiorari we have deliberately and effectively obscured the rationale underlying the decisions. It comes as no surprise that judicial attempts to follow our lead conscientiously have often ended in hopeless confusion.

Of course, the vagueness problem would be largely of our own creation if it stemmed primarily from our failure to reach a consensus on any one standard. But after 16 years of experimentation and debate I am reluctantly forced to the conclusion that none of the available formulas, including the one announced today, can reduce the vagueness to a tolerable level while at the same time striking an acceptable balance between the protections of the First and Fourteenth Amendments, on the one hand, and on the other the asserted state interest in regulating the dissemination of certain sexually oriented materials. . . .

The vagueness of the standards in the obscenity area produces a number of separate problems, and any improvement must rest on an understanding that the problems are to some extent distinct. First, a vague statute fails to provide adequate notice to persons who are engaged in the type of conduct that the statute could be thought to proscribe. The Due Process Clause of the Fourteenth Amendment requires that all criminal laws provide fair notice of "what the State commands or forbids." . . .

In addition to problems that arise when any criminal statute fails to afford fair notice of what it forbids, a vague statute in the areas of speech and press creates a second level of difficulty. We have indicated that "stricter standards of permissible statutory vagueness may be applied to a statute having a potentially inhibiting effect on speech; a man may the less be required to act at his peril here, because the free dissemination of ideas may be the loser." . . .

As a result of our failure to define standards with predictable application to any given piece of material, there is no probability of regularity in obscenity decisions by state and lower federal courts. That is not to say that these courts have performed badly in this area or paid insufficient attention to the principles we have established. The problem is, rather, that one cannot say with certainty that material is obscene until at least five members of this Court, applying inevitably obscure standards, have pronounced it so. The number of obscenity cases on our docket gives ample testimony to the burden that has been placed upon this Court. . . .

More important . . . the practice effectively censors protected expression by leaving lower court determinations of obscenity intact even though the status of the allegedly obscene material is entirely unsettled until final review here. In addition, the uncertainty of the standards creates a continuing source of tension between state and federal courts, since the need for an independent determination by this Court seems to render superfluous even the most conscientious analysis by state tribunals. And our inability to justify our decisions with a persuasive rationale—or indeed, any rationale at all—necessarily creates the impression that we are merely second-guessing state court judges.

The severe problems arising from the lack of fair notice, from the chill on protected expression, and from the stress imposed on the state and federal judicial machinery persuade me that a significant change in direction is urgently required. . . .

In short, while I cannot say that the interests of the State—apart from the question of juveniles and unconsenting adults—are trivial or nonexistent, I am compelled to conclude that these interests cannot justify the substantial damage to constitutional rights and to this Nation's judicial machinery that inevitably results from state efforts to bar the distribution even of unprotected material to consenting adults. . . . I would hold, therefore, that at least in the absence of distribution to juveniles or obtrusive exposure to unconsenting adults, the First and Fourteenth Amendments prohibit the State and Federal Governments from attempting wholly to suppress sexually oriented materials on the basis of their allegedly "obscene" contents.

Hazelwood School District v. Kuhlmeier
56 U.S.L.W. 4079 (1988)

In 1983, Cathy Kuhlmeier and other former staff members of *Spectrum*, the school newspaper at Hazelwood East High School, filed suit in district court against officials of the Hazelwood School District in St. Louis County, Missouri. The principal had deleted two pages from the paper that included two articles, one describing students' experiences with pregnancy and the other discussing the impact of divorce on students and the school. *Spectrum* was written and edited by a journalism class. When the teacher in charge of the paper submitted page proofs to the principal, as was customarily done, the principal objected to the first article because the pregnant students might be identified from the text even though their names had not been used and because the references to sexual activity and birth control were inappropriate for younger students. He objected to the second article because it contained the name of a student who complained of her father's conduct. The principal believed that the parent should have been given an opportunity to respond. This was the last issue of the paper, and there seemed to be no time to correct the articles. The district court found no constitutional violation, but the Court of Appeals for the Eighth Circuit reversed. Under *Tinker* v. *Des Moines Independent Community School District* (1969), the appeals court held, the contents of the paper could not be censored except when "necessary to avoid material and substantial interference with school work or discipline . . . or the rights of others." Majority: White, O'Connor, Rehnquist, Scalia, Stevens. Dissenting: Brennan, Blackmun, Marshall.

JUSTICE WHITE delivered the opinion of the Court.

This case concerns the extent to which educators may exercise editorial control over the contents of a high school newspaper produced as part of the school's journalism curriculum. . . .

We deal first with the question whether Spectrum may appropriately be characterized as a forum for public expression. The public schools do not possess all of the attributes of streets, parks, and other traditional public forums that "time out of mind, have been used for purposes of assembly, communicating thoughts between citizens, and discussing public questions." Hence, school facilities may be deemed to be public forums only if school authorities have "by policy or by practice" opened those facilities "for indiscriminate use by the general public," or by some segment of the public, such as student organizations. . . .

The policy of school officials toward Spectrum was reflected in Hazelwood School Board Policy 348.51 and the Hazelwood East Curriculum Guide. Board Policy 348.51 provided that "[s]chool sponsored publications are developed within the adopted curriculum and its educational implications in regular classroom activities." The Hazelwood East Curriculum Guide described the Journalism II course as a "laboratory situation in which the students publish the school newspaper applying skills they have learned in Journalism I." The lessons that were to be learned from the Journalism II course, according to the Curriculum Guide, included development of journalistic skills under deadline pressure, "the legal, moral, and ethical restrictions imposed upon journalists within the school community," and "responsibility and acceptance of criticism for articles of opinion." Journalism II was taught by a faculty member during regular class hours. Students received grades and academic credit for their performance in the course.

School officials did not deviate in practice from their policy that production of Spectrum was to be part of the educational curriculum and a "regular classroom activit[y]." The District Court found that Robert Stergos, the journalism teacher during most of the 1982-1983 school year, "both had the authority to exercise and in fact exercised a great deal of control over *Spectrum*." . . . Moreover, after each Spectrum issue had been finally approved by Stergos or his successor, the issue still had to be reviewed by Principal Reynolds prior to publication.

The evidence relied upon by the Court of Appeals in finding Spectrum to be a public forum is equivocal at best. For example, Board Policy 348.51, which stated in part that "[s]chool sponsored student publications will not restrict free expression or diverse viewpoints within the rules of responsible journalism," also stated that such publications were "developed within the adopted curriculum and its educational implications." . . .

The question whether the First Amendment requires a school to tolerate particular student speech—the question that we addressed in *Tinker*—is different from the question whether the First Amendment requires a school affirmatively to promote particular student speech. The former question addresses educators' ability to silence a student's personal expression that happens to occur on the school premises. The latter question concerns educators' authority over school-sponsored publications, theatrical productions, and other expressive activities that students, parents, and members of the public might reasonably perceive to bear the imprimatur of the school. These activities may fairly be characterized as part of the school curriculum, whether or not they occur in a traditional classroom setting, so long as they are supervised by faculty members and designed to impart particular knowledge or skills to student participants and audiences.

Educators are entitled to exercise greater control over this second form of student expression to assure that participants learn whatever lessons the activity is designed to teach, that readers or listeners are not exposed to material that may be inappropriate for their level of maturity, and that the views of the individual speaker are not erroneously attributed to the school. . . .

Accordingly, we conclude that the standard articulated in *Tinker* for determining when a school may punish student expression need not also be the standard for determining when a school may refuse to lend its name and resources to the dissemination of student expression. Instead, we hold that educators do not offend the First Amendment by exercising editorial control over the style and content of student speech in school-sponsored expressive activities so long as their actions are reasonably related to legitimate pedagogical concerns.

This standard is consistent with our oft-expressed view that the education of the Nation's youth is primarily the responsibility of parents, teachers, and state and local school officials, and not of federal judges. . . . It is only when the decision to censor a school-sponsored publication, theatrical production, or other vehicle of student expression has no valid educational purpose that the First Amendment is so "directly and sharply implicate[d]," as to require judicial intervention to protect students' constitutional rights. . . .

In sum, we cannot reject as unreasonable Principal Reynolds' conclusion that neither the pregnancy article nor the divorce article was suitable for publication in Spectrum. Reynolds could reasonably have concluded that the students who had written and edited these articles had not sufficiently

mastered those portions of the Journalism II curriculum that pertained to the treatment of controversial issues and personal attacks, the need to protect the privacy of individuals whose most intimate concerns are to be revealed in the newspaper, and "the legal, moral, and ethical restrictions imposed upon journalists within [a] school community" that includes adolescent subjects and readers. Finally, we conclude that the principal's decision to delete two pages of Spectrum, rather than to delete only the offending articles or to require that they be modified, was reasonable under the circumstances as he understood them. Accordingly, no violation of First Amendment rights occurred.

The judgment of the Court of Appeals for the Eighth Circuit is therefore

Reversed.

JUSTICE BRENNAN, with whom JUSTICE MARSHALL and JUSTICE BLACKMUN join, dissenting. . . .

Free student expression undoubtedly sometimes interferes with the effectiveness of the school's pedagogical functions. Some brands of student expression do so by directly preventing the school from pursuing its pedagogical mission: The young polemic who stands on a soapbox during calculus class to deliver an eloquent political diatribe interferes with the legitimate teaching of calculus. And the student who delivers a lewd endorsement of a student-government candidate might so extremely distract an impressionable high school audience as to interfere with the orderly operation of the school. Other student speech, however, frustrates the school's legitimate pedagogical purposes merely by expressing a message that conflicts with the school's, without directly interfering with the school's expression of its message: A student who responds to a political science teacher's question with the retort, "Socialism is good," subverts the school's inculcation of the message that capitalism is better. Even the maverick who sits in class passively sporting a symbol of protest against a government policy, or the gossip who sits in the student commons swapping stories of sexual escapade could readily muddle a clear official message condoning the government policy or condemning teenage sex. Likewise, the student newspaper that, like Spectrum, conveys a moral position at odds with the school's official stance might subvert the administration's legitimate inculcation of its own perception of community values.

If mere incompatibility with the school's pedagogical message were a constitutionally sufficient justification for the suppression of student speech, school officials could censor each of the students or student organizations in the foregoing hypotheticals, converting our public schools into "enclaves of totalitarianism" that "strangle the free mind at its source." The First Amendment permits no such blanket censorship authority. . . .

In *Tinker,* this Court struck the balance. We held that official censorship of student expression—there the suspension of several students until they removed their armbands protesting the Vietnam War—is unconstitutional unless the speech "materially disrupts classwork or involves substantial disorder or invasion of the rights of others. . . ."

This Court applied the *Tinker* test just a Term ago . . . upholding an official decision to discipline a student for delivering a lewd speech in support of a student-government candidate. The Court today casts no doubt on *Tinker's* vitality. Instead it erects a taxonomy of school censorship, concluding that *Tinker* applies to one category and not another. On the one hand is censorship "to silence a student's personal expression that happens to occur on the school premises." On the other hand is censorship of expression that arises in the context of "school-sponsored . . . expressive activities that students, parents, and members of the public might reasonably perceive to bear the imprimatur of the school."

The Court does not, for it cannot, purport to discern from our precedents the distinction it creates. . . .

Even if we were writing on a clean slate, I would reject the Court's rationale for abandoning *Tinker* in this case. The Court offers no more than an obscure tangle of three excuses to afford educators "greater control" over school-sponsored speech than the *Tinker* test would permit: the public educator's prerogative to control curriculum; the pedagogical interest in shielding the high school audience from objectionable viewpoints and sensitive topics; and the school's need to dissociate itself from student expression. None of the excuses, once disentangled, supports the distinction that the Court draws. *Tinker* fully addresses the first concern; the second is illegitimate; and the third is readily achievable through less oppressive means. . . .

Finally, even if the majority were correct that the principal could constitutionally have censored the objectionable material, I would emphatically object to the brutal manner in which he did so. Where "[t]he separation of legitimate from illegitimate speech calls for more sensitive tools" the principal used a paper shredder. He objected to some material in two articles, but excised six entire articles. He did not so much as inquire into obvious alternatives, such as precise deletions or additions (one of which had already been made), rearranging the layout, or delaying publication. Such unthinking contempt for individual rights is intolerable from any state official. It is particularly insidious from one to whom the public entrusts the task of inculcating in its youth an appreciation for the cherished democratic liberties that our Constitution guarantees.

The Court opens its analysis in this case by purporting to reaffirm *Tinker's* time-tested proposition that public school students " 'do not shed their constitutional rights to freedom of speech or expression at the schoolhouse gate.' " That is an ironic introduction to an opinion that denudes high school students of much of the First Amendment protection that *Tinker* itself prescribed. . . . The young men and women of Hazelwood East expected a civics lesson, but not the one the Court teaches them today.

VI. RELIGIOUS FREEDOM

Minersville School District v. *Gobitis*
310 U.S. 586, 60 S.Ct. 1010, 84 L.Ed. 1375 (1940)
West Virginia State Board of Education v. *Barnette*
319 U.S. 624, 63 S.Ct. 1178, 87 L.Ed. 1628 (1943)

One of the most dramatic reversals of a Court decision occurred in 1943 when a precedent of only three years' standing was overruled. Both cases presented the same issue: Could schoolchildren, members of the sect known as Jehovah's Witnesses, be required to salute the flag, a practice forbidden by their religious tenets? In the earlier case, the Court in an 8-to-1 decision reversed the district court and upheld the action of a Pennsylvania school board expelling two pupils; but in the later case the Court held a similar action unconstitutional. It should be noted that this about-face was the result partly of personnel changes (which brought *Justices Jackson* and *Rutledge* to the bench) and partly of the change of viewpoint of *Justices Black, Douglas,* and *Murphy.* Court records misspelled the Gobitas and Barnett family names, hence the landmark decisions continue the error. Majority in *Gobitis:* Frankfurter, Black, Douglas, Hughes, McReynolds, Murphy, Reed, Roberts. Dissenting: Stone.

Minersville School District v. *Gobitis* (1940)

MR. JUSTICE FRANKFURTER delivered the opinion of the court. . . .

Lillian Gobitis, aged twelve, and her brother William, aged ten, were expelled from the public schools of Minersville, Pennsylvania, for refusing to salute the national flag as part of a daily school exercise. . . .

The Gobitis children were of an age for which Pennsylvania makes school attendance compulsory. Thus they were denied a free education, and their parents had to put them into private schools. To be relieved of the financial burden thereby entailed, their father, on behalf of the children and in his own behalf, brought this suit. He sought to enjoin the authorities from continuing to exact participation in the flag-salute ceremony as a condition of his children's attendance at the Minersville school. . . .

We must decide whether the requirement of participation in such a ceremony, exacted from a child who refuses upon sincere religious grounds, infringes without due process of law the liberty guaranteed by the Fourteenth Amendment.

Centuries of strife over the erection of particular dogmas as exclusive or all-comprehending faiths led to the inclusion of a guarantee for religious freedom in the Bill of Rights. The First Amendment, and the Fourteenth through its absorption of the First, sought to guard against repetition of those bitter religious struggles by prohibiting the establishment of a state religion and by securing to every sect the free exercise of its faith. So pervasive is the acceptance of this precious right that its scope is brought into question, as here, only when the conscience of individuals collides with the felt necessities of society.

Certainly the affirmative pursuit of one's convictions about the ultimate mystery of the universe and man's relation to it is placed beyond the reach of law. Government may not interfere with organized or individual expression of belief or disbelief. Propagation of belief—or even of disbelief in the supernatural—is protected, whether in church or chapel, mosque or synagogue, tabernacle or meetinghouse. . . .

But the manifold character of man's relations may bring his conception of religious duty into conflict with the secular interests of his fellow-men. When does the constitutional guarantee compel exemption from doing what society thinks necessary for the promotion of some great common end, or from a penalty for conduct which appears dangerous to the general good? To state the problem is to recall the truth that no single principle can answer all of life's complexities. The right to freedom of religious belief, however dissident and however obnoxious to the cherished beliefs of others—even of a majority—is itself the denial of an absolute. But to affirm that the freedom to follow conscience has itself no limits in the life of a society would deny that very plurality of principles which, as a matter of history, underlies protection of religious toleration. . . . Our present task then, as so often the case with courts, is to reconcile two rights in order to prevent either from destroying the other. But, because in safeguarding conscience we are dealing with interests so subtle and so dear, every possible leeway should be given to the claims of religious faith. . . .

The religious liberty which the Constitution protects has never excluded legislation of general scope not directed against doctrinal loyalties of particular sects. Judicial nullification of legislation cannot be justified by attributing to the framers of the Bill of Rights views for which there is no historic warrant. Conscientious scruples have not, in the course of the long struggle for religious toleration, relieved the individual from obedience to a general law not aimed at the promotion or restriction of religious beliefs. The mere possession of religious convictions which contradict the relevant concerns of a political society does not relieve the citizen from the discharge of political responsibilities. The necessity for this adjustment has again and again been recognized. In a number of situations the exertion of political authority has been sustained,

while basic considerations of religious freedom have been left inviolate.

. . . [T]he question remains whether school children, like the Gobitis children, must be excused from conduct required of all the other children in the promotion of national cohesion. We are dealing with an interest inferior to none in the hierarchy of legal values. National unity is the basis of national security. . . .

Situations like the present are phases of the profoundest problems confronting a democracy—the problem which Lincoln cast in memorable dilemma: "Must a government of necessity be too *strong* for the liberties of its people, or too *weak* to maintain its own existence?" No mere textual reading or logical talisman can solve the dilemma. And when the issue demands judicial determination, it is not the personal notion of judges of what wise adjustment requires which must prevail.

Unlike the instances we have cited, the case before us is not concerned with an exertion of legislative power for the promotion of some specific need or interest of secular society—the protection of the family, the promotion of health, the common defense, the raising of public revenues to defray the cost of government. But all these specific activities of government presuppose the existence of an organized political society. The ultimate foundation of a free society is the binding ties of cohesive sentiment. Such a sentiment is fostered by all those agencies of the mind and spirit which may serve to gather up the traditions of a people, transmit them from generation to generation, and thereby create that continuity of a treasured common life which constitutes a civilization. "We live by symbols." The flag is the symbol of our national unity, transcending all internal differences, however large, within the framework of the Constitution. . . .

The precise issue, then, for us to decide is whether the legislatures of the various states and the authorities in a thousand counties and school districts of this country are barred from determining the appropriateness of various means to evoke that unifying sentiment without which there can ultimately be no liberties, civil or religious. To stigmatize legislative judgment in providing for this universal gesture of respect for the symbol of our national life in the setting of the common school as a lawless inroad on that freedom of conscience which the Constitution protects, would amount to no less than the pronouncement of pedagogical and psychological dogma in a field where courts possess no marked and certainly no controlling competence. The influences which help toward a common feeling for the common country are manifold. Some may seem harsh and others no doubt are foolish. Surely, however, the end is legitimate. And the effective means for its attainment are still so uncertain and so unauthenticated by science as to preclude us from putting the widely prevalent belief in flag-saluting beyond the pale of legislative power. It mocks reason and denies our whole history to find in the allowance of a requirement to salute our flag on fitting occasions the seeds of sanction for obeisance to a leader.

The wisdom of training children in patriotic impulses by those compulsions which necessarily pervade so much of the educational process is not for our independent judgment. Even were we convinced of the folly of such a measure, such belief would be no proof of its unconstitutionality. For ourselves, we might be tempted to say that the deepest patriotism is best engendered by giving unfettered scope to the most crotchety beliefs. Perhaps it is best, even from the standpoint of those interests which ordinances like the one under review seek to promote, to give to the least popular sect leave from conformities like those here in issue. But the courtroom is not the arena for debating issues of educational policy. It is not our province to choose among competing considerations in the subtle process of securing effective loyalty to the traditional ideals of democracy, while respecting at the same time individual idiosyncrasies among a people so diversified in racial origins and religious allegiances. So to hold would in effect make us the school board for the country. That authority has not been given to this Court, nor should we assume it. . . .

Judicial review, itself a limitation on popular government, is a fundamental part of our constitutional scheme. But to the legislature no less than to courts is committed the guardianship of deeply cherished liberties. . . . Where all the effective means of inducing political changes are left free from interference, education in the abandonment of foolish legislation is itself a training in liberty. To fight out the wise use of legislative authority in the forum of public opinion and before legislative assemblies rather than to transfer such a contest to the judicial arena, serves to vindicate the self-confidence of a free people.

Reversed.

MR. JUSTICE STONE, dissenting. . . .

Concededly the constitutional guaranties of personal liberty are not always absolutes. Government has a right to survive and powers conferred upon it are not necessarily set at naught by the express prohibitions of the Bill of Rights. . . . But it is a long step, and one which I am unable to take, to the position that government may, as a supposed educational measure and as a means of disciplining the young, compel public affirmations which violate their religious conscience. . . .

The guaranties of civil liberty are but guaranties of freedom of the human mind and spirit and of reasonable freedom and opportunity to express them. They presuppose the right of the individual to hold such opinions as he will and to give them reasonably free expression, and his freedom, and that of the state as well, to teach and persuade others by the communication of ideas. The very essence of the liberty which they guarantee is the freedom of the individual from compulsion as to what he shall think and what he shall say, at least where the compulsion is to bear false witness to his religion. If these guaranties are to have any meaning they must, I think, be deemed to withhold from the state any authority to compel belief or the expression of it where that expression violates religious convictions, whatever may be the legislative view of the desirability of such compulsion.

History teaches us that there have been but few infringements of personal liberty by the state which have not been justified, as they are here, in the name of righteousness and the public good, and few which have not been directed, as they are now, at politically helpless minorities. The framers were not unaware that under the system which they created most governmental curtailments of personal liberty would have the support of a legislative judgment that the public interest would be better served by its curtailment than by its constitutional protection. I cannot conceive that in prescribing, as limitations upon the powers of government, the freedom of the mind and spirit secured by the explicit guaranties of freedom of speech and religion, they intended or rightly could have left any latitude for a legislative judgment that the compulsory expression of belief which violates religious convictions would better serve the public interest than their protection. The Constitution may well elicit expressions of loyalty to it and to the government which it created, but it does not command such expressions or otherwise give any indication that compulsory expressions of loyalty play any such part in our scheme of government as to override the constitutional protection of freedom of speech and religion. And while such expressions of loyalty, when voluntarily given, may promote national unity, it is quite another matter to say that their compulsory expression by children in violation of their own and their parents' religious convictions can be regarded as playing so important a part in our national unity as to leave school boards free to exact it despite the constitutional guarantee of freedom of religion. The very terms of the Bill of Rights preclude, it seems to me, any reconciliation of such compulsions with the constitutional guaranties by a legislative declaration that they are more important to the public welfare than the Bill of Rights.

But even if this view be rejected and it is considered that there is some scope for the determination by legislatures whether the citizen shall be compelled to give public expression of such sentiments contrary to his religion, I am not persuaded that we should refrain from passing upon the legislative judgment "as long as the remedial channels of the democratic process remain open and unobstructed." This seems to me no more than the surrender of the constitutional protection of the liberty of small minorities to the popular will. We have previously pointed to the importance of a searching judicial inquiry into the legislative judgment in situations where prejudice against discrete and insular minorities may tend to curtail the operation of those political processes ordinarily to be relied on to protect minorities. See *United States v. Carolene Products Co.,* note 4. And until now we have not hesitated similarly to scrutinize legislation restricting the civil liberty of racial and religious minorities although no political process was affected.

. . . Here we have such a small minority entertaining in good faith a religious belief, which is such a departure from the usual course of human conduct, that most persons are disposed to regard it with little toleration or concern. In such circumstances careful scrutiny of legislative efforts to secure conformity of belief and opinion by a compulsory affirmation of the desired belief, is especially needful if civil rights are to receive any protection. Tested by this standard, I am not prepared to say that the right of this small and helpless minority, including children having a strong religious conviction, whether they understand its nature or not, to refrain from an expression obnoxious to their religion, is to be overborne by the interest of the state in maintaining discipline in the schools.

The Constitution expresses more than the conviction of the people that democratic processes must be preserved at all costs. It is also an expression of faith and a command that freedom of mind and spirit must be preserved, which government must obey, if it is to adhere to that justice and moderation without which no free government can exist. For this reason it would seem that legislation which operates to repress the religious freedom of small minorities, which is admittedly within the scope of the protection of the Bill of Rights, must at least be subject to the same judicial scrutiny as legislation which we have recently held to infringe the constitutional liberty of religious and racial minorities.

With such scrutiny I cannot say that the inconveniences which may attend some sensible adjustment of school discipline in order that the religious convictions of these children may be spared, presents a problem so momentous or pressing as to outweigh the freedom from compulsory violation of religious faith which has been thought worthy of constitutional protection.

Justice Frankfurter to Justice Stone, May 27, 1940: A *Qualified* Plea for Judicial Self-Restraint

Students of constitutional interpretation have wondered why it took Black and Douglas, two of the sharpest minds on the Court, both of them ardent liberals, so long to discover their error in joining Frankfurter's well-nigh unanimous opinion in the first Flag Salute Case. A clue may be found in the letter Frankfurter wrote Stone in trying to win his vote. Hitler's armies were then on the march, threatening to envelop Europe. In this struggle America could not escape involvement.

SUPREME COURT OF THE UNITED STATES WASHINGTON, D.C.

CHAMBERS
OF JUSTICE FELIX FRANKFURTER

May 27, 1940

Dear Stone:

Were No. 690 an ordinary case, I should let the opinion speak for itself. But that you should entertain doubts has naturally stirred me to an anxious reexamination of my own views, even though I can assure you that nothing has weighed as much on my conscience, since I have come on this Court, as has this case. Your doubts have stirred me to a reconsideration of the whole matter, because I am not happy that you should entertain doubts that I cannot share or meet in a domain where constitutional power is on one side and my private notions of liberty and toleration and good sense are on the other. After all, the vulgar intrusion of law in the domain of conscience is for me a very sensitive area. For various reasons—I suspect the most dominant one is the old colored man's explanation that Moses was just raised that way—a good part of my mature life has thrown whatever weight it has had against foolish and harsh manifestations of coercion and for the amplest expression of dissident views, however absurd or offensive these may have been to my own notions of rationality and decency. I say this merely to indicate that all my bias and predisposition are in favor of giving the fullest elbow room to every variety of religious, political, and economic view.

But no one has more clearly in his mind than

you, that even when it comes to these ultimate civil liberties, insofar as they are protected by the Constitution, we are not in the domain of absolutes. Here, also, we have an illustration of what the Greeks thousands of years ago recognized as a tragic issue, namely, the clash of rights, not the clash of wrongs. For resolving such clash we have no calculus. But there is for me, and I know also for you, a great makeweight for dealing with this problem, namely, that we are not the primary resolvers of the clash. We are not exercising an independent judgment; we are sitting in judgment upon the judgment of the legislature. I am aware of the important distinction which you so skillfully adumbrated in your footnote 4 (particularly the second paragraph of it) in the *Carolene Products Co.* case.* I agree with that distinction; I regard it as basic. I have taken over that distinction in its central aspect, however inadequately, in the present opinion by insisting on the importance of keeping open all those channels of free expression by which undesirable legislation may be removed, and keeping unobstructed all forms of protest against what are deemed invasions of conscience, however much the invasion may be justified on the score of the deepest interests of national well-being.

What weighs with me strongly in this case is my anxiety that, while we lean in the direction of the libertarian aspect, we do not exercise our judicial power unduly, and as though we ourselves were

* See Chapter Eight.—Ed.

legislators by holding with too tight a rein the organs of popular government. In other words, I want to avoid the mistake comparable to that made by those whom we criticized when dealing with the control of property. I hope I am aware of the different interests that are compendiously summarized by opposing "liberty" to "property." But I also know that the generalizations implied in these summaries are also inaccurate and hardly correspond to the complicated realities of an advanced society. I cannot rid myself of the notion that it is not fantastic, although I think foolish and perhaps worse, for school authorities to believe—as the record in this case explicitly shows the school authorities to have believed—that to allow exemption to some of the children goes far towards disrupting the whole patriotic exercise. And since certainly we must admit the general right of the school authorities to have such flag-saluting exercises, it seems to me that we do not trench on an undebatable territory of libertarian immunity to permit the school authorities a judgment as to the effect of this exemption in the particular setting of our time and circumstances.

For time and circumstances are surely not irrelevant considerations in resolving the conflicts that we do have to resolve in this particular case. . . . [C]ertainly it is relevant to make the adjustment that we have to make within the framework of present circumstances and those that are clearly ahead of us. . . . After all, despite some of the jurisprudential "realists," a decision decides not merely the particular case. Just as *Adkins* v. *Children's Hospital* had consequences not merely as to the minimum wage laws but in its radiations and in its psychological effects, so this case would have a tail of implications as to legislative power that is certainly debatable and might easily be invoked far beyond the size of the immediate kite, were it

to deny the very minimum exaction, however foolish as to the Gobitis children, of an expression of faith in the heritage and purposes of our country.

For my intention—and I hope my execution did not lag too far behind—was to use this opinion as a vehicle for preaching the true democratic faith of not relying on the Court for the impossible task of assuring a vigorous, mature, self-protecting and tolerant democracy by bringing the responsibility for a combination of firmness and toleration directly home where it belongs—to the people and their representatives themselves.

I have tried in this opinion really to act on what will, as a matter of history, be a lodestar for due regard between legislative and judicial powers, to wit, your dissent in the Butler case. For please bear in mind how very little this case authorizes and how wholly free it leaves us for the future. This is not a case where confinement either of children or of parents is the consequence of nonconformity. It is not a case where conformity is exacted for something that you and I regard as foolish—namely, a gesture of respect for the symbol of our national being—even though we deem it foolish to exact it from Jehovah's Witnesses. . . . The duty of compulsion being as minimal as it is for an act, the normal legislative authorization of which certainly cannot be denied, and all channels of affirmative free expression being open to both children and parents, I cannot resist the conviction that we ought to let the legislative judgment stand and put the responsibility for its exercise where it belongs. In any event, I hope you will be good enough to give me the benefit of what you think should be omitted or added to the opinion.

Faithfully yours
s/Felix Frankfurter

Mr. Justice Stone.

West Virginia State Board of Education v. Barnette (1943)

Majority: Jackson, Black, Douglas, Murphy, Rutledge, Stone. Dissenting: Frankfurter, Reed, Roberts.

Mr. Justice Jackson delivered the opinion of the Court: . . .

This case calls upon us to reconsider a precedent decision, as the Court throughout its history often has been required to do. Before turning to the Gobitis case, however, it is desirable to notice certain characteristics by which this controversy is distinguished. . . .

The sole conflict is between authority and rights of the individual. The State asserts power to condition access to public education on making a prescribed sign and profession and at the same time to coerce attendance by punishing both parent and child. The latter stand on a right of self-determination in matters that touch individual opinion and personal attitude. . . .

There is no doubt that, in connection with the pledges, the flag salute is a form of utterance. Symbolism is a primitive but effective way of communicating ideas. . . .

It is also to be noted that the compulsory flag salute and pledge requires [sic] affirmation of a belief and an attitude of mind. . . . To sustain the compulsory flag salute we are required to say that a Bill of Rights which guards the individual's right to speak his own mind, left it open to public authorities to compel him to utter what is not in his mind.

Whether the First Amendment to the Constitution will permit officials to order observance of ritual of this nature does not depend upon whether as a voluntary exercise we would think it to be good, bad or merely innocuous. . . .

Nor does the issue as we see it turn on one's possession of particular religious views or the sincerity with which they are held. While religion supplies appellees' motive for enduring the discomforts of making the issue in this case, many citizens who do not share these religious views hold such a compulsory rite to infringe constitutional liberty of the individual. It is not necessary to inquire whether nonconformist beliefs will exempt from the duty to salute unless we first find power to make the salute a legal duty.

The Gobitis decision, however, *assumed,* as did the argument in that case and in this, that power exists in the State to impose the flag salute discipline upon school children in general. The Court only examined and rejected a claim based on religious beliefs of immunity from an unquestioned general rule. The question which underlies the flag salute controversy is whether such a ceremony so touching matters of opinion and political attitude may be imposed upon the individual by official authority

under powers committed to any political organization under our Constitution. . . .

In weighing arguments of the parties it is important to distinguish between the due process clause of the Fourteenth Amendment as an instrument for transmitting the principles of the First Amendment and those cases in which it is applied for its own sake. The test of legislation which collides with the Fourteenth Amendment because it also collides with the principles of the First, is much more definite than the test when only the Fourteenth is involved. Much of the vagueness of the due process clause disappears when the specific prohibitions of the First become its standard. The right of a State to regulate, for example, a public utility may well include, so far as the due process test is concerned, power to impose all of the restrictions which a legislature may have a "rational basis" for adopting. But freedoms of speech and of press, of assembly, and of worship may not be infringed on such slender grounds. They are susceptible of restriction only to prevent grave and immediate danger to interests which the State may lawfully protect. It is important to note that while it is the Fourteenth Amendment which bears directly upon the State it is the more specific limiting principles of the First Amendment that finally govern this case.

Nor does our duty to apply the Bill of Rights to assertions of official authority depend upon our possession of marked competence in the field where the invasion of rights occurs. True, the task of translating the majestic generalities of the Bill of Rights, conceived as part of the pattern of liberal government in the eighteenth century, into concrete restraints on officials dealing with the problems of the twentieth century, is one to disturb self-confidence. . . . But we act in these matters not by authority of our competence but by force of our commissions. We cannot, because of modest estimates of our competence in such specialties as public education, withhold the judgment that history authenticates as the function of this Court when liberty is infringed. . . .

The case is made difficult not because the principles of its decision are obscure but because the flag involved is our own. Nevertheless, we apply the limitations of the Constitution with no fear that freedom to be intellectually and spiritually diverse or even contrary will disintegrate the social organization. To believe that patriotism will not flourish if patriotic ceremonies are voluntary and spontaneous instead of a compulsory routine is to make an unflattering estimate of the appeal of our institutions to free minds. We can have intellectual individualism and the rich cultural diversities that we owe to exceptional minds only at the price of occasional eccentricity and abnormal attitudes. When they are so harmless to others or to the State as those we deal with here, the price is not too great. But freedom to differ is not limited to things that do not matter much. That would be a mere shadow of freedom. The test of its substance is the right to differ as to things that touch the heart of the existing order.

If there is any fixed star in our constitutional constellation, it is that no official, high or petty, can prescribe what shall be orthodox in politics, nationalism, religion, or other matters of opinion or force citizens to confess by word or act their faith therein. If there are any circumstances which permit an exception, they do not now occur to us. . . .

MR. JUSTICE FRANKFURTER, dissenting.

One who belongs to the most vilified and persecuted minority in history is not likely to be insensible to the freedoms guaranteed by our Constitution. Were my purely personal attitude relevant I should wholeheartedly associate myself with the general libertarian views in the Court's opinion, representing as they do the thought and action of a lifetime. But as judges we are neither Jew nor Gentile, neither Catholic nor agnostic. We owe equal attachment to the Constitution and are equally bound by our judicial obligations whether we derive our citizenship from the earliest or the latest immigrants to these shores. As a member of this Court I am not justified in writing my private notions of policy into the Constitution, no matter how deeply I may cherish them or how mischievous I may deem their disregard. The duty of a judge who must decide which of two claims before the Court shall prevail, that of a State to enact and enforce laws within its general competence or that of an individual to refuse obedience because of the demands of his conscience, is not that of the ordinary person. It can never be emphasized too

much that one's own opinion about the wisdom or evil of a law should be excluded altogether when one is doing one's duty on the bench. The only opinion of our own even looking in that direction that is material is our opinion whether legislators could in reason have enacted such a law. In the light of all the circumstances, including the history of this question in this Court, it would require more daring than I possess to deny that reasonable legislators could have taken the action which is before us for review. . . .

There is no warrant in the constitutional basis of this Court's authority for attributing different rôles to it depending upon the nature of the challenge to the legislation. Our power does not vary according to the particular provision of the Bill of Rights which is invoked. The right not to have property taken without just compensation has, so far as the scope of judicial power is concerned, the same constitutional dignity as the right to be protected against unreasonable searches and seizures, and the latter has no less claim than freedom of the press or freedom of speech or religious freedom. In no instance is this Court the primary protector of the particular liberty that is invoked. . . .

Of course patriotism cannot be enforced by the flag salute. But neither can the liberal spirit be enforced by judicial invalidation of illiberal legislation. Our constant preoccupation with the constitutionality of legislation rather than with its wisdom tends to preoccupation of the American mind with a false value. The tendency of focussing attention on constitutionality is to make constitutionality synonymous with wisdom, to regard a law as all right if it is constitutional. Such an attitude is a great enemy of liberalism. Particularly in legislation affecting freedom of thought and freedom of speech much which should offend a free-spirited society is constitutional. Reliance for the most precious interests of civilization, therefore, must be found outside of their vindication in courts of law. Only a persistent positive translation of the faith of a free society into the convictions and habits and actions of a community is the ultimate reliance against unabated temptations to fetter the human spirit.

Sherbert v. *Verner*
374 U.S. 398, 83 S.Ct. 1790, 10 L.Ed. 2d 965 (1963)

Adell Sherbert was a member of the Seventh-day Adventist Church who was discharged by her employer in South Carolina because she would not work on Saturday, the Sabbath of her religion. After looking for other work and finding none because of her strictures against Saturday work, she filed a claim for unemployment compensation under South Carolina law. Her claim was denied because she failed to accept "suitable work when offered . . . by the employment office or the employer. . . ." This ruling of the Employment Security Commission was sustained by the Court of Common Pleas of Spartanburg County. The South Carolina Supreme Court affirmed. Majority: Brennan, Black, Clark, Douglas, Goldberg, Stewart, Warren. Dissenting: Harlan, White.

MR. JUSTICE BRENNAN delivered the opinion of the Court. . . .

We turn first to the question whether the disqualification for benefits imposes any burden on the free exercise of appellant's religion. We think it is clear that it does. In a sense the consequences of such a disqualification to religious principles and practices may be only an indirect result of welfare legislation within the State's general competence to enact; it is true that no criminal sanctions directly compel appellant to work a six-day week. But this is only the beginning, not the end, of our inquiry. For "[i]f the purpose or effect of a law is to impede the observance of one or all religions or is to discriminate invidiously between religions, that law is constitutionally invalid even though the burden may be characterized as being only indirect." Here not only is it apparent that appellant's declared ineligibility for benefits derives solely from the practice of her religion, but the pressure upon her to forgo that practice is unmistakable. The ruling forces her to choose between following the precepts of her religion and forfeiting benefits, on the one hand, and abandoning one of the precepts of her religion in order to accept work, on the other hand. Governmental imposition of such a choice puts the same kind of burden upon the free exercise of religion as would a fine imposed against appellant for her Saturday worship. . . .

We must next consider whether some compelling state interest enforced in the eligibility provisions of the South Carolina statute justifies the substantial infringement of appellant's First Amendment right. . . . No such abuse or danger has been advanced in the present case. The appellees suggest no more than a possibility that the filing of fraudulent claims by unscrupulous claimants feigning religious objections to Saturday work might not only dilute the unemployment compensation fund but also hinder the scheduling by employers of necessary Saturday work. But that possibility is not apposite here because no such objection appears to have been made before the South Carolina Supreme Court, and we are unwilling to assess the importance of an asserted state interest without the views of the state court. Nor, if the contention had been made below, would the record appear to sustain it; there is no proof whatever to warrant such fears of malingering or deceit as those which the respondents now advance. . . .

In holding as we do, plainly we are not fostering the "establishment" of the Seventh-day Adventist religion in South Carolina, for the extension of unemployment benefits to Sabbatarians in common with Sunday worshippers reflects nothing more than the governmental obligation of neutrality in the face of religious differences, and does not represent that involvement of religious with secular institutions which it is the object of the Establishment Clause to forestall. . . .

The judgment of the South Carolina Supreme Court is reversed and the case is remanded for further proceedings not inconsistent with this opinion.

It is so ordered.

MR. JUSTICE STEWART, concurring in the result.

Although fully agreeing with the result which the Court reaches in this case, I cannot join the Court's opinion. . . .

I am convinced that no liberty is more essential to the continued vitality of the free society which our Constitution guarantees than is the religious liberty protected by the Free Exercise Clause explicit in the First Amendment and imbedded in the Fourteenth. And I regret that on occasion . . . the Court has shown what has seemed to be a distressing insensitivity to the appropriate demands of this constitutional guarantee. By contrast I think that the Court's approach to the Establishment Clause has on occasion, and specifically in *Engel, Schempp,* and *Murray,* been not only insensitive, but positively wooden, and that the Court has accorded to the Establishment Clause a meaning which neither the words, the history, nor the intention of the authors of that specific constitutional provision even remotely suggests.

But my views as to the correctness of the Court's decisions in these cases are beside the point here. The point is that the decisions are on the books. And the result is that there are many situations where legitimate claims under the Free Exercise Clause will run into head-on collision with the Court's insensitive and sterile construction of the Establishment Clause. The controversy now before us is clearly such a case.

Because the appellant refuses to accept available jobs which would require her to work on Saturdays, South Carolina has declined to pay unemployment compensation benefits to her. Her refusal to work on Saturdays is based on the tenets of her religious faith. The Court says that South Carolina cannot under these circumstances declare her to be not "available for work" within the meaning of its statute because to do so would violate her constitutional right to the free exercise of her religion.

Yet what this Court has said about the Establishment Clause must inevitably lead to a diametrically opposite result. If the appellant's refusal to work on Saturdays were based on indolence, or on a compulsive desire to watch the Saturday television programs, no one would say that South Carolina could not hold that she was not "available for work" within the meaning of its statute. That

being so, the Establishment Clause as construed by this Court not only *permits* but affirmatively *requires* South Carolina equally to deny the appellant's claim for unemployment compensation when her refusal to work on Saturdays is based upon her religious creed. . . .

Mr. Justice Harlan, whom Mr. Justice White joins, dissenting. . . .

The South Carolina Supreme Court has uniformly applied this law in conformity with its clearly expressed purpose. It has consistently held that one is not "available for work" if his unemployment has resulted not from the inability of industry to provide a job but rather from personal circumstances, no matter how compelling. . . .

Thus in no proper sense can it be said that the State discriminated against the appellant on the basis of her religious beliefs or that she was denied benefits *because* she was a Seventh-day Adventist. She was denied benefits just as any other claimant would be denied benefits who was not "available for work" for personal reasons.

With this background, this Court's decision comes into clearer focus. What the Court is holding is that if the State chooses to condition unemployment compensation on the applicant's availability for work, it is constitutionally compelled to *carve out an exception*—and to provide benefits— for those whose unavailability is due to their religious convictions.

. . . [T]he implications of the present decision are far more troublesome than its apparently narrow dimensions would indicate at first glance. The State . . . must *single out* for financial assistance those whose behavior is religiously motivated, even though it denies such assistance to others whose identical behavior (in this case, inability to work on Saturdays) is not religiously motivated. . . .

. . . My own view is that at least under the circumstances of this case it would be a permissible accommodation of religion for the State, if it *chose* to do so, to create an exception to its eligibility requirements for persons like the appellant. The constitutional obligation of "neutrality" . . . is not so narrow a channel that the slightest deviation from an absolutely straight course leads to condemnation. . . .

Wallace v. *Jaffree*
472 U.S. 38, 105 S.Ct. 2479, 86 L.Ed. 2d 29 (1985)

In 1978, the Alabama legislature authorized a one-minute period of silence in public schools "for meditation" (Alabama Code, Section 16-1-20). Section 16-1-20.1, enacted in 1981 authorized a similar period of silence "for meditation or voluntary prayer." Section 16-1-20.2, passed in 1982, authorized teachers to lead "willing students" in a prescribed prayer to "Almighty God . . . the Creator and Supreme Judge of the world." By 1984, some 25 other states had laws providing for some kind of "moment of silence" in their public school systems.

In May 1982, Ishmael Jaffree, father of three children in the public schools of Mobile County, challenged the constitutionality of these statutes as violations of the First and Fourteenth Amendments. The United States District Court for the Southern District of Alabama found Section 16-1-20 constitutionally unobjectionable, and in later litigation Jaffree abandoned his claim that the "meditation" statute was unconstitutional. Judge Hand of the district court admitted that 16-1-20.1 and 16-1-20.2 were efforts "to encourage a religious activity," but in an extraordinary step concluded that these two laws were also constitutional because "this Court's review of the relevant legislative history surrounding the adoption of the Fourteenth Amendment, together with the plain language of those amendments, leaves no doubt that those amendments were not intended to forbid religious prayers in the schools. . . ." Moreover, Hand found "little historical support for the view that the states were prohibited by the establishment clause of the First Amendment from establishing a religion."

The Court of Appeals for the Eleventh Circuit reversed the district court, finding both 16-1-20.1 and 16-1-20.2 violations of the First and Fourteenth Amendments. The Supreme Court summarily affirmed the court of appeals with respect to 16-1-20.2 and limited argument solely to the constitutionality of 16-1-20.1, the provision for a moment of silence "for meditation or voluntary prayer." Majority: Stevens, Blackmun, Brennan, Marshall, O'Connor, Powell. Dissenting: Rehnquist, Burger, White.

JUSTICE STEVENS delivered the opinion of the Court. . . .

[T]he narrow question for decision is whether § 16-1-20.1, which authorizes a period of silence for "meditation or voluntary prayer," is a law respecting the establishment of religion within the meaning of the First Amendment. . . .

As is plain from its text, the First Amendment was adopted to curtail the power of Congress to interfere with the individual's freedom to believe, to worship, and to express himself in accordance with the dictates of his own conscience. Until the Fourteenth Amendment was added to the Constitution, the First Amendment's restraints on the exercise of federal power simply did not apply to the States. But when the Constitution was amended to prohibit any State from depriving any person of liberty without due process of law, that Amendment imposed the same substantive limitations on the States' power to legislate that the First Amendment had always imposed on the Congress' power. This Court has confirmed and endorsed this elementary proposition of law time and time again. . . .

At one time it was thought that this right merely proscribed the preference of one Christian sect over another, but would not require equal respect for the conscience of the infidel, the atheist, or the adherent of a non-Christian faith such as Mohammedism or Judaism. But when the underlying principle has been examined in the crucible of litigation, the Court has unambiguously concluded that the individual freedom of conscience protected by the First Amendment embraces the right to select any religious faith or none at all. This conclusion derives support not only from the interest in respecting the individual's freedom of conscience, but also from the conviction that religious beliefs worthy of respect are the product of free and voluntary choice by the faithful, and from recognition of the fact that the political interest in forestalling intolerance extends beyond intolerance among Christian sects—or even intolerance among "religions"—to encompass intolerance of the disbeliever and the uncertain. . . .

When the Court has been called upon to construe the breadth of the Establishment Clause, it has examined the criteria developed over a period of many years. Thus, in *Lemon* v. *Kurtzman* . . . we wrote:

"Every analysis in this area must begin with consideration of the cumulative criteria developed by the Court over many years. Three such tests may be gleaned from our cases. First, the statute must have a secular legislative purpose; second, its principal or primary effect must be one that neither advances nor inhibits religion . . . ; finally, the statute must not foster 'an excessive government entanglement with religion.' . . ."

It is the first of these three criteria that is most plainly implicated by this case. . . . [T]he record . . . reveals that the enactment of § 16-1-20.1 was not motivated by any clearly secular purpose—indeed, the statute had *no* secular purpose.

The sponsor of the bill that became § 16-1-20.1, Senator Donald Holmes, inserted into the legislative record—apparently without dissent—a statement indicating that the legislation was an

"effort to return voluntary prayer" to the public schools. Later Senator Holmes confirmed this purpose before the District Court. In response to the question whether he had any purpose for the legislation other than returning voluntary prayer to public schools, he stated, "No, I did not have no other purpose in mind." The State did not present evidence of *any* secular purpose. . . .

The legislative intent to return prayer to the public schools is, of course, quite different from merely protecting every student's right to engage in voluntary prayer during an appropriate moment of silence during the school day. The 1978 statute already protected that right, containing nothing that prevented any student from engaging in voluntary prayer during a silent minute of meditation. Appellants have not identified any secular purpose that was not fully served by § 16-1-20 before the enactment of § 16-1-20.1. Thus, only two conclusions are consistent with the text of § 16-1-20.1: (1) the statute was enacted to convey a message of State endorsement and promotion of prayer; or (2) the statute was enacted for no purpose. No one suggests that the statute was nothing but a meaningless or irrational act. . . . The Legislature enacted § 16-1-20.1 despite the existence of § 16-1-20 for the sole purpose of expressing the State's endorsement of prayer activities for one minute at the beginning of each school day. The addition of "or voluntary prayer" indicates that the State intended to characterize prayer as a favored practice. Such an endorsement is not consistent with the established principle that the Government must pursue a course of complete neutrality toward religion. . . .

For whenever the State itself speaks on a religious subject, one of the questions that we must ask is "whether the Government intends to convey a message of endorsement or disapproval of religion." Keeping in mind, as we must, "both the fundamental place held by the Establishment Clause in our constitutional scheme and the myriad, subtle ways in which Establishment Clause values can be eroded," we conclude that § 16-1-20.1 violates the First Amendment.

The judgment of the Court of Appeals is affirmed.

It is so ordered.

JUSTICE O'CONNOR, concurring in the judgment. . . .

[T]he religious liberty protected by the Establishment Clause is infringed when the government makes adherence to religion relevant to a person's standing in the political community. Direct government action endorsing religion or a particular religious practice is invalid under this approach because it "sends a message to nonadherents that they are outsiders, not full members of the political community, and an accompanying message to adherents that they are insiders, favored members of the political community." . . . Under this view, *Lemon*'s inquiry as to the purpose and effect of a statute requires courts to examine whether government's purpose is to endorse religion and whether the statute actually conveys a message of endorsement.

The endorsement test is useful because of the analytic content it gives to the *Lemon*-mandated inquiry into legislative purpose and effect. In this country, church and state must necessarily operate within the same community. Because of this coexistence, it is inevitable that the secular interests of Government and the religious interests of various sects and their adherents will frequently intersect, conflict, and combine. A statute that ostensibly promotes a secular interest often has an incidental or even a primary effect of helping or hindering a sectarian belief. Chaos would ensue if every such statute were invalid under the Establishment Clause. For example, the State could not criminalize murder for fear that it would thereby promote the Biblical command against killing. The task for the Court is to sort out those statutes and government practices whose purpose and effect go against the grain of religious liberty protected by the First Amendment.

The endorsement test does not preclude government from acknowledging religion or from taking religion into account in making law and policy. It does preclude government from conveying or attempting to convey a message that religion or a particular religious belief is favored or preferred. . . .

A state sponsored moment of silence in the public schools is different from state sponsored vocal prayer or Bible reading. First, a moment of silence is not inherently religious. Silence, unlike prayer or Bible reading, need not be associated with a religious exercise. Second, a pupil who participates in a moment of silence need not compromise his or her beliefs. During a moment of silence, a student who objects to prayer is left to his or her own thoughts, and is not compelled to listen to the

prayers or thoughts of others. For these simple reasons, a moment of silence statute does not stand or fall under the Establishment Clause according to how the Court regards vocal prayer or Bible reading. Scholars and at least one member of this Court have recognized the distinction and suggested that a moment of silence in public schools would be constitutional. . . .

[Justice O'Connor next makes reference to Justice Rehnquist's dissent.]

The United States, in an *amicus* brief, suggests a less sweeping modification of Establishment Clause principles. In the Federal Government's view, a state sponsored moment of silence is merely an "accommodation" of the desire of some public school children to practice their religion by praying silently. Such an accommodation is contemplated by the First Amendment's guaranty that the Government will not prohibit the free exercise of religion. Because the moment of silence implicates free exercise values, the United States suggests that the *Lemon*-mandated inquiry into purpose and effect should be modified. . . .

The challenge posed by the United States' argument is how to define the proper Establishment Clause limits on voluntary government efforts to facilitate the free exercise of religion. On the one hand, a rigid application of the *Lemon* test would invalidate legislation exempting religious observers from generally applicable government obligations. By definition, such legislation has a religious purpose and effect in promoting the free exercise of religion. On the other hand, judicial deference to all legislation that purports to facilitate the free exercise of religion would completely vitiate the Establishment Clause. Any statute pertaining to religion can be viewed as an "accommodation" of free exercise rights. . . .

The solution to the conflict between the religion clauses lies not in "neutrality," but rather in identifying workable limits to the Government's license to promote the free exercise of religion. The text of the Free Exercise Clause speaks of laws that prohibit the free exercise of religion. On its face, the Clause is directed at government interference with free exercise. Given that concern, one can plausibly assert that government pursues free exercise clause values when it lifts a government-imposed burden on the free exercise of religion. If a statute falls within this category, then the standard Establishment Clause test should be modified accordingly. It is disingenuous to look for a purely secular purpose when the manifest objective of a statute is to facilitate the free exercise of religion by lifting a government-imposed burden. Instead, the Court should simply acknowledge that the religious purpose of such a statute is legitimated by the Free Exercise Clause. I would also go further. In assessing the effect of such a statute—that is, in determining whether the statute conveys the message of endorsement of religion or a particular religious belief—courts should assume that the "objective observer" . . . is acquainted with the Free Exercise Clause and the values it promotes. Thus individual perceptions, or resentment that a religious observer is exempted from a particular government requirement, would be entitled to little weight if the Free Exercise Clause strongly supported the exemption. . . .

JUSTICE REHNQUIST, dissenting.

Thirty-eight years ago this Court, in *Everson* v. *Board of Education* (1947), summarized its exegesis of Establishment Clause doctrine thus:

"In the words of Jefferson, the clause against establishment of religion by law was intended to erect 'a wall of separation between church and State.' "

This language . . . quoted from Thomas Jefferson's letter to the Danbury Baptist Association [1805] the phrase "I contemplate with sovereign reverence that act of the whole American people which declared that their legislature should 'make no law respecting an establishment of religion, or prohibiting the free exercise thereof,' thus building a wall of separation between church and State." . . .

It is impossible to build sound constitutional doctrine upon a mistaken understanding of constitutional history, but unfortunately the Establishment Clause has been expressly freighted with Jefferson's misleading metaphor for nearly forty years. . . .

Jefferson's fellow Virginian James Madison, with whom he was joined in the battle for the enactment of the Virginia Statute of Religious Liberty of 1786, did play as large a part as anyone in the drafting of the Bill of Rights. He had two advantages over Jefferson in this regard: he was present in the United States, and he was a leading member of the First Congress. But when we turn to the record of the proceedings in the First Congress leading up to the adoption of the Establishment Clause of

the Constitution, including Madison's significant contributions thereto, we see a far different picture of its purpose than the highly simplified "wall of separation between church and State." . . .

[Justice Rehnquist next discusses the proceedings surrounding adoption of the First Amendment in the First Congress.]

On the basis of the record of these proceedings in the House of Representatives, James Madison was undoubtedly the most important architect among the members of the House of the amendments which became the Bill of Rights, but it was James Madison speaking as an advocate of sensible legislative compromise, not as an advocate of incorporating the Virginia Statute of Religious Liberty into the United States Constitution. . . .

It seems indisputable from these glimpses of Madison's thinking, as reflected by actions on the floor of the House in 1789, that he saw the amendment as designed to prohibit the establishment of a national religion, and perhaps to prevent discrimination among sects. He did not see it as requiring neutrality on the part of government between religion and irreligion. Thus the Court's opinion in *Everson*—while correct in bracketing Madison and Jefferson together in their exertions in their home state leading to the enactment of the Virginia Statute of Religious Liberty—is totally incorrect in suggesting that Madison carried these views onto the floor of the United States House of Representatives when he proposed the language which would ultimately become the Bill of Rights.

The repetition of this error in the Court's opinion in *Illinois ex rel. McCollum* v. *Board of Education* and *Engel* v. *Vitale* does not make it any sounder historically. Finally, in *Abington School District* v. *Schempp* . . . the Court made the truly remarkable statement that "the views of Madison and Jefferson, preceded by Roger Williams came to be incorporated not only in the Federal Constitution but likewise in those of most of our States". . . . On the basis of what evidence we have, this statement is demonstrably incorrect as a matter of history. And its repetition in varying forms in succeeding opinions of the Court can give it no more authority than it possesses as a matter of fact; *stare decisis* may bind courts as to matters of law, but it cannot bind them as to matters of history.

None of the other Members of Congress who spoke during the August 15th debate expressed the slightest indication that they thought the language before them from the Select Committee, or the evil to be aimed at, would require that the Government be absolutely neutral as between religion and irreligion. The evil to be aimed at, so far as those who spoke were concerned, appears to have been the establishment of a national church, and perhaps the preference of one religious sect over another; but it was definitely not concern about whether the Government might aid all religions evenhandedly. . . .

Joseph Story, a member of this Court from 1811 to 1845, and during much of that time a professor at the Harvard Law School, published by far the most comprehensive treatise on the United States Constitution that had then appeared. Volume 2 of Story's Commentaries on the Constitution of the United States discussed the meaning of the Establishment Clause of the First Amendment this way:

"Probably at the time of the adoption of the Constitution, and of the amendment to it now under consideration [First Amendment], the general if not the universal sentiment in America was, that Christianity ought to receive encouragement from the State so far as was not incompatible with the private rights of conscience and the freedom of religious worship. An attempt to level all religions, and to make it a matter of state policy to hold all in utter indifference, would have created universal disapprobation, if not universal indignation.

"The real object of the [First] [A]mendment was not to countenance, much less to advance, Mahometanism, or Judaism, or infidelity, by prostrating Christianity; but to exclude all rivalry among Christian sects, and to prevent any national ecclesiastical establishment which should give to a hierarchy the exclusive patronage of the national government. It thus cut off the means of religious persecution (the vice and pest of former ages), and of the subversion of the rights of conscience in matters of religion, which had been trampled upon almost from the days of the Apostles to the present age. . . ."

It would seem from this evidence that the Establishment Clause of the First Amendment had acquired a well-accepted meaning: it forbade establishment of a national religion, and forbade preference among religious sects or denominations. . . . The Establishment Clause did not re-

quire government neutrality between religion and irreligion nor did it prohibit the federal government from providing non-discriminatory aid to religion. There is simply no historical foundation for the proposition that the Framers intended to build the "wall of separation" that was constitutionalized in *Everson*. . . .

The Court has more recently attempted to add some mortar to *Everson's* wall through the three-part test of *Lemon* v. *Kurtzman* . . . which served at first to offer a more useful test for purposes of the Establishment Clause than did the "wall" metaphor. . . .

[D]ifficulties arise because the *Lemon* test has no more grounding in the history of the First Amendment than does the wall theory upon which it rests. The three-part test represents a determined effort to craft a workable rule from an historically faulty doctrine; but the rule can only be as sound as the doctrine it attempts to service. The three-part test has simply not provided adequate standards for deciding Establishment clause cases, as this Court has slowly come to realize. Even worse, the *Lemon* test has caused this Court to fracture into unworkable plurality opinions . . . depending upon how each of the three factors applies to a certain state action. The results from our school services cases show the difficulty we have encountered in making the *Lemon* test yield principled results. . . .

If a constitutional theory has no basis in the history of the amendment it seeks to interpret, is difficult to apply and yields unprincipled results, I see little use in it. . . .

The true meaning of the Establishment Clause can only be seen in its history. . . . As drafters of our Bill of Rights, the Framers inscribed the principles that control today. Any deviation from their intentions frustrates the permanence of that Charter and will only lead to the type of unprincipled decisionmaking that has plagued our Establishment Clause cases since *Everson*. . . .

The Court strikes down the Alabama statute . . . because the State wished to "endorse prayer as a favored practice." . . . It would come as much of a shock to those who drafted the Bill of Rights as it will to a large number of thoughtful Americans today to learn that the Constitution, as construed by the majority, prohibits the Alabama Legislature from "endorsing" prayer. George Washington himself, at the request of the very Congress which passed the Bill of Rights, proclaimed a day of "public thanksgiving and prayer, to be observed by acknowledging with grateful hearts the many and signal favors of Almighty God." History must judge whether it was the father of his country in 1789, or a majority of the Court today, which has strayed from the meaning of the Establishment Clause.

Aguilar v. Felton
473 U.S. 402, 105 S.Ct. 3232, 87 L.Ed 2d 290 (1985)

Under Title I of the Elementary and Secondary Education Act of 1965, New York City used federal funds to pay the salaries of public school employees who taught remedial subjects on the premises of private schools to educationally deprived children from low-income families in those situations where the remedial instruction was not offered by the private school. Of the eligible students in 1981–1982, 13.2 percent were enrolled in private schools. Of that group, 84 percent were enrolled in schools affiliated with the Roman Catholic Archdiocese of New York and the Diocese of Brooklyn, and 8 percent were enrolled in Hebrew day schools. The record indicated that 78 percent of Title I instructors who taught in sectarian schools visited more than one school each week and that about one-quarter of the instructors shared the religious affiliation of the schools in which they taught. The district court upheld the constitutionality of the program, but the Court of Appeals for the Second Circuit reversed. In its view the establishment clause "constitutes an insurmountable barrier to the use of federal funds to send public school teachers and other professionals into religious schools to carry on instruction, remedial or otherwise, or to provide clinical and guidance services of the sort at issue here." The Supreme Court decided this case on the same day as *School Districts of Grand Rapids* v. *Ball,* which invalidated a similar program not involving Title I funds. Majority: Brennan, Blackmun, Marshall, Powell, Stevens. Dissenting: O'Connor, Burger, Rehnquist, White.

JUSTICE BRENNAN delivered the opinion of the Court. . . .

In *School Districts of the City of Grand Rapids* v. *Ball,* the Court has today held unconstitutional under the Establishment Clause two remedial and enhancement programs operated by the Grand Rapids Public School District, in which classes were provided to private school children at public expense in classrooms located in and leased from the local private schools. The New York programs challenged in this case are very similar to the programs we examined in *Ball.* In both cases, publicly funded instructors teach classes composed exclusively of private school students in private school buildings. In both cases, an overwhelming number of the participating private schools are religiously affiliated. In both cases, the publicly funded programs provide not only professional personnel, but also all materials and supplies necessary for the operation of the programs. Finally, the instructors in both cases are told that they are public school employees under the sole control of the public school system.

The appellants attempt to distinguish this case on the ground that the City of New York, unlike the Grand Rapids Public School District, has adopted a system for monitoring the religious content of publicly funded Title I classes in the religious schools. At best, the supervision in this case would assist in preventing the Title I program from being used, intentionally or unwittingly, to inculcate the religious beliefs of the surrounding parochial school. But appellants' argument fails in any event, because the supervisory system established by the City of New York inevitably results in the excessive entanglement of church and state, an Establishment Clause concern distinct from that addressed by the effects doctrine. Even where state aid to parochial institutions does not have the primary effect of advancing religion, the provision of such aid may nonetheless violate the Establishment Clause owing to the nature of the interaction of church and state in the administration of that aid.

The principle that the state should not become too closely entangled with the church in the administration of assistance is rooted in two concerns. When the state becomes enmeshed with a given denomination in matters of religious significance, the freedom of religious belief of those who are not adherents of that denomination suffers, even when the governmental purpose underlying the involvement is largely secular. In addition, the freedom of even the adherents of the denomination is limited by the governmental intrusion into sacred matters. . . .

In *Lemon* v. *Kurtzman* (1971), the Court held that the supervision necessary to ensure that teachers in parochial schools were not conveying religious messages to their students would constitute the excessive entanglement of church and state:

"A comprehensive, discriminating, and continuing state surveillance will inevitably be required to ensure that these restrictions are obeyed and the First Amendment otherwise respected. Unlike a book, a teacher cannot be inspected once so as to determine the extent and intent of his or her personal beliefs and subjective acceptance of the limitations imposed by the First Amendment. These prophylactic contacts will involve excessive and enduring entanglement between state and church."

Similarly, in *Meek* v. *Pittenger* (1975), we invalidated a state program that offered, *inter alia,* guidance, testing, remedial and therapeutic services performed by public employees on the premises of the parochial schools. As in *Lemon,* we observed that though a comprehensive system of supervision might conceivably prevent teachers from having the primary effect of advancing religion, such a system would inevitably lead to an unconstitutional administrative entanglement between church and state. . . .

The critical elements of the entanglement proscribed in *Lemon* and *Meek* are thus present in this case. First, as noted above, the aid is provided in a pervasively sectarian environment. Second, because assistance is provided in the form of teachers, ongoing inspection is required to ensure the absence of a religious message. In short, the scope and duration of New York's Title I program would require a permanent and pervasive State presence in the sectarian schools receiving aid.

This pervasive monitoring by public authorities in the sectarian schools infringes precisely those Establishment Clause values at the root of the prohibition of excessive entanglement. Agents of the State must visit and inspect the religious school regularly, alert for the subtle or overt presence of religious matter in Title I classes. . . . In addition, the religious school must obey these same agents when they make determinations as to what is and what is not a "religious symbol" and thus off limits in a Title I classroom. In short, the religious school, which has as a primary purpose the advancement and preservation of a particular religion must endure the ongoing presence of state personnel whose primary purpose is to monitor teachers and students in an attempt to guard against the infiltration of religious thought.

The administrative coöperation that is required to maintain the educational program at issue here entangles Church and State in still another way that infringes interests at the heart of the Establishment Clause. Administrative personnel of the public and parochial school systems must work together in resolving matters related to schedules, classroom assignments, problems that arise in the implementation of the program, requests for additional services, and the dissemination of information regarding the program. Furthermore, the program necessitates "frequent contacts between the regular and the remedial teachers (or other professionals), in which each side reports on individual student needs, problems encountered, and results achieved."

We have long recognized that underlying the

Establishment Clause is "the objective . . . to prevent, as far as possible, the intrusion of either [Church or State] into the precincts of the other." . . .

Despite the well-intentioned efforts taken by the City of New York, the program remains constitutionally flawed owing to the nature of the aid, to the institution receiving the aid, and to the constitutional principles that they implicate—that neither the State nor Federal Government shall promote or hinder a particular faith or faith generally through the advancement of benefits or through the excessive entanglement of church and state in the administration of those benefits.

Affirmed.

JUSTICE O'CONNOR, with whom JUSTICE REHNQUIST joins, dissenting. . . .

Recognizing the weakness of any claim of an improper purpose or effect, the Court today relies entirely on the entanglement prong of *Lemon* to invalidate the New York City Title I program. The Court holds that the occasional presence of peripatetic public schoolteachers on parochial school grounds threatens undue entanglement of church and state because (1) the remedial instruction is afforded in a pervasively sectarian environment; (2) ongoing supervision is required to assure that the public schoolteachers do not attempt to inculcate religion; (3) the administrative personnel of the parochial and public school systems must work together in resolving administrative and scheduling problems; and (4) the instruction is likely to result in political divisiveness over the propriety of direct aid. . . .

This analysis of entanglement, I acknowledge, finds support in some of this Court's precedents. . . .

I would accord these decisions the appropriate deference commanded by the doctrine of *stare decisis* if I could discern logical support for their analysis. . . . It is not intuitively obvious that a dedicated public school teacher will tend to disobey instructions and commence proselytizing students at public expense merely because the classroom is within a parochial school. *Meek* is correct in asserting that a teacher of remedial reading "remains a teacher," but surely it is significant that the teacher involved is a professional, full-time public school employee who is unaccustomed to bringing religion into the classroom. Given that not a single incident of religious indoctrination has been identified as

occurring in the thousands of classes offered in Grand Rapids and New York over the past two decades, it is time to acknowledge that the risk . . . was greatly exaggerated.

Just as the risk that public schoolteachers in parochial classrooms will inculcate religion has been exaggerated, so has the degree of supervision required to manage that risk. In this respect the New York Title I program is instructive. What supervision has been necessary in New York to enable public school teachers to help disadvantaged children for 19 years without once proselytizing? Public officials have prepared careful instructions warning public schoolteachers of their exclusively secular mission, and have required Title I teachers to study and observe them. Under the rules, Title I teachers are not accountable to parochial or private school officials; they have sole responsibility for selecting the students who participate in their class, must administer their own tests for determining eligibility, cannot engage in team teaching or cooperative activities with parochial school teachers, must make sure that all materials and equipment they use are not otherwise used by the parochial school, and must not participate in religious activities in the schools or introduce any religious matter into their teaching. To ensure compliance with the rules, a field supervisor and a program coordinator, who are full-time public school employees, make unannounced visits to each teacher's classroom at least once a month.

The Court concludes that this degree of supervision of public school employees by other public school employees constitutes excessive entanglement of church and state. I cannot agree. . . . Even if I remained confident of the usefulness of entanglement as an Establishment Clause test, I would conclude that New York's efforts to prevent religious indoctrination in Title I classes have been adequate and have not caused excessive institutional entanglement of church and state.

The Court's reliance on the potential for political divisiveness as evidence of undue entanglement is also unpersuasive. There is little record support for the proposition that New York's admirable Title I program has ignited any controversy other than this litigation. . . .

It is curious indeed to base our interpretation of the Constitution on speculation as to the likelihood of a phenomenon which the parties may create merely by prosecuting a lawsuit. My reservations about the entanglement test, however, have come to encompass its institutional aspects as well. As JUSTICE REHNQUIST has pointed out, many of the inconsistencies in our Establishment Clause decisions can be ascribed to our insistence that parochial aid programs with a valid purpose and effect may still be invalid by virtue of undue entanglement. . . .

Pervasive institutional involvement of church and state may remain relevant in deciding the *effect* of a statute which is alleged to violate the Establishment Clause, but state efforts to ensure that public resources are used only for nonsectarian ends should not in themselves serve to invalidate an otherwise valid statute. The State requires sectarian organizations to cooperate on a whole range of matters without thereby advancing religion or giving the impression that the government endorses religion. . . . If a statute lacks a purpose or effect of advancing or endorsing religion, I would not invalidate it merely because it requires some ongoing cooperation between church and state or some state supervision to ensure that state funds do not advance religion.

Lyng v. Northwest Indian Cemetery Protective Association
56 U.S.L.W. 4292 (1988)

To connect the California towns of Gasquet and Orleans with a paved road, the U.S. Forest Service decided to build a six-mile segment of roadway (the G-O road) through the Chimney Rock section of the Six Rivers National Forest. That section of the forest was located between two completed stretches of the road. The Chimney Rock area has historically been used for religious purposes by the Yurok, Karok, and Tolowa Indians. In 1979 a study commissioned by the Forest Service concluded that construction of the roadway along any available route "would cause serious and irreparable damage to the sacred areas which are an integral and necessary part of the belief systems and lifeway of Northwest California Indian peoples." The Forest Service nonetheless decided in 1982 to proceed with construction and also approved a plan allowing the harvesting of 733 million board feet of timber over an 80-year period. (A large part of the lumbering was banned by Congress in 1984, however.) After exhausting their administrative remedies, the Indian Cemetery Protective Association and other parties filed suit in United States district court, claiming violation of the free exercise clause. In 1983 the district court agreed and issued a permanent injunction forbidding the government from constructing the Chimney Rock segment of the road and from harvesting timber. In 1986 the Court of Appeals for the Ninth Circuit affirmed. Majority: O'Connor, Rehnquist, Scalia, Stevens, White. Dissenting: Brennan, Blackmun, Marshall. Not participating: Kennedy.

JUSTICE O'CONNOR delivered the opinion of the Court.

This case requires us to consider whether the First Amendment's Free Exercise Clause forbids the Government from permitting timber harvesting in, or constructing a road through, a portion of a

National Forest that has traditionally been used for religious purposes by members of three American Indian tribes in northwestern California. . . .

It is undisputed that the Indian respondents' beliefs are sincere and that the Government's proposed actions will have severe adverse effects on the practice of their religion. Respondents contend that the burden on their religious practices is heavy enough to violate the Free Exercise Clause unless the Government can demonstrate a compelling need to complete the G-O road or to engage in timber harvesting in the Chimney Rock area. We disagree.

In *Bowen* v. *Roy* (1986), we considered a challenge to a federal statute that required the States to use Social Security numbers in administering certain welfare programs. Two applicants for benefits under these programs contended that their religious beliefs prevented them from acceding to the use of a Social Security number for their two-year-old daughter because the use of a numerical identifier would " 'rob the spirit' of [their] daughter and prevent her from attaining greater spiritual power." Similarly, in this case, it is said that disruption of the natural environment caused by the G-O road will diminish the sacredness of the area in question and create distractions that will interfere with "training and ongoing religious experience of individuals using [sites within] the area for personal medicine and growth . . . and as integrated parts of a system of religious belief and practice which correlates ascending degrees of personal power with a geographic hierarchy of power." The Court rejected this kind of challenge in *Roy:*

"The Free Exercise Clause simply cannot be understood to require the Government to conduct its own internal affairs in ways that comport with the religious beliefs of particular citizens. Just as the Government may not insist that [the Roys] engage in any set form of religious observance, so [they] may not demand that the Government join in their chosen religious practices by refraining from using a number to identify their daughter. . . .

". . . The Free Exercise Clause affords an individual protection from certain forms of governmental compulsion; it does not afford an individual a right to dictate the conduct of the Government's internal procedures."

The building of a road or the harvesting of timber on publicly owned land cannot meaningfully be distinguished from the use of a Social Security number in *Roy*. In both cases, the challenged government action would interfere significantly with private persons' ability to pursue spiritual fulfillment according to their own religious beliefs. In neither case, however, would the affected individuals be coerced by the Government's action into violating their religious beliefs; nor would either governmental action penalize religious activity by denying any person an equal share of the rights, benefits, and privileges enjoyed by other citizens. . . .

. . . It is true that this Court has repeatedly held that indirect coercion or penalties on the free exercise of religion, not just outright prohibitions, are subject to scrutiny under the First Amendment. Thus, for example, ineligibility for unemployment benefits, based solely on a refusal to violate the Sabbath, has been analogized to a fine imposed on Sabbath worship. This does not and cannot imply that incidental effects of government programs, which may make it more difficult to practice certain religions but which have no tendency to coerce individuals into acting contrary to their religious beliefs, require government to bring forward a compelling justification for its otherwise lawful actions. . . . [T]he Constitution simply does not provide a principle that could justify upholding respondents' legal claims. However much we might wish that it were otherwise, government simply could not operate if it were required to satisfy every citizen's religious needs and desires. A broad range of government activities—from social welfare programs to foreign aid to conservation projects—will always be considered essential to the spiritual well-being of some citizens, often on the basis of sincerely held religious beliefs. Others will find the very same activities deeply offensive, and perhaps incompatible with their own search for spiritual fulfillment and with the tenets of their religion. The First Amendment must apply to all citizens alike, and it can give to none of them a veto over public programs that do not prohibit the free exercise of religion. The Constitution does not, and courts cannot, offer to reconcile the various competing demands on government, many of them rooted in sincere religious belief, that inevitably arise in so diverse a society as ours. That task, to the extent that it is feasible, is for the legislatures and other institutions. . . .

Perceiving a "stress point in the longstanding conflict between two disparate cultures," the dissent attacks us for declining to "balanc[e] these competing and potentially irreconcilable interests, choosing instead to turn this difficult task over to the federal legislature." Seeing the Court as the arbiter, the dissent proposes a legal test under which it would decide which public lands are "central" or "indispensable" to which religions, and by implication which are "dispensable" or "peripheral," and would then decide which government programs are "compelling" enough to justify "infringement of those practices." We would accordingly be required to weigh the value of every religious belief and practice that is said to be threatened by any government program. Unless a "showing of 'centrality' " is nothing but an assertion of centrality, the dissent thus offers us the prospect of this Court holding that some sincerely held religious beliefs and practices are not "central" to certain religions, despite protestations to the contrary from the religious objectors who brought the lawsuit. In other words, the dissent's approach would require us to rule that some religious adherents misunderstand their own religious beliefs. We think such an approach cannot be squared with the Constitution or with our precedents, and that it would cast the judiciary in a role that we were never intended to play.

The decision of the court below, according to which the First Amendment precludes the Government from completing the G-O road or from permitting timber harvesting in the Chimney Rock area, is reversed. . . .

It is so ordered.

JUSTICE BRENNAN, with whom JUSTICE MARSHALL and JUSTICE BLACKMUN join, dissenting. . . .

As the Forest Service's commissioned study . . . explains, for Native Americans religion is not a discrete sphere of activity separate from all others, and any attempt to isolate the religious aspects of Indian life "is in reality an exercise which forces Indian concepts into non-Indian categories." Thus, for most Native Americans, "[t]he area of worship cannot be delineated from social, political, cultural and other aspects of Indian life-style." . . . A pervasive feature of this life-style is the individual's relationship with the natural world; this relationship, which can accurately though somewhat incompletely be characterized as one of stewardship, forms the core of what might be called, for want of a better nomenclature, the Indian religious experience. While traditional western religions view creation as the work of a deity "who institutes natural laws which then govern the operation of physical nature," tribal religions regard creation as an ongoing process in which they are morally and religiously obligated to participate. . . . Where dogma lies at the heart of western religions, Native American faith is inextricably bound to the use of land.

For respondent Indians, the most sacred of lands is the high country where, they believe, pre-human spirits moved with the coming of humans to the earth. Because these spirits are seen as the source of religious power, or "medicine," many of the tribes' rituals and practices require frequent journeys to the area. . . .

The Court does not for a moment suggest that the interests served by the G-O road are in any way compelling, or that they outweigh the destructive effect construction of the road will have on respondents' religious practices. Instead, the Court embraces the Government's contention that its prerogative as landowner should always take precedence over a claim that a particular use of federal property infringes religious practices. Attempting to justify this rule, the Court argues that the First Amendment bars only outright prohibitions, indirect coercion, and penalties on the free exercise of religion. All other "incidental effects of government programs," it concludes, even those "which may make it more difficult to practice certain religions but which have no tendency to coerce individuals into acting contrary to their religious beliefs," simply do not give rise to constitutional concerns. Since our recognition nearly half a century ago that restraints on religious conduct implicate the concerns of the Free Exercise Clause, we have never suggested that the protections of the guarantee are limited to so narrow a range of governmental burdens. The land-use decision challenged here will restrain respondents from practicing their religion as surely and as completely as any of the governmental actions we have struck down in the past, and the Court's efforts simply to define away respondents' injury as non-constitutional is both unjustified and ultimately unpersuasive. . . .

Ultimately, the Court's coercion test turns on a distinction between governmental actions that compel affirmative conduct inconsistent with religious belief, and those governmental actions that prevent conduct consistent with religious belief. In my view, such a distinction is without constitutional significance. . . .

Both common sense and our prior cases teach us . . . that governmental action that makes the practice of a given faith more difficult necessarily penalizes that practice and thereby tends to prevent adherence to religious belief. The harm to the practitioners is the same regardless of the manner in which the Government restrains their religious expression, and the Court's fear that an "effects" test will permit religious adherents to challenge governmental actions they merely find "offensive" in no way justifies its refusal to recognize the constitutional injury citizens suffer when governmental action not only offends but actually restrains their religious practices.

In the final analysis, the Court's refusal to recognize the constitutional dimension of respondents' injuries stems from its concern that acceptance of respondents' claim could potentially strip the Government of its ability to manage and use vast tracts of federal property. In addition, the nature of respondents' site-specific religious practices raises the specter of future suits in which Native Americans seek to exclude all human activity from such areas. These concededly legitimate concerns lie at the very heart of this case, which represents yet another stress point in the longstanding conflict between two disparate cultures—the dominant western culture, which views land in terms of ownership and use, and that of Native Americans, in which concepts of private property are not only alien, but contrary to a belief system that holds land sacred. . . .

I believe it appropriate, therefore, to require some showing of "centrality" before the Government can be required either to come forward with a compelling justification for its proposed use of federal land or to forego that use altogether. . . . [W]hile Native Americans need not demonstrate,

as respondents did here, that the Government's land-use decision will assuredly eradicate their faith, I do not think it is enough to allege simply that the land in question is held sacred. Rather, adherents challenging a proposed use of federal land should be required to show that the decision poses a substantial and realistic threat of frustrating their religious practices. Once such a showing is made, the burden should shift to the Government to come forward with a compelling state interest sufficient to justify the infringement of those practices. . . .

The Court today suggests that such an approach would place courts in the untenable position of deciding which practices and beliefs are "central" to a given faith and which are not, and invites the prospect of judges advising some religious adherents that they "misunderstand their own religious beliefs." In fact, however, courts need not undertake any such inquiries: like all other religious adherents, Native Americans would be the arbiters of which practices are central to their faith, subject only to the normal requirement that their claims be genuine and sincere. The question for the courts, then, is not whether the Native American claimants understand their own religion, but rather, whether they have discharged their burden of demonstrating . . . that the land-use decision poses a substantial and realistic threat of undermining or frustrating their religious practices. Ironically, the Court's apparent solicitude for the integrity of religious belief and its desire to forestall the possibility that courts might second-guess the claims of religious adherents leads to far greater inequities than those the Court postulates: today's ruling sacrifices a religion at least as old as the Nation itself, along with the spiritual well-being of its approximately 5,000 adherents, so that the Forest Service can build a six-mile segment of road that two lower courts found had only the most marginal and speculative utility, both to the Government itself and to the private lumber interests that might conceivably use it.

ELEVEN

Privacy

The makers of our Constitution . . . conferred,
as against the government, the right to be
let alone—the most comprehensive of rights
and the right most valued by civilized men.

—JUSTICE LOUIS D. BRANDEIS (1928)

The word *privacy* appears not once in the Constitution, yet the right of privacy has become a vital concept in American constitutional law. Some aspects of privacy were recognized by the framers of the Constitution as fundamental—an integral element of civilization. Yet privacy is also an idea with few apparent limits. Paul Freund once called it a "greedy legal concept." What is privacy? How do questions of privacy involve the Constitution? How are judges supposed to decide what the right of privacy includes?

DIMENSIONS OF PRIVACY

Privacy denotes different things. For some it is a broad right "to be let alone." So put, privacy is almost synonomous with freedom. Accordingly, individuals should be allowed to make decisions about their lives without undue interference from others. Carried to an extreme, however, privacy would make organized society impossible. Every day, laws impinge on the liberty of individuals in numerous ways. Being in society means that most people are by no means "let alone" to go their own direction entirely in their own way.

More narrowly conceived, privacy may mean physical separation from others. People enter their homes, close the door, and pull the blinds for the express purpose of keeping themselves and their belongings hidden from public view. Such ordinary actions make it plain that people intend to shield the interior from the prying eyes of neighbors, as well as those of the state.

Protecting one's reputation from defamatory public comment is another dimension of privacy. As Chapter Ten explained, courts must reconcile the privacy interest, recognized by the law of libel, with a competing interest—a free press—recognized by the First Amendment. A third and related dimension is control over information about oneself. Credit records, bank statements, employers' evaluations, letters of recommendation, and tax returns all contain information that the persons about whom the information is compiled may not intend to become public. *Informational privacy* fosters a dual concern: accuracy and access. Are the data correct, and who is allowed to see and use them? These are questions made more urgent in an age of computers.

Privacy may also denote security from intrusion on the intimacies of life, a dimension that is the focus of this chapter. Certain decisions regarding companionship, marriage, and child rearing may not be entirely free of government restrictions, but they should preserve a core of freedom from outside restraint. This suggests a zone of autonomy, which the government may not penetrate without justification.

PRIVATE LAW AND PUBLIC LAW BEGINNINGS

Not all dimensions of privacy involve the Constitution. Some are regulated by statute alone. From the beginning, American law has offered redress from physical trespass and intrusion, and libel actions have allowed damages when one's reputation has been besmirched. (Both are examples of *private law* at work: legal rules governing relations among individuals. *Public law* involves regulations overseeing the operations of government as well as relations between individuals and their governments. Constitutional law, for example, is a field of public law.)

Threats to privacy or autonomy are the focus of several provisions of the Constitution. By banning religious tests for public office, Article VI protects the sanctity of personal religious beliefs, and the First Amendment guards rights of individual expression, religious and otherwise. The Third Amendment virtually proscribes the quartering of troops in homes. The Fourth Amendment prohibits "unreasonable searches and seizures" of one's "persons, houses, papers, and effects." The Fifth Amendment protects the integrity of the individual by curtailing the state's power to force people to be witnesses against themselves in criminal proceedings. The Fifth and the Fourteenth remove government's power to take away a person's "life, liberty, or property without due process of law." Spiritual and bodily integrity are important as well in the ban on "cruel and unusual punishments" in the Eighth Amendment. In its own way, each of these provisions addresses some dimension of personality or autonomy.

Yet it was not until after the 1890s that "privacy" began to take on life as a subject of its own. In 1890 Boston attorneys Samuel Warren and Louis Brandeis published a seminal article called "The Right to Privacy." Their immediate concern was nondefamatory, but nonetheless offensive, gossip in the newspapers. Although existing law provided redress for libel and slander, Warren and Brandeis believed that persons should be able to sue for damages when certain kinds of unwanted, unpleasant information appeared in the press.

The goal of Warren and Brandeis was law to guard "an inviolate personality," to enforce "the right of the individual to be left alone." The article was partly successful in stemming some of the abuses that troubled its authors. But the article's more lasting impact lay in stimulating thinking about the concept of privacy generally.

Privacy was at least a peripheral concern in several decisions by the United States Supreme Court before 1965. In *Meyer* v. *Nebraska* (1923), eight justices overturned a state statute that both prohibited the teaching of subjects in any language other than English and forbade the teaching of foreign languages to any pupil who had not passed the eighth grade. According to Justice McReynolds, liberty "denotes not merely freedom from bodily restraint but also the right of any individual to contract, to engage in any of the common occupations of life, to acquire useful knowledge, to marry, establish a home and bring up children . . . and generally to enjoy those privileges long recognized at common law as essential to the orderly pursuit of happiness by free men." Similarly, the Court in *Pierce* v. *Society of Sisters* (1925) invalidated an Oregon law forbidding parents from sending their children to private schools. The "liberty" of the Fourteenth Amendment was construed to include the right of the parents to direct the upbringing of their children.

In *Skinner* v. *Oklahoma* (1942), the Court struck down a compulsory sterilization scheme mandated by Oklahoma for certain classes of habitual criminals. Although the decision rested mainly on equal protection grounds (see the following chapter), Justice Douglas's majority opinion suggested a broader basis: "the Oklahoma legislation . . . involves one of the basic civil rights of man. Marriage and procreation are fundamental to the very existence and survival of the race." The foreign language and private school decisions had arguably been related to the First Amendment, although the Court construed them in traditional terms of "calling" and property. Yet in *Skinner* the right infringed was tied neither to the First Amendment nor to any other express constitutional provision, for that matter. Barely half a decade after discrediting judicial creation of substantive rights in the wake of President Roosevelt's court-packing plan, the justices created another.

Justice Douglas was persistent. When a divided Court in *Public Utilities Commission* v. *Pollack* (1952) refused to recognize a right not be disturbed by music in public conveyances, his dissent reflected Brandeis's influence: "Liberty in the constitutional sense must mean more than freedom from unlawful governmental restraint; it must include privacy as well, if it is to be a repository of freedom. The right to be left alone is indeed the beginning of all freedom."

The 1961 decision in ***Mapp*** v. ***Ohio*** (see Chapter Nine), in which the Court applied the exclusionary rule to the states as a way of putting "teeth" into the Fourth Amendment, was also proclaimed in the context of protecting privacy. Without the suppression of illegally acquired evidence, said Justice Clark, "the freedom from state invasions of privacy would be so ephemeral and so neatly severed from its conceptual nexus with the freedom from all brutish means of coercing evidence as not to merit this Court's high regard as a freedom 'implicit in the concept of ordered liberty.' " The same term witnessed an unsuccessful challenge to the Connecticut birth control law, later invalidated in ***Griswold*** v. ***Connecticut*** (1965). Dissenting in *Poe* v. *Ullman*, Justice Harlan drew an analogy between the Connecticut law and the protections of the Fourth Amendment.

> Certainly the safeguarding of the home does not follow merely from the sanctity of property rights. The home derives its preeminence as the seat of family life. And the integrity of that life is something so fundamental that it has been found to draw to its protection the principles of more than one explicitly granted Constitutional right. . . . Of this whole 'private realm of family life' it is difficult to imagine what is more private or more intimate than a husband and wife's marital relations.

By 1961, thinking about privacy had evolved well beyond Warren and Brandeis's article of 1890. The rudiments of a new constitutional right were at hand.

CONSTITUTIONAL PENUMBRAS

The Connecticut anticontraceptive statute came before the Court again in 1965 in *Griswold* **v. *Connecticut*.** "Any person who uses any drug, medicinal article or instrument for the purpose of preventing conception," declared the act, "shall be fined not less than fifty dollars or imprisoned not less than sixty days nor more than one year or be both fined and imprisoned." The law had been on the books since 1879, but this was apparently only the second time anyone had been charged. Arrested and convicted were the state director of Planned Parenthood and a medical professor at Yale. Both had given instruction and advice to married persons.

Though it violated no express provision in the Constitution, the law foundered on the right of privacy. For the majority, Justice Douglas announced that no fewer than eight amendments (he named the First, Third, Fourth, Fifth, Sixth, Eighth, Ninth, and Fourteenth) "have penumbras, formed by emanations from those guarantees that give them life and substance." In other words, the specific guarantees in the Constitution implied others, equally important though unenumerated. By impinging on "an intimate relation of husband and wife . . ." the statute violated "a right of privacy older than the Bill of Rights. . . ." (Originally an astronomical term, *penumbra* is the partial shadow surrounding a complete shadow in an eclipse.)

If privacy is a penumbral right, how far does it extend? Two years later in *Loving* v. *Virginia* the Court struck down Virginia's law banning interracial marriages. Relying mainly on the equal protection clause, Chief Justice Warren also drew authority from the constitutionally protected "freedom to marry"—"one of the vital personal rights essential to the orderly pursuit of happiness by free men." Then a 1968 decision, *Stanley* v. *Georgia,* invalidated a state law forbidding private possession of obscene material. Combining privacy as well as First Amendment interests, Justice Marshall reasoned, "Whatever may be the justifications for other statutes regulating obscenity, we do not think they reach into the privacy of one's home."

Griswold was directly involved in *Eisenstadt* v. *Baird,* a 1972 challenge to a Massachusetts statute that confined distribution of contraceptive devices to married persons. According to Justice Brennan,

> If under Griswold the distribution of contraceptives to married persons cannot be prohibited, a ban on distribution to unmarried persons would be equally impermissible. It is true that in Griswold the right of privacy in question inhered in the marital relationship. Yet the marital couple is not an independent entity with a mind and heart of its own, but an association of two individuals each with a separate intellectual and emotional makeup. If the right of privacy means anything, it is the right of the *individual,* married or single, to be free from unwarranted governmental intrusion into matters so fundamentally affecting a person as the decision whether to bear or beget a child.

ABORTION

The landmark decision ***Roe* v. *Wade*** came early in the following year. (The name Roe is fictitious; in cases of this sort "Roe" or "Doe" is used to protect the true identity of the parties.) The 7–2 decision stoked the flames of a national political blaze that shows no sign of diminishing.

Justice Blackmun's majority opinion acknowledged a right to abortion as an aspect of the constitutionally protected right of privacy. "[W]hether it be founded in the Fourteenth Amendment's concept of personal liberty and restrictions upon state action, as we feel it is, or . . . in the Ninth Amendment's reservation of rights to the people, [it] is broad enough to encompass a woman's decision whether or not to terminate her pregnancy." Yet the right to abortion was not absolute. According to Justice Blackmun,

> [A] state may properly assert important interests in safeguarding health, in maintaining medical standards, and in protecting potential life. At some point in pregnancy, these respective interests become sufficiently compelling to sustain regulation of the factors that govern the abortion decision. The privacy right involved, therefore, cannot be . . . absolute. . . . These interests are separate and distinct. Each grows in substantiality as the woman approaches term and, at a point during pregnancy, each becomes "compelling."

The decision called into question the abortion laws of virtually all the states. Furthermore, by finding a protection for abortion in the Constitution, the Court nationalized the abortion debate. No longer would a state's abortion laws be the product of clashing interests within its own legislature. From now on, much of the battle between those who believed *Roe* was right and those who believed it was wrong would shift to Congress and the federal courts. Moreover, *Roe* reinvigorated debate over the proper role of the Court as expositor of the Constitution.

Those who opposed the new abortion right began almost at once to press for regulations limiting the availability of abortion and discouraging its use. *Planned Parenthood of Central Missouri* v. *Danforth* (1976) knocked down the parts of a statute (1) requiring a married woman to obtain consent of her spouse in most instances before undergoing an abortion; (2) requiring parental consent for an abortion if an unmarried woman was under 18 years of age; (3) banning abortion by saline amniocentesis; and (4) criminalizing a physician's failure to preserve the life and health of a fetus, whatever the stage of pregnancy. Nonetheless, a Utah statute requiring physicians to "notify, if possible" the parents of minor women seeking abortions received six affirmative votes in 1981 (*H.L.* v. *Matheson*).

Aside from cases on when and how abortions might be performed, litigation has also centered on government's discretion to fund some abortions but not others. In *Maher* v. *Roe* (1977) a majority found no constitutional defect in Connecticut's policy of granting Medicaid support for therapeutic abortions (those deemed necessary for any one of several reasons) but not for nontherapeutic or elective ones. Against the state's argument that it could constitutionally discourage abortions in this fashion because of its rational interest in promoting normal childbirth, opponents charged that paying for childbirth but not for elective abortions burdened the exercise of a constitutional right, financially forcing poor women to carry a pregnancy full term.

The Court extended the *Maher* reasoning to Congress in 1980. The Hyde Amendment (so named because of its sponsor, Representative Henry Hyde of Illinois) went a step beyond Connecticut's restriction and barred federal Medicaid funds from being spent even on some medically necessary abortions. Only abortions necessary to save the life of the mother qualified. A majority of five concluded that a state was not required to pay for those Medicaid abortions for which federal reimbursement under the Hyde Amendment was unavailable. Neither was the Hyde Amendment itself unconstitutional. It placed no government obstacle, concluded the majority, in the way of an abortion. A poor woman was no worse off than if no Medicaid funds were available for any medical needs.

A decade after *Roe*, six justices declined to reconsider *Roe* and explicitly reaffirmed the 1973 abortion decision. On review in *Akron* v. *Akron Center for Reproductive Health, Inc.* (1983) was a municipal abortion ordinance governing location, notice and consent, informed consent, waiting period, and disposal of remains. None of the provisions survived constitutional challenge. Of particular interest was the first, that all abortions performed after the first trimester of pregnancy be performed in a hospital. Under the balancing of interests formula which Justice Blackmun employed in *Roe,* that requirement seemed constitutional. But a majority in *Akron* thought otherwise. Although noting that "a State's interest in health regulation becomes compelling at approximately the end of the first trimester," Justice Powell observed that medical techniques since *Roe* had progressed to the extent that even some second trimester abortions could safely be done in facilities other than regular hospitals. The Akron ordinance thus had the effect of "unreasonably infring[ing]" a woman's right to an abortion.

In her first opinion on abortion, Justice O'Connor dissented. Joined by Justices White and Rehnquist, she found

> it . . . apparent . . . that neither sound constitutional theory nor our need to decide cases based on the application of neutral principles can accommodate an analytical framework that varies according to the "stages" of pregnancy, where those stages, and their concomitant standards of review, differ according to the level of medical technology available when a particular challenge to state regulation occurs.

Recalling *Roe*'s approval of bans on abortion in the third trimester because of the state's interest in protecting potential life at the point of viability, she saw the majority on a collision course.

> Just as improvements in medical technology inevitably will move *forward* the point at which the State may regulate for reasons of maternal health, different technological improvements will move *backward* the point of viability at which the State may proscribe abortions except when necessary to preserve the life and health of the mother.

Thornburgh* v. *American College of Obstetricians and Gynecologists (1986) symbolizes much of the contemporary abortion debate. At stake was a comprehensive Pennsylvania statute regarding consent, information, record keeping, determination of viability, care of the fetus, and a second-physician requirement in postviability abortions. A majority of five struck down all challenged sections in the law. Justice Blackmun was openly impatient with regulations "seemingly designed to prevent a woman, with the advice of her physician, from exercising her freedom of choice." States "are not free, under the guise of protecting maternal health or potential life, to intimidate women into continuing pregnancies."

The 7–2 majority for *Roe* in 1973 had shrunk to 5–4 by 1986. Retiring immediately after *Thornburgh,* Chief Justice Burger had already let it be known that he thought *Roe* was wrongly decided. The division on the bench in 1987 therefore made Justice Powell's retirement and the designation of a successor all the more critical. More than anything else, the widely held conviction that Judge Robert Bork would undermine the 1973 abortion decision led to his rejection by the Senate when President Reagan nominated him to take Powell's seat. (Bork's confirmation battle is reviewed in the Introduction.) "Prochoice" and "prolife" activists alike awaited the views of Justice Kennedy.

A DEVELOPING CONCEPT

As the previous sections demonstrate, a right once acknowledged invites application to new situations. For example, for over 60 years the Court has recognized the broad powers states and localities possess in establishing land-use regulations for residential areas. In 1974, against a claim based on privacy and other grounds, seven justices upheld a zoning ordinance in the Village of Belle Terre, New York, near the Stony Brook campus of the State University. Prohibited was occupancy of a dwelling by more than two unrelated persons as a "family." Permitted was occupancy by any number of persons related by blood, marriage, or adoption. The Court was willing to accept the community's judgment that in "families" larger than two, relationship rather than numbers chiefly determined the quality of life in a neighborhood.

Deference to local authorities was not dispositive three years later in *Moore* v. *East Cleveland*. Confronting the Court was an ordinance limiting occupancy of a dwelling unit to members of a family, where a "family" included only some categories of related persons. Specifically, Inez Moore lived with her two grandsons who were cousins, a category not within East Cleveland's definition of "family." In the city's eyes, one of the grandsons was an illegal occupant. In the eyes of five justices, the city's zoning rule impermissibly trod on a constitutional right. "Our decisions establish that the Constitution protects the sanctity of the family . . . ," wrote Justice Powell in a plurality opinion, and "prevents East Cleveland from standardizing its children—and its adults—by forcing all to live in certain narrowly defined family patterns."

Sexual orientation and practice also involve a dimension of privacy or autonomy. The Supreme Court squarely confronted this issue in 1986 in **Bowers v. Hardwick**. Five justices upheld the constitutionality of Georgia's sodomy statute, which made criminal certain combinations of private parts. The law applied to heterosexual as well as homosexual behavior, but Justice White's opinion of the Court, perhaps deliberately, regarded the act as if it made only the latter criminal.

The 5–4 split revealed that no consensus existed on the Court concerning what privacy encompassed. Since *Griswold,* privacy's "scorecard" in the Supreme Court had been good. Many observers were surprised that five balked at an extension. Close reading of Justice White's majority opinion and the principal dissent by Justice Blackmun provides insight.

To discover what rights, though not expressly mentioned, are constitutionally protected, White looked to two sources: those "implicit in the concept of ordered liberty" and those "deeply rooted in the nation's history and tradition." Framing the investigation in this way, White concluded "that neither of these formulations would extend a fundamental right to homosexuals to engage in acts of consensual sodomy."

For Blackmun, the majority was asking the wrong question. The case was not "about 'a fundamental right to engage in homosexual sodomy.' . . . Rather, this case is about 'the most comprehensive of rights . . . the right to be let alone.' [W]hat the Court really has refused to recognize is the fundamental interest all individuals have in controlling the nature of their intimate associations with others." White scanned a category of rights. Blackmun focused on a constitutionally protected realm of intimate association.

Undoubtedly questions of sexual practice and orientation, like other privacy issues, will continue to arise. Heightened sensitivity throughout the United States to issues of individual privacy, a tradition of legal protection for privacy, and concepts of privacy with few clearly discernible boundaries virtually guarantee a continued involvement by judges in marking the dimensions of the constitutional right "to be let alone."

KEY TERMS

privacy	public law	Hyde Amendment
informational privacy	penumbra	
private law	Ninth Amendment	

QUERIES

1. Do cases involving the right to privacy present problems of interpretation not encountered when the justices rule in disputes over free speech and free press?

2. Civil libertarian Justice Black dissented in *Griswold* v. *Connecticut.* Why?

3. Does *Thornburgh* mark a change in the Supreme Court's view of the right to abortion as first announced in *Roe* v. *Wade?*

4. Dissenting in *Bowers* v. *Hardwick,* Justice Blackmun contended that the majority "distorted the question this case presents." What did Blackmun mean?

SELECTED READINGS

BAKER, TYLER. "*Roe* and *Paris:* Does Privacy Have a Principle?" 26 *Stanford Law Review* 1161 (1974).

BEANEY, WILLIAM M. "The Constitutional Right to Privacy in the Supreme Court." 1962 *Supreme Court Review* 212.

————. "The Griswold Case and the Expanded Right to Privacy," 1966 *Wisconsin Law Review* 979 (1966).

DIXON, ROBERT G., Jr. "The Griswold Penumbra: Constitutional Charter for an Expanded Law of Privacy?" 64 *Michigan Law Review* 197 (1965).

ERNST, MORRIS L., and ALAN U. SCHWARTZ. *Privacy: The Right to Be Let Alone.* New York: Macmillan, 1961.

FAUX, MARIAN. *Roe v. Wade.* New York: Macmillan, 1988.

FRIED, CHARLES. "Privacy." 77 *Yale Law Journal* 475 (1968).

O'BRIEN, DAVID M. *Privacy, Law, and Public Policy.* New York: Praeger, 1979.

RHODEN, NANCY K. "Trimesters and Technology: Revamping *Roe* v. *Wade.*" 95 *Yale Law Journal* 639 (1986).

RICHARDS, DAVID A. "Constitutional Legitimacy and Constitutional Privacy." 61 *New York University Law Review* 800 (1986).

————. *Toleration and the Constitution.* New York: Oxford University Press, 1986.

WARREN, SAMUEL, and LOUIS D. BRANDEIS. "The Right to Privacy." 4 *Harvard Law Review* 220 (1890).

Griswold v. Connecticut
381 U.S. 479, 85 S.Ct. 1678, 14 L.Ed. 2d 510 (1965)

A Connecticut statute made the use of contraceptives a criminal offense. Griswold, executive director of the Planned Parenthood League of Connecticut, was convicted on a charge of having violated the statute as an accessory by giving information, instruction, and advice to married persons as a means of preventing conception. A professor at the Yale Medical School, serving as medical director for the league, was a codefendant. The Appellate Division of the Circuit Court and the Supreme Court of Errors of Connecticut affirmed the conviction. Majority: Douglas, Brennan, Clark, Goldberg, Harlan, Warren, White. Dissenting: Black, Stewart.

MR. JUSTICE DOUGLAS delivered the opinion of the Court. . . .

Coming to the merits, we are met with a wide range of questions that implicate the Due Process Clause of the Fourteenth Amendment. Overtones of some arguments suggest that *Lochner* v. *New York* . . . should be our guide. But we decline that invitation. . . . We do not sit as a super-legislature to determine the wisdom, need, and propriety of laws that touch economic problems, business affairs, or social conditions. This law, however, operates directly on an intimate relation of husband and wife and their physician's role in one aspect of that relation. . . .

. . . [S]pecific guarantees in the Bill of Rights have penumbras, formed by emanations from those guarantees that help give them life and substance. . . . Various guarantees create zones of privacy. The right of association contained in the penumbra of the First Amendment is one. . . . The Third Amendment in its prohibition against the quartering of soldiers "in any house" in time of peace without the consent of the owner is another facet of that privacy. The Fourth Amendment explicitly affirms the "right of the people to be secure in their persons, houses, papers, and effects against unreasonable searches and seizures." The Fifth Amendment in its Self-Incrimination Clause enables the citizen to create a zone of privacy which government may not force him to surrender to his detriment. The Ninth Amendment provides: "The enumeration in the Constitution, of certain rights, shall not be construed to deny or disparage others retained by the people." . . .

The present case, then, concerns a relationship lying within the zone of privacy created by several fundamental constitutional guarantees. And it concerns a law which, in forbidding the *use* of contraceptives rather than regulating their manufacture or sale, seeks to achieve its goals by means having a maximum destructive impact upon that relationship. Such a law cannot stand in light of the familiar principle, so often applied by this Court, that a "governmental purpose to control or prevent activities constitutionally subject to state regulation may not be achieved by means which sweep unnecessarily broadly and thereby invade the area of protected freedom." Would we allow the police to search the sacred precincts of marital bedrooms for telltale signs of the use of contraceptives? The very idea is repulsive to the notions of privacy surrounding the marriage relationship.

We deal with a right of privacy older than the Bill of Rights—older than our political parties, older than our school system. Marriage is a coming together for better or for worse, hopefully enduring, and intimate to the degree of being sacred. It is an association that promotes a way of life, not causes; a harmony in living, not political faiths; a bilateral loyalty, not commercial or social projects. Yet it is an association for as noble a purpose as any involved in our prior decisions.

Reversed.

MR. JUSTICE GOLDBERG, whom the CHIEF JUSTICE and MR. JUSTICE BRENNAN join, concurring. . . .

The Ninth Amendment to the Constitution may be regarded by some as a recent discovery and may be forgotten by others, but since 1791 it has been a basic part of the Constitution which we are sworn to uphold. To hold that a right so basic and fundamental and so deep-rooted in our society as the right of privacy in marriage may be infringed because that right is not guaranteed in so many words by the first eight amendments to the Constitution is to ignore the Ninth Amendment and to give it no effect whatsoever. . . .

Nor am I turning somersaults with history in arguing that the Ninth Amendment is relevant in a case dealing with a *State's* infringement of a fundamental right. While the Ninth Amendment—and indeed the entire Bill of Rights—originally concerned restrictions upon *federal* power, the subsequently enacted Fourteenth Amendment prohibits the States as well from abridging fundamental personal liberties. And, the Ninth Amendment, in indicating that not all such liberties are specifically mentioned in the first eight amendments, is surely relevant in showing the existence of other fundamental personal rights, now protected from state, as well as federal, infringement. In sum, the Ninth Amendment simply lends strong support to the view that the "liberty" protected by the Fifth and Fourteenth Amendments from infringement by the Federal Government or the States is not restricted to rights specifically mentioned in the first eight amendments. . . .

MR. JUSTICE HARLAN, concurring in the judgment.

I fully agree with the judgment of reversal, but find myself unable to join the Court's opinion. The reason is that it seems to me to evince an approach to this case very much like that taken by my Brothers Black and Stewart in dissent, namely: the Due Process Clause of the Fourteenth Amendment does not touch this Connecticut statute unless the enactment is found to violate some right assured by the letter or penumbra of the Bill of Rights.

In other words, what I find implicit in the Court's opinion is that the "incorporation" doctrine may be used to *restrict* the reach of Fourteenth Amendment Due Process. For me this is just as unacceptable constitutional doctrine as is the use of the "incorporation" approach to *impose* upon the States all the requirements of the Bill of Rights as found in the provision of the first eight amendments and in the decisions of this Court interpreting them. . . .

In my view, the proper constitutional inquiry in this case is whether this Connecticut statute infringes the Due Process Clause of the Fourteenth Amendment because the enactment violates basic values "implicit in the concept of ordered liberty." . . .

MR. JUSTICE BLACK, with whom MR. JUSTICE STEWART joins, dissenting. . . .

The Court talks about a constitutional "right of privacy" as though there is some constitutional provision or provisions forbidding any law ever to be passed which might abridge the "privacy" of individuals. But there is not. . . .

One of the most effective ways of diluting or expanding a constitutionally guaranteed right is to substitute for the crucial word or words of a constitutional guarantee another word, more or less flexible and more or less restricted in its meaning. This fact is well illustrated by the use of the term "right of privacy" as a comprehensive substitute for the Fourth Amendment's guarantee against "unreasonable searches and seizures." "Privacy" is a broad, abstract and ambiguous concept which can easily be shrunken in meaning but which can also, on the other hand, easily be interpreted as a constitutional ban against many things other than searches and seizures. . . . For these reasons I get nowhere in this case by talk about a constitutional "right of privacy" as an emanation from one or more constitutional provisions.[1] I like my privacy as well as the next one, but I am nevertheless compelled to admit that government has a right

---

[1] The phrase "right to privacy" appears first to have gained currency from an article written by Messrs. Warren and (later Mr. Justice) Brandeis in 1890 which urged that States should give some form of tort relief to persons whose private affairs were exploited by others. Largely as a result of this article, some States have passed statutes creating such a cause of action, and in other States courts have done the same thing by exercising their powers as courts of common law. Thus the Supreme Court of Georgia, in granting a cause of action for damages to a man whose picture had been used in a newspaper advertisement without his consent, said that "A right to privacy in matters purely private is . . . derived from natural law" and that "The conclusion reached by us seems to be . . . thoroughly in accord with natural justice, with the principles of the law of every civilized nation, and especially with the elastic principles of the common law. . . ." Observing that "the right of privacy . . . presses for recognition here," today this Court, which I did not understand to have power to sit as a court of common law, now appears to be exalting a phrase which Warren and Brandeis used in discussing grounds for tort relief, to the level of a constitutional rule which prevents state legislatures from passing any law deemed by this Court to interfere with "privacy."

to invade it unless prohibited by some specific constitutional provision. For these reasons I cannot agree with the Court's judgment and the reasons it gives for holding this Connecticut law unconstitutional. . . .

I think that if properly construed neither the Due Process Clause nor the Ninth Amendment, nor both together, could under any circumstances be a proper basis for invalidating the Connecticut law. I discuss the due process and Ninth Amendment arguments together because on analysis they turn out to be the same thing—merely using different words to claim for this Court and the federal judiciary power to invalidate any legislative act which the judges find irrational, unreasonable or offensive.

The due process argument which my Brothers Harlan and White adopt here is based, as their opinions indicate, on the premise that this Court is vested with power to invalidate all state laws that it considers to be arbitrary, capricious, unreasonable, or oppressive, or because of this Court's belief that a particular state law under scrutiny has no "rational or justifying purpose," or is offensive to a "sense of fairness and justice." If these formulas based on "natural justice," or others which mean the same thing, are to prevail, they require judges to determine what is or is not constitutional on the basis of their own appraisal of what laws are unwise or unnecessary. The power to make such decisions is of course that of a legislative body. Surely it has to be admitted that no provision of the Constitution specifically gives such blanket power to courts to exercise such a supervisory veto over the wisdom and value of legislative policies and to hold unconstitutional those laws which they believe unwise or dangerous. I readily admit that no legislative body, state or national, should pass laws that can justly be given any of the invidious labels invoked as constitutional excuses to strike down state laws. But perhaps it is not too much to say that no legislative body ever does pass laws without believing that they will accomplish a sane, rational, wise and justifiable purpose. While I completely subscribe to the holding of *Marbury* v. *Madison* . . . and subsequent cases, that our Court has constitutional power to strike down statutes, state or federal, that violate commands of the Federal Constitution, I do not believe that we are granted power by the Due Process Clause or any other

constitutional provision or provisions to measure constitutionality by our belief that legislation is arbitrary, capricious or unreasonable, or accomplishes no justifiable purpose, or is offensive to our own notions of "civilized standards of conduct." Such an appraisal of the wisdom of legislation is an attribute of the power to make laws, not of the power to interpret them. The use by federal courts of such a formula or doctrine or whatnot to veto federal or state laws simply takes away from Congress and States the power to make laws based on their own judgment of fairness and wisdom and transfers that power to this Court for ultimate determination—a power which was specifically denied to federal courts by the convention that framed the Constitution.[2] . . .

---

[2] This Court held in *Marbury* v. *Madison* . . . that this court has power to invalidate laws on the ground that they exceed the constitutional power of Congress or violate some specific prohibition of the Constitution. But the Constitutional Convention did on at least two occasions reject proposals which would have given the federal judiciary a part in recommending laws or in vetoing as bad or unwise the legislation passed by the Congress. Edmund Randolph of Virginia proposed that the President "and a convenient number of the National Judiciary, ought to compose a council of revision with the authority to examine every act of the National Legislature before it shall operate, & every act of a particular Legislature before a Negative thereon shall be final; and that the dissent of the said Council shall amount to a rejection, unless the Act of the National Legislature be again passed, or that of a particular Legislature be again negatived by [3] of the members of each branch."

In support of a plan of this kind James Wilson of Pennsylvania argued:

"It had been said that the Judges, as expositors of the Laws would have an opportunity of defending their constitutional rights. There was weight in this observation; but this power of the Judges did not go far enough. Laws may be unjust, may be unwise, may be dangerous, may be destructive; and yet not be so unconstitutional as to justify the Judges in refusing to give them effect. Let them have a share in the Revisionary power, and they will have an opportunity of taking notice of these characters of a law, and of counteracting, by the weight of their opinions the improper views of the Legislature."

Nathaniel Gorham of Massachusetts "did not see the advantage of employing the Judges in this way. As Judges they are not to be presumed to possess any peculiar knowledge of the mere policy of public measures."

Elbridge Gerry of Massachusetts likewise opposed the proposal for a council of revision:

"He relied for his part on the Representatives of the people as the guardians of their Rights & interests. It [the proposal] was making the Expositors of the Laws, the Legislators which ought never to be done." And at another point:

"Mr. Gerry doubts whether the Judiciary ought to form a

My Brother Goldberg has adopted the recent discovery that the Ninth Amendment as well as the Due Process Clause can be used by this Court as authority to strike down all state legislation which this Court thinks violates "fundamental principles of liberty and justice," or is contrary to the "traditions and collective conscience of our people." He also states, without proof satisfactory to me,

that in making decisions on this basis judges will not consider "their personal and private notions." One may ask how they can avoid considering them. Our Court certainly has no machinery with which to take a Gallup Poll. And the scientific miracles of this age have not yet produced a gadget which the Court can use to determine what traditions are rooted in the "collective conscience of our people." Moreover, one would certainly have to look far beyond the language of the Ninth Amendment to find that the Framers vested in this Court any such awesome veto powers over lawmaking, either by the States or by the Congress. . . . If any broad, unlimited power to hold laws unconstitutional because they offend what this Court conceives to be "the collective conscience of our people" is vested in this Court by the Ninth Amendment, or any other provision of the Constitution, it was not given by the Framers, but rather has been bestowed on the Court by the Court. . . .

---

part of it [the proposed council of revision], as they will have a sufficient check agst. encroachments on their own department by their exposition of the laws, which involved a power of deciding on their Constitutionality. . . . It was quite foreign from the nature of ye. office to make them judges of the policy of public measures."

Madison supported the proposal on the ground that "a Check [on the legislature] is necessary." John Dickinson of Delaware opposed it on the ground that "the Judges must interpret the Laws; they ought not to be legislators." The proposal for a council of revision was defeated.

Roe v. Wade
410 U.S. 113, 93 S.Ct. 705, 35 L.Ed. 2d 147 (1973)

An unmarried, pregnant woman who wished to terminate her pregnancy by abortion instituted an action in the United States District Court for the Northern District of Texas, seeking a declaratory judgment that the Texas criminal abortion statutes, which prohibited abortions except with respect to those procured or attempted by medical advice for the purpose of saving the life of the mother, were unconstitutional. She also sought an injunction against their continued enforcement. A physician, who alleged that he had been previously arrested for violations of the Texas statutes and that two prosecutions were presently pending against him in the state courts, sought and was granted permission to intervene. A separate action, similar to that filed by the unmarried, pregnant woman, was filed by a married, childless couple, who alleged that should the wife become pregnant at some future date, they would wish to terminate the pregnancy by abortion. The two actions were consolidated and heard by a three-judge district court, which held that the Texas criminal abortion statutes were void on their face because they were unconstitutionally vague and overbroad. Majority: Blackmun, Brennan, Burger, Douglas, Marshall, Powell, Stewart. Dissenting: Rehnquist, White.

MR. JUSTICE BLACKMUN delivered the opinion of the Court.

. . . We forthwith acknowledge our awareness of the sensitive and emotional nature of the abortion controversy, of the vigorous opposing views, even among physicians, and of the deep and seemingly absolute convictions that the subject inspires. One's philosophy, one's experiences, one's exposure to the raw edges of human existence, one's religious training, one's attitudes toward life and family and their values, and the moral standards one establishes and seeks to observe, are all likely to influence and to color one's thinking and conclusions about abortion.

In addition, population growth, pollution, poverty, and racial overtones tend to complicate and not to simplify the problem.

Our task, of course, is to resolve the issue by constitutional measurement free of emotion and of predilections. We seek earnestly to do this, and, because we do, we have inquired into, and in this opinion place some emphasis upon, medical and medical-legal history and what that history reveals about man's attitudes toward the abortive procedure over the centuries. We bear in mind, too, Mr. Justice Holmes's admonition in his now vindicated dissent in *Lochner* v. *New York*. . . .

> It [the Constitution] is made for people of fundamentally differing views, and the accident of our finding certain opinions natural and familiar or novel and even shocking ought not to conclude our judgment upon the question whether statutes embodying them conflict with the Constitution of the United States.

The Texas statutes that concern us here . . . make it a crime to "procure an abortion," as therein defined, or to attempt one, except with respect to "an abortion procured or attempted by medical advice for the purpose of saving the life of the mother." Similar statutes are in existence in a majority of the States. . . .

The principal thrust of the appellant's attack on the Texas statutes is that they improperly invade a right, said to be possessed by the pregnant woman, to choose to terminate her pregnancy. Appellant would discover this right in the concept of personal "liberty" embodied in the Fourteenth Amendment's Due Process Clause; or in personal, marital, familial, and sexual privacy said to be protected by the Bill of Rights or its penumbras. . . . Before addressing

this claim, we feel it desirable briefly to survey, in several aspects, the history of abortion, for such insight as that history may afford us, and then to examine the state purposes and interests behind the criminal abortion laws.

It perhaps is not generally appreciated that the restrictive criminal abortion laws in effect in a majority of States today are of relatively recent vintage. Those laws, generally proscribing abortion or its attempt at any time during pregnancy except when necessary to preserve the pregnant woman's life, are not of ancient or even of common law origin. Instead, they derive from statutory changes effected, for the most part, in the latter half of the 19th century. . . .

It is thus apparent that at common law, at the time of the adoption of our Constitution, and throughout the major portion of the 19th century, abortion was viewed with less disfavor than under most American statutes currently in effect. . . .

Three reasons have been advanced to explain historically the enactment of criminal abortion laws in the 19th century and to justify their continued existence.

It has been argued occasionally that these laws were the product of a Victorian social concern to discourage illicit sexual conduct. Texas, however, does not advance this justification in the present case, and it appears that no court or commentator has taken the argument seriously. . . .

A second reason is concerned with abortion as a medical procedure. When most criminal abortion laws were first enacted, the procedure was a hazardous one for the woman. This was particularly true prior to the development of antisepsis. . . . Abortion mortality was high. . . .

Modern medical techniques have altered this situation. Appellants and various amici refer to medical data indicating that abortion in early pregnancy, that is, prior to the end of first trimester, although not without its risk, is now relatively safe. Mortality rates for women undergoing early abortions, where the procedure is legal, appear to be as low or lower than the rates for normal childbirth. . . . Of course, important state interests in the area of health and medical standards do remain. The State has a legitimate interest in seeing to it that abortion, like any other medical procedure, is performed under circumstances that insure maximum safety for the patient. . . . Moreover, the risk to the woman increases as her pregnancy continues. Thus the State retains a definite interest in protecting the woman's own health and safety when an abortion is proposed at a late stage of pregnancy.

The third reason is the State's interest—some phrase it in terms of duty—in protecting prenatal life. Some of the argument for this justification rests on the theory that a new human life is present from the moment of conception. The State's interest and general obligation to protect life then extends, it is argued, to prenatal life. Only when the life of the pregnant mother herself is at stake, balanced against the life she carries within her, should the interests of the embryo or fetus not prevail. Logically, of course, a legitimate state interest in this area need not stand or fall on acceptance of the belief that life begins at conception or at some other point prior to live birth. In assessing the State's interest, recognition may be given to the less rigid claim that as long as at least *potential* life is involved, the State may assert interests beyond the protection of the pregnant woman alone. . . .

It is with these interests, and the weight to be attached to them, that this case is concerned.

The Constitution does not explicitly mention any right of privacy. In a line of decisions, however, going back perhaps as far as *Union Pacific R. Co. v. Botsford* (1891), the Court has recognized that a right of personal privacy, or a guarantee of certain areas or zones of privacy, does exist under the Constitution. In varying contexts the Court or individual Justices have indeed found at least the roots of that right in the First Amendment . . . in the Fourth and Fifth Amendments . . . in the penumbras of the Bill of Rights . . . in the Ninth Amendment . . . or in the concept of liberty guaranteed by the first section of the Fourteenth Amendment. . . . These decisions make it clear that only personal rights that can be deemed "fundamental" or "implicit in the concept of ordered liberty" . . . are included in this guarantee of personal privacy. They also make it clear that the right has some extension to activities relating to marriage . . . procreation, contraception, family relationships, and child rearing and education.

This right of privacy, whether it be founded in the Fourteenth Amendment's concept of personal liberty and restrictions upon state action, as we feel it is, or, as the District Court determined, in the Ninth Amendment's reservation of rights to the people, is broad enough to encompass a woman's decision whether or not to terminate her pregnancy. The detriment that the State would impose upon the pregnant woman by denying this choice altogether is apparent. Specific and direct harm medically diagnosable even in early pregnancy may be involved. Maternity, or additional offspring, may force upon the woman a distressful life and future. Psychological harm may be imminent. Mental and physical health may be taxed by child care. There is also the distress, for all concerned, associated with the unwanted child, and there is the problem of bringing a child into a family already unable, psychologically and otherwise, to care for it. In other cases, as in this one, the additional difficulties and continuing stigma of unwed motherhood may be involved. All these are factors the woman and her responsible physician necessarily will consider in consultation. . . .

We therefore conclude that the right of personal privacy includes the abortion decision, but that this right is not unqualified and must be considered against important state interests in regulation. . . .

The appellee and certain amici argue that the fetus is a "person" within the language and meaning of the Fourteenth Amendment. . . .

The Constitution does not define "person" in so many words. Section 1 of the Fourteenth Amendment contains three references to "person." The first, in defining "citizens," speaks of "persons born or naturalized in the United States." The word also appears both in the Due Process Clause and in the Equal Protection Clause. "Person" is used in other places in the Constitution. . . . But in nearly all these instances, the use of the word is such that it has application only postnatally. None indicates, with any assurance, that it has any possible prenatal application. . . .

Texas urges that, apart from the Fourteenth Amendment, life begins at conception and is present throughout pregnancy, and that, therefore, the State has a compelling interest in protecting that life from and after conception. We need not resolve the difficult question of when life begins. When those trained in the respective disciplines of medicine, philosophy, and theology are unable to arrive at any consensus, the judiciary, at this point in the development of man's knowledge, is not in a position to speculate as to the answer. . . .

We do not agree that, by adopting one theory

of life, Texas may override the rights of the pregnant woman that are at stake. We repeat, however, that the State does have an important and legitimate interest in preserving and protecting the health of the pregnant woman, whether she be a resident of the State or a nonresident who seeks medical consultation and treatment there, and that it has still *another* important and legitimate interest in protecting the potentiality of human life. These interests are separate and distinct. Each grows in substantiality as the woman approaches term and, at a point during pregnancy, each becomes "compelling."

With respect to the State's important and legitimate interest in the health of the mother, the "compelling" point, in the light of present medical knowledge, is at approximately the end of the first trimester. This is so because of the now established medical fact . . . that until the end of the first trimester mortality in abortion is less than mortality in normal childbirth. It follows that, from and after this point, a State may regulate the abortion procedure to the extent that the regulation reasonably relates to the preservation and protection of maternal health. Examples of permissible state regulation in this area are requirements as to the qualifications of the person who is to perform the abortion; as to the licensure of that person; as to the facility in which the procedure is to be performed, that is, whether it must be a hospital or may be a clinic or some other place of less-than-hospital status; as to the licensing of the facility; and the like.

This means, on the other hand, that, for the period of pregnancy prior to this "compelling" point, the attending physician, in consultation with his patient, is free to determine, without regulation by the State, that in his medical judgment the patient's pregnancy should be terminated. If that decision is reached, the judgment may be effectuated by an abortion free of interference by the State. . . .

With respect to the State's important and legitimate interest in potential life, the "compelling" point is at viability. This is so because the fetus then presumably has the capability of meaningful life outside the mother's womb. State regulation protective of fetal life after viability thus has both logical and biological justifications. If the State is interested in protecting fetal life after viability, it may go so far as to proscribe abortion during that period except when it is necessary to preserve the life or health of the mother.

Measured against these standards . . . Texas, in restricting legal abortion to those "procured or attempted by medical advice for the purpose of saving the life of the mother," sweeps too broadly. The statute makes no distinction between abortions performed early in pregnancy and those performed later, and it limits to a single reason, "saving" the mother's life, the legal justification for the procedure. The statute, therefore, cannot survive the constitutional attack made upon it here. . . .

Mr. Justice Rehnquist, dissenting.

. . . I would reach a conclusion opposite to that reached by the Court. I have difficulty in concluding, as the Court does, that the right of "privacy" is involved in this case. Texas by the statute here challenged bars the performance of a medical abortion by a licensed physician on a plaintiff such as Roe. A transaction resulting in an operation such as this is not "private" in the ordinary usage of that word. Nor is the "privacy" which the Court finds here even a distant relative of the freedom from searches and seizures protected by the Fourth Amendment to the Constitution which the Court has referred to as embodying a right to privacy. . . .

If the Court means by the term "privacy" no more than that the claim of a person to be free from unwanted state regulation of consensual transactions may be a form of "liberty" protected by the Fourteenth Amendment, there is no doubt that similar claims have been upheld in our earlier decisions on the basis of that liberty. I agree with the statement of Mr. Justice Stewart in his concurring opinion that the "liberty," against deprivation of which without due process the Fourteenth Amendment protects, embraces more than the rights found in the Bill of Rights. But that liberty is not guaranteed absolutely against deprivation, but only against deprivation without due process of law. The test traditionally applied in the area of social and economic legislation is whether or not a law such as that challenged has a rational relation to a valid state objective. . . . But the Court's sweeping invalidation of any restrictions on abortion during the first trimester is impossible to justify under that standard, and the conscious weighing of competing factors which the Court's opinion apparently substitutes for the established test is far more appropriate to a legislative judgment than to a judicial one.

The Court eschews the history of the Fourteenth

Amendment in its reliance on the "compelling state interest" test. . . . But the Court adds a new wrinkle to this test by transposing it from the legal considerations associated with the Equal Protection Clause of the Fourteenth Amendment to this case arising under the Due Process Clause of the Fourteenth Amendment. Unless I misapprehend the consequences of this transplanting of the "compelling state interest test," the Court's opinion will accomplish the seemingly impossible feat of leaving this area of the law more confused than it found it.

While the Court's opinion quotes from the dissent of Mr. Justice Holmes in *Lochner* v. *New York* . . . the result it reaches is more closely attuned to the majority opinion of Mr. Justice Peckham in that case. As in *Lochner* and similar cases applying substantive due process standards to economic and social welfare legislation, the adoption of the compelling state interest standard will inevitably require this Court to examine the legislative policies and pass on the wisdom of these policies in the very process of deciding whether a particular state interest put forward may or may not be "compelling." The decision here to break the term of pregnancy into three distinct terms and to outline the permissible restrictions the State may impose in each one, for example, partakes more of judicial legislation than it does of a determination of the intent of the drafters of the Fourteenth Amendment.

The fact that a majority of the States, reflecting after all the majority sentiment in those States, have had restrictions on abortions for at least a century seems to me as strong an indication there is that the asserted right to an abortion is not "so rooted in the traditions and conscience of our people as to be ranked as fundamental." . . . Even today, when society's views on abortion are changing, the very existence of the debate is evidence that the "right" to an abortion is not so universally accepted as the appellants would have us believe.

To reach its result the Court necessarily has had to find within the scope of the Fourteenth Amendment a right that was apparently completely unknown to the drafters of the Amendment. As early as 1821, the first state law dealing directly with abortion was enacted by the Connecticut legislature. . . . By the time of the adoption of the Fourteenth Amendment in 1868 there were at least 36 laws enacted by state or territorial legislatures limiting abortion. While many States have amended or updated their laws, 21 of the laws on the books in 1868 remain in effect today. Indeed, the Texas statute struck down today was, as the majority notes, first enacted in 1857 and "has remained substantially unchanged to the present time." . . .

There apparently was no question concerning the validity of this provision or of any of the other state statutes when the Fourteenth Amendment was adopted. The only conclusion possible from this history is that the drafters did not intend to have the Fourteenth Amendment withdraw from the States the power to legislate with respect to this matter. . . .

For all of the foregoing reasons, I respectfully dissent.

Thornburgh v. *American College of Obstetricians and Gynecologists*
476 U.S. 747, 106 S.Ct. 2169, 90 L.Ed. 2d 779 (1986)

Appellees brought an action in the United States District Court for the Eastern District of Pennsylvania, claiming that the Pennsylvania Abortion Control Act of 1982 violated the Constitution. The district court denied a motion for a preliminary injunction against enforcement of the statute except for the provision, which it held unconstitutional, mandating a 24-hour waiting period between a woman's receipt of certain information about abortions and the performance of her abortion. The Court of Appeals for the Third Circuit then enjoined enforcement of the entire statute and held unconstitutional provisions relating to consent, information, record keeping, determination of viability of the fetus, postviability abortions, and the presence of a second physician. The provisions of the Pennsylvania law challenged in this case are explained in Justice Blackmun's opinion for the majority. That part of his opinion discussing the Court's jurisdiction in the case is omitted. Majority: Blackmun, Brennan, Marshall, Powell, Stevens. Dissenting: White, Burger, O'Connor, Rehnquist.

JUSTICE BLACKMUN delivered the opinion of the Court. . . .

Less than three years ago, this Court, in *Akron, Ashcroft,* and *Simopoulos,* reviewed challenges to state and municipal legislation regulating the performance of abortions. In *Akron,* the Court specifically reaffirmed *Roe* v. *Wade.* . . . Again today, we reaffirm the general principles laid down in *Roe* and in *Akron.*

In the years since this Court's decision in *Roe,* States and municipalities have adopted a number of measures seemingly designed to prevent a woman, with the advice of her physician, from exercising her freedom of choice. *Akron* is but one example. But the constitutional principles that led this Court to its decisions in 1973 still provide the compelling reason for recognizing the constitutional dimensions of a woman's right to decide whether to end her pregnancy. "[I]t should go without saying that the vitality of these constitutional principles cannot be allowed to yield simply because of disagreement with them." . . . The States are not free, under the guise of protecting maternal health or potential life, to intimidate women into continuing pregnancies. Appellants claim that the statutory provisions before us today further legitimate compelling interests of the Commonwealth. Close analysis of those provisions, however, shows that they wholly subordinate constitutional privacy interests and concerns with maternal health in an effort to deter a woman from making a decision that, with her physician, is hers to make.

We turn to the challenged statutes:

1. Section 3205 ("informed consent") and § 3208 (printed information). Section 3205(a) requires that the woman give her "voluntary and informed consent" to an abortion. . . .

Seven explicit kinds of information must be delivered to the woman at least 24 hours before her consent is given, and five of these must be presented by the woman's physician. The five are: (a) the name of the physician who will perform the abortion, (b) the "fact that there may be detrimental physical and psychological effects which are not accurately foreseeable," (c) the "particular medical risks associated with the particular abortion procedure to be employed," (d) the probable gestational age, and (e) the "medical risks associated with carrying her child to term." The remaining two categories are (f) the "fact that medical assistance benefits may be available for prenatal care, childbirth and neonatal care," and (g) the "fact that the father is liable to assist" in the child's support, "even in instances where the father has offered to pay for the abortion." . . . The woman also must be informed that materials printed and supplied by the Commonwealth that describe the fetus and that list agencies offering alternatives to abortion are available for her review. If she chooses to review the materials but is unable to read, the materials, "shall be read to her," and any answer she seeks must be "provided her in her own language." . . . She must certify in writing, prior to the abortion, that all this has been done. . . . The printed materials "shall include the following statement":

"There are many public and private agencies willing and able to help you to carry your child to term, and to assist you and your child after your child is born, whether you choose to keep your child or place her or him for adoption. The Commonwealth of Pennsylvania strongly urges you to contact them before making a final decision about abortion. The law requires that your physician or his agent give you the opportunity to call agencies like these before you undergo an abortion." . . .

The materials must describe the "probable anatomical and physiological characteristics of the unborn child at two-week gestational increments from fertilization to full term, including any relevant information on the possibility of the unborn child's survival." . . .

The informational requirements in the *Akron* ordinance were invalid for two "equally decisive" reasons. . . . The first was that "much of the information required is designed not to inform the woman's consent but rather to persuade her to withhold it altogether." . . . The second was that a rigid requirement that a specific body of information be given in all cases, irrespective of the particular needs of the patient, intrudes upon the discretion of the pregnant woman's physician and thereby imposes the " 'undesired and uncomfortable straitjacket' " with which the Court in *Danforth* . . . was concerned.

These two reasons apply with equal and controlling force to the specific and intrusive informational prescriptions of the Pennsylvania statutes. The printed materials required by §§ 3205 and 3208 seem to us to be nothing less than an outright attempt to wedge the Commonwealth's message discouraging abortion into the privacy of the informed-consent dialogue between the woman and her physician. The mandated description of fetal characteristics at 2-week intervals, no matter how objective, is plainly overinclusive. This is not medical information that is always relevant to the woman's decision, and it may serve only to confuse and punish her and to heighten her anxiety, contrary to accepted medical practice. Even the listing of agencies in the printed Pennsylvania form presents serious problems; it contains names of agencies that well may be out of step with the needs of the particular woman and thus places the physician in an awkward position and infringes upon his or her professional responsibilities. Forcing the physician or counselor to present the materials and the list to the woman makes him or her in effect an agent of the State in treating the woman and places his or her imprimatur upon both the materials and the list. . . . All this is, or comes close to being, state medicine imposed upon the woman, not the professional medical guidance she seeks, and it officially structures—as it obviously was intended to do—the dialogue between the woman and her physician. . . .

2. Sections 3214(a) and (h) (reporting) and § 3211(a) (determination of viability). . . . Section 3211(a) requires the physician to report the basis for his determination "that a child is not viable." It applies only after the first trimester. The report required by §§ 3214(a) and (h) is detailed and must include, among other things, identification of the performing and referring physicians and of the facility or agency; information as to the woman's political subdivision and State of residence, age, race, marital status, and number of prior pregnancies; the date of her last menstrual period and the probable gestational age; the basis for any judgment that a medical emergency existed; the basis for any determination of nonviability; and the method of payment for the abortion. The report is to be signed by the attending physician. . . .

The scope of the information required and its availability to the public belie any assertions by the Commonwealth that it is advancing any legitimate interest. . . .

A woman and her physician will necessarily be more reluctant to choose an abortion if there exists a possibility that her decision and her identity will become known publicly. Although the statute does not specifically require the reporting of the woman's name, the amount of information about her and the circumstances under which she had an abortion are so detailed that identification is likely. Identification is the obvious purpose of these extreme reporting requirements. . . .

We note, as we reach this conclusion, that the Court consistently has refused to allow government to chill the exercise of constitutional rights by requiring disclosure of protected, but sometimes unpopular, activities. . . . Pennsylvania's reporting requirements raise the spectre of public exposure and harassment of women who choose to exercise their personal, intensely private, right, with their physician, to end a pregnancy. Thus, they pose an unacceptable danger of deterring the exercise of that right, and must be invalidated.

3. Section 3210(b) (degree of care for postviability abortions) and § 3210(c) (second-physician requirement when the fetus is possibly viable). Section 3210(b) sets forth two independent requirements for a postviability abortion. First, it demands the exercise of that degree of care "which such person would be required to exercise in order to preserve the life and health of any unborn child

intended to be born and not aborted." Second, "the abortion technique employed shall be that which would provide the best opportunity for the unborn child to be aborted alive unless," in the physician's good-faith judgment, that technique "would present a significantly greater medical risk to the life or health of the pregnant woman." . . .

The Court of Appeals ruled that § 3210(b) was unconstitutional because it required a "trade-off" between the woman's health and fetal survival, and failed to require that maternal health be the physician's paramount consideration. . . .

Appellants do not take any real issue with this proposition. . . . They argue instead, as did the District Court . . . that the statute's words "significantly greater medical risk" for the life or health of the woman do not mean some additional risk (in which case unconstitutionality apparently is conceded) but only a "meaningfully increased" risk. That interpretation, said the District Court, renders the statute constitutional. . . . The Court of Appeals disagreed, pointing out that such a reading is inconsistent with the statutory language and with the legislative intent reflected in that language; that the adverb "significantly" modifies the risk imposed on the woman; that the adverb is "patently not surplusage"; and that the language of the statute "is not susceptible to a construction that does not require the mother to bear an increased medical risk in order to save her viable fetus." . . . We agree with the Court of Appeals and therefore find the statute to be facially invalid.

Section 3210(c) requires that a second physician be present during an abortion performed when viability is possible. The second physician is to "take control of the child and . . . provide immediate medical care for the child, taking all reasonable steps necessary, in his judgment, to preserve the child's life and health."

In *Planned Parenthood Assn. v. Ashcroft*, . . . the Court, by a 5–4 vote, but not by a controlling single opinion, ruled that a Missouri statute requiring the presence of a second physician during an abortion performed after viability was constitutional. JUSTICE POWELL, joined by THE CHIEF JUSTICE, concluded that the State had a compelling interest in protecting the life of a viable fetus and that the second physician's presence provided assurance that the State's interest was protected more fully than with only one physician in attendance. . . . JUSTICE POWELL recognized that, to

pass constitutional muster, the statute must contain an exception for the situation where the health of the mother was endangered by delay in the arrival of the second physician. Recognizing that there was "no clearly expressed exception" on the face of the Missouri statute for the emergency situation, JUSTICE POWELL found the exception implicit in the statutory requirement that action be taken to preserve the fetus "provided it does not pose an increased risk to the life or health of the woman." . . .

Like the Missouri statute, § 3210(c) of the Pennsylvania statute contains no express exception for an emergency situation. While the Missouri statute, in the view of JUSTICE POWELL, was worded sufficiently to imply an emergency exception, Pennsylvania's statute contains no such comforting or helpful language and evinces no intent to protect a woman whose life may be at risk. Section 3210(a) provides only a defense to criminal liability for a physician who concluded, in good faith, that a fetus was nonviable "or that the abortion was necessary to preserve maternal life or health." It does not relate to the second-physician requirement and its words are not words of emergency. . . .

Our cases long have recognized that the Constitution embodies a promise that a certain private sphere of individual liberty will be kept largely beyond the reach of government. . . . That promise extends to women as well as to men. Few decisions are more personal and intimate, more properly private, or more basic to individual dignity and autonomy, than a woman's decision—with the guidance of her physician and within the limits specified in *Roe*—whether to end her pregnancy. A woman's right to make that choice freely is fundamental. Any other result, in our view, would protect inadequately a central part of the sphere of liberty that our law guarantees equally to all.

The Court of Appeals correctly invalidated the specified provisions of Pennsylvania's 1982 Abortion Control Act. Its judgment is affirmed.

It is so ordered.

JUSTICE WHITE, with whom JUSTICE REHNQUIST joins, dissenting. . . .

. . . Because the Constitution itself is ordained and established by the people of the United States, constitutional adjudication by this Court does not, in theory at any rate, frustrate the authority of the people to govern themselves through institutions of their own devising and in accordance with principles of their own choosing. But decisions that find in the Constitution principles or values that cannot fairly be read into that document usurp the people's authority, for such decisions represent choices that the people have never made and that they cannot disavow through corrective legislation. For this reason, it is essential that this Court maintain the power to restore authority to its proper possessors by correcting constitutional decisions that, on reconsideration, are found to be mistaken. . . .

In my view, the time has come to recognize that *Roe* v. *Wade,* no less than the cases overruled by the Court in the decisions I have just cited, "departs from a proper understanding" of the Constitution and to overrule it. . . .

Roe v. *Wade* posits that a woman has a fundamental right to terminate her pregnancy, and that this right may be restricted only in the service of two compelling state interests: the interest in maternal health (which becomes compelling only at the stage in pregnancy at which an abortion becomes more hazardous than carrying the pregnancy to term) and the interest in protecting the life of the fetus (which becomes compelling only at the point of viability). A reader of the Constitution might be surprised to find that it encompassed these detailed rules, for the text obviously contains no references to abortion, nor, indeed, to pregnancy or reproduction generally; and, of course, it is highly doubtful that the authors of any of the provisions of the Constitution believed that they were giving protection to abortion. As its prior cases clearly show, however, this Court does not subscribe to the simplistic view that constitutional interpretation can possibly be limited to the "plain meaning" of the Constitution's text or to the subjective intention of the Framers. The Constitution is not a deed setting forth the precise metes and bounds of its subject matter; rather, it is a document announcing fundamental principles in value-laden terms that leave ample scope for the exercise of normative judgment by those charged with interpreting and applying it. In particular, the Due Process Clause of the Fourteenth Amendment, which forbids the deprivation of "life, liberty, or property without due process of law," has been read by the majority of the Court to be broad enough to provide substantive protection against State infringement of a broad range of individual interests. . . .

In most instances, the substantive protection afforded the liberty or property of an individual

by the Fourteenth Amendment is extremely limited: State action impinging on individual interests need only be rational to survive scrutiny under the Due Process Clause, and the determination of rationality is to be made with a heavy dose of deference to the policy choices of the legislature. Only "fundamental" rights are entitled to the added protection provided by strict judicial scrutiny of legislation that impinges upon them. . . . I can certainly agree with the proposition—which I deem indisputable—that a woman's ability to choose an abortion is a species of "liberty" that is subject to the general protections of the Due Process Clause. I cannot agree, however, that this liberty is so "fundamental" that restrictions upon it call into play anything more than the most minimal judicial scrutiny.

Fundamental liberties and interests are most clearly present when the Constitution provides specific textual recognition of their existence and importance. Thus, the Court is on relatively firm ground when it deems certain of the liberties set forth in the Bill of Rights to be fundamental and therefore finds them incorporated in the Fourteenth Amendment's guarantee that no State may deprive any person of liberty without due process of law. When the Court ventures further and defines as "fundamental" liberties that are nowhere mentioned in the Constitution (or that are present only in the so-called "penumbras" of specifically enumerated rights), it must, of necessity, act with more caution, lest it open itself to the accusation that, in the name of identifying constitutional principles to which the people have consented in framing their Constitution, the Court has done nothing more than impose its own controversial choices of value upon the people.

Attempts to articulate the constraints that must operate upon the Court when it employs the Due Process Clause to protect liberties not specifically enumerated in the text of the Constitution have produced varying definitions of "fundamental liberties." One approach has been to limit the class of fundamental liberties to those interests that are "implicit in the concept of ordered liberty" such that "neither liberty nor justice would exist if [they] were sacrificed." . . . Another, broader approach is to define fundamental liberties as those that are "deeply rooted in this Nation's history and tradition." . . . [N]ot subject to debate, however, is that either of the basic definitions of fundamental liberties, taken seriously, indicates the illegitimacy of the Court's decision in *Roe* v. *Wade*. . . .

Both the characterization of the abortion liberty as fundamental and the denigration of the State's interest in preserving the lives of nonviable fetuses are essential to the detailed set of constitutional rules devised by the Court to limit the State's power to regulate abortion. If either or both of these facets of *Roe* v. *Wade* were rejected, a broad range of limitations on abortion (including outright prohibition) that are now unavailable to the States would again become constitutional possibilities.

In my view, such a state of affairs would be highly desirable from the standpoint of the Constitution. Abortion is a hotly contested moral and political issue. Such issues, in our society, are to be resolved by the will of the people, either as expressed through legislation or through the general principles they have already incorporated into the Constitution they have adopted. *Roe* v. *Wade* implies that the people have already resolved the debate by weaving into the Constitution the values and principles that answer the issue. As I have argued, I believe it is clear that the people have never—not in 1787, 1791, 1868, or at any time since—done any such thing. I would return the issue to the people by overruling *Roe* v. *Wade*.

As it has evolved in the decisions of this Court, the freedom recognized by the Court in *Roe* v. *Wade* and its progeny is essentially a negative one, based not on the notion that abortion is a good in itself, but only on the view that the legitimate goals that may be served by state coercion of private choices regarding abortion are, at least under some circumstances, outweighed by the damage to individual autonomy and privacy that such coercion entails. In other words, the evil of abortion does not justify the evil of forbidding it. . . . But precisely because *Roe* v. *Wade* is not premised on the notion that abortion is itself desirable (either as a matter of constitutional entitlement or of social policy), the decision does not command the States to fund or encourage abortion, or even to approve of it. Rather, we have recognized that the States may legitimately adopt a policy of encouraging normal childbirth rather than abortion so long as the measures through which that policy is implemented do not amount to direct compulsion of the woman's choice regarding abortion. . . . The provisions before the Court today quite obviously represent the State's effort to implement such a policy.

The majority's opinion evinces no deference toward the State's legitimate policy. Rather, the majority makes it clear from the outset that it simply disapproves of any attempt by Pennsylvania to legislate in this area. The history of the state legislature's decade-long effort to pass a constitutional abortion statute is recounted as if it were evidence of some sinister conspiracy. . . .

One searches the majority's opinion in vain for a convincing reason why the apparently laudable policy of promoting informed consent becomes unconstitutional when the subject is abortion. The majority purports to find support in *Akron*. . . . But *Akron* is not controlling. The informed consent provisions struck down in that case, as characterized by the majority, required the physician to advance tendentious statements concerning the unanswerable question of when human life begins, to offer merely speculative descriptions of the anatomical features of the fetus carried by the woman seeking the abortion, and to recite a "parade of horribles" suggesting that abortion is "a particularly dangerous procedure." . . . I have no quarrel with the general proposition, for which I read *Akron* to stand, that a campaign of state-promulgated disinformation cannot be justified in the name of "informed consent" or "freedom of choice." But the Pennsylvania statute before us cannot be accused of sharing the flaws of the ordinance at issue in *Akron*. As the majority concedes, the statute does not, on its face, require that the patient be given any information that is false or unverifiable. Moreover, it is unquestionable that all of the information required would be relevant in many cases to a woman's decision whether or not to obtain an abortion.

Why, then, is the statute unconstitutional? The majority's argument, while primarily rhetorical, appears to offer three answers. First, the information that must be provided will in some cases be irrelevant to the woman's decision. This is true. Its pertinence to the question of the statute's constitutionality, however, is beyond me. . . .

Second, the majority appears to reason that the informed consent provisions are invalid because the information they require may increase the woman's "anxiety" about the procedure and even "influence" her in her choice. Again, both observations are undoubtedly true; but they by no means cast the constitutionality of the provisions into question. It is in the very nature of informed consent provisions that they may produce some anxiety in the patient and influence her in her choice. This is in fact their reason for existence, and—provided that the information required is accurate and nonmisleading—it is an entirely salutary reason. . . .

Third, the majority concludes that the informed consent provisions are invalid because they "intrud[e] upon the discretion of the pregnant woman's physician" . . . violate "the privacy of the informed-consent dialogue between the woman and her physician" . . . and "officially structur[e]" that dialogue. . . .

Were the Court serious about the need for strict scrutiny of regulations that infringe on the "judgment" of medical professionals, "structure" their relations with their patients, and amount to "state medicine," there is no telling how many state and federal statutes (not to mention principles of state tort law) governing the practice of medicine might be condemned. . . .

The majority resorts to linguistic nit-picking in striking down the provision requiring physicians aborting viable fetuses to use the method of abortion most likely to result in fetal survival unless that method would pose a "significantly greater medical risk to the life or health of the pregnant woman" than would other available methods. The majority concludes that the statute's use of the word "significantly" indicates that the statute represents an unlawful "trade-off" between the woman's health and the chance of fetal survival. Not only is this conclusion based on a wholly unreasonable interpretation of the statute, but the statute would also be constitutional even if it meant what the majority says it means. . . .

The Court's ruling in this respect is not even *consistent* with its decision in *Roe* v. *Wade*. In *Roe*, the Court conceded that the State's interest in preserving the life of a viable fetus is a compelling one, and the Court has never disavowed that concession. The Court now holds that this compelling interest cannot justify *any* regulation that imposes a quantifiable medical risk upon the pregnant woman who seeks to abort a viable fetus: if attempting to save the fetus imposes any additional risk of injury to the woman, she must be permitted to kill it. . . .

The Court's ruling today that any trade-off between the woman's health and fetal survival is impermissible is not only inconsistent with *Roe*'s recognition of a compelling state interest in viable fetal life; it directly contradicts one of the essential holdings of *Roe*—that is, that the State may forbid *all* post-viability abortions except when *necessary* to protect the life or health of the pregnant woman. As is evident, this holding itself involves a trade-off between maternal health and protection of the fetus, for it plainly permits the State to forbid a postviability abortion even when such an abortion may be statistically safer than carrying the pregnancy to term, provided that the abortion is not medically necessary. The trade-off contained in the Pennsylvania statute, even as interpreted by the majority, is no different in kind: the State has simply required that when an abortion of some kind is medically necessary, it shall be conducted so as to spare the fetus (to the greatest degree possible) unless a method less protective of the fetus is itself to some degree medically necessary for the woman. That this choice may involve the imposition of some risk on the woman undergoing the abortion should be no more troublesome than that a prohibition on nonnecessary post-viability abortions may involve the imposition of some risk on women who are thereby forced to continue their pregnancies to term; yet for some reason, the Court concludes that whereas the trade-offs it devises are compelled by the Constitution, the essentially indistinguishable trade-off the State has attempted is foreclosed. This cannot be the law. . . .

Bowers v. Hardwick
478 U.S. 186, 106 S.Ct. 2841, 92 L.Ed. 2d 140 (1986)

In 1982, police officers in Atlanta, Georgia, went to the home of Michael Hardwick because of a previous offense of public drunkenness. Someone at the home admitted the officers, saying that Hardwick was probably in the bedroom. When police entered, they found Hardwick in bed with another man committing acts that police concluded violated the state's sodomy statute: "A person commits the offense of sodomy when he performs or submits to any sexual act involving the sex organs of one person and the mouth or anus of another" (Official Code of Georgia Annotated, Section 16–2–2). Violation of the statute is punishable by imprisonment for not less than one nor more than 20 years. At the time, approximately half the states in the Union had statutes similar to Georgia's.

Authorities declined to prosecute Hardwick, but in 1983 he filed suit in the United States District Court for the Northern District of Georgia, seeking a declaratory judgment that the law was unconstitutional as applied to private sexual conduct between consenting adults. The district court dismissed Hardwick's complaint on the ground that his constitutional claims had been rejected without opinion by the Supreme Court in *Doe* v. *Commonwealth's Attorney* (1976). In 1985, the United States Court of Appeals for the Eleventh Circuit reversed the district court, concluding that Georgia's sodomy statute infringed on Hardwick's fundamental rights of privacy and association and that the state would have to demonstrate a compelling interest in proscribing the conduct in order to validate the statute. Majority: White, Burger, O'Connor, Powell, Rehnquist. Dissenting: Blackmun, Brennan, Marshall, Stevens.

JUSTICE WHITE delivered the opinion of the Court. . . .

Because other Courts of Appeals have arrived at judgments contrary to that of the 11th Circuit in this case, we granted the state's petition for certiorari questioning the holding that its sodomy statute violates the fundamental rights of homosexuals. We agree with the state that the Court of Appeals erred, and hence reverse its judgment.

This case does not require a judgment on whether laws against sodomy between consenting adults in general, or between homosexuals in particular, are wise or desirable. It raises no question about the right or propriety of state legislative decisions to repeal their laws that criminalize homosexual sodomy, or of state court decisions invalidating those laws on state constitutional grounds. The issue presented is whether the Federal Constitution confers a fundamental right upon homosexuals to engage in sodomy and hence invalidates the laws of the many states that still make such conduct illegal and have done so for a very long time. The case also calls for some judgment about the limits of the court's role in carrying out its constitutional mandate.

We first register our disagreement with the Court of Appeals and with respondent that the Court's prior cases have construed the Constitution to confer a right of privacy that extends to homosexual sodomy and for all intents and purposes have decided this case. Three cases were interpreted as construing the Due Process Clause of the 14th Amendment to confer a fundamental individual right to decide whether or not to beget or bear a child. . . .

Accepting the decisions in these cases and the

above description of them, we think it evident that none of the rights announced in those cases bears any resemblance to the claimed constitutional right of homosexuals to engage in acts of sodomy that is asserted in this case. No connection between family, marriage, or procreation on the one hand and homosexual activity on the other has been demonstrated, either by the Court of Appeals or by respondent. Moreover, any claim that these cases nevertheless stand for the proposition that any kind of private sexual conduct between consenting adults is constitutionally insulated from state proscription is unsupportable.

Precedent aside, however, respondent would have us announce, as the Court of Appeals did, a fundamental right to engage in homosexual sodomy. This we are quite unwilling to do. It is true that despite the language of the Due Process Clauses of the Fifth and 14th Amendments, which appears to focus only on the processes by which life, liberty, or property is taken, the cases are legion in which those clauses have been interpreted to have substantive content, subsuming rights that to a great extent are immune from Federal or state regulation or proscription. Among such cases are those recognizing rights that have little or no textual support in the constitutional language. . . .

Striving to assure itself and the public that announcing rights not readily identifiable in the Constitution's text involves much more than the imposition of the Justices' own choice of values on the states and the Federal Government, the Court has sought to identify the nature of the rights qualifying for heightened judicial protection. In *Palko* v. *Connecticut* . . . it was said that this category includes those fundamental liberties that are "implicit in the concept of ordered liberty," such that "neither liberty nor justice would exist if (they) were sacrificed." A different description of fundamental liberties appeared in *Moore* v. *East Cleveland* . . . where they are characterized as those liberties that are "deeply rooted in the nation's history and tradition." . . .

It is obvious to us that neither of these formulations would extend a fundamental right to homosexuals to engage in acts of consensual sodomy. Proscriptions against that conduct have ancient roots. Sodomy was a criminal offense at common law and was forbidden by the laws of the original 13 states when they ratified the Bill of Rights. In 1868,

when the 14th Amendment was ratified, all but 5 of the 37 states in the Union had criminal sodomy laws. In fact, until 1961, all 50 states outlawed sodomy, and today, 24 states and the District of Columbia continue to provide criminal penalties for sodomy performed in private and between consenting adults. Against this background, to claim that a right to engage in such conduct is "deeply rooted in this nation's history and tradition" or "implicit in the concept of ordered liberty" is, at best, facetious.

Nor are we inclined to take a more expansive view of our authority to discover new fundamental rights imbedded in the Due Process Clause. The Court is most vulnerable and comes nearest to illegitimacy when it deals with judge-made constitutional law having little or no cognizable roots in the language or design of the Constitution. That this is so was painfully demonstrated by the face-off between the Executive and the Court in the 1930's, which resulted in the repudiation of much of the substantive gloss that the Court had placed on the Due Process Clause of the Fifth and 14th Amendments. There should be, therefore, great resistance to expand the substantive reach of those clauses, particularly if it requires redefining the category of rights deemed to be fundamental. Otherwise, the judiciary necessarily takes to itself further authority to govern the country without express constitutional authority. The claimed right pressed on us today falls far short of overcoming this resistance. . . .

Respondent, however, asserts that the result should be different where the homosexual conduct occurs in the privacy of the home. He relies on *Stanley* v. *Georgia* . . . where the Court held that the First Amendment prevents conviction for possessing and reading obscene material in the privacy of his home. . . .

Stanley did protect conduct that would not have been protected outside the home, and it partially prevented the enforcement of state obscenity laws; but the decision was firmly grounded in the First Amendment. The right pressed upon us here has no similar support in the text of the Constitution, and it does not qualify for recognition under the prevailing principles for construing the 14th Amendment. Its limits are also difficult to discern. Plainly enough, otherwise illegal conduct is not always immunized whenever it occurs in the home.

Victimless crimes, such as the possession and use of illegal drugs do not escape the law where they are committed at home. *Stanley* itself recognized that its holding offered no protection for the possession in the home of drugs, firearms, or stolen goods. And if respondent's submission is limited to the voluntary sexual conduct between consenting adults, it would be difficult, except by fiat, to limit the claimed right to homosexual conduct while leaving exposed to prosecution adultery, incest, and other sexual crimes even though they are committed in the home. We are unwilling to start down that road.

Even if the conduct at issue here is not a fundamental right, respondent asserts that there must be a rational basis for the law and that there is none in this case other than the presumed belief of a majority of the electorate in Georgia that homosexual sodomy is immoral and unacceptable. This is said to be an inadequate rationale to support the law. The law, however, is constantly based on notions of morality, and if all laws representing essentially moral choices are to be invalidated under the Due Process Clause, the courts will be very busy indeed. Even respondent makes no such claim, but insists that majority sentiments about the morality of homosexuality should be declared inadequate. We do not agree, and are unpersuaded that the sodomy laws of some 25 states should be invalidated on this basis.

Accordingly, the judgment of the Court of Appeals is

Reversed.

JUSTICE BLACKMUN, with whom JUSTICES BRENNAN, MARSHALL, and STEVENS join, dissenting.

This case is no more about "a fundamental right to engage in homosexual sodomy," as the court purports to declare, than *Stanley* v. *Georgia* was about a fundamental right to watch obscene movies, or *Katz* v. *United States* . . . was about a fundamental right to place interstate bets from a telephone booth. Rather, this case is about "the most comprehensive of rights and the most valued by civilized men," namely "the right to be let alone." . . .

In its haste to reverse the Court of Appeals and hold that the Constitution does not "confe(r) a fundamental right upon homosexuals to engage in sodomy," the Court relegates the actual statute being challenged to a footnote and ignores the

procedural posture of the case before it. A fair reading of the statute and of the complaint clearly reveals that the majority has distorted the question this case presents. . . .

The sex or status of the persons who engage in the act is irrelevant as a matter of state law. In fact, to the extent I can discern a legislative purpose . . . that purpose seems to have been to broaden the coverage of the law to reach heterosexual as well as homosexual activity. . . .

The Court concludes today that none of our prior cases dealing with various decisions that individuals are entitled to make free of governmental interference "bears any resemblance to the claimed constitutional right of homosexuals to engage in acts of sodomy that is asserted in this case." While it is true that these cases may be characterized by their connection to protection of the family, the Court's conclusion that they extend no further than this boundary ignores the warning in *Moore* v. *East Cleveland* . . . against "clos-(ing) our eyes to the basic reasons why certain rights associated with the family have been accorded shelter under the 14th Amendment's Due Process Clause." . . .

We protect those rights not because they contribute, in some direct and material way, to the general public welfare, but because they form so central a part of an individual life. We protect the decision whether to marry precisely because marriage "is an association that promotes a way of life, not causes; a harmony in living, not political faiths; a bilateral loyalty, not commercial or social projects." . . . We protect the decision whether to have a child because parenthood alters so dramatically an individual's self-definition, not because of demographic considerations or the Bible's command to be fruitful and multiply. And we protect the family because it contributes so powerfully to the happiness of individuals, not because of a preference for stereotypical households. . . .

In a variety of circumstances we have recognized that a necessary corollary of giving individuals freedom to choose how to conduct their lives is acceptance of the fact that different individuals will make different choices. For example, in holding that the clearly important state interest in public education should give way to a competing claim by the Amish to the effect that extended formal schooling threatened their way of life, the Court declared: "There can be no assumption that today's majority is 'right' and the Amish and others like them are 'wrong.' A way of life that is odd or even erratic but interferes with no rights or interests of others is not to be condemned because it is different." . . . The Court claims that its decision today merely refuses to recognize a fundamental right to engage in homosexual sodomy; what the Court really has refused to recognize is the fundamental interest all individuals have in controlling the nature of their intimate associations with others.

The behavior for which Hardwick faces prosecution occurred in his own home, a place to which the Fourth Amendment attaches special significance. The Court's treatment of this aspect of the case is symptomatic of its overall refusal to consider the broad principles that have informed our treatment of privacy in specific cases. Just as the right to privacy is more than the mere aggregation of a number of entitlements to engage in specific behavior, so too, protecting the physical integrity of the home is more than merely a means of protecting specific activities that often take place there.

The Court's interpretation of the pivotal case of *Stanley* v. *Georgia* . . . is entirely unconvincing. *Stanley* held that Georgia's undoubted power to punish the public distribution of constitutionally unprotected, obscene material did not permit the state to punish the private possession of such material. According to the majority here, *Stanley* relied entirely on the First Amendment, and thus, it is claimed, sheds no light on cases not involving printed materials. But that is not what *Stanley* said. Rather, the *Stanley* Court anchored its holding in the Fourth Amendment's special protection for the individual in his home. The right of an individual to conduct intimate relationships in the intimacy of his or her own home seems to me to be the heart of the Constitution's protection of privacy. . . .

Petitioner and the Court fail to see the difference between laws that protect public sensibilities and those that enforce private morality. Statutes banning public sexual activity are entirely consistent with protecting the individual's liberty interest in decisions concerning sexual relations: the same recognition that those decisions are intensely private which justifies protecting them from governmental interference can justify protecting individuals from unwilling exposure to the sexual activities of others. But the mere fact that intimate behavior may be punished when it takes place in public cannot dictate how states can regulate intimate behavior that occurs in intimate places.

This case involves no real interference with the rights of others, for the mere knowledge that other individuals do not adhere to one's value system cannot be a legally cognizable interest, let alone an interest that can justify invading the houses, hearts, and minds of citizens who choose to live their lives differently.

I can only hope that the Court soon will reconsider its analysis and conclude that depriving individuals of the right to choose for themselves how to conduct their intimate relationships poses a far greater threat to the values most deeply rooted in our nation's history than tolerance of nonconformity could ever do. Because I think the Court today betrays those values, I dissent.*

* Press reports following this decision indicated that Georgia authorities would not prosecute Hardwick for sodomy. The state's four-year statute of limitations ran its course in August 1986.—ED.

TWELVE

Equal Protection of the Laws

In order to get beyond racism, we must first take account of race.
There is no other way. And in order to treat some persons equally,
we must treat them differently. We cannot—we dare not—
let the Equal Protection Clause perpetrate racial supremacy.

—JUSTICE HARRY A. BLACKMUN (1978)

The Founding Fathers, Madison in particular, were wedded to the notion that unequal distribution of wealth is the natural result in a society where individuals of differing capacities are free. Accordingly, any affirmative government action on behalf of those less fortunate, ignoring merit, was suspect. For whatever reason, a conspicuous omission from the original document, as well as the Bill of Rights, is a provision guarding against a denial of *equal protection of the laws*. This provision now so conspicuous in a wide range of Supreme Court decisions dates only from 1868, when it was made part of the Fourteenth Amendment, along with two other provisions designed to safeguard individual rights against encroachment by the states.

The equal protection clause applies when states make distinctions among people and treat them differently. The meaning the Supreme Court gives the clause largely determines what differences among people will be allowed to matter in public policy.

In the **Slaughterhouse Cases** (1873) (see Chapter Eight), when the Court first considered the clause, Justice Miller suggested that it was doubtful whether "this sweeping injunction would ever be invoked against any state action" not directed by way of discrimination against blacks as a class. "It is," he wrote, "so clearly a provision for that race and that emergency, that a strong case would be necessary for its application to any other." Yet it was not until the 1940s that the equal protection clause began to take shape as a formidable weapon against racial and other kinds of discrimination. The dramatic change in the standards of equal protection—from constitutional omission to constitutional nullity to constitutional prominence—carries within itself a fascinating story.

"SEPARATE BUT EQUAL"

After the Civil War it was essential for the states to have an acceptable legal principle to support the policy of holding blacks in their former status. The answer was found in laws requiring segregation of whites and blacks under the formula "separate but equal," which received the Supreme Court's formal approval in *Plessy* v. *Ferguson* (1896).

When the equal protection clause was invoked on behalf of blacks against Louisiana's law requiring racial segregation on trains, the Court refused to allow the provision to serve even the limited purpose that Justice Miller had earlier acknowledged. In *Plessy*, Justice Brown's majority opinion drew an important distinction between political and social equality. The Fourteenth Amendment demanded only the former, and the state law merely gave recognition to the latter. Deploring this emasculation, ex-slave owner Justice Harlan observed in dissent: "Our Constitution is color-blind, and neither knows nor tolerates classes among citizens. In respect to civil rights all citizens are equal before the law." Denouncing the majority's separate-but-equal formula, Harlan predicted that "the judgment this day rendered will in time prove to be quite as pernicious as the decision made by this tribunal in the Dred Scott case." (See Chapter Two.)

It was not until the late 1930s that the Court began to give serious attention to the equality requirement. In 1938 the Court invalidated a law under which Gaines, a black applicant, was refused admission to the School of Law of the University of Missouri (*Missouri ex rel. Gaines* v. *Canada*). Missouri made funds available to Gaines and other qualified black applicants to finance their legal education in schools of adjacent states that offered unsegregated educational facilities, and argued that by this action it was meeting the separate-but-equal requirement. Chief Justice Hughes, for the majority of seven, disposed of the state's contention emphatically.

> By the operation of the laws of Missouri a privilege has been created for white law students which is denied to negroes by reason of their race. The white resident is afforded legal education within the State; the negro resident having the same qualifications is refused it there and must go outside the State to obtain it. That is a denial of equality of legal right to the enjoyment of the privilege which the State has set up, and the provision for the payment of tuition fees in another State does not remove the discrimination. . . .

A cluster of cases between 1948 and 1950 indicated that the separate-but-equal doctrine would in the future be more difficult to apply in practice. *Sipuel* v. *University of Oklahoma* (1948) held that qualified blacks must be admitted to a state law school or be furnished equivalent professional education within the state. *McLaurin* v. *Oklahoma State Regents* (1950) nullified state efforts to segregate the scholastic activities of a black student who had been admitted to the graduate school of the University of Oklahoma pursuant to a federal court order. Finally, a direct challenge to segregated education was presented in *Sweatt* v. *Painter* (1950), where an applicant who had been denied admission to the University of Texas Law School solely on the basis of color claimed that the instruction available in the newly established state law school for blacks was markedly inferior to the instruction at the university, and that equal protection of laws was thus denied. In a unanimous decision the Supreme Court ordered his admission to the white school, indicating that it was virtually impossible in practice, at least in professional education, for a state to comply with the separate-but-equal formula. Taking into account professional and psychological considerations, thus anticipating the thrust of Chief Justice Warren's opinion in *Brown*, Chief Justice Vinson of Kentucky left that judicial creation hanging by a hair.

The law school, the proving ground for legal learning and practice, cannot be effective in isolation from the individuals and institutions with which the law interacts. Few students and no one who has practiced law would choose to study in an academic vacuum, removed from the interplay of ideas and the exchange of views with which the law is concerned. The law school to which Texas is willing to admit petitioner excludes from its student body members of the racial groups which number 85% of the population of the State and include most of the lawyers, witnesses, jurors, judges and other officials with whom petitioner will inevitably be dealing when he becomes a member of the Texas Bar. With such a substantial and significant segment of society excluded, we cannot conclude that the education offered petitioner is substantially equal to that which he would receive if admitted to the University of Texas Law School.

Following the decision in *Sweatt* the National Association for the Advancement of Colored People and other organizations pressed the fight against segregation in public elementary and secondary schools. Would the Court retract the principle of separate but equal, or alternatively, would it construe the requirement of equality so strictly that segregation in practice would be constitutionally impossible? After hearing arguments in a group of public school segregation cases presented at the 1952 term, the justices were unable to reach a decision. In setting the cases for reargument during the 1953 term, the Court took the unusual step of requesting counsel to provide answers to a long list of questions, some seeking information concerning the intention of the Congress that proposed, and the states that ratified, the Fourteenth Amendment, and others requesting advice concerning the kind of orders that the Court should issue if it were to hold segregated school arrangements unconstitutional.

The Court's caution, though unusual, was understandable. Its decision would affect the school systems of 17 states and the District of Columbia, where segregation was required by law, and four states where segregation was permitted by local option. The pattern of education for more than 8 million white children and 2½ million black children would be drastically changed if segregation practices were found unconstitutional. Even greater issues were involved: If segregation in public schools were deemed a denial of equal protection of the laws, it would be difficult, if not impossible, to defend segregation in other sectors of public life. The legal underpinnings of the social structure of a great part of the nation were under attack.

On May 17, 1954, the Court handed down its decision in **Brown** v. **Board of Education.** Speaking for a unanimous bench, Chief Justice Earl Warren declared that "in the field of public education the doctrine of 'separate but equal' has no place. Separate educational facilities are inherently unequal." The opinion was remarkable not only for its brevity but also for its references to sociological and psychological factors. Reduced to a footnote, these were gratuitous. Earlier decisions had eroded the constitutional foundations of the separate-but-equal formula to the vanishing point. Nor did the historical evidence, furnished at the Court's request and available to it in briefs of counsel, influence the decision. "In approaching this problem," said the chief justice, "we cannot turn the clock back to 1868, when the Amendment was adopted, or even to 1896, when *Plessy* v. *Ferguson* was written. We must consider public education in the light of its full development and its present place in American life throughout the nation."

With *Brown,* from Kansas, the Court combined cases from South Carolina, Virginia, and Delaware. *Bolling* v. *Sharpe* was the companion case from the District of Columbia and was decided separately on the same day. In the District of Columbia Case, the Court came to a similar conclusion, finding an equal protection component in the due process clause of the Fifth Amendment. "Segregation in public education," said the Court, ". . .

imposes on Negro children of the District of Columbia a burden that constitutes an arbitrary deprivation of their liberty in violation of the Due Process Clause." Having achieved unanimity on this difficult issue, the Court postponed formulation of a decree until the 1954–1955 term and called for additional argument.

In the following term the Court handed down its decree in the second Brown Case, expressing the conclusion that desegregation in public education would necessarily take place at varying speeds and in different ways, depending on local conditions. Federal district court judges, employing the flexible principles of equity, were given the task of determining when and how desegregation should take place. In a historic pronouncement, the Court said, "The judgments below . . . are remanded to the district courts to take such proceedings and enter such orders and decrees consistent with this opinion as are necessary and proper to admit to public schools on a racially nondiscriminatory basis *with all deliberate speed*" the parties to these cases (italics added).

Although the border states showed a disposition to comply with the Supreme Court's mandate, states in the Deep South began a campaign of active and passive resistance. Several legislatures passed resolutions declaring the desegregation decisions "unlawful." State sovereignty was "interposed" against this alleged encroachment on their reserved powers. Almost all southern senators and representatives joined in 1956 in issuing a "Declaration of Constitutional Principles" and advocated resistance to compelled desegregation by "all lawful means."

Certain states adopted various legal tactics and devices that delayed the implementation of *Brown*. Since the recalcitrant states and communities refused to desegregate, it was necessary for black citizens to bring individual suits in each school district asking the federal court to compel the school authorities to take steps toward desegregated schools. Interminable hearings followed, with local officials asking for delay because of local conditions, which in their view were unfavorable to prompt action. After several years, a plan for one-grade-a-year desegregation might be proposed and accepted by a district court. Or certain states would enact "pupil placement" and "transfer privilege" laws. Such laws were designed to achieve token integration by permitting black pupils to apply for admission to normally all-white schools or to permit parents to request transfer of their children to a school other than the assigned one. In any event, these and other devices were successful for a time in maintaining mostly segregated educational facilities. By 1963, the centennial of the Emancipation Proclamation, most school districts had no plan at all or one that produced very little desegregation.

Where there was litigation, the Supreme Court staunchly upheld lower federal court decisions ordering steps toward desegregated schools, either by denying certiorari or by *per curiam* decisions. The executive branch, which took an essentially neutral position in the 1950s, took strong steps in 1958 to support the orders of a federal court in Arkansas, actions that were upheld by a powerful decision of the Supreme Court (*Cooper* v. *Aaron*). In 1962 Mississippi troops were used to meet resistance to the desegregation order.*

The pace of integration quickened after 1965, when the combination of two congressional enactments brought both administrative and financial pressure to bear on school districts. The mid-1960s witnessed the first mass infusion of federal funds into local school coffers,

---

* Decisions in the school segregation cases not only invalidated the concept of "separate but equal" in education but also set forth a rationale that made the local continuance of other segregated public facilities and services doubtful. Segregation was outlawed in intrastate buses (*Gayle* v. *Browder*, 1956) and in public recreation facilities (*Baltimore* v. *Dawson*, 1955). Among the last state-imposed segregation laws and policies to fall were a statute prohibiting interracial marriages (*Loving* v. *Virginia*, 1967) and a court order denying a mother custody of her child because of remarriage to someone of a different race (*Palmore* v. *Sidoti*, 1984). Racial discrimination today is less overt.

and the Civil Rights Act of 1964 in several ways made continued receipt of Washington largess conditional on integrated education. Whereas litigation often took years to effect even small changes in the schools, bureaucrats with their hands on the federal faucet could accomplish substantial changes in months. Their efforts were reinforced by the Court.

In 1964, the justices were faced with a complete shutdown of public schools in Prince Edward County, Virginia, one of the school districts involved in the original *Brown* litigation a decade before. To avoid compliance with the 1954 decision, county officials contributed support to private, segregated white schools that took the place of public schools. Upholding the district court, the justices ordered the reopening of the public school system (*Griffin* v. *School Board*).

Four years after *Griffin,* the Court confronted a "freedom-of-choice" integration plan from New Kent County, Virginia (*Green* v. *School Board,* 1968). Here, there was no longer an official "white" or "black" label for schools, but all the white children in this rural district elected to remain in the school they had previously attended, and 85 percent of the black children chose to stay at the school they had previously attended. Labels aside, the school populations were "racially identifiable." What the Constitution required, said Justice Brennan, was a plan that produced compliance with *Brown*—a "unitary" as opposed to a "dual" school system. "The burden on a school board today is to come forward with a plan that promises realistically to work, and promises realistically to work *now.*"

Following President Richard Nixon's election in 1968, political observers predicted that the new president's appointees to the Court would retreat from holdings like *Green.* New justices, it was thought, would take positions supportive instead of the so-called "southern strategy," designed to woo southern whites into the ranks of the Republican Party. Those observers were poor prophets.

Dramatic evidence that the Burger Court was not willing to turn back the clock came in a pair of 1971 decisions, after Justice Blackmun's appointment. In one, the justices invalidated a state statute prohibiting assignment or busing of students on the basis of race or for the purpose of creating a racial balance (*North Carolina State Board of Education* v. *Swann,* 1971). At the same time, the Court upheld a desegregation plan that involved busing within a single metropolitan school district (*Swann* v. *Charlotte-Mecklenburg Board of Education,* 1971).

In Mecklenburg County, North Carolina, a previous desegregation plan had left large numbers of predominantly one-race schools. Not surprisingly, this residual segregation in the schools was caused partly by racially segregated neighborhoods, themselves shaped over the years by a system of legally enforced school segregation. "The objective today," declared Chief Justice Burger, "remains to eliminate from the public schools all vestiges of state-imposed segregation."

> Absent a constitutional violation there would be no basis for judicially ordering assignment of students on a racial basis. All things being equal, with no history of discrimination, it might well be desirable to assign pupils to schools nearest their homes. But all things are not equal in a system that has been deliberately constructed and maintained to enforce racial segregation. The remedy for such segregation may be administratively awkward, inconvenient, and even bizarre in some situations and may impose burdens on some; but all awkwardness and inconvenience cannot be avoided in the interim period when remedial adjustments are being made to eliminate the dual school systems.

The target of these judicial efforts to apply *Brown* was *de jure* segregation—segregation that existed because of law and public policy. The most obvious place to find de jure segregation was in the school systems of the southern states, and through the *Swann* litigation in 1971, segregation cases in the Supreme Court had a southern focus. Not reached by the Constitution and not at issue in these cases was *de facto* segregation—segregation that was a product of nongovernment actions and practices.

In 1973 the Court's attention was drawn to the problem of school segregation outside the South. *Keyes* v. *School District* (1973) did not involve statutes or other obvious official actions to create segregated schools. One section of Denver, Colorado, contained a heavy concentration of black schoolchildren, and the wrongdoing of the school officials consisted largely of various administrative decisions in the 1960s that were found by the federal district court to constitute a deliberate plan to maintain segregated schools in that part of the city. The Supreme Court agreed and ruled that where one part of a school system was segregated, the remedy could take the form of a decree involving busing of students from one part of the district to another to reduce the number of racially identifiable (that is, mainly one-race) schools. Attendance zones drawn by school boards that resulted in racial imbalances in the classroom could be a constitutional violation just as if old-style southern segregation laws had been in effect.

Although continuing to insist that a distinction be made between de facto and de jure segregation, the former being lawful, the latter unconstitutional, *Keyes* signaled northern communities that federal courts would give close scrutiny to all official decisions affecting the racial composition of schools, and that absence of statutory provisions requiring segregation would not prevent judicial action. In other words, the justices were enlarging the concept of de jure segregation in *Keyes,* and correspondingly shrinking what they considered de facto segregation.

By this time, a much larger percentage of black pupils attended desegregated schools in the South than in the North. As the flight of whites to the suburbs accelerated and blacks and other racial minorities became the dominant population in cities, the question of how to achieve racially integrated schools in multidistrict metropolitan areas became acute. More and more the argument was made that the state governments should bear ultimate responsibility for achieving desegregation. By a vote of 5 to 4 in 1974, however, the Supreme Court in *Milliken* v. *Bradley* rejected a multidistrict remedy for a single-district segregation problem.

Recall that the judicial remedies the Court upheld in both *Keyes* and *Swann* did not extend beyond the bounds of the single school district involved. *Milliken* began in Detroit as litigation similar to *Keyes*. In an effort to remove racial imbalances within the city school district, the federal judge concluded that a school district with a black majority would still have mainly black schools, even with extensive busing within Detroit. Suburban areas, in contrast, had heavily white school populations. The district judge's remedy thus became metropolitan, encompassing 53 separate suburban school districts since the segregation he observed was metropolitan in scope.

Building on the logic in the 1973 Denver decision, the Court in 1979 approved judicially ordered integration on a massive scale in the public school systems of Dayton and Columbus, Ohio (*Columbus Board of Education* v. *Penick; Dayton Board of Education* v. *Brinkman*). Where schools in a district were largely segregated by race in 1954—not necessarily by law or even by school board policy such as in the way attendance zones were drawn—and where racially segregated schools persist, the presumption now is that the schools are segregated intentionally. The burden of proof shifts to the school board to explain that it is not responsible for the existing segregation. For single school districts, therefore, *Penick* and *Brinkman* almost entirely erase the distinction between de jure and de facto. A combination of the 1974 Detroit decision and the 1979 Ohio cases appears to mean that the Fourteenth Amendment in school segregation cases normally stops at the school district line.

VOTING

Equally complex is discrimination in voting. After the Civil War, national legislation implementing the Fourteenth and Fifteenth Amendments was occasionally invoked successfully to protect black efforts to vote in congressional elections (*Ex parte Yarbrough,* 1884). In *Guinn* v. *United States* (1915) the Court invalidated state efforts to use a "grandfather clause," exempting from a literacy test for voting all persons and their lineal descendants who had voted on or before January 1, 1866. These decisions did not, however, discourage states intent on disfranchising blacks. For one thing, the Supreme Court held in *Newberry* v. *United States* (1921) that primaries were not "elections" in the constitutional sense; clearly if blacks could be excluded from participation in primaries in one-party states, their political influence would be destroyed. Nevertheless, the equal protection clause was successfully invoked both against a state law setting up a "white primary" for the Texas Democratic Party (*Nixon* v. *Herndon,* 1927) and against a similar resolution by the Democratic State Executive Committee acting under authority of statute (*Nixon* v. *Condon,* 1932). But in *Grovey* v. *Townsend* (1935) a resolution forbidding black participation adopted by the state convention of the Democratic Party was held to be private action, and therefore not within the protective range of "equal protection." Along with the white primary, other states had already adopted literacy tests, poll taxes, and similar devices to prevent blacks from voting.

The story was not, however, to end on this note. In 1941 the Court held that the right to vote in a primary election in a one-party state, in this instance Louisiana, where the primary was a step in the election of members of Congress, was a right or privilege secured by the Constitution since the actions at the primary were officially accepted by the state. Hence, the failure of state officials, acting under "color" of state law, to count ballots properly was held a violation of the provision of the United States Criminal Code that prohibited such "state" action (*United States* v. *Classic*). In *Smith* v. *Allwright* (1944) the Court overruled *Grovey* v. *Townsend* and held that the right to vote guaranteed by the Fifteenth Amendment applied to primaries as well as general elections. Later efforts by Texas to evade the principle of that case by accepting the candidates of the Jaybird Party, a Democratic political organization that conducted an unofficial primary in which blacks could not vote, were also held invalid (*Terry* v. *Adams,* 1953).

It stood to reason that blacks would never be able to look out for their own interests without the vote. Much of the delay in implementing *Brown* after 1954, for example, resulted from the political powerlessness of those who had the most to gain from the decision. Effective access to the ballot box was thus an important condition for equality under the law. Indeed, loss of the vote a half-century earlier had helped to make possible the rigid and pervasive system of de jure segregation under attack in *Brown* and other cases.

Black organizations and their white allies became increasingly aware of the hitherto undeveloped potential of the black vote in the South. In 1961 only one in four eligible voters was registered. Further measures were therefore sought to achieve a dramatic increase in electoral strength. Adoption of the Twenty-fourth Amendment (1964), prohibiting use of a poll tax in federal elections, was a notable success. The poll tax as a requirement in state elections was invalidated in *Harper* v. *Virginia Board of Elections* (1966). The Court emphasized the economic discrimination in the $1.50 tax requisite for voting, not racial discrimination. "To introduce wealth or payment of a fee," Justice Douglas wrote for the majority, "as a measure of a voter's qualifications is to introduce a capricious or irrelevant factor. The degree of discrimination is irrelevant." Almost 30 years earlier the Court had upheld the tax against constitutional attack (*Breedlove* v. *Suttles,* 1937).

Of great significance in increasing voter registration and participation was the Voting Rights Act of 1965, amended and extended in 1982. Its measures (such as a ban on literacy tests) were extreme, but so were the evils it sought to correct. (The constitutionality of the act was unsuccessfully challenged in *South Carolina* v. *Katzenbach,* 1966.)

Three sections of the 1965 act merit attention here. *Section 2* repeats the Fifteenth Amendment's prohibition against racial discrimination in voting and applies throughout the United States. *Section 4* sets up a triggering mechanism for determining which parts of the country (mostly in the South) are subject to Section 5. *Section 5* requires that any change in a "standard, practice, or procedure with respect to voting" can take effect only after being cleared by the attorney general or by the United States District Court for the District of Columbia. The Supreme Court has interpreted "standard, practice, or procedure" to include any changes in a locale's electoral system. This preclearance requirement is satisfied only if the jurisdiction proposing the change can demonstrate that the change neither has the purpose nor will have the effect of "denying or abridging the right to vote on account of race or color." Black voting strength, therefore, cannot be weakened or diluted by a change in local election practices. For example, the Supreme Court decided that Section 5 is violated if a city covered by the act enlarges its boundaries in such a way that blacks become a smaller percentage of the voting population (*Rome* v. *United States,* 1980). Discriminatory *effect* alone is enough to violate Section 5.

Understanding the difference between "purpose" (or intent) and "effect" is necessary to grasp the significance of the change that occurred in 1982 in Section 2 of the act. Section 2 applies to existing practices (not changes). Section 5 applies to changes, but only to changes in certain parts of the country. The Supreme Court had earlier interpreted Section 2 so that a person challenging an existing electoral arrangement had to prove a discriminatory *intent* (*Mobile* v. *Bolden,* 1980). What Congress did in 1982 was essentially to say that a discriminatory *effect* in existing arrangements *in any part of the United States* now constitutes a violation of Section 2.

The Court's first opportunity to interpret the 1982 amendments came in *Thornburg* v. *Gingles* (1986), which upheld a district court ruling that the use of multimember legislative districts in North Carolina violated Section 2. According to Justice Brennan, to demonstrate that multimember districts impair a group's rights, the group (1) must be sufficiently large and geographically compact to constitute a majority in a single-member district, (2) must be politically cohesive, and (3) must have its preferred candidate out-voted in most instances by a majority that votes as a block. He added that the election of some minority candidates does not foreclose a claim under Section 2.

STATE ACTION AND EQUAL ACCESS

The Supreme Court made it clear over a century ago in the **Civil Rights Cases** that the Fourteenth Amendment does not forbid racial discrimination by everyone, but only by states and their political subdivisions. Confronted with congressional legislation guaranteeing equal access to public accommodations, it balked at giving the clause positive meaning. By reading the first and fifth sections of the Fourteenth Amendment to mean merely that Congress could pass legislation to supersede discriminatory state legislation and official acts (a power similar to that of judicial review), it preserved the existing federal system at the expense of implementing equal treatment. Bradley's opinion for the Court naively assumed that the then existing laws of all states required innkeepers and public carriers to furnish accommodations to all unobjectionable persons who applied for them, and further, that anyone refused accommodations had an adequate remedy under state law.

Private discrimination is therefore not touched by the Constitution. The line between public and private discrimination, however, is sometimes blurred. How much state involvement must there be in particular situations before the strictures of the equal protection clause apply? During the last 50 years, the Court has expanded the state action principle so that if a state becomes so "entwined" with private affairs that the action of private citizens becomes tantamount to "state action," the provisions of the Fourteenth Amendment then become applicable. Moreover, the Court has also energized the Thirteenth Amendment as authority for Congress in reaching private discrimination.

Housing. Just as laws restricting the right to vote were readily challenged, so were laws prohibiting persons from residing in certain areas because of race or color (*Buchanan* v. *Warley,* 1917). The way around this difficulty was to rely on widespread use of restrictive covenants in property deeds by which several owners promised not to sell to nonwhites, with subsequent purchasers similarly bound by the restrictive provision. In 1948, after several decades of these covenants, the Supreme Court in **Shelley v. Kraemer** severely weakened their legal importance by holding that state courts could not issue orders enforcing such covenants against a property owner who decided not to be bound by the agreement. State court action was "state action" of a kind prohibited by the equal protection clause.

Perhaps the high-water mark in thwarting state action in support of private discrimination was *Reitman* v. *Mulkey* (1967). Following a number of California legislative enactments prohibiting discrimination in the sale or rental of private property, Proposition 14, forbidding the state to deny the right of any person to sell or rent his property to anyone at his absolute discretion, was adopted by a two-to-one majority of the voters. A five-justice majority concluded that Proposition 14 was "intended to authorize, and does authorize, racial discrimination in the housing market."

In 1968, Congress enacted a "Fair Housing" title, part of a broad Civil Rights Act, outlawing discrimination in the sale or rental of federally owned or assisted housing but excluding single-family dwellings sold by an owner. In the same year, the Supreme Court discovered an alternative way of barring private discrimination in housing, based on an act of 1866. The crucial section of that act reads, "All citizens of the United States shall have the same right, in every State and Territory, as is enjoyed by white citizens thereof to inherit, purchase, lease, sell, hold and convey real and personal property." Acting on its own in *Jones* v. *Mayer* (1968) the Court upheld the right of a black complainant to sue a white housing development company for refusing to sell him a house. The lower federal courts had assumed that the 1866 statute at issue in the case, like those based on the Fourteenth Amendment, outlawed only state-required or -authorized discrimination, but the Supreme Court, relying on the Thirteenth Amendment, found it applicable to all forms of discrimination in housing, public or private.

Establishing racially discriminatory intent is nonetheless important in housing cases in which government agencies are involved. In *Arlington Heights* v. *Metropolitan Housing Development Corporation* (1977), a nonprofit development corporation desired to build racially integrated, multifamily housing on a plot zoned for single-family units. The village denied the request for rezoning, and the housing corporation brought suit. After a defeat in district court, the Court of Appeals for the Seventh Circuit reversed, citing the racially discriminatory *effects* of the refusal to rezone. The Supreme Court held otherwise. "Our decision last Term in *Washington* v. *Davis* . . ." wrote Justice Powell for the majority, "made it clear that official action will not be held unconstitutional solely because it results in a racially discriminatory impact. . . . Proof of racially discriminatory intent or purpose is required to show a violation of the Equal Protection Clause." History and current circumstances might be helpful guides in divining intent, Powell suggested.

Intent vs. Effect. As Justice Powell explained in *Arlington Heights,* the reach of the Fourteenth Amendment is less than the reach of statutes protecting civil rights. Government policy challenged as a violation of the Fourteenth Amendment must exhibit evidence of an intent to discriminate. Statutes may ban policies that have a discriminatory effect. Demonstrating the latter is easier than the former, since intent entails the mental attitudes of those who proposed or enacted a law. In situations in which a discriminatory effect is sufficient, laws are able to reach more subtle forms of discrimination.

Restaurants, Private Schools, and Clubs. In 1964 Congress passed the highly significant Civil Rights Act. Title II outlawed discrimination in hotels, restaurants, theaters, gas stations, and other public facilities affecting interstate commerce. The statutory coverage was intended to be pervasive since "affect commerce" was defined to include both establishments serving interstate travelers and those serving or selling products that had "moved" in interstate commerce. Contrary to the Court's position in the Civil Rights Cases of 1883, Congress had also invoked its powers to enforce the Fourteenth Amendment as justification for this provision of the 1964 act.

In *Heart of Atlanta Motel* v. *United States* (see Chapter Six), the Court chose to rely only on the power to regulate interstate commerce in upholding application of the new statute to motels that catered to interstate travelers. Congressional power even reached to a restaurant in Birmingham, which annually used about $70,000 worth of food that had moved in interstate commerce (*Katzenbach* v. *McClung*). In view of this extended statutory coverage, discrimination in any public accommodation became plainly unlawful.

The potency of the Thirteenth Amendment, which does not present a state action problem, was shown by a 1976 decision, *Runyan* v. *McCrary*. Here *Jones* v. *Mayer*, upholding the right to purchase property free from discrimination, was the precedent for protecting the contractual rights of black parents against commercially operated, nonsectarian private schools that refused admission to black applicants solely on grounds of race. The Court rejected arguments based on the right of association, parental rights, and the right to privacy and upheld congressional power to enforce the Thirteenth Amendment. "The majority's belated discovery of a congressional purpose," dissenting Justice White observed derisively, "which escaped this Court only a decade after the statute was passed and which escaped all other federal courts for almost a hundred years is singularly unpersuasive."

Though the judicial tendency has been to resolve doubts against racial barriers, social clubs are still free under the national Constitution to close their doors to anyone, for reasons of race, religion, or otherwise. The issue in such cases involves conflict between two constitutionally recognized values—the rights of association and of equal protection of the law. In 1972 *Moose Lodge* v. *Irvis* asked the justices to consider whether the Loyal Order of Moose forfeited its liquor license when it refused to admit K. Leroy Irvis, black majority leader of the Pennsylvania House of Representatives, as a guest of one of its members. Irvis conceded that Moose members have a constitutional right of privacy and association, permitting them to exclude him from their club. But, he argued, their club cannot hold a liquor license if they do. Allowing the club to do so would amount to state licensing of racial discrimination, in violation of the Fourteenth Amendment.

Six justices led by Rehnquist rejected the sweeping argument, instead resolving the case by severing the most objectionable tie between the state and the Harrisburg lodge: the Pennsylvania Liquor Control Board's rule that private clubs adhere to their membership rules as a condition for holding a liquor license. Justice Douglas's dissent, however, mentioned another peculiarity of state licensing—a geographical quota for clubs, which made it virtually impossible for a newly organized all-black club or a racially integrated one to obtain a liquor license in that area at the time. For Douglas, "state action" promoting racial discrimination remained.

More recently, state and local governments have attempted to eliminate sexual as well as racial discrimination in private organizations and clubs. So far the Supreme Court has upheld these laws even though the justices recognize a First Amendment right of association (see *New York State Club Association* v. *New York City,* 1988, in Chapter Ten).

GENDER, ALIENAGE,
AND THE "NEW" EQUAL PROTECTION

Since virtually all legislation involves classification, it is not surprising that the equal protection clause should be invoked frequently by those challenging state acts under the police power. For a while, the Court used a two-tier model for deciding cases under the equal protection clause. For most classifications, the justices applied the old "rational basis test," asking only whether the classification in question had a *rational* (or reasonable) *relation* to a *legitimate* state interest. For "suspect classifications" such as race, they turned to the "strict scrutiny test." Here, the classification had to be *necessarily* related to a *compelling* government interest. If a law measured by the first test was almost certain to pass constitutional muster, a law measured by the second was almost certain to fail.

Recently, the justices have added a third tier to the scheme. Used especially for gender-based classifications and those involving illegitimate children, the Court applies what might be called the "moderate scrutiny test." Here, the question is whether the challenged statute is *substantially related* to an *important* state interest.

The equal protection clause has also become a far-reaching tool for judicial protection of fundamental rights specified or implicit in the Constitution. In *Skinner* v. *Oklahoma* (1942), for example, the Court struck down a compulsory sterilization scheme mandated by Oklahoma for certain, but not all, classes of habitual criminals. The classification threatened "marriage and procreation," wrote Justice Douglas, which "are fundamental to the very existence and survival of the race." Laws that infringe on rights the Court deems fundamental are judged by the strict scrutiny test. This use of the equal protection clause to shield particular rights is called the "new equal protection" or "substantive equal protection."

An instructive illustration of the new equal protection is **Shapiro** v. **Thompson** (1969). Held invalid were one-year residence requirements states imposed on all persons seeking welfare assistance. Justice Brennan for the majority spoke of the "right" of freedom to travel throughout the states: "Thus, the purpose of deterring the in-migration of indigents cannot serve as justification for the classification created by the one-year waiting period, since that purpose is constitutionally impermissible. Because the classification here touches on the fundamental right of interstate movement, its constitutionality must be judged by the stricter standard—whether it promotes a compelling state interest. Under this standard, the waiting period requirement clearly violates the Equal Protection Clause."

Is education a "fundamental right"? If so, financing of public schools by a property tax stands in constitutional jeopardy because of the substantial inequalities present between property-rich and property-poor districts. But in *San Antonio Independent School District* v. *Rodriguez* (1972), five justices declared that education is "not among the rights afforded explicit protection under our Constitution." It does not fall within any of the categories calling for strict judicial scrutiny. Accordingly, the Texas local property tax funding law for public schools does not deny equal protection to schoolchildren residing in districts with a low property tax base. The majority agreed that the tax system needed reform, but this "must come from the law makers and from the pressures of those who elect them."

In *Rodriguez* the Court might have held that education is a fundamental right and poverty a suspect classification. Either finding would have placed a burden on the state to show a compelling interest. Instead, the Court rejected both possible grounds in upholding the Texas scheme for financing public schools, which admittedly permitted substantial disparities in expenditures per pupil between districts.

Gender. Because the Constitution has been the battleground for so many years in the struggle for racial equality, one might suppose that sexual equality has occupied the attention of Congress and the courts for just as long. It has not. Until recently, the legal (and constitutional) status of women in the United States was one of substantial inequality.

Making the nation free of discrimination based on gender has been a national priority for less than three decades. There have been some citizens fighting gender-based discriminations since the earliest years of the Republic, but for a long time justices of the Supreme Court were not among them. Even in 1948, the year of the Court's ruling banning enforcement of racially restrictive covenants in deeds and the year of the first insertion since Reconstruction of a strong civil rights plank in a national party platform, six justices found no constitutional defect in a Michigan bartender law: Although men could be licensed as bartenders, a woman could be licensed only if she were the wife or daughter of the owner of the bar. But women could still work as *waitresses* in the bar. Declared Justice Frankfurter, "The fact that women may now have achieved the virtues that men have long claimed as their prerogatives and now indulge in vices that men have long practiced, does not preclude the States from drawing a sharp line between the sexes . . ." (*Goesaert* v. *Cleary,* 1948).

As late as 1961 (seven years after the *Brown* school segregation decision and the first year of President John Kennedy's "New Frontier"), the Court unanimously upheld a Florida law that excluded women from jury duty unless they affirmatively requested to be added to the list of potential jurors. At that time, three states flatly prohibited women from serving on juries, and 17 other states plus the District of Columbia had laws similar to Florida's. Justice Harlan did not think such laws were unreasonable. "Despite the enlightened emancipation of women from the restrictions and protections of bygone years, and their entry into many parts of community life formerly considered to be reserved to men, woman is still regarded as the center of home and family life" (*Hoyt* v. *Florida,* 1961).

Today, gender-based distinctions run a high risk of unconstitutionality. In 1973, in **Frontiero** v. **Richardson,** four justices were willing to consider gender a suspect category. A fifth justice for this view has not come forth. Challenged under the equal protection component of the Fifth Amendment was a Defense Department policy that treated male and female personnel differently when obtaining support for dependent spouses. Even without the tough standard of strict scrutiny, however, four other justices probed the "rationality" of the statute and reached the same result.

Justice Brennan's opinion in **Craig** v. **Boren** (1976), spells out the level of scrutiny the Court now seems to be giving to gender-based distinctions. In this case, an Oklahoma statute prohibiting the sale of 3.2 percent beer to males under 21 and to females under 18 was found to fall short constitutionally. "[T]o withstand constitutional challenge, previous cases establish that classifications by gender must serve important governmental objectives and must be substantially related to achievement of those objectives." In other words, the purpose of the statute must be valid, and the justices must be convinced that another law treating the sexes equally would not do as well. As *Craig* demonstrates, males can use the "new" equal protection to attack gender-based discrimination. The Constitution cuts both ways.

Although the Fourteenth Amendment has been useful in attacking sex-based restrictions, Congress has played an important part through enactment of Title VII of the Civil Rights Act of 1964, which bans gender as well as racial and religious discrimination in employment, salary matters, promotions, and the like. Indeed, in terms of the volume of litigation alone, there have been more suits initiated under Title VII than under the Fourteenth Amendment. Cases brought under Title VII differ from those brought under the Fourteenth Amendment in at least two major respects. First, the Fourteenth Amendment constrains only state governments and their political subdivisions, whereas Title VII includes private employers. Second, discriminatory intent is a necessary element of a violation of the Fourteenth Amendment; for Title VII, only discriminatory effect need be demonstrated.

Another significant statutory provision, especially for colleges and universities, is Title IX of the Education Amendments of 1972, prohibiting sex discrimination in "any education program or activity receiving Federal financial assistance." In *Grove City College* v. *Bell* (1984), the Court determined that the law applied to an institution with students who received direct federal financial aid even though the institution itself accepted no funds from the government. Under the statute, institutions not in compliance with regulations written by the Department of Education implementing Title IX would be denied federal aid. The cutoff of funds would also apply, the Court said, to an institution's students receiving direct support, such as Basic Educational Opportunity Grants. Although that interpretation left virtually no American campus outside the reach of Title IX, the Court then held that federal assistance to *one part* of a college's program did not trigger *institution-wide* coverage, thus limiting the impact of institutional sanctions under Title IX. In the Civil Rights Restoration Act of 1988, Congress overturned the Court's narrow reading of Title IX, leaving no doubt that it intended the cutoff of aid to be institution-wide.

In other cases, a majority of the Court has relied on the fact that sometimes the sexes are not "similarly situated." This conclusion led to *Michael M.* v. *Superior Court* (1981), which upheld California's statutory rape law against an equal protection attack. Males alone were made criminally liable. Since only the female can become pregnant, the state constitutionally could elect to punish the party to sexual intercourse on whom fewer natural burdens would fall should a pregnancy result. Reliance on the same principle was even more pronounced and important in **Rostker** v. **Goldberg** (1981). In this case, six justices expressed considerable deference to Congress and sustained the constitutionality of the Military Selective Service Act, which authorizes the president to require draft registration for males but not females.

Whatever the status of male-only draft registration, single-sex education in state-supported institutions of higher education now seems almost certainly a violation of the Fourteenth Amendment. At least the Court said as much with respect to nursing instruction in *Mississippi University for Women* v. *Hogan* (1982). Joe Hogan could enroll in two state-supported coeducational nursing schools in Mississippi but not the nursing school at MUW, said the state, because he was male. "Our decisions . . . establish that the party seeking to uphold a statute that classifies individuals on the basis of their gender must carry the burden of showing an 'exceedingly persuasive justification' for the classification," wrote Justice O'Connor for the majority. The justices found unpersuasive the state's argument that a female-only nursing school served a substantial government interest by compensating for discrimination against women. Instead, the majority concluded that the Mississippi policy only tended to perpetuate the stereotyped view of nursing as exclusively a woman's job. Furthermore, even though Title IX of the Education Amendments of 1972 expressly authorized traditionally single-sex state universities to continue admitting only men or women, Congress could not permit by statute something the Fourteenth Amendment forbids.

Whether the justices employ the "moderate scrutiny test" or discuss differences in treatment in terms of who is "similarly situated," it is clear that the Court has ample discretion in picking and choosing between those gender considerations that should be allowed to matter and those that should not.

Alienage. Laws that discriminate against aliens do not fit into neat categories. As early as 1886, the Court invalidated a local ordinance in California that discriminated against Chinese laundry workers by requiring permits for all wooden buildings used for laundrying

(*Yick Wo* v. *Hopkins*). In 1915, the Court struck down an Arizona law that discriminated against aliens in employment by requiring that at least 80 percent of any firm's employees be U.S. citizens (*Truax* v. *Raich*).

Today, congressional statutes aimed at aliens are generally judged under the rational basis test, meaning that the Court recognizes wide discretion for national policies in this area, provided they are not "arbitrary." But state laws are a different matter. Although the Court has not been completely consistent, these statutes are usually judged by the tough "strict scrutiny test," with the justices regarding "alienage" as a "suspect classification."

For example, a Connecticut law requiring U.S. citizenship for admission to the practice of law was held invalid in *In re Griffiths* (1973). In contrast, *Foley* v. *Connelie* (1978) upheld against an equal protection challenge the New York statute limiting to U.S. citizens appointment as members of the state police force. The standard was that citizenship may be a relevant qualification for fulfilling "important nonelective executive, legislative, and judicial positions held by officers who participate directly in the formulation, execution, or review of broad public policy." Five justices the following term were persuaded that *Foley* was controlling with respect to teachers in public schools (*Ambach* v. *Norwick,* 1979).

Even children who are aliens not "legally admitted" into the United States cannot be discriminated against when it comes to getting an education. In *Plyler* v. *Doe* (1982), the Court considered a Texas statute that authorized local school districts to deny enrollment to such children. Admitting that "undocumented aliens" (unlike other aliens) were not a "suspect class" and still holding that education was not a "fundamental right," the justices concluded that the Texas law, without furthering some substantial state goal, imposed a lifetime hardship on a class of children not accountable for their status.

Uncertainty surrounding the constitutionality of such laws continues. As Justice Powell acknowledged in *Ambach,* "decisions of this Court regarding the permissibility of statutory classifications involving aliens have not formed an unwavering line over the years."

AFFIRMATIVE ACTION

As parts of this chapter illustrate, much litigation under the equal protection clause has been aimed at halting practices deemed harmful to certain minorities. The focus in these cases has been on what the Constitution *prohibits*.

In a parallel development, various institutions—themselves not necessarily guilty of racial discrimination—have voluntarily established remedial programs. Their efforts are broadly aimed at correcting "societal discrimination." This affirmative action (also termed "reverse discrimination" or "preferential treatment") has been hauled into court as itself being a violation of the Constitution's ban on racial discrimination. So the question becomes one of what the Constitution *permits*. For instance, if a state university makes a special effort to recruit and to admit members of certain racial groups and to apply different criteria in assessing their qualifications, has the equal protection clause been compromised? Opponents of affirmative action argue that such programs are certainly not in the spirit of keeping the Constitution "color-blind." Proponents reply that a cessation of discrimination is not enough. Positive measures are needed, they say, to overcome the residual effects of generations of discrimination.

In other situations, institutions have practiced discrimination, and courts have ordered remedial programs in hiring and promotions. Opponents have attacked these plans as well because they are said to be too extreme: They reward those who may not have been actual victims of prior discrimination and deny rights to racial majorities.

The catch is that jobs and seats in medical school classes, for instance, are finite. To give to one means to withhold from someone else. It may also be the case that those "nonminority" individuals who claim to be hurt by affirmative action are in many situations those least able to bear the burden. They are probably also those who have benefited least from the effects of invidious discrimination that do remain. Given the extent of the controversy surrounding both voluntary and involuntary affirmative action, it is not surprising that the issue has reached the Supreme Court. Decisions have involved both public and private employers and both the Fourteenth Amendment and the Civil Rights Act of 1964.

The Supreme Court first squarely confronted affirmative action in *Regents* v. *Bakke* (1978). The medical school at the University of California at Davis operated a special admissions program in which 16 of the 100 seats in the entering class were set aside for qualifying minority students. No white had ever been admitted through the special admissions program. After his rejection in 1974, Allan Bakke, a white male, challenged the program on equal protection grounds, and the California Supreme Court ordered his admission. For those hoping for a clear, forthright, thunderbolt pronouncement by the High Court, the decision in *Bakke* was a disappointment. Bakke won (and so gained admission to medical school) but so did advocates of affirmative action. These seemingly conflicting results came about because the justices were divided into three camps.

Justices Brennan, White, Marshall, and Blackmun found no constitutional violation in the admissions program at Davis. Neither did they see it as being in conflict with Title VI of the Civil Rights Act of 1964, which outlaws racial discrimination in programs receiving federal funding. Four others (Stevens, Burger, Stewart, and Rehnquist) considered the Davis plan a violation of Title VI and so did not decide the constitutional question. Left was Justice Powell. The Davis plan was flawed, he thought, because race was used in effect as an exclusionary factor. Race, however, could be taken into account as an informing factor, especially to achieve racial diversity in the student body for educational reasons. So, combining Powell's conclusion with that of the Brennan group, one finds that race can constitutionally be used in evaluating applications for admission. Combining Powell's view with the position put forth by the Stevens group, the particular plan in question at Davis was unlawful. Significantly, Powell noted the absence in this case "of judicial, legislative, or administrative findings of constitutional or statutory violations. . . . After such findings have been made, the governmental interest in preferring members of the injured groups at the expense of others is substantial, since the legal rights of the victims must be vindicated."

A legislative determination was present in *Fullilove* v. *Klutznick* (1980), where six justices found constitutional a statutory requirement that "absent an administrative waiver, 10 percent of the federal funds granted for local public works projects must be used by the state or local grantee to procure services or supplies from businesses owned and controlled by members of statutorily identified minority groups." Finding ample constitutional authority under the spending and commerce powers and the enforcement provision (Section 5) of the Fourteenth Amendment, Chief Justice Burger for a plurality was "satisfied that Congress had abundant historical basis from which it could conclude that traditional procurement practices, when applied to minority businesses, could perpetuate the effects of prior discrimination."

Title VII of the Civil Rights Act of 1964 authorizes "make whole" remedies for victims of past discrimination, but may employers voluntarily give preferential treatment to minorities? *United Steelworkers of America* v. *Weber* (1979) upheld the legality of an affirmative action plan agreed to by a union and a corporation. *Weber* shows that even if the Supreme Court someday were to lose its power of judicial review, statutory interpretation would nonetheless allow the justices considerable influence on the course of public policy. In this case, the union and a plant in Gramercy, Louisiana, operated by the Kaiser Aluminum & Chemical Corporation entered into a collective bargaining agreement, part of which was designed to increase the number of blacks in craft jobs. Although no solid evidence of intentional discrimination in hiring or in admission to craft apprenticeships was part of the record, the Office of Federal Contract Compliance, acting under executive order, had encouraged the union and the company to develop a plan. At stake were federal contracts and therefore jobs and profits. In operation, the plan meant choosing blacks with less seniority over white workers with more. One of the latter was Brian Weber, who thought the plan violated Title VII. In part the statute declares, "It shall be an unlawful employment practice for any employer [or] labor organization . . . to discriminate against any individual because of his race, color, religion, sex, or national origin in admission to, or employment in, any program established to provide apprenticeship or other training."

For the majority of five (neither Powell nor Stevens participated), Justice Brennan reviewed the legislative history of the act. It did not speak precisely to this question, for the simple reason that discrimination against blacks and other minorities was uppermost in the minds of members of Congress when the law was passed 15 years before. Since the statute was enacted for the purpose of helping minorities, "the natural inference is that Congress chose not to forbid all voluntary race-conscious affirmative action," Brennan concluded.

Weber was reaffirmed and applied by six justices to a gender-based affirmative action plan in *Johnson* v. *Transportation Agency* (1987). Officials in Santa Clara County, California, had a long-range goal of building a work force that reflected the proportion of women and racial minorities in the area. Seven people qualified for a road dispatcher's job, and the agency selected a female even though a male candidate had scored higher on the promotion test. Justice Brennan's majority opinion drew a parallel with *Weber*. Perhaps critical in the Court's eye was the temporary nature of the program. "[T]here is ample assurance that the [county] does not . . . [plan] to maintain a permanent racial and sexual balance." Dissenting, Justice Scalia contended that Title VII should not be allowed to "overcome the effect not of the employer's own discrimination, but of societal attitudes that have limited entry of certain races, or of a particular sex, into certain jobs."

If *Weber* and *Johnson* display wide judicial tolerance for voluntary affirmative action plans under Title VII, two cases in 1986 were a significant victory for affirmative action in situations with a history of discrimination. Against the position taken by the Department of Justice, *Sheet Metal Workers* v. *E.E.O.C.* and *Firefighters* v. *Cleveland* approved race-based hiring and promotion where the beneficiaries of the policies were not victims of the discrimination the remedial plan was designed to correct. Contrary rulings in these cases would have limited the effectiveness of the remedial steps. Moreover, the latter decision found nothing in Title VII to bar such remedies as part of a *consent decree* (a judicial order embodying terms agreed to by the opposing parties). Consent decrees facilitate settlement of Title VII disputes: Lengthy litigation is avoided, it is unnecessary to prove many facts that would otherwise have to be shown, and enforcement is often easier.

The Court's acceptance of most affirmative action, whether under Title VII or the Fourteenth Amendment, may end when layoffs result. In **Wygant** v. **Jackson Board of Education** (1986), five justices overturned a collective bargaining agreement that provided for retention of the most senior teachers during layoffs "except that at no time will there be a greater percentage of minority personnel laid off than the current percentage of minority personnel employed at the time of the layoff." The board and the union wanted to retain the more recently hired minority teachers. The Court's view seemed to be that race-based layoffs would be acceptable only to correct prior discrimination, not present in this case. This view prevailed even though voluntary race-based hiring is constitutionally permitted in the absence of proven discrimination.

When discrimination is present, however, the Court continues to approve stringent measures. In *United States* v. *Paradise* (1987), a bare majority upheld a court-ordered plan that set up a one-for-one racial quota for promotions in the Alabama highway patrol. The Justice Department had argued that the plan was too extreme and violated the Fourteenth Amendment. According to Justice Brennan's plurality opinion, "the relief ordered survives even strict scrutiny analysis: it is 'narrowly tailored' to serve a 'compelling governmental purpose.' " In reaching this conclusion Brennan relied on four criteria: (1) the necessity for the relief and the efficacy of other measures, (2) the flexibility and duration of the relief, (3) the relationship of the numerical goals to the relevant labor market, and (4) the impact of the relief on third parties. Chief Justice Rehnquist and Justices O'Connor, Scalia, and White maintained in dissent that the plan went too far because it was not essential to a discrimination-free promotion policy.

The *Paradise* dissenters' concerns prevailed in *Richmond* v. *J. A. Croson Co.* (1989), a high significant decision. Here, six justices invalidated the city's 30 percent minority set-aside quota for contractors. "Under Richmond's scheme," wrote Justice O'Connor for the majority, "a successful black, Hispanic or Oriental entrepreneur from anywhere in the country enjoys an absolute preference over other citizens based solely on their race." Distinguishing *Fullilove*, O'Connor applied the strict scrutiny test because the city had not established a convincing record of purposeful municipal discrimination. The policy fell because it was "not narrowly tailored to remedy the effects of prior discrimination." *Croson* calls into question similar policies in 36 states and in at least 190 cities.

Affirmative action, whether voluntary or involuntary, will undoubtedly continue to trouble the Court. As the record demonstrates, the justices have not spoken unequivocally. This may be both wise and expected, in view of the divisiveness and complexity of the issue. Changes in the personnel of the Court may also keep these questions in flux. Nonetheless, the power of precedent remains on the side of those favoring substantial remedies. An ineffective barrier against discrimination for so long, the Fourteenth Amendment and the Civil Rights Act in the main have not been allowed to block extraordinary measures to right past wrongs.

KEY TERMS

equal protection

separate but equal

unitary school system

dual school system

de jure segregation

de facto segregation

racially identifiable
  schools

grandfather clause

white primary

poll tax

state action

discriminatory intent

discriminatory effect

substantive equal
  protection

rational basis test

strict scrutiny test

moderate scrutiny test

affirmative action

Civil Rights Act of
  1964

consent decree

QUERIES

1. Evaluate the views on the meaning of the Fourteenth Amendment in the Civil Rights Cases, *Plessy* v. *Ferguson,* and *Brown* v. *Board of Education.*

2. In *Milliken* v. *Bradley,* why did Justice Marshall believe that the segregation in Detroit was de jure segregation? Why did Marshall think the majority had retreated from its historic position in defense of racial justice?

3. Have the justices made gender a "suspect classification"?

4. Appraise the exchange between Justices Harlan and Brennan in *Shapiro* v. *Thompson.* What are the implications of each position for the role of the Court?

SELECTED READINGS

ACKERMAN, BRUCE A. "Beyond Carolene Products." 98 *Harvard Law Review* 713 (1985).

BARDOLPH, RICHARD, ed. *The Civil Rights Record: Black Americans and the Law, 1849–1970.* New York: Crowell, 1970.

BULLOCK, CHARLES S., III, and CHARLES M. LAMB. *Implementing Civil Rights Policy.* Monterey, Calif.: Brooks/Cole, 1984.

COTT, NANCY F. "Women's Rights: Unspeakable Issues in the Constitution." 77 *Yale Review* 382 (1988).

ELY, JOHN HART. "The Constitutionality of Reverse Discrimination." 41 *University of Chicago Law Review* 723 (1974).

FREEDMAN, ANN E. "Sex Equality, Sex Differences, and the Supreme Court." 92 *Yale Law Journal* 913 (1983).

GLAZER, NATHAN. *Affirmative Discrimination: Ethnic Inequality in Public Policy.* New York: Basic Books, 1975.

GRAGLIA, L. A. *Disaster by Decree: The Supreme Court's Decisions on Race and Schools.* Ithaca, N.Y.: Cornell University Press, 1976.

HARRIS, ROBERT J. *The Quest for Equality.* Baton Rouge: Louisiana State University Press, 1960.

HULL, ELIZABETH. *Without Justice for All: The Constitutional Rights of Aliens.* Westport, Conn.: Greenwood, 1985.

KITCH, EDMUND W. "The Return of Color-Consciousness to the Constitution: Weber, Dayton and Columbus." 1979 *Supreme Court Review* 1.

KLUGER, RICHARD F. *Simple Justice: The History of Brown v. Board of Education and Black America's Struggle for Equality.* New York: Knopf, 1976.

LOFGREN, CHARLES A. *The Plessy Case.* New York: Oxford University Press, 1987.

PELTASON, J. W. *Fifty-eight Lonely Men.* New York: Harcourt, Brace and World, 1961 (focuses on federal judges in the South in the years immediately after *Brown*).

SALOMONE, ROSEMARY C. *Equal Education under the Law: Legal Rights and Federal Policy in the Post-Brown Era.* New York: St. Martin's, 1986.

SCHWARTZ, BERNARD. *Swann's Way: The School Busing Case and the Supreme Court.* New York: Oxford University Press, 1986.

SCHWARTZ, HERMAN. "The 1986 and 1987 Affirmative Action Cases: It's All Over but the Shouting." 86 *Michigan Law Review* 524 (1987).

STEINER, GILBERT Y. *Constitutional Inequality.* Washington, D.C.: Brookings Institute, 1985 (reviews the Equal Rights Amendment).

STEPHENSON, D. GRIER, JR. "Weber, Affirmative Action, and Restorative Justice." 108 *USA Today* 48 (May 1980).

THERNSTRONE, ABIGAIL M. *Whose Votes Count? Affirmative Action and Minority Voting Rights.* Cambridge, Mass.: Harvard University Press, 1987.

VOSE, CLEMENT. *Caucasians Only: The Supreme Court, the NAACP, and the Restrictive Covenant Cases.* Berkeley: University of California Press, 1959.

WILLIAMS, WENDY M. "Sex Discrimination: Closing the Law's Gender Gap." In Herman Schwartz, ed. *The Burger Years.* New York: Penguin, 1988.

Civil Rights Cases
109 U.S. 3, 3 S.Ct. 18, 27 L.Ed. 835 (1883)

Five cases involving the Civil Rights Act passed by Congress in 1875 were settled by this decision. The act, which was intended to implement the Thirteenth and Fourteenth Amendments, made it a misdemeanor to deny any person equal rights and privileges in inns, theaters and amusement places, and transportation facilities, regardless of color or previous conditions of servitude. Majority: Bradley, Blatchford, Field, Gray, Matthews, Miller, Waite, Woods. Dissenting: Harlan.

MR. JUSTICE BRADLEY delivered the opinion of the Court. . . .

The essence of the law is, not to declare broadly that all persons shall be entitled to the full and equal enjoyment of the accommodations, advantages, facilities, and privileges of inns, public conveyances, and theatres; but that such enjoyment shall not be subject to any conditions applicable only to citizens of a particular race or color, or who had been in a previous condition of servitude. . . .

Has congress constitutional power to make such a law? Of course, no one will contend that the power to pass it was contained in the Constitution before the adoption of the last three amendments. The power is sought, first, in the Fourteenth Amendment. . . .

It is State action of a particular character that is prohibited. Individual invasion of individual rights is not the subject matter of the amendment. It has a deeper and broader scope. It nullifies and makes void all State legislation, and State action of every kind, which impairs the privileges and immunities of citizens of the United States, or which injures them in life, liberty or property without due process of law, or which denies to any of them the equal protection of the laws. It not only does this, but, in order that the national will, thus declared, may not be a mere *brutum fulmen*, the last section of the amendment invests Congress with power to enforce it by appropriate legislation. To enforce what? To enforce the prohibition. To adopt appropriate legislation for correcting the effects of such prohibited State laws and State acts, and thus to render them effectually null, void, and innocuous. This is the legislative power conferred upon Congress, and this is the whole of it. It does not invest Congress with power to legislate upon subjects which are within the domain of State legislation; but to provide modes of relief against State legislation, or State action, of the kind referred to. It does not authorize Congress to create a code of municipal law for the regulation of private rights; but to provide modes of redress against the operation of State laws, and the action of State officers, executive or judicial, when these are subversive of the fundamental rights specified in the amendment.

. . . Until some State law has been passed, or some State action through its officers or agents has been taken, adverse to the rights of citizens sought to be protected by the Fourteenth Amendment, no legislation of the United States under said amendment nor any proceeding under such legislation, can be called into activity: for the prohibitions of the amendment are against State laws and acts done under State authority. Of course, legislation may, and should be, provided in advance to meet the exigency when it arises; but it should be adapted to the mischief and wrong which the amendment was intended to provide against; and that is, State laws, or State action of some kind, adverse to the rights of the citizen secured by the amendment. Such legislation cannot properly cover the whole domain of rights appertaining to life, liberty and property, defining them and providing for their vindication. That would be to establish a code of municipal law regulative of all private rights between man and man in society. It would be to make Congress take the place of the State legislatures and to supersede them. . . .

If this legislation is appropriate for enforcing the prohibitions of the amendment, it is difficult to see where it is to stop. Why may not Congress with equal show of authority enact a code of laws for the enforcement and vindication of all rights of life, liberty, and property? . . . The truth is, that the implication of a power to legislate in this manner is based upon the assumption that if the States are forbidden to legislate or act in a particular way on a particular subject, and power is conferred upon Congress to enforce the prohibition, this gives Congress power to legislate generally upon that subject, and not merely power to provide modes of redress against such State legislation or action. The assumption is certainly unsound. It is repugnant to the Tenth Amendment of the Constitution, which declares that powers not delegated to the United States by the Constitution, nor prohibited by it to the States, are reserved to the States respectively or to the people. . . .

But the power of Congress to adopt direct and primary, as distinguished from corrective legislation, on the subject in hand, is sought, in the second place, from the Thirteenth Amendment, which abolishes slavery. This amendment declares "that neither slavery, nor involuntary servitude, except as a punishment for crime, whereof the party shall have been duly convicted, shall exist within the United States, or any place subject to their jurisdiction"; and it gives Congress power to enforce the amendment by appropriate legislation. . . .

. . . There were thousands of free colored people in this country before the abolition of slavery, enjoying all the essential rights of life, liberty and property the same as white citizens; yet no one, at that time, thought that it was any invasion of his personal status as a freeman because he was not admitted to all the privileges enjoyed by white citizens, or because he was subjected to discriminations in the enjoyment of accommodations in inns, public conveyances and places of amusement. Mere discriminations on account of race or color were not regarded as badges of slavery. If, since that time, the enjoyment of equal rights in all these respects has become established by constitutional enactment, it is not by force of the Thirteenth Amendment (which merely abolishes slavery), but by force of the Fourteenth and Fifteenth Amendments. . . .

MR. JUSTICE HARLAN dissenting. . . .

I am of the opinion that such discrimination practiced by corporations and individuals in the exercise of their public or quasi public functions is a badge of servitude the imposition of which Congress may prevent under its power, by appropriate legislation, to enforce the Thirteenth Amendment; and, consequently, without reference to its enlarged power under the Fourteenth Amendment, the act of March 1, 1875, is not, in my judgment, repugnant to the Constitution. . . . The assumption that this amendment [the Fourteenth] consists wholly of prohibitions upon State laws and State proceedings in hostility to its provisions, is unauthorized by its language. [Its] first clause. . . . "All persons born or naturalized in the United States, and subject to the jurisdiction thereof, are citizens of the United States, and of the State wherein they reside"—is of a distinctly affirmative character. In its application to the colored race . . . it created and granted, as well as citizenship of the United States, citizenship of the State in which they respectively resided. It introduced all of that race, whose ancestors had been imported and sold as slaves, at once, into the political community known as the "People of the United States." They became, instantly, citizens of the United States, and of their respective States. Further, they were brought, by this supreme act of the nation, within the direct operation of that provision of the Constitution which declares that "the citizens of each State shall be entitled to all privileges and immunities of citizens in the several States."

The citizenship thus acquired by that race, in virtue of an affirmative grant from the nation, may be protected, not alone by the judicial branch of the government, but by congressional legislation of a primary direct character; this, because the power of Congress is not restricted to the enforcement of prohibitions upon State laws or State action. It is, in terms distinct and positive, to enforce "the *provisions of this article*" of amendment; not simply those of a prohibitive character, but the provisions—*all* of the provisions—affirmative and prohibitive, of the amendment. . . .

It is said that any interpretation of the Fourteenth Amendment different from that adopted by the majority of the court, would imply that Congress had authority to enact a municipal code for all the States, covering every matter affecting the life, liberty, and property of the citizens of the several States. Not so. . . . The personal rights and immunities recognized in the prohibitive clauses of the amendment were, prior to its adoption, under the protection, primarily, of the States, while rights, created by or derived from the United States, have always been, and, in the nature of things, should always be, primarily, under the protection of the general government. Exemption from race discrimination in respect of the civil rights which are fundamental in *citizenship* in a republican government, is, as we have seen, a new right, created by the nation, with express power in Congress, by legislation, to enforce the constitutional provision from which it is derived. If, in some sense, such race discrimination is, within the letter of the last clause of the first section, a denial of that equal protection of the laws which is secured against State denial to all persons, whether citizens or not, it cannot be possible that a mere prohibition upon such State denial, or a prohibition upon State laws abridging the privileges and immunities of citizens of the United States, takes from the nation the power which it has uniformly exercised of protecting, by direct primary legislation, those privileges and immunities which existed under the Constitution before the adoption of the Fourteenth Amendment, or have been created by that amendment in behalf of those thereby made *citizens* of their respective States. . . .

Plessy v. *Ferguson*
163 U.S. 537, 16 S.Ct. 1138, 41 L.Ed. 256 (1896)

A Louisiana statute of 1890 required railroad companies carrying passengers within the state to provide "equal but separate" accommodations for white and "colored" persons, empowered train officials to enforce the law, and provided penalties for those who refused to obey segregation orders. The statute was upheld by the Supreme Court of Louisiana, and Homer Plessy, a black passenger who had been charged with violating the act, brought the case to the Supreme Court. Majority: Brown, Field, Fuller, Gray, Peckham, Shiras, White. Dissenting: Harlan. Not participating: Brewer.

MR. JUSTICE BROWN . . . delivered the opinion of the Court. . . .

The constitutionality of this act is attacked upon the ground that it conflicts both with the Thirteenth Amendment of the Constitution, abolishing slavery, and the Fourteenth Amendment, which prohibits certain restrictive legislation on the part of the States.

1. That it does not conflict with the Thirteenth Amendment, which abolished slavery and involuntary servitude, except as a punishment for crime, is too clear for argument. . . .

2. By the Fourteenth Amendment, all persons born or naturalized in the United States, and subject to the jurisdiction thereof, are made citizens of the United States and of the State wherein they reside; and the States are forbidden from making or enforcing any law which shall abridge the privileges or immunities of citizens of the United States, or shall deprive any person of life, liberty, or property without due process of law, or deny to any person within their jurisdiction the equal protection of the laws. . . .

The object of the amendment was undoubtedly to enforce the absolute equality of the two races before the law, but in the nature of things it could not have been intended to abolish distinctions based upon color, or to enforce social, as distinguished from political equality, or a commingling of the two races upon terms unsatisfactory to either. Laws permitting, and even requiring, their separation in places where they are liable to be brought into contact do not necessarily imply the inferiority of either race to the other, and have been generally, if not universally, recognized as within the competency of the state legislatures in the exercise of their police power. The most common instance of this is connected with the establishment of separate schools for white and colored children, which has been held to be a valid exercise of the legislative power even by courts of States where the political rights of the colored race have been longest and most earnestly enforced.

One of the earliest of these cases is that of *Roberts* v. *City of Boston* [1849], in which the Supreme Judicial Court of Massachusetts held that the general school committee of Boston had power to make provisions for the instruction of colored children in separate schools established exclusively for them, and to prohibit their attendance upon the other schools. . . .

. . . Similar laws have been enacted by Congress under its general power of legislation over the District of Columbia . . . as well as by the legislatures of many of the States, and have been generally, if not uniformly, sustained by the courts. . . .

The distinction between laws interfering with the political equality of the negro and those requiring the separation of the two races in schools, theatres, and railway carriages has been frequently drawn by this court. . . .

So far, then, as a conflict with the Fourteenth Amendment is concerned the case reduces itself to the question whether the statute of Louisiana is a reasonable regulation, and with respect to this there must necessarily be a large discretion on the part of the legislature. In determining the question of reasonableness it is at liberty to act with reference to the established usages, customs and traditions of the people, and with a view to the promotion of their comfort, and the preservation of the public peace and good order. Gauged by this standard, we cannot say that a law which authorizes or even requires the separation of the two races in public conveyances is unreasonable, or more obnoxious to the Fourteenth Amendment than the acts of Congress requiring separate schools for colored children in the District of Columbia, the constitutionality of which does not seem to have been questioned, or the corresponding acts of state legislatures.

We consider the underlying fallacy of the plaintiff's argument to consist in the assumption that the enforced separation of the two races stamps the colored race with a badge of inferiority. If this be

so, it is not by reason of anything found in the act, but solely because the colored race chooses to put that construction upon it. The argument necessarily assumes that if, as has been more than once the case, and is not unlikely to be so again, the colored race should become the dominant power in the state legislature, and should enact a law in precisely similar terms, it would thereby relegate the white race to an inferior position. We imagine that the white race, at least, would not acquiesce in this assumption. The argument also assumes, that social prejudices may be overcome by legislation, and that equal rights cannot be secured to the negro except by an enforced commingling of the two races. We cannot accept this proposition. If the two races are to meet upon terms of social equality, it must be the result of natural affinities, a mutual appreciation of each other's merits and a voluntary consent of individuals. . . . Legislation is powerless to eradicate racial instincts or to abolish distinctions based upon physical differences, and the attempt to do so can only result in accentuating the differences of the present situation. If the civil and political rights of both races be equal one cannot be inferior to the other civilly or politically. If one race be inferior to the other socially, the Constitution of the United States cannot put them upon the same plane. . . .

The judgment of the court below is, therefore,

Affirmed.

MR. JUSTICE HARLAN, dissenting. . . .

. . . [I]n view of the Constitution, in the eye of the law, there is in this country no superior, dominant, ruling class of citizens. There is no caste here. Our Constitution is color-blind, and neither knows nor tolerates classes among citizens. In respect of civil rights, all citizens are equal before the law. The humblest is the peer of the most powerful. The law regards man as man, and takes no account of his surroundings or of his color when his civil rights as guaranteed by the supreme law of the land are involved. It is, therefore, to be regretted that this high tribunal, the final expositor of the fundamental law of the land, has reached the conclusion that it is competent for a state to regulate the enjoyment by citizens of their civil rights solely upon the basis of race. . . .

In my opinion, the judgment this day rendered will, in time, prove to be quite as pernicious as the decision made by this tribunal in the *Dred Scott* case. . . . The present decision, it may well be apprehended, will not only stimulate aggressions, more or less brutal and irritating, upon the admitted rights of colored citizens, but will encourage the belief that it is possible, by means of state enactments, to defeat the beneficent purposes which the people of the United States had in view when they adopted the recent amendments of the Constitution, by one of which the blacks of this country were made citizens of the United States and of the States in which they respectively reside, and whose privileges and immunities, as citizens, the States are forbidden to abridge. Sixty millions of whites are in no danger from the presence here of eight millions of blacks. The destinies of the two races, in this country, are indissolubly linked together, and the interests of both require that the common government of all shall not permit the seeds of race hate to be planted under the sanction of law. . . .

If evils will result from the commingling of the two races upon public highways established for the benefit of all, they will be infinitely less than those that will surely come from state legislation regulating the enjoyment of civil rights upon the basis of race. We boast of the freedom enjoyed by our people above all other people. But it is difficult to reconcile that boast with a state of the law which, practically, puts the brand of servitude and degradation upon a large class of our fellow-citizens, our equals before the law. The thin disguise of "equal" accommodations for passengers in railroad coaches will not mislead any one, nor atone for the wrong this day done. . . .

For the reasons stated, I am constrained to withold my assent from the opinion and judgment of the majority.

Korematsu v. United States
323 U.S. 214, 65 S.Ct. 193, 89 L.Ed. 194 (1944)

(This case is reprinted in Chapter Three, beginning on page 100).

Shelley v. Kraemer
334 U.S. 1, 68 S.Ct. 836, 92 L.Ed. 1161 (1948)

The Supreme Courts of Michigan and Missouri upheld the validity of restrictive covenants, which were provisions in contracts between private parties declaring that they, and those to whom they might sell, would not permit the acquisition or use of their property by non-Caucasians for a stated period of time. Majority: Vinson, Black, Burton, Douglas, Frankfurter, Murphy. Not participating: Jackson, Reed, Rutledge.

MR. CHIEF JUSTICE VINSON delivered the opinion of the Court. . . .

It cannot be doubted that among the civil rights intended to be protected from discriminatory state action by the Fourteenth Amendment are the rights to acquire, enjoy, own and dispose of property.

Equality in the enjoyment of property rights was regarded by the framers of that Amendment as an essential precondition to the realization of other basic civil rights and liberties which the Amendment was intended to guarantee. . . .

It is likewise clear that restrictions on the right

of occupancy of the sort sought to be created by the private agreements in these cases could not be squared with the requirements of the Fourteenth Amendment if imposed by state statute or local ordinance. . . .

But the present cases, unlike those just discussed, do not involve action by state legislatures or city councils. Here the particular patterns of discrimination and the areas in which the restrictions are to operate, are determined, in the first instance, by the terms of agreements among private individuals. Participation of the State consists in the enforcement of the restrictions so defined. The crucial issue with which we are here confronted is whether this distinction removes these cases from the operation of the prohibitory provisions of the Fourteenth Amendment.

Since the decision of this Court in the *Civil Rights Cases,* the principle has become firmly imbedded in our constitutional law that the action inhibited by the first section of the Fourteenth Amendment is only such action as may fairly be said to be that of the States. That Amendment erects no shield against merely private conduct, however discriminatory or wrongful.

We conclude, therefore, that the restrictive agreements standing alone cannot be regarded as violative of any rights guaranteed to petitioners by the Fourteenth Amendment. So long as the purposes of those agreements are effectuated by voluntary adherence to their terms, it would appear clear that there has been no action by the State and the provisions of the amendment have not been violated. . . .

But here there was more. . . .

. . . [T]hese are cases in which the States have made available to such individuals the full coercive power of the government to deny to petitioners, on the grounds of race or color, the enjoyment of property rights in premises which petitioners are willing and financially able to acquire and which the grantors are willing to sell. The difference between judicial enforcement and nonenforcement of the restrictive covenants is the difference to petitioners between being denied rights of property available to other members of the community and being accorded full enjoyment of those rights on an equal footing. . . .

We hold that in granting judicial enforcement of the restrictive agreements in these cases, the States have denied petitioners the equal protection of the laws and that, therefore, the action of the state courts cannot stand. . . .

The historical context in which the Fourteenth Amendment became a part of the Constitution should not be forgotten. Whatever else the framers sought to achieve, it is clear that the matter of primary concern was the establishment of equality in the enjoyment of basic civil and political rights and the preservation of those rights from discriminatory action on the part of the States based on considerations of race or color. Seventy-five years ago this Court announced that the provisions of the Amendment are to be constructed with this fundamental purpose in mind. Upon full consideration, we have concluded that in these cases the States have acted to deny petitioners the equal protection of the laws guaranteed by the Fourteenth Amendment. . . .

Reversed.

Brown v. Board of Education
(First Case)
347 U.S. 483, 74 S.Ct. 686, 98 L.Ed. 873 (1954)

On May 17, 1954, the Supreme Court handed down its long-awaited decision in the public school segregation cases. Although the cases directly involved only South Carolina, Virginia, Delaware, Kansas, and the District of Columbia, the answer to the question of whether segregation of races was permissible under the Constitution affected a total of 17 states and the District of Columbia, which required segregation in public schools, and four states that permitted segregation at the option of local communities. The chief justice spoke for a unanimous Court, which postponed issuing a decree until the October 1954 term. Majority: Warren, Black, Burton, Clark, Douglas, Frankfurter, Jackson, Minton, Reed.

MR. CHIEF JUSTICE WARREN delivered the opinion of the court.

These cases come to us from the States of Kansas, South Carolina, Virginia, and Delaware. They are premised on different facts and different local conditions, but a common legal question justifies their consideration together in this consolidated opinion.

In each of the cases, minors of the Negro race, through their legal representatives, seek the aid of the courts in obtaining admission to the public schools of their community on a nonsegregated basis. In each instance, they had been denied admission to schools attended by white children under laws requiring or permitting segregation according to race.

This segregation was alleged to deprive the plaintiffs of the equal protection of the laws under the Fourteenth Amendment. In each of the cases other than the Delaware case, a three-judge Federal District Court denied relief to the plaintiffs on the so-called "separate but equal" doctrine, announced by this court in *Plessy* v. *Ferguson.* . . .

The plaintiffs contend that segregated public schools are not "equal" and cannot be made "equal," and that, hence, they are deprived of the equal protection of the laws. Because of the obvious importance of the question presented, the Court took jurisdiction. Argument was heard in the 1952 term, and reargument was heard this term on certain questions propounded by the Court.

Reargument was largely devoted to the circumstances surrounding the adoption of the Fourteenth Amendment in 1868. It covered, exhaustively, consideration of the Amendment in Congress, ratification by the states, then existing practices in racial segregation, and the views of proponents and opponents of the Amendment.

This discussion and our own investigation convince us that, although these sources cast some light, it is not enough to resolve the problem with which we are faced.

At best, they are inconclusive. The most avid proponents of the postwar Amendments undoubtedly intended them to remove all legal distinctions among "all persons born or naturalized in the United States."

Their opponents, just as certainly, were antagonistic to both the letter and the spirit of the Amendments and wished them to have the most limited effect. What others in Congress and the State legislatures had in mind cannot be determined with any degree of certainty.

An additional reason for the illusive nature of the Amendment's history, with respect to segregated schools, is the status of public education at that time. In the South, the movement toward free common schools, supported by general taxation, had not yet taken hold. Education of white children was largely in the hands of private groups. Education of Negroes was almost nonexistent, and practically all of the race was illiterate. In fact, any education of Negroes was forbidden by law in some states. . . .

As a consequence, it is not surprising that there should be so little in the history of the Fourteenth Amendment relating to its intended effect on public education. . . .

In approaching this problem, we cannot turn the clock back to 1868, when the Amendment was adopted, or even to 1896, when *Plessy* v. *Ferguson* was written. We must consider public education in the light of its full development and its present place in American life throughout the nation. Only in this way can it be determined if segregation in public schools deprives these plaintiffs of the equal protection of the laws.

Today, education is perhaps the most important function of state and local governments. Compulsory school attendance laws and the great expenditures for education both demonstrate our recognition of the importance of education to our democratic society. It is required in the performance of our most basic public responsibilities, even service in the armed forces. It is the very foundation of good citizenship.

Today, it is a principal instrument in awakening

the child to cultural values, in preparing him for later professional training, and in helping him to adjust normally to his environment.

In these days, it is doubtful that any child may reasonably be expected to succeed in life if he is denied the opportunity of an education. Such an opportunity, where the state has undertaken to provide it, is a right which must be made available to all on equal terms.

We come then to the question presented: Does segregation of children in public schools solely on the basis of race, even though the physical facilities and other "tangible" factors may be equal, deprive the children of the minority group of equal educational opportunities? We believe that it does.

In *Sweatt* v. *Painter* . . . in finding that a segregated law school for Negroes could not provide them equal educational opportunities, this court relied in large part on "those qualities which are incapable of objective measurement but which make for greatness in a law school."

In *McLaurin* v. *Oklahoma State Regents* . . . the court, in requiring that a Negro admitted to a white graduate school be treated like all other students, again resorted to intangible considerations: " . . . his ability to study, engage in discussions and exchange views with other students, and, in general, to learn his profession."

Such considerations apply with added force to children in grade and high schools. To separate them from others of similar age and qualifications solely because of their race generates a feeling of inferiority as to their status in the community that may affect their hearts and minds in a way unlikely ever to be undone. . . .

Whatever may have been the extent of psychological knowledge at the time of *Plessy* v. *Ferguson*,

this finding is amply supported by modern authority.*

. . . Any language in *Plessy* v. *Ferguson* contrary to this finding is rejected.

We conclude that in the field of public education the doctrine of "separate but equal" has no place. Separate educational facilities are inherently unequal. Therefore, we hold that the plaintiffs and others similarly situated for whom the actions have been brought are, by reason of the segregation complained of, deprived of the equal protection of the laws guaranteed by the Fourteenth Amendment. . . .

We have now announced that such segregation is a denial of the equal protection of the laws. In order that we may have the full assistance of the parties in formulating decrees the cases will be restored to the docket, and the parties are requested to present further argument on Questions 4 and 5 previously propounded by the court for the reargument this Term. [These pertained to the form of decree to be issued if segregated schools were outlawed.] . . .

*It is so ordered.***

*Citing: K.B. Clark, *Effect of Prejudice and Discrimination on Personality Development* (Mid-century White House Conference); Witmer and Kotinsky, *Personality in the Making* (1952), ch. VI; Deutscher and Chein, "The Psychological Effects of Enforced Segregation: A Survey of Social Science Opinion," 26 *J. Psychol.* 259 (1948); Chein, "What Are the Psychological Effects of Segregation Under Conditions of Equal Facilities?" 3 *Int. J. Opinion and Attitude Res.* 229 (1949); Brameld, "Educational Costs," in *Discrimination and National Welfare* (MacIver, ed., 1949), 44-48; Frazier, *The Negro in the United States* (1949), 674-681. And see generally Myrdal, *An American Dilemma* (1944).

**In *Bolling* v. *Sharpe*, decided the same day as *Brown*, the Court unanimously held that the due process clause of the Fifth Amendment prohibited racially segregated public schools in the District of Columbia.—Ed.

Brown v. Board of Education
(Second Case)
349 U.S. 294, 75 S.Ct. 753, 99 L.Ed. 1083 (1955)

In the term following the first *Brown* decision the Court handed down its decree to guide lower courts in future litigation involving desegregation. In reaching the following views, the justices heard representatives of the black parties, the states concerned, and the United States. Majority: Warren, Black, Burton, Clark, Douglas, Frankfurter, Harlan, Minton, Reed.

MR. CHIEF JUSTICE WARREN delivered the opinion of the Court.

These cases were decided on May 17, 1954. The opinions of that date, declaring the fundamental principle that racial discrimination in public education is unconstitutional, are incorporated herein by reference. All provisions of federal, state, or local law requiring or permitting such discrimination must yield to this principle. There remains for consideration the manner in which relief is to be accorded. . . .

In fashioning and effectuating the decrees, the courts will be guided by equitable principles. Traditionally, equity has been characterized by a practical flexibility in shaping its remedies and by a facility for adjusting and reconciling public and private needs. These cases call for the exercise of these traditional attributes of equity power. At stake is the personal interest of the plaintiffs in admission to public schools as soon as practicable on a non-discriminatory basis. To effectuate this interest may call for elimination of a variety of obstacles in making the transition to school systems operated in accordance with the constitutional principles set forth in our May 17, 1954, decision. Courts of equity may properly take into account the public interest in the elimination of such obstacles in a systematic and effective manner. But it should go without saying that the vitality of these constitutional principles cannot be allowed to yield simply because of disagreement with them.

While giving weight to these public and private considerations, the courts will require that the defendants make a prompt and reasonable start toward full compliance with our May 17, 1954, ruling. Once such a start has been made, the courts may find that additional time is necessary to carry out the ruling in an effective manner. The burden rests upon the defendants to establish that such time is necessary in the public interest and is consistent with good faith compliance at the earliest practicable date. To that end, the courts may consider problems related to administration, arising from the physical condition of the school plant, the school transportation system, personnel, revision of school districts and attendance areas into compact units to achieve a system of determining admission to the public schools on a nonracial basis, and revision of local laws and regulations which may be necessary in solving the foregoing problems. They will also consider the adequacy of any plans the defendants may propose to meet these problems and to effectuate a transition to a racially nondiscriminatory school system. During this period of transition, the courts will retain jurisdiction of these cases. The judgments below . . . are accordingly reversed and the cases are remanded to the District Courts to take such proceedings and enter such orders and decrees consistent with this opinion as are necessary and proper to admit to public schools on a racially nondiscriminatory basis with all deliberate speed the parties to these cases. . . .

It is so ordered.

Milliken v. Bradley
418 U.S. 717, 94 S.Ct. 3112, 41 L.Ed. 2d 1069 (1974)

This case represents a class action instituted in the United States District Court for the Eastern District of Michigan against certain state officials and the Detroit Board of Education seeking desegregation of the city's public schools. The district court ordered submission of desegregation plans for the city proper, as well as for the three-county metropolitan area, even though the 53 suburban school districts were not parties to the action and there was no claim that they had committed any constitutional violations. The United States Court of Appeals, Sixth Circuit, affirmed findings of de jure segregation in the greater Detroit area. Majority: Burger, Blackmun, Powell, Rehnquist, Stewart. Dissenting: Marshall, Brennan, Douglas, White.

MR. CHIEF JUSTICE BURGER delivered the opinion of the Court.

We granted certiorari in these consolidated cases to determine whether a federal court may impose a multi-district, areawide remedy to a single district de jure segregation problem absent any finding that the other included school districts have failed to operate unitary school systems within their districts, absent any claim or finding that the boundary lines of any affected school district were established with the purpose of fostering racial segregation in public schools, absent any finding that the included districts committed acts which effected segregation within the other districts, and absent a meaningful opportunity for the included neighboring school districts to present evidence or be heard on the propriety of a multi-district remedy or on the question of constitutional violations by those neighboring districts. . . .

The target of the *Brown* holding was clear and forthright: the elimination of state mandated or deliberately maintained dual school systems with certain schools for Negro pupils and others for white pupils. This duality in racial segregation was held to violate the Constitution in the cases subsequent to 1954. . . .

Viewing the record as a whole, it seems clear that the District Court and the Court of Appeals shifted the primary focus from a Detroit remedy to the metropolitan area only because of their conclusion that total desegregation of Detroit would not produce the racial balance which they perceived as desirable. Both courts proceeded on an assumption that the Detroit schools could not be truly desegregated—in their view of what constituted desegregation—unless the racial composition of the student body of each school substantially reflected the racial composition of the population of the metropolitan area as a whole. The metropolitan area was then defined as Detroit plus 53 of the outlying school districts. . . .

Here the District Court's approach to what constituted "actual desegregation" raises the fundamental question, not presented in *Swann*, as to the circumstances in which a federal court may order desegregation relief that embraces more than a single school district. The court's analytical starting point was its conclusion that school district lines are no more than arbitrary lines on a map "drawn for political convenience." . . .

The Michigan educational structure involved in this case, in common with most States, provides for a large measure of local control and a review of the scope and character of these local powers indicates the extent to which the interdistrict remedy approved by the two courts could disrupt and alter the structure of public education in Michigan. The metropolitan remedy would require, in effect, consolidation of 54 independent school districts historically administered as separate units into a vast new super school district. . . . Entirely apart from the logistical and other serious problems attending large-scale transportation of students, the consolidation would give rise to an array of other problems in financing and operating this new school system. Some of the more obvious questions would be: What would be the status and authority of the present popularly elected school boards? Would the children of Detroit be within the jurisdiction and operating control of a school board elected by the parents and residents of other districts? What board or boards would levy taxes for school operations in these 54 districts constituting the consolidated metropolitan area? What provisions could be made for assuring substantial equality in tax levies among the 54 districts, if this were deemed requisite? What provisions would be made for financing? Would the validity of long-term bonds be jeopardized unless approved by all of the component districts as well as the State? What body would determine that portion of the curricula now left to the discretion of local school boards? Who would establish attendance zones, purchase school equipment, locate and construct new schools, and indeed attend to all the myriad day-to-day decisions that are necessary to school operations affecting potentially more than three quarters of a million pupils? . . .

Of course, no state law is above the Constitution. School district lines and the present laws with respect to local control, are not sacrosanct and if they conflict with the Fourteenth Amendment, federal courts have a duty to prescribe appropriate remedies. . . .

But our prior holdings have been confined to violations and remedies within a single school district. We therefore turn to address, for the first time, the validity of a remedy mandating cross-district or inter-district consolidation to remedy a condition of segregation found to exist in only one district.

The controlling principle consistently expounded in our holdings is that the scope of the remedy is determined by the nature and extent of the constitutional violation. . . . Before the boundaries of separate and autonomous school districts may be set aside by consolidating the separate units for remedial purposes or by imposing a cross-district remedy, it must first be shown that there has been a constitutional violation within one district that produces a significant segregative effect in another district. Specifically it must be shown that racially discriminatory acts of the state or local school districts, or of a single school district have been a substantial cause of inter-district segregation. Thus an inter-district remedy might be in order where the racially discriminatory acts of one or more school districts caused racial segregation in an adjacent district, or where district lines have been deliberately drawn on the basis of race. In such circumstances an inter-district remedy would be appropriate to eliminate the inter-district segregation directly caused by the constitutional violation. Conversely, without an inter-district violation and inter-district effect, there is no constitutional wrong calling for an inter-district remedy. . . .

We conclude that the relief ordered by the District Court and affirmed by the Court of Appeals was based upon an erroneous standard and was unsupported by record evidence that acts of the outlying districts affected the discrimination found to exist in the schools of Detroit. Accordingly, the judgment of the Court of Appeals is reversed and the case is remanded for further proceedings consistent with this opinion leading to prompt formulation of a decree directed to eliminating the segregation found to exist in Detroit city schools, a remedy which has been delayed since 1970.

Reversed and remanded.

MR. JUSTICE MARSHALL, with whom MR. JUSTICE DOUGLAS, MR. JUSTICE BRENNAN, and MR. JUSTICE WHITE join, dissenting. . . .

After 20 years of small, often difficult steps toward that great end, the Court today takes a giant step backwards. . . . Ironically purporting to base its result on the principle that the scope of the remedy in a desegregation case should be determined by the nature and the extent of the constitutional violation, the Court's answer is to provide no remedy at all for the violation proved in this case, thereby guaranteeing that Negro children in Detroit will receive the same separate and inherently unequal education in the future as they have been unconstitutionally afforded in the past.

. . . Our precedents, in my view, firmly establish that where, as here, state-imposed segregation has been demonstrated, it becomes the duty of the State to eliminate root and branch all vestiges of racial discrimination and to achieve the greatest possible degree of actual desegregation. I agree with both the District Court and the Court of Appeals that, under the facts of this case, this duty cannot be fulfilled unless the State of Michigan involves outlying metropolitan area school districts in its desegregation remedy. Furthermore, I perceive no basis either in law or in the practicalities of the situation justifying the State's interposition of school district boundaries as absolute barriers to the implementation of an effective desegregation remedy. Under established and frequently used Michigan procedures, school district lines are both flexible and permeable for a wide variety of purposes, and there is no reason why they must now stand in the way of meaningful desegregation relief.

The rights at issue in the case are too fundamental to be abridged on grounds as superficial as those relied on by the majority today. We deal here with the right of all our children, whatever their race, to an equal start in life and to an equal opportunity to reach their full potential as citizens. Those children who have been denied that right in the past deserve better than to see fences thrown up to deny them that right in the future. Our Nation, I fear, will be illserved by the Court's refusal to remedy separate and unequal education, for unless our children begin to learn together, there is little hope that our people will ever learn to live together.

The great irony of the Court's opinion and, in my view, its most serious analytical flaw may be gleaned from its concluding sentence, in which the Court remands for "prompt formulation of a decree directed to eliminating the segregation found to exist in Detroit city schools, a remedy which has been delayed since 1970." . . . The majority, however, seems to have forgotten the District Court's explicit finding that a Detroit-only decree, the only remedy permitted under today's decision, "would not accomplish desegregation." . . .

Desegregation is not and was never expected to be an easy task. Racial attitudes ingrained in our nation's childhood and adolescence are not quickly thrown aside in its middle years. But just as the inconvenience of some cannot be allowed to stand in the way of the rights of others, so public opposition, no matter how strident, cannot be permitted to divert this Court from the enforcement of the constitutional principles at issue in this case. Today's holding, I fear, is more a reflection of a perceived public mood that we have gone far enough in enforcing the Constitution's guarantee of equal justice than it is the product of neutral principles of law. In the short run, it may seem to be the easier course to allow our great metropolitan areas to be divided up each into two cities—one white, the other black—but it is a course, I predict, our people will ultimately regret. I dissent.

Shapiro v. Thompson
394 U.S. 618, 89 S.Ct. 1322, 22 L.Ed. 2d 600 (1969)

Welfare laws in Connecticut, Pennsylvania, and the District of Columbia required applicants for benefits to show one-year residence. The rules were authorized but not required by the Social Security Act of 1935. Three-judge federal district courts held the residency provision unconstitutional. Majority: Brennan, Douglas, Fortas, Marshall, Stewart, White. Dissenting: Harlan, Black, Warren.

MR. JUSTICE BRENNAN delivered the opinion of the Court.

. . . [T]he Connecticut Welfare Department invoked § 17-2d of the Connecticut General Statutes to deny the application of appellee Vivian Marie Thompson for assistance under the program for Aid to Families with Dependent Children (AFDC). She was a 19-year-old unwed mother of one child and pregnant with her second child when she changed her residence in June 1966 from Dorchester, Massachusetts, to Hartford, Connecticut, to live with her mother, a Hartford resident. She moved to her own apartment in Hartford in August 1966, when her mother was no longer able to support her and her infant son. Because of her pregnancy, she was unable to work or enter a work training program. Her application for AFDC assistance, filed in August, was denied in November solely on the ground that . . . she had not lived in the State for a year before her application was filed. She brought this action in the District Court for the District of Connecticut where . . . the majority held that the waiting-period requirement is unconstitutional because it "has a chilling effect on the right to travel." . . . The majority also held that the provision was a violation of the Equal Protection Clause of the Fourteenth Amendment because the denial of relief to those resident in the State for less than a year is not based on any permissible purpose but is solely designed, as "Connecticut states quite frankly," "to protect its fiscal integrity by discouraging entry of those who come needing relief." . . .

There is no dispute that the effect of the waiting-period requirement in each case is to create two classes of needy resident families indistinguishable from each other except that one is composed of residents who have resided a year or more, and the second of residents who have resided less than a year, in the jurisdiction. On the basis of this sole difference the first class is granted and the second class is denied welfare aid upon which may depend the ability of the families to obtain the very means to subsist—food, shelter, and other necessities of life. . . .

There is weighty evidence that exclusion from the jurisdiction of the poor who need or may need relief was the specific objective of these provisions. In the Congress, sponsors of federal legislation to eliminate all residence requirements have been consistently opposed by representatives of state and local welfare agencies who have stressed the fears of the States that elimination of the requirements would result in a heavy influx of individuals into States providing the most generous benefits. . . .

We do not doubt that the one-year waiting period device is well suited to discourage the influx of poor families in need of assistance. An indigent who desires to migrate, resettle, find a new job, start a new life will doubtless hesitate if he knows that he must risk making the move without the possibility of falling back on state welfare assistance during his first year of residence when his need may be most acute. But the purpose of inhibiting migration by needy persons into the State is constitutionally impermissible.

This Court long ago recognized that the nature of our Federal Union and our constitutional concepts of personal liberty unite to require that all citizens be free to travel throughout the length and breadth of our land uninhibited by statutes, rules, or regulations which unreasonably burden or restrict this movement. . . .

We have no occasion to ascribe the source of this right to travel interstate to a particular constitutional provision. . . . It is a right that has been firmly established and repeatedly recognized. . . ."

Appellants next advance as justification certain administrative and related governmental objectives allegedly served by the waiting-period requirement. They argue that the requirement (1) facilitates the planning of the welfare budget; (2) provides an objective test of residency; (3) minimizes the opportunity for recipients fraudulently to receive payments from more than one jurisdiction; and (4)

encourages early entry of new residents into the labor force. . . .

The argument that the waiting-period requirement facilitates budget predictability is wholly unfounded. . . .

The argument that the waiting period serves as an administratively efficient rule of thumb for determining residency similarly will not withstand scrutiny. . . .

Similarly, there is no need for a State to use the one-year waiting period as a safeguard against fraudulent receipt of benefits; far less drastic means are available, and are employed, to minimize that hazard. . . .

We conclude therefore that appellants in these cases do not use and have no need to use the one-year requirement for the governmental purposes suggested. Thus, even under traditional equal protection tests a classification of welfare applicants according to whether they have lived in the State for one year would seem irrational and unconstitutional. But, of course, the traditional criteria do not apply in these cases. Since the classification here touches on the fundamental right of interstate movement, its constitutionality must be judged by the stricter standard of whether it promotes a *compelling* state interest. Under this standard, the waiting period requirement clearly violates the Equal Protection Clause. . . .

Affirmed.

MR. JUSTICE HARLAN, dissenting. . . . .

In upholding the equal protection argument, the Court has applied an equal protection doctrine of relatively recent vintage: the rule that statutory classifications which either are based upon certain "suspect" criteria or affect "fundamental rights" will be held to deny equal protection unless justified by a "compelling" governmental interest. . . .

The "compelling interest" doctrine, which today is articulated more explicitly than ever before, constitutes an increasingly significant exception to the long-established rule that a statute does not deny equal protection if it is rationally related to a legitimate governmental objective. The "compelling interest" doctrine has two branches. The branch which requires that classifications based upon "suspect" criteria be supported by a compelling interest apparently had its genesis in cases involving racial classifications, which have . . . been regarded as inherently "suspect." . . .

I think that this branch of the "compelling interest" doctrine is sound when applied to racial classifications, for historically the Equal Protection Clause was largely a product of the desire to eradicate legal distinctions founded upon race. However, I believe that the more recent extensions have been unwise. . . .

The second branch of the "compelling interest" principle is even more troublesome. For it has been held that a statutory classification is subject to the "compelling interest" test if the result of the classification may be to affect a "fundamental right," regardless of the basis of the classification. This rule was foreshadowed in *Skinner* v. *Oklahoma*. . . .

I think this branch of the "compelling interest" doctrine particularly unfortunate and unnecessary. It is unfortunate because it creates an exception which threatens to swallow the standard equal protection rule. Virtually every state statute affects important rights. This Court has repeatedly held, for example, that the traditional equal protection standard is applicable to statutory classifications affecting such fundamental matters as the right to pursue a particular occupation, the right to receive greater or smaller wages or to work more or less hours, and the right to inherit property. Rights such as these are in principle indistinguishable from those involved here, and to extend the "compelling interest" rule to all cases in which such rights are affected would go far toward making this Court a "super-legislature." This branch of the doctrine is also unnecessary. When the right affected is one assured by the federal Constitution, any infringement can be dealt with under the Due Process Clause. But when a statute affects only matters not mentioned in the federal Constitution and is not arbitrary or irrational, I must reiterate that I know of nothing which entitles this Court to pick out particular human activities, characterize them as "fundamental," and give them added protection under an unusually stringent equal protection test. . . .

Today's decision, it seems to me, reflects to an unusual degree the current notion that this Court possesses a peculiar wisdom all its own whose capacity to lead this Nation out of its present troubles is contained only by the limits of judicial ingenuity in contriving new constitutional principles to meet each problem as it arises. For anyone who, like myself, believes that it is an essential function of this Court to maintain the constitutional divisions between state and federal authority and among the three branches of the Federal Government, today's decision is a step in the wrong direction. This resurgence of the expansive view of "equal protection" carries the seeds of more judicial interference with the state and federal legislative process, much more indeed than does the judicial application of "due process" according to traditional concepts . . . about which some members of this Court have expressed fears as to its potentialities for setting us judges "at large."

Moose Lodge v. *Irvis*
407 U.S. 163, 92 S.Ct. 1965, 32 L.Ed. 2d 627 (1972)

A white member of the national organization of Moose took Pennsylvania legislator K. Leroy Irvis as his guest to the dining room of the Harrisburg lodge and requested food and beverage. Irvis was refused service solely because he was black. The lodge is a private club, which permits only members and their guests to frequent the clubhouse. Irvis brought action, claiming that refusal of service to him was "state action" in violation of the Fourteenth Amendment's equal protection clause. Significantly, the Pennsylvania Liquor Control Board had granted the lodge a license with the requirement that it "adhere to the provisions of its own constitution and bylaws." The

United States District Court required the state liquor board to revoke the lodge's license as long as it continued its discriminatory practices. Following the district court's decision, the national organization altered its bylaws, making applicable to guests the same racial restrictions as those placed on members. Majority: Rehnquist, Blackmun, Burger, Powell, Stevens, White. Dissenting: Brennan, Douglas, Marshall.

MR. JUSTICE REHNQUIST delivered the opinion of the Court. . . .

Moose Lodge is a private club in the ordinary meaning of that term. It is a local chapter of a national fraternal organization having well defined requirements for membership. It conducts all of its activities in a building that is owned by it. It is not publicly funded. Only members and guests are permitted in any lodge of the order; one may become a guest only by invitation of a member or upon invitation of the house committee.

Appellee, while conceding the right of private clubs to choose members upon a discriminatory basis, asserts that the licensing of Moose Lodge to serve liquor by the Pennsylvania Liquor Control Board amounts to such State involvement with the club's activities as to make its discriminatory practices forbidden by the Equal Protection Clause of the Fourteenth Amendment. The relief sought and obtained by appellee in the District Court was an injunction forbidding the licensing by the liquor authority of Moose Lodge until it ceased its discriminatory practices. We conclude that Moose Lodge's refusal to serve food and beverages to a guest by reason of the fact that he was a Negro does not, under the circumstances here presented, violate the Fourteenth Amendment.

In 1883, this Court in The Civil Rights Cases . . . set forth the essential dichotomy between discriminatory action by the State, which is prohibited by the Equal Protection clause, and private conduct, "however discriminatory or wrongful," against which that clause "erects no shield." . . .

While the principle is easily stated, the question of whether particular discriminatory conduct is private, on the one hand, or amounts to "State action," on the other hand, frequently admits of no easy answer. . . .

Our cases make clear that the impetus for the forbidden discrimination need not originate with the State if it is state action that enforces privately originated discrimination. . . . The Court held in *Burton* v. *Wilmington Park Authority* . . . that a private restaurant owner who refused service because of a customer's race violated the Fourteenth Amendment, where the restaurant was located in a building owned by a state-created parking authority and leased from the authority. . . .

Here there is nothing approaching the symbiotic relationship between lessor and lessee that was present in Burton, where the private lessee obtained the benefit of locating in a building owned by the state-created parking authority, and the parking authority was enabled to carry out its primary public purpose of furnishing parking space by advantageously leasing portions of the building constructed for that purpose to commercial lessees such as the owner of the Eagle Restaurant. Unlike Burton, the Moose Lodge building is located on land owned by it, not by any public authority. Far from apparently holding itself out as a place of public accommodation, Moose Lodge quite ostentatiously proclaims the fact that it is not open to the public at large. Nor is it located and operated in such surroundings that although private in name, it discharges a function or performs a service that would otherwise in all likelihood be performed by the State. In short, while Eagle was a public restaurant in a public building, Moose Lodge is a private social club in a private building.

. . . The only effect that the state licensing of Moose Lodge to serve liquor can be said to have on the right of any other Pennsylvanian to buy or be served liquor on premises other than those of Moose Lodge is that for some purposes club licenses are counted in the maximum number of licenses which may be issued in a given municipality. Basically each municipality has a quota of one retail license for each 1,500 inhabitants. Licenses issued to hotels, municipal golf courses and airport restaurants are not counted in this quota, nor are club licenses, until the maximum number of retail licenses is reached. Beyond that point, neither additional retail licenses nor additional club licenses may be issued so long as the number of issued and outstanding retail licenses remains above the statutory maximum. . . .

However detailed this type of regulation may be in some particulars, it cannot be said to in any way foster or encourage racial discrimination. . . .We therefore hold that, with the exception hereafter noted, the operation of the regulatory scheme enforced by the Pennsylvania Liquor Control Board does not sufficiently implicate the State in the discriminatory guest policies of Moose Lodge so as to make the latter "State action" within the ambit of the Equal Protection Clause of the Fourteenth Amendment.

The District Court found that the regulations of the Liquor Control Board adopted pursuant to the statute affirmatively require that "every club licensee shall adhere to all the provisions of its constitution and bylaws." . . .

Even though the Liquor Control Board regulation in question is neutral in its terms, the result of its application in a case where the constitution and bylaws of a club required racial discrimination would be to invoke the sanctions of the State to enforce a concededly discriminatory private rule. State action, for purposes of the Equal Protection Clause, may emanate from rulings of administrative and regulatory agencies as well as from legislative or judicial action. . . . *Shelley* v. *Kramer* . . . makes it clear that the application of state sanctions to enforce such a rule would violate the Fourteenth Amendment. Although the record before us it not as clear as one would like, appellant has not persuaded us that the District Court should have denied any and all relief.

Appellee was entitled to a decree enjoining the enforcement of . . . the regulations promulgated by the Pennsylvania Liquor Control Board insofar as that regulation requires compliance by Moose Lodge with provisions of its constitution and bylaws containing racially discriminatory provisions. He was entitled to no more. The judgment of the District Court is reversed, and the cause remanded with instructions to enter a decree in conformity with this opinion.

Reversed and remanded.

MR. JUSTICE DOUGLAS, with whom MR. JUSTICE MARSHALL joins, dissenting.

My view of the First Amendment and the related guarantees of the Bill of Rights is that they create a zone of privacy which precludes government from interfering with private clubs or groups. The associational rights which our system honors permit all white, all black, all brown, and all yellow clubs to be formed. They also permit all Catholic, all Jewish, or all agnostic clubs to be established. Government may not tell a man or woman who his or her associates must be. The individual can be as selective as he desires. So the fact that the Moose Lodge allows only Caucasians to join or come as guests is constitutionally irrelevant, as is the decision of the Black Muslims to admit to their services only members of their race. . . .

Pennsylvania has a state store system of alcohol distribution. Resale is permitted by hotels, restaurants, and private clubs which all must obtain licenses from the Liquor Control Board. The scheme of regulation is complete and pervasive; and the state courts have sustained many restrictions on the licensees. . . . Among these requirements is regulation No. 113.09 which says "Every club licensee shall adhere to all the provisions of its Constitution and Bylaws." This regulation means, as applied to Moose Lodge, that it must adhere to the racially discriminatory provision of the Constitution of its Supreme Lodge that "The membership of the lodge shall be composed of male persons of the Caucasian or White race above the age of twenty-one years, and not married to someone other than the Caucasian or White race, who are of good moral character, physically and mentally normal who shall profess a belief in a Supreme Being." . . .

Were this regulation the only infirmity in Pennsylvania's licensing scheme, I would perhaps agree with the majority that the appropriate relief would be a decree enjoining its enforcement. But there is another flaw in the scheme not so easily cured. Liquor licenses in Pennsylvania, unlike driver's licenses, or marriage licenses, are not freely available to those who meet racially neutral qualifications. . . .What the majority neglects to say is that the Harrisburg quota, where Moose Lodge No. 107 is located, has been full for many years. No more club licenses may be issued in that city.

This state-enforced scarcity of licenses restricts the ability of blacks to obtain liquor, for liquor is commercially available *only* at private clubs for a significant portion of each week. Access by blacks to places that serve liquor is further limited by the fact that the state quota is filled. A group desiring to form a nondiscriminatory club which would serve blacks must purchase a license held by an existing club, which can exact a monopoly price for the transfer. The availability of such a license is speculative at best, however, for, as Moose Lodge itself concedes, without a liquor license a fraternal organization would be hard-pressed to survive.

Thus, the State of Pennsylvania is putting the weight of its liquor license, concededly a valued and important adjunct to a private club, behind racial discrimination. . . .

Frontiero v. Richardson
411 U.S. 677, 93 S.Ct. 1764, 36 L.Ed. 2d 583 (1973)

A servicewoman's application for increased quarters allowances and medical and dental benefits for her husband was disallowed because she failed, as required by law, to demonstrate that her husband was dependent on her for more than one-half of his support. The servicewoman instituted action, contending that the statutes that allowed a serviceman to claim his wife as a dependent for such benefits, without regard to whether she was in fact dependent on him for any part of her support, were discriminatory on the basis of sex and in violation of the Fifth Amendment's due process clause. A three-judge district court upheld the constitutionality of the statutes. Majority: Brennan, Blackmun, Burger, Douglas, Marshall, Powell, Stewart, White. Dissenting: Rehnquist.

MR. JUSTICE BRENNAN announced the judgment of the Court in an opinion in which MR. JUSTICES DOUGLAS, MARSHALL, and WHITE joined.

At the outset, appellants contend that classifications based upon sex, like classifications based upon race, alienage, and national origin, are inherently suspect and must therefore be subjected to close judicial scrutiny. We agree and, indeed, find at least implicit support for such an approach in our unanimous decision only last term in *Reed* v. *Reed.* . . .

In *Reed,* the Court considered the constitutionality of an Idaho statute providing that, when two individuals are otherwise equally entitled to appointment as administrator of an estate, the male applicant must be preferred to the female. . .

. . . [T]he Court held the statutory preference for male applicants unconstitutional. In reaching this result, the Court implicitly rejected appellee's apparently rational explanation of the statutory scheme, and concluded that, by ignoring the individual qualifications of particular applicants, the

challenged statute provided "dissimilar treatment for men and women who are . . . similarly situated." The Court therefore held that, even though the State's interest in achieving administrative efficiency "is not without some legitimacy," "[t]o give a mandatory preference to members of either sex over members of the other, merely to accomplish the elimination of hearings on the merits, is to make the very kind of arbitrary legislative choice forbidden by the [Constitution]. . . ." This departure from "traditional" rational basis analysis with respect to sex-based classifications is clearly justified.

There can be no doubt that our Nation has had a long and unfortunate history of sex discrimination. Traditionally, such discrimination was rationalized by an attitude of "romantic paternalism" which, in practical effect, put women not on a pedestal, but in a cage. . . .

As a result of notions such as these, our statute books gradually became laden with gross, stereotypical distinctions between the sexes and, indeed, throughout much of the 19th century the position of women in our society was, in many respects, comparable to that of blacks under the pre-Civil War slave codes. Neither slaves nor women could hold office, serve on juries, or bring suit in their own names, and married women traditionally were denied the legal capacity to hold or convey property or to serve as legal guardians of their own children. . . . And although blacks were guaranteed the right to vote in 1870, women were denied even that right—which is itself "preservative of other basic and civil and political rights"—until adoption of the Nineteenth Amendment half a century later.

It is true, of course, that the position of women in America has improved markedly in recent decades. Nevertheless, it can hardly be doubted that, in part because of the high visibility of the sex characteristic, women still face pervasive, although at times more subtle, discrimination in our educational institutions, on the job market and, perhaps most conspicuously, in the political arena. . . .

Moreover, since sex, like race and national origin, is an immutable characteristic determined solely by the accident of birth, the imposition of special disabilities upon the members of a particular sex because of their sex would seem to violate "the basic concept of our system that legal burdens should bear some relationship to individual responsibility. . . ." And what differentiates sex from such nonsuspect statutes as intelligence or physical disability, and aligns it with the recognized suspect criteria, is that the sex characteristic frequently bears no relation to ability to perform or contribute to society. As a result, statutory distinctions between the sexes often have the effect of invidiously relegating the entire class of females to inferior legal status without regard to the actual capabilities of its individual members. . . .

With these considerations in mind, we can only conclude that classifications based upon sex, like classifications based upon race, alienage, or national origin, are inherently suspect, and must therefore be subjected to strict judicial scrutiny. Applying the analysis mandated by that stricter standard of review, it is clear that the statutory scheme now before us is constitutionally invalid.

The sole basis of the classification established in the challenged statutes is the sex of the individuals involved. . . . Thus . . . a female member of the uniformed services seeking to obtain housing and medical benefits for her spouse must prove his dependency in fact, whereas no such burden is imposed upon male members. In addition, the statutes operate so as to deny benefits to a female member, such as appellant Sharron Frontiero, who provides less than one-half of her spouse's support, while at the same time granting such benefits to a male member who likewise provides less than one-half of his spouse's support. Thus, to this extent at least, it may fairly be said that these statutes command "dissimilar" treatment for men and women who are . . . "similarly situated.". . .

Moreover, the Government concedes that the differential treatment accorded men and women under these statutes serves no purpose other than mere "administrative convenience." In essence, the Government maintains that, as an empirical matter, wives in our society frequently are dependent upon their husbands, while husbands rarely are dependent upon their wives. Thus, the Government argues that Congress might reasonably have concluded that it would be both cheaper and easier simply conclusively to presume that wives of male members are financially dependent upon their husbands, while burdening female members with the task of establishing dependency in fact.

The Government offers no concrete evidence, however, tending to support its view that such differential treatment in fact saves the Government any money. In order to satisfy the demands of strict judicial scrutiny, the Government must demonstrate, for example, that it is actually cheaper to grant increased benefits with respect to *all* male members, than it is to determine which male members are in fact entitled to such benefits and to grant increased benefits only to those members whose wives actually meet the dependency requirement. . . .

. . . On the contrary, any statutory scheme which draws a sharp line between the sexes, *solely* for the purpose of achieving administrative convenience, necessarily commands "dissimilar treatment for men and women who are . . . similarly situated," and therefore involves the "very kind of arbitrary legislative choice forbidden by the [Constitution]. . . ." We therefore conclude that, by according differential treatment to male and female members of the uniformed services for the sole purpose of achieving administrative convenience, the challenged statutes violate the Due Process Clause of the Fifth Amendment insofar as they require a female member to prove the dependency of her husband.

Reversed.

MR. JUSTICE POWELL, with whom THE CHIEF JUSTICE and MR. JUSTICE BLACKMUN join, concurring in the judgment.

. . . It is unnecessary for the Court in this case to characterize sex as a suspect classification, with all of the far-reaching implications of such a holding. . . . In my view, we can and should decide this case on the authority of *Reed* and reserve for the future any expansion of its rationale.

There is another, and I find compelling, reason for deferring a general categorizing of sex classifications as invoking the strictest test of judicial scrutiny. The Equal Rights Amendment, which if adopted will resolve the substance of this precise question, has been approved by the Congress and submitted for ratification by the States. . . . By acting prematurely and unnecessarily, as I view it, the Court has assumed a decisional responsibility at the very time when state legislatures, functioning within the traditional democratic process, are debating the proposed Amendment. It seems to me that this reaching out to pre-empt by judicial action a major political decision which is currently in process of resolution does not reflect appropriate respect for duly prescribed legislative process. . . .

Craig v. Boren
429 U.S. 190, 97 S.Ct. 451, 50 L.Ed. 2d 397 (1976)

Two sections (241 and 245) of an Oklahoma statute combined to prohibit the sale of 3.2 percent beer to males under the age of 21 and to females under the age of 18. Craig (a male between 18 and 21 years of age) and Whitener (a licensed vendor of 3.2 percent beer) sought injunctive relief against the statute in the United States District Court for the Western District of Oklahoma. They contended that the gender-based differential constituted an invidious discrimination against males 18-20 years old, in violation of the equal protection clause. The three-judge panel upheld the classification and dismissed the action. Justice Brennan's opinion for the Court begins with reference to *Reed* v. *Reed* (1971), where a unanimous bench voided an Idaho statutory probate scheme giving a mandatory preference for appointment as administrator to male applicants over equally qualified female applicants. Majority: Brennan, Blackmun, Marshall, Powell, Stevens, Stewart, White. Dissenting: Rehnquist, Burger.

MR. JUSTICE BRENNAN delivered the opinion of the Court. . . .

Analysis may appropriately begin with the reminder that Reed emphasized that statutory classifications that distinguish between males and females are "subject to scrutiny under the Equal Protection Clause.". . . To withstand constitutional challenge, previous cases establish that classifications by gender must serve important governmental ob-

jectives and must be substantially related to achievement of those objectives. Thus, in Reed, the objectives of "reducing the workload on probate courts" . . . and "avoiding intrafamily controversy" . . . were deemed of insufficient importance to sustain use of an overt gender criterion in the appointment of administrators of intestate decedents' estates. Decisions following Reed similarly have rejected administrative ease and convenience as sufficiently important objectives to justify gender-based classifications. . . .

We accept for purposes of discussion the District Court's identification of the objective underlying §§241 and 245 as the enhancement of traffic safety. Clearly, the protection of public health and safety represents an important function of state and local governments. However, appellees' statistics in our view cannot support the conclusion that the gender-based distinction closely serves to achieve that objective and therefore the distinction cannot under Reed withstand equal protection challenge.

The appellees introduced a variety of statistical surveys. . . .

Even were this statistical evidence accepted as accurate, it nevertheless offers only a weak answer to the equal protection question presented here. The most focused and relevant of the statistical surveys, arrests of 18-20 year-olds for alcohol-related driving offenses, exemplifies the ultimate unpersuasiveness of this evidentiary record. Viewed in terms of the correlation between sex and the actual activity that Oklahoma seeks to regulate—driving while under the influence of alcohol—the statistics broadly establish that .18 percent of females and 2 percent of males in that age group were arrested for that offense. While such a disparity is not trivial in a statistical sense, it hardly can form the basis for employment of a gender line as a classifying device. Certainly if maleness is to serve as a proxy for drinking and driving, a correlation of 2 percent must be considered an unduly tenuous "fit.". . .

There is no reason to belabor this line of analysis. It is unrealistic to expect either members of the judiciary or state officials to be well versed in the rigors of experimental or statistical technique. But this merely illustrates that proving broad sociological propositions by statistics is a dubious business, and one that inevitably is in tension with the normative philosophy that underlies the Equal Protection Clause. Suffice to say that the showing offered by the appellees does not satisfy us that sex represents a legitimate, accurate proxy for the regulation of drinking and driving. In fact, when it is further recognized that Oklahoma's statute prohibits only the selling of 3.2% beer to young males and not their drinking the beverage once acquired (even after purchase by their 18-20-year-old female companions), the relationship between gender and traffic safety becomes far too tenuous to satisfy Reed's requirement that the gender-based difference be substantially related to achievement of the statutory objective.

We hold, therefore, that under Reed, Oklahoma's 3.2% beer statute invidiously discriminates against males 18-20 years of age. . . .

MR. JUSTICE REHNQUIST, dissenting.

The Court's disposition of this case is objectionable on two grounds. First is its conclusion that *men* challenging a gender-based statute which treats them less favorably than women may invoke a more stringent standard of judicial review than pertains to most other types of classifications. Second is the Court's enunciation of this standard, without citation to any source, as being that "classifications by gender must serve *important* governmental objectives and must be *substantially* related to achievement of those objectives.". . . The only redeeming feature of the Court's opinion, to my mind, is that it apparently signals a retreat by those who joined the plurality opinion in *Frontiero* v. *Richardson* . . . from their view that sex is a "suspect" classification for purposes of equal protection analysis. I think the Oklahoma statute challenged here need pass only the "rational basis" equal protection analysis . . . and I believe that it is constitutional under that analysis.

In *Frontiero* v. *Richardson* . . . the opinion for the plurality sets forth the reasons of four Justices for concluding that sex should be regarded as a suspect classification for purposes of equal protection analysis. These reasons center on our Nation's "long and unfortunate history of sex discrimination" . . . which has been reflected in a whole range of restrictions on the legal rights of women, not the least of which have concerned the ownership of property and participation in the electoral process. . . .

. . . However, the Court's application here of an elevated or "intermediate" level scrutiny, like that invoked in cases dealing with discrimination against females, raises the question of why the statute here should be treated any differently from countless legislative classifications unrelated to sex which have been upheld under a minimum rationality standard. . . .

Most obviously unavailable to support any kind of special scrutiny in this case, is a history or pattern of past discrimination, such as was relied on by the plurality in Frontiero to support is invocation of strict scrutiny. There is no suggestion in the Court's opinion that males in this age group are in any way peculiarly disadvantaged, subject to systematic discriminatory treatment, or otherwise in need of special solicitude from the courts. . . .

The Court's conclusion that a law which treats males less favorably than females "must serve important governmental objectives and must be substantially related to achievement of those objectives" apparently comes out of thin air. The Equal Protection Clause contains no such language, and none of our previous cases adopt that standard. I would think we have had enough difficulty with the two standards of review which our cases have recognized—the norm of "rational basis," and the "compelling state interest" required where a "suspect classification" is involved—so as to counsel weightily against the insertion of still another "standard" between those two. How is this Court to divine what objectives are important? How is it to determine whether a particular law is "substantially" related to the achievement of such objective, rather than related in some other way to its achievement? Both of the phrases used are so diaphanous and elastic as to invite subjective judicial preferences or prejudices relating to particular types of legislation, masquerading as judgments whether such legislation is directed at "important" objectives or, whether the relationship to those objectives is "substantial" enough.

I would have thought that if this Court were to leave anything to decision by the popularly elected branches of the Government, where no constitutional claim other than that of equal protection is invoked, it would be the decision as to what governmental objectives to be achieved by law are "important," and which are not. As for the second part of the Court's new test, the Judicial Branch is probably in no worse position than the Legislative or Executive Branches to determine if there is *any* rational relationship between a classification and the purpose which it might be thought to serve. But the introduction of the adverb "substantially" requires courts to make subjective judgments as to operational effects, for which neither their expertise nor their access to data fits them. And even if we manage to avoid both confusion and the mirroring of our own preferences in the development of this new doctrine, the thousands of judges in other courts who must interpret the Equal Protection Clause may not be so fortunate. . . .

Rostker v. *Goldberg**
453 U.S. 57, 101 S.Ct. 2646, 69 L.Ed. 2d 478 (1981)

The Military Selective Service Act (referred to in the following opinions as the MSSA) authorizes the president to require draft registration for males but not females. Actual conscription was ended in 1973, and a presidential proclamation discontinued registration in 1975. As a result of the invasion of Afghanistan by the Soviet Union, President Carter decided in early 1980 to reinstate draft registration as a national display of strength. In seeking funds from Congress for registration, Carter requested that the statute be amended to permit registration of women as well. In the appropriation, however, Congress provided only enough money to register males and expressly declined to amend the statute to permit the registration of women. On July 2, 1980, President Carter by proclamation ordered the registration of certain groups of young men, a process to begin on July 21. Carter's action breathed new life into an old lawsuit, dating from 1971, against a

* This case should also be read in connection with Chapter Three.

gender-based draft. On July 18, the District Court for the Eastern District of Pennsylvania invalidated the draft statute under the due process clause of the Fifth Amendment and permanently enjoined the government from conducting registration under the act. On July 19, at the government's request, Justice Brennan, as circuit justice, stayed the district court's order. Majority: Rehnquist, Blackmun, Burger, Powell, Stevens, Stewart. Dissenting: Marshall, Brennan, White.

JUSTICE REHNQUIST delivered the opinion of the Court.

The question presented is whether the Military Selective Service Act violates the Fifth Amendment to the United States Constitution in authorizing the President to require the registration of males and not females. . . .

. . . The case arises in the context of Congress's authority over national defense and military affairs, and perhaps in no other area has the Court accorded Congress greater deference. . . .

Not only is the scope of Congress's constitutional power in this area broad, but the lack of competence on the part of the courts is marked. . . .

None of this is to say that Congress is free to disregard the Constitution when it acts in the area of military affairs. In that area as any other Congress remains subject to the limitations of the Due Process Clause . . . but the tests and limitations to be applied may differ because of the military context. We of course do not abdicate our ultimate responsibility to decide the constitutional question, but simply recognize that the Constitution itself requires such deference to congressional choice. In deciding the question before us we must be particularly careful not to substitute our judgment of what is desirable for that of Congress, or our own evaluation of evidence for a reasonable evaluation by the Legislative Branch. . . .

Nor can it be denied that the imposing number of cases from this Court previously cited suggest that judicial deference to such congressional exercise of authority is at its apogee when legislative action under the congressional authority to raise and support armies and make rules and regulations for their governance is challenged. . . .

The foregoing clearly establishes that the decision to exempt women from registration was not the "accidental by-product of a traditional way of thinking about women.". . . In *Michael M.* . . . we rejected a similar argument because of action by

the California Legislature considering and rejecting proposals to make a statute challenged on discrimination grounds gender-neutral. The cause for rejecting the argument is considerably stronger here. The issue was considered at great lengths, and Congress clearly expressed its purpose and intent. . . .

Congress determined that any future draft, which would be facilitated by the registration scheme, would be characterized by a need for combat troops. The Senate Report explained, in a specific finding later adopted by both Houses, that "if mobilization were to be ordered in a wartime scenario, the primary manpower need would be for combat replacements.". . .

Women as a group, however, unlike men as a group, are not eligible for combat. The restrictions on the participation of women in combat in the Navy and Air Force are statutory. . . . The Army and Marine Corps preclude the use of women in combat as a matter of established policy. Congress specifically recognized and endorsed the exclusion of women from combat in exempting women from registration. . . .

The reason women are exempt from registration is not because military needs can be met by drafting men. This is not a case of Congress arbitrarily choosing to burden one of two similarly situated groups, such as would be the case with an all-black or all-white, or an all-Catholic or all-Lutheran, or all-Republican or all-Democratic registration. Men and women, because of the combat restrictions on women, are simply not similarly situated for purposes of a draft or registration for a draft.

Congress's decision to authorize the registration of only men, therefore, does not violate the Due Process Clause. The exemption of women from registration is not only sufficiently but closely related to Congress's purpose in authorizing registration. See *Michael M.,* . . . *Craig* v. *Boren, Reed* v. *Reed.* . . . The fact that Congress and the Executive have decided that women should not serve in combat fully justifies Congress in not authorizing their registration, since the purpose of registration is to develop a pool of potential combat troops. . . .

Most significantly, Congress determined that staffing noncombat positions with women during a mobilization would be positively detrimental to the important goal of military flexibility. . . . The District Court was quite wrong in undertaking an independent evaluation of this evidence, rather than adopting an appropriately deferential examination of *Congress's* evaluation of that evidence.

In light of the foregoing, we conclude that Congress acted well within its constitutional authority when it authorized the registration of men, and not women, under the Military Selective Service Act. The decision of the District Court holding otherwise is accordingly

Reversed.

MR. JUSTICE MARSHALL, with whom MR. JUSTICE BRENNAN joins, dissenting.

The Court today places its imprimatur on one of the most potent remaining public expressions of "ancient canards about the proper role of women.". . . .

In the first place, although the Court purports to apply the *Craig* v. *Boren* test, the "similarly situated" analysis the Court employs is in fact significantly different from the *Craig* v. *Boren* approach. . . . The Court essentially reasons that the gender classification employed by the MSSA is constitutionally permissible because nondiscrimination is not necessary to achieve the purpose of registration to prepare for a draft of combat troops. In other words, the majority concludes that women may be excluded from registration because they will not be needed in the event of a draft.

This analysis, however, focuses on the wrong question. The relevant inquiry under the *Craig* v. *Boren* test is not whether a *gender-neutral* classification would substantially advance important governmental interests. Rather, the question is whether the gender-based classification is itself substantially related to the achievement of the asserted governmental interest. Thus, the Government's task in this case is to demonstrate that excluding women from registration substantially furthers the goal of preparing for a draft of combat troops. Or to put it another way, the Government must show that registering women would substantially impede its efforts to prepare for such a draft. Under our

precedents, the Government cannot meet this burden without showing that a gender neutral statute would be a less effective means of attaining this end. . . . In this case, the Government makes no claim that preparing for a draft of combat troops cannot be accomplished just as effectively by *registering* both men and women but *drafting* only men if only men turn out to be needed. . . .

The fact that registering women in no way obstructs the governmental interest in preparing for a draft of combat troops points up a second flaw in the Court's analysis. The Court essentially reduces the question of the constitutionality of male-only *registration* to the validity of a hypothetical program for *conscripting* only men. The Court posits a draft in which *all* conscripts are either assigned to those specific combat posts presently closed to women or must be available for rotation into such positions. . . .

But even addressing the Court's reasoning on its own terms, its analysis is flawed because the entire argument rests on a premise that is demonstrably false. As noted, the majority simply assumes that registration prepares for a draft in which *every* draftee must be available for assignment to combat. But the majority's draft scenario finds no support in either the testimony before Congress, or more importantly, in the findings of the Senate Report. Indeed, the scenario appears to exist only in the Court's imagination, for even the Government represents only that "in the event of mobilization, *approximately two-thirds* of the demand on the induction system would be for *combat skills*.". . . For my part, rather than join the Court in imagining hypothetical drafts, I prefer to examine the findings in the Senate Report and the testimony presented to Congress. . . .

This review of the findings contained in the Senate Report and the testimony presented at the congressional hearings demonstrates that there is no basis for the Court's representation that women are ineligible for *all* the positions that would need to be filled in the event of a draft.

After reviewing the discussion and findings contained in the Senate Report, the most I am able to say of the Report is that it demonstrates that drafting *very large numbers* of women would frustrate the achievement of a number of important governmental objectives that relate to the ultimate goal of maintaining "an adequate armed strength . . . to insure the security of this Nation.". . . .

Or to put it another way, the Senate Report establishes that induction of a large number of men but only a limited number of women, as determined by the military's personnel requirements, would be substantially related to important governmental interests. But the discussion and findings in the Senate Report do not enable the Government to carry its burden of demonstrating that *completely* excluding women from the draft by excluding them from registration substantially furthers important governmental objectives.

. . . Congressional enactments in the area of military affairs must, like all other laws, be *judged* by the standards of the Constitution. For the Constitution is the supreme law of the land and *all* legislation must conform to the principles it lays down. As the Court has pointed out, "the phrase 'war power' cannot be invoked as a talismanic incantation to support any exercise of congressional power which can be brought within its ambit.". . .

I would affirm the judgment of the District Court.

Regents of the University of California v. Bakke
438 U.S. 265, 98 S.Ct. 2733, 57 L.Ed. 2d 750 (1978)

The University of California at Davis opened its medical school in 1968 and soon began a special admissions program for certain minorities. The application for admission in 1974 asked candidates if they wanted to be considered as "Blacks," "Chicanos," "Asians," or "American Indians." Applications so marked were sent to a special committee. Sixteen of the 100 seats in the entering class were reserved for members of the four groups. These minority applicants could also compete for the remaining 84 seats. No white was ever admitted to the medical school through the special admissions program. In 1973 Allan Bakke applied late to the Davis medical school and was rejected. In 1974 he applied again, was again rejected, and filed suit on equal protection grounds. Bakke claimed that applicants with entrance examination scores and scholastic averages substantially lower than his had been admitted under the special program. The Superior Court of Yolo County agreed that the program violated the federal and state constitutions and Title VI of the 1964 Civil Rights Act, which proscribes racial discrimination in programs receiving federal financial assistance. The trial court, however, refused to order Bakke's admission because he had not proved that he would have been admitted except for the existence of the special program. The Supreme Court of California upheld the lower court on the invalidity of the program but ordered Bakke's admission to medical school. In the United States Supreme Court, alignment on the case was complex. The division that follows was on the issue of whether Bakke should be admitted to medical school. Majority: Powell, Stevens, Burger, Rehnquist, Stewart. Dissenting: Brennan, Blackmun, Marshall, White.

MR. JUSTICE POWELL announced the judgment of the Court. . . .

Petitioner urges us to . . . hold that discrimination against members of the white "majority" cannot be suspect if its purpose can be characterized as "benign." The clock of our liberties, however, cannot be turned back to 1868. It is far too late to argue that the guarantee of equal protection to *all* persons permits the recognition of special wards entitled to a degree of protection greater than that accorded others. . . .

Once the artificial line of a "two-class theory" of the Fourteenth Amendment is put aside, the difficulties entailed in varying the level of judicial review according to a perceived "preferred" status of a particular racial or ethnic minority are intractable. The concepts of "majority" and "minority" necessarily reflect temporary arrangements and political judgments. As observed above, the white "majority" itself is composed of various minority groups, most of which can lay claim to a history of prior discrimination at the hands of the State and private individuals. . . . Courts would be asked to evaluate the extent of the prejudice and consequent harm suffered by various minority groups. Those whose societal injury is thought to exceed some arbitrary level of tolerability then would be entitled to preferential classifications at the expense of individuals belonging to other groups. Those classifications would be free from exacting judicial scrutiny. As these preferences began to have their desired effect, and the consequences of past discrimination were undone, new judicial rankings would be necessary. The kind of variable sociological and political analysis necessary to produce such rankings simply does not lie within the judicial competence—even if they otherwise were politically feasible and socially desirable.

Moreover, there are serious problems of justice connected with the idea of preference itself. First, it may not always be clear that a so-called preference is in fact benign. . . . Second, preferential programs may only reinforce common stereotypes holding that certain groups are unable to achieve success without special protection based on a factor having no relationship to individual worth. Third, there is a measure of inequity in forcing innocent persons in respondent's position to bear the burdens of redressing grievances not of their making.

By hitching the meaning of the Equal Protection Clause to these transitory considerations, we would be holding, as a constitutional principle, that judicial scrutiny of classifications touching on racial and ethnic background may vary with the ebb and flow of political forces. . . .

We have held that in "order to justify the use of a suspect classification, a State must show that its purpose or interest is both constitutionally permissible and substantial, and that its use of the classification is 'necessary . . . to the accomplishment' of its purpose or the safeguarding of its interest." The special admissions program purports to serve the purposes of: (i) "reducing the historic deficit of traditionally disfavored minorities in medical schools and in the medical profession;" (ii) countering the effects of societal discrimination; (iii) increasing the number of physicians who will practice in communities currently underserved; and (iv) obtaining the educational benefits that flow from an ethnically diverse student body. It is necessary to decide which, if any, of these purposes is substantial enough to support the use of a suspect classification.

If petitioner's purpose is to assure within its student body some specified percentage of a particular group merely because of its race or ethnic origin, such a preferential purpose must be rejected not as insubstantial but as facially invalid. Preferring members of any one group for no reason other than race or ethnic origin is discrimination for its own sake. This the Constitution forbids. . . .

We have never approved a classification that aids persons perceived as members of relatively victimized groups at the expense of other innocent individuals in the absence of judicial, legislative, or administrative findings of constitutional or statutory violations. . . . Petitioner does not purport to have made, and is in no position to make, such findings. Its broad mission is education, not the formulation of any legislative policy or the adjudication of particular claims of illegality. . . . Petitioner simply has not carried its burden of demonstrating that it must prefer members of particular ethnic groups over all other individuals in order to promote better health-care delivery to deprived citizens. Indeed, petitioner has not shown that its preferential classification is likely to have any significant effect on the problem.

The fourth goal asserted by petitioner is the attainment of a diverse student body. This clearly is a constitutionally permissible goal for an institution of higher education.

. . . The diversity that furthers a compelling state interest encompasses a far broader array of qualifications and characteristics of which racial or ethnic origin is but a single though important element. Petitioner's special admissions program, focused *solely* on ethnic diversity, would hinder rather than further attainment of genuine diversity. Nor would the state interest in genuine diversity be served by expanding petitioner's two-track system into a multitrack program with a prescribed number of seats set aside for each identifiable category of applicants. Indeed, it is inconceivable that a university would thus pursue the logic of petitioner's two-track program to the illogical end of insulating each category of applicants with certain desired qualifications from competition with all other applicants. The experience of other university admissions programs, which take race into account in achieving the educational diversity valued by the First Amendment, demonstrates that the assignment of a fixed number of places to a minority group is not a necessary means toward that end. . . .

[R]ace or ethnic background may be deemed a "plus" in a particular applicant's file, yet it does not insulate the individual from comparison with all other candidates for the available seats. The file of a particular black applicant may be examined for his potential contribution to diversity without the factor of race being decisive when compared, for example, with that of an applicant identified as an Italian-American if the latter is thought to exhibit qualities more likely to promote beneficial educational pluralism. Such qualities could include exceptional talents, unique work or service experience, leadership potential, maturity, demonstrated compassion, a history of overcoming disadvantage, ability to communicate with the poor, or other qualifications deemed important. . . .

This kind of program treats each applicant as an individual in the admissions process. The applicant who loses out on the last available seat to another candidate receiving a "plus" on the basis of ethnic background will not have been foreclosed from all consideration for that seat simply because he was not the right color or had the wrong surname. It would mean only that his combined qualifications, which may have included similar nonobjective factors, did not outweigh those of the other applicant. His qualifications would have been weighed fairly and competitively, and he would have no basis to complain of unequal treatment under the Fourteenth Amendment. . . .

The fatal flaw in petitioner's preferential program is its disregard of individual rights as guaranteed by the Fourteenth Amendment. Such rights are not absolute. But when a State's distribution of benefits or imposition of burdens hinges on ancestry or the color of a person's skin or ancestry, that individual is entitled to a demonstration that the challenged classification is necessary to promote a substantial state interest. Petitioner has failed to carry this burden. For this reason, that portion of the California court's judgment holding petitioner's special admissions program invalid under the Fourteenth Amendment must be affirmed.

In enjoining petitioner from ever considering the race of any applicant, however, the courts below failed to recognize that the State has a substantial interest that legitimately may be served by a properly devised admissions program involving the competitive consideration of race and ethnic origin. For this reason, so much of the California court's judgment as enjoins petitioner from any consideration of the race of any applicant must be reversed. . . . Joint opinion of MR. JUSTICE BRENNAN, MR. JUSTICE WHITE, MR. JUSTICE MARSHALL, and MR. JUSTICE BLACKMUN, concurring in part and dissenting in part . . .

[B]ecause of the significant risk that racial classifications established for ostensibly benign purposes can be misused, causing effects not unlike those created by invidious classifications, it is inappropriate to inquire only whether there is any conceivable basis that might sustain such a classification. Instead, to justify such a classification an important and articulated purpose for its use must be shown. In addition, any statute must be stricken that stigmatizes any group or that singles out those least well represented in the political process to bear the brunt of a benign program. Thus, our review under the Fourteenth Amendment should be strict—not "'strict' in theory and fatal in fact," because it is stigma that causes fatality—but strict and searching nonetheless.

Davis' articulated purpose of remedying the effects of past societal discrimination is, under our cases, sufficiently important to justify the use of race-conscious admissions programs where there is a sound basis for concluding that minority underrepresentation is substantial and chronic, and that the handicap of past discrimination is impeding access of minorities to the Medical School. . . .

Certainly, on the basis of the undisputed factual submissions before this Court, Davis had a sound basis for believing that the problem of underrepresentation of minorities was substantial and chronic and that the problem was attributable to handicaps imposed on minority applicants by past and present racial discrimination. Until at least 1973, the practice of medicine in this country was, in fact, if not in law, largely the prerogative of whites. In 1950, for example, while Negroes constituted 10% of the total population, Negro physicians constituted only 2.2% of the total number of physicians. . . . By 1970, the . . . number of Negroes employed in medicine remained frozen at 2.2% while the Negro population had increased to 11.1%. The number of Negro admittees to predominantly white medical schools, moreover, had declined in absolute numbers during the years 1955 to 1964. . . .

The second prong of our test—whether the Davis program stigmatizes any discrete group or individual and whether race is reasonably used in light of the program's objectives—is clearly satisfied by the Davis program. It is not even claimed that Davis' program in any way operates to stigmatize or single out any discrete and insular, or even any identifiable, nonminority group. . . . True, whites are excluded from participation in the special admissions program, but this fact only operates to reduce the number of whites to be admitted in the regular admissions program in order to permit admission of a reasonable percentage—less than their proportion of the California population—of otherwise underrepresented qualified minority applicants.

. . . [With] respect to any factor (such as poverty or family educational background) that may be used as a substitute for race as an indicator of past discrimination, whites greatly outnumber racial minorities simply because whites make up a far larger percentage of the total population and therefore far outnumber minorities in absolute terms at every socioeconomic level. For example, of a class of recent medical school applicants from families with less than $10,000 income, at least 71% were white. Of all 1970 families headed by a person *not* a high school graduate which included related children under 18, 80% were white and 20% were racial minorities. Moreover, while race is positively correlated with differences in GPA and MCAT scores, economic disadvantage is not. Thus, it appears that economically disadvantaged whites do not score less well than economically advantaged whites, while economically advantaged blacks score less well than do disadvantaged whites. These statistics graphically illustrate that the University's purpose to integrate its classes by compensating for past discrimination could not be achieved by a general preference for the economically disadvantaged or the children of parents of limited education unless such groups were to make up the entire class.

Finally, Davis' special admissions program cannot be said to violate the Constitution simply because it has set aside a predetermined number of places for qualified minority applicants rather than using minority status as a positive factor to be considered in evaluating the applications of disadvantaged minority applicants. For purposes of constitutional adjudication, there is no difference between the two approaches. In any admissions program which accords special consideration to disadvantaged racial minorities, a determination of the degree of preference to be given is unavoidable, and any given preference that results in the exclusion of a white candidate is no more or less constitutionally acceptable than a program such as that at Davis. . . .

MR. JUSTICE STEVENS, with whom the CHIEF JUSTICE, MR. JUSTICE STEWART, and MR. JUSTICE REHNQUIST join, concurring in the judgment in part and dissenting in part.

It is always important at the outset to focus precisely on the controversy before the Court. . . . Section 601 of the Civil Rights Act of 1964 provides:

> No person in the United States shall, on the ground of race, color, or national origin, be excluded from participation in, be denied the benefits of, or be subjected to discrimination under any program or activity receiving Federal financial assistance.

The University, through its special admissions policy, excluded Bakke from participation in its program of medical education because of his race. The University also acknowledges that it was, and still is, receiving federal financial assistance. The plain language of the statute therefore requires affirmance of the judgment below. . . .

Wygant v. Jackson Board of Education
476 U.S. 267, 106 S.Ct. 1842, 90 L.Ed. 2d 260 (1986)

Article XII of a collective bargaining agreement (referred to in the following opinions as CBA) between the school board of Jackson, Michigan, and a teachers' union provided that the principle of seniority would govern the layoff of teachers should that become necessary. The exception was that at no time would there be a greater percentage of minority personnel laid off than the current percentage of minority personnel employed at the time of the layoff. When layoffs became necessary, nonminority teachers were let go ahead of minority teachers with less seniority. The former sued in United States district court, claiming violations of the Fourteenth Amendment's equal protection clause, as well as certain state and federal statutes. The district court upheld the constitutionality of the layoff provision, concluding that the racial distinctions it drew did not have to be grounded in a finding of prior discrimination but instead were permissible as an attempt to remedy societal discrimination by providing "role models" for minority schoolchildren. The Court of Appeals for the Sixth Circuit affirmed. Majority: Powell, Burger, O'-Connor, Rehnquist, White. Dissenting: Marshall, Blackmun, Brennan, Stevens.

JUSTICE POWELL announced the judgment of the Court and delivered an opinion in which THE CHIEF JUSTICE and JUSTICE REHNQUIST joined, and which JUSTICE O'CONNOR joined in part. . . .

This case presents the question whether a school board, consistent with the Equal Protection Clause, may extend preferential protection against layoffs to some of its employees because of their race or national origin. . . .

In this case, Article XII of the CBA operates against whites and in favor of certain minorities, and therefore constitutes a classification based on race. . . .We must decide whether the layoff provision is supported by a compelling state purpose and whether the means chosen to accomplish that purpose are narrowly tailored.

The Court of Appeals, relying on the reasoning and language of the District Court's opinion, held that the Board's interest in providing minority role models for its minority students, as an attempt to alleviate the effects of societal discrimination, was sufficiently important to justify the racial classification embodied in the layoff provision. . . .

This Court never has held that societal discrimination alone is sufficient to justify a racial classification. Rather, the Court has insisted upon some showing of prior discrimination by the governmental unit involved before allowing limited use of racial classifications in order to remedy such discrimination. . . .

Societal discrimination, without more, is too amorphous a basis for imposing a racially classified remedy. The role model theory announced by the District Court and the resultant holding typify this indefiniteness. There are numerous explanations for a disparity between the percentage of minority students and the percentage of minority faculty, many of them completely unrelated to discrimination of any kind. In fact, there is no apparent connection between the two groups. Nevertheless, the District Court combined irrelevant comparisons between these two groups with an indisputable statement that there has been societal discrimination, and upheld state action predicated upon racial classifications. No one doubts that there has been serious racial discrimination in this country. But as the basis for imposing discriminatory *legal* remedies that work against innocent people, societal discrimination is insufficient and over expansive. In the absence of particularized findings, a court could uphold remedies that are ageless in their reach into the past, and timeless in their ability to affect the future.

Respondents also now argue that their purpose in adopting the layoff provision was to remedy prior discrimination against minorities by the Jackson School District in hiring teachers. Public schools, like other public employers, operate under two interrelated constitutional duties. They are under a clear command from this Court, starting with *Brown v. Board of Education* . . . to eliminate every vestige of racial segregation and discrimination in the schools. Pursuant to that goal, race-conscious remedial action may be necessary. . . . On the other hand, public employers, including public schools, also must act in accordance with a "core purpose of the Fourteenth Amendment" which is to "do away with all governmentally imposed distinctions based on race.". . . These related constitutional duties are not always harmonious; reconciling them requires public employers to act with extraordinary care. In particular, a public employer like the Board must ensure that, before it embarks on an affirmative action program, it has convincing evidence that remedial action is warranted. That is, it must have sufficient evidence to justify the conclusion that there has been prior discrimination. . . .

Despite the fact that Article XII has spawned years of litigation and three separate lawsuits, no such determination ever has been made. Although its litigation position was different, the Board in *Jackson I* and *Jackson II* denied the existence of prior discriminatory hiring practices. . . . This precise issue was litigated in both those suits. Both courts concluded that any statistical disparities were the result of general societal discrimination, not of prior discrimination by the Board. The Board now contends that, given another opportunity, it could establish the existence of prior discrimination. Although this argument seems belated at this point in the proceedings, we need not consider the question since we conclude below that the layoff provision was not a legally appropriate means of achieving even a compelling purpose. . . .

Here . . . the means chosen to achieve the Board's asserted purposes is that of laying off non-minority teachers with greater seniority in order to retain minority teachers with less seniority. We have previously expressed concern over the burden that a preferential layoffs scheme imposes on innocent parties. See *Firefighters* v. *Stotts*. . . .

While hiring goals impose a diffuse burden, often foreclosing only one of several opportunities, layoffs impose the entire burden of achieving racial equality on particular individuals, often resulting in serious disruption of their lives. That burden is too intrusive. We therefore hold that, as a means of accomplishing purposes that otherwise may be legitimate, the Board's layoff plan is not sufficiently narrowly tailored. Other, less intrusive means of accomplishing similar purposes—such as the adoption of hiring goals—are available. For these reasons, the Board's selection of layoffs as the means to accomplish even a valid purpose cannot satisfy the demands of the Equal Protection Clause.

We accordingly reverse the judgment of the Court of Appeals for the Sixth Circuit.

It is so ordered.

JUSTICE O'CONNOR, concurring in part and concurring in the judgment. . . .

In the final analysis, the diverse formulations and the number of separate writings put forth by various members of the Court in these difficult cases do not necessarily reflect an intractable fragmentation in opinion with respect to certain core principles. Ultimately, the Court is at least in accord in believing that a public employer, consistent with the Constitution, may undertake an affirmative action program which is designed to further a legitimate remedial purpose and which implements that purpose by means that do not impose disproportionate harm on the interests, or unnecessarily trammel the rights, of innocent individuals directly and adversely affected by a plan's racial preference. . . .

The courts below ruled that a particularized, contemporaneous finding of discrimination was not necessary and upheld the plan as a remedy for "societal" discrimination, apparently on the assumption that in the absence of a specific, contemporaneous finding, any discrimination addressed by an affirmative action plan could only be termed "societal." . . . I believe that this assumption is false and therefore agree with the Court that a contemporaneous or antecedent finding of past discrimination by a court or other competent body is not a constitutional prerequisite to a public employer's voluntary agreement to an affirmative action plan. . . .

If contemporaneous findings were *required* of public employers in every case as a precondition to the constitutional validity of their affirmative action efforts, however, the relative value of these evidentiary advantages would diminish, for they could be secured only by the sacrifice of other vitally important values.

The imposition of a requirement that public employers make findings that they have engaged in illegal discrimination before they engage in affirmative action programs would severely undermine public employers' incentive to meet voluntarily their civil rights obligations. . . .

JUSTICE MARSHALL, with whom JUSTICE BRENNAN and JUSTICE BLACKMUN join, dissenting. . . .

The sole question posed by this case is whether the Constitution prohibits a union and a local school board from developing a collective-bargaining agreement that apportions layoffs between two racially determined groups as a means of preserving the effects of an affirmative hiring policy, the constitutionality of which is unchallenged. . . .

Despite the Court's inability to agree on a route, we have reached a common destination in sustaining affirmative action against constitutional attack. In *Bakke,* we determined that a state institution may take race into account as a factor in its decisions . . . and in *Fullilove,* the Court upheld a congressional preference for minority contractors because the measure was legitimately designed to ameliorate the present effects of past discrimination. . . .

In this case, it should not matter which test the Court applies. What is most important, under any approach to the constitutional analysis, is that a reviewing court genuinely consider the circumstances of the provision at issue. The history and application of Article XII, assuming verification upon a proper record, demonstrate that this provision would pass constitutional muster, no matter which standard the Court should adopt.

The principal state purpose supporting Article XII is the need to preserve the levels of faculty integration achieved through the affirmative hiring policy adopted in the early 1970's. . . .

The second part of any constitutional assessment of the disputed plan requires us to examine the means chosen to achieve the state purpose. Again,

the history of Article XII, insofar as we can determine it, is the best source of assistance. . . .

Article XII is a narrow provision because it allocates the impact of an unavoidable burden proportionately between two racial groups. It places no absolute burden or benefit on one race, and, within the confines of constant minority proportions, it preserves the hierarchy of seniority in the selection of individuals for layoff. Race is a factor, along with seniority, in determining which individuals the school system will lose; it is not alone dispositive of any individual's fate. . . . Moreover, Article XII does not use layoff protection as a tool for *increasing* minority representation; achievement of that goal is entrusted to the less severe hiring policies. And Article XII is narrow in the temporal sense as well. The very bilateral process that gave rise to Article XII when its adoption was necessary will also occasion its demise when remedial measures are no longer required. Finally, Article XII modifies contractual expectations that do not themselves carry any connotation of merit or achievement. . . . [N]either petitioners nor any Justice of this Court has suggested an alternative to Article XII that would have attained the stated goal in any narrower or more equitable a fashion. Nor can I conceive of one.

JUSTICE STEVENS, dissenting. . . .

It is argued . . . that the purpose should be deemed invalid because, even if the Board of Education's judgment in this case furthered a laudable goal, some other boards might claim that their experience demonstrates that segregated classes, or segregated faculties, lead to better academic achievement. There is, however, a critical difference between a decision to *exclude* a member of a minority race because of his or her skin color and a decision to *include* more members of the minority in a school faculty for that reason.

The exclusionary decision rests on the false premise that differences in race, or in the color of a person's skin, reflect real differences that are relevant to a person's right to share in the blessings of a free society. . . . [T]hat premise is "utterly irrational" . . . and repugnant to the principles of a free and democratic society. Nevertheless, the fact that persons of different races do, indeed, have differently colored skin, may give rise to a belief that there is some significant difference between such persons. The inclusion of minority teachers in the educational process inevitably tends to dispel that illusion whereas their exclusion could only tend to foster it. The inclusionary decision is consistent with the principle that all men are created equal; the exclusionary decision is at war with that principle. One decision accords with the Equal Protection Clause of the Fourteenth Amendment; the other does not. Thus, consideration of whether the consciousness of race is exclusionary or inclusionary plainly distinguishes the Board's valid purpose in this case from a race-conscious decision that would reinforce assumptions of inequality. . . .

Finally, we must consider the harm to the petitioners. Every layoff, like every refusal to employ a qualified applicant, is a grave loss to the affected individual. However, the undisputed facts in this case demonstrate that this serious consequence to the petitioners is not based on any lack of respect for their race, or on blind habit and stereotype. Rather, petitioners have been laid off for a combination of two reasons: the economic conditions that have led Jackson to lay off some teachers, and the special contractual protections intended to preserve the newly integrated character of the faculty in the Jackson schools. Thus, the same harm might occur if a number of gifted young teachers had been given special contractual protection because their specialties were in short supply and if the Jackson Board of Education faced a fiscal need for layoffs. . . . [T]he harm would be generated by the combination of economic conditions and the special contractual protection given a different group of teachers—a protection that, as discussed above, was justified by a valid and extremely strong public interest.

APPENDIX

The Constitution
of the United States of America

We the people of the United States, in order to form a more perfect Union, establish Justice, insure domestic Tranquility, provide for the common defence, promote the general Welfare, and secure the Blessings of Liberty to ourselves and our Posterity, do ordain and establish this CONSTITUTION for the United States of America.

Article I

SECTION 1

All legislative Powers herein granted shall be vested in a Congress of the United States, which shall consist of a Senate and House of Representatives.

SECTION 2

The House of Representatives shall be composed of Members chosen every second Year by the People of the several States, and the Electors in each State shall have the Qualifications requisite for Electors of the most numerous Branch of the State Legislature.

No Person shall be a Representative who shall not have attained to the Age of twenty-five Years,

and been seven Years a Citizen of the United States, and who shall not, when elected, be an Inhabitant of that State in which he shall be chosen.

[Representatives and direct Taxes shall be apportioned among the several States which may be included within this Union, according to their respective Numbers, which shall be determined by adding to the whole Number of Free Persons, including those bound to Service for a Term of Years, and excluding Indians not taxed, three fifths of all other persons.][1] The actual Enumeration shall be made within three Years after the first Meeting of the Congress of the United States, and within every subsequent Term of ten Years, in such Manner as they shall by Law direct. The Number of Representatives shall not exceed one for every thirty thousand, but each State shall have at least one Representative; and until such enumeration shall be made, the State of New Hampshire shall be entitled to chuse three, Massachusetts eight, Rhode

[1] This provision was modified by the Sixteenth Amendment. The three-fifths reference to slaves was rendered obsolete by the Thirteenth and Fourteenth Amendments.

528

Island and Providence Plantations one, Connecticut five, New York six, New Jersey four, Pennsylvania eight, Delaware one, Maryland six, Virginia ten, North Carolina five, South Carolina five, and Georgia three.

When vacancies happen in the Representation from any State, the Executive Authority thereof shall issue Writs of Election to fill such Vacancies.

The House of Representatives shall chuse their Speaker and other Officers; and shall have the sole Power of Impeachment.

SECTION 3

The Senate of the United States shall be composed of two Senators from each State, chosen by the Legislature thereof,[2] for six Years; and each Senator shall have one Vote.

Immediately after they shall be assembled in Consequence of the first Election, they shall be divided as equally as may be into three Classes. The Seats of the Senators of the first Class shall be vacated at the Expiration of the second Year, of the Second Class at the Expiration of the fourth Year, and of the third Class at the Expiration of the sixth Year, so that one-third may be chosen every second Year; and if Vacancies happen by Resignation, or otherwise, during the Recess of the Legislature of any State, the Executive therefore may make temporary Appointments until the next Meeting of the Legislature, which shall then fill such Vacancies.

No Person shall be a Senator who shall not have attained to the Age of thirty Years, and been nine Years a Citizen of the United States, and who shall not, when elected, be an Inhabitant of that State in which he shall be chosen.

The Vice President of the United States shall be President of the Senate, but shall have no vote, unless they be equally divided.

The Senate shall chuse their other Officers, and also a President pro tempore, in the absence of the Vice President, or when he shall exercise the Office of President of the United States.

The Senate shall have the sole Power to try all Impeachments. When sitting for that Purpose, they shall be on Oath or Affirmation. When the President of the United States is tried, the Chief Justice shall

preside; And no Person shall be convicted without the Concurrence of two thirds of the Members present.

Judgment in Cases of Impeachment shall not extend further than to removal from Office, and disqualification to hold and enjoy any Office of honor, Trust or Profit under the United States; but the Party convicted shall nevertheless be liable and subject to Indictment, Trial, Judgment, and Punishment, according to Law.

SECTION 4

The Times, Places and Manner of holding Elections for Senators and Representatives, shall be prescribed in each State by the Legislature thereof; but the Congress may at any time by Law make or alter such Regulations, except as to the Places of chusing Senators.

The Congress shall assemble at least once in every Year, and such Meeting shall be on the first Monday in December, unless they shall by Law appoint a different Day.[3]

SECTION 5

Each House shall be the Judge of the Elections, Returns and Qualifications of its own Members, and a Majority of each shall constitute a Quorum to do Business; but a smaller Number may adjourn from day to day, and may be authorized to compel the Attendance of absent Members, in such Manner, and under such Penalties, as each House may provide.

Each House may determine the Rules of its Proceedings, punish its Members for disorderly Behavior, and, with the Concurrence of two thirds, expel a Member.

Each House shall keep a Journal of its Proceedings and from time to time publish the same, excepting such Parts as may in their Judgment require Secrecy; and the Yeas and Nays of the Members of either House on any question shall, at the Desire of one fifth of those Present, be entered on the Journal.

Neither House, during the Session of Congress, shall without the Consent of the other, adjourn for more than three days, nor to any other Place than that in which the two Houses shall be sitting.

---

[2] See the Seventeenth Amendment.

[3] See the Twentieth Amendment.

SECTION 6

The Senators and Representatives shall receive a Compensation for their Services, to be ascertained by Law, and paid out of the Treasury of the United States. They shall in all Cases, except Treason, Felony, and Breach of the peace, be privileged from Arrest during their Attendance at the Session of their respective Houses, and in going to and returning from the same; and for any Speech or Debate in either House, they shall not be questioned in any other Place.

No Senator or Representative shall, during the Time for which he was elected, be appointed to any civil Office under the Authority of the United States, which shall have been created, or the Emoluments whereof shall have been encreased during such time; and no Person holding any Office under the United States shall be a Member of either House during his continuance in Office.

SECTION 7

All Bills for raising Revenue shall originate in the House of Representatives; but the Senate may propose or concur with Amendments as on other Bills.

Every Bill which shall have passed the House of Representatives and the Senate, shall, before it become a Law, be presented to the President of the United States; if he approve he shall sign it, but if not he shall return it, with his Objections to that House in which it shall have originated, who shall enter the Objections at large on their Journal, and proceed to reconsider it. If after such Reconsideration two thirds of that House shall agree to pass the Bill it shall be sent, together with the Objections, to the other House, by which it shall likewise be reconsidered, and if approved by two thirds of that House, it shall become a Law. But in all such Cases the Votes of both Houses shall be determined by Yeas and Nays, and the Names of the Persons voting for and against the Bill shall be entered on the Journal of each House respectively. If any Bill shall not be returned by the President within ten Days (Sundays excepted) after it shall have been presented to him, the Same shall be a Law, in like Manner as if he had signed it, unless the Congress by their Adjournment prevent its Return, in which Case it shall not be a Law.

Every Order, Resolution, or Vote to which the Concurrence of the Senate and House of Representatives may be necessary (except on a question of Adjournment) shall be presented to the President of the United States; and before the Same shall take Effect, shall be approved by him, or being disapproved by him, shall be repassed by two thirds of the Senate and House of Representatives, according to the Rules and Limitations prescribed in the Case of a Bill.

SECTION 8

The Congress shall have Power To lay and collect Taxes, Duties, Imposts and Excises, to pay the Debts and provide for the common Defence and general Welfare of the United States; but all Duties, Imposts and Excises shall be uniform throughout the United States;

To borrow money on the Credit of the United States;

To regulate Commerce with foreign Nations, and among the several States, and with the Indian Tribes;

To establish an uniform Rule of Naturalization, and uniform Laws on the subject of Bankruptcies throughout the United States;

To coin Money, regulate the Value thereof, and of foreign Coin, and fix the Standard of Weights and Measures;

To provide for the Punishment of counterfeiting the Securities and current Coin of the United States;

To Establish Post Offices and Post Roads;

To promote the Progress of Science and useful Arts, by securing for limited Times to Authors and Inventors the exclusive Right to their respective Writings and Discoveries;

To constitute Tribunals inferior to the supreme Court;

To define and punish Piracies and Felonies committed on the high Seas, and Offenses against the Law of Nations;

To declare War, grant Letters of Marque and Reprisal, and make Rules concerning Captures on Land and Water;

To raise and support Armies, but no Appropriation of Money to that Use shall be for a longer Term than two Years;

To provide and maintain a Navy;

To make Rules for the Government and Regulation of the land and naval Forces;

To provide for calling forth the Militia to execute

the Laws of the Union, suppress Insurrections and repel Invasions;

To provide for organizing, arming, and disciplining the Militia, and for governing such Part of them as may be employed in the Service of the United States, reserving to the States respectively, the Appointment of the Officers, and the Authority of training the Militia according to the discipline prescribed by Congress;

To exercise exclusive Legislation in all Cases whatsoever, over such District (not exceeding ten Miles square) as may, by Cession of particular States, and the acceptance of Congress, become the Seat of the Government of the United States, and to exercise like Authority over all Places purchased by the Consent of the Legislature of the State in which the Same shall be, for the Erection of Forts, Magazines, Arsenals, dock-Yards, and other needful Buildings;—And

To make all Laws which shall be necessary and proper for carrying into Execution the foregoing Powers, and all other Powers vested by this Constitution in the Government of the United States, or in any Department or Officer thereof.

SECTION 9

The Migration or Importation of such Persons as any of the States now existing shall think proper to admit, shall not be prohibited by the Congress prior to the Year, one thousand eight hundred and eight, but a tax or duty may be imposed on such Importation, not exceeding ten dollars for each person.

The privilege of the Writ of Habeas Corpus shall not be suspended, unless when in Cases of Rebellion or Invasion the public Safety may require it.

No Bill of Attainder or ex post facto Law shall be passed.

No capitation, or other direct Tax shall be laid, unless in Proportion to the Census or Enumeration herein before directed to be taken.[4]

No Tax or Duty shall be laid on Articles exported from any State.

No Preference shall be given by any Regulation of Commerce or Revenue to the Ports of one State over those of another: nor shall Vessels bound to,

or from one State, be obliged to enter, clear, or pay Duties in another.

No Money shall be drawn from the Treasury, but in Consequence of Appropriations made by Law; and a regular Statement and Account of the Receipts and Expenditures of all public Money shall be published from time to time.

No Title of Nobility shall be granted by the United States:—And no Person holding any Office of Profit or Trust under them, shall, without the Consent of the Congress, accept of any present, Emolument, Office, or Title, of any kind whatever, from any King, Prince or foreign State.

SECTION 10

No State shall enter into any Treaty, Alliance, or Confederation; grant Letters of Marque and Reprisal; coin Money; emit Bills of Credit; make any Thing but gold and silver Coin a Tender in Payment of Debts; pass any Bill of Attainder, ex post facto Law, or Law impairing the Obligation of Contracts, or grant any Title of Nobility.

No State shall, without the Consent of the Congress, lay any Imposts or Duties on Imports or Exports, except what may be absolutely necessary for executing its inspection Laws: and the net Product of all Duties and Imposts, laid by any State on Imports or Exports, shall be for the Use of the Treasury of the United States and all such Laws shall be subject to the Revision and Controul of the Congress.

No State shall, without the Consent of Congress, lay any duty of Tonnage, keep Troops, or Ships of War in time of Peace, enter into any Agreement or Compact with another State, or with a foreign Power, or engage in War, unless actually invaded, or in such imminent Danger as will not admit of delay.

Article II

SECTION 1

The executive Power shall be vested in a President of the United States of America. He shall hold his Office during the Term of four Years, and, together with the Vice-President, chosen for the same term, be elected, as follows.

Each State shall appoint, in such Manner as the Legislature thereof may direct, a number of Electors,

---

[4] See the Sixteenth Amendment.

equal to the whole number of Senators and Representatives to which the State may be entitled in the Congress; but no Senator or Representative, or Person holding an Office of Trust or Profit under the United States, shall be appointed an Elector.

The Electors shall meet in their respective States, and vote by Ballot for two persons, of whom one at least shall not be an Inhabitant of the same State with themselves. And they shall make a List of all the Persons voted for, and of the Number of Votes for each; which List they shall sign and certify, and transmit sealed to the Seat of the Government of the United States, directed to the President of the Senate. The President of the Senate shall, in the Presence of the Senate and House of Representatives, open all the Certificates, and the Votes shall then be counted. The Person having the greatest Number of Votes shall be the President, if such Number be a Majority of the whole Number of Electors appointed; and if there be more than one who have such Majority, and have an Equal Number of Votes, then the House of Representatives shall immediately chuse by Ballot one of them for President; and if no Person have a Majority, then from the five highest on the List the said House shall in like Manner chuse the President, but in chusing the President, the Votes shall be taken by States, the Representation from each State having one Vote; a quorum for this Purpose shall consist of a Member or Members from two-thirds of the States, and a Majority of all the States shall be necessary to a Choice. In every Case, after the Choice of the President, the Person having the greatest Number of Votes of the Electors shall be the Vice-President. But if there should remain two or more who have equal Votes, the Senate shall chuse from them by Ballot the Vice-President.[5]

The Congress may determine the Time of chusing the Electors, and the Day on which they shall give their Vote; which Day shall be the same throughout the United States.

No person except a natural born Citizen, or a Citizen of the United States, at the time of the Adoption of this Constitution, shall be eligible to the Office of President; neither shall any Person be eligible to that Office who shall not have attained to the Age of thirty-five Years, and been fourteen Years a Resident within the United States.

[5] This paragraph was superseded by the Twelfth Amendment.

In Case of the Removal of the President from Office, or of his Death, Resignation, or Inability to discharge the Powers and Duties of the said Office, the same shall devolve on the Vice-President, and the Congress may by Law provide for the Case of Removal, Death, Resignation, or Inability, both of the President and Vice-President, declaring what Officer shall then act as President, and such Officer shall act accordingly, until the Disability be removed, or a President shall be elected.

The President shall, at stated Times, receive for his Services, a Compensation, which shall neither be encreased nor diminished during the Period for which he shall have been elected, and he shall not receive within that Period any other Emolument from the United States, or any of them.

Before he enters on the Execution of his Office, he shall take the following Oath or Affirmation: "I do solemnly swear (or affirm) that I will faithfully execute the Office of President of the United States, and will to the best of my Ability, preserve, protect and defend the Constitution of the United States."

SECTION 2

The President shall be Commander in Chief of the Army and Navy of the United States, and of the Militia of the several States, when called into the actual Service of the United States; he may require the Opinion in writing, of the principal Officer in each of the executive Departments, upon any subject relating to the Duties of their respective Offices, and he shall have Power to grant Reprieves and Pardons for Offenses against the United States, except in Cases of Impeachment.

He shall have Power, by and with the Advice and Consent of the Senate, to make Treaties, provided two-thirds of the Senators present concur; and he shall nominate, and by and with the Advice and Consent of the Senate, shall appoint Ambassadors, other public Ministers and Consuls, Judges of the supreme Court, and all other Officers of the United States, whose Appointments are not herein otherwise provided for, and which shall be established by Law: but the Congress may by Law vest the Appointment of such inferior Officers, as they think proper, in the President alone, in the Courts of Law, or in the Heads of Departments.

The President shall have Power to fill up all Vacancies that may happen during the Recess of the Senate, by granting Commissions which shall expire at the End of their next Session.

SECTION 3

He shall from time to time give to the Congress Information of the State of the Union, and recommend to their Consideration such Measures as he shall judge necessary and expedient; he may, on extraordinary Occasions, convene both Houses, or either of them, and in Cases of Disagreement between them, with Respect to the Time of Adjournment, he may adjourn them to such Time as he shall think proper; he shall receive Ambassadors and other public Ministers; he shall take Care that the Laws be faithfully executed, and shall Commission all the Officers of the United States.

SECTION 4

The President, Vice-President and all civil Officers of the United States, shall be removed from Office on Impeachment for, and Conviction of, Treason, Bribery, or other high Crimes and Misdemeanors.

Article III

SECTION 1

The judicial Power of the United States, shall be vested in one supreme Court, and in such inferior Courts as the Congress may from time to time ordain and establish. The Judges, both of the supreme and inferior Courts, shall hold their offices during good Behaviour, and shall, at stated Times, receive for their Services a Compensation, which shall not be diminished during their Continuance in Office.

SECTION 2

The judicial Power shall extend to all Cases, in Law and Equity, arising under this Constitution, the Laws of the United States and Treaties made, or which shall be made, under their Authority;— to all Cases affecting Ambassadors, other public Ministers and Consuls;—to all Cases of admiralty and maritime Jurisdiction;—to Controversies to which the United States shall be a Party;—to Controversies between two or more States;—between a State and Citizens of another State;[6]— Between Citizens of different States;—between Citizens of the same State claiming Lands under Grants of different States, and between a State, or the

6 See the Eleventh Amendment.

Citizens thereof, and foreign States, Citizens or Subjects.

In all Cases affecting Ambassadors, other public Ministers and Consuls, and those in which a State shall be a Party, the supreme Court shall have original Jurisdiction. In all the other Cases before mentioned, the supreme Court shall have appellate Jurisdiction, both as to Law and Fact, with such Exceptions, and under such Regulations as the Congress shall make.

The trial of all Crimes, except in Cases of Impeachment, shall be by Jury, and such Trial shall be held in the State where the said Crimes shall have been committed; but when not committed within any State, the Trial shall be at such Place or Places as the Congress may by Law have directed.

SECTION 3

Treason against the United States, shall consist only in levying War against them, or, in adhering to their Enemies, giving them Aid and Comfort. No Person shall be convicted of Treason unless on the Testimony of two Witnesses to the same overt Act, or on Confession in open Court.

The Congress shall have Power to declare the Punishment of Treason, but no Attainder of Treason shall work Corruption of Blood, or Forfeiture except during the Life of the Person attained.

Article IV

SECTION 1

Full Faith and Credit shall be given in each State to the public acts, Records, and judicial Proceedings of every other State. And the Congress may by general Laws prescribe the Manner in which such Acts, Records and Proceedings shall be proved, and the Effect thereof.

SECTION 2

The Citizens of each State shall be entitled to all Privileges and Immunities of Citizens in the several States.

A Person charged in any State with Treason, Felony, or other Crime, who shall flee from Justice, and be found in another State, shall on demand of the executive Authority of the State from which he fled, be delivered up, to be removed to the State having Jurisdiction of the Crime.

No Person held to Service or Labour in one State, under the Laws thereof, escaping into another, shall, in Consequence of any Law or Regulation therein, be discharged from such Service or Labour, but shall be delivered up on Claim of the Party to whom such Service or Labour may be due.[7]

SECTION 3

New States may be admitted by the Congress into this Union; but no new States shall be formed or erected within the Jurisdiction of any other State; nor any State be formed by the Junction of two or more States, or parts of States, without the Consent of the Legislatures of the States concerned as well as of the Congress.

The Congress shall have Power to dispose of and make all needful Rules and Regulations respecting the Territory or other Property belonging to the United States; and nothing in this Constitution shall be so constructed as to Prejudice any Claims of the United States, or of any particular State.

SECTION 4

The United States shall guarantee to every State in this Union a Republican Form of Government, and shall protect each of them against Invasion; and on Application of the Legislature, or of the Executive (when the Legislature cannot be convened) against domestic Violence.

Article V

The Congress, whenever two-thirds of both Houses shall deem it necessary, shall propose Amendments to this Constitution, or, on the Application of the Legislatures of two-thirds of the several States, shall call a Convention for proposing Amendments, which, in either Case, shall be valid to all Intents and Purposes, as part of this Constitution, when ratified by the Legislatures of three-fourths of the several

States, or by Conventions in three-fourths thereof, as the one or the other Mode of Ratification may be proposed by the Congress; Provided that no Amendment which may be made prior to the Year One thousand eight hundred and eight shall in any Manner affect the first and fourth Clauses in the Ninth Section of the first Article; and that no State, without its Consent, shall be deprived of its equal Suffrage in the Senate.

Article VI

All Debts contracted and Engagements entered into, before the Adoption of this Constitution, shall be as valid against the United States under this Constitution, as under the Confederation.

This Constitution, and the Laws of the United States which shall be made in Pursuance thereof; and all Treaties made, or which shall be made, under the Authority of the United States, shall be the supreme Law of the Land; and the Judges in every State shall be bound thereby, any Thing in the Constitution or Laws of any State to the Contrary notwithstanding.

The Senators and Representatives before mentioned, and the Members of the several State Legislatures, and all executive and judicial Officers, both of the United States and of the several States, shall be bound by Oath or Affirmation, to support this Constitution; but no religious Test shall ever be required as a Qualification to any Office or public Trust under the United States.

Article VII

The Ratification of the Conventions of nine States shall be sufficient for the Establishment of this Constitution between the States so ratifying the Same.

Done in Convention by the Unanimous Consent of the States Present the Seventeenth Day of September in the Year of our Lord one thousand seven hundred and eighty-seven and of the Independence of the United States of America the Twelfth. In Witness whereof We have hereunto subscribed our Names.

---

[7] Obsolete. See the Thirteenth Amendment.

Geo. WASHINGTON
Presid't and Deputy from Virginia

Delaware
Geo: Read
John Dickinson
Jaco: Broom
Gunning Bedford jun
Richard Bassett

Maryland
James McHenry
Danl Carroll
Dan: of St. Thos. Jenifer

South Carolina
J. Rutledge
Charles Pinckney
Charles Cotesworth Pickney
Pierce Butler

Georgia
William Few
Abr Baldwin

New York
Alexander Hamilton

New Jersey
Wil: Livingston
David Brearley
Wm. Paterson
Jona: Dayton

New Hampshire
John Langdon
Nicholas Gilman

Massachusetts
Nathaniel Gorham
Rufus King

Connecticut
Wm Saml Johnson
Roger Sherman

Virginia
John Blair
James Madison, Jr.

North Carolina
Wm Blount
Hu Williamson
Richd Dobbs Spaight

Pennsylvania
B. Franklin
Robt. Morris
Thos. Fitzsimons
James Wilson
Thomas Mifflin
Geo. Clymer
Jared Ingersoll
Gouv Morris

Attest:
WILLIAM JACKSON, Secretary

AMENDMENTS[8]

Amendment I

Congress shall make no law respecting an establishment of religion, or prohibiting the free exercise thereof; or abridging the freedom of speech, or of the press; or the right of the people peaceably to assemble, and to petition the Government for a redress of grievances.

Amendment II

A well regulated Militia, being necessary to the security of a free State, the right of the people to keep and bear Arms, shall not be infringed.

[8] The first ten Amendments were adopted in 1791.

Amendment III

No Soldier shall, in time of peace be quartered in any house, without the consent of the Owner, nor in time of war, but in a manner to be prescribed by law.

Amendment IV

The right of the people to be secure in their persons, houses, papers, and effects, against unreasonable searches and seizures, shall not be violated, and no Warrants shall issue, but upon probable cause, supported by Oath or affirmation, and particularly describing the place to be searched, and the persons or things to be seized.

Amendment V

No person shall be held to answer for a capital, or otherwise infamous crime, unless on a presentment or indictment of a Grand Jury, except in cases arising in the land or naval forces, or in the Militia, when in actual service in time of War or public danger; nor shall any person be subject for the same offense to be twice put in jeopardy of life or limb, nor shall be compelled in any criminal case to be a witness against himself, nor be deprived of life, liberty, or property, without due process of law; nor shall private property be taken for public use, without just compensation.

Amendment VI

In all criminal prosecutions, the accused shall enjoy the right to a speedy and public trial, by an impartial jury of the State and district wherein the crime shall have been committed, which district shall have been previously ascertained by law, and to be informed of the nature and cause of the accusation; to be confronted with the witnesses against him; to have compulsory process for obtaining witnesses in his favor, and to have the Assistance of Counsel for his defence.

Amendment VII

In suits at common law, where the value in controversy shall exceed twenty dollars, the right of trial by jury shall be preserved, and no fact tried by jury, shall be otherwise reexamined in any Court of the United States, than according to the rules of the common law.

Amendment VIII

Excessive bail shall not be required, nor excessive fines imposed, nor cruel and unusual punishments inflicted.

Amendment IX

The enumeration in the Constitution, of certain rights, shall not be construed to deny or disparage others retained by the people.

Amendment X

The powers not delegated to the United States by the Constitution, nor prohibited by it to the States, are reserved to the States respectively, or to the people.

Amendment XI[9]

The Judicial power of the United States shall not be construed to extend to any suit in law or equity, commenced or prosecuted against one of the United States by Citizens of another State, or by Citizens or Subjects of any Foreign States.

Amendment XII[10]

The Electors shall meet in their respective states and vote by ballot for President and Vice-President, one of whom, at least, shall not be an inhabitant of the same state with themselves; they shall name in their ballots the person voted for as President, and in distinct ballots the person voted for as Vice-President, and they shall make distinct lists of all persons voted for as president, and all persons voted for as Vice-President, and of the number of votes for each, which lists they shall sign and certify, and transmit sealed to the seat of the government of the United States, directed to the President of the Senate;—The President of the Senate shall, in

[9] Adopted in 1798.
[10] Adopted in 1804.

the presence of the Senate and House of Representatives, open all the certificates and the votes shall then be counted;—The person having the greatest number of votes for President, shall be the President, if such number be a majority of the whole number of Electors appointed; and if no person have such majority, then from the persons having the highest numbers not exceeding three on the list of those voted for as President, the House of Representatives shall choose immediately, by ballot, the President. But in choosing the President, the votes shall be taken by states, the representation from each state having one vote; a quorum for this purpose shall consist of a member or members from two-thirds of the states, and a majority of all the states shall be necessary to a choice. And if the House of Representatives shall not choose a President whenever the right of choice shall devolve upon them, before the fourth day of March next following, then the Vice-President shall act as President, as in the case of the death or other constitutional disability of the President.—The person having the greatest number of votes as Vice-President, shall be the Vice-President, if such number be a majority of the whole number of Electors appointed, and if no person have a majority, then from the two highest numbers on the list, the Senate shall choose the Vice-President; a quorum for the purpose shall consist of two-thirds of the whole number of Senators, and a majority of the whole number shall be necessary to a choice. But no person constitutionally ineligible to the office of the President shall be eligible to that of Vice-President of the United States.

Amendment XIII[11]

SECTION 1

Neither slavery nor involuntary servitude, except as a punishment for crime whereof the party shall have been duly convicted, shall exist within the United States, or any place subject to their jurisdiction.

SECTION 2

Congress shall have power to enforce this article by appropriate legislation.

[11] Adopted in 1865.

Amendment XIV[12]

SECTION 1

All persons born or naturalized in the United States and subject to the jurisdiction thereof, are citizens of the United States and of the State wherein they reside. No State shall make or enforce any law which shall abridge the privileges or immunities of citizens of the United States; nor shall any State deprive any person of life, liberty, or property, without due process of law; nor deny to any person within its jurisdiction the equal protection of the laws.

SECTION 2

Representatives shall be apportioned among the several States according to their respective numbers, counting the whole number of persons in each State, excluding Indians not taxed. But when the right to vote at any election for the choice of electors for President and Vice-President of the United States, Representatives in Congress, the Executive and Judicial Officers of a State, or the members of the Legislature thereof, is denied to any of the male inhabitants of such State, being twenty-one years of age, and citizens of the United States, or in any way abridged, except for participation in rebellion, or other crime, the basis of representation therein shall be reduced in the proportion which the number of such male citizens shall bear to the whole number of male citizens twenty-one years of age in such State.

SECTION 3

No person shall be a Senator or Representative in Congress, or elector of President and Vice-President, or hold any office, civil or military, under the United States, or under any State, who, having previously taken an oath, as a member of Congress, or as an officer of the United States, or as a member of any State legislature, or as an executive or judicial officer of any State, to support the Constitution of the United States, shall have engaged in insurrection or rebellion against the same, or given aid or comfort to the enemies thereof. But Congress may by a vote of two-thirds of each House, remove such disability.

[12] Adopted in 1868.

SECTION 4

The validity of the public debt of the United States, authorized by law, including debts incurred for payment of pensions and bounties for services in suppressing insurrection or rebellion, shall not be questioned. But neither the United States nor any State shall assume or pay any debt or obligation incurred in aid of insurrection or rebellion against the United States, or any claim for the loss or emancipation of any slave; but all such debts, obligations, and claims shall be held illegal and void.

SECTION 5

The Congress shall have power to enforce, by appropriate legislation, the provisions of this article.

Amendment XV[13]

SECTION 1

The right of citizens of the United States to vote shall not be denied or abridged by the United States or by any State on account of race, color, or previous condition of servitude.

SECTION 2

The Congress shall have the power to enforce this article by appropriate legislation.

Amendment XVI[14]

The Congress shall have power to lay and collect taxes on incomes, from whatever source derived, without apportionment among the several States, and without regard to any census or enumeration.

Amendment XVII[15]

The Senate of the United States shall be composed of two Senators from each State, elected by the people thereof, for six years, and each Senator shall have one vote. The electors in each State shall have the qualifications requisite for electors of the most numerous branch of the State legislatures.

When vacancies happen in the representation of any State in the Senate, the executive authority of such State shall issue writs of election to fill such vacancies: *Provided,* That the legislature of any State may empower the executive thereof to make temporary appointments until the people fill the vacancies by election as the legislature may direct.

This amendment shall not be so construed as to affect the election or term of any Senator chosen before it becomes valid as part of the Constitution.

Amendment XVIII[16]

SECTION 1

After one year from the ratification of this article the manufacture, sale, or transportation of intoxicating liquors within, the importation thereof into, or the exportation thereof from the United States and all territory subject to the jurisdiction thereof for beverage purposes is hereby prohibited.

SECTION 2

The Congress and the several States shall have concurrent power to enforce this article by appropriate legislation.

SECTION 3

This article shall be inoperative unless it shall have been ratified as an amendment to the Constitution by the legislatures of the several States, as provided in the Constitution, within seven years from the date of the submission hereof to the States by the Congress.

Amendment XIX[17]

The right of citizens of the United States to vote shall not be denied or abridged by the United States or by any State on account of sex.

Congress shall have power to enforce this article by appropriate legislation.

---

[13] Adopted in 1870.
[14] Adopted in 1913.
[15] Adopted in 1913.

[16] Adopted in 1919. Repealed by the Twenty-first Amendment.
[17] Adopted in 1920.

Amendment XX[18]

SECTION 1

The terms of the President and Vice-President shall end at noon on the 20th day of January, and the terms of Senators and Representatives at noon on the 3rd day of January, of the years in which such terms would have ended if this article had not been ratified; and the terms of their successors shall then begin.

SECTION 2

The Congress shall assemble at least once in every year, and such meeting shall begin at noon on the 3rd day of January, unless they shall by law appoint a different day.

SECTION 3

If, at the time fixed for the beginning of the term of the President, the President elect shall have died, the Vice-President elect shall become President. If a President shall not have been chosen before the time fixed for the beginning of his term, or if the President elect shall have failed to qualify, then the Vice-President elect shall act as President until a President shall have qualified; and the Congress may by law provide for the case wherein neither a President elect nor a Vice-President elect shall have qualified, declaring who shall then act as President, or the manner in which one who is to act shall be selected, and such person shall act accordingly until a President or Vice-President shall have qualified.

SECTION 4

The Congress may by law provide for the case of the death of any of the persons from whom the House of Representatives may choose a President whenever the right of choice shall have developed upon them, and for the case of the death of any of the persons from whom the Senate may choose a Vice-President whenever the right of choice shall have devolved upon them.

SECTION 5

Sections 1 and 2 shall take effect on the 15th day of October following the ratification of this article.

SECTION 6

This article shall be inoperative unless it shall have been ratified as an amendment to the Constitution by the legislatures of three-fourths of the several States within seven years from the date of its submission.

Amendment XXI[19]

SECTION 1

The eighteenth article of amendment to the Constitution of the United States is hereby repealed.

SECTION 2

The transportation or importation into any State, Territory, or possession of the United States for delivery or use of intoxicating liquors, in violation of the laws thereof, is hereby prohibited.

SECTION 3

This article shall be inoperative unless it shall have been ratified as an amendment to the Constitution by conventions in the several States, as provided in the Constitution, within seven years from the date of the submission hereof to the States by the Congress.

Amendment XXII[20]

SECTION 1

No person shall be elected to the office of the President more than twice, and no person who has held the office of President, or acted as President, for more than two years of a term to which some other person was elected President shall be elected to the office of President more than once. But this Article shall not apply to any person holding the office of President when this Article was proposed

[18] Adopted in 1933.

[19] Adopted in 1933.
[20] Adopted in 1951.

by the Congress, and shall not prevent any person who may be holding the office of President, or acting as President, during the term within which this Article becomes operative from holding the office of President, or acting as President during the remainder of such term.

SECTION 2

This article shall be inoperative unless it shall have been ratified as an amendment to the Constitution by the legislatures of three-fourths of the several States within seven years from the date of its submission to the States by the Congress.

Amendment XXIII[21]

SECTION 1

The District constituting the seat of Government of the United States shall appoint in such manner as the Congress may direct:

A number of electors of President and Vice-President equal to the whole number of Senators and Representatives in Congress to which the District would be entitled if it were a State, but in no event more than the least populous State; they shall be in addition to those appointed by the States, but they shall be considered, for the purposes of the election of President and Vice-President, to be electors appointed by a state; and they shall meet in the District and perform such duties as provided by the twelfth article of amendment.

SECTION 2

The Congress shall have power to enforce this article by appropriate legislation.

Amendment XXIV[22]

SECTION 1

The right of citizens of the United States to vote in any primary or other election for President or Vice-President, for electors for President or Vice-President, or for Senator or Representative in Congress, shall not be denied or abridged by the United States or any State by reason of failure to pay any poll tax or other tax.

SECTION 2

The Congress shall have power to enforce this article by appropriate legislation.

Amendment XXV[23]

SECTION 1

In case of the removal of the President from office or his death or resignation, the Vice-President shall become President.

SECTION 2

Whenever there is a vacancy in the office of the Vice-President, the President shall nominate a Vice-President who shall take the office upon confirmation by a majority vote of both houses of Congress.

SECTION 3

Whenever the President transmits to the President pro tempore of the Senate and the Speaker of the House of Representatives his written declaration that he is unable to discharge the powers and duties of his office, and until he transmits to them a written declaration to the contrary, such powers and duties shall be discharged by the Vice-President as Acting President.

SECTION 4

Whenever the Vice-President and a majority of either the principal officers of the executive departments or of such other body as Congress may by law provide, transmit to the President pro tempore of the Senate and the Speaker of the House of Representatives their written declaration that the President is unable to discharge the powers and duties of his office, the Vice-President shall immediately assume the powers and duties of the office as Acting President.

Thereafter, when the President transmits to the President pro tempore of the Senate and the Speaker of the House of Representatives his written dec-

---

[21] Adopted in 1961.
[22] Adopted in 1964.

[23] Adopted in 1967.

laration that no inability exists, he shall resume the powers and duties of his office unless the Vice-President and a majority of either the principal officers of the executive department or of such other body as Congress may by law provide, transmit within four days to the President pro tempore of the Senate and the Speaker of the House of Representatives their written declaration that the President is unable to discharge the powers and duties of his office. Thereupon Congress shall decide the issue, assembling within 48 hours for that purpose if not in session. If the Congress, within 21 days after receipt of the latter written declaration, or, if Congress is not in session, within 21 days after Congress is required to assemble, determines by two-thirds vote of both houses that the President is unable to discharge the powers and duties of his office, the Vice-President shall continue to discharge the same as Acting President; otherwise, the President shall resume the powers and duties of his office.

Amendment XXVI[24]

SECTION 1

The Right of Citizens of the United States, who are eighteen years of age or older, to vote shall not be denied or abridged by the United States or any State on account of age.

SECTION 2

The Congress shall have the power to enforce this article by appropriate legislation.

---

[24] Adopted in 1971.

Table 1: Justices of the Supreme Court 1789–1989

1789	Jay	Rutledge, J.	Cushing	Wilson	Blair					
1790–91	Jay	Rutledge, J.	Cushing	Wilson	Blair	Iredell				
1792	Jay	Johnson, T.	Cushing	Wilson	Blair	Iredell				
1793–94	Jay	Paterson	Cushing	Wilson	Blair	Iredell				
1795	Rutledge, J.	Paterson	Cushing	Wilson	Blair	Iredell				
1796–97	Ellsworth	Paterson	Cushing	Wilson	Chase, S.	Iredell				
1789–99	Ellsworth	Paterson	Cushing	Washington	Chase, S.	Iredell				
1800	Ellsworth	Paterson	Cushing	Washington	Chase, S.	Moore				
1801–03	Marshall, J.	Paterson	Cushing	Washington	Chase, S.	Moore				
1804–05	Marshall, J.	Paterson	Cushing	Washington	Chase, S.	Johnson, W.				
1806	Marshall, J.	Paterson	Cushing	Washington	Chase, S.	Johnson, W.				
1807–10	Marshall, J.	Livingston	Cushing	Washington	Chase, S.	Johnson, W.	Todd			
1811–22	Marshall, J.	Livingston	Story	Washington	Duvall	Johnson, W.	Todd			
1823–25	Marshall, J.	Livingtson	Story	Washington	Duvall	Johnson, W.	Todd			
1826–28	Marshall, J.	Thompson	Story	Washington	Duvall	Johnson, W.	Trimble			
1829	Marshall, J.	Thompson	Story	Washington	Duvall	Johnson, W.	McLean			
1830–34	Marshall, J.	Thompson	Story	Baldwin	Duvall	Johnson, W.	McLean			
1835	Marshall, J.	Thompson	Story	Baldwin	Duvall	Wayne	McLean			
1836	Taney	Thompson	Story	Baldwin	Barbour	Wayne	McLean			
1837–40	Taney	Thompson	Story	Baldwin	Barbour	Wayne	McLean	Catron	McKinley	
1841–44	Taney	Thompson	Story	Baldwin	Daniel	Wayne	McLean	Catron	McKinley	
1845	Taney	Nelson	Woodbury		Daniel	Wayne	McLean	Catron	McKinley	
1846–50	Taney	Nelson	Woodbury	Grier	Daniel	Wayne	McLean	Catron	McKinley	
1851–52	Taney	Nelson	Curtis	Grier	Daniel	Wayne	McLean	Catron	McKinley	
1853–57	Taney	Nelson	Curtis	Grier	Daniel	Wayne	McLean	Catron	Campbell	
1858–60	Taney	Nelson	Clifford	Grier	Daniel	Wayne	McLean	Catron	Campbell	
1861	Taney	Nelson	Clifford	Grier		Wayne	McLean	Catron	Campbell	
1862	Taney	Nelson	Clifford	Grier	Miller	Wayne	Swayne	Catron	Davis	
1863	Taney	Nelson	Clifford	Grier	Miller	Wayne	Swayne	Catron	Davis	Field
1864–65	Chase, S. P.	Nelson	Clifford	Grier	Miller	Wayne	Swayne	Catron	Davis	Field
1866–67	Chase, S. P.	Nelson	Clifford	Grier	Miller	Wayne	Swayne		Davis	Field
1868–69	Chase, S. P.	Nelson	Clifford	Grier	Miller		Swayne		Davis	Field
1870–71	Chase, S. P.	Nelson	Clifford	Strong	Miller	Bradley	Swayne		Davis	Field
1872–73	Chase, S. P.	Hunt	Clifford	Strong	Miller	Bradley	Swayne		Davis	Field
1874–76	Waite	Hunt	Clifford	Strong	Miller	Bradley	Swayne		Davis	Field
1877–79	Waite	Hunt	Clifford	Strong	Miller	Bradley	Swayne		Harlan	Field

1880	Waite	Hunt	Clifford	Woods	Miller	Bradley	Swayne	Harlan	Field
1881	Waite	Hunt	Gray	Woods	Miller	Bradley	Matthews	Harlan	Field
1882–87	Waite	Blatchford	Gray	Woods	Miller	Bradley	Matthews	Harlan	Field
1888	Fuller	Blatchford	Gray	Lamar, L.	Miller	Bradley	Matthews	Harlan	Field
1889	Fuller	Blatchford	Gray	Lamar, L.	Miller	Bradley	Brewer	Harlan	Field
1890–91	Fuller	Blatchford	Gray	Lamar, L.	Brown	Bradley	Brewer	Harlan	Field
1892	Fuller	Blatchford	Gray	Lamar, L.	Brown	Shiras	Brewer	Harlan	Field
1893	Fuller	Blatchford	Gray	Jackson, H.	Brown	Shiras	Brewer	Harlan	Field
1894	Fuller	White, E.	Gray	Jackson, H.	Brown	Shiras	Brewer	Harlan	Field
1895–97	Fuller	White, E.	Gray	Peckham	Brown	Shiras	Brewer	Harlan	Field
1898–1901	Fuller	White, E.	Gray	Peckham	Brown	Shiras	Brewer	Harlan	McKenna
1902	Fuller	White, E.	Gray	Peckham	Brown	Shiras	Brewer	Harlan	McKenna
1903–05	Fuller	White, E.	Holmes	Peckham	Brown	Day	Brewer	Harlan	McKenna
1906–08	Fuller	White, E.	Holmes	Peckham	Moody	Day	Brewer	Harlan	McKenna
1909	Fuller	White, E.	Holmes	Lurton	Moody	Day	Brewer	Harlan	McKenna
1910–11	White, E.	Van Devanter	Holmes	Lurton	Lamar, J.	Day	Hughes	Harlan	McKenna
1912–13	White, E.	Van Devanter	Holmes	Lurton	Lamar, J.	Day	Hughes	Pitney	McKenna
1914–15	White, E.	Van Devanter	Holmes	McReynolds	Lamar, J.	Day	Hughes	Pitney	McKenna
1916–20	White, E.	Van Devanter	Holmes	McReynolds	Brandeis	Day	Clarke	Pitney	McKenna
1921	Taft	Van Devanter	Holmes	McReynolds	Brandeis	Day	Clarke	Pitney	McKenna
1922	Taft	Van Devanter	Holmes	McReynolds	Brandeis	Day	Sutherland	Pitney	McKenna
1923–24	Taft	Van Devanter	Holmes	McReynolds	Brandeis	Butler	Sutherland	Sanford	McKenna
1925–29	Taft	Van Devanter	Holmes	McReynolds	Brandeis	Butler	Sutherland	Sanford	Stone
1930–31	Hughes	Van Devanter	Holmes	McReynolds	Brandeis	Butler	Sutherland	Roberts	Stone
1932–36	Hughes	Van Devanter	Cardozo	McReynolds	Brandeis	Butler	Sutherland	Roberts	Stone
1937	Hughes	Black	Cardozo	McReynolds	Brandeis	Butler	Sutherland	Roberts	Stone
1938	Hughes	Black	Cardozo	McReynolds	Douglas	Butler	Reed	Roberts	Stone
1939	Hughes	Black	Frankfurter	McReynolds	Douglas	Butler	Reed	Roberts	Stone
1940	Hughes	Black	Frankfurter	McReynolds	Douglas	Murphy	Reed	Roberts	Stone
1941–42	Stone	Black	Frankfurter	Byrnes	Douglas	Murphy	Reed	Roberts	Jackson, R.
1943–44	Stone	Black	Frankfurter	Rutledge, W.	Douglas	Murphy	Reed	Roberts	Jackson, R.
1945	Stone	Black	Frankfurter	Rutledge, W.	Douglas	Murphy	Reed	Burton	Jackson, R.
1946–48	Vinson	Black	Frankfurter	Rutledge, W.	Douglas	Murphy	Reed	Burton	Jackson, R.
1949–52	Vinson	Black	Frankfurter	Minton	Douglas	Clark	Reed	Burton	Jackson, R.
1953–54	Warren	Black	Frankfurter	Minton	Douglas	Clark	Reed	Burton	Jackson, R.
1955	Warren	Black	Frankfurter	Minton	Douglas	Clark	Reed	Burton	Harlan

(Continued)

Table 1: (cont.)

Year									
1956	Warren	Black	Frankfurter	Brennan	Douglas	Clark	Reed	Burton	Harlan
1957	Warren	Black	Frankfurter	Brennan	Douglas	Clark	Whittaker	Burton	Harlan
1958–61	Warren	Black	Frankfurter	Brennan	Douglas	Clark	Whittaker	Stewart	Harlan
1962–65	Warren	Black	Goldberg	Brennan	Douglas	Clark	White, B.	Stewart	Harlan
1965–67	Warren	Black	Fortas	Brennan	Douglas	Clark	White, B.	Stewart	Harlan
1967–69	Warren	Black	Fortas	Brennan	Douglas	Marshall, T.	White, B.	Stewart	Harlan
1969	Burger	Black	Fortas	Brennan	Douglas	Marshall, T.	White, B.	Stewart	Harlan
1969–70	Burger	Black	Blackmun	Brennan	Douglas	Marshall, T.	White, B.	Stewart	Harlan
1970–71	Burger	Black	Blackmun	Brennan	Douglas	Marshall, T.	White, B.	Stewart	Harlan
1971–75	Burger	Powell	Blackmun	Brennan	Douglas	Marshall, T.	White, B.	Stewart	Rehnquist
1975–81	Burger	Powell	Blackmun	Brennan	Stevens	Marshall, T.	White, B.	Stewart	Rehnquist
1981–86	Burger	Powell	Blackmun	Brennan	Stevens	Marshall, T.	White, B.	O'Connor	Rehnquist
1986–87	Rehnquist	Powell	Blackmun	Brennan	Stevens	Marshall, T.	White, B.	O'Connor	Scalia
1987	Rehnquist		Blackmun	Brennan	Stevens	Marshall, T.	White, B.	O'Connor	Scalia
1988–	Rehnquist	Kennedy	Blackmun	Brennan	Stevens	Marshall, T.	White, B.	O'Connor	Scalia

544

Table 2: Presidents and Justices*

President	Justices Appointed	Years of Service	Age at Start of Term
Washington (F)		1789–1797	52
	Jay (F)**	1789–1795	44
	Rutledge (F)@	1789–1791	50
	Cushing (F)	1789–1810	57
	Wilson (F)	1789–1798	47
	Blair (F)	1789–1796	57
	Iredell (F)	1790–1799	38
	Johnson (F)	1791–1793	58
	Paterson (F)	1793–1806	47
	Rutledge (F)**	1795	55
	Chase (F)	1796–1811	54
	Ellsworth (F)**	1796–1800	50
Adams J. (F)		1797–1801	61
	Washington (F)	1798–1829	36
	Moore (F)	1799–1804	44
	Marshall (F)**	1801–1835	45
Jefferson (DR)		1801–1809	57
	Johnson (DR)	1804–1834	32
	Livingston (DR)	1806–1823	49
	Todd (DR)	1807–1826	42
Madison (DR)		1809–1817	57
	Duval (DR)	1812–1835	58
	Story (DR)	1811–1845	32
Monroe (DR)		1817–1825	58
	Thompson (DR)	1823–1843	55
Adams, J. Q. (DR)		1825–1829	57
	Trimble (DR)	1826–1828	49
Jackson (D)		1829–1837	61
	McLean (D)	1829–1861	43
	Baldwin (D)	1830–1844	49
	Wayne (D)	1835–1867	45
	Taney (D)**	1836–1864	58
	Barbour (D)	1836–1841	52
	Catron (D)	1837–1865	51
Van Buren (D)			54
	McKinley (D)	1837–1852	57
	Daniel (D)	1841–1860	56
Harrison, W. (W)#		1841	68
Tyler (W)		1841–1845	50
	Nelson (W)	1845–1872	52
Polk (D)		1845–1849	49
	Woodbury (D)	1845–1851	56
	Grier (D)	1846–1870	52
Taylor (W)#		1849–1850	65
Fillmore (W)		1850–1853	50
	Curtis (W)	1851–1857	42

(Continued)

President	Justices Appointed	Years of Service	Age at Start of Term
Pierce (D)		1853–1857	48
	Campbell (D)	1853–1861	41
Buchanan (D)		1857–1861	65
	Clifford (D)	1858–1881	54
Lincoln (R)		1861–1865	52
	Swayne (R)	1862–1881	57
	Miller (R)	1862–1890	46
	Davis (R)	1862–1877	47
	Field (R)	1863–1897	46
	Chase (R)**	1864–1873	56
Johnson, A. (D)#		1865–1869	56
Grant (R)		1869–1877	46
	Strong (R)	1870–1880	61
	Bradley (R)	1870–1892	56
	Hunt (R)	1872–1882	62
	Waite (R)**	1874–1888	57
Hayes (R)		1877–1881	54
	Harlan (R)	1877–1911	44
	Woods (R)	1880–1887	56
Garfield (R)		1881	49
	Matthews (R)	1881–1889	56
Arthur (R)		1881–1885	50
	Gray (R)	1881–1902	53
	Blatchford (R)	1882–1893	62
Cleveland (D)		1885–1889	47
	Lamar (D)	1888–1893	62
	Fuller (D)**	1888–1910	55
Harrison (R)		1889–1893	55
	Brewer (R)	1889–1910	52
	Brown (R)	1891–1906	54
	Shiras (R)	1892–1903	60
	Jackson (D)	1893–1895	60
Cleveland (D)		1893–1897	55
	White (D)@	1894–1910	48
	Peckham (D)	1896–1909	57
McKinley (R)		1897–1901	54
	McKenna (R)	1898–1925	54
Roosevelt, T. (R)		1901–1909	42
	Holmes	1902–1932	61
	Day (R)	1903–1922	53
	Moody (R)	1906–1910	52
Taft (R)		1909–1913	51
	Lurton (D)	1909–1914	65
	Hughes (R)@	1910–1916	48
	White+ (D)**	1910–1921	65
	Van Devanter (R)	1910–1937	51
	Lamar (D)	1910–1916	53
	Pitney (R)	1912–1922	54

President	Justices Appointed	Years of Service	Age at Start of Term
Wilson (D)		1913–1921	56
	McReynolds (D)	1914–1941	52
	Brandeis (R)	1916–1939	59
	Clarke (D)	1916–1922	59
Harding (R)		1921–1923	55
	Taft (R)**	1921–1930	63
	Sutherland (R)	1922–1938	60
	Butler (D)	1922–1939	56
	Sanford (R)	1923–1930	57
Coolidge (R)		1923–1929	50
	Stone (R)@	1925–1941	52
Hoover (R)		1929–1933	54
	Hughes (R)**	1930–1941	68
	Roberts (R)	1930–1945	55
	Cardozo (D)	1932–1938	61
Roosevelt, F. (D)		1933–1945	51
	Black (D)	1937–1971	51
	Reed (D)	1938–1957	53
	Frankfurter (I)	1939–1962	56
	Douglas (D)	1939–1975	40
	Murphy (D)	1940–1949	49
	Byrnes (D)	1941–1942	62
	Stone+ (R)**	1941–1946	68
	Jackson (D)	1941–1954	49
	Rutledge (D)	1943–1949	48
Truman (D)		1945–1953	60
	Burton (R)	1945–1958	57
	Vinson (D)**	1946–1953	56
	Clark (D)	1949–1967	49
	Minton (D)	1949–1956	58
Eisenhower (R)		1953–1961	62
	Warren (R)**	1953–1969	62
	Harlan (R)	1955–1971	55
	Brennan (D)	1956–	50
	Whittaker (R)	1957–1962	56
	Stewart (R)	1958–1981	43
Kennedy (D)		1961–1963	43
	White (D)	1962–	44
	Goldberg (D)	1962–1965	54
Johnson, L. (D)		1963–1969	55
	Fortas (D)	1965–1969	55
	Marshall (D)	1967–	58
Nixon (R)		1969–1974	56
	Burger (R)**	1969–1986	61
	Blackmun (R)	1970–	61
	Powell (D)	1971–1987	64
	Rehnquist (R)@	1971–1986	47

(Continued)

Table 2: *(cont.)*

President	Justices Appointed	Years of Service	Age at Start of Term
Ford (R)		1974–1977	61
	Stevens (R)	1975–	55
Carter (D)#		1977–1981	52
Reagan (R)		1981–1989	70
	O'Connor (R)	1981–	51
	Rehnquist+ (R)**	1986–	61
	Scalia (R)	1986–	50
	Kennedy (R)	1988–	51
Bush (R)		1989–	64

*Letter following name indicates political party affiliation.

    (F) – Federalist

    (DR) – Democrat-Republican

    (D) – Democratic

    (W) – Whig

    (R) – Republican

    (I) – Independent

**Denotes appointment as chief justice.

@Later appointed as chief justice.

+Indicates appointment from associate to chief justice.

#Indicates no appointments to Supreme Court.

Noteworthy Decisions:
1988–1989 Term

AFFIRMATIVE ACTION

Richmond v. J.A. Croson Co.
57 U.S.L.W. 4132 (1989)

In 1983, the city of Richmond, Virginia, adopted a Minority Business Utilization Plan requiring prime contractors awarded city construction contracts to subcontract at least 30% of the dollar amount of each contract to one or more "Minority Business Enterprises" (MBEs). According to the plan, MBEs included a business from anywhere in the country at least 51% of which was owned and controlled by black, Spanish-speaking, Oriental, Indian, Eskimo, or Aleut citizens. At the time the plan was adopted, approximately 51% of the population of Richmond was black, as were five of the nine members of the city council. Although the plan declared that it was "remedial" in nature, it was adopted after a public hearing at which no direct evidence was presented that the city had discriminated on the basis of race in letting contracts or that its prime contractors had discriminated against minority contractors. The city's legal counsel concluded that the plan was constitutional on the basis of the United States Supreme Court's decision in *Fullilove* v. *Klutznick* (1980), which upheld a congressional program requiring that 10% of certain federal construction grants be awarded to minority contractors. Under the Richmond plan, the city adopted rules requiring individualized consideration of each bid or request for a waiver of the 30% set-aside, and providing that a waiver could be granted only upon proof that enough qualified MBEs were unavailable or unwilling to participate. When the J.A. Croson Co., a plumbing supplier and the sole bidder on a city contract, was denied a waiver and lost its contract, it brought suit in U.S. district court claiming that the plan violated the equal protection clause of the Fourteenth Amendment. The district court upheld the plan, and the Court of Appeals for the Fourth Circuit affirmed. The Supreme Court then vacated the decision of the appeals court in light of its decision in *Wygant* v. *Jackson Board of Education* (1986), in which a plurality applied a strict scrutiny standard in voiding a race-based layoff program agreed to by the school board and the teachers' union. On remand, the court of appeals concluded that the Richmond plan violated the Fourteenth

Amendment because the plan was not narrowly tailored to serve a compelling governmental interest (the two prongs of the strict scrutiny test). Majority: O'Connor, Kennedy, Rehnquist, Scalia, Stevens, White. Minority: Blackmun, Brennan, Marshall. (The justices in the majority, except Justice Scalia, agreed to the parts of Justice O'Connor's opinion reprinted below.)

JUSTICE O'CONNOR delivered the opinion of the Court.

In this case, we confront once again the tension between the Fourteenth Amendment's guarantee of equal treatment to all citizens, and the use of race-based measures to ameliorate the effects of past discrimination on the opportunities enjoyed by members of minority groups in our society. . . .

The Equal Protection Clause of the Fourteenth Amendment provides that "[N]o State shall . . . deny to *any person* within its jurisdiction the equal protection of the laws" (emphasis added). As this Court has noted in the past, the "rights created by the first section of the Fourteenth Amendment are, by its terms, guaranteed to the individual. The rights established are personal rights." The Richmond Plan denies certain citizens the opportunity to compete for a fixed percentage of public contracts based solely upon their race. To whatever racial group these citizens belong, their "personal rights" to be treated with equal dignity and respect are implicated by a rigid rule erecting race as the sole criterion in an aspect of public decisionmaking.

Absent searching judicial inquiry into the justification for such race-based measures, there is simply no way of determining what classifications are "benign" or "remedial" and what classifications are in fact motivated by illegitimate notions of racial inferiority or simple racial politics. Indeed, the purpose of strict scrutiny is to "smoke out" illegitimate uses of race by assuring that the legislative body is pursuing a goal important enough to warrant use of a highly suspect tool. The test also ensures that the means chosen "fit" this compelling goal so closely that there is little or no possibility that the motive for the classification was illegitimate racial prejudice or stereotype. . . .

Appellant argues that it is attempting to remedy various forms of past discrimination that are alleged to be responsible for the small number of minority businesses in the local contracting industry. Among these the city cites the exclusion of blacks from skilled construction trade unions and training programs. This past discrimination has prevented them "from following the traditional path from laborer to entrepreneur." The city also lists a host of nonracial factors which would seem to face a member of any racial group attempting to establish a new business enterprise, such as deficiencies in working capital, inability to meet bonding requirements, unfamiliarity with bidding procedures, and disability caused by an inadequate track record.

While there is no doubt that the sorry history of both private and public discrimination in this country has contributed to a lack of opportunities for black entrepreneurs, this observation, standing alone, cannot justify a rigid racial quota in the awarding of public contracts in Richmond, Virginia. Like the claim that discrimination in primary and secondary schooling justifies a rigid racial preference in medical school admissions, an amorphous claim that there has been past discrimination in a particular industry cannot justify the use of an unyielding racial quota.

It is sheer speculation how many minority firms there would be in Richmond absent past societal discrimination, just as it was sheer speculation how many minority medical students would have been admitted to the medical school at Davis absent past discrimination in educational opportunities. Defining these sorts of injuries as "identified discrimination" would give local governments license to create a patchwork of racial preferences based on statistical generalizations about any particular field of endeavor.

These defects are readily apparent in this case. The 30% quota cannot in any realistic sense be tied to any injury suffered by anyone. The District Court relied upon five predicate "facts" in reaching its conclusion that there was an adequate basis for the 30% quota: (1) the ordinance declares itself to be remedial; (2) several proponents of the measure stated their views that there had been past discrimination in the construction industry; (3) minority businesses received .67% of prime contracts from the city while minorities constituted 50% of the city's population; (4) there were very few minority contractors in local and state contractors' associations; and (5) in 1977, Congress made a determination that the effects of past discrimination had stifled minority participation in the construction industry nationally.

None of these "findings," singly or together, provide the city of Richmond with a "strong basis in evidence for its conclusion that remedial action was necessary." There is nothing approaching a prima facie case of a constitutional or statutory violation by *anyone* in the Richmond construction industry. . . .

Reliance on the disparity between the number of prime contracts awarded to minority firms and the minority population of the city of Richmond is similarly misplaced. There is no doubt that "[w]here gross statistical disparities can be shown, they alone in a proper case may constitute prima facie proof of a pattern or practice of discrimination" under Title VII. But it is equally clear that "[w]hen special qualifications are required to fill particular jobs, comparisons to the general population (rather than to the smaller group of individuals who possess the necessary qualifications) may have little probative value." . . .

In the employment context, we have recognized that for certain entry level positions or positions requiring minimal training, statistical comparisons of the racial composition of an employer's workforce to the racial composition of the relevant population may be probative of a pattern of discrimination. . . . But where special qualifications are necessary, the relevant statistical pool for purposes of demonstrating discriminatory exclusion must be the number of minorities qualified to undertake the particular task.

In this case, the city does not even know how many MBEs in the relevant market are qualified to undertake prime or subcontracting work in public construction projects.

The city and the District Court also relied on evidence that MBE membership in local contractors' associations was extremely low. Again, standing alone this evidence is not probative of any discrimination in the local construction industry. There are numerous explanations for this dearth of minority participation, including past societal discrim-

ination in education and economic opportunities as well as both black and white career and entrepreneurial choices. Blacks may be disproportionately attracted to industries other than construction. . . .

For low minority membership in these associations to be relevant, the city would have to link it to the number of local MBEs eligible for membership. If the statistical disparity between eligible MBEs and MBE membership were great enough, an inference of discriminatory exclusion could arise. In such a case, the city would have a compelling interest in preventing its tax dollars from assisting these organizations in maintaining a racially segregated construction market. . . .

Finally, the city and the District Court relied on Congress' finding in connection with the set-aside approved in *Fullilove* that there had been nationwide discrimination in the construction industry. The probative value of these findings for demonstrating the existence of discrimination in Richmond is extremely limited. By its inclusion of a waiver procedure in the national program addressed in *Fullilove,* Congress explicitly recognized that the scope of the problem would vary from market area to market area. . . .

Moreover, as noted above, Congress was exercising its powers under §5 of the Fourteenth Amendment in making a finding that past discrimination would cause federal funds to be distributed in a manner which reinforced prior patterns of discrimination. While the States and their subdivisions may take remedial action when they possess evidence that their own spending practices are exacerbating a pattern of prior discrimination, they must identify that discrimination, public or private, with some specificity before they may use race-conscious relief. Congress has made national findings that there has been societal discrimination in a host of fields. If all a state or local government need do is find a congressional report on the subject to enact a set-aside program, the constraints of the Equal Protection Clause will, in effect, have been rendered a nullity. . . .

In sum, none of the evidence presented by the city points to any identified discrimination in the Richmond construction industry. We, therefore, hold that the city has failed to demonstrate a compelling interest in apportioning public contracting opportunities on the basis of race. To accept Richmond's claim that past societal discrimination alone can serve as the basis for rigid racial preferences would be to open the door to competing claims for "remedial relief" for every disadvantaged group. The dream of a Nation of equal citizens in a society where race is irrelevant to personal opportunity and achievement would be lost in a mosaic of shifting preferences based on inherently unmeasurable claims of past wrongs. . . .

Nothing we say today precludes a state or local entity from taking action to rectify the effects of identified discrimination within its jurisdiction. If the city of Richmond had evidence before it that nonminority contractors were systematically excluding minority businesses from subcontracting opportunities it could take action to end the discriminatory exclusion. Where there is a significant statistical disparity between the number of qualified minority contractors willing and able to perform a particular service and the number of such contractors actually engaged by the locality or the locality's prime contractors, an inference of discriminatory exclusion could arise. . . .

Because the city of Richmond has failed to identify the need for remedial action in the awarding of its public construction contracts, its treatment of its citizens on a racial basis violates the dictates of the Equal Protection Clause. Accordingly, the judgment of the Court of Appeals for the Fourth Circuit is

Affirmed.

JUSTICE SCALIA, concurring in the judgment.

I agree with much of the Court's opinion, and, in particular, with its conclusion that strict scrutiny must be applied to all governmental classification by race, whether or not its asserted purpose is "remedial" or "benign." . . .

We have in some contexts approved the use of racial classifications by the Federal Government to remedy the effects of past discrimination. I do not believe that we must or should extend those holdings to the States. . . . As the Court acknowledges, it is one thing to permit racially based conduct by the Federal Government—whose legislative powers concerning matters of race were explicitly enhanced by the Fourteenth Amendment—and quite another to permit it by the precise entities against whose conduct in matters of race that Amendment was specifically directed. . . .

In my view there is only one circumstance in which the States may act *by race* to "undo the

effects of past discrimination": where that is necessary to eliminate their own maintenance of a system of unlawful racial classification. If, for example, a state agency has a discriminatory pay scale compensating black employees in all positions at 20% less than their nonblack counterparts, it may assuredly promulgate an order raising the salaries of "all black employees" by 20%. This distinction explains our school desegregation cases, in which we have made plain that States and localities sometimes have an obligation to adopt race-conscious remedies. . . .

A State can, of course, act "to undo the effects of past discrimination" in many permissible ways that do not involve classification by race. In the particular field of state contracting, for example, it may adopt a preference for small businesses, or even for new businesses—which would make it easier for those previously excluded by discrimination to enter the field. Such programs may well have racially disproportionate impact, but they are not based on race. And, of course, a State may "undo the effects of past discrimination" in the sense of giving the identified victim of state discrimination that which it wrongfully denied him— for example, giving to a previously rejected black applicant the job that, by reason of discrimination, had been awarded to a white applicant, even if this means terminating the latter's employment. In such a context, the white job-holder is not being selected for disadvantageous treatment because of his race, but because he was wrongfully awarded a job to which another is entitled. That is worlds apart from the system here, in which those to be disadvantaged are identified solely by race.

It is plainly true that in our society blacks have suffered discrimination immeasurably greater than any directed at other racial groups. But those who believe that racial preferences can help to "even the score" display, and reinforce, a manner of thinking by race that was the source of the injustice and that will, if it endures within our society, be the source of more injustice still. The relevant proposition is not that it was blacks, or Jews, or Irish who were discriminated against, but that it was individual men and women, "created equal," who were discriminated against. And the relevant resolve is that that should never happen again. Racial preferences appear to "even the score" (in some small degree) only if one embraces the proposition that our society is appropriately viewed as divided into races, making it right that an injustice rendered in the past to a black man should be compensated for by discriminating against a white. Nothing is worth that embrace. Since blacks have been disproportionately disadvantaged by racial discrimination, any race-neutral remedial program aimed at the disadvantaged *as such* will have a disproportionately beneficial impact on blacks. Only such a program, and not one that operates on the basis of race, is in accord with the letter and the spirit of our Constitution. . . .

JUSTICE MARSHALL, with whom JUSTICE BRENNAN and JUSTICE BLACKMUN join, dissenting.

It is a welcome symbol of racial progress when the former capital of the Confederacy acts forthrightly to confront the effects of racial discrimination in its midst. In my view, nothing in the Constitution can be construed to prevent Richmond, Virginia, from allocating a portion of its contracting dollars for businesses owned or controlled by members of minority groups. Indeed, Richmond's set-aside program is indistinguishable in all meaningful respects from—and in fact was patterned upon—the federal set-aside plan which this Court upheld in *Fullilove* v. *Klutznick.*

A majority of this Court holds today, however, that the Equal Protection Clause of the Fourteenth Amendment blocks Richmond's initiative. The essence of the majority's position is that Richmond has failed to catalogue adequate findings to prove that past discrimination has impeded minorities from joining or participating fully in Richmond's construction contracting industry. I find deep irony in second-guessing Richmond's judgment on this point. As much as any municipality in the United States, Richmond knows what racial discrimination is; a century of decisions by this and other federal courts has richly documented the city's disgraceful history of public and private racial discrimination. In any event, the Richmond City Council *has* supported its determination that minorities have been wrongly excluded from local construction contracting. Its proof includes statistics showing that minority-owned businesses have received virtually no city contracting dollars and rarely if ever belonged to area trade associations; testimony by municipal officials that discrimination has been widespread in the local construction industry; and the same exhaustive and widely publicized federal studies relied on in *Fullilove,* studies which showed that pervasive discrimination in the Nation's tight-knit construction industry had operated to exclude minorities from public contracting. These are precisely the types of statistical and testimonial evidence which, until today, this Court had credited in cases approving of race-conscious measures designed to remedy past discrimination.

More fundamentally, today's decision marks a deliberate and giant step backward in this Court's affirmative action jurisprudence. Cynical of one municipality's attempt to redress the effects of past racial discrimination in a particular industry, the majority launches a grapeshot attack on race-conscious remedies in general. The majority's unnecessary pronouncements will inevitably discourage or prevent governmental entities, particularly States and localities, from acting to rectify the scourge of past discrimination. This is the harsh reality of the majority's decision, but it is not the Constitution's command. . . .

"Agreement upon a means for applying the Equal Protection Clause to an affirmative-action program has eluded this Court every time the issue has come before us." My view has long been that race-conscious classifications designed to further remedial goals "must serve important governmental objectives and must be substantially related to achievement of those objectives" in order to withstand constitutional scrutiny. . . . Analyzed in terms of this two-prong standard, Richmond's set-aside, like the federal program on which it was modeled, is "plainly constitutional." . . .

Today, for the first time, a majority of this Court has adopted strict scrutiny as its standard of Equal Protection Clause review of race-conscious remedial measures. This is an unwelcome development. A profound difference separates governmental actions that themselves are racist, and governmental actions that seek to remedy the effects of prior racism or to prevent neutral governmental activity from perpetuating the effects of such racism.

Racial classifications "drawn on the presumption that one race is inferior to another or because they put the weight of government behind racial hatred and separatism" warrant the strictest judicial scrutiny because of the very irrelevance of these rationales. By contrast, racial classifications drawn for the purpose of remedying the effects of discrimination that itself was race-based have a highly pertinent basis: the tragic and indelible fact that discrimination against blacks and other racial minorities in this Nation has pervaded our Nation's history and continues to scar our society. As I stated in *Fullilove:* "Because the consideration of race is relevant to remedying the continuing effects of past racial discrimination, and because governmental programs employing racial classifications for remedial purposes can be crafted to avoid stigmatization, . . . such programs should not be subjected to conventional 'strict scrutiny'—scrutiny that is strict in theory, but fatal in fact."

In concluding that remedial classifications warrant no different standard of review under the Constitution than the most brute and repugnant forms of state-sponsored racism, a majority of this Court signals that it regards racial discrimination as largely a phenomenon of the past, and that government bodies need no longer preoccupy themselves with rectifying racial injustice. I, however, do not believe this Nation is anywhere close to eradicating racial discrimination or its vestiges. In constitutionalizing its wishful thinking, the majority today does a grave disservice not only to those victims of past and present racial discrimination in this Nation whom government has sought to assist, but also to this Court's long tradition of approaching issues of race with the utmost sensitivity. . . .

Nothing in the Constitution or in the prior decisions of this Court supports limiting state authority to confront the effects of past discrimination to those situations in which a prima facie case of a constitutional or statutory violation can be made out. By its very terms, the majority's standard effectively cedes control of a large component of the content of that constitutional provision to Congress and to state legislatures. If an antecedent Virginia or Richmond law had defined as unlawful the award to nonminorities of an overwhelming share of a city's contracting dollars, for example, Richmond's subsequent set-aside initiative would then satisfy the majority's standard. But without such a law, the initiative might not withstand constitutional scrutiny. The meaning of "equal protection of the laws" thus turns on the happenstance of whether a State or local body has previously defined illegal discrimination. Indeed, given that racially discriminatory cities may be the ones least likely to have tough antidiscrimination laws on their books, the majority's constitutional incorporation of state and local statutes has the perverse effect of inhibiting those States or localities with the worst records of official racism from taking remedial action.

SEPARATION OF POWERS

Mistretta v. United States
57 U.S.L.W. 4102 (1989)

Because of serious disparities among sentences imposed by federal judges upon similarly situated offenders, Congress passed the Sentencing Reform Act of 1984 which, among other things, established the United States Sentencing Commission as an independent body in the Judicial Branch. The act empowered the commission to promulgate binding sentencing guidelines, including a range of determinate sentences for all categories of federal offenses and defendants according to specific and detailed factors. The sentencing law applies to all persons convicted of federal crimes committed after November 1, 1987.

On December 10, 1987, John M. Mistretta was indicted in the United States District Court for the Western District of Missouri on three counts centering in a sale of cocaine. Mistretta moved to have the promulgated guidelines declared unconstitutional on the grounds that the commission was constituted in violation of the principle of separation of powers and that Congress delegated excessive authority to the commission to create the guidelines. After the district court rejected Mistretta's argument, he pleaded guilty to one count of his indictment. The remaining counts were dropped. The court sentenced him under the guidelines to a $1000 fine and to 18 months' imprisonment, to be followed by a three-year term of supervised release. Mistretta then filed a notice of appeal to the Court of Appeals for the Eighth Circuit, and both Mistretta and the United States petitioned the United States Supreme Court for certiorari before judgment. Mistretta's attack on the commission and the guidelines was only one of many throughout the nation. At least 150 district judges had declared the sentencing act unconstitutional, and 115 district judges had upheld its constitutionality, leading Justice Blackmun in his opinion of the Court to acknowledge "the disarray among the Federal District Courts. . . ." Majority: Blackmun, Brennan, Kennedy, Marshall, O'Connor, Rehnquist, Stevens, White. Dissenting: Scalia.

JUSTICE BLACKMUN delivered the opinion of the Court. . . .

Background

For almost a century, the Federal Government employed in criminal cases a system of indeterminate sentencing. Statutes specified the penalties for crimes but nearly always gave the sentencing judge wide discretion to decide whether the offender should be incarcerated and for how long, whether he should be fined and how much, and whether some lesser restraint, such as probation, should be imposed instead of imprisonment or fine. This indeterminate-sentencing system was supplemented by the utilization of parole, by which an offender was returned to society under the "guidance and control" of a parole officer. . . .

Serious disparities in sentences, however, were common. Rehabilitation as a sound penological theory came to be questioned and, in any event, was regarded by some as an unattainable goal for most cases. In 1958, Congress authorized the creation of judicial sentencing institutes and joint councils to formulate standards and criteria for sentencing. In 1973, the United States Parole Board adopted guidelines that established a "customary range" of confinement. Congress in 1976 endorsed this initiative through the Parole Commission and Reorganization Act, an attempt to envision for the

Parole Commission a role, at least in part, "to moderate the disparities in the sentencing practices of individual judges." That Act, however, did not disturb the division of sentencing responsibility among the three Branches. The judge continued to exercise discretion and to set the sentence within the statutory range fixed by Congress, while the prisoner's actual release date generally was set by the Parole Commission.

This proved to be no more than a way station. Fundamental and widespread dissatisfaction with the uncertainties and the disparities continued to be expressed. Congress had wrestled with the problem for more than a decade when, in 1984, it enacted the sweeping reforms that are at issue here. . . .

The Act

The Act, as adopted, revises the old sentencing process in several ways:

1. It rejects imprisonment as a means of promoting rehabilitation, and it states that punishment should serve retributive, educational, deterrent, and incapacitative goals.

2. It consolidates the power that had been exercised by the sentencing judge and the Parole Commission to decide what punishment an offender should suffer. This is done by creating the United States Sentencing Commission, directing that Com-

mission to devise guidelines to be used for sentencing, and prospectively abolishing the Parole Commission.

3. It makes all sentences basically determinate. A prisoner is to be released at the completion of his sentence reduced only by any credit earned by good behavior while in custody.

4. It makes the Sentencing Commission's guidelines binding on the courts, although it preserves for the judge the discretion to depart from the guideline applicable to a particular case if the judge finds an aggravating or mitigating factor present that the Commission did not adequately consider when formulating guidelines. The Act also requires the court to state its reasons for the sentence imposed and to give "the specific reason" for imposing a sentence different from that described in the guideline.

5. It authorizes limited appellate review of the sentence. It permits a defendant to appeal a sentence that is above the defined range, and it permits the Government to appeal a sentence that is below that range. It also permits either side to appeal an incorrect application of the guideline. . . .

Delegation of Power

Petitioner argues that in delegating the power to promulgate sentencing guidelines for every federal criminal offense to an independent Sentencing Commission, Congress has granted the Commission excessive legislative discretion in violation of the constitutionally based nondelegation doctrine. We do not agree.

The nondelegation doctrine is rooted in the principle of separation of powers that underlies our tripartite system of government. The Constitution provides that "[a]ll legislative Powers herein granted shall be vested in a Congress of the United States," and we long have insisted that "the integrity and maintenance of the system of government ordained by the Constitution," mandate that Congress generally cannot delegate its legislative power to another Branch. . . . So long as Congress "shall lay down by legislative act an intelligible principle to which the person or body authorized to [exercise the delegated authority] is directed to conform, such legislative action is not a forbidden delegation of legislative power."

Applying this "intelligible principle" test to congressional delegations, our jurisprudence has been driven by a practical understanding that in our increasingly complex society, replete with ever changing and more technical problems, Congress simply cannot do its job absent an ability to delegate power under broad general directives. . . . Accordingly, this Court has deemed it "constitutionally sufficient if Congress clearly delineates the general policy, the public agency which is to apply it, and the boundaries of this delegated authority." . . .

In light of our approval of these broad delegations, we harbor no doubt that Congress' delegation of authority to the Sentencing Commission is sufficiently specific and detailed to meet constitutional requirements. . . .

Developing proportionate penalties for hundreds of different crimes by a virtually limitless array of offenders is precisely the sort of intricate, labor-intensive task for which delegation to an expert body is especially appropriate. Although Congress has delegated significant discretion to the Commission to draw judgments from its analysis of existing sentencing practice and alternative sentencing models, "Congress is not confined to that method of executing its policy which involves the least possible delegation of discretion to administrative officers." We have no doubt that in the hands of the Commission "the criteria which Congress has supplied are wholly adequate for carrying out the general policy and purpose" of the Act. . . .

Separation of Powers

Having determined that Congress has set forth sufficient standards for the exercise of the Commission's delegated authority, we turn to Mistretta's claim that the Act violates the constitutional principle of separation of powers.

This Court consistently has given voice to, and has reaffirmed, the central judgment of the Framers of the Constitution that, within our political scheme, the separation of governmental powers into three coordinate Branches is essential to the preservation of liberty. . . .

In applying the principle of separated powers in our jurisprudence, we have sought to give life to Madison's view of the appropriate relationship among the three coequal Branches. Accordingly, we have recognized, as Madison admonished at the founding, that while our Constitution mandates that "each of the three general departments of government [must remain] entirely free from the control or coercive influence, direct or indirect, of either of the others," the Framers did not require—and indeed rejected—the notion that the three Branches must be entirely separate and distinct. . . .

In adopting this flexible understanding of separation of powers, we simply have recognized Madison's teaching that the greatest security against tyranny—the accumulation of excessive authority in a single branch—lies not in a hermetic division between the Branches, but in a carefully crafted system of checked and balanced power within each Branch. . . .

It is this concern of encroachment and aggrandizement that has animated our separation-of-powers jurisprudence and aroused our vigilance against the "hydraulic pressure inherent within each of the separate Branches to exceed the outer limits of its power." . . .

In *Nixon* v. *Administrator of General Services,* upholding, against a separation-of-powers challenge, legislation providing for the General Services Administration to control Presidential papers after resignation, we described our separation-of-powers inquiry as focusing "on the extent to which [a provision of law] prevents the Executive Branch from accomplishing its constitutionally assigned functions." In cases specifically involving the Judicial Branch, we have expressed our vigilance against two dangers: first, that the Judicial Branch neither be assigned nor allowed "tasks that are more appropriately accomplished by [other] branches," and, second, that no provision of law "impermissibly threatens the institutional integrity of the Judicial Branch." . . .

Mistretta argues that the Act suffers from each of these constitutional infirmities. He argues that Congress, in constituting the Commission as it did, effected an unconstitutional accumulation of power within the Judicial Branch while at the same time undermining the Judiciary's independence and integrity. Specifically, petitioner claims that in delegating to an independent agency within the Judicial Branch the power to promulgate sentencing guidelines, Congress unconstitutionally has required the Branch, and individual Article III judges, to exercise not only their judicial authority, but legislative authority—the making of sentencing policy—as well. Such rulemaking authority, petitioner contends, may be exercised by Congress, or delegated by Congress

to the Executive, but may not be delegated to or exercised by the Judiciary.

At the same time, petitioner asserts, Congress unconstitutionally eroded the integrity and independence of the Judiciary by requiring Article III judges to sit on the Commission, by requiring that those judges share their rulemaking authority with nonjudges, and by subjecting the Commission's members to appointment and removal by the President. According to petitioner, Congress, consistent with the separation of powers, may not upset the balance among the Branches by co-opting federal judges into the quintessentially political work of establishing sentencing guidelines, by subjecting those judges to the political whims of the Chief Executive, and by forcing judges to share their power with nonjudges. . . .

Location of the Commission

The Sentencing Commission unquestionably is a peculiar institution within the framework of our Government. Although placed by the Act in the Judicial Branch, it is not a court and does not exercise judicial power. Rather, the Commission is an "independent" body comprised of seven voting members including at least three federal judges, entrusted by Congress with the primary task of promulgating sentencing guidelines. Our constitutional principles of separated powers are not violated, however, by mere anomaly or innovation. . . .

According to express provision of Article III, the judicial power of the United States is limited to "Cases" and "Controversies." In implementing this limited grant of power, we have refused to issue advisory opinions or to resolve disputes that are not justiciable. These doctrines help to ensure the independence of the Judicial Branch by precluding debilitating entanglements between the Judiciary and the two political Branches, and prevent the Judiciary from encroaching into areas reserved for the other Branches by extending judicial power to matters beyond those disputes "traditionally thought to be capable of resolution through the judicial process." . . .

Nonetheless, we have recognized significant exceptions to this general rule and have approved the assumption of some nonadjudicatory activities by the Judicial Branch. In keeping with Justice Jackson's *Youngstown* admonition that the separation of powers contemplates the integration of dispersed powers into a workable government, we have recognized the constitutionality of a "twilight area" in which the activities of the separate Branches merge. . . .

That judicial rulemaking, at least with respect to some subjects, falls within this twilight area is no longer an issue for dispute. None of our cases indicate that rulemaking *per se* is a function that may not be performed by an entity within the Judicial Branch, either because rulemaking is inherently nonjudicial or because it is a function exclusively committed to the Executive Branch. On the contrary, we specifically have held that Congress, in some circumstances, may confer rulemaking authority on the Judicial Branch. . . .

Our approach to other nonadjudicatory activities that Congress has vested either in federal courts or in auxiliary bodies within the Judicial Branch has been identical to our approach to judicial rulemaking: consistent with the separation of powers, Congress may delegate to the Judicial Branch nonadjudicatory functions that do not trench upon the prerogatives of another Branch and that are appropriate to the central mission of the Judiciary. Following this approach, we specifically have upheld not only Congress' power to confer on the Judicial Branch the rulemaking authority contemplated in the various enabling acts, but also to vest in judicial councils authority to "make 'all necessary orders for the effective and expeditious administration of the business of the courts.' " Though not the subject of constitutional challenge, by established practice we have recognized Congress' power to create the Judicial Conference of the United States, and the Rules Advisory Committees that it oversees, and the Administrative Office of the United States Courts whose myriad responsibilities include the administration of the entire probation service. These entities, some of which are comprised of judges, others of judges and nonjudges, still others of nonjudges only, do not exercise judicial power in the constitutional sense of deciding cases and controversies, but they share the common purpose of providing for the fair and efficient fulfillment of responsibilities that are properly the province of the Judiciary.

Given the consistent responsibility of federal judges to pronounce sentence within the statutory range established by Congress, we find that the role of the Commission in promulgating guidelines for the exercise of that judicial function bears considerable similarity to the role of this Court in establishing rules of procedure under the various enabling acts. Such guidelines, like the Federal Rules of Criminal and Civil Procedure, are court rules— rules . . . for carrying into execution judgments that the judiciary has the power to pronounce. Just as the rules of procedure bind judges and courts in the proper management of the cases before them, so the Guidelines bind judges and courts in the exercise of their uncontested responsibility to pass sentence in criminal cases. In other words, the Commission's functions, like this Court's function in promulgating procedural rules, are clearly attendant to a central element of the historically acknowledged mission of the Judicial Branch.

Petitioner nonetheless objects that the analogy between the Guidelines and the rules of procedure is flawed: Although the Judicial Branch may participate in rulemaking and administrative work that is "procedural" in nature, it may not assume, it is said, the "substantive" authority over sentencing policy that Congress has delegated to the Commission. . . .

We agree with petitioner that the nature of the Commission's rulemaking power is not strictly analogous to this Court's rulemaking power under the enabling acts. . . .

We do not believe, however, that the significantly political nature of the Commission's work renders unconstitutional its placement within the Judicial Branch. Our separation-of-powers analysis does not turn on the labelling of an activity as "substantive" as opposed to "procedural," or "political" as opposed to "judicial." . . .

First, although the Commission is located in the Judicial Branch, its powers are not united with the powers of the Judiciary in a way that has meaning for separation-of-powers analysis. Whatever constitutional problems might arise if the powers of the Commission were vested in a court, the Commission is not a court, does not exercise judicial power, and is not controlled by or accountable to members of the Judicial Branch. . . .

Second, although the Commission wields rulemaking power and not the adjudicatory power exercised by individual judges when passing sentence, the placement of the Sentencing Commission in the Judicial Branch has not increased the Branch's authority. Prior to the passage of the Act, the Judicial Branch, as an aggregate, decided precisely the questions assigned to the Commission: what sentence is appropriate to what criminal conduct under what circumstances. It was the everyday business of judges, taken collectively, to evaluate and weigh the various aims of sentencing and to apply those aims to the individual cases that came before them. The Sentencing Commission does no more than this, albeit basically through the methodology of sentencing guidelines, rather than entirely individualized sentencing determinations. Accordingly, in placing the Commission in the Judicial Branch, Congress cannot be said to have aggrandized the authority of that Branch or to have deprived the Executive Branch of a power it once possessed. . . .

Composition of the Commission

We now turn to petitioner's claim that Congress' decision to require at least three federal judges to serve on the Commission and to require those judges to share their authority with nonjudges undermines the integrity of the Judicial Branch. . . .

The text of the Constitution contains no prohibition against the service of active federal judges on independent commissions such as that established by the Act. The Constitution does include an Incompatibility Clause applicable to national legislators. . . .

No comparable restriction applies to judges, and we find it at least inferentially meaningful that at the Constitutional Convention two prohibitions against plural officeholding by members of the judiciary were proposed, but did not reach the floor of the Convention for a vote.

Our inferential reading that the Constitution does not prohibit Article III judges from undertaking extrajudicial duties finds support in the historical practice of the Founders after ratification. . . .

Subsequent history, moreover, reveals a frequent and continuing, albeit controversial, practice of extrajudicial service. . . .

In light of the foregoing history and precedent, we conclude that the principle of separation of powers does not absolutely prohibit Article III judges from serving on commissions such as that created by the Act. The judges serve on the Sentencing Commission not pursuant to their status

and authority as Article III judges, but solely because of their appointment by the President as the Act directs. Such power as these judges wield as Commissioners is not judicial power; it is administrative power derived from the enabling legislation. Just as the nonjudicial members of the Commission act as administrators, bringing their experience and wisdom to bear on the problems of sentencing disparity, so too the judges, uniquely qualified on the subject of sentencing, assume a wholly administrative role upon entering into the deliberations of the Commission. In other words, the Constitution, at least as a *per se* matter, does not forbid judges from wearing two hats; it merely forbids them from wearing both hats at the same time.

This is not to suggest, of course, that every kind of extrajudicial service under every circumstance necessarily accords with the Constitution. That the Constitution does not absolutely prohibit a federal judge from assuming extrajudicial duties does not mean that every extrajudicial service would be compatible with, or appropriate to, continuing service on the bench; nor does it mean that Congress may require a federal judge to assume extrajudicial duties as long as the judge is assigned those duties in an individual, not judicial, capacity. The ultimate inquiry remains whether a particular extrajudicial assignment undermines the integrity of the Judicial Branch. . . .

Finally, we reject petitioner's argument that the mixed nature of the Commission violates the Constitution by requiring Article III judges to share judicial power with nonjudges. As noted earlier, the Commission is not a court and exercises no judicial power. Thus, the Act does not vest Article III power in nonjudges or require Article III judges to share their power with nonjudges.

Presidential Control

The Act empowers the President to appoint all seven members of the Commission with the advice and consent of the Senate. The Act further provides that the President shall make his choice of judicial appointees to the Commission after considering a list of six judges recommended by the Judicial Conference of the United States. The Act also grants the President authority to remove members of the Commission, although "only for neglect of duty or malfeasance in office or for other good cause shown."

Mistretta argues that this power of Presidential

appointment and removal prevents the Judicial Branch from performing its constitutionally assigned functions. Although we agree with petitioner that the independence of the Judicial Branch must be "jealously guarded" against outside interference, and that, as Madison admonished at the founding, "neither of [the branches] ought to possess directly or indirectly, an overruling influence over the others in the administration of their respective powers," we do not believe that the President's appointment and removal powers over the Commission afford him influence over the functions of the Judicial Branch or undue sway over its members. . . .

In other words, since the President has no power to affect the tenure or compensation of Article III judges, even if the Act authorized him to remove judges from the Commission at will, he would have no power to coerce the judges in the exercise of their judicial duties. . . .

We conclude that in creating the Sentencing Commission—an unusual hybrid in structure and authority—Congress neither delegated excessive legislative power nor upset the constitutionally mandated balance of powers among the coordinate Branches. The Constitution's structural protections do not prohibit Congress from delegating to an expert body located within the Judicial Branch the intricate task of formulating sentencing guidelines consistent with such significant statutory direction as is present here. Nor does our system of checked and balanced authority prohibit Congress from calling upon the accumulated wisdom and experience of the Judicial Branch in creating policy on a matter uniquely within the ken of judges. Accordingly, we hold that the Act is constitutional.

The judgment of United States District Court for the Western District of Missouri is affirmed.

It is so ordered.

JUSTICE SCALIA, dissenting. . . .

I dissent from today's decision because I can find no place within our constitutional system for an agency created by Congress to exercise no governmental power other than the making of laws. . . .

I fully agree with the Court's rejection of petitioner's contention that the doctrine of unconstitutional delegation of legislative authority has been violated because of the lack of intelligible, congressionally prescribed standards to guide the Commission.

Precisely because the scope of delegation is largely uncontrollable by the courts, we must be particularly rigorous in preserving the Constitution's structural restrictions that deter excessive delegation. The major one, it seems to me, is that the power to make law cannot be exercised by anyone other than Congress, except in conjunction with the lawful exercise of executive or judicial power.

The whole theory of *lawful* congressional "delegation" is not that Congress is sometimes too busy or too divided and can therefore assign its responsibility of making law to someone else; but rather that a certain degree of discretion, and thus of lawmaking, *inheres* in most executive or judicial action, and it is up to Congress, by the relative specificity or generality of its statutory commands, to determine—up to a point—how small or how large that degree shall be. Thus, the courts could be given the power to say precisely what constitutes a "restraint of trade," or to adopt rules of procedure, or to prescribe by rule the manner in which their officers shall execute their judgments, because that "lawmaking" was ancillary to their exercise of judicial powers. And the Executive could be given the power to adopt policies and rules specifying in detail what radio and television licenses will be in the "public interest, convenience or necessity," because that was ancillary to exercise of its executive powers in granting and policing licenses and making a "fair and equitable allocation" of the electromagnetic spectrum. . . .

The focus of controversy, in the long line of our so-called excessive delegation cases, has been whether the *degree* of generality contained in the authorization for exercise of executive or judicial powers in a particular field is so unacceptably high as to *amount to* a delegation of legislative powers. I say "so-called excessive delegation" because although that convenient terminology is often used, what is really at issue is whether there has been *any* delegation of legislative power, which occurs (rarely) when Congress authorizes the exercise of executive or judicial power without adequate standards. Strictly speaking, there is *no* acceptable delegation of legislative power. . . . In the present case, however, a pure delegation of legislative power is precisely what we have before us. It is irrelevant whether the standards are adequate, because they are not standards related to the exercise of executive or judicial powers; they are, plainly and simply, standards for further legislation.

The lawmaking function of the Sentencing Commission is completely divorced from any responsibility for execution of the law or adjudication of private rights under the law. It is divorced from responsibility for execution of the law not only because the Commission is not said to be "located in the Executive Branch" (as I shall discuss presently, I doubt whether Congress can "locate" an entity within one Branch or another for constitutional purposes by merely saying so); but, more importantly, because the Commission neither exercises any executive power on its own, nor is subject to the control of the President who does. . . .

The delegation of lawmaking authority to the Commission is, in short, unsupported by any legitimating theory to explain why it is not a delegation of legislative power. To disregard structural legitimacy is wrong in itself—but since structure has purpose, the disregard also has adverse practical consequences. In this case, as suggested earlier, the consequence is to facilitate and encourage judicially uncontrollable delegation. Until our decision last Term in *Morrison* v. *Olson,* it could have been said that Congress could delegate lawmaking authority only at the expense of increasing the power of either the President or the courts. Most often, as a practical matter, it would be the President, since the judicial process is unable to conduct the investigations and make the political assessments essential for most policymaking. Thus, the need for delegation would have to be important enough to induce Congress to aggrandize its primary competitor for political power, and the recipient of the policymaking authority, while not Congress itself, would at least be politically accountable. But even after it has been accepted, pursuant to *Morrison,* that those exercising executive power need not be subject to the control of the President, Congress would still be more reluctant to augment the power of even an independent executive agency than to create an otherwise powerless repository for its delegation. Moreover, assembling the full-time senior personnel for an agency exercising executive powers is more difficult than borrowing other officials (or employing new officers on a short-term basis) to head an organization such as the Sentencing Commission.

By reason of today's decision, I anticipate that Congress will find delegation of its lawmaking powers much more attractive in the future. If rulemaking can be entirely unrelated to the exercise of judicial or executive powers, I foresee all manner of "expert" bodies, insulated from the political process, to which Congress will delegate various portions of its lawmaking responsibility. How tempting to create an expert Medical Commission (mostly MDs, with perhaps a few PhDs in moral philosophy) to dispose of such thorny, "no-win" political issues as the withholding of life-support systems in federally funded hospitals, or the use of fetal tissue for research. This is an undemocratic precedent that we set—not because of the scope of the delegated power, but because its recipient is not one of the three Branches of Government. The only governmental power the Commission possesses is the power to make law; and it is not Congress.

The strange character of the body that the Court today approves, and its incompatibility with our constitutional institutions, is apparent from that portion of the Court's opinion entitled "Location of the Commission." . . .

It would seem logical to decide the question of which Branch an agency belongs to on the basis of who controls its actions: If Congress, the Legislative Branch; if the President, the Executive Branch; if the courts (or perhaps the judges), the judicial branch. In *Humphrey's Executor* v. *United States,* we approved the concept of an agency that was controlled by (and thus within) none of the Branches. We seem to have assumed, however, that that agency (the old Federal Trade Commission, before it acquired many of its current functions) exercised no governmental power whatever, but merely assisted Congress and the courts in the performance of their functions. Where no governmental power is at issue, there is no strict constitutional impediment to a "branchless" agency, since it is only "[a]ll legislative Powers," Art. I, §1, "[t]he executive Power," Art. II, §1, and "[t]he judicial Power," Art. III, §1, which the Constitution divides into three departments. (As an example of a "branchless" agency exercising no governmental powers, one can conceive of an Advisory Commission charged with reporting to all three Branches, whose members are removable only for cause and are thus subject to the control of none of the Branches.) Over the years, however, *Humphrey's Executor* has come in general contemplation to stand for something quite different—not an "independent agency" in the sense of an agency independent of all three Branches, but an "independent agency" in the sense of an agency *within* the Executive

Branch (and thus authorized to exercise executive powers) independent of the control of the President. . . .

Today's decision may aptly be described as the *Humphrey's Executor* of the Judicial Branch, and I think we will live to regret it. Henceforth there may be agencies "within the Judicial Branch" (whatever that means), exercising governmental powers, that are neither courts nor controlled by courts, nor even controlled by judges. If an "independent agency" such as this can be given the power to fix sentences previously exercised by district courts, I must assume that a similar agency can be given the powers to adopt Rules of Procedure and Rules of Evidence previously exercised by this Court. The bases for distinction would be thin indeed.

Today's decision follows the regrettable tendency of our recent separation-of-powers jurisprudence to treat the Constitution as though it were no more than a generalized prescription that the functions of the Branches should not be commingled too much—how much is too much to be determined, case-by-case, by this Court. The Constitution is not that. Rather, as its name suggests, it is a prescribed structure, a framework, for the conduct of government. . . . Consideration of the degree of commingling that a particular disposition produces may be appropriate at the margins, where the outline of the framework itself is not clear; but it seems to me far from a marginal question whether our constitutional structure allows for a body which is not the Congress, and yet exercises no governmental powers except the making of rules that have the effect of laws.

I think the Court errs, in other words, not so much because it mistakes the degree of commingling, but because it fails to recognize that this case is not about commingling, but about the creation of a new branch altogether, a sort of junior-varsity Congress. It may well be that in some circumstances such a branch would be desirable; perhaps the agency before us here will prove to be so. But there are many desirable dispositions that do not accord with the constitutional structure we live under. And in the long run the improvisation of a constitutional structure on the basis of currently perceived utility will be disastrous.

Index of Cases*

A

Abington Township School District v. *Schempp.* 374 U.S. 203 (1963), 385–86

Ableman v. *Booth.* 62 U.S. (21 How.) 506 (1859), 127

Abortion Cases (see **Roe v. Wade,** and **Thornburgh v. American College of Obstetricians and Gynecologists**)

Abrams v. *United States.* 250 U.S. 616 (1919), 373–74

Adams v. *Williams.* 407 U.S. 143 (1972), 311

Adamson v. California, 332 U.S. 46 (1947), 305, **326**

Adkins v. *Children's Hospital.* 261 U.S. 525 (1923), 253–54

Affirmative Action Cases (see **Regents v. Bakke,** and **Wygant v. Jackson Board of Education**)

Aguilar v. Felton, 473 U.S. 402 (1985), 387, **445**

Ake v. *Oklahoma.* 470 U.S. 68 (1985), 315

Akron v. *Akron Center for Reproductive Health.* 462 U.S. 416 (1983), 456–57

Albertson v. *Subversive Activities Control Board.* 383 U.S. 70 (1965), 375

Amalgamated Food Employees v. *Logan Valley Plaza.* 391 U.S. 308 (1968), 378

Ambach v. *Norwick.* 441 U.S. 68 (1979), 491

American Trucking Association Inc. v. *Scheiner.* 483 U.S. 266 (1987), 167

Amish School Case (see *Wisconsin* v. *Yoder*)

Anastaplo. In re. 366 U.S. 82 (1961), 375

Argersinger v. *Hamlin.* 407 U.S. 25 (1972), 314

Arizona Train Limit Case (see **Southern Pacific v. Arizona**)

Arizona v. *Mauro.* 481 U.S. 520 (1987), 317

Arizona v. *Youngblood.* 57 U.S.L.W. 4013 (1988), 309

Arlington Heights v. *Metropolitan Housing Dev. Corp..* 429 U.S. 252 (1977), 486

Ashton v. *Cameron County District.* 298 U.S. 513 (1936), 192

Ashwander v. *T. V. A..* 297 U.S. 288 (1936), 19

Aurora. The v. *United States.* 11 U.S. (7 Cranch) 382 (1813), 73

B

Bailey v. *Drexel Furniture Co..* 259 U.S. 20 (1922), 221, 223

Baker v. Carr, 369 U.S. 186 (1962), 20, 38, **55**

Bake Shop Case (see **Lochner v. New York**)

Baltimore v. *Dawson.* 350 U.S. 877 (1955), 481

Barenblatt v. United States, 360 U.S. 109 (1959), 74, **89,** 401

* **Boldface** type indicates opinions included in this volume. *Lightface italic* type is used for case citations in the essays.

Index of Names*

---

* **Boldface** names and numbers indicate Justices whose opinions are reprinted in this book and the pages where their opinions can be found. Lightface type indicates references in the essays.